COMPREHENSIVE HANDBOOK

OF

PSYCHOTHERAPY

COMPREHENSIVE HANDBOOK

OF

PSYCHOTHERAPY

VOLUME 2

COGNITIVE-BEHAVIORAL APPROACHES

Editor-In-Chief   FLORENCE W. KASLOW

Volume Editor   TERENCE PATTERSON

WILEY

JOHN WILEY & SONS, INC.

Library of Congress Cataloging-in-Publication Data:

Comprehensive handbook of psychotherapy / [editor-in-chief] Florence W. Kaslow.
     p.   cm.
  Includes bibliographical references and index.
  Contents: v. 1. Psychodynamic/object relations / [edited by] Jeffrey J. Magnavita — v.
2. Cognitive-behavioral approaches / [edited by] Terence Patterson — v. 3.
Interpersonal/humanistic/existential / [edited by] Robert F. Massey, Sharon Davis Massey — v. 4.
Integrative/eclectic / [edited by] Jay Lebow.
   ISBN 0-471-01848-1 (set) — ISBN 0-471-38319-8 (cloth : alk. paper : v. 2); ISBN
0-471-65327-6 (pbk.) — ISBN 0-471-65332-2 (set : pbk.)
   1. Psychotherapy—Handbooks, manuals, etc. 2. Cognitive therapy—Handbooks,
manuals, etc. 3. Behavior therapy—Handbooks, manuals, etc. I. Kaslow, Florence
Whiteman. II. Magnavita, Jeffrey J. III. Patterson, Terence. IV. Massey, Robert F. V.
Massey, Sharon Davis. VI. Lebow, Jay.

RC480 .C593 2002
616.89'14—dc21

2001045636

Contributors

Stewart Agras, MD, is professor emeritus at Stanford University School of Medicine. His research interests include eating disorders, comprising basic laboratory work, prospective developmental studies, and outcome studies.

James F. Alexander, PhD, is a professor at the University of Utah and the founder of Functional Family Therapy with B.V. Parsons. He is a prolific author, researcher, and lecturer, and is a past president of the APA Division of Family Psychology.

Robin F. Apple, PhD, is a staff psychologist in the Stanford Psychiatry Department, Behavioral Medicine Clinic. She is actively involved in evaluating and treating a wide range of eating- and weight-disordered individuals including adolescents and their families. She participates in eating disorders research studies and engages in teaching and training of postdoctoral fellows and psychiatry residents. This is one of a number of treatment cases that she has had published.

Sonja V. Batten is a doctoral student in clinical psychology at the University of Nevada, Reno.

Karen Bearss, MA, is an advanced doctoral student at the University of Florida College of Health Professions.

Dana Becker, PhD, is assistant professor, Bryn Mawr Graduate School of Social Work and Social Research. Research areas include family therapy with adolescents, psychopathology and gender, and gender and psychotherapy. Dr. Becker has been a practicing clinician for 20 years and has acted as clinical director on several federally funded family therapy intervention and prevention studies.

Laura S. Brown, PhD, has had a private practice of clinical and forensic psychology with an emphasis on trauma since 1979. She is currently professor of psychology, Argosy University in Seattle. She was the 1997 recipient of the Sarah Haley Memorial Award for Clinical Excellence from the International Society for Traumatic Stress Studies, and she served as a member of the APA Working Group on Recovered Memories of Childhood Abuse.

David W. Coon, PhD, is a licensed psychologist who received his doctoral training in counseling psychology at Stanford University with a specialization in geropsychology. He is a research scientist at the Goldman Research Center of the Goldman Institute on Aging in San Francisco, and the associate director of the Older Adult and Family Center of the VA Palo Alto Health Care System and Stanford University. His professional interests focus on the experience of family caregivers and the development of effective psychosocial interventions for distressed older adults and family caregivers to frail elders.

Marcelle Crain is completing her doctoral degree at California School of Professional Psychology–Alliant International University (San Diego) and is a staff clinician at Children's Hospital Outpatient Psychiatry, San Diego. Her clinical interests include ADHD, conduct disorder, and childhood depression.

Mark Dadds, PhD, is currently professor of psychology, codirector of the Griffith Adolescent Forensic Assessment and Treatment Centre, and director of research in the School of Applied Psychology, Griffith University. He directs several national intervention programs for children, youth, and their families at risk for mental health problems. These programs have been implemented in each state in Australia and in Canada, the United States, Belgium, and Holland. In the past decade, he has been awarded over $1 million in research funding for his work in clinical child and family mental health. He has been national president of the Australian Association for Cognitive and Behavioural Therapy, director of research for the Abused Child Trust of Queensland, and a recipient of several awards including an Early Career Award from the division of Scientific Affairs of the Australian Psychological Society. He has authored three books and over 100 papers on child and family psychology. In the past few years, he has given keynote addresses to international conferences in Mexico, Canada, the United Kingdom, the United States, Denmark, Hungary, Austria, and Australia, including multiple invitations to the World Congress of Cognitive and Behavioral Therapies.

Helen M. DeVries, PhD, is an associate professor of psychology at Wheaton College, Wheaton, Illinois. She completed postdoctoral training in clinical geropsychology at Stanford University School of Medicine and the Department of Veterans Affairs Medical Center, Palo Alto, California, and in neuropsychology at the Medical College of Virginia. Her areas of interest include adaptation and functioning in midlife and late-life families and training issues in clinical geropsychology.

Keith Dobson, PhD, is a professor of clinical psychology at the University of Calgary. His research interests focus on cognitive models and therapies for depression. He has published in other related areas, such as on empirically supported treatments in psychology and on professional psychology, particularly in the Canadian context. He is a fellow of several organizations, and has won a number of scientific and professional awards, including the 2001 Canadian Psychological Association Award for Distinguished Contributions to Professional Psychology.

Windy Dryden, PhD, is professor of counselling at Goldsmiths College, University of London, where he is founder and coordinator of the world's only masters course in REBT. He is Fellow of the British Psychological Society and of the British Association of Counselling and Psychotherapy and is author and editor of over 125 books.

Sheila M. Eyberg, PhD, is professor of clinical and health psychology and director of the Child Study Laboratory at the University of Florida. She has served as associate editor of the *Journal of Clinical Child Psychology and Behavior Therapy* and has been a member of the NIMH Child Psychopathology and Treatment review group. She has been president of the Society of Pediatric Psychology, the Society of Clinical Child and Adolescent Psychology, and the Southeastern Psychological Association. She is currently president of the Division of Child, Youth, and Family Services of the American Psychological Association.

Gregory A. Fabiano, MA, is an advanced graduate student at the University at Buffalo. Research interests include developing effective psychosocial, pharmacological, and combined treatments for children and adolescents with attention-deficit/hyperactivity disorder.

Frank Fincham, PhD, received his degree from the University of Oxford. He is professor and director of clinical training in the psychology department at the University at Buffalo, The State University of New York. His research focuses on the conceptualization and assessment of marital quality, cognition in close relationships, the impact of interparental conflict on child adjustment, and forgiveness. Dr. Fincham has received numerous awards for his research, including the President's Award for Distinguished Contributions to Psychological Knowledge from the British Psychological Society and the Berscheid-Hatfield Award for "distinguished contributions to the field of personal relationships" from the International Network on Personal Relationships. His work has placed him among the top 25 psychologists in the world in terms of impact (number of citations per published article, APS Observer, January 1996).

Sharon L. Foster, PhD, is a professor at the California School of Professional Psychology at the San Diego Campus of Alliant International University. She is the coauthor of two books and numerous journal articles and chapters. Her scholarly interests include children's peer relations, aggression in girls, and research methodology.

Alan E. Fruzzetti, PhD, is associate professor of psychology and director of the Dialectical Behavior Therapy and Research Program at the University of Nevada in Reno, Nevada. His research focuses on developing models of severe behavior problems (e.g., borderline personality disorder, partner violence) in the context of couple and family interaction, with emphasis on the further development, evaluation, and training of Dialectical Behavior Therapy with individuals, couples, and families.

Elizabeth V. Gifford is a doctoral student in clinical psychology at the University of Nevada, Reno.

Michael C. Gottlieb, PhD, is family and forensic psychologist in independent practice in Dallas, Texas. He is board certified (ABPP) in family psychology, a fellow of the American Psychological Association, and an associate clinical professor at the University of Texas Health Science Center. A past president of the Texas Psychological Association, the American Board of Family Psychology, and the Academy of Family Psychology, his research interests are in applied ethics and the psychology/law interface.

John M. Gottman, PhD, is James Mifflin professor of psychology at the University of Washington. Research areas include statistical and mathematical research methodology for interaction, observational research methodology, marital relationships, gay and lesbian relationships, parent-child relationships, children's peer relationships, emotional development, and meta-emotion. He has received NIMH Research Scientist Awards from 1979_1995 and the NIMH Merit Award. He has written prolifically on couples' relationships, and his lectures, workshops, and publications are frequently cited in the national media.

Kim Halford, PhD, is professor of clinical psychology in the School of Applied Psychology at Griffith University in Brisbane, Australia. His research interests are in couple relationships, particularly the determinants of relationship satisfaction, aggression, and stability; the association of individual and couple well-being; couples and coping with cancer; couple-based interventions to prevent relationship problems and to assist life transitions and coping; and couple therapy. He has attracted over $3 million dollars of competitive research funding, published over 100 research articles, 3 books, and has been an advisor on couple relationship to the Australian, United States, and German governments.

Steven C. Hayes, PhD, is foundation professor and chair in the department of psychology, University of Nevada, Reno. He is a prolific author and lecturer in the field of behavior therapy and a past president of the American Association for Behavior Therapy.

Aaron Hogue, PhD, is an assistant professor in the division of Applied Developmental Psychology at Fordham University. He is a licensed clinical psychologist who received his doctorate from Temple University in 1994 and completed a postdoctoral fellowship in family-based intervention research at the Center for Treatment Research on adolescent drug abuse. His research interests include development of family-based interventions for adolescent drug use and delinquency, risk and resiliency in high-risk youth, adherence and process research on family intervention models, and program evaluation of family- and community-based interventions.

Amy Holtzworth-Munroe, PhD, received her degree in clinical psychology in 1988 from the University of Washington. She is a professor of psychology at Indiana University in Bloomington. She has conducted research on husband violence for over 15 years, most recently developing and testing a typology of male batterers. Dr. Holtzworth-Munroe trains therapists in couple therapy and batterer treatment. She is an associate editor for the *Journal of Consulting and Clinical Psychology* and has served on National Institute of Health grant review panels in the areas of family violence and aggression.

Thomas E. Land, PsyD, received his degree in counseling psychology from the Florida Institute of Technology in 1986. He is a clinical instructor at the University of Washington and maintains a cognitive-behavioral practice in Seattle. Dr. Land has conducted workshops nationally on sexual minority issues.

Rona L. Levy, MSW, PhD, MPH, is professor of social work at the University of Washington, Seattle, Washington. She has published and presented extensively in the fields of behavioral medicine, women's health issues, and clinical research methodology.

Howard Liddle, EdD, is professor of epidemiology and public health, and director of the NIDA-funded Center for Treatment Research on Adolescent Drug Abuse at the University of Miami School of Medicine. Dr. Liddle's research on the efficacy of multidimensional family therapy has been recognized with career achievement awards from the American Association for Marriage and Family Therapy and the American Family Therapy Academy, and the Division of Family Psychology (Family Psychologist of the Year Award).

Carol Markie-Dadds, MA, is the deputy director of the Parenting and Family Support Centre at The University of Queensland. She is a clinical psychologist with a masters in clinical psychology, and she has specialist clinical and research experience in working with families of young children with behavior problems. She is the state coordinator for the Triple P–Positive Parenting Program in Queensland, which involves coordinating the training, accreditation, and supervision of service providers in government-funded agencies across the state.

Amy Marshall is a doctoral student in clinical psychology at Indiana University. Her research has examined husband-to-wife sexual coercion and violence.

Christopher Martell, PhD, is a private practitioner and researcher in Seattle. He has published widely in the field of behavioral couple therapy, with a focus on the treatment of gay couples.

Louise Maxfield, MA, is a doctoral candidate in clinical psychology at Lakehead University in Canada and is a certified trauma specialist. A recipient of a doctoral fellowship from the Social Sciences and Humanities Research Council of Canada, she has been an investigator in four EMDR research studies. Research interests include the development, course, and treatment of PTSD; mechanisms of action in EMDR; emotional dysregulation; the processing of traumatic events; and clinical research methodology.

Jeffrey C. Meehan is an advanced doctoral student in clinical psychology at Indiana University. His research addresses the possible biological correlates of male intimate violence. His work has examined the psychophysiological responding (i.e., heart rate reactivity) of violent husbands during marital interactions and has compared violent and nonviolent men on neuropsychological test performance. He also has been involved in the testing of a typology of male batterers in several study samples.

David L. Meichenbaum, MA, is an advanced graduate student at the University at Buffalo. Research interests include investigating the nature of attention-deficit/hyperactivity disorder through adolescence and young adulthood and developing effective psychosocial and combined treatment approaches for adolescents with attention-deficit/hyperactivity disorder.

Julieann Pankey is a doctoral student in clinical psychology at the University of Nevada, Reno.

Terence Patterson, EdD, is director of training in the counseling psychology doctoral program at the University of San Francisco, a diplomate in family psychology (ABPP), and 2001 president of the division of family psychology of the American Psychological Association. His professional focus includes behavioral couple therapy, ethics, and theoretical paradigms.

Barbara Ann Perry, PhD, is a licensed psychologist in private practice. She has served in adjunct and courtesy assistant professor capacities in the department of psychology at the University of Oregon.

Jane Querido, MA, is an advanced doctoral student at the University of Florida College of Health Professions.

Rene Quiñones is a doctoral student in clinical psychology at the University of Nevada, Reno.

Uzma Rehman is an advanced doctoral student in clinical psychology at Indiana University. Her research has compared subtypes of maritally violent men on their attitudes toward violence and women, their communication skills, and their levels of anger and hostility. She is currently conducting cross-cultural research on the relationship of marital communication to marital satisfaction and violence in Caucasian and Pakistani couples.

Matthew Sanders, PhD, is professor at the University of Queensland in Australia and has developed behavioral training programs for young children in conjunction with the Australian government. He writes and lectures extensively throughout the world.

Jason M. Satterfield, PhD, is an assistant professor and director of behavioral medicine in the division of General Internal Medicine at the University of California in San Francisco. He is the co-director of the behavioral sciences curriculum for UCSF medical students and primary care residents including training in cultural competence, behavioral medicine, and psychiatric services in primary care settings. His current research interests include evaluation of cultural competency programs, medical provider well-being groups, and emotional intelligence in medical care.

Thomas L. Sexton, PhD, is a professor of counseling psychology and the director of the Center for Adolescent and Family Studies at Indiana University. His research interests include family therapy change process and the study of effective treatment interventions for at-risk adolescents and their families.

Francine Shapiro, PhD, originator of EMDR, is a senior research fellow at the Mental Research Institute in Palo Alto, California, and a recipient of the Distinguished Scientific Achievement in Psychology Award of the California Psychological Association. She is founder and president emeritus of the EMDR Humanitarian Assistance Programs, a global network of volunteer clinicians providing services to traumatized populations worldwide. Her research interests include the integration of salient elements of diverse psychotherapies to provide robust treatment across the entire clinical spectrum, with an emphasis on stopping the cycle of violence by eliminating perpetrator behavior and affording the most severe cases of abuse and neglect the ability to achieve healthy intrapsychic development and interpersonal relations.

Elizabeth Snyker, MSW, is in private practice and is a certified expert in traumatic stress. She has awards from Human Affairs International and from the U.S. Department of Veteran Affairs for clinical excellence. Ms. Snyker is an EMDR Institute senior facilitator, an EMDR Humanitarian Assistance Programs trainer, and an EMDR International Association approved consultant.

Mandy Steiman, MS, is a graduate student in the clinical psychology program at the University of Washington, Seattle, Washington. Research areas include cognitive-behavioral treatment, marital conflict, and parenting.

Michael A. Tompkins, PhD, is the director of professional training at the San Francisco Bay Area Center for Cognitive Therapy, assistant clinical professor at the University of California, Berkeley, and a founding fellow of the Academy of Cognitive Therapy. Dr. Tompkins specializes in empirically supported treatments for depression and anxiety disorders in adults, adolescents, and children. He is the author or coauthor of numerous articles and chapters on cognitive-behavior therapy and presents widely on the topic of cognitive-behavior therapy.

Lauren M. Weinstock, MS, is currently a graduate student in the department of psychology at the University of Colorado at Boulder. Her interests include the application of cognitive-behavioral and interpersonal approaches to the study of depression and relationship discord.

Robert L. Weiss, PhD, is professor emeritus, psychology, at the University of Oregon. He is closely identified with developing behavioral assessments and interventions within the cognitive behavioral model for couples in distress.

Mark A. Whisman, PhD, is an associate professor at the University of Colorado at Boulder. His primary interests are in understanding the onset, maintenance, and treatment of relationship discord and depression. In particular, he is interested in evaluating how relationship functioning influences the course and treatment of depression.

Foreword

Thirty years ago, when I began graduate school, it was possible to buy one book, read it carefully, and pretty much know all that was going on in the field of what was then called "behavior modification." Albert Bandura's 1969 book, his blue book, *Principles of Behavior Modification*, did that for the field and for my cohort of graduate students eagerly seeking to learn about this new, scientific approach to behavioral disorders.

Of course, we needed to supplement this book with original research articles, but they did not take up more than one large file drawer. So here was the field 30 years ago: Bandura's book and one file drawer. What a sense of mastery to know everything in the field. And with a couple of trips to conferences such as the Association for Advancement of Behavior Therapy (AABT), a little luck, and a dash of courage, we could personally meet most of the major players in the field.

Compare that idyllic past with the conditions today. So much has happened and is happening in the field of cognitive and behavior psychotherapies that one book could hardly pull it all together, and what of the supporting, original articles? My bulging file drawers and stacks of unfiled papers aren't even the tip of the iceberg of research and scholarship taking place in the field today. How can you master all the research and know all the players? Mastering one's own segment of the field is demanding enough.

Of course, the past quarter-century did bring some compensatory changes. With literature search engines, I can find relevant articles faster than thumbing through my one file drawer of years ago. And with more and more articles being available electronically, I can store more material on my hard drive than I could in a roomful of file cabinets. But what about a book that could survey the field?

To be true to the field today, such a book would have to cover interventions for a variety of *DSM-IV* disorders. When I entered graduate school, behaviorists pretty much scoffed at the *DSM* of the day (II), because it was notoriously unreliable and infiltrated with what was for us the enemy theory: psychoanalysis. With the advent of behavioral criteria for disorders that came about with the *DSM-III* and its successors and the explosion of research on psychopathology, behaviorally oriented people have become more sympathetic to the existing categories and have oriented their treatment research around these disorders.

In those early days of behavioral approaches, interventions were seen as directly emanating from basic research on classical and operant conditioning. Strategies were limited to techniques such as systematic desensitization, operant reinforcement, shaping, modeling, and behavior rehearsal. Today, a book would have to cover not only the traditional behavioral strategies, but also the array of cognitive and systems approaches that are part of the field.

To reflect the existing research, the book would have to cover treatments across the life span. It would have to address couple, family, and group treatments as well as individual treatment. It would need to reflect the diversity of clients that treatments today are oriented to serve, such as ethnic minorities and gay and lesbian clients. It could not be limited to intervention when a problem or disorder had fully declared itself, but would have to cover the exciting developments in prevention and early intervention. Finally, it would need to cover the ethical issues that treatment raises.

Amazingly, the current book achieves this kind of comprehensive coverage of the field of cognitive, behavioral, and functional approaches to psychotherapy. Furthermore, many of the leaders in the field are senior authors of the pieces. For example, Matthew Sanders and Carol Markie-Dadds write the chapter on behavioral family interventions, Stewart Agras and Robin Apple write on eating disorders, Keith Dobson and Mandy Steiman write on cognitive-behavioral approaches to depression, and Robert Weiss and Barbara Perry write on behavioral couple therapy, to name a few (and not to minimize the names of others not mentioned).

I think this book will be a "should have" for empirically oriented practitioners as well as scientists in the field. Its chapters provide a useful overview for graduate students and professionals who want an overview of cognitive-behavioral approaches to a particular problem.

I plan to put my copy right next to my aging 1969 blue book by Bandura.

ANDREW CHRISTENSEN, PhD

Preface

The world of psychotherapy theory and practice has changed markedly in the past 30 years. During this time, many forces have converged, leading to major alterations in the therapeutic landscape. Therefore, it seemed essential to produce this four-volume *Comprehensive Handbook of Psychotherapy* to illuminate the state of the art of the field, and to encompass history, theory, practice, trends, and research at the beginning of the twenty-first century.

These volumes are envisioned as both comprehensive in terms of the most current extant knowledge and as thought-provoking, stimulating in our readers new ways of thinking that should prove generative of further refinements, elaborations, and the next iteration of new ideas. The volumes are intended for several audiences, including graduate students and their professors, clinicians, and researchers.

In these four volumes, we have sought to bring together contributing authors who have achieved recognition and acclaim in their respective areas of theory construction, research, practice, and/or teaching. To reflect the globalization of the psychotherapy field and its similarities and differences between and among countries and cultures, authors are included from such countries as Argentina, Australia, Belgium, Canada, Italy, Japan, and the United States.

Regardless of the theoretical orientation being elucidated, almost all of the chapters are written from a biopsychosocial perspective. The vast majority present their theory's perspective on dealing with patient affects, behaviors or actions, and cognitions. I believe these volumes provide ample evidence that any reasonably complete theory must encompass these three aspects of living.

Many of the chapters also deal with assessment and diagnosis as well as treatment strategies and interventions. There are frequent discussions of disorders classified under the rubric of Axis I and Axis II in the fourth edition of the *Diagnostic and Statistical Manual of Mental Disorders* with frequent concurrence across chapters as to how treatment of these disorders should be approached. There are other chapters, particularly those that cluster in the narrative, postmodern, and social constructivist wing of the field, that eschew diagnosis, based on the belief that the only reality of concern is the one being created in the moment-to-moment current interaction: in this instance, the therapeutic dialogue or conversation. In these therapies, goals and treatment plans are coconstructed and co-evolved and generally are not predicated on any formal assessment through psychological testing. Whereas most of the other philosophical/theoretical schools have incorporated the evolving knowledge of the brain-behavior connection and the many exciting and illuminating findings emanating from the field of neuroscience, this is much less true in the postmodern wing of the field, which places little value on facts objectively verified by consensual validation and replication.

One of the most extraordinary developments in the past few decades has been that barriers between the theoretical schools have diminished, and leading theoreticians, academicians, researchers, and clinicians have listened to and learned from each other. As a result of this cross-fertilization, the *move toward integration* among and between theoretical approaches has been definitive. Many of the chapters in Volumes 1, 2, and 3 also could fit in Volume 4. Some of the distance between psychodynamic/object-relations therapies and cognitive-behavioral therapies has decreased as practitioners of each have gained more respect for the other and incorporated ideas that expand their theory base and make it more holistic. This is one of the strongest trends that emerges from reading these volumes.

A second trend that comes to the fore is the recognition that, at times, it is necessary to combine judicious psychopharmacological treatment with psychotherapy, and that not doing so makes the healing process more difficult and slower.

Other important trends evident in these volumes include greater sensitivity to issues surrounding gender, ethnicity, race, religion, and socioeconomic status; the controversy over empirically validated treatments versus viewing and treating each patient or patient unit as unique; the importance of the brain-behavior connection mentioned earlier; the critical role assigned to developmental history; the foci on outcome and efficacy; and the importance of process and outcome research and the use of research findings to enhance clinical practice. There is a great deal of exciting ferment going on as our psychotherapeutic horizons continue to expand.

These volumes would not have come to fruition without the outstanding collaboration and teamwork of the fine volume editors, Drs. Jeffrey Magnavita, Terence Patterson, Robert and Sharon Massey, and Jay Lebow, and my gratitude to them is boundless. To each of the contributing authors, our combined thank you is expressed.

We extend huge plaudits and great appreciation to Jennifer Simon, Associate Publisher at John Wiley & Sons, for her guidance, encouragement, and wisdom. Thanks also to Isabel Pratt, Editorial Assistant, for all her efforts. It has been a multifaceted and intense enterprise.

We hope the readers, for whom the work is intended, will deem our efforts extremely worthwhile.

FLORENCE W. KASLOW, PhD, ABPP
Editor-in-Chief

Palm Beach Gardens, Florida

Contents

SECTION ONE

PSYCHOTHERAPY WITH CHILDREN

SECTION TWO

PSYCHOTHERAPY WITH ADOLESCENTS AND YOUNG ADULTS

SECTION THREE

PSYCHOTHERAPY WITH ADULTS

SECTION FOUR

PSYCHOTHERAPY WITH FAMILIES AND COUPLES

SECTION FIVE

GROUP PSYCHOTHERAPY

SECTION SIX

SPECIAL TOPICS

SECTION ONE

PSYCHOTHERAPY WITH CHILDREN

CHAPTER 1

Behavioral Family Interventions with Children

MATTHEW R. SANDERS AND CAROL MARKIE-DADDS

HISTORY OF BEHAVIORAL FAMILY INTERVENTION

Behavioral family intervention (BFI) is a generic term used to define an intervention process that targets family interaction patterns assumed to contribute to the development or maintenance of disturbances in children's functioning or relapse of functioning. Consequently, the model of intervention is based on an assumption that many child behavioral and emotional problems arise, at least in part, because of disturbances in parent-child relationships, which in turn are related to deficits in parenting skills. BFI has emerged from the parent training (PT) movement as a broad-based, empirically established treatment of dysfunctional parenting practices and family relationships. This model of intervention is an educative one, involving the active training of parents in the use of child management and parenting skills. The intervention model aims to help parents acquire a variety of skills known to influence children's development. The skills taught aim to modify children's problem behavior by promoting their social competence.

THE ORIGINS OF BEHAVIORAL FAMILY INTERVENTION

The application of behavioral and social learning theory to the family began as an attempt to apply the laboratory-derived principles of operant learning to marital and parent-child problems (Patterson, 1982; Wahler, 1969). Early studies were devoted to demonstrating that contingencies of reinforcement and punishment are reliably associated with child and marital problem behavior. For example, Williams (1959) demonstrated that a 21-month-old boy's bedtime tantrum behavior could be eliminated by changing the way parents responded to that behavior. These early applications of learning theory focused on relatively circumscribed problem behaviors in families with some considerable success. During the 1960s and 1970s, research mushroomed to encompass an increasing range of complex clinical problems in families. These early parent training studies were firmly rooted in the broader field of behavior modification and applied behavior analysis (Baer, Wolf, & Risley, 1968) and represented the extension of basic principles of learning and behavior change to parent-child interactions. Consequently, early programs tended to involve training parents to alter contingent consequences following problem behavior and to provide positive consequences following appropriate behavior. Treatment was generally individually administered (Forehand & McMahon, 1981; O'Dell, 1974). Much of this research supported the basic conclusion that positive changes in specific adult behavior results in a corresponding improvement in the marital relationship and in children's behavior and adjustment.

As research and clinical experience with the behavioral model increased and the technology became more widely disseminated, the limitations of a narrowly focused operant model became apparent. Theorists increasingly stressed the importance of a broader view of the family's social environment in determining behavior, and the utilization of more ecologically oriented models has been a strong trend within the behavioral family area. Variables such as a couple's marital interaction, occupational demands and stresses, interactions with relatives and neighbors, psychological state, and the family's financial resources influence, either directly or indirectly, parents' behavior toward their children. For example, a father who works 80 hours a week has very little time to devote to child rearing. A mother who experiences frequent criticism from a mother-in-law who looks after her child three days a week is exposed to a hostile environment that may be difficult to avoid if alternative care is not readily available.

CONTEMPORARY MODELS OF BEHAVIORAL
FAMILY INTERVENTION

Contemporary behavioral approaches thus emphasize the integration of micro- and macroprocesses. For example, in child-oriented work, the microprocesses focus heavily on parent-child interactions and the contingencies of reinforcement that occur between parent and child.

The macroprocesses focus on how these reinforcement patterns are functionally related to the broader family and social characteristics, such as marital relations, communication skills, and social support.

Contemporary models also include a range of delivery formats to improve the cost-efficiency and accessibility of parenting programs. In addition to individual face-to-face consultations, BFI is now available in self-help, telephone, and group delivery formats. Over the past decade, BFI has become widely used as a prevention program. A distinguishing feature of the BFI approach has been its commitment to empirical evaluation and refinement of its hypotheses and methods.

BFI has a central role to play in the treatment of most forms of behavior and emotional disturbances in children. These interventions focus on changing patterns of family interaction by teaching family members skills that promote more effective functioning and prosocial behavior. There is considerable evidence that educationally oriented BFI programs involving active skills training are particularly beneficial in helping families change. There are now a number of empirically supported parenting and family interventions, including programs by Webster-Stratton (1994) and Forehand and McMahon (1981). In recent years, some attempt has been made to move from individual parenting programs to multilevel systems of family intervention such as Triple P—Positive Parenting Program (see "Methods of Assessment and Intervention," later in this chapter).

THEORETICAL BASIS OF
BEHAVIORAL FAMILY
INTERVENTION

The theoretical basis of BFI derives from viewing the family as a crucial agent of socialization. The family provides the first and most important social, emotional, interpersonal, economic, and cultural context for human development; as a result, family relationships have a profound influence on the well-being of children. The parent-child relationship in particular has a pervasive influence on the psychological, physical, social, and economic well-being of children. Disturbed interpersonal relationships within the family are generic risk factors and positive interpersonal relationships are protective factors that are related to a wide variety of mental health problems from infancy to old age (Sanders, 1995). Many significant mental health, social, and economic problems are linked to disturbances in family functioning and the breakdown of family relationships (Chamberlain & Patterson, 1995; Patterson, 1982; Sanders & Duncan, 1995).

Epidemiological studies indicate that family risk factors such as poor parenting, family conflict, and marriage breakdown strongly influence children's development (e.g., Cummings & Davies, 1994; Dryfoos, 1990; Robins, 1991). Specifically, lack of a warm positive relationship with parents; insecure attachment; harsh, inflexible, rigid, or inconsistent discipline practices; inadequate supervision of and involvement with children; marital conflict and breakdown; and parental psychopathology (particularly maternal depression) increase the risk that children will develop major behavioral and emotional problems, including substance abuse, antisocial behavior, and juvenile crime (e.g., Coie, 1996; Loeber & Farrington, 1998). Consequently, improved family functioning has the potential to reduce the prevalence of mental health problems in the community.

Contemporary models of BFI draw on several different theoretical approaches, including the following:

1. Social learning models of parent-child interaction that highlight the reciprocal and bidirectional nature of parent-child interactions (e.g., Patterson, 1982). This model identifies learning mechanisms that maintain coercive and dysfunctional patterns of family interaction and predict future antisocial behavior in children (Patterson, Reid, & Dishion, 1992).

2. Research in child and family behavior therapy and applied behavior analysis that has developed many useful behavior change strategies, particularly research that focuses on rearranging antecedents of problem behavior through designing more positive, engaging environments for children (Risley, Clarke, & Cataldo, 1976; Sanders, 1992, 1996).

3. Developmental research on parenting in everyday contexts that identifies children's competencies in naturally occurring situations, particularly work that traces the origins of social and intellectual competence to early parent-child relationships (e.g., Hart & Risley, 1995; White, 1990). Children's risk of developing severe behavioral and emotional problems is reduced by teaching parents to use naturally occurring daily interactions to teach children language, social skills, developmental competencies, and problem-solving skills in an emotionally supportive environment. Particular emphasis is placed on using child-initiated interactions as a context for the use of incidental teaching (Hart & Risley, 1975). Children are at greater risk for adverse developmental outcomes, including behavior problems, if they fail to acquire core language competencies and impulse control during early childhood (Hart & Risley, 1995).

4. Social information-processing models that highlight the important role of parental cognitions such as attributions, expectancies, and beliefs as factors that contribute to parental self-efficacy, decision making, and behavioral intentions (e.g., Bandura, 1977, 1995). In BFIs, parents are encouraged to identify alternative social interactional explanations for their child's behavior.

5. Research from the field of developmental psychopathology that has identified specific risk and protective factors linked to adverse

developmental outcomes in children (e.g., Emery, 1982; Grych & Fincham, 1990; Hart & Risley, 1995; Rutter, 1985). The modifiable risk factors of poor parent management practices, couple relationship conflict, and parental distress (e.g., stress, depression) are targeted by BFI. Coercive parenting practices are addressed through a process of active skills training, enabling parents to break negative escalating cycles of parent-child interaction. As parental discord is a risk factor for many forms of child and adolescent psychopathology (Grych & Fincham, 1990; Rutter, 1985; Sanders, Nicholson, & Floyd, 1997), BFI typically fosters collaboration and teamwork between caretakers in raising children. Improving couples' communication is an important vehicle to reduce parental conflict over child-rearing issues and to reduce personal distress of parents and children in conflictual relationships (Jacobson & Margolin, 1979; Sanders et al., 1997). BFI also targets parental distress, including depression, anger, anxiety, and high levels of stress, especially with the parenting role (Sanders & McFarland, 2000). Distress can be alleviated through parents developing better parenting skills, subsequently reducing feelings of helplessness, depression, and stress. Intensive BFI approaches have used cognitive behavior therapy techniques of mood monitoring, challenging dysfunctional cognitions and attributions, and developing specific coping skills for high-risk parenting situations (Sanders & McFarland, 2000).

6. A public health perspective to family intervention involving the explicit recognition of the role of the broader ecological context for human development (e.g., Biglan, 1995; Mrazek & Haggerty, 1994; National Institute of Mental Health, 1998). As pointed out by Biglan, the reduction of antisocial behavior in children requires a community context for parenting to change. This can be achieved by normalizing parenting experiences (particularly the process of participating in parent education), breaking down parents' sense of social isolation, increasing social and

emotional support from others in the community, and validating and publicly acknowledging the importance and difficulties of parenting. It also involves actively seeking community involvement and support for BFI parenting programs by the engagement of key community stakeholders (e.g., community leaders, businesses, schools, and voluntary organizations).

SELF-REGULATION AND PARENTAL COMPETENCE

Sanders (1999) recently argued that the development of a parent's capacity for self-regulation needs to be viewed as a central skill in BFI. This involves teaching parents skills that enable them to become independent problem solvers and decision makers. Karoly (1993) defined self-regulation as follows:

> Self-regulation refers to those processes, internal and/or transactional, that enable an individual to guide his/her goal-directed activities over time and across changing circumstances (contexts). Regulation implies modulation of thought, affect, behavior, and attention via deliberate or automated use of specific mechanisms and supportive metaskills. The processes of self-regulation are initiated when routinized activity is impeded or when goal directedness is otherwise made salient (e.g., the appearance of a challenge, the failure of habitual patterns, etc.). (p. 25)

This definition emphasizes that self-regulatory processes are embedded in a social context that not only provides opportunities and limitations for individual self-directedness, but implies a dynamic reciprocal interchange between the internal and the external determinants of human motivation. From a therapeutic perspective, self-regulation is a process whereby individuals are taught skills to modify their own behavior. For parents, these skills include selecting developmentally appropriate goals for their child or personal goals as a parent, monitoring a child's or their own behavior, choosing an appropriate method of intervention for a particular problem, implementing the solution, self-monitoring their implementation of solutions (e.g., via checklists relating to the areas of concern), and identifying strengths or limitations in their performance and setting future goals for action. In turn, parents aim to promote self-regulation skills in children. This self-regulatory framework is operationalized to include the following.

Self-Sufficiency

As a parenting program is time-limited, parents need to become independent problem solvers so that they trust their own judgment and become less reliant on others in carrying out basic parenting responsibilities. Self-sufficient parents have the resilience, resourcefulness, knowledge, and skills to parent with confidence. When confronted with a new problem, they use their knowledge, skills, and personal resources to resolve the problem.

Encouraging parents to become self-sufficient also means that parents become more connected to social support networks (e.g., partners, extended family, friends, child care supports). However, the broader ecological context within which a family lives cannot be ignored (e.g., the media, poverty, dangerous neighborhoods, community, ethnicity, culture). It is hypothesized that the more self-sufficient parents become, the more likely they are to seek appropriate support when they need it, advocate for their children, become involved in their child's schooling, and protect children from harm (e.g., by effectively managing conflict with partners and creating a secure, low-conflict environment).

Parental Self-Efficacy

A sense of parenting self-efficacy is an important component of self-sufficiency (Bandura, 1995). This refers to parents' belief in their capacity to overcome or solve a parenting or child management problem. Parents with high self-efficacy have the resilience, resourcefulness, knowledge, and skills to parent with confidence and have positive expectations about the possibility of change. The well-being of children has a high priority, and their family relationships are an important part of their lives.

Self-Management

The tools or skills that parents can use to become more self-sufficient include self-monitoring, self-determination of goals and performance standards, self-evaluation of their own performance against a performance criterion, and self-selection of change strategies. As all parents are responsible for the way they choose to raise their children, parents select those aspects of their own and their child's behavior they wish to work on, set goals, choose specific parenting and child management techniques to implement, and self-evaluate their success with their chosen goals against self-determined criteria. BFIs help parents make informed decisions by sharing knowledge and skills derived from contemporary research into effective child-rearing practices. An active skill training process is incorporated into BFIs to enable skills to be modeled and practiced. Parents receive feedback regarding their implementation of skills learned in a supportive context, using a self-regulatory framework.

Personal Agency

Here, parents increasingly attribute changes or improvements in their situation to their own or their child's efforts rather than to chance, age, maturational factors, or other uncontrollable events such as children's genetic makeup. This outcome is achieved by prompting parents to identify causes or explanations for their child's or their own behavior.

Problem Solving

A final aspect of self-regulation is in the parents' ability to apply the skills and knowledge they have acquired to issues beyond the presenting

Table 1.1 Principles of effective parenting skills programs.

Principle	Description
Programs should empower families.	Parenting skills programs aim to enhance families' ability to solve problems for themselves. Programs that promote dependency are destructive. In most instances, families have lesser need for support over time.
Programs should build on existing strengths of families.	Successful parenting programs build on the existing competencies of family members. It is assumed that individuals are capable of becoming active problem solvers, even though their previous attempts to resolve problems may not have been successful.
Program goals should address known risk variables.	Parenting skills programs vary according to the focus or goals of intervention. The focus of the intervention depends on the theoretical underpinning of the approach used. Some programs focus on behavioral change; others concentrate on cognitive, affective, or attitude change. However, a common goal in most effective programs is to improve family communication, problem solving, conflict resolution, and specific parenting skills. Interventions that have proven most successful address variables that may increase the risk of individual psychopathology.
Programs should be designed to facilitate access.	It is essential that programs are delivered in ways to increase rather than restrict parents' access to services. Professional practices can sometimes restrict access to services; for example, inflexible clinic hours may prevent working parents from participating in parenting programs. To address this problem, programs may take place in many different settings, such as clinics, hospitals, homes, kindergartens, preschools, schools, and worksites. The type of setting should vary depending on the goals of the intervention and the needs of the target group.
Programs should be timed developmentally to optimize impact.	Parenting programs should be timed to the age and developmental level of the target group. Programs can be delivered prebirth, or during infancy, toddlerhood, middle childhood, or adolescence. Developmentally targeted programs for particular problems may have a greater impact than if delivered at another time in the life cycle. For example, a prevention program for young children at risk of developing conduct disorders would be more effective than a program for older children or adolescents delivered after the onset of the conduct problems.
Programs should emphasize the importance of the therapeutic relationship.	The therapeutic relationship between the clinician and relevant family members is critical to the effectiveness of parenting programs. Clinical skills such as empathy, rapport building, effective communication, and session structuring are necessary for establishing a good therapeutic relationship. Such skills are important in programs that involve face-to-face contact and in models of intervention that involve minimal contact, such as telephone counseling or correspondence programs.
Programs should be gender sensitive.	Parenting skills programs have the potential to promote more equitable gender relationships within the family. Interventions should avoid promoting traditional gender stereotypes and power relationships and aim to promote equality between partners.
Programs should be based on scientifically validated theories.	Parenting skills programs should be based on coherent and explicit theoretical principles. It is not sufficient just to demonstrate that an intervention results in improvements in family interaction, although this is a

Table 1.1 *(Continued)*

	necessary first step. The mechanisms purported to underlie the improvement must also be demonstrated to change and be responsible for the observed improvements.
Programs should be culturally appropriate.	Programs should be tailored in such a way as to respect and not undermine the cultural values, aspirations, and needs of different ethnic groups. Although there is much to learn about how to achieve this objective, there is increasing evidence that sensitively tailored parenting programs can be effective with a variety of cultural groups.

concern. It refers to parents' ability to flexibly adapt or generalize what they have learned to new problems, at later developmental phases, with different children, and for a variety of child behavior problems and family concerns. This means that the test of whether a parenting intervention is truly successful is not simply the ability of parents to resolve current issues, but their capacity to address a diverse range of family challenges over time, with relative autonomy.

DISTINGUISHING FEATURES OF BEHAVIORAL FAMILY INTERVENTION

Several features of BFI distinguish it from other approaches to family intervention. These features can enhance the reach, acceptability, flexibility, and usefulness of programs. Table 1.1 presents the principles of effective parenting skills programs that optimize the effectiveness of BFI work. Overall, BFI has developed into a sophisticated multilevel intervention strategy that draws on social learning theory, applied behavior analysis, research on child development and developmental psychopathology, social information-processing models, and public health principles. It has many distinguishing features in its flexibility, varied delivery modalities, multidisciplinary approach, and focus on self-regulation and generalization of parenting skills.

METHODS OF ASSESSMENT AND INTERVENTION

ASSESSMENT METHODS

With BFI's commitment to a scientist-practitioner model of service delivery, the evaluation of outcome is an integral part of providing services to families. Consequently, the management of childhood behavior problems begins with a comprehensive assessment, which is essential for determining what intervention is warranted and to allow for the appropriate tailoring of the intervention to the family's individual needs.

A comprehensive assessment of an intervention program should cover the following areas: family demographics, children's behavior and adjustment, parenting skills and competence, personal adjustment of parents, parent-child interaction, participants' satisfaction with the program, participant attendance at sessions, participant dropout, and practitioners' adherence to the program protocol.

The assessment process has four main objectives: (1) to describe the primary concerns and associated features presented by the child; (2) to describe the parent-child, family, and community context within which the child's behavior occurs; (3) to provide a coherent formulation of the presenting problem, its origins, and maintaining factors; and (4) to evaluate whether the intervention program has achieved its objectives or further intervention is indicated.

Behavioral and emotional problems in children must be viewed within a developmental and sociocultural context. Practitioners need to develop an understanding of the nature of the behavioral or emotional problem the child is experiencing and determine whether there is a significant deviation from normal development. A working knowledge of normal development, familiarity with different types of child psychopathology, and experience in working with children and families are important in making such judgments. The extent to which a child's behavior deviates from normal development is based on interview and self-report data, direct observation, and behavioral monitoring. An interview with a child's parents and teacher (where indicated) will normally give the practitioner a clear idea of the primary concerns of significant others. Interviewing the child (for children around 8 years or more) enables the practitioner to gauge the child's view of the problem. Self-report questionnaires provide information about child and family adjustment that can be compared to community norms. Direct observation of the child and of parent-child interaction allows for independent verification of parent and child reports. Behavioral monitoring allows for tracking of behavior over time and helps to verify parents' estimates of the frequency and intensity of the problem behavior. Based on this assessment data, hypotheses can be formulated concerning factors that may explain the onset and/or maintenance of the child's problem behaviors.

The Clinical Interview

The intake interview plays a central role in the assessment and diagnosis of conduct problems. This interview aims to delineate the target problems, their onset, chronicity, and severity, and any associated features. An understanding of the developmental context is critical when conducting interviews with parents and children. The child's developmental stage dictates the range of normal behavior and determines the level and quality of symptoms that are indicative of psychopathology. The child's family environment is also a crucial area of inquiry. The nature of the parent-child interaction, quality of the home environment, and parental psychological well-being have been identified as risk factors in the development and maintenance of conduct problems in children. In light of the large number of families who experience transitions such as remarriage and divorce and the complex structure of many households, care should be taken to ensure that these areas are adequately assessed. The clinical interview is also the context within which the therapeutic relationship is established. The manner in which the practitioner conveys understanding and carefully listens to the problems presented by the parents and child will affect how well rapport is established.

Self-Report Measures

The use of reliable self-report measures in the assessment and evaluation of BFI occurs in two phases: prior to commencing a program and immediately following termination. The thorough assessment process includes family background details and measures of child behavior, parenting style and confidence, conflict over parenting, and relationship and personal adjustment. At postintervention, assessment should also include a measure of client satisfaction with the program.

Several useful self-report measures for assessing family functioning are outlined in Table 1.2, and many of these are described in detail in Sanders, Markie-Dadds, and Turner (2001). Other assessment tools may also be appropriate, depending on the availability of resources and current assessment practices. However, it is recommended that, at a minimum, assessment include some measurement of child adjustment, parenting style, conflict over parenting (in two-parent families), and parental adjustment. It is important not to overburden families with assessment tasks. Each

Table 1.2 Commonly used measures of child adjustment, parenting skills, and parental adjustment.

Measure	Description	Scores Produced	Reference
Child Adjustment			
Child Behavior Checklist	A 118-item measure of behavioral and psychopathological symptoms, for children 2–18 years, in parent report, teacher report, and youth self-report forms.	In addition to several subscales, this measure can provide scores for total problem behaviors, externalizing and internalizing problems, and social competence.	Achenbach (1991, 1992)
Child Depression Inventory	A 27-item self-report measure of symptoms of child depression for children 8–17 years.	Total depression score with individual items that examine suicidal ideology.	Kovacs (1981)
Child Manifest Anxiety Scale–Revised	A 37-item self-report measure of child anxiety.	Total anxiety score, with three narrow range factors and a scale to detect possible confound from social desirability.	Reynolds & Richmond (1978)
Coopersmith Self-Esteem Inventory	A 58-item self-report measure of child self-esteem for children 8–16 years.	Total self-esteem, four sub-areas of self-esteem (general, academic, social, home), and a scale to detect possible confound from social desirability.	Coopersmith (1981)
Eyberg Child Behavior Inventory; Sutter-Eyberg Student Behavior Inventory	These are 36-item measures of disruptive child behavior for parents and teachers of children 2–16 years.	(1) Intensity score: frequency of problem behaviors; (2) problem score: number of behaviors that are problems for parents.	Eyberg & Pincus (1999)
Parent Daily Report Checklist	Consists of 34 children problem behaviors that are rated by parents as present or absent over a 7-day period. Suitable for children 2–10 years.	(1) Total problem score: number of behavior problems present; (2) Targeted problem score: number of specific behaviors previously identified by parent as problematic.	Chamberlain & Reid (1987)
Strengths and Difficulties Questionnaire	A 25-item self-report measure of frequency of positive and negative child behaviors for children 3–16 years.	(1) Total difficulties score: number of difficult behaviors; (2) Five scale scores: emotional symptoms, conduct problems, inattention/hyperactivity, peer problems, and prosocial behavior.	Goodman (1997, 1999)
Parenting Skills and Competence			
The Parenting Scale	A 30-item measure of dysfunctional discipline practices in parents of young children.	A total score and three subscales: (1) Laxness (permissive discipline); (2) Overreactivity (displays of anger, meanness, and irritability); (3) Verbosity (overly long verbal reprimands).	Arnold, O'Leary, Wolff, & Acker (1993)

(continued)

Table 1.2   *(Continued)*

Measure	Description	Scores Produced	Reference
Parenting Sense of Competence Scale	A 16-item scale that taps efficacy and satisfaction dimensions of parenting self-esteem.	(1) Efficacy score (competency, problem-solving ability, and capability in parenting role); (2) Satisfaction score (parenting frustration, anxiety, and motivation).	Johnston & Mash (1989)
Parental Adjustment			
Relationship Quality Index	A 6-item measure of marital or relationship quality and satisfaction.	Total score: rating of happiness in relationship.	Norton (1983)
Parent Problem Checklist	A 16-item measure of interparental conflict that examines parents' ability to cooperate and work together as a team in their parenting roles.	Problem score: number of sources of parental disagreement.	Dadds & Powell (1991)
Depression Anxiety Stress Scale	A 42-item measure of three affective dimensions. Yields information on a broad range of symptoms of depression, anxiety, and stress in adults.	Total score and three subscales: Depression score, Anxiety score, Stress score.	Lovibond & Lovibond (1993)

measure needs to be carefully explained and justified to each parent to enhance cooperation with the task.

Observation of Family Interaction

Direct observation of parent-child interaction is used to determine the relationship between the child's problem behavior and the parents' interactional style and specific parenting behaviors. The main goals for conducting a formal observation of family interaction are to (1) assess the form, frequency, duration, and intensity of the identified problem behaviors; (2) identify the immediate antecedents and consequences of the problem behaviors; and (3) assess the broader ecological context of the problem behaviors (e.g., the physical environment, family routines and activities, tasks, noise level, time of day).

Target behaviors may include the concerns that have prompted the referral and other child, parent, or sibling behaviors that are hypothesized to be involved in the problem's maintenance. These should be stated in concrete terms conducive to direct observation (e.g., "shouting in a loud voice when mother is on the telephone," rather than "being rude"). Different behaviors vary greatly in their amenability to direct observation. Oppositional behavior in young children (e.g., crying, noncompliance, aggression) can be readily observed in the family home or clinic, if the setting is arranged appropriately. In the home, such behavior tends to escalate when parents attempt to engage young children in routine activities such as bathing, bedtime, getting ready to go out, and mealtimes (Sanders, Dadds, & Bor, 1989). In clinic settings, oppositional behavior will similarly tend to occur when the parent tries to engage the child in structured teaching tasks or when compliance requests are made (e.g., tidying up toys).

Many problem behaviors, however, cannot be so readily observed. For example, stealing, truancy, and fire setting tend to be secretive and relatively infrequent behaviors. Similarly, anxious or depressed behaviors may not occur in the presence of the practitioner. Where problem behaviors are secretive or very low in frequency, direct observation of natural interactions is less likely to provide useful data, and clinic-based family tasks (such as a family problem-solving discussion) or sole use of self-report may need to be employed.

Selecting an appropriate observation procedure involves deciding on the task to be given to the family members, the means of instructing the family to engage in this task, and the activities of the practitioner throughout the process. Ideally, the procedure is designed to elicit the child's problem behaviors and the associated family interaction patterns (Patterson & Reid, 1984). This needs to be done in a way that best approximates the natural occurrence of these patterns and yet provides sufficient procedural structure to prevent conflict or aggression that may escalate to a level that may be unusually distressing for participants.

With young children, a series of structured parent-child interaction tasks is particularly useful for sampling parent-child interactions. Table 1.3 summarizes several activities where parents interact with children. The observer can make qualitative observations of both parents' and child's behavior as well as use more formal coding procedures such as the Family Observation Schedule (FOS; Sanders, 2000) for coding parent-child interactions in such settings. Where the goal is to sample the immediate antecedents and consequences of child behavior in a short time, such structure is warranted, as it deliberately directs the parent to interact with the child. Where the practitioner is more interested in the natural topography of parent-child interaction, less structure can be useful in providing data on the extent to which

the parent sets up activities for the child, provides ground rules, and gives attention.

As children approach middle childhood, they become far more conscious of an observer's presence and are less likely to engage in open conflict with parents and siblings. With older children (8 years and over), it is more important to provide structured activities or select settings that promote family interaction. Examples of such settings are family mealtimes and family problem-solving discussions in which current issues or concerns are discussed and attempts are made to solve the problem. Problem-solving competence is an important protective factor for a family to avoid conflict. Observation of these interactions provides information about the extent to which family members actively listen to each other's point of view, reach agreement about defining the problem to be discussed, keep to the topic at hand, generate solutions and action strategies, or conversely, interrupt each other, criticize, talk tangentially, and prevent problem solving through vagueness, concreteness and expressions of hopelessness, irritation, and despair. Table 1.3 summarizes the procedure used for holding family problem-solving discussions in a clinic setting as well as other suggested observation tasks.

Behavioral Monitoring
The most obvious purpose of monitoring is to collect data. Where problem behaviors are of low intensity, are secretive, or cannot be directly observed (e.g., cognitions, affective states), self-monitoring may be the only method of data collection available. Monitoring also provides a means of validating data collected by interview, questionnaire measures, or direct observation. In designing a monitoring procedure, three points need to be considered. First, the form must be designed to be simple and easy to complete in a short time. Instructions should be clear and definitions of target behaviors must be specific, simple, and easily

Table 1.3 Sample observation tasks for assessing parent-child interaction.

Task	Details	Target Behavior
Compliance Problems		
Free play	Show the family to a room equipped with age-appropriate toys. Ask parents to engage the child in free play.	*Child:* Independent play, creative or imaginative play, sustained attention, appropriate exploration of the environment, manipulation of objects and materials in a purposeful goal-directed manner, responsiveness to adult attention, spontaneous use of language and other communicative gestures. *Parents:* Extent of interaction with the child, prompting play, suggesting activities, use of praise and encouragement, response to child initiations (e.g., questions, requests for assistance).
Structured task	Ask parents and child to complete a jigsaw puzzle or some other goal-directed activity appropriate to the child's developmental level.	*Child:* Responses to parental instructions (e.g., complaining, ignoring, complying). *Parents:* Use of instructions and prompts, praise and encouragement, incidental teaching.
Tidying up	Ask parents to supervise the tidying up of the toys.	*Child:* Compliance with parental instructions, cooperation, associate affect, latency of compliance after instruction given. *Parents:* Use of instructions, praise and encouragement, response to noncompliance.
Feeding Problems		
Mealtime interaction	Ask parents to provide the child with an age-appropriate, nutritionally adequate meal (preferably with all family members who would usually be present for the meal) and get the child to eat the meal provided.	*Child:* Food refusal and disruptive mealtime behavior. *Parents:* Use of instructions, prompts, physical guidance, and attention in an effort to get the child to eat.
School Work		
Homework completion	Ask parents to get the child to bring in a typical homework task or activity with which the child has difficulty.	*Child:* Attempts to complete homework tasks, requests for help from parents, sustained attention, fidgeting, off-task behavior. *Parents:* Explanation of task, provision of attention or help, use of incidental teaching.
Peer or Sibling Relationship Difficulties		
Play with a friend or sibling	Ask parents to invite a sibling or friend to a special play session (with the consent of the other child's parents, if not a sibling).	*Child:* Sharing, turn taking, appropriate waiting, parallel play, social skills. *Parents:* Discussion of ground rules, modeling of appropriate turn taking or other social skills.

Table 1.3 *(Continued)*

Task	Details	Target Behavior
Family Discussion		
Planning a family activity	Ask the family to select and then plan in detail a pleasant family activity that will involve all family members.	*Child:* Contribution to the discussion, appropriate expression of ideas or point of view, response to difference of opinion with parents or other family members.
		Parents: How the parents involve the child, response to the child's expression of ideas, acknowledgment of the child's contribution, use of praise and encouragement, management of turn taking.
Conflict Management		
Family problem-solving discussion	Ask both child and parents to nominate a topic or issue that is a current source of conflict or tension and ask them to discuss the issue and come up with a solution.	*Child:* Responses (both verbal and nonverbal) to parents' statement of the problem and attempts to solve the problem, participation, withdrawal, appearance (e.g., angry, sad, anxious), contribution of useful ideas or suggestions.
		Parents: Responses (both verbal and nonverbal) to the child's statement of the problem and attempts to solve the problem, invitations for the child to participate, use of problem-solving skills such as clearly defining the problem, generating possible solutions, appearance (e.g., angry, sad, anxious), use of criticism, staying on the topic, contribution of useful ideas or suggestions.

Source: From *Practitioner's Manual for Standard Triple P* (pp. 53–54), by M. R. Sanders, C. Markie-Dadds, and K. M. T. Turner, 2001, Brisbane, Australia: Families International Publishing. Copyright 2001 by the authors and The University of Queensland. Reprinted with permission.

observable. Second, the procedure for completing the form must be designed with the ongoing activities of the person in mind; for example, a teacher cannot stop every two minutes in class to fill out a form; a parent with young children cannot be expected to cease all activity for a few minutes during the busy time before dinner each night. Adherence to monitoring can be increased by ensuring that times set down for completion of the form concur with naturally occurring breaks in the person's ongoing activities (e.g., after completing a task or chore). Finally, the choice of time sampling units is crucial to the application of the previous two points.

A range of observation strategies is available and should be selected according to the nature of the problem behavior. Each monitoring instrument has its advantages and limitations. However, practical constraints often mean reaching a compromise between selecting a measure that might be ideal and selecting one that a parent can use consistently throughout the assessment and treatment phase. A number of useful observation strategies are outlined below:

1. *Episodic Record.* A behavior diary involves writing a description of the problem behavior, when and where it occurred, what happened before the problem behavior, and

what happened afterward. This type of monitoring helps to clarify the antecedents and consequences of a problem behavior (e.g., tantrums, hitting, swearing).

2. *Event Record.* Each occurrence of a behavior is recorded in a frequency tally. This form is most useful for behaviors that are low frequency and have a clear beginning and end (e.g., out of seat in classroom, pants soiling, smoking cigarettes).

3. *Duration Record.* This form tracks how long a behavior lasts in hours, minutes, or seconds. This is useful when the primary concern is the duration of the behavior (e.g., crying after being put to bed, screaming in time-out, time to complete a task) rather than frequency of its occurrence.

4. *Permanent Product.* This involves recording the specific outcome of a behavior or series of behaviors (e.g., number of exams passed, windows broken, chores completed, beds wet) over a defined time period.

5. *Momentary Time Sample.* This form of time sampling records the occurrence of a behavior if it is occurring at the moment a given time interval ends. It is useful for long-duration or high-frequency behaviors (e.g., rocking or self-stimulatory behavior, thumb sucking, on-task behavior in the classroom).

6. *Partial Interval Time Sampling.* This method is used to record the presence or absence of a behavior if it occurs once or more in a specified time interval. It is most appropriate for high-frequency behaviors and behaviors that do not have a clear beginning or end or that come and go quickly over a short time (e,g., crying, noncompliance, whining, arguing, answering back).

Functional Assessment of Problem Behavior
The type of functional assessment advocated in the Triple P-Positive Parenting Program system of intervention draws on the conceptual model developed by Kanfer and Saslow (1969). On the

basis of data collected, each relevant family member's behaviors can be classified in terms of excesses, deficits, and assets. Excesses are behaviors that occur at such high frequency, intensity, or duration that they are problematic in the setting in which they occur. In contrast, deficits are behaviors that occur at such low frequency, intensity, or duration that they are problematic. Assets are behaviors that are developmentally and socially appropriate and constructive. Once a comprehensive classification of problem behaviors has been generated, the list can be prioritized for intervention. Subsequently, for each problem behavior, a functional analysis can be used to analyze patterns of antecedents and consequent events that serve to maintain problem behavior. Refer to Sanders (2000) for more information on integrating assessment information and conducting a functional analysis to guide the development of intervention plans.

INTERVENTION METHODS

The Triple P-Positive Parenting Program is a unique example of a contemporary multilevel model of BFI that aims to prevent severe behavioral, emotional, and developmental problems in children by enhancing the knowledge, skills, and confidence of parents. It incorporates five levels of intervention on a tiered continuum of increasing strength (see Table 1.4) for parents of preadolescent children from birth to 12 years. Level 1, a universal parent information strategy, provides all interested parents with access to useful information about parenting through a coordinated media and promotional campaign using print and electronic media, as well as user-friendly parenting tip sheets and videotapes that demonstrate specific parenting strategies. This level of intervention aims to increase community awareness of parenting resources and receptivity of parents to participating in parenting programs, and to create a

Table 1.4　The Triple P model of parenting and family support.

Level of Intervention	Target Population	Intervention Methods	Program Resources	Possible Target Areas
1. *Universal Triple P:* Media-based parenting information campaign	All parents interested in information about parenting and promoting their child's development.	A coordinated information campaign using print and electronic media and other health promotion strategies to promote awareness of parenting issues and normalize participation in parenting programs such as Triple P. May include some contact with professional staff (e.g., telephone information line).	• *Triple P: A Guide to the System* • Media and promotions kit (including promotional poster, flyer, brochure, radio announcements, newspaper columns) • *Every Parent: A Positive Approach to Children's Behavior*	• General parenting issues • Common, everyday behavioral and developmental issues
2. *Selected Triple P:* Information and advice for a specific parenting concern	Parents with specific concerns about their child's behavior or development.	Provision of specific advice on how to solve common child developmental issues and minor child behavior problems. May involve face-to-face or telephone contact with a practitioner (about 20 minutes over two sessions) or seminars (60–90 minutes).	• Level 1 materials • *Positive Parenting* booklet • *Triple P Tip Sheet Series* • *Every Parent Video Series* • *Triple P Video Series* • *Five Steps to Positive Parenting* wall chart	• Common behavior difficulties or developmental transitions, such as toilet training, bedtime problems
3. *Primary Care Triple P:* Narrow focus parenting skills training	Parents with specific concerns about their child's behavior or development who require consultations or active skills training.	A brief program (about 80 minutes over four sessions) combining advice with rehearsal and self-evaluation as required to teach parents to manage a discrete child problem behavior. May involve face-to-face or telephone contact with a practitioner.	• Level 2 materials • *Practitioner's Manual for Primary Care Triple P* • *Consultation Flip Chart for Primary Care Triple P*	• Discrete child behavior problems, such as tantrums, whining, fighting with siblings
4. *Standard Triple P, Group Triple P, Self-Directed Triple P:* Broad focus parenting skills training	Parents wanting intensive training in positive parenting skills. Typically targets parents of children with more severe behavior problems.	A broad focus program (about 10 hours over 8–10 sessions) for parents requiring intensive training in positive parenting skills and generalization enhancement strategies. Application of parenting skills to a broad range of target behaviors, settings, and children. Program variants include individual, group, and self-directed (with or without telephone assistance) options.	• Level 1 to 3 materials • *Practitioner's Manual for Standard Triple P* and *Every Parent's Family Workbook* • *Facilitator's Manual for Group Triple P* and *Every Parent's Group Workbook* • *Every Parent's Self-Help Workbook*	• Multiple child behavior problems • Aggressive behavior • Oppositional Defiant Disorder • Conduct Disorder • Learning difficulties

(continued)

Table 1.4   *(Continued)*

Level of Intervention	Target Popularion	Intervention Methods	Program Resources	Possible Target Areas
5. *Enhanced Triple P:* Behavioral family intervention	Parents of children with concurrent child behavior problems and family dysfunction.	An intensive, individually tailored program (up to 11, 60–90-minute sessions) for families with child behavior problems and family dysfunction. Program modules include practice sessions to enhance parenting skills, mood management strategies and stress coping skills, and partner support skills.	• Level 1 to 4 materials • *Practitioner's Manual for Enhanced Triple P* and *Every Parent's Supplementary Workbook*	• Concurrent child behavior problems and parent problems (e.g., relationship conflict, depression, stress)

Source: From *Practitioner's Manual for Standard Triple P* (p. 4), by M. R. Sanders, C. Markie-Dadds, and K. M. T. Turner, 2001, Brisbane, Australia: Families International Publishing. Copyright 2001 by the authors and The University of Queensland. Reprinted with permission.

sense of optimism by depicting solutions to common behavioral and developmental concerns. Level 2 is a brief, one- to two-session primary health care intervention providing early anticipatory developmental guidance to parents of children with mild behavior difficulties. Level 3, a four-session intervention, targets children with mild to moderate behavior difficulties and includes active skills training for parents. Level 4 is an intensive 10-session individual or 8-session group training program for parents of children with more severe behavioral difficulties. Level 5 is an enhanced BFI program for families where parenting difficulties are complicated by other sources of family distress (e.g., relationship conflict, parental depression, or high levels of stress).

Triple P teaches parents strategies to encourage their child's social and language skills, emotional self-regulation, independence, and problem-solving ability. These skills are listed in Table 1.5. Attainment of these skills promotes family harmony, reduces parent-child conflict, fosters successful peer relationships, and prepares children for the commencement of school.

Parents are taught a variety of child management skills, including monitoring problem behavior, providing brief contingent attention following appropriate behavior; arranging engaging activities in high-risk parenting situations; using directed discussion and planned ignoring for minor problem behavior; giving clear, calm instructions; and backing up instructions with logical consequences, quiet time (nonexclusionary time-out), and time-out. Parents learn to apply these skills both at home and in the community. Specific strategies such as planned activities training are used to promote the generalization and maintenance of parenting skills across settings and over time. Table 1.6 summarizes some of the specific parenting skills introduced in Triple P.

Triple P interventions combine the provision of information with active skills training and support. Active skills training methods include modeling, rehearsal, feedback, and homework tasks. Segments from the *Every Parent's Survival Guide* video (Sanders, Markie-Dadds, & Turner, 1996) can be used to demonstrate positive parenting skills. Several generalization enhancement strategies are incorporated (e.g., training with sufficient exemplars until parents can generalize skills to an untrained situation, and training loosely with varied target behaviors and children) to promote the transfer of parenting skills across settings, siblings, and time. Practice

Table 1.5   Child skills promoted through Triple P.

Social and Language Skills	• Expressing views, ideas, and needs appropriately. • Requesting assistance or help when needed. • Cooperating with adult requests. • Playing cooperatively with others. • Being aware of the feelings of others. • Being aware of how one's own actions affect others.
Emotional Skills	• Expressing feelings in ways that do not harm others. • Controlling aggression and impulsiveness. • Developing positive feelings about oneself and others. • Accepting rules and limits.
Independence Skills	• Learning to do things for oneself. • Keeping busy without constant adult attention. • Being responsible for one's own actions.
Problem-Solving Skills	• Showing an interest and curiosity in everyday things. • Asking questions and developing ideas. • Considering alternative solutions. • Negotiating and compromising. • Making decisions and solving problems.

Source: From *Practitioner's Manual for Standard Triple P* (p. 7), by M. R. Sanders, C. Markie-Dadds, and K. M. T. Turner, 2001, Brisbane, Australia: Families International Publishing. Copyright 2001 by the authors and The University of Queensland. Reprinted with permission.

sessions can be conducted at home or in the clinic, during which parents self-select goals to practice, are observed interacting with their child and implementing parenting skills, and subsequently review their performance and receive feedback from the practitioner. For families with additional risk factors, intervention can be expanded to include a focus on marital communication, partner support, mood management, and stress coping skills for parents.

MAJOR SYMPTOMS AND PROBLEMS TREATED

BFI has been most commonly employed as a treatment for conduct problems in children with Oppositional Defiant Disorder, Conduct Disorder, or Attention-Deficit/Hyperactivity Disorder (ADHD). However, BFI has also been used to manage depression, anxiety, pain, sleep and habit disorders, and academic learning problems (see Sanders, 1996 for a review).

BFI methods have also been used successfully with children with somatic complaints or physical illnesses that may or may not have an organic basis. These children typically present to pediatric settings, and intervention is often multidisciplinary. BFI has shown promise as part of a child's intervention for recurrent abdominal pain (Sanders, Shepherd, Cleghorn, & Woolford, 1994), persistent feeding difficulties (Turner, Sanders, & Wall, 1994), sleep disturbance (France & Hudson, 1990), and chronic illness (Stark, Bowen, Tyc, Evans, & Passero, 1990).

CASE EXAMPLE

PRESENTING PROBLEM

Andrew was referred by his mother due to her inability to manage his behavior and following reports from his preschool that he would have to leave if his behavior did not improve. Andrew was the 5-year-old son of Paula and Mark, a professional couple, and had two younger siblings, Cassie and Morgan. Paula presented in a highly distressed state with her partner. Paula talked about a number of Andrew's problem behaviors, the most troublesome of which were

Table 1.6 Parenting skills promoted through Triple P.

Strategy	Description	Recommended Age	Applications
Developing Positive Relationships			
Spending quality time with children	Spending frequent, brief amounts of time (as little as 1 or 2 minutes) involved in child-preferred activities.	All ages	Opportunities for children to self-disclose and practice conversational skills.
Talking to children	Having brief conversations with children about an activity or interest of the child.	All ages	Promoting vocabulary, conversational, and social skills.
Showing affection	Providing physical affection (e.g., hugging, touching, cuddling, tickling, patting).	All ages	Opportunities for children to become comfortable with intimacy and physical affection.
Encouraging Desirable Behavior			
Using descriptive praise	Providing encouragement and approval by describing the behavior that is appreciated.	All ages	Encouraging appropriate behavior (e.g., speaking in a pleasant voice, playing cooperatively, sharing, drawing pictures, reading, cooperating).
Giving attention	Providing positive nonverbal attention (e.g., a smile, wink, pat on the back, watching).	All ages	As above.
Providing engaging activities	Arranging the child's physical and social environment to provide interesting and engaging activities, materials, and age-appropriate toys (e.g., board games, paints, tapes, books, construction toys).	All ages	Encouraging independent play and promoting appropriate behavior when in the community (e.g., shopping, traveling).
Teaching New Skills and Behaviors			
Setting a good example	Demonstrating desirable behavior through parental modeling.	All ages	Showing children how to behave appropriately (e.g., speak calmly, wash hands, tidy up, solve problems).
Using incidental teaching	Using a series of questions and prompts to respond to child-initiated interactions and to promote learning.	1 to 12 years	Promoting language, problem solving, cognitive ability, and independent play.
Using Ask, Say, Do	Using verbal, gestural, and manual prompts to teach new skills.	3 to 12 years	Teaching self-care skills (e.g., brushing teeth, making bed) and other new skills (e.g., cooking, using tools).
Using behavior charts	Setting up a chart and providing social attention and back-up rewards contingent on the absence of a problem behavior or the presence of an appropriate behavior.	2 to 12 years	Encouraging children for appropriate behavior (e.g., doing homework, playing cooperatively, asking nicely) and for the absence of problem behavior (e.g., swearing, lying, stealing, tantrums).

Table 1.6 *(Continued)*

Strategy	Description	Recommended Age	Applications
Managing Misbehavior			
Establishing ground rules	Negotiating in advance a set of fair, specific, and enforceable rules.	3 to 12 years	Clarifying expectations (e.g., for watching TV, shopping trips, visiting relatives, going out in the car).
Using directed discussion for rule breaking	The identification and rehearsal of the correct behavior following rule breaking.	3 to 12 years	Correcting occasional rule breaking (e.g., leaving school bag on the kitchen floor, running through the house).
Using planned ignoring for minor problem behavior	The withdrawal of attention while the problem behavior continues.	1 to 7 years	Ignoring attention seeking behavior (e.g., answering back, protesting after a consequence, whining, making faces).
Giving clear, calm instructions	Giving a specific instruction to start a new task or to stop a problem behavior and start an appropriate alternative behavior.	2 to 12 years	Initiating an activity (e.g., getting ready to go out, coming to the dinner table) or terminating a problem behavior (e.g., fighting over toys, pulling hair) and saying what to do instead (e.g., share, keep your hands to yourself).
Backing up instructions with logical consequences	Using a specific consequence that involves removing an activity or privilege from the child or the child from an activity for a set time.	2 to 12 years	Dealing with disobedience and mild problem behaviors that do not occur often (e.g., not taking turns).
Using quiet time for misbehavior	Removing a child from an activity in which a problem has occurred and having the child sit on the edge of the activity for a set time.	18 months to 10 years	Dealing with disobedience and children repeating a problem behavior after a logical consequence.
Using time-out for serious misbehavior	Taking a child to an area away from others for a set time when problem behavior occurs.	2 to 10 years	Dealing with temper outbursts, serious misbehavior (e.g., hurting others), and children not sitting quietly in quiet time.

Source: From *Practitioner's Manual for Standard Triple P* (pp. 10–11), by M. R. Sanders, C. Markie-Dadds, and K. M. T. Turner, 2001, Brisbane, Australia: Families International Publishing. Copyright 2001 by the authors and The University of Queensland. Reprinted with permission.

his defiance, physical aggression (hitting), throwing tantrums (crying, screaming, yelling, stamping feet, and rolling around on the floor), swearing and name calling, and an inability to play independently and concentrate on activities. Paula reported that she was feeling tired and irritable and felt she could no longer cope with Andrew's behavior. On weekends, Mark would spend a lot of time with Andrew doing things he enjoyed, such as bike riding, playing ball games, and swimming. During these activities, aggressiveness and tantrums would occur when Andrew did not get his own way or when he did not win the game. Paula and Mark reported that they were happy in their relationship but disagreed about how they should deal with Andrew's behavior. Paula reported a tendency to reason and debate misbehavior with Andrew, whereas Mark was more likely to shout and smack when problem behavior occurred.

INITIAL ASSESSMENT

Assessment involved an interview with both parents, a clinic-based observation of structured activities with Andrew and both parents, a telephone conversation with Andrew's preschool teacher, and parental completion of a number of self-report and monitoring forms.

Self-Report Measures
According to both parents, Andrew's disruptive behavior fell within the clinical range on the Eyberg Child Behavior Inventory. On the Parenting Scale, Paula had elevated scores on the Laxness and Verbosity subscales, and Mark had an elevated score on the Overreactivity subscale. Although both parents reported that they were happy in their couple relationship, their scores on the Parent Problem Checklist were within the clinical range, indicating conflict over parenting issues. Paula also had an elevated score on the Depression subscale on the Depression Anxiety Stress Scale. The remaining data from these self-report measures were within the nonclinical range.

Date	Behavior	How often did it occur?	Total
5/19	Tantrums	► ► ► ►	4
	Disobedience	► ► ► ► ► ►	6
5/20	Tantrums	► ► ►	3
	Disobedience	► ► ► ► ► ► ►	8
5/21	Tantrums	► ► ► ►	4
	Disobedience	► ► ► ► ► ►	6
5/22	Tantrums	► ►	2
	Disobedience	► ►	2
5/23	Tantrums		0
	Disobedience	► ►	2
5/24	Tantrums	► ► ► ►	4
	Disobedience	► ► ► ► ►	5
5/25	Tantrums	► ► ►	3
	Disobedience	► ► ► ► ► ►	6

Figure 1.1   Frequency tally completed by mother.

Behavioral Monitoring

Following the initial interview, Paula kept a record of temper outbursts and episodes of defiance using the monitoring forms in Figure 1.1. Mark maintained a record of hitting and swearing between 4:30 and 7:30 each evening (see Figure 1.2). The parents were asked not to change anything during this time but to simply become more observant about how Andrew behaved when he was being difficult, and what their reaction was to his behavior.

Observation

At the second appointment, the parents and Andrew were observed doing some puzzles together and a tidying-up task. These tasks were chosen to assess Andrew's responses to parental instructions and the parents' use of instructions, prompts, praise and encouragement, and incidental teaching and their response to noncompliance.

Interview with Preschool Teacher

In a 10-minute telephone interview, the teacher reported that Andrew did not get on well with the other children at school. He disrupted the activities of others and used aggression to get his own way. The teacher was also concerned about his defiance. She reported that he became frustrated with activities quickly and reacted with aggressive and destructive behavior when he experienced difficulties. For example, he threw a pair of scissors across the room when he was unable to complete a cutting-out activity.

Date	Behavior	How often did it occur?	Total
5/19	Hitting	► ►	2
	Swearing	►	1
5/20	Hitting	► ► ►	3
	Swearing	►	1
5/21	Hitting	► ► ►	3
	Swearing	► ►	2
5/22	Hitting	►	1
	Swearing	►	1
5/23	Hitting	►	1
	Swearing		0
5/24	Hitting	► ► ►	3
	Swearing	► ► ►	3
5/25	Hitting	► ►	2
	Swearing	► ►	2

Figure 1.2 Frequency tally completed by father.

FUNCTIONAL ASSESSMENT

Table 1.7 shows a classification of each family member's behavior. For Andrew, the behaviors conform closely to his parents' description, with the notable addition of whining. This behavior is common in children with oppositional behavior and is often the first step in an escalation into aggression and tantrums. However, parents often fail to report it as a problem, perhaps having habituated to its occurrence and not realizing its role in the problem.

For the mother, excesses centered around use of vague instructions, the most common form being to simply repeat her son's name over and over in increasingly aggressive tones.

In response to Andrew's problem behavior, Paula tended to either use overly lengthy reprimands or to simply ignore it. There was a deficit in providing positive attention for appropriate child behavior.

For Mark, excesses included shouting and smacking Andrew when tantrums and aggression occurred. He gave little praise for appropriate behavior and would often undermine Paula's attempts to discipline Andrew by intervening with a smack.

On the basis of these data, Andrew was diagnosed as having an Oppositional Defiant Disorder (American Psychiatric Association, 1994) in the context of maternal depression and couple conflict over parenting issues.

Table 1.7 Behavioral classificaton for each family member.

Andrew	Mother	Father
Excesses		
Tantrums: crying, screaming, yelling, stamping feet, rolling around on the floor.	Lengthy reprimands (reasoning/debating).	Shouting and smacking.
Definance.	Ignoring Andrew's misbehavior.	Undermining mother's attempts to discipline (e.g., intervening with a smack).
Physical aggression: hitting.	Vague instructions (e.g., "Andrew!").	
Swearing.		
Name calling.		
Whining.		
Deficits		
Independent play and activities.	Positive attending to Andrew's appropriate behavior.	Praise for appropriate behavior.
Concentration.	Disagreement with partner about how to deal with Andrew's behavior.	Disagreement with partner about how to deal with Andrew's behavior.
Assets		
Normal intelligence.	Happiness in relationship with partner.	Happiness in relationship with partner.
Physically coordinated in accordance with age and stage of development.	Normal intelligence.	Normal intelligence.
Affectionate to parents.		

DISCUSSION OF ASSESSMENT RESULTS

Following completion of the observational task, a discussion of the assessment results was held. Paula and Mark were provided with feedback on the assessment results from the interview, self-report forms, observational task, and monitoring forms. With the practitioner, the parents then formulated factors contributing to Andrew's behavior. Possible causal factors identified in this discussion included genetic factors, family factors, and community factors. Both parents recalled that Andrew probably had a difficult temperament, as evidenced by the difficulties they had experienced with him from early on. In terms of causal factors that are modifiable, the following factors from within the family environment were identified: (1) accidental rewards for misbehavior; (2) coercive escalation cycles; (3) modeling of inappropriate behavior (e.g., yelling, smacking by Mark); (4) poor instruction giving; (5) inconsistent responses to discipline between partners; and (6) lack of attention for appropriate prosocial child behavior. Conflict between the parents over child-rearing practices and Paula's depressed affect were also noted as causal factors.

GOALS FOR INTERVENTION

As a result of the discussion of assessment findings, the parents set the following goals for change in Andrew's behavior: more cooperation with instructions, more independent play, fewer tantrums, and less swearing, hitting, and kicking. Further, the data indicated that these behaviors were interrelated, occurring in a cluster. Paula noted that she would like to give more attention for appropriate behavior and clear specific instructions, backed up with consequences; similarly, Mark wished to give more calm instructions, back-up consequences, and attention for appropriate behavior. The parents

noted that they also needed to develop a shared parenting plan to promote consistency between themselves as parents. The conflict between partners over parenting and Paula's depressed affect were openly discussed with the parents, and they agreed to target partner support and maternal depression for change. However, the first priority was to target change in parent-child interactions and then follow up with a focus on the couple relationship and mother's adjustment if required.

INTERVENTION PROGRAM

Paula and Mark completed a Standard Triple P intervention in eight 60-minute sessions. In the first two sessions, the parents were taught the 17 child management strategies presented in Table 1.6. Ten of the strategies are designed to promote children's competence and development (e.g., quality time, praise, incidental teaching, behavior charts), and seven strategies are designed to help parents manage misbehavior (e.g., clear direct instructions, logical consequences, quiet time, time-out). The next three sessions were completed in the family's home. Paula and Mark were observed implementing the parenting skills with Andrew and received feedback from the practitioner on their strengths and weaknesses. Planned activities training was completed in Sessions 7 to 9. In this section, Paula and Mark were taught a 6-step planned activities routine to enhance the generalization and maintenance of parenting skills (i.e., plan ahead, decide on rules, select engaging activities, decide on rewards and consequences, and hold a follow-up discussion with child). Overall, Paula and Mark were taught to apply parenting skills to a broad range of target behaviors in both home and community settings with Andrew and his siblings. Following this, the parents completed two further sessions, focusing on partner support issues and backing up one another's attempts to discipline. Issues of maintenance and closure were covered in Session 12. Throughout the program, the parents completed exercises in their workbook, *Every Parent's Family Workbook* (Markie-Dadds, Sanders, & Turner, 2000), and learned to set and monitor their own goals for behavior change and enhance their skills in observing their children's and their own behavior.

FOLLOW-UP ASSESSMENT

Monitoring and questionnaires were administered at the end of the intervention program and again six months later. By the end of the program and at follow-up, Andrew's behavior was within normal limits. According to the questionnaire measures, Paula and Mark used less coercive discipline strategies and had high levels of self-efficacy in parenting. There was less conflict over parenting issues and the couple were highly satisfied in their relationship. Although the program had not specifically targeted Paula's depression, Paula reported that she felt happy and content in her life, and this was reflected in the self-report questionnaire. The depressed affect lifted once Andrew's behavior had improved and the parents had a shared parenting plan. Both Paula and Mark expressed satisfaction with the program and its outcome.

SUMMARY

The positive response to BFI suggests that even when numerous risk factors are evident (e.g., child behavior, parenting conflict, maternal depression), improvements in parenting style result not only in reduced disruptive behavior problems of children but also in improved aspects of the family system, such as maternal adjustment. In this case, there was no need to directly address the mother's depression to alleviate her distress; Paula's depression was alleviated through improved parenting practices and development of a shared parenting plan.

RESEARCH EVALUATING EFFICACY AND EFFECTIVENESS

BFI has had a major influence in the field of child psychopathology and has become a dominant paradigm in the treatment of many childhood disorders (Lochman, 1990; Sanders, 1996; Taylor & Biglan, 1998). There have been several recent comprehensive reviews that have documented the efficacy of BFI as an approach to helping children and their families (Lochman, 1990; McMahon, 1999; Sanders, 1996, 1998; Taylor & Biglan, 1998). There is clear evidence that BFI can benefit many children with disruptive behavior disorders, particularly children with Oppositional Defiant Disorder, and their parents (Forehand & Long, 1988; Webster-Stratton, 1994). The empirical basis of BFI is strengthened by evidence that the approach can be successfully applied to many other clinical problems and disorders, including ADHD (Barkley, Guevremont, Anastopoulos, & Fletcher, 1992), persistent feeding difficulties (Turner et al., 1994), pain syndromes (Sanders et al., 1994), anxiety disorders (Barrett, Dadds, & Rapee, 1996), autism and developmental disabilities (Schreibman, Kaneko, & Koegel, 1991), achievement problems, habit disorders, and everyday problems of normal children (see Sanders, 1996; Taylor & Biglan, 1998, for reviews of this literature). Good maintenance of treatment gains and the generalization of treatment effects to school and community settings have been demonstrated (Forehand & Long, 1988; Sanders & Glynn, 1981). Parents participating in these programs are generally satisfied consumers. However, the treatment is not a panacea, and in some studies, 30 to 50% of children after intervention have remained clinically disturbed on measures of child adjustment (Patterson, Dishion, & Chamberlain, 1993).

SUMMARY

BFI has its historical routes firmly grounded in social learning approaches to family problems (e.g., Patterson, 1982). This skills training approach to the treatment and prevention of a range of childhood disorders has the strongest empirical support of any intervention with children (see Kazdin, 1995; Sanders, 1996; Webster-Stratton & Hammond, 1997). Triple P is an example of a contemporary model of BFI. Triple P is a coordinated, multilevel prevention/early intervention strategy that draws on social learning theory, applied behavior analysis, research on child development and developmental psychopathology, social information-processing models, and public health principles. It has many distinguishing features in its flexibility, varied delivery modalities, multidisciplinary approach, and focus on self-regulation and generalization of parenting skills across all levels of intervention.

Besides being theoretically and empirically grounded, BFI has developed extensive assessment and intervention protocols. From a BFI perspective, the management of child behavior problems begins with a comprehensive assessment, which is essential for determining whether a parenting intervention is warranted and allows for the appropriate tailoring of the intervention to the family's individual needs. This chapter provided a description of the primary areas of assessment and the techniques used to determine the nature of the presenting problem in its developmental, family, and broader social and cultural context. Subsequently, intervention involves the teaching of positive family interaction and child management skills via the provision of verbal, video, and written information and modeling. Typically, intervention is conducted in clinic and home environments to promote the generalization and maintenance of skills across behaviors, settings, siblings, and time.

A current challenge facing the field of BFI involves the development of empirically derived decision rules for determining which families require differing strengths of intervention. At present, the empirical literature cannot clearly elucidate what these rules should be; this area would be fruitful for further investigation.

REFERENCES

Achenbach, T. M. (1991). *Manual for the child behavior checklist/4–18 and 1991 profile.* Burlington: University of Vermont Department of Psychiatry.

Achenbach, T. M. (1992). *Manual for the child behavior checklist/2–3 and 1992 profile.* Burlington: University of Vermont Department of Psychiatry.

American Psychiatric Association. (1994). *Diagnostic and statistical manual for mental disorders* (4th ed.). Washington, DC: Author.

Arnold, D. S., O'Leary, S. G., Wolff, L. S., & Acker, M. M. (1993). The Parenting Scale: A measure of dysfunctional parenting in discipline situations. *Psychological Assessment, 5,* 137–144.

Baer, D. M., Wolf, M. M., & Risley, T. D. (1968). Some current dimensions of applied behavior analysis. *Journal of Applied Behavior Analysis, 1,* 91–97.

Bandura, A. (1977). *Social learning theory.* Englewood Cliffs, NJ: Prentice-Hall.

Bandura, A. (1995). *Self-efficacy in changing societies.* New York: Cambridge University Press.

Barkley, R. A., Guevremont, D. C., Anastopoulos, A. D., & Fletcher, K. E. (1992). A comparison of three family therapy programs for treating family conflicts in adolescents with Attention-Deficit Hyperactivity Disorder. *Journal of Consulting and Clinical Psychology, 60,* 450–462.

Barrett, P. M., Dadds, M. R., & Rapee, R. M. (1996). Family treatment of childhood anxiety: A controlled trial. *Journal of Consulting and Clinical Psychology, 64,* 333–342.

Biglan, A. (1995). Translating what we know about the context of antisocial behavior into a lower prevalence of such behavior. *Journal of Applied Behavior Analysis, 28,* 479–492.

Chamberlain, P., & Patterson, G. R. (1995). Discipline and child compliance in parenting. In M. H. Bornstein (Ed.), *Handbook of parenting: Vol. 4. Applied and practical parenting* (pp. 205–225). Mahwah, NJ: Erlbaum.

Chamberlain, P., & Reid, J. B. (1987). Parent observation and report of child symptoms. *Behavioral Assessment, 9*, 97–109.

Coie, J. D. (1996). Prevention of violence and antisocial behavior. In R. D. Peters & R. J. McMahon (Eds.), *Preventing childhood disorders, substance abuse, and delinquency* (pp. 1–18). Thousand Oaks, CA: Sage.

Coopersmith, S. (1981). *SEI–Self-Esteem Inventories*. Palo Alto, CA: Consulting Psychologists Press.

Cummings, E. M., & Davies, P. T. (1994). Maternal depression and child development. *Journal of Child Psychology and Psychiatry and Allied Disciplines, 35*, 73–112.

Dadds, M. R., & Powell, M. B. (1991). The relationship of interparental conflict and global marital adjustment to aggression, anxiety, and immaturity in aggressive nonclinic children. *Journal of Abnormal Child Psychology, 19*, 553–567.

Dryfoos, J. G. (1990). *Adolescents at risk: Prevalence and prevention*. New York: Oxford University Press.

Emery, R. E. (1982). Interparental conflict and the children of discord and divorce. *Psychological Bulletin, 9*, 310–330.

Eyberg, S. M., & Pincus, D. (1999). *Eyberg Child Behavior Inventory and Sutter-Eyberg Student Behavior Inventory–Revised: Professional manual*. Odessa, FL: Psychological Assessment Resources.

Forehand, R., & Long, N. (1988). Outpatient treatment of the acting out child: Procedures, long term follow-up data, and clinical problems. *Advances in Behavior Research and Therapy, 10*, 129–177.

Forehand, R. L., & McMahon, R. J. (1981). *Helping the non-compliant child: A clinician's guide to parent training*. New York: Guilford Press.

France, K. G., & Hudson, S. M. (1990). Behavior management of infant sleep disturbance. *Journal of Applied Behavior Analysis, 23*, 91–98.

Goodman, R. (1997). The Strengths and Difficulties Questionnaire: A research note. *Journal of Child Psychology and Psychiatry, 38*, 581–586.

Goodman, R. (1999). The extended version of the Strengths and Difficulties Questionnaire as a guide to child psychiatric caseness and consequent burden. *Journal of Child Psychology and Psychiatry 40*(5), 791–799.

Grych, J. H., & Fincham, F. D. (1990). Marital conflict and children's adjustment: A cognitive-contextual framework. *Psychological Bulletin, 108*, 267–290.

Hart, B. M., & Risley, T. R. (1975). Incidental teaching of language in the preschool. *Journal of Applied Behavior Analysis, 8*, 411–420.

Hart, B. M., & Risley, T. R. (1995). *Meaningful differences in the everyday experience of young American children*. Sydney, Australia: Brookes.

Jacobson, N. S., & Margolin, G. (1979). *Marital therapy: Strategies based on social learning and behavior exchange principles*. New York: Brunner/Mazel.

Johnston, C., & Mash, E. J. (1989). A measure of parenting satisfaction and efficacy. *Journal of Clinical Child Psychology, 18*, 167–175.

Kanfer, F. H., & Saslow, G. (1969). Behavioral diagnosis. In C. Franks (Ed.), *Behavior therapy: Appraisal and status* (pp. 417–444). New York: McGraw-Hill.

Karoly, P. (1993). Mechanisms of self-regulation: A systems view. *Annual Review of Psychology, 102*, 23–52.

Kazdin, A. E. (1995). *Conduct disorders in childhood and adolescence*. Thousand Oaks, CA: Sage.

Kovacs, M. (1981). Rating scales to assess depression in school-aged children. *Acta Paedopsychiatrica, 46*, 305–315.

Lochman, J. E. (1990). Modification of childhood aggression. In M. Hersen & P. M. Miller (Eds.), *Progress in behavior modification* (Vol. 25, pp. 47–85). New York: Academic Press.

Loeber, R., & Farrington, D. P. (1998). Never too early, never too late: Risk factors and successful interventions for serious and violent juvenile offenders. *Studies on Crime and Crime Prevention, 7*, 7–30.

Lovibond, S. H., & Lovibond, P. F. (1993). *Manual for the Depression Anxiety Stress Scales* (2nd ed.). Sydney, NSW: Psychology Foundation of Australia

Markie-Dadds, C., Sanders, M. R., & Turner, K. M. T. (2000). *Every parent's family workbook*. Brisbane, Australia: Families International.

McMahon, R. J. (1999). Parent training. In S. W. Russ & T. H. Ollendick (Eds.), *Handbook of psychotherapies with children and families* (pp. 153–180). New York: Kluwer Academic/Plenum Press.

Mrazek, P., & Haggerty, R. J. (1994). *Reducing the risks for mental disorders.* Washington, DC: National Academy Press.

National Institute of Mental Health. (1998). *Priorities for prevention research at NIHM: A report by the National Advisory Mental Health Council Workgroup on mental disorders prevention research* (NIH Publication No. 98–4321). Washington, DC: U.S. Government Printing Office.

Norton, R. (1983). Measuring marital quality: A critical look at the dependent variable. *Journal of Marriage and the Family, 45,* 141–151.

O'Dell, S. (1974). Training parents in behavior modification: A review. *Psychological Bulletin, 81,* 418–433.

Patterson, G. R. (1982). *Coercive family process.* Eugene, OR: Castalia.

Patterson, G. R., Dishion, T. J., & Chamberlain, P. (1993). Outcomes and methodological issues relating to treatment of antisocial children. In T. R. Giles (Ed.), *Handbook of effective psychotherapy: Plenum behavior therapy series* (pp. 43–88). New York: Plenum Press.

Patterson, G. R., & Reid, J. B. (1984). Social interactional processes within the family: The study of the moment-by-moment family transactions in which human social development is imbedded. *Journal of Applied Developmental Psychology, 5,* 237–262.

Patterson, G. R., Reid, J. B., & Dishion, T. J. (1992). *Antisocial boys.* Eugene, OR: Castalia.

Reynolds, C. R., & Richmond, B. O. (1978). What I think and feel: A revised measure of children's manifest anxiety. *Journal of Abnormal Child Psychology, 6,* 271–280.

Risley, T. R., Clark, H. B., & Cataldo, M. F. (1976). Behavioral technology for the normal middle class family. In E. J. Mash, L. A. Hamerlynch, & L. C. Handy (Eds.), *Behavior modification and families* (pp. 34–60). New York: Brunner/Mazel.

Robins, L. N. (1991). Conduct Disorder. *Journal of Child Psychology and Psychiatry and Allied Disciplines, 32,* 193–212.

Rutter, M. (1994). Family discord and Conduct Disorder: Cause, consequence, or correlate? *Journal of Family Psychology, 8,* 170–186.

Sanders, M. R. (1992). *Every parent: A positive guide to children's behavior.* Sydney, Australia: Addison-Wesley.

Sanders, M. R. (Ed.). (1995). *Healthy families, healthy nation: Strategies for promoting family mental health in Australia.* Brisbane, QLD: Australian Academic Press.

Sanders, M. R. (1996). New directions in behavioral family intervention. In T. H. Ollendick & R. J. Prinz (Eds.), *Advances in clinical child psychology* (Vol. 18, pp. 283–330). New York: Plenum Press.

Sanders, M. R. (1998). The empirical status of psychological interventions with families of children and adolescents. In L. L'Abate (Ed.), *Family psychopathology: The relational roots of dysfunctional behavior* (pp. 427–465). New York: Guilford Press.

Sanders, M. R. (1999). Triple P–Positive Parenting Program: Towards an empirically validated multilevel parenting and family support strategy for the prevention of behavior and emotional problems in children. *Clinical Child and Family Psychology Review, 2*(2), 71–90.

Sanders, M. R. (2000). *Family Observation Schedule.* Brisbane, Australia: University of Queensland, Parenting and Family Support Centre.

Sanders, M. R., Dadds, M. R., & Bor, W. (1989). A contextual analysis of oppositional child behavior and maternal aversive behavior in families of conduct disordered children. *Journal of Clinical Child Psychology, 18,* 72–83.

Sanders, M. R., & Duncan, S. B. (1995). Empowering families: Policy, training, and research issues in promoting family mental health in Australia. *Behaviour Change, 12,* 109–121.

Sanders, M. R., & Glynn, E. L. (1981). Training parents in behavioural self management: An analysis of generalization and maintenance effects. *Journal of Applied Behavior Analysis, 14,* 223–237.

Sanders, M. R., Markie-Dadds, C., & Turner, K. M. T. (Producers/Directors). (1996). *Every parent's survival guide* [Videotape and booklet]. Brisbane: Families International Pty Ltd. Also published by the Victorian Department of Human Services and the Health Department of Western Australia.

Sanders, M. R., Markie-Dadds, C., & Turner, K. M. T. (2001). *Practitioner's manual for Standard Triple P.* Brisbane, Australia: Families International.

Sanders, M. R., & McFarland, M. L. (2000). The treatment of depressed mothers with disruptive children: A controlled evaluation of cognitive behavioral family intervention. *Behavior Therapy, 31,* 89–112.

Sanders, M. R., Nicholson, J. M., & Floyd, F. J. (1997). Couples' relationships and children. In W. K. Halford & H. J. Markman (Eds.), *Clinical handbook of marriage and couples intervention* (pp. 225–253). Chichester, England: Wiley.

Sanders, M. R., Shepherd, R. W., Cleghorn, G., & Woolford, H. (1994). The treatment of recurrent abdominal pain in children: A controlled comparison of cognitive-behavioral family intervention and standard pediatric care. *Journal of Consulting and Clinical Psychology, 62,* 306–314.

Schreibman, L., Kaneko, W. M., & Koegel, R. L. (1991). Positive affect of parents of autistic children: A comparison across two teaching techniques. *Behavior Therapy, 22,* 479–490.

Stark, L. J., Bowen, A. M., Tyc, V. L., Evans, S., & Passero, M. A. (1990). A behavioral approach to increasing calorie consumption in children with cystic fibrosis. *Journal of Pediatric Psychology, 15,* 309–326.

Taylor, T. K., & Biglan, A. (1998). Behavioral family interventions for improving child-rearing: A review of the literature for clinicians and policy makers. *Clinical Child and Family Psychology Review, 1,* 41–60.

Turner, K., Sanders, M. R., & Wall, C. (1994). A comparison of behavioral parent training and standard education in the treatment of persistent feeding difficulties in children. *Behavior Change, 11,* 105–111.

Wahler, R. G. (1969). Oppositional children: A quest for parental reinforcement control. *Journal of Applied Behavior Analysis, 2,* 159–170.

Webster-Stratton, C. (1994). Advancing videotape parent training: A comparison study. *Journal of Consulting and Clinical Psychology, 62,* 583–593.

Webster-Stratton, C., & Hammond, M. (1997). Treating children with early-onset conduct problems: A comparison of child and parent training interventions. *Journal of Consulting and Clinical Psychology, 65,* 93–109.

White, B. L. (1990). *The first three years of life.* New York: Prentice-Hall.

Williams, C. D. (1959). The elimination of tantrum behavior by extinction procedures. *Journal of Abnormal and Social Psychology, 59,* 269.

CHAPTER 2

Social Skills and Problem-Solving Training

SHARON L. FOSTER AND MARCELLE M. CRAIN

HISTORY OF SOCIAL SKILLS AND PROBLEM-SOLVING TRAINING

Social skills training and problem-solving training are broad terms used to encompass a variety of approaches designed to help children behave effectively in their social environments. In this chapter, we use the terms more narrowly to describe approaches designed specifically to teach children particular behavioral (social) and cognitive (problem-solving) skills to improve their social functioning with peers.

Although isolated reports of successful attempts to modify children's social behavior appeared as early as the 1940s (e.g., Chittenden, 1942), research on social skills training began to gain momentum in the late 1960s and 1970s (Asher & Renshaw, 1990). Social skills interventions during this period were designed to improve the interactions of children who were socially isolated and withdrawn (e.g., O'Conner, 1969) or who were disliked or rejected by their peers (e.g., Oden & Asher, 1977). Around the same time, Spivak, Platt, and Shure's (1976) landmark book, *The Problem-Solving Approach to Adjustment*, spurred a related line of research examining the effects of teaching children social-cognitive problem-solving skills with the goal of improving adjustment (e.g., Weissberg et al., 1981). Since that time, social skills and problem-solving training approaches have been widely adopted and adapted both as treatment strategies and preventive interventions. Many of these prevention programs have focused in particular on reducing risk for antisocial behavior (e.g., Conduct Problems Prevention Research Group, 1999a, 1999b) and drug use (e.g., Botvin, Baker, Dusenbury, Tortu, & Botvin, 1990).

This expansion of social skills approaches follows logically from literature associating peer relationship difficulties with a variety of clinically relevant behavior problems in children and adolescents. Aggression is perhaps the single strongest correlate of peer rejection (e.g.,

The work of the first author was supported in part by the National Institutes of Health grant number BCS 960 1236 and the Robert Wood Johnson Foundation grant number 034 248.

Newcomb, Bukowski, & Pattee, 1993), and some of the criteria for diagnoses of Conduct Disorder imply difficulties with social interactions (e.g., "bullies, threatens, or intimidates others"; American Psychiatric Association, 1994, p. 90); so do the criteria used to diagnose Oppositional Defiant Disorder ("deliberately annoys people"; p. 94). Peer relationship and social skills problems have also been implicated in Attention Deficit Disorder; children with this diagnosis are more likely than nondiagnosed classmates to be rejected by peers (Erhardt & Hinshaw, 1994; Johnston, Pelham, & Murphy, 1985) and to behave in annoying and socially inappropriate ways, such as talking excessively, interrupting, and failing to pay attention to work and play tasks. Depression in children and adolescents has also been linked to poor interpersonal and problem-solving skills (e.g., Rudolph, Hammen, & Burge, 1994).

THEORETICAL
UNDERPINNINGS

Many social skills training approaches operate from a skills deficit model, which proposes that children handle social situations poorly because they lack the skills to perform in more appropriate ways (Asher & Renshaw, 1990; Bierman & Welsh, 1997). This assumption is buttressed by numerous findings indicating that children who are rejected by peers frequently display lower rates of prosocial behaviors and are more withdrawn than their better-accepted peers (Newcomb et al., 1993). Their aversive repertoire also alienates peers. In particular, rejected children behave in more physically aggressive ways and disrupt others' activities more often than well-accepted peers (Newcomb et al., 1993). They have particular difficulties joining ongoing peer activities (Putallaz & Wasserman, 1989) and managing conflict (Shantz, 1986). These difficulties emerge even when rejected children are

placed in groups of previously unacquainted children, giving them a fresh start without an established reputation (Coie & Kupersmidt, 1983). Rejected children also actively attempt to harm others' relationships by excluding others, conveying negative gossip, and behaving in other relationally aggressive ways (Crick & Grotpeter, 1995). Based on the skills deficit model, one logical intervention to promote more skillful performance is to teach children better skills for handling the situations in which they behave inappropriately.

Why do children behave in socially maladaptive and unskilled ways? Social information-processing theory (Crick & Dodge, 1994), a decision-making and response enactment approach to explaining children's social behavior, offers a particularly comprehensive cognitive model. Crick and Dodge (1994) hypothesize that children's interpersonal responses are the outcome of a series of six cognitive steps that are influenced by both the child's personal history and individual cognitive style. Specifically, children (1) encode external and internal cues; (2) interpret and mentally represent those cues; (3) clarify or select a goal; (4) access or construct potential responses to the situation; (5) decide which response to enact; and (6) behaviorally enact the response. Crick and Dodge suggest that this process follows a cyclical pattern, such that the steps reoccur in response to feedback from ongoing environmental events and that steps can occur simultaneously. They also propose that emotional arousal can have significant impact on functioning at each of the social information-processing steps, although limited research has directly investigated this conjecture.

Crick and Dodge (1994) hypothesize that social information processing can explain both competent and deviant or maladaptive social behaviors, and that aggression in particular is the result of faulty functioning at one or more of the processing steps described above. A great deal of empirical evidence supports this hypothesis with aggression, although fewer studies have examined social information processing in relation to other social skill assets and problems. In response to hypothetical situations, aggressive boys are particularly likely to interpret ambiguous provocations as motivated by hostile intent, whereas their nonaggressive peers are more likely to think that the provocation was an accident (see Crick & Dodge, 1994, for review). When asked how to handle hypothetical problem situations, aggressive and poorly accepted children generate fewer alternative responses than their nonaggressive or better-accepted classmates (Asarnow & Callan, 1985; Slaby & Guerra, 1988). They are less likely to choose appropriate responses (Slaby & Guerra, 1998) and more likely to endorse aggression (Chung & Asher, 1996) when evaluating the possible ways of reacting to problems. Their goals for handling situations fit the aggressive strategies they endorse: Children who report goals relating to controlling others tend to report a higher likelihood of using aggressive strategies for achieving those goals (Chung & Asher, 1996). Consistent with this research, a number of intervention programs have developed methods for building cognitive problem-solving skills as a method of reducing negative behavior and promoting socially adaptive responses.

Emerging research also has examined family influences on social behavior and peer processes, although this research has not yet found its way into the design of interventions specifically aimed at promoting positive peer interactions. In general, positive social adjustment has been linked with more positive maternal communication and warmth and with use of authoritative discipline styles. In contrast, parents of rejected children use the kinds of harsh disciplinary practices that also characterize the families of aggressive children (see Rubin, Bukowski, & Parker, 1998, for review). In addition, parents of young children with good peer relations are more likely than parents of less well-accepted children to arrange opportunities for their children to play with others, to supervise this play unobtrusively, and to coach their children about peer problems (Parker, Rubin, Price, & DeRosier, 1995).

MAJOR PROBLEMS ADDRESSED BY SOCIAL SKILLS AND PROBLEM-SOLVING TRAINING

Given the many problems associated with peer rejection and poor social problem solving, it is not surprising that investigators have developed social skills and problem-solving programs to ameliorate or prevent a range of youth behavior problems. Approaches vary in their scope, specific content, procedures, and intended populations. Many were designed to reduce aggressive behavior and were aimed at populations such as incarcerated adolescents (e.g., Spence & Marzillier, 1981) and children and teens with high rates of antisocial behavior and/or diagnosed with Oppositional Defiant Disorder or Conduct Disorder (e.g., Kazdin, Siegel, & Bass, 1992; Webster-Stratton & Hammond, 1997). Social skills training has also been implemented with children diagnosed with Attention-Deficit/Hyperactivity Disorder (e.g., Pfiffner & McBurnett, 1997). Other types of specialized social skills programs teach skills for handling particular sorts of situations; examples include assertiveness training and anger control training. Finally, many prevention interventions combine social skills or problem-solving training with approaches such as parent training (e.g., Conduct Problems Prevention Group, 1999a), with the goal of preventing aggression, delinquency, or drug abuse. Some prevention programs specifically target high-risk youth; others direct the interventions toward general populations of children or adolescents.

ASSESSMENT AND INTERVENTION METHODS

Social skills assessment can have several goals, and the methods selected to assess the child's social functioning depend in part on the goal of assessment. In particular, mental health professionals can use assessment to (1) screen children to determine whether social skills training is appropriate; (2) characterize the social behavior of a particular child for the purpose of determining the situations and behaviors that should be addressed during intervention; (3) identify presumed determinants of social behavior problems that warrant attention during treatment (e.g., social-cognitive biases, peer group process problems); and (4) monitor the effects of treatment both on the child's skills and on the quality of the child's peer relations, which presumably will improve as a result of improved social skills.

Social skills assessment methods assess three general domains relevant to social functioning: (1) prosocial and maladaptive behavior with peers; (2) problem-solving and social-cognitive skills; and (3) social status (acceptance, rejection) and friendships in their peer group. Identifying a child's social skills and skill deficits clearly requires assessment of the child's behavior with peers. In addition, cognitive interventions hypothesize that social-cognitive variables should be assessed because they presumably undergird children's social performance. Finally, investigators advocate assessing peer acceptance and rejection both because these are important correlates of children's social behavior and because frequently one goal of social skills training is to help children improve their acceptability to peers. This in turn should enable the child to become involved with prosocial friendship networks instead of the more antisocial peers that characterize the networks of rejected and aggressive children. Assessment of acceptance and rejection can provide an important check on the clinical significance or social validity of the results of social skills training by examining whether improved peer relationships accompany behavioral or social-cognitive changes.

ASSESSING SOCIAL BEHAVIOR

Available methods for assessing social behavior include questionnaires completed by teachers or parents, peer nominations and ratings, and observational systems. A small number of self-report questionnaires are also available.

Teacher and Parent Questionnaires

Many teacher report measures assess problem behaviors, but few also include items assessing adaptive behaviors. One exemplary instrument is the Child Behavior Scale, which Ladd and Profilet (1996) developed for 5- and 6-year-olds. The Child Behavior Scale contains six subscales that assess various behaviors in the peer group: aggression, prosocial behavior, asocial behavior, peer exclusion, anxious and fearful behavior, and hyperactive-distractible behavior. Other instruments are relevant to wider age groups. One of several teacher questionnaires with reasonable evidence for the reliability and validity of their scores is the Teacher Rating of Social Skills (Gresham & Elliott, 1990), which contains subscales assessing social skills, problem behaviors, and academic competence. Different forms are available for preschool, elementary school, and secondary school students. Another instrument, the Matson Evaluation of Social Skills with Youngsters (MESSY; Matson, Rotatori, & Helsel, 1983), can be used with children 4 to 18 years; it assesses positive and negative behaviors that load on two factors: appropriate social skills and inappropriate assertiveness/impulsiveness. Other similar teacher report measures that assess social behavior include the Walker-McConnell Scale of Social Competence and School Adjustment (Walker & McConnell, 1988) and the Teacher-Child Rating Scale (Hightower et al., 1986). A teacher report measure with a slightly different focus is the Taxonomy of Problematic Social Situations (Dodge, McClaskey, & Feldman, 1985), which assesses the extent to which elementary school children have difficulty with six social tasks: entering peer groups, responding to provocations, responding to success, conforming to social expectations, responding to failure, and meeting teacher expectations.

Teacher measures have several assets. First, teachers in elementary school typically view children over long periods of time and may therefore be quite familiar with their social interactions in school settings. Second, teachers are often important "consumers" of social skills training in that they refer children for assistance based on classroom or playground difficulties, and therefore their views can provide important indicators of whether treatment makes a noticeable difference in the child's behavior. Third, most teacher measures are relatively convenient and rarely take more than 30 minutes to complete for an individual child.

Teacher measures have limitations as well. First, teacher measures differ widely in how they operationalize social skills; whether they assess behavior with peers, adults, or both; and how well their content mirrors behaviors that are associated with peer acceptance and rejection. Second, correspondence between teacher reports and direct observation of child behavior has rarely been examined, particularly with more widely used teacher measures. Finally, teachers of younger children may have more opportunities to observe their students than teachers of adolescents, who may be less familiar with a child's social functioning because children typically change classes at this stage and interact with others in many situations that are not available to adult observation.

As with teacher measures, many parent measures assess child behavior problems, but few address social skills per se. The exceptions generally involve parent versions of instruments developed for teachers, such as the parent version of the Teacher Rating of Social Skills. The utility of these measures, however, depends on the extent to which parents observe their children's peer interactions. Because much of a child's day is spent in school, teachers or peers may be in a better position than parents to make these observations. However, parents may be useful reporters of the child's peer contacts and activities outside of school (Bierman & Welsh, 1997), which can be assessed using the Social Competence scale of the Child Behavior Checklist (Achenbach, 1991).

Peer Nominations

Peer measures provide an alternative or supplement to teacher measures for assessing social behavior. These typically take the form of peer nominations in which children circle names of those in their class or grade who fit specific behavioral descriptors. The number of nominations a child receives is tallied and then standardized within classrooms, and behavioral items are often grouped into scales based on results of factor analytic studies. For example, the Pupil Evaluation Inventory (Pekarik, Prinz, Liebert, Weintraub, & Neale, 1976) contains 35 items that make up three subscales: Likability, Withdrawal-Ostracism, and Aggression. Children select peers who fit each descriptor. For the Revised Class Play (Masten, Morrison, & Pelligrini, 1985), a similar instrument, children select peers who are best suited to play particular hypothetical roles (e.g., "the bully"). Items are grouped into scales labeled Sociability-Leadership, Aggressive-Disruptive, and Sensitive-Isolated.

Peer nominations have two major advantages. First, peers have many opportunities to interact with and observe their classmates, often in situations in which adults are not present. Second, using nominations or ratings of many peers permits reliable assessment with many fewer items than the number required when only one rater is used.

Peer measures of behavior have disadvantages as well. Many peer nomination schemes require that children nominate a limited number of peers for behavioral descriptors (e.g., "Circle the names of three kids who hit others"). This process requires that children be selected for each descriptor, regardless of their level of performance. This forced selection may result in scores that are not particularly sensitive to behavior change over time. This insensitivity can be overcome by using unlimited nomination procedures in which children can choose as many or as few peers as fit the descriptor, then scoring the percentage who select a child as being characterized by the item. Unlimited nominations have been used less frequently than limited nomination procedures, however.

Another drawback to peer nominations lies in controversies about their use: Teachers and parents may object to asking children to "say bad things" about their peers. This in turn may require that parents of all participating children, not just the target child, provide informed consent for their children to participate in peer assessment—a cumbersome process when a clinician is treating only a single child in a classroom. In addition, peer nominations of behavior may be developmentally inappropriate for very young children such as preschoolers with limited verbal and cognitive skills for differentiating complex behaviors among their peers (Bierman & Welsh, 1997). Finally, whether peer ratings are biased by halo effects (i.e., nominating others for positive or negative items based on overall liking or general impressions) has not been established.

Direct Observations of Behavior

Observational procedures can be applied either in the natural environment or in analog situations. In natural environment observations, trained observers usually record the child's behavior in the classroom or on the playground using specific behavioral codes, often using an interval coding or time-sampling procedure.

Typical observation categories might assess aggression or negative social interaction, positive or prosocial behavior, solitary/unoccupied behavior, and positive or negative initiations to and from peers (Bierman & Welsh, 1997); more fine-grained categories can also be included. In vivo observations have the obvious advantages of being less prone to possible bias than teacher or peer report and therefore of providing a particularly objective index of behavior change. Limitations come from the time, code development, and personnel required to establish reliable observational coding. Considerable observation time may be required to establish stable samples of behaviors that occur infrequently, as is the case with many negative behaviors. In addition, capturing behaviors that occur only in particular situations is difficult unless the observers are present and collecting data during those situations. Finally, observations are often most feasible with young children, and may become increasingly intrusive and potentially reactive as children become older.

One alternative to in vivo observation involves creating analog situations that mirror the types of situations that are problematic for the child or adolescent, then asking the child to role-play his or her typical way of handling the situation. Trained observers code or rate audio- or videotaped recordings of the child's performance using categories appropriate for the situation assessed by the analog. Analog situations include peer group entry situations, play situations, conversations, and interactions calling for anger control or assertiveness (Foster, Inderbitzen, & Nangle, 1993).

Analog situations allow the mental health professional to select particular situations to observe, thereby making this assessment method more efficient than direct observation in the natural environment. This asset can limit the scope of analog observation, however. In addition, observations in analog situations have frequently been criticized for their failure to produce data that correspond with observation in the natural environment (Foster et al., 1993), although the degree of correspondence may depend on the nature of the analog situation. One particularly promising analog with children involves creating situations in which small groups of previously unacquainted children come together for a series of short groups that involve play activities. These situations are particularly relevant for assessing the behavior of rejected children, who reestablish their rejected status in new groups very quickly and who generally show behavior profiles similar to the ones they display in classroom settings when they interact with acquainted peers (Coie & Kupersmidt, 1983).

Self-Report Measures

Generally, child self-report measures assess children's general perceptions of their friendships and peer relations rather than their social behavior per se. With adolescents, however, self-reports may become more important as opportunities to observe interactions directly become less feasible. The Teenage Inventory of Social Skills (Inderbitzen-Pisaruk & Foster, 1992) is one instrument that assesses teens' self-report of social behavior. The MESSY also has a self-report version for children. A number of measures assess children's and adolescents' views of their interactions within specific friendships (see Furman, 1996, for review).

Self-report measures are convenient and capture children's views of their own behavior. However, data indicate that rejected children in particular fall into two groups, one that recognizes their social difficulties and one that does not (Boivin & Begin, 1989), indicating that measures of children's views should be supplemented by data from other, presumably more objective, sources.

ASSESSING SOCIAL COGNITION

Many treatment programs for improving children's peer relationships attempt to do so at least in part by improving children's problem-solving skills. This in turn requires assessment of children's social cognitive styles or processes. Typically, investigators assess these processes by presenting the child with a series of vignettes, then asking a series of questions that address steps in the social information-processing model described earlier. Vignettes vary in number and type, depending on the population of interest. Assessments of aggressive children, for example, often use vignettes that depict provocation situations in which the intent of the provocateur is ambiguous, based on repeated findings that overtly aggressive children tend to interpret the provocateur's intent in these situations as hostile (Crick & Dodge, 1994). Other situations used in this type of assessment include peer group entry situations, in which a child contemplates joining a group of peers who are engaged in an activity (Crick & Dodge, 1996), and peer conflicts (Chung & Asher, 1996). Alternatively, vignettes can be created specifically for individual children based on interviews with teachers or parents about the situations in which the child has difficulties (e.g., Guevremont & Foster, 1993).

After hearing each vignette, the examiner commonly asks the child to respond to open-ended or rating scale questions assessing social information-processing or problem-solving steps. Trained coders later evaluate any open-ended responses. Questions can assess the cues to which children attend in the situation (e.g., Dodge & Price, 1994), children's social goals (e.g., relationship versus control versus avoidance goals; Chung & Asher, 1996), the attributions children make about the intent of others in the situation (e.g., Crick, 1995), the number and type of solutions children generate for handling the situation (e.g., Dodge & Price, 1994; Quiggle, Garber, Panak, & Dodge, 1992), the child's preferred or first-choice solution (e.g., Slaby & Guerra, 1988), and the child's skill at enacting the solution (Dodge & Price, 1994).

These analog social-cognitive assessment strategies presumably provide a window into children's thinking in the natural environment. As such, they are subject to many of the same strengths and concerns expressed earlier about analog direct observational assessment. On the positive side, many of the types of vignettes used to gather information on goals and outcome expectancies have been rated by participants as reflecting situations that commonly occur in the natural environment (Chung & Asher, 1996), suggesting that they have some degree of content validity and external validity to real-life social situations. In addition, several different types of vignettes (e.g., peer group entry, instrumental conflict) can be presented using a variety of modalities (e.g., oral, written, videotape, audiotape) over a relatively short period of time. On the other hand, one concern with the use of hypothetical situations is the uncertainty of whether reports of children's cognitions provide accurate depictions of their true cognitive processes. Even if children do accurately report their thoughts, the responses given to hypothetical situation vignettes may vary from what actually occurs during real social interactions. Also, the quality of open-ended responses gained using this methodology can be confounded with verbal intelligence, unless the task is simplified so that it does not require complex verbal expression. Despite these potential limitations, empirical evidence that children are indeed able to respond to the questions and that their responses relate to other variables in meaningful ways suggests that the hypothetical situation methodology provides valid information (Asher, Chung, & Hopmeyer, 1995; Crick & Dodge, 1996; Cuddy & Frame, 1991; Rabiner & Gordon, 1992).

Assessing Peer Acceptance, Rejection, and Friendship

One common way of identifying children who may benefit from social skills training involves assessing children's social status or peer acceptance, typically using peer sociometric ratings or nominations. Investigators also sometimes use these procedures to assess the outcomes of social skills training, in particular, whether a child's changed behavior translates into improved acceptance with peers. With peer ratings, participating children in a classroom or other social group rate how much they like (or like to play with) each of their classmates using a roster of names and a rating scale. This procedure can be simplified for use with preschool children, for example, by asking children to sort pictures into piles anchored with faces that show a frown, a neutral expression, or a smile that depict the child's feelings about the peer. Each child who is rated receives a score that represents the average of the peers' ratings.

Peer nominations provide an alternative way of assessing social status or peer acceptance. With the typical peer nomination procedure, children circle names of peers that they like from a roster of participating classmates, then repeat the procedure with a new roster by circling names of disliked peers. Number of "like" and "dislike" nominations are standardized within each nominating group (typically, a classroom or grade) to provide peer acceptance and rejection scores. These scores can be combined using cutoffs (the most common being those suggested by Coie, Dodge, & Coppotelli, 1982) to place the child into one of several social status categories: accepted or popular children (liked by many, disliked by few), rejected children (disliked by many, liked by few), controversial children (liked by some, disliked by some), neglected children (infrequently mentioned as either liked or disliked), and average children (mentioned by peers, but neither strongly liked nor strongly disliked).

Peer nomination and rating procedures have been widely used and have exceptionally strong psychometric properties, especially for identifying rejected and accepted children (Foster et al., 1993). However, these procedures generally require that at least 50% of children in the classroom participate: Nomination categories become less stable as fewer children participate, particularly when the procedure asks children to identify a limited and not an unlimited number of liked and disliked peers (Crick & Ladd, 1989). In addition, as with peer ratings of behavior, these procedures can be controversial. Some adults object to asking children to state negative choices about others; some are concerned that voicing negative nominations will lead children to ostracize disliked peers even further. Questionnaire and observational studies assessing potentially negative outcomes of these procedures have not documented negative effects with preschool and elementary school children (Bell-Dolan, Foster, & Christopher, 1992; Bell-Dolan, Foster, & Sikora, 1989; Hayvren & Hymel, 1981; Iverson, Barton, & Iverson, 1997). Although occasionally, children report momentary negative feelings when completing negative peer nominations, most go on to state that they enjoyed participating in the research project (Bell-Dolan et al., 1992). Nonetheless, investigators suggest that adults try to prevent potential negative repercussions by refraining from administering peer nomination procedures right before a free-play situation, and by embedding nominations in other, more salient measures that are likely to distract children's attention from the nominations. Another suggestion is to obtain children's written agreement to keep their responses confidential (e.g., Foster et al., 1993).

Variations on sociometric measures can be used to identify friendships, another aspect of peer acceptance. Friendship measures have not been as widely used to assess the impact of social skills training as nominations that assess social status. Nonetheless, investigators increasingly have distinguished friendships from peer acceptance and rejection (Asher, Parker, & Walker, 1996), perhaps because rejected children frequently do have friends (George & Hartmann, 1996). Absence of mutual friendships predicts feelings of loneliness over and above peer rejection (Parker & Asher, 1993), supporting the notion that friendship

assessments capture phenomena that are distinct and important in children's peer relations. Assessment of friendships typically provides children with a definition of "friend," then asks the children to identify their friends from a classroom roster. Sometimes, children also rate how much they like each of their friends. These measures can be scored in different ways, the most stringent determining the number of friends a child has by counting the number of reciprocated nominations a child receives in which both parties indicated a high degree of liking for the other.

Several self-report questionnaires also assess children's perceptions of the general quality of their peer relations. Examples of these are Asher, Hymel, and Renshaw's (1984) Loneliness and Social Dissatisfaction Scale and the Social Competence subscale of Harter's (1982) Perceived Competence Scale for Children. Although instruments such as these indicate children's perceptions of their peer acceptance, it is important to note that a subgroup of rejected children do not report being disliked or experiencing distress about their peer relations, whereas others are more cognizant of their difficulties (Boivin & Begin, 1989).

TREATMENT APPROACHES

Social skills and problem-solving interventions have been evaluated as treatment methods for children with serious behavior problems and as part of more general preventive interventions that are usually implemented with high-risk youth. Specific details of the populations addressed, targets of intervention, and concurrent interventions have varied from study to study. Nonetheless, many of these interventions contain core commonalities.

Social Skills Training
Social skills training approaches have as their goal to teach children prosocial or adaptive

methods of handling potentially problematic social situations. Some programs focus on a limited number of specific skills and situations (e.g., assertiveness training); others address more varied skills and situations. Skills and situations that have been included in social skills training include entering peer group activities, playing cooperatively with peers, handling conflictual situations nonaggressively, conversing skillfully, asserting one's opinions and rights, and resisting peer pressure to engage in problem behavior such as tobacco or alcohol use. Most commonly, an adult trainer teaches skills using explanations, demonstrations and modeling, rehearsal, feedback, and opportunities to practice the skills in the natural environment, all employed in the context of activities that are age-appropriate and engaging for the children or teenagers. Methods for helping children generalize what they have learned to ongoing in vivo situations may be included, such as homework assignments, prompts by adults, and reward systems for behaving appropriately in social skills training groups or in the natural environment. Social skills training can be delivered to individual children or to groups of children. Groups in some studies consist solely of children identified as needing skill training; other studies use mixtures of skilled and unskilled children.

Problem-Solving Training
Problem-solving training is based on the assumption that children perform ineffectively because they lack the cognitive or problem-solving skills required to think through difficult situations. Therefore, the goal of problem-solving training is to teach children a thoughtful, deliberative, sequential approach to reaching good solutions for handling problematic social situations. This generally involves instructing children to (1) identify problem situations; (2) stop and think when confronted by a problem situation; (3) define the nature of the problem; (4) generate ideas for how to solve the problem;

(5) evaluate the ideas and pick the idea most likely to produce positive outcomes and minimize negative outcomes; and (6) plan and implement the idea behaviorally. Like social skills training, problem-solving training can be done individually or in groups, and involves instruction, modeling, behavior rehearsal, and feedback to the child, often in the context of games, activities, or stories that address difficult social situations. Interventions sometimes also include activities designed to promote generalization of problem-solving skills.

CASE EXAMPLE

Mark, an 8-year-old male, was brought to the clinic by his father and stepmother. He had been diagnosed with Attention-Deficit/Hyperactivity Disorder (predominantly Hyperactive type) three years earlier, and was being treated with Ritalin by his pediatrician. Mark's parents reported that the medication had been partially successful in decreasing Mark's hyperactivity and impulsivity. However, he continued to have difficulties with peer relationships, problem-solving skills, and anger management. Most troubling to Mark's parents was his controlling and demanding interactional style with both peers and adults.

To assess Mark's difficulties, the therapist interviewed Mark, his parents, and his teacher; administered the Child Behavior Checklist to Mark's parents; and directly observed Mark's behavior at school. Mark's parents reported that he had a history of poor peer relationships; he preferred to interact with adults or with younger children. Mark had also injured other children inadvertently during play when he was overexcited (i.e., throwing a ball too hard, placing a peer in a tight headlock during rough play). Mark's parents also described him as being unable to accept others' points of view or recognize their feelings. He seemed unaware of the impact of his own behavior on other people and rarely accepted responsibility for wrongdoing. When describing Mark's controlling behavior, his father stated, "He always wants it his way" and "He argues about everything." Mark also dominated conversations, frequently interrupting others, speaking very loudly, and giving no indication that he was listening to the other person.

Mark's teacher reported similar problems at school. Although Mark excelled academically, he experienced numerous social difficulties in the classroom and had been placed in a self-contained special education classroom. Mark's teacher reported that he had not made any friends in the two years he had spent in her classroom. She described his behavior as "bossy" and "overbearing," and stated that the other children rejected him outright. Mark's teacher stated that he easily became overly excited and acted "goofy" (i.e., talking very loudly, dancing around, falling to the ground laughing). His anger outbursts (i.e., yelling, clenching fists and teeth, knocking over desks) also troubled her.

The therapist noted many of these behaviors during her school observation. During instructional time, Mark accurately answered nearly every question the teacher asked, but frequently interrupted her or failed to raise his hand. He also made many off-task remarks. During the playground observation, Mark unsuccessfully attempted to enter various peer activities. For instance, he burst into a basketball game without requesting entry from his peers, took the ball from another child, and began dribbling it around the court, loudly taunting the other children by verbally challenging them to get the ball away from him. Mark's peers reacted with anger. When they were eventually able to get the ball back after a struggle, they told Mark they did not want him to play.

The assessment revealed three general problem areas that the therapist targeted for Mark's treatment. First, she confirmed Mark's ADHD diagnosis and concluded that his impulsivity promoted his maladaptive behavior with peers.

Second, Mark experienced difficulties recognizing, regulating, and expressing his own negative and positive emotions. His poor emotional regulation was problematic because it generally provoked a state of overarousal and lack of behavioral control. In particular, his expression of anger and frustration with loud and sometimes violent outbursts resulted in both social rejection and tangible negative consequences (i.e., loss of privileges, suspension from school). Third, Mark's insistence on dominating and controlling others both in conversation and in physical interactions was particularly troublesome due to its effects on his relationships. Furthermore, due to his impulsivity, poor regulation of emotions, and lack of empathy, Mark consistently failed to consider the impact of his behavior on others. He also missed social cues indicating how his words and behaviors were affecting others, and he continued to engage in annoying behaviors despite obvious signs of displeasure by others. At the same time, he displayed two specific strengths that treatment could capitalize on: his high intelligence and his general desire to please adults. He also recognized his lack of peer friendships and was interested in learning new ways to make friends.

To address Mark's ADHD-related difficulties, the therapist referred him to the staff psychiatrist, who adjusted his medication dosage. Mark's impulsive behavior significantly declined. To address Mark's difficulties with emotion regulation, the therapist provided training in recognizing, regulating, and expressing feelings. Finally, the therapist implemented empathy training and problem solving and social skills building with the goal of reducing Mark's controlling behavior by promoting alternative strategies and helping him to understand the impact of his behavior on others.

Treatment had three components: individual skill-building sessions with Mark, parent training, and group treatment. Although some children can benefit from group social skills training without additional intervention, Mark required initial training and preparation in individual sessions before being immersed in a peer group. Additionally, training Mark's parents in behavioral management techniques to use in the home was required to reduce his demanding behavior in that setting.

In the individual sessions, the therapist used role playing and modeling to teach Mark appropriate peer group entry and problem-solving techniques. She coached Mark on basic social skills such as maintaining eye contact, allowing other people to finish speaking, and making "listening noises" (comments that communicate that he is attending to others). She also used more structured activities such as psychoeducational board games to address social skills, anger management, and expression of feelings. The therapist provided Mark with frequent feedback about how his behavior affected her.

To target Mark's difficulty with emotional regulation, a part of his treatment was dedicated to learning how to recognize, process, and express emotions. Typically, the therapist prompted Mark to identify (1) how he felt when initially confronted with a recent real-life situation; (2) how his feelings translated into physiological responses (i.e., flushed face, rapid breathing, sweaty palms); (3) how he expressed his feelings behaviorally (i.e., increased vocal loudness, jumping around, laughing excessively, or yelling, throwing things); (4) what consequences his behavioral responses produced; and (5) how he felt about the events after they occurred. Initially, Mark had a hard time recognizing each component of the process. With direct prompting and repeated use of this exercise, however, he began to be able to articulate answers to these questions in appropriate ways.

Mark also responded with strong physiological reactions in many situations. To help him manage these reactions, the therapist trained Mark to use deep breathing exercises, counting exercises, and self time-out procedures (e.g., "I need a break"). The therapist instructed Mark's parents and teacher to prompt him verbally to attend to his physiological state by asking, "Mark, how fast is your engine running?" With training, Mark learned to attend to his responses and use appropriate skills to wind his "engine" down. When this technique occasionally failed (primarily because Mark refused to stop what he was doing and respond to adult prompts), he was instructed to take a break and look at his face in the mirror. Seeing his red face and rapid breathing in the mirror was helpful in getting him to attend to these symptoms, and also provided a break from the activity that was eliciting this state of overarousal.

During the first phase of treatment, the therapist trained Mark's parents to design and implement a behavioral modification program to reduce Mark's interrupting ("taking turns in conversations") and arguing ("allowing others to have their own ideas") at home. Mark's parents redirected his problem behavior and provided rewards based on check marks he earned each day that his behavior improved. Mark responded well to this intervention and enjoyed being involved in planning both the intervention and the rewards.

After Mark's emotional regulation, conversational, empathic, and problem-solving skills began to improve in his individual sessions, he joined a social skills group with five other 8- to 9-year-old boys and girls. Although Mark could clearly articulate the "right answers" in his therapy sessions, observations of the group quickly revealed that his newly learned skills had not generalized to the peer environment.

Mark selected behavioral goals to address in the social skills group (e.g., "I will be a good listener"). Children completed structured and unstructured tasks that required the use of cooperation and problem-solving techniques and participated in role-playing activities to provide training in empathy, problem solving, and anger management. Children provided feedback to each other during and at the end of each group (e.g., "I liked when you . . ."; "When you . . . I felt . . .").

Mark was initially controlling, disruptive, and dominating in the social skills group. However, he quickly began to respond to feedback from his peers and redirection from the therapist leaders. He began to take breaks from activities when he or a therapist identified this as a need. Furthermore, Mark made a friend in the group with whom he continued to have a positive relationship after the termination of the group.

Overall, Mark's treatment was successful. On termination of treatment, he had developed two friendships with peers at his school and had successfully begun activities such as karate and band. Mark's parents reported positive behavioral changes in the home as well, with a marked decrease in interrupting and arguing behaviors.

Mark returned to the clinic twice for booster sessions. Both times, he had slipped back into some of his old behaviors, such as arguing and becoming overly excited. The therapist instructed Mark's parents to resume a behavioral program at home for a brief period to reestablish his previous behavioral changes. Additionally, Mark had become embarrassed by verbal cues to check his engine and needed a new cue. A nonverbal hand signal was selected to replace the verbal cue and was successful in decreasing his emotional outbursts once again. Mark was recently reintegrated into regular education classes and at the last assessment was doing well in this new setting.

This case illustrates several general points that emerge from the social skills literature. First, Mark, like many children who have poor peer relations and social skills, had received a formal diagnosis involving an externalizing behavior problem. Second, assessment using several different ways of collecting information allowed the therapist to pinpoint Mark's problems, to formulate hypotheses about factors responsible for these difficulties, and to develop a treatment plan. Third, Mark's interpersonal style and ways of handling conflict and group entry situations clearly alienated both peers and adults. Fourth, his social skills problems were related to cognitive deficits: Despite high intelligence, he showed remarkably little ability to think through or to articulate his feelings, his behavior, or others' reactions to his behavior. Difficulties regulating his emotional reactions also contributed to his problems. Fifth, treatment required a sequential approach that first built his cognitive, emotional, and behavioral skills repertoire, then employed specific strategies to promote generalization of these skills to the natural environment. Involving Mark in a social skills group provided a particularly worthwhile way both to assess and to promote skills generalization. The use of booster sessions also helped the therapist assess maintenance of Mark's gains and to interrupt recurrences of old problems before they became severe. Finally, treatment success was evident not only in reduced behavior problems and improved skills, but also in Mark's peer relationships when he made and kept friends for the first time.

EVALUATIONS OF SOCIAL SKILLS AND PROBLEM-SOLVING TRAINING

General statements about the effects of social skills and problem-solving training are difficult to make for several reasons. First, the generic term social skills training has been used to encompass a variety of approaches with children selected in various ways. Second, the specific social skills included in training have varied widely, with varied empirical support for what is termed their social validity: the extent to which the behavioral skills, if enacted, will actually help the child become better accepted by peers, build adaptive friendships, or resist negative peer influences. Third, studies have varied widely in the duration, format, and types of primary and adjunctive techniques used in combination with social skills training. Fourth, meta-analyses and reviews of problem-solving and social skills approaches often do not separate these approaches, instead grouping them into the generic category of social skills training. This may be because some interventions that teach problem solving also include social skills training components and coach children on how to enact the behavioral responses they select for handling problem situations.

Several qualitative and meta-analytic reviews have examined the effects of social skills training. Authors have reached somewhat different conclusions. This may be due not only to the variety of populations and approaches that fall under the social skills rubric, but also to the different criteria reviewers used to select studies to include in their reviews and the different ways they coded and contrasted studies. For example, Schneider (1992) conducted a meta-analysis of 79 controlled studies of social skills training, including social-cognitive interventions that provided problem-solving training. His data generally indicated moderate short-term effect sizes across outcome measures and targets, populations, and types of training procedures. In contrast, Quinn, Kavale, Mathur, Rutherford, and Forness (1999) calculated effect sizes for social skills interventions from studies involving children likely to be classified as emotionally or behaviorally disordered, found them to be lower than those reported by Schneider, and concluded that social skills training has more modest effects with children with serious behavior disorders than with children selected in other ways. Erwin's (1994) meta-analysis also supports the view that some children may benefit more than others from social skills training. He found larger effect sizes for classroom-based interventions that targeted withdrawn children than for interventions that did not target this population. It is quite possible that these comparisons were confounded with other intervention parameters that accounted for the effects,

as no meta-analyses have simultaneously controlled for participant, intervention, and methodological characteristics that could be related to the obtained effects.

Three consistencies in these reviews are worth noting. First, Quinn et al. (1999) and Taylor, Eddy, and Biglan (1999) concluded that the overall effects of social skills training on aggressive behavior, particularly longer-term effects with children who enter the study with severe aggressive behavior, are limited. Schneider's (1992) data are consistent with this conclusion. Second, the largest effect sizes detected by Schneider and by Erwin (1994) when they examined different types of measures were for measures of social interaction, with smaller effect sizes for measures of peer acceptance and rejection, suggesting that peer acceptance may not change as markedly as children's social interaction skills as a result of social skills training. Third, both Erwin and Schneider reported a significant degree of heterogeneity in effect sizes across the studies they surveyed, indicating that not all social skills approaches have the same effects.

This heterogeneity underscores the need to identify particularly effective intervention programs for producing specific, meaningful changes in well-defined populations. In addition, most research using social skills training to treat clinical populations can best be considered efficacy research, testing the intervention under ideal circumstances in which clinicians were closely supervised to ensure consistent implementation of the approach. Research that tests the most efficacious approaches under conditions typical of clinical practice is an important next step in evaluating social skills and problem-solving training.

The reviews just cited generally examined social skills and problem-solving training used as a sole intervention strategy to benefit children with peer relationship or aggressive behavior problems. Social skills and problem-solving training also have been used in combination with strategies to prevent later delinquency or drug use. Some of these approaches have targeted general populations; others have been aimed specifically at high-risk youth.

Prevention programs that include social skills and problem-solving training fall into two general groups. The first group includes programs that are implemented in early elementary school, with the general goals of reducing aggressive behavior and preventing various negative outcomes associated with aggression and rejection. Most of these also involve parent training in child management as well as a social skills curriculum. The second set of programs includes interventions that begin during the transition from elementary school to junior high school. The most effective of these focus on teaching children skills for resisting peer instigation to use tobacco, drugs, or alcohol. These intervention programs often also provide information about drug use norms, involve peer leaders in the curriculum, and involve families and communities in reducing teens' access to drugs and alcohol. Teachers deliver social skills and problem-solving training in many of these interventions, which package the training as part of classroom curricula.

Isolating the sole effects of social skills and problem-solving training in these approaches is impossible because, as mentioned, these prevention studies have involved intervention components in addition to the training. Nonetheless, many of these approaches have produced impressive long-term as well as immediate effects. For example, Tremblay, Pagani-Kurtz, Masse, Vitaro, and Pihl (1995) and Reid and colleagues (Eddy, Reid, & Fetrow, 2000; Reid, Eddy, Fetrow, & Stoolmiller, 1999) evaluated the effects of combined interventions that included behavioral parent training with school-based social skills training. Tremblay et al.'s (1995) intervention also included problem-solving training and was delivered to disruptive boys between the ages of 7 and 9. Tremblay et al. followed up these boys when they reached ages 10 to 15. Treated

boys consistently reported significantly less delinquency than control boys who did not receive the intervention over this time period. Reid et al.'s (1999) program included teacher training in behavior management strategies and was implemented in first- and fifth-grade classrooms. Three-year follow-up of the fifth-graders indicated that treated children were less likely than controls to have been arrested and to have initiated drug and alcohol use (Eddy et al., 2000).

Several prevention programs implemented as children near adolescence include social skills training. Most of these teach adolescents to handle specific situations relevant to the prevention goal. For example, social skills and problem-solving training approaches for handling risky sexual situations in combination with relevant sexual information have been used with some success to reduce risky sexual behavior such as unprotected intercourse (e.g., St. Lawrence, Jefferson, Alleyne, & Brasfield, 1995). Other programs focus specifically on skills for refusing peers' invitations to use drugs, tobacco, or alcohol. One program with positive effects that has been widely replicated is Life Skills Training, a school-based program that teaches seventh-graders social and problem-solving skills that focus on decision making, resisting media influences, coping with negative affect, managing their own behavior, communicating effectively with others, behaving appropriately in situations that require assertiveness, and resisting peer pressure to smoke or use drugs or alcohol. Numerous studies indicate that youth who have received Life Skills Training report less use of tobacco, alcohol, marijuana, and other drugs, relative to teens who have not received the training (Botvin, Baker, Botvin, Filazzola, & Millman, 1984; Botvin, Baker, Dusenbury, Botvin, & Diaz, 1995; Botvin & Eng, 1982; Botvin et al., 1992), and that poor implementation of the curriculum is associated with poorer outcomes (Tortu & Botvin, 1989). Other programs that include social skills training as one of several preventive efforts have also shown positive effects on tobacco, alcohol, and drug use (e.g., Pentz et al., 1989; Perry et al., 1996).

Although social skills and problem-solving prevention programs have produced generally positive outcomes, a small number of iatrogenic effects have been reported and are worth noting. These are particularly important because they occurred in the context of studies in which teens were randomly assigned to intervention conditions, increasing the likelihood that the negative effects were due to the treatment and not to preexisting characteristics of the sample. In one of the most striking examples of this, Dishion and Andrews (1995) found that high-risk teens who had received a group intervention that emphasized selection of friends who would encourage positive behavior, teen self-management, and improved problem solving and communication with parents and peers reported more smoking one year later compared to teens in various other intervention conditions. Teachers also rated these teens higher in externalizing behavior problems. Dishion, McCord, and Poulin (1999) speculated that peer reinforcement of deviant behavior and conversation content in the intervention groups may have been responsible for the effect. Similarly, Palinkas, Atkins, Miller, and Ferreira (1996) found that pregnant or parenting teens at high risk for drug use who reported never having previously used drugs were significantly more likely to begin using drugs after receiving a version of social skills training plus a "Facts of Life" educational curriculum, compared with similar teens who had been randomly assigned to receive only the curriculum. Further analyses indicated that this group also showed significant increases in the number of peers in their social networks who used drugs or were delinquent, implying that the group social skills training treatment may have inadvertently led these teens to make friends with peers who were bad influences on them. Botvin, Baker, Filazzola, and Botvin (1990)

found that teens in teacher-led Life Skills Training groups who received booster sessions reported significantly *more*, not *less*, substance use on several measures than the control participants, and that these effects were associated with poor teacher implementation of the curriculum. Together, these findings underscore the need to attend closely to both the content and the process of social skills training to ensure that peers and teachers are encouraging appropriate skill use in the interest of prosocial development.

SUMMARY

Social skills and problem-solving training attempt to improve children's interpersonal style by expanding their positive repertoire, teaching them skills for handling problem situations, and helping them take a thoughtful, reflective approach to troublesome situations. When successful, these interventions result in improved social behavior and reductions in aggression and other negative responses. These changes in turn help the child to become better accepted by peers and to form friendships with prosocial peers. As a result, the child is less likely to follow developmental trajectories linked with adolescent problem behavior.

Social skills and problem-solving programs have been designed and implemented to address problems of withdrawal, rejection, and aggression in different populations. Preventive approaches have focused largely on resisting negative peer influences to use drugs, tobacco, and alcohol. These interventions have varied considerably in content, length, measures used to assess effects, and results. In addition, social skills and problem-solving training as clinical interventions have rarely been evaluated in the context of effectiveness studies. Studies using social skills and problem-solving training approaches to prevent the emergence of behavior problems have been broader in scope and have often involved large school and community-wide efforts, thus better approximating studies of effectiveness. Although these interventions have often been successful, most have included components other than social skills training and do not evaluate the effects of social skills training or problem-solving training in isolation. In addition, a few prevention studies evaluating social skills training as a prevention strategy with high-risk youth have documented iatrogenic findings, but the intervention processes responsible for these effects are not yet well understood.

Taken as a whole, these findings suggest that clinicians who use social skills and problem-solving training approaches should carefully monitor the quality of the intervention and the peer processes that transpire if the child is involved in social skills groups. In addition, clinicians should monitor the effects of intervention on child behavior in the natural environment and peer acceptance, supplementing the approaches when needed with additional interventions such as parent training.

REFERENCES

Achenbach, T. M. (1991). *Manual for the Child Behavior Checklist/4–18 and 1991 profile.* Burlington: University of Vermont, Department of Psychiatry.

American Psychiatric Association. (1994). *Diagnostic and statistical manual of mental disorders* (4th ed.). Washington, DC: Author.

Asarnow, J. R., & Callan, J. W. (1985). Boys with peer adjustment problems: Social cognitive processes. *Journal of Consulting and Clinical Psychology, 53,* 80–87.

Asher, S. R., Chung, T. Y., & Hopmeyer, A. (1995, March). *Children's goals and strategies in conflict situation.* Paper presented at the meeting of the Society for Research in Child Development, Indianapolis, IN.

Asher, S. R., Hymel, S., & Renshaw, P. D. (1984). Loneliness in children. *Child Development, 55,* 1456–1464.

Asher, S. R., Parker, J. G., & Walker, D. L. (1996). Distinguishing friendship from acceptance: Implications for assessment and intervention. In W. M. Bukowski, A. F. Newcomb, & W. W. Hartup (Eds.), *The company they keep: Friendship in childhood and adolescence* (pp. 366–405). New York: Cambridge University Press.

Asher, S. R., & Renshaw, P. D. (1990). Children without friends: Social knowledge and social skills training. In S. R. Asher & J. D. Coie (Eds.), *Peer rejection in childhood* (pp. 273–296). New York: Cambridge University Press.

Bell-Dolan, D. J., Foster, S. L., & Christopher, J. S. (1992). Children's reactions to participating in a peer relations study: Child, parent, and teacher reports. *Child Study Journal, 22,* 137–156.

Bell-Dolan, D. J., Foster, S. L., & Sikora, D. M. (1989). Effects of sociometric testing on children's behavior and loneliness in school. *Developmental Psychology, 25,* 306–311.

Bierman, K. L., & Welsh, J. A. (1997). Social relationship deficits. In E. J. Mash & L. G. Terdal (Eds.), *Assessment of childhood disorders* (3rd ed., pp. 328–365). New York: Guilford Press.

Boivin, M., & Begin, G. (1989). Peer status and self-perception among early elementary school children: The case of the rejected children, *Child Development, 60,* 591–596.

Botvin, G. J., Baker, E., Botvin, E. M., Dusenbury, L., Cardwell, J., & Diaz, T. (1993). Factors promoting cigarette smoking among Black youth: A causal modeling approach. *Addictive Behaviors, 18,* 397–405.

Botvin, G. J., Baker, E., Botvin, E. M., Filazzola, A. D., & Millman, R. B. (1984). Prevention of alcohol misuse through the development of personal and social competence: A pilot study. *Journal of Studies on Alcohol, 45*(6), 550–552.

Botvin, G. J., Baker, E., Dusenbury, L., Botvin, E. M., & Diaz, T. (1995). Long term follow-up results of a randomized drug abuse trial in a White middle class population. *Journal of the American Medical Association, 273,* 1106–1112.

Botvin, G. J., Baker, E., Dusenbury, L., Tortu, S., & Botvin, E. M. (1990). Preventing adolescent drug abuse through a multimodal cognitive-behavioral approach: Results of a 3-year study. *Journal of Consulting and Clinical Psychology, 58,* 437–446.

Botvin, G. J., Baker, E., Filazzola, A. D., & Botvin, E. M. (1990). A cognitive-behavioral approach to substance abuse prevention: One-year follow-up. *Addictive Behaviors, 15*, 47–63.

Botvin, G. J., Dusenbury, L., Baker, E., James-Ortiz, S., Botvin, E. M., & Kerner, J. (1992). Smoking prevention among urban minority youth: Assessing effects on outcome and mediating variables. *Health Psychology, 11*, 290–299.

Botvin, G. J., & Eng, A. (1982). The efficacy of a multicomponent approach to the prevention of cigarette smoking. *Preventive Medicine, 11*, 199–211.

Chittenden, G. F. (1942). An experimental study in measuring and modifying assertive behavior in young children. *Monographs of the Society for Research in Child Development, 7*(1, Serial No. 31).

Chung, T. Y., & Asher, S. R. (1996). Children's goals and strategies in peer conflict situations. *Merrill-Palmer Quarterly, 42*, 125–147.

Coie, J. D., Dodge, K. A., & Coppotelli, H. (1982). Dimensions and types of social status: A cross-age perspective. *Developmental Psychology, 18*, 557–570.

Coie, J. D., & Kupersmidt, J. B. (1983). A behavioral analysis of emerging social status in boys' groups. *Child Development, 54*, 1400–1416.

Conduct Problems Prevention Research Group. (1999a). Initial impact of the Fast Track prevention trial for conduct problems: I. The high-risk sample. *Journal of Consulting and Clinical Psychology, 67*, 631–647.

Conduct Problems Prevention Research Group. (1999b). Initial impact of the Fast Track prevention trial for conduct problems: II. Classroom effects. *Journal of Consulting and Clinical Psychology, 67*, 648–657.

Crick, N. R. (1995). Relational aggression: The role of intent attribution, feelings of distress, and provocation type. *Development and Psychopathology, 7*, 313–322.

Crick, N. R., & Dodge, K. A. (1994). A review and reformulation of social information-processing mechanisms in children's social adjustment. *Psychological Bulletin, 115*, 74–101.

Crick, N. R., & Dodge, K. A. (1996). Social information-processing mechanisms in reactive and proactive aggression. *Child Development, 67*, 993–1002.

Crick, N. R., & Grotpeter, J. K. (1995). Relational aggression, gender, and social information-processing mechanisms in children's social adjustment. *Child Development, 66*, 710–722.

Crick, N. R., & Ladd, G. W. (1989). Nominator attrition: Does it affect the accuracy of children's sociometric classifications? *Merrill-Palmer Quarterly, 35*, 197–207.

Cuddy, E. M., & Frame, C. (1991). Comparison of aggressive and nonaggressive boys' self-efficacy and outcome expectancy beliefs. *Child Study Journal, 21*, 135–151.

Dishion, T. J., & Andrews, D. W. (1995). Preventing escalation in problem behaviors with high-risk young adolescents: Immediate and 1-year outcomes. *Journal of Consulting and Clinical Psychology, 63*, 538–548.

Dishion, T. J., McCord, J., & Poulin, F. (1999). When interventions harm: Peer groups and problem behavior. *American Psychologist, 54*, 755–764.

Dodge, K. A., McClaskey, C. L., & Feldman, E. (1985). Situational approach to the assessment of social competence in children. *Journal of Consulting and Clinical Psychology, 53*, 344–353.

Dodge, K. A., & Price, J. M. (1994). On the relation between social information processing and socially competent behavior in early school-aged children. *Child Development, 65*, 1385–1397.

Eddy, J. M., Reid, J. B., & Fetrow, R. A. (2000). An elementary school-based program targeting modifiable antecedents of youth delinquency and violence: Linking Interests of Families and Teachers (LIFT). *Journal of Emotional and Behavioral Disorders, 8*, 165–176.

Erhardt, D., & Hinshaw, S. P. (1994). Initial sociometric impressions of attention-deficit hyperactivity disorder and comparison boys: Predictions from social behaviors and from nonverbal variables. *Journal of Consulting and Clinical Psychology, 62*, 833–842.

Erwin, P. (1994). Effectiveness of social skills training with children: A meta-analytic study. *Counselling Psychology Quarterly, 7*, 305–310.

Foster, S. L., Inderbitzen, H., & Nangle, D. W. (1993). Assessing acceptance and social skills with peers in childhood: Current issues. *Behavior Modification, 17*, 255–286.

Furman, W. (1996). The measurement of friendship perceptions: Conceptual and methodological issues. In W. M. Bukowski, A. F. Newcomb, & W. W. Hartup (Eds.), *The company they keep:*

Friendship in childhood and adolescence (pp. 41–65). New York: Cambridge University Press.

George, T. P., & Hartmann, D. P. (1996). Friendship networks of unpopular, average, and popular children. *Child Development, 67*, 2301–2316.

Gresham, F. M., & Elliott, S. N. (1990). *Social skills rating system.* Circle Pines, MN: American Guidance Service.

Guevremont, D. C., & Foster, S. L. (1993). Impact of social problem-solving training on aggressive boys: Skill acquisition, behavior change, and generalization. *Journal of Abnormal Child Psychology, 21*, 13–27.

Harter, S. (1982). The Perceived Competence Scale for Children. *Child Development, 53*, 87–92.

Hayvren, M., & Hymel, S. (1981). Ethical issues in sociometric testing: The impact of sociometric measures on interaction behavior. *Developmental Psychology, 20*, 844–849.

Hightower, A. D., Work, W. C., Cowen, E. L., Lotyczewski, B. S., Spinell, A. P., Guare, J. C., et al. (1986). The Teacher-Child Rating Scale: A brief objective measure of elementary school children's school problem behaviors and competencies. *School Psychology Review, 15*, 393–409.

Inderbitzen, H., & Foster, S. L. (1992). The Teenage Inventory of Social Skills: Development, reliability and validity. *Psychological Assessment: A Journal of Consulting and Clinical Psychology, 4*, 451–459.

Iverson, A. N., Barton, E. A., & Iverson, G. L. (1997). Analysis of risk to children participating in a sociometric task. *Developmental Psychology, 33*, 104–112.

Johnston, C. J., Pelham, W. E., & Murphy, H. A. (1985). Peer relationships in ADHD and normal children: A developmental analysis of peer and teacher ratings. *Journal of Abnormal Child Psychology, 13*, 89–100.

Kazdin, A. E., Siegel, T. C., & Bass, D. (1992). Cognitive problem-solving skills training and parent management training in the treatment of antisocial behavior in children. *Journal of Consulting and Clinical Psychology, 60*, 733–747.

Ladd, G. W., & Profilet, S. M. (1996). The Child Behavior Scale: A teacher-report measure of young children's aggressive, withdrawn, and prosocial behaviors. *Developmental Psychology, 32*, 1008–1024.

Masten, A. S., Morrison, P., & Pelligrini, D. (1985). A revised class play method of peer assessment. *Developmental Psychology, 21*, 523–533.

Matson, J. L., Rotatori, A. F., & Helsel, W. J. (1983). Psychometric properties of the Matson Evaluation of Social Skills with Youngsters (MESSY) with emotional problems and self-concept in deaf children. *Journal of Behavior Therapy and Experimental Psychiatry, 16*, 117–123.

Newcomb, A. F., Bukowski, W. M., & Pattee, L. (1993). Children's peer relations: A meta-analytic review of popular, rejected, controversial, and average sociometric status. *Psychological Bulletin, 113*, 91–128.

O'Conner, R. D. (1969). Modification of social withdrawal through symbolic modeling. *Journal of Applied Behavior Analysis, 2*, 15–22.

Oden, S., & Asher, S. R. (1977). Coaching children in social skills for friendship making. *Child Development, 48*, 495–506.

Palinkas, L. A., Atkins, C. J., Miller, C., & Ferreira, D. (1996). Social skills training for drug prevention in high-risk female adolescents. *Preventive Medicine, 25*, 692–701.

Parker, J. G., & Asher, S. R. (1993). Friendship and friendship quality in middle childhood: Links with peer group acceptance and feeling of loneliness and social dissatisfaction. *Developmental Psychology, 29*, 611–621.

Parker, J. G., Rubin, K. H., Price, J. M., & DeRosier, M. E. (1995). Peer relationships, child development, and adjustment: A developmental psychopathology perspective. In D. Cicchetti & J. D. Cohen (Eds.), *Developmental psychopathology* (Vol. 2, pp. 96–144). New York: Wiley.

Pekarik, E. G., Prinz, R. J., Liebert, D. E., Weintraub, S., & Neale, J. M. (1976). The Pupil Evaluation Inventory: A sociometric technique for assessing children's social behavior. *Journal of Abnormal Child Psychology, 4*, 83–97.

Pentz, M. A., Dwyer, J. H., MacKinnon, D. P., Flay, B. R., Hansen, W. B., Wang, E., et al. (1989). A multicommunity trial for primary prevention of adolescent drug abuse. *Journal of the American Medical Association, 261*, 3259–3266.

Perry, C. L., Williams, C. L., Veblen-Mortenson, S., Toomey, T. L., Komro, K. A., Anstine, P. S., et al. (1996). Project Northland: Outcomes of a communitywide alcohol use prevention program during early adolescence. *American Journal of Public Health, 86,* 956–965.

Pfiffner, L. J., & McBurnett, K. (1997). Social skills training with parent generalization: Treatment effects for children with Attention Deficit Disorder. *Journal of Consulting and Clinical Psychology, 65,* 749–757.

Putallaz, M., & Wasserman, A. (1989). Children's naturalistic entry behavior and sociometric status: A developmental perspective. *Developmental Psychology, 25,* 297–305.

Quiggle, N. L., Garber, J., Panak, W. F., & Dodge, K. A. (1992). Social information processing in aggressive and depressed children. *Child Development, 63,* 1303–1320.

Quinn, M. M., Kavale, K. A., Mathur, S. R., Rutherford, R. B., & Forness, S. R. (1999). A meta-analysis of social skill interventions for students with emotional or behavioral disorders. *Journal of Emotional and Behavioral Disorders, 7,* 54–64.

Rabiner, D. L., & Gordon, L. V. (1992). The coordination of conflicting social goals: Differences between rejected and nonrejected boys. *Child Development, 63,* 1344–1350.

Reid, J. B., Eddy, J. M., Fetrow, R. A., & Stoolmiller, M. (1999). Description and immediate impacts of a preventative intervention for conduct problems. *American Journal of Community Psychology, 24,* 483–517.

Rubin, K. H., Bukowski, W., & Parker, J. (1998). Peer interactions, relationships and groups. In W. Damon (Series Ed.) & N. Eisenberg (Vol. Ed.), *Handook of child psychology: Vol. 3. Social, emotional, and personality development* (pp. 619–700). New York: Wiley.

Rudolph, K. D., Hammen, C., & Burge, D. (1994). Interpersonal functioning and depressive symptoms in childhood: Addressing the issues of specificity and comorbidity. *Journal of Abnormal Child Psychology, 22,* 355–371.

Schneider, B. H. (1992). Didactic methods for enhancing children's peer relations: A quantitative review. *Clinical Psychology Review, 12,* 363–382.

Shantz, D. W. (1986). Conflict, aggression, and peer status: An observational study. *Child Development, 57,* 1322–1332.

Slaby, R. G., & Guerra, N. G. (1988). Cognitive mediators of aggression in adolescent offenders: I. Assessment. *Developmental Psychology, 24,* 580–588.

Spence, S. H., & Marzillier, J. S. (1981). Social skills training with adolescent male offenders: II. Short-term, long-term, and generalized effects. *Behavior Research and Therapy, 19,* 349–368.

Spivak, G., Platt, J. J., & Shure, M. B. (1976). *The problem-solving approach to adjustment.* San Francisco: Jossey-Bass.

St. Lawrence, J. S., Jefferson, K. W., Alleyne, E., & Brasfield, T. L. (1995). Cognitive-behavioral intervention to reduce African American adolescents' risk for HIV infection. *Journal of Consulting and Clinical Psychology, 63,* 221–237.

Taylor, T. K., Eddy, J. M., & Biglan, A. (1999). Interpersonal skills training to reduce aggressive and delinquent behavior: Limited evidence and the need for an evidence-based system of care. *Clinical Child and Family Psychology Review, 2,* 169–182.

Tortu, S., & Botvin, G. J. (1989). School-based smoking prevention: The teacher training process. *Preventive Medicine, 18,* 280–289.

Tremblay, R. E., Pagani-Kurtz, L., Masse, L. C., Vitaro, F., & Pihl, R. O. (1995). A bimodal preventive intervention for disruptive kindergarten boys: Its impact through mid-adolescence. *Journal of Consulting and Clinical Psychology, 63,* 560–568.

Walker, H., & McConnell, S. (1988). *Scale of Social Competence and School Adjustment.* Austin, TX: ProEd.

Webster-Stratton, C., & Hammond, M. (1997). Treating children with early-onset conduct problems: A comparison of child and parent training interventions. *Journal of Consulting and Clinical Psychology, 65,* 93–109.

Weissberg, R. P., Gesten, E. L., Carnrike, C. L., Toro, P. A., Rapkin, B. D., Davidson, E., et al. (1981). Social problem-solving training: A competence-building intervention with second- to fourth-grade children. *American Journal of Community Psychology, 9,* 411–423.

CHAPTER 3

Early Intervention Approach for Children and Families at Risk for Psychopathology

Mark R. Dadds

HISTORY AND THEORETICAL CONSTRUCTS

Early intervention (EI) programs target individuals at risk of developing a disorder or showing early or mild signs of the problem. Yet, prevention programs in the purest sense do not require that an individual be either at risk or showing any signs of a disorder. As it is common to hear terms such as "primary prevention" and "universal programs," it is useful to be clear where these terms come from and to what they refer. Understanding the difference between these types of prevention programs is also important, as they each involve a different set of procedures for screening and evaluation.

Traditionally, the system for describing prevention programs examined prevention from the perspective of the onset of the disorder and distinguished among primary, secondary, and tertiary prevention (Caplan, 1964). *Primary prevention* refers to interventions that target individuals

before they show any signs of a disorder; the focus is on preventing its development. *Secondary prevention* refers to interventions that target individuals showing symptoms of a disorder who do not meet diagnostic criteria for that disorder but may go on to display full-blown symptoms, and is close to the idea of EI; the focus is on ensuring that problems do not become more serious. *Tertiary prevention,* or tertiary intervention, refers to interventions targeting individuals with a diagnosed condition; the focus here is to prevent suffering by limiting the intensity of the problem, limiting the duration of an episode of the problem, increasing the interval between episodes (e.g., between depressive episodes, or the frequency and/or intensity of panic attacks), and preventing relapse.

A second and subsequent model organizes prevention initiatives based on sample catchment boundaries within at-risk populations (Mrazek & Haggerty, 1994) and distinguishes three types of prevention programs: universal, selective, and indicated. These models may be useful in determining a method for selecting participants who best fit the goals of a program. Should all children be included, or only those identified to be at risk, or only those with some signs or symptoms? There is no simple answer to this question, and in practice, the model used may include elements of each.

There are advantages and disadvantages associated with the use of different types of intervention. For example, an advantage of universal programs is that no selection procedures are needed and thus stigmatization is unlikely to result. However, such programs are likely to be more expensive from both a financial and a human resource perspective and, without careful and thoughtful design, risk the possibility of doing harm to healthy people. Shochet and O'Gorman (1995) argued that the first guiding principle of any universal intervention must be to quarantine harm. Especially in initial trials when outcomes of prevention initiatives remain uncertain, it is imperative that, above all, people are not worse off as a result of participating in the program. For example, concern is often expressed about possible iatrogenic effects of suicide prevention programs when applied universally to young people. Similarly, there is growing evidence that universal programs for preventing eating problems in schoolchildren can be associated with increases in eating and body image concerns (O'Dea, 2000).

Selected programs target individuals most likely to be in need of assistance and optimize the use of financial and human resources. Such programs increase the probability of identifying and intervening with individuals who otherwise may have gone unnoticed and progressed to a more severe level of dysfunction. In some contexts, selected programs are termed "early intervention," especially if some level of dysfunction already exists in the sample. However, the selection procedures associated with selected and indicated programs carry the risk of stigmatizing or labeling individuals.

Clearly, there is much overlap in the various categories of preventive and EI models and technologies. Throughout the remainder of this chapter, the term *prevention* is used broadly to indicate any intervention program designed to build resilience and reduce risk and/or suffering prior to the establishment of clear-cut psychological disorders. *EI* also is used broadly, but focuses more on strategies that target groups in which some risk or problems are already evident. This chapter is limited to covering those programs that focus primarily on the child and/or family. Programs that prevent psychological problems by modifying community and school factors are not covered, nor are programs that are entirely *universal* unless they also assess change in at-risk subgroups.

Spence and Dadds (1996) outlined several prerequisites for the establishment of effective EI programs: (1) an empirically tested model of the etiology of the target problem that identifies risk and protective factors; (2) a reliable and valid method of identifying children at risk; (3) effective strategies for reducing risk and enhancing protective factors; and (4) the opportunity to apply these methods in practice. Similarly, Simeonsson (1994) argued that to develop a program, one must begin with a clear understanding of risk factors, protective factors, and characteristics of the targeted population, all of which inform the formulation of the prevention program. Clearly, the selection criteria apply more to EI than to universal preventive programs. By targeting the entire group, the need for identifying children at risk is largely overcome. Further, if the goal is to increase resilience in the group, a model of specific problems may not be needed as much as a clear model of protective factors and their relationship to health.

However, most EI and prevention programs aim to reduce the incidence of specific problems. In the area of child psychopathology, externalizing disorders (EDs) of aggression, impulsivity, and delinquency and internalizing disorders

(IDs) of anxiety and depression are the most common both in terms of clinical costs and self-reported suffering in young people. The aim of the following is to look at models of how these problems develop, their risk and protective factors, and targeted interventions. Throughout this chapter, studies from around the world are reviewed. Although some of the findings are based on research conducted in Australia, these samples have been found to be quite similar to samples studied in the midwestern United States.

ASSESSMENT AND INTERVENTION

EXTERNALIZING PROBLEMS

Diagnostically, EDs consist of Oppositional Defiant Disorder (ODD), characterized by persistent defiant and disruptive behavior, Conduct Disorder (CD), which includes ODD features plus more severe violations of society rules, and Attention-Deficit/Hyperactivity Disorder (ADHD), which refers to persistent levels of inattention and impulsivity (American Psychiatric Association [APA], 1994). Alone or in clusters, these problems occur in approximately 5 to 10% of school-age individuals. The onset is variable but occurs typically in early childhood for ODD and ADHD, and later in the school years for CD. Throughout history, this cluster of behaviors has attracted various names, such as delinquency and antisocial behavior, and has been approached from a variety of perspectives, from a failure of moral development to a sociopolitical problem. Current parlance assumes that these behaviors can be thought of as psychological or behavioral disorders; thus, the phenomena have largely now become the domain of mental health professionals. However, categorical diagnoses have inherent problems, especially for prevention and EI science, due to the fact that disruptive behavior is a dimensional phenomenon.

Many children are referred for treatment of disruptive behavior problems who do not meet the formal diagnostic criteria, and only a subset of recent studies has used formally diagnosed children. A review limited to these latter studies would lose much of the richness of accumulated evidence about the characteristics of disruptive children. Thus, this review considers the wide range of disruptive behavior. In this chapter, conduct problems and disruptive behavior problems (EDs) refer to problems in the general population of children referred for disruptive behavior problems.

A reasonably clear picture of the developmental course of EDs has developed (Conduct Problems Prevention Research Group [CPRG], 1992; Loeber & Dishion, 1983; Patterson, De-Barshye, & Ramsey, 1989; Reid & Eddy, 1997). In their most severe and persistent forms, EDs take an identifiable path from childhood to adulthood. Along this path, different causal factors emerge. The prescription of a developmental course refers to a commonality among groups of ED children, and it is easy to identify exceptions to the general pattern. These include youths who, after years of being well behaved, showed the first signs of conduct problems in adolescence and children who were highly oppositional and difficult as children but "grew out of it" by adolescence. Notwithstanding these individual differences, it is crucial that EDs are conceptualized as a developmental sequence and as involving the interplay of multiple causative factors.

The developmental causes of EDs are viewed as a set of systems, subsystems, and components of systems interacting at the biological, interpersonal, family, and social levels. Further, the importance of any one factor varies according to the developmental stage of the child. Developmentally, the literature indicates clusters of risk that may be seen as windows of opportunity for guiding the establishment of comprehensive intervention programs. Table 3.1 summarizes the developmental sequence of risk with some

Table 3.1 Developmental risk factors for externalizing disorders and associated intervention opportunities.

Development Phase		Risk Factors	Potential Interventions
Prenatal to infancy	Child:	Environmental toxicity. Temperamental difficulties.	Environmental safety (e.g., lead minimization). Early identification of children at risk through temperamental and behavioral problems, and families at high risk through socioeconomic adversity and psychopathology. Provision of adequate health care/parental and infant support programs, home visiting programs. Promotion of social equality/support/community connectedness. provision of family support, education and therapy services, premarital and preparenting education programs. Promotion of nonviolent cultures and communities.
	Family:	Poverty/low SES/social isolation. Family violence/conflict/ separation. Parental psychopathology. Poor health/nutrition.	
	Social:	Economic hardship/ unemployment. Family breakdown/isolation. Cultures of violence.	
Toddler to late childhood	Child:	Learning and language difficulties. Impulsivity.	Early remediation of learning and language difficulties. Provision of parent training and broader family interventions. Family and marital support programs. After-school care and monitoring of children. Peer social skills programs. Provision of positive school environments and educational opportunities. Promotion of quality parent-school relationships.
	Family:	Coercive family processes/ violence. Low care and nurturance. Inadequate monitoring of child.	
	Social:	Inadequate child care and parental support. Lack of educational opportunities. Negative parent-school relationship.	
Adolescence	Child:	School/employment failure. Cognitive bias to threat/ hostility. Peer rejection/deviant peer group. Substance abuse/depression.	Cognitive-behavioral skills programs for teenagers. Academic and work transition skills programs. Crisis support for family/youth individuation problems, breakdown, and homelessness. Family-adolescent therapy services. Substance abuse prevention programs. Cultures of community respect and connectedness.
	Family:	Conflict/individuation problems. Rejection/homelessness.	
	Social:	Lack of education/employment. Culture of violence.	

potential interventions at each point. In the next section, interventions are reviewed within this developmental framework, highlighting the impediments and difficulties faced by clinicians in typical clinical practice.

Tertiary Interventions for Externalizing Disorders

Considerable work has been done on the development and evaluation of tertiary treatments for EDs. The most successful are parent training and family interventions and individual or group social-cognitive work with the child.

Family Intervention. Research evaluating treatments for child EDs has supported the efficacy of behavioral family interventions (BFIs) in the short term and over follow-up periods of years after the termination of treatment (Miller & Prinz, 1990). The past few decades have witnessed continuous refinement of the BFI approach. Empirical evidence and clinical experience suggest that not all parents or families benefit to the same extent from treatment (Miller & Prinz, 1990), and difficulties are commonly encountered when there are concurrent family problems, parental psychopathology, and economic hardship. Several authors have made various proposals to improve the outcome of treatment by expanding the focus of treatment to the multiple systems that provide the context for family life (Henggeler, Melton, Brondino, Scherer, & Hanley, 1997; Miller & Prinz, 1990). Of particular interest to EI is the Triple P approach (Sanders, 1999), which offers various levels of intervention intensity, from simple provision of information to a multisystemic, individually tailored intervention. Of the different approaches encompassed by BFI, parent training for the treatment of younger ODD children has the most accumulated evidence regarding its therapeutic value. There is less evidence to suggest that BFI is effective in altering the course of the more severe CD children, especially beyond the years of early childhood.

Social-Cognitive Interventions with ED Children. Social-cognitive interventions are based on the finding that EDs are characterized by a tendency to overinterpret threat and hostility in others and poor social problem-solving skills. Thus, these interventions aim to help children to more accurately interpret the behavior of others and formulate nonaggressive, prosocial responses in common social situations that would usually provoke them to aggression.

Given this emphasis on abstract cognitive and social analysis, social-cognitive interventions with ED youth are generally limited to older children and youth who can operate at abstract cognitive levels (i.e., approximately 7 to 8 years and older). According to Kazdin (1993), variations on social-cognitive interventions are numerous, but they share some central features: (1) a focus on the cognitive processes; (2) teaching a step-by-step approach to solving interpersonal problems; (3) using a range of activities to train children in these skills that are engaging and understandable for the developmental level of the target children; and (4) emphasizing learning of skills via the provision of clear information, modeling of skills, role playing with the provision of feedback, and shaping strategies.

Social-cognitive interventions are a relatively recent development, and less research into therapeutic outcomes and processes has been undertaken compared to that for BFI. Reviews of treatment outcome (e.g., Baer & Nietzel, 1991; Durlack, Furhman, & Lampman, 1991; Kazdin, 1993) are generally positive. However, treatment effect sizes associated with social-cognitive interventions are often not clinically significant, interventions are limited to older children who can benefit from abstract social problem solving, and the putative relationship between therapeutic change and the development of cognitive skills has not been clearly established.

A range of well-known problems are associated with tertiary treatments for EDs in the real world. These have been reviewed in depth by Dadds (1995). Many families may not seek help as part of a larger marginalization from traditional health services associated with low socioeconomic status (SES), low education, poverty, cultural and racial isolation, the lack of services in rural regions and urban areas of poverty, and general disempowerment in society. Thus, the very families that are at highest risk for EDs may be the ones least likely or able to access the services that can potentially help.

When EDs, comprehensive assessments and treatments need to take a broader parent training and family focus. Mental health services require the physical structures (e.g., child care facilities, group work consultation rooms, home visit services) and the political structures that allow clinicians to consult with the entire family. Family breakdown is also a major impediment to successful treatment, often associated with frequent geographical moves, disrupted routines, multiple caregivers and schools, and changes of family composition. Dropout from treatment is a common problem for clinicians working with EDs, dropout rates can be as high as 50% of initial starters (Kazdin, 1993; Miller & Prinz, 1990).

Due to the fact that EDs are associated with multiple problems in families, schools, and society, the delivery of comprehensive interventions presents a major challenge to the skill level of the clinician. Most especially, the provision of a state-of-the-art BFI requires multiple therapist skills involving individual and family assessment, behavior change strategies, family engagement and therapy process skills, and communication and interagency liaison skills (Sanders & Dadds, 1993). It cannot be guaranteed that a particular mental health setting employs clinicians who can provide these interventions. Given that the development and effective treatment of EDs can involve the interplay of multiple child, family, school, and societal factors, another common impediment to intervention is lack of communication and coordination between different health and educational agencies.

Family interventions for EDs have the strongest research support. With younger children, the evidence for these interventions is strong. However, as children move into the teen years, the evidence for the effectiveness of these interventions becomes weaker. Thus, early detection and intervention is a major factor in the prevention and treatment of EDs. Clinical settings in which the most common referral of EDs is for teenagers, especially those who have a well-established pattern of antisocial behavior, will have relatively little success with just the sole use of family interventions.

These problems show that the existence of an effective treatment does not guarantee that the child and family will receive it. Tertiary models of treatment, though necessary, are probably not the best way to tackle the majority of EDs in their early stages. Thus, we now consider programs that attempt to reduce the incidence of EDs using an EI approach.

Early Intervention for EDs
A number of prevention programs aim to reduce aggression and promote social skills in children via universal curriculum-based programs in schools. These may have some impact on EDs but are outside the scope of this review (see Greenberg, Domitrovich, & Bumbarger, 2000). Greenberg et al. located 10 EI programs that have shown success in reducing EDs or their risk factors. Similar to tertiary models, the majority of these utilize child cognitive skills training, parent training, or both. Only the most recent and well-evaluated are reviewed here.

As an example of a child-focused program, Lochman, Coie, Underwood, and Terry (1993) evaluated a 26-session social skills training program focusing on peer relations, problem solving, and anger management, with a sample ($n = 52$) of 9- to 11-year-old aggressive-rejected children. Compared to controls, the program children were rated as significantly less aggressive by teachers and more socially accepted by peers at posttreatment and at one-year follow-up. In contrast, in Lochman's (1985) program, children who had received an anger coping program were, three years after the intervention, no different from controls in terms of parent ratings of aggression and observations of disruptive-aggressive behavior or in terms of self-reported delinquency. Tierney, Grossman, and Resch (Big Brother/Big Sister Program, 1995) randomly assigned 959 10- to 16-year-old adolescents to a mentor or a wait-list control condition. Those with a mentor reported that they engaged in significantly less fighting, were less likely to initiate the use of drugs and alcohol, and perceived their family relationships more positively than controls. However, there were no significant differences between groups in terms of self-reported delinquency. Although encouraging, these data are based solely on self-report.

One problem with the use of group interventions for indicated ED youth is that iatrogenic effects have been found in programs where antisocial youth were grouped together (Dishion, Andrews, Kavanagh, & Soberman, 1996). In contrast, studies have found that ED youth benefit from being in groups with nonproblem children. For example, Hudley and Graham (1993, 1995) paired aggressive 10- to 12-year-old boys with nonaggressive peers in a 12-lesson school-based intervention focusing on improving the accuracy of children's perceptions and interpretations of others' actions. Compared to controls, teacher ratings indicated that the program successfully reduced aggressive behavior immediately following the intervention. There have been no follow-up data to date. A similar 22-session integration program by Prinz, Blechman, and Dumas (1994) was evaluated up to six months following the intervention. Children in the program were rated by teachers as significantly less aggressive than controls at posttest and follow-up. Significant improvements were also noted in the intervention children's prosocial coping and teacher-rated social skills.

Overall, the evidence is not strong that child-focused EI interventions are effective with EDs. In general, their results are modest and not durable, the sample sizes are small, and due to the nature of the interventions, they are limited to older children and adolescents. However, child-focused interventions remain a component of more comprehensive programs that are showing more impressive results.

Parent-focused interventions generally have produced more clinically significant outcomes. As noted earlier, there have been numerous demonstrations of the effectiveness of social learning based parent-training programs for families of children with EDs. Numerous independent replications in community settings have produced significant results (Sanders, 1999). Although most of these programs developed as tertiary treatments and have been evaluated on clinical populations, a number of authors have argued that they are excellent EI strategies, in that they effectively reduce EDs early in their growth to later delinquency (e.g., Sanders, 1999). As noted earlier, however, one limitation of a referral-based approach is that it leaves initiatives for intervention in the hands of parents, who may not seek help even in extreme situations.

Parent interventions also have been recently applied in both universal prevention and EI formats. Webster-Stratton has recently used a parent training model with young Head Start children (Webster-Stratton & Hammond, 1998). The program can thus be regarded as *selected*, and the entry procedure is not dependent on parent referrals. Parents of Head Start children were randomly assigned to receive the intervention or to serve as a control and receive only the usual services. The nine-week intervention consisted of parent training groups and a teacher training program. Results at posttest and 12 to 18 months follow-up indicate significant improvements in parent behavior, parental involvement in school, child conduct problems, and child school-based behavior.

Recently, a number of EI programs have been evaluated that adopt developmental models of Eds and, as such, utilize multiple interventions across settings and time. This is consistent with a general view that a more comprehensive approach is necessary to alter the developmental trajectories of children who live in high-risk environments and show early signs of EDs (CPRG, 1992; Reid & Eddy, 1997). In the Montreal Prevention Experiment, Tremblay and colleagues (McCord, Tremblay, Vitaro, & Desmarais-Gervais, 1994; Tremblay, Masse, Pagani, & Vitaro, 1996; Tremblay et al., 1992) combined parent training and child skill training. Primary school boys rated high on aggressive and disruptive behavior ($n = 166$) were randomly assigned to a two-year intervention or placebo control condition. Children worked with normative peers to develop more prosocial and adaptive social behavior, and parents worked with family consultants approximately twice a month to learn positive discipline techniques and how to support their child's positive behavior. Initial results did not reveal clear group differences. At the three-year follow-up, when the boys were age 12 years, the treatment group was significantly less likely than control boys to engage in fighting aggression, or delinquent activity and to be classified as having serious adjustment difficulties. These results came from a variety of self-, teacher-, peer-, and parent-report measures. Effects of the treatment on other forms of antisocial behavior (e.g., self-reported stealing) and substance use continued into early adolescence. Other EI programs have found durable effects that did not emerge until follow-up assessments (see Dadds, Spence, Holland, Barrett, & Laurens, 1997). Intervention effects were reported by multiple informants across multiple domains of adjustment (i.e., behavioral, social, school/academic).

The First Steps Program (Walker et al., 1998) intervenes with both parents and children, the latter having been identified at kindergarten for exhibiting elevated levels of antisocial behavior. Families with an at-risk child receive a six-week home and children participate in a classroom-based skill building and reinforcement program that lasts two months. The program has been evaluated with 42 subjects in two cohorts using a randomized-control design. Positive treatment effects were found for both adaptive and academic behavior at postintervention and at follow-up into early primary school. A replication (Golly, Stiller, & Walker, 1998) with a new sample of 20 kindergarten students has produced similar results. Positive results also have been found for a program for students age 6 to 12 years exhibiting aggressive and disruptive behavior that targets the child,

the parents, and the classroom (Pepler, King, & Byrd, 1991; Pepler, King, Craig, Byrd, & Bream, 1995). In this program, the parent training is optional. It is important to note that significant group differences were found only on teacher ratings; parents failed to see significant behavior changes in the intervention children.

The Conduct Problems Prevention Research Group (1992) implemented Fast Track, a school-wide program that integrates universal, selective, and indicated models of prevention into a comprehensive longitudinal model for the prevention of conduct disorders and associated adolescent problem behaviors. A randomized-control trial of 50 elementary schools in four U.S. urban and rural locations is still underway. The universal intervention includes teacher consultation in the use of a series of grade-level versions of the PATHS Curriculum throughout the elementary years. The targeted intervention package includes a series of family (e.g., home visiting, parenting skills, case management), child (e.g., academic tutoring, social skills training), school, peer group, and community interventions. Targeted children were identified by multigate screening for externalizing behavior problems during kindergarten; these were children with the most extreme behavior problems in schools (10%) in neighborhoods with high crime and poverty rates (selected aspect). At present, evaluations are available for the first three years (CPPRG, 1999a, 1999b). There have been significant reductions in special education referrals and aggression both at home and at school for the targeted children. The initial results provide evidence for improved social and academic development, including lower sociometric reports of peer aggression and improved observer ratings of the classroom atmosphere in the intervention sample. Evaluations will continue through middle school as Fast Track adopts an ecological-developmental model that assumes that, for high-risk groups, prevention of antisocial behavior will be achieved by enhancing and linking protective factors within the child, family, school, and community.

Summary

It can be seen that only recently have community trials been conducted that use randomized-control designs to evaluate multicomponent programs based on comprehensive ecological and developmental models of EDs. A number of characteristics appear to be associated with successful EI for externalizing problems in children: (1) early identification and intervention beginning not later than preschool or early primary school years; (2) incorporation of family-based intervention as a core target for change; (3) adoption of a comprehensive model that emphasizes a broad ecology (child, family, school, community); (4) adoption of a longitudinal-developmental approach to risk and protective factors and windows of opportunity for intervention; and (5) use of a comprehensive mix of selected (e.g., poor neighborhoods), indicated (identification of aggressive children), and universal (e.g., classroom program) strategies.

INTERNALIZING PROBLEMS

In contrast to EDs, less is known about the developmental pathways and risk and protective factors characteristic of internalizing disorders (IDs) in young people. However, such knowledge is rapidly accumulating, especially for anxiety disorders (e.g., Vasey & Dadds, 2000), and these are the main focus of this review. A summary of the risk and protective factors of anxiety problems during early childhood, middle childhood, and adolescence are outlined in Table 3.2, together with associated prevention or early intervention strategies. The most salient risk factors emerging in the literature are temperamental predispositions to be shy and fearful of novel people, objects, or situations (behavior inhibition or reticence; Biederman et al., 1993; Gest, 1997), the existence of parental anxiety or depressive problems (Beidel & Turner, 1997), and exposure to traumatic environmental events (Marans, Berkowitz, & Cohen, 1998). Secure attachment to caregivers

(e.g., Warren, Huston, Egeland, & Sroufe, 1997), an easy temperament, and good social skills stand out as ongoing protective mechanisms. These risk and protective factors switch in and out at various developmental points; thus, a series of windows of opportunity for prevention and early intervention can be identified.

Early Intervention Strategies for IDs

Early Childhood. Evidence is inconclusive regarding the effectiveness of prevention of anxiety disorders in early childhood. One of the obstacles to determining the effectiveness of preventive efforts is the lack of established assessment criteria within this young age group that are suitable for use at the community level. Additionally, many of the cognitive-restructuring aspects of reducing anxiety are beyond the cognitive capacities of very young children; therefore, adult modeling and shaping are the primary avenues of protection. It is generally considered that, for infants and preschoolers, the best treatment approach is working with parents (Bernstein & Borchardt, 1991). Knowledge of developmental needs, including differences in temperament, parental support, fostering secure attachment, and parental acquisition/modeling of coping strategies are broad areas of prevention. These strategies provide opportunities for parents to learn patterns of interaction that support children's well being as well as skills to manage parental stress.

LaFreniere and Capuano (1997) implemented a six-month intensive home-based indicated prevention program for mothers and preschoolers. Children receiving high teacher ratings on anxious-withdrawn behavior were invited to be in the program. The project offered information on child development, including booklets on development, behavior, security, the body, and parental needs. Additional sessions were provided to address core skills in parenting, as well as any additional personal or parental concerns, to alleviate stress within the parent-child relationship. Finally, parents were assisted in building a social support network. As assessed

Table 3.2 Developmental risk for anxiety disorders and associated intervention strategies.

Development Phase		Risk Factors	Potential Mechanisms of Prevention
Infancy	*Child:*	Shy temperament, behavioral inhibition.	Early identification of high-risk children and anxious parents.
	Family:	Neglect or overprotection. Parental psychopathology, especially anxiety.	Parental support and parent training to foster responsive parenting, secure attachment, and positive parental coping strategies.
	Society:	Environmental stress.	
Childhood	*Child:*	Reticence/behavioral/inhibition/shyness. Social isolation.	Social problem-solving training encouraging proactive solutions. Increasing focus on cognitive strategies as child matures. Exposure programs to overcome fears.
	Family:	Parental psychopathology. Overprotection of child in face of challenges, selective attention to threat, and avoidant solutions. Parental overcontrol or criticism.	Enhancement of social skills and opportunities for peer interaction. Training parents to model effective cognitive and behavioral coping.
	Society:	Social isolation, insularity.	Positive parental strategies to manage child avoidance. Responsive parenting. Family connections to school and community.
Adolescence	*Child:*	As above. Possibility of comorbid disorders, especially depression and substance use.	As above. Cognitive-behavioral training with increasing focus on adolescent and related issues (depression, substance use).
	Family:	As above.	Increasing focus on issues of autonomy for family.
	Society:	Peer pressure. Regarding comorbidity: Prevalence of substance use.	Parental training in balancing autonomy and independence with family support.

by teachers at the conclusion of the program, anxious-withdrawn preschoolers showed significant gains in social competence, but reduction in anxious-withdrawn behavior only approached significance. Parenting stress in the intervention group did not show a significant reduction relative to controls, although a subjective positive bias was noted in mothers who participated in the intervention.

A parent-teacher universal prevention program for children age 4 to 5 years aimed at reducing the incidence of IDs later in childhood has been evaluated (Roth & Dadds, 1999). REACH for Resilience aimed to teach parents and teachers strategies and ways of thinking that can increase children's ability to cope with

challenges, especially through adult modeling of these strategies and encouragement of children's efforts. Results showed that the most distressed parents tended to attend the intervention, and their distress reduced at post-treatment and follow-up. However, this self-selection confound made reaching definitive conclusions difficult, and, similar to LaFreniere and Capuano (1997), the overall results were not impressive.

Middle Childhood. Middle childhood appears to be an especially advantageous time for anxiety prevention and EI. Developmentally, this is the time when most anxiety disorders emerge (Bernstein & Borchardt, 1991). As children's cognitive abilities mature, cognitive-behavioral techniques (CBT) are able to be utilized in helping at-risk children positively attribute the meaning of aversive events and experiences. Recent trials of individual and group format tertiary treatments for children and adolescents with anxiety disorders have shown impressive results up to six years postintervention (Barrett, Dadds, & Rapee, 1996; Barrett, Duffy, Dadds, & Rapee, 2001; Kendall & Southam-Gerow, 1996). These interventions have formed the basis of the EI programs reviewed below.

An indicated EI program in Australia targeted children ($N = 1,786$) age 7 to 14 years (Dadds et al., 1997). Those included in the project ranged from children who were exhibiting mildly anxious features but remained disorder-free, to those who were in the less severe range of a *DSM-IV* anxiety disorder. An intensive screening process incorporated parent, child, and teacher reports, telephone calls, and face-to-face interviews. Excluded from the sample were children (1) with disruptive behaviors (impulsive, aggressive, hyperactive, noncompliant); (2) for whom English was not the first language in the home; (3) with a developmental delay or other problems; (4) who had no anxiety problem according to teacher reports; and (5) with invalid child reports (ticked "yes" for all items). The final sample consisted of 128 children. Any child with severe symptoms or whose parents requested individual help for their child's anxiety was referred for individual treatment and no longer included in follow-up assessments.

The intervention was based on an adaptation of Kendall's Coping Cat Workbook (Coping Koala; Barrett, Dadds, & Holland, 1994), a 10-session program presented in group format for teaching children strategies to cope with anxiety. The sessions were conducted weekly for one hour at the child's school, in groups of 5 to 12 children. In addition, parents periodically attended three sessions covering child management skills, modeling and encouraging the

strategies children were learning through the Coping Koala Prevention Program, and how to use Kendall's FEAR plan to manage their own anxiety. The monitoring group received no intervention but were contacted at planned intervals for follow-up assessments.

At postintervention, no significant differences were found between the monitoring and the intervention groups. Yet, at six months follow-up, the intervention group showed a significant reduction in the onset of disorder relative to the control group. Most important, the success of the program in reducing the existing rate of anxiety disorders and preventing the onset of new anxiety disorders was successfully maintained at a two-year follow-up (Dadds et al., 1999). These results are very promising. Given that over half of the at-risk children in the monitoring group progressed from mild anxious symptoms into a full-blown anxiety disorder, middle childhood and early adolescence appear to provide an important window of opportunity for prevention initiatives.

Considering a broader framework than anxiety prevention, a number of studies have focused on building resilience rather than overcoming disorders. The Rochester Child Resilience Project (Cowen, Wyman, & Work, 1996) contrasted stress-affected and stress-resilient children living in a highly stressed urban context. A number of other prevention and early intervention projects that aim to build resilience across time or that have targeted problems other than anxiety have demonstrated promising results, including reductions in anxiety (Marans et al., 1998; McDonald et al., 1997).

Adolescence. With respect to IDs, the prevention of depression has gained prominence in research investigations with adolescents. To date, one of the most successful programs for reduction of depressive symptoms in young people has been the Pennsylvania Depression Program for adolescents age 10 to 13 years (Jaycox, Reivich, Gillham, & Seligman, 1994). The study included three separate programs focusing on teaching cognitive skills, social problem-solving skills, and a combination of cognitive and social problem-solving skills. Training in assertiveness, negotiation, and coping skills was also included. After finding no significant difference among the three intervention modalities, the groups were combined, resulting in a treatment sample of 69 participants and a wait-list control group of 74 participants. Significant improvements in depressive symptoms were obtained for the intervention group compared to controls at posttest, six-month follow-up, and two-year follow-up (Gillham, Reivich, Jaycox, & Seligman, 1994). This innovative study indicates that psychoeducational prevention efforts to build resilience to depression are promising during early adolescence. A limitation of the study was the possible biasing effect of a self-selected sample in conjunction with the low initial recruitment rate (between 13% and 19%) and high attrition rate (30%).

Clarke et al. (1995) reported significant improvements in depression for an indicated intervention group compared to wait-list for 14- to 15-year-olds. The program was more successful than Jaycox et al. (1994) at recruiting adolescents; however, it still succeeded in engaging fewer than 50% of the adolescents identified at being at risk for depression. There was also a reasonably high attrition rate, particularly in the intervention group (21 out of 76). In another indicated trial, Hains and Ellmann (1994) reported positive results for their program, which consisted of problem solving, cognitive restructuring, and anxiety management, reducing depression scores in volunteer adolescents who had been classified as having high arousal levels. These authors also experienced difficulty with possible self-selection bias.

Beardslee and colleagues (Beardslee, 1989; Beardslee & MacMillan, 1993; Beardslee et al., 1992, 1993) evaluated a selective program for adolescents and parents, where one or both parents had a major affective disorder, often in combination with other serious psychiatric disorders. The authors used family therapy and psychoeducational approaches to help families develop a shared perspective on the depressive illness and to change parents' behavior in relation to their children. In a randomized trial of 20 families, parents who received family-based interventions reported significantly more improvements in behavior and attitudes than parents who received information alone. Recruitment was conducted through Medical Health Fund advertising, so no information is available regarding recruitment rates and self-selection processes.

The above studies provide evidence for the usefulness of selective and indicated prevention programs. They also highlight the well-known difficulties associated with recruitment and retention of adolescents. Adolescents may see such programs as singling them out from their peer group at an age when peer group acceptance is especially important. This problem might be substantially reduced if intervention programs for adolescent depression were implemented routinely as part of the school curriculum, either as an alternative or a complement to indicated programs.

The Resourceful Adolescent Program (RAP; Shochet, Holland, & Whitefield, 1997) was developed to meet this need. It consists of components for adolescents (RAP-A) and their families (RAP-F). The RAP-A is a 10-week group treatment run in groups of approximately 8 to 10 participants per group and focuses on building resilience in adolescents as a way of preventing depression. Given its universal delivery, participation rates were 80% or higher for the adolescents, although recruitment of families has remained a problem. Results indicate that participation in RAP is associated with reductions in self-reported depression, especially for adolescents with preexisting depression at pretreatment (Shochet et al., in press). Replication of these effects is needed, as Clarke, Hawkins, Murphy, and

Sheeber (1993) also used a universal approach and failed to find any significant effects.

Summary

Middle childhood is the age of onset of most anxiety disorders and appears to be an optimum time to provide prevention and early intervention initiatives. Indicated prevention programs have demonstrated the effectiveness of anxiety prevention and early intervention in middle childhood to adolescence. Evidence that such interventions can be scheduled earlier is difficult to find. For depression, indicated and selected programs have shown success in reducing depressive symptoms, but participation numbers have been a problem. Universal programs for depression in adolescence achieve more acceptable participation rates, but the outcomes are unclear at this point. The programs for anxiety and depression are similar in content, and the middle childhood programs for anxiety need to be evaluated for their potential to prevent later depressive disorders. Family involvement has been shown to facilitate successful treatment of childhood anxiety disorders. However, due to their school-based delivery, the role of parental involvement in these programs is not clear.

Home Visiting Programs for New At-Risk Parents

Home visiting programs focus on improving the capacity of at-risk parents to provide a nurturing, healthy environment for their children in the early years of life. Parents are usually selected into such programs via the neonatal health care systems on the basis of multiple risk factors such as poverty, teenage mother, low birthweight child, and history of abuse. Models of intervention generally revolve around the formation of a trusting, empathic relationship with the home visitor (usually a nurse), who promotes parenting efficacy and an ensuing increase in healthy parenting behaviors and secure attachment with the infant. These programs have been implemented throughout the world for many years. However, controlled designs have only recently been used to evaluate their effectiveness. The most comprehensive evaluation of such a program has been reported by Olds et al. (1998), who now have data up to 15 years follow-up from their original intervention.

In the original trial, 400 women who met criteria for either low income, single-parent status, or teenage pregnancy were recruited during pregnancy and randomized to standard well-child-infant care or two levels of home visiting by a trained nurse. In the most intense condition, the visiting continued until the child's second birthday. A range of positive outcomes have been shown to be associated with the intensive visiting; perhaps the most impressive findings are the recent data showing reductions in delinquency, substance use, and numbers of sexual partners for the children at 15 years of age (Olds et al., 1998). Olds and Kitzman (1993) reviewed similar well-designed studies and concluded that there is substantial evidence to support the effectiveness of these home visiting EI programs in promoting a range of healthy outcomes for children at risk. Further, sufficient research has been reported in this area to allow for analyses of factors moderating intervention outcomes (e.g., Cole, Kitzman, Olds, & Sidora, 1998).

Given the effects attributable to interventions in most other EI research, it is difficult to understand how a nonspecific intervention in the first two years of life can lead to such powerful effects 15 years later. Replications and results from other communities are needed because most of the evidence supporting home visitations comes from this single study. A recent trial of a similar program for at-risk mothers in Australia was also successful in producing immediate gains for mothers and infants (Armstrong, Fraser, Dadds, & Morris, 1999); however, the results were not impressive in terms of differences from the control group at two-year follow-up (Fraser, Armstrong, Morris, & Dadds, 2000).

Overall, these results are impressive. They are also consistent with the literature on EDs previously reviewed showing that the most impressive findings come from programs that target children early in the first few years of life within a broad ecological framework. Waiting until the school years, especially adolescence, may be too late to affect delinquency and violence.

PREVENTION OF SUBSTANCE USE DISORDERS

Data from clinical samples point to a high overlap between substance abuse disorders (SADs) and psychopathology, independent of whether the referred problem is the SAD (Kessler & Price, 1993) or the psychopathology (Bibb & Chambless, 1986). One has approximately three times the chance of suffering a SAD if one has an ID, and vice versa, compared to a disorder-free person. These odds reflect means collapsed across specific IDs and SADs. They would be considerably higher if calculated according to the presence of *any* type of ID, and may be higher for social phobia and panic/depression in particular. Thus, there is an opportunity for joint preventive efforts depending on the nature of the causal links between them (see Kessler & Price, 1993).

One of the best studies showing a developmental sequence linking IDs and SADs comes from Catalano, Koslerman, Hawkins, and Newcomb (1996), who showed that a social development model that emphasizes social competence through late childhood and adolescence was the best predictor of SAD in the late teen years. Few other longitudinal studies exist, but there is enough indirect evidence to make some useful speculations. Apart from transient distress directly resulting from the abuse of specific substances, both IDs and EDs tend to precede SADs developmentally. In terms of comorbidity with EDs and IDs, several studies have shown that both anxiety problems and conduct problems typically precede and are risk factors for depressive disorders, but the reverse has not been found (Angst, Vollrath, Merikangas, & Ernst, 1990; D. Cole, Peeke, Martin, Truglio, & Seroczynski, 1998; Hagnell & Graesbeck, 1990). The early signs of conduct and anxiety problems can be identified in childhood, and many emerge as clear disorders in late childhood and early adolescence. Depression is relatively rare before middle adolescence and shares its initial onset period with SAD in the teen years.

Thus, it is likely that SAD may be preceded by anxiety disorders and depression. Early intervention for IDs may hold potential for reducing SADs in the community. This is in contrast to the commonly recognized pathway to SADs as coming through conduct and attention-deficit problems, high sensation seeking, and social adversity. It is likely that alternative pathways to SADs—through IDs, on the one hand, and EDs on the other—are in fact interweaving. Recent research has shown that anxiety and depression may coexist with externalizing problems in young people far more significantly than has been traditionally acknowledged. Measures of attention deficit, for example, are highly confounded by the presence of anxiety problems (Perrin & Last, 1992), and internalizing problems can enhance externalizing problems through adolescence (Loeber, Russo, Stouthamer-Loeber, & Lahey, 1994). Unfortunately, longitudinal studies that simultaneously consider early IDs and EDs as predictors of later SADs are not available; these should become a research priority.

Research reviewed earlier clearly showed the potential of programs to reduce the incidence and severity of both EDs and IDs in children. Given the comorbidity of these with concurrent and later SADs, it is tempting to conclude that reductions in the former should result in reductions in SADs. However, few studies explicitly tested whether SADs could be reduced by intervening to reduce EDs and IDs and thus build resilience in young people. However, indirect evidence can be found that helps inform the area. First, many school-based studies exist that tried to directly change adolescents' drug behavior by training them in drug-related social skills (e.g., saying no, managing stress without drugs). Although many have reported positive short-term benefits, the overall success rate is not impressive (Gorman, 1996).

The majority of SAD prevention studies for adolescents have focused on EDs and social adversity risk factors. Several programs of research reviewed above have demonstrated reductions in EDs through the primary school years (see Greenberg et al., 2000), and several of these have shown effective reductions in SADs from the targeting of externalizing behavior (e.g., The Anger Coping Programme, Lochman, 1992; Big Brother/Sister, Tierney et al., 1995).

There are also studies in which the promotion of general resilience in primary school children has been shown to reduce substance use into adolescence. For example, Schinke and Tepavac (1995) showed that a universal school-based intervention that focuses on personal and social decision-making and assertiveness skills reduced actual and potential substance use in 8- to 11-year-olds. The Seattle Social Development Project is a universal program that combines parent and teacher training throughout the primary school years. Controlled trials have compared early versus late scheduling of the intervention in large samples. Secondary school intervention was not effective, but the early intervention model (i.e., targeting social competence in the primary school years and continuing across developmental phases) has been shown to effectively reduce SADs at 18 years of age (Hawkins, Catalano, Kosterman, Abbott, & Hill, in press). Similarly, a number of well-designed studies that have targeted improved parent-child relationships have shown positive long-term benefits in reductions or delays in

drug taking (e.g., Kosterman, Hawkins, Spoth, Haggerty, & Zhu, 1997).

CASE EXAMPLE

The extent to which intervention technologies can actually make a difference in the community is influenced by a number of pragmatic, methodological, and theoretical issues. The aim of this section is to discuss important applied issues and to present a specific case example of an early intervention program. Most of the intervention studies reviewed were a combination of effectiveness and efficacy trials. That is, although they were conducted in real-world settings, they evaluated the intervention under optimal delivery conditions (e.g., in the context of a funded research program, using careful experimental designs and measures) and were implemented by highly trained and motivated staff. The question remains as to the community effectiveness of such interventions when implemented in the less than optimal conditions of existing mental health and educational systems.

Recruitment of participants is one of the major obstacles to preventive interventions, regardless of the type of prevention. Because participants have not self-referred for treatment and may not even believe they have any problems, especially in early childhood, the sense of urgency and motivation that drives clinical interventions is often absent. With childhood anxiety problems, parents and teachers often have not noticed anxiety problems or assume that children will "grow out of it." In the LaFreniere and Capuano (1997) study of selected children, fewer than one-third of identified participants were successfully recruited. The Roth and Dadds (1999) trial of a parenting intervention applied universally to preschool children has maintained contact with approximately half of those invited to participate. Indicated prevention projects in middle childhood show similar rates of recruitment, and selected and indicated programs for depression in adolescents have typically achieved very low participation rates. The Shochet et al. (in press) school-based universal prevention of depression program received parental consent for over 80% of potential students; however, when an additional parental component was added, attendance by parents at three evening sessions was very low, with 36% attending one session and only 10% attending all three sessions.

In the Roth and Dadds (1999) study, the most stressed parents were more likely to attend the intervention than those who felt good about their child. However, in many cases, the children, adolescents, and families that do not attend will be those who may most need the intervention. Interventions that are built into other routines, such as curriculum-based programs in schools, will achieve the highest participation rates. However, such integration is not always possible, and creative solutions for improving participation by high-risk samples are sorely needed.

An additional issue concerns the administrative systems that control the resource allocations and structures for mental health services. As we have seen, substantial evidence to date that childhood psychopathology can be prevented comes from school-based intervention trials. However, the responsibility for mental health promotion is typically within statutory *health* rather than *education* departments, and program designers may find their efforts frustrated by a lack of communication between the two groups. Intersectorial jurisdictions relating to the overlapping structure and functions of the various agencies that have responsibility for health and education of young people are a major concern for the science and practice of prevention.

Ethical considerations are of prime importance in EI as well. If a selective or indicated intervention is chosen, implementors must be aware of the danger of creating a stigma for at-risk children and families. Thus, strategies must be used to maximize chances that selection into a program is handled discreetly and is communicated in a way that minimizes distress and stigma (see case example below). Accuracy of identification is another concern when using selective or indicated intervention models. There is always the possibility of not detecting and so excluding children who actually are at risk and instead including those who are not at risk. These errors are very difficult to avoid; careful consideration must be given to determining a comprehensive and flexible process for deciding which individuals will be offered the program. In general, the best strategies involve collating information from multiple informants on multiple measures at various times.

The nature of informed consent and confidentiality will depend on local legal and administrative processes. However, a crucial consent issue is how the identification of acute risk is dealt with. For example, most mental health screening measures have the potential to identify children who are acutely distressed and at risk. In EI programs for anxiety and depression, a small number of children in each school are found to be highly depressed, engaging in risky behaviors, and sometimes suicidal. It is important that methods for dealing with such situations are established prior to screening. This is most commonly achieved through screening materials using predetermined cutoffs, resulting in scores that will be used to consider whether a child or adolescent is at immediate risk. Backup support systems to provide interventions for children identified as in need of individual counseling is an important step in planning a program. A strategy should be organized with school staff and parents and children informed in advance that, where such risk is detected, the school mental health worker will follow up. However, in some settings, such as rural or remote areas, organizing appropriate backup support may be more difficult and should be negotiated prior to implementation of the group. Thus, participants must be informed, prior to screening, about conditions that will cause confidentiality to be broken and of the processes that will be followed in such a situation.

The early intervention and prevention trial described by Dadds et al. (1997, 1999) provides a useful case example of these applied issues. It assessed the effectiveness of a school-based intervention to reduce the incidence of anxiety disorders in 7- to 14-year-olds. Previous research had established the effectiveness of tertiary treatment for anxiety problems in children and adolescents (Barrett et al., 1996). However, because most children with anxiety problems are not referred to outpatient treatment, the question was thus formulated: Could such an intervention be delivered to vulnerable children in a normal school environment?

The first challenge was to recruit the support of schools. The project was framed in positive terms, de-emphasizing pathology and focusing on a positive resilience-building program. Schools were approached via principals, school psychology staff, teachers, and any existing parent organizations. Talks were given to raise knowledge, deal with concerns, and build enthusiasm. Half of the schools were offered the intervention. For the control schools, an ongoing monitoring process was used. Any behavioral or emotional difficulties detected in the children were carefully assessed, and, in consultation with the parents, the child was withdrawn from the study and offered individual help by project staff free of charge. Thus, the provision of backup clinical services was essential to cooperation in the control conditions. Further, should the intervention prove to be successful, the control schools were promised the receipt of the interventions at a later time. Most schools were cooperative and enthusiastic, but a small number of schools did decline.

Once initial agreement was established, the practical issues of room and participant scheduling were addressed to ensure that the schools were not overly burdened by the presence and procedures of the study. Teachers were involved extensively in this planning.

Screening children to identify risk factors is complex in terms of theory and practice. A selected approach was chosen that utilized a screening procedure to identify children already showing signs of anxiety problems. Mindful of the need to utilize multiple informants, measures of anxiety were taken from both children and teachers. Many measures exist for self-report of anxiety in children, but finding a measure that could be used by teachers to report on large samples of children was problematic. A sheet containing simple descriptors of an anxious child and a conduct problem child were given to teachers. They were asked to nominate up to three children in each class who matched these descriptions. The aim was to channel the conduct problem children into other services and include in the intervention the children who scored high on either their own or the teacher's report.

Flexibility is needed in applied research. Almost no overlap was found between the children's and the teachers' reports. To include all the children who appeared on either list meant greatly increasing the number of children being offered the intervention. No evidence was available indicating the relative superiority of the teachers' or the children's reports, so all children were included. Later diagnostic interviews confirmed the wisdom of this decision, as children recruited from either list were equally likely to have an anxiety disorder.

After the lists of vulnerable children were prepared, the difficult challenge of contacting parents to request interviews was undertaken. This had to be approached with great persistence and sensitivity, the former because it was so difficult to establish contact with many parents, and the latter because of the danger of creating distress in parents and children. During contact with parents, the intervention was described as an innovative program to build skills in children. Interviewers emphasized that the children had been selected because the measures had shown them to be the sensitive sort of child who may benefit from a confidence-building program. Few problems were encountered. Problems that did occur arose mainly in two areas: (1) children who appeared anxious according to the measures, but whose parents regarded them as having no problems and thus refused permission for their child to participate; and (2) detection of children who had multiple psychosocial problems but were not receiving services. Several of the latter were removed from the program and given individual help. For example, one girl showed evidence of depression, anxiety, suicidality, and eating disordered behavior but was considered healthy by her parents.

Parents were interviewed at the school using a structured anxiety interview, with much care given to information sharing, reassurance about any concerns, and dealing with practical issues, such as what were the best afternoons for their child to attend. Once the parents had been interviewed, the intervention started with groups run after school in a classroom. Healthy and appealing snacks were provided as well as certificates and other rewards for attendance. Children received practice in how to describe their involvement in nonstigmatizing ways to other children.

The intervention ran for 10 weeks during the school term, and follow-up assessments continued for two years. Overall, the feedback was very positive and complemented the quantitative data on program success. In such a large study, individual problems always occur. Some of the most salient included the following: (1) a few schools from the control condition obtained a copy of the intervention program and implemented it themselves during the follow-up period; (2) one or two parents contacted program staff almost daily to complain of their child's problems and how the program was not working; these families were offered individual help; and (3) reports increased through follow-up that the children were tired of completing the same measures and thus had difficulties maintaining high response rates. There were also a high number of requests to provide the intervention to hosts of schools once the fame of the program spread.

Otherwise, the program was incident-free and resulted in substantial reduction in both existing anxiety problems and the development of new problems. Since this initial evaluation trial, the program has been widely disseminated and has the potential to help a wide spectrum of children who would not otherwise receive help early in the development of problems.

SUMMARY

Many effective tertiary treatments for child psychopathology have been developed in the past few decades. However, many children who need help do not benefit from these because they are not referred to appropriate services. If they are referred, their problems have often become severe, generalized, and difficult to treat. EI programs target individuals at risk of developing a disorder or showing early or mild signs of the problem. They thus have advantages over referral-based interventions by intervening before problems become severe and entrenched and by not being dependent on clinical referral. The best EI programs are based on development models of how disorders emerge over time, the changing patterns of risk and protective factors, and windows of opportunity for identification and intervention. Such programs have been successfully used to prevent the development of conduct problems, anxiety, and depression, and substance use problems in young people. For conduct problems, the most effective EI programs intervene early in childhood using a broad ecological approach to family and school adjustment. For anxiety and depression, brief school-based programs are effective that provide skills training in emotion regulation in the middle childhood to adolescent years. Both of these EI approaches to conduct problems and anxiety/depression have potential to reduce the incidence of substance use problems later in adolescence and adulthood. A range of practical and ethical issues associated with the use of these programs has been identified. These include concerns about processes of informed consent and confidentiality, stigmatization, accuracy of identification of at-risk children, recruitment processes and participation rates, and intersectorial overlap among health care jurisdictions.

REFERENCES

American Psychiatric Association. (1994). *Diagnostic and statistical manual of mental disorders* (4th ed.). Washington, DC: Author.

Angst, J., Vollrath, M., Merikangas, K. R., & Ernst, C. (1990). Comorbidity of anxiety and depression in the Zurich Cohort Study of Young Adults. In J. D. Maser & R. C. Cloninger (Eds.), *Comorbidity of mood and anxiety disorders* (pp. 123–137). Washington, DC: American Psychiatric Press.

Armstrong, K. L., Fraser, J. A., Dadds, M. R., & Morris, J. (1999). A randomised controlled trial of nurse home visiting to vulnerable families with newborns. *Journal of Pediatrics and Child Health, 35*, 237–244.

Baer, R. A., & Nietzel, M. T. (1991). Cognitive and behavior treatment of impulsivity in children: A meta-analytic review of the outcome literature. *Journal of Clinical Child Psychology, 20*, 400–412.

Barrett, P. M., Dadds, M. R., & Holland, D. E. (1994). *The Coping Koala: Prevention manual.* Unpublished manuscript, Brisbane, Australia, University of Queensland.

Barrett, P. M., Dadds, M. R., & Rapee, R. M. (1996). Family treatment of childhood anxiety: A controlled trial. *Journal of Consulting and Clinical Psychology, 64*, 333–342.

Barrett, P. M., Duffy, A. L., Dadds, M. R., & Rapee, R. M. (2001). Cognitive-behavioral treatment of anxiety disorders in children: Long-term (6-year) follow up. *Journal of Consulting and Clinical Psychology, 69*, 135–141.

Beardslee, W. R. (1989). The role of self-understanding in resilient individuals: The development of a perspective. *American Journal of Orthopsychiatry, 59*(2), 266–278.

Beardslee, W. R., Hoke, L., Wheelock, I., Rothberg, P. C., van der Velde, P., & Swatling, S. (1992). Initial findings on preventive interaction for families with parental affective disorders. *American Journal of Psychiatry, 149*, 1335–1340.

Beardslee, W. R., & MacMillan, H. L. (1993). Preventive intervention with the children of depressed parents: A case study. *Psychoanalytic Study of the Child, 48*, 249–276.

Beardslee, W. R., Salt, P., Porterfield, K., Rothberg, P. C., van der Velde, P., Swatling, S., et al. (1993). Comparison of preventative interventions for families with parental affective disorder. *Journal of the American Academy of Child and Adolescent Psychiatry, 32*, 254–263.

Beidel, D. C., & Turner, S. M. (1997). At risk for anxiety: I. Psychopathology in the offspring of anxious parents. *Journal of the American Academy of Child and Adolescent Psychiatry, 36*, 918–924.

Bernstein, G. A., & Borchardt, C. M. (1991). Anxiety disorders of childhood and adolescence: A critical review. *Journal of the American Academy of Child and Adolescent Psychiatry, 30*, 519–532.

Bibb, J. L., & Chambless, D. L. (1986). Alcohol use and abuse among diagnosed agoraphobics. *Behavior Research and Therapy, 24*, 49–58.

Biederman, J., Rosenbaum, J. F., Bolduc-Murphy, E. A., Faraone, S. V., Chaloff, J., Hirshfeld, D. R., et al. (1993). A 3-year follow-up of children with and without behavioural inhibition. *Journal of the American Academy of Child and Adolescent Psychiatry, 32*, 814–821.

Caplan, G. (1964). *Principles of preventative therapy.* New York: Basic Books.

Catalano, R. F., Kosterman, R., Hawkins, D. J., & Newcomb, M. D. (1996). Modeling the etiology of adolescent substance use: A test of the social development model. *Journal of Drug Issues, 26*, 429–455.

Clarke, G. N., Hawkins, W., Murphy, M., & Sheeber, L. B. (1993). School-based primary prevention of depressive symptomology in adolescents: Results from two studies. *Journal of Adolescent Research, 8*(2), 183–204.

Clarke, G. N., Hawkins, W., Murphy, M., Sheeber, L. B., Lewinshon, P. M., & Seeley, J. R. (1995). Targeted prevention of Unipolar Depressive Disorder in an at-risk sample of high school adolescents: A randomised trial of a group cognitive intervention. *Journal of the American Academy of Child Adolescent Psychiatry, 34,* 312–321.

Cole, D. A., Peeke, L. G., Martin, J. M., Truglio, R., & Seroczynski, A. D. (1998). A longitudinal look at the relation between depression and anxiety in children and adolescents. *Journal of Consulting and Clinical Psychology, 66*(3), 451–460.

Cole, R., Kitzman, H., Olds, D., & Sidora, K. (1998). Family context as a moderator of program effects in prenatal and early childhood home visitation. *Journal of Community Psychology, 26*(1), 37–48.

Conduct Problems Prevention Research Group. (1992). A developmental and clinical model for the prevention of Conduct Disorder: The FAST Track Program. *Development and Psychopathology, 4,* 509–527.

Conduct Problems Prevention Research Group. (1999a). Initial impact of the FastTrack prevention trial for conduct problems: I. The high risk sample. *Journal of Consulting and Clinical Psychology, 67,* 631–647.

Conduct Problems Prevention Research Group. (1999b). Initial impact of the FastTrack prevention trial for conduct problems: II. Classroom effects. *Journal of Consulting and Clinical Psychology, 67,* 648–657.

Cowen, E. L., Wyman, P. A., & Work, W. C. (1996). Resilience in highly stressed urban children: Concepts and findings. *Bulletin of the New York Academy of Medicine, 73*(2), 267–284.

Dadds, M. R. (1995). *Families, children, and the development of dysfunction.* New York: Sage.

Dadds, M. R., Holland, D. E., Laurens, K. R., Mullins, M., Barrett, P. M., & Spence, S. H. (1999). Early intervention and prevention of anxiety disorders: Results at two year follow-up. *Journal of Consulting and Clinical Psychology, 67,* 145–150.

Dadds, M. R., Spence, S. H., Holland, D. E., Barrett, P. M., & Laurens, K. R. (1997). Prevention and early intervention for anxiety disorders: A controlled trial. *Journal of Consulting and Clinical Psychology, 65*(4), 627–635.

Dishion, T. J., Andrews, D. W., Kavanagh, K., & Soberman, L. H. (1996). Preventive interventions for high-risk youth: The adolescent transition project. In R. D. Peters & R. J. McMahon (Eds.), *Preventing childhood disorders, substance abuse and delinquency* (pp. 184–214). Thousand Oaks, CA: Sage.

Durlak, J. E., Furhman, T., & Lampman, C. (1991). Effectiveness for cognitive-behavioral therapy for maladapting children: A meta-analysis. *Psychological Bulletin, 110,* 204–214.

Fraser, J. A., Armstrong, K. L., Morris, J., & Dadds, M. R. (2000). Home visiting intervention for vulnerable families with newborns: Follow-up results of a randomised controlled trial. *Child Abuse and Neglect, 24,* 1399–1429.

Gest, S. D. (1997). Behavioral inhibition: Stability and associations with adaptation from childhood to early adulthood. *Journal of Personality and Social Psychology, 72*(2), 467–475.

Gillham, J. E., Reivich, K. J., Jaycox, L. H., & Seligman, M. E. P. (1994). Prevention of depressive symptoms in school children: Two-year follow-up. *Psychological Science, 6*(6), 343–350.

Golly, A., Stiller, B., & Walker, H. (1998). First step to success: Replication and validation. *Journal of Emotional and Behavioral Disorders, 6,* 243–250.

Gorman, D. M. (1996). Do school-based social skills programs prevent alcohol use among young people? *Addiction Research, 4,* 191–210.

Greenberg, M. T., Domitrovich, C., & Bumbarger, B. (2000). *Preventing mental disorders in school-aged children: A review of the effectiveness of prevention programs.*

Hagnell, O., & Graesbeck, A. (1990). Comorbidity of anxiety and depression in the Lundby 25-Year Prospective Study: The pattern of subsequent episodes. In J. D. Maser & C. R. Cloninger (Eds.), *Comorbidity of mood and anxiety disorders* (pp. 139–152). Washington, DC: American Psychiatric Press.

Hains, A. A., & Ellmann, S. W. (1994). Stress inoculation training as a preventative intervention for high school youths. *Journal of Cognitive Psychotherapy, 8*(3), 219–232.

Hawkins, J., Catalano, R., Kosterman, R., Abbott, R., & Hill, K. (in press). Preventing adolescent health risk behaviors by strengthening protection during childhood. *Archives of Pediatrics and Adolescent Medicine.*

Henggeler, S. W., Melton, G. B., Brondino, M. J., Scherer, D. G., & Hanley, J. H. (1997). Multisystemic therapy with violent and chronic juvenile offenders and their families: The role of treatment fidelity in successful dissemination. *Journal of Consulting and Clinical Psychology, 65,* 821–833.

Hudley, C., & Graham, S. (1993). An attributional intervention to reduce peer-directed aggression among African-American boys. *Child Development, 64,* 124–138.

Hudley, C., & Graham, S. (1995). School-based interventions for aggressive African-American boys. *Applied and Preventive Psychology, 4,* 185–195.

Jaycox, L. H., Reivich, K. J., Gillham, J. E., & Seligman, M. E. P. (1994). Prevention of depressive symptoms in school children. *Behaviour Research Therapy, 32*(8), 801–816.

Kazdin, A. E. (1993). Treatment of conduct disorder: Progress and directions in psychotherapy research. *Development and Psychopathology, 5,* 277–310.

Kendall, P. C., & Southam-Gerow, M. A. (1996). Long-term follow-up of a cognitive-behavioral therapy for anxiety-disordered youth. *Journal of Consulting and Clinical Psychology, 64,* 724–730.

Kessler, R. C., & Price, R. H. (1993). Primary prevention of secondary disorders: A proposal and agenda. *American Journal of Community Psychology, 21*(5), 607–633.

Kosterman, R., Hawkins, J., Spoth, R., Haggerty, K. P., & Zhu, K. (1997). Effects of a preventive parent-training intervention on observed family interactions: Proximal outcomes from preparing for the drug free years. *Journal of Community Psychology, 25,* 337–352.

LaFreniere, P. J., & Capuano, F. (1997). Preventive intervention as means of clarifying direction of effects in socialization: Anxious-withdrawn preschoolers case. *Development and Psychopathology, 9,* 551–564.

Lochman, J. E. (1985). Effects of different length treatments in cognitive-behavioral interventions with aggressive boys. *Child Psychiatry and Human Development, 16,* 45–56.

Lochman, J. E. (1992). Cognitive-behavioral intervention with aggressive boys: Three year follow-up and preventative efforts. *Journal of Consulting and Clinical Psychology, 60,* 426–432.

Lochman, J. E., Coie, J. D., Underwood, M. K., & Terry, R. (1993). Effectiveness of a social relations intervention for aggressive and nonaggressive, rejected children. *Journal of Consulting and Clinical Psychology, 61,* 1053–1058.

Loeber, R., & Dishion, T. (1983). Early predictors of male delinquency: A review. *Psychological Bulletin, 93,* 68–99.

Loeber, R., Russo, M. F., Stouthamer-Loeber, M., & Lahey, B. B. (1994). Internalizing problems and their relation to the development of disruptive behaviors in adolescence. *Journal of Research on Adolescence, 4,* 615–637.

Marans, S., Berkowitz, S. J., & Cohen, D. J. (1998). Police and mental health professionals: Collaborative responses to the impact of violence on children and families. *Child and Adolescent Psychiatric Clinics of North America, 7,* 635–640.

McCord, J., Tremblay, R. E., Vitaro, F., & Desmarais-Gervais, L. (1994). Boys' disruptive behavior, school adjustment, and delinquency: The Montreal Prevention Experiment. *International Journal of Behavioral Development, 17,* 739–752.

McDonald, L., Billingham, S., Conrad, T., Morgan, A., Payton, N. O., & Payton, E. (1997). Families and schools together (FAST): Integrating community development with clinical strategies. *Families in Society, 78,* 140–155.

Miller, G. E., & Prinz, R. J. (1990) Enhancement of social learning family interventions for childhood conduct disorder. *Psychological Bulletin, 108,* 291–307.

Mrazek, P. J., & Haggerty, R. J. (1994). *Reducing risks for mental disorders: Frontiers for preventive intervention research.* Washington, DC: National Academy Press.

O'Dea, J. (2000). School-based interventions to prevent eating problems: First do no harm. *Eating Disorders: The Journal of Treatment and Prevention, 8,* 123–130.

Olds, D., Henderson, C. R., Cole, R., Eckenrode, J., Kitzman, H., Luckey, D., et al. (1998). Long-term effects of nurse home visitation on children's criminal and antisocial behavior: 15-year follow-up of a randomized controlled trial. *Journal of the American Medical Association, 280*(14), 1238–1244.

Olds, D., & Kitzman, H. (1993). Review of research on home visiting for pregnant women and parents of young children. *Future of Children, 3*(3), 53–92.

Patterson, G. R., DeBarshye, B. D., & Ramsey, E. (1989). A developmental perspective on antisocial behavior. *American Psychologist, 44,* 329–335.

Pepler, D. J., King, G., & Byrd, W. (1991). A socially cognitive-based social skills training program for aggressive children. In D. J. Pepler & K. Rubin (Eds.), *The development and treatment of childhood aggression* (pp. 361–379). Hillsdale, NJ: Erlbaum.

Pepler, D. J., King, G., Craig, W., Byrd, B., & Bream, L. (1995). The development and evaluation of a multisystem social skills training program for aggressive children. *Child and Youth Care Forum, 24,* 297–313.

Perrin, S., & Last, C. G. (1992). Do childhood anxiety measures measure anxiety? *Journal of Abnormal Child Psychology, 20,* 567–578.

Prinz, R. J., Blechman, E. A., & Dumas, J. E. (1994). An evaluation of peer coping-skills training for childhood aggression. *Journal of Clinical Child Psychology, 23,* 193–203.

Reid, J. B., & Eddy, J. M. (1997). The prevention of antisocial behavior: Some considerations in the search for effective interventions. In D. Staff, J. Breiling, & J. D. Maser (Eds.), *Handbook of antisocial behavior.* New York: Wiley.

Roth, J., & Dadds, M. R. (1999). *Reach for resilience: Evaluation of a universal programme for the prevention of internalising problems in young children.* Brisbane, Australia: Griffith University, School of Applied Psychology, Griffith Early Intervention Project.

Sanders, M. R. (1999). Triple P–Positive Parenting Program: Towards an empirically validated multilevel parenting and family support strategy for the prevention of behavior and emotional problems in children. *Clinical Child and Family Psychology Review, 2*(2), 71–90.

Sanders, M. R., & Dadds, M. R. (1993). *Behavioral family intervention.* New York: Allyn & Bacon.

Schinke, S. P., & Tepavac, L. (1995). Substance abuse prevention among elementary school students. *Drugs and Society, 8*(3/4), 15–27.

Shochet, I. M., Dadds, M. R., Holland, D., Whitefield, K., Harnett, P., & Osgarby, S. M. (in press). Short-term effects of a universal school-based program to prevent adolescent depression. *Journal of Clinical Child Psychology.*

Shochet, I. M., Holland, D., & Whitefield, K. (1997). *The Resourceful Adolescent Program: Group leader's manual.* Brisbane, Australia: Griffith University, Griffith Early Intervention Project.

Shochet, I. M., & O'Gorman, J. (1995). Ethical issues in research on adolescent depression and suicidal behaviour. *Australian Psychologist, 30,* 183–187.

Simeonsson, R. J. (1994). Toward an epidemiology of developmental, educational, and social problems of childhood. In R. J. Simeonsson (Ed.), *Risk, resilience and prevention: Promoting the well-being of all children* (pp. 13–32). Sydney, Australia: Brookes.

Spence, S. H., & Dadds, M. R. (1996) Preventing childhood anxiety disorders. *Behaviour Change, 13*(4), 241–249.

Tierney, J. P., Grossman, J. B., & Resch, N. L. (1995). *Making a difference: The impact study of Big Brother/Sister.* Philadelphia: Public/Private Ventures.

Tremblay, R. E., Masse, L. C., Pagani, L., & Vitaro, F. (1996). From childhood aggression to adolescent maladjustment: The Montreal Prevention Experiment. In R. D. Peters & R. J. McMahon (Eds.), *Preventing childhood disorders, substance abuse and delinquency* (pp. 268–298). Thousand Oaks, CA: Sage.

Tremblay, R. E., Masse, L. C., Perron, D., LeBlanc, M., Schwartzman, A. E., & Ledingham, J. E. (1992). Early disruptive behavior, poor school achievement, delinquent behavior, and delinquent personality: Longitudinal analyses. *Journal of Consulting and Clinical Psychology, 60,* 64–72.

Vasey, M., & Dadds, M. R. (2000). *Developmental psychopathology of anxiety disorders.* Oxford, England: Oxford University Press.

Walker, H., Kavanagh, K., Stiller, B., Golly, S., Severson, H., & Feil, E. (1998). First step to success: An early intervention approach for preventing school antisocial behavior. *Journal of Emotional and Behavioral Disorders, 6,* 66–80.

Warren, S. L., Huston, L., Egeland, B., & Sroufe, L. A. (1997). Child and adolescent anxiety disorders and early adjustment. *Journal of the American Academy of Child and Adolescent Psychiatry, 36*(5), 637–644.

Webster-Stratton, C., & Hammond, M. (1998). Conduct problems and level of social competence in Head Start children: Prevalence, pervasiveness, and associated risk factors. *Clinical Child and Family Psychology Review, 1*(2), 101–124.

CHAPTER 4

Delayed Recall of Childhood Trauma

LAURA S. BROWN

The impact of trauma on memory has been documented for almost a century. Janet's (1904, 1907) descriptions of "hysterics," written in the earliest part of the twentieth century, are detailed pictures of individuals who, unable to have a cognitive memory of a painful or traumatic life experience, enacted the trauma symptomatically. Next, the British psychiatrists tending to the "shell-shocked" soldiers of the First World War described persons who had no ability to recall the traumatic battlefield events to which they had been exposed, but who suffered from nightmares, behavioral reenactments, and what would now be called flashbacks. Freud's early work (1896) contains detailed portraits of individuals who, he hypothesized, had repressed memories of early traumata that were evident in neurotic symptomatology.

That trauma has a profound impact on memory is consistent with everything known about memory, learning, and changes in levels of physiological arousal. Trauma, defined as experiences that threaten safety and personal integrity (American Psychiatric Association, 1994), as well as those events in which one's perception of a just world is shattered (Janoff-Bulman, 1992) or one's close personal relationships are destroyed by betrayal (Freyd, 1996), invariably creates changes in the body's level of arousal, which in turn affects learning and memory of events surrounding the traumatic event or process.

Two states of arousal are most commonly associated with traumatic stressors. Hyperarousal, in which the body is flooded with affect and the accompanying rush of neurohormones, occurs when the trauma leads to feelings of terror and panic. Hypoarousal, or peritraumatic dissociation, also frequently occurs during trauma exposure (Shalev, 1996), with a complementary change in stress hormones. Both hyper- and hypoarousal may occur within the experience of the same traumatic event or process, with vast fluctuations in the individual's ability to attend and recall.

Either heightened or lowered levels of arousal affect how information is perceived, stored, and retrieved. Both the arousal process itself and the changes to brain chemistry that occur as a result may lead to overlearning or, conversely, to weakened memory traces. It may also contribute to confusion or distortion of information placed into memory storage. Thus, a memory for a traumatic event can be compromised or strengthened at various points of the learning process, but as with other aspects of learning that are affected by low or high levels of arousal, it is unlikely to be left undisturbed by the trauma. Particularly when a memory trace is weak or the material contained in the memory is highly aversive, very specific, affect-laden or somatosensory cues may be required to access it, leading to a subjective experience of delay in recall.

When trauma occurs during childhood, the developmental factors influencing emotional and cognitive development also come into play. Children's capacity for recall is affected by such factors as language development and the ability to find words to describe an event (Howe, Courage, & Peterson, 1994), as well as by the presence or absence of supportive adults who will assist a child in encoding an event into memory (Fivush, 1994). Children, particularly those younger than 4, are somewhat more suggestible as a group. If an aspect of a trauma is the provision of suggestions by a perpetrator of interpersonal violence, then a child's inability to distinguish between suggestion and reality may act to impair memory. Children who have suffered traumata prior to the offset of infantile amnesia (which occurs around age 3) or who lack vocabulary to describe their experiences may never "recall" an event in the usual way that adults remember, but may demonstrate knowledge of what has happened to them via play reenactments of the trauma (see Terr, 1994, for a powerful description of the behavior of toddlers who are forced to be depicted in child pornography). Consequently, adults' memories for childhood traumata are subject to a variety of factors that can result in recollections that are impaired, fuzzy, distorted, incomplete, and/or delayed in their availability to conscious recollection.

The effects of trauma on the psyche were first incorporated into a defined diagnosis under the title of Posttraumatic Stress Disorder (PTSD) in the third edition of the *Diagnostic and Statistical Manual of Mental Disorders* (*DSM-III*; American Psychiatric Association, 1980). In this initial description of PTSD, and in all of the minor revisions to the diagnosis that have followed in the subsequent two decades, the impact of trauma on memory is a clear and important part of the diagnostic picture. Inescapable memories, in the form of intrusive thoughts and flashbacks, as well as posttraumatic amnesia, in which the PTSD sufferer cannot recall all or some part of the trauma, are among the criteria for PTSD. Thus, the diagnosis recognizes the biphasic nature of arousal disturbances during trauma exposure and the consequent bimodal memory disturbances.

In the general area of posttraumatic amnesia, the phenomenon of delayed recall for trauma (also known as repressed memory, recovered memory, or dissociated memory) has received a good deal of attention, both professional and popular, in the past decade and a half. Some of this attention arose in the context of the social movement for adult survivors of childhood sexual abuse. Some of these individuals described their recollection of the trauma of incest being suddenly available to them in adult life after lengthy periods in which the memory was unavailable to conscious recollection (Armstrong, 1978; Bass & Davis, 1988; Bass & Thornton, 1983; Brady, 1979; Butler, 1978; Herman, 1981; McNaron & Morgan, 1982; Rush, 1980). Professionals working with adult survivors also began to document these cases (Briere & Conte, 1993; Briere & Zaidi, 1989; Feldman-Summers & Pope, 1994; Herman & Schatzow, 1987; Loftus, Fullilove, & Polansky, 1994) in such diverse populations as psychiatric emergency room admissions, poor women of color in early recovery from substance abuse, and practicing psychologists who were members of the APA. Although many adult survivors of childhood maltreatment had continuous recollections of what had been done to them, a substantial minority reported either a complete absence of recall for extended periods of time or significant impairments in their memories of the events. Others reported an ability to recall factual details but not their affect.

In 1992, a backlash against the concept of delayed recall for childhood sexual abuse emerged in the form of the so-called false memory movement. Spurred in part by the proliferation of successful civil litigation undertaken by adult survivors against their alleged perpetrators, as well as by a groundswell of legislation that allowed people with delayed recall of trauma to toll the statute of limitations in a lawsuit from the time of remembering rather than from the childhood event (see Pope & Brown, 1996, for discussion of this phenomenon), the false memory movement focused its attention on two topics. First, the movement and its proponents alleged that most reports of delayed recall of childhood sexual abuse were false, representing confabulations developed under the tutelage of therapists who were at best misinformed about the nature of memory and suggestibility, and at worst engaged in a malevolent conspiracy to undermine families (Loftus & Ketcham, 1994; Ofshe & Watters, 1994). The memories were assumed false for various reasons, including denial of culpability by alleged perpetrators (Pendergast, 1995) and an assertion by some in the false memory movement that most people would recall a traumatic event, so searing would it be.

Second, the false memory movement called the entire phenomenon of delayed recall of trauma into question. This questioning largely stemmed from standard research on memory and suggestibility, and they argued that it was impossible for an event as searing (and often, as repetitive) as childhood sexual abuse to be forgotten, given the normal rules of memory (Ornstein, Ceci, & Loftus, 1998). This argument has also had various subthemes. These have included the notion that repression, as a mechanism of defense, cannot be proven to exist, with

the consequent conclusion that repressed memories cannot exist. Another argument against delayed recall has been the theory that it is simple to suggest to people that they have had experiences that did not occur (Loftus, 1993), supporting the false memory movement hypothesis that reports of long-forgotten sexual abuse arose from suggestive therapeutic techniques. Attempts were made to document the presence of such techniques (Poole, Lindsay, Menon, & Bull, 1995), leading to counterarguments regarding the validity of the studies (Olio, 1996).

In the mid-1990s, several professional groups, including the American Psychological Association and the British Psychology Society, set up scholarly working groups to address the problem. The APA Working Group arrived at the consensus conclusion that it is possible for memories of childhood abuse to be delayed for lengthy periods of time, although the cognitive mechanism by which this occurs cannot be identified. The Working Group also agreed that it is possible that a person could come to believe in a personal history of abuse due solely or primarily to suggestive influences (Alpert et al., 1996).

The intervening years since the inception of the debate over delayed recall have led to a softening of positions on all sides. Solid empirical research by cognitive scientists has demonstrated a variety of normal memory mechanisms that could lead to a delayed recall of a traumatic event (Freyd, 1996). Neuroimaging research has studied the brain structure and function of adult survivors of known childhood sexual abuse and discovered damage to neural mechanisms implicated in the integration, storage, and retrieval of complex memories (Bremner et al., 1995). Several prospective studies, consisting of longitudinal follow-up interviews of adults whose childhood molestations were medically or legally documented, have demonstrated that meaningful proportions of these known survivors of childhood sexual abuse are unable, as adults, to recall and/or report this childhood trauma (Widom & Morris, 1997; Williams, 1994). That therapists may suggest abuse to clients, although believed to be a rare event, has been acknowledged as possible by leaders in the field of incest treatment (Briere, 1996; Courtois, 1999), and the standards of psychotherapy practice with adults who report having delayed recall of childhood trauma have changed as a result (Courtois, 1999).

This chapter does not explore in greater depth the debate over delayed recall of childhood trauma. For the purposes of this chapter, the author assumes that such delayed recall is possible, that it can be as accurate or inaccurate as continuous memory for events, both traumatic and ordinary, and that it is unlikely in most cases to be a product of suggestion or confabulation. (For a more complete review, see Pope & Brown, 1996; D. Brown, Scheflin, & Hammond, 1998). Rather, the emphasis here is on treatment considerations. When a therapist is confronted with a client who believes that she or he is recovering memories of childhood trauma, what issues must that therapist consider? What are the special considerations for treatment when the client is outside of the population mainstream? When the remembered perpetrator is a close family member (as is frequently the case), what considerations must be made regarding family treatment? Because of the high visibility of several cases brought against therapists by family members or former clients alleging implantation of false memories by a therapist, what are risk management considerations for working with this population?

HISTORY OF THE THERAPEUTIC APPROACH

Treatment of individuals who are recovering memories of trauma has never occurred within the framework of a particular psychotherapeutic approach. This author's library contains volumes on treatment that derive from the gamut of psychotherapies, including psychodynamic, cognitive-behavioral, systemic, hypnotherapeutic, and various technically eclectic modalities such as trauma treatment and feminist therapy.

This eclecticism has been both a strength and a problem in the field of trauma treatment, which has proceeded from no systematic unified theory, regardless of the specific type of trauma under consideration. Instead, there have been various attempts to understand the phenomenon of delayed recall and to treat it according to those conceptual paradigms.

As noted previously, early clinical descriptions of delayed recall occured in the context of the development of psychodynamic psychotherapy. Freud and Janet both proposed various uncovering techniques in which the patient who was suffering from "hysterical" (e.g., dissociative) symptoms was encouraged to speak about, and thus consciously recollect, the underlying trauma. However, after Freud changed his model for neurosis, the presentation of materials related to childhood sexual abuse was framed in psychodynamic theory as fantasy material. This paradigm remained prevalent until the mid-1970s, when the study of trauma once again became a focus for mental health professionals (Herman, 1992) and the credibility of these productions as actual memories of childhood sexual abuse was heightened.

The rediscovery of childhood sexual abuse and of individuals with delayed recall has led to a new set of treatment paradigms. Initially, during most of the 1970s and 1980s, treatment focused on the uncovering of memory, with the expressed goal of making conscious that which had been repressed (Briere, 1989; Courtois, 1988). Exposure therapies, in which the trauma survivor told the story of the trauma, appeared to be successful with the other large group of identified traumatees, that is, combat veterans. Thus, an exposure model was typically adopted by those working with clients remembering sexual abuse.

Largely in reaction to the psychoanalytic framework that had branded all such materials as fantasy, the early treatment models proposed believing, without question, the memories reported by clients. This was the case even when such memories seemed implausible or highly unlikely; for example, a small number of individuals reported being abused in cult settings in which ritualized abuse occurred. Remembering per se was construed as helpful and curative, in line with the early psychodynamic posture that making the unconscious conscious would lead to remission of symptoms.

Over the decade of the 1980s, two factors began to become apparent that informed a change in the therapeutic approach to adults who reported delayed recall of childhood trauma. First, clinicians, researchers, and theorists began to more closely scrutinize the impact of developmental stage on the acquisition, storage, and retrieval of memories. This inquiry highlighted the possibility that, although a patient might be accurately reporting what she or he had stored in memory, the details themselves might have been subject to a variety of distorting influences during the formation of the memory itself. As an example, one patient treated by this author made an initial report of recalling being forced to drink blood and being made sleepy and confused by the ingestion of the sweet-tasting substance. The author encouraged the client to consider what other red, sweet drinks might cause drowsiness. The patient was able to reason that, although her perpetrators told her that she was drinking blood (which was later used as a rationale for other sorts of maltreatment in the guise of "punishment" for this alleged "cannibalism"), it was most likely that she had drunk wine or some other alcoholic beverage. Her memory had been distorted by the suggestions made at the time of the abuse, as well as, probably, by the alcohol in the drink and by her developmental inability, at the age of 6, to easily separate out suggestion, fact, and fantasy.

Sexual abuse by itself may act as a distorting factor. Dalenberg (1996) has found that, in cases where the sexual abuse of a child has been incontrovertibly corroborated by forensic medical evidence, the memories of the abuse that are produced by the children are more laden with fantastic and improbable details. She suggests that these findings raise the consideration that, in addition to normative developmental factors, there is something cognitively disorganizing about sexual abuse. Such cognitive effects of abuse could in turn lead to distortions in how the abuse is stored in memory. The possibility that an event could have been distorted by age-related cognitive and affective factors and/or by the suggestions made by a sexual abuse perpetrator (e.g., that the abuse was a dream or something to be forgotten), led to a reconsideration of how this material should be responded to in therapy.

A first standard of practice that has evolved from the discourse over delayed recall is to remove the clinician from the role of believing or validating the accuracy of a client's productions (Briere, 1996; D. Brown, Scheflin, & Hammond, 1998; Courtois, 1999; Gold, 2000; Pope & Brown, 1996). Rather, the focus is on assisting clients to become credible to themselves and to become their own source of validation and belief. Clients are neither encouraged to seek nor discouraged from seeking external corroboration of the material that they perceive to be memories of childhood abuse (Briere, 1996; D. Brown et al., 1998; Courtois, 1999; Gold, 2000; Pope & Brown, 1996). The goal of therapy, as Harvey (1996) and Harvey and Herman (1994) note, is recovery of functioning, not archaeology, whose goal is to dig up all possible fragments of memory. Remembering per se is no longer seen as curative and now is frequently made a secondary focus of therapy (Gold, 2000).

Second, and more important, the trauma-focused exposure model that had informed the first stage of treatment with this population has been set aside. The experimental data are strong that exposure therapies are extremely helpful for individuals with adult-onset, single-event traumas. However, the clinical data emerging from the first stage of sexual abuse recovery work made it clear that, for survivors of childhood sexual abuse, there was frequently an absence of core coping strategies that would create the safety and containment necessary for doing exposure therapy. Simply put, too many important developmental tasks in the area of emotion regulation, self-soothing, and self-care are frequently interfered with when a child is sexually abused. In cases that present clinically with reports of delayed recall, clients often describe other, concurrent forms of maltreatment, including physical and emotional abuse and neglect. Clients who attempted exposure therapies were observed to suffer serious impairments in functioning and an increase in symptoms and symptom severity (see Gold, 2000, for an eloquent description of this problem).

THE PHASE AND STAGE MODEL OF TREATMENT

In response to this, the model for treating adult survivors (not only those with reports of delayed recall) has changed significantly. Currently, the standard of practice is a phase and stage model (Briere, 1996; D. Brown et al., 1998; Courtois, 1999; Gold, 2000; Harvey & Herman, 1994; Pope & Brown, 1996). The first stage of therapy is a focus on *containment,* teaching skills of self-soothing, emotion regulation, and self-care. The goal of this phase of treatment is to reduce symptoms and stabilize the client's functioning. Memory materials are likely to be produced involuntarily by clients during this phase of treatment, but the emphasis is not, as it was in the past, on exploring the memory. Rather, it is on assisting the client to cope with frightening intrusions in a positive and non-self-destructive manner (Gold & Brown, 1997).

The next phase of treatment is the *integration* of memories, both continuous and delayed. This differs from any prior focus on recovering memory in that remembering per se is not emphasized. Rather, the emphasis is on integrating new information about one's life history into the current autobiographical narrative. In the past, there was an emphasis on the abreaction of emotion associated with the memory; the current standard focuses on being able to transform the experience of the memory from unprocessed affective and somatosensory forms into a more cognitive, integrated structure. This model does not discourage the expression of feelings; rather, the emphasis is on understanding the feeling and being able to look at it through the adult eyes of the patient, using some of the emotion regulation and containment skills developed in the initial phase of treatment.

A final stage of therapy is that of *trauma resolution,* in which the task is confronting the existential and meaning-making issues that arise for the adult survivor. Even for those persons with continuous memories of childhood sexual abuse, the process of therapy frequently changes the cognitive appraisal of the memories and, thus, their meaning. This is even more the case for persons who had previously seen a family member/perpetrator in a positive or neutral light and must now make sense of this new understanding of the person and of the relationship between themselves as children and the individuals who harmed them. As with all survivors of trauma, the question Why did this happen to me? emerges at this stage of treatment.

The three stages of treatment are not distinct; memory integration and meaning-making work may occur in the midst of a focus on containment and emotion regulation, and it is almost always necessary to frequently revisit work on containment, self-care, and self-soothing when addressing memory integration and meaning making. However, the emphasis is on improving client functioning and on assisting clients in creating a coherent life narrative.

For some individuals, an important component of treatment will also include some kind of family and couples work. It is not unusual for persons who are addressing a history of childhood sexual abuse to experience disruptions in their adult intimate relationships. Sexual dysfunctions, reenactments of problems of trust, and the inadvertent triggering of posttraumatic materials by a partner can be challenging to even the most loving and stable of couples. There is no current standard model for working with the survivor in a couples therapy context. However, couples treatment is most likely to be successful only after the containment phase of treatment, when emotion regulation and self-soothing skills are well established. Referral of a partner for supportive psychotherapy, largely to assist in normalizing the difficulties being experienced, is not necessary but can be extremely helpful.

In early stages of sexual abuse treatment, some therapists encouraged patients to invite perpetrators into the therapy office for "confrontations." In some cases, these experiences were cathartic for the patient; more often, they were frustrating and frequently led to serious estrangement between adult survivors and their family of origin. Some of the complaints against therapists generated by the false memory movement arose from such confrontation sessions; one such session led to the first successful lawsuit by an allegedly sexually abusive parent against his daughter's therapist (*Ramona v. Ramona*, 1991). For all of these reasons, confrontation sessions are now strongly discouraged by leaders in the field of sexual abuse treatment.

However, sessions with alleged perpetrators within the family of origin can at times be helpful to the adult survivor. These sessions are not focused on the truth of what occurred, as it is more common than not for family members accused of sexual abuse to deny the charges (this is true for almost all people accused of criminal acts, and denials should never be construed as evidence that the abuse did not occur). Rather, the focus is on attempting to develop a modus vivendi for the adult survivor and her or his family of origin; to affirm that which was good and positive in the relationship, if such existed; and to find strategies for relating in the present

that will respect the feelings and boundaries of all parties.

THEORETICAL CONSTRUCTS

As noted earlier, initial treatment models for adults recovering memories of childhood abuse derived vaguely from psychodynamic notions of uncovering and exposure to repressed materials. Few of the early authors on this topic were strictly psychodynamic in their conceptualizations of treatment, yet all proposed models that were indirectly dynamic in their assumptions.

Currently, the theoretical models underlying treatment are eclectic and integrative, drawing on psychodynamic formulations (Alpert, 1995), cognitive therapies, particularly the dialectical behavior therapy approach of Linehan (1993a), and trauma treatment models (D. Brown et al., 1998; Courtois, 1999). A strong feminist perspective, which attends to issues of gender and power as they inform both the experience of childhood abuse and its outcomes, can be seen throughout the field, even when the authors are not themselves explicitly feminist (Contratto & Gutfreund, 1996; Enns, McNeilly, Corkery, & Gilbert, 1994; Gold & Brown, 1997). However, given the extreme range of theoretical orientations espoused by authors and teachers in the field of sexual abuse treatment, no one theoretical model can be said to predominate. Models for working with adult survivors experiencing delayed recall are most commonly both theoretically and technically eclectic, although most currently converge on the phase and stage model described above.

MAJOR SYMPTOMS AND SYNDROMES TREATED

A history of childhood maltreatment, particularly childhood sexual abuse, has been implicated as a risk factor in a wide range of diagnoses. PTSD, Dissociative Identity Disorder and other dissociative disorders, and Borderline Personality Disorder (APA, 1994) are the diagnoses most commonly found among adult survivors of severe and repetitive childhood sexual abuse, particularly in those cases where the configuration of the abuse is likely to lead to delayed recall of the events (e.g., abuse by a caregiver, frequently within the family, often with other co-occurring maltreatment; Briere, 1996; Courtois, 1999). Herman (1992) has proposed an overarching diagnosis of Complex Posttraumatic Stress Disorder, also referred to by van der Kolk (1994) as Disorder of Extreme Stress Not Otherwise Specified (DESNOS). High rates of childhood sexual abuse are also found in individuals with Major Depression, Bulimia, and Chronic Pain Disorder.

Patients who report having delayed recall of childhood sexual abuse are often highly and severely symptomatic, regardless of their formal diagnosis. This frequently reflects the dynamics hypothesized to lead to delayed recalls (e.g., repetitive abuse by a caregiver, issues of betrayal, interference with normal development of self-regulation skills). Suicidality, nonlethal self-harm (e.g., cutting, burning, head banging), substance abuse, and sexually compulsive behaviors are common, particularly when the individual has been engaging in frantic efforts to stop the onset of intrusive materials into consciousness. Patients with a history of childhood sexual abuse are frequently impaired in their interpersonal skills, with deficits in their ability to assess trustworthiness. Educational and vocational problems are common because posttraumatic symptoms may interfere with concentration, academic performance, and abilities to function in the workplace.

The range and variability of diagnoses and symptoms commonly found in adults who report delayed recall of childhood sexual abuse underscore the possibility that a patient entering treatment with a wide range of presenting problems may at some point begin to experience and report the onset of intrusive, delayed memories.

CASE EXAMPLE

The following case illustrates a common presentation of delayed or impaired recall of childhood trauma. (All potentially identifying details have been disguised and materials from several different clients have been combined to generate a composite picture.)

Angeline is a Caucasian woman in her early thirties. She came to therapy with the author because "I keep having these odd images. I think I might have been sexually abused, but I don't know. I just feel lousy. I can't seem to stop doing stupid things." She comes from a middle-class family in the central Midwest. She is the middle of three siblings and the only girl. Her parents are both alive and married to one another. She reported that her mother had been severely depressed "for as long as I can remember" and would frequently lie on the couch for days. Her father was an episodic binge drinker; she described him at intake as "warm, but strange. He was my buddy."

She had never been married and had had multiple sexual partners of both sexes, although she identified herself as heterosexual; her longest relationship lasted six months. She is a chain-smoker and had been bulimic during her late adolescence, now reporting bouts of binge eating when upset. She abuses methamphetamine, reporting that she needs it for energy and that it helps her to control her weight. She completed a degree in liberal arts after seven years in college, and had started and dropped out of a master's program in creative writing. Since then, she worked in a series of low-paying, low-skilled jobs, most recently as a barista at a large coffee chain. She reported that she dealt "badly" with stress. On inquiry, she described episodes of cutting on herself, head banging, and drinking to pass out. During one of the most recent episodes of passing out, she had been sexually assaulted by several men in a bar. She did not recall the assault, but had been told of it by the bartender, who was an acquaintance.

Angeline reported that since the sexual assault, at the urging of several women friends, she had tried to stop drinking and using methamphetamines. She found this attempt at sobriety severely challenged by the emergence of "odd images" that were disturbing to her. When the therapist inquired, Angeline stated, "I get this weird sensation, like I'm a kid. My body feels small. I look down, and it's a kid's body. And then I see his hand. I know it's my dad's hand. It's on my crotch. I don't feel scared. I don't feel anything. I just think, how odd, my dad's hand is on my crotch." Angeline reported that these images appeared during the day when her attention was not otherwise taken and often when she tried to go to sleep at night. She reported severe sleep disturbance, decreased appetite, and sexual aversion. She was surprised at these symptoms because "I've been raped before. You know, as long as I don't remember it, I always figured, what's the big deal." Her affectless expression of this fact was notable.

Angeline was able to identify that on one prior occasion, just after she had moved to Seattle, she had tried to stop drinking and using to please a girlfriend and that during that brief period of sobriety, she had also had the "odd images." She reported that her return to drinking had been motivated partly by a desire to stop having the images appear; alcohol effectively stopped their emergence. She reported that she was afraid that she would lose her best friend if she did not succeed at getting sober this time: "She's tired of bailing me out." Additionally, for the first time in her life, her substance abuse was putting at risk a job that she had come to value for its relatively benign hours and excellent benefit structure. "I'm coming in hung over and screwing up orders. The crystal is slowing me down, not speeding

me up." Angeline reported being chronically suicidal since middle adolescence and that her suicidality was becoming more acute as the disturbing images escalated.

Angeline represents a common clinical presentation of early recollection of delayed childhood trauma material, in which the cessation of numbing strategies leads to access to recollections of sexual abuse. She describes a history of various numbing coping behaviors, including disordered eating, alcohol and drug use, compulsive sexuality, persistent suicidal fantasies, and nonsuicidal self-harm. She has a history of repeated sexual victimization in adulthood, for which she experiences little or no affect. When attempting sobriety, she describes the onset of intrusive images, for which she also experiences little or no affect. However, she reports a number of symptoms that could be classified as either depressive or posttraumatic.

In addition to taking a complete psychosocial history from Angeline, the author administered one formal assessment measure, Briere's Trauma Symptom Inventory (TSI; Briere, 1995), which was specifically developed to assess the range of posttraumatic symptoms, both acute and long term. On the TSI, Angeline's valid profile was marked by elevations on scales measuring intrusive experiences, dissociative and overtly defensive avoidant strategies, depressed mood, and long-standing core problems of sexuality, identity, and emotion regulation. A working diagnosis of PTSD and Major Depression was made by the author based on these findings. Angeline's problems of substance abuse and disordered eating were formulated as secondary aspects of the PTSD. However, these problems, as manifestation of her difficulties with emotion regulation, became the initial focus of treatment.

As discussed earlier, therapy with an adult who presents as did Angeline progresses through three identifiable, although not necessarily sequential, phases: *containment,* which focuses on the development of self-care and emotion regulation skills, *memory integration,* and *meaning making*. When confronted with an adult who may be remembering childhood sexual abuse for the first time, the primary consideration during that first phase of therapy must be the establishment of adequate containment, self-care, and emotion regulation skills before any work is done to process trauma and/or ascertain whether these are memories or other kinds of material (e.g., obsessive compulsive intrusions, hallucinations, or fantasies; Gold & Brown, 1997, 1999). Even when, or perhaps especially when the client expresses an urgency to do uncovering work and focus on the intrusive material, therapy must focus on giving the client adequate skills with which to approach trauma resolution. There are several rationales for taking this approach. First, in most such cases, the client has been engaging in a variety of self-defeating and often dangerous strategies for emotional regulation in attempts to ward off the now intruding materials. The failure of those strategies, or a conscious attempt at cessation (as was true for Angeline, who was trying to give up drugs and alcohol), is extremely disorganizing. The onslaught of intrusive memories feels unmanageable and creates enormous risk for relapse into self-harm. If the client has few or no affirmative coping strategies, she or he will default to the known territory of numbing at any cost. Any attempts to directly deal with the intrusive materials at this stage are likely only to escalate destructive strategies and lead to crisis after crisis. These crises impair the client's actual physical safety, which must be a primary consideration at the early stage of treatment.

With Angeline, the therapist used a number of approaches concurrently to assist her client in becoming more competent at containment, self-soothing, and emotion regulation. The therapist told Angeline that the question of what had happened to her was important, and that the best way to address it was to provide her with enough comfort and safety inside herself to be able to look carefully at these images. In this way, she validated the importance of examining the intrusive materials for Angeline. She did not

dismiss them as unimportant or confabulated, nor did she make them overimportant. She told Angeline that it was worth taking the time to learn self-care, and then continually reinforced that message.

The self-care strategies that the therapist introduced to Angeline included a number of the skills described by Linehan (1993b). Leaving aside questions of whether the diagnosis of Borderline Personality Disorder or Complex PTSD is the more accurate label for this clinical presentation (see L. S. Brown, 1994, 2000; Herman, 1992, for a discussion of this question), Linehan's skill-based approach is extremely empowering to clients whose inner and outer lives have felt, and been, out of their own control. Angeline learned to practice mindfulness, meditation, and relaxation as strategies for calming and centering herself. The therapist used Eye Movement Desensitization Reprocessing (EMDR; Shapiro, 1995) to assist Angeline in developing an image of an internal helper to whom she could turn for self-soothing, using Leeds's (1998) Resource Installation protocol. At the therapist's urging, she joined and regularly attended a support group for women who were trying to stay clean and sober.

The therapist taught Angeline the concepts of relapse prevention so that she could learn to observe herself and take steps to avert self-destructive behaviors before they occurred. This had the additional effect of heightening Angeline's sense of mastery as she began to see her destructive coping strategies as predictable and controllable rather than out-of-control behaviors that would strike her seemingly at random. As another component of the containment phase of treatment, Angeline also learned a variety of active self-soothing skills. These included learning positive self-talk, getting regular massages, and getting a pet cat. Clinical lore in the treatment of trauma survivors suggests that having a companion animal creates a safe context for affectionate relating in the survivor of childhood maltreatment and provides an incentive to avoid suicide.

As is true for many individuals with a history of both substance abuse and childhood maltreatment (Walker, Katon, Roy-Byrne, Jemlka, & Russo, 1993; Walker et al., 1988), Angeline had a number of serious medical problems. She had neglected obtaining medical care, in part because of lack of funds, but more important, because getting medical care, especially gynecological care, had always led to an upsurge in symptoms. As an aspect of the containment phase of therapy, Angeline used self-hypnosis, relaxation, and role play to prepare herself for seeking medical attention. The therapist assisted with a referral to a primary care physician who had extensive experience in working with childhood trauma survivors. Making accurate and targeted referrals for adjunctive care is an important part of therapy with childhood sexual abuse survivors. Therapists need to know, and carefully screen, physicians, dentists, massage therapists, and other health care providers who might become involved in the client's care, as the risk is high that the dynamics of a health care setting can be retraumatizing. This is particularly the case when a childhood sexual abuse survivor is confronting reproductive issues (Seng, 1999).

As therapy progressed through this initial phase, Angeline became increasingly capable of identifying the precursor symptoms to the intrusion of new materials. In her case, these consisted of a sudden onset of feelings of hopelessness and suicidality. She was able to identify that, in the past, she had used some of the self-destructive numbing strategies to deal with incipient intrusions of memory whenever she felt this combination of emotions. The therapist taught her to use this awareness of her precursor state to act so as to create safety and protection for herself before the frightening images emerged (Gold & Brown, 1997), rather than feeling as if she were the helpless target of intrusions from her unconscious mind. She learned to go to a safe and comforting place, call a friend, write in her journal, or, if needed, call the therapist when she knew that intrusive

materials were on their way. She found that holding and stroking her pet cat was a particularly effective way to help herself through such a passage. This acquisition of skill at predicting and responding to intrusive images of childhood sexual abuse had the effect, in turn, of increasing Angeline's perception of herself as someone who could competently care for and protect herself.

Acquisition of these skills and the initial phase of treatment took several turbulent years. During that time, Angeline struggled with her depressed mood and with the advent of more intrusive images in the form of flashbacks and nightmares. Her memories became more vivid, laden with affect and sensory memories of smell and touch. She learned to apply her skills to both her mood and the intrusive images. As she did so, the intrusive materials became more affect-laden and more extensive. By the end of a year of treatment, she had clear and detailed images, which she had come to believe were her memories rather than other kinds of material, of her father repeatedly touching her genitals and having her masturbate him to orgasm. The memory integration phase of treatment thus began in the midst of the containment phase, a common occurrence in therapy with adults who are experiencing delayed recall. Intrusive materials emerge with increasing frequency and become grist for the mill of the containment phase, with new skills being practiced in the management of new intrusions.

The sexual abuse frequently occurred in the context of shared father-daughter activities that she had never forgotten, such as day trips to a park, overnight stays at the homes of his relatives, or simply being tucked into bed at night. Thus, the sexual abuse was repeatedly mixed with experiences of nurturance, connection, and parental care. She was able to report mixed feelings of confusion, arousal, and fear, with the latter predominating, as she became older. As far as she knew, the touching began when she was preschool age and continued until early adolescence, when she was able to recall telling her father "This feels bad," at which point he stopped approaching and touching her. She remembered that her father usually smelled of alcohol during these episodes and that the touching was often accompanied by his assertions that "This is how Daddy shows you that he loves you." Angeline also identified an occasion, around age 8, when she had attempted to talk to her mother about her father's actions, and her mother had acted uninterested, annoyed, and disengaged.

Although none of this detail was proof of the accuracy of Angeline's memories, her narrative was highly consistent with both research and theories about which sexually abused persons are likely to experience a delayed recall. Freyd's (1996) betrayal trauma (BT) model was particularly useful for both the therapist and Angeline in helping her to make sense of why and how she might have lost access to this knowledge about her father. As the primary nurturing parent, Angeline's father represented her main attachment figure and caregiver. As Freyd posits, when a child is faced with the untenable choice of losing attachment and care or knowing and acknowledging betrayal, most children will follow their evolutionary imperative to attach. In Angeline's life experience, there was only one loving, caring parent: her father. Her mother's depression, and perhaps other factors, made her unavailable to Angeline, thus depriving Angeline of the option of forming a positive connection with her other parent.

The second stage of therapy, which lasted for several years, focused on Angeline's processing of her memories of sexual abuse. This process included several components: reducing and removing self-blame, allowing expression of affect, and dealing with her changed view of her father. She also needed to come to terms with her mother's role in the family system as an aspect of the abuse experience. During this stage, Angeline was repeatedly required to use the self-care and containment skills that she had developed in the first stage of therapy, as the affect that was stimulated during trauma

resolution work was intense. Grieving the loss of the image of her loving father, raging at both parents for, respectively, abusing and neglecting her, and then further grieving the loss of childhood safety all challenged her ability to maintain without reverting to self-harm. During this time, the therapist focused on reinforcement of the newly acquired containment skills, frequently slowing down the work of memory integration to ensure that Angeline could safely tolerate the affect and information that she was retrieving from memory.

Doing the work of trauma resolution, the third step in therapy, can be a lengthy process because it not only requires an integration of cognition and affect, but also challenges the sexual abuse survivor to tolerate knowing that which was formerly unknowable and intolerable. Clients at this point in treatment struggle with issues that can best be described as existential or spiritual: What does it mean to be someone whose father did this to her? How can I love someone who hurt me in this way? How could God have let this happen to a child? These were common themes of Angeline's therapy. During this phase of treatment, she learned to make connections between the abuse and her adult dysfunctional behaviors. For example, she developed an awareness of how she had learned to conflate attachment with sexual exploitation, leading to the many exploitative relationships she had had as an adult. With this knowledge in hand, she was able to make changes in her intimate life that had previously eluded her, leading to the first nonabusive, stable, intimate relationship of her life. She was able to look at how her chronic underemployment had been yet another numbing strategy, and to look for work that was more commensurate with her skills and intelligence.

The therapist once again employed a range of strategies to assist Angeline in the work of trauma resolution. This technical eclecticism is a requirement of trauma treatment, particularly when the trauma has been one of interpersonal violation. For the therapist to shoehorn clients into a favored theory or treatment modality rather than meet them where they are is likely to create a reenactment of victimization (Pearlman & Saakvitne, 1995) rather than lead to effective trauma resolution (Pope & Brown, 1996).

In the fifth year of treatment, with her symptoms stable, Angeline decided that she wanted to approach her father directly with her belief that she had been sexually abused by him. She used the therapy sessions to role-play her presentation and to work through writing a letter to her father. The therapist assisted her in identifying a neutral party who agreed to act as the mediator for this meeting, avoiding creating a situation where the father might feel confronted or ganged up on by his daughter and her therapist. This part of the therapy reawakened many of the existential issues for Angeline, as well as setting the stage for her to do further work on her grief over this betrayal by her beloved father.

The session with the father went extremely well. He had become sober in the year prior to the meeting, and in the context of his own 12-Step recovery program took responsibility for his behaviors and for making amends to his daughter for his sexual abuse of her. This initially was confusing for Angeline, who had been emotionally prepared for denial and hostility, but not for his confession and desire to make restitution. Her confusion over the relationship resurfaced, and she experienced a period of profound depression in which she doubted her memories once again, even though they had now been corroborated by her father. This revisitation of the task of memory integration and the continued revision of her autobiographical narrative occupied a considerable period of time and led to a resurgence of symptoms. Her task became to learn to hold both her anger at her father for his abuse and use of her and her love for and attachment to him for his care of her. She had to find a way of taking in his amends without rationalizing away his behavior on the grounds of his alcoholism. Learning to contain all of these contradictions and

ambiguities in her relationship with her father was challenging for Angeline, as is true for many adult survivors.

Treatment ended after seven years, with the option for Angeline to return if life events evoked a recurrence of difficulties. This open-ended termination is a common component of treatment with adult survivors of childhood sexual abuse. In her case, she came in for a six-month "refresher course" when, three years after termination, she entered a new intimate relationship with a man and began to experience difficulties in sexual functioning. Two years later, she returned to therapy when her father's liver cancer was diagnosed and his death became imminent. The likelihood of a client's return to therapy in this kind of case underscores the importance of clear therapeutic boundaries in the treatment.

Angeline had a successful outcome of her therapy. She had sufficient love and care available to her while she was growing up to have an internal framework on which to build skills at containment, self-soothing, and self-care. Her perpetrator was not otherwise abusive, but provided some love and nurturance and was able, ultimately, to admit to and take responsibility for his behaviors. All of these factors assisted in creating the good therapy outcome. However, many individuals with delayed recall of childhood sexual trauma will have little or no experiences in their life histories that build inner resilience. As a tertiary effect of the abuse, they may have present-day environments that are themselves retraumatizing, such as dangerous living situations, abusive partners, extreme poverty, or chronic illness. Any of these factors can make the course of treatment longer and the prognosis less favorable (Courtois, 1999; Gold, 2000.)

One of the greatest challenges to the therapist in this case, as in many cases where the client presents with an influx of intrusive material, was to stay focused on the stage and phase treatment model. It can be seductive to move away from the intensive and repetitive work of skills development and instead focus on the more affect-laden and thus potentially more exciting territory of the intrusive materials themselves. However, the therapist's own experience with attempting to do trauma and memory-focused work two decades earlier had been a powerful incentive to stay with the focus on containment and self-care in the first part of therapy. The therapist had observed firsthand the difficulties engendered by moving too soon to work with memories and neglecting to build the foundation of the containment phase of treatment.

When first working with this population, it is tempting to try to rescue clients from their pain and terror by imposing a premature closure on the issue of whether or not sexual abuse occurred. Pope and Brown (1996) comment that to work with the remembering adult, therapists must have not only a foundation of competence in their knowledge and skills base, but also the emotional competence to contain the ambiguity of not knowing what "really happened." Therapists must be able to soothe themselves to remain emotionally engaged and present and to serve as a witness to a client who, especially at the initial stages of treatment, is highly symptomatic and at risk of harm to self.

RESEARCH AND EFFECTIVENESS

To date, little research has been done specifically on the matter of psychotherapy with adults experiencing delayed recall of trauma. The phase and stage model reflects a clinical consensus arising from two decades of practice and the observation, mostly in uncontrolled clinical settings, of the results of certain approaches to working with this population.

A number of the treatment strategies commonly used in the stage and phase model, such as Linehan's (1993a) skills-building approach of dialectical behavior therapy, EMDR (Shapiro,

1995), cognitive therapy, and various prolonged exposure therapies (Foa, Rothbaum, Riggs, & Murdock, 1991), have been studied and found to be effective in some circumstances and with some subpopulations, including remembering adults. Shapiro strongly suggests that the use of EMDR with survivors of repeated trauma be done only by therapists who have completed the second level of EMDR training, given the risk that this client population may experience dissociative symptoms.

Gold (2000) describes the results of long-term data collection on the treatment of adult survivors in a comprehensive trauma treatment outpatient program, including the results of research on various subcomponents of comprehensive treatment. He reports, citing Bisbey (1995), that a trauma-resolution strategy known as traumatic incident reduction is particularly effective in working with survivors of repeated, similar traumas.

However, the nature of practice with this population is that there is no one-size-fits-all model of therapy. It would be presumptuous to attempt to define one treatment paradigm to assess for its effectiveness or efficacy. Rather, in working with each patient who is experiencing delayed recall, therapists must take care to choose from the menu of available interventions, keeping in mind the stage and phase treatment model. Currently, programmatic research regarding each of the components of the phase and stage model of treatment is underway in several settings, but data are unavailable, with the exception of Gold's (2000) findings. Specific research regarding the long-term effectiveness of treatment is needed to buttress clinical observations regarding the most appropriate strategies for working with sexual abuse survivors.

SUMMARY

A wide range of clients, with a plethora of formal diagnoses, may present to therapy with the subjective experience that they are experiencing delayed recall of childhood sexual abuse. Therapy with this population requires a range of skills and competencies. Therapists must be knowledgeable about models of memory and the ways in which trauma impacts memory and learning. They must also have a clear understanding of how cognitive and emotional development impact acquisition and storage of traumatic materials. Therapists working with these patients must demonstrate flexibility in their choice of interventions. The goal of treatment should be the improvement of functioning. Therapists must make the integration, rather than the retrieval, of memory primary.

Finally, the issue of childhood sexual abuse must be addressed in the broader context in which it occurs. For example, the person molested once by a stranger, who is then cared for and protected by her or his family, is likely to be able to integrate that fact and fit it into her or his personal narrative. In such a context, the cascade of interference with developmental tasks is less likely to happen, and attachment to caregivers is less likely to be threatened. But individuals experiencing delayed recall are more likely to have experienced sexual abuse by someone close to them, someone on whom they depended for care, and someone whose actions were confusing and frightening (Freyd, 1996). The molestation will frequently have occurred in the context of other, severe family dysfunction (Gold, 2000), which by itself will be a risk factor for emotional problems and deficits in self-care skills. Sexual abuse is a complex, nonunitary phenomenon that carries different meaning and impact for each person who has been its target. Consequently, therapists working with these clients must eschew formulas and protocols in favor of the creation of individualized treatment plans in which the specific functional impairments of clients are addressed and remediated.

The complexity of meaning attached to sexual abuse when it occurs in the context of family and care increases the likelihood that the memory will be difficult to access and thus may be delayed in coming into conscious recollection and understanding. The mental mechanisms by which persons numb themselves and attempt to ward off the knowledge of the abuse will, in turn, create higher and more impairing levels of symptoms. Consequently, therapists who work with these patients must be prepared for a lengthy and challenging course of treatment.

Additional contextual factors can also add layers of complexity to the treatment. For example, sexual abuse in ethnic and religious minority communities is often denied by the community as a whole as a means of warding off racist stereotypes about the group (Wyatt, 1985; Wyatt, Newcomb, & Riederle, 1993). African American or Jewish survivors abused by a parent may experience a particular kind of silencing related to the rule about "not washing dirty laundry" in front of the majority culture. Arab Muslim sexual abuse survivors may find themselves stigmatized in their communities for sexual impurity rather than seen as the victims of violence. Therapists working with adult survivors must equip themselves with multicultural competencies to adequately address the interlocking layers of complexity that can occur at the intersection of cultural oppression and sexual violation.

Although the stereotype is that adult survivors are female, the reality is that a significant percentage of boys are also the victims of sexual abuse. Gender issues and questions of sexual identity and orientation are likely to emerge when the victim is male (Gonsiorek, Bera, & LeTourneau, 1994). Therapists working with male survivors must be particularly attentive during the trauma resolution phase of treatment to attend to the manner in which gender and sexual orientation issues intensify questions of the meaning of the abuse, particularly questions of whether abuse of a boy at the hands of a man implies that the abused boy is, or should be, other than heterosexual.

Therapy with sexual abuse survivors also affects the therapist. Pearlman and Saakvitne (1995) have eloquently described "vicarious traumatization" (VT) as a common experience arising from working regularly with sexual abuse survivors. Different from secondary PTSD, VT is a profound change in the therapist's own worldview and sense of safety and justice arising from repetitive exposure to the realities of adults' cruelty to the children who grew up into our clients. The practice of therapist self-care (Pope & Brown, 1996) is a further essential component of successful work with the adult survivor population.

Sexual abuse can have profound, pervasive, and long-lasting impacts on its targets. Ultimately, however, many of these individuals can and do learn to care for themselves, to integrate the fact of the abuse into their lives, and to go on to make meaning and thrive. Therapy that focuses on the stage and phase model, with its emphasis on containment, integration, and meaning making, appears to give these individuals the greatest chance for that desired favorable outcome.

REFERENCES

Alpert, J. L. (Ed.). (1995). *Sexual abuse recalled: Treating trauma in the era of the recovered memory debate.* Northvale, NJ: Aronson.

Alpert, J. L., Brown, L. S., Ceci, S. J., Courtois, C. A., Loftus, E. F., & Ornstein, P. A. (1996). *Final report of the working group on investigation of memories of childhood abuse.* Washington, DC: American Psychological Association.

American Psychiatric Association. (1980). *Diagnostic and statistical manual of mental disorders* (3rd ed.). Washington, DC: Author.

American Psychiatric Association. (1994). *Diagnostic and statistical manual of mental disorders* (4th ed.). Washington, DC: Author.

Armstrong, L. (1978). *Kiss daddy goodnight: A speakout on incest.* New York: Pocket Books.

Bass, E., & Davis, L. (1988). *The courage to heal: A guide for women survivors of child sexual abuse.* New York: Perennial/HarperCollins.

Bass, E., & Thornton, L. (Eds.). (1983). *I never told anyone: Writings by women survivors of child sexual abuse.* New York: Harper Colophon.

Bisbey, L. B. (1995). No longer a victim: A treatment outcome study for crime victims with Post-Traumatic Stress Disorder. (Doctoral dissertation, California School of Professional Psychology, 1995). *Dissertation Abstracts International, 5,* 1692.

Brady, K. (1979). *Father's days.* New York: Seaview Books.

Bremner, J. D., Randall, P., Scott, T. M., Bronen, R. A., Seibyl, J. P., Southwick, S. M., et al. (1995). MRI-based measurement of hippocampal volume in patients with combat-related Posttraumatic Stress Disorder. *American Journal of Psychiatry, 152,* 973–981.

Briere, J. (1989). *Therapy for adults molested as children.* New York: Springer.

Briere, J. (1995). *Trauma symptom inventory: Professional manual.* Odessa, FL: Psychological Assessment Resources.

Briere, J. (1996). *Therapy for adults molested as children: Beyond survival* (2nd ed.). New York: Springer.

Briere, J. N., & Conte, J. (1993). Self-reported amnesia for abuse in adults molested as children. *Journal of Traumatic Stress, 6,* 21–31.

Briere, J., & Zaidi, L. Y. (1989). Sexual abuse histories and sequelae in female psychiatric emergency room patients. *American Journal of Psychiatry, 146,* 1602–1606.

Brown, D., Scheflin, A. W., & Hammond, D. C. (1998). *Memory, trauma, treatment and the law.* New York: Norton.

Brown, L. S. (1994). *Subversive dialogues: Theory in feminist therapy.* New York: Basic Books.

Brown, L. S. (2000). Discomforts of the powerless: Feminist constructions of distress. In J. D. Raskin & R. A. Neimeyer (Eds.), *Constructions of disorder* (pp. 297–308). Washington, DC: American Psychological Association.

Butler, S. (1978). *Conspiracy of silence: The trauma of incest.* San Francisco: New Glide.

Contratto, S., & Gutfreund, J. (Eds.). (1996). *A feminist clinician's guide to the memory debate.* New York: Haworth Press.

Courtois, C. (1988). *Healing the incest wound: Adult survivors in therapy.* New York: Norton.

Courtois, C. (1999). *Recollections of sexual abuse: Treatment principles and guidelines.* New York: Norton.

Dalenberg, C. J. (1996). Accuracy, timing and circumstances of disclosure in therapy of recovered and continuous memories of abuse. *Journal of Psychiatry and Law, 24,* 229–275.

Enns, C. Z., McNeilly, C., Corkery, J., & Gilbert, M. (1994). The debate about delayed memories of child sexual abuse: A feminist perspective. *The Counseling Psychologist, 22,* 181–279.

Feldman-Summers, S., & Pope, K. S. (1994). The experience of "forgetting" childhood abuse: A national survey of psychologists. *Journal of Consulting and Clinical Psychology, 62,* 636–639.

Fivush, R. (1994). Young children's event recall: Are memories constructed through discourse? *Consciousness and Cognition, 3,* 356–373.

Foa, E. B., Rothbaum, B. O., Riggs, D. S., & Murdock, T. B. (1991). Treatment of Posttraumatic Stress Disorder in rape victims: A comparison between cognitive-behavioral procedures and counseling. *Journal of Consulting and Clinical Psychology, 5,* 715–723.

Freud, S. (1896). The etiology of hysteria. In J. Strachey (Ed. and Trans.), *The standard edition of the complete psychological works of Sigmund Freud* (Vol. 3, pp. 191–221). New York: Norton.

Freyd, J. J. (1996). *Betrayal trauma: The logic of forgetting abuse.* Cambridge, MA: Harvard University Press.

Gold, S. N. (2000). *Not trauma alone: Therapy for child abuse survivors in family and social context.* Philadelphia: Brunner/Routledge.

Gold, S. N., & Brown, L. S. (1997). Therapeutic responses to delayed recall: Beyond recovered memory. *Psychotherapy: Theory, Research, Practice, Training, 34,* 182–191.

Gold, S. N., & Brown, L. S. (1999). Assessing survivors of sexual abuse: Adult survivors of sexual abuse. In R. T. Ammerman & M. Hersen (Eds.), *Assessment of family violence: A clinical and legal sourcebook* (2nd ed., pp. 390–412). New York: Wiley.

Gonsiorek, J. C., Bera, W. H., & LeTourneau, D. (1994). *Male sexual abuse: A trilogy of intervention strategies.* Newbury Park, CA: Sage.

Harvey, M. R. (1996). An ecological view of psychological trauma and trauma recovery. *Journal of Traumatic Stress, 9,* 3–24.

Harvey, M. R., & Herman, J. L. (1994). Amnesia, partial amnesia and delayed recall among adult survivors of childhood trauma. *Consciousness and Cognition, 3,* 295–306.

Herman, J. L. (1981). *Father-daughter incest.* Cambridge, MA: Harvard University Press.

Herman, J. L. (1992). *Trauma and recovery.* New York: Basic Books.

Herman, J. L., & Schatzow, E. (1987). Recovery and verification of memories of childhood sexual trauma. *Psychoanalytic Psychology, 4,* 1–14.

Howe, M. L., Courage, M. L., & Peterson, C. (1994). How can I remember when "I" wasn't there? Long-term retention of traumatic experiences and emergence of the cognitive self. *Consciousness and Cognition, 3,* 327–355.

Janet, P. (1904). Amnesia and the dissociation of memories. *Journal de Psychologie, 1,* 417–453.

Janet, P. (1907). *The major symptoms of hysteria.* New York: Macmillan.

Janoff-Bulman, R. (1992). *Shattered assumptions: Toward a new psychology of trauma.* New York: Free Press.

Leeds, A. M. (1998). Lifting the burden of shame: Using EMDR resource installation to resolve a therapeutic impasse. In P. Manfield (Ed.), *Extending EMDR: A case book of innovative applications.* New York: Norton.

Linehan, M. M. (1993a) *Cognitive-behavioral treatment of Borderline Personality Disorder.* New York: Guilford Press.

Linehan, M. M. (1993b) *Skills training manual for treating Borderline Personality Disorder.* New York: Guilford Press.

Loftus, E. F. (1993). The reality of repressed memories. *American Psychologist, 48,* 518–537.

Loftus, E. F., Fullilove, M. T., & Polonsky, S. (1994). Memories of childhood abuse: Remembering and repressing. *Psychology of Women Quarterly, 18,* 67–84.

Loftus, E. F., & Ketcham, K. (1994). *The myth of repressed memory: False memories and allegations of sexual abuse.* New York: St. Martin's Press.

McNaron, T., & Morgan, Y. (Eds.). (1982). *Voices in the night: Women speaking out about incest.* Minneapolis, MN: Cleis Press.

Ofshe, R., & Watters, E. (1994). *Making monsters: False memories, psychotherapy, and sexual hysteria.* New York: Scribners.

Olio, K. (1996). Are 25% of clinicians using potentially risky therapeutic practices? A review of the logic and methodology of the Poole, Lindsay, et al. study. *Journal of Psychiatry and Law, 24,* 277–299.

Ornstein, P. A., Ceci, S. J., & Loftus, E. F. (1998). Adult recollections of childhood abuse: Cognitive and developmental perspectives. *Psychology, Public Policy, and Law, 4,* 1025–1051.

Pearlman, L. A., & Saakvitne, K. (1995). *Trauma and the therapist.* New York: Norton.

Pendergast, M. (1995). *Victims of memory: Incest accusations and shattered lives.* Hinesburg, VT: Upper Access.

Poole, D. A., Lindsay, D. S., Menon, A., & Bull, R. (1995). Psychotherapy and the recovery of memories of childhood sexual abuse: U.S. and British practitioners' opinions, practices and experiences. *Journal of Consulting and Clinical Psychology, 63,* 426–437.

Pope, K. S., & Brown, L. S. (1996). *Recovered memories of abuse: Assessment, therapy, forensics.* Washington, DC: American Psychological Association.

Ramona v. Ramona (September 12, 1991). Sup. Ct., Napa Co., CA. (No. 61898).

Rush, F. (1980). *The best-kept secret: The sexual abuse of children.* New York: McGraw-Hill.

Seng, J. (1999, November). *Turning a trauma lens on pregnancy: Theory, research and cases.* Workshop presented at the 15th annual meeting of the International Society for Traumatic Stress Studies, Miami, FL.

Shalev, A. (1996). Stress versus traumatic stress: From acute homeostatic reactions to chronic psychopathology. In B. A. van der Kolk, A. C. McFarlane, & L. Weisath (Eds.), *Traumatic stress* (pp. 77–101). New York: Guilford Press.

Shapiro, F. (1995). *Eye movement desensitization reprocessing.* New York: Guilford Press.

Terr, L. (1994). *Unchained memories: True stories of traumatic memories lost and found.* New York: Basic Books.

van der Kolk, B. A. (1994). The body keeps score: Memory and the evolving psychobiology of traumatic stress. *Harvard Review of Psychiatry, 1,* 253–265.

Walker, E. A., Katon, W. J., Harop-Griffith, J., et al. (1988). Relationship of chronic pelvic pain to psychiatric diagnoses and childhood sexual abuse. *American Journal of Psychiatry, 147,* 75–80.

Walker, E. A., Katon, W. J., Roy-Byrne, P. P., Jemlka, R. P., & Russo, J. (1993). Histories of sexual victimization in patients with irritable bowel syndrome or inflammatory bowel disease. *American Journal of Psychiatry, 150,* 1502–1506.

Widom, C. S., & Morris, S. (1997). Accuracy of recollections of childhood victimization: Part II. Childhood sexual abuse. *Psychological Assessment, 8,* 412–421.

Williams, L. M. (1994). Recall of childhood trauma: A prospective study of women's memories of child sexual abuse. *Journal of Consulting and Clinical Psychology, 62,* 1167–1176.

Wyatt, G. E. (1985). The sexual abuse of Afro-American and White American women in childhood. *Child Abuse and Neglect, 9,* 231–240.

Wyatt, G. E., Newcomb, M. D., & Riederle, M. H. (1993). *Sexual abuse and consensual sex: Women's developmental patterns and outcomes.* Newbury Park, CA: Sage.

CHAPTER 5

Parent/Child Interaction Therapy

JANE G. QUERIDO, KAREN BEARSS, AND SHEILA M. EYBERG

THE DEVELOPMENT OF PARENT-CHILD INTERACTION THERAPY

Parent training for children with conduct problem behavior has historically taken either a relationship enhancement approach, as used by Guerney (1964), or a behavioral approach, as used by Patterson (1974) and Wahler and colleagues (Wahler, Winkel, Peterson & Morrison, 1965). In relationship enhancement therapies, parents are trained to use nondirective play therapy skills with their child at home. The goals of therapy are to foster increased intimacy between parent and child, greater independence and self-acceptance on the part of the child, and a greater acceptance of the child by the parent. In contrast, early behavioral approaches to parent training focused on modifying specific child behaviors using principles of learning. In behavioral therapies, the progress of therapy is guided by changes in targeted child behaviors.

Hanf (1969) developed a two-stage treatment model based on operant principles that involved coaching parents in vivo while they played with their child. In the first stage of treatment, mothers were taught to change their child's behavior by giving attention to appropriate behavior and ignoring inappropriate behavior. The second stage focused on teaching parents how to give direct commands, praise obedience, and punish disobedience using time-out.

Parent-child interaction therapy (PCIT) is a treatment for behavior problems in young children that integrates relationship enhancement and behavioral approaches. Based on the Hanf model, PCIT includes two primary phases in which parents are coached in the treatment skills as they play with their child. The PCIT program is distinguishable from other Hanf-model programs in its emphasis on teaching parental responsiveness and improving the quality of the parent-child relationship. In PCIT, parents are taught skills to establish a nurturing and secure relationship with their child while increasing their child's prosocial behavior and decreasing negative behavior. Treatment progresses through two basic phases: (1) child-directed interaction (CDI) resembles traditional play

91

therapy and focuses on strengthening the parent-child bond, increasing positive parenting, and improving child social skills; (2) parent-directed interaction (PDI) resembles clinical behavior therapy and focuses on improving parents' expectations, ability to set limits, consistency, and fairness in discipline and reducing child noncompliance and other negative behavior.

THEORETICAL UNDERPINNINGS

PCIT was influenced by Baumrind's (1967) developmental research associating parenting styles with child outcomes. Baumrind formulated the authoritative-authoritarian-permissive parenting theory and later transformed her typology of parenting styles into one based on two orthogonal constructs: parent responsiveness and parent demandingness (Baumrind, 1991). She demonstrated that parents who do not adequately meet young children's needs for nurturance and limits are less likely to have successful and healthy adolescents. The strong and consistent relation between certain parenting styles and problematic child outcomes has been shown in many studies (e.g., Azar & Wolfe, 1989; Calzada & Eyberg, 2001; Franz, McClelland, & Weinberger, 1991; Olson, Bates, & Bayles, 1990). Based on this literature, PCIT assumes that treatment must focus on promoting optimal parenting styles and parent-child interactions to achieve optimal child outcomes. To define this focus, PCIT draws on both attachment and social learning theories (Foote, Eyberg, & Schuhmann, 1998).

ATTACHMENT THEORY

A secure, stable attachment relationship and healthy parent-child interactions play key roles in promoting optimal social, emotional, and behavioral development in children (Hobbs, 1982;

Kazdin, 1985). Attachment theory asserts that sensitive and warm parenting leads infants to develop the belief that a caregiver will respond accurately and promptly to their needs. These children will develop a secure attachment to their caregiver. In contrast, children who develop a maladaptive attachment with their caregiver will show more severe levels of aggressive behavior, low social competence, poor coping skills, low self-esteem, and poor peer relationships (Coie, Watt, West, & Hawkins, 1993; Earls, 1980; Jenkins, Bax, & Hart, 1980; Richman, Stevenson, & Graham, 1982; Rutter, 1980). Maladaptive attachment relationships are also associated with increased maternal stress and the occurrence of child abuse and neglect (Crowther, Bond, & Rolf, 1981; Richman et al., 1982). The combination of maladaptive parent-child attachment and poor child management skills has been consistently linked to the severity of conduct disordered behavior (Loeber & Schmaling, 1985; Patterson, 1982). Based on such findings, CDI aims to develop a secure parent-child relationship and stable attachment.

SOCIAL LEARNING THEORY

Patterson's (1982) coercion theory provides a transactional account of early conduct problems (Eyberg, Schuhmann, & Rey, 1998) in which children's behavior problems are inadvertently established or maintained by parent-child interactions. Social learning theorists emphasize the contingencies that shape dysfunctional interactions of children and their parents. Aversive interactions must be interrupted by a change in parent behavior, which involves clear limit setting that is firmly and consistently enforced early in the child's life (Baumrind, 1996; Patterson, 1982). PDI addresses these processes by establishing consistent contingencies for child behaviors that are implemented in the context of the positive parent-child relationship established through CDI interactions.

METHODS OF ASSESSMENT AND INTERVENTION

ASSESSMENT

Few would argue that initial assessment of a child's presenting problems is critical in determining the appropriate course of treatment. The structure of the assessment, however, can range from a brief interview to several days of testing. The intake assessment for PCIT seeks to obtain an accurate representation of the child's behavior by using multiple informants and methods, including interviews with parents and teachers, behavior rating scales, and behavioral observation in clinic and school settings. This allows the therapist to assess the frequency, intensity, and duration of the child's behavior problems across settings and from the perspective of different individuals.

Because of the interactional nature of conduct problem behavior, assessment in PCIT also appreciates the behavior of individuals in the child's environment. For this reason, primary areas that are assessed are not limited to the child's behavior, but also include familial and extrafamilial factors (e.g., parent personality, the parenting and marital relationship, and health, educational, and socioeconomic factors). This assessment information is integrated in PCIT to delineate the treatment needs, guide the course of treatment, and evaluate treatment outcome.

The PCIT intake assessment begins with a semistructured clinical interview with the parent that is designed to obtain information about the child's behavior problems and the contexts in which they occur, to identify child and family adversities and strengths that will impact treatment, to understand the family's goals and expectations for treatment, and to describe for the parents the assessment process and the structure of PCIT. The interview is also used as a time to establish an alliance with the parents and enables them to ask questions they may have and help them decide if they are ready to commit to the demands of treatment.

The therapist can then guide parents in their discussion of the presenting problems by incorporating a behavioral analysis, which involves assessing the nature of typical problematic parent-child interactions by determining the antecedent stimulus conditions under which problem behaviors occur and the consequences that typically accompany such behaviors. The evaluator then obtains the child's developmental, social, medical (including current and past medication), and educational history. This information helps to determine whether any of these factors are associated with the development and/or maintenance of the child's behavior problems. For example, the interview may uncover the presence of factors that suggest difficulties with the child's temperament that were present at an early age (e.g., early sleep problems, difficulty soothing as an infant). These difficulties may, in turn, have contributed to the development of a coercive style of parent-child interactions.

Also of interest is an assessment of discipline strategies, including descriptions of how they are used, their frequency, perceived efficacy, and parental attitude toward their use. Finally, the interview is designed to illustrate family structure and functioning among parents and children, including assessment of the parent-parent, parent-child, and sibling relationships. As children below the age of 10 are not considered reliable reporters of their own behavioral symptoms (Edelbrock, Costello, Dulcan, Kalas, & Conover, 1985), such young children are typically not relied on as major informants in the PCIT assessment.

At the end of the semistructured clinical interview, the therapist administers a structured diagnostic interview, such as the Diagnostic Interview Schedule for Children IV (NIMH DISC-IV-P; Shaffer, Fisher, Lucas, Dulcan, & Schwab-Stone, 2000), to determine whether the child meets diagnostic criteria for Oppositional

Defiant Disorder and whether there are comorbid disorders that also need to be considered in treatment planning. Children with subclinical expressions of disruptive disorders can be treated effectively with PCIT, but these children and their families may also do well in less intensive treatments. Consequently, the therapist may suggest alternative treatment options to the parents, particularly if the child is age 4 or younger and can return to PCIT at a later time if the problems persist. One situation in which children may show subclinical behavior problems but where PCIT is often an appropriate treatment option is when the child has been physically abused and the most critical element in treatment is parent behavior change (Urquiza & McNeil, 1996). Children with primary diagnoses of Attention-Deficit/Hyperactivity Disorder (ADHD) and internalizing disorders are also treated clinically using PCIT, but these applications have not yet been empirically examined.

After completion of the initial interview, parents are asked to complete several parent rating scales to assess important behaviors or characteristics of the child that have been suggested by the interview. Behavior rating scales are useful because they allow the assessment of a broad range of behaviors, including low-frequency behaviors, and require relatively little time to administer, score, and interpret. One behavior rating scale always used in PCIT is the Eyberg Child Behavior Inventory (ECBI; Eyberg & Pincus, 1999). This 36-item instrument permits a fine-grained analysis of the child's disruptive behavior. The ECBI contains two scales: The Intensity scale measures the frequency of current behavior problems similar to most behavior rating scales; the Problem scale measures the extent to which the child's behavior is problematic for the parent, which is highly related to parent tolerance (Brestan, Eyberg, Algina, Johnson, & Boggs, 2001). The Intensity and Problem scales of the ECBI have been found to be highly reliable (e.g., internal consistency

coefficients of .95 and .93; interrater [mother-father] reliability coefficients of .69 and .61; test-retest stability coefficients of .80 and .85 across 12 weeks and .75 across 10 months). Studies have also supported the construct and discriminative validity of the ECBI. Results from several treatment outcome studies have shown that the ECBI is a sensitive measure of treatment change in clinic-referred children (Taylor, Schmidt, Pepler, & Hodgins, 1998; Webster-Stratton & Hammond, 1997). In the program at the University of Florida, the Intensity score cutoff of 132 is used as one index in determining whether a child's behavior problems are severe enough to warrant PCIT. If PCIT is deemed suitable at this point, the full PCIT assessment is conducted.

The PCIT assessment takes into account the transactional nature of psychological functioning in the parent-child relationship and other family relationships. For this reason, parents are asked to complete self-report scales of individual, parent, and family functioning, such as the Parenting Stress Index (PSI; Abidin, 1995), Parenting Alliance Measure (PAM; Abidin & Konold, 1999), Parenting Locus of Control-Short Form (PLOC-SF; Rayfield et al., 1995), Personality Styles Inventory (PSI; Lilienfeld & Andrews, 1996), and Beck Depression Inventory II (BDI-II; Beck, Steer, & Brown, 1996). These scales extend and quantify information from the interview and enable the therapist to anticipate ways in which treatment may need to be tailored to the family.

Finally, to determine whether the child's problems are consistent across informants and situations, data are collected from the child's teacher or day care provider. The teacher/provider is asked to complete the Sutter-Eyberg Student Behavior Inventory-Revised (SESBI-R; Eyberg & Pincus, 1999), which is a 38-item teacher rating scale of disruptive behaviors at school. Like the ECBI, it contains an Intensity scale and a Problem scale that yield similar information from the school setting. Studies have shown internal consistency coefficients of .98 and .96, and test-retest correlations of .87 and .93 for the two scales, respectively. The SESBI-R scales also correlate significantly with classroom observational measures. The intensity and problem scores have been shown to predict school conduct referrals and suspensions during the subsequent one and two years (Schuhmann, 1999).

The final component of the PCIT intake assessment involves the behavioral observations of parent-child interactions conducted unobtrusively in the clinic playroom and the behavioral observations conducted in the child's classroom. These observations provide information about the severity and extent of the child's behavior problems, provide the therapist with a clearer understanding of the parent and teacher reports, and clarify the most important ways in which the child's interactions with important adults may need to be modified.

The Dyadic Parent-Child Interaction Coding System II (DPICS-II; Eyberg, Bessmer, Newcomb, Edwards, & Robinson, 1994) is a behavioral coding system that is used in the clinic to measure the quality of parent-child social interactions. The interactions are coded twice, on separate days, during three 5-minute standard situations (child-directed interaction, parent-directed interaction, cleanup) that vary in the degree of parental control required. The coded behaviors include child and parent verbalizations as well as selected vocalizations (e.g., whine, yell) and physical behaviors (e.g., positive and negative touch). Several sequences of behavior are also coded; these emphasize parental antecedents (e.g., commands) and consequences (e.g., praise) for important child behaviors. One advantage of the DPICS-II during the pretreatment assessment is that it can efficiently elicit salient interactions that will be targeted during treatment.

The Revised Edition of the School Observation Coding System (REDSOCS; Jacobs et al., 1999) is used to assess the child's disruptive behavior in the classroom. REDSOCS is an interval coding system that measures inappropriate, noncompliant, and off-task behaviors. The system allows for a variable number of children to be coded alternately during an observation session and results in 10 minutes of observed behavior per child during each session. A child is observed on three different school days, yielding 30 minutes of observation time in total. Kappa reliability coefficients for the REDSOCS categories are high (all above .77). The REDSOCS categories show significant correlations with the SESBI-R and the Revised Conners Teacher Rating Scale (Goyette, Conners, & Ulrich, 1978), and the system successfully discriminates children referred for treatment of school behavior problems from their randomly selected classmates.

After the interview, parent and teacher report measures, and behavioral observations are completed, the PCIT therapist integrates the information for initial treatment planning. The data also serve as a baseline against which treatment progress can be compared. Progress in PCIT is assessed continuously using DPICS-II to determine the parents' skill acquisition and guide the course of treatment. Parents also complete the ECBI at regular intervals to track the changes in child behavior outside the clinic setting. When these measures show that the parents have mastered the interaction skills and the child's behavior problems have come to within the normal range, the standard treatment is successfully completed. Many of the measures administered at treatment intake are then repeated to assess the generalized effects of treatment and to plan for follow-up.

Intervention

PCIT sessions are conducted once a week and are one hour in length. During the first phase of treatment, the emphasis is on developing CDI skills; during the second phase of treatment, the emphasis is on parents' use of PDI skills. The principles and skills of each phase are first presented to the parents alone using modeling and role play during a didactic session. At the end of each didactic session, handouts summarizing the basic CDI or PDI techniques are given to parents for their review. In subsequent coaching sessions, parents take turns being coached interacting with their child and observing their spouse being coached with the child. The average length of PCIT treatment is 13 sessions (Werba, Eyberg, Boggs, & Algina, 2000).

Child-Directed Interaction
CDI emphasizes changing the quality of the parent-child interaction by creating or strengthening a positive parent-child relationship. CDI incorporates the techniques of differential social attention and nondirective play therapy with the parent in the role of the therapist. During CDI, parents learn to follow the child's lead in play by using the nondirective PRIDE skills: *P*raising the child, *Re*flecting the child's statements, *I*mitating the child's play, *D*escribing the child behavior, and using *E*nthusiasm in the play. Differential reinforcement of child behavior, by directing the PRIDE skills to the child's appropriate play and consistently ignoring any undesirable behavior, provides a positive form of behavior management throughout this phase. Table 5.1 shows the CDI handout, which includes all CDI rules, their rationale, and examples of each rule, along with illustrations designed to be appealing to parents. Parents are asked to practice CDI skills at home during daily 5-minute play sessions with their child. Additional handouts addressing general behavior management skills, social support, and modeling of appropriate behavior are provided to parents during the course of CDI if discussion indicates that these would be applicable to the family's areas of concern.

During CDI coaching sessions, therapists coach parents in their use of the PRIDE skills until parents meet criteria for skill mastery, as assessed during a 5-minute coding interval at the start of each session. Criteria include 10 behavioral descriptions, 10 reflective statements, 10 labeled praises, and no more than 3 questions, commands, or criticisms. Parents must also ignore nonharmful inappropriate behavior. It is through the CDI coaching that therapists convey important developmental expectations for child behavior and point out specific effects of the parents' behavior on the child.

Parent-Directed Interaction
PDI emphasizes decreasing inappropriate behaviors that are too harmful to be ignored, are controlled by reinforcers other than parental attention, or do not extinguish easily. During PDI, parents continue to give positive attention to appropriate behavior and to ignore inappropriate behavior. However, they learn to direct the child's behavior when necessary with effective commands and specific consequences for compliance and noncompliance.

In PDI, parents first learn to teach their child to mind when given a "running command": a command to perform a specific behavior immediately, or "on the run." Parents are taught the Eight Rules of Effective Commands (Table 5.2) and a simple algorithm of precise steps to follow after a command is given. Specifically, they are taught to pay attention only to whether the child obeys or disobeys, and to give a labeled praise if the child obeys or initiate the time-out procedure if the child disobeys.

The time-out procedure begins with a warning and may proceed to a time-out chair and then to a time-out room. The time-out room is used only when the child gets off the time-out chair without permission; as the family progresses in treatment, use of the time-out room decreases. At specific points in the time-out procedure, the child is given the opportunity to end time-out, which continues until the child obeys the original command. The therapist describes and role-plays the time-out procedure with parents alone during the didactic session of the PDI phase, and the parents are encouraged to memorize the

Table 5.1 CDI rules handout.

Parent-Child Interaction Therapy
Child Directed Interaction

Pride Rules	Reason	Examples
PRAISE your child's appropriate behavior.	• Causes your child's good behavior to increase. • Lets your child know what you like. • Increases your child's self-esteem. • Makes you and your child feel good.	• Good job of putting the toys away! • I like the way you're playing so gently with the toys. • Great idea to make a fence for the horses. • Thank you for sharing with me.
REFLECT appropriate talk.	• Lets your child lead the conversation. • Shows your child that you are listening. • Demonstrates that you accept and understand your child. • Improves your child's speech. • Increases verbal communication between you.	• Child: I drew a tree. Parent: Yes, you made a tree. • Child: The doggy has a black nose. Parent: The dog's nose is black. • Child: I like to play with the blocks. Parent: These blocks are fun.
IMITATE appropriate play.	• Lets your child lead. • Shows your child that you approve of the activity. • Shows that you're involved. • Teaches your child how to play with others and take turns. • Increases the child's imitation of the things that you do.	• Child: I put a nose on the potato head. Parent: I'm putting a nose on Mr. Potato Head too. • (Child is drawing circles on a piece of paper.) Parent: I'm going to draw circles on my paper just like you.
DESCRIBE appropriate behavior.	• Lets your child lead. • Shows your child that you are interested. • Teaches your child concepts. • Models speech for your child. • Holds your child's attention on the task. • Organizes your child's thoughts about the activity.	• You're making a tower. • You drew a square. • You are putting together Mr. Potato Head. • You put the girl inside the fire truck.
Be ENTHUSIASTIC.	• Lets your child know that you are enjoying the time you are spending together. • Increases the warmth of the play.	• (Child carefully places a blue Lego on a tower.) Parent: (gently touching the child's back) You are *really* being gentle with the toys.

(continued)

Table 5.1 (Continued)

More Rules	Reason	Examples
Avoid *COMMANDS*.	• Takes the lead away from your child. • Can cause unpleasantness.	*Indirect Commands:* • Let's play with the farm next. • Could you tell me what animal this is? *Direct Commands:* • Give me the pigs. • Please sit down next to me. • Look at this.
Avoid *QUESTIONS*.	• Leads the conversation. • Many questions are commands and require an answer. • May seem like you aren't listening to your child or that you disagree.	• We're building a tall tower, aren't we? • What sound does the cow make? • What are you building? • Do you want to play with the train? • You're putting the girl in the red car?
Avoid *CRITICAL STATEMENTS*.	• Often increases the criticized behavior. • May lower your child's self-esteem. • Creates an unpleasant interaction.	• That wasn't nice. • I don't like it when you make that face. • Do not play like that. • No, sweetie, you shouldn't do that. • That animal doesn't go there.

Behavior Management	Reason	Examples

IGNORE negative behavior (unless it is dangerous or destructive).
  a. Avoid looking at the child, smiling, frowning, etc.
  b. Be silent.
  c. Ignore every time.
  d. Expect the ignored behavior to increase at first.
  e. Continue ignoring until your child is doing something appropriate.
  f. Praise your child immediately for appropriate behavior.
 	
Behaviors to ignore include:
• Crying for no good reason.
• Whining.
• Playing roughly.
	• Helps your child to notice the difference between your responses to good and bad behavior.
	• Although the ignored behavior may increase at first, *consistent* ignoring decreases many behaviors.
		• (Child sasses parent and picks up toy.)
		(Parent ignores sass; praises picking up.)

STOP THE PLAYTIME for aggressive and destructive behavior. Aggressive and destructive behaviors include: • Hitting. • Biting.	• Teaches your child that good behavior is required during special playtime. • Shows your child that you are beginning to set limits.	• (Child hits parent.) Parent: (CDI STOPS. This can't be ignored.) Special playtime is stopping because you hit me. Child: Oh, oh, oh Mom. I'm sorry. Please, I'll be good. Parent: Special playtime is over now. Maybe next time you will be able to play nicely during special playtime.

Table 5.2 Eight rules of effective commands in PDI.

Rule	Reason	Examples
1. Commands should be *direct* rather than indirect.	• Leaves no question that the child is being told to do something. • Does not imply a choice, or suggest the parent might do the task for the child. • Is not confusing for young children.	• Please hand me the block. • Put the train in the box. • Draw a circle. **Instead of** • Will you hand me the block? • Let's put the train in the box. • Would you like to draw a circle?
2. Commands should be *positively* stated.	• Tells child what *to do* rather than what *not to do*. • Avoids criticism of the child's behavior. • Provides a clear statement of what the child can or should do.	• Come sit beside me. **Instead of** • Don't run around the room! • Put your hands in your pocket. **Instead of** • Stop touching the crystal.
3. Commands should be given *one at a time.*	• Helps child to remember the whole command. • Helps parent to determine if child completed entire command.	• Put your shoes in the closet. **Instead of** • Put your shoes in the closet, take a bath, and brush your teeth. • Put your shirt in the hamper. **Instead of** • Clean your room.
4. Commands should be *specific* rather than vague.	• Permits children to know exactly what they're supposed to do.	• Get down off the chair. **Instead of** • Be careful. • Talk in a quiet voice. **Instead of** • Behave!
5. Commands should be age-appropriate.	• Makes it possible for children to understand the command and be able to do what they are told to do.	• Put the blue Lego in the box. **Instead of** • Change the location of the azure plastic block from the floor to its container. • Draw a square. **Instead of** • Draw a hexagon.
6. Commands should be given *politely and respectfully.*	• Increases the likelihood that the child will listen better. • Teaches children to obey polite and respectful commands. • Avoids child learning to obey only if yelled at. • Prepares child for school	• (Child is banging block on table.) Parent: (in a normal tone of voice) Please hand me the block. **Instead of** • Parent: (said loudly) Hand me that block this instant!

(continued)

Table 5.2 *(Continued)*

Rule	Reason	Examples
7. Commands should be explained *before* they are given or *after* they are obeyed.	• Avoids encouraging child to ask "why" after a command as a delay tactic. • Avoids giving child attention for not obeying.	Parent: Go wash your hands. Child: Why? (Parent ignores, or uses time-out warning if child disobeys.) (Child obeys.) Parent: Now your hands look so clean! It is so good to be all clean when you go to school!
8. Commands should be used *only when necessary*.	• Decreases the child's frustration (and the amount of time spent in the time-out chair).	(Child is running around.) • Please sit in this chair. (Good time to use command.) **Instead of** • Please hand me my glass from the counter. (Not a good time to use a direct command.)

procedure using handouts that are provided, but they are instructed not to practice it with the child until the next therapy session. Parents are coached through their first PDI with their child in the clinic so that parents will have emotional support from the therapist if they find the procedure difficult.

Subsequent PDI sessions are tailored to the child's unique problems as described by the parents. If a treatment goal includes increasing certain behavior, the therapist coaches the parents to give commands for that behavior. For example, to increase a child's use of manners, the parent might give commands directing the child to say "Thank you" or "Please" during the interaction, and follow with an enthusiastic labeled praise that explains the reason the behavior is important, such as "I'm glad that you said please because that made me want to help you even more!" In PDI coaching sessions, parents work toward meeting mastery criteria of PDI skills that serve as an indicator of their consistency. During the 5-minute coding at the beginning of the session, at least 75% of parent commands must be effective, and parents must

show 75% correct follow-through after commands (labeled praise after obey and warning after disobey).

Throughout the PDI phase of treatment, the therapist guides the parent in applying the principles and procedures of CDI and PDI to the child's behavior at home and in other settings. Initially, parents are instructed to practice the PDI skills in brief, 5- to 10-minute daily practice sessions after the daily CDI play session. Homework assignments proceed gradually to use of the PDI procedure only at times when it is important that the child obey a specific command. Parents are then often taught House Rules, a "standing command" variation of the PDI algorithm that is primarily used to deal with aggressive behavior. Other variations of the basic PCIT procedures for problems encountered in public situations are reviewed with parents in the last few sessions of treatment as parents assume increasing responsibility for applying the principles creatively to new situations and practice problem solving future situations as their children become older.

MAINTENANCE STRATEGIES

Two strategies are used to maintain treatment gains following PCIT. The first, which is always included in PCIT, is to teach and use a problem-solving technique when specific problems arise. This technique can then be applied to assist the families in generalizing skills and in maintaining treatment gains after treatment has ended. The second strategy, which is currently being studied empirically, is to continue therapist-patient contact following completion of the formal treatment program, with brief, monthly telephone checkup calls and booster sessions as needed. To understand and improve further the durability of change following PCIT, maintenance strategies must be undertaken and tested for long-term effects. Although several strategies designed to promote maintenance are available, little research has been conducted examining the effectiveness of maintenance strategies in improving long-term outcome of PCIT.

CLINICAL DISORDERS TREATED WITH PCIT

OPPOSITIONAL DEFIANT DISORDER

The essential feature of Oppositional Defiant Disorder (ODD) is a repetitive pattern of defiant, disobedient, and negative behavior toward authority figures, such as parents or teachers. According to the *Diagnostic and Statistical Manual of Mental Disorders IV* (*DSM-IV*; American Psychiatric Association [APA], 1994), ODD is characterized by the presence of at least four of the following eight behaviors: losing temper, arguing with adults, defying adults' requests, annoying others, blaming others, being easily annoyed by others, being angry and resentful, and being spiteful and vindictive. These behaviors must be present for at least six months, must have a higher frequency than is generally seen in children of similar developmental level

and age, and must lead to meaningful impairment in social or academic functioning. ODD is strongly associated with risk for eventual childhood Conduct Disorder (Lahey & Loeber, 1997; Patterson, 1982; Patterson, Reid, & Dishion, 1992). Most PCIT outcome studies have been conducted with young children whose primary diagnosis is ODD (Eyberg et al., in press; Schuhmann, Foote, Eyberg, Boggs, & Algina, 1998).

CONDUCT DISORDER

According to *DSM-IV* (APA, 1994), the essential feature of Conduct Disorder (CD) is a recurrent, persistent pattern of behavior that violates the rights of others or major age-appropriate societal norms or rules. CD, the more severe counterpart of ODD, is characterized by behaviors that may include aggression toward people and animals, destruction of property, deceitfulness or theft, and serious violation of rules, such as running away. The age of onset of ODD and CD symptoms has been shown to be an important predictor of the presence, severity, and stability of delinquency (Loeber, 1990; Patterson et al., 1992). CD is relatively rare among preschoolers. In a recent PCIT study, 20% of the referred children received a diagnosis of CD (Schuhmann et al., 1998). Much more study is needed before the long-term effects of PCIT on children with such early CD can be established definitively.

OTHER APPLICATIONS OF PCIT

ADHD is the comorbid condition most commonly associated with ODD or CD (McMahon & Wells, 1998). According to *DSM-IV* (APA, 1994), ADHD is characterized by deficiencies in behavioral inhibition, sustained attention, resistance to distraction, and regulation of activity level. Among young children with ODD referred to PCIT, approximately 70% have comorbid ADHD; often, the primary reason for referral of young children with ADHD is for treatment of behavior problems. Interestingly, PCIT outcome research has demonstrated statistically and clinically significant improvements on measures of hyperactivity and attention problems in children referred for behavior problems (Eisenstadt, Eyberg, McNeil, Newcomb, & Funderburk, 1993). Current research (Eyberg et al., in press) suggests that PCIT may result in long-term gains for a significant proportion of preschoolers with ADHD.

PCIT has also been used to treat families of children who have experienced physically abusive parent-child relationships. Borrego, Urquiza, Rasmussen, and Zebell (1999) described the first case study documenting the application of PCIT to a family at high risk for physical abuse. Results showed that PCIT was effective in reducing the child's behavior problems and parental stress, and increasing positive parent-child interactions. It will be important for future research to examine further the potential application of PCIT to this population.

CASE EXAMPLE

Background Information

Bradley C. is a 5-year-old boy who was referred by his pediatrician for treatment of oppositional and aggressive behaviors at home. He was diagnosed with ODD and ADHD-Combined Type at age 4.

Bradley lives at home with his mother and his 3-year-old sister, Amy. Ms. C. is 32 years old and is employed as an insurance salesperson. She divorced Bradley's father when Bradley was 3 years old. Bradley has not had contact with his father in two years.

Ms. C. described her relationship with Bradley as satisfactory, but indicated that he requires constant supervision. Her primary methods of discipline are time-out and loss of privileges, although she reported that both are ineffective in achieving positive changes in his behavior. She described Bradley as aggressive with his sister and bossy with his peers.

Ms. C. described Bradley's development as normal. He walked alone at 13 months and combined two words before his second birthday. During the intake evaluation, Bradley was active and had difficulty staying focused on the task at hand. Results of the evaluation showed average intellectual functioning with average verbal skills and low average performance skills. Ms. C.'s responses during the *DSM-IV* Structured Interview showed that Bradley met criteria for ODD at the time of the evaluation. The ECBI yielded an Intensity scale score of 197 and a Problem scale score of 20, indicating significant conduct problem behavior, almost 3 standard deviations above the mean. Ms. C. identified several behavior problems on the ECBI, including whining, sassing, getting angry when he doesn't get his way, arguing, throwing temper tantrums, and hitting. Bradley was observed in his classroom for 10 minutes on three separate days during learning circle time using the REDSOCS. He showed inappropriate and off-task behavior approximately half of the time he was observed and did not obey most of his teacher's commands. Ms. L., Bradley's teacher, was also asked to complete the SESBI-R, a rating scale of children's classroom behavior. Her scores were consistent in showing significant behavior problems at school. She noted a variety of classroom behavior problems exhibited by Bradley, including acting defiantly, blaming others, disobeying, teasing and provoking other children, and fighting with other students.

During the clinic evaluation, Ms. C. was observed with Bradley in three play situations. They played well with each other and seemed to enjoy their interactions. In the CDI, where Ms. C. was instructed to follow Bradley's lead in play, she allowed Bradley to choose the games and played alongside her son. She asked Bradley several questions during the playtime. In the PDI, when Ms. C. was asked to lead Bradley's play and get him to play along with her, she asked him to do several things and he did not obey her. Notably, as PDI continued, Ms. C. began to follow Bradley's lead in play once she realized that he refused to play along with her games. During cleanup, Bradley requested a few more minutes of playtime before he began to clean up, and Ms. C. agreed. After a few minutes of play, Ms. C. again asked Bradley to put away the toys. He said that he wasn't ready, and although Ms. C. pleaded with him to begin cleaning up the playroom, he continued playing until the end of the situation. Ms. C. reported that the structured interactions were typical of Bradley's behavior at home. She described him as argumentative and noncompliant when it is time to put away his toys.

At the end of the evaluation, feedback was provided to Ms. C. concerning Bradley's behavior and treatment options. PCIT was described to her as a program that would help her teach Bradley how to get her attention in positive ways. The program would also provide her with skills to use consistently when she needed to discipline him for being disruptive. Ms. C. was motivated to begin PCIT. The first session was scheduled the following week. Ms. C. was asked if she could make arrangements to come by herself so that she could focus all of her attention on our discussion of the first part of the program. She said that she would have to check whether her mother was available to watch the kids because her regular babysitter recently told her that she could babysit only Amy from now on because Bradley was so hard to control. Ms. C. was informed that our clinic provides free sibling services to all families; she agreed that she would use these services if she needed to bring the children to the session.

CHILD-DIRECTED INTERACTION

Ms. C. arrived promptly for the CDI didactic session without her children. She paid close attention as the therapist described the reasons for using each of the PRIDE skills, and her questions indicated that she was anticipating practicing the skills with Bradley. During the role-play practice with the therapist, Ms. C. spoke very little, which seemed in part due to concern about making a "mistake," but also due to fatigue. She mentioned not having slept well, but was responsive to feedback from the therapist and increased her involvement in the exercises. She demonstrated good understanding of CDI in describing the specific toys she planned to use in her practice sessions with Bradley at home. The therapist gave Ms. C. a handout summarizing the CDI skills and a homework sheet to check off her daily practice sessions and record any problems or questions that might come up during the practice sessions at home.

Ms. C. returned to the clinic with Bradley one week later for the first CDI coaching session. In the therapy room, Bradley played with toys that were set out on the table while the therapist spoke to Ms. C. about the past week. Ms. C. reported that she forgot to bring her homework sheet with her, so the therapist took a new sheet and reviewed the days, completing the sheet with her. She reported that Bradley had smashed his action figures into the other toys each time they tried to practice and that ignoring didn't seem to help. The therapist praised Ms. C. for trying to ignore Bradley when he was being rough with the toys and discussed ways that Ms. C. could offer choices for CDI only from toys suitable for quiet play. After this discussion, the therapist described the structure of this session and future CDI sessions. The therapist told Ms. C. that she and Bradley would be observed for 5 minutes while the therapist coded her skills, and then the therapist would spend the majority of the session coaching her through the bug-in-ear device. During the coding, Ms. C. described Bradley's behavior continuously, although she gave no labeled praises or reflections. Following the coding, the therapist coached her on turning her behavior descriptions into labeled praises by simply adding a positive descriptor. Ms. C. caught on to this quickly and gave Bradley several well-crafted praises for behaviors incompatible with destructive play. Bradley responded positively to the praises by smiling and sharing with his mother, and the therapist pointed out these behaviors as they were happening. At the end of the session, Ms. C. stated that the coaching had really helped and that she was pleased with her progress, although she said that avoiding questions was difficult for her. The therapist praised Ms. C. for her effort and advised her that, with continued practice, all of the skills would become easier.

Ms. C. and Bradley came to their second coaching session with Amy. Before the session began, the therapist introduced the sibling coordinator to Ms. C. and the children. Amy immediately took the sibling coordinator's hand, and Ms. C. told Amy that she and Bradley would be back to get her in about an hour when it was time to go home. Ms. C. and Bradley then walked with the therapist to the playroom. Ms. C. proudly showed the therapist her homework sheet, which showed that they had practiced all seven days since their last session. She said that she had one day off during the week so she took the children to a fun park after school that day. She said that they all had a good time there, and she had a chance to talk with some other parents while the children were playing. When asked about her skills, Ms. C. said that she was still having problems avoiding questions. The therapist talked with her about ways to turn questions into statements, and she seemed motivated to practice this during the session. The therapist told Ms. C. that each time she asked Bradley a question during today's coaching, the therapist would quickly say "Question" over the bug to prompt her to restate her question as a statement. The therapist discussed how practicing this together would make it easier for Ms. C. to turn her questions into statements during her practice sessions with Bradley at home. Ms. C. seemed motivated to practice this skill during the session. During coding, she gave several behavior descriptions and labeled praises. The therapist noted that

most of her questions this week seemed to occur when she was attempting to reflect Bradley's statements. During coaching, the therapist focused on identifying Ms. C.'s questions and prompting her to restate them. As a result, in addition to decreasing her questions, Ms. C. made several excellent reflections. She expressed surprise at the realization of how many questions she had been asking until then. For homework, Ms. C. felt that it would be most helpful for her to focus on her reflections, now that she recognized how her previous attempts had not succeeded because of inadvertent questioning.

Ms. C. called to cancel the third coaching session due to an unexpected change in her schedule at work. The therapist was able to reschedule her session in the same week. Ms. C. and Bradley arrived early for the appointment. On entering the therapy room, Bradley immediately went toward the toys, as Ms. C. sat with the therapist to discuss the previous week. She reported that it had been a tough week because of inventory at work. She reported coming home from work exhausted and being unable to get adequate rest because of the needs of her two young children. The therapist asked about ways that she could get support from her family and friends so that she could get some time for herself during the week. The therapist gave Ms. C. a Parent Survival Tip Sheet on social support and then turned attention to Ms. C.'s practice sessions with Bradley at home. Ms. C. brought in her homework sheet, which showed that she practiced 8 days out of 10. On her homework sheet, Ms C. wrote that she had to use her ignoring skills during four of the practice sessions because Bradley had played roughly with the toys. She reported that he quickly calmed down when she turned away. She noticed herself beginning to praise him more often throughout the day and found the PRIDE skills were becoming easier. During coding, Ms. C. was very close to meeting mastery criteria. She needed only one more behavior description and three more praises to meet criteria.

She did not give Bradley any commands, although she did reflect one of Bradley's negative self-statements, thus forming an unintentional critical statement. For example, when Bradley said, "I drew an ugly bird," Ms. C. said, "An ugly canary." During the coaching portion of the session, the therapist concentrated on increasing Ms. C.'s awareness of the verbalizations that she was reflecting. She was coached to ignore Bradley's negative self-talk and, instead, to use a behavior description to describe what he was doing. At the end of coaching, while the therapist was reviewing with Ms. C. the graph of weekly changes in each skill, Ms. C. reacted at seeing her critical statement, which the therapist had jotted down beside the graph point, saying "This is why Bradley has all these problems." The therapist looked at Ms. C. briefly without commenting, to assess if she was serious. The therapist felt their alliance was strong and decided to use gentle humor to help her to view the event from a different perspective. The therapist pulled out the picture of the bird, looked at it intently, and said in a thoughtful, serious tone, "You may be right. You really should have known that was a duckling." After a moment, Ms. C. and the therapist burst into laughter and then reviewed the graph in a positive, realistic light. The therapist praised Ms. C. for her progress and encouraged her to spend the upcoming week refining her skills during the practice sessions.

At the fourth coaching session, Ms. C. reported that Bradley had been especially aggressive during the past week, throwing toys at his sister, hitting, and biting. She was tearful while she described Bradley's behavior. She reported that she was afraid that he would hurt his sister. The therapist listened and reflected her fear and frustration, and wondered aloud if there were any days when he didn't throw, hit, or bite. Ms. C. reported that Bradley did have some good days during the past week and that he may have acted up more because his sister was getting a lot of attention from relatives because

of her birthday. She said that she was preparing a big party for Amy's birthday, and so she did not have time for any practice sessions with Bradley during the week. She did report, however, that she found herself practicing the PRIDE skills all day long with relatives as well as the children. During coding, Ms. C.'s skills were exceptionally good and she met mastery criteria. She appeared proud of her accomplishment. During coaching, Bradley was cheerful and played nicely with his mother. The therapist described to Ms. C. how much Bradley seemed to enjoy her attention. After the coaching, the therapist congratulated Ms. C. for her success and handed her a midtreatment ECBI to complete during the week, along with a CDI homework sheet. The PDI didactic session was scheduled for the following week. The therapist told Ms. C. that Bradley would not need to come to the next session, but that if she needed to bring the children, the clinic's sibling services would be available.

PARENT-DIRECTED INTERACTION

Ms. C. came to this first PDI session alone. Before starting the PDI didactic session, the therapist collected the ECBI and scored it so that the therapist and Ms. C. could compare it with the pretreatment ECBI and discuss Bradley's general progress briefly before starting the next phase of treatment. Ms. C., who obtained an Intensity score of 147 and a Problem score of 12, was surprised to see how many behaviors she now marked better than before CDI. She mentioned that her babysitter had begun to watch both children again. The therapist then suggested they start reviewing PDI. Ms. C. listened attentively as the therapist explained the Eight Rules of Effective Commands and the steps of the PDI procedure. The therapist modeled the PDI scenarios and then asked Ms. C. to role-play the scenarios with her. Ms. C. picked up the skills quickly during the role-play and said she was eager to begin using the skills with Bradley. The therapist explained that the first PDI practice session with Bradley would not occur until next week in the therapy session so that Ms. C. and the therapist could explain it to Bradley together and so that the therapist could coach her to ensure that their first experience with the new procedure would go well. At the end of the session, Ms. C. was given the PDI summary handouts to review during the following week. The therapist explained that this next week would be the most important week to practice CDI faithfully because it would help to make Bradley's first "time-outs from CDI" especially salient.

At the first PDI coaching session, Ms. C. reported that they had practice sessions each day during the past week. The therapist praised Ms. C. for taking time to practice CDI despite her busy week. Ms. C. reported that she had reviewed the time-out procedure during her lunch breaks at work but still felt nervous about actually doing time-out because she wasn't sure how Bradley would react. The therapist reviewed the procedure with her briefly, and then they described it to Bradley so that he would understand what would be happening during the session. Bradley sat quietly for a brief period and then began playing with his shirt as the therapist talked to him about the time-out chair. The therapist continued describing the time-out procedure, and afterward, commented to Ms. C. that, although it seemed as though Bradley wasn't paying attention, he was probably listening to the entire discussion.

During the session, Bradley chose to play with the Legos and Ms. C. was coached for about 2 minutes of CDI until she and Bradley were engaged in the play. Then Ms. C. was coached to tell Bradley that it was time to switch to her game. Bradley began to whine, but Ms. C. was coached to ignore his whining and state a simple and easy direct command for a behavior that Bradley might like to do. The therapist said, "Tell Bradley 'I think I'll build a garage for your

house. Please hand me a red Lego.'" Bradley complied with his mother's command, and Ms. C. immediately said, "Thank you so much for handing me the Lego just like I asked." The therapist praised Ms. C. for her great follow-through with labeled praise, and told her to switch back to just using her CDI skills. Approximately 30 seconds later, the therapist said, "Now give Bradley another simple direct command." Bradley ignored her command to hand her the blue Lego, and the therapist prompted Ms. C. to give the warning.

After the chair warning, Bradley still did not show any movement toward the blue Lego, and the therapist quickly directed Ms. C. "Get ready to tell him 'You didn't hand me the blue Lego so you have to sit on the chair' while you are taking him to the time-out chair. Okay, his 5 seconds are up." For this first implementation of time-out, the therapist directed Ms. C. in every step, even before checking whether she knew it by heart, as the therapist and she had planned. Bradley remained on the chair for approximately 1 minute before he got up. At that point, Ms. C. went to him to give him the time-out room warning.

Immediately following the room warning, Bradley yelled "No" and defiantly hopped off of the chair, and Ms. C. took him to the time-out room. The therapist did the timing for Ms. C. so that she could concentrate on staying calm and relaxed. After 1 minute, Ms. C. was reminded to wait for Bradley to demonstrate 5 seconds of quiet time. She waited for approximately 2 additional minutes because Bradley was extremely noisy in the room, throwing his shoes against the walls, hitting the door, and yelling. After 5 seconds of quiet time passed, Ms. C. resumed the procedure and placed Bradley back on the time-out chair.

Bradley sat quietly for 15 seconds, but then turned around in his chair and began screaming at his mother. He yelled that she was unfair, he screamed her name, and began crying and yelling her name. Ms. C. was visibly upset by

Bradley's behavior, and the therapist spoke to her over the bug about the possible feelings she might be experiencing while listening to Bradley's angry words. The therapist reminded her of the choices Bradley had made and praised her for her consistency at this critical time when he was first learning the procedure. The therapist then began reminding her of the next steps in the time-out procedure.

Throughout the time-out periods, the therapist talked calmly and continuously to Ms. C., both to distract and calm her and to help her understand the reason for Bradley's behavior and the principles underlying her own behavior. Following 5 seconds of quiet, Ms. C. approached Bradley in the chair. She asked him if he was ready to pick up the blue Lego, and Bradley said yes. As they approached the blue Lego, however, Bradley whisked it across the room. The therapist quickly directed Ms. C. to take him back to the time-out chair and let her know that the 3-minute timing would begin again. This time Bradley stayed quietly in the chair and the therapist commented on how differently he behaved after only a few trials in which she was consistent. After 3 minutes, Ms. C. approached the time-out chair and asked Bradley if he was ready to hand her the blue Lego. Bradley said he was sorry and went to hand her the blue Lego. He complied quickly with her next command and appeared pleased when his mother gave him a big hug for obeying her. During the rest of the session, Bradley complied with Ms. C.'s commands and required only two warnings.

At the end of the session, Ms. C. talked about how hard it had been to ignore him when he was crying. The therapist acknowledged how difficult it must have been not to comfort Bradley while he was upset. Ms. C. stated, however, that she knew that he wasn't physically hurt in any way and that he was probably crying so that she would let him out of the time-out chair. She reflected that she would have ended the time-out in the past if he started crying and

that she was somewhat pleased with her ability to ignore him. When asked her thoughts about practicing PDI at home, Ms. C. said that she felt comfortable practicing time-out at home, although she was not sure if she would be able to practice it often because of her hectic work schedule. She was asked to practice PDI after her regular CDI sessions, but only when she had sufficient time to follow through with a lengthy time-out procedure in case Bradley tested the limits at home this first week. The therapist asked Ms. C. to think about where the time-out chair and time-out room would be in their home, and they discussed safety preparations for using Bradley's bedroom as the time-out room. Ms. C. was asked to contact the therapist if any problems arose before the next session so that they could problem solve difficult situations as soon as they happened.

The therapist called Ms. C. midweek to check on their home practice sessions. Ms. C. stated that these had been going okay so far, and that she had started using her PDI skills to get Bradley to put the toys away after their sessions. She reported that over half of her commands required warnings and that she had needed to send him to the time-out chair two or three times during their first two practice sessions. She reported, however, that she had not needed to use the time-out room.

Ms. C. and Bradley came to the second PDI coaching session in a positive mood. Ms. C. reported that they had had a good week and that they had practiced on five days. She reported that Bradley had not had to go to the time-out chair during the last three days that they practiced. Bradley told the therapist that he did what his mom said so he didn't have to sit on the chair. Ms. C. was encouraged by their progress.

During this session, Bradley complied with Ms. C.'s first three commands. He did not obey the fourth command or the warning. The time-out procedure was initiated, and Bradley stayed on the chair quietly. When Ms. C. approached the chair, Bradley immediately agreed to comply with her command. Throughout the session, Ms. C. demonstrated the use of effective commands, and she remembered to follow Bradley's compliance with labeled praise about half of the time. She also seemed more enthusiastic in her play than in previous weeks.

During the third PDI coaching session, Ms. C. began by reporting that Bradley had started scooting the time-out chair in their first practice session, and then he kept it up each time, scooting the chair to wherever she was. As a result, she practiced only three times at home. The therapist advised Ms. C. to implement a new, "no scooting the time-out chair" rule. When coaching began, the therapist helped Ms. C. describe the new rule to Bradley. She told Bradley that if he scooted the time-out chair, he would be sent immediately to the time-out room. Bradley did not have to be sent to the time-out chair or room during the entire session, however, because he complied with all of his mother's commands. She seemed very proud of Bradley, and the therapist encouraged her to tell Bradley how she felt about his good behavior.

During the fourth PDI coaching session, Ms. C. reported that the "no scooting the time-out chair" rule had been effective. Bradley had been sent to the time-out room for scooting once and had not scooted the chair since. She reported feeling confident in her skills and noted that even her friends had begun to notice improvements in Bradley's behavior. In this session, the therapist coded Ms. C. in both CDI and PDI and observed maintenance of her skills in both situations. Once again, Bradley complied with all of her commands during the session. At the end, Ms. C. was asked if she felt comfortable using her PDI skills for four or five selected commands throughout the day, using the PDI procedure to follow through. She reported that she was ready to begin giving him real-life commands, but that she wasn't sure how often she would be able to practice because she didn't always have that much time to spare. She was ad-

vised to use indirect commands during times she would not be able to follow through with the time-out procedure and to use direct commands only when Bradley's obedience was really necessary and she would be able to follow through with time-out if necessary.

The fifth PDI coaching session was spent introducing the house rules procedure. Ms. C. stated that the first house rule she wanted to implement was "no bad words." The therapist also asked Ms. C. to generate ideas for future house rules that might be needed. Ms. C. reported confidence in her ability to label the target behavior and implement the house rule. She reported that her daughter would also have to abide by the house rule. She reported that Bradley had shown good overall behavior during the entire week, and that now only 10 to 20% of her commands required warnings. She reported that he did not have to go to the time-out chair even once.

Prior to the final session, the therapist asked Ms. C. to fill out the ECBI while in the waiting room. Ms. C. obtained an Intensity score of 101 and a Problem score of 4, which are within normal limits. The therapist administered the *DSM-IV* Structured Interview for Disruptive Behavior Disorders, which indicated that Bradley no longer met criteria for ODD. Ms. C. reported that Bradley had to be sent to the time-out chair three times for saying bad words, each time seeming to "remember" the rule just after the words came out, and that he may have begun to "think ahead" because he seemed to be saying fewer bad words. She said he was also hitting his sister less, and hadn't hit her at all in the prior week, but she decided to make "no hitting" the next house rule "just in case." She reported that he again complied with all of her running commands.

The therapist then introduced the topic of public behavior. Ms. C. reported that only the grocery store was a problem now, but that she had started a plan that seemed to be working. Her plan was to reward Bradley at the end of each aisle with a sticker if he was able to keep his hands to himself. If he got seven stickers by the time they reached the check-out line, he would get to choose a piece of candy. The therapist praised Ms. C. for her excellent problem-solving skills and encouraged her to continue applying and adapting positive discipline strategies when future problems come up. The therapist then coded Ms. C.'s CDI and PDI skills. Bradley was compliant throughout the session. Ms. C. showed mastery of CDI and PDI criteria and reported being confident in her ability to manage his behavior. Therefore, the therapist gave her a handout outlining other discipline techniques that would be useful for maintaining their progress as Bradley grew older. After the therapist and Ms. C. discussed the handout, therapy was terminated with the assurance that the therapist could be contacted again in the future if the need arose.

EMPIRICAL SUPPORT FOR PCIT

PCIT outcome research has demonstrated a number of findings in the treatment of conduct disordered behavior of preschool children, including statistically significant improvements in children's behavior at the end of treatment on rating scales and direct observation measures, as well as clinically significant changes for the child and family. Specifically, these studies have documented the superiority of PCIT to wait-list controls (McNeil, Capage, Bahl, & Blanc, 1999; Schuhmann et al., 1998), to classroom controls (McNeil et al., 1991), and to parent group didactic training (Eyberg & Matarazzo, 1980). PCIT outcome studies have demonstrated important changes in parents' interactions with their child in play situations, such as increased reflective listening, physical proximity, and prosocial verbalization and decreased criticism and sarcasm at treatment completion (Eisenstadt et al., 1993; Schuhmann

et al., 1998). Significant changes on parents' self-report measures of psychopathology, personal distress, and parenting locus of control have also been demonstrated (Schuhmann et al., 1998).

Studies have also supported the generalizability of PCIT by showing that behavioral changes extend to other family members and other settings. Brestan, Eyberg, Boggs, and Algina (1997) found that the behaviors of untreated siblings improved relative to wait-list siblings, suggesting generalization of treatment effects on parent behavior to interactions with other children in the family. The behaviors of the referred children have also been shown to generalize to the school setting (McNeil et al., 1991). McNeil et al. found that after PCIT, children showed significantly greater improvements than two control groups on all teacher rating scales and observational measures of conduct problem behavior in the classroom.

The studies cited above show that child and family problems are brought to within normal limits at the end of PCIT, but conduct problem behaviors in young children often recur with time (Kazdin, 1990). Research examining the maintenance of treatment effects for children with conduct problems is quite limited, and the recent increase in violent crime by children makes rigorous maintenance studies a research priority. A few recent studies have begun to address the issue of maintenance following completion of PCIT (Edwards, Eyberg, Rayfield, Jacobs, & Hood, 2001; Eisenstadt et al., 1993; Eyberg et al., in press; Funderburk et al., 1998; Hood & Eyberg, 2001). The first study to examine follow-up data after PCIT involved 24 families six weeks following treatment completion (Eisenstadt et al., 1993). The researchers found that all families maintained short-term gains on observational measures of compliance, parent rating scale measures of conduct problems, internalizing problems, activity level, and maternal stress, and child self-report of self-esteem. Eyberg and colleagues (in press) examined outcome of these families one and two years later. Two years after completion of PCIT, parents continued to report child behavior problems, child activity level, and parenting stress at posttreatment levels, while the majority of children remained free of diagnoses of disruptive behavior disorders. Further, parents reported high satisfaction with the process and outcome of PCIT.

Evidence of long-term maintenance of treatment effects at school was provided by Funderburk and colleagues (1998), who conducted 12- and 18-month follow-up school assessments after completion of PCIT with 12 boys referred for behavioral problems at home and school. Treated children were compared to classroom control children on teacher ratings and classroom observations of behavior, attention, and social adjustment. At posttreatment, the children had shown significant improvements on teacher ratings of classroom behavior and classroom observational measures of noncompliant and inappropriate behaviors, but not observed off-task behaviors or teacher ratings of social skills (McNeil et al., 1991). At the 12-month follow-up, 11 of the 12 boys maintained all posttreatment improvements on observational and teacher rating measures of classroom conduct problems. At the 18-month follow-up, children maintained improvements in compliance, but demonstrated declines on other measures of school behavior into their pretreatment range. Funderburk et al. also gathered information on the children's behavior at home. Interestingly, parents' ratings of child behavior at home remained within normal limits at both follow-ups, suggesting that the school problems evident at the 18-month follow-up did not appear to be due to a decline in parenting skills or increased behavior problems at home.

Differences in long-term outcomes associated with either completing or dropping out of PCIT were documented by Edwards et al. (2001). They conducted telephone follow-up assessments of 23 children from the Eyberg, Boggs, and Algina (1995) study who had com-

pleted treatment and 23 children who had dropped out. The length of follow-up for both groups ranged from 10 to 30 months after the pretreatment assessment. Both mothers and teachers of children who dropped out of PCIT reported significantly more symptoms of the disruptive behavior disorders at follow-up than did mothers or teachers of children in families that completed treatment. Decreased parenting stress and higher satisfaction with treatment were also associated with treatment completion. These data provide evidence that PCIT can alter the developmental path of conduct disordered behavior for those young children and families who complete treatment.

Finally, Hood and Eyberg (2001) extended the examination of maintenance of treatment gains for the families who completed PCIT and assessed the Eyberg et al. (1995) families three to six years following treatment completion. Overall, they found that the frequency of child conduct problems was unchanged when compared to posttreatment levels, as was the confidence of the mothers in their ability to control their child's behavior. Further, they found that the length of time since treatment was significantly related to better behavior. The improvements in child behavior from posttreatment to follow-up suggest that parent and child behaviors function reciprocally in a spiral of positively reinforcing behaviors that promote positive changes for years after PCIT.

SUMMARY

This chapter has described the history, theory, research, and clinical application of PCIT, an empirically supported intervention for young children with disruptive behavior disorders. PCIT is a theoretically grounded intervention that provides a framework for understanding the development of interactional and behavioral patterns within family systems. It is also an assessment-driven intervention designed to meet the individual needs of families experiencing behavioral and emotional difficulties. Short- and long-term outcome research with families who have completed PCIT provides strong evidence for the effectiveness of PCIT in affecting the stability, chronicity, and persistent nature of child behavior problems and provides an impetus for continued clinical applications with diverse populations.

REFERENCES

Abidin, R. R. (1995). *Parenting Stress Index–Manual* (3rd ed.). Odessa, FL: Psychological Assessment Resources.

Abidin, R. R., & Konold, T. R. (1999). *Parenting alliance measure: Professional manual.* Odessa, FL: Psychological Assessment Resources.

American Psychiatric Association. (1994). *Diagnostic and statistical manual of mental disorders* (4th ed.). Washington, DC: Author.

Azar, S. T., & Wolfe, D. A. (1989). Child abuse and neglect. In E. J. Mash & R. A. Barkley (Eds.), *Treatment of childhood disorders* (pp. 451–489). New York: Guilford Press.

Baumrind, D. (1967). Child care practices anteceding three patterns of preschool behavior. *Genetic Psychology Monographs, 75,* 43–88.

Baumrind, D. (1991). The influence of parenting style on adolescent competence and substance use. *Journal of Early Adolescence, 11,* 56–95.

Baumrind, D. (1996). The discipline controversy revisited. *Family Relations: Journal of Applied Family and Child Studies, 45,* 405–414.

Beck, A. T., Steer, R. A., & Brown, G. K. (1996). *Manual for the Beck Depression Inventory–II.* San Antonio, TX: Psychological Corporation.

Borrego, J., Urquiza, A., Rasmussen, R., & Zebell, N. (1999). Parent-child interaction therapy with a family at high risk for physical abuse. *Child Maltreatment: Journal of the American Professional Society on the Abuse of Children, 4,* 331–342.

Brestan, E. V., Eyberg, S. M., Algina, J., Johnson, S. B., & Boggs, S. R. (2001). *How annoying is it? Defining parental tolerance for childhood misbehavior.* Manuscript submitted for publication.

Brestan, E. V., Eyberg, S. M., Boggs, S. R., & Algina, J. (1997). Parent-child interaction therapy: Parents' perceptions of untreated siblings. *Child and Family Behavior Therapy, 19,* 13–28.

Calzada, E., & Eyberg, S. M. (2001). *Normative parenting in a sample of Dominican and Puerto Rican mothers of young children.* Manuscript submitted for publication.

Coie, J. D., Watt, N. F., West, S. G., & Hawkins, J. D. (1993). The science of prevention: A conceptual framework and some directions for a national research program. *American Psychologist, 48,* 1013–1022.

Crowther, J. H., Bond, L. A., & Rolf, J. E. (1981). The incidence, prevalence, and severity of behavior disorders among preschool-aged children in day care. *Journal of Abnormal Child Psychology, 9,* 23–42.

Earls, F. (1980). Prevalence of behavior problems in 3-year-old children: A cross-national replication. *Archives of General Psychiatry, 37,* 1153–1157.

Edelbrock, C., Costello, A. J., Dulcan, M. K., Kalas, D., & Conover, N. (1985). Age differences in the reliability of the psychiatric interview of the child. *Child Development, 56,* 265–275.

Edwards, D. L., Eyberg, S. M., Rayfield, A., Jacobs, J., & Hood, K. (2001). *Long-term treatment outcome: A comparison of treatment completers and treatment dropouts from Parent-child interaction therapy.* Manuscript submitted for publication.

Eisenstadt, T. H., Eyberg, S. M., McNeil, C. B., Newcomb, K., & Funderburk, B. W. (1993). Parent-child interaction therapy with behavior problem children: Relative effectiveness of two stages and overall treatment outcome. *Journal of Clinical Child Psychology, 22,* 42–51.

Eyberg, S. M., Bessmer, J., Newcomb, K., Edwards, D., & Robinson, E. (1994). *Dyadic Parent-Child Interaction Coding System: II. A manual.* Social and Behavioral Sciences Documents (Ms. No. 2897). San Rafael, CA: Select Press.

Eyberg, S. M., Boggs, S. R., & Algina, J. (1995). Parent-child interaction therapy: A psychosocial model for the treatment of young children with conduct problem behavior and their families. *Psychopharmacology Bulletin, 31,* 83–91.

Eyberg, S. M., Funderburk, B. W., Hembree-Kigin, T. L., McNeil, C. B., Querido, J. G., & Hood, K. (in press). Parent-child interaction therapy with behavior problem children: One and two year maintenance of treatment effects in the family. *Child and Family Behavior Therapy.*

Eyberg, S. M., & Matarazzo, R. G. (1980). Training parents as therapists: A comparison between individual parent-child interaction training and parent group didactic training. *Journal of Clinical Psychology, 36,* 492–499.

Eyberg, S. M., & Pincus, D. (1999). *Eyberg Child Behavior Inventory and Sutter-Eyberg Student Behavior Inventory: Professional manual.* Odessa, FL: Psychological Assessment Resources.

Eyberg, S. M., Schuhmann, E. M., & Rey, J. (1998). Child and adolescent psychotherapy research: Developmental issues. *Journal of Abnormal Child Psychology, 26,* 71–82.

Foote, R., Eyberg, S., & Schuhmann, E. (1998). Parent-child interaction approaches to the treatment of child behavior problems. *Advances in Clinical Child Psychology, 20,* 125–151.

Franz, C. E., McClelland, D. C., & Weinberger, J. (1991). Childhood antecedents of conventional social accomplishment in midlife adults: A 36-year prospective study. *Journal of Personality and Social Psychology, 60,* 586–595.

Funderburk, B. W., Eyberg, S. M., Newcomb, K., McNeil, C. B., Hembree-Kigin, T. L., & Capage, L. (1998). Parent-child interaction therapy with behavior problem children: Maintenance of treatment effects in the school setting. *Child and Family Behavior Therapy, 20,* 17–38.

Goyette, C. H., Conners, C. K., & Ulrich, R. F. (1978). Normative data on Revised Conners Parent and Teacher Rating Scales. *Journal of Abnormal Child Psychology, 6,* 221–236.

Guerney, B. G., Jr. (1964). Filial therapy: Description and rationale. *Journal of Consulting Psychology, 28,* 303–310.

Hanf, C. (1969). *A two-stage program for modifying maternal controlling during mother-child (M-C) interaction.* Paper presented at the meeting of the Western Psychological Association, Vancouver, BC, Canada.

Hobbs, N. (1982). *The troubled child and troubling child.* San Francisco: Jossey-Bass.

Hood, K., & Eyberg, S. M. (2001). *Long-term treatment effects of parent-child interaction therapy.* Manuscript submitted for publication.

Jacobs, J., Boggs, S. R., Eyberg, S. M., Edwards, D., Durning, P., Querido, J., et al. (2000). Psychometric properties and reference point data for the revised edition of the School Observation Coding System. *Behavior Therapy, 31,* 695–712.

Jenkins, S., Bax, M., & Hart, H. (1980). Behaviour problems in pre-school children. *Journal of Child Psychology and Psychiatry and Allied Disciplines, 21,* 5–17.

Kazdin, A. (1985). *Treatment of antisocial behavior in children and adolescents.* Homewood, IL: Dorsey Press.

Kazdin, A. (1990). Premature termination from treatment among children referred for antisocial behavior. *Journal of Child Psychology and Psychiatry and Allied Disciplines, 31,* 415–425.

Lahey, B., & Loeber, R. (1997). Attention-Deficit/Hyperactivity Disorder, Oppositional Defiant Disorder, Conduct Disorder, and adult antisocial behavior: A life span perspective. In D. Stoff, J. Breiling, & J. Maser (Eds.), *Handbook of antisocial behavior* (pp. 51–59). New York: Wiley.

Lilienfeld, S. O., & Andrews, B. P. (1996). Development and preliminary validation of a self-report measure of psychopathic personality traits in noncriminal populations. *Journal of Personality Assessment, 66,* 488–524.

Loeber, R. (1990). Development and risk factors of juvenile antisocial behavior and delinquency. *Clinical Psychology Review, 10,* 1–41.

Loeber, R., & Schmaling, K. B. (1985). The utility of differentiating between mixed and pure forms of antisocial child behavior. *Journal of Abnormal Child Psychology, 13,* 315–335.

McMahon, R. J., & Wells, K. C. (1998). Conduct problems. In E. J. Mash & R. A. Barkley (Eds.), *Treatment of childhood disorders* (2nd ed., pp. 111–207). New York: Guilford Press.

McNeil, C. B., Capage, L., Bahl, A., & Blanc, H. (1999). Importance of early intervention for disruptive behavior problems: Comparison of treatment and waitlist-control groups. *Early Education and Development, 10,* 445–454.

McNeil, C. B., Eyberg, S. M., Eisenstadt, T. H., Newcomb, K., & Funderburk, B. W. (1991). Parent-child interaction therapy with behavior problem children: Generalization of treatment effects to the school setting. *Journal of Clinical Child Psychology, 20,* 140–151.

Olson, S. L., Bates, J. E., & Bayles, K. (1990). Early antecedents of childhood impulsivity: The role of parent/child interaction, cognitive competence, and temperament. *Journal of Abnormal Child Psychology, 18,* 317–334.

Patterson, G. R. (1974). Interventions for boys with conduct problems: Multiple settings, treatments, and criteria. *Journal of Consulting and Clinical Psychology, 42,* 471–481.

Patterson, G. R. (1982). *A social learning approach to family intervention: III. Coercive family process.* Eugene, OR: Castalia.

Patterson, G. R., Reid, J. B., & Dishion, T. J. (1992). *Antisocial boys.* Eugene, OR: Castalia.

Rayfield, A., Eyberg, S. M., Boggs, S. R., Foote, R. C., Monaco, L., & Roberts, M. W. (1995). *The Parenting Locus of Control Scale: Development, reliability, and validity of a short form.* Unpublished manuscript, University of Florida, Gainesville.

Richman, N., Stevenson, J., & Graham, P. J. (1982). *Pre-school to school: A behavioural study.* London: Academic Press.

Rutter, M. (1980). *Changing youth in a changing society.* Cambridge, MA: Harvard University Press.

Schuhmann, E. (1999). *Predictive validity of the Sutter-Eyberg Student Behavior Inventory–revised and the Teacher Report Form.* Unpublished doctoral dissertation, University of Florida, Gainesville.

Schuhmann, E. M., Foote, R. C., Eyberg, S. M., Boggs, S. R., & Algina, J. (1998). Efficacy of parent-child interaction therapy: Interim report of a randomized trial with short-term maintenance. *Journal of Clinical Child Psychology, 27,* 34–45.

Shaffer, D., Fisher, P., Lucas, C. P., Dulcan, M. K., & Schwab-Stone, M. E. (2000). NIMH Diagnostic Interview Schedule for Children Version IV (NIMH DISC-IV): Description, differences from previous versions, and reliability of some common diagnoses. *Journal of the American Academy of Child and Adolescent Psychiatry, 39,* 28–38.

Taylor, T. K., Schmidt, F., Pepler, D., & Hodgins, C. (1998). A comparison of eclectic treatment with Webster-Stratton's parents and children series in a children's mental health center: A controlled trial. *Behavior Therapy, 29,* 229–240.

Urquiza, A. J., & McNeil, C. B. (1996). Parent-child interaction therapy: An intensive dyadic intervention for physically abusive families. *Child Maltreatment: Journal of the American Professional Society on the Abuse of Children, 1,* 134–144.

Wahler, R. G., Winkel, G. H., Peterson, R. F., & Morrison, D. C. (1965). Mothers as behavior therapists for their own children. *Behavior Research and Therapy, 3,* 113–124.

Webster-Stratton, C., & Hammond, M. (1997). Treating children with early-onset conduct problems: A comparison of child and parent training interventions. *Journal of Consulting and Clinical Psychology, 65,* 93–109.

Werba, B., Eyberg, S. M., Boggs, S. R., & Algina, J. (2000). *Predicting outcome in parent-child interaction therapy: Responsiveness and attrition.* Manuscript submitted for publication.

SECTION TWO

PSYCHOTHERAPY WITH ADOLESCENTS AND YOUNG ADULTS

CHAPTER 6

Functional Family Therapy for At-Risk Adolescents and Their Families

THOMAS L. SEXTON AND JAMES F. ALEXANDER

Functional family therapy (FFT) is one of the best examples of the current generation of family-based, empirically supported treatments for adolescent behavior problems. FFT is a multisystemic approach focusing on relevant systems at several levels (individual, family, and community) and all domains of client experience (biological, behavioral, affective, cognitive, cultural, and relational). As a *treatment* program, FFT has been applied successfully to a wide range of problem youth and their families in various contexts (Alexander, Sexton, & Robbins, 2001; Elliott, 1998). As a *prevention* program, FFT has demonstrated its effectiveness as a way to divert the trajectory of at-risk adolescents away from entering the mental health and justice systems (Alexander, Robbins, & Sexton, 2000). In both contexts, the target populations are generally youth age 11 to 18, although younger siblings of referred adolescents also may be seen. Thus, the youth range from preadolescents who are at-risk to older youth with very serious problems such as Conduct Disorder, drug involvement, risky sexual behaviors, or truancy. The families represent multiethnic,

multicultural populations living in diverse communities. FFT is a short-term intervention averaging 8 to 12 sessions for mild to moderate cases and up to 30 hours of clinical service for more difficult situations.

FFT cannot be classified in one of the traditional "theoretical school" categories of family therapy (e.g., behavioral, systemic, cognitive) or exclusively as an integrative model. Instead, FFT consists of an integrated theoretical base, well-developed clinical assessment and intervention techniques, and an ongoing research program, which for over three decades has focused on clinically relevant process and outcome research. FFT also has added a strong component of training, supervision, and community implementation. The systematic implementation and training program has been developed in conjunction with the Center for the Study and Prevention of Violence, the Office of Juvenile Justice and Delinquency Prevention, and numerous state and local community initiatives. This implementation program is articulated in a clinical manual (Alexander, Pugh, Parsons, & Sexton, 2000) and numerous additional training materials (Sexton & Alexander, 1999). To ensure accountability, FFT systematically assesses clients, outcomes, the process of the intervention, and adherence to the model embedded within a common tracking and monitoring system (Sexton & Wilkenson, 1999).

HISTORY OF FUNCTIONAL FAMILY THERAPY

Since its inception in 1969, FFT has been informed by three primary threads: directly from clinical need and the clinical experience in meeting that need; deductively from an integrated view of psychological theory; and inductively from empirical evidence produced by process and outcome studies (described in a later section). Figure 6.1 describes the relationship among these threads.

FFT grew out of a need to serve a population of at-risk adolescents and families who were underserved, had few resources, and were difficult to treat. These clients often entered the treatment system resistant, fearful, disrespectful, and angry, having experienced failure in many of their previous change attempts. Traditional treatment providers often required individuals and families to be "motivated" as a

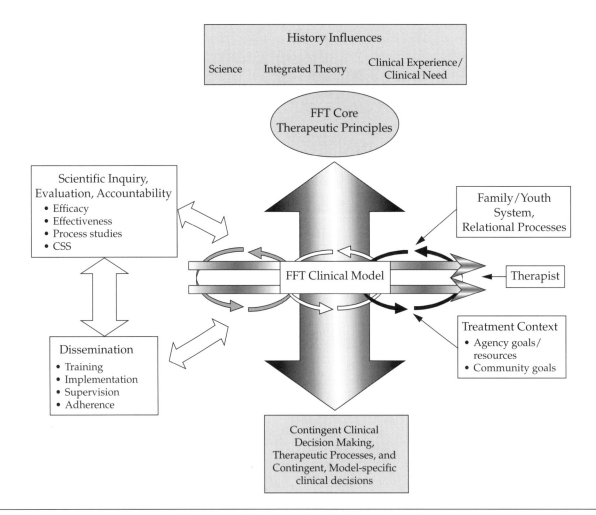

Figure 6.1 Functional family therapy model.

prerequisite for change; thus, the helping professions often viewed these families as treatment resistant, and they were notoriously unsuccessful in addressing the needs of this population. In contrast, FFT attended to this underserved population in a way that focused on understanding the source of the resistance and providing the type of intervention that would motivate them, reduce their negativity, and give them hope. Early clinical experience showed that it was helpful to provide a road map for change for the individual family and provide the tools necessary to navigate their changes and overcome roadblocks in the future. Clinical experience also suggested that long-term change needed to focus not only on stopping the maladaptive behavior, but also on developing the unique strengths of the family in a culturally sensitive way and enhancing their ability to make future changes. Finally, it became clear with this population that incorporating community resources to help support changes made by the family is essential. For an expanded description of the FFT developmental history, see Alexander and Sexton (Volume 4: Integrative Approaches).

FFT began in an era in which adherence to schools of therapy was common, if not expected. However, FFT took a different approach by *integrating* behavioral techniques, systems perspectives, and cognitive theory, and at the same time remaining informed by intrapsychic perspectives. In some early family therapy texts, FFT is classified as a behavioral approach; others characterized it as *systems-behavioral.* The former was based on our utilization of specific behavioral technologies, such as communication training (Parsons & Alexander, 1973). Unfortunately, although technologically sound, during this time, behavioral approaches rarely if ever spoke of ways to understand and implement change within the relational context of multi-problem, unmotivated families who often expressed severely maladaptive emotional and cognitive styles.

The *systemic* component of FFT emphasized dynamic and reciprocal processes in troubled families (Watzlawick, Weakland, & Fisch, 1974). Early theoretical discussions of FFT (Barton & Alexander, 1981) relied heavily on work of early communication theorists (e.g., Watzlawick, Beavin, & Jackson, 1967) and incorporated the notion that behavior serves to define and create interpersonal relationships and has meaning only in its relational context. *Cognitive* approaches, particularly attribution and information-processing theories, helped explain some of the mechanisms of meaning and emotion often manifested as blaming and negativity in family interactional patterns (Jones & Nisbett, 1972; Kelley, 1973; Taylor & Fiske, 1978). More recently, *constructivist* ideas have informed FFT through a focus on the constructed nature of therapeutic problem definitions that can organize therapy (Friedlander & Heatherington, 1998; Gergen, 1985).

THEORETICAL CONSTRUCTS AND FUNDAMENTAL PRINCIPLES

FFT is built on a set of core theoretical constructs that represent the natural dialectic tension that exists between clinical reality and the axioms of theory and science. For FFT, this tension is addressed by accepting the need for both rigor and clinical sensitivity. The guiding principles that emerge from this acceptance set the parameters of every program element, every clinical decision, and every implementation plan. The principles give direction to the unavoidable, necessary, and desirable contingent clinical decisions that must be made in response to immediate within-therapy events. The clinical decisions made within the core principles of the model represent the responsive and flexible end of the dialectic, and theory and science inform a structured and directional aspect of the dialectic. Together, they constitute a "clinical map" that is both structured and individually responsive (see Figure 6.1).

A MULTISYSTEMIC FOCUS WITHIN MULTIPLE DOMAINS

FFT overcomes the inherent tension of attending to individual, contextual, and family issues by focusing on each of the experiential domains of the family (cognitive, behavioral, emotional) while attempting to impact multiple relational systems of the family in a way that is both systematic (nomothetic: producing treatment fidelity) and clinically responsive (ideographic: client-focused). To do so, FFT focuses on each of the relevant elements that comprise a multisystemic treatment approach: the client, the therapist, and the treatment context (see Figure 6.1).

THE YOUTH, FAMILY SYSTEM, AND INTERVENTION PROCESS VIEWED THROUGH A RELATIONAL LENS

FFT views the family as the primary source from which it understands the clinical meaning of the behaviors of each family member and as the primary entry point for clinical intervention. The structural makeup of what is considered family varies widely; therefore, FFT defines the family as the primary psychosocial system in which the adolescent may spend most of his or her family time. By following this definition, FFT works with families characterized by a wide variety of structural arrangements, such as two parents ("natural," adoptive, step, foster) and an adolescent; an adolescent and his or her uncle/aunt (grandparent, etc.) caretaker; and single parent/adolescent families. Families may also include full biological siblings, stepsiblings, and other formally or informally adopted sibs. And families may include a variety of other adults, such as boyfriends, developmentally delayed siblings of a parent, and another family sharing living expenses. Most important, FFT focuses on the primary psychosocial unit of the adolescent

as our major source of information to understand regularities in interpersonal behavior that explain the existence of various risk and/or protective factors that characterize the daily life of families.

The family-focused approach is supported by various sociological studies that find similarities in family processes (Barton & Alexander, 1981), parent and adolescent prosocial behavior (Patterson, 1976), and verbal exchanges (Murrell & Stachowiak, 1967). More recent work has focused on the notion of risk and protective factors that identify the family as a primary relational system that influences family members (Hawkins, Catalano, & Miller, 1992; Lipsey, 1992) and has shown that families have identifiable patterns of behavior, that those patterns distinguish among types of families, and that these types of families can be distinguished by the likelihood of being at risk or being protected from various factors in the environment (Tolan, Guerra, & Kendall, 1995).

As a mulitsystemic model, FFT acknowledges the clinical importance of serious problems with individuals as well as the interactions among the youth, family, school, peer, justice, and neighborhood systems (Liddle, 1995; Szapocznik et al., 1997). However, FFT views these influences as mediated by the family relational system. By taking a family-first philosophy, our goal is to engage the family context that empowers and motivates the family to work at problems, regardless of their origin.

INTERVENTIONISTS AS PART OF THE TREATMENT/PREVENTION SYSTEM

Like families, therapists bring a personal history, unique set of skills and abilities, and a relational style to their clinical work. FFT is successfully implemented when therapists apply these strengths through the lens of the FFT model. Thus, therapists apply their unique strengths through the model rather than adjusting the model to fit their unique strengths. In this way, clinicians maintain their individuality while working within the structure of the model. Successful application of FFT requires that therapists use the clinical model to make the myriad clinical decisions necessary both strategically and moment by moment.

The service delivery and administrative structures in which FFT is practiced form a *treatment context* that is an important factor in both successful implementation and long-term sustainability of the model. A successful treatment context provides the coordination of services through the family therapist, the time necessary to staff cases, the scheduling flexibility to work with these families intensively when needed, and support for program implementation, including the elimination of unnecessary barriers. Many FFT programs are home-based services.

THE FUNCTIONAL OUTCOME OF BEHAVIOR WITHIN FAMILY RELATIONAL SYSTEMS

Families enter therapy with self-defeating cycles and malevolent emotional reactions, which result in emotionally destructive and often volatile relationships. Therapists and researchers often know which changes family members should make to successfully solve these problems. However, getting families to make seemingly simple and clearly apparent changes is the clinical challenge. FFT believes that this is because the problems of at-risk adolescents and their families are relational rather than technical. As a result, working with families requires that the therapist find the meaning of individual adolescent and parent behaviors in the family relational system so that reliable and valid clinical interventions that produce lasting and meaningful change can be developed that fit the unique nature of the family.

FFT has adopted a circular model of causes and effects in which the relational processes of the family are the primary unit of analysis. The goal is to derive meaning through the identification of sequential behavioral patterns and the regularities in those patterns (Barton & Alexander, 1981). From this perspective, the meaning of individual behaviors (e.g., drug abuse, delinquency, acting-out behaviors) is derived from an examination of the way these behaviors are inexorably tied to the relational process in which they are embedded. FFT assumes that people direct their actions toward achieving a particular end or outcome from others; simultaneously, those actions are mediated by the actions of others. From this perspective, behaviors become the vehicle for both creating and obtaining certain specific outcomes from interpersonal encounters. FFT uses the term *functional outcomes* to describe these patterns and their effects.

This focus on the functional outcomes of relational patterns rather than individual behaviors has helped FFT develop an ideographic and relationally focused approach to understanding families. Regardless of their form, the common, repetitive, and highly entrenched behavioral sequences apparent in families lead to consistent relational outcomes that can be understood only from an ideographic perspective.

FFT characterizes functional outcomes along two dimensions: relatedness (closeness-distance) and hierarchy (one-up versus one-down). Based on the theoretical concept of equifinality proposed by the early communication and systemic theorists (Watzlawick et al., 1974) and clinical experience, FFT learned that very different family relational patterns (e.g., anger and fighting versus warmth and cooperation) can produce the same functional outcomes (such as a high degree of interconnectedness). In contrast, very similar interactional sequences (warm communication and intimacy behaviors) can produce entirely different relational outcomes (e.g., enhancing contact in one relationship and increasing distance in another relationship). Thus, from this perspective, these dimensions represent the functional outcomes of patterned behavioral sequences, not specific behaviors in themselves.

Functional outcomes can be difficult to identify, as they must be inferred by an observer from what is produced by the interactional process of the family rather than being phenomena that can be observed directly. In other words, functional outcomes must be understood as an end result of varying and often arbitrarily punctuated relational sequences. It is important to note that FFT views these outcomes as the *state of the relationship* when the dust settles. To get a sense of this state, the therapist must understand how the behaviors characterize the family over time and across situations.

Understanding functional outcomes can be further complicated by the fact that family members often misrepresent and can even be unaware of the instrumental purpose of their own behavior. The complexity and temporal span of relational patterns leading to functional outcomes often lead family members to make other, mostly external, attributions for the cause, purpose, and explanation of their own and others' actions. The functional outcomes in the relationships between adolescents and their parents also are complicated because they are subject to the developmental trajectory of the adolescent. A once stable hierarchial relationship between a parent and child is likely to change in adolescence, and it is the negotiation of this change that is a difficult transition for both. FFT views the family as a relational web of interrelated behavioral patterns, individual expectations and motivations, and intertwined emotional systems in which the behavior patterns of each individual either proximally or distally functions to promote or limit certain behaviors in other members. It is this relational system that is also the primary entry point for therapeutic intervention.

Clinical Problems in Family Relational Systems

The task of the family therapist is to use the etiological system of the model to explain the problem behavior that families present. FFT considers the clinical problems of families to represent individual, family, and community risk factors within *ineffective but functional* interpersonal processes (Hawkins et al., 1992). FFT assumes that the symptom is both mediated by and embedded in complex relational sequences involving all other family members and that it has come to serve some legitimate relational outcome (closeness, distance, hierarchy). FFT therapists help family members find different, more effective, less painful, and nonharmful ways of achieving the functional goals.

The Change Process: A Structured, Phasic, but Contingent Path

The FFT clinical model is built on the notion that change occurs in phases that unfold over time. Each phase involves clinically relevant and scientifically based interventions that are organized in a coherent manner and allow clinicians to maintain focus in the context of considerable family and individual disruption. Each phase has a set of therapeutic goals, related change mechanisms that help accomplish those goals, and therapist interventions most likely to activate those change mechanisms.

It is important to note that the phasic nature of FFT is more than a linear protocol for intervention. FFT survives within the dialectic tension between theoretical and clinical realities because of its foundation on guiding principles that serve as the parameters within which the practitioners make immediate clinical decisions when faced with the unique features of the family.

Contingent clinical decisions are guided by the principle of matching therapeutic activities to the phase, the client, and the sample. Matching is a way to negotiate the dialectic between the theoretical and clinical goals of a model and the individual differences of specific clients. Matching to the phase guides therapists to consider the goals of the change phase in determining which direction to go, how to respond, and where to focus intervention or assessment activities. Matching to the client directs the therapist to achieve the phase goals in a way that fits the clients' relational needs, problem definition, or abilities of the family. Matching to the client also allows FFT to respect, value, and work within the important cultural, racial, religious, and gender-based values of the client. Matching to sample suggests that the therapist should target outcomes and changes that fit a particular client, in a particular situation, acknowledging the client's specific abilities and unique values. Matching to sample also allows the therapist to target obtainable and therefore lasting change. It enables therapists to avoid imposing their own value systems, social agenda, and interpersonal needs on the youth and family.

The matching principle allows FFT therapists to negotiate the dialectic of structure through an a priori change process, at the same time being respectful of the unique features of individual families. This position asserts that although families are different and may not fit the typical societal stereotype, they still have the potential to function acceptably. The match to principle also allows therapists to view resistance as a situation that exists when the offered activity, intervention, or belief does not seem as if it will be in the best interest of the receiver. Thus, resistance occurs when therapy does not fit the client or his or her perceived circumstances.

OBTAINABLE AND LASTING CHANGES

The primary objective of FFT is to make changes that will have a lasting impact on the family. In this regard, FFT seeks to pursue obtainable outcomes that fit the values, capability, and style of the family rather than to make "healthy" families or to reconstruct the personality of the family or individual therein. The goal is to focus on obtainable behavioral changes for the specific family, with the

resources they have and the values that they believe in, in the circumstances in which they live. Changes are lasting when they enhance the relevant protective factors and decrease the important risk factors in the individual family in treatment.

One of the great strengths of FFT is that in the multiproblem families with whom we work, we are able to find ways to make changes that become meaningful for the family. Some of the obtainable changes that occur not only have an immediate effect of changing a specific problem but have an additional impact of actually empowering a family to continue applying changes to future circumstances. In this way, what currently seems like a small change becomes, over time, a significant and lasting alteration in the functioning of the family.

FFT CLINICAL MODEL: ASSESSMENT AND INTERVENTION OVER THE PHASES OF CHANGE

The guiding principles of FFT serve as the foundation of clinical intervention and assessment. The clinical map, Phase Task Analysis model (PTA; Sexton & Alexander, 1999), includes specific goals, change mechanisms, therapist activities, and expected outcomes at each phase. Each phase of the model involves clinically rich assessment and intervention components that are organized in a coherent manner and allow clinicians to maintain focus in the context of considerable family and individual disruption. The clinical activities in each phase occur in multiple domains of client experience (cognitive, behavioral, and relational) and are aimed at different systems (individual, family, community). Figure 6.2 is a graphic representation of the FFT clinical model and its components.

A number of points are important to note before a specific discussion of the goals and techniques of each phase. First, FFT considers every action of the therapist to have therapeutic

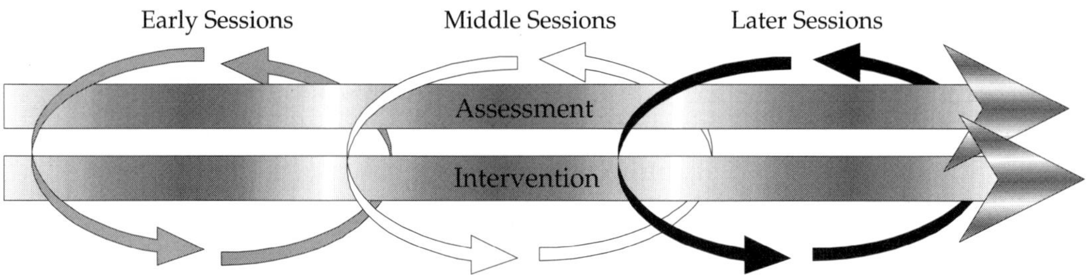

Intervention Phase

Engagement/Motivation	*Behavior Change*	*Generalization*
	Phase Goal	
• Reduce negativity. • Reduce blaming. • Redefine problem with a family focus. • Create therapeutic alliance.	• Identify targets of change. • Identify implementation path for change.	• Generalize change. • Manitain change. • Support change by incorporating community resources.
	Targeted Change Mechanisms	
• Alliance with therapist through support and structure. • Engagement through acceptance of the therapist and the intervention. • Reattribbution of the intent and menaing of conflicted problems, intentions, emotions, and behaviors.	• Behavioral competence to reduce risk factors and promote protective factors. • Mastery in dealing with problematic situations.	• Generalizing behavioral changes across situations. • Efficacy to overcome setbacks and relapse. • Use of community resources.
	Primary Interventions	

• Reframing.
• Interpersonal support.
• Process structuring.
• Clinical responsiveness.
	Behavioral technologies:
	  • Communication training.
	  • Problem solving.
	  • Conflict management.
	  • Parent skills training.
		• Relapse prevention.
		• Integration and incorporation of necessary community resources.

Figure 6.2 FFT clinical change model: phases, goals, change mechanisms, and interventions.

potential. Thus, interventions are redefined to include all of the activities of the therapist throughout each phase of therapy. Second, assessment, too, is an activity that takes place in each phase: It is the focus of assessment that changes across the phases. Finally, the circular depiction of the FFT phase is important. Accomplishment of the phase goals, though structured and directional, is neither linear nor direct. As such, the conversations between therapist and client may actually revolve around similar content areas as the therapist takes advantage of the opportunities that occur to accomplish the goals of the phase. In this regard, the model represents the reality of the therapist and exists as a process map that guides him or her in determining how to respond during the course of the interview. For example, in early phases, the therapist takes opportunities to respond in ways that promote engagement and motivation.

In the second phase, the primary goal of intervention is to target and implement behavior changes. In the third phase, the primary goal is maintaining and generalizing change. In this way, the clinical model becomes the primary source of guidance in how to respond within a less than linear and direct relational context of family therapy. The phase-based responses called for in the model are intended to promote specific change mechanisms associated with each phase of the FFT clinical model and are represented in Figure 6.2.

ENGAGEMENT AND MOTIVATION PHASE

The engagement and motivation phase of therapy begins with the first contact between therapist and family. Engagement is defined as involving the family in the immediate activities of the session such that they become interested in taking part in and accepting therapy. Motivation is a state that families develop through the initial phase in which they come to see hope that the problem can change, and a belief that the therapist and therapy can help promote those changes, that things can be different, and that they, along with other members of the family, will have to change. Both engagement and motivation are important internal client states that must be developed if families are going to be willing to return to and participate in therapy and accept and take part in any behavior change interventions (see Figure 6.2). Engagement and motivation opportunities and interventions most often occur simultaneously.

For engagement and motivation to occur, families must experience the individual- and family-focused support that engages them in the process of therapy. In addition, they must experience a change in interpersonal behavior among family members in the initial sessions, particularly in regard to negative and blaming interactions. When negativity and blaming are reduced, hope can emerge and the therapist can

demonstrate that he or she is capable and competent to be a helpful influence. Reduction of blaming and negativity also creates more positive interactions among family members, contributing to a sense of hope. Reattribution of the causes, emotions, and intent of the behaviors of family members helps frame the problem in a family-focused way in which each member retains some responsibility but no blame. In the alliance thus developed, each family member believes that the therapist supports and understands his or her position, beliefs, and values.

Engagement and motivation also require that a mutual and family-focused definition of the problem emerge. Having struggled with the behavior problems of the adolescent or parent for some time, it is only natural that each family member comes to therapy with well-defined explanations for the problems they experience. These definitions may exist in emotional ("It hurts and I am angry"), behavioral ("Stay away from me"; "You don't deserve a break"), or cognitive terms ("You are just trying to hurt me"; "Why does he/she intentionally do this?"). The cognitive sets, or problem definitions, are the meanings that contribute to the emotional intensity that is often behind the anger, blaming, and negativity seen in the interpersonal interactions among family members. In the engagement and motivation phase, a family-focused problem definition can be constructed through the conversation of therapy. A family-focused problem definition is one in which everyone in the family has some responsibility and thus, some part in the problem. However, no family member bears the blame for the state of affairs in the family. The difficult goal is the reduction of blame while each one retains a sense of responsibility for his or her own actions.

A family-focused problem definition has a number of important therapeutic functions. First, it contributes to the reduction of blaming and negative interactions among family members and thus produces hope and a sense of motivation. Second, it helps individual family members reattribute the intent and causes of behaviors from malevolent to benevolent intent and thus alters the emotional attributions associated with problem behavior. Third, the family-focused problem definition helps identify potential solutions that otherwise may have been difficult to identify. Finally, this constructed family-focused problem definition helps organize therapy and becomes the major theme that explains the problems of the family and thus organizes behavior change efforts. In fact, without this redefinition to include all family members, it is almost impossible to get everyone in the family involved in the behavior change phase.

Assessment is an ongoing activity throughout the engagement and motivation phase in two primary areas. First, the therapist assesses the process issues of the phase, attempting to judge the progress of each of the phase goals to determine what interventions need to occur. Second, the therapist begins to develop a multisystemic understanding of the individuals, family, and relational context of the family. The assessment is focused on identifying the problem sequences that unite the issues presented and the underlying relational system of the family. Assessing these issues helps the therapist understand the family well enough to match to them and begin to plan for the behavior change phase. It is important to note that unlike some models, assessment at this phase is usually based on observation rather than direct questioning or intervention.

Probably the most common and universal therapeutic technique, reframing has a particularly important place in the engagement and motivation phase. Reframing helps family members find a way out of the defensive, blaming, and negative emotionally spiraling behavior patterns that dominate the family. When events, emotions, and behavior are reframed, an alternative route to emotional expression is created. In addition, an alternative cognitive and attributional set is created that helps redefine the meaning of events and thus reduce the negativity and redirect the emotionality surrounding them. Reframing also creates confusion and thus provides some distance and protection from the automatic negative processing and relational patterns that have developed in families over time.

Reframing is a therapeutic process that is systematic, relationally contingent, and responsive. On being presented with a reframing opportunity, the therapist first finds a way to validate the position, statement, emotion, or primary meaning of the speaker. The validation response supports and engages the client. Validation is followed by a reattribution, which presents an alternative theme or meaning to the event, which must be plausible and believable to the client. For example, it is possible to reframe anger as the hurt the individual feels in response to the trouble in the family. The reattribution is helpful because it changes the focus of the behavior from being directed to another person to being inside the speaker. Thus, the blame inherent in anger is now redefined as hurt, which removes negative emotions while retaining behavioral responsibility.

Reframing is not an isolated intervention conducted by the therapist aimed at making the client feel better by finding the positive, nor is it an attempt to say "It's okay, things will be better," or provide another interpretation to an event. Instead, reframing is a *process* conducted by the therapist that acknowledges the position of the client (validation) while at the same time reattributing the event to an alternative yet plausible explanation that fits the client without being negative or blaming (reframe). In this process, therapist and client are actually constructing a mutually agreed upon and jointly acceptable alternative explanation for an emotional set of events or series of behaviors. Because it is jointly constructed, it is real and relevant to both client and therapist. Over time, the small, individual reframes become thematic, involving many family members, a series of events, and a complex alternative explanation for the problem. In this way, the reframing process helps organize and provide a therapeutic thread to the engagement and motivation phase.

This phase is successful when family members begin to believe that, although everyone in the family has a different and unique contribution to the primary concerns, everyone shares in the emotional struggle that is occurring. The family comes to trust in the therapist; they believe that the therapist has an understanding of their unique position, although they may not agree with it, and that the therapist has the ability to help. They come to know that regardless of what they may have done, the therapist will protect and help them. They become engaged in the process and come to believe that it will benefit them personally and the family as a whole and that the solution will require changes from each of them. In a sense, each family member will be more hopeful that a solution is possible and feel motivated to take responsibility to try new behaviors and techniques in search of this solution (see Figure 6.2).

BEHAVIOR CHANGE PHASE

The behavior change phase begins a purposeful refocusing of the therapeutic conversation from reframing and redirecting to focusing on specific changes in targeted behavior. The hope and involvement generated in the earlier phase provides the motivation, and the family-focused definition of the problem provides a rationale that makes the behavior change interventions logical and thus more likely to be carried out by the family. The relational understanding of the family gained in the engagement and motivation phase provides a clear path to deliver the technologies of improved communication, problem solving, or parenting to the specific family. Specific behavior change interventions commonly used in FFT can be found elsewhere

(Alexander, Pugh, et al., 2000; Barton & Alexander, 1981). The specific goals and change mechanisms are detailed in Figure 6.2.

The primary goal of the behavior change phase is to cement the attributional changes made in the engagement and motivation phase by helping the family increase their ability to competently perform the myriad tasks that contribute to successful family functioning. This is accomplished by developing an individualized change plan that targets the risk and protective factors evident in the family and achieves those goals using the unique relational pathways to change that fit the family. The emphasis in this phase is on building protective family skills that will improve the factors that put the family and adolescent at risk. The desired outcomes are the competent performance of the primary activities associated with risk factors: parenting, rewards and punishments, communication between adolescent and parent, negotiation of limits and rules, and problem solving and conflict management in a way that matches the relational capabilities of the particular family, that is developmentally appropriate, and that is possible for this family with their abilities in this context.

The targets of a behavior change plan are somewhat common (e.g., improved communication, parenting, problem solving) in the population of at-risk adolescents, but the implementation of change is unique to each family relational system. Implementation of behavior change is unique because the paths to behavior change are through the relational functions and patterns of the individual family. The goal is to increase competent performance of, for example, parenting, but in a way that matches the relational functions of the particular parent and adolescent. In one family, the implementation of parenting change might take the form of close and connected negotiation of consequences so that both parents feel a part of a collaborative relationship with one another. In another family, with a different relational profile, the same parenting changes would look more disconnected and distanced, with information exchanged via notes instead of conversation. The independence-oriented adolescent is unlikely to complete making behavior changes that involve high levels of contact with the family. FFT targets improved communication, for example, while maintaining a degree of family contact that still guarantees autonomy, independence, and distance for the adolescent.

FFT makes the assumption that change is accomplished only when the change plan is consistent with the problem definitions of the family, their relational processes, and the functions of behaviors, and fits with the strengths and weaknesses of individuals. Therefore, the goal of our behavioral intervention is not to change the relational functions of behaviors but to encourage the manifestation of these outcomes. By focusing on the expression of functional outcomes and not the outcomes themselves, FFT individualizes the changes of behavior to fit the existing relational functioning of the family. Making behavioral technologies fit the family relational system allows the family therapist to take the path of least resistance.

The targeted changes are implemented both in sessions and through assigned family tasks accomplished between sessions. The themes from the previous stages help provide the rationale for these new behaviors. As behavior change sessions progress, the therapist may model new skills, ask the family to practice, or provide guidance in the successful accomplishment of these new behaviors. Through the use of therapeutic directives, the therapist may structure activities that the family practices. The implementation of these changes draws on many of the typical technical aids that help to increase the likelihood of success in changing behaviors. For example, communication might be enhanced through message boards or reminders.

Assessment in the behavior change phase is directed at two areas: The therapist must identify the targets of behavior change (e.g., the risk factors to be addressed) and identify a path to implement changes in those behaviors that fit the family relational system. Developing and implementing individualized change plans are based on an assessment of interpersonal functions, culture, capacities, and context that targets the presenting problem and the risk and protective factors. Themes from the previous stages help provide the rationale for new behaviors; however, it is a complete understanding of the relational functioning of the family members that helps the therapist identify pathways to implement the changes in a way that matches the family.

GENERALIZATION PHASE

In this phase, the focus of attention turns from changing family behaviors to the future and extended application of these behaviors by the family members. There are three primary goals in this phase. First, the therapist attempts to generalize changes that have occurred in the behavior change and engagement/motivation phase. The goal of generalization is to systematically focus the family perspective on moving the changes into other, similar family situations. A second goal is to work to maintain change by helping families overcome the natural roller coaster of change. Maintenance of change occurs through using relapse prevention techniques to help develop the expectation that things will get worse, but can get better again and to build confidence that the newly acquired skills will work in different situations over time. Finally, the goal of supporting change is usually accomplished by bringing the necessary community resources and support to the family. In general, long-term change is accomplished when the family is helped to use their own skills to obtain these changes with the guidance of the therapist. In other situations, supporting change requires the therapist to move into the role of family case manager (see Figure 6.2).

The desired outcomes of the generalization stage are to stabilize emotional and cognitive shifts made by the family in engagement and motivation and the specific behavior changes made to alter risk and enhance protective factors. This is done by having the family develop a sense of mastery in their ability to address future and different situations (generalize). In addition, the goal is to maintain the changes through the roller coaster of life events using relapse prevention techniques. Finally, the hope is that the family is able to act in self-reliant ways by identifying and using relevant community resources.

FFT also recognizes that to support the changes made by families, therapists must give attention to the community, extended family, peer, and cultural context in which they live. These contexts often provide valuable resources to help the family maintain the positive change trajectory developed during therapy. There are community organizations that help with positive mentoring, agencies that provide economic assistance, community sites that provide positive and prosocial activities for children, to name a few. Consequently, in the generalization phase, another goal of the therapist is to help the family learn to access these resources to further support change. To accomplish this, the therapist often must adopt the role of family resource manager; thus, family therapists best accomplish this job because they understand the relational system of the family and can match it to available resources (Alexander, Pugh, et al., 2000).

DYNAMIC NATURE OF THE PHASES OF FUNCTIONAL FAMILY THERAPY

The dialectic struggle between a systematic treatment program and a contingently responsive clinical process is evident in the application of these phases to families in treatment. The description of FFT phases of treatment in the previous discussion and in Figure 6.2 may seem to imply that FFT is a linear process applied in equal amounts and in rote ways regardless of the family. This perception is misleading. FFT is both systematic in its approach and contingently directed and dynamic in its application. The clinical model and accompanying treatment manual is a map that details the specific goals and strategies of each phase of change. However, recognizing individual differences and the need to be responsive, the clinical model applies these strategies and approaches these goals in ways that are unique to each family.

Application of the model may require differential attention to the phases. For example, in one family, the negativity and blaming may be so intense that the therapist spends significant time (three to five sessions) during the early phase realizing that without the requisite level of motivation, any move into behavior change will likely produce noncompliance and not allow the family to accomplish change. In another family, the initial motivation level, family focus on the problem, and negativity may take very little time to address. In this case, the therapist may move more quickly to the behavior change phase, where it may be the development of competencies and the building of skills that take significant time (four to five sessions). In yet another family, both of the early phases may be accomplished relatively quickly, and maintaining change in the difficult peer and community environment of the family may take the most energy. In each of these examples, the model retains its direction and the goals of each phase are accomplished; however, the distribution of these efforts are contingent on the needs of the family.

Application of the model may also require that the phases overlap to different degrees. For example, in one family, the engagement and motivation changes may seem very distinct from behavior changes. Thus, it would feel as if engagement and motivation ended in one session and behavior change began in another. However, in another family, the attention to motivation may continue through many of the behavior change interventions as the therapist continues to reframe negativity while simultaneously implementing a behavior change plan. The dynamic nature of the FFT model is one of its most unique features. By embracing the dialectic among structure, direction, systematic intervention, and contingent, individually focused, and clinically responsive treatment, the model has clinical relevance and widespread application.

CLINICAL ASSESSMENT WITHIN THE PHASES OF FFT

FFT takes a relational approach to understanding the problems experienced by families and adolescents (Alexander & Pugh, 1996). To do so, FFT relies on three types of assessment: (1) formal assessment (self-report assessment inventories) that help identify the family characteristics at the beginning of therapy that may become behavior change targets, (2) clinical observation aimed at understanding the relational dynamics that help the therapist identify the unique intervention path, and (3) constant monitoring of the process of therapy, particularly in regard to adherence and competent application of the model.

Two levels of relational assessment constitute the clinical assessment domain. At the *sequence* level, the primary goal is to identify the relatively stable and lawful sequences of behavior in the family. These behavioral sequences are the reliable and meaningful sequences that help the therapist understand how everyone is connected. FFT makes a key assumption that the problems experienced by the family are embedded in a few common behavior patterns or problem sequences that promote certain risk factors. The *functional* level of clinical assessment leads

the therapist to understand how these relational patterns contribute to adaptive and legitimate relational outcomes. The primary goal here is to determine the functional payoffs for each family member. As noted above, functional outcomes are a post hoc hypothesis based on numerous observations by the therapist organized around two dimensions: relatedness (distance and closeness) and hierarchy. These two dimensions help provide structure to the clinical assessment of the space between the family members.

MAJOR SYNDROMES, SYMPTOMS, AND PROBLEMS TREATED IN FUNCTIONAL FAMILY THERAPY

Disruptive behaviors and conduct problems are the most common reasons that adolescents are referred for mental health care (Kazdin, 1991). Similarly, the most common referrals to FFT are for adolescents demonstrating the wide range of behaviors included under the heading of Disruptive Behavior Disorders (Costello & Angold, 1993). These behaviors include delinquency, impulse-control problems (typical of Attention-Deficit/Hyperactivity Disorder), substance abuse problems, and family and social problems associated with the aggressive and oppositional behaviors common in this group. These behaviors are classified in the *DSM-IV* as diagnostic of Oppositional Defiant and Conduct Disorders. Unfortunately, the *DSM-IV* classification represents a narrowly defined set of behaviors that misses the clinically rich constructs regarding etiology, course, prognosis, and treatment that are necessary to understand adolescent problems (Alexander & Pugh, 1996).

Like others (Kazdin, Siegel, & Bass, 1992), we suggest that these behavior patterns of adolescents referred to FFT represent a package that includes biological, relational, family, socioeconomic, and environmental factors. Thus, regardless of whether the behavior of the adolescent is diagnosable or fits the developmental trajectory of early or late onset (Loeber, 1991), we attend to the role of the family, parents, peers, school, and environment in understanding the adolescents referred to us.

CASE EXAMPLE

Janis, a 16-year-old African American female, was a mandatory referral to the FFT program from a local juvenile justice court. She lived with her mother (Sarah), stepfather (Bill), and two younger siblings (3 and 4 years old). Both mother and stepfather worked as nurses in a local hospital. Janis had been suspended from high school for truancy, fighting, and disorderly conduct in the late fall semester and had lost all of her junior year academic credits. She had a long history of conduct problems, a history of other delinquency-related behaviors (truancy, drug use, oppositional and defiant behavior, etc.), and a recent domestic violence charge that finally brought her and her family into contact with the court system. Janis had been evaluated by a clinical psychologist and diagnosed with Conduct and Attention Deficit Disorders. The psychiatrist recommended a residential treatment program. The court and Janis's parents considered the FFT program to be the last hope before removing her from her home. The senior author and a cotherapist saw Janis and her family for nine visits over a four-month period. A one-year follow-up visit was also conducted.

ENGAGEMENT AND MOTIVATION

During the initial phone call, Sarah reported that Janis refused to attend counseling with her stepfather and that it might be best if she met alone with the therapists to present the many psychiatric and psychological reports and help

the therapists understand the important issues in her daughter's case. In typical FFT fashion, we listened carefully, thanked her for her effort and concern, and asked that she, her daughter, and her stepfather attend the first session, where we would make sure that she had an opportunity to help us better understand the problems she, her husband, and her daughter faced. We thanked her for her help and asked her to think carefully about everything we might need to know from her perspective, so that we could get to the heart of the issue that Janis and her family were struggling with. The cotherapist talked with Janis, who was noncommittal but willing to attend the first session.

First phone calls represent important opportunities to engage the family and to begin the process of establishing a family focus. These calls also reveal the way the family attributes cause to the problems they face. In this case, it was clear that the causes of the problem were focused on the adolescent. The adolescent-focused problem definition was further supported by a history of psychological reports, problems at home and at school, and now, trouble with the court system. This is a typical way that families present for treatment. In an attempt to engage families, we accept this position while making it clear that FFT is a family-focused intervention that will involve everyone. In the phone call described above, we accomplished this by supporting the mother's concern about the seriousness of the case, asking for her to share her expertise with us, relying on her and her husband's care and concern for Janis, while quietly standing firm in our requirement to meet with the family. We rarely, if ever, agree to see either parents or adolescents alone during the early sessions. From our perspective, establishing a family and relational focus to the problem is more important than anything we might gain from individual contacts with family members.

The first two family sessions were conducted during the next week and were attended by

Janis, her mother, and stepfather. Both of these sessions were marked by angry, emotional, and blaming interactions among them. The intensity and emotional nature of these interactions are difficult to convey in text form; however, we describe them here to give the reader a sense of the *primary focus* of FFT in the early sessions of treatment. Early sessions usually reveal the behavioral sequences that characterize the family relationships, the problem definitions held by family members, and the emotionality connected to these issues. In this case, the negativity began in the waiting room of the clinic prior to the first session, where Janis and her stepfather got into an argument. Sarah jumped into the quickly escalating argument by espousing Bill's care and concern, noting the great effort it required for him to even attend, given how Janis had treated him. Sarah explained to the therapists that the reason Janis was arrested was because of domestic violence resulting from an incident in which Janis had hit Bill with a shovel when he attempted to block her from leaving the house. In an escalating set of interchanges, Janis and her mother argued about the details of the domestic violence charge. When Bill finally spoke, he declared that Janis's behavior, both in the session and at home, would need to stop if she were going to live in the family. Sarah responded quickly by angrily attacking Bill, suggesting that he was very much to blame for what had gone on. Janis's only response was that the behavior displayed by Bill was the reason she was unable to be in the same room with him. Janis defended her mother, saying that the real problem in the family was Bill and the way he treated her mother. Janis and Bill sat quietly defiant; Sarah cried. With almost every issue that was discussed, whether it was school, behavior at home, the influence of peers, or Janis's drug use, a similar pattern of interaction resulted.

Additional background emerged during these early sessions. FFT therapists are usually more interested in the way the clients' history plays out in present relational patterns and functional outcomes; however, background information does provide an important context for understanding the emotionality of the family's response to these patterns. During the first session, Sarah told the therapist that the *real* problem was that Janis had yet to overcome and adequately grieve her father's death. Five years earlier, Janis's father had committed suicide. His suicide came at a time when Sarah and Bill were having an affair and Sarah was preparing to divorce her former husband. Not long after the suicide, Sarah discovered that she was pregnant by Bill with her son.

The discussion above is presented to give the reader a sense of the interdependent nature of the behavior sequences in the family. In the actual session, the therapists were very active, frequently reframing, attempting to interrupt the sequences noted above, and redirecting the conversation. In matching our interventions to the phase of treatment, our primary goals were to establish a sense of alliance, reduce the negativity and blaming, and establish a family focus and interdependent definition of the problem. We accomplished these goals by actively reframing the statements of each family member. Reframing interventions were developed over the course of the session and not just delivered to the family. The themes and reframes were constantly adjusted, altered, and made to fit the family. As the themes developed, they were repeated numerous times during the conversation, becoming the thread linking the conversation together. Finally, each reframe was an attempt to help establish some sense of individual responsibility, validation, and relational interdependence and family focus, while reattributing the cause of the behavior to benign sources.

As the negativity and blaming decreased, the family began to experience the interdependent nature of their problems. We had supported each member enough to develop an alliance with each while clearly establishing a family focus.

Throughout the engagement and motivation phase, we also formulated an individualized treatment plan. We targeted the interruption of the escalating behavioral sequences, problem solving, and conflict management as early goals. Our relational assessment developed over numerous observations and led us to hypothesize that Sarah and her stepfather shared a distant relational connection that was symmetrical. Janis was midpointing (both contacting and distant) in relation to her mother, who was a distant relative to her. Janis was one-up relative to her mother. Sarah and Bill had discrepant functions, with Sarah being more distant than Bill, who was more contacting toward her. From our FFT perspective, we see these as the functional outcomes of the behavioral sequences we observed. We view these functional outcomes not as behavior change targets, but as pathways to use in matching our behavior change interventions to the client, which creates the path of least resistance.

BEHAVIOR CHANGE

We used these relational assessment hypotheses to craft a set of within-session and out-of-session directives to attempt to change the behavioral targets noted above. In the sessions, we targeted communication skills, asking Janis and her mother to reply to each other with short responses along the lines of "I don't agree, but I understand." As their ability to successfully interrupt the escalation in session increased, we asked that they continue this strategy at home. We also asked Janis to take charge of helping Sarah know what issues needed to be solved at home during the afternoon. To accommodate the distant relational position of Sarah, we asked Janis to do this by daily afternoon phone calls that were short in duration but intended to prevent the development of problems that Sarah would face when she came home. As the family became increasingly successful at preventing the escalating sequences of behavior, we introduced a simple problem-solving technique to be used for struggles over schoolwork, disputes between Janis and Bill, and even challenges with the younger boys. We used the specific behavioral issues identified by the family in subsequent sessions as opportunities to have the family practice the problem-solving technique. Over the course of three sessions, we helped the family use this technique to struggle with a number of specific problems. In particular, we discussed educational alternatives for Janis, helping the family negotiate her attendance at a local opportunity school. In each case, the orientation was one of coming up with a solution that was minimally acceptable in the shortest possible time.

It is typical for FFT therapists to focus on obtainable behavioral goals. In this case, we experienced behavior sequences that were rigid, stable, and filled with emotionally powerful negativity and anger. We thought it most useful to make small but lasting changes in the emotional tone of the family and reinforce those changes with obtainable success in managing small but important behaviors. Our goal is to help the family on the path of working together and using their own resources to promote obtainable changes into lasting ones through generalization of the change to various content areas. Although the behavior change plan seems very linear, its implementation was marked by constant movement between a behavioral change focus and additional reframing to counteract the ever-emerging negativity and escalating behavioral sequences.

At the beginning of the sixth session, Janis began to cry, wouldn't talk, and wanted to speak to the therapists alone. We asked the parents to leave and spoke briefly with her alone. Janis told us that she was pregnant. She was understandably scared and worried about her parents' reaction and her future. While being emotionally responsive, we also used the same problem-solving orientation introduced earlier to help her think about ways to talk to her parents. When Sarah and Bill returned to the session, Janis told her story. Both were angry and yet, over the course of an additional hour, each came to support Janis. Bill was most outspoken in his commitment to support Janis through both pregnancy and motherhood. Eventually, Janis, Sarah, and Bill all rallied to the challenge and united to help provide a supportive environment. Even though many of the subsequent conversations focused on issues of pregnancy, the escalating sequences of behavior continued and were the primary therapeutic focus.

It is not uncommon for the session plans of FFT therapists to be interrupted by unexpected and important events. The FFT clinical model is a useful guide even during critical and crisis events. In this case, Janis's pregnancy required us to be clinically and interpersonally responsive to the impact of the problem but not to change direction or goals. It was clear that such an event would promote an escalation of negativity and blaming. In fact, out of fear, both Sarah and Bill were quite blaming. We viewed this as indicating a need to increase our attention to reframing and negativity reduction. However, we quickly moved ahead, using the behavior change plan with the crisis events, seeing them as an opportunity for the family to make additional behavioral changes. By continuing to *match to the phase* and respond to the important individual issues presented by the client, FFT can be both client-focused and directional.

GENERALIZATION

During the last two sessions, the therapists turned their attention to issues of the generalization phase. To generalize the changes, we promoted the simple problem-solving method introduced in the behavior change phases as a technique that could be used with many of the issues they confronted regarding Janis's

pregnancy. We also discussed relapse prevention. In that discussion, our focus was on the natural desire each would have to give up on those days when one or the other would seemingly revert back to his or her old behavior. Much of our attention was focused on finding ways for Bill and Sarah to remind each other of Janis's quite natural emotional roller coaster, learning to respond by saying "I don't agree, but I understand." Against her parents' advice, Janis decided to keep the baby. Both Sarah and Bill were supportive and helpful, even though they did not like her decision.

One year after termination, the therapists interviewed the family as part of our usual follow-up evaluation. Janis and her baby boy were living at home, and she was attending night school. She had made up her lost year of school and was on track to graduate from high school on time. She and her mother continued to argue, but seemed able to prevent the fights from going beyond "blowing off steam." Janis and Bill were civil, occasionally disagreed, but did not have either physical or verbal fights. Sarah remained steadfastly committed to supporting Janis in her role as a mother, and continued to work with Bill to support Janis. Bill and Sarah continued to struggle with their own relationship, and at the follow-up visit considered marriage counseling as potentially useful in their continued growth as a couple.

COMMENT

Although unique in many of its content details, the case presented above is typical of the process of an FFT intervention. The initial focus was on reframing the negativity and blaming embedded within the behavior sequences of the family to develop a sense of motivation to become involved in therapy. Over time, the themes that emerged began to organize the work, providing a new, nonpathological and nonblaming explanation for the struggles of the family.

These new explanations served as the rationale for pursuing specific behavior change targets, which were addressed in ways that fit the relational functions of the family dyads to increase the chances of successful change. We cemented the obtainable changes through generalization and attention to relapse prevention. By attending to the process of change outlined in the clinical model we were able to address many of the important change mechanism active in therapy.

SCIENTIFIC FOUNDATION OF FUNCTIONAL FAMILY THERAPY: RESEARCH INTO PRACTICE

FFT is based on a long-term, systematic, and independently replicated series of outcome and process research. The research overcomes many of the criticisms of traditional clinical research (Henry, 1998) by investigating real youth (e.g., multiproblem, ethnically diverse, representing a wide range of SES) in real settings (e.g., home, community) by real therapists (practicing professionals) with diverse training backgrounds. These results have led the Center for Substance Abuse Prevention and the Office of Juvenile Justice and Delinquency Prevention to identify FFT as a model program for both substance abuse and delinquency prevention (Alverado, Kendall, Beesley, & Lee-Cavaness, 2000). Similarly, the Center for the Study and Prevention of Violence designated FFT as one of 11 (out of over 500 reviewed) "blueprint" programs (Elliott, 1998). FFT is an evidence-based intervention model that meets all of the current benchmarks of empirically validated treatments (Sexton & Alexander, 2001).

The results of published studies suggest that FFT is effective in reducing recidivism between 26% and 73% with status offending, moderate, and seriously delinquent youth as compared to both no treatment and juvenile court probation services (Alexander, Pugh, et al., 2000). (See Table 6.1.) Of most interest is the range of community settings and client ethnicities that have composed these studies (a more complete list can be found in Alexander, Pugh, et al., 2000). These positive outcomes remain relatively stable even at follow-up times as long as five years (Gordon, Arbuthnot, Gustafson, & McGreen, 1988). The positive impact also affects siblings of the identified adolescent (Klein, Alexander, & Parsons, 1977). These studies typically used recidivism as the dependent measure, yet a recent community-based effectiveness study of violent and drug abusing youth in a large urban setting with a multiethnic and multicultural population found that those adolescents in the FFT treatment condition not only had significantly lower recidivism rates but also committed significantly fewer crimes that were much less severe, even when pretreatment crime history was factored into the analysis (Sexton, Ostrom, Bonomo, & Alexander, 2000).

FFT has also proven to be a cost-effective intervention. Sexton and Alexander (2000) found FFT to be significantly more effective in reducing recidivism, $5,000 per case less costly than an equivalent juvenile detention intervention, and $12,000 less expensive than residential treatment of a similar course. In the most comprehensive investigation of the economic outcomes of family-based interventions to date, the state of Washington found that FFT had among the highest cost savings when compared to other juvenile offender programs. The cost of implementing the program was approximately $2,000 per family, with a cost savings (taxpayer and crime victim cost) of $13,908 (Aos & Barnoski, 1998).

FFT also has a long history of process studies aimed at understanding therapeutic change mechanisms. What is unique about this line of research is that it has systematically verified many of the theoretically identified change mechanisms of the model. For example, Alexander, Barton, Schaivo, and Parsons (1976) found that the ratio of negative to supportive

Table 6.1 Functional family therapy outcome studies.

Alexander & Parsons (1973), Parsons & Alexander (1973)

Clients:	Court-referred juvenile delinquent adolescents, 13 to 16 years old, randomly assigned to FFT, no treatment, or two ongoing alternative treatment conditions ($n = 99$).
Outcome:	At 6 to 8 month follow-up, FFT families had a reoffense rate of 26%, compared to 50% for no-treatment controls, 47% for client-centered family groups therapy controls, and 73% for eclectic psychodynamic family therapy.
Risk/Protective factors:	FFT families displayed greater equality in interaction and talk time, less silence, and more positive interruptions for clarification and feedback.

Klein, Alexander, & Parsons (1977)

Clients:	Sibling of adolescents in Alexander & Parsons, 1973 (see above).
Outcome:	Two to three years after initial treatment, siblings in the families that received FFT had only a 20% rate of court referral following FFT. Siblings of adolescents in the other treatment groups had significantly higher recidivism: no treatment 40%; client-centered family therapy 59%; eclectic-dynamic family therapy 63%.
Risk/Protective factors:	At initial posttreatment evaluation, families who received FFT were significantly improved in the process of their family interaction compared to those who received other treatments, and these family processes differentiated families who ultimately experienced a sibling referral from those who did not.

Hansson (1998)

Clients:	Youth arrested by police in Lund, Sweden, for serious offenses randomly assigned to FFT ($n = 45$), case management, and treatment as usual ($n = 50$).
Outcome:	At two-year follow-up, the FFT group had significantly less recidivism (48% versus 82%) than the family case management and individual counseling treatment as usual group.
Risk/Protective factors:	Maternal improvements on depression, anxiety, and somatization on self-report symptom checklist in FFT group only.

Barton, Alexander, Waldron, Turner, & Warburton (1985)

Clients:	Status delinquent youth (runaway, truancy, sexual promiscuity, possession of alcohol, and ungovernability), treatment by trained undergraduate paraprofessionals and compared to similar delinquents on probation.
Outcome:	Recidivism at one year was 26% for the FFT group, compared to a population base rate of 51%.
Risk/Protective factors:	Changes in the family processes, most notably decreases in family defensiveness, were seen with this sample, just as they were with more senior therapists.
Clients:	Children and adolescents (status delinquent offenses, school problems, and custody issues/ineffective parenting) at risk for foster care placement, referred by workers who investigate cases for protective or alternative custody, compared to similar adolescents receiving treatment as usual.
Outcome:	Comparisons of cases treated by the trained workers before and after their FFT training showed significant decreases in rates of out-of-home placements (from 48% to 11%). Coworkers not trained in FFT continued to reflect very high out-of-home placement rates (4%) and required roughly twice the number of family contacts per case.
Risk/Protective factors:	Maintenance of parental contact and preservation of family.
Clients:	Conduct disordered adolescents with multiple felonies, heavy substance abuse, and considerable violence, incarcerated in a state facility for serious and repeated offenses (an average of 20 prior adjudicated offenses).

Table 6.1   *(Continued)*

Outcome:	The FFT group (with average of only 30 hours of FFT per family) had a 60% recidivism rate at 16-month follow-up compared to 93% of comparison youth released to alternative reentry programs (primarily group homes) and an 89% average annual institutional base rate. In addition, those from the FFT group who did reoffend did do with significantly less frequency and severity than reoffenders in the non-FFT group.

Gordon, Arbuthnot, Gustafson, & McGreen (1988); Gordon (1995)

Clients:	Delinquents with multiple offenses at risk for out-of-home placement, court ordered into treatment in rural setting with low SES, compared to similar adolescents receiving probation services as usual.
Outcome:	Two years following treatment, the FFT group ($n = 27$) had an 11% recidivism rate compared to juveniles who received regular probation services ($n = 27$, 67% recidivism rate). In any given 12-month period, the FFT group committted 1.29 offenses and the treatment as usual group committed 10.29 offenses.
	At five-year follow-up (Gordon, 1995), the FFT group had a 9% recidivism rate as adults; the control group had a 41% recidivism rate as adults.

Sexton, Ostrom, Bonomo, & Alexander (2000)

Clients:	Court-referred adolescents from a multicultural, urban setting with various offenses (delinquency, drug abuse, and violent crimes) compared with a statistically equivalent group of adolescents receiving probation services as usual.
Outcome:	One year following treatment, the FFT group ($n = 166$) had a 22% recidivism rate, significantly lower than those juveniles who received regular probation services ($n = 133$, 38% recividism). The FFT group also committed fewer crimes that were less severe, even when precirme history was considered.

statements made by family members was significantly higher in cases that dropped out of therapy than among cases that completed treatment. In turn, premature termination predicted recidivism in adolescents. Newell, Alexander, and Turner (1996) confirmed that levels of family member negativity could successfully predict program dropouts. Newberry, Alexander, and Turner (1991) found that in the engagement and motivation phase, therapist supportiveness increased the likelihood of a positive response and thus the reduction of negativity by family members. Negativity reduction is a primary objective of the engagement and motivation phase.

THE DISSEMINATION OF FUNCTIONAL FAMILY THERAPY: TRAINING, IMPLEMENTATION, SUPERVISION, AND THE PRACTICE-RESEARCH NETWORK

FFT has been implemented as the primary intervention model in over 50 community sites in more than 15 states between 1998 and 2000. At those sites, approximately 200 therapists have helped approximately 5,000 families through FFT. The same therapeutic and scientific principles that guide the clinical model direct the implementation process. The specifics of the implementation process, detailed in the Center for the Study and Prevention of Violence *Blueprints* (Alexander, Pugh, et al., 2000), are briefly reviewed here.

Model fidelity is achieved by a specific training model and a systematic client assessment, tracking, and monitoring system that provides for specific clinical assessment and outcome accountability. FFT supervision focuses on two issues: adherence to the model and competent delivery of the core elements of the model. Follow-up training helps overcome unique implementation challenges in a way that retains the essence of the model. Weekly phone supervision targets specific clinical issues and helps maintain clinical continuity. To monitor implementation, therapist adherence and competence scales were developed to identify training and supervision needs for individual sites and therapists (Sexton & Alexander, 1999).

Sexton and colleagues (Sexton & Alexander, 1999; Sexton & Wilkenson, 1999) developed a computer-based monitoring and tracking system to serve as an additional tool to aid in the training and adherence of community practice sites. The Functional Family Therapy Clinical Services System (FFT-CSS) is an intuitive, user-friendly computer program used by community-based FFT therapists to record client information (e.g., contact information, demographic information, previous history), client contacts (visits, scheduled visits, phone contacts), assessment information (individual, family, and behavioral assessment), adherence measures, and outcomes measurements. The goal of the CSS is to increase therapist competence and skill by keeping clinicians focused on the relevant goals, skills, and interventions necessary for each of the phases of FFT.

The FFT Practice Research Network (FFT-PRN) links the various community practice sites and provides a constant flow of outcome and process data to practitioners. Through the FFT-PRN, community sites can participate in the development and dissemination of the FFT model by contributing nonconfidential practice data that is then published and sent back to sites, allowing them to compare clients (e.g., problem type, family structure), clinical practice (e.g., number of sessions, dropouts), adherence ratings, and outcomes. What is unique about this system is that therapists at each participating site were trained and supervised using a similar protocol, all are implementing the same clinical model, and thus, the comparative information can be used to improve practice.

SUMMARY

Over its thirty years, FFT has evolved from a set of theoretically integrated and clinically based principles to a well-articulated model of clinical intervention firmly rooted in science. Throughout that evolution, FFT has demonstrated and maintained its clinical, theoretical, and scientific integrity. The concept of function has been a central organizing feature of FFT. Unlike other behaviorally or cognitively focused models, the FFT functional approach considers the meaning of multiple domains of experience (cognition, emotion, and behavior) across multiple perspectives (individual, family, contextual) within a relational context. By focusing on function as an organizing principle, FFT has been able to embrace the inherent dialectic tension in family therapy, adopting both an ideographic and nomothetic perspective. FFT has emerged from its history as an example of a new generation of mature clinical models because of its systematic attention to theoretical and conceptual development, clinical practice, ongoing research and development, and systematic training, supervision, and implementation.

REFERENCES

Alexander, J. F., Barton, C., Schaivo, R. S., & Parsons, B. V. (1976). Behavioral intervention with families of delinquents: Therapist characteristics and outcome. *Journal of Consulting and Clinical Psychology, 44,* 656–664.

Alexander, J. F., & Parsons, B. V. (1973). Short-term behavior interventions with delinquent families: Impact on family process and recidivism. *Journal of Abnormal Psychology, 81,* 219–225.

Alexander, J. F., & Pugh, C. A. (1996). Oppositional behavior and conduct disorders of children and youth. In F. W. Kaslow (Ed.), *Handbook of relational diagnosis and dysfunctional family patterns.* New York: Wiley.

Alexander, J. F., Pugh, C. A., Parsons, B. V., & Sexton, T. L. (2000). Functional family therapy. In D. Elliott (Series Ed.), *Book three: Blueprints for violence prevention* (2nd ed.). Golden, CO: Venture.

Alexander, J. F., Robbins, M. S., & Sexton, T. L. (2000). Family-based interventions with older, at-risk youth: From promise to proof to practice. *Journal of Primary Prevention, 42,* 185–205.

Alexander, J. F., & Sexton, T. L. (in press). Functional family therapy (FFT) as an integrative, mature clinical model for treating high risk, acting out youth. In F. Kaslow (Series Ed.) & J. Lebow (Vol. Ed.), *Comprehensive handbook of psychotherapy* (Vol. 4). New York: Wiley.

Alexander, J. F., Sexton, T. L., & Robbins, M. S. (2001). The developmental status of family therapy in family psychology intervention science. In H. A. Liddle (Ed.), *Family psychology intervention science.* Washington, DC: American Psychological Association.

Alverado, R., Kendall, K., Beesley, S., & Lee-Cavaness, C. (2000). *Strengthening America's families.* Washington, DC: U. S. Department of Justice, Office of Juvenile Justice and Delinquency Preventions.

Aos, S., & Barnoski, R. (1998). *Watching the bottom line: Cost-effective interventions for reducing crime in Washington.* Washington State Institute for Public Policy: RCW 13.40.500.

Barton, C., & Alexander, J. F. (1981). Functional family therapy. In A. S. Gurman & D. P. Kniskern (Eds.), *Handbook of family therapy* (pp. 403–443). New York: Brunner/Mazel.

Barton, C., Alexander, J. F., Waldron, H., Turner, C. W., & Warburton, J. (1985). Generalizing treatment effects of functional family therapy: Three replications. *American Journal of Family Therapy, 13,* 16–26.

Costello, J. E., & Angold, A. (1993). Toward a developmental epidemiology of the disruptive behavior disorders. *Development and Psychopathology, 5,* 91–101.

Elliott, D. S. (1998). Editor's introduction: In D. Elliott (Series Ed.) *Book three: Blueprints for violence prevention.* Golden, CO: Venture.

Friedlander, M. L., & Heatherington, L. (1998). Assessing client's constructions of their problems in family therapy discourse. *Journal of Marital and Family Therapy, 24,* 289–303.

Gergen, K. (1985). The social constructionist movement in modern psychology. *American Psychologist, 40,* 266–273.

Gordon, D. A., Arbuthnot, J., Gustafson, K. E., & McGreen, P. (1988). Home-based behavioral-systems family therapy with disadvantaged juvenile delinquents. *American Journal of Family Therapy, 16*(3), 243–255.

Gordon, D. A., Graves, K., & Arbuthnot, J. (1996). The effect of functional family therapy for delinquents on adult criminal behavior. *Criminal Justice and Behavior, 22,* 6–73.

Hansson, K. (1998, February). *Functional family therapy replication in Sweden: Treatment outcome with juvenile delinquents.* Paper presented to the eighth conference on treating addictive behaviors, Santa Fe, NM.

Hawkins, J. D., Catalano, R. F., & Miller, J. Y. (1992). Risk and protective factors for alcohol and other drug problems in adolescence and early adulthood: Implications for substance abuse preventions. *Psychological Bulletin, 112,* 64–105.

Henry, W. (1998). Science, politics, and the politics of science: The use and misuse of empirically validated treatment research. *Psychotherapy Research, 8,* 126–140.

Jones, E. E., & Nisbett, R. E. (1972). The actor and the observer: Divergent perceptions of the causes of behavior. In E. E. Jones, D. E. Kanouse, H. H. Kelley, R. E. Nisbett, S. Valins, & B. Weiner (Eds.), *Attribution: Perceiving the causes of behavior* (pp. 79–94). Morristown, NJ: General Learning Press.

Kazdin, A. E. (1991). Effectiveness of psychotherapy with children and adolescents. *Journal of Consulting and Clinical Psychology, 59,* 785–798.

Kazdin, A. E., Siegel, T. C., & Bass, D. (1992). Cognitive problem-solving skills training and parent management training in the treatment of antisocial behavior in children. *Journal of Consulting and Clinical Psychology, 60,* 733–747.

Kelley, H. H. (1973). The process of causal attribution. *American Psychologist, 28,* 107–128.

Klein, N., Alexander, J., & Parsons, B. (1977). Impact of family systems intervention on recidivism and sibling delinquency: A model of primary prevention and program evaluation. *Journal of Consulting and Clinical Psychology, 45,* 469–474.

Liddle, H. A. (1995). Conceptual and clinical dimensions of a multidimensional, multisystems engagement strategy in family-based adolescent treatment [Special issue: Adolescent Psychotherapy]. *Psychotherapy: Theory, Research and Practice, 32,* 39–58.

Lipsey, M. W. (1992). Juvenile delinquency treatment: A meta-analytic inquiry into the variability of effects. In T. Cook, H. Cooper, D. Corbray, H. Hartman, L. Hedges, R. Light, et al. (Eds.), *Meta-analysis for explanation: A casebook.* New York: Russell Sage Foundation.

Loeber, R. (1991). Antisocial behavior: More enduring than changeable? *Journal of the American Academy of Child and Adolescent Psychiatry, 30,* 393–397.

Murrell, S. A., & Stachowiak, J. G. (1967). Consistency, rigidity, and power in the interaction patterns of clinic and non-clinic families. *Journal of Abnormal Psychology, 72,* 265–272.

Newberry, A. M., Alexander, J. F., & Turner, C. W. (1991). Gender as a process variable in family therapy. *Journal of Family Psychology, 5,* 158–175.

Newell, R. M., Alexander, J. F., & Turner, C. W. (1996, June). *The effects of therapist divert and interrupt on family members' reciprocity of negativity in delinquent families.* Poster session presented at the annual convention of the American Family Therapy Academy, San Francisco.

Parsons, B., & Alexander, J. (1973). Short-term family intervention: A therapy outcome study. *Journal of Consulting and Clinical Psychology, 48,* 195–201.

Patterson, G. R. (1976). The aggressive child: Victim and architect or a coercive system. In E. J. Marsh, L. A. Hamerlynck, & L. C. Handy (Eds.), *Behavior modification and families.* New York: Brunner/Mazel.

Sexton, T. L., & Alexander, J. F. (1999). *Functional family therapy: Principles of clinical intervention, assessment, and implementation.* Henderson, NV: RCH Enterprises.

Sexton, T. L., & Alexander, J. F. (2000). *Functional family therapy* [Juvenile Justice Bulletin]. Washington, DC: U.S. Department of Justice.

Sexton, T. L., & Alexander, J. F. (in press). Family based empirically supported interventions. *Counseling Psychologist.*

Sexton, T. L., Ostrom, N., Bonomo, J., & Alexander, J. F. (2000, November). *Functional family therapy in a multicultural, multiethnic urban setting.* Paper presented at the annual conference of the American Association of Marriage and Family Therapy, Denver, CO.

Sexton, T. L., & Wilkenson, J. (1999). *The Functional Family Therapy Clinical Services System.* Henderson, NV: RCH Enterprises.

Szapocznik, J., Kurtines, W., Santisteban, D. A., Pantin, H., Scopetta, M., Mancilla, Y., et al. (1997). The evolution of structural ecosystemic theory for working with Latino families. In J. Garcia & M. C. Zea (Eds.), *Psychological interventions and research with Latino populations.* Boston: Allyn & Bacon.

Taylor, S. E., & Fiske, S. T. (1978). Salience, attention, and attribution: Top of the head phenomena. In L. Berkowitz (Ed.), *Advances in experimental social psychology* (Vol. 11, pp. 250–288). New York: Academic Press.

Tolan, P. H., Guerra, N. G., & Kendall, P. C. (1995). Introduction to special section: Prediction and prevention of antisocial behavior in children and adolescents. *Journal of Consulting and Clinical Psychology, 63,* 515–517.

Watzlawick, P., Beavin, J. H., & Jackson, D. D. (1967). *Pragmatics of human communication: A study of interactional patterns, pathologies, and paradoxes.* New York: Norton.

Watzlawick, P., Weakland, J., & Fisch, R. (1974). *Change: Principles of problem formation and problem resolution.* New York: Norton.

CHAPTER 7

Multidimensional Family Prevention for At-Risk Adolescents

AARON HOGUE, HOWARD A. LIDDLE, AND DANA BECKER

The science of mental health prevention has made significant conceptual and empirical advances over the past two decades (Bryant, Windle, & West, 1997). During that time, prevention has emerged as a major focus of programmatic, research, and policy work in the mental health arena (Munoz, Mrazek, & Haggerty, 1996). These efforts are aimed at preventing, delaying, or moderating the onset of psychological disorders in the general population and within high-risk subgroups. Specifically, mental health prevention is concerned with (1) investigating the etiology, developmental course, and psychosocial correlates of psychological disorders; (2) identifying risk factors that predict future disorders and protective factors that buffer against psychological dysfunction in given populations; and (3) developing interventions for insulating persons against the onset of disorder and ameliorating risk factors and incipient behavioral symptoms. This last focus of prevention is known as *preventive intervention*. Preventive interventions are directed at preventing or delaying the onset of behavioral problems, whereas *treatment interventions* attempt to alleviate or eliminate disorders in persons who meet criteria for psychiatric diagnosis or have significant impairment in functioning (Institute of Medicine, 1994).

Substance use and antisocial behavior problems such as aggression, delinquency, and violence have received the greatest attention in the prevention field. Recent national surveys provide strong evidence that adolescent drug use and delinquency are prevalent and on the rise. For example, the National Household Survey of Drug Abuse (Gfroerer, 1995) found that 16% of teens age 12 to 17 reported marijuana use and 2% reported cocaine use. The Monitoring the Future study (Johnston, O'Malley, & Bachman, 1995) found that among eighth-graders, 59%

Correspondence concerning this article should be addressed to Aaron Hogue, Department of Psychology, 441 E. Fordham Road, Fordham University, Bronx, NY, 10458, or to Howard A. Liddle, Center for Treatment Research on Adolescent Drug Abuse, University of Miami School of Medicine, Department of Epidemiology and Public Health, 1400 Northwest 10th Ave, 11th floor, Miami, FL, 33136. Electronic mail may be sent via the Internet to athogue@aol.com or hliddle@med.miami.edu.

had used alcohol, 46% cigarettes, 17% marijuana, and 20% inhalants; moreover, between 1992 and 1995, rates of use increased 37% for marijuana, 60% for hallucinogens, and 115% for cocaine. A recent household probability study (Kilpatrick et al., 2000) sampled teenagers age 12 to 17 who had five or more drinks at one sitting or had used an illicit drug on at least four occasions. Among this subpopulation of nonincidental drug users, 4% reported disorder-level symptoms of alcohol or marijuana abuse/dependence and 1% reported abuse/dependence on harder drugs. National rates of delinquency and violence are alarmingly high as well; arrests for juvenile violent offenses rose over 60% between 1988 and 1994 (Loeber & Stouthamer-Loeber, 1998; Osofsky, 1997). Drug use and antisocial behavior exert a tremendous toll on the families and communities in which troubled youth reside, and the financial costs of interdiction, institutionalization, and treatment are substantial. For these reasons, the dissemination of effective programs for preventing antisocial behavior in adolescence has become a top priority in the prevention field (Elias, 1997).

This chapter describes a family-based, developmental-ecological preventive intervention for drug use and delinquency: multidimensional family prevention (MDFP; Liddle & Hogue, 2000). MDFP has two characteristics that set it apart from most family-based preventions for antisocial behavior. First, it is an individualized model implemented exclusively in one-to-one (versus parent group or multifamily) settings. This allows for development of a prevention agenda that reflects the unique needs and goals of each family. Second, it targets a population that is notoriously difficult to treat: at-risk adolescents and their families. Adolescents are among the most underserved populations in both prevention and treatment settings (Kazdin, 1993), and families of at-risk teens present multiple challenges to recruitment and intervention design (Prinz & Miller, 1996).

As an individualized prevention model for at-risk youth and families, MDFP is something of a hybrid between traditional preventive and treatment interventions. This is no accident. The conceptual framework and intervention components of MDFP were adapted directly from our experience in developing a family-based treatment for adolescent substance abuse: multidimensional family therapy (MDFT; Liddle, 2000). It was reasoned that the basic intervention principles of an empirically supported family therapy model would be highly effective if revised for use in prevention settings, wherein at-risk youth are in earlier and (theoretically) more malleable stages of problematic behavior (Reid, 1993). In this spirit, MDFP combines the curriculum-based and protection-focused methods of standard prevention models with the assessment-based and symptom-focused methods of psychotherapy. Such an approach may offer the best hope for working with multiproblem adolescents who have not yet developed clinical disorders.

HISTORY OF THE INTERVENTION APPROACH

TREATMENT AND PREVENTION: THE MENTAL HEALTH INTERVENTION SPECTRUM

Multidimensional family therapy has been recognized as one of a handful of multicomponent, theoretically derived treatments for adolescent drug abuse with empirical evidence of treatment efficacy (Stanton & Shadish, 1997; Weinberg, Rahdert, Colliver, & Glantz, 1998). MDFT is an outpatient, multisystemic intervention that focuses on changing both within-family interactional patterns and interactions between the family and relevant social systems. Research support has come from controlled outcome studies of drug-using adolescents (Liddle et al., in press) and process research studies investigating mechanisms of therapeutic change (G. S. Diamond & Liddle, 1996; G. M. Diamond, Liddle, Hogue, & Dakof, 1999; Schmidt, Liddle, & Dakof, 1996).

MDFT's solid empirical record for treating adolescent substance use and conduct problems made it an appealing model of preventive intervention for these symptoms. Two additional factors strengthened this appeal. First, MDFT treatment principles and techniques are grounded in basic developmental theory regarding mechanisms of risk and protection (Liddle, Rowe, Dakof, & Lyke, 1998; Liddle et al., 2000). MDFT targets the multiple ecologies of adolescent development and, within these ecologies, the various developmental processes known to produce adaptation versus dysfunction as they are manifested in any adolescent and family. This focus on risk and protection within multiple ecologies is also a central organizing principle of contemporary prevention science (Masten & Coatsworth, 1995). Thus, the core theories constituting MDFT's developmental base—risk and protection theory, developmental psychopathology, and developmental-ecological theory—are also guiding frameworks of MDFP.

Second, prevention science has recently made great theoretical strides in articulating the link between prevention and treatment; these approaches are now seen as two poles defining a single continuum of mental health intervention services. As depicted in Figure 7.1, the mental health intervention spectrum (see also Institute of Medicine, 1994; National Advisory Mental Health Council [NAMHC], 1998) spans the range of mental health services from preintervention epidemiological research on mechanisms of risk and protection, to preventive interventions for nonsymptomatic or subclinical populations, to prevention services that are concurrent with treatment interventions (comorbidity, disability, and relapse prevention), to treatment for clinical disorders and maintenance of treatment gains. It thereby formalizes a theoretical continuity between preventive and treatment interventions—they are members of the same species, so to speak. This theoretical connection allows for fluid adaptation of principles and practices from one tradition to the other. Intervention techniques, training and supervision procedures, and methodological innovations can be productively shared back and forth between the prevention and treatment

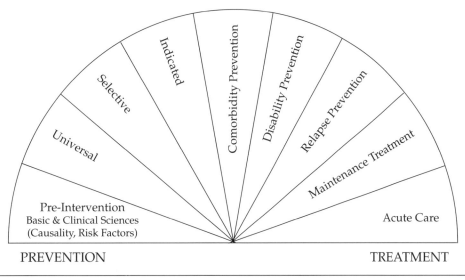

Figure 7.1   The mental health intervention spectrum.

sciences. Of course, the feasibility and utility of a knowledge-practice transfer between any two particular models can be demonstrated only through rigorous developmental work and empirical testing. This was our challenge in developing MDFP.

There are also important, indelible distinctions between preventive and treatment interventions, two of which are salient to MDFP. First, there is a population distinction. Preventive intervention is directed at preventing or delaying the onset of mental health problems in persons who do not have a psychiatric disorder, whereas treatment intervention targets persons who meet (or almost meet) clinical diagnostic criteria. As a result, prevention populations on average exhibit less severe and less entrenched psychological symptoms, if any, than treatment populations. Second, there is an intentional distinction. The ultimate aim of prevention is to lessen the likelihood of possible or anticipated symptoms. Thus, for individual cases and entire samples, intervention goals are expressed in terms of outcome probabilities (i.e., odds that targeted persons will eventually develop a given disorder; Institute of Medicine, 1994). The ultimate aim of treatment is to alleviate symptoms or reduce their severity immediately, so that therapeutic progress can be judged in large measure at termination.

Finally, as Figure 7.1 shows, there are important distinctions in target populations within the prevention field itself.* *Universal* preventions are designed for the general population or a specific subpopulation in which all members are included (e.g., advertising campaigns about the dangers of drug use). *Selective* preventions target subgroups identified as having higher-than-average risk based on group characteristics with empirically established links to a given disorder (e.g., children of adult drug users). *Indicated* preventions are for persons identified as high risk based on an individual risk assessment that detects prediagnostic levels of behavioral problems (e.g., children who have experimented with drugs). MDFP is an indicated preventive intervention; this has concrete implications for model design and implementation, as discussed below.

FAMILY-BASED PREVENTIVE INTERVENTION

Family-based preventive interventions such as MDFP seek to promote healthy functioning in individual children primarily through addressing the risk and protective factors that characterize their parents and families (Hogue & Liddle, 1999). Family-based prevention is widely endorsed as a key component of comprehensive prevention planning for adolescent drug abuse (Etz, Robertson, & Ashery, 1998) and antisocial behavior (Kazdin, 1993). The emergence of the family-based approach has been buoyed by studies underscoring the significance of family socialization processes for the onset and course

---

*The terminology for describing mental health prevention efforts has changed in recent years. Prevention efforts have traditionally been classified according to the following system developed in medicine and public health (Caplan, 1964; Commission on Chronic Illness, 1957). *Primary* preventions are intended for healthy populations and are aimed at preventing the occurrence of disease. *Secondary* preventions are intended for persons with early symptoms of disease and are aimed at forestalling its progression. *Tertiary* preventions are intended for persons with an existing disease and are aimed at reducing its duration and the amount of associated disability. However, this classification system has been criticized on two counts: for its overemphasis on the causes and mechanisms of disease, at the expense of risk-benefit decisions about who should receive prevention services (Institute of Medicine, 1994); and for its confusion about differences among tertiary prevention, treatment, and rehabilitation (Durlak, 1997). Most mental health preventionists have therefore adopted the terminology recommended by the Institute of Medicine: universal, selective, and indicated prevention.

of youth problem behaviors (Brook, Brook, Gordon, Whiteman, & Cohen, 1990; Hawkins, Catalano, & Miller, 1992). Research on the efficacy of family-based prevention models offers limited but credible support for this approach. Such programs have demonstrated noteworthy successes in the difficult primary task of engaging and retaining parents in program activities (Hogue, Johnson-Leckrone, & Liddle, 1999; Spoth, Redmond, Hockaday, & Shin, 1996). Outcome studies provide convergent evidence of prevention effects across several family-based models: parenting skills workshops (Kosterman, Hawkins, Spoth, Haggerty, & Zhu, 1997; Spoth, Reyes, Redmond, & Shin, 1999), parent training alone and in combination with child skills training (Dishion & Andrews, 1995; Tremblay, Pagani-Kurtz, Masse, Vitaro, & Pihl, 1995), and family skills training (Kumpfer & Alvarado, 1995; Spoth et al., 1999). Moreover, empirically supported family prevention programs have been promoted and disseminated at the national level (National Institute on Drug Abuse [NIDA], 1997; Substance Abuse and Mental Health Services Administration [SAMHSA], 1998).

MDFP: An Individualized Approach to Family Prevention

Akin to its psychotherapy cousin MDFT, MDFP is an individualized intervention model. Individualized models are predicated on client-specific assessment and intervention planning. For this reason, they appear well-suited for working with high-risk populations in particular (Hogue & Liddle, 1999; Tolan & McKay, 1996). In contrast to standardized psychoeducational models, individualized counseling models employ a flexible intervention format that features (1) sessions held primarily in one-to-one (versus group) settings; (2) clinical assessment of the unique profile of risk and protection factors for every client;

(3) collaborative formulation and periodic revision of counseling needs and goals. The individualized format has many potential benefits for prevention work with at-risk families. It promotes specification and monitoring of a family-specific prevention agenda, allows each family member to articulate personally relevant goals, and provides opportunities for extensive interaction between counselor and family around multiple issues.

Empirical support for an individualized approach to family-based prevention can be found in two sources. First, family-based psychotherapies, almost all of which use an individualized format, have an excellent track record for treating substance abuse (Stanton & Shadish, 1997) and antisocial behavior (Henggeler, 1996) in children and adolescents. Some family therapy models have even shown preventive effects in siblings of the targeted youths (e.g., Klein, Alexander, & Parsons, 1977). Second, a few studies have tested the efficacy of family prevention counseling for at-risk youths. Fast Track (Conduct Problems Prevention Research Group, 1999) has demonstrated good prevention outcomes for a national sample of high-risk first-graders. As one feature of a multicomponent intervention plan, each family received home-based family counseling that included biweekly sessions and weekly phone contacts. Catalano and associates (described in Bry, Catalano, Kumpfer, Lochman, & Szapocznik, 1998) reported small prevention gains following an intensive counseling prevention for children of substance users that included a five-hour family retreat, a 32-session parent training module, and a nine-month home-based case management module. Santisteban et al. (1997) found that brief structural/strategic family counseling (12 to 16 sessions over four to six months) reduced early-stage behavior problems and improved family functioning for indicated-risk, inner-city African American and Hispanic young adolescents.

THEORETICAL CONSTRUCTS OF MDFP

MDFP is a behaviorally oriented prevention model grounded in three theoretical frameworks: risk and protection theory, developmental psychopathology, and developmental-ecological theory. It incorporates research knowledge from these theories about adaptive developmental trajectories and ecological risk into prevention work with individual families. Also, as a behavioral prevention model with a family focus, this approach adheres to the basic tenets of behavioral family intervention.

RISK AND PROTECTION THEORY

Risk and protection theory is the dominant framework in the prevention field (Jessor, Van Den Bos, Vanderryn, Costa, & Turbin, 1995). Psychological dysfunction is thought to be determined by the interaction between risk factors, which predispose an individual to the development of disorder, and protective factors, which predispose positive outcomes and buffer individuals against disorder. Thus, complex behavior problems such as substance abuse and delinquency do not stem from a single set of specifiable precursors; instead, there are several pathways to genesis of these disorders, and various risk and protective influences can be identified in the psychological, biological, and environmental realms. Risk factors are thought to have a multiplicative effect, such that overall risk increases exponentially with the addition of each risk factor, whereas protective factors exert both a direct positive influence on behavior and a moderating influence on the relation between risk factors and behavior.

Profiles of risk and protective factors are used to identify individuals who are at risk for behavioral problems so that appropriate intervention steps can be taken. Family-based preventions focus on risk and protective factors in the family arena. There are several family factors that create serious vulnerabilities for problem behavior: deficiencies in parental monitoring and discipline practices, high rates of family conflict and low rates of communication and involvement, poor parental attachment to children, and parental attitudes about and history of drug use (Dishion, French, & Patterson, 1995; Hawkins et al., 1992). The quality of the parent-child relationship is a particularly critical factor. Emotional support from family members and the perceived quality of the affective relationship with parents are strong predictors of adolescent well-being that insulate youths from drug use and negative environmental influences (Baumrind, 1985; Resnick et al., 1997).

DEVELOPMENTAL PSYCHOPATHOLOGY

The goal of developmental psychopathology is to examine the course of individual adaptation and dysfunction through the lens of normative development, so that truly maladaptive behavior patterns can be distinguished from expectable variations within the normative range (Sroufe & Rutter, 1984). Developmental psychopathology is concerned not so much with specific symptoms in a given youth as with the youth's ability to cope with the developmental tasks at hand and the implications of stressful experiences in one developmental period for (mal)adaptation in future periods. Because multiple pathways of adjustment and deviation may unfold from any given point, emphasis is placed equally on understanding competence and resilience in the face of great risk. Developmental psychopathology underscores the advantages of designing prevention programs for high-risk children before the onset of mental health disorders, so that developmental trajectories may be changed while more adaptive pathways remain available. Normative developmental issues most relevant to drug use prevention include self-regulation and exploratory behavior (Hill & Holmbeck, 1986), autonomy seeking and emotional stress within the family (Steinberg, 1990), and involvement with peer groups (B. Brown, 1990).

DEVELOPMENTAL-ECOLOGICAL THEORY

Developmental-ecological theory is concerned with understanding the intersecting web of social influences that form the context of human development (Bronfenbrenner, 1986; Tolan, Guerra, & Kendall, 1995). Developmental-ecological theory regards the family as the principal social system for human development, but in addition, it emphasizes how individual development is directly and indirectly affected by many extrafamilial factors. Therefore, developmental-ecological preventions seek to intervene simultaneously in multiple social systems that are salient to adolescent functioning, so that developmental contexts outside the family (e.g., school, peer, neighborhood) are routinely subject to assessment and intervention. Specifically, interventions aim to influence how family members relate to (i.e., think about and interact with) these extrafamilial systems (Liddle, 1995).

BEHAVIORAL FAMILY INTERVENTION

Behavioral family interventions have received a wealth of empirical support for treating childhood conduct problems and improving child-rearing practices (Taylor & Biglan, 1998). Likewise, in the prevention field, family-based interventions that follow a behavioral approach have demonstrated greater success than interventions that simply educate parents about recommended parenting techniques (Etz et al., 1998; Kosterman et al., 1997). Behavioral family interventions teach families about principles of behavioral reinforcement and address both parent management skills, such as discipline techniques and child monitoring, and family

relationship characteristics, such as emotional climate, communication, and parent-child bonding (Alexander & Parsons, 1982; Patterson, Reid, & Dishion, 1992). The hallmark of behavioral family intervention is use of practitioner modeling and feedback to participants following attempts to practice specific skills in the home or office setting. Behavioral family approaches foster a collaborative, interactive atmosphere that encourages family members to critique, refine, and modify learned strategies based on their observed applicability and effectiveness (Taylor & Biglan, 1998).

MDFP PRINCIPLES OF ASSESSMENT AND INTERVENTION

The distinctive character of any given intervention model is defined by two separate features: intervention *parameters* and intervention *techniques* (Kazdin, 1994). Intervention parameters are program-delivery aspects of the intervention that determine its timing, intensity, duration, and persons targeted. Intervention techniques are the essential counselor behaviors utilized during case contacts: the various interventions, combinations, and phases of work that are implemented in response to given client problems. The intervention parameters and techniques of MDFP are summarized in this section: service delivery and recruitment strategies, assessment procedures, and multimodule intervention guidelines. The section that follows describes the target population and the fundamental intervention goals of MDFP.

INTERVENTION PARAMETERS

Service Delivery
MDFP is both a home-based and community-based intervention. Sessions occur primarily in the home of the family. Home-based delivery

offers several advantages over office-based models: It circumvents transportation barriers (especially for economically disadvantaged families), affords flexibility in scheduling sessions that can enhance recruitment and participation rates, allows the counselor to make use of all available resources in the home and community (including family members not predisposed to clinic visits), and supports the acceptability and generalizability of interventions in the everyday environment of the family. MDFP counselors also function as de facto case managers who make visits to schools, places of worship, and other local institutions to broker services for the family. The overarching goal of case management is to facilitate the family's increased involvement with local agencies and competence in acquiring various supportive services.

Sessions occur with single families, not in group format. Decisions about session composition are made on a case-by-case and session-by-session basis. Both individual and conjoint sessions are regularly used, and it is common for a given session to contain a blend of individual and conjoint minisessions. Families typically receive services for three to four months, and counselors make an average of three substantive contacts per week for every case. Each family receives a total of 15 to 25 sessions that take place either in person or (occasionally) by phone and last 30 to 90 minutes. Counselors also make in-person contacts with extrafamilial resources on behalf of the family as needed. Depending on the exigencies of the case, the intensity of program delivery varies: Families that present relatively few distressing issues may be scheduled for one session per week; those that present with greater needs or are in crisis during counseling may receive two in-person sessions and several phone contacts per week.

Recruitment Strategies

The prevention model's commitment to home-based, intensive intervention is extended to its program recruitment procedures (see Hogue et al., 1999). Recruitment is conducted by the MDFP counselors themselves, rather than by adjunctive staff, so that sophisticated clinical skills are brought to bear on the manifold challenges of family recruitment. Counselors recruit families using empirically based systemic engagement techniques (Szapocznik et al., 1988) that include phone contact(s) with functional parents followed by an in-home recruitment visit. The recruitment process is marked by counselor flexibility and persistence, sensitivity to the unique circumstances of each family, and readiness to allocate substantial program resources to enlist families.

Assessment Procedures

Assessing Multiple Domains of Functioning
MDFP utilizes a multidomain, multisystems assessment strategy for evaluating various dimensions of the adolescent's and family's psychosocial functioning. MDFP focuses on seven domains of functioning that are linked to the development of risk and protective mechanisms in adolescent populations and that represent critical foci of concern for families with high-risk youth, who typically demonstrate elevated risk levels in more than one domain (Hawkins et al., 1992; Jessor, 1993; Petraitis, Flay, & Miller, 1995). Counselors assess each domain of functioning to identify major problem areas and protective supports in the life of the adolescent and to map out the nature of parent/family involvement in each domain. These include:

1. *Family relationships:* History and patterns of positive and negative interactions, strength of attachment bonds between members, roles played by extended or estranged members in family life, child caretaking and monitoring arrangements, family coping and communication style.

2. *School involvement:* School grades and conduct, educational goals, homework habits, learning disabilities, relationships with teachers or school mentors.
3. *Prosocial activities:* Involvement in extracurricular youth activities and community institutions such as sporting and social clubs, tutoring and academic enrichment programs, leadership and vocational programs, and religious institutions.
4. *Peer relationships:* Friendship attitudes and experiences, identification with peer values, activities favored by close friends and larger peer groups, parental contact with friends and the parents of friends.
5. *Drug issues:* Parental and adolescent attitudes about and exposure to drugs, drug involvement by other family members, drug use by peers, drug-related activity in school and neighborhood.
6. *Cultural themes:* Family values regarding racial/ethnic history, emergence of the adolescent's cultural identity, hardships and coping mechanisms related to racial/ethnic bias.
7. *Adolescent health and sexuality:* Physical problems (e.g., diabetes, weight issues), psychological problems (e.g., depression, anxiety, aggression, impulsivity), self-concept and self-care, family attitudes about adolescent dating and sex, and sexual activities of the adolescent.

An informal assessment of the family's risk and protective factors within each of these domains occurs in the program's initial sessions. Domains are not assessed in a predetermined, programmatic fashion. Instead, the idiosyncratic characteristics of the family determine the priority, timing, and depth with which each domain is explored. As the assessment progresses, some domains may loom large in the family landscape and become a focal area of work, whereas other domains with lesser relevance may recede into the background. In assessing each domain, the counselor pursues three avenues of inquiry simultaneously: history and perspective of the adolescent, history and perspective of the functional parents, and history and status of the adolescent-parents relationship. The assessment is managed so that sensitive issues can be addressed in a respectful manner; careful consideration is given to when topics should be raised with individuals alone, raised with all members present, or raised first in private and then again (with preparation) in a conjoint setting. In all situations, the counselor is interested in identifying risk and protective factors that bear directly on the adolescent's key developmental challenges.

Crafting the Counseling Agenda

The main goal of assessing risk and protection domains during initial sessions is to crystallize family-specific issues that will become the focus of intervention. MDFP is an individualized model whose assessment and intervention techniques are applied according to counselor judgment about the status and needs of a given family. As such, MDFP centralizes the unique history, values, identified problems, interactional patterns, and socialization goals of the family and its members in crafting a counseling agenda. To set a tone of counselor-family collaboration, it is made clear that parental investment in counseling is the cornerstone of program success. Attention is paid to dispelling any preconceptions that the program is meant to "straighten out" the adolescent, and the importance of continued parental influence and parent-adolescent communication for adolescent development is underscored. Also, connections among parent well-being, parenting competence, and adolescent adjustment are discussed.

Especially with at-risk prevention populations, assessment of risk and protection domains often uncovers one or more risk factors that exert a significant negative influence on the family and are perceived as highly stressful, resistant to change, and requiring immediate intervention. In short, high-risk prevention populations often present with difficulties in adaptation that command a treatment-like urgency (Tolan, 1996). It is therefore imperative that practitioners who work with high-risk populations have sufficient training and skills, flexibility within the model in choosing and adapting interventions, and supervisory support from the program to address clinical-level problems in a competent manner.

What if the assessment phase reveals that a family has few problems or concerns of alarming magnitude? Even at-risk adolescents and their families may present with relatively mild risk factors and stable coping mechanisms in some or most domains. For such cases, protection-oriented themes receive the bulk of attention in counseling. Protection-oriented themes are generated from the counselor's expertise in general risk and protective mechanisms and normative family psychology, coupled with knowledge of the particular family gained from the assessment process. Protection-oriented themes take the generic form: What every family should know and do to manage normative adolescent transitions. They assume the functions of curbing mild symptoms or nascent problems and building individual and family coping skills as an inoculation against future risk. This is intended to foster a more protective family context in which developmental needs are recognized and integrated within the governing family system. Note that protection-oriented themes are pursued with all families, including those with few coping skills and a multitude of daily stressors.

Intervention Modules

MDFP features four integrated modules of intervention, each associated with core intervention goals and techniques. Counselors rely on training, experience, and knowledge of the family to coordinate intervention efforts within and among the modules. Depending on the family's risk and protection profile, more time may be devoted to some modules than to others. Modules are not meant to be implemented in a sequential or prearranged fashion; instead, progress in one module is used to support or potentiate work in others, and critical themes are cycled throughout different modules and sometimes recycled within a given module over the course of intervention.

Adolescent Module

This module focuses on the role of the individual adolescent within the family system as well as his or her membership in other social systems, principally school and peer groups. Normative developmental issues such as school achievement, family support and stress, emotional and physical maturation, friendship and romantic interests, and prosocial and antisocial influences in the peer group and neighborhood are discussed for their personal relevance to the teen and their suitability as focal topics for family sessions. This module also includes social competence training for adolescents with deficiencies in social processing and interaction skills. Anxieties or social problems in relationships within and outside the family are targeted for individual skills building activities (e.g., relaxation training, problem-solving exercises) that can be used in multiple sessions.

It is crucial that the counselor help adolescents paint a detailed picture of personally meaningful issues in their everyday social life: how they make decisions about family and peer relations, how stable and supportive their social network is, how they are adjusting to achievement and maturity demands. In doing so, the counselor gains better access to the ecological world of the adolescent and the risk and protective factors found there, and this information becomes the basis for designing practical and relevant prevention strategies. In addition, these details are natural building blocks for establishing a strong working alliance with the teenager (G. M. Diamond et al., 1999). Adolescents should be convinced that prevention counseling can be worthwhile, a vehicle for thinking about their unique issues and working on self-defined goals that may be quite different from those of parents and other adults. This realization facilitates work with the adolescent and increases motivation to participate in conjoint sessions.

Parent Module

The parent module uses individual sessions with parents to establish a counselor-parent working alliance, review their history of perceived successes and failures as parents, and present a developmentally informed perspective on adolescent functioning. When indicated, parenting skills are enhanced in the areas of monitoring, limit setting, fostering a supportive emotional climate, and modeling coping strategies. Counselors endeavor to translate established principles of effective parenting into practical strategies that mesh with the ecological niche and everyday parenting routine of the family (Liddle et al., 1998). The main goal of this work is to clarify how parents can, and cannot, affect their teen's behavior. Parents need to receive accurate information about how much influence they actually wield on adolescent behavior and about the most efficient means for using this influence.

In addition, intrapersonal and interpersonal experiences apart from the parenting realm are explored so that impediments to effective parenting can be addressed. Parents of high-risk adolescents are often under considerable stress from a variety of sources. Many are single parents with multiple children, some struggle with considerable relationship problems or economic hardships, and some exhibit depression or other forms of psychopathology, all of which can precipitate and/or exacerbate symptoms in the adolescent and constitute part of the adolescent's risk profile (Robinson & Garber, 1995). In such cases, a significant portion of the parent

module may be devoted to (1) identifying how these stressors affect the parenting environment; (2) determining how the adolescent (and other children) can be better shielded from their effects; and (3) helping parents access various social (and, if needed, psychiatric) resources for themselves and their families. Also, parents sometimes harbor strong negative feelings about the parenting they received in their own family of origin; these historical issues usually need to be addressed prior to, or concurrent with, helping them transform the current parenting climate.

Family Interaction Module

The family interaction module facilitates change in family relationship patterns by providing an interactional context for families to develop the motivation, skills, and experience to modify interpersonal bonds and interact in more adaptive ways. Family members are helped to understand and validate the values and perspectives of other members. Adolescents and parents are asked to evaluate their attachment bonds and the balance they have achieved between autonomy and connectedness. Also, siblings, older-generation adults, and influential family members not living in the home (including estranged parents) are invited to take part in family sessions, when appropriate.

Family relationships and interactional patterns are the main foci of intervention in MDFP, with greatest emphasis placed on the parent-adolescent relationship. Counselors seek to understand and ultimately modify the parent-adolescent relationship by evaluating and coaching their interactions in session. Conversations are sometimes prompted by the counselor in direct attempts to change interactional patterns, and thus to change the relationship; at other times, the conversations occur spontaneously. The counselor watches how parents and adolescent communicate, how they solve or fail to solve problems, and how the viewpoint of each is validated or thwarted. The counselor then shapes interactions in an attempt to provide new experiences within existing relationships and to develop more functional relationship habits. As families practice adaptive relationship behaviors in session, they become better able to recognize what good conversations feel like; this fosters the generalizability of these behaviors to novel situations.

Parents and adolescents generally spend a small amount of daily time together in conversation (Larson & Richards, 1994), and the task of conversing "naturally" about emotional or conflictual topics in the alien environment of a counseling session can be formidable (G. S. Diamond & Liddle, 1996). Especially for families with a history of negative or impoverished communication, teenagers and parents may need considerable coaching from the counselor before they can begin productive in-session conversations. This coaching is carried out in one-to-one sessions dedicated to preparing participants for later, mutually planned interactions in session. The overall objectives of preparatory individual coaching include helping each participant to formulate the content and tone of what is to be said, prepare for potential reactions by other participants, and solidify a mutual agreement that enables the counselor to challenge participants to follow through as planned once the interaction begins.

Extrafamilial Module
In this module, the counselor seeks to develop a high level of collaboration between the family and other social systems to which the adolescent is connected, such as school, peer, and recreational. Interventions take one of two basic forms: discussion about the parents' contacts with and knowledge of the adolescent's life outside the family, with emphasis on the protective benefits of parents remaining personally involved in those systems; helping parents appreciate the importance of remaining knowledgeable about the adolescent's subjective

experience of those systems. MDFP counselors work to boost parental involvement by encouraging parents to attend school conferences, arrange independent meetings with teachers, visit the sites of extracurricular activities, meet best friends, and meet the parents of best friends. For parents who are already active in the adolescent's school and peer networks, counselors discuss strategies for remaining engaged in these systems even as new demands for independence and responsibility emerge in later years. Counselors also routinely accompany family members in meeting with mentoring adults invested in the adolescent, and they investigate community resources available to both teens and parents. In this way, the counselor acts as a direct support for the family and helps parents become more competent advocates on behalf of the adolescent.

POPULATIONS AND PROBLEMS TARGETED

RISK FACTORS FOR ADOLESCENT DRUG USE AND ANTISOCIAL BEHAVIOR

Multidimensional family prevention is designed to prevent substance abuse and delinquency in young and middle adolescents (ages 11 to 15) exhibiting nascent psychosocial problems that are empirically established precursors to drug use and antisocial behavior disorders, such as declining school performance, significant aggression and negative emotionality, minor delinquent acts, association with drug-using or antisocial peers, and early drug experimentation (Masten et al., 1999; Newcomb & Felix-Ortiz, 1992; O'Donnell, Hawkins, & Abbott, 1995). The challenge of preventing drug use and antisocial behavior in adolescents is considerable, given the complex and entrenched individual and environmental risk factors that predispose development of these disorders. Epidemiological, clinical, and basic research studies confirm that adolescent drug use is a multidimensional problem. Both experimental substance use by adolescents not yet committed to continued use (Petraitis et al., 1995) and clinical substance abuse and dependence (Weinberg et al., 1998) result from a confluence of etiological factors. Contemporary studies on the correlates of drug use and abuse typically encompass several domains of functioning: individual, family, peer, school, community, and societal. Both macrolevel, distal factors such as economic deprivation and neighborhood influences and proximal ones such as family conflict and parental antisocial behavior (Hawkins et al., 1992; Jessor, 1993) are implicated. Individual adolescent factors such as school disengagement and failure, emotional dysregulation, and poor social skills are also risk factors (Jessor et al., 1995; Newcomb & Felix-Ortiz, 1992). In addition, substance abuse portends myriad negative consequences for the adolescent, including physical health risks (Daily, 1992), delayed emotional development and problem-solving ability (Baumrind & Moselle, 1985), impaired interpersonal relations (Newcomb & Bentler, 1988), and poor investment in prosocial activities (Steinberg, 1991), to name a few. In short, there are multiple pathways to, and multiple consequences of, adolescent drug problems.

Likewise, serious conduct problems in adolescence—aggression, Conduct Disorder, delinquency and violence—are known to arise from an amalgamation of biological, dispositional, and environmental factors. Genetic and temperament traits, cognitive and interpersonal skills deficits, coercive and highly inconsistent parenting practices, poor attachments with prosocial adults, and antisocial peer relations all predispose antisocial behavior (Dishion et al., 1995). Along with substance abuse, these behavioral problems belong to the externalizing dimension of childhood psychopathology, the class of outer-directed psychological problems whose core symptoms are associated with socially disruptive behavior (Achenbach, Howell, Quay, & Conners, 1991). Moreover, at the most severe levels, these problems make up a cluster of co-occurring symptoms that exacerbate one another and endure as an "antisocial trait" that assumes various age-specific guises across the developmental span (Patterson, 1993). The co-occurrence of conduct problems, school failure, social skills deficits, and substance use has been labeled "problem behavior syndrome" (Jessor et al., 1995) to emphasize the overlapping risk profiles and multifaceted behavioral problems that typically afflict youths with significant externalizing symptoms.

TARGETING AT-RISK ADOLESCENTS

At-risk adolescents might be the most difficult population for family prevention to address. Parents in the highest-risk groups are least likely to access family-based programs because they are less involved in their children's lives and less capable of utilizing extrafamilial resources (Resnik & Wojcicki, 1991). Also, family-based models have traditionally taken a narrow-band approach that underplays the broader ecological stresses experienced by high-risk families (Miller & Prinz, 1990). Most programs do not consistently address extrafamilial stressors that high-risk populations encounter in multiple contexts and that inevitably compromise youth and family functioning. Finally, there is some evidence that parent training, the most widely used model in family prevention, is less effective with adolescents than with younger children. Families with adolescents are more likely to drop out of parent training (Dishion & Patterson, 1992), require specialized engagement procedures (Dishion, Andrews, Kavanagh, & Soberman, 1996), and require extensive alterations in program implementation (Bank, Marlowe, Reid, Patterson, & Weinrott, 1991).

Several concrete recommendations can be made for developing family-based prevention programs specifically for at-risk adolescents (Hogue & Liddle, 1999). First, such programs should feature individualized assessment and intervention planning. Most family prevention programs favor standardized intervention curricula that are suitable for a broad constituency and are expected to generalize to a variety of situations. Standardized curricula contain a fixed roster of generic skills and rely on a structured, didactic presentation (Pizzolongo, 1996). However, as described above, families of at-risk youths benefit from more flexible planning that attends to their unique profile of deficits and strengths. Second, programs should intervene in extrafamilial social systems. Family prevention programs have traditionally focused on intrafamilial issues such as problem solving, communicating, and bonding. However, we know that multiple social systems outside the family affect the course of externalizing behavior. To protect against or counteract these risks, prevention counselors should look to build and reinforce prosocial support systems that are available to the teen. Third, several developmentally geared prevention techniques have been endorsed particularly for families with at-risk adolescents (Bank et al., 1991; Dishion et al., 1996; McMahon, Slough, & CPPRG, 1996). These involve less focus on behavior management and more focus on parent-child interactional skills, establishment of an appropriately egalitarian parent-child relationship, attention to the unique perspective and autonomy needs of the adolescent, and promotion of parental involvement in peer activities.

FUNDAMENTAL PREVENTION GOALS

The previous two sections highlight the difficult task of aiming prevention efforts toward adolescents at greatest risk for developing substance abuse and conduct problems. Given what we know about risk and resiliency in adolescents, it follows that two general prevention goals are essential for boosting protective factors in this population: helping the adolescent achieve a redefined, interdependent attachment bond to parents and the family, and helping the adolescent forge durable connections with prosocial institutions. These fundamental prevention goals serve to direct and organize the diverse intervention activities for every family in MDFP.

Regarding bonding to the family, MDFP counselors help families negotiate the changing but continuing bond that exists between adolescents and parents. As adolescents mature, their relationship with their parents should graduate from emotional dependence to an increasing emotional interdependence that respects both the autonomy and connectedness needs of adolescents (Silverberg & Gondoli, 1996). This transformation unfolds in conjunction with adolescent striving for increased responsibility and self-determination, which gives rise to increases in parent-teen bickering and minor conflict (Steinberg, 1990). However, emotional detachment from parents is not a developmentally sound status for teenagers, even those in highly conflicted families. Evidence clearly indicates that families marked by negative emotional expression and disengaged parent-child relationships are associated with antisocial outcomes (Volk, Edwards, Lewis, & Sprenkle, 1989). In contrast, strong parent-adolescent attachment bonds are known to provide a secure base from which adolescents can build psychosocial competency and self-reliance in novel behavioral and emotional environments (Resnick et al., 1997).

Regarding bonding to prosocial institutions, counselors are especially concerned with the role that parents take in securing adolescent involvement in positive extrafamilial environments. Parents who actively participate in school and extracurricular activities boost the performance of their children in these areas (Epstein, 1987; Fletcher, Elder, & Mekos, 2000). Also, parents who maintain contact with the adolescent's closest friends and their friends' parents are able to build an informal "parenting community" that enhances the effectiveness of their own parenting efforts (Fletcher, Darling, Steinberg, & Dornbusch, 1995). MDFP counselors therefore attempt to help parents become a more knowledgeable and active presence in the adolescent's various extrafamilial contexts; in other words, parents are asked to engage in regular prevention activities for their own teens.

CASE EXAMPLE

ENGAGEMENT AND ASSESSMENT

Ms. J., an African American single mother with five children, volunteered to participate in the MDFP program with her daughter, Taisha, age 14. In the process of recruitment, Ms. J. understood that the purpose of the program was to help keep her daughter "on the right track." Prior to the first session, she spoke with the counselor who would work with her and Taisha for approximately four months—a young, White man who had recently received his master's degree in family therapy and had just completed the first phase of his training in the MDFP model.

The First Session

In the first session, the counselor, as he does throughout the course of counseling, validates Ms. J.'s story of parental hardship and resilience. The children's father had died eight years earlier, leaving Ms. J. with five young children and little money. Ms. J.'s own father had died when she was young, leaving her mother with five children as well. However, in contrast to her mother, who, after her husband's death, began to drink and frequently neglected her children, Ms. J. describes herself as someone who wants to "be there" for her children in a way that her mother was not. This discussion

about the contrasts between Ms. J.'s parenting and that of her mother serves an important assessment function at this early stage, yielding information about her care and concern for her children and demonstrating her capacity to articulate her ideas about parenting. She explains how she monitors Taisha's behavior and how she discusses important subjects with her.

During this first session, the counselor asks Ms. J. about her concerns for Taisha. She is clear that she does not want her daughter to get pregnant, to drop out of school, or to get high. However, she states that she really has "no problems" with Taisha, apart from the fact that Taisha's grades are falling and that she occasionally has a "spunky" attitude. As he will do in future sessions, in addition to meeting with mother and daughter together, the counselor also meets with Taisha alone to gain a more thorough understanding of her world and its challenges and, at times, to help work through impediments to difficult but important conversations with her mother. As the two talk, Taisha refers back to the school problem that her mother had identified, telling the counselor that she wants to attend one of the city's better high schools, but that her grades have been poor lately. In answer to the counselor's question about what she makes of this, Taisha talks about how difficult she finds it when the teachers "go too fast." "Do you talk to your mother about these difficulties at school?" the counselor asks. Taisha responds that she "gets smart" with her mother. The counselor uses this conversation about school performance as a gateway to exploring the adolescent's unique point of view, thereby furthering the process of alliance building, while he simultaneously gains information about interactions between mother and daughter. He does not attempt to help Taisha solve problems at this time; he is just beginning to learn something about the mother-daughter and family-school relationships. However, he is aware that it will be important by the end of the session to remind Ms. J. that he is available to give the family support and assistance in working with the school.

The Second Session

By the second session, it is evident that mother and daughter are capable of talking to each other respectfully and about difficult topics, although it is not clear how they approach difficult subjects when they are on their own. It has also become apparent that Ms. J. is quite isolated socially, that she has endured chronic poverty, and that her relationships with her own family are sometimes volatile and frequently unsupportive. In addition, it is clear that the counselor's alliance with the family is not yet solid. The family has already missed one appointment. When mother and daughter arrive, the counselor, who senses Taisha's disaffection with the process, attempts to initiate a discussion with her about dissatisfactions she has with the program or her part in it. He lets Taisha know that he realizes that coming to these meetings may not be her favorite activity and, to his surprise, Ms. J. states that she feels the same way. The counselor decides first to meet with Taisha alone in an attempt to establish a stronger relationship with her. Taisha, who seems to take on the role of mother's protector, quickly lets him know that her mother does not want to go back into the past, that "the past is gone." She and her mother do not discuss the past when they are together. When asked what she likes to talk about with her mother, she says she likes discussing her mother's problems. Although she mentions a recent incident in which a girl at school "picked on" her, she insists that she does not want to discuss this event because it, too, occurred in the past.

For Ms. J., discussion of painful events in the past, including the hardships of parenting, the loss of the children's father, and her own difficult childhood, is not part of what the prevention program seemed to promise. Asked about her reluctance to revisit the past, she declares plainly, "I buried it." When the counselor applauds the courage she displayed in returning for another session, she tells him that she would not have come back had he not stopped by the house and left her a note and bus tokens. A number of sessions later, when the counselor asked Ms. J. what had caused her to decide to return to counseling, she replies, "It seemed like you cared, so that's why I came back." For all his caring behavior, however, had the counselor failed to ask in sufficient detail the reasons for her disaffection with counseling and the subjects that had caused her particular pain, Ms. J.'s return might have been short-lived. Although the counselor is tempted to promise that no painful subjects will be broached in the future, such a promise could well compromise the work ahead and limit the scope of exploration of several key areas of family life. Instead, he states that there might be times when, to proceed in the present, it will be necessary to revisit the past, and he asks if, on those occasions, he might request her consent to proceed. Ms. J. is able to agree to this more limited use of the past. Discussion of the past for its own sake is not a part of the MDFP approach, but the past is often explored in the service of illuminating the present.

COURSE OF PREVENTION COUNSELING

Beginning Phase

In the first few sessions of counseling, care is taken to explore a number of facets of Taisha's and Ms. J.'s experiences, both as individuals and as members of a family. This exploration is accompanied by great attention to the nature and quality of the relationship between the two and between each of them and the counselor. Increasingly, the counselor seeks detail in those areas revealed by the assessment to have particular salience for the family as well as strong protective value for Taisha as she enters her later adolescent years. In this case, assessment in the risk and protective factor domains point the way to a primary focus on the connections among parental well-being, the parent-adolescent relationship, and adolescent adjustment.

The problem of Taisha's declining grades and her being teased by a classmate pose less of a challenge for the counselor than addressing other contextual factors that might adversely affect Taisha as she faces entry to high school. Ms. J. requires only minimal to moderate support to maintain contact with school personnel and to discuss school-related matters with her daughter. Ms. J. is aware that supervising her children, monitoring their homework, enrolling them in after-school activities, and expressing interest in their lives both in and outside of school are tasks essential to good parenting. However, Taisha's worry about her mother's well-being and Ms. J.'s depression and sense of social isolation are more difficult to tackle. For example, Ms. J. is not accustomed to considering the effect of her moods on her children. In the fourth session, with Ms. J. present, the counselor helps Taisha to articulate this connection for the first time:

COUNSELOR: I was just wondering how that is for you—seeing your mom and your older sister get into a little argument. How was that for you?

TAISHA: They was just arguin'. . . .

COUNSELOR: It just sounded like your mom was upset with her; she was sad because she didn't come [for Christmas dinner]. I was wondering, maybe, were you sad also; were you sad that your mom was upset with your sister. . . .

TAISHA: I was sad because she took it out on me.

MOM: Yeah . . . How? (Taisha giggles)

MOM: You can say, go ahead. . . . Maybe I didn't realize I was taking it out on you.

TAISHA: (unclear) . . . your attitude.

MOM: Well, what'd I say?

TAISHA: I don't know. I forgot (unintelligible). But you was just. . . . You was just hollering

stuff . . . not all like that, but every time someone said something you disapproved of, you just started hollering.

COUNSELOR: So that probably made it hard for you, then.

The counselor has taken every opportunity to emphasize Ms. J.'s importance in her daughter's life, and at this point, he and Ms. J. are in agreement that the quality of the relationship between her and her daughter will largely determine the amount of influence she will retain as Taisha faces the challenges of later adolescence. They are beginning to discuss the fact that sometimes Ms. J. feels quite depressed, that she has a habit of hiding away in her room when she is upset, and that she lacks social supports, all of which may prevent her from attaining the personal goals she has mentioned in previous sessions: returning to school and living in better surroundings.

Middle Phase

Over a period of weeks, a shared understanding begins to take root that these and other factors have and will continue to have an impact on Ms. J.'s relationship with her daughter. Taisha worries about finances. For example, what will mother do when the youngest child turns 18 and she can no longer collect Social Security? Taisha worries that her mother is not enjoying life and that she has no friends and a difficult relationship with her own mother and sister. She reports that it is difficult to study in the house when there is no heat other than that provided by the stove. If her mother is unable to work, no other housing will be provided. Discussions on these subjects build on each other, and conversations with the counselor and Taisha alone about her worries for mother develop into mother-daughter dialogues in which Taisha is encouraged to reveal her worries and her mother is asked to listen and respond to them. Alone with Ms. J., the counselor suggests that Taisha's sensitivity to mother's distress may sometimes prevent her from approaching Ms. J. with her own concerns. Mother, too, is concerned about this and recalls an instance when she was depressed and withdrew to her room. Shortly thereafter, she heard Taisha's footsteps on the stairs, but heard her quickly retreat. Ms. J. did not call out to her daughter. The counselor suggests that Ms. J. might have to encourage Taisha repeatedly to come to her if this pattern of protectiveness is to change. This conversation with mother leads to an in-session dialogue between mother and daughter.

The counselor takes care never to imply that, in her depression, Ms. J. is failing her children. It is important for Ms. J. to be consistently validated for what is working well, and to know that the counselor understands the constraints and burdens she has in mothering. He lets her know that he does not want the counseling to be yet another burden for her and repeatedly inquires about how she is experiencing the difficult emotional moments in counseling. During one session, after he encourages her to tell Taisha how she always wants to "be there" for her, he asks what this experience was like for her. Ms. J. has gradually become a convert to this way of talking. She replies that it is getting easier to express herself: "It felt good to come out and really say how I was feeling." Despite this transformation, however, Ms. J. finds it difficult to hear her daughter's frustrations and disappointments about matters that cannot be readily resolved, such as the impact of the family's chronic poverty on her life.

In addition to helping Ms. J. and Taisha open up new content areas for discussion and increase the emotional range of their exchanges, the counselor works with Ms. J. alone to address some critical problems. Having made the connection between care for her children and care for herself, mother and counselor can proceed to discuss her depression and reclusiveness as impediments to self-care. The counselor encourages Ms. J. to consider calling him when she gets "in the hole." Doing so would represent

a dramatic change in behavior for Ms. J., who resolutely maintained early in counseling, "I don't want to put my problems on anybody else." The counselor repeatedly discusses with her the dilemma posed by the lack of social support. In family prevention work, increasing protective factors through the shoring up of an existing social network or the creation of new ones is deemed essential.

Ms. J. states, "I've just been on my own all my life." The counselor asks, "Who's out there to help you out?" "Just me," she responds. She says that she has spent most of her adulthood in the house and it feels strange to come out of the house when she has been inside it for so long. She has stopped going to church, and the counselor asks about her plans to return, encouraging her both to state her fears about stepping out in public and to consider what she can do to work through them. Toward the later stages of counseling, Ms. J. goes to her neighborhood church and contemplates returning to the church that most of her family attends. This represents not only an acceptance of the need to move out into the world, but also her growing willingness to revisit some unfinished family business. Already, Ms. J. is talking to her own mother more often and differently; instead of merely tolerating her mother's negativity and stewing about it later or withdrawing from all contact with her, she tells her mother to listen and "Don't be giving me that negative stuff." Ms J. signs up for a job training program that offers the opportunity for her to obtain her high school equivalency diploma, and her eyes sparkle as she recounts the details of her involvement.

The counselor also tracks in detail those behaviors, cognitions, emotions, and interactions that contribute to or accompany positive outcomes. On the day Ms. J. triumphantly hands the counselor Taisha's report card to read, telling him that Taisha has brought up every grade, the counselor asks Taisha in great detail how she managed to accomplish this feat. When

Taisha gives a global response, answering that she was just "taking care of business," the counselor continues to question her: "Were you doing your work more? Were you studying more?" He asks whether she studied in the same way and in the same place, and whether she wants to study. He asks Ms. J. what she felt when she saw the report card and how she thinks her daughter did it. When the counselor asks Ms. J. how she thinks she helped her, her response demonstrates some real faith in the process of talking with her daughter: "I just talked with her; yeah, told her how important this is." The counselor then turns to Taisha, asking her if this helped. Her response: "Yeah. And coming here talking with you." Ms. J. chimes in, "And now that we talk more too, so that probably has a lot to do with it too. And plus coming up here."

Ending Phase

With only a few counseling sessions left, Taisha brings to the counselor a problem that has recently cropped up between her mother and older sister. Ms. J. slumps in her chair, tearful and deflated. It soon becomes evident that she would not have discussed the incident with the counselor had Taisha not brought it up. The counselor remarks that Taisha has sometimes been the vehicle for bringing up material that her mother did not want to discuss. He talks about the connection between Taisha's raising these subjects and her worry for her mother, and goes on to state that the antidote to Taisha's worry lies in Ms. J.'s taking care of herself. He says that Ms. J. is always quick to reassure her daughter that she can take care of herself, but he doesn't know if it will be so easy: "It doesn't seem like it's working for you, doing everything for yourself. . . . It's taking a toll; the kids are worrying about you."

It is clear that, despite the considerable investment made by Ms. J. in the process of counseling, it remains difficult for her to find and use social supports that will benefit her personally and help her meet her stated goal of "being there" for Taisha as she faces the challenges of later adolescence. Her social network is still very small, venturing into the world is still new to her, and she can be easily discouraged by even relatively minor setbacks. As counseling nears an end, the counselor asks Ms. J. to consider the possibility of continuing to talk to another counselor on her own. By the final session, she has agreed, and the therapist will accompany her to the first meeting. A few sessions earlier, when the counselor remarked to her, "You know how it is. You don't get through much when you're by yourself," Ms. J. had responded emphatically, "You don't get through nothing."

EMPIRICAL SUPPORT FOR MDFP

IMMEDIATE OUTCOMES

MDFP has been tested in a demonstration trial that evaluated immediate postintervention outcomes for a group of at-risk, inner-city young adolescents and their families (Hogue, Liddle, Becker, & Johnson-Leckrone, in press). Adolescents were recruited from a community youth program in which every member completed a risk factor screening measure that assessed individual risk in four areas: adolescent drug use history and attitudes and history of delinquent behavior; peer drug use history and attitudes; family drug use history and attitudes and history of police involvement; and adolescent school attendance, performance, and behavior. Youths were then randomly assigned to an MDFP ($n = 61$) or control ($n = 63$) condition. The study sample comprised early adolescents (mean age 12.5 years), predominantly girls (56%), almost entirely African American (97%), and mostly lower income (57% of families reported annual income less than $15,000, and 53% received public assistance).

Intervention effects were examined for nine targeted outcomes in four domains of functioning: self-competence, family functioning, school involvement, and peer associations. These domains are considered to be proximal mediators (indices of risk and protection) of the ultimate behavioral symptoms to be prevented: substance use and antisocial behavior. The immediate efficacy of MDFP was investigated by testing the within-subjects interaction (group × time) term of repeated measures ANOVA. Testing the interaction term indicates whether there is a significant difference between groups in change over time on the target variable. Intervention cases showed greater gains than controls on four of the nine outcomes. This represents one outcome apiece within each of the four domains: increased self-concept [$F(1,112) = 6.44$, $p < .05$], a trend toward increased family cohesion [$F(1,122) = 3.21$, $p < .10$], increased bonding to school [$F(1,122) = 5.60$, $p < .05$], and decreased antisocial behavior by peers [$F(1,122) = 7.29$, $p < .01$]. Effect size estimates for these improvements were in the small to moderate range ($\eta^2 = .03 – .06$).

These results offer preliminary evidence for the short-term efficacy of family-based prevention counseling for at-risk young adolescents. In comparison to controls, adolescents and their families who received MDFP showed gains in four key indicators of adolescent well-being. Results also suggest that MDFP enjoyed some success in reversing negative developmental trends. Whereas controls experienced decreases in family cohesion and school bonding and an increase in peer delinquency, those receiving MDFP reported strengthened family and school bonds and reduced peer delinquency. Overall, these gains were small to moderate in magnitude, and they were evident regardless of the adolescent's sex, age, or initial severity of behavioral symptoms. This initial study demonstrates that an individually tailored, family-based prevention model can be successfully implemented with at-risk minority youth.

Furthermore, family prevention counseling can foster change in multiple behavioral domains that represent critical mediational influences on the ultimate development of problem behaviors.

INTERVENTION FIDELITY

Intervention fidelity—the degree to which an intervention is implemented in accordance with essential theoretical and procedural aspects of the model—is a particularly salient issue for studies that utilize manualized treatments (Hogue, Liddle, & Rowe, 1996). Treatment manuals are intended to facilitate internal consistency and model specificity in the delivery of interventions. The intervention fidelity of MDFP in the demonstration trial described above was examined using observationally based adherence process evaluation procedures (Hogue, Johnson-Leckrone, & Liddle, 2001). The fidelity evaluation compared interventions utilized in MDFP sessions to those utilized in two empirically based treatment interventions for adolescent substance abuse: MDFT (Liddle & Hogue, in press) and cognitive-behavioral therapy (CBT; Turner, 1992). The goal was to determine whether MDFP counselors emphasized signature family-based intervention techniques prescribed by MDFP and avoided individual-based cognitive-behavioral techniques proscribed by MDFP, in comparison to two psychotherapy models with established intervention fidelity (Hogue et al., 1998). The MDFT and CBT models were implemented in the same inner-city community as the MDFP model. However, in accord with their status as treatment (versus prevention) models, MDFT and CBT were used with a sample that was older (mean age 15 years), more male (72%), and troubled by more severe behavioral symptoms (all had substance abuse disorders and 53% were on juvenile court probation).

Every available MDFP case from the demonstration study was included in the fidelity evaluation (10 cases were unavailable because the family attended no sessions or refused to be videotaped). The final study pool included 110 MDFP sessions from 51 cases, 57 MDFT sessions from 28 cases, and 32 CBT sessions from 16 cases. Sessions were rated by trained nonparticipant judges according to the thoroughness and frequency with which counselors used 20 model-specific intervention techniques throughout the entire session, with each item anchored on a 7-point Likert scale ranging from 1 (never) to 7 (extensively). Factor analysis of the 20 items supported a three-factor solution: 7-item CBT scale (sample items: utilizes behavioral reward systems and structured protocols, helps client amend cognitive distortions), 8-item Family Intervention scale (coaches multiparticipant interactions, works on family communication), and 4-item Prevention scale (explores connection between parent and adolescent ecosystem, helps develop a future orientation). The scales showed acceptable internal consistency (Cronbach's α = .74 for CBT, .74 for Family, .49 for Prevention) and interrater reliability (ICC$_{(1,2)}$ = .84 for CBT, .74 for Family, and .73 for Prevention).

Analyses of variance tested how counselors trained in the three models compared in their utilization of interventions from the three factor scales. On the CBT scale, CBT counselors (M = 3.72, SD = 1.06) used significantly more interventions than either MDFT (M = 1.93, SD = .52) or MDFP (M = 1.81, SD = .46) counselors, who did not differ from one another [$F(2,196)$ = 126.58, $p < .001$]. On the Family scale, MDFT (M = 3.93, SD = .70) and MDFP (M = 3.84, SD = .89) counselors again did not differ from one another, and both used these interventions to a greater extent than did CBT counselors (M = 3.16, SD = .59; $F(2,196)$ = 10.78, $p < .001$). On the Prevention scale, surprisingly, MDFT counselors (M = 2.44, SD = .81) were stronger than MDFP counselors (M = 2.05, SD = .76), with CBT counselors (M = 2.12, SD = .63) performing in the middle [$F(2,196)$ = 5.04, $p < .01$]. These results attest to the basic fidelity of MDFP as a family-based intervention model, in that

MDFP counselors emphasized core family-based techniques and eschewed individual cognitive-behavioral interventions. However, results also suggest that much more must be learned about what intervention techniques are uniquely *preventive* when contrasting family prevention models with family therapy models.

SUMMARY

Relatively intensive, individually tailored preventions such as MDFP may have a natural home in the mental health intervention spectrum. Contemporary prevention theories favor a stratified, assessment-based strategy for determining the scope and intensity of prevention programs offered to various populations. According to this strategy, known as a unified or multiple gating model of prevention (C. Brown & Liao, 1999; Dishion et al., 1996), all persons within a given population are screened for the presence of known risk and protective factors salient for the disorder being prevented. Then, those with higher-risk profiles—a greater number of risk factors or risk factors of greater severity—are targeted to receive selective or indicated preventions that provide more intensive and multifaceted services. In some cases, prevention programs initially implement a universal model and then look to implement an additional selective or indicated model for subgroups of participants who demonstrate greater need.

In this scheme, individualized prevention models appear well-suited for meeting the idiosyncratic prevention goals of high-risk adolescents and their caretakers. Family-based counseling models such as MDFP may therefore be a valuable third option within a unified prevention initiative. Family prevention counseling offers an acute alternative for adolescents with indicated risk profiles or for those who do not respond to universal or selective prevention efforts. In addition, this approach also has an excellent theoretical and strategic fit with comprehensive, ecological prevention strategies that seek to intervene in an integrated manner across multiple systems of influence on the development of problem behavior in adolescence. Of course, it remains to be seen whether prevention counseling models for indicated populations will stand the tests of empirical validation, clinical practicality, and cost-effectiveness over time. If they do, MDFP and similar models can become integral components of a mental health services agenda that strives to provide the right intervention for the right client at the right time.

REFERENCES

Achenbach, T. M., Howell, C., Quay, H. C., & Conners, C. K. (1991). National survey of problems and competencies among four- to sixteen-year-olds. *Monographs of the Society for Research in Child Development, 56*(No. 225).

Alexander, J. F., & Parsons, B. V. (1982). *Functional family therapy: Principles and procedures.* Carmel, CA: Brooks/Cole.

Bank, L., Marlowe, J. H., Reid, J. B., Patterson, G. R., & Weinrott, M. R. (1991). A comparative evaluation of parent-training interventions for families of chronic delinquents. *Journal of Abnormal Child Psychology, 19,* 15–33.

Baumrind, D. (1985). Familial antecedents of adolescent drug use: A developmental perspective. In C. L. Jones & R. J. Battjes (Eds.), *Etiology of drug abuse: Implications for prevention* (NIDA Research Monograph 56, pp. 13–44). Rockville, MD: National Institute on Drug Abuse.

Baumrind, D., & Moselle, K. A. (1985). A developmental perspective on adolescent drug abuse. *Advances in Alcohol and Substance Abuse: Alcohol and Substance Abuse in Adolescence, 4,* 41–67.

Bronfenbrenner, U. (1986). Ecology of the family as a context for human development. *Developmental Psychology, 22,* 723–742.

Brook, J. S., Brook, D. W., Gordon, S., Whiteman, M., & Cohen, P. (1990). The psychosocial etiology of adolescent drug use: A family interactional approach. *Genetic, Social, and General Psychology Monographs, 116,* 111–267.

Brown, B. B. (1990). Peer groups and peer cultures. In S. S. Feldman & G. R. Elliot (Eds.), *At the threshold: The developing adolescent* (pp. 171–196). Cambridge, MA: Harvard University Press.

Brown, C. H., & Liao, J. (1999). Principles for designing randomized prevention trials in mental health: An emerging developmental epidemiology paradigm. *American Journal of Community Psychology, 27,* 673–710.

Bry, B. H., Catalano, R. F., Kumpfer, K. L., Lochman, J. E., & Szapocznik, J. (1998). Scientific findings from family prevention intervention research. In R. S. Ashery, E. B. Robertson, & K. L. Kumpfer (Eds.), *Drug abuse prevention through family interventions* (NIDA Research Monograph 177, pp. 103–129). Rockville, MD: National Institute on Drug Abuse.

Bryant, K. J., Windle, M., & West, S. G. (Eds.). (1997). *The science of prevention.* Washington, DC: American Psychological Association.

Caplan, G. (1964). *The principles of preventive psychiatry.* New York: Basic Books.

Commission on Chronic Illness. (1957). *Chronic illness in the United States: Vol. 1.* Published for the Commonwealth Fund. Cambridge, MA: Harvard University Press.

Conduct Problems Prevention Research Group. (1999). Initial impact of the FastTrack prevention trial for conduct problems: I. The high-risk sample. *Journal of Consulting and Clinical Psychology, 67,* 631–647.

Daily, S. G. (1992). Suicide solution: The relationship of alcohol and drug abuse to adolescent suicide. In G. W. Lawson & A. W. Lawson (Eds.), *Adolescent substance abuse: Etiology, treatment, and prevention* (pp. 233–250). Gaithersburg, MD: Aspen.

Diamond, G. M., Liddle, H. A., Hogue, A., & Dakof, G. A. (1999). Alliance-building interventions with adolescents in family therapy: A process study. *Psychotherapy, 36,* 355–368.

Diamond, G. S., & Liddle, H. A. (1996). Resolving a therapeutic impasse between parents and adolescents in multidimensional family therapy. *Journal of Consulting and Clinical Psychology, 64*(3), 481–488.

Dishion, T. J., & Andrews, D. W. (1995). Preventing escalation in problem behaviors with high-risk young adolescents: Immediate and 1-year outcomes. *Journal of Consulting and Clinical Psychology, 63,* 538–548.

Dishion, T. J., Andrews, D. W., Kavanagh, K., & Soberman, L. H. (1996). Preventive interventions for high-risk youth: The Adolescent Transitions Program. In R. D. Peters & R. J. McMahon (Eds.), *Preventing childhood disorders, substance abuse, and delinquency* (pp. 184–214). Thousand Oaks, CA: Sage.

Dishion, T. J., French, D. C., & Patterson, G. R. (1995). The development and ecology of antisocial behavior. In D. Cicchetti & D. J. Cohen (Eds.), *Developmental psychopathology: Risk, disorder, and adaptation* (Vol. 2, pp. 421–471). New York: Wiley.

Dishion, T. J., & Patterson, G. R. (1992). Age effects in parent training outcome. *Behavior Therapy, 23,* 719–729.

Durlak, J. A. (1997). *Successful prevention programs for children and adolescents.* New York: Plenum Press.

Elias, M. J. (1997). Reinterpreting dissemination of prevention programs as widespread implementation with effectiveness and fidelity. In R. P. Weissberg, T. P. Gullotta, R. L. Hampton, B. A. Ryan, & G. R. Adams (Eds.), *Issues in children's and families' lives: Vol. 9. Establishing preventive services* (pp. 253–289). Thousand Oaks, CA: Sage.

Epstein, J. (1987). Parent involvement: What research says to administrators. *Education and Urban Society, 19,* 119–136.

Etz, K. E., Robertson, E. B., & Ashery, R. S. (1998). Drug abuse prevention through family-based interventions: Future research. In R. S. Ashery, E. B. Robertson, & K. L. Kumpfer (Eds.), *Drug abuse prevention through family interventions* (NIDA Research Monograph 177, pp. 1–11). Rockville, MD: National Institute on Drug Abuse.

Fletcher, A. C., Darling, N. E., Steinberg, L., & Dornbusch, S. M. (1995). The company they keep: Relation of adolescents' adjustment and behavior to their friends' perceptions of authoritative parenting in the social network. *Developmental Psychology, 31,* 300–310.

Fletcher, A. C., Elder, G. H., & Mekos, D. (2000). Parental influences on adolescent involvement in community activities. *Journal of Research on Adolescence, 10,* 29–48.

Gfroerer, J. (1995). *1994 national household survey of drug abuse* (Advance Report No. 10). Washington, DC: Office of Applied Studies, Substance Abuse and Mental Health Services Administration.

Hawkins, J. D., Catalano, R. F., & Miller, J. Y. (1992). Risk and protective factors for alcohol and other drug problems in adolescence and early adulthood: Implications for substance abuse prevention. *Psychological Bulletin, 112,* 64–105.

Henggeler, S. W. (1996). Treatment of violent juvenile offenders–We have the knowledge: Comment on Gorman-Smith et al. *Journal of Family Psychology, 10,* 137–141.

Hill, J. P., & Holmbeck, G. N. (1986). Attachment and autonomy during adolescence. In G. J. Whitehurst (Ed.), *Annals of child development* (Vol. 3, pp. 145–189). Greenwich, CT: JAI Press.

Hogue, A., Johnson-Leckrone, J., & Liddle, H. A. (1999). Recruiting high-risk families into family-based prevention and prevention research. *Journal of Mental Health Counseling, 21,* 337–351.

Hogue, A., Johnson-Leckrone, J., & Liddle, H. A. (2001). *Intervention fidelity of a family-based, ecological preventive intervention for antisocial behavior in high-risk adolescents.* Manuscript submitted for publication.

Hogue, A., & Liddle, H. A. (1999). Family-based preventive intervention: An approach to preventing substance use and antisocial behavior. *American Journal of Orthopsychiatry, 69,* 278–293.

Hogue, A., Liddle, H. A., Becker, D., & Johnson-Leckrone, J. (in press). Family-based prevention counseling for high-risk young adolescents: Immediate outcomes. *Journal of Community Psychology.*

Hogue, A., Liddle, H. A., & Rowe, C. (1996). Treatment adherence process research in family therapy: A rationale and some practical guidelines. *Psychotherapy, 33,* 332–345.

Hogue, A., Liddle, H. A., Rowe, C., Turner, R. M., Dakof, G. A., & LaPann, K. (1998). Treatment adherence and differentiation in individual versus family therapy for adolescent substance abuse. *Journal of Counseling Psychology, 45,* 104–114.

Institute of Medicine. (1994). *Reducing risks for mental disorders: Frontiers for preventive intervention research.* Washington, DC: National Academy.

Jessor, R. (1993). Successful adolescent development among youth in high risk settings. *American Psychologist, 48,* 117–126.

Jessor, R., Van Den Bos, J., Vanderryn, J., Costa, F. M., & Turbin, M. S. (1995). Protective factors in adolescent problem behavior: Moderator effects and developmental change. *Developmental Psychology, 31,* 923–933.

Johnston, L. D., O'Malley, P. M., & Bachman, J. G. (1995). *National survey results on drug use from the Monitoring the Future Study (1975–1994): Vol. 1. Secondary school students* (NIH Publication No. 96–4027). Rockville, MD: National Institute on Drug Abuse.

Kazdin, A. E. (1993). Adolescent mental health: Prevention and treatment programs. *American Psychologist, 48,* 127–141.

Kazdin, A. E. (1994). Methodology, design, and evaluation in psychotherapy research. In A. Bergin & S. Garfield (Eds.), *Handbook of psychotherapy and behavior change* (4th ed., pp. 19–71). New York: Wiley.

Kilpatrick, D. G., Acierno, R., Saunders, B., Resnik, H. S., Best, C. L., & Schnurr, P. P. (2000). Risk factors for adolescent substance abuse and dependence: Data from a national sample. *Journal of Consulting and Clinical Psychology, 68,* 19–30.

Klein, N., Alexander, J. F., & Parsons, B. V. (1977). Impact of family systems on recidivism and sibling delinquency: A model of primary prevention and program evaluation. *Journal of Consulting and Clinical Psychology, 45,* 469–474.

Kosterman, R., Hawkins, J. D., Spoth, R., Haggerty, K. P., & Zhu, K. (1997). Preparing for the drug free years: Effects of a preventive parent-training intervention on observed family interactions. *Journal of Community Psychology, 25,* 337–352.

Kumpfer, K. L., & Alvarado, R. (1995). Strengthening families to prevent drug use in multiethnic youth. In G. J. Botvin, S. Schinke, & M. A. Orlandi (Eds.), *Drug abuse prevention with multiethnic youth* (pp. 255–294). Thousand Oaks, CA: Sage.

Larson, R., & Richards, M. H. (1994). *Divergent realities: The emotional lives of mothers, fathers, and adolescents.* New York: Basic Books.

Liddle, H. A. (1995). Conceptual and clinical dimensions of a multidimensional, multisystems engagement strategy in family-based adolescent treatment. *Psychotherapy, 32,* 39–58.

Liddle, H. A. (2000). *Multidimensional family therapy treatment (MDFT) for adolescent cannabis users* (Cannabis Youth Treatment [CYT] manual series, Vol. 5, pp. 244). Rockville, MD: Substance Abuse and Mental Health Services Administration, Center for Substance Abuse Treatment. Available from www.samhsa.gov/csat/csat.htm

Liddle, H. A., Dakof, G. A., Parker, K., Diamond, G. S., Barrett, K., & Tejeda, M. (in press). Multidimensional family therapy of substance abusing adolescents. *American Journal of Drug and Alcohol Abuse.*

Liddle, H. A., & Hogue, A. (2000). A family-based, developmental-ecological preventive intervention for high-risk adolescents. *Journal of Marital and Family Therapy, 26,* 265–279.

Liddle, H. A., & Hogue, A. (in press). Multidimensional family therapy: Establishing empirical support through systematic treatment development. In H. Waldron & E. Wagner (Eds.), *Adolescent substance abuse.* Needham Heights, MA: Allyn & Bacon.

Liddle, H. A., Rowe, C., Dakof, G. A., & Lyke, J. (1998). Translating parenting research into clinical interventions. *Clinical Child Psychology and Psychiatry, 3*(3), 419–443.

Liddle, H. A., Rowe, C., Diamond, G. M., Sessa, F. M., Schmidt, S., & Ettinger, D. (2000). Toward a developmental family therapy: The clinical utility of research on adolescence. *Journal of Marital and Family Therapy, 26,* 485–500.

Loeber, R., & Stouthamer-Loeber, M. (1998). Development of juvenile aggression and violence: Some common misconceptions and controversies. *American Psychologist, 53,* 242–259.

Masten, A. S., & Coatsworth, J. D. (1995). Competence, resilience, and psychopathology. In D. Cicchetti & D. J. Cohen (Eds.), *Developmental psychopathology: Risk, disorder, and adaptation* (Vol. 2, pp. 715–752). New York: Wiley.

Masten, A. S., Hubbard, J. J., Gest, S. G., Tellegen, A., Garmezy, N., & Ramirez, M. (1999). Competence in the context of adversity: Pathways to resilience and maladaption from childhood to late adolescence. *Development and Psychopathology, 11,* 143–169.

McMahon, R. J., Slough, N. M., & Conduct Problems Prevention Research Group. (1996). Family-based intervention in the Fast Track Program. In R. D. Peters & R. J. McMahon (Eds.), *Preventing childhood disorders, substance abuse, and delinquency* (pp. 90–110). Thousand Oaks, CA: Sage.

Miller, G. E., & Prinz, R. J. (1990). Enhancement of social learning family interventions for childhood Conduct Disorder. *Psychological Bulletin, 108,* 291–307.

Munoz, R. F., Mrazek, P. J., & Haggerty, R. J. (1996). Institute of Medicine report on prevention of mental disorders: Summary and commentary. *American Psychologist, 51,* 1116–1122.

National Advisory Mental Health Council. (1998). *Priorities for prevention research at NIMH.* A report by the National Advisory Mental Health Council Workgroup on Mental Disorders Prevention Research. Washington, DC: U.S. Government Printing Office.

National Institute on Drug Abuse. (1997). *Preventing drug use among children and adolescents: A research-based guide.* (NIH Publication No. 97–4212). Washington, DC: U.S. Government Printing Office.

Newcomb, M. D., & Bentler, P. M. (1988). Impact of adolescent drug use and social support on problems of young adults: A longitudinal study. *Journal of Abnormal Psychology, 97,* 64–75.

Newcomb, M. D., & Felix-Ortiz, M. (1992). Multiple protective and risk factors for drug use and abuse: Cross-sectional and prospective findings. *Journal of Personality and Social Psychology, 63,* 280–296.

O'Donnell, J., Hawkins, J. D., & Abbott, R. A. (1995). Predicting serious delinquency and substance use among aggressive boys. *Journal of Consulting and Clinical Psychology, 63,* 529–537.

Osofsky, J. D. (1997). Children and youth violence: An overview of the issue. In J. D. Osofsky (Ed.), *Children in a violent society* (pp. 3–8). New York: Guilford Press.

Patterson, G. R. (1993). Orderly change in a stable world: The antisocial trait as a chimera. *Journal of Consulting and Clinical Psychology, 61,* 911–919.

Patterson, G. R., Reid, J. B., & Dishion, T. J. (1992). *A social interactional approach: Vol. 4. Antisocial boys.* Eugene, OR: Castalia.

Petraitis, J., Flay, B. R., & Miller, T. Q. (1995). Reviewing theories of adolescent substance use: Organizing pieces in the puzzle. *Psychological Bulletin, 117,* 67–86.

Pizzolongo, P. J. (1996). The comprehensive child development program and other early intervention program models. In R. D. Peters & R. J. McMahon (Eds.), *Preventing childhood disorders, substance abuse, and delinquency* (pp. 48–64). Thousand Oaks, CA: Sage.

Prinz, R. J., & Miller, G. E. (1996). Parental engagement in interventions for children at risk for Conduct Disorder. In R. D. Peters & R. J. McMahon (Eds.), *Preventing childhood disorders, substance abuse, and delinquency* (pp. 161–183). Thousand Oaks, CA: Sage.

Reid, J. B. (1993). Prevention of Conduct Disorder before and after school entry: Relating interventions to developmental findings. *Development and Psychopathology, 5,* 243–262.

Resnick, M. D., Bearman, P. S., Blum, R. W., Bauman, K. E., Harris, K. M., Jones, J., et al. (1997). Protecting adolescents from harm: Findings from the National Longitudinal Study on Adolescent Health. *Journal of the American Medical Association, 278,* 823–832.

Resnik, H., & Wojcicki, M. (1991). Reaching and retaining high-risk youth and their parents in prevention programs. In E. N. Goplerud (Ed.), *Preventing adolescent drug use: From theory to practice* (OSAP Prevention Monograph No. 8, pp. 91–126). Rockville, MD: Office for Substance Abuse Prevention.

Robinson, N. S., & Garber, J. (1995). Social support and psychopathology across the lifespan. In D. Cicchetti & D. J. Cohen (Eds.), *Developmental psychopathology: Risk, disorder, and adaptation* (Vol. 2, pp. 162–209). New York: Wiley.

Santisteban, D. A., Coatsworth, J. D., Perez-Vidal, A., Mitrani, V., Jean-Gilles, M., & Szapocznik, J. (1997). Brief structural/strategic family therapy with African-American and Hispanic high-risk youth. *Journal of Community Psychology, 25,* 453–471.

Schmidt, S. E., Liddle, H. A., & Dakof, G. A. (1996). Changes in parenting practices and adolescent drug abuse during multidimensional family therapy. *Journal of Family Psychology, 10,* 12–27.

Silverberg, S. B., & Gondoli, D. M. (1996). Autonomy in adolescence: A contextualized perspective. In G. R. Adams, R. Montemayor, & T. P. Gullotta (Eds.), *Advances in adolescent development: Psychosocial development during adolescence* (Vol. 8, pp. 12–60). Thousand Oaks, CA: Sage.

Spoth, R., Redmond, C., Hockaday, C., & Shin, C. Y. (1996). Family programs: Barriers to participation in family skills preventive interventions and their evaluations: A replication and extension. *Family Relations, 45,* 247–254.

Spoth, R., Reyes, M. L., Redmond, C., & Shin, C. (1999). Assessing a public health approach to delay onset and progression of adolescent substance use: Latent transition and log-linear analyses of longitudinal family preventive intervention outcomes. *Journal of Consulting and Clinical Psychology, 67,* 619–630.

Sroufe, L. A., & Rutter, M. (1984). The domain of developmental psychopathology. *Child Development, 55,* 17–29.

Stanton, M. D., & Shadish, W. R. (1997). Outcome, attrition, and family-couples treatment for drug abuse: A meta-analysis and review of the controlled, comparative studies. *Psychological Bulletin, 122*(2), 170–191.

Steinberg, L. (1990). Autonomy, conflict, and harmony in the family relationship. In S. Feldman & G. Elliot (Eds.), *At the threshold: The developing adolescent* (pp. 255–276). Cambridge, MA: Harvard University Press.

Steinberg, L. (1991). Adolescent transitions and alcohol and other drug use prevention. In E. Goplerud (Ed.), *Preventing adolescent drug use: From theory to practice* (OSAP Monograph No. 8, pp. 13–51, DHHS Publication No. ADM 91–1725). Rockville, MD: Office of Substance Abuse Prevention.

Substance Abuse and Mental Health Services Administration. (1998). *Preventing substance abuse among children and adolescents: Family-centered approaches* (Prevention Enhancement Protocols System [PEPS] series). Washington, DC: U.S. Government Printing Office.

Szapocznik, J., Perez-Vidal, A., Brickman, A. L., Foote, F. H., Santisteban, D., Hervis, O., et al. (1988). Engaging adolescent drug abusers and their families in treatment: A strategic structural systems approach. *Journal of Consulting and Clinical Psychology, 56,* 552–557.

Taylor, T. K., & Biglan, A. (1998). Behavioral family interventions for improving child-rearing: A review of the literature for clinicians and policy makers. *Clinical Child and Family Psychology Review, 1,* 41–60.

Tolan, P. H. (1996). Characteristics shared by exemplary child clinical interventions for indicated populations. In M. C. Roberts (Ed.), *Model programs in child and family mental health* (pp. 91–108). Mahwah: NJ: Erlbaum.

Tolan, P. H., Guerra, N. G., & Kendall, P. C. (1995). A developmental-ecological perspective on antisocial behavior in children and adolescents: Toward a unified risk and intervention framework. *Journal of Consulting and Clinical Psychology, 63,* 579–584.

Tolan, P. H., & McKay, M. M. (1996). Preventing serious antisocial behavior in inner-city children. *Family Relations, 45,* 148–155.

Tremblay, R. E., Pagani-Kurtz, L., Masse, L. C., Vitaro, F., & Pihl, R. O. (1995). A bimodal preventive intervention for disruptive kindergarten boys: Its impact through mid-adolescence. *Journal of Consulting and Clinical Psychology, 63,* 560–568.

Turner, R. M. (1992). Launching cognitive-behavioral therapy for adolescent depression and drug abuse. In S. Budman, M. Hoyt, & S. Friedman (Eds.), *Casebook of brief therapy* (pp. 135–156). New York: Guilford Press.

Volk, R. J., Edwards, D. W., Lewis, R. A., & Sprenkle, D. H. (1989). Family systems of adolescent substance abusers. *Family Relations, 38,* 266–272.

Weinberg, N. Z., Rahdert, E., Colliver, J. D., & Glantz, M. D. (1998). Adolescent substance abuse: A review of the past 10 years. *Journal of the American Academy of Child and Adolescent Psychiatry, 37,* 252–261.

CHAPTER 8

Communication in Relationships with Adolescents

DAVID L. MEICHENBAUM, GREGORY A. FABIANO, AND FRANK FINCHAM

Ever since G. S. Hall (1904) described adolescence as a period of "storm and stress," researchers have attempted to describe the specific physiological, emotional, cognitive, and social changes that characterize this developmental period. Recently, Arnett (1999) noted that conflict with parents is a major contributor to the turbulence of this period. Adolescents' and parents' contrasting desires and experiences contribute to increased conflict. Adolescents' desire for independence and peer acceptance often contributes to the tendency to conform to peer group norms and influences and to resist and challenge parental directives and adult authorities. At the same time that adolescents are seeking more autonomy, many parents have difficulties relinquishing control, resulting in conflictual parent-adolescent communication pathways and potentially escalating negative consequences for all involved (Laurson, Coy, & Collins, 1998; Steinberg, 1990).

Although adolescents may also have difficulty communicating with their peers, siblings, teachers, and other adults, this chapter focuses on communication in parent-adolescent relationships. This focus is determined by theoretical and empirical considerations. At the theoretical level, adolescence is a developmental phase that requires a restructuring of the parent-child relationship in which communication necessarily plays a central role. At the empirical level, research has demonstrated that how parents and adolescents negotiate the developmental tasks of adolescence can take an emotional toll on mothers, fathers, and adolescents (Larson & Richards, 1994). There is also evidence to show that the incidence of dysfunctional parent-adolescent communication is quite high. Using naturalistic observations, Montemayor and Hanson (1985) found that conflicts between parents and their adolescent children occurred at a rate of two conflicts every three days, or an average of 20 per month. Paikoff and Brooks-Gunn (1991) report that such conflicts increase in early adolescence, compared with preadolescence, with conflict intensity highest in midadolescence. While the number of daily conflictual episodes increases and becomes more intense, the amount of time that adolescents spend with their parents declines (Larsen & Richards, 1994). As a result, parents report that adolescence is the "most difficult stage" of their children's development (Buchanan, Eccles, Flanagan, Midgley, Feldlaufer, & Harold, 1990).

Most parent-adolescent conflict tends to be about apparently mundane issues such as personal appearance, curfews, telephone usage, completing chores, and homework (Rae, 1992). Arnett (1999) cautions, however, that such conflict may *not* be as trivial as it seems on the surface. These seemingly mundane conflicts may be "proxies" for concerns over more complex and sensitive issues involving trust, independence, peer influences, risky behaviors, and sexuality. Conflicts about appearance, curfew, friends, and dating may represent parents' attempts to restrict and control their adolescents. The parents' agenda can come into conflict with the adolescents' yearnings for independence and peer acceptance, thus contributing to familial distress (Robin & Foster, 1989; Smetana, 1996). Several investigators have found that frequent and often intense relationship breakdowns between parents and adolescents can have severe effects contributing to adolescent problems, including delinquency, running away from home, substance abuse, adjustment disorders, low self-esteem, and depression (Adams, Gullotta, & Clancy, 1985; Dekovic, 1999a; Schwartz, Dorer, Beardslee, Lavor, & Keller, 1990). On the parents' side, such ongoing conflict has been found to contribute to parental dissatisfaction, depression, anger, and marital distress (Montemayor, 1983, 1986; Robin & Foster, 1989). Steinberg and Steinberg (1994) found that 40% of parents experienced two or more of the following over the family's transition into adolescence: lowered self-esteem, diminished life-satisfaction, or increased anxiety and depression. Such parental distress was worse among parents whose adolescent was actively involved in the individuation process, whose adolescent is the same sex, who have invested relatively less energy in work and marriage, and who have been divorced.

Not all youth and their parents experience adolescence as a tumultuous period of storm and stress. In fact, most adolescents and their parents are able to satisfactorily negotiate, and even enjoy, the many challenges and developmental tasks of this period (Offer & Offer, 1975; Offer & Schonert-Reichl, 1992). Steinberg (2000) reports that studies among samples of adolescents, drawn from schools rather than clinics, revealed that around 75% of teenagers reported having "happy and pleasant" relationships with their parents. Of the remaining 25% who evidence problematic parent-adolescent relationships, most had histories of family difficulties that *preceded* the child's entry into adolescence. Thus, adolescence can act as a catalyst to exacerbate long-standing familial distress (Rutter, Graham, Chadwick, & Yule, 1976). For example, conflictual parent-adolescent relationships have been found to contribute to later developmental and adjustment difficulties; adolescent delinquency is associated with families being less emotionally warm, less active in resolving problems, and more conflictual (Borduin, Henggeler, Hanson, & Pruitt, 1985). Furthermore, Paternite and Loney (1980, as cited in Marshall, Longwell, Goldstein, & Swanson, 1990) report that the single best familial predictor of teenager aggressive tendencies and future aggressive-antisocial behavior were ratings of conflictual parent-child relationships.

Given the likelihood of negative consequences resulting from dysfunctional parent-adolescent relationships, the goal of treatment is to improve communication between parents and adolescents and to promote a successful transition into adult roles and responsibilities. Investigators who have developed interventions designed to reduce parent-adolescent distress have highlighted the need to assess the nature of interpersonal conflict to improve parent-adolescent communication and negotiation skills (e.g., Barkley, Edwards, & Robin, 1999; Robin & Foster, 1989; Szapocznik et al., 1988). It is not clear, however, whether it is the quantity, intensity, source, perceived discrepancy, or emotional impact of the conflict between parents and adolescent that contributes most to poor parent-adolescent relations. Thus, it is critical that clinicians concentrate their efforts on understanding the nature of negative familial interactions to develop procedures that can assess and alleviate familial conflict.

The goal of this chapter, therefore, is to outline a comprehensive cognitive-behavioral family systems therapeutic approach that will be useful in guiding clinical decision making and interventions.

HISTORY OF THE THERAPEUTIC APPROACH

Parent-adolescent communication problems may be only one aspect of the presenting clinical problem. The therapist must be sensitive to selecting adjunct treatments that address the many needs of all family members. For example, when a syndrome such as Conduct Disorder, Attention-Deficit/Hyperactivity Disorder (ADHD), or Depression is a major source of parent-adolescent conflict, several integrative adjunctive therapeutic techniques should be employed. As Dekovic (1999b) concluded:

> An intervention that aims at only one component is *not* likely to be effective. Such fragmented interventions have poor long-term outcome and often lead to unnecessary duplication of efforts. Current knowledge suggests that instead of dealing with separate, independent and isolated problems, it is necessary to design more complex interventions characterized by more comprehensive and simultaneous efforts to alter multiple domains of functioning and to intervene in each of the relevant settings (e.g., family, school and peer groups). (p. 668)

A great deal of converging research underscores the need for a comprehensive, intensive, and integrated treatment approach for clinicians to effectively intervene in conflictual parent-adolescent relationships (Henggeler & Borduin, 1990; Meichenbaum, Pelham, Gnagy, & Chronis, 2000).

The need to focus on extrafamilial influences, such as the adolescents' associations with deviant peers, is highlighted by the findings that from late childhood to adolescence, factors outside of the family become increasingly more predictive of adolescent problem behaviors (Dekovic, 1999b; Dishion, Andrews, & Crosby, 1995; Patterson, Reid, & Dishion, 1992). As therapists formulate intervention strategies that focus on parent-adolescent conflict, there is a need to keep in mind how these extrafamilial factors impact not only the nature and course of treatment, but also the maintenance and generalization of treatment gains and adherence to treatment regimens.

The need for such a comprehensive systemic approach is underscored by the data reporting limited effectiveness of treatment outcome studies based on conjoint therapy with parents and youngsters who are already adolescents. Barkley et al. (1999) observe in their recent book, *Defiant Teens*, that the overall treatment efficacy with this population is only a 35% *improvement* rate. In contrast, the improvement rate for conjoint parent-preadolescent interventions is 60 to 65%. In fact, the most effective interventions are for children younger than 6 years of age. With these qualifying findings in mind, the remaining focus of this chapter is on assessing and treating parent-adolescent conflict.

A number of clinical researchers have proposed psychoeducational and cognitive-behavioral training programs for alleviating parent-adolescent conflict (Barkley et al., 1999; Patterson & Forgatch, 1987; Robin & Foster, 1989; Smith, Molina, & Eggers, 1993; Steinberg, 2000). Table 8.1 enumerates the various program skills that have been taught to reduce parent-adolescent conflict. However, focusing on acquisition of skills may in part be responsible for the

Table 8.1 Illustrative skills taught to family members in therapy to reduce parent-adolescent conflict.

Educate about teen misbehavior and the nature of conflict.

Teach to recognize and deal with unreasonable beliefs and expectations.

Improve listening and attending skills.

Improve deliverance of request, commands, transitional warnings.

Teach authoritative parenting skills (warmth, involvement, firmness, consistency, nurturing adolescent independence).

Improve communication, problem solving; negotiate solution-specific solutions.

Instruct how to "notice, catch, interrupt, and alter" coercive interactions.

Set reasonable limits and establish behavioral contracts.

Nurture effective discipline strategies.

Educate about monitoring and supervising adolescents.

Instruct how to appropriately praise.

Increase parent involvement in adolescent's school and after-school activities and peer associations.

Improve social supports.

Support parents' sense of acceptance.

limited efficacy of some programs because simply teaching skills is often insufficient. Robin and Foster propose that some family members experience a performance deficit rather than a skills deficit. Family members can, at times, communicate positively, resolve conflicts, and suppress negative behaviors, but they fail to do so in conflicting and affectively charged situations. Cognitive barriers such as dysfunctional conflict-engendering beliefs, affective barriers such as anger, and interpersonal barriers such as triangulation, cross-generation coalitions, and shifting parental coalitions (Szapocznik & Williams, 2000) often get in the way of family members responding and negotiating in a constructive fashion.

Robin and Foster (Foster & Robin, 1997, 1998; Robin, 1979, 1981; Robin & Foster, 1984, 1989), who are considered major contributors in the field of parent-adolescent conflict, propose that family problem solving, communication patterns, belief systems, and family structures mediate the intensity, frequency, and pervasiveness of family conflict. Therefore, to treat family conflict, they have developed a behavioral family systems therapeutic approach that includes the following components:

1. Educating and teaching family members how to negotiate conflict, focusing on solution-specific disputes by means of psychoeducation.
2. Remediating negative communication patterns and nurturing self-regulatory affective and cognitive skills such as learning how to communicate without antagonizing.
3. Cognitively restructuring dysfunctional conflict-engendering beliefs and attributions such as helping families notice, catch, understand, and alter their overdetermined, often exaggerated and irrational beliefs about autonomy, entitlement, rumination, fairness, perfection, respect, and intentionality.
4. Engaging family members in problem solving and behavioral contracting.
5. Engaging in self-monitoring and practicing applying these skills.
6. Learning to challenge their belief systems through personal experiments at home.

Such a behavioral family systems approach considers and addresses both skills and performance (motivational) deficits.

THEORETICAL CONSTRUCTS OF THE APPROACH

AN INFORMATION-PROCESSING MODEL OF COMMUNICATION

Theoretical frameworks are beneficial for clinicians to assist in guiding clinical decision making and interventions. In this section, we offer an information-processing model that highlights the central constructs of communication and conflict, but that is also influenced by the adolescents' emerging self-identity; the family members' cognitions, emotions, and associated communicative behaviors; ecological extrafamilial factors, such as peers; and contextual influences, such as neighborhood and workplace factors. Two central theoretical constructs, *communication* and *conflict,* are fundamental to any understanding of parent-adolescent relationships.

The Nature of Communication

An analysis of how the communication process works provides a framework for understanding the nature of dysfunctional conflict-engendering communication. The goal of initiating communication is to express, either verbally or nonverbally, some form of intention. This communicated *intent* will have an *impact* on the recipient of the communication, and, as a result of feedback from the recipient, there will be an impact on the sender of the communication. At this most basic level, miscommunication may take place if the message sent is not the message the partner receives. Thus, communication breakdowns may arise as a result of the ongoing failure to effectively communicate intentions. For example, adolescents may miscommunicate to their parents their desires and needs for greater autonomy by skipping their curfew (intent = need for autonomy). Parents may attribute their adolescent's skipping curfew as being a deliberate attempt to annoy them (impact = attempt to annoy), rather than perceiving it as being an inherent need of the adolescent for autonomy. Repeated instances of such miscommunication, where the intent and

impact differ, will result in an increased frequency and intensity of parent-adolescent conflict. This circular pattern can all too readily escalate.

Intent and impact serve as the basic goals and outcomes of communication—but much more takes place. If we delve deeper into exploring other facets of communication that exist between the communicating of intent and the receiving of impact, we can explore ways in which miscommunication occurs and determine a significant source of conflict. To help examine communication in greater detail, a model of communication is presented that is similar to that described in Fincham, Fernandes, and Humphreys (1993). Figure 8.1 displays the theoretical pathways of communication. Although one may conceptualize effective communication in terms of specific behavioral skills (i.e., appropriate voice level, eye contact, and attention), the model proposed by Fincham et al. illustrates that cognitive processes such as encoding and decoding messages, expectations, cognitive appraisal, and attributions are also critical to understand the nature of communication failures. This view is consistent with that held by Robin and Foster (1989) and others (Barkley et al., 1999) who emphasize the importance of addressing irrational beliefs to ameliorate parent-adolescent conflict.

The first cognitive step, according to the proposed model, is *encoding.* Encoding involves turning one's intent into words and conveying those words to the recipient in a way that is consistent with the intent. Encoding is influenced by one's self-identity, communication goals, cognitions such as expectations and attributions, and behaviors, all of which are shaped and tempered by such factors as one's past experiences, present mood, and current concerns.

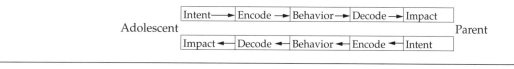

Figure 8.1 Theoretical pathways of communication.

Miscommunication may result when the communicator chooses the wrong or vague words, uses contradictory tones such as sarcasm, or undermines the message intent by nonverbal behavior, such as folded arms or glaring.

The second cognitive process, *decoding*, requires the recipient of the message to accurately interpret (decode) the message so that it reflects the communicator's intent. As with encoding, decoding is influenced by one's self-identity, communicated goals, cognitions (defined above), and behaviors. Similarly, these communication functions are shaped and tempered by the recipient's past experiences, present mood, and current thoughts. Accurate decoding may be marred by these same influences, particularly by the attributions and perceptions held by the listener.

This communication model is recursive and cyclical. It is recursive in that each of the members of the communicating unit has a continual impact in influencing the ways in which messages are encoded and decoded. It is cyclical in that each member bidirectionally influences the behavior of the others as a repetitive interactional coercive pattern occurs, as described by Patterson and Forgatch (1987). Moreover, the history of communication experiences between parent and adolescent, their current goals, and emotional and cognitive states interact in determining communication effectiveness. An example of this bidirectional and cyclical pattern was offered by Steinberg (2000) in his analysis of a parent-adolescent conflict that involves the failure of an adolescent to keep his room clean. Such noncompliance may hold very different meaning and elicit very different emotional reactions in parents and adolescents. Steinberg notes that parents may be bothered more intently by this noncompliance and are more likely to hold onto the affective aftermath because they view the issue as "right or wrong," whereas the teenager is likely to view the decision to not clean up his room more dismissively, as a "personal choice and his own business."

This clash of views and values and violation of parental expectations has all the ingredients for escalating parental-adolescent conflict. Behind the conflict is a clash of outlooks, meanings, and intents.

The Nature of Conflict

The above model of communication can be used to explain the context of parent-adolescent conflict. When communication fails, conflict is likely to result, and such conflict can contribute to further communication failures. A key component of the model is that conflict arises when incompatible and dysfunctional cognitions or behaviors occur along any of the theoretical communication pathways depicted in Figure 8.1, and thereby thwart the communication process between parents and adolescents. For example, an adolescent may have a normative developmental goal, such as the desire to be more independent. Using the proposed model, it is clear that a situation may arise in which this goal, though appropriate and not in itself confrontational, may result in a communication breakdown. The extent of the eventual conflict depends on the ways the parents and the adolescent encode and decode communication and behaviors. When an adolescent exerts his or her autonomy by staying out past curfew, parents may decode and interpret this behavior as a defiant act, as a personal threat to their authority, and as a deliberate attempt to provoke them. Thus, the initial autonomous-seeking behavior can result in an escalating chain reaction of hostile attributions, a violation of parental expectations, and thwarted communication goals on the part of the parents and the adolescent. These may be expressed through negative communication behaviors, such as arguing followed by withdrawal. Regardless of how the negative behaviors are expressed, the end result is likely to be parent-adolescent conflict. Over time, this conflict can change the parents' and adolescent's goals so that they become more self-serving and hostile, thus leading to even more in-grained and irrevocable conflict and ultimately to increased avoidance and further escalation.

A good example of this parent-adolescent distress is offered in Szapocznik and Williams's (2000) study of parent-adolescent conflict in Hispanic families in Miami. They found that the process of acculturation disrupted the family unit and led to parent-adolescent conflict. The adolescents' normal striving for independence combined with their acculturation to the American values of individualism was in conflict with their Hispanic parents' tendencies to preserve their family's integrity by adhering to cultural values of strong family cohesion and parental control. This culturally based conflict of individualism and independence versus cohesion and control resulted in ongoing parent-adolescent "battles," with accompanying attributions, expectations, and conflictual communication breakdowns. Family-based interventions were required to address these bicultural differences.

FACTORS INFLUENCING COMMUNICATION PATHWAYS

Other components of the present information-processing communication model are the role of self-identity, cognitions, behaviors, and the ecological context in which the communication takes place. Each of these is examined before we consider the assessment and treatment implications.

Emerging Self-Identity

Adolescence is a period rife with new challenges. Associated with this developmental time period are rapidly changing demands regarding academic achievement, social relationships, independence, and intimacy. Acknowledging that this is an important transitional period, Erikson (1968) suggested that adolescence is characterized by a need to assume a unique and autonomous role in society. The extent to which an adolescent is unable to develop an acceptable "adult" identity may result in impairment in various domains, including interpersonal communication.

The study of Hispanic adolescents (Szapocznik & Williams, 2000) illustrates the general desire by adolescents in this culture to develop a self-identity that is autonomous. This process of developing autonomy may begin by adolescents increasing their affiliation with peers and by their challenging adults' directives. The adolescent's desires for autonomy and motivation to gain acceptance by others are often experienced at the expense of parental supervision. The avoidance of such adult supervision raises parental concerns about the adolescent's increased opportunities for engaging in high-risk behaviors such as substance use, sexual activity, and antisocial behaviors, many of which may co-occur (Hawkins, Catalano, & Miller, 1992; Jessor, 1991). The adolescent's expression of autonomy is often appraised by parents as being "risky" and "reckless" and can thus result in conflict. The fear of possible negative consequences for their child's behaviors may result in the parents' reluctance to relinquish control.

In many parent-adolescent relationships, the conflicts are functional. That is, in the safe haven of a family, an adolescent may learn negotiation and compromise strategies over time. However, the absolute imposition of a parental "will" that is contrary to their adolescent's desire for autonomy can put a child at even greater risk for experiencing negative consequences. For example, the failure to successfully negotiate such differences of opinion may contribute to familial distress, communication breakdowns, avoidance, and parent-adolescent conflict, as adolescents decode their parents' enforcement of rules as being unfair. Research by Ary, Duncan, Duncan, and Hops (1999) found that the imposition of the parents' will and the associated resulting conflict led families to experience even higher levels of conflict and lower levels of parent-child involvement. Ary et al. further noted that these conflictual family interactions are related to adolescent association with deviant peer groups one year later. Thus, the change in self-identity associated with the transitional stage of adolescence, along with parents absolutely imposing their will on the adolescent, may inadvertently inhibit the natural development of negotiation skills. Obviously, these skills are adaptive, and a failure to learn how to compromise may result in negative repercussions for the adolescent in later life. This process highlights the need for treatment protocols of parents and adolescents to involve cognitive restructuring of conflicting beliefs and expectations.

Parent and Adolescent Cognitions

Along with the emerging self-identity of adolescents, the beliefs and attributions of adolescents and their parents are integral factors in leading to miscommunication and conflict. As noted earlier, Robin and Foster (1989) proposed that irrational beliefs and attributions are central components that mediate the frequency, intensity, and pervasiveness of family conflict. According to Robin and Foster and Barkley et al. (1999), both parents and adolescents may develop conflict-engendering belief systems. These beliefs can color the ways participants interpret (i.e., encode/decode) information. For parents, these fixated beliefs most commonly include (1) the notion that their adolescent behaves intentionally and maliciously to annoy them; (2) expectations of perfect obedience and compliant behavior; (3) thoughts that they should *not* give their adolescents freedom because they will abuse it and endanger their lives; (4) feelings of self-blame for their adolescents' behaviors; and (5) thoughts that their adolescents should appreciate all that the parents do for them.

The most common types of conflict-engendering beliefs adopted by adolescents include (1) feelings that their parents' restrictions are unfair and are intentionally designed to thwart them; (2) thoughts that they should

have complete autonomy and be accountable only to themselves; and (3) thoughts that love and appreciation are associated with receiving material goods.

Research on parents' and adolescents' beliefs and attributions underscores the role that such affectively charged cognitions play in the conflict process. For example, differences in the beliefs held by parents and adolescents about autonomy have been found to differentiate between normal and clinic-referred adolescents and their parents (Robin & Koepke, 1990). Reed and Dubow (1997) found that adolescents' negative beliefs about their parents significantly and uniquely predicted negative communication beyond the effects of directly observed communication behavior. Grace, Kelley, and McCain (1993) reported that negative attributions by mothers and their teenage daughters contributed to the increased rate of conflict. The beliefs that the other's behavior was intentional, selfishly motivated, and blameworthy exaggerated the level of their parent-adolescent conflict.

The proposed information-processing model highlights that breakdowns in communication can contribute to such maladaptive beliefs and to distressing emotions such as anger. These, in turn, can further contribute to conflictual communication. For example, repeated errors of encoding and decoding can lead to increased negative attributions that become self-fulfilling prophecies. As both Barkley et al. (1999) and Foster and Robin (1998) highlight, interventions with parent-adolescent conflict need to address dysfunctional beliefs, changing expectations, conflict-engendering attributions, and accompanying emotions and behaviors. Thus, it is important for clinicians to understand not only the nature of the current conflict, but also the history of the conflictual relationship.

Behavior

A number of researchers have highlighted the importance of both the nonverbal and behavioral features of communication (Barton &

Alexander, 1981; Fincham et al., 1993; Kaslow, 1996). Not only *what* is said, but how and when it is said can undermine or enhance communication. Whether a message is conveyed with sarcasm or affirmation, with begrudging compliance or enthusiasm is a critical factor in the communication process. In short, when people communicate, their words, tone, gestures, and behaviors influence the way messages are interpreted (decoded). For example, an adolescent saying to his parent "I'll be home by 10:00 P.M." in a scoffing tone of voice while rolling his eyes conveys a completely different message from an adolescent who says "I'll be home by 10:00 P.M." in a neutral tone of voice while making eye contact. The information-processing model therefore highlights that the way messages are sent and received (encoded/decoded) and the various cognitive and affective factors associated with the messages contribute to the overall success of communication and to parent-adolescent conflict.

Contextual and Ecological Factors
The focus of the discussion thus far has been on parents and adolescents. Researchers who have adopted an ecological developmental perspective following the lead of Bronfenbrenner (1979) have highlighted the need to consider extrafamilial factors in explaining and treating parent-adolescent conflict. They highlight that a family is "nested" in an ecological context of other settings such as school, the neighborhood, and the larger cultural community. Research indicates that the parents' dissatisfaction with their workplace, the absence of social supports, the influence of deviant peers, the absence of after-school activities, and the absence of parent involvement with peers and the school have each been found to contribute to parent-adolescent conflict (Szapocznik & Coatsworth, 1999). Moreover, contextual factors such as ethnic, racial, and socioeconomic status (SES) may play a role in the nature of parent-adolescent conflict. For example, Szapocznik and Coatsworth reported that African American and Asian

American families who raise their adolescent offspring in high-risk urban areas are much more likely to use authoritarian rather than authoritative parenting styles. In contrast, parents with a European or Hispanic background were more likely to employ authoritative parenting practices. Considering Steinberg's (2000) claim of the importance of parenting style on the nature of conflict in the home, Szapocznik and Coatsworth's findings suggest that the quantity, type, and effects of conflict may differ among ethnic groups as a function of parenting styles. As McGoldrick, Giordano, and Pearce (1996) highlight, there is a need to consider the family's ethnicity and other cross-domain influences in any assessment strategy and family therapy approach of parent-adolescent conflict.

METHODS OF ASSESSMENT AND INTERVENTION

Before delineating specific assessment strategies, it is necessary to identify important parameters of parent and adolescent communication. Three general classes of factors have been identified as contributing to the incidence and intensity of parent-adolescent conflict. These include characteristics of the *adolescent*, the *parents*, and *relationship factors*. A brief consideration of these varied factors will provide a framework for understanding what information should be obtained in the assessment process. In considering adolescent factors, research indicates that parent-adolescent conflict tends to be more frequent when the following components are present: the adolescent is experiencing early maturation (especially in adolescent daughters); the adolescent has externalizing and internalizing problems and related mental and physical difficulties; the adolescent is caught up in the individuation process; the adolescent evidences low academic achievement and associates with deviant peers; and the adolescent experiences high exposure to stressors (Ary et al., 1999; Colten & Gore, 1991; Dekovic, 1999b; Hawkins et al., 1992; Steinberg, 2000; Szapocznik & Coatsworth, 1999).

Parental factors such as marital status (divorce), parenting style (authoritative, authoritarian, permissive), parenting behaviors (parental involvement, supervision, monitoring), parental psychopathology (depression, substance abuse, history of antisocial behavior), and parental stressors (marital distress, job stressors that spill over into the home) have been found to influence parent-adolescent conflict (Dekovic, 1999a; Galambos, Sears, Almeida, & Kolaric, 1995; Steinberg, 1990; Steinberg, Mounts, Lamborn, & Dornbusch, 1991). Such parental factors may have a negative impact on the children that extends beyond parent-adolescent conflict. For example, Schwartz et al. (1990), reported that mothers who are highly critical, hostile, and emotionally overinvolved have a three times greater risk of raising a child who will develop a depressive disorder, substance abuse disorder, or Conduct Disorder.

In considering these parental factors, there are two important observations to keep in mind. First, as Smetana and Gaines (1999) caution, most studies of parent-adolescent conflict have involved Caucasian, middle-class, two-parent families. They emphasize that the meaning of conflict may be different for parents and adolescents, depending on their ethnic, racial, and SES status. The second observation concerning parental influences is that some parental factors may prove more important than other types of factors in mediating outcome, depending on the developmental stage of the child. For example, Rey and Plapp (1990) reported that parental overprotectiveness and lack of caring occurred more frequently in children diagnosed with Oppositional Defiant Disorder and Conduct Disorder compared to a control group of children without disruptive behavior disorders. In adolescence, poor parental supervision and poor communication have been associated with oppositional and risky behaviors (Miller, Forehand, & Kotchick, 1999). Research has also

demonstrated that family management style plays a key role in mediating the nature of the parent-adolescent relationship and outcome. For instance, poor family management practices, especially coercive interactions, lack of parental involvement, and poor parental supervision, contribute to youth's association with deviant peers and to parent-adolescent conflict (Dishion et al., 1995; Patterson, DeBarshye, & Ramsey, 1989; Patterson et al., 1992). Thus, parents and adolescents with conflictual relationships may be negatively reinforced by avoiding problems in the short run, but this avoidance may exacerbate problems in and out of the family system over the long run.

The nature of the relationship between the adolescent and his or her parents has also been found to be critical. For instance, more intense conflicts have been found between mothers and daughters than with any other dyads (Smetana, 1996). The sex of the family members is only one background factor that influences parent-adolescent conflict. Dekovic (1999b) reported that the history of the parent-adolescent relationship proved more important in influencing such outcome measures as the level of adolescent depression and self-esteem than did the parent-adolescent interaction behaviors in specific conflict situations. Research has indicated that the level of parent attachment and emotional closeness also plays an important role in influencing parent-adolescent conflict (Dekovic, 1999b; Holmbeck, 1996; Steinberg, 2000).

It is also critical to evaluate the nature of the parent-adolescent negotiation and conflict-resolution processes. For instance, Smetana and Gaines (1999) found that in the minority of parent-adolescent conflict situations, the conflict is resolved by the adolescent submitting to the parents. In the majority of disagreements, the parent concedes, uses threats and punishments, compromises, seeks a mutual solution, or lets the issue go unresolved. Parents and adolescents from clinically referred distressed

Table 8.2 Domains to assess in a functional analysis.

Adolescent Variables

Age (early/late maturing).

Gender.

Race and ethnicity.

Family constellation, density of siblings, birth order.

Sexual preference.

Diagnosable classification and comorbidity (present/past; age of onset).

Physical and mental health (early maturing; externalizing and/or internalizing problems).

Intellectual level.

Academic performance (current/past).

Involvement in supervised after-school activities.

Sense of belonging to the school.

Attachment history.

Peer associations (prosocial, deviant).

Talents and hobbies.

Coping skills and strengths.

Career plans (amount of current after-school work).

Exposure to present stressors (major stressors, daily hassles).

Experience of past stress (loss, maltreatment, victimization).

Past treatment/services received.

Motivation to change/level of involvement.

Parent Variables

Current age and age at which had child.

Marital status (present/past).

Sex.

Race and ethnicity.

Level of acculturation.

SES.

Highest level of education.

Occupation, employment status, job satisfaction.

Diagnosable disorder (present/past).

Level of marital distress.

Parental stressors (financial, legal, health, burden of care).

Level of family functioning.

Parenting style (authoritative, authoritarian, permissive).

Parenting behaviors (involvement, supervision, monitoring).

History of own child rearing.

History of previous treatment/services.

Motivation to change/level of involvement.

Relationship Variables

Communication, negotiation, conflict-resolution and problem-solving skills.

Table 8.2 *(Continued)*

Evidence of coercive process and evidence of "exceptions" (i.e., skills deficits versus performance deficits).

Beliefs, attributions, expectations, dysfunctional feelings (anger) for both parent and adolescent.

Interpersonal skills evidence with others (generality).

Emotional context and affective climate.

Ecological/Contextual Variables

Residence (neighborhood factors, crime, number of moves).

Work stressors.

Racial stressors.

Social supports.

Peer influences on adolescent.

Possible agency barriers (waiting list, insurance, transportation, child care).

families, compared to nondistressed families, have been found to have communication and negotiation skills deficits, as well as cognitive (beliefs) and emotional (anger) barriers that get in the way of their effectively resolving such conflicts (Foster & Robin, 1998). These results underscore the need for clinicians to assess the history of familial relationships, as well as the negotiation skills that occur during the current parent-adolescent conflict.

Given that dysfunctional relationships can be influenced by and affect so many aspects of the family system, it is critical to perform a comprehensive *functional assessment* prior to intervening, as enumerated in Table 8.2. A functional analysis (Mash & Terdal, 1998) during the assessment phase will remind clinicians to attend to key factors that may influence communication and contribute to parent-adolescent conflict, including antecedents and consequences of the conflict. This analysis involves obtaining information from multiple informants (parents, adolescents, siblings, peers, and teachers), through various methods:

1. Structured and unstructured interviews.
2. Self-report measures of family functioning completed by both the parents and the adolescent.
3. Naturalistic reports and self-monitoring of behavioral frequencies of home-based conflict.
4. Clinic-based observations of dyadic and familial interactions.
5. Responses to hypothetical scenarios, as obtained from interviews and questionnaires.
6. Reflective sampling (listening and reacting to audiotapes of their observations).
7. Assessment of related ecological factors.

Given the present space limitations and the fact that comprehensive reviews already exist, we will not enumerate the specific self-report measures that can be used to assess parent-adolescent conflict (see Foster & Robin, 1998, for a comprehensive review).

The major focus of the assessment is to help the participants (1) specify and define as clearly as possible (operationalize) examples of the parent-adolescent conflict that brought them in; (2) identify the times when, antecedents of, and situations where these behaviors occur; and (3) consider the functions or reinforcing properties of these behaviors. As part of the functional analysis, the clinician should determine the setting events that influence the occurrence of the conflictual behaviors (who is present; where and when the conflict occurs and over what issues); the antecedents (parental demands; poor school performance, telephone call from the principal); and the consequences (how resolved; imposition of consequences; escalation). There is also a need to map the nature of the parent-adolescent coercive cycle that Patterson and his colleagues (Patterson & Forgatch, 1987) have described. Such tracking on a collaborative basis with family members not only serves assessment purposes, but will also educate and engage the family members on how to anticipate, recognize, interrupt, and alter conflict-engendering behavioral patterns.

The functional analysis, however, must go beyond the focus on directly observable behaviors and assess, as noted in the model, the role that the parents' and adolescents' cognitions (beliefs, expectations, attributions) and feelings (motivational goals, emotional reactions) play in conflict situations. As noted, it is not only what the participants do in a conflictual situation, but also the meaning (present and past) that they ascribe to others and to their own behaviors that contributes to communication breakdowns. Effective interventions need to target not only the alteration in communication patterns, but also the cognitions that precede, accompany, and follow such interactions.

In summary, the assessment process needs to determine the degree to which the parent-adolescent conflict is a reflection of a *skills deficit* in the areas of communication, negotiation, conflict resolution, problem solving, and parent management, and also the degree to which the parent-adolescent conflict reflects *performance deficits* where a variety of barriers (beliefs, expectations, attributions, dysfunctional emotions, cross-domain social influences such as peer pressure, marital distress, and job dissatisfaction) contribute to the parent-adolescent conflict.

The assessment process would not be complete, however, if it focused only on deficits and excesses, barriers, and stressors. It should also focus on *potential strengths* that family members possess, as these may prove valuable in treatment planning. These strengths may include individual, social, and extrafamilial contextual factors that can be accessed and strengthened. The level of affectional ties, shared beliefs, specific talents, the degree of social supports, the readiness to change, the degree of parental involvement, the availability of social services, and other potential moderating or mediating factors should be part of the assessment process. The role of protective factors that can buffer families from negative outcomes should be built into assessment and treatment regimens.

We do not consider assessment to be distinct from treatment. Using a detailed functional analytic approach, clinicians integrate the assessment with treatment. The focus of the assessment should be to identify behaviors and cognitions that will be targeted by the treatment. Treatment should be multifaceted and individually tailored to account for the antecedents, consequences, and setting events that influence the target behaviors. Assessment then continues throughout treatment, and progress toward treatment goals is continually monitored. Based on the ongoing functional analysis, multisystemic interventions are added, deleted, or modified, with the goal of providing the most effective treatment for the needs of the individual family.

MAJOR SYMPTOMS, SYNDROMES, AND PROBLEMS TREATED USING A MULTIFACETED APPROACH

The impairing nature of parent-adolescent conflict noted earlier has received attention from the fourth edition of the *Diagnostic and Statistical Manual of Mental Disorders (DSM-IV)* under the category of Parent-Child Relational Problems (V61.20), highlighting the need for clinical attention (American Psychiatric Association [APA], 1994). Because parent-adolescent conflict is not a *DSM-IV* Axis I diagnostic category, we view it from the perspective of a relational diagnosis of dysfunctional family patterns (Kaslow, 1996). When assessment identifies diagnosable disorders or problems in family members that exacerbate parent-adolescent conflict, specific assessment procedures and interventions tailored to address those disorders and problem areas should be added to the clinical regimen (as demonstrated in the following case example).

A number of diverse intervention programs have been developed to treat parent-adolescent conflict in the presence of comorbid psychopathology. Many of these programs target specific adolescent problems such as reducing delinquent, aggressive, and substance-abusing behaviors (functional family therapy developed by Alexander & Parsons, 1982; Barton & Alexander, 1981; multisystemic therapy developed by Borduin et al., 1985; Henggeler & Borduin, 1990; and strategic therapy as implemented by Szapocznik & Kurtines, 1989; Szapocznik & Williams, 2000). Other targeted problems include adolescents with disruptive behavior disorders (Barkley et al., 1999; Barkley, Guevremont, Anastopoulos, & Fletcher, 1992; McCleary & Ridley, 1999; Robin, 1998), depression (Kazdin & Mariano, 1998; Lewisohn, Clarke, Rhode, Hops, & Seeley, 1996), and eating disorders (Foreyt, Poston, Winebarger, & McGavin, 1998; Robin, Bedway, Siegel, & Gilroy, 1996). As a result of parent-adolescent conflict often being accompanied by comorbid psychopathology and its associated problems, treatment must be comprehensive and integrative. Henggeler and Borduin highlight the importance and effectiveness of treating behavior problems in children and adolescents through a multifaceted approach, whereby individual, familial, and social systems are addressed.

The following case illustrates a comprehensive integrative approach to treating parent-adolescent communication problems and accompanying behavioral problems in a clinical setting. It conveys how a multifaceted model can guide treatment planning.

CASE EXAMPLE OF MULTIFACETED TREATMENT OF PARENT-ADOLESCENT CONFLICT

Todd is 14 years and 2 months old. He was referred by his pediatrician because of the high level of parent-adolescent conflict, parent-adolescent defiance, and problems associated with his diagnosis of ADHD. Todd's difficulties included inattention, constant fidgeting, low frustration tolerance, and poor peer interactions, and these problems contributed to a high stress level in the home. Todd was the middle of three children and he would often get into fights with his older and younger brothers.

Initially, a detailed functional assessment was performed, and Todd and his parents were interviewed. They engaged in self-monitoring behavior and completed self-report measures. In addition, behavioral ratings were completed by Todd's teacher. According to the parents' and teacher's report on the Conners' Rating Scales (Conners, 1969; Pelham, Milich, Murphy, & Murphy, 1989) Disruptive Behavior Disorders Rating Scale (Pelham, Gnagy, Greenslade, & Milich, 1992), and the parents' reports on the Child Behavior Checklist (Achenbach & Edelbrock, 1981), Todd met the *DSM-IV* criteria for ADHD (combined type) and Oppositional Defiant Disorder. Todd's behavioral difficulties were evident across situations and were further complicated by his accompanying academic failures and peer rejection. Although his oppositional behavior led to coercive parental interactions, he had not gotten into trouble with the law, nor engaged in any antisocial behaviors. His preoccupation with his computer seemed to keep him out of trouble, but not out of conflict with his parents. Todd had been treated for the prior year with methylphenidate. His parents reported that although the medication "got him through the school day," he was a "terror to deal with" at home. Although medication ameliorated some of his disruptive behavior at school, intensive psychosocial treatment was clearly needed to remediate maladaptive parent-adolescent interactions.

Parent-adolescent conflict was directly assessed with the Issues Checklist (Prinz, Foster, Kent, & O'Leary, 1979), which measures the frequency and intensity of specific family issues; the Conflict Behavior Questionnaire (Robin & Weiss, 1980), which measures parent and adolescent communication patterns; and a family session, during which the family had to negotiate and solve a familial problem (bedtime). The results of the assessment revealed a family in marked distress. The major issues raised on the Issues Checklist included Todd's not fulfilling his responsibilities, having trouble in school and with homework, and sibling fighting. Items concerning drugs and lying were not endorsed. The Conflict Behavior Questionnaire and the family negotiation session allowed for observation of Todd's and his parents' cognitions and communication behaviors. In terms of cognitions, Todd expressed that his parents were "bossy" and "nag" and did not trust him to be alone, treating him like a "little kid." Todd's parents felt that their son acted intentionally to annoy them and "drive us crazy" and did not deserve to be trusted because he could not take care of himself or follow directions. In addition to these cognitions, it was noticed during their discussion that each member of the family frequently interrupted the others, rarely made eye contact, had difficulty controlling their anger, and regularly wandered off-topic.

It should be noted further that Todd's mother was mildly clinically depressed, as evidenced on the Beck Depression Inventory. Her husband's distancing behaviors, intermittently mixed with an aggressive confrontational style, contributed to a moderately high level of marital distress.

Case Formulation/Treatment Plan

Todd's family represents a typical case that is treated using a multifaceted intervention approach. Treatment included the following components:

1. An eight-week behavioral summer treatment program (STP) (Pelham, Greiner, & Gnagy, 1997; Pelham & Hoza, 1996) for adolescents. The goal of the program was to help Todd learn to manage his ADHD symptoms, oppositionality, and anger, and to foster social skills with peers via an intensive cognitive-behavioral treatment

program. A central component of the program was daily social skills and conflict-resolution skills training. Equally important was a daily jobs period. Todd's interest in computers provided a means to have him perform a summer job in which computer skills were necessary and in which he could engage in coached and supervised peer and adult interactions.

2. A concurrent eight-session group parent-training program. Parent training focused on educating Todd's parents about the nature of their son's ADHD and teaching them behavioral strategies and parenting skills that could help them avoid coercive interactions in the future. The material covered involved selected components from a number of psychoeducational and cognitive-behavioral training programs (see Table 8.1; Barkley et al., 1999; Patterson & Forgatch, 1987; Robin & Foster, 1989; Smith et al., 1993). The group sessions included such topics as understanding teen misbehavior and ADHD, reviewing the principles of behavior management, teaching parents effective problem-solving and negotiation strategies, addressing ways to deal with unreasonable beliefs and expectations, and providing strategies for disciplining and rewarding their adolescents.

3. Three parent-teenager negotiation training sessions. These sessions were implemented following Todd's first four weeks of participation in the STP. The negotiation training sessions involved Todd and his parents learning and practicing communication and negotiation skills. The ultimate goal of this training is to "promote developmentally appropriate communication, problem-solving, and personal responsibility" (Smith et al., 1993, p. 1). These goals are achieved by having parents and their teenagers practice discussing conflictual topics, proposing solutions, evaluating suggestions, and reaching a compromise in the presence of a clinical facilitator. Once a compromise is reached, the discussants write a contract that reflects their compromise and indicates the consequences for both abiding by and violating the contract. Following each interaction, the facilitator engages the family members in a discussion of their effectiveness in negotiating. In each subsequent session, the facilitator fades his or her involvement in leading this discussion.

4. Follow-up booster sessions in which the therapist (DLM) met with Todd and his parents. The purpose of these sessions was to ensure maintenance of the skills taught, followed by meetings with Todd's parents and teachers to establish an individualized behavioral plan to address Todd's academic and behavioral problems at school.

The need to go beyond simply a parent management approach and a skills training program with children such as Todd was underscored in an experimental study by Barkley et al. (1992), who found that although adolescents with ADHD improved following treatment, most did *not* show significant improvement relative to the functioning of children in a control group.

The authors of this chapter have experience that indicates that there is a need to directly target the parent-adolescent conflict as in the treatment plan above. But, before targeting the parent-adolescent conflict, therapists need to engage parents in the therapy process to reduce the high likelihood of dropout (Foster & Robin, 1998). Szapocznik and Williams (2000) have described, from a brief strategic family therapy perspective, a variety of techniques that can be used to engage parents, to elicit their commitment, and to improve their motivation to change and remain involved. Clinicians need to be as concerned about these engagement procedures as they are about the specific skills they wish to teach (Kazdin, Holland, & Crowley, 1997). Given the recalcitrant nature of Todd's behavior, the long history of parent-adolescent conflict, and the multiple other stressors (mother's depression, marital discord, Todd's ADHD and ODD, the high stress level at home with the other children, and the limited social supports available to the family), there was a need to focus on the engagement processes of therapy. For example, Foster and Robin highlight the potential value of having parents discuss extrafamilial stressors, their own child-rearing experiences, and strengths and behaviors that they would like to see continued. Clarifying the parents' misconceptions about treatment and discussing the potential benefits of treatment will nurture the hope and effort required to undertake the challenging tasks of altering the parent-adolescent pattern of interactions.

"Engagement is probably a necessary but *not* a sufficient condition for treatment success" (Foster & Robin, 1998, p. 634). After engagement was addressed, the strategy of focusing on Todd's ADHD behavior and educating his parents about ADHD and on ways to improve their parenting skills led to improvement sufficient enough that the family could now work on improving their communication and problem-solving skills (as enumerated in Table 8.2). The skills training program, especially the focus on ways that Todd's father could control his anger and work collaboratively with his wife, was critical. An examination was also made of the father's conflict-engendering beliefs and attributions that acted as anger triggers. For example, the transition from viewing Todd's behavior as intentionally motivated to viewing his behavior as a by-product of his ADHD was a major step in the therapy process. These cognitive and affective changes were then strengthened with daily practice and feedback.

The family also came together in formulating a mutual family plan (with the help of the therapist) to become a more active team and stay involved in helping Todd improve his school performance and further develop his computer skills.

POSTTERMINATION SYNOPSIS

The initial task of treatment that involved skills training for Todd and psychoeducational skills training for his parents was supplemented by a plan to enhance the family's commitment and involvement in treatment by using a number of engagement procedures. The second major task of treatment focused directly on the parent-adolescent conflict after the initial high level of oppositional behavior and coercive family interactions was reduced. The third task of treatment focused on generalization training by ensuring that Todd and his parents practiced skills, anticipated possible barriers, and worked as a team to effect change in Todd's school (develop a parent-school recording program with behavioral contracting built in). Booster sessions were added to the treatment regimen to ensure maintenance of the treatment effects over time.

RESEARCH ON EFFICACY AND EFFECTIVENESS

Although the long-term effectiveness of this program has yet to be evaluated, parents and STP staff completed improvement and satisfaction ratings at posttreatment. These ratings indicated that all four of Todd's clinical counselors and his parents felt that he had improved in his communication and problem-solving skills. Moreover, Todd's parents indicated that their son was pleasant to interact with at posttreatment, that they were extremely satisfied with the program, and that this program was much more effective in changing their adolescent's problems than were other programs. At least for this case, the high rate of satisfaction and improvement speaks to the program's effectiveness.

As for the program's efficacy, although our case study does not constitute grounds that this is an empirically supported treatment, components of this program have been empirically demonstrated elsewhere to foster significant changes. For example, conducting problem-solving communication training (teaching negotiation skills, cognitive restructuring, and practicing problem-solving skills) has been widely noted to reduce the degree of conflict in the home between parents and adolescents (Barkley et al., 1992; Foster, Prinz, & O'Leary, 1983; Robin, 1981; Robin & Foster, 1989). In addition, providing parents with psychoeducational training and skills training has also been demonstrated to be effective in decreasing reported conflict (McCleary & Ridley, 1999).

SUMMARY

It is difficult to provide "hard" summative evaluation data on the efficacy of various intervention programs because clinicians have advocated so many different treatment formats (see Foster & Robin, 1998, for a discussion of alternative treatment approaches). For example, some therapists have proposed initially seeing the family members alone, with cotherapists seeing the adolescent, especially when the initial level of conflict is high; family members are seen together (Everett, 1976) only after some improvement. Some therapists have advocated seeing the family members together from the outset (Szapocznik & Williams, 2000). Some therapists have posited that adolescents would benefit most from group treatment with other adolescents (J. A. Hall & Rose, 1987), yet other therapists, such as Dishion, McCord, and Poulin (1999), have reported on the dangers of putting high-risk adolescents in the same treatment group because adolescent misbehaviors may be inadvertently exacerbated by association with deviant peers. Still other combinations of treatment formats have been proposed.

Because there are so many different approaches to the treatment of parent-adolescent conflict and because such psychosocial treatments have not

been adequately evaluated, the authors have adapted the strategy of enumerating the "core task " of treatment that should be incorporated in treatment approaches of parent-adolescent conflict (see Table 8.3). Families seen in a clinical setting typically have a history that includes years of conflict; thus, treatment of this conflict has to be intensive and long-term. After initial treatment, programs for maintenance and relapse prevention (booster sessions during important developmental transitions) are essential. Table 8.3 highlights the variety of components that need to be addressed in the treatment of parents and adolescents, as illustrated in the case study.

Future research will need to specify the algorithms that allow for the development of standardized treatments that can be empirically validated. At this point, Dekovic's (1999) observation that single-component interventions are unlikely to prove effective with parent-adolescent populations who have dysfunctional communication patterns is most appropriate. Whether those interventions focus on relationship enhancement, social skills and communication training, parent training, or family therapy in its various forms, they are likely to result in statistical but *not* clinically significant changes. More is not always better,

Table 8.3   Core tasks of treatment with parent-adolescent conflict.

Establish a therapeutic alliance.
Foster engagement and involvement in treatment.
Provide psychoeducation.
Nurture hope.
Teach skills.
Foster generalization.
Anticipate and address possible barriers.
Have participants "take credit" (self-attributions) for changes.
Conduct relapse prevention.
Foster maintenance of improvement (use booster sessions and follow-through).

but a comprehensive, focused intervention approach will likely prove to be the most effective. It is asserted in this chapter that the best approach to parent-adolescent conflict involves the following components: thorough functional assessment of the nature and scope of parent-adolescent conflict; consideration of barriers and strengths to treatment; engagement of all family members in the program; maintenance of family engagement; addressing of distorted cognitions and dysfunctional communication and problem-solving skills; continual monitoring of progress; and building in relapse prevention.

REFERENCES

Achenbach, T. M., & Edelbrock, C. S. (1981). Behavioral problems and competencies reported by parents of normal and disturbed children aged four through sixteen. *Monographs of the Society for Research in Child Development, 46*, 82.

Adams, G. R., Gullotta, T., & Clancy, M. A. (1985). Homeless adolescents: A descriptive study of similarities and differences between runaways and throwaways. *Adolescence, 20*, 715–724.

Alexander, J. F., & Parsons, B. V. (1982). *Functional family therapy.* Monterey, CA: Brooks/Cole.

American Psychiatric Association. (1994). *Diagnostic and statistical manual of mental disorders* (4th ed.). Washington, DC: Author.

Arnett, J. J. (1999). Adolescent storm and stress reconsidered. *American Psychologist, 54*, 317–326.

Ary, D. V., Duncan, T. E., Duncan, S. C., & Hops, H. (1999). Adolescent problem behavior: The influence of parents and peers. *Behavior Research and Therapy, 37*, 217–230.

Barkley, R. A., Edwards, G. H., & Robin, A. L. (1999). *Defiant teens: A clinician's manual for assessment and family intervention.* New York: Guilford Press.

Barkley, R. A., Guevremont, D. C., Anastopoulos, A. D., & Fletcher, K. E. (1992). A comparison of three family therapy programs for treating family conflicts in adolescents with Attention-Deficit Hyperactivity Disorder. *Journal of Consulting and Clinical Psychology, 60*, 450–462.

Barton, C., & Alexander, J. F. (1981). Functional family therapy. In A. S. Gurman & D. P. Kniskern (Eds.), *Handbook of family therapy* (pp. 403–443). New York: Brunner/Mazel.

Borduin, C. M., Henggeler, S. W., Hanson, C. L., & Pruitt, J. A. (1985). Verbal problem solving in families of father-absent and father-present delinquent boys. *Child and Family Behavior Therapy, 7*, 51–63.

Bronfenbrenner, U. (1979). *The ecology of human development: Experiments by nature and design.* Cambridge, MA: Harvard University Press.

Buchanan, C. M., Eccles, J. S., Flanagan, C., Midgley, C., Feldlaufer, H., & Harold, R. D. (1990). Parents' and teacher's beliefs about adolescence. *Journal of Youth and Adolescence, 19*, 363–394.

Colten, M. E., & Gore, S. (Eds.). (1991). *Adolescent stress: Causes and consequences.* New York: Aldine De Gruyter.

Conners, C. K. (1969). A teacher rating scale for use in drug studies with children. *American Journal of Psychiatry, 126*, 152–156.

Dekovic, M. (1999a). Parent-adolescent conflict: Possible determinants and consequences. *International Journal of Behavioral Development, 23*, 977–1000.

Dekovic, M. (1999b). Risk and protective factors in the development of problem behavior during adolescence. *Journal of Youth and Adolescence, 28*, 667–685.

Dishion, T. J., Andrews, D. W., & Crosby, L. (1995). Antisocial boys and their friends in early adolescence: Relationship characteristics, quality, and interactional process. *Child Development, 66*, 139–151.

Dishion, T. J., McCord, J., & Poulin, F. (1999). When interventions harm: Peer groups and problems. *American Psychologist, 9*, 755–764.

Erikson, E. H. (1968). *Identity: Youth and crisis.* New York: Norton.

Everett, C. A. (1976). Family assessment and intervention for early adolescent problems. *Journal of Marriage and Family Counseling, 2*, 155–165.

Fincham, F. D., Fernandes, L., & Humphreys, K. (1993). *Communicating in relationships: A guide for couples and professionals.* Champaign, IL: Research Press.

Foreyt, J. P., Poston, W. S. C., Winebarger, A. A., & McGavin, J. K. (1998). Anorexia nervosa and bulimia nervosa. In E. J. Mash & R. A. Barkley (Eds.), *Treatment of childhood disorders* (2nd ed., pp. 647–691). New York: Guilford Press.

Foster, S. L., Prinz, R. J., & O'Leary, K. D. (1983). Impact of problem-solving communication training and generalization procedures on family conflict. *Child and Family Behavior Therapy, 5,* 1–23.

Foster, S. L., & Robin, A. L. (1997). Family conflict and communication in adolescence. In E. J. Mash & L. G. Terdal (Eds.), *Assessment of childhood disorders* (3rd ed., pp. 627–682). New York: Guilford Press.

Foster, S. L., & Robin, A. L. (1998). Parent-adolescent conflict and relationship discord. In E. J. Mash & R. A. Barkley (Eds.), *Treatment of childhood disorders* (2nd ed., pp. 601–646). New York: Guilford Press.

Galambos, N. L., Sears, H. A., Almeida, D. M., & Kolaric, G. C. (1995). Parents' work overload and problem behavior in young adolescents. *Journal of Research on Adolescence, 5,* 201–223.

Grace, N. C., Kelley, M. L., & McCain, A. P. (1993). Attribution processes in mother-adolescent conflict. *Journal of Abnormal Child Psychology, 21,* 199–211.

Hall, G. S. (1904). *Adolescence* (Vols. 1/2). Englewood Cliffs, NJ: Prentice Hall.

Hall, J. A., & Rose, S. D. (1987). Evaluation of parent training in groups for parent-adolescent conflict. *Social Work Research and Abstracts, 23,* 3–8.

Hawkins, J. D., Catalano, R. F., & Miller, J. Y. (1992). Risk and protective factors for alcohol and other drug problems in adolescence and early childhood: Implication for substance abuse prevention. *Psychological Bulletin, 112,* 64–105.

Henggeler, S. L., & Borduin, C. M. (1990). *Family therapy and beyond: A multisystemic approach to treating behavior problems of children and adolescents.* Pacific Grove, CA: Brooks/Cole.

Holmbeck, G. N. (1996). A model of family relational transformations during the transition to adolescence: Parent-adolescent conflict and adaptation. In J. A. Graber & J. Brooks-Gunn (Eds.), *Transitions through adolescence: Interpersonal domains and context.* Mahwah, NJ: Erlbaum.

Jessor, R. (1991). Risk behavior in adolescence: A psychological framework for understanding and action. *Journal of Adolescent Health, 48,* 117–126.

Kaslow, F. (Ed.). (1996). *Handbook of relational diagnosis and dysfunctional family patterns.* New York: Wiley.

Kazdin, A. E., Holland, L., & Crowley, M. (1997). Family experience of barriers to treatment and premature termination from child therapy. *Journal of Consulting and Clinical Psychology, 65,* 453–463.

Kazdin, A. E., & Mariano, P. L. (1998). Childhood and adolescent depression. In E. J. Mash & R. A. Barkley (Eds.), *Treatment of childhood disorders* (2nd ed., pp. 211–248). New York: Guilford Press.

Larson, R., & Richards, M. (1994). *Divergent realities: The emotional lives of mothers, fathers, and adolescents.* New York: Basic Books.

Laursen, B., Coy, K., & Collins, W. A. (1998). Reconsidering changes in parent-child conflict across adolescence: A meta-analysis. *Child Development, 69,* 817–832.

Lewisohn, P. M., Clarke, G. N., Rhode, P., Hops, H., & Seeley, J. R. (1996). A course in coping: A cognitive-behavioral approach to the treatment of adolescent depression. In E. D. Hibbs & P. Jensen (Eds.), *Psychosocial treatments for child and adolescent disorders* (pp. 109–135). Washington, DC: American Psychological Association.

Marshall, V. G., Longwell, L., Goldstein, M. J., & Swanson, J. M. (1990). Family factors associated with aggressive symptomatology in boys with Attention Deficit Hyperactivity Disorder: A research note. *Journal of Child Psychology and Psychiatry, 31,* 629–636.

Mash, E. J., & Terdal, L. G. (1998). Assessment of child and family disturbance: A behavioral-systems approach. In E. J. Mash & L. G. Terdal (Eds.), *Assessment of childhood disorders* (pp. 3–68). New York: Guilford Press.

McCleary, L., & Ridley, T. (1999). Parenting adolescents with ADHD: Evaluation of a psychoeducation group. *Patient Education and Counseling, 38,* 3–10.

McGoldrick, M., Giordano, J., & Pearce, J. K. (Eds.). (1996). *Ethnicity and family therapy* (2nd ed.). New York: Guilford Press.

Meichenbaum, D. L., Pelham, W. E., Gnagy, E. M., & Chronis, A. M. (2000, November). *Explaining and treating "Blue Mondays" for an ADHD/ODD adolescent through a multisystemic approach.* Paper presented at the Association for the Advancement of Behavior Therapy 34th annual conference, New Orleans, LA.

Miller, K. S., Forehand, R., & Kotchick, B. A. (1999). Adolescent sexual behavior in two ethnic minority samples: The role of family variables. *Journal of Marriage and the Family, 61,* 85–98.

Montemayor, R. (1983). Parents and adolescents in conflict: All families some of the time and some families most of the time. *Journal of Early Adolescence, 3,* 83–103.

Montemayor, R. (1986). Family variation in parent-adolescent storm and stress. *Journal of Adolescent Research, 1,* 15–31.

Montemayor, R., & Hanson, E. (1985). A naturalistic view of conflict between adolescents and their parents and siblings. *Journal of Early Adolescence, 5,* 23–30.

Offer, D., & Offer, J. B. (1975). *From teenage to young manhood.* New York: Brooks/Cole.

Offer, D., & Schonert-Reichl, K. A. (1992). Debunking the myths of adolescence: Findings from recent research. *Journal of the American Academy of Child and Adolescent Psychiatry, 31,* 1003–1014.

Paikoff, R., & Brooks-Gunn, J. (1991). Do parent-child relationships change during puberty? *Psychological Bulletin, 110,* 47–66.

Patterson, G. R., DeBarshye, B. D., & Ramsey, E. (1989). A developmental perspective on antisocial behavior. *American Psychologist, 44,* 329–335.

Patterson, G. R., & Forgatch, M. S. (1987). *Parents and adolescents living together: The basics* (Vol. 1). Eugene, OR: Castalia.

Patterson, G. R., Reid, J., & Dishion, T. J. (1992). *Antisocial boys.* Eugene, OR: Castalia.

Pelham, W. E., Gnagy, E. M., Greenslade, K. E., & Milich, R. (1992). Teacher ratings of *DSM-II-R* symptoms for the disruptive behavior disorders. *Journal of the American Academy of Child and Adolescent Psychiatry, 31,* 210–218.

Pelham, W. E., Greiner, A. R., & Gnagy, E. M. (1997). *Children's summer treatment program manual.* Buffalo, NY: Comprehensive Treatment for Attention Deficit Disorder, Inc.

Pelham, W. E., & Hoza, B. (1996). Intensive treatment: A summer treatment program for children with ADHD. In E. Hibbs & P. Jensen (Eds.), *Psychosocial treatments for child and adolescent disorders:*

Empirically based strategies for clinical practices (pp. 311–340). New York: Associated Press.

Pelham, W. E., Milich, R., Murphy, D. A., & Murphy, H. A. (1989). Normative data on the IOWA Conners' Teacher Rating Scale. *Journal of Clinical Child Psychology, 18,* 259–262.

Prinz, R. J., Foster, S., Kent, R. N., & O'Leary, K. D. (1979). Multivariate assessment of conflict in distressed and non-distressed mother-adolescent dyads. *Journal of Applied Behavioral Analysis, 12,* 691–700.

Rae, W. A. (1992). Common adolescent-parent problems. In C. E. Walker & M. C. Roberts (Eds.), *Handbook of clinical child psychology* (2nd ed.). New York: Wiley.

Reed, J. S., & Dubow, E. F. (1997). Cognitive and behavioral predictors of communication in clinic-referred and nonclinical mother-adolescent dyads. *Journal of Marriage and the Family, 59,* 91–102.

Rey, J. M., & Plapp, J. M. (1990). Quality of perceived parenting in oppositional and conduct disordered adolescents. *Journal of the American Academy of Child and Adolescent Psychiatry, 29,* 382–385.

Robin, A. L. (1979). Problem-solving communication training: A behavioral approach to the treatment of parent-adolescent conflict. *American Journal of Family Therapy, 7,* 69–82.

Robin, A. L. (1981). A controlled evaluation of problem-solving communication training with parent-adolescent conflict. *Behavior Therapy, 12,* 593–609.

Robin, A. L. (1998). Training families with ADHD children. In R. A. Barkley (Ed.), *Attention-Deficit Hyperactivity Disorder: A handbook for diagnosis and treatment* (2nd ed., pp. 413–457). New York: Guilford Press.

Robin, A. L., Bedway, M., Siegel, P. T., & Gilroy, M. (1996). Therapy for adolescent anorexia nervosa: Addressing cognitions, feelings, and the family's role. In E. D. Hibbs & P. S. Jensen (Eds.), *Psychosocial treatments for child and adolescent disorders: Empirically based strategies for clinical practice* (pp. 239–262). Washington, DC: American Psychological Association.

Robin, A. L., & Foster, S. L. (1984). Problem-solving communication training: A behavioral-family systems approach to parent-adolescent conflict.

Advances in Child Behavior Analysis and Therapy, 3, 195–240.

Robin, A. L., & Foster, S. L. (1988). Issues Checklist. In M. Hersen & A. S. Bellack (Eds.), *Dictionary of behavioral assessment techniques.* New York: Pergamon Press.

Robin, A. L., & Foster, S. L. (1989). *Negotiating parent-adolescent conflict: A behavioral, family systems approach.* New York: Guilford Press.

Robin, A. L., & Koepke, T. (1990). Behavioral assessment and treatment of parent-adolescent conflict. *Annual Review of Psychology, 25,* 178–215.

Robin, A. L., & Weiss, J. G. (1980). Criterion-related validity of behavioral and self-report measures of problem-solving communication skills in distressed and non-distressed parent-adolescent dyads. *Behavioral Assessment, 2,* 339–352.

Rutter, M., Graham, P., Chadwick, O. F., & Yule, W. (1976). Adolescent turmoil: Fact or fiction? *Journal of Child Psychology and Psychiatry and Allied Disciplines, 17,* 35–56.

Schwartz, C. E., Dorer, D. J., Beardslee, W. R., Lavor, P. W., & Keller, M. B. (1990). Maternal expressed emotion and parental Affective Disorder: Risk of childhood Depressive Disorder, substance abuse, or Conduct Disorder. *Journal of Psychiatric Research, 24,* 231–250.

Smetana, J. G. (1996). Adolescent-parent conflict: Implications of adaptive and nonadaptive development. In D. Cicchetti & S. L. Toth (Eds.), *Adolescence: Opportunities and challenges* (Vol. 7, pp. 1–46). Rochester, NY: University of Rochester Press.

Smetana, J. G., & Gaines, C. (1999). Adolescent-parent conflict in middle-class African American families. *Child Development, 70,* 1447–1463.

Smith, B. H., Molina, B., & Eggers, S. E. (1993). *Parent-Teenager Negotiation manual.* Unpublished manual.

Steinberg, L. (1990). Interdependency in the family: Autonomy, conflict and harmony in the parent-adolescent relationship. In S. S. Feldman & G. R. Elliot (Eds.), *At the threshold: The developing adolescent* (pp. 255–276). Cambridge, MA: Harvard University Press.

Steinberg, L. (2000). The family at adolescence: Transition and transformation. *Journal of Adolescent Health, 27,* 170–178.

Steinberg, L., Mounts, N. S., Lamborn, S. D., & Dornbusch, S. M. (1991). Authoritative parenting and adolescent adjustment across varied ecological niches. *Journal of Research in Adolescence, 1,* 19–36.

Steinberg, L., & Steinberg, W. (1994). *Crossing paths: How your child's adolescence triggers your own crisis.* New York: Simon & Schuster.

Szapocznik, J., & Coatsworth, J. D. (1999). An eco-developmental framework for organizing the influences on drug abuse: A developmental model of risk and protection. In M. D. Glantz & C. R. Hartel (Eds.), *Drug abuse: Origins and intervention.* Washington, DC: American Psychological Association.

Szapocznik, J., & Kurtines, W. M. (1989). *Breakthroughs in family therapy with drug abusing problem youth.* New York: Springer.

Szapocznik, J., Perez-Vidal, A., Brickman, A., Foote, F. H., Santisteban, D., Hervis, O. E., et al. (1988). Engaging adolescent drug abusers and their families into treatment: A strategic structural systems approach. *Journal of Consulting and Clinical Psychology, 56,* 552–557.

Szapocznik, J., & Williams, R. A. (2000). Brief strategic family therapy. *Clinical Child and Family Psychology Review, 3,* 117–135.

CHAPTER 9

Understanding and Treating Eating Disorders

W. STEWART AGRAS AND ROBIN F. APPLE

The eating disorders usually emerge during adolescence. The rarest of the disorders, Anorexia Nervosa (AN), presents in full clinical form in two peaks of onset, the first around 14 years of age and the second around 18 years of age (Lucas, Beard, et al., 1991). Both Bulimia Nervosa (BN) and Binge Eating Disorder (BED) onset at a mean age of 18 years, preceded by concerns regarding weight, shape, and dieting, which increase in frequency during adolescence, and may set the scene for the development of binge eating and eventually purging in the individual at risk. This chapter focuses on the use of cognitive-behavioral therapy (CBT), primarily in the treatment of BN and BED, the two disorders for which there is the best evidence for the specific utility of this form of treatment. The relative effectiveness of alternative methods of treatment for the three eating disorders will also be considered.

THE DEVELOPMENT OF COGNITIVE-BEHAVIORAL THERAPY

Although the eating disorders, particularly AN, have been described for centuries, the application of empirically based psychotherapeutic treatments to these disorders is a more recent development. In the case of AN, there have been few studies of CBT and none with an adequate sample size. Hence, the research to date does not allow for definitive conclusions regarding the efficacy of CBT in this disorder. The stimulus for the development of CBT for BN was the rapid increase in the number of individuals with this condition presenting to clinics in the Western world during the mid-1970s (Garner, Olmsted, & Garfinkel, 1985). Because the literature on treatment at the time was based on a few case reports, there was little guidance available for the clinician. Fairburn (1981) at Oxford University first described a form of CBT specifically aimed at treating BN. The treatment drew on the general principles of behavior change and was aimed at reducing excessive dieting and correcting maladaptive cognitions regarding diet, weight, and shape concerns. This treatment approach was applied to BN by a number of researchers, first in uncontrolled and then in controlled studies. As these studies progressed, the treatment underwent modification and has now been manualized (Agras & Apple, 1997; Apple & Agras, 1997; Fairburn, Marcus, & Wilson, 1993).

As research into the nature and treatment of BN progressed, it became clear that a parallel eating disorder existed, characterized by binge eating not associated with compensatory behaviors such as purging, and often associated with obesity (Spitzer et al., 1993). This led to two developments: First, BED was added to the fourth edition of the *Diagnostic and Statistical Manual of Mental Disorders (DSM-IV)* as a disorder requiring further study; second, the therapies developed for BN, including CBT, were applied in controlled studies to BED.

THEORETICAL CONSTRUCTS

The cognitive-behavioral model of BN on which the treatment is based includes several interacting factors that perpetuate the disorder. The core components of the model have been demonstrated through both clinical observation and laboratory studies (Fairburn & Hay, 1992).

At the center of the model is an overvaluation of thinness (which may be derived from a number of sources, including low self-esteem during childhood and adolescence; a family environment characterized by high achievement expectations, lack of warmth, or a genetic predisposition toward overweight; and growing up in a culture that overvalues a slim body

shape and low weight). Whatever the cause(s), BN usually includes rejection of the natural body shape and appropriate weight range.

This drive for thinness leads to a pattern of dietary restriction, supported by a number of erroneous beliefs regarding weight, eating, exercise, and metabolism, which becomes self-perpetuating. Prolonged efforts to diet by reducing the number of eating episodes, calories taken in, or types of foods eaten eventually result in states of physiological and psychological deprivation (Keys, Brozek, & Henschel, 1950; Polivy & Herman, 1987; Rossiter, Agras, Losch, & Telch, 1988). Over time, these deprivation states give way to out-of-control binge eating followed by compensatory behaviors such as purging through vomiting, laxative use, or excessive exercise. Purging is initially reinforcing because of its ability to decrease the physical discomfort associated with overeating as well as anxiety about weight gain; it also becomes symbolic of reversing many of the other negative feeling states (e.g., loss of control, shame, extreme fullness) that occur in response to binge eating (Kenardy, Arnow, & Agras, 1996). The gratifying aspects of purging, however, tend to be short-lived. Typically, soon after purging is completed, a resurgence of emotional distress (e.g., worsening of negative views of the body and the self and intensification of the same deprivation states caused by dieting) resurface (Kenardy et al., 1996). As these feelings and attitudes lower the threshold for future binge and purge episodes, a vicious cycle of binge eating and purging is established.

The treatment of BN and BED derive from this model. CBT for BN is conducted in three phases: (1) normalizing the meal pattern (i.e., overcoming dietary restraint); (2) addressing additional binge triggers, including faulty cognitions about weight and shape; and (3) maintaining change and preventing relapse. Treatment duration is usually about six months. With an agenda including review of food records, introduction of relevant topics, summary, and assignment of homework, sessions are typically held on a weekly basis, with the exception of the first four and last three sessions, which are held twice weekly and every other week, respectively. Like any other effective treatment, CBT for BN requires the presence of a collaborative and supportive therapeutic alliance that should begin to take form during the first few sessions. Given the interpersonal sensitivity of many individuals with eating disorders, the establishment of a strong therapy relationship is a key first step in treatment.

METHODS OF ASSESSMENT AND INTERVENTION

ASSESSMENT

The clinical approach to the assessment of an eating disordered patient should focus on a detailed description of the core eating disorder symptoms and the history of their development, including the relationship of particular life events or stressors that may have been associated with the onset and worsening of these symptoms. Periods during which amelioration of the eating disorder symptoms occurred may also be of interest and should be reviewed for any changes in dieting or psychosocial factors associated with the remission. The core eating disordered behaviors to be explored include binge eating; compensatory behaviors such as purging, excessive exercise, dieting or fasting, diuretic use, the use of enemas, and chewing and spitting out food; and perceptions and concerns about weight and body shape. Patients with AN are the most difficult to assess because of their denial of the severity of the illness.

The key characteristics of a binge are loss of the sense of control over eating and consumption of a large amount of food. To meet criteria for an objective binge, the amount of food usually exceeds what would be eaten in two meals, a minimum of approximately 1,500 kilo-calories (kcal). Binges characterized by loss of control with the consumption of smaller amounts of food are classified as subjective binges. Compensatory behaviors are engaged in to counterbalance excessive caloric consumption or to alter weight and shape. The type and extent of dieting and purging should be carefully reviewed by taking a detailed history of food consumption and compensatory activities during the prior few days. Typically, the eating disordered patient will eat little during regular meals, will eat fewer meals than usual, and will choose foods low in calories.

It is also important to take a detailed developmental history focusing on life events that may have led to low self-esteem. Such factors may include physical and sexual abuse, competition with siblings, maternal or paternal rejection, or reactions to parental divorce or relationship failures. In addition, there may be factors specific to the development of an eating disorder, for example, maternal concern over the patient's weight, shape, or eating during childhood and adolescence; teasing by peers about weight and shape; or engaging in particularly competitive sports or ballet a great deal.

In addition to the elicitation of specific eating disordered psychopathology, it is important to investigate associated general psychopathology both past and present, including depression, anxiety disorders such as social phobia and panic disorder, substance use and abuse, and the existence of personality disorder. Such psychopathology is frequently associated with all three of the eating disorders, with about half of eating disordered patients having a past major depressive episode, one-fifth having a current depression, and a third having a past anxiety disorder (Agras, Walsh, Fairburn, Wilson, & Kraemer, 2000b; Telch & Stice, 1998). Evaluation should include a medical examination with accompanying blood tests (e.g., for electrolytes and anemia), and for those who binge and purge, a dental examination if they are not receiving regular dental care, because of the deleterious effect of sugars and acid in the mouth on dental enamel. More complex medical assessments are necessary for patients with AN who have substantial weight loss and for the obese patient with BED, the latter to assess conditions comorbid with obesity such as hypertension, Type-II diabetes, and hypercholesterolemia.

Useful questionnaires include the Three Factor Eating Questionnaire (TFEQ), which measures dietary restraint, disinhibition of eating, and hunger (Stunkard & Messick, 1985); the Questionnaire on Eating and Weight Patterns-Revised (Spitzer, Yanovski, & Marcus, 1993), which assesses eating disorder symptoms and is useful to give to patients with an eating disorder before the initial interview; and the Binge Eating Scale (BES), which assesses severity of binge eating (Gormally, Black, Daston, & Rardin, 1982). In addition, because of the prevalence of depression associated with eating disorders, the Beck Depression Inventory (Beck, 1987) is useful in the assessment of eating disorder patients. Both the TFEQ and the BES are useful indicators of clinical progress, although the principal indicators are the changes in binge eating and purging behavior, which are best assessed through continuous self-monitoring.

From a research viewpoint, the gold standard for the assessment of eating disorders has become the Eating Disorder Examination (EDE; Z. Cooper, Cooper, & Fairburn, 1989). This structured interview with rules for coding responses has good validity and reliability and is useful for predictive purposes. The interview objectively documents binge eating and purging rates over a 28-day period, as well as dietary restraint, weight concern, shape concern, and eating concern. In addition, the EDE generates *DSM-IV* diagnoses for the eating disorders. (For those interested in a more detailed approach to evaluation of the various facets of the eating disorders, see Allison, 1995.)

COGNITIVE-BEHAVIORAL THERAPY

The First Phase of Treatment

For most patients, a primary focus on normalizing the meal pattern extends through session 8 or so, when most who will respond to CBT have demonstrated some signs of improvement (Agras, Crow, et al., 2000). Introduction to the CBT model for BN and BED (see Figure 9.1) sets the stage for the interventions that are included in this phase, which utilize behavioral, psychoeducational, and supportive elements to consistently but gently encourage change.

Patients are first shown the figure that illustrates the model (which may be drawn for them in session), and the links between low self-esteem, negative emotions, overvaluation of low weight and slim shape, dietary restriction, binge eating and purging are pointed out. They are then asked to reflect on any parallels they have noted between the model and their own experience with BN or BED. In this way, the importance of regularly consuming planned meals and snacks to decrease the cycle of strict dieting, binge eating, and purging is highlighted.

The therapist then explains the need to keep records of food intake, including such details as the content and amounts of foods and liquids consumed; the time, place, and context in which the eating occurred; associated thoughts and feelings; characterization of the episode as a meal, snack, or binge; and the occurrence of purging. In keeping records, the aim is to better inform patients and their therapists about the problem patterns of eating and the factors that contribute to them as well as episodes of eating that are handled successfully. To begin the process of regularizing their meal patterns, patients are initially instructed to "eat by the clock," going for no more than three to four hours without food. Adopting this schedule of eating will interrupt dieting that involves skipping or delaying meals or snacks. Dieting involving limiting the

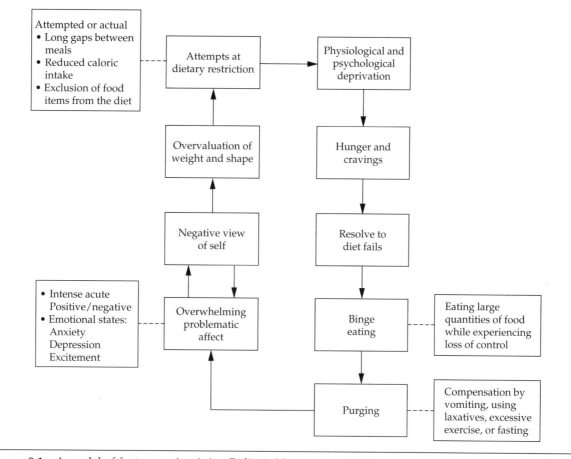

Figure 9.1 A model of factors maintaining Bulimia Nervosa on which cognitive-behavioral therapy is based.

contents and quantities of foods consumed is addressed later in treatment.

In the first few sessions, a regimen of weekly weighing to combat tendencies toward compulsive overweighing or scale avoidance is prescribed. This intervention helps patients to desensitize themselves to the numbers on the scale and to keep track of their weight during a time when they are experimenting with changes in food intake as well as purging behaviors. For patients who have been using laxatives, a "cold turkey" approach to discontinuing is recommended because there is no evidence that prolonging the process is useful. Patients are educated about any side effects that may occur and are supported through the experience. Finally, encouragement of participation in pleasurable alternative activities incompatible

with eating helps patients to soothe and distract themselves from becoming preoccupied with the issues of their eating disorder. Simultaneously, recommendations to eat only in appropriate settings (such as the kitchen and dining room, rather than the bedroom or car) can decrease the number and strength of food cues originating in situations that have become associated with eating. Similarly, practice in eating in a planful but relaxed fashion can reacquaint patients with the enjoyment of eating and help them get back in touch with natural hunger and satiety signals.

The Second Phase of Treatment
Once the patient is eating more regularly, with fewer binge and purge episodes, the second phase of treatment can begin. This phase is

more cognitively oriented, with a focus on identifying and working through the triggers to binge and purge episodes, bouts of restriction, and other aspects of the eating disorder. Whereas in the first phase, the role of hunger as a trigger is explained and addressed through prescription of the regular pattern of eating, in the second phase, there is an emphasis on the problematic situations, thoughts, or emotions that might be detrimental to healthy eating. Often, these are first identified in the context column of the food record.

Problem solving, often introduced early in this phase, involves first helping patients to identify a problem situation linked to binge eating or another aspect of the eating disorder. The second step teaches brainstorming about solutions to this problem. In the third step, patients are taught skills for evaluating the desirability of each solution based on likely outcomes. In the last step, based on this evaluation, they are instructed to choose one or more of the solutions that will lead to adaptive rather than maladaptive behavior. A related intervention is challenging problem thoughts, a tool that helps patients counter distorted attitudes or thoughts that may serve as precipitants to certain eating disordered behaviors such as binge eating or purging. This skill involves identifying the core problem thought, gathering data to first support and then refute the thought, and coming up with a reasoned and balanced conclusion that can guide the patient to healthy behavior.

The feared foods list intervention is used to help patients become more comfortable and flexible in consuming foods that they may have long avoided due to concerns about their effect on shape and weight. It requires that patients first create a list of these "bad" or "fattening" foods and rank order them according to difficulty on a scale of 1 to 4. Then, beginning with the food items rated as easiest, the patient attempts to consume moderate-size portions on a weekly or biweekly basis. This experimentation is done only in contexts that are considered safe, that is, free of risk factors for binge eating or purging (e.g., absence of negative mood and no access to excessively large quantities of food or opportunities to purge).

In certain cases, when a patient is overweight and in need of nutritional guidance to prevent weight concerns from exacerbating the eating disorder via resumption of strict dieting, examination of and suggestions about food contents and quantities for purposes of weight management can be included. With these patients, for whom strict dieting is not recommended, taking a reasonable amount of responsibility for food choices, along the lines of a "heart healthy" approach to reducing portion sizes and fat intake, is acceptable. Patients are encouraged to view prescriptions of this nature as preventive in the sense that stabilizing their weight in a comfortable range can offset a temptation to resume restrictive dieting. Recommendations for moderate, regular exercise can be equally helpful to the overweight subgroup for similar reasons, in addition to enhancing both body image and mood. Other strategies, such as breathing retraining, progressive muscle relaxation, and guided imagery can be used to help patients regulate their emotions, including negative feelings about the body (Wiser & Telch, 1999).

The Third Phase of Treatment

During the final phase of treatment, which usually comprises two or three sessions held every other week, patients are encouraged to create a maintenance plan. They are also asked to anticipate and problem-solve about upcoming events or situations that might prove to be stressful or challenging to the progress they have made. Patients are educated about differentiating between short-term lapses and longer-term relapses, with a goal of applying the tools they've learned to short-circuit problems before they get out of hand. If confronted with eating-related difficulties, they are encouraged to apply these tools first before recontacting their therapist for additional assistance.

CASE EXAMPLE

Several factors led to our presenting this treatment case, which illustrates some of the issues that are common to adolescent-onset BED and BN. First, the patient's problems began as "recreational" indulgences in the context of her social group. Only later, when these problems became more extreme and preoccupying, was it clear that they warranted consultation with a professional. Second, she began therapy at a slightly higher than average weight and gained a few pounds during treatment. This heightened her sensitivity to weight and shape concerns and kept her at continued risk for resuming a pattern of restrictive dieting that could restart the bulimic cycle, requiring the therapist to make the gentle, "heart healthy" recommendations regarding nutrition and exercise described above. Finally, because she experienced a number of significant life events throughout the course of treatment, the case exemplified the challenge of staying within the parameters of CBT for bulimia when a patient has other important, but only indirectly linked issues.

BACKGROUND INFORMATION AND HISTORY OF PRESENTING PROBLEM

Meryl, a 21-year-old recent college graduate, came to the clinic requesting treatment for BN of approximately five years duration. The first session of CBT involved a clinical interview that covered the current symptom picture and relevant history, as well as psychosocial, family, and medical history. Meryl was straightforward and at times tearful, demonstrating an understanding that many complex factors had contributed to her eating disorder. She described feeling as if she had "never fit in" either at home or at school. With respect to her family, she was three years younger than a favored brother, who apparently was valued by their parents because he was "tall, lean, intelligent,

and even-keeled like them," whereas she was "shorter, pudgier, unattractive, too sensitive, and overly emotional." Meryl also compared herself unfavorably to her peers, believing that she was noticeably "more clumsy and ugly" and had to "work much harder" to obtain acceptable grades.

However, the onset of Meryl's eating disorder at age 14 was unremarkable in that her occasional overeating episodes occurred only in the context of group activities where such eating indulgences were the norm and therefore were not a source of significant concern. Rather, "pigging out" occasionally on junk foods, including pizza, chips, ice cream, and sweets, represented an easily obtainable source of pleasure and fun for her and her friends, despite their shared, mild concerns about weight (which also seemed normative for their age group).

When Meryl turned 17, however, and began her senior year of high school, her perception of her shape, weight, and eating behavior changed as she became more interested in boys and began to date. Although still within the high-average range for her height, she was particularly concerned about having put on 10 pounds in the preceding year and became determined to lose the weight before leaving for college. Together with two equally weight-conscious girlfriends, she embarked on a "crash diet" with a goal of losing 20 pounds—which was probably 10 pounds too many, given her body type and weight history. She was able to reach her weight goal following several weeks on a very strict regimen of diet and exercise. Although initially ecstatic at her success, she soon realized that without continuing to severely restrict her diet, maintaining this new, low weight would be impossible. Resolving to stick with her diet, she began to succumb to urges to overeat when extreme hunger, as well as a host of other negative feelings (e.g., irritability, anxiety, fatigue, some of which were associated with the ongoing frustrations of dieting), got the best of her. Soon, she became caught in a cycle of "eating next to nothing" and "totally overdoing it."

This pattern of uncontrolled overeating and restriction wreaked havoc on Meryl's emotional state and self-esteem. Although binge eating helped to distract her from these feelings momentarily, generally, they worsened afterward, particularly if she started to worry about the eventuality of weight gain with continued bingeing. Once, when overwrought after bingeing, she attempted to make herself vomit, having read about different methods of purging in a magazine article on BN. Although not successful in inducing vomiting the first time, after several rounds of "experimentation" with various foods, liquids, and periods of delay after eating, she eventually discovered a formula that worked. In discovering this "eating strategy" that would allow her to "have her cake and eat it too," she felt both elated and disgusted. She noticed, as do others who purge, that both the frequency and size of her binges began to increase. To compensate for the increased caloric intake, she began to use laxatives to ensure that "everything got out."

Like other bulimic individuals, Meryl was demoralized to discover after several months of bingeing and purging that her weight had not decreased as expected but had actually increased by about 10 pounds. Still not wanting to accept the futility of dieting, she wrongly attributed her weight gain to "not dieting well enough" and persevered with her weight loss effort, continuing to binge and purge at least once a day. The anxiety and stress associated with preparing to leave for college—a state school on the opposite coast from her family—resulted in a worsening of her disordered eating behaviors. Fortunately, though, the exacerbation of her symptoms prompted her to consider treatment. After a presentation about campus mental health services, she contacted a therapist, with whom she then worked for a few months. However, when her schedule became too busy, she discontinued her regular, individual sessions and instead experimented with a variety of treatments, intermittently attending individual sessions, a self-help eating disorders group, and self-growth workshops. As none of these short-term treatments were helpful, she remained fairly hopeless about resolving her eating disorder and eventually gave up on treatment, opting instead for self-help books and rationalizing that her symptoms, with the exception of a higher-than-ideal weight, were not that bothersome.

When she finished college, having achieved "barely acceptable" grades, she felt fortunate to obtain a job offer in her field and eagerly accepted, even though it would require an interstate move. The transition proved to be more stressful than she expected, particularly as she quickly began to have some misgivings about her capacity to perform well in her position. She felt disliked and disrespected by her colleagues, sensed that her higher-ups were scrutinizing her work, and worried that she might be asked to leave. These concerns took a toll on her mental state, and again, her eating disorder became much worse. Recognizing that things could only get worse in her life if the eating disorder continued untreated, she contacted our clinic.

ASSESSMENT AND DIAGNOSIS

Through participating in a semistructured clinical interview, along with the EDE, Meryl reported symptoms suggestive of a primary Axis I diagnosis of Bulimia Nervosa (with Atypical Depression representing a secondary diagnosis). She described recurrent episodes of binge eating during which she experienced a loss of control. To reduce her fears of weight gain, she compensated for these episodes by purging, using both vomiting and laxatives. Her self-concept was shaky and influenced unduly by her body shape and weight. In addition to the BN, she also described low mood, tearfulness, poor concentration, irritability, anhedonia, and some tendency toward social isolation.

The full 5-axis diagnosis for Meryl when she started treatment was as follows:

Axis I: 307.51, Bulimia Nervosa and 311 Depression NOS.

Axis II: 71.09, No diagnosis.

Axis III: Asthma.

Axis IV: Occupational problems (threat of job loss); Social problems (limited local social support network).

Axis V: GAF = 60 (current).

CASE FORMULATION

In many ways, Meryl represents a "classic" example of an individual first developing and then "getting stuck" in a cycle of BN in that the elements of poor self-concept, sensitive temperament, strained relationships and a tendency to weigh more than what was considered to be "ideal" were all present. She had struggled from an early age with a poor self-concept, a problem that was amplified by a family environment characterized by a distant relationship with her parents and competition with a brother, whom her parents seemed to favor. Within the context of family and later in school, she felt marginalized and excluded, attributing this to an array of self-described "personal defects" that ranged from an "overly sensitive and emotional" temperament to physical appearance and weight concerns.

During her adolescence, when she first became interested in boys, she began to diet in an attempt to master these feelings. She was initially successful in losing weight, experiencing herself as slender and more attractive after her weight loss. However, when her resolve to diet was worn down due to increasingly strong cues to eat (stemming from the physiological and psychological deprivation associated with dieting), she began to binge. Even though prior to her weight loss she had been able to enjoy the occasional "out-of-control" eating episode as a social and recreational outlet with friends, it became increasingly linked, after her successful experience of dieting, with the anxiety of weight gain.

Eventually, Meryl learned to purge after bingeing, first using vomiting and later also using laxatives, to reduce this anxiety by ridding her body of the excess food and calories she had consumed. Although as her weight slowly increased, she quickly became aware that restrictive dieting, binge eating, and purging was not proving to be an effective weight management strategy, she was soon entrenched in the cycle of BN. Then, as she confronted a variety of significant life events and transitions (e.g., starting college and then her first job after college), which yielded a number of strong emotions, her eating problems worsened. She began to binge eat and purge to numb or distract herself from all kinds of experiences and sensations: hunger as well as intense feeling states involving anxiety, loneliness, and depression. Overwhelmed by her symptoms and not knowing how to begin the process of breaking free of the eating disordered cycle, she once again sought treatment.

TREATMENT APPROACH AND RATIONALE FOR ITS SELECTION

Data on efficacy suggest that CBT is more effective, or more rapidly effective, than other psychotherapies in the treatment of BN (see "Efficacy" below). In addition, CBT is more effective than antidepressant medication (Agras et al., 1992; Mitchell et al., 1990). These considerations led to the selection of CBT as the first line treatment for BN. An additional consideration was the patient's history, which fit well with the theoretical rationale underlying CBT. Specifically, her early history of low self-esteem and sensitivity about a weight problem compounded by aberrant eating patterns and dieting efforts provided a clear parallel with the CBT model. This impression was solidified in the initial session, when she "saw herself" in the CBT model and expressed a willingness to make a commitment to treatment, despite some ambivalent feelings based on her mixed experiences with prior therapies. She understood that an agreement to participate in CBT meant acceptance of the basic session structure (e.g., a review of records, agenda setting, introduction of new topics, and assignment of homework), and also openness to experimenting with the range of model-driven interventions.

COURSE OF TREATMENT

In the first session, Meryl was asked to draw parallels between her own experience with bulimia and the CBT model. While easily endorsing the contributions of low self-esteem, poor body image, and strong emotions to the binge-purge cycle, she was surprised to learn about the central role of eating too little, as she had not recently thought of herself as a "dieter." Based on a review of her food intake patterns in the few days prior to the session, however, she concluded that she had been displaying multiple forms of dieting behavior. These included delaying or skipping meals and snacks, reducing portion sizes, and attempting to limit or avoid certain food groups, such as sweets and high-fat snacks—the very foods that she craved and succumbed to during binges.

Based on the information gleaned during the record review, a prescription was made of a regular pattern of eating including, ideally, three meals and two snacks a day. She was both willing and "terrified" to eat more frequently, sharing the commonly held fear that "I'll only gain weight if I eat more and I already weigh too much." However, by adopting an attitude of experimentation together with a "small steps" approach, she agreed to "test out" some part of the recommended pattern

for the few days between sessions. She started with the reasonable goal of "getting something in at lunchtime," a meal she had often avoided despite frequent invitations from colleagues to join them for lunch.

Meryl arrived at the next session with completed food records documenting her success at eating something for lunch. She then briefly engaged in a productive records review before suddenly becoming tearful and upset, commenting that "a lot of stuff is coming up for me right now." She elaborated that making even these minor improvements in her eating had ignited a fear of "moving forward and experiencing life after the eating disorder . . . because my eating problems might have been a way to avoid other issues." The other issues apparently included ongoing dissatisfaction with her job and worries about being fired. Given that this was just session 2, the therapist at this juncture was faced with a dilemma. Although she wanted to empathize with Meryl, validate her feelings, and enable her to feel understood and safe to express herself in therapy, she was also mindful of the need to remain in the CBT frame. She recognized that further, in-depth exploration of these issues could distract from fully communicating the nature and primary objectives of this early stage of CBT. Specifically, it would be more difficult to establish the session structure and organization, review the model, examine in detail the most important aspects of the food record, and clarify the necessity of working toward a regular pattern of eating. In weighing several options for responding, the therapist chose the following:

It sounds like you're going through a really hard time right now and that you're feeling sad and somewhat overwhelmed by your work life and some other situations. I'd like to help you work through feelings, but rather than continue to talk about them directly, I wonder if you would be willing to experiment with staying on track and following the session agenda that we'd set to discuss the issues of your eating? In the same way that the recommendation to structure your eating has been helpful during the past few days, my hope is that our continuing along with the session agenda as planned will be equally helpful in teaching you a new way to handle a variety of difficult situations. In time, we'll be able to talk more specifically about the issues you're concerned with, particularly those that trigger some of your problem eating episodes, but for today, are you willing to go with me on sticking with our agenda for the session?

Meryl appeared somewhat more calm and reassured following this response, sharing her perspective that the need to focus on her eating problems before working on other concerns was understandable. She then added that her distress might have been more closely linked to the eating disorder than she first realized, acknowledging, "Mostly, I'm just afraid to gain weight because I'm already 10 pounds higher than my goal." In response, a brief discussion ensued about the need to put weight loss "on the back burner" during CBT. The therapist offered this perspective:

> At this early stage of treatment, it is important to put weight loss goals in the background and focus instead on stabilizing your eating so that you are no longer bingeing and purging. The only way to do this is to give up dieting for now. I want to reassure you, though, that we will not lose sight of your weight concerns. Rather, in time we can expand our discussion beyond the focus on normalizing your pattern of eating to include attention to food contents and quantities with an emphasis on helping you eat the foods you like in moderation, and with a sense of mastery and control. These general principles should help you land in a stable and comfortable weight range. If not, we can tinker with your eating patterns later to help you get closer to that range. That way you won't be tempted to resume a pattern of restrictive dieting, which would put you at continued risk for resuming the binge-purge cycle.

The remainder of the session proceeded smoothly. Meryl acknowledged the conflict between her ongoing weight gain concerns and related urges to diet and her newfound appreciation of the need to "eat more" since learning that "starving myself" had only worsened the bulimic cycle. Wishing that she could rely on herself to "eat when I'm hungry and stop when I'm full," she also accepted the need to start with "mechanical" eating as a temporary means for reinstating a more normal meal pattern based on the therapist's explanation:

> The prescription of regular meals and snacks is done to interrupt the cycle of binge eating and purging. Once you have that down, and are no longer binge eating and purging, you can become more flexible and adapt it to suit your individual needs.

Toward the end of the session, the issue of discontinuing laxatives was addressed in relation to Meryl's describing her discomfort at having a full stomach and a related fear that "food is never going to leave my body." She was educated about the costs of using laxatives, encouraged to discontinue laxatives in "cold turkey" fashion, and informed of the typical side-effects of laxative withdrawal. Admirably, at the conclusion of the session, she agreed to try the two challenging interventions that were introduced: withdrawing from laxatives and, although she had been avoiding the scale, weighing herself once before the next meeting.

With pride, Meryl reported at the beginning of session 3 that she had discontinued laxatives entirely despite some bloating and discomfort. (From that point in treatment she remained laxative-free.) She also had weighed herself and was able to accept a 3-pound gain, attributing it appropriately to pronounced fluid retention associated with eating more regularly and withdrawing from laxatives. She had continued to make strides toward normalizing her meal pattern, still taking in something at noontime.

But her records revealed a persistent problem of nighttime eating: "Although hunger is not the problem and food is not the solution, I eat out of boredom because there is nothing else to do." To help Meryl target this and related high-risk situations (e.g., due to boredom, other strong emotions, or feelings of fullness or "fatness"), she was asked to create a list of pleasurable alternative activities that were incompatible with eating, to be used for distraction or self-soothing. Although she expressed difficulty in "finding the right things to do," she was willing to try to compile a list that would include a number of activities put on hold during the years when her eating disorder had dominated much of her time.

Considerable gains were demonstrated during the next few sessions (3 through 5) extending over two weeks. Meryl reported that her binge eating and purging decreased from more than once a day to daily, to just three times a week, and that how she had ceased purging altogether. She described ongoing efforts to "accept my hunger as normal" as well as the need to eat regularly and by the clock, a pattern that she had been successful in maintaining on most days. She disclosed, "I already feel better, more in control, less guilty about eating, and since the treatment is working, more confident in my attitude about finding another job and handling other things." She had created an appropriately varied pleasurable alternative activities list comprised of sleeping, taking a walk, buying flowers, working in the garden, taking a bubble bath, doing her nails, or "for times when I'm full, just reminding myself that it's okay to feel full after eating."

Still, she admitted ongoing frustration with her weight, which now fell within the high-average range, approximately 3 pounds higher than when treatment began, "but 18 pounds over what I weighed when I was really skinny several years ago," a fact she continued to ruminate about. These issues were addressed by retaining a psychoeducational and supportive focus

that spanned a number of areas. The first was education about the origins and likely temporary nature of her weight gain during treatment, including discussion of the impact of regularizing her meal pattern and discontinuing all forms of purging. Second was examination of the costs and benefits of *weighing somewhat less and remaining bulimic* compared *with weighing slightly more and recovering from her eating disorder*. Third was a discussion of triggers to "feelings of fatness" (e.g., keeping items of clothing that were too small and too tight). Fourth was an exploration of the meaning attached to weighing a few pounds more than what was considered "ideal" and options regarding succumbing to or fighting back against the tendency to overvalue thinness and the slim body ideal. Finally, encouragement was offered to remain inconclusive about her body shape and size "for now," until she had recovered even more fully from her eating disorder.

Meryl raised the issue of physical exercise at this time, admitting that it could help her manage her weight and improve her body image but acknowledging a simultaneous hesitance to get started, which resulted in her concluding, "If I want to change it enough, I'll start exercising."

Session 6 began with Meryl reporting that she had had no binge or purge episodes in the prior week, despite the fact that her food records continued to reveal occasional, fairly long gaps between meals. These were important in that they indicated a lack of planning and also seemed linked to her sensitivity to feeling full after meals (i.e., when she allowed herself to become overly hungry, she was prone to eat beyond the point of satiety). Apparently, stress was also playing a role in hindering Meryl's efforts to normalize her pattern of eating. She noticed a general tendency to undereat in response to stress, which she "paid for later" by overeating. Also, she acknowledged a number of current stressors (e.g., worries about being fired from her job and associated financial strain). These negatively affected her mood, interrupted her use of pleasurable activities, and adversely affected both the pattern and the content of her meals.

Despite these areas of difficulty, Meryl had made considerable and obvious progress in normalizing her eating. For this reason, and also because she had already demonstrated a natural facility in tracking her thoughts and conjuring up alternative perspectives regarding her eating, the treatment at this point shifted into phase 2. This phase is more cognitively oriented, focusing on identifying and working through triggers to various aspects of the eating problem. In session 6, Meryl was introduced to a formal technique for challenging problem thoughts (CPT), as shown in Figure 9.2, along with an excerpt from her food record, which reveals the potentially problematic thought.

From this session on, Meryl began to use the CPT exercise regularly to examine thoughts associated with problem eating episodes and times when she concluded that she was fat. She began to persistently question her reasoning when she formed strong and negative conclusions about her body weight and shape. She also began to reconsider her strategy of using certain items of clothing (many of which were tight or too small) to determine the acceptability of her weight, coming up in one case with this conclusion: "There are certain clothes that

Daily Food Record Problem Thoughts

Day _____   Date _____

Time	Food Intake	Location	Binge	Purge	Situation
6:30 A.M.	Bowl of cereal with milk, medium size	Kitchen			Breakfast—hungry!
9:30 A.M.	2 peanut butter and honey sandwiches				Craving this and hungry but shouldn't have it!

Challenging Problem Thoughts

Step 1. Identify the underlying problem thought.

Peanut butter should be consumed only at lunch or dinner and never eaten as a snack in the morning—that means I've blown it for the day!

Step 2. List objective evidence to support.

• Maybe not ideal to eat 2 PB sandwiches at once—seems like an overly large portion for a snack.

Step 3. List objective evidence to dispute.

• I was craving PB and sometimes okay to satisfy a craving.
• There is no rule that PB is an afternoon or evening food only.
• Others use PB as a midmorning snack.

Step 4. Develop a reasoned conclusion based on lists of evidence.

I can eat PB in moderation at any time and I don't need to beat up on myself by bingeing and purging, or in any other way, for eating it this morning.

Step 5. Determine a course of action based on your logical conclusion.

Eat normally for the rest of the day and try to do a bit more physical activity if worried; also keep mind occupied with other topics to distract from preoccupation with the PB snack.

Figure 9.2   An excerpt from a food record and a challenging exercise based on the record.

don't fit, but those might have been bought too small because there are others that still do fit and those are in an appropriate size for my height."

Shortly thereafter (session 8), the feared foods assignment was introduced. Meryl was asked to construct a list of all the foods she deemed bad, off-limits, scary, or fattening, and for that reason attempted to avoid. Having devised and rank ordered the food items on her list (regular soda, cheeseburgers, french fries, ice cream, cake, and cookies), she agreed to try to incorporate normal portions into her diet once or twice a week, starting with the least difficult items first, at times when she felt safe and unlikely to eat too much or purge.

At about this point in the treatment (sessions 9 to 10), Meryl's weight decreased to just slightly above where it had been when treatment began. Even so, she was still frustrated by what she perceived to be a "heavier than ideal" weight and an unattractive shape and occasionally lapsed into questioning the CBT model and the continued value of eating regularly. Nevertheless, she retained awareness of the fact that all facets of her eating disorder had improved. She had lost a few pounds, was no longer bingeing or purging, had continued to eat regularly scheduled meals and snacks (that included a much wider array of foods, even those formerly feared), and had finally begun a moderate exercise program. When she did begin to second-guess the treatment, she productively utilized a shorthand form of the CPT exercise to counteract any distortions: "In spite of these feelings, I know I am doing the right thing and it just takes some time for the results of eating better and exercising more to show."

Because she was doing so well, the therapist chose at this point (session 11) to discuss issues of portion control and food content. As described earlier, Meryl's sensitivity to weight and shape concerns, compounded by a predisposition toward overweight, could put her at risk for resuming a restrictive dieting pattern that might restart the bulimic cycle if she did

not learn to use healthier strategies for weight control during treatment. Using the CBT model to support these points, the therapist initiated a discussion about weight management, food intake moderation, and physical activity.

Without discussing calories or fat grams per se, examples of commonly accepted one-serving portion sizes for several of the foods that Meryl was consuming frequently (e.g., cereal: one cup; sandwich: one; peanut butter: two tablespoons) were provided along with some loose guidelines about a "heart healthy" approach to eating. This included highlighting the importance of establishing flexible and reasonable guidelines for consuming "indulgence" foods while including other healthy foods such as fruits, vegetables, and whole grains. The material was presented to Meryl in a positive and confident manner, to reassure her that taking more responsibility for aspects of her food intake that were contributing to weight gain could diminish her frustration and decrease her vulnerability to resuming the cycle of dieting, bingeing, and purging. Meryl reported that she felt empowered by this discussion, which she viewed as "offering permission to choose foods carefully and cut back as needed, without being labeled eating disordered." She then reflected specifically on her tendency to eat peanut butter to excess and discussed her excitement that in the context of CBT, she could also work on this type of "generic overeating."

In contrast to session 11, during which she was feeling confident and strong, Meryl started session 12 in tears, noting that she had lost her job and was feeling demoralized, depressed, alone, and worried about the implications of unemployment. She also admitted feeling despondent about a 4-pound weight gain, apparently the result of having done some "emotional overeating" on high-calorie foods such as hamburgers and fries during regularly scheduled meals and snacks. The concerns about this weight gain provided an opportunity to use formal problem solving to revisit the benefits of adopting a "heart healthy" style of eating. Meryl generated the example shown in Figure 9.3.

Although she continued to struggle with the perception that her weight was too high and her shape unattractive, Meryl consistently applied the principles of treatment for the next several sessions (13 to 16). She demonstrated increasing facility for responding to her weight and shape concerns by utilizing both CPT and problem-solving strategies. For example, at one point when battling "feelings of fatness" and concerns about overeating that threatened her attendance at an eagerly anticipated neighborhood barbecue, she was able to use prior examples of working through "fat feelings" to come to a speedy and adaptive conclusion.

> Based on my weight, which is within or near the average range, I am not really fat. Furthermore, by eating regularly during the hours prior to the barbecue and visualizing myself engaging in

healthy eating behaviors once there, I will be less likely to overeat. Moreover, attending the barbecue and socializing with my friends and neighbors will probably decrease my vulnerability to overeating compared with staying home and dwelling on my weight and other problems.

Meryl also applied the CPT exercise to this situation by working through her tendency to assume that other party-goers were likely to negatively judge or dislike her based on her weight, shape, and physical appearance.

Following this session, the remainder of treatment (sessions 17 to 19) focused on issues of relapse prevention and creation of a maintenance plan, for which Meryl was ready. She had not binged or purged in several weeks and had made considerable progress in adopting a healthy, normalized eating pattern as prevention against resuming the bulimic cycle. Still quite sensitive about her body weight (which

Step 1. Identify the problem. Be specific.

I want to experiment with eating certain "energy-dense" foods that I've avoided for a long time, but seem to gain weight when I do.

Step 2. Brainstorm all possible solutions. No screening!
- Could eat these anyway without worrying so much about weight.
- Could eat these and purge later if I'm worried about weight gain.
- Could omit several of these foods again, in an attempt to lose weight.
- Could try to be more moderate in consumption of these foods, as we discussed last time.
- Could exercise more and do more active pleasurable activities to offset the increased calories.

Step 3. Evaluate the practicality and effectiveness of each solution.
- No. Can't "not worry" about my weight.
- No. Don't want to resume purging.
- No. This did not work before—felt deprived and binged.
- Yes. Need to establish the edible guidelines for myself with these tempting foods, such as twice a week maximum.
- Yes. Do need to exercise more and stay more active. Would help with weight.

Step 4. Choose one or a combination of solutions.

Try to eat these foods just once or twice a week maximum, while also making a concerted effort to get more physical activity.

Step 5. Use solutions to guide your behavior.

Step 6. Review the outcome and entire problem-solving method.

This should work if I stick with it.

Figure 9.3 The problem-solving exercise as used in cognitive-behavioral therapy.

had stabilized at 2 pounds over her treatment start weight) and shape, she had made considerable progress in accepting her natural physique, although she admitted that ideally she would still like to weigh less. She continued to exercise regularly, trusting that it would lead to ongoing improvement in her body image.

A few weeks before the final phase of treatment, she had begun a new job that was progressing fairly well. She was, however, struggling with some feelings of anxiety about an upcoming one-week conference in another city that would require her to make several oral presentations to large groups. Following the conference, she would visit her family for the Christmas holidays. Recognizing both situations as "risky" for her eating, she was enthusiastic about developing a relapse prevention and maintenance plan that would include strategies to keep her on track during these upcoming stressful events and help her maintain her progress once treatment was concluded.

In creating her plan, she began with a review of the primary components of treatment that had been and would likely continue to be most helpful. These included (1) adherence to a regular pattern of eating that could be modified flexibly as needed; (2) checking her weight weekly; (3) taking some responsibility for making healthy food choices; and (4) paring down amounts if her weight was going up. Second, strategies for managing her emotions were listed, such as accepting her needs for self-care by committing to regular participation in pleasurable activities and enjoyable physical exercise. She reflected on the importance of using some format to record her food intake and associated feelings and situations, partly to "stay aware and mindful of the need for structure, flexibility, and self-acceptance" with respect to her eating and weight concerns. Fourth, she listed using her mind to reason through potentially problematic situations (e.g., conjuring up alternative, adaptive perspectives and solutions using the CPT and problem-solving exercises as needed to prevent a setback).

Her weight stability over the course of treatment (in the end, her weight had fluctuated by only about 5 pounds in either direction) reassured her that occasional indulgences in tempting foods caused only temporary, minimal weight gain. This finding led to her acceptance of a regular eating pattern as a more straightforward method of weight maintenance compared with the cycle of restrictive dieting, bingeing, and purging. From this observation she was able to conclude that her weight would probably stabilize within a healthy range if she followed the basic principles of moderation in food intake and physical exercise. When she did struggle with strong desires to be thinner, she fought back by mustering up alternative perspectives and using a cost-benefit analysis to examine the perceived advantages of thinness compared with the consequences of remaining bulimic. She forced herself to consider the liabilities of weighing too little, including strong food cravings and urges to binge that would likely restart the cycle of bulimia. She actively challenged "old" ways of thinking, such as "If I was thin I would be more outgoing and live a happier life," by conjuring up examples from her and others' lives to support a more balanced view of thinness. At those moments, she was able to recognize that thinness would not ensure her happiness. She retained the perception that although not currently at her weight goal, she had finally begun to enjoy her *life*—in both professional and social spheres—more than ever before. Displaying a newfound acceptance of herself at her current weight, she bought some new and flattering clothes. Altogether, she was able to use the skills of therapy to distance somewhat from her overinvestment in thinness by reflecting,

I'm proud of my accomplishment in treatment, in that I'm no longer binge eating and purging and I now adhere to a regular program of exercise. In time, I know these will lead to the healthiest weight for me, and meanwhile, there's a lot more to my life.

EFFICACY

Because research into the treatment of BN now has a 20-year history, there is much information about both psychotherapeutic and psychopharmacologic treatments for this disorder, with more than 50 controlled trials published (Agras, 1998; Mitchell, Hoberman, Peterson, Mussell, & Pyle, 1996; Wilson et al., 1999). Psychotherapy research was paralleled by psychopharmacologic research, eventually leading to comparative studies of antidepressants and CBT, as well as additive studies. Fewer studies exist for BED, although it appears that treatments effective for BN are also effective for BED. Overall, it is fair to conclude that CBT is the treatment of choice for both BN and BED. Because AN is a relatively rare condition, the number of studies with an adequate sample size is small. Two additional reasons account for the small sample sizes in many studies. First, it is difficult to recruit sufficient eligible participants with AN at any one center. Second, unlike patients with BN and BED, the patient with AN is ambivalent about treatment, leading to low entry rates and high dropout rates. Many of the studies of AN focus on inpatient rather than outpatient treatment; in addition, there is a lack of standardization of psychotherapeutic approaches by means of treatment manuals. Overall, one can conclude that there is evidence for the effectiveness of a particular type of family therapy for the younger anorexic (Robin et al., 1999; Russell, Szmukler, Dare, & Eisler, 1987). Apart from family therapy, it is not possible to conclude that any other form of outpatient psychotherapy is specifically effective for the treatment of AN.

BULIMIA NERVOSA

Cognitive-Behavioral Therapy
The initial uncontrolled studies of CBT, both individual and group, were convincing enough about the effectiveness to lead to controlled outcome studies (Fairburn, 1981; Schneider, 1985).

In the group treatment study, 54% of patients were no longer binge eating and purging at the end of treatment, and 45% were abstinent at a six-month follow-up (Schneider, 1985). Several studies comparing different forms of CBT with waiting list control groups either in individual or group format found CBT to be superior to the waiting list controls (Huon & Brown, 1985; Lee & Rush, 1986; Ordman & Kirschenbaum, 1985), leading to the next stage of research, namely, comparing CBT to other forms of psychotherapy. An early comparison of CBT and a nonspecific psychotherapy combined with self-monitoring of food intake, binge eating, and purging, found that CBT reduced purging rates by a mean of 95% compared with 69% for the nondirective therapy group (Kirkley, Schneider, Agras, & Bachman, 1985). Self-monitoring is a key component of CBT, and was used in the nondirective group, thus strengthening its effect. Later comparisons with focal psychotherapy (combined with self-monitoring) (Fairburn, Kirk, O'Connor, & Cooper, 1986), manualized supportive-expressive psychotherapy (Garner, Rockert, Garner, Olmsted, & Eagle, 1993), and, most recently, a form of psychodynamic psychotherapy (Walsh et al., 1997) all found CBT superior to other psychotherapies. However, in one study, there was no difference in the reduction of binge eating between the two therapies (Garner et al., 1993); in another, there was considerable improvement with both treatments (Fairburn et al., 1986).

An alternative treatment, exposure and response prevention, was also compared to CBT (Leitenberg, Rosen, Gross, Nudelman, & Vara, 1988). This treatment is based on the hypothesis that purging is maintained by the anxiety generated by binge eating. Following the methods used in the treatment of obsessive-compulsive disorder, patients are encouraged to eat enough binge food to generate anxiety during treatment sessions, and are then kept in session until the urge to induce vomiting has dissipated. In this way, patients expose themselves to anxiety-generating stimuli and are prevented from carrying out purging, which is hypothesized to reduce anxiety. In the first controlled study, exposure plus response prevention was superior to CBT in reducing binge eating and purging (Leitenberg et al., 1988). However, the abstinence rates achieved in the CBT group were lower than usual. In a second study, an additive design was used, namely, a waiting list condition, self-monitoring of caloric intake and purging behaviors with supportive psychotherapy, CBT, and CBT plus response prevention (Agras, Schneider, Arnow, Raeburn, & Telch, 1989). In the latter group, response prevention was added after session 7 of CBT. In this study, although the results of CBT plus response prevention were comparable to those reported in the earlier study, CBT was superior to the waiting list condition, but CBT plus response was not. It can be argued that waiting until session 7 to add response prevention did not give the response prevention condition enough time to work. A third study also found that exposure with response prevention did not add to the effectiveness of CBT, although no deleterious effects of the addition were found (Wilson, Eldridge, Smith, & Niles, 1991). Overall, there is no evidence that exposure and response prevention add to the effectiveness of CBT in the treatment of BN, and conflicting evidence as to whether it is as effective as CBT. Hence, the utility of this approach requires further research.

The only form of psychotherapy that may be as effective as CBT is interpersonal therapy (IPT). The first controlled study included three groups: CBT, IPT, and behavior therapy (BT; Fairburn et al., 1991). The BT group included the behavioral and educational components of CBT, but did not include the cognitive component. The study was particularly convincing because IPT contained none of the elements of CBT (e.g., self-monitoring). Instead, in the first four sessions of treatment, interpersonal factors associated with maintenance of the eating disorder were investigated, leading to the elucidation of one or two clearly defined interpersonal problems. In the

next phase of treatment, the therapist became less active, ensuring that therapy remained focused on the defined problem areas and exerting a pressure for change in these areas. When eating disorder symptoms were referred to by the patient, the interpersonal context of the symptoms was examined. In the last two or three sessions, relapse prevention procedures pertinent to the interpersonal problems addressed were applied. In the first, relatively small-scale study, CBT was found superior to IPT in reducing purging but not binge eating at the end of treatment, and a greater proportion of participants receiving CBT was abstinent compared with those treated with IPT. At follow-up, both at one year (Fairburn, Jones, Peveler, Hope, & O'Connor, 1993) and five years (Fairburn et al., 1995), there were no significant differences between the two treatments because the abstinence rates for IPT continued to improve after the first year of follow-up, and those for CBT leveled off. Importantly, both CBT and IPT were superior to BT at follow-up, suggesting that both IPT and CBT have a specific therapeutic effect in BN, although the effects of IPT are significantly slower to develop.

The most recent comparison of IPT and CBT for BN involved a multisite study with 220 bulimic participants randomly allocated to either CBT or IPT (Agras, Walsh, et al., 2000). CBT was superior to IPT at the end of treatment in reducing binge eating, purging, and dietary restraint. However, by the one-year follow-up, there were no significant differences between the results of the two treatments on any measure. Those treated with IPT continued to improve; those treated with CBT showed no further improvement. This again suggests that the two treatments are equivalent in effectiveness, but that IPT is much slower to work. Therefore, CBT should continue to be regarded as the psychotherapeutic treatment of choice.

A further question is whether the cognitive component of CBT is necessary. As mentioned earlier, this component is added in the latter half of therapy. In the comparison with IPT and CBT, behavior therapy stripped of the cognitive component was associated with a high rate of relapse posttreatment (Fairburn, Jones, et al., 1993). This finding was replicated in a further study (P. Cooper & Steere, 1995). These studies suggest that the cognitive component of treatment does not enhance initial outcome, but that it is important in the maintenance of treatment improvements.

Abbreviated Forms of CBT

Bibliotherapy, alone or therapist-supervised, has been used successfully in several mental health conditions. A few studies of these abbreviated approaches to treatment for BN have now been published. In the first study, a self-help manual without therapist assistance and used for eight weeks was compared with eight weeks of CBT and a waiting list control group (Treasure et al., 1994). Full remission for the intent to treat group was obtained for 24% of the group assigned to CBT, 22% of those assigned to the manual, and 11% of the waiting list control. It should be remembered that CBT usually consists of 18 to 20 sessions. The authors concluded that the manual produced somewhat smaller symptomatic improvement than CBT. A larger-scale study found similar results (Treasure et al., 1996). In a large, uncontrolled study, 82 patients with BN were treated with therapist-supervised self-help (Cooper, Coker, & Fleming, 1996). In this study, 27% of participants in an intent to treat analysis were recovered at the end of treatment, improving to 39% at one-year follow-up. Therapy was provided by a social worker with no specialized training in eating disorders, with patients receiving an average of eight sessions. These results tentatively suggest that self-help with or without therapist supervision can be useful in a sizable proportion of patients with BN. It has been suggested that such treatment might form the first step in the treatment of BN with treatment failures then receiving CBT (Treasure et al., 1996).

Comparison of CBT with Medication

Studies of the effectiveness of medication for the treatment of BN began at the same time as studies of CBT. Antidepressant medication was first studied because it was hypothesized that BN was a form-*fruste* of depression (Pope, Hudson, Jonas, & Yurgelin-Todd, 1983). This view is no longer held. However, antidepressant medication, including tricyclic antidepressants, monoamine-oxidase inhibitors, and serotonin reuptake inhibitors, has been found in numerous studies to be more effective than placebo, and is effective irrespective of level of depression (Agras, 1998; Walsh & Devlin, 1995). The development of two effective treatments, antidepressant medication and CBT, ultimately led to their comparison. In the first of these studies, participants with BN were randomly allocated to one of four groups: placebo, imipramine, imipramine combined with CBT in group format, and placebo combined with group CBT (Mitchell et al., 1990). Imipramine and both CBT groups were more effective than placebo in reducing binge eating and purging, and CBT was more effective than imipramine. Adding imipramine to CBT produced little extra benefit in terms of reducing eating disorder symptoms, although depression was reduced more effectively in the CBT group combined with medication than in CBT combined with placebo. Other studies essentially replicated these results, with CBT being more effective than desipramine in reducing eating disorder symptoms, and the combination being no more effective in reducing eating disorder symptoms than CBT alone (Agras et al., 1992). In one study, however, it appeared that a sequence of two medications, substituting fluoxetine if the initial medication, desipramine, was not effective, was as effective as CBT (Walsh et al., 1997). This study is important because most practicing physicians would use a second medication if the first were not effective. However, the dropout rates in most of the comparison studies are higher for medication than for

CBT; hence, one might argue that CBT should remain the first choice of therapy in the treatment of BN.

A further question is whether a second therapy would be effective if CBT or IPT is not, as happens in a quarter to half of all patients. At this point, only one study has addressed this issue (Walsh et al., 2000). In this study, patients who did not respond to manualized CBT or IPT were allocated at random to either fluoxetine or placebo. In the fluoxetine group, 38% of participants became abstinent compared with none in the placebo group, suggesting that fluoxetine is useful when psychotherapy fails.

This raises a final question regarding BN: Is it possible to predict with reasonable certainty those who will fail CBT before the end of treatment? This issue was addressed in a recent multisite trial in which 194 women with BN were treated with manualized CBT (Agras, Crow, et al., 2000). Although treatment failures were characterized by poor social adjustment and a lower body mass index (the latter probably indicating greater dietary restriction), these predictors did not differentiate those who would do better or worse in a clinically significant manner. However, when the rate of progress in treatment was examined, it was found that those who decreased purging by at least 70% at treatment session 6 were likely to become abstinent by the end of treatment. This suggests that triage to a second treatment (e.g., adding an antidepressant medication) could take place early in treatment with CBT. Data from this study suggest that if such triage were to take place, 70% of participants would receive the correct treatment (either continued CBT alone or CBT with the added second treatment), 6% would receive the second treatment unnecessarily, and 24% who continued CBT but did not receive the second treatment would fail treatment. The last group could, of course, be treated with the second therapy at the end of CBT. Thus, it appears that a slow response to CBT predicts treatment failure for a substantial proportion of patients well before the end of CBT.

BINGE EATING DISORDER

As noted above, because BED has only recently been recognized as an eating disorder distinct from BN, treatment research is less advanced than for BN. The first study in this series compared group CBT with a waiting list control (Telch, Agras, Rossiter, Wilfley, & Kenardy, 1990). The results were promising, with over 70% of participants abstinent at the end of treatment. Abstinence in this case was defined as no binge eating for a period of one week. Hence, the results of this study undoubtedly overstated the efficacy of CBT in the treatment of BED. In the next study, group CBT was compared with group IPT and a wait-list control (Wilfley et al., 1993): 33% of participants in the CBT group dropped out compared with 11% in the IPT group, a difference that was not statistically significant. However, members of the IPT group completed significantly more sessions (14) than those in the CBT group (11.5). These data suggest that IPT may be more acceptable than CBT in the treatment of BED. Using an intent to treat analysis (i.e., including all participants in the study in the analysis), both CBT and IPT were significantly superior to the wait-list condition, with no differences between CBT and IPT: 44% of participants became abstinent in the IPT group, 28% in the CBT group, and none in the wait-list group. In the third study, an additive design was used: weight loss treatment (WL), CBT plus WL, and CBT plus WL plus the tricyclic antidepressant desipramine (Agras et al., 1994). After three months of treatment, before either WL or the antidepressant had been added to the CBT groups, CBT was significantly superior in reducing binge eating, and WL was significantly superior in inducing weight loss. At the end of 36 weeks of treatment, 37% of those receiving CBT were abstinent compared with 19% receiving WL, a nonstatistically significant difference. As with BN, the addition of desipramine did not add to the effectiveness of CBT in reducing binge eating. However, at three-month follow-up, those receiving CBT had lost no weight compared with a weight loss of 4.8kg in the group also receiving desipramine, a statistically significant difference. In a subsequent study, individuals with BED treated with CBT followed by WL were followed one year posttreatment (Agras, Telch, Arnow, Eldridge, & Marnell, 1997). Those who had maintained abstinence from binge eating had lost 14 pounds since beginning treatment, compared with those who were never abstinent during treatment or follow-up, who gained 7.25 pounds. This suggests that abstinence from binge eating is essential to the maintenance of weight loss.

Placebo controlled trials of antidepressants in BED have yielded mixed results. In one study, 23 women with BED were allocated to either desipramine or placebo in a short-term trial. At the end of treatment, 60% of those receiving desipramine were abstinent compared with 15% of those receiving placebo (McCann & Agras, 1990). However, in a further study, no differences were found for reduction in binge frequency between imipramine and placebo, perhaps due to a fairly large placebo response (Alger, Schwalberg, & Bigaouette, 1991). There was, however, a significant difference in duration of binge eating, with those receiving imipramine reducing their duration. It is noteworthy, however, that in the same study, there were no differences found in reduction of binge eating and purging between imipramine and placebo in subjects with BN. This finding is unusual given the large number of studies in which antidepressants have been found superior to placebo in this disorder. In a third study, fluvoxamine, a serotonin reuptake inhibitor, was found to be significantly superior to placebo in reducing binge eating and weight (Hudson et al., 1998).

These initial studies reveal some interesting similarities and differences in the response of BN and BED to different treatments. CBT appears effective in both conditions. However, unlike the research in BN, no study has compared CBT to a nonspecific psychotherapy condition in the treatment of BED. It is therefore possible that the response to CBT in BED is nonspecific. IPT appears to be equally and as rapidly effective as CBT in BED, unlike the findings in BN, where CBT was significantly more rapid in its effects. As with CBT, the effects of IPT in BED could be nonspecific. Finally, both tryciclic antidepressants and a serotonin uptake inhibitor appear more effective than placebo in BED, similar to the findings in BN, although the one discrepant finding of no effect of imipramine in reducing binge eating rates is noted. Similar to the findings in BN, antidepressant medication does not add to the efficacy of CBT in reducing binge eating, but such medication does appear to be beneficial in facilitating weight reduction. With the various caveats in mind, one can conclude that CBT and IPT are equally effective in the treatment of BED, and that medication is also useful both in reducing binge eating and in enhancing weight loss.

SUMMARY

Despite the relatively short period of time during which the majority of the controlled research on the treatment of the eating disorders has occurred, much progress has been made. The effect sizes for CBT in the treatment of BN and BED are similar to those seen for the treatment of depression and panic disorder. At the present time, CBT can be regarded as the preferred approach to the treatment of BN, with psychopharmacologic agents forming a second-level treatment, depending, of course, on the informed preferences of the individual patient. In the case of BED, it appears that CBT and IPT are equivalent in effectiveness and again should be regarded as the preferred approach to treatment. Although the recovery rates for BN and BED have been found to be respectable, further research is needed to enhance the effectiveness of treatment. Not only are new procedures needed, but we need to understand how best to sequence the effective treatments now available, both from the viewpoint of therapeutic effectiveness and cost effectiveness.

REFERENCES

Agras, W. S. (1998). Treatment of eating disorders. In A. F. Schatzberg & C. B. Nemeroff (Eds.), *The American Psychiatric Press textbook of psychopharmacology* (2nd ed., pp. 869–880). Washington, DC: American Psychiatric Press.

Agras, W. S., & Apple, R. F. (1997). *Overcoming eating disorders: A cognitive-behavioral treatment for bulimia nervosa and binge eating disorder. Therapist guide.* San Antonio, TX: Psychological Corporation.

Agras, W. S., Crow, S. J., Halmi, K. A., Mitchell, J. E., Wilson, G. T., & Kraemer, H. C. (2000). Outcome predictors for the cognitive-behavioral treatment of bulimia nervosa: Data from a multisite study. *American Journal of Psychiatry, 157,* 1302–1308.

Agras, W. S., Rossiter, E. M., Arnow, B., Schneider, J. A., Telch, C. F., Raeburn, S. D., et al. (1992). Pharmacologic and cognitive-behavioral treatment for bulimia nervosa: A controlled comparison. *American Journal of Psychiatry, 149*(1), 82–87.

Agras, W. S., Schneider, J. A., Arnow, B., Raeburn, S. D., & Telch, C. F. (1989). Cognitive-behavioral therapy and response prevention treatments for bulimia nervosa. *Journal of Consulting and Clinical Psychology, 57,* 215–221.

Agras, W. S., Telch, C. F., Arnow, B., Eldridge, K., & Marnell, M. (1997). One-year follow-up of cognitive-behavioral therapy for obese individuals with binge eating disorder. *Journal of Consulting and Clinical Psychology, 65,* 343–347.

Agras, W. S., Telch, C. F., Arnow, B., Eldredge, K., Wilfley, D. E., Raeburn, S. D., et al. (1994). Weight loss, cognitive-behavioral, and desipramine treatments in binge eating disorder: An additive design. *Behavior Therapy, 25,* 209–238.

Agras, W. S., Walsh, B. T., Fairburn, C. G., Wilson, G. T., & Kraemer, H. C. (2000). A multicenter comparison of cognitive-behavioral therapy and interpersonal psychotherapy for bulimia nervosa. *Archives of General Psychiatry, 57,* 459–466.

Alger, A., Schwalberg, D., & Bigaouette, J. M. (1991). Effect of a tricyclic antidepressant and opiate antagonist on binge eating behavior in normoweight bulimic, and obese, binge eating subjects. *American Journal of Clinical Nutrition, 53,* 865–871.

Allison, D. B. (Ed.). (1995). *Handbook of assessment methods for eating behaviors and weight related problems.* Thousand Oaks, CA: Sage.

Apple, R. F., & Agras, W. S. (1997). *Overcoming eating disorders: A cognitive-behavioral treatment for bulimia nervosa and binge eating disorder. Client workbook.* San Antonio, TX: Psychological Corporation.

Beck, A. T. (1987). *Beck Depression Inventory.* San Antonio, TX: Psychological Corporation.

Cooper, P. J., Coker, S., & Fleming, C. (1996). An evaluation of the efficacy of supervised cognitive behavioral self-help for bulimia nervosa. *Journal of Psychosomatic Research, 40,* 281–287.

Cooper, P. J., & Steere, J. (1995). A comparison of two psychological treatments for bulimia nervosa: Implications for models of maintenance. *Behaviour Research and Therapy, 33,* 875–885.

Cooper, Z., Cooper, P. J., & Fairburn, C. G. (1989). The validity of the eating disorder examination and its subscales. *British Journal of Psychiatry, 154,* 807–812.

Fairburn, C. G. (1981). A cognitive behavioural approach to the treatment of bulimia. *Psychological Medicine, 11,* 707–711.

Fairburn, C. G., & Hay, P. J. (1992). The treatment of bulimia nervosa. *Annals of Medicine, 24,* 297–302.

Fairburn, C. G., Jones, R., Peveler, R. C., Carr, S. J., Solomon, R. A., O'Connor, M. E., et al. (1991). Three psychological treatments for bulimia nervosa: A comparative trial. *Archives of General Psychiatry, 48,* 463–469.

Fairburn, C. G., Jones, R., Peveler, R. C., Hope, R. A., & O'Connor, M. E. (1993). Psychotherapy and bulimia nervosa: Longer-term effects of interpersonal psychotherapy, behavior therapy, and cognitive behavior therapy. *Archives of General Psychiatry, 50,* 419–428.

Fairburn, C. G., Kirk, J., O'Connor, M., & Cooper, P. J. (1986). A comparison of two psychological treatments for bulimia nervosa. *Behaviour Research and Therapy, 24,* 629–643.

Fairburn, C. G., Marcus, M. D., & Wilson, G. T. (1993). Cognitive-behavioral therapy for binge eating and bulimia nervosa: A comprehensive treatment manual. In C. G. Fairburn & G. T. Wilson (Eds.), *Binge eating: Nature, assessment, and treatment* (pp. 361–404.). New York: Guilford Press.

Fairburn, C. G., Norman, P. A., Welch, S. L., O'Connor, M. E., Doll, H. A., & Peveler, R. C. (1995). A prospective study of outcome in bulimia nervosa and the long-term effects of three psychological treatments. *Archives of General Psychiatry, 52,* 304–312.

Garner, D. M., Olmsted, M. P., & Garfinkel, P. E. (1985). Similarities among bulimic groups selected by weight and weight history. *Journal of Psychiatric Research, 19,* 129–134.

Garner, D. M., Rockert, W. R. D., Garner, M. V., Olmsted, M. P., & Eagle, M. (1993). Comparison between cognitive-behavioral and supportive-expressive therapy for bulimia nervosa. *American Journal of Psychiatry, 150,* 37–46.

Gormally, J., Black, S., Daston, S., & Rardin, D. (1982). The assessment of binge eating severity among obese persons. *Addictive Behaviors, 7,* 47–55.

Hudson, J. I., McElroy, S. L., Raymond, N. C., Crow, S., Keck, P. E., Jr., Carter, W. P., et al. (1998). Fluvoxamine in the treatment of binge-eating disorder: A multicenter placebo-controlled, double-blind trial. *American Journal of Psychiatry, 155,* 1756–1762.

Huon, G. F., & Brown, L. (1985). Evaluating group treatment for bulimia. *Journal of Psychiatric Research, 19,* 479–483.

Kenardy, J., Arnow, B., & Agras, W. S. (1996). The aversiveness of specific emotional states associated with binge eating in obese subjects. *Australian and New Zealand Journal of Psychiatry, 30,* 839–844.

Keys, A., Brozek, J., & Henschel, A. (1950). *The biology of human starvation.* Minneapolis: University of Minnesota Press.

Kirkley, B. G., Schneider, J. A., Agras, W. S., & Bachman, J. A. (1985). Comparison of two group treatments for bulimia. *Journal of Consulting and Clinical Psychology, 53,* 43–48.

Lee, N., & Rush, A. J. (1986). Cognitive-behavioral group therapy for bulimia. *International Journal of Eating Disorders, 5,* 599–615.

Leitenberg, H., Rosen, J. C., Gross, J., Nudelman, S., & Vara, L. S. (1988). Exposure plus response-prevention treatment of bulimia nervosa. *Journal of Consulting and Clinical Psychology, 56,* 535–541.

Lucas, A. R., Beard, C. M., & O'Fallon, W. M. (1991). 50-Year trends in the incidence of anorexia nervosa in Rochester, MN: A population-based study. *American Journal of Psychiatry, 148,* 917–929.

McCann, U. D., & Agras, W. S. (1990). Successful treatment of nonpurging bulimia nervosa with desipramine: A double-blind, placebo-controlled study. *American Journal of Psychiatry, 147,* 1509–1513.

Mitchell, J. E., Hoberman, H. N., Peterson, C. B., Mussell, M., & Pyle, R. L. (1996). Research on the psychotherapy of bulimia nervosa: Half empty or half full? *International Journal of Eating Disorders, 20,* 219–229.

Mitchell, J. E., Pyle, R. L., Eckert, E. D., Hatsukami, D., Pomeroy, C., & Zimmerman, R. (1990). A comparison study of antidepressants and structured intensive group psychotherapy in the treatment of bulimia nervosa. *Archives of General Psychiatry, 47,* 149–157.

Ordman, A., & Kirschenbaum, D. (1985). Cognitive-behavioral therapy for bulimia: An initial outcome study. *Journal of Consulting and Clinical Psychology, 53,* 305–313.

Polivy, J., & Herman, C. P. (1987). Diagnosis and treatment of normal eating. *Journal of Consulting and Clinical Psychology, 55,* 635–644.

Pope, H. G., Hudson, J. I., Jonas, J. M., & Yurgelin-Todd, D. (1983). Bulimia treated with impramine: A placebo-controlled, double-blind study. *American Journal of Psychiatry, 140,* 554–558.

Robin, A. L., Siegel, P. T., Moye, A. W., Gilroy, M., Dennis, A. B., & Sikand, A. (1999). A controlled comparison of family versus individual therapy for adolescents with anorexia nervosa. *Journal of the American Academy of Child and Adolescent Psychiatry, 38,* 1482–1489.

Rossiter, E. M., Agras, W. S., Losch, M., & Telch, C. F. (1988). Dietary restraint of bulimic subjects following cognitive-behavioral therapy or pharmacological treatment. *Behavior Therapy, 26,* 495–498.

Russell, G. F. M., Szmukler, G. I., Dare, C., & Eisler, M. A. (1987). An evaluation of family therapy in anorexia nervosa and bulimia nervosa. *Archives of General Psychiatry, 44,* 1047–1056.

Schneider, J. A. (1985). A cognitive behavioral group treatment of bulimia. *British Journal of Psychiatry, 146,* 473–484.

Spitzer, R. L., Yanovski, S. Z., & Marcus, M. D. (1993). *The Questionnaire on Eating and Weight Patterns–revised.* New York: New York State Psychiatric Institute.

Spitzer, R. L., Yanovski, S. Z., Wadden, T., Wing, R., Marcus, M. D., Stunkard, A., et al. (1993). Binge eating disorder: Its further validation in a multisite study. *International Journal of Eating Disorders, 13,* 137–153.

Stunkard, A. J., & Messick, S. (1985). The three-factor eating questionnaire to measure dietary restraint, disinhibition and hunger. *Journal of Psychosomatic Research, 29,* 71–83.

Telch, C. F., Agras, W. S., Rossiter, E. M., Wilfley, D. E., & Kenardy, J. (1990). Group cognitive-behavioral treatment for the non-purging bulimic: An initial evaluation. *Journal of Consulting and Clinical Psychology, 58,* 629–635.

Telch, C. F., & Stice, E. (1998). Psychiatric comorbidity in women with binge eating disorder: Prevalence rates from a non-treatment seeking sample. *Journal of Consulting and Clinical Psychology, 66,* 768–776.

Treasure, J., Schmidt, U., Troop, N., Tiller, J., Todd, G., Keilen, M., et al. (1994). First step in managing bulimia nervosa: Controlled trial of therapeutic manual. *British Medical Journal, 308,* 686–689.

Treasure, J., Schmidt, U., Troop, N., Tiller, J., Todd, G., & Turnbull, S. (1996). Sequential treatments for bulimia nervosa incorporating a self-care manual. *British Journal of Psychiatry, 168,* 94–98.

Walsh, B. T., Agras, W. S., Devlin, M. J., Fairburn, C. G., Wilson, G. T., Kahn, C., et al. (2000). Fluoxetine in bulimia nervosa following poor response to psychotherapy. *American Journal of Psychiatry, 157,* 1332–1334.

Walsh, B. T., & Devlin, M. J. (1995). Pharmacotherapy of bulimia nervosa and binge eating disorder. *Addictive Behaviors, 20,* 757–764.

Walsh, B. T., Wilson, G. T., Loeb, K. L., Devlin, M. J., Pike, K. M., Roose, S. P., et al. (1997). Medication and psychotherapy in the treatment of bulimia nervosa. *American Journal of Psychiatry, 154,* 523–531.

Wilfley, D. E., Agras, W. S., Telch, C. F., Rossiter, E. M., Schneider, J. A., Cole, A. B., et al. (1993). Group cognitive-behavioral therapy and group interpersonal psychotherapy for the non-purging bulimic: A controlled comparison. *Journal of Consulting and Clinical Psychology, 61,* 296–305.

Wilson, G. T., Eldridge, K. L., Smith, D., & Niles, B. (1991). Cognitive-behavioral treatment with and without response prevention for bulimia. *Behavior Research and Therapy, 29,* 575–583.

Wilson, G. T., Loeb, K. L., Walsh, B. T., Labouvie, E., Petkova, E., Liu, X., et al. (1999). Psychological versus pharmacological treatments of bulimia nervosa: Predictors and process of change. *Journal of Consulting and Clinical Psychology, 67,* 451–459.

Wiser, S., & Telch, C. F. (1999). Dialectical behavior therapy for binge eating disorder. *Journal of Clinical Psychology/In Session: Psychotherapy in Practice, 55,* 755–768.

SECTION THREE

PSYCHOTHERAPY WITH ADULTS

CHAPTER 10

Dialectical Behavior Therapy for Borderline Personality and Related Disorders

ALAN E. FRUZZETTI

Dialectical behavior therapy (DBT) is at the leading edge of the "new wave" of behavior therapies that emphasize utilizing the principles of behavior change in treatment rather than providing a more structured, "one size fits all" approach. Furthermore, this approach attempts to balance change principles and strategies with acceptance principles and strategies across the domains of treatment.

DBT was developed by Marsha Linehan at the University of Washington specifically to treat the complex, often refractory clinical problems of chronically suicidal patients with Borderline Personality Disorder (BPD). The problems of BPD are many and varied. Rare is the individual who meets criteria for BPD without meeting criteria for multiple other disorders. Specifically, Depression and other affective disorders, Posttraumatic Stress Disorder, other anxiety disorders (e.g., Panic Disorder, Social Phobia), eating disorders, substance abuse disorders, and other personality disorders are all commonly comorbid with BPD. Moreover, individuals with BPD have among the highest lifetime prevalence of completed suicide, about 10%, a rate comparable to individuals with Major Depressive Disorder or Schizophrenia.

Perhaps as a consequence of the multiple problems associated with BPD, along with often high levels of anger toward others (including treatment providers), low levels of treatment adherence, and high levels of risk of suicide, individuals with borderline problems are difficult to treat successfully. Similarly, borderline clients utilize mental health services at rates that are far greater than their representation in the clinical population. For example, although borderline clients constitute approximately 10% to 12% of outpatients and about 20% of inpatients, they utilize services and cost mental health systems at least twice these proportions (Linehan & Heard, 1999). Thus, because of the severe nature of the disorder and its concomitant systemic costs, the need for effective treatments for this population is great.

DBT has been shown to be an effective treatment particularly for borderline, multiproblem, parasuicidal, and suicidal women. Founded on a biosocial or transactional theory of the development of BPD and related disorders, DBT integrates or synthesizes both change-based strategies (traditional behavior therapy) and acceptance-based strategies (validation) into a multidimensional treatment package. The various components of DBT are explicated in the following section.

HISTORY OF THIS THERAPEUTIC APPROACH

Behaviorists were slow to develop treatments for personality disorders for many reasons. First, behaviorists have historically eschewed *DSM* diagnoses in general, and the diagnosis of personality disorders in particular, preferring instead to focus on specific problem behaviors. Thus, early behaviorists emphasized overt behaviors such as suicide attempts as targets of treatment and often focused on modifying environmental variables as a means of intervention. For example, Marsha Linehan focused on treating suicidal behaviors specifically until the 1980s, when she began to assess and treat BPD more broadly.

Linehan developed the first treatment manual for DBT, which focused on the treatment of suicidal behavior and evolved into her published treatment manuals (Linehan 1993a, 1993b), following successful outcomes in the first randomized clinical trial (Linehan, Armstrong, Suarez, Allmon, & Heard, 1991). Since their publication, Linehan's treatment manuals have been studied extensively in the United States and Europe and increasingly employed in both public and private mental health delivery systems with notable success. More recently, DBT has been applied or extended to treatment for problems and populations related to BPD, which is discussed next. The increasing popularity of DBT seems likely to be due to two related factors: outcome evidence and practitioner preferences. Not only has DBT been shown to be effective in multiple studies, but prior to the development of DBT, no other treatment had garnered much empirical support for treating chronically suicidal, self-injurious borderline clients. Moreover, cost-effectiveness data suggest that, despite being a comprehensive and often expensive treatment, DBT is quite efficient compared to existing alternatives. Perhaps just as important as good client outcomes, DBT also targets avoiding or ameliorating therapist burnout in the treatment of difficult-to-treat borderline clients. Thus, although no randomly controlled data address the impact of therapist DBT practice on therapist burnout and job satisfaction, delivering a treatment that has better outcomes while still taking the level of burnout in the providers seriously may enhance its popularity. By targeting both parts of the reciprocal relationship between therapist burnout and patient outcome in DBT, both may be affected positively and synergistically.

THEORETICAL CONSTRUCTS

TRANSACTIONAL OR BIOSOCIAL MODEL

Marsha Linehan and her colleagues (e.g., Fruzzetti & Linehan, 2001; Linehan, 1993a) have proposed a biosocial model for the development of BPD and related disorders. In this model, borderline personality is considered to result from a *transaction* between an individual's level of *emotion vulnerability* and the social environment's *invalidating* responses. In a transactional model, factors are seen to exert mutual influence. This is different from an interactional model, in which factors are typically considered to be static and independent. For example, many interactional models for the development of psychopathology maintain that genetic and biological factors (often referred to as predispositions, or as a diathesis) interact with the environment (often viewed as a "stressor") to result in a particular disorder. In the biosocial or transactional model, biological, genetic, and social/environmental variables may all be relevant, but are assumed to influence each other over time (Fruzzetti & Linehan, 2001).

For example, a child may be born with a particularly difficult temperament, be difficult to sooth, and very sensitive and reactive to emotional stimuli. The child's social or family environment may respond to the child in ways that minimize his or her sensitivity or exacerbate it over time. Similarly, an ordinary child may become increasingly sensitive to emotional stimuli and develop temperamental or other difficulties in response to pervasive emotional neglect, abuse, or other maladaptive patterns of parenting. Thus, vulnerability to negative emotion by adulthood may be the result of genetic or biological factors and/or may be learned over time. The idea of the biosocial/transactional model is that if either factor (individual emotion vulnerability or environmental invalidation) is sufficiently extreme, it can create the other extreme factor over time. A very difficult child can "create" a hostile, less nurturing, or invalidating family environment, and a very invalidating family environment can "create" a very emotionally sensitive and reactive child. In a situation in which both factors are somewhat extreme in the beginning, both will be exacerbated over time.

Emotional Vulnerability and Emotion Dysregulation

Vulnerability to negative emotional experiences and emotion dysregulation is the essence of the individual factor in the biosocial model. According to Linehan, this vulnerability has three parts, all of which must be present to create serious difficulties: (1) high sensitivity to emotional stimuli; (2) high reactivity to emotional stimuli; and (3) a slow return to baseline following emotion dysregulation. It is important to clarify that emotional arousal per se is not the

same as emotion dysregulation; by definition, dysregulation describes a situation in which high emotional arousal disrupts effective self-management. Being upset may not (and likely seldom does in normative populations) lead to problematic actions (suicidal urges or actions, substance abuse, obsessive-compulsive behavior, etc.).

Emotion dysregulation includes extreme difficulties in (1) modulating arousal, including psychophysiological arousal, compared with norms; (2) orienting, maintaining, and/or reorienting attention and maintaining effective cognitive processing; (3) inhibiting dysfunctional (impulsive) mood-dependent actions; (4) titrating emotional intensity (i.e., the person may either escalate or blunt emotions); and (5) organizing behavior in the service of long-term goals rather than in the service of alleviating short-term emotional arousal.

Invalidating Family or Social Environment

The other factor in the biosocial/transactional model is the invalidating social environment. In this model, to be considered an *invalidating* social environment, the responses of the social environment must *pervasively* invalidate (criticize, punish, ignore, respond inconsistently, pathologize, etc.) the *valid* behaviors of the target person, including the wants or desires, emotions, thoughts, and other behaviors or responses of the person. That is, a broad range of the person's valid behaviors (especially core "self behaviors" such as desires and emotions) must be the object of criticism, misunderstanding, inattention, and/or punitive action. Stated differently, an invalidating social environment is highly incompatible with the behavioral repertoire of the individual, and there is a resulting poor fit (Hoffman, Fruzzetti, & Swenson, 1999).

In principle, an invalidating environment may have been present for an individual's entire life, or may have developed or been exacerbated over time, in transaction with the individual's vulnerabilities and early emotion dysregulation. Regardless, such an environment is characterized by its likelihood to punish or respond in an erratic way to an individual's "private" experiences (behaviors such as wants, emotions, sensations, and thoughts that do not necessarily have a clear public corollary). In such an environment, others typically respond to emotions or interpretations of events with derision, dismissal, or disregard. In addition, the individual's responses may be pathologized or attributed to "negative" characteristics such as being "too emotional" or overreactive, not being motivated to take care of oneself, being motivated to manipulate or harm or control others, having a lack of discipline, having a bad attitude, or simply being a bad person.

It is important to discriminate between a social or family environment that is invalidating and one that is simply critical or in which trauma has occurred. Aside from its pervasive nature, an invalidating environment specifically may ignore or punish an individual's expression of pain or negative affect, may reinforce (or respond only to) extreme levels of pain or entreaties for help, may consistently oversimplify the difficulty of tasks or the ease of solving problems, and may emphasize controlling or suppressing natural emotional experiences instead of accurate expression.

Given the high rates (estimates of 65% or more) of physical and sexual abuse in this population (e.g., Herman, Perry, & van der Kolk, 1989), it may be useful to consider abuse, along with invalidating responses to disclosures of abuse, as examples of invalidating environments. However, other pervasive invalidating responses may have an impact similar to that of abuse on the development of emotional vulnerability. Consequently, individuals developing and living in an invalidating environment often do not develop the ability to identify accurately various private experiences (e.g., accurately discriminate different emotions), may

not trust their own experiences (having consistently been told they are faulty or wrong), and may instead learn to actively self-invalidate. They may develop an extreme style of expression, vacillating between inhibiting emotion and extreme displays, as a result of family response patterns. For example, cutting and overdosing are likely both to regulate emotion and to elicit at least some helping behaviors from a family environment that typically ignores or punishes emotional expression and pain.

In addition, children growing up in invalidating environments may not learn how to regulate their emotional arousal or tolerate negative emotion or even moderate levels of emotional distress, and may instead rely on others for information about what to feel and think and how to respond. This external search for private information may similarly result in an unstable sense of self or identity (Koerner, Kohlenberg, & Parker, 1996). In turn, having difficulties regulating emotion and relying on the environment both for cues to private experiences and for help in regulating emotions interferes with the development of stable adult relationships. Thus, the transaction (emotional vulnerability ←→ invalidating environment) continues.

DIALECTICS

Dialectics provides the theoretical underpinnings of both the transactional model of the development of BPD and the structure and treatment strategies of DBT. Historically, dialectics provided a rationale for adding together and then synthesizing acceptance and validation strategies with procedures to change behaviors and reduce suicidal crises. Ultimately, this synthesis resulted in a treatment theory and structure that we now call dialectic behavior therapy. Dialectical principles in DBT were derived and adapted from both Western contemplative and Eastern meditative practices as well as from dialectical philosophy (Linehan, 1993a; Pinkard, 1988). Theoretically, dialectics in DBT refers to both an understanding of the nature of reality and behavior change and to a method of engaging in persuasion, providing both an ontological and an epistemological framework for the theory and the treatment. The dialectical position informs specific applications and intervention strategies.

In a dialectical worldview, wholeness and interrelatedness are emphasized over logical positivism and separateness, consistent with a transactional or contextual behavioral theory of the development of BPD and related disorders. Similarly, change is accepted as an ongoing process and a fundamental characteristic of reality (the only consistency is change). This view, although consistent with spiritual practice in both Eastern and Western traditions, may also be considered a contextual worldview (Fruzzetti & Linehan, 2001). That is, any specific behavior may be considered only in its context and in the context of the question being asked. Both the context of the object under study (e.g., a client's given behavior) and the context for the observer (e.g., the therapist or treatment team; their rationale or goal for the analysis) must be considered to be effective. Thus, as in systems theory, the part must be related to the whole for a fuller understanding of any phenomenon.

Moreover, dialectics suggests that in trying to identify any part of a behavioral analysis (or any subpart of a system), there is necessarily tension, or polarity. For example, for every proposition (or thesis) about the cause of a target behavior (e.g., cutting), there will be one or more alternatives naturally generated (antitheses) that expose the limitations of the original explanation and add potential explanatory power. This ongoing transaction of ideas (thesis and antithesis) forges new syntheses, which are in turn the next theses. These polarities include, but are not limited to, understanding from the perspective of historical versus present factors in causality;

biological versus environmental factors; individual versus family environment factors; client versus therapist; good versus bad; and acceptance versus change. This process of analysis continues until an *effective* (not right or wrong) understanding or explanation is achieved, one from which a promising intervention may be attempted. For example, if a client's mother frequently cut herself as a means of emotional self-management, and the client was regularly exposed to this, it is reasonable to see the explanation for her behavior historically, as learned through modeling. Whatever face validity this explanation may hold, this thesis naturally generates a critical question: But why did she cut herself on Thursday morning, not Wednesday evening or Thursday afternoon? This question about current factors exposes the limitations of the first explanation or proposition. Arriving at some synthesis, one might conclude that both early learning and current emotional factors (e.g., she had just been criticized in a phone call with a family member) were relevant in the present cutting behavior. This proposition might naturally generate another alternative proposition (antithesis) that exposes the limitations of the synthesis (new proposition)—When criticized, she gets deeply ashamed and cannot tolerate this aversive arousal—which leads the therapist and team to consider internal, not just external, factors. This process continues until some intervention strategy, consistent with agreed on treatment targets and the data collected, is developed. Data collected from this new intervention strategy are incorporated into the analysis subsequently, if the intervention is not successful. It is therefore essential to recognize that, in a dialectical worldview, there is no "right" answer or explanation, but rather many possible effective ones, those that lead to successful interventions.

Similarly, dialectics provides a rationale and a method for targeting increasing *effective* (more functional) client behaviors: those that not only provide immediate emotional or instrumental improvements, but are also consistent with long-term goals and a life worth living. Thus, dialectics also describes a method of persuasion or engagement in behavior change in which the therapist and client (or team members) utilize and embrace the contradictions in opposing positions, rather than attempt to use logic to refute opposing points of view. New meanings are synthesized through this process, and the dialogue becomes one of collaboration rather than merely confrontation. All parties to a discussion embrace the question, What is missing, what is being left out from our consideration? and collaborate toward a fuller meaning or explanation, one with a new synthesis and new implications for intervention.

Finally, a dialectic approach informs the structure and the strategies of treatment. The fundamental dialectic in DBT revolves around the tension between acceptance and change. Thus, acceptance and validation strategies are balanced and synthesized with problem-solving and change strategies. Similarly, other treatment strategies necessarily have at least two polarities, and treatment providers endeavor to balance or synthesize these polarities. These strategies are described next.

MAJOR SYNDROMES, SYMPTOMS, AND PROBLEMS TREATED

Because of the heterogeneous nature of BPD, the client population for whom DBT has been successful has varied tremendously in terms of presenting problems and other diagnoses. DBT specifically targets emotion dysregulation and its associated problems, which is hypothesized to be the core problem in borderline personality and its related disorders. Thus, on the one hand, DBT has been utilized primarily for borderline women; on the other, it takes a problem focus as opposed to a diagnostic one.

The problem focus for which DBT was developed is suicidal and parasuicidal behavior. The term *parasuicidal* is used to provide a description of behavior on a continuum with suicide, without making assumptions about the function or intention of that behavior. Many terms used to describe suicidal and self-injurious behavior, or that are associated with parasuicidal behavior, lead practitioners (and others) to take more pejorative positions due to the implied assumptions of these terms. For example, the term "suicidal gesture" is often used as a synonym for parasuicidal behavior (e.g., cutting that did not require sutures), without assessing the intent of the individual or the function of the cutting. On further assessment, it may be determined that cutting in this instance was quite private and functioned to ameliorate intense emotional distress and not to communicate suicidality to others or to seek help or attention. Descriptive terms are generally preferred in DBT, thereby promoting careful assessment of the function, intention, and meaning of given behaviors. Because this kind of assessment information is not included in any diagnostic criteria, assessment must extend well beyond diagnosis.

Despite the problems associated with *DSM* diagnostic nosology (e.g., W. C. Follette & Houts, 1996; Fruzzetti, 1996), accurate diagnosis may be important when it informs treatment choices (Hayes, Nelson, & Jarrett, 1987). DBT clearly has amassed the most support as a treatment for BPD (e.g., Koerner & Dimeff, 2000; Linehan, 2000). Nevertheless, it is important to understand how and why BPD, per se is a means of organizing the large and heterogeneous set of problems demonstrated by clients who also meet criteria for BPD.

Linehan (1993a) has reorganized the *DSM-IV* (American Psychiatric Association [APA], 1994) criteria for BPD into multiple areas of *dysregulation*. Specifically, emotion dysregulation includes the *DSM* criteria of emotional lability and problems with anger; interpersonal dysregulation includes chronic fears of abandonment and interpersonal chaos; behavioral dysregulation includes parasuicidal behaviors and other impulsive behaviors; self dysregulation includes feelings of emptiness; and cognitive dysregulation includes transient paranoia and difficulty thinking. The advantage of this reorganization is that the problem behaviors that define the disorder are identified as treatment targets in a theoretically consistent way. Moreover, the treatment is then organized around skill acquisition to ameliorate each of these areas of dysregulation.

Perhaps more important than theoretical consistency, this reorganization accounts for the multiple problems of comorbidity found in BPD. For example, several cross-sectional studies have shown very high rates of depression or other affective disorders, Panic Disorder, Posttraumatic Stress Disorder, eating disorders, substance abuse disorders, Dissociative Disorder, and other personality disorders (cf. Linehan, 1993a). Many of the behavioral deficits or excesses of these other diagnoses may reasonably be seen as emotion, cognitive, interpersonal, self, or behavioral dysregulation as well. Consequently, these comorbid disorders may be viewed theoretically as overlapping with BPD for some patients; therefore, treating BPD effectively may concomitantly treat these comorbid disorders.

Because DBT was developed to treat multi-problem clients with emotion dysregulation problems, it has recently been applied to patients with diagnoses other than BPD whose difficulties may reasonably be considered to revolve around emotion dysregulation. These problems include suicidality among adolescents (Miller, 1999; Rathus & Miller, 2000), aggression and violence (Fruzzetti & Levensky, 2000; McCann, Ball, & Ivanoff, 2000), eating disorders (Telch, Agras, & Linehan, 2000; Wiser & Telch, 1999), and substance abuse (Linehan et al., 1999). Ongoing research will determine the efficacy of DBT for these populations.

METHODS OF ASSESSMENT

Assessment in DBT may have three purposes (Fruzzetti & Levensky, 2000), as is the case with most cognitive and behavior therapies. Assessment determines appropriateness for treatment (identifying inclusion and exclusion criteria), identifies and measures ongoing treatment targets, and allows the effectiveness of the treatment to be determined (pretreatment, posttreatment, and perhaps during a follow-up period). The assessment method used may vary to some extent depending on its purpose.

INCLUSION/EXCLUSION CRITERIA AND APPROPRIATENESS FOR TREATMENT

Because most of the data supporting the effectiveness of DBT have utilized BPD as an essential inclusion criterion, it is often desirable to assess whether or not clients meet these criteria. The most common assessments for BPD are the Structured Clinical Interview for *DSM-IV*, Axis II (SCID-II; First, Gibbon, Spitzer, & Williams, 1995), the Diagnostic Interview for Borderline Personality Disorder (Zanarini, Gunderson, Frankenburg, & Chauncey, 1989), or an unstructured clinical interview employing the *DSM-IV* criteria. Although reliability is often only modest, these are the best available methods to date for assessing the presence or absence of BPD.

One promising assessment tool is the Life Problems Inventory (LPI), developed by Rathus and Miller (1995). The LPI is a 60-item self-report that measures each of the four subtypes of dysregulation central to borderline personality from a DBT perspective. Thus, the LPI creates subscales that correspond to the treatment model and provides both a measurement of severity of BPD and a face valid method of treatment outcome. Moreover, this method provides a test of the underlying treatment model as well as the treatment itself (W. C. Follette, 1995). The

LPI has acceptable internal consistency (subscale alphas ranging from .82 to .90) and criterion validity.

TREATMENT TARGETS

Treatment targets are very specifically defined in DBT, and the use of daily diary or self-monitoring cards allows for regular assessment of these targets. For example, life-threatening behaviors such as suicide attempts and parasuicidal behaviors are the highest-level target in DBT, and patients who currently or recently have had suicidal or parasuicidal thoughts, urges, or actions would monitor all three of these behaviors on at least a daily basis. Thus, the therapist efficiently assesses patient functioning since the previous session and sets an agenda for the present session simply by going over the diary card with the patient.

In addition, because borderline clients in DBT are often suicidal, it may be useful to assess their reasons for living to identify motivating factors in times of distress. The Reasons for Living Inventory serves this purpose (Ivanoff, Jang, Smyth, & Linehan, 1994; Linehan, Goodstein, Nielson, & Chiles, 1983) and may also be employed as a measure of change at the end of treatment.

Diary Cards

In addition to assessing targets for treatment, the use of diary cards also affords a cost-effective means of evaluating treatment success and treatment outcome. Clinicians in nonresearch settings may easily compile diary card data over regular intervals (weekly, monthly, quarterly, etc.) to determine the extent to which client problem behaviors (e.g., parasuicide, substance use, emergency room visits) change over time.

However, assessment of treatment targets does not stop with simple measurement of frequency or severity. Careful behavioral or chain analyses are conducted to understand the function of problem behaviors, to identify factors that inhibit the use of new, more functional behaviors, and to identify specific behaviors (secondary targets such as emotion dysregulation or self-invalidation) that lead to the primary problems or targets of treatment (e.g., life-threatening behaviors, substance abuse). Identifying antecedents and consequences of any problem behavior therefore also highlights specific behaviors "along the chain" that can be modified to result in more adaptive, less dysfunctional client behavior.

TREATMENT OUTCOMES

In addition to summarizing data collected on diary cards and the use of the LPI, various self-report questionnaires, structured or semistructured interviews, observational data, system data (e.g., resource utilization, costs), and reports by others may be employed to measure treatment outcome along one dimension or another.

With respect to client outcomes specifically, clients may complete self-reports of general psychopathology (e.g., Brief Symptom Inventory; Derogatis & Melisatatos, 1985) or of specific problems (e.g., the Beck Depression Inventory to assess depression; Beck, 1979). Although a comprehensive review of all the reliable or valid measures of psychopathology is beyond the scope of this chapter, any valid index of patient problems may be employed to measure treatment outcomes.

In addition, it may be more valid to assess certain kinds of problems in multiple ways and perhaps to employ more than one method. For example, measuring the acquisition of social skills may be accurately assessed using direct observation or the reports of friends or family members, and not solely via paper-and-pencil skill tests. Similarly, measuring resource utilization (inpatient days, number of emergency room visits, overall patient costs in a year) may be done efficiently with cooperation from management information systems. Level of therapist burnout should be ascertained via assessment of the therapist. Regardless of method, assessment of outcomes is an essential component of DBT.

METHODS OF INTERVENTION

TREATMENT TARGETS: STAGES OF DISORDER, STAGES OF TREATMENT

The first step in DBT is structuring the treatment frame in a way that is informed both by the biosocial/transactional theory and by a model of the stages of disorder to create a hierarchy of treatment targets (Linehan, 1993a, 1999). This hierarchy requires that more severe and/or out-of-control behaviors be addressed before less severe behaviors, and promotes clarity and precision of case conceptualization and treatment targets.

The overarching goal of DBT is helping clients create and maintain a life worth living according to their own core values. Treatment targets are lined up hierarchically according to how severely they interfere with creating a life worth living. Specifically, treatment is organized according to stages that correspond to stages of disorder. Each stage primarily targets those behaviors that most interfere with the goals of each stage. In turn, each *primary target* (e.g., cutting) is assessed to determine which specific patient behaviors, environmental events, or behaviors of others are "on the chain" toward the primary targets. These other behaviors are called *secondary targets,* and may be similar or different across primary targets. Secondary targets may also vary when assessing the same primary target across different episodes (see Case Example later in this chapter).

Pretreatment Stage of Treatment

Prior to beginning treatment formally, DBT requires a clear orientation of the patient to the nature of the treatment (e.g., how it is conducted and evaluated, the modes of treatment available), treatment target hierarchy, assessment procedures, agreed upon length of treatment (and the factors that would result in more or less treatment), and any rules of the treatment setting. During this orienting and committing phase of treatment, the pros and cons of entering DBT (and of other available treatments or no treatment) are evaluated by the client and therapist. Clients begin to complete daily self-monitoring sheets, the therapist demonstrates the process of treatment, and together they evaluate (and try to reduce or resolve) factors that are likely to interfere with active participation and commitment to the treatment program. The primary targets during this phase, which typically lasts from two to four sessions in an outpatient setting, are orienting and committing to the treatment. Once an agreement is reached, treatment moves on to the first stage of treatment.

Stage 1

The main difficulty in stage 1 is behavioral dyscontrol, so the goal here is for the patient to achieve behavioral control across all relevant contexts. More specifically, behavioral safety and stability across three domains are targeted: (1) life-threatening behaviors, including suicidal and parasuicidal behaviors, aggression and violence (as a perpetrator or victim), and child abuse and neglect; (2) therapy-interfering behaviors, or behaviors that interfere with the patient receiving the treatment (e.g., client does not come to session, noncollaborative behaviors of the patient or therapist), behaviors that interfere with other patients receiving the treatment (e.g., verbal criticism toward other patients, giving drugs to other patients), or behaviors that would likely "burn out" the therapist or treatment team or decrease the therapist's motivation to treat the client; and (3) severe quality of life-interfering behaviors, such as severe drug abuse, a severe eating disorder, being homeless or in jail, or other out-of-control behaviors that preclude or limit an acceptable quality of life. Treatment in this stage, therefore, focuses on achieving stability and bringing out of control behaviors into control. This is achieved by teaching clients self-management skills, strengthening those skills, and helping them to generalize new skills to their natural environment. Similarly, treatment may also help clients to change their environments to make them safer, more stable, and more compatible with skillful living (Fruzzetti & Fruzzetti, in press; Hoffman et al., 1999). When safety and stability are achieved, treatment moves on to stage 2.

Stage 2
The main difficulty in the second stage is emotional misery, which is hypothesized to be related to deficits in emotional experiencing. The prototype problem for this stage is Posttraumatic Stress Disorder (PTSD), in which the individual suffers primarily due to emotional pain associated with traumatic cues and has overgeneralized or overlearned avoidance and escape behaviors, which function to keep emotional misery lower. Although not all borderline patients have PTSD, any pervasive or generalized emotional misery (including problems escaping or avoiding emotions or emotional stimuli) may be treated in this stage. Thus, the individual treatment target for this stage of treatment is effective emotional experiencing (without escalating or blunting).

It is important to note that patients often respond to trauma treatment with increased arousal and frequently have renewed thoughts or urges to engage in stage 1 behaviors once again. Sometimes, patients do relapse into old, problematic behaviors. This is anticipated in DBT, and relapse prevention is a frequent target in stage 2. If stage 1 behaviors reemerge, treatment again focuses on these targets until stability and safety are established once again, and then treatment moves back to stage 2 targets. Successful treatment of trauma-related affect and other trauma-related behaviors sometimes involves moving back and forth between stage 1 and stage 2 targets quite fluidly.

To experience and express emotions effectively, one must have the requisite skills to do so and a supportive or validating environment to support or reinforce effective expression (Fruzzetti & Linehan, 2001); a validating social environment may be a therapist (e.g., for exposure treatment for trauma) or good relationships with family members or friends.

Stage 3
The main difficulty in stage 3 is considered to be life problems; thus, ameliorating major life problems are now the main treatment targets. Because safety and stability have been achieved and emotional experiencing is possible for the client, the focus in stage 3 turns to problems in living: problem solving (change) or problem management (problem acceptance that minimizes associated difficulties). Typically, stage 3 targets include resolving education- or employment-related difficulties and improving relationships.

Stage 4
Finally, a last stage of treatment has been described (Fruzzetti & Fruzzetti, in press; Linehan, 1999) in which the main target involves "incompleteness," or the recognition that even after significant or even ordinary life problems have been solved, human beings sometimes struggle with meaning, isolation, and intimacy. The presence of stage 4 is less a well-articulated set of treatment strategies or options than a recognition of ongoing life struggles that virtually everyone encounters, even in the absence of difficulties with safety, stability, emotional misery, or significant life problems. Thus, enhancing the capacity for sustained contentment and joy is the main target here.

MODES AND FUNCTIONS OF TREATMENT

DBT is not defined by the way it is delivered, but by the functions of the treatment and the goals it tries to accomplish. Although the mode of delivery may vary widely, five different functions of the treatment must be delivered to define a treatment as comprehensive DBT: (1) capability enhancement, (2) skill generalization, (3) patient motivation, (4) therapist capability enhancement and motivation, and (5) structuring the environment. Providing only a subset of these five necessary functions is similar to offering cardiac surgery without anesthesia, skilled nursing, or a sterile operating environment: A reasonable and important target is addressed, but the absence of necessary treatment components likely renders the treatment either useless, impossible, or suboptimal.

Capability enhancement typically centers around skill acquisition or skill training and may also include pharmacotherapy targeting specific symptom reduction (Linehan, 1993a). An assumption of the treatment model is that patients have psychological and social skill deficits and need to learn skills in all relevant contexts of their lives. Often, pharmacotherapy is employed to make skill training more effective by reducing specific problem behaviors that would otherwise interfere with skill acquisition.

Skill training typically follows the guidelines presented in Linehan's skill training manual (1993b), which includes mindfulness skills, emotion regulation skills, distress tolerance skills, and interpersonal effectiveness skills. Each of these is designed to ameliorate difficulties associated with BPD. For example, mindfulness provides training in attention control and awareness of self and others, helps to reduce emotional reactivity, and provides a foundation for self-validation (helping to reduce feelings of emptiness and self and cognitive dysregulation). Emotion regulation provides skills to identify and label emotions, to reduce vulnerability to negative emotion, to reduce suffering associated with negative emotion, and to help change negative emotion (reducing emotional lability and problems associated with anger and other negative emotions). Distress tolerance skills provide a counterbalance to impulsivity, teaching clients how to inhibit dysfunctional

actions (such as parasuicide or substance abuse), to tolerate intense emotional pain and urges to engage in problematic responses, and not to exacerbate whatever suffering or misery they may have. Finally, interpersonal effectiveness skills teach clients how to achieve their objectives interpersonally, to manage relationships effectively, and to maintain self-respect in interpersonal situations. Moreover, DBT interpersonal effectiveness skills teach clients how to balance and juggle effectively their specific situational objectives with their relationship objectives while maintaining or enhancing self-respect.

As a behavioral treatment, it is not assumed that learning basic skills will generalize to the environment without focusing on transferring these skills from one setting to another. Thus, skill generalization is an essential function of this treatment. Generalization is typically accomplished through a combination of planning or programming (homework, planned practice) and the use of in vivo coaching in situations in which clients need skills in their daily lives. For example, clients may call the therapist for help in identifying or employing skills between sessions while they work on a primary target.

Attending to patient motivation is another essential function of DBT. In this instance, motivation is defined behaviorally: identifying and modifying the conditions (antecedents and consequences) that create or maintain dysfunctional behaviors, or that inhibit, punish, or fail to reinforce more functional and skillful alternative behaviors. Thus, once a primary target is identified for treatment in a session, the antecedents and consequences of the problem behavior are analyzed, and alternatives are identified (typically using skills from one of the four skill modules). If employed in the future, these skillful alternatives would promote more functional behaviors and outcomes.

Typically, this function is achieved in individual therapy, particularly when clients have life-threatening behaviors. However, motivation per se is the primary target, and alternative modes (e.g., group therapy, family therapy) have been employed for nonlife-threatening behavioral targets (e.g., Fruzzetti & Fruzzetti, in press; Telch et al., 2000).

DBT requires therapists to acquire necessary treatment skills and maintain a high level of motivation (Fruzzetti, Waltz, & Linehan, 1997). It is a difficult treatment to deliver, and borderline, suicidal, multiproblem clients are often difficult to treat in any modality. Thus, it is assumed that therapists need constantly to enhance their skills and attend to their own motivation. A typical way to accomplish this is for therapists to form a consultation team that meets regularly (typically, once per week for outpatient treatment programs). During the team meeting, case conceptualization is discussed, treatment is reviewed, behavioral analyses are scrutinized, and the motivation of the therapist is assessed and treated. With the exception of some family therapies and some treatments for severe psychosis (for some of the same reasons: trying to maintain a balance), few other treatments require ongoing consultation even after achieving a high level of expertise. For these clients and this therapy, however, ongoing consultation is required.

Other activities also function to enhance therapist skills and motivation to treat. For example, any continuing education on topics relevant to treating borderline or multiproblem clients might enhance skills. Similarly, providing staff incentives for effective treatment, making available program follow-up data, and providing opportunities for case consultation may also address issues of therapist motivation and reduce burnout.

Finally, a DBT treatment team must also be able to structure a patient's environment. Typically, environmental structuring falls into one of two categories: administrative or family/social environment. The objective is to increase the likelihood that when clients make progress, their environment will not punish their increasingly functional behavior. For example, if an agency has a rule that individual therapy is available only to suicidal patients and that they must move to group-only treatment after stabilization, clients may lose their individual therapist at this point (perhaps punishing a client for his or her success). In such a setting, structuring the environment would involve changing the rules so that a patient could continue working with his or her individual therapist as long as other criteria were met (e.g., staying out of hospital) or for a fixed length of time (not dependent on *not* making progress).

Similarly, if a patient learns new interpersonal effectiveness skills but is beaten up by a partner or family member when trying to implement them (or told to find a new place to live), these skills will effectively be punished. Structuring the environment in this case would involve social or family intervention or therapy to help the client reinforce significant others for reinforcing the patient's progress.

All five of these functions are what define DBT. Although to date, no comprehensive study has systematically established that each component or function is equally important, at least one study indicates that offering less than comprehensive treatment may not be effective. In her initial outcome study, Linehan and colleagues (Linehan et al., 1991) found that skill training plus uncontrolled (non-DBT) individual therapy resulted in fewer treatment effects than did comprehensive DBT. Thus, unless and until subsequent research specifically demonstrates that a subset of these functions is sufficient for good outcomes, all five functions must be provided to call a treatment DBT.

ACCEPTANCE AND VALIDATION STRATEGIES

Acceptance strategies have an important role in DBT. As part of the new wave in behavior therapy that emphasizes acceptance as well as change, Linehan and colleagues have pioneered the addition and application of acceptance principles and strategies to augment behavior therapy (Linehan, 1993a, 1994). Acceptance is found in multiple ways in DBT. It may be a treatment target for a client (in contrast to client nonacceptance), a therapist behavior employed to reinforce progress, or a team target to balance emphasis on change or to combat judgmental behavior.

Acceptance as a treatment target is taught via mindfulness skills. In mindfulness, patients learn to observe, describe, or participate, and to do so nonjudgmentally, one thing at a time, and effectively (in the service of long-term goals). This is important because it is so much in contrast to the pervasive, problematic, nonaccepting/nonmindful behavior that is the hallmark of borderline clients. Similarly, by embracing a nonjudgmental therapeutic stance, DBT clinicians more easily avoid the common pitfalls of treatment with difficult clients.

Linehan has described a set of ways that therapists may communicate acceptance toward clients using validation strategies (Linehan, 1998). Validation in DBT means communicating, in a genuine and honest way, an understanding of the legitimacy of a client's behavior at the level or in the way(s) in which it is legitimate. Specifically, therapists may validate verbally in six different ways or at six different levels of validity: (1) attentive listening; (2) reflecting the client's observable (via actions or verbal statements) emotions, thoughts, wants, or goals; (3) articulating the client's unverbalized emotions, thoughts, wants, or goals; (4) acknowledging the legitimacy of a given behavior in light of the client's learning history (life experiences, behavioral or biological dysfunction or disorder); (5) acknowledging the legitimacy of a given behavior in the present circumstances (normalizing the behavior); and (6) responding in a radically genuine way (i.e., not treating the client as fragile). Of course, simply being responsive to a patient, or to his or her requests, may also be validating in a functional (not necessarily verbal) way.

DBT puts a premium on validating behavior at the highest possible level to counterbalance the pervasive invalidation that borderline patients have experienced. High levels of validation also reduce the likelihood that treatment providers will pathologize "normative" behaviors simply because the client may have a large repertoire of problem behaviors. Moreover, validating valid behaviors (or the parts that are valid) may subsequently make it possible to invalidate the invalid parts of a given behavior, resulting in a kind of discrimination training.

In Linehan's conceptualization, acceptance and validation almost always may be employed for one or more targets. For example, even when targeting dysfunctional behaviors such as substance abuse or parasuicide, the emotional suffering experienced may be validated, as may the difficulty of the task of engaging in more functional and skillful but less well-learned alternatives. It is important to note that validation is provided only in response to valid behaviors at the level at which they are valid. For example, if a patient is told by her boyfriend that he wants to break up, the client may feel hurt, sad, disappointed, afraid, and/or angry, and her emotion may escalate to very high, aversive levels of arousal. She may drink alcohol and, later in the day, cut herself as a means of reducing negative emotional arousal. When analyzing this chain of behavior, perhaps in the subsequent therapy session, her therapist may note how normal it is to feel sad, disappointed, hurt, afraid, or angry when a boyfriend or girlfriend breaks up with the other person (level 5 validation). However, the therapist likely would also point out that cutting is an overlearned response to emotional arousal for this client (level 4 validation) and is problematic (thereby also pointing out the invalid/ineffective part of the given behavior).

Finally, acceptance is also a team target. That is, not only is acceptance of the client an essential part of DBT, but every effort is made to accept and validate therapists' views and feelings about clients and the process of treatment. Members of the treatment team are encouraged to participate in discussions about clients, each other, and the treatment free from fears of a judgmental response from team members. Thus, the notion of acceptance permeates the treatment at multiple levels.

Problem-Solving and Change Strategies

Change strategies in DBT reflect its behavioral roots. After determining the appropriate target for intervention using the treatment target hierarchy, the therapist performs a careful behavioral analysis and helps the client to employ more skillful solutions as alternatives to problematic behaviors. Finally, the therapist orients the client to the solution(s) and together they strengthen the patient's commitment to the solution. Each of these steps is discussed briefly below.

Behavioral or Chain Analysis

Performing an effective behavioral analysis or chain analysis of the target behavior is the first step toward effective solutions. In a dialectical or contextual behavioral worldview, no one analysis of the causes is considered to be "correct." Rather, an effective chain analysis results in identifying targets for treatment that can be implemented and, if accomplished, reduce the likelihood of the target behavior and increase the likelihood of skillful alternatives. Consequently, early learning or very distal factors are not included in a chain analysis even when there is agreement that they were influential in the development of a dysfunctional behavior or behavior pattern. Instead, vulnerability factors (e.g., insufficient sleep or nutrition, too much caffeine), triggers (specific events in the environment or behaviors of others), and the chain of events that lead to the target behavior (thoughts, emotions, urges, actions, responses of others, etc.) are noted, and the reinforcing

consequences for the target behavior are similarly identified.

For example, if an incident of cutting was identified from the diary card on Saturday, the following chain might be identified: Vulnerability factors might have included drinking on Friday night, which contributed to poor sleep that night, a hangover in the morning, staying in bed until noon, and eating no breakfast Saturday. A trigger might have been a phone call from the client's father, who scolded her for "still being in bed at noon on a Saturday." He also told her he was ashamed of her. After hanging up from the phone call, the client felt a lot of shame, self-invalidated (e.g., "I'm a bad person for this, I'm no good, I deserve to be treated like shit"), and felt escalating shame. She then had urges to drink more, then felt overwhelming shame, along with fear (of others' responses to her), sat on the floor of her bathroom crying while having urges to harm herself, and a few minutes later cut the inside of her thigh with a razor blade. She cleaned up her cut and the blood off the floor, felt less negatively aroused, took a shower, got dressed, ate lunch, and went on with her day.

Solution Analysis

A solution analysis involves identifying one or more alternative behaviors that could be implemented on a chain of behaviors that would likely alter the outcome, and then weaving one or more of these skillful solutions into the chain. For example, in the previous behavioral analysis, the client could focus energy on reducing her vulnerabilities (emotion regulation skills that target drinking less, treating a hangover more effectively, or balancing her eating better). Or the therapist and client could focus on helping the client to self-manage more effectively when vulnerable. For example, she could remember to screen her calls and talk with her father on the phone only when she is emotionally less vulnerable (using mindfulness and accurate emotion identification). The therapist could focus on helping the client learn how to assert or defend herself more when being criticized (using interpersonal effectiveness skills), reduce excessive shame through "opposite action" (an emotion regulation skill), or tolerate her misery while engaging in alternative activities, allowing her arousal to subside without self-harm (distress tolerance skills). Other links and other skillful alternatives could be identified.

Skill Training

One of the assumptions DBT makes is that borderline clients lack skillful behaviors in their repertoires, especially in emotionally difficult situations. As noted, DBT emphasizes the training of mindfulness, emotion regulation, distress tolerance, and interpersonal effectiveness skills in the service of self-management. Each of these skills is taught from skill modules that include teaching outlines, skill handouts, and homework exercises (Linehan, 1993b). Each module includes multiple skills designed specifically to ameliorate one or more of the skill deficits hypothesized to result from the transaction between emotion vulnerability and an invalidating environment.

As noted, skill acquisition is one of the core functions of this treatment. More than just describing a skill, good skill acquisition includes finding a rationale for clients that is motivating, typically by connecting learning a given skill to one or more of a client's actual goals, providing clear instruction at the level of sophistication of the client, giving relevant examples, providing clear modeling, and encouraging client practice. Skills must also be strengthened through rehearsal and corrective feedback and then generalized or transferred to daily life.

Commitment Strategies

Learning a skill and understanding or appreciating how useful it might be to employ that skill as an alternative to dysfunctional target behaviors is not necessarily sufficient to result in the person's actually using the skill when needed. Many different commitment strategies are employed in DBT to enhance the probability that the person will use the skill, and do so effectively as needed. For example, verbal commitment to do something different may help. However, verbal intent is often not sufficient to result in complex or difficult behavior change (e.g., intending or wanting to diet or exercise has minimal behavioral impact for most people). Evaluating the pros and cons of doing the new versus old behavior can result in enhancing motivation, as can playing devil's advocate, in which the client is asked to identify the disadvantages of new, often difficult, behavioral change. Role playing or practice may help, as may anticipating interfering factors and working through them or shaping stronger and stronger commitments over time.

General Behavior Therapy and Cognitive Therapy Strategies

Virtually every behavior therapy or cognitive therapy intervention strategy may be employed in DBT. For example, stimulus control strategies are often used in DBT. Mindfulness, with its emphasis on attention control, may be considered a stimulus control strategy. In addition, DBT therapists may use stimulus control techniques to help make genuine positive verbal feedback function more normatively for clients (i.e., as a reinforcer) for whom positive response of others has a negative (punishing) impact. Avoiding certain cues to keep arousal at moderate levels is another common use of stimulus control.

Similarly, contingency management strategies are routinely employed in DBT. The most important rule in DBT may simply be Do not reinforce dysfunctional behavior, which is, of course, an example of contingency management (extinction of target behaviors). Also, the 24-hour rule in DBT suggests that the individual therapist not have any unplanned contact with a client within 24 hours after parasuicide to minimize the chance that the therapist will provide any attentional/social reinforcement (of course, the client would continue to have access to crisis intervention staff through a different means during this "therapy blackout," similar to that which is available during a therapist's vacation). In addition, DBT therapists utilize in-session differential responding in ways similar to that found in functional analytic psychotherapy (Kohlenberg & Tsai, 1991) not to reinforce dysfunctional behaviors but instead reinforce more collaborative, functional in-session behaviors.

Exposure and response prevention is employed in DBT in any stage of treatment. However, with clients who have PTSD, these strategies may be at the core of stage 2 interventions that focus on alleviating emotional misery, reducing emotional avoidance, and enhancing emotional experiencing. These strategies may be used formally in stage 2 for trauma (cf. Foa & Rothbaum, 1998; V. M. Follette, Ruzek, & Abueg, 1998) and also may be employed more informally to treat and reduce in-session emotional reactivity by blocking escape responses and simultaneously coaching skillful self-management while repeatedly presenting the emotional stimulus until it loses some of its potency.

Cognitive modification strategies are also utilized in DBT. However, cognitive strategies are less common in the early stages of treatment because they are less effective when a client is emotionally (and therefore cognitively) dysregulated. As clients become more regulated, cognitive interventions provide a balance to emotion regulation strategies.

Thus, the entirety of behavior therapy and cognitive therapy may be employed in the service of helping clients to change problematic behaviors. However, just as little change seems to occur when acceptance and validation are the only modes of treatment and change itself is not targeted, clients often feel invalidated and less motivated to change if change strategies are used alone. *In DBT, the balance of acceptance and change strategies is the primary treatment dialectic,* which will be addressed further following.

DIALECTICAL STRATEGIES

Treatments that focus primarily on change may not be experienced only as invalidating for borderline clients, but clients may become dysregulated, hopeless, and noncollaborative as a result of not feeling understood (e.g., Swann, 1997). Conversely, focusing exclusively on acceptance and validation likely will leave the chronically suicidal borderline patient stuck in his or her misery and dysfunctional behavior patterns, without any new skills or behaviors that are more functional. Thus, balancing or synthesizing acceptance and change strategies is the first dialectic treatment strategy.

It is important to consider what "balancing treatment strategies" (acceptance/validation with change/problem solving) actually means in practice. First of all, dialectical balance does not mean equal parts, nor does it suggest that both acceptance and change strategies must be employed all the time. Rather, balance refers both to the process of choosing and delivering different treatment strategies and to the goal of enacting whatever treatment balance is necessary to be effective. A dialectical position is one in which the therapist and other treatment team members pay virtually constant attention to emphasizing both acceptance and change, if not in a synthesis (i.e., using a single intervention that includes parts of both), then at least in harmony. A dialectical position also assumes that acceptance by the client can be facilitated by emphasizing change, and that change can be accomplished by emphasizing acceptance. Of course, in the absence of balance, emphasizing either may facilitate neither acceptance nor change.

Furthermore, an emphasis on dialectics also provides therapists with a beginning question when they are starting to get stuck with a client: What am I leaving out, or what is out of balance? Thus, the therapist (along with the client and/or treatment team members) keeps the focus on effective outcomes, not on being "right," and views balancing validation with change strategies as the primary means of achieving an effective treatment outcome. For example, if a client's cutting (or substance use or any other target) has been a target for change, but no change has occurred for months, the therapist may ask: What is missing? What am I not understanding? What am I not validating? These questions may lead to a more careful assessment, perhaps of the function of the target behavior or of the antecedents. Finding, accepting, and validating new links on the chain may be an important step in helping to reduce the target behavior. Similarly, trying to help a client self-validate self-worth more (acceptance) in the context of criticism from others may not yield much success. Alternatively, helping clients to be more skillful (accepting certain deficits and working to change them) may in turn reduce criticisms from others and make it possible to self-validate or "accept" themselves more.

In addition to taking a dialectical position throughout the treatment, DBT also employs specific dialectical strategies for use in different treatment situations (cf. Linehan, 1993a). The aim of these strategies is to provide the therapist with ways to achieve, or maintain, a dialectical position of balance from which treatment can be effective. For example, using metaphors (taking the observing role; reducing reactivity), trying to help the client act from a "wise mind" (a synthesis of reason and emotion in mindfulness practice), or "making lemonade out of lemons" (acknowledging undesirable parts of the situation but enhancing motivation to change anyway) all orient the therapist and client to balance. This is the essence of dialectical balance: accepting what is and changing what is necessary for an effective outcome.

OTHER CORE STRATEGIES

Communication Strategies

The style with which therapists communicate with clients may also be viewed from a dialectical perspective (Linehan, 1993a). For example, a therapist may express *reciprocal* communication, which is often gentle, highly genuine and accepting in tone, and typified by humanistic or client-centered therapies. Alternatively, a therapist may express *irreverent* communication, a style that often represents an abrupt change in tone or is unexpected or even unorthodox in the moment or context in which it is used. Irreverent communication may often be found in rational-emotive-behavior therapy and in strategic therapies.

Reciprocal communication minimizes the role difference between therapist and client for the moment because the therapist is being genuine, responsive, often disclosing (his or her own reactions in the moment), reflecting warmth and acceptance. This style of communication inherently validates the client's experience in the moment and his or her goals and agenda. However, although often warm and always genuine, reciprocal communication also requires that the therapist not treat the client as a fragile person. That is, warmth and caring are communicated in a context of equality, not fragility.

In contrast, irreverent communication accentuates the role difference between therapist and client for that moment because the therapist is specifically trying to push the client off balance, as a means to help him or her become "unstuck." This strategy is designed to change the tone and get the client's attention and may be directly confrontational, may reframe the client's statement in an unorthodox way, and may even include an element of humor. Although irreverent communication highlights the therapist's role via its change orientation, it also requires treating the client as a competent, equal human being, one who can stand a push now and then. Importantly, irreverent communication should not be sarcastic or disrespectful.

Case Management Strategies

Borderline patients often live very chaotic lives that include multiple environmental stressors. When environmental factors interfere with client progress, case management strategies are employed. These strategies include two general (apparently opposite) sets of interventions: *consultation to the client* and *environmental intervention*. In essence, these strategies attempt to empower clients (consultation to the client) to manage their own social environment (including treatment providers), while employing a kind of safety net (environmental intervention) when specifically needed. The case management principle is that DBT therapists do not intervene directly in a client's environment, nor do they consult with other professionals concerning how to interact with or treat the client. Rather, clients are viewed as their own agents, who, with consultation from the therapist, attempt to manage effectively their own social and professional network.

It is desirable for clients to learn to act effectively on their own behalf both because it is consistent with DBT's empowerment approach to helping clients manage their own lives and because this approach may inhibit or reduce staff splitting around patient management issues. For example, in most situations where clients have difficulties with another professional (inside or outside the DBT treatment team), the therapist will consult with them about how to be effective in dealing with the other provider to meet their objectives (including balancing respect for others and self-respect with the objectives).

There may also be times when consulting to patients is not possible or would not be effective, and in which the alternative strategy, environmental intervention, would be employed. Typically, therapists would intervene in the environment only if clients cannot do it themselves *and* the outcome is very important (e.g., if substantial harm would be likely without direct intervention). Thus, if the outcome were not important, even if the client did not have the skills to be effective, environmental intervention would not be enacted. Similarly, if clients have the skills, they would be coached on how to approach the situation skillfully.

There may be dialectical consequences to this approach. For example, on the one hand, it may take more effort from the therapist to help empower the client to act effectively in a given situation than to simply intervene directly, but intervening on the client's behalf would result in a large cost to long-term learning and ultimately disempower the client. On the other hand, to the patient consulting means that over time he or she can develop a larger and larger self-management repertoire, taxing the therapist less over time. Evaluating the pros and cons of both sides of this equation in the interest of balance is an important function of the treatment team.

Crisis Strategies

Although far too complex to review here, DBT includes a large and comprehensive approach to client crisis behavior, including suicidal crises (Linehan, 1993a). By definition, chronically suicidal borderline clients have many crises, often life-threatening. It is very difficult for therapists to handle these crises in a way that keeps the client alive, ideally without hospitalization, without reinforcing dysfunctional behaviors, without burning out the therapist (or other members of the treatment team), and in a way that reinforces client skills. Ultimately, crisis strategies must be balanced with all the other strategies for optimal treatment. The job of balancing all of these strategies and interventions falls to the treatment or consultation team.

Team Consultation Strategies

The *team consultation* strategy is the means by which the balance among all the other strategies in DBT is achieved and maintained (Fruzzetti et al., 1997; Linehan, 1993a). As noted above, the treatment team allows therapists to attend both to improving their own skills and to their motivation, and to keep the treatment as effective as possible for the client without burning out the therapist. To balance the consultation to the patient strategy described above, the consultation to the therapist strategy is employed on the treatment team. This strategy allows the therapist to consult with the treatment team on how to manage the client and provides balance with the therapist to allow the treatment to proceed. Thus, other providers support the therapist a great deal while simultaneously targeting what the therapist can do more effectively. Team members adopt a dialectical philosophy (as well as other team agreements) and constantly attempt to balance issues within and between strategies, and to search for "what is missing" and for valid alternative perspectives that might shed new light on intransigent problems.

CASE EXAMPLE

DIAGNOSIS AND ASSESSMENT

Melissa was 31 years old when she was referred to our DBT program from the local state hospital. She was the eldest of three children and had regular, albeit conflictual, contact with her siblings and her parents, who lived nearby. She lived with her partner of two years and had no children. She had not held a job for nearly eight years and had been designated disabled due to depression. At the time of her initial assessment, she reported having had at least six psychiatric admissions in the previous 12 months for a total of at least 41 inpatient days, all following suicidal or parasuicidal behavior (either cutting or overdosing on prescription medications, sometimes with alcohol). In addition to the parasuicidal behaviors that prompted these admissions, she reported cutting an average of once a week over the previous six months (ranging from five times per week to once in two weeks) and overmedicating several times per week in order to "numb out."

The SCID-I and SCID-II were administered and showed that she met criteria for BPD, Major Depression with anhedonia (unipolar, recurrent), PTSD, Panic Disorder, Bulimia, Social Phobia, polysubstance abuse (primarily alcohol and marijuana), and Antisocial Personality Disorder.

CASE FORMULATION

Behavioral analyses of Melissa's parasucidal episodes just prior to the start of treatment and those early in treatment revealed some fairly consistent behavioral patterns. First, Melissa tended to have highly conflictual relationships and to engage in stage 1 out-of-control behaviors (e.g., cutting, using drugs, purging) within hours of very aversive interpersonal interactions. These interactions may be with her partner, Gary, or with a family member, and sometimes with acquaintances or even strangers. She reported becoming so emotionally aroused during these conflicts that she felt "overwhelmed, lost, empty, and ashamed." Further exploration identified that in these situations, she often had urges to drink or use marijuana and often did use, which resulted in decreased emotional arousal (negatively reinforcing substance use). Bingeing and purging seemed to serve the same function. When substances were not readily available to her, she had urges to strike out verbally or physically against the other person, but often imagined cutting herself (and committed to doing so) as a means of interrupting her assaultive urges. When she did cut herself, her arousal abated.

She reported two episodes in the prior two years that differed. On these two occasions, she overdosed on prescription medication with alcohol, specifically intending to kill herself. Both of these suicide attempts followed fights with Gary. In one, she had accused him of sleeping with another woman, which he confirmed. She physically attacked him; he hit her repeatedly and left their apartment, saying he would not return. She overdosed within a couple of hours. He did return home later that night, found her unconscious, called an ambulance, and stayed with her until she recovered.

He broke off the affair he had been having and recommitted to Melissa. In the other episode (about a year later), he told her he was unhappy in their relationship and was thinking of leaving. When he did not return her calls to him at work the next day, she became extremely emotionally aroused and again overdosed. When he came home from work, he again found her and took her to the emergency room. He again recommitted to stay in the relationship. One hypothesis was that her suicide attempts were reinforced by Gary's changing his mind and staying with her.

These assessments revealed two fairly distinct patterns, one for parasuicidal behavior[1] and another for both assaultive behaviors and suicide attempts. Other stage 1 behaviors, such as bingeing and purging and substance use, seemed to function similarly to that of parasuicidal behavior. These behavioral analyses informed treatment targets directly: Both antecedents and consequences of her problem behaviors were targeted for change to help Melissa manage her relationships more effectively, self-manage her emotions more effectively, and improve the quality of her life.

TREATMENT APPROACH AND RATIONALE FOR ITS SELECTION

Because Melissa met criteria for BPD and had a chronic and recent history of parasuicide, she seemed a perfect candidate for DBT. Moreover, she met no exclusion criteria and had not been successfully treated in other therapies. In fact, she had been in almost continuous treatment since the age of 15, and was functioning at about the same level (with more frequent parasuicidal behavior) as she had been at age 21. Thus, she was considered appropriate for our DBT program.

Melissa was accepted for DBT following commitment to the various parts of the treatment program (treatment hierarchy, modes of treatment and assessment, etc.). For Melissa, the biggest obstacle to committing to treatment was agreeing to work on reducing cutting. She described it as "often the only thing I can do so I don't punch someone out" and was very afraid of losing control. We agreed, however, to help her find alternative, more skillful ways to maintain control without either cutting or being aggressive. She agreed to a one-year contract, and treatment commenced.

Treatment during the first several months focused on Melissa's learning DBT skills and applying them to her common chains of problem behavior. Melissa worked hard to use skills instead of cutting and sought therapist support by phone to coach her in skillful alternatives when she had high urges to harm herself. Certain distress tolerance skills seemed to help her through her highest urges, and then she was able to use mindfulness skills to reengage in her daily activities. Also, not eating well emerged as a significant vulnerability for Melissa. Not eating enough increased both the chances of her bingeing and purging and of her having highly negative interpersonal interactions.

However, her difficulties in her relationship with her partner and ongoing criticisms from her family continued to be related to emotional distress and dysregulation, cutting, and substance use. Gary attended several sessions in which the therapist targeted helping Melissa validate how difficult it was at times for him to live with her (but also highlighting its benefits and joys). The therapist also targeted helping (pushing) Gary to join a men's group to commit to not being violent and to learning how to slow down in conflict situations so that each of them could avoid out-of-control behavior.

Melissa's in-session behavior was similarly changeable. She was often quiet, collaborative, and hard working, but at other times, she would skip sessions, become very angry, and yell loudly at the therapist. Some members of the treatment team became somewhat judgmental of Melissa, in part because she could present so differently from one day to another. One of the skill group leaders was quite angry and judgmental of her, saying, "She shouldn't be belligerent with us. It's obvious she can pull it together when she wants to." The therapist, of course, targeted her yelling and other disruptive in-session behaviors as therapy-interfering, and the team sought more phenomenologically empathic ways of understanding her dichotomous behavior.

Several sessions were also held with Melissa and her family of origin (Hoffman et al., 1999), targetimg reducing invalidation among family members. Melissa's relationship with her siblings improved significantly, although little improvement was reported by Melissa or her parents in their relationship.

After six months of treatment, Melissa had not cut herself for more than a month, although she still had urges to do so at least once a week. In addition, she had stopped abusing prescription medication. Her missed sessions and yelling at the therapist continued intermittently through the end of the contract year.

Over time, other links in the chain toward dysfunctional behaviors were identified. For example, Melissa often self-invalidated when someone initially treated her badly by thinking she "deserved it" because she was a "bad person" or invalidated a moderate anger response by cutting it off and saying to herself that she "did not have the right to be angry." The pattern seemed to be one where the more she invalidated the "legitimate" anger in such a situation, the more likely she would end up in a rage and subsequently became quite ashamed. Using emotion regulation and mindfulness skills, she learned to identify her emotion accurately and nonjudgmentally, which virtually eliminated both her aggressive urges and outbursts. Also, in addition to treating her depression with behavioral activation strategies, mindfulness skills were employed to counterbalance her anhedonia. Because treatment targets showed consistent improvement, Melissa and her therapist

(after consulting with the treatment team) committed to a second year of treatment.

The biggest crisis in treatment occurred after about one year, when Gary decided again to leave Melissa. She was flooded with urges to kill herself and to engage in vindictive behaviors toward him, but by this point, she had managed to build two friendships (one new and the other renewed) and relied on these two friends for support. Gary actually did leave, nonviolently, and Melissa moved in with one of her friends because she could not afford the apartment herself.

Eventually, Melissa returned to school part time. She entered stage 2 of treatment and addressed her PTSD, resulting from multiple sexual assaults between the ages of 14 and 19. As she started the exposure treatment, her urges to self-harm increased, and she returned to the systematic use of skills that had originally enhanced her stability. She continued the exposure treatment and was successful over time. Ultimately, she got off disability and continued in school and got a part-time job. By the end of the second year of treatment, she decreased therapy sessions to every other week, targeting improving relationships (she had a new boyfriend) and effective management at work. Melissa terminated formal DBT after two and one half years, although she keeps in contact with her therapist and schedules an occasional visit every few months or so.

SYNOPSIS AND REFLECTION

Melissa's case was a very successful one, chosen to illustrate the potential for focused, intensively delivered DBT to appropriately matched clients. Parts of her case are quite typical: She gained a lot of behavioral stability in the first year of treatment, yet still had many serious difficulties. Improving relationships and reducing family/partner instability had a big impact on her outcomes; her therapy-interfering behavior was a challenge for the treatment team at times; and a lot of hard work by the therapist, treatment team, and client over a long period of time was necessary to achieve these outcomes.

Many clients do not benefit at all from DBT; some are helped to achieve behavioral stability but little else; and others make great strides, as Melissa did. But rarely is therapy easy for client or therapist. The seriousness of the problems and sometimes seeming intractability, the intensity of clients' pain, judgments about clients and ourselves, and the potential for therapists and clients to get demoralized or hopeless all threaten optimal outcomes. However, the comprehensive nature of the treatment, the fact that it is delivered in a team format, its use of basic principles and strategies, and its emphasis on constantly trying to improve provide effective tools for the treatment of patients like Melissa.

RESEARCH ON DBT: EFFICACY AND EFFECTIVENESS DATA

Considerable evidence points to the efficacy of DBT in randomized clinical trials, and other data indicate its effectiveness when delivered outside research centers and in the community. Studies include those conducted by Marsha Linehan herself, as well as many other researchers in a variety of settings.

First, Linehan's original research demonstrated that DBT was superior to treatment as usual (TAU) in the community (Linehan, Heard, & Armstrong, 1993; Linehan, Tutek, Heard, & Armstrong, 1994; Linehan et al., 1991) in terms of reducing parasuicide, decreasing psychiatric hospitalization days, improving social functioning, reducing anger, enhancing treatment retention, and global improvements, which were essentially maintained at six-month and one-year follow-up. Moreover, Linehan, Kanter, and Comtois (1999) showed that DBT cost about half as much as TAU over the course of one year. These results have been replicated in large

measure by other researchers in outpatient settings. For example, in a study of female veterans with BPD (but not necessarily a recent history of parasuicide), researchers found that DBT produced better outcomes than TAU on measures of suicidal ideation, depression, anger, and hopelessness, with a trend toward fewer psychiatric hospitalization days (Koons et al., 2001). Other researchers have reported similar findings. For example, Stanley, Ivanoff, Brodsky, and Oppenheim (1998) found that DBT was superior to TAU (in a nonrandomized pilot project) in measures of parasuicide (self-mutilation), suicidal ideation and urges, and urges to self-mutilate. Similarly, in the Stockholm Psychotherapy Study for Suicidal Women, DBT is being compared (in a randomized design) to object relations psychotherapy and to TAU in the community. Patients in the DBT condition during the training phase of this study demonstrated significant improvements in suicidal and parasuicidal behaviors and significantly fewer psychiatric and medical costs in the year following the initiation of treatment than they had in the previous year (Nilsonne, Berndtson, Kåver, & Götmark, 1999).

Linehan and colleagues (Linehan et al., 1999) replicated her original study with a sample of borderline clients dually diagnosed with substance abuse. Again compared to TAU, DBT showed significantly greater reductions in substance abuse, as measured by both structured interviews and urinalyses at posttest and at follow-up. DBT was also superior in treatment retention and produced greater improvements in social and global adjustment at follow-up. Van den Bosch (1999) has reported similarly good outcomes for borderline, substance-abusing women.

Several inpatient studies have found support for DBT. Barley et al. (1993) in a quasi-experimental design (effectiveness study) found that DBT resulted in lower rates of parasuicide on the unit with both men and women. Martin Bohus and colleagues (Bohus et al., 2000) found significant improvements at one-month postdischarge in depression, dissociation, anxiety, and global functioning with DBT.

In addition, a nonrandomized controlled pilot study of suicidal adolescents (Rathus & Miller, in press) found that DBT was more effective than TAU in reducing hospitalization and in treatment retention, despite the fact that the DBT group was significantly more impaired than the TAU group at pretreatment. In a study of 33 suicidal adolescents consecutively admitted to a DBT treatment program, researchers (Miller, Wyman, Huppert, Glassman, & Rathus, 2000) found significant improvements across all DBT problem domains. Telch et al. (2000) found DBT to be highly successful in treating Binge Eating Disorder in a study of 11 women; there were no dropouts from treatment and 82% of subjects reported no longer binge eating by the end of treatment. These results were essentially maintained at follow-up (80% maintenance at three months, 70% maintenance at six months posttreatment).

Finally, two other studies address the generalizability or effectiveness of DBT when it is practiced in the community. The Mental Health Center of Greater Manchester, New Hampshire (Gold Award, 1998), showed a 77% decrease in psychiatric hospitalization days, 76% decrease in partial hospitalization days, 56% decrease in crisis bed days, and an 80% decrease in emergency service contacts in the first year after instituting DBT. Moreover, they showed a 58% decrease in total treatment costs over one year. Turner (2000) compared DBT to client-centered therapy in a community mental health center setting. DBT was superior to the client-centered treatment on most measures, including showing greater changes in suicide/self-harm behaviors, impulsiveness, anger, depression, psychiatric hospitalization days, and global functioning.

Taken together, this set of studies demonstrates a great deal of research support for DBT, especially given that the first published study testing DBT was in 1991. Data suggest that DBT consistently is very effective in helping borderline clients achieve greater stability (lower rates of parasuicide, impulsivity, etc.) and is quite cost-effective. More recent data suggest that DBT may be effective for some problems even when clients do not meet criteria for BPD. Further study will elucidate both the specific strengths and limitations of DBT, creating the opportunity to improve efforts to treat this group of clients that, until quite recently, was often considered untreatable.

SUMMARY

The problems of clients with BPD are both severe and difficult to treat, with generally poor outcomes and frequently high therapist frustration and burnout. Until the past decade, there was little or no established efficacy for treatments for borderline clients. Recently, however, Marsha Linehan and colleagues have developed, refined, and tested DBT, a treatment for suicidal borderline patients. DBT is based on a comprehensive model of the development of this disorder that centers around client emotion dysregulation, hypothesized to result from a transaction between an individual's disposition (or emotional vulnerabilities) and pervasive invalidation from his or her social and family environment. This treatment utilizes both established change interventions from behavior therapy and acceptance strategies from humanistic therapy and Eastern and Western meditative practice. Both acceptance and change strategies are dialectically balanced or synthesized into a multicomponent treatment program. Results to date from both Linehan's research and a variety of other researchers in the United States and Europe have demonstrated that DBT is effective in reducing the problem behaviors of suicidal borderline patients across a variety of domains and is cost-effective and that treatment gains are maintained over time. In addition, DBT is currently being adapted to new populations with promising results, offering some hope to clients with seemingly refractory clinical problems, their therapists, and family members.

REFERENCES

American Psychiatric Association. (1994). *Diagnostic and statistical manual of mental disorders* (4th ed.). Washington, DC: Author.

Barley, W. D., Buie, S. E., Peterson, E. W., Hollingsworth, A. S., Griva, M., Hickerson, S. C., et al. (1993). The development of an inpatient cognitive-behavioral treatment program for Borderline Personality Disorder. *Journal of Personality Disorders, 7,* 232–240.

Beck, A. T. (1979). *Cognitive therapy for depression.* New York: Guilford Press.

Bohus, M., Haaf, B., Stiglmayr, C., Pohl, U., Bohme, R., & Linehan, M. (2000). Evaluation of inpatient dialectical behavioral therapy for Borderline Personality Disorder: A prospective study. *Behaviour Research and Therapy, 38,* 875–887.

Derogatis, L. R., & Melisatatos, N. (1985). The Brief Symptom Inventory: An introductory report. *Psychological Medicine, 13,* 595–605.

First, M. B., Gibbon, M., Spitzer, R. L., & Williams, J. B. W. (1995). *User's guide for the Structured Clinical Interview for DSM-IV Axis II personality disorders (SCID-II).* Washington, DC: American Psychiatric Press.

Foa, E. B., & Rothbaum, B. O. (1998). *Treating the trauma of rape: Cognitive-behavioral therapy for PTSD.* New York: Guilford Press.

Follette, V. M., Ruzek, J. I., & Abueg, F. R. (Eds.). (1998). *Cognitive-behavioral therapies for trauma.* New York: Guilford Press.

Follette, W. C. (1995). Correcting methodological weaknesses in the knowledge base used to derive practice standards. In S. C. Hayes, V. M. Follette, R. M. Dawes, & K. E. Grady (Eds.), *Scientific standards of psychological practice: Issues and recommendations.* Reno, NV: Context Press.

Follette, W. C., & Houts, A. C. (1996). Models of scientific progress and the role of theory in taxonomy development: A case study of the *DSM. Journal of Consulting and Clinical Psychology, 64,* 1120–1132.

Fruzzetti, A. E. (1996). Causes and consequences: Individual distress in the context of couple interactions. *Journal of Consulting and Clinical Psychology, 64,* 1192–1201.

Fruzzetti, A. E., & Fruzzetti, A. R. (in press). Partners with Borderline Personality Disorder: Dialectical behavior therapy with couples. In D. K. Snyder & M. Whisman (Eds.), *Treating difficult couples: Managing emotional, behavioral, and health problems in couple therapy.* New York: Guilford Press.

Fruzzetti, A. E., & Levensky, E. R. (2000). Dialectical behavior therapy for domestic violence: Rationale and procedures. *Cognitive and Behavioral Practice, 7,* 435–447.

Fruzzetti, A. E., & Linehan, M. M. (2001). *Toward a behavioral understanding of borderline personality and related disorders.* Manuscript in preparation.

Fruzzetti, A. E., Waltz, J. A., & Linehan, M. M. (1997). Supervision in dialectical behavior therapy. In C. E. Watkins Jr. (Ed.), *Handbook of psychotherapy supervision* (pp. 84–100). New York: Wiley.

Gold Award. (1998). The Mental Health Center of Greater Manchester, New Hampshire: Integrating dialectical behavior therapy into a community mental health program. *Psychiatric Services, 49,* 1338–1340.

Hayes, S. C., Nelson, R. O., & Jarrett, T. (1987). Treatment utility of assessment: A functional approach to evaluating quality of assessment. *American Psychologist, 42,* 963–974.

Herman, J. L., Perry, J. C., & van der Kolk, B. A. (1989). Childhood trauma in Borderline Personality Disorder. *American Journal of Psychiatry, 146,* 490–495.

Hoffman, P. D., Fruzzetti, A. E., & Swenson, C. R. (1999). Dialectical behavior therapy: Family skills training. *Family Process, 38,* 399–414.

Ivanoff, A., Jang, S. J., Smyth, N. J., & Linehan, M. M. (1994). Fewer reasons for staying alive when you are thinking of killing yourself: The Brief Reasons for Living Inventory. *Journal of Psychopathology and Behavioral Assessment, 6,* 1–13.

Koerner, K., & Dimeff, L. A. (2000). Further data on dialectical behavior therapy. *Clinical Psychology: Science and Practice, 7,* 104–112.

Koerner, K., Kohlenberg, R. J., & Parker, C. (1996). Diagnosis of personality disorder: A radical behavioral alternative. *Journal of Consulting and Clinical Psychology, 64,* 1169–1176.

Kohlenberg, R. J., & Tsai, M. (1991). *Functional analytic psychotherapy.* New York: Plenum Press.

Koons, C. R., Robins, C. J., Tweed, J. L., Lynch, T. R., Gonzalez, A. M., Morse, J. Q., et al. (2001). Efficacy of dialectical behavior therapy in women veterans with Borderline Personality Disorder. *Behavior Therapy, 32,* 371–390.

Linehan, M. M. (1993a). *Cognitive-behavioral treatment of Borderline Personality Disorder.* New York: Guilford Press.

Linehan, M. M. (1993b). *Skills training manual for treating Borderline Personality Disorder.* New York: Guilford Press.

Linehan, M. M. (1994). Acceptance and change: The central dialectic in psychotherapy. In S. C. Hayes, N. S. Jacobson, V. M. Follette, & M. J. Dougher (Eds.), *Acceptance and change: Content and context in psychotherapy.* Reno, NV: Context Press.

Linehan, M. M. (1998). Validation and psychotherapy. In A. Bohart & L. S. Greenberg (Eds.), *Empathy and psychotherapy: New directions to theory, research, and practice.* Washington, DC: American Psychological Association.

Linehan, M. M. (1999). Development, evaluation, and dissemination of effective psychosocial treatments: Levels of disorder, stages of care, and stages of treatment research. In M. G. Glantz & C. R. Hartel (Eds.), *Drug abuse: Origins and interventions.* Washington, DC: American Psychological Association.

Linehan, M. M. (2000). The empirical basis of dialectical behavior therapy: Development of new treatments versus evaluation of existing treatments. *Clinical Psychology: Science and Practice, 7,* 113–119.

Linehan, M. M., Armstrong, H. E., Suarez, A., Allmon, D., & Heard, H. (1991). Cognitive-behavioral treatment of chronically suicidal borderline patients. *Archives of General Psychiatry, 48,* 1060–1064.

Linehan, M. M., Goodstein, J. L., Nielson, S. L., & Chiles, J. A. (1983). Reasons for staying alive when you're thinking of killing yourself: The Reasons for Living Inventory. *Journal of Consulting and Clinical Psychology, 51,* 276–286.

Linehan, M. M., & Heard, H. L. (1999). Borderline Personality Disorder: Costs, course, and treatment outcomes. In N. Miller & K. Magruder (Eds.), *The cost-effectiveness of psychotherapy: A guide for practitioners, researchers and policy-makers.* New York: Oxford University Press.

Linehan, M. M., Heard, H. L., & Armstrong, H. E. (1993). Naturalistic followup of a behavioral treatment for chronically parasuicidal borderline patients. *Archives of General Psychiatry, 50,* 971–974.

Linehan, M. M., Kanter, J. W., & Comtois, K. A. (1999). Dialectical behavior therapy for Borderline Personality Disorder: Efficacy, specificity, and cost-effectiveness. In D. S. Janowsky (Ed.), *Psychotherapy: Indications and outcomes* (pp. 93–118). Washington, DC: American Psychiatric Press.

Linehan, M. M., Schmidt, H., III, Dimeff, L. A., Craft, J. C., Kanter, J. W., & Comtois, K. A. (1999). Dialectical behavior therapy for patients with Borderline Personality Disorder and drug-dependence. *American Journal on Addictions, 8,* 279–292.

Linehan, M. M., Tutek, D. A., Heard, H. L., & Armstrong, H. E. (1994). Interpersonal outcome of cognitive behavioral treatment for chronically suicidal borderline patients. *American Journal of Psychiatry, 151,* 1771–1776.

McCann, R. A., Ball, E. M., & Ivanoff, A. (2000). DBT with an inpatient forensic population: The CMHIP forensic model. *Cognitive and Behavioral Practice, 7,* 447–456.

Miller, A. E. (1999). Dialectical behavior therapy: A new treatment approach for suicidal adolescents. *American Journal of Psychotherapy, 53,* 413–417.

Miller, A. E., Wyman, S. E., Huppert, J. D., Glassman, S. L., & Rathus, J. H. (2000). Analysis of behavioral skills utilized by adolescents receiving dialectical behavior therapy. *Cognitive and Behavioral Practice, 7,* 183–187.

Nilsonne, Å., Berndtson, T., Kåver, A., & Götmark, H. (1999, November). *DBT training patients the year before and after start of therapy: Preliminary data.* Paper presented at the annual meeting of the Association for Advancement of Behavior Therapy, Toronto, Canada

Pinkard, T. (1988). *Hegel's dialectic: The explanation of possibility.* Philadelphia: Temple University Press.

Rathus, J. H., & Miller, A. E. (1995). *The Life Problems Inventory.* Unpublished manuscript, Bronx, NY, Montefiore Medical Center.

Rathus, J. H., & Miller, A. E. (2000). DBT for adolescents: Dialectical dilemmas and secondary targets. *Cognitive and Behavioral Practice, 7,* 425–434.

Rathus, J. H., & Miller, A. L. (in press). DBT adapted for suicidal adolescents. A pilot study. *Journal of Suicide and Life Threatening Behavior.*

Stanley, B., Ivanoff, A., Brodsky, B., & Oppenheim, S. (1998, November). *Comparison of DBT and "treatment as usual" in suicidal and self-mutilating behavior.* Paper presented at the annual meeting of the Association for Advancement of Behavior Therapy, Washington, DC.

Swann, W. B. (1997). The trouble with change: Self-verification and allegiance to the self. *Psychological Science, 8*(3), 177–180.

Telch, C. F., Agras, W. S., & Linehan, M. M. (2000). Group dialectical behavior therapy for Binge-Eating Disorder: A preliminary, uncontrolled trial. *Behavior Therapy, 31,* 569–582.

Turner, R. M. (2000). Naturalistic evaluation of dialectical behavior therapy-oriented treatment for Borderline Personality Disorder. *Cognitive and Behavioral Practice, 7,* 413–419.

van den Bosch, L. M. C. (1999, November). *A study of the effectiveness of DBT in the treatment of substance and non-substance abusing women in Holland.* Paper presented at the annual meeting of the Association for Advancement of Behavior Therapy, Toronto, Canada.

Wiser, S., & Telch, C. F. (1999). Dialectical behavior therapy for Binge-Eating Disorder. *In Session: Psychotherapy in Practice, 55,* 755–768.

Zanarini, M. C., Gunderson, J. G., Frankenburg, F. R., & Chauncey, D. L. (1989). The revised diagnostic interview for borderlines: Discriminating BPD from other Axis II disorders. *Journal of Personality Disorders, 3,* 10–18.

CHAPTER 11

EMDR: Eye Movement Desensitization and Reprocessing

FRANCINE SHAPIRO, ELIZABETH SNYKER, AND LOUISE MAXFIELD

HISTORY OF EMDR

Rather than the logical outcome of a theoretical position, the development of Eye Movement Desensitization and Reprocessing (EMDR) was based on Shapiro's (1989a, 1991, 1999) accidental discovery of the apparent ability of eye movements to defuse negative emotions and cognitions. A subsequent examination of the literature, however, revealed that this was not the first time such a role for oculomotor behavior had been observed. Many years earlier, Antrobus and his colleagues (Antrobus, 1973; Antrobus, Antrobus, & Singer, 1964) demonstrated in systematic experiments that spontaneous eye movements are associated with unpleasant emotions and cognitive changes. It was noted that characteristics of eye movements appeared to correspond significantly with certain cognitive responses. They reported, for instance, "The attempt to break up a thought sequence when it is unpleasant or anxiety provoking may very well lead to a series of almost desperate rapid shifts in cognitive activity with consequent ocular motility"

(Antrobus, Antrobus, & Singer, 1964, p. 251). In the course of an experiment, Antrobus questioned a subject on the nature of her thoughts after he observed a series of saccades (rapid, back-and-forth eye movements as might occur in reading) during a 1.5-second interval. He was informed that the eye movements had followed a highly unpleasant thought. The saccades appeared correlated with shifts in cognitive content.

Shapiro (1989a) made a similar observation, first on the basis of her own experience, and then by deliberately experimenting with others by means of induced saccades at a speed approximately equivalent to those noticed by Antrobus and colleagues. Thus, Shapiro's findings that inhibition of unpleasant thoughts and shifts in cognitive content are associated with spontaneous multiple saccades suggest that she had simply rediscovered in a naturalistic setting a phenomenon that had already been conducted in the laboratory.

During open-ended experiments with approximately 70 people, Shapiro (1989a) evolved a procedure that was initially thought of as a variation of systematic desensitization (Wolpe, 1990) and that she called Eye Movement Desensitization (EMD). Although clearly having a pronounced effect with a subclinical population, particularly in the treatment of disturbing memories, it was unknown whether the effects of EMD would be as consistent with traumatic memories. To ascertain the applicability to clinical populations, Shapiro (1989a; Shapiro & Fonest, 1997) treated a veteran counselor from a local Veterans Outreach Center for a recurring memory, which had paralyzed him for 20 years. The memory regarded one of the soldiers he was taking out of a rescue helicopter. After a set of eye movements, the veteran reported that the auditory portion of the memory was gone; all he saw was the moving mouth of the person who had spoken to him. As treatment continued, he continued to report that the image of the original memory was shrinking, so that it now was beginning to look like "a paint chip under water." He also reported experiencing a different feeling that he verbalized as "I can finally say that the war is over and everyone can go home."

When asked to think about Vietnam again, rather than describing the original image of dead bodies, which had haunted him, he now reported his first impression of Vietnam as "a garden paradise." He now remembered the way it had looked when he first flew over the country, a memory not recalled in 20 years. At a two year follow-up, the original memory, which had lost its disturbing qualities, was still being experienced as "a paint chip under water."

In the behaviorist tradition, Shapiro (1989a) conducted a randomized controlled study to evaluate the efficacy of EMD in the treatment of traumatic memories. All but 4 of the 22 participants were diagnosed as having Posttraumatic Stress Disorder (PTSD). They were referred from Parents United, a veterans outreach group, a rape crisis group, and independent therapists in Mendocino County, California. The participants ranged in age from 11 to 53 years, had received 2 months to 25 years of prior therapy, and had traumatic memories persisting from 1 to 47 years. Participants were randomly assigned to receive one session of either EMD treatment or a placebo control in which they were asked to concentrate on their disturbing memory and describe it in detail. Both groups were interrupted the same number of times with the same questions to control for expectancy effects and exposure.

Three variables were measured by this small study: level of emotional disturbance, face validity of beliefs about the self as a result of participation in the event, and relief from a primary behavioral indicator of PTSD (nightmares, flashbacks, intrusive thoughts). Employing the Subjective Units of Distress (SUD) scale developed by Joseph Wolpe (1990) for use in systematic desensitization, Shapiro rated levels of emotional disturbance associated with the patient's traumatic memory. The patient was asked to bring up the memory, hold it in mind, and rate how disturbing it felt—from 0 (meaning no disturbance/neutral) to 10 (highest level of disturbance). The participant rated the level of distress using the SUD scale before and after the treatment and at one-month and three-month follow-up.

In the EMD group, Shapiro (1989a) found that the SUD level decreased from a mean of 7.45 at the beginning of treatment to 0.13 at the end of treatment. In the placebo group, which merely concentrated and described the memory (i.e., a modified flooding procedure), the average SUD level changed from 6.77 to 8.31. This increase rather than decrease in anxiety is a common occurrence in clinical practice and is often noticed when clients concentrate on or simply talk about their trauma (Rogers & Silver, in press). Unwilling to leave the controls in an agitated, anxious state, Shapiro provided them with delayed EMD treatment. Their mean level of disturbance was reduced to a SUD level of

0.18. At one- and three-month follow-up, the participants' positive treatment effects were maintained.

After the SUD measurement, the second variable Shapiro (1989a) studied was the face validity of beliefs commonly held by persons suffering from PTSD. An example is the rape victim, overpowered by her attacker, who then thinks, "I'm to blame; I should have done something." The assumption is that these beliefs are irrational, and if the PTSD is healed, then a change to a more rational set of beliefs and cognitions, such as "I'm blameless; I did the best I could," would emerge. An increase in self-acceptance and movement from a negative to a more positive belief would be indicative of traumatic information being resolved and integrated.

To measure validity, Shapiro developed a semantic differential scale, the Validity of Cognition (VOC) scale. First, subjects were asked to bring up the memory of the traumatic event and describe the negative belief associated with it. Then they were asked to identify what they would prefer to believe about themselves instead (i.e., I am fine; I am in control; I am safe). Next, subjects were asked to focus on this positive cognition and rate how true it felt on the validity scale, where 1 is completely false and 7 is completely true. It is essential to the VOC that the question is answered on a feeling or "gut level" rather than intellectually. Shapiro found that the mean of the VOC for the EMD participants was 3.95 pretreatment and 6.75 posttreatment. In the placebo control condition, the mean of the VOC scores was 2.95 pretreatment and 2.36 posttreatment. A delayed treatment for this group resulted in a mean of the VOC scores at the start of treatment of 2.36 and 6.77 at the end of treatment.

The third variable investigated was relief from the major symptoms of PTSD (nightmares, flashbacks, and intrusive thoughts). For 18 of the 22 participants, Shapiro (1989a) had external corroboration from a spouse, other family member, or the referring therapist that symptoms related to the treated memory had stopped completely or decreased. For instance, when the molestation victim recalled being attacked, she did not experience the high degree of emotionality that had been elicited previously. In one case, a psychiatrist with a lifelong history of violent, fearful nightmares (confirmed by his wife) reported a dream the night of the treatment in which he was being chased by Samurai warriors. This time, without fear, he turned to them and bowed in a ritual manner. They returned his bow. They then joined forces and went off together. His violent nightmares ended. In another case, a Vietnam vet reported recurrent nightmares of someone slipping into his bunker and cutting his throat prior to treatment. The night after EMD, the veteran recognized his own face on the assailant and did not have this dream again. It was concluded that dream images were excellent targets to reach disturbing material contributing to current complaints (see Shapiro, 2001).

Shapiro's preliminary findings also served to answer an earlier clinical issue raised by Kilpatrick, Veronen, and Resick (1982) as to whether one could desensitize appropriate fears. A rape victim whose SUD level of 8 had decreased to 0 was discovered to have an elevated SUD level (4) at one-month follow-up, potentially signifying that the treatment effect had not maintained. Further inquiry revealed that the woman had learned the rapist was still in the area where she lived and she feared another attack. It was concluded that this SUD level was appropriate to the client's current situation.

A second important finding involved generalization of treatment effects. In follow-up with a victim of molestation, the participant was asked to think about the molestation memory treated. She reported it as desensitized, although there was still some emotion connected with it. On being asked to bring up another, similar incident by the same perpetrator, this second memory was found to be desensitized down to the same level as the one originally treated; it too had the same admixture of emotions. From this finding, it was concluded that one does not have to treat every single disturbing memory: It is possible to cluster similar memories, elicit one memory that represents the entire cluster, target that one, and obtain the generalization effect (see Shapiro, 1989a, 1989b, 2001). In 1989, Shapiro's research was published in the *Journal of Traumatic Stress,* and the method was introduced to the behavioral therapy community in 1990 by Joseph Wolpe, who cochaired a symposium with Shapiro about EMD at the annual meeting of the Association for the Advancement of Behavior Therapy. Further clinical investigation and procedural refinement resulted in the treatment being renamed Eye Movement Desensitization and Reprocessing or EMDR in 1990 to reflect a change in application and theory.

Shapiro's initial study is considered to have a number of problems. It lacked standardized measures and adequate control for demand characteristics and expectancy effects, and researcher and therapist were the same person. However, prior to this study on EMD's treatment effects, there had been only one published controlled study (Peniston, 1986) that investigated treatment of PTSD. Given the paucity of controlled treatment outcome literature with people suffering from PTSD (Hyer, 1994; Shapiro, 1996; S. D. Solomon, Gerrity, & Muff, 1992), the effectiveness of the procedure in treating this population was subject to intense scrutiny, leading in a relatively short period to over a dozen additional independent controlled evaluations (see Chemtob, Tolin, van der Kolk, & Pitman, 2000; Maxfield & Hyer, in press; Shapiro, 1999, 2001, in press; Spector & Read, 1999; Van Etten & Taylor, 1998). Following a pattern common to most research, seriously flawed early studies of PTSD treatment

procedures (Foa & Meadows, 1997; Maxfield & Hyer, in press; Shapiro, 1999, in press) have been superceded by studies that involve greatly improved methodology, procedures, and experimental designs (see Research section below; Maxfield & Hyer, in press). EMDR has been designated as an effective form of treatment in the *Practice Guidelines* of the International Society for Traumatic Stress Studies (Foa, Keane, & Friedman, 2000), and a meta-analysis of all PTSD treatments designated EMDR as one of the most effective and most efficient (Van Etten & Taylor, 1998).

THEORIES

ADAPTIVE INFORMATION-PROCESSING MODEL

Because Shapiro (1989a) initially viewed the resultant treatment effects as merely a "desensitization of anxiety," she called her method EMD. After observation and analysis of hundreds of treatment sessions, it was realized that desensitization was simply a by-product of the more global reprocessing of the experiential material that was taking place (Shapiro, 1991, in press). Consequently, the desensitization model was changed to an information-processing paradigm (Shapiro, 1991, 1995), and the overall paradigm is now termed the adaptive information-processing (AIP) model (Shapiro, 2001).

The AIP model draws on the language of neurobiology and is generally consistent with other information-processing models that have been advanced in the field (Chemtob, Roitblat, Hamada, Carlson, & Twentyman, 1988; Foa & Kozak, 1986; Lang, 1979; Teasdale, 1999). Its tenets are applicable to a broad-based understanding of psychopathology, personality development, and clinical change processes (Shapiro, 2001, in press). Systematic observation of EMDR sessions allowed the identification of patterns of information processing and memory association that successfully predict a wide range of treatment effects and clinical outcomes. These, in turn, led to further development and refinement of specific EMDR practice, protocols, and procedures. To reflect the change of paradigm and the complexity of the refined procedures, the treatment was renamed EMDR (Shapiro, 1991).

MEMORY NETWORKS

Significant differences appear to occur in the ways a nontraumatized and a traumatized person remember disturbing events. Most people who become upset or frightened by an event, such as an argument with a relative or hearing a loud fireworks display, are able to easily assimilate and integrate the experience internally by sharing it, thinking about what happened, dreaming, or even confronting directly what was distressing. After a while, details of the memory may fade and the person may not remember it, or, if recalled, it may have little or no emotional charge. For those who have been traumatized by their experiences, the sensory elements (sights, sounds, smells, thoughts, and physical sensations) may continue to intrude into awareness in the form of nightmares, flashbacks, and intrusive recollections. They may experience altered states of consciousness, states of hyperarousal, and exaggerated startle responses. There may be extremes of retention such that some aspects may seem fixed in the mind with exceptionally vivid detail (van der Kolk, in press), whereas other aspects may be dissociated and forgotten. Any number of internal or external cues can trigger the unresolved traumatic experience, resulting in a distressful reexperiencing of the event in nightmares, flashbacks, or intrusive recollections.

The symptoms of PTSD are considered to be a result of information stored in state-dependent form in implicit/motoric memory Shapiro (1991, 2001). The diagnostic criteria of PTSD require that the person has experienced a criterion A incident, which Shapiro refers to as a "big T" trauma, but any event that has a lasting negative effect on self or psyche can be considered a "small t" trauma. Such events, which may be ubiquitous throughout childhood, are hypothesized to be the basis of many experientially based pathologies. It is believed that these, with their disturbing affects, cognitions, and somatic responses, are similarly stored in implicit memory, and that successful treatment effects are dependent on adaptive processing.

The AIP model (Shapiro, 1995, 2001), which guides EMDR practice, incorporates the physiological notion of network activation, counterconditioning, assimilation of the emotionally corrective, and adaptive information. During EMDR treatment, the neurophysiological network that contains the memory to be targeted is accessed in a focused manner, initiating information processing, which is enhanced by the eye movements (EMs) or alternative dual attention (e.g., auditory and tactile) stimuli. As processing continues, the negative information is integrated with more adaptive, positive, and realistic information, and then functionally stored in memory.

As with all psychotherapy procedures, the exact underlying mechanism for the effect of the dual attention stimulation is currently unknown and is unnecessary for an appreciation of the procedures or principles governing EMDR's application. Likewise, although a number of models have contributed to our understanding of anxiety disorders, they have offered no substantive theoretical framework to account for EMDR's apparently rapid treatment results (see Rogers & Silver, in press). Rather than an extinction/habituation model (e.g., Keane, Zimering, & Caddell, 1985; Marks, Lovell, Noshirvani, Livanou, & Thrasher, 1998), the AIP model is closer to the more recent neurocognitive conceptual models, because it underscores assimilation and accommodation through an integration of memory networks.

Shapiro (1995) maintains that inherent in everyone is a system physiologically geared to process information to a state of mental health and to "adaptive resolution":

> This adaptive resolution means that negative emotions are relieved and that learning takes place, is appropriately integrated, and is available for future use. The system may become unbalanced due to a trauma or through stress engendered during a developmental period, but once it is appropriately activated and maintained in a dynamic state by means of EMDR, it transmutes information to a state of therapeutically appropriate resolution. Desensitization and cognitive restructuring are viewed as byproducts of the adaptive reprocessing taking place on a neurophysiological level. (p. 13)

Many of the procedural elements of EMDR contribute to the appropriate accessing of the dysfunctionally stored information and dynamic activation of this information-processing system. As noted, Shapiro proposed that most pathology is derived from earlier life experiences that were dysfunctionally stored in the brain in a state-dependent form and thus set in motion a repetitive pattern of affect, behavior, cognition, and a consequent identity structure. Recurring, present-day stimuli can elicit the negative affect and beliefs embodied in these memories and cause the client to continue acting in ways consistent with the earlier events.

Psychoanalysts might consider this line of thinking analogous to Freud's repetition compulsion, whereas behaviorists would view it as operant conditioning based on variable interval reinforcement. However, the clinical application of EMDR was not conceived as breaking a patterned response, but rather as allowing the appropriate processing of the stored affects, cognitions, and sensations to take place, leading to the previously described adaptive resolution. Appropriate behaviors, emotions, and beliefs can then spontaneously emerge.

This model views not only overt psychological symptoms but also nonadaptive personality characteristics as similarly rooted in dysfunctionally stored memories that have been insufficiently processed. The use of EMDR catalyzes a learning process that allows the appropriate assimilation of the events. What is useful is learned and stored with appropriate affect and therefore guides the person adaptively in the future. What is useless (negative emotions, affects, beliefs) is discarded. All of EMDR's procedures are geared to assist the appropriate accessing of the stored information, stimulation of the information-processing system, and moving the information to adaptive resolution. The assimilation of the experience and resultant accommodation of emotional, somatic, and cognitive structures are the basis of both personality development and clinical change.

Neurobiological Conjectures

As of this writing, theories to explain specific mechanisms of action involved in the phenomenology of trauma, EMDR, and their joint interactions are speculative. Research on the physiology of PTSD indicates that it is accompanied by a distinct, complex pattern of biological alterations (Orr & Roth, 2000; Yehuda & McFarlane, 1995). PTSD patients have developed exaggerated and finely tuned biological responses both to stimuli that are reminders of the traumatic event (Post, Weiss, & Smith, 1995) and to other stressors such as loud noise (Shalev, Peri, et al., 2000). Brain imaging studies have shown differential patterns of activation in persons with PTSD (e.g., Rauch et al., 1996). Several preliminary studies have investigated the effects of EMDR on brain activation. In 1999, P. Levin, Lazrove, and van der Kolk used SPECT (single photon emission computed tomography) neuroimaging both before and after EMDR treatment. They noted definitive changes in two areas of the brain that were more active post-EMDR treatment relative to pretreatment: the anterior cingulate gyrus and the left frontal lobe. Lansing, Amen, and Klindt (2000) report SPECT scans post-EMDR treatment that reveal patterns of change and recovery involving the limbic system. With the advent of SPECT scans, MRI, and a greater understanding of neurotransmitters, preliminary data indicate that biological changes do take place subsequent to EMDR processing, in a manner that would be expected after any successful therapy.

It has been hypothesized that inadequately processed traumatic memories may be dysfunctionally stored in dissociated fragments in implicit/motoric memory rather than in explicit/narrative memory (e.g., Shobe & Kihlstrom, 1997; van der Kolk, 1994; van der Kolk, Hopper, & Osterman, in press). The effects of extreme stress on memory processes may in fact be related to hippocampal function (Bremner, 1999). On the basis of current neurobiological findings, Stickgold (in press) suggested that EMDR elicits an orienting response, inducing REM-like neurobiological mechanisms that facilitate the activation of episodic memories and their integration into cortical semantic memory. Support for this theory is found in independent research by Christman and Garvey (2000), who determined that alternating leftward and rightward eye movements produced a beneficial effect for episodic, but not semantic, retrieval memory tasks.

There is much conjecture about the possible neurobiological role of eye movements and other dual attention stimuli. Correlations between eye movements and shifts in cognitive content and attribution have been documented since the 1960s (e.g., Antrobus, 1973; Antrobus et al., 1964). Several theories attempt to explain how these may contribute to information processing within the EMDR procedures. These include: (1) disruption of the function of the visuospatial sketchpad and interference with working memory (Andrade, Kavanagh, & Baddeley, 1997); (2) elicitation of an orienting response that stimulates an instinctive affect of interest or excitement (Armstrong & Vaughan, 1996; Lipke, 1992, 2000; MacCulloch & Feldman, 1996); (3) evocation of a relaxation response (D. L. Wilson, Silver, Covi, & Foster, 1996), or a new set of physiological states; (4) activation of neurological processes that mimic REM sleep-type function and its information-processing mechanisms (Stickgold, in press); and (5) distraction that acts as an unreinforced extinction trial (Dyck, 1993) or in other ways encourages client engagement.

Although research is needed to investigate these neurobiological speculations, science has not yet developed the precise tools needed to identify and measure the specific physiological elements that contribute to psychological change for EMDR or any other form of psychotherapy. Research is needed to evaluate the contributions of the multiple components of EMDR and to test various hypothetical mechanisms of action (for a comprehensive discussion, see Shapiro, 2001).

METHOD OF ASSESSMENT AND INTERVENTION

EMDR is a complex treatment methodology. On the surface, it might appear as though the method entails simple dual attention stimulation, but this is a misperception. Clinicians are cautioned at all trainings that EMDR is an integrated form of therapy requiring all the expertise in the therapist's armamentarium of clinical skills.

The cognitive-behavioral elements of EMDR are apparent in its use of quantitative scales for clients to report in-session changes, the positive and negative cognitions, and the evaluation of behavioral indices postsession (see also Smyth & Poole, in press). In addition, Shapiro (1989a, 1995, 1999, 2001) has consistently and frequently encouraged the investigation of EMDR with empirical research. However, EMDR is an integrative treatment that incorporates elements of many other therapeutic approaches, including psychodynamic (R. M. Solomon, Neborsky, McCullough, Alpert, Shapiro, & Malan, 2001; Wachtel, in press), person-centered (Bohart & Greenberg, in press; L. S. Brown, in press; Krystal et al., in press), body-based (Siegel, in press; van der Kolk, in press), and interactional (Kaslow, Nurse, & Thompson, in press; C. Levin, Shapiro, & Weakland, 1996) therapies.

One of the principal reasons that many traditional psychological approaches are easily integrated with EMDR is its ability to shift information on emotional, cognitive, and physiological levels. Psychodynamic therapists will recognize free association to childhood experiences, transference, and reconversion of somatic disorders (Wachtel, in press). Cognitive therapists will observe shifts in beliefs (J. E. Young, Zangwill, & Behary, in press); behaviorists, shifts in original learning, generalization effects, and stimulus response (Smyth & Poole, in press); gestaltists, changes in figure and ground relationships. Many clinicians will recognize shifts in physical sensation (see Shapiro, in press; van der Kolk, in press).

EMDR has undergone significant modifications as a result of clinical observations over the past decade and has evolved into a complex integrative approach (Norcross & Shapiro, in press; Shapiro, in press; Zabukovec, Lazrove, & Shapiro, 2000). Although the name of the method may emphasize eye movements, the emphasis over the past decade (Shapiro, 1991, 1994a, 1995, 2001, in press) is on the complex procedural elements and dual attention stimulation that may include eye movements and auditory and/or tactile stimulation. Previous research has reported that both participants and clinicians prefer the addition of stimulation (Boudewyns & Hyer, 1996) to the use of procedures alone. Further research is necessary to determine if optimal levels of stimulation attenuate disturbances and result in greater client compliance or accelerated

treatment effects are engendered because of cognitive loading (Becker, Nugent, & Tinker, 2000; Becker, Todd-Overmann, Stoothoff, & Lawson, 1998).

EIGHT PHASES OF EMDR TREATMENT

A brief review of procedures is offered below (see Shapiro, 2001, for comprehensive procedures and protocols). EMDR uses a standardized eight-phase approach.

Phase 1: Comprehensive History and Treatment Planning

Clinicians are expected to complete a comprehensive history of their clients, consistent with good clinical practice. Clients should be routinely assessed for presenting complaints as well as the following: substance abuse, domestic violence, forensic and other legal concerns, ego strength, dissociative phenomena, current life situation and quality of support system, secondary gains, differences between reality-based and irrational fears, impulse control, hospitalizations and risk of self-harming behaviors, medication use and other substance abuse, and medical conditions.

Clients are assessed to handle the strain of a possible abreaction experience (i.e., high level of emotional and physical disturbance in response to the elicitation of the targeted memory), especially if they have a history of seizure disorder, cardiac problems, pregnancy, organic brain syndrome, or other serious condition. Medical conditions warrant careful evaluation and often consultation with the client's physician, but they may not necessarily be a contraindication for the use of EMDR. If the client has a severe history of torture, was hit by lightning, woke up in the middle of surgery, or had similar trauma, will he or she be able to withstand physical sensations similar to the original experience? With clients who have had these types of experiences, it might be wiser to conduct sessions in a safe environment with adequate monitoring, such as a hospital, rather than in the clinician's office.

The client must be educated about EMDR and the possibility that highly emotional states may occur during processing, and that unresolved issues from the past related to presenting complaints may also emerge. Informed consent and other ethical requirements as mandated by individual state licensing laws and professional codes of conduct must be followed. As with all trauma treatments, a strong therapeutic alliance and truth-telling agreements are important, particularly with complex PTSD and child abuse cases. EMDR treatment should be integrated within the standard phase-oriented model as described by Herman (1992), and reprocessing should take place only after appropriate stabilization and trust has occurred.

After completing a comprehensive history to gather all the information needed to implement the full EMDR protocol, the clinician then identifies with the patient specific issues to be addressed. In an attempt to proceed more comprehensively, EMDR emphasizes use of the three-pronged approach with a past, present, and future protocol. Earlier memories, which have set the groundwork for present dysfunction, are identified and become the initial targets for EMDR (first prong) processing. After this is completed, present stimuli that trigger disturbances are processed (second prong). The future template (third prong), which incorporates and enhances skills and behaviors necessary for optimal functioning, becomes the target of processing.

Phase 2: Preparation
According to Shapiro (1999, p. 40) the preparation phase of EMDR involves establishing an appropriate therapeutic relationship, setting reasonable levels of expectation, educating the client regarding his or her symptoms, establishing an appropriate client perspective to the active processing of the trauma, training the client

in the use of a set of specific coping skills and self-control techniques for the purpose of rapidly eliminating disturbance, and accessing positive affects. Consistent with clients' age, background, experiences, and levels of sophistication, they are next given an explanation of EMDR similar to the following:

> Often, when something traumatic happens it seems to get locked in the nervous system with the original picture, sounds, thoughts, feelings and so on. Since the experience is locked there, it continues to be triggered whenever a reminder comes up. It can be the basis for a lot of discomfort and sometimes a lot of negative emotions, such as fear and helplessness that we can't seem to control. These are really the emotions connected with the old experience that are being triggered. The eye movements we use in EMDR seem to unlock the nervous system and allow your brain to process the experience. That may be what is happening in REM, or dream, sleep: The eye movement may be involved in processing the unconscious material. The important thing to remember is that it is your own brain that will be doing the healing and that you are the one in control. (Shapiro, 1995, p. 120)

Because EMDR is a highly interactive, collaborative, and client-centered method, the clinician needs to facilitate healing and adopt an attitude of respect and flexibility in meeting client needs for safety, reassurance, and pacing of the treatment.

Appropriate distance and direction and speed of eye movement or use of alternative dual attention stimulation are evaluated in this stage. Metaphors are regularly used to teach the concept of dual attention necessary for successful processing. The client may be told to "imagine riding on a train and just watching the scenery go by." Metaphors are also helpful as a means of creating emotional distance between the client and the very painful experiences that might otherwise be overwhelming (Shapiro, 1995, 2001).

Another strategy, establishing a safe place in imagination, is particularly useful in assisting clients to cope with high levels of emotional disturbance during or between sessions. The safe place is an eight-step exercise especially useful with clients who are hypervigilant, have great difficulty relaxing, and need to have a means of recovering quickly after experiencing any disturbance. The safe place is selected by the client, is uncontaminated by negative associations (danger, betrayal, rejection, abandonment, fear, etc.), has significant diagnostic value, requires a full sensory experience to be linked to it, and is an adult location of safety rather than a childhood memory. Other skills a client might be taught during the preparation phase include structured relaxation and guided imagery techniques.

Phase 3: Assessment
During the history taking, symptoms, problems, patterns of response, areas of conflict, and traumatic events the person experienced are identified. In the assessment phase, movement is toward more precise identification of what will be processed with EMDR during that session and the establishment of baseline measure using VOC and SUD (Wolpe, 1990). The basic procedural elements include selection of the image, negative cognition, positive cognition, emotions, physical sensations, SUD, and VOC.

Once clients select the incident to be treated, they are asked to select the image that best represents that event: "What picture represents the most traumatic part of the incident? What is the worse part of that memory?" If a person has multiple, similar memories (of being hit, criticized, molested), these can be clustered by location, type, person involved, and so on. Clients are then asked to choose one memory that best represents the cluster.

The negative cognition (NC) is selected next. It represents a belief that discloses an irrational, dysfunctional, or maladaptive self-assessment and is connected to the client's participation in the event. The NCs are elicited by asking the question, "What words go best with that image/picture/incident that expresses your negative belief about yourself now?" Examples of such statements are: "I am powerless/insignificant/unlovable."

NCs function to focus the presenting issue, generalize to related events or areas of concern, and resonate well with the client's associated affect. It is important to realize that a cognition that is true will not change: There is validity for the belief of a person recollecting a childhood incident of physical abuse who says "I was powerless. I was in danger." The search is for objectively untrue and inappropriate self-appraisals in the present, such as "I *am* powerless." It is a valid description of a past event. Shapiro writes, "Clinical observations consistently indicate that EMDR cannot be used to remove a true negative cognition or to instill a false one" (1995, p. 57).

Next, a positive cognition (PC) is selected that incorporates an internal locus of control, focuses the client on the desired direction of change, and is able to address the same schemas identified in the NCs. The client is asked, "When you bring up that image, what would you like to believe about yourself now?" Examples of positive responses include statements such as: "I am worthwhile/strong/lovable/in control/capable of learning." Having stated the desired belief, the client is then asked to rate the PC on a semantic differential scale where 1 equals completely false and 7 equals completely true. The PC is rated not on how true the client thinks it is, but rather, on how true it feels emotionally.

The goal in selection of the PC is to find one that enhances feelings of self-worth and redefines one's own capacity regardless of the behavior of others, over which we have no control. An inappropriate PC will stall processing. If the PC is appropriate, the VOC will increase as information processing takes place, until it reaches 7 or the level ecologically valid for the client. Examples of ecological reasons wherein the PC is not expected to reach a 7 include the need for completion of a task, such as moving out of the house or securing a new job or recognition that the client's goal is unattainable (becoming the perfect parent/mate).

Emotions are evoked with the question "When you bring up that picture and those words (repeat the NC), what emotions do you feel now?" The emphasis is on the feelings elicited in the present, not emotions felt at the time of the occurrence. A significant level of distress indicates unresolved material when the client brings it into current consciousness. Level of intensity of emotions is measured by using the SUD scale and asking clients to rate their emotion on a scale from 0 to 10, where 0 equals no disturbance and 10 is the highest disturbance imaginable. It is not unusual for SUD ratings to decrease and then increase again as different emotional states are reprocessed by the dual attention stimulation of the treatment.

The last piece of information requested during the assessment phase is that of the location of the physical sensations experienced in the body when the person thinks of the disturbing or traumatic event. Physical sensations may be associated with tension and anxiety or represent part of the sensory experience at the time of the event. NCs can also evoke strong physical impressions. The key is the location of the sensation, not its description. Emotional thinking reflected in physical sensation statements, such as "I feel numb/blocked/nothing/empty," is equally incorporated into the event for processing. Treatment then proceeds to the desensitization phase.

Phase 4: Desensitization
At this stage, processing of the traumatic or disturbing material is ready to begin. Because the next three phases combine the procedural components and dual attention stimulation via eye movements, hand taps, or tone, the instructions given during the preparation phase now become

valuable for a variety of reasons. These instructions allow for maximum client direction and feedback. From the very beginning, clients are instructed to give as accurate feedback as they can. Demand characteristics are reduced when they are alerted to the fact there are no "supposed to's," and that sometimes changes take place and sometimes nothing different occurs. An attitude of open acceptance is encouraged by informing clients to "let whatever happens happen and just notice whatever type of internal material may emerge."

The client maintains dual attention, simultaneously attending to the present stimuli (e.g., eye movements or tones, clinician reassurance, present safety) while engaged in thinking about the event being targeted. This dual focus promotes the ability to observe and reflect on internal states, and appears to facilitate the processing of dysfunctionally stored information. This in turn permits the natural emergence of insights, changes in related sensory experience and associations, and an increased sense of self-efficacy experienced with EMDR.

At the beginning of the desensitization phase, the client is instructed to hold together in consciousness the image, the NC, and the body sensations while attending to the dual attention stimulation (eye movement, taps, tones). During each set of stimulation the client generally reports changes in some component of the memory. Alternatively, new memories, associations, or insights emerge. At the end of each set, "What do you get now?" is asked. The expectation is for clients to share in a free-associative manner whatever might have emerged. During this stage, clinicians are strongly discouraged from repeating clients' statements, offering interpretations, engaging in conversation to elicit other information, or distracting clients from their current focus. SUD or VOC ratings are not elicited midsession but are guided instead by the changes in clients' report.

Periods of clients' attention to internal foci along with dual attention stimulation are alternated with a verbalizing of outcome to the clinician. The clinician suggests the next focus of attention depending on the clients' responses. Variations in attention and procedures are used to ensure that processing is evident in subsequent sets of stimulation (Shapiro, 1995, 2001; Shapiro & Forrest, 1997).

Clinical observations over time indicate that during successful processing, the client response to each set of dual stimulation will produce some type of change in the memory being treated. Feedback by the client will then determine the therapist's next intervention. If processing is continuing smoothly, the clinician can expect to see shifts in the visual components of the memory, for example, changes in the picture (faded, blurry, absent, more distant); in content (angry face change to a loving face); and in appearance (darker, lighter, more/less vivid). Changes in the progression of thinking from negative to increasingly more adaptive and insightful can also be anticipated. As the client experiences emotional shifts, SUD levels may spike up and down, at times becoming higher than originally rated as processing goes through the different emotions associated with the targeted event. Alterations in physical sensations are common as well. The feeling can shift from tight to relaxed and can move from one location (chest) to another (throat) or increase or decrease. It is crucial for clinicians to know when information is changing and the type of changes that are occurring. Flow charts have been developed to guide clinicians in the course of action to follow when reprocessing stops at pictorial, auditory/cognitive, affective, or somatic/kinesthetic levels.

To assist with blocked responses, insufficient information, lack of generalization, and time pressures, Shapiro (1995) developed specialized interventions called *cognitive interweaves*. These proactive strategies are best used when working with populations characterized by more complicated pathologies (personality disorders, dissociative disorders, multiple abuse histories, and educational deficits):

> The term *cognitive interweave* refers to the process of offering the client strategies to "jump-start" blocked processing by introducing certain material rather than depending on the client to provide all of it. The term *interweave* refers to the fact that this strategy calls for the clinician to offer statements that therapeutically weave together the appropriate neuro networks and associations. (1995, p. 244)

When the client reaches a level where no disturbance is reported or no meaningful associations are continuing to emerge, and the SUD has reached a level of 0, the client is then ready for the installation of the PC.

Phase 5: Installation
Installation is the process of linking the desired PC with the original memory, incident, or picture. The goal is to incorporate and strengthen the new positive self-assessment and replace the originally stated negative belief. The initially chosen PC is checked to determine if it is still suitable or if a more positive self-statement has emerged. It is not unusual to find that, along with shifts in image, cognition, emotion, and sensation, there may also be shifts from the original PC to a more enhanced or more applicable and valid statement. The most positive and self-empowering cognition is then chosen and paired with the original incident and assessed on the VOC scale.

Sequential sets of stimulation are then added and their effects assessed until a VOC level of 7 is reached. If the VOC rating does not rise above 5 or 6, it may be necessary to determine if there is need for a better PC than the original one, if a blocking belief is interfering, or if some future action is required. As examples of these, a client may respond to the question "What prevents it from being a 7?" with "Seven means I am perfect; that is unrealistic" or "I need to file for divorce/leave home first."

Phase 6: The Body Scan

Therapeutic treatment is considered incomplete as long as there is any physical or somatic residue associated with the original targeted event. At this stage, the client is instructed: "Close your eyes, concentrate on the incident and the positive cognition, and mentally scan your entire body. Tell me where you feel anything." If any sensation is reported, another set of eye movements is done. If the sensation is a positive or comfortable one, the eye movements tend to strengthen it. If the sensation is uncomfortable, it may be that it is linked to other ancillary targets that need reprocessing. At this time, the processing continues until it diminishes or the session is closed down using a variety of other strategies and considered incomplete. A disturbing event is considered to be completely processed when the VOC is 7 and SUD level is 0.

Phase 7: Closure

Comments often stated at the end of completed sessions include: "I feel totally different. I feel like I dropped a hundred pounds. I feel lighter. I can do it, I'm not afraid anymore." The clinician next informs the client as follows:

> The processing we have done today may continue after the session. You may or may not notice new insights, thoughts, memories, or dreams; if so, just notice what you are experiencing—take a snapshot of it (what you are seeing, feeling, thinking and the trigger), and keep a log. We can work on this new material next time. If you feel it is necessary, call me. (see Shapiro, 1995, 2001)

Incomplete sessions (SUD greater than 1, VOC less than 6) result when material is still unresolved at the end of the session. Incompletion may be due to multiple reasons (e.g., time has run out, complex memories cannot realistically be completed in a single session, client is highly dissociative). It is important to debrief all clients, as processing can continue between sessions. Whether or not a session is deemed complete, other ancillary material may arise that needs to be addressed. For incomplete sessions, additional steps, demonstrated and practiced during the preparation phase (relaxation, safe place, guided imagery), may need to be employed. These are clinically and ethically sound practices and ensure that clients are functioning well in present time and safe to return to their home/office or engage in necessary activities (driving, child care) after leaving the treatment setting.

Phase 8: Reevaluation

The final phase, reevaluation, begins at the start of each succeeding session. Previously targeted material is reaccessed to ensure that treatment effects have been maintained and to determine if the client needs further processing on memories from the previous week. It is not unusual for new information related to the previously treated material to emerge between sessions. Healing does not necessarily follow a linear progression, especially with more highly traumatized populations.

The log clients are asked to keep between sessions is an essential source of information for the clinician. The triggers and components of the event (i.e., image, cognition, emotion, and sensation) are used to record disturbances and to organize information inside/outside of sessions in a similar pattern. Through the log changes in baseline rates of symptoms, evidence of new behaviors or emotional responses, reactions to persons, places, or situations, insights developed, and emergent progress are documented. It is from the log and verbal client reports that new targets for the next session are selected; previous material is reaccessed and processed as necessary, unanticipated issues are planned for, and, when appropriate, termination takes place.

It is important to integrate the progress made during individual sessions into the overall treatment plan:

> The goal of EMDR therapy is to produce the most substantial treatment effects possible in the shortest period of time, while simultaneously maintaining client stability (i.e., preventing emotional overload) while maintaining a balanced system (e.g., appropriately integrated with his/her larger family and social systems). (Shapiro, 1999, p. 45)

The Standard EMDR Protocol

The standard EMDR protocol is a three-pronged approach incorporating changes related to the past, present, and future. Upon completion of phase 1, client history, the number of problems and degree of pathology that need to be addressed are evident to the clinician. The work of therapy may include resolution of a single trauma or disturbing memory (one traffic accident, or assault, or failed examination); multiple traumas (of the same type, e.g., multiple traffic accidents; or of different types, e.g., an accident plus an assault); or a lifelong history of dysfunctional living secondary to personality disorder, complex PTSD, medical or psychiatric illness, poverty, and other conditions. The processing of ancillary events and triggers contributing to their dysfunctional schema, behaviors, and affects is particularly important with multiply traumatized persons. Developmental and social deficits are addressed through templates for appropriate future action (Shapiro, 1995, 2001, in press). Whereas resolution of a single trauma may take only one to three 90-minute sessions (Ironson, Freund, Strauss, & Williams, in press; Marcus, Marquis, & Sakai, 1997; Rothbaum, 1997; Scheck, Schaeffer, & Gillette, 1998; S. A. Wilson, Becker, & Tinker, 1995, 1997), resolution of multiple traumas may take multiple sessions.

Because treatment effects can generalize, not all traumas or events initially identified may have to be processed. Clustering targets, as mentioned previously, saves clinical time (Shapiro, 1995, 2001). When treatment progresses to the stage where the dysfunctionally stored information from the past is reprocessed, improved client functioning in the present becomes more noticeable. The process of recycling through treated targets is recommended during the reevaluation phase.

The first prong of EMDR therapy relates to the processing of earlier events that set the groundwork for the presenting dysfunction. As these are resolved, the clinician moves into the second prong of EMDR processing, which attends to any present-day fears and anxieties. Current behaviors, situations, issues that continue to distress the client are targeted in the same manner as any other event. Current targets are also reevaluated for maintenance of treatment effects and recycled and reprocessed when necessary. Treatment of other memories and associative links to other disturbing information ensures maximum overall benefits. With certain clients, it may be pertinent to provide education in a variety of areas (parenting classes, assertiveness training, and referral for vocational evaluation) for present functioning to improve. These adjunctive procedures fill in existing gaps or deficits in social, interpersonal, and occupational functioning.

The final prong of the EMDR protocol relates to future concerns and problems. It addresses the additional training and skills the client will need to be successful in the future. This part of the protocol examines the need to target anticipatory fears related to failure, success, loss of control, abandonment, rejection, and performance issues, as well as positive templates that incorporate desired and appropriate future behaviors. Incorporation of a detailed positive template is not attempted until earlier dysfunctional material liable to affect specific areas of functioning has been reprocessed.

Treatment is considered incomplete until there is installation of a positive template: specific, alternative behavioral responses for appropriate future action. The objectives are increases in mastery of specific skills (e.g., assertiveness, anxiety or anger management, success in intimidating tasks) or improved performances in the workplace, career, professional activities, or athletic contests. Initially, the therapist will have clients practice skills and identify potential problems in the clinical setting rather than encounter disturbances, fears, and other resistance on their own in the actual situation. Imagery of positive outcomes is a visualization technique similar to that used by star athletes (Foster & Lendl, 1995, 1996, in press).

Education, modeling, and visualization, in conjunction with EMDR processing, are used to enable the client to respond differently in future situations. For abuse victims, the future may involve contacts with former perpetrator(s). For this type of situation, after appropriate preparation, the client might be asked to imagine a future encounter with the abuser and report whatever comes spontaneously to mind and body. The resulting information addresses whether additional reprocessing is necessary. Feeling fear in the presence of a violent offender may be indicative that consensus reality needs to be taken into account, and the client's reaction of fear is sanctioned as appropriate to the situation at hand. Inappropriate fears (e.g., when the perpetrator is aged, infirm, or living out of the area) may indicate the need for additional processing of the relationship issues before the future template can be appropriately installed. A client assaulted in an enclosed space may have processed memories related to the assailant, yet not fully processed feelings that have generalized to other similar places (airplanes, boats, cars, elevators, amusement park rides, closets). Clients can be asked to visualize themselves in these types of places and situations or to watch a movie or videotape of how situations from current life would evolve in the future and process the emergent significant information. Specific protocols are used appropriate to the presenting clinical complaint (e.g., phobias, somatic disorders).

After areas of dysfunction have been comprehensively processed and a sense of joy and success are the baseline experiences in the client's life, it may be appropriate to consider termination. However, as the client engages in new behaviors, other previously unrevealed issues may arise that may influence the client to return to therapy. The best goal is to achieve a state of health and equilibrium congruent with the client's current developmental stage, as well as to enhance the level of self-knowledge, self-esteem, and behavioral and cognitive self-control. The need for subsequent therapeutic assistance may arise if situations overcome the client's ability to cope. It is important to empower clients and simultaneously teach them that personal growth is an ongoing process of social and self-revelation.

MAJOR SYNDROMES, SYMPTOMS, AND PROBLEM POPULATIONS

Major Syndromes and Symptoms

PTSD

The effectiveness of EMDR with people suffering from PTSD is now well documented by over a dozen independent controlled evaluations. The *Practice Guidelines* of the International Society for Traumatic Stress Studies (Chemtob et al., 2000; Shalev, Friedman, Foa, & Keane, 2000) have declared EMDR to be effective in the treatment of PTSD. Controlled studies on the use of EMDR with civilian (nonmilitary personnel) PTSD have been conducted by a variety of investigators (Ironson et al., in press; Marcus et al., 1997; Rothbaum, 1997; Scheck et al., 1998; S. A. Wilson et al., 1995, 1997). These studies consistently found that after the equivalent of three 90-minute treatment sessions, 84 to 100% of single-trauma subjects were no longer diagnosed with PTSD. One study by Carlson, Chemtob, Rusnak, Hedlund, and Muraoka (1998) on multiply traumatized combat veterans found EMDR to be an efficacious treatment when an appropriate number of sessions (12) for this clinical population were provided; 77% of this group was no longer diagnosed with PTSD at nine-month follow-up. The standard PTSD protocol (Shapiro, 1995, 2001) includes reprocessing the primary incident, intrusive symptoms (e.g., nightmares, flashbacks), present triggers, and a template for future action to overcome avoidance behavior.

Complex PTSD

Preliminary research has also indicated the potential utility of Resource Development and Installation (Korn & Leeds, in press) for use with complex PTSD and borderline clients in the stabilization phase of treatment. More extensive research needs to be conducted to fully evaluate its effects. This protocol uses EMDR to increase access to positive affects and memories before trauma processing is inaugurated.

Phobias

Shapiro (1995, 2001) developed a specific protocol of 8 to 11 steps for treatment of phobias that clinical observations supported as efficacious (De Jongh, Ten Broeke, & Renssen, 1999; Fenster-heim, 1996; Lipke, 1994, 1995; Marquis, 1991). Other studies, however, have reported less positive outcomes. To evaluate this range of outcomes, a blind evaluation of all published phobia research was conducted. The findings (reported in Shapiro, 1999) concluded that studies lacking in procedural fidelity and protocol adherence (i.e., misapplied, truncated, inexact application of standardized protocol or elimination or inappropriately structured targets) achieved negligible or modest effects (e.g., Acierno, Tremont, Last, & Montgomery, 1994; Bates, McGlynn, Montgomery, & Mattke, 1996; Lohr, Tolin, & Kleinknecht, 1995, 1996; Muris & Merckelbach, 1997; Muris, Merkelbach, Holdrinet, & Sijsenaar,

1998; Muris, Merckelbach, Van Haaften, & Nayer, 1997; Sanderson & Carpenter, 1992). Phobia studies utilizing all of the procedures including the appropriate number of sessions achieved positive results (e.g., De Jongh & Ten Broeke, 1998; De Jongh, van den Oord, & Ten Broeke, in press; De Jongh et al., 1999; Goldstein & Feske, 1994).

Panic Disorders

Case studies and limited controlled research have reported promising results on the use of EMDR with panic disorders (Feske & Goldstein, 1997; Goldstein & Feske, 1994; Nadler, 1996; Shapiro & Forrest, 1997). However, a study of panic disorder with agoraphobia (Goldstein, de Beurs, Chambless, & Wilson, 2000) reported negligible results, possibly due to insufficient preparation time (see Shapiro, 2001). The application to panic disorder is based on the 11-step phobia protocol (Shapiro, 1995, 2001).

Somatoform Disorders

Promising results have also been reported with the use of EMDR for somatoform disorders, including chronic pain (Grant & Threlfo, in press), phantom limb pain (Shapiro & Forrest, 1997; S. A. Wilson, Tinker, Becker, Hofmann, & Cole, 2000), and Body Dysmorphic Disorder (BDD); K. W. Brown, McGoldrick, and Buchanan (1997). Brown et al. successfully eliminated symptoms of body dysmorphia by processing the etiological memory in five of seven consecutive cases in one to three sessions. The protocol for BDD includes reprocessing the etiological event, triggers, and templates as in the standard PTSD protocol. The applications to phantom limb and chronic pain utilize the standard three-pronged protocol, along with a variety of techniques that concentrate on the physical sensations.

Other Disorders

There are no well-established, empirically validated treatments for many complex pathologies according to an efficacy and validation review

(Chambless et al., 1998), yet the EMDR treatment of dissociative disorders (Lazrove & Fine, 1996; Paulsen, 1995; Twombly, 2000) personality disorders (Fensterheim, 1996; Manfield, 1998), and substance abuse (Shapiro, Vogelmann-Sine, & Sine, 1994) indicate positive outcomes when EMDR has been utilized in combination with traditional methods with these disorders. Over 100 articles have reported that EMDR appears effective in the treatment of a wide range of experientially based disorders. (See Shapiro, 2001, for a full delineation of protocols, research, and published case reports.)

PROBLEM POPULATIONS

EMDR is not an appropriate treatment for every client. A comprehensive and detailed history is necessary to determine who is suitable, with whom it can be used, and who needs to be excluded. Because of the accelerated processing that takes place, there is no way to predict how a client will react to the targeting of a specific event. Responses range from mild emotional responses to full-blown abreactions. Emergent information can readily surface with emotions and physical sensations connected to the original event in the form of new, associated, or dissociated material of which the client was unaware.

Information processing may continue between sessions and clients may experience discomfort as material is stimulated. In all of these situations, clients must be able to handle whatever emotions (despair, rage, helplessness, or sense of vulnerability) are connected with their memories. Additionally, during a full-blown abreaction (i.e., the experiencing of the stimulated memory at high levels of disturbance), the intensity of physical sensations and emotions may be frightening to the client. As an example, Shapiro (1995) cites the case of a client who began to emit choking sounds, turned color, and had marked difficulty breathing when processing a

childhood memory of being captured by friends, tied with a rope, and hung by the neck. The memory was successfully processed, resulting in a decline of current dysfunction, because certain conditions facilitated positive treatment effects (see also Shapiro, 2001).

The following factors require careful assessment to ensure client safety and treatment suitability:

1. *The therapeutic alliance:* EMDR requires a strong therapeutic relationship sufficient to engender trust and truth telling by the client. Insufficient trust, high susceptibility to demand characteristics, and/or desire to avoid painful material will cause clients to inaccurately report what they are experiencing. As with all trauma treatments, clients are at higher risk for suicidal behaviors when they feel greatly disturbed and withhold this information from the therapist.

2. *Inability/difficulty in use of self-control/self-soothing techniques:* To reduce disturbances arising from processing, clients must be able to use self-control strategies (relaxation, safe place, hypnosis, guided imagery, etc.). As with all trauma treatments, an inability to self-sooth may be a contraindication to processing.

3. *Questionable stability secondary to crisis-oriented lifestyle:* Major life pressures (e.g., legal, job, financial, family problems), difficulties remembering instructions because of emotional or physical impairment, and lack of a supportive environment indicate the need for caution and possible postponement of treatment until the life crisis is resolved or under control.

4. *Physical health issues:* Clients must be assessed for ability to withstand the physical rigors of processing. This is especially important for clients with complex PTSD and histories of severe abuse, torture, and similar trauma. Caution is required in the

treatment of pregnant women and persons with medical problems (e.g., cardiac, respiratory, and neurological problems, alcohol and drug dependency). Medication management may require consultation with the patient's physician.

5. *Victims of crime, witnesses, police officers, and critical incident debriefing personnel:* There is a possibility that the client's testimony may be significantly modified by EMDR treatment; such changes can include diminished emotional distress, elimination of PTSD, and blurring or loss of visual details. This may have ramifications for any legal proceedings in which the client is involved. Consultation with attorneys is advised and videotaping of sessions may be required to preserve evidence; otherwise, postponing treatment may be indicated.

6. *Secondary gains:* Issues related to this category need to be addressed prior to trauma processing. The compensated veteran who lacks occupational skills to support self and family adequately may first need to be reassured and involved in vocational rehabilitation before getting well, which can mean losing pension benefits. The alcoholic may be threatened by being asked to give up the only support group he has ever had, his drinking buddies. It is important to assess the impact of loss of secondary gains for the individual and others dependent on him or her.

7. *Drug and alcohol abuse:* In some clients, cravings have decreased while undergoing EMDR treatment, whereas others have transiently reported an increased desire to use as old painful material associated with past use is stimulated and/or the need to self-medicate reappears. Recent crack cocaine addicts may require stimulation by other than eye movements. There is one report of a daily amphetamine abuser who required hospitalization post-EMDR treatment after becoming highly agitated.

8. *Dissociative disorders:* Treatment planning issues become extremely important with dissociative disorders (especially Dissociative Identity Disorder). Clinicians are strongly urged not to proceed without supervised training in dissociative disorders and a thorough knowledge of appropriate EMDR protocols (see Lazrove & Fine, 1996; Paulsen, 1995; Shapiro, 1995, 2001).

CASE EXAMPLE

The client, a successful businessman, was a 45-year-old ex-Marine with a 20-year history of PTSD and a history of multiple traumas treated by one of the authors (E. S.). The case exemplifies the efficacy of EMDR for resolution of complex PTSD and multiple traumatic events beginning in infancy.

The client was referred for EMDR therapy by the clinician he saw for marital counseling. His presenting complaints included nightmares related to his helicopter crash, frequent intrusive thoughts of the suicide of his ex-girlfriend, and unresolved feelings about having been adopted. A comprehensive history was completed during the first and second sessions. Significant information obtained included general details regarding a helicopter crash on training maneuvers in the United States. This event led to the death of three crewmen. He survived with multiple injuries and burns, requiring painful treatment procedures and a three-month hospitalization. Though informed of his condition, his parents failed to visit during his long convalescence. They had been opposed to his going into the military. While he was hospitalized, he also learned that his entire squadron stationed in Vietnam had been destroyed in a two-day period. Other losses included the suicide death of his ex-girlfriend when he was in his late 20s, and the death of his father when the client was 40. The client described a highly conflicted relationship with his parents, whom he portrayed as emotionally distant and very strict. During childhood, his father was frequently physically abusive and punished the client at times by hitting him with the buckle end of a belt. The pattern was that his mother would say she was going to tell his father of misbehaviors. He would experience long episodes of dread as he waited to be beaten. Mother would then attempt to console him. The client expressed confusion and a lack of understanding as to why anyone would adopt a child and then be as physically abusive as they were.

An avid reader, he had gone on the Internet and educated himself on EMDR and PTSD. At the second session, he described himself as "the Poster Child for PTSD." He described how his family had to fling cotton balls at him to wake him. "Otherwise, I'm too dangerous." The client was instructed in the mechanical aspects of EMDR. He chose visual processing, as he was hearing impaired in the right ear. A safe place was established. Because of his long history of multiple traumas and the high probability of incomplete sessions, a method of containment for traumatic memories was also developed. He owned a cedar chest and used it as an imaginary place to store traumatic material that might require further processing between the weekly 90-minute sessions. The standard EMDR trauma protocol (Shapiro, 1995, 2001) was used.

During the assessment phase (third session), the veteran chose to deal with the death of his ex-girlfriend as the first EMDR trauma target. He remembered a phone call from her. She was very depressed and wanted him to visit her. He declined. Gas was being rationed at the time and he did not have enough for the visit. After obtaining gas the next day and having a premonition something was wrong, he made the visit only to discover her dead from an overdose. The client blamed himself for her suicide because he did not visit as she had requested of him. He states he did not cry at her funeral. He recalled the phone call as the worst part of the memory. His negative cognition was: "I am self-centered.

I am responsible for her death." The positive cognition was: "I am only partially responsible for her death." The VOC was 1. Caution is recommended with VOCs of 1, as they may turn out to be wishful thinking or impossible positive self-statements to achieve. In this case, the therapist let it stand. The predominant emotion described was guilt (SUD of 10).

Emergent information during the desensitization phase revealed that his girlfriend had a history of depression and previous suicide attempts that he did not learn about until after her death. Remembering this fact during processing helped him to accept a lesser degree of responsibility for her death. However, the level of self-blame remained high. In an effort to reduce his guilt and given his religious upbringing, a cognitive interweave with a Christian reference was used. The client knew that for many years, through the repeated experiencing of guilt, he continued to punish himself for her death. He was informed that even the thief on Calvary had been forgiven by Jesus and that most prisoners eventually served their sentence and their debt to society was considered paid. He was asked how much longer he planned to continue to endure his guilt. A positive insight regarding his need to take care of himself and his girlfriend's responsibility for taking care of herself emerged. A feeling of calm followed. After continued processing, at the end of the session the guilt reduced to a SUD level of 3. This level is indicative of incomplete processing, so the client was asked to put the memories of the death of his ex-girlfriend in the cedar chest for further processing at the next session.

Upon reevaluation at the next session, the client shared feeling differently toward his girlfriend and expressed a sense of "missing her." Because he reported a sense of tightness about the temples when thinking of the phone call, additional reprocessing was needed. The negative cognitions were similar to the previous session: "I'm selfish and irresponsible." His desired belief began with the statement "I want to believe I didn't know she was going to commit suicide, and had I known, I would have done whatever was necessary." This was shortened to "I did the best I could." It had no validity (VOC of 1). The emotions of sadness and guilt were now experienced at a SUD level of 6.

He began to cry as soon as processing started and described a sense of "my life being sucked away" when speaking to her on the phone, a feeling also described as old and familiar. The session was very emotional for him, as there was acknowledgment of times he had wished her dead. He voiced considerable guilt and shame for these thoughts. He then began to say "This is the first time I have seen a dead person" and spontaneously associated to the helicopter crash and the death of his crew, an event that had preceded his girlfriend's death. Given the little time remaining in the session, the decision was made to process the crash on another occasion. He contained this information in the cedar chest as before. The material related to the death of his girlfriend seemed completely processed. No VOC or SUD levels were used to avoid restimulating the crash material.

At the end of this session, he stated that he would be unable to return for several weeks as he was going out of town on business. Normally, to forestall any negative effects, treatment of a major trauma is delayed until there is certainty the work can be started and finished with no interruptions. It was fortunate in this case that no significant negative reactions took place. The between-session processing often observed in EMDR treatment proceeded in a beneficial manner as after the previous visit.

At the reevaluation phase of the fifth session, the client announced that he had not thought of his ex-girlfriend for the prior two weeks and that he no longer held himself responsible for her death. The trauma of her death was now in his past. He reported that these realizations were very unusual for him.

He now reported as major concerns, a fear of flying, something frequently required in his job, and of dying in a plane crash. He additionally shared having had a nightmare regarding the crash. Part of the nightmare involved injury to his leg and seeing the dead pilot cut in half. Initially, he stated that this was probably a false memory. He also shared that a common theme for him from early childhood was not being able to trust his perceptions and recollections.

During this assessment phase, it was decided to target his nightmare as a primary representation of the presenting problem. In EMDR, it is assumed that a nightmare is a manifestation of incompletely processed experiences, particularly helpful when it is consistent with the client's previous session. The negative belief "I cannot be afraid" developed from his statement "I'm a Marine, I cannot be scared." The PC was "It's okay to be scared." Once again, he rated the PC as completely false and having no validity (VOC of 1), though intellectually he knew this not to be the case. The emotion was a very high level of fear (SUD of 10) and felt in the stomach. As processing of the nightmare took place, he imagined the dead pilot trying to reach for him. Initially, he reported the event as though happening to someone else and then spontaneously realized it had indeed happened to him. The client described episodes of resisting the urge to cry and how sometimes at night he would bang his head on the headboard of his bed. It seemed that by causing himself pain he could momentarily stop or distract himself from the anguish of the pilot's death and his own fears of burning to death. The session was closed with insights emerging as described. Additional processing of this particular material would continue at the next meeting.

At the next session, the client announced that the nightmares had stopped and he described this as highly unusual. Further inquiry revealed that his father had been so opposed to his son joining the Corps that he refused to visit and disowned him. The worst part of these memories was recalling his mother's admonition to "stop feeling sorry" for himself, an old and familiar response from her. The negative belief was "It's my fault they didn't visit. I'm responsible." "I'm proud of what I did" emerged as the PC (VOC of 1). He described his emotions as "I'm imbedded in a fog; immense loneliness" (SUD of 10). Further details of the crash emerged along with information regarding the pilot's behavior, his inability to extricate his legs from the helicopter's struts, the ensuing fire, eventual rescue, and hospitalization.

He associated the impact of this trauma with present-day behaviors. He described a sense of horror and significant startle response at football games when the cannon was fired after a touchdown. Habitually he found himself diving under the seats, often to his friends' amusement. Processing his hospital experience activated memories about treatment for his burns and the excruciating pain experienced. Peter Levin in *Waking the Tiger* (1997) writes that traumatized people have a need to complete behaviors the body would have naturally executed had that been possible or allowed. Shapiro (1995, 2001) has also reported on the utility of inviting a blocked physical response. Therefore, a cognitive interweave was introduced to the client in the form of "What action(s) would your body have liked to have taken regarding the daily wound-cleaning procedures?" The veteran visualized himself screaming, something he had been unable to do. At the end of this session, he was again asked to contain the traumatic material in the cedar chest, and relaxation techniques were used to calm his state of hyperarousal.

The client began the seventh session by stating happily, "I'm a believer!" He reported being on "the flight from hell" (Denver to Chicago during a hurricane alert). The plane was struck by lightning, and although there was no serious damage, there was considerable turbulence and at least 25 people threw up. He, on the other hand, experienced himself as handling the entire flight quite well and feeling very calm during the ordeal. Generalization effects are fairly common in EMDR treatment and it was obvious this is what had happened. Except for dealing with the helicopter crash in previous sessions, no targeting of his fear of flying in airplanes had been attempted. We briefly processed the plane flight and his resistance to feeling proud of his behavior. The NC was "I don't deserve compliments." At installation, the PC of "I can feel proud. I can do it" had a VOC of 7 and his feeling of resistance was a SUD of 0, down from 6.

We returned to the material of the previous session, including his hospitalization and his parents' lack of involvement in his care, particularly the anticipation of hearing his mother telling him to stop feeling sorry for himself. The client associated to earlier childhood experiences of illness and his mother's refusal to let friends visit him. The NC was "It's my fault they didn't visit. I'm responsible." The PC was "I am proud of what I did (acted assertively)" (VOC of 4). Emotionally he felt considerable sadness (SUD of 10). During the desensitization phase, he began to associate to his parents' tendency to exclude him from contact with friends and how very important this childhood network of companions had been for him.

In subsequent sessions, the client reported having no more nightmares, a decrease in startle response, and that he was beginning to dream positively. An avid football fan who regularly attended games, he had additionally become aware that he was no longer "diving under the seats." During processing, after which he linked fireworks sounds to machine gun fire and rotating helicopter blades, he no longer experienced a sense of terror during fireworks displays. Because of EMDR's generalizing effects, other present-day changes spontaneously emerged. The client reported being aware that after moving his office, there was no longer a need to guard his back (desk positioning), have bells on doors (or the cat) to warn him of "anyone entering the area," or have "all the lights on in order to not be surprised." As far as he could tell, his startle response seemed gone.

The final piece of work related to his military experiences took place during the session on November 9, coincidentally, the day before the birth date of the U.S. Marine Corps. The eve of this date triggered memories related to the loss of his squadron overseas. He found himself able to grieve their loss through recollections of previous visits to The Wall, the Vietnam War Memorial in Washington, D.C., where he touched the names of those he needed to remember. More recently, he has made plans to ride in a helicopter and has toured a military base housing helicopters similar to the one he crashed in to more fully identify any residual PTSD-related reactions. With regard to his other issues (death of ex-girlfriend, adoption, and physical and emotional abuse experienced growing up), these too have been fully resolved. He reports more positive feelings toward his deceased father and of longing to have known him better. The feeling toward his mother is one of acceptance of her inability to change who she is and how she continues to behave. He no longer feels intimidated by her and is more trusting of his own perceptions.

RESEARCH ON THE APPROACH: EFFICACY AND EFFECTIVENESS DATA

CONTROLLED STUDIES EVALUATING PTSD TREATMENT

Efficacy
As indicated previously, controlled studies (Ironson et al., in press; Marcus et al., 1997; Rothbaum, 1997; Scheck et al., 1998; Wilson et al., 1995, 1997) that provided three to five hours of treatment to civilian populations with PTSD have consistently found that after EMDR, 84 to 100% of single-trauma subjects came within one standard deviation of the norm on multiple measures and/or were no longer diagnosed with PTSD. Treatment effects have been maintained with follow-up assessment of 3 to 15 months. Outcomes with combat veterans have been mixed, due to an insufficient amount of treatment time. However, the one study (Carlson et al., 1998) offering a full treatment regime (i.e., 12 sessions) to multiply traumatized veterans found EMDR efficacious. Treatment effects were maintained at nine-month follow-up, with 77% of the EMDR participants no longer meeting diagnostic criteria for PTSD.

There has been only one controlled EMDR study treating children with PTSD (Chemtob, Nakashima, Hamada, & Carlson, in press). This is the first randomized treatment study of any kind of psychotherapy for children with PTSD. Participants were children with PTSD related to a hurricane that had occurred three years previously; these children had not responded to a course of prior psychosocial treatment and had PTSD at a one-year follow-up. After three EMDR sessions, 53% of these children no longer met diagnostic criteria for PTSD, and there were significant decreases of symptoms on many measures, with gains maintained at six-month follow-up.

Effectiveness
There have been several field studies, using randomized designs, that examined the effectiveness of EMDR in natural settings with PTSD populations. The children's study described above (Chemtob et al., in press) was a field study, with treatment provided in school settings. Researchers found that after EMDR treatment, in addition to improvements on clinical measures, the frequency of health visits to the school nurse was significantly reduced. Ironson et al. (in press) randomly assigned 22 patients from a university-based clinic serving the outside community to either EMDR or prolonged exposure therapy; these participants were predominantly rape and crime victims. The efficiency of EMDR treatment appeared to be an advantage with this population; 7 of the 10 EMDR clients finished treatment after three active sessions, but only 2 of the 9 exposure clients did so. Although extra sessions were offered to

the noncompleters, 3 of the continuing 7 exposure clients dropped out, apparently because of time considerations and/or inconvenience.

Scheck et al. (1998) compared EMDR and active listening for a group of young women engaging in high-risk behaviors, with treatment provided by community agencies. This short intervention was helpful, with most clients moving into the normative range on multiple measures. Marcus et al. (1997) provided EMDR in a health maintenance organization (HMO) and compared EMDR to the standard treatments used in the facility (cognitive, psychodynamic, or behavioral). EMDR resulted in significantly lower scores than standard HMO treatment, after three sessions and at posttreatment, on measures of PTSD symptoms, depression, and anxiety. This field study has high external validity and indicates that EMDR may be superior to commonly used forms of treatment.

Comparison of EMDR and Exposure-Based and Other Cognitive-Behavioral Treatments for PTSD

A meta-analysis of PTSD treatment observed that EMDR was more efficient than other psychotherapies (Van Etten & Taylor, 1998). Exposure-based cognitive-behavioral therapies (e.g., Brom, Kleber, & Defares, 1989; Foa et al., 1999; Keane, Fairbank, Caddell, & Zimering, 1989; Marks et al., 1998; Resick & Schnicke, 1992; Tarrier et al., 1999) provide 8 to 15 hours of treatment, often supplemented by homework of 25 to 100 hours. These studies have typically reported a 50 to 80% decrease in PTSD diagnosis. In comparison, several EMDR studies documented that 77 to 100% of single-trauma victims no longer had PTSD after three to five hours of treatment and/or had reduced symptoms to within one standard deviation of normal on multiple measures (e.g., Ironson et al., in press; Marcus et al., 1997; Rothbaum, 1997; Scheck et al., 1998; S. A. Wilson et al., 1995, 1997; for detailed reviews see Chemtob et al., 2000; Maxfield & Hyer, in press; Shapiro, 2001).

Determinations of relative efficacy require head-to-head comparisons using the same populations in the same treatment centers. To date, there have been four controlled studies directly comparing EMDR and traditional exposure therapies. Three of these studies (Ironson et al., in press; Lee, Gavriel, Drummond, Richards, & Greenwald, in press; Vaughan et al., 1994) have generally found equivalent effects, with EMDR producing better outcomes on measures of intrusive symptoms. In all cases, EMDR was reported as more efficient and needing fewer sessions or homework. The fourth nonrandomized study (Devilly & Spence, 1999) compared EMDR to a cognitive-behavior therapy created and administered by the first author and found that treatment more successful. Controlled studies of EMDR and exposure have been confined to civilian populations.

FUTURE RESEARCH

One of the difficulties in designing comparative studies is that there is no standardized method for conducting cognitive-behavioral treatment of PTSD; different research teams have used different methods and/or combinations. Recommendations for future research include some standardization of exposure and cognitive therapies so that the same protocols can be tested in multiple, independent studies. Comparative evaluations of exposure therapy, cognitive therapy, and EMDR should include measures of efficacy, effectiveness, efficiency, attrition, clinician acceptance, and client preference (e.g., tolerance and comfort), and, when possible, neurophysiological and neurobiological data. Studies should utilize the methodological gold standards advocated by Foa and Meadows (1997), with blind independent assessors and expert treatment fidelity assessments. A course of treatment adequate to the needs of the population (Maxfield & Hyer, in press) should be provided.

Other Anxiety Disorders

Phobias and Panic Disorders

As mentioned previously in the "Syndrome" section, much of the research investigating EMDR treatment of phobias and panic disorders has been limited by problems with truncated procedures and poor treatment fidelity. Many studies did not provide a full course of treatment, and so may represent an inadequate test of EMDR's effectiveness with these disorders. For example, when Feske and Goldstein (1997) provided four active EMDR sessions to participants with Panic Disorder, the positive treatment effects dissipated after three months. Interpretations of these findings should consider that "even 10 to 16 sessions of the most powerful treatments rarely result in normalization of panic symptoms" (Feske & Goldstein, 1997, p. 1034).

Additionally, many studies did not test EMDR's phobia protocol but used procedures modified and adapted by the researcher; such studies have generally reported poor results. However, promising results have been reported in case studies where the protocols were employed (e.g., complete elimination of symptoms based on behavioral measures; De Jongh & Ten Broeke, 1998; De Jongh et al., 1999, in press). Future research to investigate these applications must use the standardized protocols, with good fidelity, in a course of treatment of sufficient duration. Until such research is completed, the efficacy of EMDR in the treatment of panic disorders and phobias is unclear.

Component Analysis Research

Well-designed and methodologically rigorous component analysis research is needed to determine the active ingredients in EMDR. Most studies conducted to date on the eye movement component have been hampered by the use of brief treatment times, samples too small to yield statistical power, inappropriate controls, and/or inappropriate participants. Some component studies have provided insufficient treatment (two sessions; Boudewyns, Stwertka, Hyer, Albrecht, & Sperr, 1993; Devilly, Spence, & Rapee, 1998) to multiply traumatized combat veterans and/or treated only one or two memories (Boudewyns & Hyer, 1996; Pitman et al., 1996). Such a truncated course of treatment with this population is inadequate and unlikely to result in significant effects. Other studies have used subclinical participants (e.g., Dunn, Schwartz, Hatfield, & Wiegele, 1996), whose problems were minor and whose ready response to treatment prevented the measurement of differential treatment effects. Other component studies provided brief interventions of only two or five minutes (e.g., Sanderson & Carpenter, 1992). Such truncated treatment does not provide an adequate test of treatment efficacy. In addition, the control condition in some studies was similar to clinical variants of EMDR (e.g., tapping; Bauman & Melnyk, 1994; Pitman et al., 1996), reducing the likelihood of a statistical and/or meaningful difference between conditions.

Almost every study has used small samples, with fewer than 10 persons per cell, providing inadequate statistical power and increasing the probability of Type II error (Cohen, 1988; Kazdin & Bass, 1989). For example, in a study (Renfrey & Spates, 1994) with PTSD participants, only 13.5% of participants in the combined eye movement conditions still met diagnostic criteria at the posttest, compared to 50% in the eye fixation condition. However, the small sample size (seven or eight per cell) did not provide adequate power for statistical significance.

Nevertheless, a consistent finding in studies using clinical participants is the significantly greater decreases in SUD levels when EMDR is compared to exposure (Boudewyns et al., 1993; Rogers et al., 1999) or to a non-eye-movement analog (Lohr et al., 1996; Montgomery & Ayllon, 1994; Shapiro, 1989a). Some controlled component analyses have obtained positive effects for the eye movement condition at posttest (Andrade et al., 1997; Feske & Goldstein, 1997; Gosselin & Matthews, 1995; D. L. Wilson, Silver, Covi, & Foster, 1996), but the findings of these studies are limited by methodological shortcomings. Positive effects for eye movements have also been found in single-subject studies (Lohr et al., 1995, 1996; Montgomery & Ayllon, 1994).

Currently, the aggregate evidence for the role of eye movements is inconclusive. This does not mean, however, that the eye movement or alternate dual attention stimuli are irrelevant to the procedure (see Chemtob et al., 2000; Feske, 1998; Shapiro, 1994a, 1995, 1999, 2001). Future research must address the above mentioned methodological problems and should be designed to test hypotheses concerning mechanisms of action. (For a thorough discussion of these issues, see Shapiro, 2001.)

OTHER CLINICAL APPLICATIONS

Positive therapeutic results have been reported using EMDR with a wide range of traumatized populations and diagnoses. These include surgery and burn victims (Hassard, 1993; McCann, 1992), crime victims and police subject to violent assaults (Kleinknecht & Morgan, 1992; Page & Crino, 1993; Shapiro & Solomon, 1995), sexual assault victims (Hyer, 1995; Parnell, 1999; Puk, 1991; Rothbaum, 1997; Shapiro, 1989a, 1991, 1994b; Wolpe & Abrams, 1991), children subjected to assault or natural disaster (Chemtob et al., in press; Cocco & Sharpe, 1993; Greenwald, 1994, 1999; Lovett, 1999; Pellicer, 1993; Puffer, Greenwald, & Elrod, 1998; Shapiro, 1991; Tinker & Wilson, 1999), excessive or pathological grief reactions, line of duty deaths to railroad engineers (Shapiro & Solomon, 1995), and persons with dissociative disorders (Lazrove & Fine, 1996; Paulsen, 1995; W. C. Young, 1994), body dysmorphic disorder (K. W. Brown et al., 1997), and chronic pain (Grant & Threlfo, in press).

Future research is needed to evaluate such applications. In addition to the methodological rigor previously recommended, it is advised that the standardized EMDR procedure and protocols be evaluated for the treatment of the particular disorder. If for some reason the protocol is adapted, such modifications should be described and the purpose for the deviation explained. The application of EMDR to various disorders may be enriched by integration with other treatment modalities. However, integration, without critical investigation, creates a risk that treatment outcomes may be diluted rather than enhanced.

SUMMARY

The effectiveness of EMDR for PTSD is now documented in over a dozen independent controlled evaluations. In 1995, a Division 12 Task Force of the American Psychological Association developed guidelines for assessing the empirical status of psychological interventions. Based on these standards, independent reviewers (Chambless et al., 1998) placed EMDR on the list of empirically validated treatments as probably efficacious for civilian PTSD. Exposure therapy (flooding) and stress inoculation therapies were also described as probably efficacious for PTSD. No other clinical interventions were judged to be empirically validated by controlled research.

More recently, on the basis of additional studies, the *Practice Guidelines* of the International Society for Traumatic Stress Studies has designated EMDR as effective for the treatment of PTSD (Chemtob et al., 2000; Shalev, Friedman, et al., 2000). A meta-analysis of all psychological and drug treatments designated EMDR as one of the most effective and efficient treatments for PTSD (Van Etten & Taylor, 1998). Additional research is needed to address the various protocols that have already been developed for treatment of other presenting complaints, such as phobias, body dysmorphic disorder, Panic Disorder, addictions, and Obsessive Compulsive Disorder. It appears that some disorders can be eliminated by utilization of the standard three-pronged protocol, including the targeting and reprocessing of key memories of the trauma or fear, whereas others require additional modification.

The goal of EMDR is to produce the most profound and comprehensive treatment effects possible in the shortest period of time, while maintaining a stable client in a balanced system. As an integrative approach to psychotherapy, EMDR has continued to benefit from the systematic integration of all the psychological modalities (see Frischholz, Kowal, & Hammond, 2001; Norcross & Shapiro, in press; Shapiro, in press; Zabukovec et al., 2000). As integration increases, it is important to conduct research to make sure that alterations of standardized protocols result in increased rather than diluted treatment effects (see Shapiro, 2001). Further, given the reported wide range of positive treatment effects, it is important to develop research tools capable of assessing changes in emotional, cognitive, somatic, and behavioral domains that can best guide the practicing clinician.

REFERENCES

Acierno, R., Tremont, G., Last, C., & Montgomery, D. (1994). Tripartite assessment of the efficacy of eye-movement desensitization in a multi-phobic patient. *Journal of Anxiety Disorders, 8,* 259–276.

Andrade, J., Kavanagh, D., & Baddeley, A. (1997). Eye-movements and visual imagery: A working memory approach to the treatment of Post-Traumatic Stress Disorder. *British Journal of Clinical Psychology, 36,* 209–223.

Antrobus, J. S. (1973). Eye movements and non-visual cognitive tests. In V. Zikmund (Ed.), *The oculomotor system and brain functions* (pp. 354–368). London: Butterworth.

Antrobus, T. S., Antrobus, J. S., & Singer, J. L. (1964). Eye movements accompanying daydreaming, visual imagery, and thought suppression. *Journal of Abnormal and Social Psychology, 69,* 244–252.

Armstrong, M. S., & Vaughan, K. (1996). An orienting response model of eye movement desensitization. *Journal of Behavior Therapy and Experimental Psychiatry, 27,* 21–32.

Bates, L., McGlynn, D., Montgomery, R., & Mattke, T. (1996). Effects of eye-movement desensitization versus no treatment on repeated measures of fear of spiders. *Journal of Anxiety Disorders, 10,* 555–569.

Bauman, W., & Melnyk, W. T. (1994). A controlled comparison of eye movement and finger tapping in the treatment of test anxiety. *Journal of Behavior Therapy and Experimental Psychiatry, 25,* 29–33.

Becker, L. A., Nugent, N. R., & Tinker, B. (2000). *What about the eye movements in EMDR?* Paper presented at the annual meeting of the EMDR International Association, Toronto, Canada.

Becker, L. A., Todd-Overmann, A., Stoothoff, W., & Lawson, T. (1998, July). *Ironic memory, PTSD, and EMDR: Do eye movements hinder the avoidance process leading to greater accessibility of traumatic memories?* Paper presented at the annual meeting of the EMDR International Association, Baltimore.

Bohart, A. C., & Greenberg, L. S. (in press). EMDR and experimental psychotherapy. In F. Shapiro (Ed.), *EMDR and the paradigm prism.* Washington, DC: American Psychological Association.

Boudewyns, P. A., & Hyer, L. A. L. (1996). Eye movement desensitization and reprocessing (EMDR) as treatment for Post-Traumatic Stress Disorder (PTSD). *Clinical Psychology and Psychotherapy, 3,* 185–195.

Boudewyns, P. A., Stwertka, S. A., Hyer, L. A. L., Albrecht, J. W., & Sperr, E. V. (1993). Eye movement desensitization for PTSD of combat: A treatment outcome pilot study. *Behavior Therapist, 16,* 29–33.

Bremner, J. D. (1999). Does stress damage the brain? *Biological Psychiatry, 45,* 797–805.

Brom, D., Kleber, R. J., & Defares, P. B. (1989). Brief psychotherapy for Posttraumatic Stress Disorders. *Journal of Consulting and Clinical Psychology, 57,* 607–612.

Brown, K. W., McGoldrick, T., & Buchanan, R. (1997). Body Dysmorphic Disorder: Seven cases treated with eye movement desensitization and reprocessing. *Behavioural and Cognitive Psychotherapy, 25,* 203–207.

Brown, L. S. (in press). Feminist therapy and EMDR: A practice meets a theory. In F. Shapiro (Ed.), *EMDR and the paradigm prism.* Washington, DC: American Psychological Association.

Carlson, J. G., Chemtob, C. M., Rusnak, K., Hedlund, N. L., & Muraoka, M. Y. (1998). Eye movement desensitization and reprocessing (EMDR) treatment for combat-related Posttraumatic Stress Disorder. *Journal of Traumatic Stress, 11,* 3–24.

Chambless, D. L., Baker, M. J., Baucom, D. H., Beutler, L. E., Calhoun, K. S., Crits-Christoph, P., et al. (1998). Update on empirically validated therapies. *The Clinical Psychologist, 51,* 3–16.

Chemtob, C., Nakashima, J., Hamada, R., & Carlson, J. (in press). Brief treatment for elementary school children with disaster-related PTSD: A field study. *Journal of Clinical Psychology.*

Chemtob, C. M., Roitblat, H., Hamada, R., Carlson, J. G., & Twentyman, C. (1988). A cognitive action theory of Posttraumatic Stress Disorder. *Journal of Anxiety Disorders, 2,* 253–275.

Chemtob, C. M., Tolin, D. F., van der Kolk, B. A., & Pitman, R. K. (2000). *Eye movement desensitization and reprocessing.* New York: Guilford Press.

Christman, S., & Garvey, K. (2000, November). *Episodic versus semantic memory: Eye movements and cortical activation.* Paper presented at the 41st annual meeting of Psychonomic Society, New Orleans, LA.

Cocco, N., & Sharpe, L. (1993). An auditory variant of eye movement desensitization in a case of childhood Post-Traumatic Stress Disorder. *Journal of Behavior Therapy and Experimental Psychiatry, 24,* 373–377.

Cohen, H. (1988). *Statistical power analysis for the behavioral sciences* (2nd ed.). Hillsdale, NJ: Erlbaum.

De Jongh, A., & Ten Broeke, E. (1998). Treatment of choking phobia by targeting traumatic memories with EMDR: A case study. *Clinical Psychology and Psychotherapy, 5,* 1–6.

De Jongh, A., Ten Broeke, E., & Renssen, M. R. (1999). Treatment of specific phobias with eye movement desensitization and reprocessing (EMDR): Protocol, empirical status, and conceptual issues. *Journal of Anxiety Disorders, 13,* 69–85.

De Jongh, A., van den Oord, H. J. M., & Ten Broeke, E. (in press). Efficacy of eye movement desensitization and reprocessing (EMDR) in the treatment of specific phobias: Four single case studies on dental phobia. *Journal of Clinical Psychology.*

Devilly, G. J., & Spence, S. H. (1999). The relative efficacy and treatment distress of EMDR and a cognitive-behavior trauma treatment protocol in the amelioration of Posttraumatic Stress Disorder. *Journal of Anxiety Disorders, 13,* 131–157.

Devilly, G. J., Spence, S. H., & Rapee, R. M. (1998). Statistical and reliable change with eye movement desensitization and reprocessing: Treating trauma within a veteran population. *Behavior Therapy, 29,* 435–455.

Dunn, T. M., Schwartz, M., Hatfield, R. W., & Wiegele, M. (1996). Measuring effectiveness of eye movement desensitization and reprocessing (EMDR) in non-clinical anxiety: A multi-subject, yoked-control design. *Journal of Behavior Therapy and Experimental Psychiatry, 27,* 231–239.

Dyck, M. J. (1993). A proposal for a conditioning model of eye movement desensitization treatment for Posttraumatic Stress Disorder. *Journal of Behavior Therapy and Experimental Psychiatry, 24,* 201–210.

Fensterheim, H. (1996). Eye movement desensitization and reprocessing with complex personality pathology: An integrative therapy. *Journal of Psychotherapy Integration, 6,* 27–38.

Feske, U. (1998). Eye movement desensitization and reprocessing treatment for Posttraumatic Stress Disorder. *Clinical Psychology: Science and Practice, 5,* 171–181.

Feske, U., & Goldstein, A. J. (1997). Eye movement desensitization and reprocessing treatment for Panic Disorder: A controlled outcome and partial dismantling study. *Journal of Consulting and Clinical Psychology, 65,* 1026–1035.

Foa, E. B., Dancu, C. V., Hembree, E. A., Jaycox, L. H., Meadows, E. A., & Street, O. P. (1999). A comparison of exposure therapy, stress inoculation training, and their combination in reducing Posttraumatic Stress Disorder in female assault victims. *Journal of Counseling and Clinical Psychology, 67,* 194–200.

Foa, E. B., Keane, T. M., & Friedman, M. J. (2000). *Effective treatments for PTSD: Practice guidelines from the International Society for Traumatic Stress Studies.* New York: Guilford Press.

Foa, E. B., & Kozak, M. J. (1986). Emotional processing of fear: Exposure to corrective information. *Psychological Bulletin, 99,* 20–35.

Foa, E. B., & Meadows, E. A. (1997). Psychosocial treatments for Posttraumatic Stress Disorder: A critical review. *Annual Review of Psychology, 48,* 449–480.

Foster, S., & Lendl, J. (1995). Eye movement desensitization and reprocessing: Initial applications for enhancing performance in athletes. *Journal of Applied Sports Psychology, 7*(Suppl. 63).

Foster, S., & Lendl, J. (1996). Eye movement desensitization and reprocessing: Four cases of a new tool for executive coaching and restoring employee performance after setbacks. *Consulting Psychology Journal: Practice and Research, 48,* 155–161.

Foster, S., & Lendl, J. (in press). Peak performance EMDR: Adapting trauma treatment to positive psychology outcomes. *EMDR International Association Newsletter: Special Issue.*

Frischholz, E. J., Kowal, J. A., & Hammond, D. C. (2001). Introduction to the special section: Hypnosis and EMDR. *American Journal of Clinical Hypnosis, 43,* 179–182.

Goldstein, A. J., de Beurs, E., Chambless, D. L., & Wilson, K. A. (2000). EMDR for Panic Disorder with agoraphobia: Comparison with waiting list and credible attention-placebo control condition. *Journal of Consulting and Clinical Psychology, 68,* 947–956.

Goldstein, A. J., & Feske, U. (1994). Eye movement desensitization and reprocessing for panic disorders: A case series. *Journal of Anxiety Disorders, 8,* 351–362.

Gosselin, P., & Matthews, W. J. (1995). Eye movement desensitization and reprocessing in the treatment of test anxiety: A study of the effects of expectancy and eye movement. *Journal of Behavioral Therapy and Experimental Psychiatry, 26,* 331–337.

Grant, M., & Threlfo, C. (in press). EMDR in the treatment of chronic pain. *Journal of Clinical Psychology.*

Greenwald, R. (1994). Applying eye movement desensitization and reprocessing (EMDR) to the treatment of traumatized children: Five case studies. *Anxiety Disorders Practice Journal, 1,* 83–97.

Greenwald, R. (1999). *Eye movement desensitization and reprocessing (EMDR) in child and adolescent therapy.* Northvale, NJ: Aronson.

Hassard, A. (1993). Eye movement desensitization of body image. *Behavioral Psychotherapy, 21,* 157–160.

Herman, J. L. (1992). Complex PTSD: A syndrome in survivors of prolonged and repeated trauma. *Journal of Traumatic Stress, 5,* 377–391.

Hyer, L. (1994). The trauma response: Its complexity and dimensions. In L. Hyer (Ed.), *Trauma victim: Theoretical issues and practical suggestions.* Muncie, IN: Accelerated Development.

Hyer, L. (1995). Use of EMDR in a "dementing" PTSD survivor. *Clinical Gerontologist, 16,* 70–73.

Ironson, G. I., Freund, B., Strauss, J. L., & Williams, J. (in press). A comparison of two treatments for traumatic stress: A pilot study of EMDR and prolonged exposure. *Journal of Clinical Psychology.*

Kaslow, F. W., Nurse, A. R., & Thompson, P. (in press). Utilization of EMDR in conjunction with family systems therapy. In F. Shapiro (Ed.), *EMDR and the paradigm prism: Experts of diverse orientation explore an integrated treatment.* Washington, DC: American Psychological Association.

Kazdin, A. E., & Bass, D. (1989). Power to detect differences between alternative treatments in comparative psychotherapy outcome research. *Journal of Consulting and Clinical Psychology, 57,* 138–147.

Keane, T. M., Fairbank, J. A., Caddell, J. M., & Zimering, R. T. (1989). Implosive (flooding) therapy reduces symptoms of PTSD in Vietnam combat veterans. *Behavior Therapy, 20,* 245–260.

Keane, T. M., Zimering, R. T., & Caddell, J. M. (1985). A behavioral formulation of Posttraumatic Stress Disorder. *Behavior Therapist, 8,* 9–12.

Kilpatrick, D. G., Veronen, L. J., & Resick, P. A. (1982). Psychological sequelae to rape: Assessment and treatment strategies. In D. M. Doleys & R. L. Meredith (Eds.), *Behavioral medicine: Assessment and treatment strategies.* New York: Plenum Press.

Kleinknecht, R. A., & Morgan, M. P. (1992). Treatment of Posttraumatic Stress Disorder with eye movement desensitization. *Journal of Behavior Therapy and Experimental Psychiatry, 23,* 43–49.

Korn, D., & Leeds, A. M. (in press). Preliminary evidence of efficacy for EMDR resource development and installation in the stabilization phase of treatment of complex Posttraumatic Stress Disorder. *Journal of Clinical Psychology.*

Krystal, S., Prendergast, J., Krystal, P., Fenner, P., Shapiro, I., & Shapiro, K. (in press). Transpersonal psychology, Eastern nondual philosophy and EMDR. In F. Shapiro (Ed.), *EMDR and the paradigm prism.* Washington, DC: American Psychological Association.

Lang, P. J. (1979). Imagery in therapy: An information processing analysis of fear. *Behavior Therapy, 8,* 862–886.

Lansing, K. M., Amen, D. G., & Klindt, W. C. (2000). *Tracking the neurological impact of CBT and EMDR in the treatment of PTSD.* Paper presented at the annual meeting of the Association for the Advancement for Behavior Therapy, New Orleans, LA.

Lazrove, S., & Fine, C. G. (1996). The use of EMDR in patients with Dissociative Identity Disorder. *Dissociation, 9,* 289–299.

Lee, C., Gavriel, H., Drummond, P., Richards, J., & Greenwald, R. (in press). Treatment of Post-Traumatic Stress Disorder: A comparison of stress inoculation training with prolonged exposure and eye movement desensitization and reprocessing. *Journal of Clinical Psychology.*

Levin, C., Shapiro, F., & Weakland, J. (1996). When the past is present: A conversation about EMDR and the MRI interactional approach. In M. F. Hoyt (Ed.), *Constructive therapies two.* New York: Guilford Press.

Levin, P., Lazrove, S., & van der Kolk, B. (1999). What psychological testing and neuroimaging tell us about the treatment of Posttraumatic Stress Disorder by eye movement desensitization and reprocessing. *Journal of Anxiety Disorders, 13,* 159–172.

Levine, P. (1997). *Waking the tiger: Healing trauma.* Berkeley, CA: North Atlantic Books.

Lipke, H. J. (1992). *Manual for teaching of Shapiro's EMDR in the treatment of combat-related PTSD.* Pacific Grove, CA: EMDR Institute.

Lipke, H. J. (1994). *Survey of practitioners trained in eye movement desensitization and reprocessing.* Paper presented at the 102nd annual meeting of the American Psychological Association, Los Angeles.

Lipke, H. J. (1995). EMDR clinician survey. In F. Shapiro (Ed.), *Eye movement desensitization and reprocessing: Basic principles, protocols and procedures* (Appendix D, pp. 376–386). New York: Guilford Press.

Lipke, H. J. (2000). *EMDR and psychotherapy integration: Theoretical and clinical suggestions with focus on traumatic stress.* Boca Raton, FL: CRC Press.

Lohr, J. M., Tolin, D. F., & Kleinknecht, R. A. (1995). Eye movement desensitization of medical phobias: Two case studies. *Journal of Behavior Therapy and Experimental Psychiatry, 26,* 141–151.

Lohr, J. M., Tolin, D. F., & Kleinknecht, R. A. (1996). An intensive investigation of eye movement desensitization of claustrophobia. *Journal of Anxiety Disorders, 10,* 73–88.

Lovett, J. (1999). *Small wonders: Healing childhood trauma with EMDR.* New York: Free Press.

MacCulloch, M. J., & Feldman, P. (1996). Eye movement desensitization treatment utilizes the positive visceral element of the investigatory reflex to inhibit the memories of Post-Traumatic Stress Disorder: A theoretical analysis. *British Journal of Psychiatry, 169,* 571–579.

Manfield, P. (1998). *Extending EMDR: A casebook of innovative applications.* New York: Norton.

Marcus, S. V., Marquis, P., & Sakai, C. (1997). Controlled study of treatment of PTSD using EMDR in an HMO setting. *Psychotherapy, 3,* 307–315.

Marks, I. M., Lovell, K., Noshirvani, H., Livanou, M., & Thrasher, S. (1998). Treatment of Posttraumatic Stress Disorder by exposure and/or cognitive restructuring: A controlled study. *Archives of General Psychiatry, 55,* 317–325.

Marquis, J. N. (1991). A report on seventy-eight cases treated by eye movement desensitization. *Journal of Behavior Therapy and Experimental Psychiatry, 22,* 187–192.

Maxfield, L., & Hyer, L. (in press). The relationship between efficacy and methodology in studies investigating EMDR treatment of PTSD. *Journal of Clinical Psychology.*

McCann, D. L. (1992). Post-Traumatic Stress disorder due to devastating burns overcome by a single session of eye movement desensitization. *Journal of Behavior Therapy and Experimental Psychiatry, 23,* 319–323.

Montgomery, R. W., & Ayllon, T. (1994). Eye movement desensitization across subjects: Subjective and physiological measures of treatment efficacy.

Journal of Behavior Therapy & Experimental Psychiatry, 25, 217–230.

Muris, P., & Merckelbach, H. (1997). Treating spider phobics with eye movement desensitization and reprocessing: A controlled study. *Behavioral and Cognitive Psychotherapy, 25,* 39–50.

Muris, P., Merckelbach, H., Holdrinet, I., & Sijsenaar, M. (1998). Treating phobic children: Effects of EMDR versus exposure. *Journal of Consulting and Clinical Psychology, 66,* 193–198.

Muris, P., Merckelbach, H., Van Haaften, H., & Nayer, B. (1997). Eye movement desensitization and reprocessing versus exposure in vivo: A single-session crossover study of spider-phobic children. *British Journal of Psychiatry, 171,* 82–86.

Nadler, W. (1996). EMDR: Rapid treatment of Panic Disorder. *International Journal of Psychiatry, 2,* 1–8.

Norcross, J. C., & Shapiro, F. (in press). Paradigms, processing and personality development. In F. Shapiro (Ed.), *EMDR and the paradigm prism.* Washington, DC: American Psychological Association.

Orr, S. P., & Roth, W. T. (2000). Psychophysiological assessment: Clinical applications for PTSD. *Journal of Affective Disorders, 61,* 225–240.

Page, A. C., & Crino, R. D. (1993). Eye-movement desensitization: A simple treatment for Post-Traumatic Stress Disorder? *Australian and New Zealand Journal of Psychiatry, 27,* 288–293.

Parnell, L. (1999). *EMDR in the treatment of adults abused as children.* New York: Norton.

Paulsen, S. (1995). Eye movement desensitization and reprocessing: Its cautious use in the dissociative disorders. *Dissociation, 8,* 32–44.

Pellicer, X. (1993). Eye movement desensitization treatment of a child's nightmares: A case report. *Journal of Behavior Therapy and Experimental Psychiatry, 24,* 73–75.

Peniston, G. E. (1986). EMG biofeedback-assisted desensitization treatment for Vietnam combat veterans' Post-Traumatic Stress Disorder. *Clinical Biofeedback Health, 9,* 35–41.

Pitman, R. K., Orr, S. P., Altman, B., Longpre, R. E., Poire, R. E., & Macklin, M. L. (1996). Emotional processing during eye movement desensitization and reprocessing therapy of Vietnam veterans with chronic Posttraumatic Stress Disorder. *Comprehensive Psychiatry, 37,* 419–429.

Post, R. M., Weiss, S. R. B., & Smith, M. A. (1995). Sensitization and kindling: Implications for the evolving neural substrates of Post-Traumatic Stress Disorder. In M. J. Friedman, D. S. Charney, & A. Y. Deutch (Eds.), *Neurobiological and clinical consequences of stress: From normal adaptation to PTSD.* Philadelphia: Lippincott-Raven.

Puffer, M. K., Greenwald, R., & Elrod, D. E. (1998). A single EMDR study with 20 traumatized children and adolescents. *Traumatology, 3*(2).

Puk, G. (1991). Treating traumatic memories: A case report on the eye movement desensitization procedure. *Journal of Behavior Therapy and Experimental Psychiatry, 22,* 149–151.

Rauch, S. L., van der Kolk, B. A., Fisler, R. E., Alpert, N. M., Orr, S. P., Savage, C. R., et al. (1996). A symptom provocation study of Posttraumatic Stress Disorder using positron emission tomography and script-driven imagery. *Archives of General Psychiatry, 53,* 380–387.

Renfrey, G. S., & Spates, C. R. (1994). Eye movement desensitization: A partial dismantling study. *Journal of Behavior Therapy and Experimental Psychiatry, 25,* 231–239.

Resick, P. A., & Schnicke, M. K. (1992). Cognitive processing therapy for sexual assault victims. *Journal of Consulting and Clinical Psychology, 60,* 748–756.

Rogers, S., & Silver, S. M. (in press). Is EMDR an exposure therapy? A review of trauma protocols. *Journal of Clinical Psychology.*

Rogers, S., Silver, S. M., Goss, J., Obenchain, J., Willis, A., & Whitney, R. L. (1999). A single session, group study of exposure and eye movement desensitization and reprocessing in treating Posttraumatic Stress Disorder among Vietnam War veterans: Preliminary data. *Journal of Anxiety Disorders, 13,* 119–130.

Rothbaum, B. O. (1997). A controlled study of eye movement desensitization and reprocessing in the treatment of Posttraumatic Stress Disordered sexual assault victims. *Bulletin of Menninger Clinic, 61,* 317–334.

Sanderson, A., & Carpenter, R. (1992). Eye movement desensitization versus image confrontation: A single-session crossover study of 58 phobic subjects. *Journal of Behavior Therapy and Experimental Psychiatry, 23,* 269–275.

Scheck, M. M., Schaeffer, J. A., & Gillette, C. (1998). Brief psychological intervention with traumatized young women: The efficacy of eye movement desensitization and reprocessing. *Journal of Traumatic Stress, 11,* 25–44.

Shalev, A. Y., Friedman, M. J., Foa, E. B., & Keane, T. M. (2000). Integration and summary. In E. B. Foa, T. M. Keane, & M. J. Friedman (Eds.), *Effective treatments for PTSD: Practice guidelines from the International Society for Traumatic Stress Studies* (pp. 359–379). New York: Guilford Press.

Shalev, A. Y., Peri, T., Brandes, D., Freeman, S., Orr, S., & Pitman, R. K. (2000). Auditory startle response in trauma survivors with Posttraumatic Stress Disorder: A prospective study. *American Journal of Psychiatry, 157,* 255–261.

Shapiro, F. (1989a). Efficacy of the eye movement desensitization procedure in the treatment of traumatic memories. *Journal of Traumatic Stress, 2,* 199–223.

Shapiro, F. (1989b). Eye movement desensitization: A new treatment for Post-Traumatic Stress Disorder. *Journal of Behavior Therapy and Experimental Psychiatry, 20,* 211–217.

Shapiro, F. (1991). Eye movement desensitization and reprocessing procedure: From EMD to EMD/R. A new treatment model for anxiety and related trauma. *Behavior Therapist, 14,* 133–135.

Shapiro, F. (1994a). Alternative stimuli in the use of EMD(R). *Journal of Behavior Therapy and Experimental Psychiatry, 25,* 89.

Shapiro, F. (1994b). Eye movement desensitization and reprocessing: A new treatment for anxiety and related trauma. In L. Hyer (Ed.), *Trauma victim: Theoretical issues and practical suggestions* (pp. 501–521). Muncie, IN: Accelerated Development.

Shapiro, F. (1995). *Eye movement desensitization and reprocessing: Basic principles, protocols, and procedures.* New York: Guilford Press.

Shapiro, F. (1996). Eye movement desensitization and reprocessing (EMDR): Evaluation of controlled PTSD research. *Journal of Behavior Therapy and Experimental Psychiatry, 27,* 209–218.

Shapiro, F. (1999). Eye movement desensitization and reprocessing (EMDR) and the anxiety disorders: Clinical and research implications of an integrated psychotherapy treatment. *Journal of Anxiety Disorders, 13,* 35–67.

Shapiro, F. (2001). *Eye movement desensitization and reprocessing: Basic principles, protocols and procedures* (2nd ed.). New York: Guilford Press.

Shapiro, F. (in press). *EMDR and the paradigm prism.* Washington, DC: American Psychological Association.

Shapiro, F., & Forrest, M. S. (1997). *EMDR: The breakthrough therapy for overcoming anxiety, stress, and trauma.* New York: Basic Books.

Shapiro, F., & Solomon, R. M. (1995). Eye movement desensitization and reprocessing: Neurocognitive information processing. In G. S. Everly (Ed.), *Innovations in disaster and trauma psychology, Volume 1: Applications in emergency services and disaster response* (pp. 216–237). Elliot City, MD: Chevron.

Shapiro, F., Vogelmann-Sine, S., & Sine, L. F. (1994). Eye movement desensitization and reprocessing: Treating trauma and substance abuse. *Journal of Psychoactive Drugs, 26,* 379–391.

Shobe, K. K., & Kihlstrom, J. F. (1997). Is traumatic memory special? *Current Directions in Psychological Science, 6,* 70–74.

Siegel, D. (in press). The developing mind and the resolution of trauma: Some ideas about information processing and an interpersonal neurobiology of psychotherapy. In F. Shapiro (Ed.), *EMDR and the paradigm prism.* Washington, DC: American Psychological Association.

Smyth, N. J., & Poole, D. (in press). EMDR and cognitive behavioral therapy. In F. Shapiro (Ed.), *EMDR and the paradigm prism.* Washington, DC: American Psychological Association.

Solomon, R. M., Neborsky, R. J., McCullough, L., Alpert, M., Shapiro, F., & Malan, D. (2001). *Short term therapy for long term change.* New York: Norton.

Solomon, S. D., Gerrity, E. T., & Muff, A. M. (1992). Efficacy of treatments for Posttraumatic Stress Disorder: An empirical review. *Journal of the American Medical Association, 268,* 633–638.

Spector, J., & Read, J. (1999). The current status of eye movement desensitization and reprocessing (EMDR). *Clinical Psychology and Psychotherapy, 6,* 165–174.

Stickgold, R. (in press). EMDR: A putative neurobiological mechanism of action. *Journal of Clinical Psychology.*

Tarrier, N., Pilgrim, H., Sommerfield, C., Faragher, M. R., Graham, E., & Barrowclough, C. (1999). A randomized trial of cognitive therapy and imaginal exposure in the treatment of chronic Posttraumatic Stress Disorder. *Journal of Consulting and Clinical Psychology, 67,* 13–18.

Teasdale, J. D. (1999). Emotional processing, three modes of mind and the prevention of relapse in depression. *Behaviour Research and Therapy, 37*(Suppl. 1), 53–77.

Tinker, R. H., & Wilson, S. A. (1999). *Through the eyes of a child: EMDR with children.* New York: Norton.

Twombly, J. H. (2000). Incorporating EMDR and EMDR adaptations into the treatment of clients with Dissociative Identity Disorder. *Journal of Trauma and Dissociation, 1,* 61–81.

van der Kolk, B. (1994). The body keeps the score: Memory and the evolving psychobiology of posttraumatic stress. *Harvard Review of Psychiatry, 1,* 253–256.

van der Kolk, B. A. (in press). Beyond the talking cure: Somatic experience and subcortical imprints in the treatment of trauma. In F. Shapiro (Ed.), *EMDR and the paradigm prism.* Washington, DC: American Psychological Association.

van der Kolk, B. A., Hopper, J. W., & Osterman, J. A. (in press). Exploring the nature of traumatic memory: Combining clinical knowledge and laboratory methods. *Journal of Aggression, Maltreatment, and Trauma.*

Van Etten, M. L., & Taylor, S. (1998). Comparative efficacy of treatments for Post-Traumatic Stress Disorder: A meta-analysis. *Clinical Psychology and Psychotherapy, 5,* 126–144.

Vaughan, K., Armstrong, M. S., Gold, R., O'Connor, N., Jenneke, W., & Tarrier, N. (1994). A trial of eye movement desensitization compared to image habituation training and applied muscle relaxation in Post-Traumatic Stress Disorder. *Journal of Behavior Therapy and Experimental Psychiatry, 25,* 283–291.

Wachtel, P. L. (in press). EMDR and psychoanalysis. In F. Shapiro (Ed.), *EMDR and the paradigm prism.* Washington, DC: American Psychological Association.

Wilson, D. L., Silver, S. M., Covi, W. G., & Foster, S. (1996). Eye movement desensitization and reprocessing: Effectiveness and autonomic correlates. *Journal of Behavior Therapy and Experimental Psychiatry, 27,* 219–229.

Wilson, S. A., Becker, L. A., & Tinker, R. H. (1995). Eye movement desensitization and reprocessing (EMDR) treatment for psychologically traumatized individuals. *Journal of Consulting and Clinical Psychology, 63,* 928–937.

Wilson, S. A., Becker, L. A., & Tinker, R. H. (1997). Fifteen-month follow-up of eye movement desensitization and reprocessing (EMDR) treatment for Posttraumatic Stress Disorder and psychological trauma. *Journal of Consulting and Clinical Psychology, 65,* 1047–1056.

Wilson, S. A., Tinker, R. H., Becker, L. A., Hofmann, A., & Cole, J. W. (2000). *EMDR treatment of phantom limb pain with brain imaging (MEG).* Paper presented at the annual meeting of EMDR International Association, Toronto, Canada.

Wolpe, J. (1990). *The practice of behavior therapy* (4th ed.). New York: Pergamon Press.

Wolpe, J., & Abrams, J. (1991). Post-Traumatic Stress Disorder overcome by eye-movement desensitization: A case report. *Journal of Behavior Therapy and Experimental Psychiatry, 22,* 39–43.

Yehuda, R., & McFarlane, A. (1995). Conflict between current knowledge about Post-Traumatic Stress Disorder and its original conceptual basis. *American Journal of Psychiatry, 152,* 1705–1713.

Young, J. E., Zangwill, W. M., & Behary, W. E. (in press). Combining EMDR and schema-focused therapy: The whole may be greater than the sum of the parts. In F. Shapiro (Ed.), *EMDR and the paradigm prism.* Washington, DC: American Psychological Association.

Young, W. C. (1994). EMDR treatment of phobic symptoms in Multiple Personality Disorder. *Dissociation, 7,* 129–133.

Zabukovec, J., Lazrove, S., & Shapiro, F. (2000). Self healing aspects of EMDR: The therapeutic change process and perspectives of integrated psychotherapies. *Journal of Psychotherapy Integration, 10,* 189–206.

CHAPTER 12

Anxiety and Panic Disorder

Michael A. Tompkins

nxiety is defined as a diffuse cognitive-affective structure characterized by somatic arousal and preparation to cope, activated by a perceived demand or threat (Barlow, 1988). As part of the preparatory response, attention is focused on a threat cue, which leads to amplification of mental and somatic responses. This intensification of mental acuity results in a further narrowing of attention and amplification of preparatory arousal. This interplay of attention and somatic arousal is common to both normal and pathological anxiety.

Pathological anxiety results when attention shifts from an external focus (such as a task or object) to an internal focus on the affective and cognitive components elicited by the context. This shift in attention contributes to a vicious cycle of anxious apprehension, in which increasing arousal contributes to further shifting and narrowing of attention, decrements in performance, and spiraling of arousal (Barlow, 1988). Current conceptualizations of anxiety disorders rely on identifying the focus of anxious apprehension to differentiate one anxiety disorder from another. For example, in the case of Obsessive Compulsive

Disorder, the focus of anxious apprehension is an obsession (e.g., thoughts of germs), whereas in the case of a specific phobia, it is a particular object (e.g., spiders).

Panic attacks, on the other hand, are discrete episodes of intense dread or fear accompanied by somatic and cognitive symptoms (American Psychiatric Association [APA], 1994). Often, panic attacks (particularly the first) occur in unexpected situations or at unexpected times. Approximately 10 to 12% of the general population has experienced at least one unexpected panic attack in the prior 12 months (Norton, Dorward, & Cox, 1986; Telch, Lucas, & Nelson, 1989). However, the incidence of Panic Disorder (PD) or Panic Disorder with agoraphobia (PDA) is only 2 to 6%, suggesting that not all individuals who experience panic attacks develop PD/PDA. As a result, the current classification of PD/PDA depends on the presence of anxiety about the recurrence of panic attacks rather than panic attacks per se (APA, 1994).

This chapter presents a brief history of cognitive-behavioral approaches to the treatment of anxiety and panic, with special emphasis on Barlow's (1988) biopsychosocial model of panic.

The chapter also presents methods for assessing PD and developing an individualized treatment plan, the components of cognitive-behavioral treatment, and a case example.

HISTORY OF THERAPEUTIC APPROACH

Prior conceptualizations of panic as free-floating anxiety led to psychosocial interventions that were generally nonspecific (Barlow et al., 1984). With the recognition of PD as a specific anxiety disorder (APA, 1980), models of PD evolved in which fearful responding to panic-related bodily sensations played a more important role (Barlow, 1988; Clark, 1986; Margraf, Ehlers, & Roth, 1986). One model attributed panic to the effects of chronic hyperventilation (Ley, 1985; Lum, 1976), which led to treatments focused on breathing control training (Kraft & Hooguin, 1984). Other models, including Barlow's biopsychosocial model, viewed panic as the result of catastrophic misinterpretations of bodily sensations, which led to treatments emphasizing cognitive restructuring of these misinterpretations (Beck, Emery, & Greenberg, 1985; Clark, Salkovskis, & Chalkley, 1985) or cognitive restructuring and exposure to somatic fear cues associated with panic (Barlow, 1988; Griez & Van den Hout, 1986).

THEORETICAL CONSTRUCTS

Barlow (1988) views the initial panic attack as an exaggerated autonomic response or "false alarm" to high life stress. Individuals are vulnerable to this false alarm because of increased physiologic reactivity (biological vulnerability) or because they are extremely sensitive to anxious states or tend to overestimate the probability and impact of negative events (psychological vulnerability). Individuals may then develop fear associations to internal fear cues (bodily sensations) through the process of interoceptive conditioning and may become apprehensive about future panic attacks. This anxious apprehension results in an increase in autonomic arousal and the amplification of bodily sensations that evoke the fear response, thereby strengthening the individual's fear of certain bodily sensations. PD is thus conceptualized as a fear of bodily sensations, particularly sensations associated with autonomic arousal.

METHODS OF ASSESSMENT AND INTERVENTION

ASSESSMENT

In the case of the treatment of anxiety and panic, the objective of assessment is fourfold: (1) to establish an accurate diagnosis that will guide choice of treatment protocol; (2) to identify issues that may complicate treatment, such as the severity of the disorder, degree of motivation, and comorbid conditions; (3) to identify specific information to develop a treatment plan involving internal and external fear cues, avoidance and safety behaviors; and (4) to develop hypotheses about the functional relationships among all treatment targets. A comprehensive assessment for PD includes a clinical interview, self-report measures, and behavioral observation.

Clinical Interview
Accurate diagnosis of PD is often difficult because panic is a feature of many psychiatric disorders (Barlow, 1988). A structured interview such as the Anxiety Disorders Interview Schedule-Revised (ADIS-R; DiNardo & Barlow, 1988) is very useful in diagnosing anxiety disorders and in gathering information about the specific features of a client's anxiety and panic that are used to develop an individualized

treatment plan. It assesses bodily sensations, such as sweating and pounding heart; feared consequences, such as fear of dying or going crazy; situations that trigger panic attacks; degree and type of avoidance, such as freeways or walking up stairs; and stressors.

It is helpful to interview family members, particularly those living with the client, as part of a comprehensive assessment. Sometimes an individual with a significant anxiety disorder such as PD is no longer fulfilling his or her responsibilities at home or at work, creating an economic and emotional stress on client and family; this stress can exacerbate the anxiety disorder. Family members may resent these individuals because they demand that family members accompany them when they leave home or even a room of the house. A comprehensive treatment plan depends on the identification of all contingencies that support the maintenance of anxiety and fear. It is unwise to assume that family members support the client's full recovery. For example, when Ed, a high-powered patent attorney, developed PD and was no longer able to work, his wife, Shawn, returned to work as an attorney. Ed assumed that Shawn would give up her job when he recovered. As Ed's symptoms improved, however, Shawn did not volunteer to quit her job, nor would she directly tell him that she wasn't happy as a full-time housewife. Instead, she cautioned Ed that his job was too stressful and that he was certain to relapse if he returned to work. Ed began to doubt his ability to manage his symptoms over time and his condition deteriorated. Shawn declined numerous invitations to meet with Ed's therapist or to take a referral for couple therapy. Eventually, Ed withdrew from treatment.

The clinical interview should include inquiry regarding medical conditions that might mimic or exacerbate anxiety or PD (Hall, 1980; Mackenzie & Popkin, 1983; McCue & McCue, 1984). These include cardiovascular disease, thyroid conditions, asthma, allergies, and hypoglycemia as well as caffeine or amphetamine intoxication and drug withdrawal. A medical evaluation and consultation with the client's physician prior to treatment is recommended.

Self-Report Measures

Standardized self-report measures are useful as indexes of therapeutic change and in developing the specifics of a treatment plan. These include the Beck Depression Inventory (Beck, Ward, Mendelson, Mock, & Erbaugh, 1961), the Beck Anxiety Inventory (Beck, Epstein, Brown, & Steer, 1988), and the Burns Anxiety Inventory (Burns, 1998). In addition, these measures have sufficient sensitivity to yield a session-by-session index of treatment progress.

The Body Sensations and Agoraphobia Cognitions Questionnaires (Chambless, Caputo, Bright, & Gallagher, 1984) provide information about anxiety-evoking bodily sensations and the common cognitive distortions. The Mobility Inventory (Chambless, Caputo, Gracely, Jasin, & Williams, 1985) lists situations commonly avoided by agoraphobic clients and the degree of their avoidance. Information from these measures can be used to design the situational exposure hierarchies introduced later in the treatment protocol.

Behavioral Avoidance Test

The behavioral avoidance test (BAT) is a contrived situation in which a fear-evoking stimulus is presented to clients so that their fearful behavior can be observed and measured. During the BAT, all three domains of the fear-response system are assessed: behavior (e.g., the minimum distance the client will stand from the object), cognitions (e.g., the client's report of fear-evoking thoughts), and somatic response (e.g., the client's report of physiological symptoms). The BAT usually involves three to five situations that the client has rated from low to extremely anxiety evoking, such as driving up a hill or walking for 10 minutes in a crowded shopping mall.

TREATMENT

Cognitive-behavior therapy for PD/PDA rests on the formulation that panic attacks result from catastrophic misinterpretations of bodily sensations. Based on this formulation, researchers have identified a set of treatment targets and interventions (see Table 12.1). In general, the treatment components are presented in this order; however, therapists are encouraged to be flexible in their application of the protocol (Kendall, Chu, Gifford, Hayes, & Nauta, 1998). An individualized formulation can assist clinicians in making decisions regarding adapting the treatment protocol (Persons, 1989). Generally, the treatment consists of 15 to 20 sessions conducted weekly, with homework to generalize what is learned in session to natural situations associated with panic attacks. Treatment includes breathing control and relaxation training, psychoeducation and cognitive restructuring, and interoceptive and situational exposure.

Self-Monitoring

Self-monitoring refers to the client's observing and recording target symptoms as they happen (Nelson, 1977). Self-monitoring corrects misperceptions about panic, provides information about the physiological, cognitive, and behavioral contributions to panic attacks, and provides an objective measure of treatment progress.

Through discussions of self-monitoring results, clients learn to identify antecedents (bodily sensations, anxious thoughts, catastrophic imagery) that trigger anxiety and fear. For example, Chuck, a 37-year-old insurance underwriter, insisted that his panic attacks "just come over me for no reason at all." Chuck and his therapist identified a recent panic attack when Chuck was driving on a stretch of freeway near his home. They identified his cognitive and behavioral responses, particularly the internal cues (dizziness and light-headedness) that triggered his fear. Although Chuck had experienced mild vertigo all his life, he was unaware that it triggered his panic attacks. Chuck also learned that certain driving situations tended to trigger his vertigo: at the crest of a hill when the freeway stretched out before him, when a section of freeway was less enclosed by hillsides or buildings, and when there were more than three or four car lengths between his auto and the one in front, which gave him the impression of open space.

Table 12.1 Treatment targets and cognitive-behavioral interventions for panic disorder.

Treatment Targets	Cognitive-Behavioral Interventions	Treatment Goals
Somatic arousal	Breathing retraining; progressive muscle relaxation	Increase awareness of low-level tension and and stress; increase ability to manage somatic arousal; correct overbreathing
Misappraisals and cognitive errors	Self-monitoring; psychoeducation; cognitive restructuring; interoceptive exposure; in vivo situational exposure	Increase awareness of contribution of anxious thinking to panic sequence; restructure misappraisals that contribute to vulnerability to panic attacks; increase tolerance to anxiety-evoking bodily sensations and real-life situations
Avoidance	Interoceptive exposure; in vivo situational exposure	Decrease phobic avoidance of bodily sensations and anxiety-evoking situation

Psychoeducation

Education is an essential component of the treatment of anxiety disorders because misappraisals of situations and bodily sensations are presumed to influence pathological anxiety and panic (Barlow, 1988). The therapist provides accurate information about anxiety and panic to help clients understand that panic attacks do not come "out of the blue," but involve identifiable cues and are influenced by a process that builds over time. Such information serves as the rationale for interventions designed to help clients intervene early in the panic sequence. In addition, education about anxiety and panic can provide clients with a sense of control over their anxiety and panic, thereby decreasing their vulnerability to panic attacks.

Correct information about anxiety and panic also helps family members respond more adaptively to the client's symptoms. For example, Bob, a 57-year-old engineer, experienced heart palpitations when even mildly anxious. He would complain to his wife, who would become quite anxious herself and insist they go to the emergency room, in spite of Bob's assurances that he was okay. Several therapy sessions with the couple helped Bob's wife understand that Bob's palpitations were a symptom of his anxiety and not of heart disease.

Psychoeducation is conducted through Socratic questioning, in which the therapist guides the client to correct information about anxiety. For example, rather than saying "Anxiety and panic are useful to us as organisms, and are natural and needed responses," the therapist might ask clients "Have you ever wondered why human beings worry and experience fear?" Such questions can lead to a collaborative discussion of the survival value of anxious apprehension and panic. Typical psychoeducation topics include a description of the panic sequence, the physiology of anxiety and panic, and the role of hyperventilation in anxiety and panic. Education about the epidemiology of anxiety and panic and about the survival value of worry and panic help to normalize the experience of panic for clients and thereby decrease their tendency to perceive certain bodily sensations as dangerous.

Psychoeducation can be facilitated through the use of reading materials (Gould, Clum, & Shapiro, 1993); a number of self-help books on the market are useful adjuncts to the treatment of PD (Barlow & Craske, 1989; Wilson, 1996). Often, clients will not read voluntarily about anxiety and panic because the information triggers anxious symptoms. Therapists can encourage clients to begin reading in session and use the tools they are learning to tolerate their anxiety and persist.

Breathing Retraining

The treatment protocol (Barlow & Cerny, 1988; Barlow & Craske, 1989) for PD/PDA presented later in this chapter includes respiratory training to counter hyperventilatory symptoms. Studies that include breathing control to treat panic have mixed results. This suggests that conceptualizations of panic that emphasize panic as a fear response to respiratory change may not adequately explain the phenomenon of panic (Garssen, de Ruiter, & van Dyck, 1992). Instead, breathing retraining may decrease panic symptoms because it distracts panickers from their anxiety-evoking bodily sensations and thoughts while providing them with a sense of control.

Breathing retraining begins with the therapist reviewing with clients the significant bodily sensations they experienced during panic attacks (shortness of breath, cold sweat, smothering sensation) and their catastrophic misinterpretations of the bodily sensations. The therapist demonstrates for the client how to hyperventilate and instructs the client to follow along. Clients are instructed to breathe slowly and regularly until their hyperventilatory symptoms decrease to demonstrate how slow diaphragmatic breathing can decrease their panicky feelings. Clients are to count up from 1 to 10 and down from 10 to 1, inhaling on each count. As they exhale, they are to subvocalize the word "relax." The therapist instructs clients to try for a respiration cycle of about six seconds (from the beginning of inhalation to the end of exhalation). After clients have induced hyperventilatory symptoms and lessened them through diaphragmatic breathing, the therapist describes the role of hyperventilation in the sequence, particularly how overbreathing can exacerbate the bodily sensations that evoke their fear response. Clients are instructed to practice diaphragmatic breathing at home and record their anxiety level, concentration level, and ease of breathing.

Following breathing retraining practice, clients are encouraged to generalize breathing control through its application in stressful situations that contribute to their anxiety and panic. With the assistance of the therapist, clients develop a list of situations that are demanding or anxiety evoking (e.g., driving alone, speaking in a small meeting, speaking in a large meeting, telephone calls to mother, meetings with supervisor). Clients rate the situations from least to most demanding, and practice breathing control in the least demanding situations first, gradually extending their practice to more demanding situations.

Relaxation Training

Most treatment protocols for PD incorporate relaxation training to reduce somatic arousal. However, the mechanism through which relaxation training contributes to the overall treatment effect for panic remains unclear. Rice and Blanchard (1982) suggest that relaxation provides the panicker with a sense of control or mastery and assists the client to identify and decrease tension that might contribute to anxiety that escalates into a full-blown panic attack. Applied relaxation training is the form most often used in the treatment of panic. It occurs over a number of sessions and is fully integrated with the other treatment components and includes progressive muscle relaxation, discrimination training, recall relaxation, cue-controlled relaxation, and generalization practice. Although a general description of applied relaxation training is presented here, the reader is referred to a step-by-step procedure in Barlow and Cerny (1988).

Applied relaxation training begins with training in 16 muscle group progressive relaxation (Jacobson, 1938), in which the client is taught to tense and then relax 16 discrete muscle groups while attending to the somatic and cognitive differences between the relaxed and tense states. Muscle groups include the right and left lower arms (1 and 2), the right and left upper arms (3 and 4), the right and left lower legs and feet (5 and 6), thighs (7), abdomen (8), chest and breathing (9), shoulders (10), lower neck (11), back of neck (12), lips (13), eyes (14), lower forehead (15), and, upper forehead (16). Therapists can make an audiotape of the relaxation sequence that clients can listen to when practicing at home.

After in-session and out-of-session 16 muscle group relaxation practice, discrimination training is added. This involves teaching clients that there is a gradient to their tension and that it is to their benefit to learn to recognize low levels of tension so they can initiate relaxation at the first sign of tension. Discrimination training begins with awareness training. Clients are instructed to tense a muscle group, such as their arm, with the same degree of tension they usually use when practicing the progressive muscle relaxation. They are then instructed to tense with half the usual tension, then with a quarter the usual tension, all the while attending to the difference. This is practiced repeatedly in and out of session. Later, discrimination training involves other muscle groups, such as the back of the neck and the eyes.

Clients are then instructed in 8 muscle group and 4 muscle group progressive muscle relaxation. The goal here is to make the relaxation more portable so that clients can initiate relaxation quickly and effectively, regardless of location or situation. As clients learn these abbreviated forms of progressive muscle relaxation, they are instructed to generalize their out-of-session practice to known stressful situations. With the assistance of their therapist, clients construct a list of stressful situations or physical positions (sitting, standing, lying) and rank them from least to most stressful. Clients are instructed to begin practicing relaxation in the least stressful situations and, over time, to extend their practice to more challenging and stressful situations. In this way, clients learn to initiate and maintain a relaxed state in situations known to increase their level of tension and anxiety and thereby lower their vulnerability to panic attacks.

After clients have mastered 4 muscle group progressive muscle relaxation and have generalized this skill to stressful situations, the therapist introduces recall relaxation. The goal of recall relaxation is to train clients in a highly portable relaxation strategy that they can use to quickly and easily initiate the relaxed state. Recall relaxation begins with the therapist instructing clients to recall the relaxed state without tensing the muscles. They are to focus and identify any sensations of tension in a particular muscle group and then to relax and recall what it felt like to release the tension when they performed progressive muscle relaxation. Again, clients are instructed to practice recall relaxation out of session and later generalize the strategy to stressful situations.

Applied relaxation training concludes with training in cue-controlled relaxation, a highly portable relaxation strategy. Clients are instructed to use cue-controlled relaxation whenever they feel tense or anxious to decrease the likelihood of panic attacks. Clients begin by focusing on their breathing. They are instructed to take a deep breath and think the word "relax" as they exhale slowly and easily. The word "relax" becomes the cue for the relaxed state. Again, clients are encouraged to generalize cue-controlled relaxation to stressful situations and physical positions. Although cue-controlled

relaxation becomes the relaxation strategy of choice, clients are encouraged to periodically practice the full 16 muscle group progressive muscle relaxation throughout treatment and after treatment has ended, as a prophylactic against a buildup of tension and stress that may increase their vulnerability to panic attacks.

Cognitive Restructuring

A number of studies have suggested that catastrophic or negative cognitions contribute to the maintenance of pathological anxiety (Beck, Laude, & Bohnert, 1974; Last & Blanchard, 1982; Wade, Malloy, & Proctor, 1977). In the case of panic and agoraphobia, cognitive strategies target the misappraisals that certain bodily sensations are dangerous or threatening.

Cognitive interventions are based on the techniques outlined by Beck et al. (1985). The cognitive therapy component of panic control treatment is presented in three phases. The first phase includes monitoring or sampling cognitions during anxious situations. The therapist reviews with the client the three-component (physiological, cognitive, behavioral) model of panic and introduces the role of cognitions in anxiety and panic. Clients are encouraged to develop their ability to observe their thoughts and consider them as hypotheses rather than foregone conclusions. Therapists can use self-monitoring procedures or thought records (Persons, Davidson, & Tompkins, 2001) for this purpose. Once clients have increased their awareness of their anxious thoughts and have learned to record them, the therapist teaches clients the contributions of these thoughts to their anxiety and panic episodes. Generally, specific anxious thoughts take three forms: (1) individuals overestimate the probability of the occurrence of a negative event such as a panic attack; (2) individuals overestimate the magnitude of the impact of that negative event should it occur (catastrophizing); and (3) individuals underestimate their ability to cope with what they perceive is a highly likely and catastrophic event should it occur. This is the triple play of anxious thinking.

For example, consider the first type of anxious thoughts or cognitive errors: the tendency to overestimate the likelihood of a negative event. The therapist assists clients to identify several situations in which they were anxious and absolutely certain that they would have a panic attack but did not, or experienced the feared bodily sensation (smothering or dizziness) but did not experience the feared outcome (suffocation or fainting):

THERAPIST: So you say you feel like you won't be able to keep breathing, is that right?

CLIENT: Yes.

THERAPIST: During this last episode, what did you do?

CLIENT: I called my husband. He was in the backyard and I screamed for him to come inside.

THERAPIST: So you were able to speak and scream for your husband. At what point did you stop breathing?

CLIENT: I guess I never really stopped breathing, but it feels like I may stop at any moment.

THERAPIST: So you feel like you will stop breathing but you continue to breathe. How many times have you felt like you may stop breathing at any moment?

CLIENT: Oh, several times per day.

THERAPIST: How many times, would you guess? Two or three times each day? Four or five times each day? More?

CLIENT: No, maybe like four times per day.

THERAPIST: How long has this been going on?

CLIENT: Oh, I guess four or five weeks now.

THERAPIST: So that makes, let's see, that must be over one hundred times. Is that right?

CLIENT: Yes, at least.

THERAPIST: So, over one hundred times you have felt like you will stop breathing but this has never happened. You continue to breathe. Is that right?

CLIENT: Yes.

THERAPIST: So now what would you rate the probability that you'll stop breathing next time you're anxious? Use a 0 to 100 scale, where 0 means that there is no chance it will happen and 100 means that it absolutely will happen.

CLIENT: Well, maybe it's 10%.

THERAPIST: Ten percent. Let's see. So that means that you have actually stopped breathing once out of the last 10 times you've felt like you couldn't breathe. Is that right?

CLIENT: Well, I guess I really haven't stopped breathing. When you put it that way, 10% sounds pretty high. Maybe it's lower than that.

THERAPIST: Yes. Perhaps it is lower, but when you're anxious, you believe the likelihood is much higher that you will stop breathing.

CLIENT: Yeah. It feels like I'm going to stop breathing for sure.

THERAPIST: Yes. But now, what do you think about your ability when you're anxious to predict with any certainty that you will stop breathing? How good do you think you are at that?

CLIENT: Well, I guess not so good. But now, I'm thinking that I might see things a little clearer. At least I hope so.

The second phase of cognitive therapy introduces a variety of cognitive coping strategies that include evaluating thoughts for evidence of catastrophizing and other forms of faulty thinking, exploring alternative explanations of anxious interpretations, testing hypotheses through behavioral experiments, and identifying adaptive ways to prevent a catastrophic event or cope with it should it happen (rescue factors). For example, clients are taught to decatastrophize, by de-emphasizing how they "feel" about a negative event and instead examining how they would cope:

CLIENT: If I have the smothering feeling, that would be horrible. I couldn't take that.

THERAPIST: What makes you think you couldn't take it?

CLIENT: I don't know. It just feels like I couldn't. It's terrible, really awful.

THERAPIST: Yes. I hear you saying that it's just awful. But could we talk about this idea you have that you can't take the smothering feeling? Would that be okay?

CLIENT: Sure.

THERAPIST: Well, let's say you weren't able to take the smothering feeling. What would that look like?

CLIENT: Huh?

THERAPIST: If I were watching you, what would I see that would tell me that you weren't taking it?

CLIENT: Well, I guess . . . I guess I'd be screaming and running around. I want to do that when I feel that way.

THERAPIST: You want to run around. Yes. And what else would I see?

CLIENT: Well, maybe I'd be pulling at my clothes, at my collar especially.

THERAPIST: Yes, and what else would I see?

CLIENT: Well, I might be turning red and sweating. That's happened before.

THERAPIST: Yes, you're anxious and you're turning red and sweating. What else would I see?

CLIENT: I guess that's it. I can't think of anything else.

THERAPIST: So, if you had the smothering feeling and you weren't taking it, I would see you screaming, running around, pulling at your collar, and turning red and sweating. Have I got it right?

CLIENT: Yes.

THERAPIST: I see. So then what happens?

CLIENT: What happens?

THERAPIST: Yes. What happens next?

CLIENT: Well . . . nothing. Just that. But that would be horrible.

THERAPIST: Yes. I hear you saying it would be horrible. How long would that last?

CLIENT: I don't know.

THERAPIST: Several weeks? Four or five weeks?

CLIENT: No. Not four or five weeks. Of course not.

THERAPIST: Well then, help me here. How long would the screaming and running around last? Several days?

CLIENT: No, not several days. Maybe a few hours. Yes, a couple of hours. But boy, would that be a horrible couple of hours.

THERAPIST: Yes. I think it would be very uncomfortable. But if it went on for a couple of hours, what would you do?

CLIENT: What would I do? I guess I would scream and run around my house. I could try to watch TV to get my mind off the feeling or call my daughter on the phone.

THERAPIST: You would do those things until the feeling went away? You would get through it somehow? Is that right?

CLIENT: Yeah. I guess I'd just do the best I could until the feeling passed.

THERAPIST: So you believe that the feeling would pass?

CLIENT: Yes. Eventually.

THERAPIST: So what does that mean, then, about your idea that you couldn't take it? You would have the smothering feeling. It would last for several hours and you would do something to get by until the feeling passed. Does this sound like someone who couldn't take it?

CLIENT: No. I guess I could take it. I just wouldn't like it.

In the final phase of cognitive therapy, the client applies the cognitive strategies during graded imaginal exposures (visualizing the feared object or situation) or in vivo (real-life) exposures to anxiety-evoking situations or bodily sensations. This is done in the same way the relaxation strategies were generalized to natural situations. For example, a client who fears he will "go blank and make a fool of myself" when making a presentation in a business meeting can be encouraged to make a presentation first to his therapist, then to a small group of trusted colleagues, and then at the business meeting to test his prediction.

Interoceptive Exposure

Interoceptive exposure involves a series of exercises designed to induce paniclike sensations such as dizziness, nausea, sweating, or heart palpitations to decondition the panicker's fear of them. It begins with the therapist presenting the rationale for interoceptive exposure. Through repeated exposure to the feared bodily sensations, clients will become less fearful of the sensations they associate with panic attacks and thereby decrease their vulnerability to the attacks themselves. The therapist then models a series of exercises (Craske & Barlow, 1993) such as breathing through a straw, spinning, running in place, and forced hyperventilation and instructs clients to practice each exercise in session while they record the bodily sensations they experience, their anxiety level, the intensity of the bodily sensations, and similarity of the sensations to those experienced during a natural panic attack. The therapist identifies the exercises that are the most anxiety evoking for the client and the most similar to the sensations the client experiences during a natural panic attack. Clients are then instructed to practice again these specific exercises in session, with the support of the therapist. Clients are encouraged to use their thinking tools to challenge anxious thoughts and their breathing tools to decrease somatic arousal to reinforce the usefulness of these strategies in moderating feelings of anxiety and panic.

It is important to generalize the effects of interoceptive exposure as much as possible to natural situations linked to previous panic attacks. For example, Ed, whose first series of panic attacks occurred in his office at work, benefited from a round of interoceptive exposure practice in his office after he had become comfortable with its effects in his therapist's office and his home. Interoceptive exposure practice continues until little or no anxiety is triggered during the exposure exercises.

Situational Exposure

Most, if not all, panic-disordered individuals exhibit some degree of agoraphobia (Barlow, 1988). In fact, the most profound consequences of PD may arise from the professional and personal limitations caused by attempts to avoid or escape panic. For this reason, situational exposure is an important component in the treatment of anxiety and panic.

Situational exposure involves the repeated approach (rather than avoidance) to the feared object or situation. Typical situations feared by panickers include crowded places (malls, theaters, public transportation), performance situations (public speaking, business meetings), driving situations (freeways, tunnels, bridges, overpasses), or any situation from which escape might be difficult in case of a panic attack. Situational exposure treatments take three forms. *In vivo exposure* is when the client approaches the fear-evoking stimulus in real life, such as driving on a specified stretch of freeway. *Imaginal exposure* is when the client approaches the fear-evoking stimulus by imagining interacting with the stimulus, such as sitting in a business meeting when a colleague notices that he is blushing and laughs at him. *In vitro exposure* is when the client approaches the fear-evoking stimulus in a structured, controlled, and artificial setting, such as the therapist's office.

Guidelines for effective exposure treatment recommend that exposures should be (1) prolonged until the anxiety generated in a session has decreased to a minimal level; (2) repeated until the maximum anxiety generated in each consecutive exposure session is minimal; (3) graduated from lowest anxiety-evoking to highest anxiety-evoking situations; (4) clearly specified, explained, and agreed upon; (5) able to evoke significant anxiety in relevant situations;

and (6) carried out so the client attends to and interacts with the fear stimuli so that anxiety symptoms are provoked (Barlow & Cerny, 1988).

Situational exposure begins by explaining the targets of situational exposures: agoraphobic situations that clients avoid because they anticipate that they will feel anxious or panicky, because they fear they will not be able to escape, or because they fear that help will not be available. After learning the anxiety management tools presented earlier in the treatment, most agoraphobic clients expect that they will not experience anxiety in the situations they fear. If not prepared, they may be surprised that they are anxious in these situations and again attempt to suppress or control their anxiety, thereby exacerbating the feelings that make them more vulnerable to panic attacks. It is important that therapists underscore for clients that the goal of situational exposures is not to control or eliminate anxiety but to accept their anxious state through an objective awareness of their cognitive and physiological reactions when anxious. To that end, therapists should watch for clients who use distraction to cope with their anxiety during exposure practice and discourage this strategy. Distraction, particularly when used exclusively to cope with anxiety, prevents clients from becoming comfortable with the bodily sensations that contribute to their anxiety and panic. Instead, therapists should encourage clients to practice observing their bodily sensations in a detached, objective manner, rather than worrying about the sensations themselves.

Therapists begin situational exposure practice by developing with clients a list of agoraphobic situations. The situations are then ranked (0 to 100) in terms of predicted difficulty or anxiety. When developing exposure hierarchies such as this, it is helpful to think of hierarchies within hierarchies. For example, Oscar and his therapist generated a situational hierarchy and ranked driving on freeways as 70, driving over bridges

as 90, and driving through tunnels as 100. Oscar worked his way up his situational hierarchy, and when he was ready to begin driving on freeways, he and his therapist developed the hierarchy shown in Table 12.2. Here, the therapist generated a range of exposure tasks involving driving on freeways by varying time, situation, and location of the task.

MAJOR SYNDROMES, SYMPTOMS, AND PROBLEMS TREATED

There have been many refinements to the description and classification of anxiety disorders over the past 50 years. The anxiety disorders were described as psychoneurotic disorders in the *DSM-I* (APA, 1952) and included anxiety and phobic reactions. There was little change in this classification until the *DSM-III* (APA, 1980), in which PD was recognized as distinct from phobic reactions. Later, as the relationship between panic and agoraphobia was clarified, agoraphobia was subsumed under PD, with the resulting diagnoses of PDA and PD without agoraphobia (*DSM-III-R*; APA, 1987). The *DSM-III-R* incorporated more cognitive features, including anticipatory anxiety (fear of having another panic attack) in addition to bodily sensations associated with panic attacks.

Further refinements in the understanding of anxiety disorders resulted in the *DSM-IV* (APA, 1994). Because panic attacks can occur in any anxiety disorder, a description of panic attacks is no longer limited to the section on PD but is presented at the beginning of the anxiety disorder section to reflect the presence of panic features in all anxiety disorders. The *DSM-IV* distinguishes subtypes of panic attacks. Unexpected (uncued) panic attacks are spontaneous panic attacks that are typical of PD. Situationally bound (cued) panic attacks occur on approach or exposure to fear stimuli. Situationally

Table 12.2 Situational (real-life) exposure hierarchy.

Rank	Avoided Situation	Rank	Avoided Situation	Rank	Avoided Situation
100	Tunnels	70.9	Highway 24		
90	Bridges	70.8	Highway 680		
80	Overpasses	70.6	Highway 101	70.59	Highway 13 (4-lane, 2 exits, therapist in back seat with eyes open)
70	Freeways	70.5	Highway 13	70.58	Highway 13 (4-lane, 1 exit, therapist in back seat with eyes open)
60	Surface streets (2-lane, business)	70.4	Highway 580	70.56	Highway 13 (4-lane, 2 exits, therapist in front seat with eyes closed)
50	Surface streets (2-lane, residential)	70.2	Highway 880	70.54	Highway 13 (4-lane, 1 exit, therapist in front seat with eyes closed)
40	Surface streets (4-lane, business)			70.52	Highway 13 (4-lane, 2 exits, therapist in front seat with eyes open)
30	Surface streets (4-lane, residential)			70.50	Highway 13 (4-lane, 1 exit, therapist in front seat with eyes open)
20	Crowded parking lots				
10	Empty parking lots				

predisposed panic attacks are typical of PD but are also seen in specific and social phobias. The *DSM-IV* includes a distinction between full panic attacks (those involving four or more symptoms) and limited panic attacks (those involving fewer than four symptoms). However, clients with PD rarely make this distinction (Rapee, Craske, & Barlow, 1990). The diagnosis of agoraphobia without history of panic attacks remains, although this disorder is rarely seen in clinical practice (Thyer, Himle, Curtis, Cameron, & Nesse, 1985). The diagnosis of PD requires that panic attacks occur repeatedly and unexpectedly, and that at least one of the attacks must be followed by at least one month of persistent concern about having additional attacks, worry about the implications or consequences of the attack, or a significant change in behavior related to the attacks.

Available studies of PD indicate high rates of comorbid diagnoses. Studies have shown that 65 to 88% of individuals with PD (de Ruiter, Rijken, Garssen, van Schaik, & Kraaimaat, 1989) and 51 to 91% of individuals with PDA (Starcevic, Uhlenhuth, Kellner, & Pathak, 1992) have coexisting disorders, most commonly another anxiety disorder. Mood disorders and alcohol abuse are common (Beck & Zebb, 1994). In 30 to 80% of samples of individuals with PD and PDA, an Axis II disorder is present, with

Cluster C (anxious, fearful) being the most prevalent.

CASE EXAMPLE

DESCRIPTION OF CASE

Gail is a 46-year-old Caucasian mother of four adult children. She and her ex-husband, Rick, are divorced but continue to live together. He is a recovering alcoholic and intermittently works as a house painter. Gail works full time as a manager of a restaurant. Over the past year, Gail has experienced increasing stress because of growing job responsibilities. She has been working long hours and frequently cares for her oldest daughter's two sons, who are difficult to manage. In addition, for three weeks prior to her first panic attack, she had been suffering from a particularly severe bout of hay fever that had made it difficult for her to breathe. About 7 A.M. one morning she awakened suddenly from a deep sleep, gasping for breath. She became acutely anxious and feared she would suffocate and die. She remembers feeling nervous and shaky inside, her legs and hands were trembling, her heart was pounding, and she felt detached from her surroundings. She called Rick at work. He came home immediately, and this settled her down. Now she insists Rick stay with her at home and that he accompany her to her appointments. She is less fearful when she is with him because he can get medical help if she can't breathe.

Gail is preoccupied with her breathing and has not been able to sleep for several days. She worries whether she'll ever be able to sleep again and whether she'll be able to function on so little sleep. She also worries about the long-term health consequences of her insomnia. Gail does not worry excessively about other situations. Her worry appears to be predominantly focused on the possibility that she will be unable to breathe, and she is sensitive to any situa-

tion that produces feelings of breathlessness, such as a change in her respiration rate when she is sleeping, exercising, or walking up stairs. She can go anywhere if accompanied by someone she trusts who will get help if she cannot breathe. At least once or twice a day when napping, she awakens abruptly, feeling short of breath and scared.

She denies previous panic attacks but reports that she has always been anxious when she is in enclosed spaces like elevators, small crowded rooms, or buses. Gail is also afraid of deep water and attributes this to a near-drowning experience when she was 11 years old. Otherwise, there is no history of medical problems or previous psychological treatment. Gail is baffled by her condition. She is the oldest of four children and is accustomed to being the strong, competent one. Both her parents suffered from depression and her youngest sister was hospitalized several times following suicide attempts.

DIAGNOSIS AND ASSESSMENT

Gail arrived on time for her appointment, accompanied by Rick. She was dressed appropriately but looked a bit disheveled and tired. The therapist met with Gail alone and reviewed the measures she had completed prior to the appointment. Her Beck Depression Inventory score was 24 (moderate depression), and she subscribed to such items as "I am disgusted with myself" and "I am very worried about physical problems and it's hard to think of much else." Her Burns Anxiety Inventory score was 43 (severe anxiety). Items she rated "a lot" included "Feeling tense, stressed, uptight or on edge"; "Apprehension or a sense of impending doom"; "Fear that something terrible is about to happen"; and physiological symptoms such as a pounding heart, sweating, trembling, and choking or smothering sensations or difficulty breathing. On the Agoraphobic Cognitions Questionnaire, she reported the following thoughts as always occurring when she is nervous: "I will choke to death"; "I will not be able to control myself"; and "I am going to go crazy." The Body Sensations Questionnaire showed that she rated as extreme heart palpitations, pressure or a heavy feeling in her chest, feeling short of breath, sweating, and dry throat. The Mobility Inventory showed that she could go to most places but was quite uncomfortable. She continued to drive to work alone but would not drive long distances from home if unaccompanied. She was able to shop alone and to do most of her routine activities, but asked others to accompany her more than in the past. The most difficult situation was when she was home alone, particularly in the evenings when she was trying to sleep.

Gail was very distressed because she had not been able to get to sleep or remain asleep most nights during the past week. As the primary breadwinner for the family, she feared that if she didn't sleep, she would lose her job, and this added to her anxiety and sleeplessness. To keep herself going, Gail had been drinking more coffee and diet sodas than usual. She agreed to switch to decaffeinated beverages to rule out caffeine as a cause of her anxiety and panic attacks. Gail's therapist spoke to her referring physician, who reported that she had ruled out any medical condition as contributing to Gail's anxiety.

Her therapist completed the ADIS-R with Gail and decided that she met the criteria for PD with mild agoraphobia. Because Gail had a lifelong dread of enclosed spaces in the absence of panic attacks, she likely met the criteria for the additional diagnosis of claustrophobia (a specific phobia). Gail also met the criteria for a Major Depressive Episode. She was not generally anxious in social settings and was not concerned about the social consequences of a panic attack. Although she described herself as a "worrier," she did not experience her worry as uncontrollable.

CASE FORMULATION

The formulation of this case begins with the nomothetic (general) biopsychosocial formulation of panic (Barlow, 1988). This formulation is then individualized by careful inquiry regarding Gail's specific (and sometimes idiosyncratic) internal and external fear cues, the situations that trigger her panic that she avoids, and information about Gail's early history that may have contributed to her psychological vulnerability. The result is the individualized formulation, or hypothesis, that attempts to explain the nature of her particular anxiety and panic.

Internal and External Fear Cues and Feared Consequences

Internal fear cues included bodily sensations such as sensations of smothering, shortness of breath, and changes in respiration depth and rate. Cognitions included thoughts of being unable to catch her breath, suffocating, dying, and going crazy. The most notable external fear cues were situations in which Gail was alone or would be unable to reach someone in an emergency. Traveling long distances from home, being at home alone, and being in enclosed spaces triggered Gail's worries about future panic attacks. Her feared consequence was that she would be unable to catch her breath and would suffocate and die.

Avoidance and Safety Signals

Gail did not increase her avoidance significantly following her panic attacks. Although she was often uncomfortable, she was able to continue her usual activities. Although she was able to tolerate being alone at home, she insisted Rick carry his cellular telephone and she called him frequently and asked that he come home immediately after work. She reported that she was avoiding sleeping on her stomach, her usual position, because she found that this position was now uncomfortable for her. Safety signals that reassured Gail that she could prevent a panic attack or get help quickly if she needed it included the presence of Rick and other family members, her allergy medicine, and a cellular telephone for emergencies.

Precipitants and Activating Situations

For several months prior to Gail's first panic attack, she experienced considerable life stress. She had been working long hours, sleeping less, and drinking more caffeinated coffee and soda to keep going. She was caring for her two grandsons, who were difficult to manage, and her unemployed adult son was living with them. She and Rick were having financial problems because he was working only part time. She was exhausted but hadn't slept well for several days because a particularly bad episode of hay fever made it difficult for her to breathe. Activating situations that trigger panic or acute episodes of anxiety for Gail included allergy attacks, breathlessness when climbing stairs or exerting herself, being alone at home, trying to sleep, and changing sleeping positions (from back to side, from side to stomach).

Origins of Biopsychosocial Vulnerability

Gail reported that her grandparents, parents, and siblings suffered from anxiety and depression, suggesting a biological vulnerability to her anxiety and panic. Gail was the oldest child of alcoholic parents who often fought, and she remembers the household being chaotic and unpredictable. Her parents were quite critical of her, saying that she was useless and stupid, and she grew to believe that she was inadequate. However, her parents praised her when she cared for them or her siblings, and she learned early to cope and get approval through hyperresponsibility and overcontrol. Throughout her life, she had trouble being assertive with others and often takes on too much. When she was 11 years old, she nearly drowned and now

remembered coughing and gasping for air after being pulled from the water. Since then, she was particularly sensitive to changes in her respiration and often experienced heaviness in her chest and smothering sensations.

Individualized Formulation

Barlow's (1988) psychosocial formulation considers panic to result from the interplay of an individual's biological and psychological vulnerabilities with external stressors. Gail learned in her family of origin that her needs are not as important as those of others, that others are unreliable, and that the world is chaotic and unpredictable. Thus, it was difficult for her to say no to the demands of others and she experienced progressively more stress as she took on more responsibilities at work and home. She worried more about her finances and health and thought that she was the only one who could manage the problems but feared she was not adequate to the task. This raised her level of general anxiety, which was exacerbated by lack of sleep and the caffeinated beverages she was drinking to keep going. She then experienced an acute allergy episode. Because Gail had developed extreme respiratory sensitivity following her near-drowning experience, the allergy episode caused her to overfocus on her breathing. When her respiration rate changed while she was sleeping, she experienced a nocturnal panic attack. Since then, Gail became extremely sensitive to bodily sensations of smothering and breathlessness and avoided situations that trigger these feelings. She was fearful of being alone and was exhausted but not sleeping well because she was anxious that she would have another panic attack while asleep and suffocate and die. Because she was exhausted, she was no longer able to cope through overcontrol and hyperresponsibility. This contributed to her worry that she would not be able to take care of her family and reinforced her beliefs that the world was dangerous and unpredictable and that she was inadequate.

TREATMENT APPROACH

Cognitive-behavior therapy for PD and agoraphobia has three phases over 15 to 20 sessions. The early phase includes self-monitoring, psychoeducation, breathing control, and relaxation training. The middle phase focuses on application of the breathing control and relaxation to anxiety-evoking natural settings, cognitive restructuring, and interoceptive exposure. The final phase of treatment emphasizes application of interoceptive exposure to anxiety-evoking natural settings and exposure to real-life situations that evoke the fear response.

Early Phase

The early phase of treatment covered four sessions and focused on instruction in self-monitoring, breathing retraining, and applied relaxation training. The therapist showed Gail how to monitor her anxiety and panic attacks and described the psychosocial model of panic. Gail and her therapist identified a recent panic attack and discussed her physiologic, cognitive, and behavioral responses, particularly the internal cues (breathlessness and smothering sensations) that triggered Gail's fear. With the help of her therapist, Gail identified the anxious thoughts she had in response to her breathlessness ("I can't breathe. I'm going to suffocate and die."). The therapist then described the physiology underlying anxiety and panic and the role anxious apprehension and interoceptive conditioning play in the process of panic. Gail was particularly concerned about her sleep difficulties and asked the therapist whether this treatment would help her sleep. The therapist explained that Gail most likely was experiencing nocturnal panic attacks and that her sleep would improve as treatment proceeded.

Over the next three sessions, Gail and her therapist focused on breathing control and applied relaxation training. The therapist explained the role of hyperventilation in exacerbating the bodily sensations that evoked Gail's fear

response and instructed her in diaphragmatic breathing. Once Gail had mastered the breathing control strategies, her therapist demonstrated how to hyperventilate and asked her to follow along. When she became anxious and stopped hyperventilating, the therapist instructed her to breathe diaphragmatically until her panicky feelings subsided. In this way, Gail learned that diaphragmatic breathing could decrease the panicky feelings that made her vulnerable to panic attacks.

Next, Gail applied her new breathing control skills in stressful situations in her life. She and her therapist developed a list of stressful situations and ranked them from least to most stressful. They focused on situations when she was separated from Rick, as Gail reported that her dependency on him had created more tension in their relationship. She was instructed to practice diaphragmatic breathing in these situations, beginning with the least stressful and working up to the most stressful. She practiced first with Rick in the room with her for the first two days, then with Rick in the next room for the next two days. On the last two days she practiced with Rick at the neighbor's house next door.

While Gail learned to control her breathing, she was also instructed in applied relaxation training, beginning with 16 muscle group progressive muscle relaxation and ending with cue-controlled relaxation. Gail's therapist taped the relaxation exercises in session so that she could listen to the tapes at home when practicing. Gail generalized her relaxation practice to a variety of stressful situations, including driving, work, and when taking care of her grandsons.

Middle Phase

The next five sessions of treatment focused on training in the use of cognitive strategies to manage her anxious thoughts and interoceptive exposure to the bodily sensations that evoke panic attacks. The therapist emphasized the importance of learning to observe rather than to react to her thoughts and to treat her thoughts as hypotheses rather than foregone conclusions. The therapist introduced the role of cognitive errors in anxiety and panic and focused on Gail's tendency to overestimate the likelihood of a negative event. Gail and her therapist identified several situations in which she was anxious and absolutely certain that something bad would happen and didn't. For example, she was certain that when she arrived at work last Monday that her supervisor would reprimand her because she was 10 minutes late. Instead, her supervisor had been supportive, asking Gail if she was feeling okay because she was never late. Similarly, with help she was able to identify other situations in which she experienced smothering sensations but did not suffocate, or anxiety, but did not have a panic attack.

Similarly, Gail was instructed in the role of catastrophic thinking in initiating and maintaining anxiety and panic. She identified several catastrophic thoughts: "The smothering feeling is horrible, I can't stand it"; "I'm going to suffocate and die"; and "If I don't get some sleep, I won't be able to work." She was then taught to decatastrophize by de-emphasizing how she "feels" about a negative event ("I'll feel horrible") and instead examine how she would cope.

The next several sessions focused on interoceptive exposure. The therapist reviewed with Gail the role of interoceptive conditioning in maintaining her avoidance of bodily sensations that evoke fear. In Gail's case, breathlessness and smothering were the most prominent feared bodily sensations. The therapist then presented the rationale for interoceptive exposure. Through repeated exposure to the feared sensations, she would become less fearful of the sensations and would also learn that experiencing the sensations did not result in real danger. The therapist also suggested that the interoceptive exposure practice might improve her sleep, as she appeared to be experiencing nocturnal panic attacks.

Not surprisingly, Gail had the most trouble with the exercises involving some aspect of respiration (holding her breath, hyperventilation, and breathing through a straw). She became very anxious when trying to breathe through a straw, and she complained of not being able to get enough air and feelings of shortness of breath and smothering. She required considerable therapist support to maintain the breathing exercises for even 10 to 15 seconds. During the in-session practice, the therapist encouraged her to use her breathing control and thinking tools to calm herself whenever she felt she had to stop the exercise. She used countering thoughts, such as "I'm getting enough air, I just feel like I'm not," and "My body knows how to breathe and take care of itself."

Once Gail was able to breathe through the straw comfortably while sitting up, the therapist suggested that she generalize her practice to other physical positions (standing, lying on her back, lying on her side). With considerable therapist support, Gail was able to breathe comfortably for two minutes in several positions (sitting up, lying on her back, and lying on her side) and to generalize this practice when at home with Rick in the room until she was able to do the full two minutes with little or no anxiety.

Gail did well with the in-session interoceptive exposure practice but found that breathing through the straw while lying on her stomach was very anxiety evoking. The therapist asked Gail about her preferred sleeping position and discovered that it was on her stomach with her head resting on one pillow and another pillow beneath her stomach. With continued practice and therapist support, she was able to breathe through the straw comfortably while lying on her stomach. Later, she added the pillows and was able to complete the exposure with moderate anxiety. Gail and her therapist designed naturalistic exposures (ride to and from work each day with the car windows rolled up and the heater on, wear a mask, close her office door and windows) to help her become more comfortable with situations that evoked the feared sensations of breathlessness or suffocation.

Late Phase
The next six sessions focused on continued interoceptive exposure, relaxation practice, and situational exposure. The therapist met with Rick and Gail together to solicit Rick's assistance in the situational exposures and to instruct him how to respond to Gail should she become anxious or panicky. Rick would help Gail decide when and where to practice each situational exposure and remind her to apply her thinking and breathing control strategies. The therapist then taught Rick how to solicit Gail's anxious thoughts and to help her counter and challenge these anxious thoughts through corrective questioning. The therapist role-played this process with Gail while Rick observed and then asked Rick to role-play the process with Gail while the therapist observed and provided corrective feedback.

After Gail, Rick, and the therapist had finalized the situational hierarchy, the first item was role-played. Gail pretended to step into an elevator while Rick stood to the side, holding the door open. The therapist encouraged Rick to solicit Gail's anxious thoughts, to provide corrective questioning, and to remind her to use her breathing control strategies. The therapist provided corrective feedback and the situation was role-played until Gail and Rick felt comfortable. They were instructed to practice this exposure three times over the next week, and at least once Gail was to practice stepping on and off an elevator alone.

The focus of the remaining sessions was the review of situational exposure homework, corrective feedback about the exposure, and setting up and rehearsing the next exposure assignment. Gail did very well and moved through her situational exposure hierarchy quickly. Near the end of treatment, the therapist met with Gail alone and introduced relapse management. They

developed her panic plan and she wrote this down. Gail was asked to refer to her panic plan any time she felt anxious or panicky or was avoiding a situation. Her panic plan included coping techniques she found helpful, such as breathing slowly and regularly and decatastrophizing. It also included principles she had learned and wanted to remember ("I tend to think I won't be able to handle things when I really can"). As the therapist discussed with Gail how to prevent relapse, he introduced the importance of managing stress that may influence her vulnerability to anxious episodes and panic attacks. The therapist noted that Gail's relationship with Rick contributed to her stress and he recommended couple therapy focused on balancing their roles and responsibilities.

POSTTERMINATION SYNOPSIS

At the end of 15 weeks of treatment, Gail had not experienced a panic attack in nine weeks and her anxiety and depression were within normal limits. She was sleeping well and seldom experienced breathlessness or smothering sensations. She continued situational exposure practice with Rick and they were attending couple therapy.

At three-month follow-up, Gail was still panic-free. She seldom thought about her anxiety and had enrolled in a master's swim class to work on her fear of deep water. She had swum in several meets and reported that swimming was a great stress release for her. She said that the couple therapy had helped her and Rick feel better about themselves and each other. Rick was working full time and doing well. They had a regular date night, and they had agreed to limit the time they spent caring for their daughter's children. Also, they had asked their adult son to move out of their home; he was now back in school and living with his girlfriend.

At six-month follow-up, Gail was still panic-free. She had been promoted and now managed the catering division of the restaurant chain for which she worked. She had placed second in a recent swim meet, and she and her ex-husband were planning a cruise to celebrate their 30th wedding anniversary. Gail had suggested a cruise to Rick because she thought it would be fun and a good way to practice facing her fear of deep water.

RESEARCH ON THE APPROACH

EFFICACY

Many studies have demonstrated the efficacy of cognitive-behavioral treatment approaches for panic. Klosko, Barlow, Tassinari, and Cerny (1990) demonstrated that 15 weeks of cognitive-behavior therapy for panic was as good as or better than 15 weeks of treatment with aprazolam (Xanax); other studies demonstrated similar advantages of cognitive-behavior therapy over medication (Clark et al., 1994; Craske, Brown, & Barlow, 1991). Several studies suggested that adding cognitive-behavior therapy to medication treatment improved outcome (Mavissakalian & Michelson, 1986; Telch, Agras, Taylor, Roth, & Gallen, 1985).

A comparison of 12 weeks of cognitive therapy (CT) versus brief supportive therapy showed that CT resulted in significantly greater reductions in panic symptoms and general anxiety after only 8 weeks of treatment. After 12 weeks, 94% of the subjects in the CT group were panic-free, and 87% of the subjects in the CT group remained panic-free at one-year follow-up (Beck, Sokol, Clark, Berchick, & Wright, 1992).

A study comparing CT, applied relaxation (AR), and imipramine (IM) demonstrated that all three treatments were effective compared to wait-list controls (Clark et al., 1994). However, at three-month follow-up, CT was superior to AR and IM on most measures; AR and IM were not significantly different from each other. The proportion of subjects who were panic-free at the end of the study was significantly greater in the CT group than in the AR and IM groups. Most interesting, however, was that, whereas at six-month follow-up the CT and IM groups had similar results and both were superior to the AR group, at 15-month follow-up, the CT group was again superior to both the AR and IM groups.

Craske et al. (1991) conducted a two-year follow-up study in which subjects were assigned to 15 weekly sessions of applied progressive muscle relaxation (AR), interoceptive exposure plus cognitive restructuring (IEC), combined treatment of AR with IEC, or a wait list. At six-month follow-up, the IEC and combined treatment subjects maintained their treatment gains, but subjects in the AR group had deteriorated significantly. In addition, 71% of the subjects in the IEC treatment and 83% of the subjects in the combined treatment were panic-free at six-month follow-up, but only 22% of the subjects in the AR group were panic-free. When dropouts were included, however, they found that 81% of the IEC subjects were panic-free, whereas 43% of the combined treatment subjects and 36% of the AR subjects were panic-free. The authors concluded that interoceptive exposure plus cognitive restructuring more effectively controlled panic attacks than applied relaxation; also, the effects of short-term cognitive-behavior therapy were maintained for up to two years following treatment completion, whereas AR subjects tended to deteriorate over this period and had high rates of attrition from the study.

Telch and colleagues (1993) studied cognitive-behavior group therapy for PD that included education, cognitive restructuring techniques, breathing retraining, and interoceptive exposure. Subjects were randomly assigned to the treatment group or the delayed-treatment group and received 12 90-minute sessions, delivered over an eight-week period. Mean recovery at posttreatment was 81% for the CBT group and 31% for the delayed-treatment controls, with little erosion of treatment gains over a six-month period.

Although clients who complete cognitive-behavioral treatment for their panic can learn to effectively control panic attacks, this does not always indicate a proportional decrease in the general level of anxiety, fear, and disability. Several studies have estimated that only 50 to 60% of clients who complete panic control protocols achieved a clinically significant benefit from therapy (Barlow, Craske, Cerny, & Klosko, 1989; Michelson et al., 1990). Investigators have speculated that severity of agoraphobic avoidance, severity of PD, and fears of anxiety sensations may play a significant role in how well clients can be expected to function in the world following cognitive-behavior therapy for PD (Brown & Barlow, 1995; Craske & Barlow, 1993; Ehlers, 1995) and that a persistent comorbid condition may predict a poorer long-term outcome for clients receiving cognitive-behavior therapy for their panic (Brown, Antony, & Barlow, 1995).

SUMMARY

Numerous studies suggest that 80 to 100% of individuals who complete cognitive-behavior therapy are panic-free at the end of treatment and remain panic-free at follow-up intervals of up to two years (Barlow et al., 1989). For this reason, cognitive-behavioral treatments for anxiety and panic, along with medications, are now recognized as the treatments of choice for anxiety disorders. This chapter has presented a treatment approach based on the biopsychosocial conceptualization that PD is a phobic response to anxiety-evoking bodily sensations (Barlow, 1988). The treatment is designed to influence the cognitive-physiological-behavioral contributions to anxiety that increase an individual's vulnerability to panic attacks. This treatment includes psychoeducation, breathing control and relaxation training, cognitive

restructuring, and interoceptive and situational exposures. Although the treatment is structured, time-limited, and protocol-driven, it is not applied inflexibly, without consideration to the uniqueness of the each client. As demonstrated in the case of Gail, the clinician considered Gail's specific anxious thoughts, her specific somatic symptoms, and the specific situations she avoided for fear of panic attacks to derive an individualized case formulation that guided treatment planning and implementation.

REFERENCES

American Psychiatric Association. (1952). *Diagnostic and statistical manual of mental disorders* Washington, DC: Author.

American Psychiatric Association. (1980). *Diagnostic and statistical manual of mental disorders* (3rd ed.). Washington, DC: Author

American Psychiatric Association. (1987). *Diagnostic and statistical manual of mental disorders* (3rd ed., rev.). Washington, DC: Author

American Psychiatric Association. (1994). *Diagnostic and statistical manual of mental disorders* (4th ed.). Washington, DC: Author

Barlow, D. H. (1988). *Anxiety and its disorders: The nature and treatment of anxiety and panic.* New York: Guilford Press.

Barlow, D. H., & Craske, M. G. (1989). *Mastery of your anxiety and panic.* Albany, NY: Graywind.

Barlow, D. H., Craske, M. G., Cerny, J. A., & Klosko, J. S. (1989). Behavioral treatment of Panic Disorder. *Behavior Therapy, 20,* 261–282.

Barlow, D. H., & Cerny, J. A. (1988). *Psychological treatment of panic.* New York: Guilford Press.

Barlow, D. H., Cohen, A., Waddell, M., Vermilyea, J., Klosko, J., Blanchard, E., et al. (1984). Panic and generalized anxiety disorders: Nature and treatment. *Behavior Therapy, 15,* 431–449.

Beck, A. T., Emery, G., & Greenberg, R. L. (1985). *Anxiety disorders and phobias: A cognitive perspective.* New York: Basic Books.

Beck, A. T., Epstein, N., Brown, G., & Steer, R. (1988). An inventory for measuring clinical anxiety: Psychometric properties. *Journal of Consulting and Clinical Psychology, 56,* 893–897.

Beck, A. T., Laude, R., & Bohnert, M. (1974). Ideational components of anxiety neurosis. *Archives of General Psychiatry, 31,* 319–325.

Beck, A. T., Sokol, L., Clark, D. A., Berchick, R., & Wright, F. (1992). A crossover study of focused cognitive therapy for Panic Disorder. *American Journal of Psychiatry, 149,* 778–783.

Beck, A. T., Ward, C. H., Mendelson, M., Mock, J., & Erbaugh, J. (1961). An inventory for measuring depression. *Archives of General Psychiatry, 4,* 561–571.

Beck, J. G., & Zebb, B. J. (1994). Behavioral assessment and treatment of Panic Disorder: Current status, future directions. *Behavior Therapy, 25,* 581–611.

Brown, T. A., Antony, M. M., & Barlow, D. H. (1995). Diagnostic comorbidity in Panic Disorder: Effect of treatment outcome and course of co-morbid diagnoses following treatment. *Journal of Consulting and Clinical Psychology, 63,* 408–418.

Brown, T. A., Barlow, D. H. (1995). Long-term outcome in cognitive-behavioral treatment of Panic Disorder: Clinical predictors and alternative strategies for assessment. *Journal of Consulting and Clinical Psychology, 63,* 754–765.

Burns, D. D. (1998). *Therapist toolkit.* Unpublished manuscript, Los Altos, CA.

Chambless, D. L., Caputo, G., Bright, P., & Gallagher, R. (1984). Assessment of fear in agoraphobics: The Body Sensations Questionnaire and the Agoraphobic Cognitions Questionnaire. *Journal of Consulting and Clinical Psychology, 52,* 1090–1097.

Chambless, D. L., Caputo, G., Gracely, S., Jasin, E., & Williams, C. (1985). The Mobility Inventory for agoraphobia. *Behaviour Research and Therapy, 23,* 35–44.

Clark, D. (1986). A cognitive approach to panic. *Behaviour Research and Therapy, 24,* 461–470.

Clark, D. M., Salkovskis, P. M., & Chalkley, A. (1985). Respiratory control as a treatment for panic attacks. *Journal of Behavior Therapy and Experimental Psychiatry, 16,* 23–30.

Clark, D. M., Salkovskis, P. M., Hackmann, A., Middleton, H., Anastasiades, P. A., & Gelder, M. (1994). A comparison of cognitive therapy, applied relaxation and imipramine in the treatment

of Panic Disorder. *British Journal of Psychiatry, 164,* 759–769.

Craske, M. G., & Barlow, D. H. (1993). Panic Disorder and agoraphobia. In D. H. Barlow (Ed.), *Clinical handbook of psychological disorders: A step-by-step treatment manual* (2nd ed., pp. 1–47). New York: Guilford Press.

Craske, M. G., Brown, T. A., & Barlow, D. H. (1991). Behavioral treatment of panic: A two year follow-up. *Behavior Therapy, 22,* 289–304.

de Ruiter, C., Rijken, H., Garssen, B., van Schaik, A., & Kraaimaat, F. (1989). Comorbidity among the anxiety disorders. *Journal of Anxiety Disorders, 3,* 57–68.

DiNardo, P. A., & Barlow, D. H. (1988). *Anxiety Disorders Interview Schedule–Revised (ADIS-R).* Albany, NY: Graywind.

Ehlers, A. (1995). A one-year prospective study of panic attacks: Clinical course and factors associated with maintenance. *Journal of Abnormal Psychology, 104,* 164–172.

Garssen, B., de Ruiter, C., & van Dyck, R. (1992). Breathing retraining: A rational placebo? *Clinical Psychology Review, 12,* 141–153.

Gould, R. A., Clum, G. A., & Shapiro, D. (1993). The use of bibliotherapy in the treatment of panic: A preliminary investigation. *Behavior Therapy, 24,* 241–252.

Griez, E., & Van den Hout, M. A. (1986). CO_2 inhalation in the treatment of panic attacks. *Behaviour Research and Therapy, 24,* 145–150.

Hall, R. C. W. (Ed.). (1980). *Anxiety in psychiatric presentation of medical illness: Somatopsychic disorders.* New York: SP Medical and Scientific Books.

Jacobson, E. (1938). *Progressive relaxation (Rev. ed.).* Chicago: University of Chicago Press.

Kendall, P. C., Chu, B., Gifford, A., Hayes, C., & Nauta, M. (1998). Breathing life into a manual: Flexibility and creativity with manual-based treatments. *Cognitive and Behavioral Practice, 5,* 177–198.

Klosko, J. S., Barlow, D. H., Tassinari, R., & Cerny, J. A. (1990). A comparison of alprazolam and behavior therapy in the treatment of Panic Disorder. *Journal of Consulting and Clinical Psychology, 58,* 77–84.

Kraft, A. R., & Hooguin, C. A. L. (1984). The hyperventilation syndrome: A pilot study on the effectiveness of treatment. *British Journal of Psychiatry, 145,* 538–542.

Last, C. G., & Blanchard, E. B. (1982). Classification of phobics versus fearful nonphobics: Procedural and theoretical issues. *Behavioral Assessment, 4,* 195–210.

Ley, R. (1985). Agoraphobia, the panic attack and the hyperventilation syndrome. *Behaviour Research and Therapy, 23,* 79–81.

Lum, L. C. (1976). The syndrome of habitual chronic hyperventilation. In O. W. Hill (Ed.), *Modern trends in psychosomatic medicine* (Vol. 3). London: Butterworth.

Mackenzie, T. B., & Popkin, M. K. (1983). Organic anxiety syndrome. *American Journal of Psychiatry, 140,* 342–344.

Margraf, J., Ehlers, A., & Roth, W. (1986). Biological models of Panic Disorder and agoraphobia: A review. *Behaviour Research and Therapy, 24,* 553–567.

Mavissakalian, M., & Michelson, L. (1986). Two-year follow-up of exposure in imipramine treatment of agoraphobia. *American Journal of Psychiatry, 143,* 1106–1112.

McCue, E. C., & McCue, P. A. (1984). Organic and hyperventilatory causes of anxiety-type symptoms. *Behavioural Psychotherapy, 12,* 308–317.

Michelson, L., Mavissakalian, M., Marchione, K., Ulrich, R., Marchione, N., & Testa, S. (1990). Psychophysiological outcome of cognitive, behavioral, and psychophysiologically based treatments of agoraphobia. *Behaviour Research and Therapy, 28,* 127–139.

Nelson, R. O. (1977). Methodological issues in assessment via self-monitoring. In J. D. Cone & R. P. Hawkins (Eds.), *Behavioral assessment: New directions in clinical psychology* (pp. 217–240). New York: Brunner/Mazel.

Norton, G., Dorward, J., & Cox, B. (1986). Factors associated with panic attacks in nonclinical subjects. *Behavior Therapy, 17,* 239–252.

Persons, J. P. (1989). *Cognitive therapy in practice: A case formulation approach.* New York: Norton.

Persons, J. P., Davidson, J., & Tompkins, M. A. (2001). *Essential components of cognitive-behavior therapy for depression.* Washington, DC: American Psychological Association.

Rapee, R. M., Craske, M. G., & Barlow, D. H. (1990). Subject described features of panic attacks using a new self-monitoring form. *Journal of Anxiety Disorders, 4,* 171–181.

Rice, K. M., & Blanchard, E. B. (1982). Biofeedback in the treatment of anxiety disorders. *Clinical Psychology Review, 2,* 557–577.

Starcevic, V., Uhlenhuth, E. H., Kellner, R., & Pathak, D. (1992). Patterns of comorbidity in Panic Disorder and agoraphobia. *Psychiatry Research, 42,* 171–183.

Telch, M. J., Agras, W. S., Taylor, C. B., Roth, W. T., & Gallen, C. (1985). Combined pharmacological and behavioral treatment for agoraphobia. *Behaviour Research and Therapy, 23,* 325–335.

Telch, M. J., Lucas, J. A., & Nelson, P. (1989). Nonclinical panic in college students: An investigation of prevalence and symptomatology. *Journal of Abnormal Psychology, 98,* 300–306.

Telch, M. J., Lucas, J. A., Schmidt, N. B., Hanna, H. H., Jaimez, T. L., & Lucas, R. A. (1993). Group cognitive behavioral treatment of Panic Disorder. *Behavior Research and Therapy, 31,* 279–287.

Thyer, B. A., Himle, J., Curtis, G. C., Cameron, O. G., & Nesse, R. M. (1985). A comparison of Panic Disorder and agoraphobia with panic attacks. *Comprehensive Psychiatry, 26,* 208–214.

Wade, T. C., Malloy, T. E., & Proctor, S. (1977). Imaginal correlates of self-reported fear and avoidance behavior. *Behaviour Research and Therapy, 22,* 393–402.

Wilson, R. R. (1996). *Don't panic: Taking control of anxiety attacks.* New York: HarperPerennial.

CHAPTER 13

Cognitive-Behavioral
Approaches to Depression

MANDY STEIMAN AND KEITH S. DOBSON

HISTORY OF THE COGNITIVE-BEHAVIORAL APPROACHES

Cognitive-behavior therapy is the generic term for a growing set of therapies that include both behavioral and cognitive interventions. Since cognitive-behavioral therapies first appeared in the 1960s with Ellis's (1962) rational emotive therapy (RET, later renamed rational-emotive-behavior therapy or REBT), cognitive-behavioral therapies have become increasingly diverse. Through the 1970s, the "cognitive revolution" took hold in psychology generally, and also in psychotherapy. During this time, researchers and clinicians continued to develop cognitive-behavioral models of psychopathology and psychotherapy and subject them to empirical scrutiny. Through this work, new approaches to understanding and treating psychological problems developed. The sheer volume of applications in this area has benefited clinicians, who can now choose among the many cognitive and behavioral clinical techniques introduced over the past few decades.

Each of the cognitive-behavioral therapies has its own methods for conceptualizing and treating clients and can be traced along its own particular historical path. In spite of this, the cognitive-behavioral approaches also share a collective history (Dobson & Dozois, 2000). This history has its early roots in radical behavioral theory and practice, which subsequently led to the development of traditional behavioral therapies. The cognitive-behavioral therapies grew out of a dissatisfaction with purely behavioral approaches that did not fit with the mediational perspective that conscious thought has a significant impact on feelings and behavior (Mahoney, 1974). Certain specific factors have been proposed as necessary for the development of the cognitive-behavioral therapies. The mediational approach to understanding psychopathology gained favor when it became evident that the behaviorist approach was too narrow for a thorough conceptualization of disorders (Meichenbaum, 1977). In terms of treatment considerations, the primary symptoms of certain disorders demanded the development

295

of cognitive interventions. Disorders with large cognitive components, such as Obsessive-Compulsive Disorder, Generalized Anxiety Disorder, Panic Disorder, and Depression, could be more easily treated if the treatment package included cognitive techniques (Brewin, 1996). Paralleling the new emphasis on cognitive factors, dissatisfaction with psychodynamic models of therapy and doubts about their efficacy contributed to a climate where there was room for the development of new approaches to therapy. Further, basic research in the 1960s and 1970s provided empirical demonstrations of cognitive mediation in psychopathology. Interest in the cognitive-behavioral approach was further encouraged as theorists and therapists began to adopt and announce a cognitive-behavioral orientation. A forum for these views was created with the establishment of the journal *Cognitive Therapy and Research* in 1977. As the cognitive-behavioral movement gained momentum, newly generated research provided empirical support for the efficacy of cognitive-behavioral approaches to treatment (Dobson, 2000). At present, a variety of cognitive-behavioral approaches to treating depression continue to generate research and influence clinical practice.

THEORETICAL CONSTRUCTS

ASSUMPTIONS UNDERLYING THE COGNITIVE-BEHAVIORAL APPROACHES

Cognitive-behavioral approaches to treatment share the perspective that internal covert processes, called thinking or cognition, play important roles in the etiology, maintenance, and treatment of psychopathology. For this reason, cognitive-behavioral treatments for depression intervene primarily at the level of cognition, with the expectation that by changing thinking, depressive mood will be alleviated and depressive behavior will be modified. Further, cognitive-behavioral models of psychopathology share

three fundamental assumptions (Dobson & Dozois, 2000). First, they share the proposition that cognitive activity affects behavior. This assumption means that the way individuals think about events affects their response to these events. A second shared assumption of the cognitive-behavioral therapies is that cognitive activity can be monitored and altered. In other words, cognitions can be directly accessed and changed, and progress can be assessed. The third common proposition is that behavior change can result from cognitive change and that changing the thinking of an individual can be clinically valuable. Although behavioral principles apply and can be useful in effecting behavioral change, cognitive change is promoted as the principal means of changing behavior.

Cognitive theory (A. T. Beck, Rush, Shaw, & Emery, 1979; Clark, Beck, & Alford, 1999) posits that depressed individuals have a cognitive vulnerability to depression. Clark and colleagues (1999) describe the research that has provided empirical support for different assumptions of the cognitive model. A number of studies lend credence to the notion that negative cognition is an important part of depression and that activation of cognitive structures and processes can be helpful in treating depression. Empirical support has also been found for the idea that cognitive factors are involved in the predisposition and maintenance of depression. These two propositions—that cognition is important in the maintenance and treatment of depression and that cognition is a vulnerability factor for depression—are respectively termed the descriptive and the vulnerability hypotheses of the cognitive model.

DIFFERENCES IN COGNITIVE AND BEHAVIORAL EMPHASIS

Despite broad advances in the field, diversity in practical applications and theoretical constructs on which the approaches are based can cause confusion. Different cognitive-behavioral approaches may put more or less emphasis on the cognitive versus the behavioral aspects of treatment. Although it must be acknowledged that most therapists want to create broad change in patients' emotional, cognitive, behavioral, and interpersonal spheres of functioning, different cognitive-behavioral theories may recommend intervention at different levels. Specifically, behavioral interventions involve attempts to change functioning by intervening at the level of behavior, whereas cognitive interventions attempt to effect change by altering perceptions and/or thinking patterns. Cognitive interventions were originally developed by theorists trained in psychodynamic models who emphasized the role of meaning, whereas cognitive-behavioral interventions were originally developed by behaviorist theorists who focused on the role of conditioning and its effect on thinking (Hollon & Beck, 1994). There continues to be controversy over the importance of behavioral interventions for the treatment of depression and when they should be employed. For example, A. T. Beck and colleagues (1979) assert that they are most useful at the beginning of therapy, when symptoms are most severe. Others have suggested that behavioral interventions alone may be sufficient for change (Jacobson et al., 1996). Although the relative emphasis placed on cognitive and behavioral aspects of treatment differs between therapy approaches, most cognitive-behavioral therapies and therapists use both classes of interventions.

CATEGORIZING THE COGNITIVE-BEHAVIORAL TREATMENTS FOR DEPRESSION

To appreciate the differences among the various cognitive-behavioral models, it is helpful to use an organizing framework. The different approaches to depression place varying amounts of emphasis on certain theoretical constructs. Indeed, the cognitive-behavioral therapies can be categorized into three broad classes with differing theoretical perspectives and clinical goals (Mahoney & Arnkoff, 1978). The assumptions and theoretical underpinnings of each class of interventions are closely tied to the specific interventions used in each approach.

The first type of cognitive-behavioral therapies focuses on *cognitive restructuring.* Therapies of this sort accept the assumption that changing maladaptive thought patterns is therapy's most essential intervention. According to cognitive restructuring models, the main goal of treatment is to replace dysfunctional cognitions with more functional cognitive appraisals. The two best-known cognitive-behavioral therapies for depression, REBT (Ellis, 1962) and Beck's cognitive therapy (A. T. Beck et al., 1979), are included in this category. The second class of cognitive-behavioral therapies includes the *coping skills therapies.* These approaches emphasize the development of a wide repertoire of skills that can facilitate adjustment to challenging circumstances. In coping skills therapies, the client is taught how to facilitate coping by using more adaptive strategies. The goal of treatment is to teach skills that will help decrease the amount of adverse emotional consequences experienced as a result of life events. The Coping with Depression (CWD) course (Lewinsohn, Antonuccio, Steinmetz, & Teri, 1984) and self-control therapy (Rehm, 1977) are examples of coping skills therapies. The final category of cognitive-behavioral models is the *problem-solving therapies.* Beyond training clients to use specific coping skills, these therapies theorize that it is best to teach clients general skills to deal with life predicaments, such as problem definition and decision making. Problem-solving therapy for depression is one such approach (Nezu, Nezu, & Perri, 1989).

Kendall and Kriss (1983) have provided a useful framework for examining the similarities and differences among the cognitive-behavioral therapies for depression. They propose five dimensions to use for comparison: (1) the theoretical orientation of the therapy and its target for change; (2) the nature of the therapeutic relationship; (3) the principal method for effecting cognitive change; (4) the type of evidence used to help change cognitions; and (5) the amount of emphasis on self-control. For instance, when evaluated according to these dimensions, Beck's cognitive therapy for depression has both cognitive and behavioral targets for change, and therapists and clients assume a collaborative relationship. This form of therapy uses rational means, or collaborative empiricism, where cognitive appraisals are judged against empirical evidence. Cognitive therapists emphasize client self-control, where persons seeking treatment learn to monitor their own cognitions and implement learned techniques.

The individual cognitive-behavioral approaches can be distinguished from each other in additional ways (Hollon & Beck, 1994). As previously mentioned, the amount of emphasis placed on behavioral components differs among individual treatment protocols. Further, certain approaches may be tied to a central model of change, whereas others adhere to a peripheral model of change. The individual cognitive-behavioral approaches also vary to the extent to which they have differentiated theories of psychopathology, where one disorder does not share the same theoretical explanation as another form of psychopathology.

COGNITIVE-BEHAVIORAL METHODS OF ASSESSMENT AND INTERVENTION

Cognitive-behavioral treatment programs for depression may focus more or less on cognitive change versus behavioral change, but all such treatments accept that cognitive events can mediate behavior change and that behavioral change can occur independent of cognitive processes. This chapter presents five of the major cognitive-behavioral treatments for depression: REBT, cognitive therapy, self-control therapy, CWD, and problem-solving therapy. We also present a novel, competing behavioral approach to depression, which has been termed behavioral activation.

RATIONAL-EMOTIVE BEHAVIOR THERAPY

Albert Ellis developed REBT over four decades ago, and thus it has the longest history of the cognitive-behavioral approaches presented in this chapter. This therapy was originally termed rational-emotive therapy, but renamed REBT when critics accused it of neglecting to attend to clients' behaviors, although REBT has always attended to behavioral aspects of clients' problems (Dryden & Ellis, 2000). There have been few changes in the theory and practice of REBT since Ellis's publication of *Reason and Emotion in Psychotherapy* (1962), and REBT continues to be used to treat a variety of psychological problems, including depression.

The REBT model of psychological functioning stresses the relationships among cognition, emotion, and behavior (Ellis, 1995). According to Ellis's ABC model, an individual evaluates activating events or experiences (A) according to his or her belief system (B); beliefs about events are presumed to cause cognitive, emotional, and behavioral consequences (C). REBT assumes that innate tendencies to make absolute and irrational evaluations of events are at the core of psychological disturbance. Ellis (1970) identified 12 types of basic irrationalities that can be considered unrealistic expectations. He also coined the term "musterbation" to account for the human tendency to cling to "musts" or "must nots" regarding life events such as failures, rejections, and frustrations; for example, a depressed man might think that he must perform perfectly as a father or he will be a failure. Such beliefs are considered to be rigid and irrational. REBT posits that when individuals fail to live up to irrational expectations, they are vulnerable to experiencing psychological symptoms, including depression.

REBT attempts to challenge, question, and forcefully debate unrealistic expectations (Dryden & Ellis, 2000). Indeed, the goal of therapy is to teach the client to consistently apply REBT's methods to change irrational thinking. Beyond symptom reduction, REBT aims to create durable changes in beliefs and living. A large variety of cognitive, emotive, and behavioral techniques can be employed in treatment. Although therapists are flexible in the types of interventions they may use, they most commonly focus on identifying and challenging clients' irrational beliefs. Toward this goal, therapists begin by breaking down the presenting problem into the ABC model. During the early stage of therapy, clients are taught how to see the links between their irrational thoughts and emotional and behavioral consequences. Once clients understand these links, therapists progress into a "disputing stage." REBT therapists employ an active-directive and psychoeducational stance toward clients. REBT puts the most emphasis on verbal persuasion of all the cognitive-behavioral approaches. Clients are expected to first gain the intellectual insight that irrational beliefs lead to psychological disturbance, and rational beliefs can lead to healthier consequences. In addition to intellectual insight, therapists use a variety of techniques to help clients achieve a deeper level of emotional insight into their problems. A client who has become proficient in REBT's self-change techniques is able to identify, challenge, and counteract irrational beliefs. In effect, clients should learn how to actively dispute their own irrational thoughts.

In the REBT framework, homework is often assigned and can include bibliotherapy, listening to audiocassettes of REBT lectures, and practicing REBT methods by using them with friends and family. Additional techniques include rational-emotive imagery, semantic methods (e.g., teaching the use of nondefeating language), self-disclosure, modeling, role playing, shame-attacking exercises, operant conditioning, desensitization exercises, and skills training. REBT was designed for brief psychotherapy, and nonsevere cases are often treated with 10 or fewer sessions, especially if the presenting problem is discrete and specific (Ellis, 1995). REBT employs many forms of individual and group psychotherapy, including encounter groups and one-day "marathons."

Cognitive Therapy

Aaron Beck's cognitive therapy is a widely studied and commonly applied treatment program for depression. Beck's conceptual model of depression and the cognitive therapy treatment protocol are outlined in a comprehensive treatment manual for depression, which remains a primary reference for both researchers and clinicians (A. T. Beck et al., 1979). Further, the Beck Depression Inventory (BDI) is one of the most common self-report questionnaires used to assess depressive symptoms and is widely used in research and practice.

Beck's cognitive model of depression states that depressed individuals demonstrate distorted information processing. According to this model, the symptoms of depression stem from the way a depressed person structures his or her world. Specifically, the cognitive model proposes that depressed individuals exhibit a consistently negative view of the self, the world, and the future. As such, depressed individuals are expected to think that they are defective or inadequate, that the world is full of demands and insurmountable obstacles, and that the future involves unrelenting suffering. This characterization of distorted schematic processes is labeled the *cognitive triad.*

A second component of the cognitive model involves the focus on relatively accessible mental content and processes that the client can learn to reveal in therapy (A. T. Beck et al.,

1979). Depressed clients are expected to exhibit cognitive patterns, or schemas, through which they filter their experiences. Several cognitive errors may occur more frequently during affective episodes, such as all-or-nothing thinking, overgeneralizing, inappropriate blaming, and jumping to conclusions. Treatment for depression aims to help the client identify, examine, and challenge such dysfunctional cognitive distortions and the schemas on which they rest.

Through the course of cognitive therapy, clients are taught how to adopt more realistic and adaptive appraisals of life events. Cognitive therapists are encouraged to assume a collaborative relationship with clients, in which both parties work together toward treatment goals. This process, termed collaborative empiricism, requires a scientific approach to the client's thoughts. Beliefs are seen as hypotheses that can be tested by examining supporting or refuting evidence. In contrast with REBT's persuasive therapeutic style, cognitive therapists are encouraged to avoid didactic persuasion or lecturing clients into adopting new beliefs. Instead, they use the method of Socratic questioning, which involves open-ended questions that encourage clients to examine their own mental processes.

Cognitive therapy can be applied in individual or group format, although the former is more common. Therapy is structured so that most sessions progress in a typical way. Sessions usually begin by reviewing progress since the previous appointment, setting an agenda, and prioritizing problems and topics. After these topics are addressed, therapists and clients collaboratively design homework to help the client apply learned concepts and skills to presenting problems. Homework is reviewed at the beginning of the following session.

Cognitive therapy is multifaceted and includes both behavioral and cognitive components (A. T. Beck et al., 1979; J. S. Beck, 1995). Early in therapy, when symptoms are most severe, the clinician may employ behavioral interventions to increase the frequency of avoided activities and provide experiences of pleasure and mastery. However, according to the model of cognitive therapy, behavioral methods are used with the primary goal of modifying dysfunctional thoughts. For example, a therapist may encourage the client to schedule pleasurable activities (behavioral intervention) to counter the belief "It's impossible for me to enjoy myself" (cognitive change goal). Typical behavioral tools involve asking the client to keep a detailed record of activities and associated moods, and helping the client to schedule and structure activities between sessions.

Cognitive techniques are the principal tools in the cognitive therapist's armamentarium. These techniques are used to identify and test automatic thoughts, as well as to identify and correct underlying distorted cognitive schemas. Automatic thoughts are easily accessible thoughts that occur in response to outside events. Underlying schemas, or core beliefs, are more deeply rooted beliefs that occur at the level of personal meaning, such as "I am fundamentally worthless" and "I am a failure."

Clients are first taught how to identify automatic thoughts through education. Next, they learn to monitor their automatic thoughts and recognize how thoughts can affect their mood. The Daily Record of Dysfunctional Thoughts (A. T. Beck et al., 1979) is often used to explore and challenge automatic thoughts. Clients use this form to identify upsetting events, automatic thoughts that occurred in response to the events, resulting emotional responses, and alternative adaptive beliefs that they could potentially adopt. Once clients learn how to identify automatic thoughts, therapists begin to help them test the validity of their beliefs by asking them to provide evidence that supports and refutes their thoughts. This intervention may include designing an actual experiment to test a given belief.

Once clients are skilled at challenging automatic thoughts, therapists use additional cognitive methods to identify clients' underlying schemas. Therapists can administer the Dysfunctional Attitudes Scale (Weissman & Beck, 1978) to tap underlying assumptions, or they may use the "downward arrow" technique, where the therapist asks successive questions to try to elicit clients' fundamental beliefs. During the final phase of cognitive therapy, the focus is on maintaining treatment gains and preventing relapse. Therapists may schedule booster sessions to help consolidate treatment gains over time. Cognitive therapy has contributed greatly to cognitive-behavioral treatment for depression and has developed many useful cognitive and behavioral techniques, as well as methods for assessment.

SELF-CONTROL THERAPY

Rehm's (1977) self-control model of depression attempts to integrate cognitive and behavioral approaches. The interventions used in self-control therapy for depression are tied to the self-control model (Fuchs & Rehm, 1977). Self-control therapy is based on Kanfer's (1970, 1971) model of self-regulation. Self-control involves a series of processes that individuals engage in to try to change the probability of their responses. These responses are maintained in the absence of immediate external reinforcement. When individuals perceive that their behavior does not result in a desired outcome, self-control processes become active. For example, a depressed man may perceive that his activity level is problematic when he notes that he has not exercised in several months and is putting on weight. Once he realizes this, he may begin to engage in self-control processes. The three processes involved in self-control are self-monitoring, self-evaluation, and self-reinforcement. Self-monitoring refers to the observation of one's own behavior, self-evaluation involves a comparison between one's own performance and some standard of performance,

and self-reinforcement refers to the administration of contingent rewards and punishments.

Rehm's (1977) model of depression conceptualizes symptoms of depression as deficits in one or more of the three self-control processes defined by Kanfer (1970, 1971): self-monitoring, self-evaluation, and self-reinforcement. Six specific deficits in self-control behavior can explain the appearance of depressive symptoms. The two deficits in self-monitoring behavior are selectively attending to negative events in the environment and selectively attending to immediate instead of long-term outcomes of behavior. Deficits in self-evaluation include setting strict and self-evaluative standards for one's own behavior and making inaccurate attributions for one's own behavior. Finally, deficits in self-reinforcement include administering too little self-reward and engaging in too much self-punishment.

The original self-control treatment program closely follows Rehm's model of depression, although the program has been revised in therapy outcome studies (Rehm, 1984). The treatment protocol is highly structured and well defined in a detailed therapist's manual (Rehm, 1977). Therapists present the self-control concepts didactically and encourage a better understanding of the concepts through in-session exercises and homework assignments. The program is presented in a group therapy format over 10 sessions, and treatment is conducted in three phases, with each module building on the last. During the self-monitoring phase of self-control therapy, clients learn to monitor their focus on negative activities and negative self-statements. They also learn to monitor positive delayed outcomes of their behavior. Clients are encouraged to conduct an ongoing assessment of their progress by keeping a daily log of their activities, self-statements, and mood. In the self-evaluation phase of therapy, clients learn how to set reasonable goals and break them down into subgoals, as well as how to make effective attributions for their behavior. In the self-reinforcement phase, clients learn to reinforce their own behavior by following a difficult goal or subgoal activity with easy and positive activities and/or positive self-statements. Self-control therapy has been successful in illuminating many common deficits in coping skills exhibited by individuals who present with depressive disorders.

THE COPING WITH DEPRESSION COURSE

The CWD course is a highly structured psychoeducational treatment approach for group treatment of depression first developed by Lewinsohn and colleagues. The CWD course is outlined in detail in an instructor's manual (Lewinsohn et al., 1984).

The theoretical foundation for the interventions in the CWD course lies in social learning theory (Bandura, 1977), which posits that all behaviors are learned responses that influence and are influenced by the environment. This course also has roots in behavioral theory, as one of its primary hypotheses is that low rates of response-contingent positive reinforcement precede the development of depression (Clarke & Lewinsohn, 1989). The idea behind the course is that depressed people do not behave in ways that elicit enough positive reinforcement to maintain positive interactions with the environment. Moreover, according to this theory, a high rate of punishing experiences further contributes to depressive symptoms. Therefore, the goal of the CWD course is to increase the quality and quantity of positively reinforcing interactions with the environment while decreasing punishing interactions.

The CWD course is a multimodal treatment program designed to be an explicit educational experience (Clarke & Lewinsohn, 1989). The course is conducted as a class, not as traditional psychotherapy, to help decrease the possibility of reluctance and resistance to seeking treatment. Treatment consists of 12 two-hour sessions conducted over eight weeks, with

follow-up sessions, termed class reunions, held one month and six months following treatment. The group leader, who is trained to be a teacher and not a therapist, typically leads groups of six to eight adults (Lewinsohn et al., 1984). Treatment providers with different levels of experience can conduct the course. In fact, advanced graduate students have led the course in the University of Oregon Depression Research Unit, where it was developed (Lewinsohn, Steinmetz-Breckenridge, Antonuccio, & Teri, 1985), and paraprofessionals also have been successfully trained as group leaders (Thompson, Gallagher, Nies, & Epstein, 1983).

The first two sessions of the CWD course involve an overview of the course, presentation of ground rules for the group, and instruction in basic self-change skills such as setting realistic goals. The next eight sessions focus on the acquisition of four skills that may be deficient in depressed individuals, with two sessions focusing on each skill. These skills, which include relaxation, increasing positive activities, decreasing negative and dysfunctional thoughts, and increasing social skills, are taught to help clients better cope with stressors that may cause or maintain depression (Clarke & Lewinsohn, 1989). Follow-up sessions focus on integration of skills, maintenance of treatment gains, and relapse. Each session involves a lecture, a review of homework assignments, discussion, and role play. Group leaders assign readings from *Control Your Depression* (Lewinsohn, Munoz, Youngren, & Zeiss, 1986); *Participant Workbook* (Brown & Lewinsohn, 1984) supplements this text and includes homework assignments.

A notable strength of the CWD course is its adaptability for use with specific populations. For example, the course has been modified for use with adolescents (Clarke, Lewinsohn, & Hops, 1990; Lewinsohn, Clarke, Hops, & Andrews, 1990), the elderly (Steinmetz-Breckenridge, Thompson, Breckenridge, & Gallagher, 1985), drug-refractory patients (Antonuccio et al.,

1984), caretakers of elderly persons (e.g., Lovett & Gallagher, 1988), and low-income and minority medical outpatients (Organista, Munoz, & Gerardo, 1994). Another promising area of intervention involves the modification of the course as a means for preventing episodes of depression in populations at high risk for developing depression (Munoz, Ying, Armas, Chan, Guzza, 1987). Ongoing work by the second author, for example, has involved modifications of the CWD course for prevention of depression in adolescents and elderly people relocating into nursing homes.

Problem-Solving Therapy

Problem-solving therapy (PST) reflects the fact that many disorders involve a reduced ability on the part of clients to manage day-to-day problems. The evidence for the efficacy of PST is strongest in the area of depression, but the approach can be applied to a variety of other clinical problems. The treatment protocol for PST for depression is detailed in Nezu et al. (1989). A more recent text on the general problem-solving approach is also available (D'Zurilla & Nezu, 1999).

The problem-solving model of depression focuses on transactional relationships among major life events, current problems, problem-solving coping, and depressive symptoms (Nezu, 1987). The model posits that the way individuals problem-solve around life circumstances influences their emotional state. Thus, depression and other forms of psychopathology result from an inability to successfully resolve problems (D'Zurilla & Goldfried, 1971). Depressive symptoms, as well as other negative consequences, may emerge as a result of inadequate attempts at solving problems. When individuals fail to resolve a stressful situation due to deficits in problem-solving skills, they experience unpleasant results, diminished personal and social reinforcement, and a resulting depressive episode.

Conceptually, the problem-solving model also views depression as a maladaptive response and a problem to be solved. Therefore, PST aims to help clients identify and resolve problems, as well as teach skills that will help them navigate future problems. Nezu and colleagues (1989; Nezu & Perri, 1989) posit that depression can result from deficiencies in any one or a combination of the five major components of problem solving: problem orientation, problem definition and formulation, generation of alternative solutions, decision making, and solution implementation and verification (see Nezu et al., 1989, for detailed explanation of the problem-solving components).

Nezu et al. (1989) propose four goals for PST for depression: (1) to help depressed individuals identify life events that precipitate depression; (2) to minimize the impact of depressive symptoms on coping; (3) to increase the effectiveness of problem-solving behaviors; and (4) to teach general coping skills. PST can operate as an independent treatment method, a maintenance strategy, or a prevention program and may be applied in individual or group format. When PST is applied in its structured, time-limited format, the program is completed in about 8 to 12 sessions divided into an assessment stage, an intervention stage, and a period focused on the maintenance and generalization of treatment gains.

The assessment phase of PST is geared toward defining clients' problem-solving skills and deficits. Assessment related to problem-solving skills may include the use of observational and self-report measures, including the Means-End Problem Solving Procedure (Platt & Spivak, 1975) and the Problem Solving Inventory (Heppner & Petersen, 1982). The intervention stage of PST focuses on training clients in the five problem-solving components. Therapeutic techniques incorporated into treatment include didactic instruction, prompting, modeling, role play, behavioral rehearsal, homework, shaping, positive reinforcement, and performance feedback (Nezu et al., 1989). Of all of the cognitive-behavioral therapies presented in this chapter, PST is the most concerned with incorporating training in more general coping skills that can be generalized to a variety of contexts.

BEHAVIORAL ACTIVATION

Behavioral activation (BA) was developed recently as an independent treatment for depression. In contrast to the aforementioned treatments, BA does not include a cognitive component in its treatment protocol. However, it is included here because it grew out of empirical investigations on Beck's cognitive therapy for depression and shares many qualities with the other cognitive-behavioral therapies, including the structuring of sessions and the use of behavioral techniques specified in Beck's treatment for depression.

BA began as a behavior therapy treatment condition for depression within a component analysis of A. T. Beck et al.'s (1979) cognitive therapy, conducted by Jacobson and colleagues (Jacobson et al., 1996). Findings from that study indicated that there were no differences in posttreatment outcome or relapse rates between the behavioral activation component of cognitive therapy and the full cognitive therapy package (Gortner, Gollan, Dobson, & Jacobson, 1998; Jacobson et al., 1996). Since that time, BA has been developed into a more comprehensive treatment program for depression (Martell, Addis, & Jacobson, 2000).

BA's theoretical roots are grounded in the behavioral literature (Jacobson, Martell, & Dimidjian, in press; Martell et al., 2000). BA shares a radical behaviorist conceptualization of depression that an increase in avoidance and escape behaviors and a decrease in positively reinforced behaviors are essential to the understanding of depression. It also emphasizes the importance of a functional analysis of the behavior of depressed individuals. The BA model

of depression assumes that depressive responses are largely controlled by external life events, not deficiencies within the individual, and that depression results from low levels of reinforcement. Much of the behavior of depressed individuals can be characterized as avoidance behaviors, which have the consequence of decreasing the accessibility to positive reinforcers. Depressive symptoms are further exacerbated by disruptions in routine. Clinicians are encouraged to adopt a contextualist philosophy, which posits that events can be understood only within the greater context in which they occur (Jacobson et al., in press).

The goal for treatment in BA is to expand opportunities for positive reinforcement through decreasing avoidance patterns, increasing reinforcing activities, and establishing routines that can be maintained in the client's natural environment (Jacobson et al., in press; Martell et al., 2000). Additional goals of therapy include teaching clients how to elicit positive reinforcement and identifying and increasing clients' pleasurable activities. Treatment proceeds over a maximum of 24 sessions for four months. Therapy involves four stages (Jacobson et al., in press): (1) establishing a therapeutic relationship with the client and presenting the BA model; (2) conducting a functional analysis of the client's behavior and determining the correlation between functional behavior and mood; (3) modifying the client's actions and assessing the effect on his or her mood; and (4) reviewing what occurred in treatment and focusing on relapse prevention.

As in cognitive therapy for depression, sessions include setting an agenda with the client, reviewing homework, and soliciting feedback from the client. BA differs most from cognitive therapy in that the primary technique in BA is a functional analysis of behavior. This involves evaluating the antecedents and consequences of behavior through activity charts and self-monitoring. BA concentrates on focused activation; it is not sufficient to increase activity, as the goal is to find activities that elicit positive reinforcement in the environment. Other commonly used techniques include graded task assignments, decreasing avoidance, establishing routines, decreasing rumination by increasing attention to experience, and relapse prevention. BA therapists may include other interventions such as role playing, modeling, acting toward goals (i.e., acting in a manner that is consistent with how one would like to feel), and skills training. BA therapists recognize that depressed clients engage in negative thinking. An important distinction between BA therapists and other cognitive-behavioral therapists is that, where other approaches involve assessment of the *content* of negative thinking and its correspondence with actual circumstance (e.g., Is it distorted or irrational?), in BA, cognitions are examined from a functional perspective (e.g., When did the thoughts emerge and what effect did they have on the client?). Consequently, the BA intervention for negative thinking is on changing the context in which it occurs or the effect of negative thinking, rather than the thoughts per se. BA represents an interesting trend in cognitive-behavioral therapies for depression in that researchers are attempting to define the active components in cognitive-behavioral therapies. As researchers determine what interventions are sufficient for change, cognitive-behavioral therapies may become more streamlined and parsimonious. As a result, improved knowledge of mechanisms and parsimony may provide a positive force in the training and dissemination of treatment approaches.

COMMON PROCEDURAL ASPECTS OF THE
COGNITIVE-BEHAVIORAL TREATMENTS
FOR DEPRESSION

The shared procedural aspects among the cognitive-behavioral therapies for depression help distinguish their approaches from other approaches (Dobson & Dozois, 2000). Most of the therapies presented in this chapter were either designed to be time-limited or can be used in time-limited formats. Brevity is an advantage, as brief treatments are more easily evaluated in research protocols. They also are lower cost than longer-term treatments, especially when administered in a group format. Because the therapies are also problem-focused and skills-focused, they are tailored specifically for the treatment of depressive symptoms and were designed with the specific deficits of depressed individuals in mind. Further, all the cognitive-behavioral therapies for depression assume an educative role, where clients learn to take control over the way they think and act. Depressed individuals often have questions about their worth and have reduced self-efficacy. By treating therapy as a means of learning specific skills and goals, perceptions of powerlessness are undermined. One goal underlying these models of therapy and their use as clinical interventions is to help clients become their own therapists. Considering the chronic nature of depressive disorders and the high relapse rate for depressive episodes, it is essential that clients leave therapy with the ability to recognize and respond to pitfalls that they will likely experience in the future. Clients are taught skills and concepts that they themselves can apply to help maintain therapeutic gains and prevent depressive relapses.

MAJOR SYNDROMES,
SYMPTOMS, AND
PROBLEMS TREATED

Cognitive-behavioral therapy is often used to treat a variety of depressive and anxiety disorders, including Major Depression, Panic Disorder, and agoraphobia. Although a wide variety of symptoms can be treated with cognitive-behavioral therapy, this chapter focuses on the treatment of depression. Depression is not easily defined, as symptoms and related problems may differ dramatically, depending on the individual client. Cognitive-behavioral treatments for depression can be used with a multiplicity of clinical presentations.

Depression has been operationalized in three different ways, including depressed mood, depressive syndromes, and depressive disorders (Angold, 1988). Depressed mood involves dysphoria, or depressed affect, while depressive syndromes involve co-occurring symptoms of depression. Depressive disorders are represented as categorical diagnoses defined by the fourth edition of the *Diagnostic and Statistical Manual of Mental Disorders* (*DSM-IV*; American Psychiatric Association, 1994) or the *International Classification of Diseases* (World Health Organization, 1996). As defined in *DSM-IV*, Major Depression involves the experience of depressed mood and/or diminished interest or pleasure in most activities nearly every day over the course of at least two weeks. In addition, Major Depression involves the presence of four or more other symptoms for two weeks or more, for a total of at least five symptoms. These symptoms include unintentional weight or appetite gain or loss, insomnia or hypersomnia, psychomotor agitation or retardation, fatigue or loss of energy, feelings of worthlessness or inappropriate guilt, reduced concentration or indecisiveness, and recurrent thoughts of death, suicidal ideation, a plan for suicide, or a suicide attempt. To meet the criteria for a diagnosis of Major Depression, the symptoms must cause clinically significant distress or impairment in functioning. Major Depression is not diagnosed if the effects of a substance, a general medical condition, or bereavement better account for the symptoms. Also, the presence of a mixed episode of mania and depression rules out this diagnosis. Subtypes of depression defined in *DSM-IV*, in addition to Major Depression, include Dysthymic Disorder, Minor Depressive Disorder, and Mixed Anxiety-Depressive Disorder. The latter two categories are provisional diagnoses in *DSM-IV*, meaning that they lack empirical support as distinct categories but

deserve future study. In addition to discussion about the different types of depression, there is also debate regarding whether depression exists on a continuum with subthreshold Major Depression or Major Depression is categorically different from subthreshold Major Depression (e.g., Lewinsohn, Solomon, Seeley, & Zeiss, 2000).

Depressive disorders are most often episodic, but high relapse and recurrence rates help characterize depression as a chronic condition for many individuals. Major depressive episodes most commonly last between 3 and 11 months (Gotlib & Hammen, 1992), with 60% of individuals recovering within six months from the onset of the episode (Coryell & Winokur, 1992). Although treatment can encourage the offset of an episode, recovery from bouts of depression can occur whether or not an individual has received treatment. In one study, treated and nontreated individuals experienced similar numbers of episodes of Major Depression (Coryell et al., 1995).

Major Depression often takes a recurring course. Although most individuals do eventually recover from a depressive episode, relapse rates are often high. People who experience one episode of Major Depression have a high risk of eventually relapsing into another episode. One review article determined that, within two years after recovering from an initial episode, half of individuals will experience a relapse (Belsher & Costello, 1988). Another review article concluded that about four-fifths of individuals who suffer from an episode of Major Depression will reexperience depression within five years (Keller, 1994). Considering the chronic nature of depression, it is clear that relapse prevention should be an essential component of any treatment for depression.

In clinical practice, the cognitive-behavioral therapies can be used to treat individuals who present with Major Depression, another type of depressive disorder, or depressive symptomology that does not meet the diagnostic criteria of any of the aforementioned *DSM-IV* categories.

Clinical practice diverges with treatment research on cognitive-behavioral therapy, which more commonly focuses on the treatment of Major Depressive Disorder. Understanding the process of how people benefit from cognitive-behavioral therapy is complicated by the diverse symptom presentations of depressive disorders. Research cannot yet tell us which symptoms are best targeted by cognitive interventions and which symptoms would be better treated through behavioral techniques. It may be ideal to individualize treatment according to symptom presentation, but such "aptitude by treatment" research has only begun. As support increases for the efficacy of cognitive-behavioral therapies for depression, more empirical pursuits are being focused on understanding the mechanisms of symptom change.

Because depressed individuals often show deficits in both cognitive and behavioral domains, cognitive-behavioral treatments for depression are particularly fitting for a mood disorder. Many of the symptoms of depression, such as feelings of worthlessness and diminished concentration, relate to disrupted thinking patterns; others, such as reduced activity levels, relate to behavioral patterns. Behavioral, cognitive, and affective change can be encouraged through the use of either cognitive or behavioral interventions. In fact, a major proposition of cognitive-behavioral therapies is that desired behavior change can be mediated through cognitive change. For example, a depressed woman may avoid going out with friends because she thinks that she will not enjoy herself; through learning how to appraise the likely outcome of avoided social situations, however, she may begin to interact more with friends. Cognitive-behavioral theorists would also agree that cognitive change may be facilitated through the use of behavioral interventions. If the woman goes out with friends (and enjoys herself), she may alter her perception that seeing friends will not be pleasurable for her. Cognitive theorists attribute the success of

their treatments to the modification of cognitive phenomena. However, research has provided mixed support for the role of cognition as a mechanism of change (Clark et al., 1999; Dimidjian & Dobson, in press). Alternatively, behaviorist explanations that point to increases in positive reinforcement may be at least equally tenable. Thus, although research cannot provide a definitive answer for why cognitive-behavioral therapies work, it seems intuitive that both cognitive and behavioral changes can reinforce each other.

CASE EXAMPLE

Frank Merriweather was a 47-year-old machinist who developed clinical depression following the untimely death of his teenage son in a motor vehicle accident, followed by an expensive but unsuccessful wrongful death lawsuit, marital problems, and ultimate divorce from his wife of 25 years. At the time of intake, he was living alone, was not managing his food and daily routines well, and was able to work only on a part-time basis. His two surviving children were married and doing well, but by his report, his ex-wife was also somewhat depressed.

It became clear that there were both short- and long term problems to address. In the short term, it was important to establish good daily health habits and to ensure more regular work attendance. In the long term, it was agreed to try to separate the influence of his son's death, the legal process that followed, and the dissolution of his marriage as potential factors in his depression to both understand his current problems and reduce the likelihood of future depressions. The cognitive-behavioral therapist was acutely aware of Frank's self-derogatory comments and his general self-assessment as being "stupid." However, it was also noted that Frank had some strengths; for example, he had not resorted to using alcohol or other substances during his stressful times and, although his work attendance was not optimal, he still maintained his position.

It was agreed that therapy would begin with some basic monitoring of Frank's activities. It was found that his eating was intermittent and that when not at work, he spent most of his time in front of the television. Although he expressed an interest in his children, he did little to act on this interest because he was afraid that his children were disappointed and angry with him. Treatment began with the assignment of modest tasks while monitoring the effects on his thinking and mood.

A regular routine was set as a goal, with a consistent time to get out of and into bed. It was agreed that Frank would eat breakfast and supper daily and let his lunch vary depending on his appetite. The therapist encouraged Frank to have an open discussion with his employer about being depressed and to negotiate a gradual return to full-time employment as his depression improved. Frank resisted this suggestion because he was afraid of his employer's negative thoughts about him. Consequently, Frank returned to full-time work the week after he started therapy.

His BDI scores dropped from 35 on his first appointment to 18 in week 3. The therapist began having Frank notice and log his thinking when his mood dipped, then explored these situations with Frank and worked with him to learn how to combat negative thinking. For example, it became clear quite early in this process that Frank's even minor disappointments would result in his feeling frustrated and helpless. His negative thinking often led him to prematurely stop certain activities, which reinforced his view of himself as a failure. He also viewed many situations as "complete failures" if his hopes were not met. Frank was taught about negative distortions (J. S. Beck, 1995) and typical ways to overcome these through examining the evidence to support or refute the thought and evaluating reasonable alternative thoughts.

As Frank became more adept at recognizing his typical negative thoughts and as he engaged in scheduling activities with his therapist, he consistently approached previously avoided situations and (generally) succeeded in getting his goals met. It became apparent through discussion and examining his thoughts that Frank viewed himself as a "social disaster" and predicted social isolation for himself. At this point in the treatment, the therapist shifted the focus to his past relationship failure. Although Frank initially held himself responsible for the events that followed his son's death, the evidence became increasingly clear that others significantly influenced decisions leading to the resulting problems. As he talked more, it came to light that his wife likely disengaged from the marriage some time before actually discussing it with Frank.

Through the review process described above, Frank's degree of responsibility was reevaluated. Further, the implications for his future were reconsidered in light of the faulty judgments he had made of himself in the past. With the encouragement of the therapist, Frank agreed to reengage with his children, a move that was met with mutual satisfaction. He began to openly state interest in dating. Toward the end of treatment, he took the "risk" to ask a coworker out. This date ended with neither wanting to go out again, but Frank felt that it had been a mutual decision, which was new and pleasurable for him.

Therapy ended with a review of cognitive and behavioral strategies Frank had learned in therapy. His remaining negative self-beliefs and the need for continued social experiments to contradict these beliefs were highlighted. He was encouraged to schedule appointments with himself to deal with specific problems using the cognitive therapy model, or to contact the therapist if his mood dipped significantly and he wanted further booster appointments. His BDI score at the final session was 6, indicating only mild depression.

EMPIRICAL STATUS OF THE COGNITIVE-BEHAVIORAL APPROACHES TO DEPRESSION

CURRENT EMPIRICAL STATUS

Overall, the cognitive-behavioral therapies have received considerable empirical support as efficacious treatments for depression. There is evidence that cognitive-behavioral interventions are at least as effective as pharmacological treatments, even in cases where depressive symptoms are severe (Antonuccio, Danton, & DeNelsky, 1995; Dobson, 1989; Hollon, Shelton, & Loosen, 1991). In terms of the specific treatment programs, Beck's cognitive therapy has the most empirical support and is the most widely researched of the cognitive-behavioral approaches (Clark et al., 1999). In several studies, cognitive therapy has been found to be as effective as (e.g., Blackburn, Bishop, Glen, Whalley, & Christie, 1981; Elkin et al., 1989; Jarrett et al., 1999; Murphy, Simons, Wetzel, & Lustman, 1984) or superior to antidepressant medication (e.g., Rush, Beck, Kovacs, & Hollon, 1977). Cognitive therapy has also been shown to outperform behavior therapy and other psychotherapies (Dobson, 1989). It remains questionable, however, whether all components of cognitive therapy are necessary for successful treatment. There is evidence that the BA component of cognitive therapy is as effective as the full cognitive therapy package in terms of treatment outcome (Jacobson et al., 1996) and long-term follow-up (Gortner et al., 1998).

Beyond cognitive therapy, the evidence for the efficacy of other cognitive-behavioral therapies for depression is encouraging, although less plentiful. REBT has received support as an effective method of psychotherapy in meta-analytic reviews (Dryden & Ellis, 2000), but qualitative reviews challenge the internal and external validity of published studies (Haaga & Davison, 1993). Moreover, the complexity of the therapy and disagreements over the definition of REBT confuse the interpretation of research findings. Nevertheless, REBT theory has greatly influenced cognitive-behavioral therapies for depression and remains a major modality within the cognitive-behavioral spectrum.

A recent meta-analysis found that the CWD course was an effective therapy for depression (Cuijpers, 1998). However, few studies make direct comparisons between the effects of the CWD course and other psychosocial and pharmacological treatments. Research on the different formats of the CWD course is needed to examine its effectiveness in all its applications.

The handful of outcome studies on self-control therapy seems promising. In two studies, self-control therapy was superior to a control condition at posttest (Fuchs & Rehm, 1977; Rehm, Fuchs, Roth, Kornblith, & Romano, 1979). Another study found that self-control therapy was superior, on some measures, to another type of cognitive therapy (based on Shaw, 1977) and a nondirective control condition (Fleming & Thornton, 1980). However, it is still unclear if all components of self-control therapy are necessary for change. Two studies failed to find a difference in outcome in comparisons between the full program and therapies that included one or two of the self-control therapy components (Kornblith, Rehm, O'Hara, & Lamparski, 1983; Rehm et al., 1981). Another study found that the program was effective at alleviating depression whether the focus was on changing behaviors, cognitions, or both (Rehm, Kaslow, & Rabin, 1987). It appears that studies have not been conducted on self-control therapy for depression since the mid-1980s, which suggests that the field has lost interest in this promising approach to depression.

PST has been found to be an effective treatment for adult unipolar depression (Mynors-Wallis, Gath, Lloyd-Thomas, & Tomlinson, 1995; Nezu, 1986; Nezu & Perri, 1989) and depression in older adult populations (Arean et al., 1993; Hussian & Lawrence, 1981). It appears, as suggested by the primary advocates of

PST (D'Zurilla & Nezu, 1999), that this approach is valid for depression as well as other conditions.

Researchers are finding a significant amount of support for the use of cognitive-behavioral treatments for depression. However, more research is needed to compare these approaches with other forms of psychotherapy or pharmacotherapy. Longitudinal studies that examine relapse rates would be especially illuminating. Research that compares the cognitive-behavioral treatments to each other would also be useful. Further, these treatments incorporate a relatively wide variety of cognitive and behavioral interventions in short-term treatment for depression. Future research could perhaps help determine which components of treatment are most helpful for clients. Suggestions for specific areas of further research follow.

EXAMINING EFFECTIVE INGREDIENTS OF CHANGE

The many outcome studies on the cognitive-behavioral therapies for depression provide evidence for their efficacy. Although it is known that the cognitive-behavioral therapies are generally effective treatments for depression, definitive answers about why and how they work remain elusive. Researchers now face the challenge of providing evidence for the hypothesized active ingredients of change within cognitive-behavioral approaches to the treatment of depression. Because the bulk of research on this topic concerns A. T. Beck and colleagues' (1979) cognitive therapy, we do not specifically address the other cognitive-behavioral approaches in this section. Still, many of the issues discussed generally apply to all the cognitive-behavioral therapies.

Like other cognitive-behavioral approaches, cognitive therapy is a multifaceted treatment for depression that includes many factors that could account for therapeutic change. The active ingredients of therapy have been conceptualized as

falling into the category of either common factors or theory-specific factors (Hollon & Kriss, 1984). Common or nonspecific factors are the general aspects of therapy that are often assumed to be necessary but not sufficient conditions for change. These factors, which include the therapeutic alliance and the provision of a treatment rationale, are generally considered to play a secondary role to theoretically specified treatment interventions (A. T. Beck et al., 1979). There has been some empirical support for the importance of nonspecific factors in cognitive therapy (Dimidjian & Dobson, in press). Despite the evidence for the importance of common factors, though, research on this topic suffers from some methodological problems. For example, most of the research in this area has been conducted by examining the data from controlled trials of psychotherapies. Unfortunately, there is little variability among the highly trained and supervised psychotherapists in these studies, making it difficult to relate therapist variables to outcome (Crits-Christoph et al., 1991). Also, when secondary studies are conducted after the completion of a controlled trial of psychotherapy, researchers often fail to attend to temporal confounds. For instance, much of the research on the therapeutic alliance is correlational, so that it cannot be established whether a good therapeutic alliance leads to symptom change or merely follows symptom improvement (Feeley, DeRubeis, & Gefland, 1999).

Beyond the common factors in cognitive therapy, efforts have focused on the role of theory-specific interventions. In particular, research has examined the relative importance of cognitive and behavioral factors in the treatment of depression. According to the theory of cognitive therapy, cognitive techniques are the active ingredients of change (A. T. Beck et al., 1979). Numerous investigators have examined whether cognitive interventions contribute to symptom change above and beyond behavioral interventions (e.g., Jacobson et al., 1996; Shaw, 1977; Wilson, Goldin, & Charbonneau-Powis, 1983). To date, the data are equivocal (Dimidjian & Dobson, in press).

Uncertainty also persists in regard to the type of cognitive interventions that are most crucial for change. Cognitive therapy specifies a number of cognitive techniques that may contribute differentially to symptom change. Yet, only a handful of studies have attempted to explore this important area of investigation. These studies have provided interesting results that link a variety of cognitive interventions to improved outcome for depressed individuals. For example, research has provided support for active modification of thoughts (Teasdale & Fennell, 1982), homework assignment (Persons, Burns, & Perloff, 1988), and logical analysis and hypothesis testing (Jarrett & Nelson, 1987). Improved outcome has also been associated with the concrete methods of cognitive therapy, such as setting and following an agenda or examining the evidence around belief. However, abstract methods of cognitive therapy, including exploring the personal meaning of thoughts and encouraging independence, have been found to be unrelated to outcome (DeRubeis & Feeley, 1990; Feeley et al., 1999). Identifying cognitive and behavioral ingredients for change represents a developing area of research that can make great contributions to both clinical practice and the theoretical understanding of cognitive-behavioral therapies.

ISSUES RELATED TO EFFICACY AND UTILITY RESEARCH

Determining whether a certain treatment has enough supporting evidence to justify its use requires delving into many different realms. The bulk of evidence indicates that cognitive-behavioral interventions are successful in the treatment of depression and represent a viable alternative to pharmacotherapy. However, strict criteria should be applied to the evaluation of the cognitive-behavioral therapies. Chambless and Hollon (1998) provide useful guidelines to

aid in the determination of whether a given treatment can be established as an empirically supported treatment (EST). ESTs are defined as "clearly specified psychological treatments shown to be efficacious in controlled research with a delineated population" (Chambless & Hollon, 1998, p. 7). They suggest that research on treatment efficacy, clinical utility or effectiveness, and cost-effectiveness should all be considered in the evaluation of a treatment. Beyond demonstrations of efficacy, the APA Task Force on Psychological Intervention Guidelines (1995) indicates that it is also important to examine whether the treatments can work in clinical practice. This determination involves considering if the research studies can be generalized across the populations, settings, and therapists involved in the efficacy studies. Client diversity is an especially salient issue, and attention to differences in age, ethnicity, sexual orientation, and socioeconomic status represents an important direction for future treatment studies.

Evaluating treatments also requires examination of issues related to client acceptance, client compliance, and ease of dissemination to treatment providers, who may not have extensive and specialized experience in a given treatment modality. Treatment outcome involves improving symptoms of depression, but also bears on many domains of functioning, including interpersonal relationships, work productivity, and general quality of life. A wider view of outcome can help us better evaluate the cognitive-behavioral treatments for depression. The cost-effectiveness of treatments also needs to be established. At present, only a small number of studies include cost components or report cost-effectiveness or cost-benefit ratios for other interventions (Hargreaves, Shumway, Hu, & Cuffel, 1998).

Attention to the effectiveness and cost-effectiveness is critical for the continuing development of the cognitive-behavioral therapies, partly due to competition with rival treatments for depression. Antidepressant medication is the most popular treatment for depression, with prescriptions being offered to clients by a variety of health practitioners and in more than 30% of visits to psychiatrists (Olfson & Klerman, 1993). Cognitive-behavioral treatments for depression represent important alternatives to medication treatment for several reasons: Pharmacological treatments can involve debilitating side effects, increased risk of overdose and suicide, and medical complications from drug interactions (Antonuccio et al., 1995; Antonuccio, Danton, DeNelsky, Greenberg, & Gordon, 1999). For these reasons, and because of research showing superior long-term outcome of cognitive-behavioral therapies for relapse prevention (see below), some researchers believe that cognitive-behavioral treatments represent the first choices in treatment for depression (Antonuccio et al., 1995).

THE TREATMENT OF ACUTE DEPRESSION VERSUS RELAPSE PREVENTION

Advocates of cognitive-behavioral treatments have suggested that a potential advantage over pharmacological treatments is that cognitive-behavioral treatments attempt to teach actual behavioral and cognitive skills that can be employed toward the prevention of future episodes. As previously mentioned, Major Depression is often episodic, and even when individuals recover from acute episodes of depression, they remain at increased risk for relapse. Out of all the cognitive-behavioral treatments for depression, there is the most evidence that Beck's cognitive therapy may reduce the risk of relapses (Clark et al., 1999). Some studies have shown that cognitive therapy is more effective at preventing relapse than pharmacological treatments (Evans et al., 1992; Kovacs, Rush, Beck, & Hollon, 1981; Simons, Murphy, Levine, & Wetzel, 1986). However, results from the well-known Treatments for Depression Collaborative Research Program indicated that there

were no significant differences between cognitive therapy and pharmacotherapy in terms of preventing relapse (Shea et al., 1992). Another area for further investigation involves short-term treatment with cognitive therapy following a trial with antidepressant medication. After successful treatment with pharmacotherapy, cognitive therapy is as effective at preventing relapse as continuing medication and more successful than clinical management without medication (Blackburn & Moore, 1997; Fava, Grandi, Zielezny, & Canestrari, 1996; Fava, Grandi, Zielezny, Canestrari, & Morphy, 1994; Fava, Rafanelli, Grandi, Conti, & Belluardo, 1998). However, more comparisons are needed between cognitive therapy and the other cognitive-behavioral treatments for depression.

SUMMARY

Cognitive-behavioral therapies for depression continue to grow in popularity and to be subjected to empirical scrutiny. Considering the symptoms of depression, which include both cognitive and behavioral deficits, a therapy approach that intervenes at the levels of both cognition and behavior seems very fitting. This chapter describes the theoretical foundations and clinical application of five of the major cognitive behavioral treatments for depression: REBT, cognitive therapy, self-control therapy, the CWD Course, and PST. These approaches share a common history, some theoretical aspects, and some methods. However, the cognitive-behavioral approaches also demonstrate variability in theoretical underpinnings and techniques.

Research provides support for the use of the cognitive-behavioral therapies with depressed populations, with cognitive therapy being the most widely researched and supported of the aforementioned therapies. However, many questions related to the efficacy of the cognitive-behavioral therapies linger: What are the effective ingredients of change? Who benefits most from cognitive-behavioral therapy? When is cognitive-behavioral therapy a preferred alternative to medication and vice versa? Issues related to effectiveness and cost-effectiveness are also relevant. These topics require further exploration so that clients achieve maximum benefit and so that the cognitive-behavioral therapies can be more easily disseminated to treatment providers.

REFERENCES

American Psychiatric Association. (1994). *Diagnostic and statistical manual of mental disorders* (4th ed.). Washington, DC: Author

American Psychological Association Task Force on Psychological Intervention Guidelines. (1995). *Template for developing guidelines: Interventions for mental disorders and psychological aspects of physical disorders.* Washington, DC: American Psychological Association.

Angold, A. (1988). Childhood and adolescent depression: I. Epidemiological and aetiological aspects. *British Journal of Psychiatry, 152,* 601–617.

Antonuccio, D. O., Akins, W. T., Chatham, P. M., Monagin, J. A., Tearnan, B. H., & Zeigler, B. L. (1984). An exploratory study: The psychoeducational group treatment of drug-refractory unipolar depression. *Journal of Behavior Therapy and Experimental Psychiatry, 15,* 309–313.

Antonuccio, D. O., Danton, W. G., & DeNelsky, G. Y. (1995). Psychotherapy versus medication for depression: Challenging the conventional wisdom with data. *Professional Psychology: Research and Practice, 26,* 574–585.

Antonuccio, D. O., Danton, W. G., DeNelsky, G. Y., Greenberg, R. P., & Gordon, J. S. (1999). Raising questions about antidepressants. *Psychotherapy and Psychosomatics, 68,* 3–14.

Arean, P. A., Perri, M. G., Nezu, A. M., Schein, R. L., Christopher, F., & Joseph, T. X. (1993). Comparative effectiveness of social problem-solving therapy and reminiscence therapy as treatments for depression in older adults. *Journal of Consulting and Clinical Psychology, 61,* 1003–1010.

Bandura, A. (1977). *A social learning theory.* Englewood Cliffs, NJ: Prentice-Hall.

Beck, A. T., Rush, A. J., Shaw, B. F., & Emery, G. (1979). *Cognitive therapy of depression.* New York: Guilford Press.

Beck, J. S. (1995). *Cognitive therapy: Basics and beyond.* New York: Guilford Press.

Belsher, G., & Costello, C. G. (1988). Relapse after recovery from unipolar depression: A critical review. *Psychological Bulletin, 104,* 84–96.

Blackburn, I. N., Bishop, S., Glen, A. I. M., Whalley, L. J., & Christie, J. E. (1981). The efficacy of cognitive therapy in depression: A treatment trial using cognitive therapy and pharmacotherapy, each alone and in combination. *British Journal of Psychiatry, 139,* 181–189.

Blackburn, I. N., & Moore, I. (1997). Controlled acute and follow-up trial of cognitive therapy and pharmacotherapy in outpatients with recurrent depression. *Behavioural and Cognitive Psychotherapy, 25,* 251–259.

Brewin, C. R. (1996). Theoretical foundations of cognitive-behavior therapy for anxiety and depression. *Annual Review of Psychology, 47,* 33–57.

Brown, R., & Lewinsohn, P. M. (1984). *The participant workbook for the Coping with Depression course.* Eugene, OR: Castalia.

Chambless, D. L., & Hollon, S. D. (1998). Defining empirically supported therapies. *Journal of Consulting and Clinical Psychology, 66,* 7–18.

Clark, D. A., Beck, A. T., & Alford, B. A. (1999). *Scientific foundations of cognitive theory and therapy of depression.* New York: Wiley.

Clarke, G. N., & Lewinsohn, P. M. (1989). The Coping with Depression course: A group psychoeducational intervention for unipolar depression. *Behavior Change, 6,* 54–69.

Clarke, G. N., Lewinsohn, P. M., & Hops, H. (1990). *Adolescent Coping with Depression course.* Eugene, OR: Castalia.

Coryell, W., Endicott, J., Winokur, G., Akiskal, H., Solomon, D., Loen, A., et al. (1995). Characteristics and significance of untreated major depressive disorders. *American Journal of Psychiatry, 152,* 1124–1129.

Coryell, W., & Winokur, G. (1992). Course and outcome. In E. S. Paykel (Ed.), *Handbook of affective disorders* (2nd ed., pp. 89–108). New York: Guilford Press.

Crits-Christoph, P., Baranackle, K., Kurcias, J. S., Beck, A. T., Carroll, K., Perry, K., et al. (1991). Meta-analysis of therapist effects in psychotherapy studies. *Psychotherapy Research, 1,* 81–91.

Cuijpers, P. (1998). A psychoeducational approach to the treatment of depression: A meta-analysis of Lewinsohn's "Coping with Depression" course. *Behavior Therapy, 29,* 521–533.

DeRubeis, R. J., & Feeley, M. (1990). Determinants of change in cognitive therapy for depression. *Cognitive Therapy and Research, 14,* 469–482.

Dimidjian, S., & Dobson, K. S. (in press). Process of change in cognitive therapy. In M. A. Reinecke & D. A. Clark (Eds.), *Cognitive therapy of emotional and behavioral disorders: Clinical and conceptual horizons.* Cambridge, MA: Cambridge University Press.

Dobson, K. S. (1989). A meta-analysis of the efficacy of cognitive therapy for depression. *Journal of Consulting and Clinical Psychology, 57,* 414–419.

Dobson, K. S. (Ed.). (2000). *Handbook of cognitive-behavioral therapies* (2nd ed.). New York: Guilford Press.

Dobson, K. S., & Dozois, D. J. A. (2000). Historical and philosophical bases of the cognitive-behavioral therapies. In K. S. Dobson (Ed.), *Handbook of cognitive-behavioral therapies* (2nd ed.). New York: Guilford Press.

Dryden, W., & Ellis, A. (2000). Rational-emotive behavior therapy. In K. S. Dobson (Ed.), *Handbook of cognitive-behavioral therapies* (2nd ed.). New York: Guilford Press.

D'Zurilla, T. J., & Goldfried, M. R. (1971). Problem solving and behavior modification. *Journal of Abnormal Psychology, 78,* 107–126.

D'Zurilla, T. J., & Nezu, A. M. (1999). *Problem solving therapy: A social competence approach to clinical intervention* (2nd ed.). New York: Springer.

Elkin, I., Shea, M. T., Watkins, J. T., Imber, S. D., Sotsky, S. M., Collins, J. F., et al. (1989). National Institute of Mental Health Treatment of Depression Collaborative Research Program: General effectiveness of treatments. *Archives of General Psychiatry, 46,* 971–982.

Ellis, A. (1962). *Reason and emotion in psychotherapy.* New York: Stuart.

Ellis, A. (1970). *The essence of rational psychotherapy: A comprehensive approach to treatment.* New York: Institute for Rational Living.

Ellis, A. (1995). Rational-emotive behavior therapy. In R. J. Corsini & D. Wedding (Eds.), *Current psychotherapies (5th ed., pp. 162–196).* Itasca, IL: Peacock.

Evans, M. D., Hollon, S. D., DeRubeis, R. J., Piasecki, J., Grove, W. B., & Tuason, V. B. (1992). Differential relapse following therapy and pharmacotherapy for depression. *Archives of General Psychiatry, 49,* 802–808.

Fava, G. A., Grandi, S., Zielezny, M. C., & Canestrari, R. (1996). Four-year outcome for cognitive behavioral treatment of residual symptoms in major depression. *American Journal of Psychiatry, 153,* 945–947.

Fava, G. A., Grandi, S., Zielezny, M. C., Canestrari, R., & Morphy, M. A. (1994). Cognitive behavioral treatment of residual symptoms in primary Major Depressive Disorder. *American Journal of Psychiatry, 151,* 1295–1299.

Fava, G. A., Rafanelli, C., Grandi, S., Conti, S., & Belluardo, P. (1998). Prevention of recurrent depression with cognitive behavioral therapy. *Archives of General Psychiatry, 55,* 816–820.

Feeley, M., DeRubeis, R. J., & Gefland, L. A. (1999). The temporal relation of adherence and alliance to symptom change in cognitive therapy for depression. *Journal of Consulting and Clinical Psychology, 64,* 578–582.

Fleming, B. M., & Thornton, D. W. (1980). Coping skills training as a component in the short-term treatment of depression. *Journal of Consulting and Clinical Psychology, 48,* 652–655.

Fuchs, C. Z., & Rehm, L. P. (1977). A self-control behavior therapy program for depression. *Journal of Consulting and Clinical Psychology, 45,* 206–215.

Gortner, E. T., Gollan, J. K., Dobson, K. S., & Jacobson, N. S. (1998). Cognitive-behavioral treatment for depression: Relapse prevention. *Journal of Consulting and Clinical Psychology, 66,* 377–384.

Gotlib, I. H., & Hammen, C. L. (1992). *Psychological aspects of depression: Toward a cognitive-interpersonal integration.* Chichester, England: Wiley.

Haaga, D. A. F., & Davison, G. C. (1993). An appraisal of rational-emotive therapy. *Journal of Consulting and Clinical Psychology, 61,* 215–220.

Hargreaves, W. A., Shumway, M., Hu, T., & Cuffel, B. (1998). *Cost-outcome methods for mental health.* San Diego, CA: Academic Press.

Cognitive-Behavioral Approaches to Depression 315

Heppner, P. P., & Petersen, C. H. (1982). The development and implications of a personal problem solving inventory. *Journal of Counseling Psychology, 29,* 66–75.

Hollon, S. D., & Beck, A. T. (1994). Cognitive and cognitive-behavioral therapies. In S. L. Garfield & A. E. Bergin (Eds.), *Handbook of psychotherapy and behavior change* (4th ed., pp. 428–466). New York: Wiley.

Hollon, S. D., & Kriss, M. R. (1984). Cognitive factors in clinical research and practice. *Clinical Psychology Review, 4,* 35–76.

Hollon, S. D., Shelton, R. C., & Loosen, P. T. (1991). Cognitive therapy and pharmacotherapy for depression. *Journal of Consulting and Clinical Psychology, 59,* 88–99.

Hussian, R. A., & Lawrence, P. S. (1981). Social reinforcement of activity and problem-solving training in the treatment of depressed institutionalized elderly patients. *Cognitive Therapy and Research, 5,* 57–69.

Jacobson, N. S., Dobson, K. S., Truax, P. A., Addis, M. E., Koerner, K., Gollan, J. K., et al. (1996). A component analysis of cognitive-behavioral treatment for depression. *Journal of Consulting and Clinical Psychology, 64,* 295–304.

Jacobson, N. S., Martell, C. R., & Dimidjian, S. (in press). Behavioral activation for depression: A contextual reformulation. *Clinical Psychology: Science and Practice.*

Jarrett, R. B., & Nelson, R. O. (1987). Mechanisms of change in cognitive therapy of depression. *Behavior Therapy, 18,* 227–241.

Jarrett, R. B., Schaffer, M., McIntire, D., Witt-Browder, A., Kraft, D., & Risser, R. C. (1999). Treatment of atypical depression with cognitive therapy or phenelzine. *Archives of General Psychiatry, 56,* 431–437.

Kanfer, F. H. (1970). Self-regulation: Research issues and speculations. In C. Neuringer & L. L. Michael (Eds.), *Behavior modification in clinical psychology* (pp. 178–220). New York: Appleton-Century-Crofts.

Kanfer, F. H. (1971). The maintenance of behavior by self-generated stimuli and reinforcement. In A. Jacob & L. B. Sachs (Eds.), *The psychology of private events: Perspectives on covert response systems* (pp. 39–59). New York: Academic Press.

Keller, M. B. (1994). Depression: A long-term illness. *British Journal of Psychiatry, 165,* 9–15.

Kendall, P. C., & Kriss, M. R. (1983). Cognitive-behavioral interventions. In C. E. Walker (Ed.), *The handbook of clinical psychology: Theory, research, and practice.* Homewood, IL: Dow Jones-Irwin.

Kornblith, S. J., Rehm, L. P., O'Hara, M. W., & Lamparski, D. M. (1983). The contribution of self-reinforcement training and behavioral assignments to the efficacy of self-control therapy for depression. *Cognitive Therapy and Research, 7,* 499–527.

Kovacs, M., Rush, A. J., Beck, A. T., & Hollon, S. D. (1981). Depressed outpatients treated with cognitive therapy or pharmacotherapy: A one-year follow-up. *Archives of General Psychiatry, 38,* 33–39.

Lewinsohn, P. M., Antonuccio, D. O., Steinmetz, J. L., & Teri, L. (1984). *The Coping with Depression course: A psychoeducational intervention for unipolar depression.* Eugene, OR: Castalia.

Lewinsohn, P. M., Clarke, G. N., Hops, H., & Andrews, J. A. (1990). Cognitive-behavioral treatment for depressed adolescents. *Behavior Therapy, 21,* 385–401.

Lewinsohn, P. M., Munoz, R. F., Youngren, M. A., & Zeiss, A. M. (1986). *Control your depression.* Englewood Cliffs, NJ: Prentice-Hall.

Lewinsohn, P. M., Solomon, A., Seeley, J. R., & Zeiss, A. (2000). Clinical implications of "subthreshold" depressive symptoms. *Journal of Abnormal Psychology, 109,* 345–351.

Lewinsohn, P. M., Steinmetz-Breckenridge, J., Antonuccio, D. O., & Teri, L. (1985). Group therapy for depression: The coping with depression course. *International Journal of Mental Health, 13,* 8–33.

Lovett, S., & Gallagher, D. (1988). Psychoeducational interventions for family caregivers: Preliminary efficacy data. *Behavior Therapy, 19,* 321–330.

Mahoney, M. J. (1974). *Cognition and behavior modification.* Cambridge, MA: Ballinger.

Mahoney, M. J., & Arnkoff, D. B. (1978). Cognitive and self-control therapies. In S. L. Garfield & A. E. Bergin (Eds.), *Handbook of psychotherapy and behavior change: An empirical analysis.* New York: Wiley.

Martell, C. R., Addis, M. E., & Jacobson, N. S. (2000). *Depression in context: Strategies for guided action.* New York: Norton.

Meichenbaum, D. (1977). *Cognitive-behavior modification.* New York: Springer.

Munoz, R. F., Ying, Y. W., Armas, R., Chan, F., & Guzza, R. (1987). The San Francisco Depression Prevention Project: A randomized trial with medical outpatients. In R. F. Munoz (Ed.), *Depression prevention: Research directions* (pp. 199–215). Washington, DC: Hemisphere.

Murphy, G. E., Simons, A. D., Wetzel, R. D., & Lustman, P. J. (1984). Cognitive therapy and pharmacotherapy: Singularly and together in the treatment of depression. *Archives of General Psychiatry, 41,* 33–41.

Mynors-Wallis, L. M., Gath, D. H., Lloyd-Thomas, A. R., & Tomlinson, D. (1995). Randomised controlled trial comparing problem solving treatment with amitrptyline and placebo for major depression in primary care. *British Medical Journal, 310,* 441–445.

Nezu, A. M. (1986). Efficacy of a social problem solving therapy approach for unipolar depression. *Journal of Consulting and Clinical Psychology, 54,* 196–202.

Nezu, A. M. (1987). A problem-solving formulation of depression: A literature review and proposal of a pluralistic model. *Clinical Psychology Review, 7,* 121–144.

Nezu, A. M., Nezu, C. M., & Perri, M. G. (1989). *Problem-solving therapy for depression: Therapy, research, and clinical guidelines.* New York: Wiley.

Nezu, A. M., & Perri, M. G. (1989). Social problem solving therapy for unipolar depression: An initial dismantling investigation. *Journal of Consulting and Clinical Psychology, 57,* 498–513.

Olfson, M. D., & Klerman, G. L. (1993). Trends in the prescription of antidepressants by office-based psychiatrists. *American Journal of Psychiatry, 150,* 571–577.

Organista, K. C., Munoz, R. F., & Gerardo, G. (1994). Cognitive-behavioral therapy for depression in low-income and minority medical outpatients: Description of a program and exploratory analyses. *Cognitive Therapy and Research, 18,* 241–259.

Persons, J. B., Burns, D. D., & Perloff, J. M. (1988). Predictors of dropout and outcome in cognitive therapy for depression in a private practice setting. *Cognitive Therapy and Research, 12,* 557–575.

Platt, J. J., & Spivak, G. (1975). *Manual for the Means-End Problem Solving procedure (MEPS): A measure of interpersonal cognitive problem-solving skills.* Hahnemann Community Health/Mental Retardation Center, Philadelphia.

Rehm, L. P. (1977). A self-control model of depression. *Behavior Therapy, 8,* 787–804.

Rehm, L. P. (1984). Self-management therapy for depression. *Advances in Behavior Research and Therapy, 6,* 83–98.

Rehm, L. P., Fuchs, C. Z., Roth, D. M., Kornblith, S. J., & Romano, J. M. (1979). A comparison of self-control and assertion skills treatments of depression. *Behavior Therapy, 10,* 429–442.

Rehm, L. P., Kaslow, N. J., & Rabin, A. S. (1987). Cognitive and behavioral targets in a self-control therapy program for depression. *Journal of Consulting and Clinical Psychology, 55,* 60–67.

Rehm, L. P., Kornblith, S. J., O'Hara, M. W., Lamparski, D. M., Romano, J. M., & Volkin, J. (1981). An evaluation of major components in a self-control behavior therapy program for depression. *Behavior Modification, 5,* 459–490.

Rush, A. J., Beck, A. T., Kovacs, J. M., & Hollon, S. D. (1977). Comparative efficacy of cognitive therapy and pharmacotherapy in outpatient depressives. *Cognitive Therapy and Research, 1,* 17–37.

Shaw, B. F. (1977). Comparison of cognitive therapy and behavior therapy in the treatment of depression. *Journal of Consulting and Clinical Psychology, 45,* 543–551.

Shea, M. T., Elkin, I., Imber, S. D., Sotsky, S. M., Watkins, J. T., Collins, J. F., et al. (1992). Course of depressive symptoms over follow-up: Findings from the National Institute of Mental Health Treatment of Depression Collaborative Research Program. *Archives of General Psychiatry, 49,* 782–787.

Simons, A. D., Murphy, G. E., Levine, J. L., & Wetzel, R. D. (1986). Cognitive therapy and pharmacotherapy for depression: Sustained improvement over one year. *Archives of General Psychiatry, 43,* 43–48.

Steinmetz-Breckenridge, J., Thompson, L. W., Breckenridge, J. N., & Gallagher, D. E. (1985). Behavioral group therapy with the elderly: A psychoeducational approach. In D. Upper & S. Ross (Eds.), *Handbook of behavioral group therapy* (pp. 275–302). New York: Plenum Press.

Teasdale, J. D., & Fennell, M. J. (1982). Immediate effects on depression of cognitive therapy interventions. *Cognitive Therapy and Research, 6,* 343–352.

Thompson, L. W., Gallagher, D., Nies, G., & Epstein, D. (1983). Evaluation of the effectiveness of professionals and nonprofessionals as instructors of Coping with Depression classes for elders. *The Gerontologist, 23,* 390.

Weissman, A. N., & Beck, A. T. (1978, November). *Development and validation of the dysfunctional attitude scale: A preliminary investigation.* Paper presented at the meeting of the American Educational Research Association, Toronto, Canada.

Wilson, P. H., Goldin, J. C., & Charbonneau-Powis, M. (1983). Comparative efficacy of behavioral and cognitive treatments of depression. *Cognitive Therapy and Research, 7,* 111–124.

World Health Organization. (1996). *Multiaxial classification of child and adolescent psychiatric disorders.* New York: Cambridge University Press.

CHAPTER 14

Acceptance and Commitment Therapy in Experiential Avoidance Disorders

Steven C. Hayes, Julieann Pankey, Elizabeth V. Gifford,
Sonja V. Batten, and Rene Quiñones

HISTORY OF THE ACCEPTANCE AND COMMITMENT THERAPY APPROACH

In psychology, psychopathology and its treatment is driven by an *assumption of healthy normality*, the belief that psychological health is the natural homeostatic state that is disturbed only by psychological illness or distress. Based on this assumption, the purpose of psychopathological models is to identify the unusual processes that result in psychological disorders and to return these processes to normal in treatment so that normal functioning will result.

Acceptance and commitment therapy (ACT; Hayes, Strosahl, & Wilson, 1999) comes from a different view: the *assumption of destructive normality*. This assumption holds that ordinary human psychological processes can themselves lead to extremely destructive and dysfunctional results and can amplify or exacerbate unusual pathological processes.

The evidence for the assumption of destructive normality is first and foremost the pervasiveness of human suffering itself. Human beings are enormously privileged creatures in material terms, and yet when one adds up major disorders categorized in the *Diagnostic and Statistical Manual of Mental Disorders (DSM)*, domestic violence, abuse, sexual concerns, poor relationship skills, severe shyness, family problems, suicidal thoughts, and so on, almost no human life is left untouched. It is, in effect, entirely normal to be abnormal. For human beings, suffering in the midst of comfort, health, and material plenty is commonplace.

Preparation of this manuscript was supported in part by a grant from the National Institute of Health, National Institute on Drug Abuse, R01 DA08634 and R01 DA13106.

If one adopts the view that what is normal is often destructive, two things happen. First, one begins to look anew at ordinary psychological processes in search of the seeds of psychopathology. Second, one begins to abandon the idea that we will eliminate such processes; instead, the goal is to work within these processes to accomplish more productive outcomes.

A normal process that is most likely at the core of a great deal of human suffering is human language and cognition. Many cultural traditions have taken the same stance (see, e.g., the biblical story of the Garden of Eden); indeed, psychopathologists implicitly do so every time they use the words "mental illness." What about human language and cognition would have destructive effects? ACT is based on a specific answer to that question.

To some degree, this question and its answer both emerge from the pragmatic behavioral tradition. It is a tenet of this tradition that fundamental processes do not differ between "normal" and "abnormal" populations. However, the answer ACT provides represents a unique expansion of the historical parameters of behavior therapy. Traditional operant behavior therapies would not have asked questions about human language and cognition as they did not emphasize issues such as language, cognition, and emotion. As behavior therapies developed into *cognitive* behavioral therapies and made efforts to deal with complex clinical phenomena, techniques and diagnostic approaches from other traditions were added (such as the information-processing models of basic cognitive science). However, these techniques and approaches did not necessarily represent systematic integration at the level of basic behavioral science (Wilson, Gifford, & Hayes, 1997). ACT has been developed as an integration of theory, technology, and experimental research. It is a cognitive-behavioral therapy that returns to its basic behavioral roots, using recent developments in behavioral science to expand on these roots in a coherent and integrated fashion to address the complex cognitive and language processes involved in human suffering.

EXPERIMENTAL LITERATURE: RELATIONAL FRAME THEORY AND EXPERIENTIAL AVOIDANCE

The ACT approach to psychopathology and its treatment is based on a 15-year program of basic research on the behavioral processes underlying language and cognition. In this section, we outline that work (for more detailed account, see Hayes, Barnes-Holmes, & Roche, 2001) and discuss an additional relevant experimental literature underlying the ACT treatment model, the literature on thought suppression.

STIMULUS EQUIVALENCE

Stimulus equivalence provides a simple example of what we believe to be the essence of human verbal behavior. The fundamental phenomenon is usually examined in a matching-to-sample paradigm. An unfamiliar stimulus (such as a graphical squiggle or a series of three consonants) is presented at the top of a computer screen. A set of perhaps three novel comparison stimuli is provided. The subject is then rewarded for selecting the correct comparison stimuli. Comparison stimuli are arbitrarily assigned as either correct or incorrect by the experimenter. There is no formal property of the stimulus that provides a basis for correctness. In this way, the organism is taught that given stimulus A1 (we are using the label A1 for ease of understanding, but in fact, the actual stimulus would be an arbitrary one such as a graphical squiggle) and comparisons B1, B2, and B3, pick B1, not B2 or B3. In further training, the organism might be taught that given the stimulus A1 and another set of comparisons, C1, C2, and C3, pick C1. The stimuli that are incorrect would be correct in the presence of other samples. Given stimulus A2 and the comparisons B1, B2, and B3, for example, the subject would be taught to pick B2, not B1 or B3.

Such conditional discriminations can be trained in any complex organism (e.g., rats, pigeons, or people). What is striking, however, are the derived performances that result. Human infants as young as 17 months (Lipkens, Hayes, & Hayes, 1993) readily select A1 without explicit feedback or training—what is called symmetry. Similarly, if presented with a trial with B1 as the sample, and with C1, C2, and C3 as the comparisons, humans readily select C1, whereas nonhumans respond at chance levels. We can think of equivalence classes this way: Train two sides of a triangle in any one direction; as a result, humans, but apparently not nonhumans (see Hayes, Barnes-Holmes, et al., 2001, for a review) will show all sides in all directions.

What makes stimulus equivalence clinically relevant is that functions given to one member of an equivalence class tend to transfer to other members. Consider a simple example. Suppose a child has never before seen or played with a cat. After learning the word → object and word → oral name relations, the child can derive four additional relations: object → word, oral name → word, oral name → object, and object → oral name. Now suppose that the child is scratched while playing with a cat. The child may cry and run away. Later, the child hears mother saying, "Oh, look! A cat." Now the child again cries and runs away even though the child was never scratched in the presence of the words "Oh, look! A cat."

These kinds of processes are not based on the simple and familiar processes of stimulus generalization because there are no formal properties that bring these stimuli together. These new forms of behavior are established through indirect means. Such effects may help explain why, for example, agoraphobics can have an initial panic attack while "trapped" in a shopping mall and soon find that they are worrying about being "trapped" in an open field, in a marital relationship, on a bridge, or in a job. What brings these situations together is not their formal properties in a simple sense, but the verbal classes in which they share membership.

RELATIONAL FRAME THEORY

Equivalence is a beginning model of word-referent relations, but it is not enough to explain the functions of verbal rules or the complexity of human language. Relational frame theory (RFT; Hayes, Barnes-Holmes, et al., 2001) expands stimulus equivalence into the larger, more general case.

RFT begins with the idea that organisms can learn to respond relationally to various stimulus events, but adds the idea that a wide variety of relations can be learned and brought under contextual control. Such contextual control has been demonstrated in stimulus equivalence research (e.g., Wulfert & Hayes, 1988) and it is obvious in natural language. For example, the spoken word "bat" has a different meaning when in a dark cave as opposed to being at a baseball game. The final key point in RFT is that the functions of events in a relational network can be mutually transformed based on the relations among events.

According to RFT, derived stimulus relations are the core of human cognition. There are three main properties of relating as a learned class of behavior. First, such relations show mutual entailment. That is, if a person learns in a particular context that A relates in a particular way to B, then this must entail some kind of relation between B and A in that context. For example, if Alan is said to be larger than Bob, then Bob must be smaller than Alan. We also call this property bidirectionality. Second, such relations show combinatorial entailment: If a person learns in a particular context that A relates in a particular way to B and B relates in a particular way to C, then this must entail some kind of mutual relation between A and C in that context. For example, if Bob is larger than Charlie, then Alan is also larger than Charlie. Finally, such relations enable a transformation of stimulus functions among related stimuli. If you need a person to fight an enemy and Charlie is known to be valuable, Alan is probably even more valuable. These kinds of derived stimulus functions have been demonstrated with consequential functions (Hayes, Brownstein, Devany, Kohlenberg, & Shelby, 1987; Hayes, Kohlenberg, & Hayes, 1991), antecedent functions (Hayes et al., 1987), and elicited emotional responses (Dougher, Augustson, Markham, & Greenway, 1994). Relational frames are learned patterns of contextually controlled and arbitrarily applicable relational responding involving mutual entailment, combinatorial entailment, and the transformation of stimulus functions.

An important finding that becomes relevant as this theory is applied is that the derived stimulus relations are extraordinarily difficult to break up, even with direct, contradictory training (Wilson & Hayes, 1996). Once verbal relations are derived, they never seem to go away; you can add to them, but you cannot eliminate them altogether. Furthermore, derived relational responding will be maintained indefinitely by "sense making." Basic research shows that once we learn how to derive relations among events, we do so constantly as long as we are able to make order out of our world by doing so (e.g., Leonhard & Hayes, 1991).

According to RFT, human language and cognition are both dependent on relational frames. When we think, reason, speak with meaning, or listen with understanding, we do so by deriving relations among events: among words and events, words and words, events and events. Because of the mutual entailment quality of relational frames, when a human interacts verbally with his or her own behavior, the psychological meaning of both the verbal symbol and the behavior itself can change. RFT argues that it is this bidirectional property that makes human self-awareness useful. For example, if an incorrect choice is made, evaluation of that choice will alter the function of the original environment when it is next encountered. This same property of human cognition, however, makes self-awareness painful.

A nonhuman animal can easily be taught a form of self-awareness, but it does not have this bidirectional quality. For example, suppose we teach a pigeon (using food as a consequence) to peck one key after it has been shocked and another after it has not been shocked. We are, in effect, asking the pigeon whether it has been shocked and the bird is "answering." These answers are not, however, bidirectionally related to the original condition. For that reason, the bird will as readily "report" about the shock as it will report about the absence of shock, and without negative emotional arousal. These reports, after all, lead to food, not shock.

Humans are quite different. For the verbally competent human, the word shock and the actual shock participate in an equivalence relation and therefore share some stimulus functions. From an RFT perspective, this is why humans often cry when reporting past hurts and traumas, even (or perhaps especially) if the report has never been made before. The crying comes because the report is mutually related to the event itself, not because the report itself has been directly associated in the past with aversive events.

This process presents an extreme challenge. A nonhuman animal trying to avoid pain can avoid the situations in which it occurs. A human cannot because language allows pain to occur in almost any situation through derived relations. In self-defense, humans begin to try to avoid the painful thoughts and feelings themselves, what we term "experiential avoidance," even though this is often tremendously destructive in the long run, as we show in a later section.

Even though this process is harmful, it is not obvious what alternatives there are. Verbal rules gradually dominate over other sources of behavioral regulation in humans (what we term "cognitive fusion"), a process extensively researched in our laboratory (see Hayes, 1989). Data from a study by Hayes, Brownstein, Haas, and Greenway (1986) provide an example. In this study, subjects learned a task either by directly following a rule or by experience. Later, the task requirements were changed, without any notice being given to the subjects. All of the subjects who learned the task by experience were sensitive to the change, compared to only half of the subjects who originally learned the task by following verbal rules.

From an RFT perspective, even such a simple rule as "I can't stand this feeling" can lead human beings into years of needless struggle. Problems with rules regarding experiential avoidance are confirmed by the experimental literature on the effects of suppression, which we will review briefly.

EXPERIMENTAL RESEARCH ON
EXPERIENTIAL AVOIDANCE

A growing body of literature indicates that, in general, attempts to suppress unwanted private experiences can be detrimental. Emotion-focused and -avoidant strategies have been found to negatively predict outcome in a variety of clinical domains, including depression (DeGenova, Patton, Jurich, & MacDermid, 1994), substance abuse (Ireland, McMahon, Malow, & Kouzekanani, 1994), and sequelae of child sexual abuse (Leitenberg, Greenwald, & Cado, 1992). The thought suppression literature provides insight into some of the processes underlying the deleterious effects of avoidance.

Work on thought suppression began with Wegner and colleagues, who found that deliberate attempts to suppress target thoughts actually increased the occurrence of these thoughts (Clark, Ball, & Pape, 1991; Clark, Winton, & Thynn, 1993; Wegner, Schneider, Carter, & White, 1987). For example, participants told to suppress thoughts of a white bear reported higher frequencies of thoughts about white bears (Wegner, 1989; Wegner & Zanakos, 1994; Wegner et al., 1987). These increases occurred in one of two ways. Some studies found an immediate enhancement effect, where suppressed thoughts immediately increase in frequency (Lavy & Van den Hout, 1990; Merckelbach, Muris, Van den Hout, & de Jong, 1991). Other studies have found that efforts to suppress succeeded in the short term but resulted in a rebound effect, that is, an increase in frequency above baseline levels when active suppression ceases (e.g., Clark et al., 1991).

Since its inception, the thought suppression literature has expanded to include the role of mood and autonomic activity in suppression conditions. For example, mood and suppressed thoughts appear to become linked in the course of suppression, such that the reactivation of one leads to the reinstatement of the other (Wenzlaff, Wegner, & Klein, 1991). In addition, autonomic arousal appears to be a common physiological reaction to the suppression of emotional thoughts (Cottington, Matthews, Talbott, & Kuller, 1986; Dimsdale, Pierce, Schoenfeld, & Brown, 1986; Wegner, Shortt, Blake, & Page, 1990; Wegner et al., 1987). Wegner et al. (1990) found that trying not to think about sex increased electrodermal responding as much as did thinking about sex. Participants instructed to suppress their emotions while watching a distressing film showed greater constriction of peripheral vasculature and greater electrodermal activity than those in the nonsuppression condition (Gross & Levenson, 1993). Individuals who suppress thoughts on a chronic basis show a pattern of physiological responses that appear to be consistent with anxiety (Lorig, Singer, Bonanno, & Davis, 1995).

Suppression studies such as those alluded to above have been applied across a wide range of content areas and experimental situations. Subjects shown a distressing movie who were asked to suppress their thoughts about the movie for 10 minutes after viewing had more intrusive thoughts about the movie than subjects who had not previously suppressed (Davies & Clark, 1998). Subjects asked to read a transcription of Freud's Ratman obsession who were asked to avoid all thoughts about the transcript reported more frequent thoughts about the transcript after one week (Muris & Merckelbach, 1997). Spider phobics who were asked to suppress thoughts about spiders showed an increase in thoughts of spiders after their efforts to suppress (Zeitlin, Netten, & Hodder, 1995). Subjects instructed not to think stereotypically about a photograph of a skinhead showed an increase in use of stereotypical constructs in a later writing task and increased priming of stereotypic constructs in a priming task and chose to sit at a greater distance from a skinhead immediately after the suppression task (Macrae, Bodenhausen, Milne, & Jetten, 1994). Subjects told to put their hands in painfully cold water and instructed to suppress their painful sensations were slower to recover and rated later innocuous stimuli as more aversive (Cioffi & Holloway, 1993).

Such findings provide a description of the ways in which rules regarding avoidance or suppression of experiential stimuli can become counterproductive. If individuals react to the presence of certain thoughts and feelings with efforts to suppress, such efforts are likely to lead to amplification. As a simple example, dieters who "try not to think about food" often find themselves completely obsessed. As a more complex clinical example, analog studies examining the suppression of thoughts with traumatic content have found that efforts to suppress such thoughts increase traumatic intrusions. These processes may contribute to the perpetuation of posttraumatic stress symptoms experienced by some individuals after a traumatic event (Davies & Clark, 1998; Harvey & Bryant, 1998).

The experimental literatures reviewed above—on suppression and on derived relations—provide us with a view into the cognitive and verbal processes that define the human condition. Where powerful stimulus functions adhere in verbal formulations (as the literature on derived relations illustrates) and these functions are organized in rules that structure the perceived world (as the literature on rules illustrates), the processes that permit verbal humans to imagine worlds unseen, to envision futures, to plan and carry out intentional activity are the same processes that produce incapacitating anxiety, hopelessness about the future, and suicidality.

Such processes are powerful enough to reshape the world. Therefore, it is perhaps unsurprising that these processes can run amok. For example, fusing with the thought "I simply can't have this feeling," that is, responding to the stimulus functions of this thought as literal truth rather than observing the thought *as a thought* emerging from one's history, can carry with it a host of problems. The literature on suppression supports the futility of efforts to avoid aspects of internal experience and some of the problematic outcomes attendant on these efforts. Unfortunately, the culture teaches many instances of these rules, and almost everyone's history contains examples of them. The means by which ACT intervenes on these processes is discussed in the following section.

ASSESSMENT AND INTERVENTION

ASSESSMENT METHODS

Assessment in ACT occurs early and continues throughout the course of treatment. In the early stages, the history and current strength of mal-adaptive behaviors are examined. Maladaptive behaviors are those that interfere with clients engaging in concrete behaviors in alignment with their values. Because the assumption is that cognitive fusion and experiential avoidance may underlie these problems, a detailed assessment is made of what the client has done to solve these problems, with an eye toward fusion and avoidance processes that may be entangled with these solution attempts.

Because the goal of ACT is to have clients choose to act effectively by engaging in concrete behaviors in alignment with their values, even in the presence of difficult or interfering private events, a careful assessment of client values is considered essential (a detailed values assessment procedure for ACT can be found in Chapter 8 of Hayes, Strosahl, et al., 1999).

Values provide an overall direction; specific goals and actions that would lead to these goals, and barriers that would prevent such actions, must also be part of this stage of assessment. In the analysis of barriers, particular emphasis is given to (1) possible avoided private events, their domains and dimensions, and possible feared consequences of experiencing avoided private events, and to (2) literally held thoughts or rules, including the client's reasons and ex-planations for behavior. Feared consequences for defusing from literally held thoughts are also explored. The assessment of values, goals, actions, and barriers most often is timed to fol-low work on cognitive defusion and experiential willingness, but to precede concrete behavior change strategies.

Finally, this specific analysis is fit into a broader functional analysis of the problem be-haviors. This adds external antecedents and consequences to the more psychological ap-proach that flows readily from the ACT model.

Several ACT-specific assessment tools have been developed, in addition to the values assess-ment tools already mentioned. These include the daily diary assessment of suffering, struggle,

and workability (see Hayes, Strosahl, et al., 1999); process assessment measures for scoring ACT sessions (e.g., Khorakiwala, 1991; Mc-Curry, 1991); and a paper-and-pencil measure of acceptance, the Acceptance and Action Ques-tionnaire (Hayes et al., 1996).

INTERVENTION METHODS

The general clinical goals of ACT are loosening the grip of the verbal content of language, aban-doning maladaptive behavior based on this ver-bal content, and focusing instead on more useful forms of behavior change. There are several more specific domains of ACT intervention, and each has its own specific methodology, exer-cises, homework, and metaphors. The following is a brief synopsis of these areas:

Creative hopelessness.

Control is the problem, not the solution.

Acceptance as an alternative agenda.

A transcendent sense of self.

Defusing language and cognition.

Values.

Willingness and commitment.

The ACT therapeutic relationship.

Creative Hopelessness

The goal of the first stage of ACT is to identify the strategies that the client has employed to this point and to assess the extent to which the current agenda has worked so far. To some ex-tent, the fact that the client is even presenting for therapy means that what the client has tried to do hasn't worked well enough. In the earliest stage of therapy, we work to identify the strategies that have been used thus far, so that we can focus on new approaches rather than spending time and energy on something that has not worked. In exploring previously used tactics, the client is asked to consider the possibility that the problem is not that the client has not tried hard enough or has not been motivated enough. Instead, perhaps it is the case that the agenda that the client is working on is part of the problem and will actually never bring the client closer to the goals that he or she values.

We should be clear here about what we mean by the term creative hopelessness. Generally, hopelessness is evaluated as a negative thing. However, in ACT, we are not trying to instill a *feeling* of hopelessness. Instead, we are trying to help clients see that maybe the things they have been trying are not working and are even hopeless. If clients can stop doing what has not been working, then perhaps there is something else to try. This type of hopelessness is creative because it allows clients to let go of the struggle and try something new.

It is important to allow individuals to come into experiential contact with the effectiveness of their change agendas without bringing therapist judgment into the conversation. The arbiter during this exploration is never the therapist's opinion, it is the client's experience (Hayes, Pankey, & Gregg, 2000).

A dialogue in this phase of ACT might look something like this:

THERAPIST: So, you are telling me you've tried quite of number of things to attempt to control your depression. You've tried ignoring it; you've tried toughing it out; you've tried withdrawing into a cocoon; you've tried prayer; you've tried to have others help. What is your sense of how these things have worked for you?

CLIENT: Well, I've tried and tried and I can't seem to find something that works. I just want to make it stop.

THERAPIST: You've certainly tried different things.

CLIENT: Yes, I'm so confused. My husband told me the other day that he thinks I want to be depressed. But it's not true. I've done everything I know how to do and nothing works.

THERAPIST: It looks like that to me. You've done all the usual things people do. I think you have tried your best. And bottom line is, it's not working. So I want you to consider this. You know it *hasn't* worked. What if it *can't* work?

CLIENT: What do you mean? I feel stuck then. Okay, so now I'm really confused.

THERAPIST: Good. Maybe we are in a place where we can do some work. Because you've already tried all the obvious stuff. You've already done what makes sense to you and yet you are here. So, perhaps these things you've tried simply *cannot* work. Maybe these so-called solutions are actually part of the problem.

Confusion is used deliberately to prevent clients from intellectualizing and compartmentalizing their dilemmas into the same solutions that have already failed (Hayes & Wilson, 1994). In this context, the therapist can introduce the idea that the client's agenda is indeed hopeless because the client has already attempted a variety of solutions to the problem and is still seeking help. Here, the great deal of effort yet minimal payoff clients have has experienced from their control strategies and avoidance attempts can be highlighted from a compassionate stance. From an ACT standpoint, the greatest ally clients have is their own pain. If the logical and reasonable strategy of avoidance worked, no one would ever question it (Hayes et al., 2000).

An important cornerstone of ACT therapy is the use of metaphor and metaphorical language to undermine language-induced struggle. Metaphors can have an impact without invoking the client's normal verbal defenses (Hayes, Strosahl, et al., 1999).

One of the core ACT metaphors introduced in the context of creative hopelessness is the *person in the hole metaphor.* This is a flexible metaphor that can be used to help clients understand on a more experiential level the unworkability of their struggle.

Clients are asked to imagine that they are a person who has been placed in an open field, blindfolded, with a tool bag to carry, and told that living a life means running around that field. Unfortunately, the field is filled with a variety of large holes. Inevitably, they fall into one of the holes and are stuck at the bottom, much as they are stuck in the current predicament. After a while, they feel inside the tool bag to see if there is something there that would help. It contains nothing but a shovel. So they dig, with big scoop or little, fast scoop or slow. But the hole is not getting smaller, it's getting bigger. And here they are, seeing a therapist, in the secret hope that therapy is a really *huge* shovel. But shovels aren't for getting out of holes—shovels make holes.

Often, clients will suggest a variety of options, including giving up and creative ways to change the tool. As clients bring up different options, the therapist has the opportunity to address them as strategies.

CLIENT: I'm going to yell for someone to help me.

THERAPIST: Right. And you've probably even tried that, haven't you? And yet, here you are, still in the depression hole.

CLIENT: I don't understand. This is crazy. There is always a solution—I need to find it.

THERAPIST: Listen to what your mind is giving you there. Isn't that a dusty, old thought? There is an answer: I must find it. And what does your experience say about how well that thought has paid off? What if no amount of digging will ever work? In that case, the first thing we may really need to do is to give up on digging, and maybe even before any alternatives present themselves.

Part of the power of metaphors is that they allow clients to explore issues in the world of common sense. It really is true that digging is a poor way to get out of a hole. The quicksand metaphor has some of that same value:

> It could be as if you were caught in quicksand. Of course, you'd try what you know how to do to get out, but almost everything you know about how to get out will only get you deeper in the quicksand. The only thing to do with quicksand is to spread out and try to get yourself fully in contact with the quicksand. Maybe your situation is like that. It may not make logical sense at first, but maybe what you need to do is to stop struggling and instead get fully in contact with what you have been struggling with.

A list of some other ACT techniques in this area is shown in Table 14.1.

Control Is the Problem

Human beings are great problem solvers. They use their logical abilities to tackle problems head-on. Often, it works. In the world outside of one's own skin, figuring out how to get rid of something and then getting rid of it work quite well. In the world inside one's skin, this is not so easy. Trying not to feel anxious is itself an anxiety-provoking thing to do. Trying not to have an urge focuses one's attention on it and makes it more likely.

In the second component of ACT, therapists target emotional and cognitive control as a core obstacle preventing successful solution of the problems in living the client faces (Hayes & Wilson, 1994). As human beings, we are taught early to control emotions and thoughts, to "stop that crying," to "handle ourselves," and to "buck up." It becomes apparent at a young age that when we are asked how we are doing or feeling, the most appropriate and reinforced social response is "Fine."

When applied to the world inside the skin, control strategies may be effective in the short run but become increasingly ineffective as time goes on. A useful metaphor for introducing

Table 14.1 Creative hopelessness/control is a problem.

Purpose: Notice that there is a change agenda in place and the basic unworkability of that system. Name the system Control and examine why this does not work.

Method: Draw out what the client has tried to make things better, examine whether they have worked, and create space for something new to happen.

When to use: As a precursor to the rest of the work in order for new responses to emerge.

Example of techniques designed to increase clients' creative hopelessness:

Creative hopelessness	Are they willing to consider that there might be another way, but it requires not knowing?
What brought you into treatment?	Bring into sessions sense of being stuck, life being off track, etc.
Person in the hole exercise	Illustrate that they are doing something and it is not working.
Chinese handcuffs metaphor	No matter how hard they pull to get out of them, pushing in is what it takes.
Noticing the struggle	Tug of war with a monster; the goal is to drop the rope, not win the war.
Driving with the rearview mirror	Even though control strategies are taught, it doesn't mean they work.
Clear out old to make room for new	Field full of dead trees that need to be burned down for new trees to grow.
Break down reliance on old agenda	"Isn't that like you? Isn't that familiar? Does something about that one feel old?"
Paradox	Telling clients their confusion is a good outcome.
Feedback screech metaphor	It's not the noise that is the problem, it's the amplification.
Control is a problem	How they struggle against it—control strategies (ways they try to control or avoid inner experience).
The paradox of control	"If you aren't willing to have it, you've got it."
Illusion of control metaphors	Fall in love, jelly doughnut, what are the numbers exercise.
Consequences of control	Polygraph metaphor.
Willingness versus control	Two scales metaphor.
Costs of low willingness	Box full of stuff metaphor, clean versus dirty discomfort.

control as a problem is the *chocolate cake exercise.* It's quite simple. The therapist tells the client the following:

> I'm going to tell you something very soon. When I do, I want you to immediately stop thinking about what I am telling you. Okay, here goes. Don't think about chocolate cake. You know how chocolate cake is: warm and smelling so good right out of the oven . . . Don't think about it! . . . The icing when you bite into the first piece, the warm moist pieces of chocolate . . . Yum. But don't think about it!

Most clients will laugh and say it is impossible to stop thinking about the cake. This exercise is a concrete example of the futility of attempting to control or suppress some thoughts. Another quick strategy to introduce control as a problem is to tell the client "I'll give you $10 million to fall in love, right here, right now. You fall in love and you've got it." Most clients will smile and say something along the lines of "I wish I could do that, a million bucks sounds great about now!" An exercise of this nature gives the therapist the opportunity to identify the inability of human beings to control private experiences and to elevate awareness of control instructions in language.

The *polygraph metaphor* is a core intervention at this stage of ACT therapy. This metaphor has utility in demonstrating the paradoxical aspects of attempts to control emotion, particularly negative emotion:

THERAPIST: Now suppose I have you hooked up to the world's most sensitive polygraph machine. I want you to imagine that this machine is incredibly effective in measuring anxiety. The task is simple. All you have to do is stay relaxed. However, I know you want to do well, to try hard, so I am going to add an extra incentive here. I will have a loaded .44 Magnum trained at your skull. You must stay calm or I'm going to shoot you. I'll kill you if you get anxious, which I'll know you are based on this polygraph. What do you think might happen here? The tiniest bit of anxiety would terrify you, wouldn't it?

CLIENT: Oh man, that is scary to think about.

THERAPIST: It is, because you know how difficult it would be to try to keep calm. This is the paradox with controlling emotion. If you aren't willing to have it, you will.

Acceptance as an Alternative Agenda

If the therapist has been able to establish the client's control agenda as destructive, it becomes useful to point to the alternative: acceptance and willingness. Metaphors such as the *two scales metaphor* are used to introduce the concept of control and its relationship to psychological distress:

Imagine there are two scales, like the volume knobs on a stereo. One is right out here in front of us and it is called Anxiety. [Use labels that fit the client's situation such as Anger, Guilt, Urges, Worry. It may also help to move your hand as if it is moving up and down a numerical scale.] It can go from 0 to 10. In the posture you're in, what brought you in here was this: "This anxiety is too

high." In other words, you have been trying to pull the pointer down on this scale [the therapist can use the other hand to pull down unsuccessfully on the anxiety hand]. But now there's also another scale. It's been hidden. It is hard to see. This other scale can also go from 0 to 10 [move the other hand up and down behind your head so you can't see it].

What we have been doing is gradually preparing the way so that we can see this other scale. We've been bringing it around to look at it [move the other hand around in front]. It is really the more important of the two, because it is this one that makes the difference and it is the only one that you can control. This second scale is called Willingness. It refers to how open you are to experiencing your own experience when you experience it—without trying to manipulate it, avoid it, escape it, change it, and so on. When Anxiety is up here at 10, and you're trying hard to control this anxiety, make it go down, make it go away, then you're *un*willing to feel this anxiety. In other words, the Willingness scale is at 0.

But that is a terrible combination. It's like a ratchet or something. You know how a ratchet wrench works? When you have a ratchet set one way, no matter how you turn the handle on the wrench, it can only tighten the bolt. It's like that. When anxiety is high and willingness is low, the ratchet is on and anxiety can't go down. That's because if you are really, really unwilling to have anxiety, then anxiety is something to be anxious about. It's as if when anxiety is high, and willingness drops down, the anxiety kind of locks into place. So, what we need to do in this therapy is shift our focus from the anxiety scale to the willingness scale. You've been trying to control anxiety for a long time, and it just doesn't work. It's not that you weren't clever enough; it simply doesn't work. Instead of working on the anxiety scale, we will turn our focus to the willingness scale. Unlike the anxiety scale, which you can't move around at will, the willingness scale is something you can set anywhere. It is not a reaction, not a feeling or a thought—it is a choice. You've had it set low. You came in here with it set low. In fact, coming in here at all may initially have been a reflection of its low setting. What we need to do is get it set high. If you do this, I can guarantee that if you stop trying to control anxiety, your anxiety will be low . . . [pause] or . . . it will be high. I promise you! And when it is low, it will be low, until it's not low and then it will be high. And when it is high it will be high until it isn't high anymore. Then it will be low again. I'm not teasing you. There just aren't good words for what it is like to have the willingness scale set high.

At this point, willingness is merely opened up briefly. It will mean much more when the therapy turns into active exposure and behavior change. Thus, we revisit willingness and acceptance later.

A Transcendent Sense of Self

It is not realistic to ask clients to expose themselves to their most feared emotions and thoughts until they can see directly that their survival will not be threatened by such exposure. There is one aspect of human experience that usually provides a fairly firm foundation: continuity of consciousness. Seeing that there is a part of themselves that is constant provides great comfort to clients being asked to do what they have avoided, often for their entire life. The *chessboard metaphor* is a central ACT metaphor for the distinction between self and avoided psychological content:

It's as if there is a chessboard that goes out infinitely in all directions. It's covered with different pieces, black pieces and white pieces. They work together in teams, as in chess: The white pieces fight against the black pieces. You can think of your thoughts and feelings and beliefs as these pieces; they sort of hang out together in teams too. For example, "bad" feelings (anxiety, depression, resentment) hang out with "bad" thoughts and "bad" memories; same thing with the "good" ones. So it seems that the way the game is played is that we select which side we want to win. We put the "good" pieces (thoughts

that are self-confident, feelings of being in control) on one side, and the "bad" pieces on the other. Then we get up on the back of the white queen and ride to battle, fighting to win the war against anxiety, depression, or thoughts about using drugs. It's a war game. But there's a logical problem here, and that is that from this posture, huge portions of yourself are your own enemy. In other words, if you need to be in this war, there is something wrong with you. And even though these pieces are in you (they are different facets of your experience), from the level of the pieces, they can be as big as or even bigger than you. Plus, even though it is not logical, the more you fight, the bigger they get. If it is true that "If you are not willing to have it, you've got it," then as you fight them, they get more central to your life, more habitual, more dominating, and more linked to every area of living. The logical idea is that you will knock enough of them off the board and eventually will dominate them, except your experience tells you that the exact opposite happens. Apparently, the black pieces can't be deliberately knocked off the board. So the battle goes on. You feel hopeless, you have a sense that you can't win, and yet you can't stop fighting. If you're on the back of that white horse, fighting is the only choice you have because the black pieces seem life-threatening. Yet living in a war zone is no way to live.

As the client connects with this metaphor, it can be turned to the issue of the self:

THERAPIST: Now, let me ask you to think about this carefully. In this metaphor, suppose you aren't the chess pieces. Who are you?

CLIENT: Am I the player?

THERAPIST: That may be what you have been trying to be. Notice, though, that a player has a big investment in how this war turns out. Besides, who are you playing against? Some other player? So, suppose you're not that either.

CLIENT: Am I the board?

THERAPIST: It's useful to look at it that way. Without a board, these pieces have no place to be. The board holds them. If you're the pieces, the game is very important. You've got to win, your life depends on it. But if you're the board, it doesn't matter if the war stops or not.

A list of some additional ACT techniques in this area is shown in Table 14.2.

Defusing Language
The ACT therapist seeks to disrupt the usual meaning functions of language so that the ongoing process of framing events relationally is evident in the moment. Cognitive defusion techniques erode the tight equivalence classes and verbal relations that establish stimulus functions through verbal processes (Hayes, Strosahl, et al., 1999).

A number of verbal conventions are adopted with ACT clients, designed to increase the psychological distance between the client and the client's private events. An example of a language convention has to do with our use of the words "but" and "and." *But* literally means that the phase that follows the word contradicts what

Table 14.2 Self as context.

Purpose: Make contact with a sense of self that is a safe and consistent perspective from which to observe and accept all changing inner experiences.

Method: Mindfulness and noticing the continuity of consciousness.

When to use: When the person needs a solid foundation to be able to experience experiences; when identifying with a conceptualized self.

Example of techniques designed to increase self as context:

Observer exercise	Notice who is noticing in various domains of experience.
Therapeutic relationship	Model unconditional acceptance of client's experience.
Metaphors for context	Box with stuff; house with furniture; chessboard.
Confidence	con = with; fidence = fidelity or faith → self-fidelity.
Riding a bicycle	You are always falling off balance, yet you move forward.
Experiential centering	Make contact with self-perspective.
Practicing unconditional acceptance	Permission to be; accept self as is.
Identifying content as content	Separating out what changes and what does not.
Identify programming	Two computers exercise.
Programming process	Content is always being generated; generate some in session together.
Process versus outcome	Practice pulling back into the present from thoughts of the future/past.
ACT-generated content	Thoughts/feelings about self (even "good" ones) don't substitute for experience.
Self as object	Describe the conceptualized self, both "good" and "bad."
Others as objects	Relationship versus being right.
Connecting at board level	Practice being a human with humans.
Getting back on the horse	Connecting to the fact that they will always move in and out of perspective of self-as-context, in session and out.
Identifying when you need it	Occasions where "getting present" is indicated (learning to apply first aid).
Contrast observer self with conceptualized self	Pick an identity exercise.
Forgiveness	Identify painful experiences as content; separate from context.

went before the word; "*but* that" means that there are two things that are inconsistent, that are literally at war with each other. In the ancient etymology of the word, one has to "be out," given the other. The ACT convention is to say *and* instead of *but* whenever possible, which reduces the psychological sense that something is wrong and must be changed whenever literally contradictory reactions are noticed. For example, a person saying "I love my spouse but I can't stand living with him" has less flexible alternatives than one saying "I love my spouse, *and* I'm having the thought that I can't stand living with him."

Another example of a defusion technique is the *milk, milk, milk* exercise, first used by Titchener (1916, p. 425). It consists of an exploration of all of the properties of milk (white, creamy, etc.), followed by two or three minutes of the client and therapist saying the word milk out loud until it loses all meaning. The point is that all words are like that: In addition to their "meanings," they are also just sounds.

A list of some ACT techniques in this area is shown in Table 14.3.

Values

It is within a context of values that action, acceptance, and defusion come together into a sensible whole. During this part of the protocol, we are really asking the client: What do you want your life to stand for? The goal is a vital compass by which clients may live their life.

In this phase of treatment, a client is asked to list values in different life domains, such as family, intimate relationships, health, and spirituality. Values ultimately cannot be evaluated

Table 14.3 Cognitive defusion (deliteralization).

Purpose: See thoughts as what they are, not as what they say they are.

Method: Expand attention to thinking and experiencing as an ongoing behavioral process, not a causal, ontological result.

When to use: When private events are functioning as barriers due to FEAR (fusion, evaluation, avoidance, reasons).

Examples of defusion techniques:

"The Mind"	Treat "the mind" as an external event; almost as a separate person.
Mental appreciation	Thank your mind; show aesthetic appreciation for its products.
Cubbyholing	Label private events as to kind or function in a back-communication.
"I'm having the thought that . . ."	Include category labels in descriptions of private events.
Commitment to openness	Ask if the content is acceptable when negative content shows up.
Just noticing	Use the language of observation (e.g., noticing) when talking about thoughts.
"Buying" thoughts	Use active language to distinguish thoughts and beliefs.
Titchener's repetition	Repeat the difficult thought until you can hear it.
Physicalizing	Label the physical dimensions of thoughts.
Put them out there	Sit next to the client and put each thought and experience out in front of you both as an object.
Open mindfulness	Watch thoughts as external objects without use or involvement.
Focused mindfulness	Direct attention to nonliteral dimensions of experience.
Sound it out	Say difficult thoughts very, very slowly.
Sing it out	Sing your thoughts.

Table 14.3   *(Continued)*

Silly voices	Say your thoughts in other voices, a Donald Duck voice, for example.
Experiential seeking	Openly seek out more material, especially if it is difficult.
Polarities	Strengthen the evaluative component of a thought and watch it pull its opposite.
Arrogance of word	Try to instruct nonverbal behavior.
Think the opposite	Engage in behavior while trying to command the opposite.
Your mind is not your friend	Suppose your mind is mindless; whom do you trust, your experience or your mind?
Who would be made wrong by that?	If a miracle happened and this cleared up without any change in (list reasons), who would be made wrong by that?
Strange loops	Point out a literal paradox inherent in normal thinking.
Thoughts are not causes	"Is it possible to think that thought, as a thought, *and* do X?"
Choose being right or choose being alive	If you have to pay with one to play for the other, which do you choose?
There are four people in here	Openly strategize how to connect when minds are listening.
Monsters on the bus	Treating scary private events as monsters on a bus you are driving.
Feed the tiger	Like feeding a tiger, you strengthen the impact of thoughts by dealing with them.
Who is in charge here?	Treat thoughts as bullies; use colorful language.
Carrying around a dead person	Treat conceptualized history as rotting meat.
Take your mind for a walk	Walk behind clients, chattering mind talk, while they choose where to walk.
How old is this? Is this just like you?	Step out of content and ask these questions.
And what is that in the service of?	Step out of content and ask this question.
Okay, you are right. Now what?	Take "right" as a given and focus on action.
Mary had a little . . .	Say a common phrase and leave out the last word; link to automaticity of thoughts the client is struggling with.
Get off your butts	Replace virtually all self-referential uses of "but" with "and."
What are the numbers?	Teach a simple sequence of numbers and then harass the client regarding the arbitrariness and yet permanence of this mental event.
Why, why, why?	Show the shallowness of causal explanations by repeatedly asking "Why?"
Create a new story	Write down the normal story, then repeatedly integrate those facts into other stories.
Find a free thought	Ask client to find a free thought, unconnected to anything.
Do not think X	Specify a thought not to think and notice that you do.
Find something that can't be evaluated	Look around the room and notice that every single thing can be evaluated negatively.
Flip cards	Write difficult thoughts on 3 × 5 cards; flip them on the client's lap versus keep them off.
Carry cards	Write difficult thoughts on 3 × 5 cards and carry them with you.
Carry your keys	Assign difficult thoughts and experiences to the clients' keys. Ask the client to think the thought as a thought each time the keys are handled, and then carry them from there.

in themselves (because evaluation requires values), so clients' values ultimately are not the problem; the problem is the failure to live them.

Various evocative exercises are used to develop more clarity about fundamental values. For example, the ACT therapist may ask clients to write what they would most like to see on their tombstone, or the eulogy they would want to hear at their own funeral.

When values are clarified, achievable goals that embody those values, concrete actions that would produce those goals, and specific barriers to performing these actions are identified. A list of some ACT techniques in this area is shown in Table 14.4.

Table 14.4   Valuing as a choice.

Purpose: To clarify what the client values for its own sake: What gives your life meaning?

General method: To distinguish choices from reasoned actions; to understand the distinction between a value and a goal; to help clients choose and declare their values, and to set behavioral tasks linked to these values.

When to use: Whenever motivation is at issue; again, after defusion and acceptance removed avoidance as a compass.

Examples of values techniques:

Coke and 7-Up	Define choice and have the client make a simple one. Then ask Why? If there is any content-based answer, repeat.
Your values are perfect	Point out that values cannot be evaluated; thus, your values are not the problem.
Tombstone	Have client write what they stand for on their tombstone.
Eulogy	Have clients write the eulogies they would most like to hear.
Values clarification	List values in all major life domains.
Goal clarification	List concrete goals that would instantiate these values.
Action specification	List concrete actions that would lead toward these goals.
Barrier clarification	List barriers to taking these actions.
Taking a stand	Stand up and declare a value without avoidance.
Pen through the board	Physical metaphor of a path, the twists and turns are not the direction.
Traumatic deflection	What pain would you have to contact to do what you value?
Pick a game to play	Define a game as "pretending that where you are not yet is more important than where you are"; define values as choosing the game.
Process/outcome and values	"Outcome is the process through which process becomes the outcome."
Skiing down the mountain metaphor	Down must be more important than up, or you cannot ski; if a helicopter flew you down, it would not be skiing.
Point on the horizon	Picking a point on the horizon is like a value; heading toward the tree is like a goal.
Choosing not to choose	You cannot avoid choice because no choice is a choice.
Responsibility	You are able to respond.
What if no one could know?	Imagine no one could know of your achievements: Then what would you value?
Sticking a pen through your hand	Suppose getting well required this. Would you do it?
Confronting the little kid	Bring back the client at an earlier age to ask the adult for something.
First you win; then you play	Choose to be acceptable.

Willingness and Commitment

The concrete actions and specific psychological barriers identified in the previous step become the final focus of ACT. In essence, the last stage of ACT is simply learning a generalized strategy of moving forward behaviorally toward valued ends, dissolving barriers through defusion and acceptance. At the point at which the client is able to do this with regularity, therapy is complete. Most clients must have several if not scores of small trials and exercises before this strategy emerges as a generalized response.

In this stage of ACT, clients begin to see that life itself is asking them this question: Given that there is a difference between you as a person and your own private experiences, are you willing to contact those experiences, fully and without defense, as they are and not as they say they are, and do what moves you in the direction of chosen values in this situation? If the answer is no, the person gets smaller. If the answer is yes, the person gets bigger.

A variety of "willingness exercises" are constructed that help frame that question. Almost any method is useful here that deliberately produces and defuses previously avoided private events that were functioning as barriers to effective action. Imaginal and in vivo exposure exercises are particularly common. These are not designed to produce situational exposure so much as exposure to thoughts, feelings, bodily sensations, and the like that have functioned as barriers. Gestalt or experiential exercises are used to evoke difficult material.

In this phase, commitment homework is identified in important life areas. Starting small and growing over time, a repeated cycle is practiced of recognizing values, goals, actions, and barriers, and then committing to action, defusion, acceptance, and actual behavior. A list of some ACT techniques in this area is shown in Table 14.5.

The Therapeutic Relationship

The techniques in the ACT protocol are multifaceted and complex, and often paradoxical and confusing to the clients because of the metaphorical and experiential nature of the therapy. It is important for the therapist to maintain a compassionate yet challenging approach, which creates a context for some difficult emotional work on the part of the client but does not feel judgmental or demeaning to them.

ACT is a collaborative effort (Hayes et al., 2000). ACT therapists are encouraged to discuss their role as a "hired hand" for the client. The ACT therapist works for the client, and in every step of the intervention the goal is to take action in service of the needs of the client.

A description of the ACT relationship is exemplified by the *two mountains metaphor:*

It's like this. You and I are both kind of climbing our own mountains of life. Imagine that these mountains are across each other in a valley. Perhaps, as I climb my mountain, I can look across the valley, and from my perspective, see you climbing your mountain. What I can offer to you as a therapist is that I can comment from my perspective, to give you my viewpoint from outside of your experience. You can look over at me and see that I am not "complete" while you are broken. We are both human beings climbing our mountains. There is no person who is "up" while the other is "down." The fact that I am on a different mountain means I have some perspective on the road you are traveling. My job is to provide that perspective in a way that helps you get where you want to go.

In the ACT approach to the therapeutic relationship, the assumption of destructive normality holds for the therapist as well as for the client. This levels any hierarchical assumptions clients may hold about fundamental differences between their status as a human being and their therapist's status (i.e., the client is not fundamentally "broken" and the therapist inherently superior or "normal"). It also illuminates two risks that a competent ACT therapist must bear in mind. One risk is that it is often tempting to discourage clients from expressing emotional or cognitive content that is painful to hear.

Table 14.5 Acceptance and willingness.

Purpose: Allow yourself to have whatever inner experiences are present when doing so fosters effective action.

Method: Reinforce approach responses to previously aversive inner experiences, reducing motivation to behave avoidantly (altering negatively reinforced avoidant patterns).

When to use: When escape and avoidance of private events prevents positive action.

Example of techniques designed to increase acceptance:

Unhook	Thoughts/feelings don't always lead to action.
Identify the problem	When we battle with our inner experience, it distracts and derails us. Use examples.
Explore effects of avoidance	Has it worked in your life?
Define the problem	What they struggle against = Barriers toward heading in the direction of their goals.
Experiential awareness	Learn to pay attention to internal experiences, and to how we respond to them.
Lean down the hill	Changing the response to material: *toward* the fear, not away.
Amplify responses	Bring experience into awareness, into the room.
Empathy	Participate with client in emotional responding.
In vivo exposure	Structure and encourage intensive experiencing in session.
The Serenity Prayer	Change what we can, accept what we can't.
Practice doing the unfamiliar	Pay attention to what happens when you don't do the automatic response.
Acceptance homework	Go out and find it.
Discrimination training	What do they feel/think/experience?
Mind reading	Help them to identify how they feel.
Journaling	Write about painful events.
Tin can monster exercise	Systematically explore response dimensions of a difficult overall event.
Distinguishing between clean and dirty emotions	Trauma = Pain + Unwillingness to have pain.
Distinguishing willingness from wanting	Bum at the door metaphor: You can welcome a guest without being happy he's there.
How to recognize trauma	Are you less willing to experience the event or more?
Distinguishing willingness the activity from willingness the feeling	Opening up is more important that feeling like it.
Choosing willingness: The willingness question	Given the distinction between you and the stuff you struggle with, are you willing to have that stuff, as it is and not as what it says it is, and do what works in this situation?
Focus on what can be changed	Two scales metaphor.
Caution against qualitatively limiting willingness	The tantruming kid metaphor: If a kid knew your limits, he'd trantrum exactly that long; jumping exercise: You can practice jumping from a book or a building, but you can step down only from the book. Don't limit willingness qualitatively.
Distinguish willing from wallowing	Moving through a swamp metaphor: The only reason to go in is because it stands between you and getting to where you intend to go.
Challenge personal space:	Sitting eye to eye.

Therapists may want to "rescue" clients from their bad feelings instead of modeling how these feelings can be embraced compassionately in the service of effective action. In the therapeutic relationship in ACT, acceptance of experiential material is practiced regardless of the content of this material.

The second and related risk when practicing ACT is that it is easy to get pulled into "buying" clients' formulations about reality, or, conversely, into rejecting their version of reality and attempting to argue them out of it. The strength of literal formulations is potent, and as verbal creatures, therapists are susceptible to fusing with their own and their client's formulations. For example, it may be tempting to buy into thoughts about the hopelessness of the client's situation, or to attempt to argue the client out of such beliefs. In particular, the therapist must be aware of the risk of fusing with any of the implicit or explicit rules regarding reasons for ineffective behavior. The goal is to help clients become aware of, and defuse from, these formulations, not to do battle with them at a content level. If therapists remain unaware of such thoughts and their struggle and/or fusion with them, it will reduce their ability to help the client identify and defuse problematic cognitions, and thus reduce the client's opportunity to create a life more in accordance with his or her values. Therapists are thus encouraged to seek supervision or consultation that permits them to address their reactions and experiences engendered by their work. Just as with clients, therapists are encouraged to practice acceptance at the level of awareness and effectiveness at the level of behavior.

Conclusion

The theoretical underpinnings of ACT as well as the strategies and goals of the intervention can be summarized in an easily remembered fashion from the word *awareness:*

Acceptance of private events.

Willingness as an alternative.

Action in a chosen direction.

Recognizing inappropriate control as the problem.

Examining and clarifying values.

Noticing that thoughts are just thoughts.

Experience, not belief, as the teacher.

Self as a transcendent context of action.

Step forward with self-fidelity (con-fidence as an action).

PROBLEMS TREATABLE WITH ACT

ACT is particularly applicable when the conscious and deliberate control of private events is highly likely to fail. These include situations such as the following.

THE PROCESS OF DELIBERATE CONTROL CONTRADICTS THE DESIRED OUTCOME

One example of this occurs when one tries not to think a specific thought. There is a significant body of evidence that deliberate thought suppression and control may actually be counterproductive in that an attempt not to think thoughts often creates these same thoughts (e.g., Wegner, Schneider, Knutson, & McMahon, 1991; Wegner et al., 1987). This is because deliberately trying to rid oneself of a thought involves following the rule Don't think of X. However, such a rule, by specifying X, produces X. This process seems to relate to psychopathology. For example, data suggest that thought suppressors are vulnerable to depression (Wegner et al., 1991).

THE PROCESS IS NOT RULE-GOVERNED

Many private events are classically conditioned. For example, if painful emotional experiences have been associated with situation X, it is likely that being in situation X will arouse negative emotions by association alone. In these circumstances, attempts at purposeful control may be futile, because the underlying process is not verbally governed. In fact, a vicious cycle can be set up that paradoxically will maintain the event the person wishes to diminish. For example, suppose a person is extremely distressed about anxiety and tries everything to eliminate the anxiety. In this case, a small bit of classically conditioned anxiety will cue both purposeful attempts to reduce anxiety as well as additional anxiety because the person is distressed by anxiety in general; thus, a vicious cycle is set up. Panic Disorder may be an example of such a phenomenon (Hayes, 1987). Change is possible, but the change effort leads to unhealthy forms of avoidance.

Suppose someone tried not to remember a given event, such as the memory of physical abuse as a child. Memories are not simple voluntary behavior because once an event has occurred, memories are associated with it. A memory might be avoided, however, by avoiding all situations that might give rise to it, or by dissociating. The problem with this strategy is that the avoidance itself creates many problems, such as constricting the person's freedom to be in otherwise valuable situations, or limiting conscious access to life events. Some forms of avoidance might be used that are themselves destructive (e.g., drug abuse). Indeed, it is known that some survivors of sexual abuse use drugs in exactly this way (Polusny & Follette, 1995).

The Event Is Not Changeable

Sometimes, emotional control is used in the service of unchangeable events. For example, a woman may take the view that she can not accept that her father was killed, and she will consume drugs to ease her grief. Grief is a natural reaction to such losses. No amount of drug consumption will alter either the situation or the loss, and no effort to reduce or alter private events is called for. When an unchangeable loss occurs, the healthy thing to do is to feel fully what one naturally feels when losses occur.

Change Is Possible but Cannot Be Pursued because Change Efforts Produce Events That Are Not Changeable

Change-oriented strategies are most often the proper approach in problems that have to do with overt behavior or overt situations. When change is the target, however, emotional barriers may still be encountered. In work with couples and families, for example, requesting changes may be suppressed by an individual due to fear of rejection by a partner or family member, and a self-amplifying cycle of suppression, isolation, and alienation may set in. It may be necessary to step back and look at the feared outcomes of change in terms of the thoughts and feelings that might be produced by such changes. Once such barriers to change are identified and treated, the commitment phase begins. The commitment part of ACT is oriented toward behavior change, and virtually any change-oriented procedure can be integrated into ACT at this stage of treatment.

In light of these considerations, ACT seems readily applicable to many types of mood and anxiety disorders, substance abuse problems, couples problems, and even thought disorders. Later, we review data that apply to all of these areas with ACT.

Problems Not Relevant to ACT

ACT is not applicable in several situations. First, some problems are purely skills deficit problems, and in some of these cases, experiential avoidance may not be a significant barrier to accessing skills development experiences. If so, ACT does not apply. Second, some problems are too minor to justify a relatively intrusive treatment such as ACT. Third, if treatments are available that have greater empirical support in a given area, and these have not yet been tried, it would be irresponsible to implement ACT without at least constructing a package that includes the better-supported intervention. Finally, there may be times when experiential avoidance and cognitive fusion are workable in the eyes of the client. If so, ACT would be of little value.

CASE EXAMPLE

Lee, a 19-year-old Caucasian, single female, presented for help reducing ongoing substance abuse and dealing with a history of child sexual abuse. Lee scored above the clinical cutoffs for depression on the Beck Depression Inventory (BDI) and general psychological distress on the Symptom Checklist-90-R (SCL-90-R), and she recorded a high score on a measure of experiential avoidance, the Acceptance and Action Questionnaire (Hayes, Bissett, et al., 2001). She also had seven subscales with T-scores above 70 on the Minnesota Multiphasic Personality Inventory II (MMPI-II). She had a seven-year history of alcohol abuse, a five-year history of drug abuse, and was using methamphetamine daily at the beginning of treatment. She had been unable to hold a job for more than two to three months over the past two years, and was in a chaotic, unstable relationship with a romantic partner with whom she lived.

RELEVANT HISTORICAL INFORMATION

Lee had an extensive history of child abuse and neglect. While she was growing up, her father was absent, and her mother had a significant drug problem. This led to notable parental neglect and set the stage for Lee to be sexually abused by her older brother. She began to have psychological problems related to her mother's drug abuse and neglect at a young age, contributing to her own early use of substances as a way of avoiding negatively evaluated private experiences. This childhood context also led Lee to drop out of high school in ninth grade, although she was very bright. Finally, due to lack of parental supervision and her spending time with other drug users, Lee was sexually assaulted multiple times by acquaintances during her adolescence.

COURSE OF THERAPY (17 MONTHS)

Because therapists using ACT are trained to systematically assess client progress throughout therapy, the treatment began with a comprehensive assessment to determine pretreatment functioning and provide a baseline by which to evaluate subsequent client change. After completing standardized self-report and interview assessments, the ACT-focused therapy began with a comprehensive values assessment process (described earlier in this chapter). Therapist and client worked together to identify Lee's values, potential life and therapy goals, and the barriers that she saw to achieving these goals. The discussion of barriers led into the creative hopelessness phase of treatment: an analysis of the ineffective strategies that she had tried in the past in the service of "feeling good" rather than living a valued life. During this time, Lee continued using alcohol and methamphetamine and had trouble making it to appointments regularly.

The usual course of ACT resumed with work on defusion and the client's sense of self. In this latter phase, and consistent with much of our work with child sexual abuse survivors, Lee had a difficult time identifying any sense of self as distinct from her private events. The therapist had to adjust the pace of therapy to prevent client dissociation during the sessions at this point, and therapist and client continued to work on exposure to painful memories related to her history of abuse. During this time, Lee gradually reduced her levels of substance abuse and got more and more in contact with the consequences of this behavior, recognizing the extent to which substance use was taking her further away from a valued life. Lee also experienced a substantial emotional loss through the death of her mother. This event gave Lee an opportunity to focus on forgiveness as a valued action and to experience grieving while concurrently working toward acceptance and commitment to self.

Approximately six months into therapy, Lee unexpectedly became pregnant. Although this event was not in the original game plan for her treatment or her life, it became an excellent opportunity to revisit the phase of determining Lee's values and working on committed action related to them. Lee chose to stop smoking within one week of finding out that she was pregnant, did not use any drugs throughout the time that she knew she was pregnant, and had only two or three glasses of wine during the pregnancy. She eventually changed jobs to avoid working with cleaning chemicals while pregnant, and quickly found a new job and worked regularly until about one month before giving birth. She moved into a larger, safer home in anticipation of needing more space for herself and her child. Finally, Lee completed therapy approximately six weeks after she gave birth to a healthy baby.

At Termination

Lee had not abused substances since having her baby. Although she reported being understandably tired from taking care of her child, she was working hard at being a good mother and attending to her child's needs. She was continuing to work on her relationship with the father of her child; although the relationship still had problems, she was communicating openly with the father and doing her best to deal with these problems directly. Self-report measures of depression, psychological distress, and experiential avoidance had all decreased since intake. With respect to the long-term problems related to her child sexual abuse history that had led her to therapy, Lee stated that although the memories were still somewhat painful to her, they did not incapacitate her anymore. Furthermore, she spontaneously noted that she no longer wished to change her history, because *all* of her experiences had contributed to her being the person she had turned out to be. Likewise, although Lee continued to miss her mother, she was able to experience painful and pleasant thoughts, feelings, and memories about her mother without having to avoid, numb, or change them.

One Year Posttherapy

Lee continued to behave responsibly with respect to taking care of herself and her child. She reported that she had used methamphetamine two times during the prior year, but that in each case, she was able to discontinue use immediately. Lee was no longer romantically involved with the father of her child, but she had been able to establish a responsible, open relationship with him, in which they shared parenting and financial responsibilities. She had earned her GED and enrolled at a vocational training school. She also had held a steady office job for six months, with hope of advancing her career. On self-report measures, levels of depression and general psychological distress had dropped well below levels of clinical significance, with experiential avoidance scores notably reduced as well. Lee no longer had any subscales elevated at critical levels on the MMPI-II.

18 MONTHS POSTTHERAPY

Lee graduated from a vocational school program where she had completed training to become an assistant in a professional field, with plans of pursuing further education in the medical field in the future.

IMPORTANT PROCESS ISSUES

As is frequently the case in psychotherapy, unexpected events (mother's death, unplanned pregnancy) other than the presenting issues occupied much of the focus of therapy with Lee. However, this development demonstrates certain issues relevant to the process of ACT. First, it highlights the flexibility of the ACT approach in dealing with diverse client issues. ACT is a coherent, theoretically grounded therapy dealing with functional classes of behavior and does not rely on maintaining an exclusive focus on topographical content areas (substance use, trauma). In addition, it demonstrates the importance of tailoring the therapy to whatever is going on in the client's life to promote the generalizability of ACT concepts and maintain clients' commitment to their therapy. As well as providing an armamentarium of techniques in manual form, the theoretical underpinnings of ACT provide a guideline with which to formulate hypotheses, identify relevant response classes, and evaluate the impact of interventions.

Finally, the importance of the therapeutic relationship in ACT should be noted. We believe that one of the primary reasons that Lee was able to make such significant gains throughout her therapy was the strong, mutual relationship that she had with her therapist. Lee's therapist saw herself on the same level as her client, and was actually reminded of this intensely when Lee's mother died suddenly. The therapist had also experienced the painful death of a parent while a teenager, and the death of Lee's mother brought many painful feelings to the surface for

the therapist at the time that she was trying to help Lee. Thus, the therapist had to use the same skills of acceptance of private events in the service of valued action in dealing with the immediate crisis and her own intense feelings. Because the therapist's supervisor had already established an open, accepting supervisory relationship, the therapist was able to express her feelings during supervision without having to suppress them, leading to a more genuine, empathic, and effective therapy process for both therapist and client.

RESEARCH

EFFICACY DATA

Controlled ACT outcome studies, though limited, provide support both for ACT as a technology and for the ACT model of psychopathology. In the early stages of the development of ACT, two small randomized trials were carried out comparing ACT to cognitive therapy in the treatment of depression. These comparison studies were performed in part because the process mechanisms thought to underpin cognitive therapy are different from those in ACT, and therefore present an opportunity for analyses of mode-specific change processes. In the first randomized controlled trial (Zettle & Hayes, 1986), 18 depressed women were assigned to a 12-week course of either cognitive therapy (Beck, Rush, Shaw, & Emery, 1979) or ACT. In both conditions, the therapy was presented in an individual format. Results indicated that ACT produced significantly greater reductions in depression than cognitive therapy, as assessed by the Hamilton Rating Scale for Depression (HRSD), a difference that existed both at posttreatment and at a follow-up assessment.

In a second study (Zettle & Raines, 1989), 31 depressed female subjects were randomly assigned to one of three group treatment conditions: a complete cognitive therapy package, a partial cognitive therapy package, or ACT. The complete cognitive therapy package consisted of the procedures outlined by Hollon and Shaw (1979). The partial cognitive therapy package consisted of the former, minus distancing procedures (e.g., similes, reattribution techniques, and alternative conceptualizations; see Hollon & Beck, 1979, for a full description of these techniques). ACT was performed according to guidelines provided by Hayes (1987).

All three groups showed significant improvement as measured by the BDI, HRSD, the Automatic Thoughts Questionnaire (ATQ), and the Dysfunctional Attitudes Scale. There were no significant differences found between the treatment conditions on any outcome measure. However, analysis of the ATQ indicated differing mechanisms of change in ACT and cognitive therapy. Subjects in both conditions reported significant decreases in the frequency of automatic negative thoughts. However, unlike subjects in the cognitive therapy condition, subjects in the ACT condition reported a rapid decrease in believability ratings from pre- to posttreatment relative to the cognitive therapy group.

Outcome research slowed in the 1990s as greater development effort was put into refining the basic research underlying ACT and the treatment manual itself. With the completion of a book-length explanation of the approach (Hayes, Strosahl, et al., 1999), several controlled outcome studies have recently been completed.

The first medium-size randomized controlled trial of ACT was conducted by Bond and Bunce (2000) on workplace anxiety and stress. In this study, workers at a large media company were randomly assigned to three conditions (30/group): ACT, Behavioral Innovation (a previously tested behavioral package designed to increase worksite stress reduction innovations), and a wait-list control. Measures of stress, anxiety, and general health improved significantly for ACT, but not the other two groups (see Figure 14.1). Actual behavioral innovations in the workplace increased significantly for both the

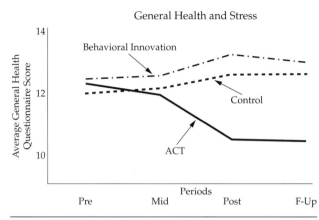

Figure 14.1 General psychological health and stress for the ACT, wait-list, and Behavioral Innovation conditions, at the pre-, mid-, posttreatment, and follow-up periods.

ACT and Behavioral Innovation subjects (see Figure 14.2). Importantly, the mechanism of action in the ACT subjects was shown to be increased acceptance of negative emotions and thoughts. In other words, by increasing acceptance, ACT reduced stress and anxiety but also increased behavior change in the workplace, an outcome not specifically targeted by ACT. Presumably, this occurred because workers were now more willing to face the negative thoughts

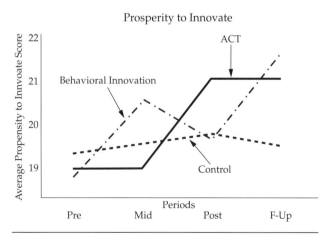

Figure 14.2 Behavioral innovations at work for the ACT, wait-list, and Behavioral Innovation conditions, at the pre-, mid-, posttreatment, and follow-up periods.

and feelings that came up in association with overt efforts to change the workplace. The Bond and Bunce study is also important because it was conducted by researchers other than the originators of the therapy, showing that the treatment is transportable at least to some degree.

A second randomized controlled trial used ACT to treat relatively chronic, hospitalized seriously mentally ill patients experiencing hallucination or delusions. Eighty patients were randomly assigned to receive four sessions of ACT or treatment as usual (TAU) while in the hospital (Bach & Hayes, in press). Patients were then followed for four months after release. ACT patients were taught to stop fighting with hallucinations or delusions, and to accept unpleasant private events if necessary to complete valued activities. Rehospitalization data (see Figure 14.3) showed that this very short version of ACT could cut nearly in half the rate of rehospitalization over a four-month period. Post hoc analyses showed that the positive benefits of ACT could not be accounted for by medication compliance, reductions in distress, or reductions in symptom

frequency. Rather, the effect seemed to be due to greater acceptance of symptoms and a decreased tendency to believe symptom content (i.e., to believe that the content of the hallucinations were reality). At follow-up, twice as many ACT as TAU subjects admitted to positive psychotic symptoms. Those that did admit to the presence of symptoms reported similar symptom frequency in both groups. Yet those in the ACT condition who admitted to symptoms were nearly four times more likely to remain out of the hospital (see Figure 14.4), suggesting that symptom reporting reflected lower levels of denial and higher levels of psychological acceptance.

We are now completing a NIDA-funded randomized controlled trial examining the impact of ACT and Intensive Twelve-Step Facilitation (ITSF) in the reduction of drug use among polysubstance abusing methadone clients. All subjects continued to receive methadone throughout treatment; 126 subjects were randomly assigned

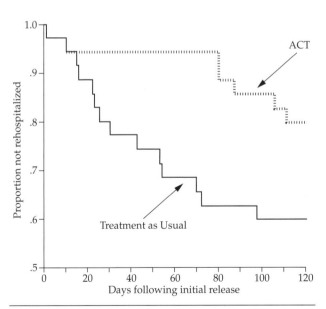

Figure 14.3 Survival curve for psychotic patients in the ACT and treatment as usual conditions during a four-month follow-up.

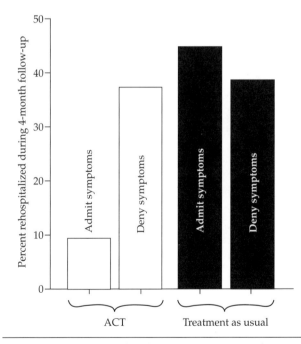

Figure 14.4 Relationship between symptom admission and rehospitalization for psychotic patients in the ACT and treatment as usual conditions during a four-month follow-up.

to the ACT, ITSF, or methadone maintenance only conditions.

The population had both extensive drug use and treatment attempt histories and high rates of serious co-occurring psychological disorders. Reported opiate use (83%) and cocaine use (40%) were common; over the prior 30 days, 88% of the subjects tested positive for drugs of abuse in baseline. Subjects on average had participated in treatment 5.3 times previously. Mood (40%), anxiety (42%), and personality (52%) disorder diagnoses occurred frequently.

Drug use was assessed through monitored urinalysis. The results for opiate use are shown in Figure 14.5. At baseline, the three groups did not differ in the percentage of subjects who tested positive for opiates, nor were differences statistically significant at the end of 16 weeks of treatment. At the six-month follow-up, however, the ACT and ITSF groups differed in the percentage of subjects testing positive for opiates. There was a strong incubation effect for

ACT (i.e., effects of treatment accumulating over time), shown by the continuing reduction in drug use from posttreatment to follow-up.

Total drug use showed a different overall pattern, as some subjects shifted drug use from opiates to other drugs. The percentages of subjects testing positive for any drug are shown in Figure 14.6. Significantly fewer ACT subjects were using drugs of abuse at follow-up than were methadone maintenance control subjects. ITSF was no longer significantly different from the control group. The incubation effect is once again very clear in the ACT condition.

Hierarchical logistic regressions suggested ACT and ITSF processes were both responsible for successful outcomes, and were occasionally even better predictors than baseline measures of drug use alone (which have traditionally been the best predictors of future drug use). These latter results confirmed the key change mechanisms proposed for the ACT and ITSF interventions.

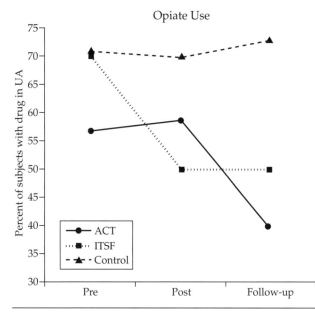

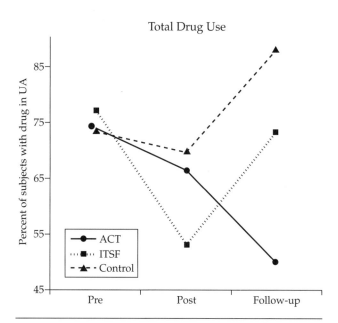

Figure 14.5 Percentage of subjects who tested positive for opiates in the ACT plus methadone, methadone, and Intensive Twelve-Step Facilitation plus methadone conditions at baseline, posttreatment, and six-month follow-up.

Figure 14.6 Percentage of subjects who tested positive for any drug in the ACT plus methadone, methadone, and Intensive Twelve-Step Facilitation plus methadone conditions at baseline, posttreatment, and six-month follow-up.

Several recent controlled studies have also successfully combined ACT interventions with other approaches in randomized controlled trials, or have tested components of the intervention with specialized populations. Roemer and Orsillo (in press) have shown positive results in a small randomized controlled trial with generalized anxiety disorder, using a protocol that is heavily based on the ACT protocol. Components of ACT have been used in controlled studies of interventions for depression in primary care (Robinson & Hayes, 1997). Modified versions of the ACT protocol have been tested successfully in controlled research on pain, both in laboratory (Hayes, Bissett, et al., 1999) and clinical settings (Geiser, 1992). ACT has also been applied to work with families of disabled children (Biglan, Lewin, & Hops, 1990), to agoraphobia (Lopez, 1999), to other anxiety disorders (Garcia, 2000), and to sexual deviation (Paul, Marx, & Orsillo, 1999).

The research on ACT is still preliminary. What is remarkable, however, is the scope of the empirical application for such a young technology. The theory on which ACT rests suggests that cognitive fusion and experiential avoidance are both psychologically troublesome and built into human language and cognition. If so, a very wide variety of problems should be treatable with ACT. The early results suggest that this is the case, not merely in efficacy trials but also in effectiveness research, a topic to which we now turn.

EFFECTIVENESS DATA

ACT is one of a small number of procedures that have been shown to be useful in field effectiveness studies and is the only procedure of which we are aware that has been shown to improve clinical outcomes for most problems referred to general outpatient clinicians (Strosahl, Hayes, Bergan, & Romano, 1998). Because this finding is important in the assessment of the

ACT approach, the study is described in some detail.

The great majority of effectiveness research has been post hoc and correlational, and some researchers (e.g., Seligman, 1996) have limited effectiveness research in these ways. The Strosahl et al. (1998) study developed a new, experimental model for effectiveness research called the manipulated training method. In this approach, clinicians are assigned to training and nontraining (or comparison training) conditions. Assessments are conducted of the effectiveness of clinicians in both groups by assessing all of their clients pre- and posttreatment for several months. After the normal treatment effects and processes have been documented adequately, training on particular clinical approaches is provided. Upon completion, assessments of the effectiveness of clinicians in both groups are once again conducted by assessing all clients pre- and posttreatment for several months.

In the manipulated training method, clinicians are not necessarily required to follow a manual. The manual of importance is that for the trainers; clinicians are free to make use of the training in a variety of ways. If important and useful treatment methods and sensitivities have been transmitted, and are sufficiently adhered to following training, then the value of training will be revealed in improved client outcomes. If clients show more improvement following clinician training, we know that the training is beneficial even if we do not know exactly how it impacted clinician behavior.

The manipulated training method is the first experimental procedure of which we are aware that assesses effectiveness without altering the key variables that distinguish effectiveness and efficacy research. Seligman (1995) describes several of these variables: heterogeneous patient samples with multiple problems, open-ended treatment, active selection and deselection of treatment by the patient, self-correcting treatment regimens, and a greater emphasis on general functioning as opposed to symptom reduction. In addition, the following variables should be considered: the use of unscreened practitioners of highly variable backgrounds, the use of outcome and process assessments that are system-friendly, the use of unstructured usual care as a minimal treatment comparison (rather than wait-list or structured placebo treatments), and the lack of adherence to a manual as a necessary condition for experimental control.

Strosahl et al. (1998) studied 17 experienced (average of 5.2 years of postdegree experience) master's-level therapists and one psychologist (those not receiving training = 10; receiving training = 8) who were treatment staff in a large-staff model health maintenance organization. Therapists were assigned to one of two conditions: training in ACT or no training. Clinicians in the training groups received a package consisting of a didactic workshop, an intensive clinical training, and monthly supervision groups.

Before training began, for one month all consecutive new intakes seen by training or control therapists were assessed pretreatment and after five months. Clients rated their presenting problems on a 1 to 5 scale according to its severity, how well they were coping with the problem, and how well they were accepting emotions, thoughts, memories, and other private reactions to the problem.

The ACT training started with a two-day experiential workshop. This workshop discussed the ACT model and then took participants through various components of the ACT technology in the form of a set of guided exercises, metaphors, and therapeutic discussions. Essentially, after the first few hours, this workshop was not *about* ACT, it *was* ACT, and clinicians themselves were invited to walk through their own pain and struggles. A few weeks later, trainees participated in a three-day intensive clinical workshop. In this workshop, a detailed ACT manual was distributed (Hayes, McCurry, Afari, & Wilson, 1993), and each of the ACT components was demonstrated, role-played,

and practiced. The intensive workshop also involved direct observation of live ACT sessions with particularly difficult clients, followed by extended group discussions. Finally, ACT therapists in training received three hours of direct supervision a month. Supervision consisted of didactic and experiential training and group observation of trainees' tapes. An important training component was to observe live ACT sessions conducted by the supervisor with difficult clients brought in by the therapists in training, followed by group discussions. Therapists were encouraged to follow the manual with one client, and then to use it as they saw fit. Specific guidelines for discriminating when treatment components were relevant were provided by the ACT model itself (e.g., when cognitive fusion is observed, use defusion techniques).

After a year of training (approximately 80 hours total, all in group formats), posttraining client data were obtained for all consecutive new intakes seen during one month in a fashion similar to the pretraining assessment. A posttreatment chart review was also completed of all patients in the study to determine a final *DSM-IV* diagnosis, the current status of the case, the use of medication referrals, and similar variables.

A total of 321 clients were assessed, divided almost equally between the baseline (N = 172) and posttraining (N = 149) cohorts; 63% of these clients had been in treatment previously. Among *DSM-IV* Axis I and Axis II diagnoses, the most common were Adjustment Disorder (16.4%), Affective Disorders (12 %), Personality Disorder (8%), and Anxiety Disorders (7.4%). V-codes were also common, including Partner Relational Problem (22%), Phase of Life Problem (8.5%), Parent-Child Problem (7.5%), and Relational Problem (7%).

The results showed that clients of ACT-trained therapists reported significantly better coping than the clients of untrained therapists in the posttraining but not the pretraining cohort.

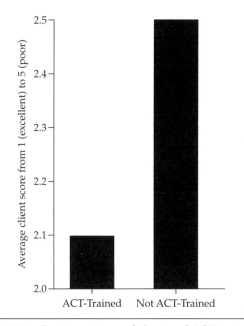

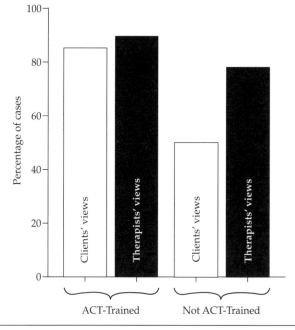

Figure 14.7   Coping ratings of clients of ACT-trained or non-ACT-trained therapists five months after the onset of treatment.

Figure 14.8   Percentage of cases completed, according to patients and therapists, in ACT-trained or non-ACT-trained groups five months after the onset of treatment.

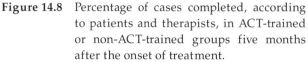

These results are shown in Figure 14.7. Further, clients of ACT-trained therapists were significantly more likely to report that treatment was completed after five months in the posttraining but not the pretraining cohort. This effect was not seen when therapists were asked whether treatment was completed (see Figure 14.8), indicating that ACT-trained therapists were more likely to share their client's view of treatment—a distinct outcome in itself. Comparing the pretraining and posttraining cohorts, ACT-trained therapists reduced their use of medication referrals (a significant cost savings; see Figure 14.9), and their clients showed higher acceptance ratings after ACT training; these effects were not seen in the control group.

In summary, ACT training produced better client outcomes across the range of cases normally seen in this HMO. These results were achieved more rapidly and at lower cost. ACT therapists viewed case progress in a fashion

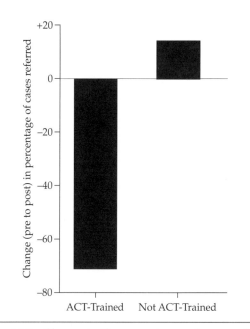

Figure 14.9   Change in the percentages of cases referred for medication consultations from pretraining to posttraining among clients of ACT-trained or non-ACT-trained therapists.

that was more similar to patients' views, and the process of change was consistent with the ACT model.

SUMMARY

As may be obvious from a reading of this chapter, ACT is a treatment that is difficult to categorize. On the one hand, it is thoroughly formulated in behavioral terms and is linked to a specific behavioral theory. On the other, the actual technology shares features with gestalt, humanistic, and other experiential traditions, in addition to its behavior therapy roots. It is a manualized treatment increasingly supported by empirical evidence, yet it is also a treatment that includes Eastern and other components drawn from relatively nonempirical sources. This mix of influences is not a weakness but a strength. Empirical clinical procedures need not isolate themselves from possible sources of wisdom merely because experimental scientists did not originate the methods that are tested. Currently, other integrative treatments include dialectical behavior therapy (Linehan, 1993), relapse prevention (Marlatt & Gordon, 1985), and integrative behavioral couples therapy (see Koerner, Jacobson, & Christensen, 1994).

ACT amplifies the scope of traditional classical and operant conditioning to the extent that it becomes a truly integrative behavioral approach. Historical criticisms such as the lack of attention to the nature of the relationship, the need for flexibility, the importance of cognition and affect, and the utility of openness to experience are thoroughly addressed and empirically substantiated in ACT. This expansion is in part a result of integrating experimental findings from current basic behavioral research on language and cognition and current research in experimental psychopathology. ACT is fundamentally a theory of human behavior that permits flexible and focused interventions in an area of extraordinary complexity and promise:

the human suffering that is the true subject of scientific psychology. What is truly new is not the technology so much as the integration of theory, technology, and experimental research. Whether or not ACT per se is ultimately viewed as a step forward, we believe that this multilevel and integrated approach to treatment development has much to offer the field, regardless of the particular treatment involved. The success of this approach to development so far is one of the more reassuring features of the ACT story.

REFERENCES

Bach, P., & Hayes, S. C. (in press). The use of acceptance and commitment therapy to prevent the rehospitalization of psychotic patients: A randomized controlled trial. *Journal of Consulting and Clinical Psychology*.

Beck, A. T., Rush, A. J., Shaw, B. F., & Emery, G. (1979). *Cognitive therapy of depression*. New York: Guilford Press.

Biglan, A., Lewin, L., & Hops, H. (1990). A contextual approach to the problem of aversive practices in families. In G. Patterson (Ed.), *Depression and aggression: Two facets of family interactions* (pp. 103–129). New York: Erlbaum.

Bond, F. W., & Bunce, D. (2000). Mediators of change in emotion-focused and problem-focused worksite stress management interventions. *Journal of Occupational Health Psychology, 5*, 156–163.

Cioffi, D., & Holloway, J. (1993). Delayed costs of suppressed pain. *Journal of Personality and Social Psychology, 64*, 274–282.

Clark, D. M., Ball, S., & Pape, K. (1991). An experimental investigation of thought suppression. *Behaviour Research and Therapy, 29*, 253–257.

Clark, D. M., Winton, E., & Thynn, L. (1993). A further experimental investigation of thought suppression. *Behaviour Research and Therapy, 31*, 207–210.

Cottington, E. M., Matthews, K. A., Talbott, E., & Kuller, L. H. (1986). Occupational stress, suppressed anger, and hypertension. *Psychosomatic Medicine, 48*, 249–260.

Davies, M. I., & Clark, D. M. (1998). Thought suppression produces rebound effect with analogue post-traumatic intrusions. *Behaviour Research and Therapy, 36,* 571–582.

DeGenova, M. K., Patton, D. M., Jurich, J. A., & MacDermid, S. M. (1994). Ways of coping among HIV-infected individuals. *Journal of Social Psychology, 134,* 655–663.

Dimsdale, J. E., Pierce, C., Schoenfeld, D., & Brown, A. (1986). Suppressed anger and blood pressure: The effects of race, sex, social class, obesity, and age. *Psychosomatic Medicine, 48,* 430–436.

Dougher, M. J., Augustson, E., Markham, M. R., & Greenway, D. E. (1994). The transfer of respondent eliciting and extinction functions through stimulus equivalence classes. *Journal of the Experimental Analysis of Behavior, 62,* 331–351.

Garcia, R. F. (2000). Application of acceptance and commitment therapy in an example of experiential avoidance. *Psicothema, 12,* 445–450.

Geiser, D. S. (1992). *A comparison of acceptance-focused and control-focused psychological treatments in a chronic pain treatment center.* Unpublished doctoral dissertation, University of Nevada, Reno.

Gross, J. J., & Levenson, R. W. (1993). Emotional suppression: Physiology, self-report, and expressive behavior. *Journal of Personality and Social Psychology, 64,* 970–986.

Harvey, A. G., & Bryant, R. A. (1998). The effect of attempted thought suppression in Acute Stress Disorder. *Behaviour Research and Therapy, 36,* 583–590.

Hayes, S. C. (1987). A contextual approach to therapeutic change. In N. Jacobson (Ed.), *Psychotherapists in clinical practice: Cognitive and behavioral perspectives* (pp. 327–387). New York: Guilford Press.

Hayes, S. C. (Ed.). (1989). *Rule-governed behavior: Cognition, contingencies, and instructional control.* New York: Plenum Press.

Hayes, S. C., Barnes-Holmes, D., & Roche, B. (Eds.). (2001). *Relational frame theory: A post-Skinnerian account of human language and cognition.* New York: Plenum Press.

Hayes, S. C., Bergan, J., Strosahl, K., Wilson, K. G., Polusny, M., Naugle, A., et al. (1996, November).

Measuring psychological acceptance: The Acceptance and Action Questionnaire. Paper presented at the meeting of the Association for Advancement of Behavior Therapy, New York.

Hayes, S. C., Bissett, R., Korn, Z., Zettle, R. D., Rosenfarb, I., Cooper, L., et al. (1999). The impact of acceptance versus control rationales on pain tolerance. *Psychological Record, 49,* 33–47.

Hayes, S. C., Bissett, R., Strosahl, K., Pistorello, J., Toarmino, D., Polusny, M., et al. (2001). *The Acceptance and Action Questionnaire.* Manuscript in preparation.

Hayes, S. C., Brownstein, A. J., Devany, J. M., Kohlenberg, B. S., & Shelby, J. (1987). Stimulus equivalence and the symbolic control of behavior. *Mexican Journal of Behavior Analysis, 13,* 361–374.

Hayes, S. C., Brownstein, A. J., Haas, J. R., & Greenway, D. E. (1986). Instructions, multiple schedules, and extinction: Distinguishing rule-governed from schedule controlled behavior. *Journal of the Experimental Analysis of Behavior, 46,* 137–147.

Hayes, S. C., Kohlenberg, B. S., & Hayes, L. J. (1991). The transfer of specific and general consequential functions through simple and conditional equivalence classes. *Journal of the Experimental Analysis of Behavior, 56,* 119–137.

Hayes, S. C., McCurry, S. M., Afari, N., & Wilson, K. G. (1993). *Acceptance and commitment therapy: A manual for the treatment of emotional avoidance.* Reno, NV: Context Press.

Hayes, S. C., Pankey, J., & Gregg, J. (2000). Anxiety and acceptance and commitment therapy. In E. A. Gosch & R. A. DiTomasso (Eds.), *Comparative treatments of anxiety disorders.* New York: Springer.

Hayes, S. C., Strosahl, K., & Wilson, K. G. (1999). *Acceptance and commitment therapy: An experiential approach to behavior change.* New York: Guilford Press.

Hayes, S. C., & Wilson, K. G. (1994). Acceptance and commitment therapy: Altering the verbal support for experiential avoidance. *Behavior Analyst, 17,* 289–303.

Hollon, S. D., & Beck, A. T. (1979). Cognitive therapy of depression. In P. C. Kendall & S. D. Hollon (Eds.), *Cognitive-behavioral interventions: Theory, research, and procedures* (pp. 153–203). New York: Academic Press.

Hollon, S. D., & Shaw, B. F. (1979). Group cognitive therapy for depressed patients. In A. T. Beck, A. J. Rush, B. F. Shaw, & G. Emery (Eds.), *Cognitive therapy of depression* (pp. 328–353). New York: Guilford Press.

Ireland, S. J., McMahon, R. C., Malow, R. M., & Kouzekanani, K. (1994). Coping style as a predictor of relapse to cocaine abuse. In L. S. Harris (Ed.), *Problems of drug dependence: 1993. Proceedings of the 55th annual scientific meeting* (NIDA Monograph Series No. 141, p. 158). Washington, DC: U. S. Government Printing Office.

Khorakiwala, D. (1991). *An analysis of the process of client change in a contextual approach to therapy.* Unpublished doctoral dissertation available from the library at the University of Nevada, Reno.

Koerner, K., Jacobson, N. S., & Christensen, A. (1994). Emotional acceptance in integrative behavioral couple therapy. In S. C. Hayes, N. S. Jacobson, V. M. Follette, & M. J. Dougher (Eds.), *Acceptance and change: Content and context in psychotherapy* (pp. 109–118). Reno, NV: Context Press.

Lavy, E. H., & Van den Hout, M. A. (1990). Thought suppression induces intrusions. *Behavioural Psychotherapy, 18,* 251–258.

Leitenberg, H., Greenwald, E., & Cado, S. (1992). A retrospective study of long-term methods of coping with having been sexually abused during childhood. *Child Abuse and Neglect, 16,* 399–407.

Leonhard, C., & Hayes, S. C. (1991, May). *Prior inconsistent testing affects equivalence responding.* Paper presented at the annual meeting of the Association for Behavior Analysis, Atlanta, GA.

Linehan, M. M. (1993). *Cognitive behavioral treatment of Borderline Personality Disorder.* New York: Guilford Press.

Lipkens, G., Hayes, S. C., & Hayes, L. J. (1993). Longitudinal study of derived stimulus relations in an infant. *Journal of Experimental Child Psychology, 56,* 201–239.

Lopez, F. J. (1999). Acceptance and commitment therapy (ACT) in Panic Disorder with agoraphobia: A case study. *Psicothema, 11,* 1–12.

Lorig, T. S., Singer, J. L., Bonanno, G. A., & Davis, P. (1995). Repressor personality styles and EEG patterns associated with affective memory and thought suppression. *Imagination, Cognition, and Personality, 1*(4), 203–210.

Macrae, C. N., Bodenhausen, G. V., Milne, A. B., & Jetten, J. (1994). Out of mind but back in sight: Stereotypes on the rebound. *Journal of Personality and Social Psychology, 67,* 808–817.

Marlatt, G. A., & Gordon, J. R. (1985). *Relapse prevention: Maintenance strategies in the treatment of addictive behaviors.* New York: Guilford Press.

McCurry, S. M. (1991). *Client metaphor use in a contextual form of therapy.* Unpublished doctoral dissertation available from the library at the University of Nevada, Reno.

Merckelbach, H., Muris, P., Van den Hout, M. A., & de Jong, P. (1991). Rebound effects of thought suppression: Instruction dependent? *Behavioural Psychotherapy, 19,* 225–238.

Muris, P., & Merckelbach, H. (1997). Suppression and dissociation. *Personality and Individual Differences, 23,* 523–525.

Paul, R. H., Marx, B. P., & Orsillo, S. M. (1999). Acceptance-based psychotherapy in the treatment of an adjudicated exhibitionist: A case example. *Behavior Therapy, 30,* 149–162.

Polusny, M. A., & Follette, V. M. (1995). Long-term correlates of child sexual abuse: Theory and review of the empirical literature. *Applied and Preventive Psychology, 4,* 143–166.

Robinson, P., & Hayes, S. C. (1997). Acceptance and commitment: A model for integration. In N. A. Cummings, J. L. Cummings, & J. N. Johnson (Eds.), *Behavioral health in primary care: A guide for clinical integration* (pp. 177–203). Madison, CT: Psychosocial Press.

Roemer, E., & Orsillo, S. (in press). Expanding our conceptualization of and treatment for Generalized Anxiety Disorder: Integrating mindfulness/acceptance-based approaches with existing cognitive-behavioral models. *Clinical Psychology: Science and Practice.*

Seligman, M. (1995). The effectiveness of psychotherapy: The Consumer Reports study. *American Psychologist, 50,* 965–974.

Seligman, M. (1996). Science as an ally of practice. *American Psychologist, 51,* 1072–1079.

Strosahl, K. D., Hayes, S. C., Bergan, J., & Romano, P. (1998). Does field based training in behavior therapy improve clinical effectiveness? Evidence from the acceptance and commitment therapy training project. *Behavior Therapy, 29,* 35–64.

Titchener, E. B. (1916). *A text-book of psychology.* New York: Macmillan.

Wegner, D. M. (1989). *White bears and other unwanted thoughts.* New York: Viking/Penguin.

Wegner, D. M., Schneider, D. J., Carter, S. R., & White, T. L. (1987). Paradoxical effects of thought suppression. *Personality and Social Psychology, 53,* 5–13.

Wegner, D. M., Schneider, D. J., Knutson, B., & McMahon, S. R. (1991). Polluting the stream of consciousness: The effect of thought suppression on the mind's environment. *Cognitive Therapy and Research, 15,* 141–152.

Wegner, D. M., Shortt, J. W., Blake, A. W., & Page, M. S. (1990). The suppression of exciting thoughts. *Journal of Personality and Social Psychology, 58,* 409–418.

Wegner, D. M., & Zanakos, S. (1994). Chronic thought suppression. *Journal of Personality, 62,* 615–640.

Wenzlaff, R. M., Wegner, D. M., & Klein, S. B. (1991). The role of thought suppression in the bonding of thought and mood. *Journal of Personality and Social Psychology, 60,* 500–508.

Wilson, K. G., Gifford, E. V., & Hayes, S. C. (1997). Cognition in behavior therapy: Agreements and differences. *Journal of Behavior Therapy and Experimental Psychiatry, 28,* 53–63.

Wilson, K. G., & Hayes, S. C. (1996). Resurgence of derived stimulus relations. *Journal of the Experimental Analysis of Behavior, 66,* 267–281.

Wulfert, E., & Hayes, S. C. (1988). The transfer of conditional sequencing through conditional equivalence classes. *Journal of the Experimental Analysis of Behavior, 50,* 125–144.

Zeitlin, S. B., Netten, K. A., & Hodder, S. L. (1995). Thought suppression: An experimental investigation of spider phobics. *Behaviour Research and Therapy, 33,* 407–413.

Zettle, R. D., & Hayes, S. C. (1986). Dysfunctional control by client verbal behavior: The context of reason giving. *Analysis of Verbal Behavior, 4,* 30–38.

Zettle, R. D., & Raines, J. C. (1989). Group cognitive and contextual therapies in treatment of depression. *Journal of Clinical Psychology, 45,* 438–445.

PSYCHOTHERAPY WITH FAMILIES AND COUPLES

CHAPTER 15

A Multidimensional
Approach to Couples

JOHN M. GOTTMAN

HISTORY OF THE
THERAPEUTIC APPROACH

In the 1970s, psychologists, mostly those who were behaviorally oriented, began entering the field of research on marital therapy and conducting basic research on marital relationships. Until then, the field had been primarily the domain of sociologists, who relied on self-report survey methods. Psychologists brought to this area a concern for the study of interaction processes, and with it, the use of observational data. The seminal paper that started this research field was a very ambitious one published in 1973 by Weiss, Hops, and Patterson. Their laboratory in Oregon was extending its primarily operant conditioning base program with families of oppositional, defiant, and delinquent children to the study of marital interaction.

Our laboratory adopted a different approach to the same problem. The approach was motivated by a paper written in 1969 by Goldfried and D'Zurilla. Richard McFall had introduced Gottman to this paper in graduate school, and

he suggested that it ought to guide clinical psychology research in the future. The major idea in this paper was that intervention programs for target clinical populations should be developed empirically by studying how other, more competent populations dealt with similar problematic situations. This very simple idea motivated basic research on marriage, from which our first intervention program was derived. Later, it took shape in a series of seven longitudinal studies of the "masters" and the "disasters" of marriage. In those studies we attempted to predict longitudinal outcomes of marriages. The masters were those couples who stayed together and were happily married on self-report measures of marital satisfaction. The disasters either separated or divorced or stayed together despite the fact that at least one person was unhappily married.

The original Goldfried and D'Zurilla (1969) paper was based on individuals; our work was influenced by the general systems theorists, who pointed out that it was the *interaction* and the *relationship* that was the proper unit of study, and that psychology needed to move beyond the study of the individual to the study of interacting systems. Mavis Hetherington had introduced Gottman to this work in graduate school, so this approach was a blending of the teaching of two mentors, McFall and Hetherington.

Gottman was also fortunate to have attracted the creative talents of two students, Cliff Notarius and Howard Markman, for this early work. We began examining two domains of measurement: interactive behavior and perception. The goal was to find theories and methodologies that examined sequences of both perception and interaction in synchronized fashion over time, as an interaction unfolded. We selected Thibaut and Kelley's (1959) behavior exchange theory that described something resembling first-order transition Markov payoff matrices, in which the matrix elements were roughly "costs" or "benefits" of behaviors exchanged.

We also selected methods for the sequential analysis of observational data for deriving transition probabilities (and z-scores comparing transition probabilities to unconditional probabilities); these methods were being developed by Sackett and later by Bakeman. We also chose methods for the time-series analysis of more continuous variables derived from observational coding (by a weighted sum of categorical codes sliding across a fixed time-window). We participated in the development of some of these methods (e.g., Bakeman & Gottman, 1986; Gottman & Roy, 1990). They were not widely used by other researchers, although Gottman and Notarius (2001) recently noted that they were being used more often in the 1990s.

To operationalize these domains of measurement, we constructed a device called the "talk table." This device was a double-sloping table that constrained one person to speak at a time; for each turn at speech, that person would rate the positivity or negativity of the "intent" of the message sent, and the recipient would rate the positivity or negativity of the "impact" of the message received. The messages themselves would be coded separately for content and

nonverbal behavior using a system developed with Notarius and Markman called the Couples Interaction Scoring System (CISS). It examined both how people dealt with conflict and how they approached more positive tasks, such as conversation and having fun (Rubin, 1977).

The same question was asked that Terman (Terman, Buttenwieser, Ferguson, Johnson, & Wilson, 1938) had asked: What is different about unhappy and happy couples? However, because we were motivated by Goldfried and D'Zurilla's (1969) paper, it was important for us to develop a methodology that actually studied how happily married couples approached *real conflicts* that they were actually having. This was not easy. The initial studies that attempted to describe the differences between happily and unhappily married couples (e.g., Birchler, Weiss, & Vincent, 1975) had couples use the Olson Inventory of Marital Conflicts (IMC). The IMC asks spouses to decide who is most at fault in an argument, the husband or the wife; the trick is that they are given slightly or greatly disparate stories about the argument. This task was also used in our first study, and we found that unhappily married couples really get involved in this task, fighting with one another and taking things very personally. However, happily married couples quickly understand the setup of the spouses getting different stories, and they laugh at the task and tend not to take things personally; on the whole, the task generates little or no conflict in happily married couples. Thus, the conclusions about differences between happily and unhappily married couples on this task do not reflect the ideas that appear in the Goldfried and D'Zurilla paper. It was important to see how happily married couples handle real conflicts that they actually have.

Toward this end, we designed our play-by-play interview and began studying the conflicts of happily married couples. We were quite confident that this approach would be fruitful because previous research had shown that the rank order correlation of problems between happily and unhappily married couples was in the high .90s. Thus, it seemed that all couples had to cope with particular developmental tasks, which could be expected to vary across the life span. This was an idea adapted from the Goldfried and D'Zurilla method (1969). The interview was successful in helping all couples to first describe their actual disagreements and then to talk about them.

In the initial two studies, couples varied widely in demographic characteristics; there were university students in the first study and a rural southern Indiana population in the second study. Nonetheless, the data replicated strikingly well across the studies. We were able to discriminate happy from unhappy couples using observational data with our CISS and with our talk table. The data were most interesting when they were synchronized. Later, Notarius, Benson, Sloane, Vanzetti, and Hornyak (1989) showed how to use log-linear analysis to study the interface between perception and behavior in their analysis of Weiss's (1980) concept of sentiment overrides.

From these studies, we developed an intervention program (Gottman, Notarius, Gonso, & Markman, 1976) and tested it in three randomized clinical trials (reported in Gottman, 1979). The results of these clinical experiments were encouraging, but also discouraging. Couples improved in all treatment groups compared to the control groups, which deteriorated without treatment. Upon follow-up, however, there was significant relapse in marital satisfaction over time. Something wasn't right with our initial basic research work.

It was necessary to go back to the drawing board and develop another intervention. That basic research work, in seven longitudinal studies, took approximately 20 years (1976 to 1996). The details of these studies are described in *The Marriage Clinic* (Gottman, 1999). The new studies were based on a collaboration with Robert Levenson, which began in 1979.

THEORETICAL CONSTRUCTS

The term "theory" is used differently in the social sciences and in the physical and biological sciences. In the physical and biological sciences, this term is reserved for a set of concepts that provide an explanation for a set of phenomena. So, to develop a theory, one first requires a replicable phenomenon; then the theory needs to provide the mechanism that explains the phenomenon. A test of a good theory is that it winds up going beyond the phenomena that generated it; it explains more than it set out to explain, and provides surprising new insights. For example, Newton's theory of gravitation explained not only the planetary orbits, but also the motion of projectiles on the earth; Einstein's general theory of relativity, which explained gravitational force as the curve of space-time, also explained the precession of Mercury's planetary orbit. Furthermore, a theory is more respected in the physical and biological sciences if it can be stated mathematically, especially if the mathematics can be considered somehow aesthetically beautiful or elegant (Davies, 1991).

In the social sciences, however, the term theory generally refers to a particular school or perspective, a more or less unified set of concepts that takes a particular point of view or emphasis. There is no prior need to establish a replicable set of phenomena whose nature is not understood.

The development of theory was approached in a manner modeled after the physical and biological sciences. This consisted of the following phases: (1) basic longitudinal research attempting to establish predictions as the replicable phenomena; (2) the construction of correlational models that might generate hypotheses that could explain these phenomena; (3) the creation of mathematical models that describe these explanations; (4) a series of proximal intervention change experiments that test linkage elements in the proposed theory; (5) clinical trials that integrate the proximal interventions into a therapy; and (6) prevention trials that show that through knowledge of the presumed etiology of dysfunction, that dysfunction can be prevented. In essence, we were influenced by many perspectives in the social sciences, which are detailed below.

FOUNDATIONS

Systems Theory

The systems perspective (e.g., von Bertalanffy, 1963) pointed the study of families away from an individual personality theory perspective and toward the study of interactive behavior. We were influenced to examine interactive behavior, particularly sequences of categorical codes between two people.

Cybernetic Theory

We were also influenced by the development of cybernetics in mathematics and engineering, particularly the early work represented by Norbert Weiner in time-series analysis and its later development by Box and Jenkins (1970).

Behavior Exchange Theory

Behavior exchange theory also emphasized the interaction or exchanges between two people, focusing on an economic view or interaction in terms of rewards and costs. We chose to interpret this theory as a theory of *perception*, not of reality; that is, we operationalized the payoff matrix of exchange as each person's perceived rewards and costs.

Social Learning Theory

Social learning theory was a very important research tradition that emphasized observational data. This theory expanded the set of processes that behaviorally oriented research clinicians considered. In particular, researchers who collaborated with Gerald Patterson at the Oregon Social Learning Center (Patterson, 1982) began studying family processes using sequential measures (primarily the conditional probability). They uncovered sequences that turned out to be central in the creation and maintenance of oppositional behavior, which they called "coercive process." These processes were then found to be predictive of the development of delinquency in adolescents and preadolescents. The models that emerged from this research were used to create a therapy intervention that has demonstrated some effectiveness. In the mid-1970s, these researchers turned their attention to marriages, and this work continued with the seminal work of Robert Weiss (e.g., Weiss, 1980).

THE THEORY WE HAVE DEVELOPED

Research Questions

The theory we have developed emerged from five very productive research questions. First, what is "dysfunctional" when a marriage is ailing? This is an important question because it provides the goals of marital therapy; it tells us what needs fixing and what does not need fixing. We have noticed that some marital therapies are designed to change patterns of interaction that are not problems in the sense that they are related to nothing negative in concurrent marital unhappiness, or they predict nothing negative in marital or child outcomes.

Second, what is functional when a marriage is going well? This question provides new answers to the first question. Our research has been informed by studies of the disasters as well as the masters of marriage. The masters are doing and thinking unique things to create and maintain intimacy and manage disagreements that are not simply the absence of negativity. The idea here is to create an intimate psychology of everyday marriage that will inform theory construction and the development of interventions.

Third, what is the etiology of marital dysfunction? For example, what is the etiology of the often critical, harsh start-up of a marital issue displayed by unhappy couples in the attack-defend mode? We have discovered that a harsh start-up can be predicted by the irritability and lack of responsiveness of the partner in nonconflict conversations about events of the day; this has pointed us away from the conflict context and to consideration of the everyday moments of potential emotional connection.

Fourth, how can we understand why it is that some couples are able to *repair* their interaction once it becomes negative, whereas other couples' repair attempts fail? Finally, how can we understand why it is that some couples have access to their sense of humor and affection even when they are disagreeing, whereas others have very little positive affect?

Mathematical Ideas

The desire to create mathematical models was inspired by the very important book *General Systems Theory* (von Bertalanffy, 1963). This book inspired many major thinkers of family systems and family therapy, including Gregory Bateson, Don Jackson, and Paul Watzlawick. Unfortunately, the mathematics of general systems theory was not utilized by most of the social scientists who were influenced by von Bertalanffy's work. Bateson and colleagues (Bateson, Jackson, Haley, & Weakland, 1956) originally envisaged making their family systems theory mathematical (for a historical review, see Gottman, 1979), but did not do so. Hence, the nonmathematical work of these theorists of family interaction kept their systems concepts at the level of metaphor. Even at the level of metaphor, these concepts were tremendously influential in the field of family therapy (see Rosenblatt, 1994). However, they were never quantified or subjected to experimental processes. We have now done the work necessary to make this thinking mathematical, and not merely metaphorical.

Von Bertalanffy clearly viewed his theory as essentially mathematical. He believed that the interaction of complex systems with many units could be characterized by a set of values that change over time, denoted Q_1, Q_2, Q_3, and so on. Each of these Qs was a variable that indexed something important about a particular unit in the system, such as mother, father, and child. He thought that the system could be best described by a set of ordinary differential equations of the form:

$$dQ_1/dt = f_1(Q_1, Q_2, Q_3, \dots)$$
$$dQ_2/dt = f_2(Q_1, Q_2, Q_3, \dots)$$
and so on.

The terms on the left of the equal sign are time derivatives, that is, rates of change of the quantitative sets of values Q_1, Q_2, and so on. The terms on the right of the equal sign are functions, f_1, f_2, and so on, of the Qs. Von Bertalanffy thought that these functions, the fs, would generally be linear, but he had no suggestions for what the Qs ought to measure, nor what the fs ought to be. His vision remained a metaphorical one without a quantitative science to back it up.

We obtained the Qs for modeling from our ability to predict the longitudinal course of marriages. Gottman and Levenson (1992) have reported that a variable that describes specific interaction patterns in terms of the balance between negativity and positivity was predictive of marital dissolution. In this work, a methodology was used for obtaining synchronized physiological, behavioral, and self-report data in a sample of 73 couples who were followed longitudinally during a four-year period. Applying observational coding of interactive behavior with the Rapid Couples Interaction Scoring System (RCISS; Krokoff, Gottman, & Haas, 1989), couples were divided into two groups; a low-risk group and a high-risk group. This classification was based on a graphical method originally proposed by Gottman (1979) for use with the CISS, a predecessor of the RCISS. On each conversational turn, the total number of positive RCISS speaker codes minus the total number of negative speaker codes was computed for each spouse. Then the cumulative total of these points was plotted for each spouse. This creates a kind of Dow-Jones industrial average for a marital conversation. The slopes of these plots, which were thought to provide a stable estimate of the difference between positive and negative codes over time, were determined using linear regression analysis.

The decision to utilize the slopes in this way was guided by a balance theory of marriage, namely, that those processes most important in predicting dissolution would involve a *balance,* or a *regulation,* of positive and negative interaction. Consistent with this theory, we decided that low-risk couples would have to be those for whom both husband and wife speaker slopes were significantly positive (there was generally more positive than negative interaction). High-risk couples would have to be those for whom at least one of the speaker slopes was either negative or not significantly positive. We found that the high/low-risk distinction was able to predict the "cascade" toward divorce, which consisted of marital dissatisfaction, persistent thoughts about divorce and separation, and actual separation and divorce. Subsequently, the ability to predict the longitudinal course of marital relationships in this manner has now been found in our laboratories in four separate longitudinal studies (see Gottman, 1993, 1994; Gottman, Coan, Carrere, & Swanson, 1998; Jacobson, Gottman, Gortner, Berns, & Shortt, 1996).

In our first paper using mathematical modeling (Cook et al., 1995), we made use of these speaker slopes as the Qs in our equations and used them to develop a mathematical model that might explain the Gottman-Levenson findings. The equations were very similar to the ones that von Bertalanffy had envisioned, except that we used discrete difference equations rather than differential equations. There is one additional difference. As noted, von Bertalanffy thought that the equations had to be linear. He presented a table in which these nonlinear

equations were classified as "impossible" (von Bertalanffy, 1968, p. 20), referring to the popular mathematical method of approximating nonlinear functions with a linear approximation. Unfortunately, linear equations are not generally stable, so they tend to give erroneous solutions, except as approximations under very local conditions near a steady state. Von Bertalanffy was not aware of the mathematics Poincaré and others had developed in the last quarter of the nineteenth century for the study of nonlinear systems. It was actually no longer the case that these nonlinear systems were impossible, even in von Bertalanffy's day. This is even more true today, when the modeling of complex deterministic (and stochastic) systems with a set of nonlinear difference or differential equations has become a productive enterprise across a wide set of phenomena in a wide range of sciences. Thus, the use of nonlinear equations formed the basis of our first attempts at modeling marital interaction (these methods are described in detail in Cook et al., 1995).

This general method of mathematical modeling with nonlinear equations has been employed with great success in the biological sciences, and many departments of applied mathematics now have a mathematical biology program (Murray, 1989). It is a quantitative approach that allows the modeler to be able to write down, in mathematical form, on the basis of some theory, the causes of change in the dependent variables. For example, in mathematical ecology, in the classic predator-prey problem, one writes down the rate of change in the population densities of the prey and of the predator as some function of their current densities (e.g., Murray, 1989). Although this is a simple representation of the predator-prey phenomenon, it has served well as an initial exploratory model. An advantage of nonlinear equations (in addition to their possibility of stability) is that by employing nonlinear terms in the equations of change, some very complex processes can be represented with very few parameters. Unfortunately, unlike many linear equations, these nonlinear equations are generally not solvable in closed functional mathematical form. For this reason, the methods are often called "qualitative," and visual graphical methods and numerical approximation must be relied on. For this purpose, numerical and graphical methods have been developed, such as phase space plots. These visual approaches to mathematical modeling can be very appealing in engaging the intuition of a scientist working in a field that has no mathematically stated theory. If the scientist has an intuitive familiarity with the data of the field, our approach may suggest a way of building theory using mathematics in an initially qualitative manner. The use of these graphical solutions to nonlinear differential equations makes it possible to talk about "qualitative" mathematical modeling. In qualitative mathematical modeling, one searches for solutions that have similarly shaped phase space plots, which provide a good qualitative description of the solution and how it varies with the parameters.

However, unlike other fields, psychology and marital therapy had no scientific basis for writing down the equations, no phenomena, no principles. Hence, the process of building the models took four years, and another three years to modify the model until it reached its present form. Basically, we dismantled each partner's Dow-Jones average into two parts: how well each person's behavior could be predicted from his or her immediate past, and another term that was the partner's influence. From that simple decomposition came the integration of affect and power in relationships.

Another advantage of this kind of modeling is that, once the model for a couple and the parameter estimates are developed, the equations permit the *simulation* of the couple's interaction under new conditions, with different parameter values, such as when a partner begins the interaction much more positively than has ever been observed. This possibility leads to natural proximal change experiments in which very specific interventions are tested with the goal of changing the second of two interactions so it does not look so dysfunctional. This is an alternative to clinical trials in which a very complex intervention is tested against a control group. Proximal change experiments can eventually lead to more complex clinical trials.

The modeling of marital interaction using the mathematical methods of nonlinear difference equations is an attempt to integrate the mathematical insights of von Bertalanffy with the general systems theorists of family systems (Bateson, Jackson, Haley, & Weakland, 1956) using nonlinear equations. The methods introduce a new language for thinking about and describing interaction.

A basic concept in this modeling is that every system of equations has one or more stable or unstable "steady states" or "attractors." These stable attractors are like the old family systems notion of homeostatic set points of the system. These are values toward which the system is drawn and, if perturbed from the stable attractor, return the system back toward it. However, in our models, there are both uninfluenced attractors and influenced attractors. The uninfluenced attractor is what each person brings to the interaction, assuming there are times of zero or near zero influence. The influenced attractor is what happens as each person influences the other in particular ways. The difference between influenced and uninfluenced attractors gives one an estimate of power, or how the interactive system pushes each person.

The Concepts of Repair and Damping

In theorizing about mother-infant interaction, Brazelton (e.g., Brazelton, Koslowski, & Main, 1974) suggested that mother-infant interaction could be the sine qua non of human interaction, and that the healthy norm was a cyclic shared rhythmicity and coordination of interaction. However, Gianino and Tronick (1988), in observing mother-infant interaction, reported that 70% of mother-infant interaction was actually miscoordinated. Hence, miscoordination is the norm, not coordination. What they found was that some mothers noticed the miscoordination and tried to repair the interaction, and other mothers did not. The mother's use of repair later predicted the infant's attachment security. Gianino and Tronick built a theory of interactive regulation and repair based on their findings. Hence, repair is a down-regulation of negative affect. In our own modeling, we also studied couples' repair of negativity. We hypothesize that in married couples, repair is the one central theoretical construct that will consistently discriminate couples whose marriages are dissatisfied and headed for divorce from those whose marriages are satisfied and stable (e.g., see Gottman, 1999).

The concept of "damping" is the analog of repair for positive affect. It is a down-regulation of positive affect. At first, we thought that damping would not be a helpful event in interaction, but our mathematical work has shown that there are many examples when down-regulating positive affect will produce a stable steady state in the positive-positive quadrant of phase space, whereas none would exist without damping. Hence, it turned out, much to our surprise, that the down-regulation of positive affect can be a good thing.

Parameters of the Modeling
Our initial modeling (Cook et al., 1995) produced five parameters. First, there was the un-influenced steady state for each partner, which represented the attractors reflecting what that partner brought to the interaction before influence began. This uninfluenced state turned out to be a function both of that partner's personality and of the immediate past history of the relationship (Gottman et al., 1998). Second, there were the emotional inertia parameters, which assess the tendency of each person's behavior to be predictable from that person's immediate past behavior. Third, there were the influenced steady states, in which each partner was drawn

to follow the social influence process. Fourth, there were the influence functions, which, for each spouse's affect value, describe the average effect of that affect value (over the entire interaction) on the partner. These influence functions provide a more detailed description of interpersonal influence or power. The power function is defined in our modeling as the ability of one person's affect to move the other partner's affect. This adds precision to the power concept. For example, one person may be more influential than the other with positive affect, and the pattern may be reversed for negative affect. Fifth, the initial model has now been modified to include a repair term, which is repair of negative interaction that is potentially triggered at a particular threshold of a partner's negativity and is effective at pushing the data in a more positive direction. The two repair terms have two parameters: the threshold of the repair and its effectiveness. The damping terms are analogous to the repair terms; they just refer to the down-regulation of positive rather than negative affect.

The Sound Marital House Theory
The sound marital house theory emerged from a search of what makes repair attempts during conflict and negative segments of the interaction effective. This theory organizes our results into seven components (see Figure 15.1). The first three components describe the marital friendship. They are (1) love maps, (2) fondness and admiration, and (3) bids and turning. Love maps refers to knowledge about one's partner's internal psychological world, about being known and showing interest in one another, and updating this knowledge periodically by asking questions. Assessment is done in our laboratory by coding our oral history interview.

Fondness and admiration refers to affection and respect in the marriage. The masters of marriage create what could be called a culture of affection and appreciation in small and genuine ways every day, and this system is the

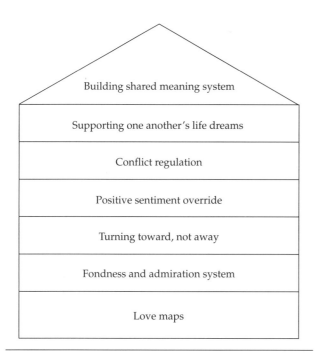

Figure 15.1   The sound marital house theory.

antidote to contempt. Bids and turning refers to our discovery of a primary sequence of emotional connection in our apartment laboratory. The bid refers to one person's direct or indirect request for some response from the partner; the responses are organized in a loose hierarchy from attention to conversation, emotional support, affection, humor, play, and so on. The partner either turns toward, turns away, or turns against the bid. Turning toward ranges from a minimal response to an enthusiastic response; turning away involves ignoring or not noticing the partner's bid; turning against is an irritable response to a partner's bid. We discovered that playful bidding and enthusiastic turning toward are strongly correlated, and we hypothesized that it is causally connected to having a sense of humor during conflict discussions and being able to be affectionate toward one's spouse even when disagreeing. On the other hand, we found that turning away is related to, and we hypothesize that it is causally connected to, an attack-defend mode during conflict. The attack-defend mode was predictive

of early divorcing (about five years after the wedding, on average) in a 14-year longitudinal study (Gottman & Levenson, 2000). Turning against was related to, and we hypothesize that it is causally connected to, an emotionally withdrawn pattern during conflict, which was predictive of later divorcing (about 16 years after the wedding, on average) in a 14-year longitudinal study (Gottman & Levenson, 2000).

The sound marital house theory suggests that when the first three levels of the sound marital house are working well, that is, the friendship in the marriage is working well, people will be in a state of positive sentiment override. Sentiment override is a concept introduced by Weiss (1980) in which he suggested that couples are in one of two states: positive sentiment override or negative sentiment override. The concept is defined by discrepancies between insider and outsider perspectives on the marriage. In positive sentiment override, people's positive sentiments about the spouse and the relationship generally override momentary irritability and emotional distance. However, in negative sentiment override, people's negative sentiments about the spouse and the relationship generally override momentary positivity, and people even view neutral statements as negative; they are hypervigilant for insults. It is our view that negative sentiment override cannot be changed directly, but that it is caused by the first three levels of the sound marital house not working well. We hypothesize that therapists cannot directly induce people to be "less sensitive," or to not be hypervigilant to negativity, or to think more positively about the partner or the relationship.

According to the theory, positive sentiment override is responsible for effective repair during conflict, and negative sentiment override is responsible for the failure of repair during conflict. There is now evidence that sentiment overrides are strongly related to the effectiveness of repair. Clinically, it also appears that the first three levels of the sound marital house are responsible for romance, passion, and good sex in the marriage, particularly the bids and turning portion. This was initially a surprise, but in hindsight, it made a great deal of sense. We now think that romance and passion are built by microsocial processes that build emotional connection and thus create a sense of intimacy. We studied this phenomenon at first with questionnaires and found that good sex, romance, and passion in the marriage were strongly related to the couple's self-report of the quality of the first three levels of the sound marital house. Further research is needed on these issues. However, Zilbergeld (in press) studied a group of marriages where couples were 45 years of age or older and claimed that they had very good sex lives. He found that, when compared to a similar group of couples who had disappointing sex lives, the common ingredient that emerged was that the group who claimed that they had good sex lives said that they were very good friends and that is what accounted for their good sex lives. They also tended to mention keeping alive romance and passion and working to ensure that this was the case.

The next level of the sound marital house is the regulation of conflict. There were some new findings when we studied couples' conflict interaction four years apart. It turned out that there was enormous stability to the marital interaction over the four-year period. Many correlations were in the .60s to the .80s. Furthermore, when we examined the *content* of the conversations, most of the couples were talking about the same issues and in the same ways (in terms of Specific Affect Coding System codes). In fact, if we were to edit the two videotapes of the same couple together, in most cases it would appear that they were talking about the same issues in the same ways. With this study, we came to realize that most marital conflicts are not solvable, but instead are *perpetual* issues. These issues are simply endemic; they arise from basic differences in personality, needs, and lifestyle preferences of the partners, and they will usually not ever be resolved. Couples will be talking about these same issues for the next 20, 30, or 40 years.

There are two kinds of couples in terms of handling perpetual issues. There are couples who make an adaptation to these problems and learn to cope with them. They are in a state we call "dialogue" about these issues. They are in conflict about them, but they generally are accepting of one another's personalities and positive about the marriage. They seem to communicate a kind of magical formula to their partners: "I love you, I love this marriage, I don't want you to change, but for God's sake, will you please change?" It is change within the context of acceptance, an idea that has formed the basis of Christensen and Jacobson's (2000) acceptance-based marital therapy. Other couples are in a state we call "gridlock" on these perpetual issues. Every time they discuss the issue, they feel hurt, alienated, and rejected by their partner. They are in one of two modes around the gridlocked conflict: an attack-defend mode or an emotionally disengaged mode. The emotionally disengaged mode is either a later stage of gridlock or a style the couple has had for some time.

The major clinical objective around conflict (these are the issues 69% of the time) is not resolving conflict: It is moving a couple from gridlock to dialogue on the issue. This is accomplished with the existentially based "dreams-within-conflict intervention," which approaches gridlocked conflict by recognizing that people cannot yield on these issues because each person's position has symbolic meaning that is core to that person's sense of self. There are two steps in this intervention: Step 1 is releasing the dreams behind each person's position on the issue; step 2 is helping the couple honor both dreams.

About 31% of the conflicts were resolved during the four-year period they were studied. The masters of marriage took a very gentle approach to these conflicts. They softened their start-up, meaning they did not present the issue as a symptom of a deeper personality flaw in their partner. They accepted influence from one another, rather than rejecting influence by escalating the conflict. They used positive affect to de-escalate the conflict and physiologically soothe one another (see Gottman et al., 1998).

METHODS OF ASSESSMENT AND INTERVENTION

ASSESSMENT

The purpose of assessment is to individualize the therapy and to further refine the theory of how marriage works. The assessment begins with the couple's narrative and each person's individual narrative; these narratives are the center of the assessment. There is one conjoint 90-minute assessment session that has the following parts: (1) the couple's narrative; (2) the oral history interview; (3) a 10-minute videotaped conflict discussion; (4) debriefing, scheduling the individual sessions, and giving each person the questionnaire packet. This session is followed by two individual sessions that assess (1) each person's individual narrative; (2) where they are in the marriage and the therapy in terms of hopes, commitment to the marriage, and fears; (3) the presence of violence and/or battering, and any ongoing extramarital affair; (4) their cost-benefit analysis of the marriage. The third conjoint session is about the assessment summary, goal setting, and therapeutic contracting.

The sound marital house is the basis for elaborating these narratives in a systematic manner for assessment. It is a strength-based assessment, in which the strengths and the areas that need improvement are assessed. A multimethod approach to assessment is used, employing questionnaires, interviews (the oral history interview, the meta-emotion interview,

and the meanings interview), a short videotape of the couple discussing an area of continuing disagreement, and questionnaires to assess the following basic central dimensions of the marriage: (1) love maps, (2) fondness and admiration, (3) bids and turning, (4) sentiment overrides, (5) the regulation of conflict (on perpetual and solvable issues), (6) honoring life dreams, and (7) the shared meaning system. We also assess marital satisfaction, persistent thoughts about divorce, physical and emotional abuse, flooding, parallel lives, loneliness, and psychopathology.

We recommend having a library of assessment tools, because in every case, there may be different dimensions of the marriage that are salient to understanding the problem.

INTERVENTION

Goals

There are six goals of this marital therapy model:

1. Move the couple from gridlock to dialogue on their perpetual issues.
2. Enable the couple to process a marital argument without the therapist. Processing a fight means that the couple can talk about the argument without starting the fight again; they can see that there are two subjective realities in every argument; they can think of one way of making the next conversation better than their last on this issue.
3. Establish six social skills: (1) label and replace the four horsemen of the apocalypse (criticism, contempt, defensiveness, and stonewalling) with their antidotes (complaining, creating a culture of appreciation in the marriage, accepting responsibility for even a part of the problem, and self-soothing, respectively); (2) softened start-up; (3) accepting influence; (4) physiological

soothing (self and other); (5) effective repair; and (6) compromise.

4. Build friendship as a base for effective repair: (1) process failed bids for connection; (2) set up meaningful rituals of connection; (3) set up methods of managing stress.
5. Fade out the therapist; plan for relapse, vacations, and follow-ups for two years after termination.
6. Build the shared meaning system.

These six goals follow directly from the sound marital house theory (which is also the basis of the assessment). *Probably the most important goal with respect to repeating conflict is the couple's being able to process a fight.* Repair is the central construct of the therapy.

Methods of the Therapy
The work of the therapy emerges from the process in each session. Couples always bring to the therapist the ways in which they are "stuck" in accomplishing the six therapeutic goals. The theory of the sound marital house is a template in the therapist's mind; it does not constitute an agenda that the therapist uses to structure therapy. Couples come into sessions with two types of issues: They either have had horrible conflict that leaves them feeling alienated from one another or they are feeling lonely due to failed bids for emotional connection, or both. They need to be able to process conflicts and failed bids for connection without the therapist.

With Respect to Conflict
The techniques of the therapy involve the dreams within conflict intervention for creating initial dramatic change (it also is used throughout therapy as one encounters conflicts with symbolic meanings). This is followed by structured change with respect to conflict. One of the important parts of the therapy is opening up the attack-defend mode. There are five ways of accomplishing this: (1) using Dan Wile's

(1992) method of introducing the internal dialectic; (2) learning how to process fights through video playback and the aftermath of a fight questionnaire; (3) creating insights into fights and repeating negative patterns: examining the anatomies of attack and defend (the internal working models of attack and defend), the repetitive negative cycles, and enduring vulnerabilities; (4) formalizing repair; and (5) having the conversation the couple never had but needed to have (which can often be determined from the fight itself).

With Respect to Building Friendship
The fundamental unit of friendship is the bid and the turning response (turning toward, away, or against). This bid and turning unit has an anatomy, just as attack and defend have an anatomy. The couple learns to process failed bids for connection. The therapist helps the couple set up meaningful rituals, formal and informal, for emotional connection. Working with the affectional system and bids and turning, the therapy integrates sex therapy with marital therapy. Based on our research with older long-term marriages, romance and passion are not considered absurd romantic ideals, but are realistic goals.

The Shared Meaning System
This is an existential marital therapy, and the most difficult conflicts in a marriage have symbolic meaning. Thus, the therapist is always helping the couple build the shared meaning system. The meanings interview is a direct approach to building the shared meaning system.

Minimizing Relapse
In the Munich marital study, Boegner and Zielenbach-Coenen (1984) discovered that massed intervention (long sessions) early in the marital therapy and phased fading later in the therapy result in larger treatment effects and less relapse than a uniform set of sessions. They delivered the same amount of therapy as

Table 15.1   Sample from the Table of Interventions.

Intervention Content	Description	Page*
Friendship, Intimacy		
Love maps	Introduce concept love map cards	185
Love maps	Generalization to everyday life	185
Fondness and admiration	Positive adjective checklist	189
Fondness and admiration	Thanksgiving exercise	190
Deepening love maps	Injury and healing	192
Deepening love maps	Mission and legacy	192
Deepening love maps	Triumphs and Strivings	193
Fondness and admiration	Generalization to everyday life	195
Emotional bank account	Areas of strength checklist	196
Emotional bank account	Generalization to everyday life	197
Emotional bank account	Stress-reducing conversation	199
Working as a team	Paper tower exercise	202
Negotiating marital power	Who does what in the marriage	203
Physiological soothing	Soothing one's partner	206
Conflict Regulation		
Softened start-up	Problem items and stems	212
Repair and de-escalate	Repair checklist	218
Flooding and self-soothing	Couple break ritual	220
Self-soothing	Five steps of self-soothing	223
Accepting influence	Find common ground	224
Compromise	Steps toward compromise	225
Meta-emotion	Your history w/basic emotion and mismatches	226
Dreams within conflict A	Acceptance and adaptations already made	227
Accept one another	Accept what you cannot change	228
Dreams within conflict B	Finding dreams in others' gridlock	229
Part 1, ending gridlock	The dreams emerge	241
Part 2, ending gridlock	Fears of accepting influence	243
Part 3, ending gridlock	Honoring both people's dreams	245
Stuck in attack-defend	Rapport conflict exercise	322
Stuck in four horsemen	Speaking and Writing Exercise	323
Individual training skills	Audiotape six pack in three skills Softened startup, accepting influence, Editing negativity	not in manual
Relapse Prevention		
Reset negativity threshold	Marital poop detector	275
Build rituals of connection	Informal and formal rituals	277
Magic five hours a week	Basic emotional connections	280
Culture of pride and praise	Antidote to contempt	281
Decision-making style	Mountain survival	288
Marital mismatches	Confront mismatches	291
Philosophy of marriage	Oral history dyadic version	292
Marital mismatches	Decision-making styles	296
Fondness and admiration	Change cognitions in 7 weeks	297
Team building	Island survival	299
Team building	Shared meanings	304
Team building	Paper tower with straws	307
Marriage contract	17 areas as a contract	310
Building solidarity	Shared values	321
Rituals of connection	Emotional communication	460
One person less committed	Cost-benefit analysis exercise	321

*Page numbers refer to clinician manual (Gottman, 1996).

the Hahlweg group (their mentors; Hahlweg, Schindler, Revenstorf, & Brengelmann, 1984), but changed the distribution of the therapy, using 90-minute sessions and structured vacations from therapy, with homework that they monitored. These results are taken very seriously. All of our sessions are 90 minutes long, and we attempt to make the therapy as dyad-focused as possible, with the therapist's methods being very clear and very public, the goal being to transfer these methods to the couple.

In addition to these general interventions, our proximal change experiments and our weekend workshop for couples have given rise to a library of very specific interventions. The library is growing over time. Table 15.1 is a brief summary of some of these interventions, which are described in detail in our clinician's manual (Gottman, 1996).

MAJOR SYNDROMES, SYMPTOMS, AND PROBLEMS TREATED

This approach seeks to treat almost all marital issues. The research evidence suggests that marital therapy is contraindicated in only two situations: where violence is being used to control and intimidate one of the partners, a pattern Neil Jacobson (Jacobson & Gottman, 1999) called "battering"; and when there is an ongoing extramarital affair. There has yet to be a randomized clinical trial outcome study on extramarital affairs. The literature on marital interventions for treating or preventing violence is not much better; otherwise, we think that all other comorbidities can be treated with marital therapy. There may be a need to supplement the marital therapy when there is a serious comorbidity. But the evidence with alcoholism suggests that the problem can be treated even more successfully when there is a marital component, and that with an individual treatment component the marital therapy is even more effective

than it normally is. This surprising result can be found in the work of both O'Farrell and McCrady (e.g., McCrady, Stout, Noel, Abrams, & Nelson, 1991; O'Farrell, 1995).

CASE EXAMPLE

The couple, Bob and Samantha, had been married for 20 years. Our first contact with them was when they attended our two-day workshop. They were very close to getting a divorce when they came to the workshop. It was a last-ditch effort before seeing a divorce lawyer, a state of affairs that is not uncommon in our workshop population. Samantha is a smart woman with a great sense of humor. She has a great way with words, is very articulate. She came from a primary family shattered by alcoholism and divorce. As a teenager, she had so many fights with her alcoholic mother that she opted to live with her father and stepmother, a decision she was later to regret. They used her as a baby sitter, chief cook, and bottle washer to the stepmother's children. Her father was away, traveling as a salesman a great deal, and her stepmother was a nurse who worked long hours. So Samantha became the Cinderella, doing all the work of the house. She felt unappreciated and also terrified of her stepmother's rages. She kept all of her anger inside for fear that she might be sent back to her own alcoholic mother.

Bob came from an emotionally unexpressive family. When he was a young boy of about 13 years, he was teased one day by his peers and walked off into the woods to cope with this horrible experience. He wrote a poem in which he described himself as someone who could not be hurt because his real self was locked deep inside of him and he was actually not responding to anything or anyone. It worked, in some ways. He stopped getting teased (because he did not respond to teasing). But it also cost him a great deal in his later relationships with his work friends, wife, and children. He became a very successful top-management executive in a large computer software company, but his job became increasingly meaningless to him. Now, after about 15 years of alienation from his wife, he wants to rebuild his marriage and become closer to his children.

After the workshop, Bob and Samantha entered marital therapy. They reported that the workshop started a dramatic change in their marriage. He said that the revelation was in the lecture and exercise on processing fights, in which we said that in every fight there are two very different subjective realities, both right. In the next conversation with his wife, he made it his job to find out her subjective reality, and started asking her a great many questions. She said she was startled by this. She said that for 15 years he had always argued that he was right in every discussion. She thought that there was nothing he could do to change how alienated she felt from him, and then, in just 15 minutes of his listening to her, she felt entirely different toward him.

Their relationship began to change after the workshop. Therapy began, as usual, with the assessment sessions. In the first conjoint session, Bob said that he thought Samantha had no idea how much he cared for her. She responded that she would like him to take the initiative in conversations and to raise issues. Bob kept saying that he didn't really know what to do. He said that he frequently felt misunderstood.

In the first individual session, each of them began talking about the shared meaning system. He said that what he wanted as his epitaph was "He helped people." He works at a large corporation as an upper-level executive. However, his job has had no meaning to him for the past two years, except when he was helping an African country. He said that he wants to be a better father and husband. He wants his helping to start with Samantha. He wants to be on boards of arts councils with her and wants to do meaningful work with her. He said that he

wants his helping to start with his family, especially his wife.

In Samantha's individual session, she said that she felt like "girl interrupted." She used to be interested in playing piano, writing, and painting, and thought, What happened to that girl? She said that she had been there for the children, but that she had lost interest in being there for Bob. She wasn't even sure that he noticed. She thought that now she might like to write a book. She said that everything had changed suddenly for her in the workshop. Both said that working on the relationship was now important to them. She worried about how she was going to deal with her resentment about the past.

In the next session, Bob repeated his desire to help people and asked Samantha if she wanted that also. She said that she had helped people all her life and that wasn't what she wanted to do now. He told her that he wanted "He helped people" to appear on his tombstone and then asked her what she might want to appear on her tombstone. She said that she wanted to write a book on her life, one that was very personal. She then asked if he wanted to help people without her or with her. He said that he definitely wanted her included. They talked about the goals for the therapy and emphasized that being able to deal with fights and being able to connect with one another was very important.

In the next session, they said that the past week had been rough. Samantha said that she woke up early on Saturday and everyone else was sleeping in, and that she had to admit that she became angry because she was ready to do things and everyone else was asleep and she was tired of having to adjust to everyone else's needs. Bob said that it felt to him that her whole world was falling apart and that it was all his fault, and when he feels like that he just wants to leave. I asked them what weekends were like in each of their families. Bob said that his father was a shift worker and that there was no set schedule, but that there was always a list of chores to do. Everyone led parallel lives and he spent lots of time alone in his radio room. She said that her dad used to watch cartoons with them on Saturday morning and her mom made pancakes, but that after her parents divorced, it was everyone for himself or herself. She said that consistency was not a big part of her childhood. We then discussed what rituals of connection they would like for their weekends. They decided to spend Saturday mornings going out for coffee. He decided he could practice his new skill of asking questions.

In the next session, Samantha said that she realized that no one had been there for her when she was trying to raise the children and Bob was working all the time. Bob said that he really wanted to be close to Samantha, and then she patted his arm in a patronizing way and said, "You just don't get it." I asked him what his thoughts were when he said that, and he said that he felt really sad that no one had been there for her when she was a kid either, and he admired the way she was toward people, always giving to them. I asked her how she felt hearing that, and she said that she felt very little. I said that it was hard for her to let Bob be close now, and I paraphrased what he said (as the therapist Dan Wile might have done). I paraphrased: "I think there's something delicate and fragile about Samantha and it's part of what I love about her. But somehow it winds up making her stuck. I don't understand how, but it does, and that makes me very sad." She said that was all very true. So I suggested that when he said it, she couldn't hear the love in it, and she agreed. He said that this moment was like recourting her, not with flowers, but by reaching out to her.

In the next session, they had had a fight, and she came in saying that she needed individual therapy and perhaps medication. They began processing the fight. They had gone out for coffee and she had gotten a drink she didn't order. He suggested that she take it back, and she said that she would prefer to just forget about it. He

became forceful about her needing to be assertive, and she ran out of the coffee house feeling overly emotional and somewhat crazy. When she told him about her subjective reality about the fight, he turned to her and said, "There's not very much that I regret in my life, but one thing I really regret was that I ever made you feel like you were crazy." He was crying when he said it. She cried also, and when she left the session, she said that she didn't think she needed any medication or a referral to a psychiatrist.

In their next session, they both said that they felt very good about the week. They had connected with one another all week, doing very simple things together, like going grocery shopping together. When she enthusiastically suggested that they buy paint to paint their daughter's room, he thought of all the other errands that they needed to do, but he heard the enthusiasm in her voice and said, "Sure, let's go." She was very moved by this response. It was the beginning of their increased sensitivity to bids and turning toward one another.

Over the next several sessions, they kept working on these twin themes of processing fights and understanding one another's perspective, and turning toward one another. He had decided to leave his job and take an early retirement. They discussed what this meant to him and to both of them, and he proceeded to leave. His adjustment to retirement was surprisingly easy, and they had much more time for one another.

Currently, they are still in therapy.

RESEARCH ON EFFICACY AND EFFECTIVENESS

Ongoing research evaluating our interventions is taking place on several levels. The first level of intervention research is proximal change experiments. These are experiments in which a brief and very specific intervention is designed to create only proximal change, making the second of two conversations the couple has better than the first. The experiments are the components of our therapy intervention library and of our weekend couples' workshop. These brief interventions have been pilot-tested for the past eight years.

The couples workshop has been evaluated in a five-group randomized experimental design. Six-month postworkshop follow-up data are currently being collected, and the study has not yet been written up for publication. Hence, the presentation of results in this chapter must be brief and incomplete.

There were five groups in the study: (1) a bibliotherapy control group; (2) a one-day workshop that focused only on conflict regulation; (3) a one-day workshop that focused only on building the couple's friendship; (4) a two-day workshop that included both components; and, (5) a two-day workshop plus eight sessions of marital therapy that sought to individualize the sound marital house interventions for each couple, and stress management. To date, only the marital satisfaction data have been analyzed. The marital satisfaction data on six-month follow-up show that the two-day workshop produced large increases that were maintained on follow-up; however, the gains leveled off. The two-day workshop plus therapy group kept significantly increasing in marital satisfaction from the end of the workshop to the six-month follow-up.

The next step in our outcome evaluation is to have the two-day workshop plus therapy group serve as the control group, and have a second experimental group which has a two-day workshop plus therapy group plus marital therapy in our marriage clinic; that study is currently being planned.

REFERENCES

Bakeman, R., & Gottman, J. (1986). *Observing interaction: An introduction to sequential analysis.* New York: Cambridge University Press.

Bateson, G., Jackson, D. D., Haley, J., & Weakland, J. (1956). Toward a theory of schizophrenia. *Behavioral Science, 1,* 251–264.

Birchler, G., Weiss, R., & Vincent, J. (1975). Multimethod analysis of social reinforcement exchange between maritally distressed and nondistressed spouse and stranger dyads. *Journal of Personality and Social Psychology, 31,* 349–360.

Boegner, I., & Zielenbach-Coenen, H. (1984). On maintaining change in behavioral marital therapy. In K. Hahlweg & N. S. Jacobson (Eds.), *Marital interaction: Analysis and modification* (pp. 27–35). New York: Guilford Press.

Box, G. E. P., & Jenkins, G. M. (1970). *Time-series analysis: Forecasting and control.* San Francisco: Holden-Day.

Brazelton, T. B., Koslowski, B., & Main, M. (1974). The origins of reciprocity: The early mother-infant interaction. In M. Lewis & L. Rosenbaum (Eds.), *The effect of the infant on its caregiver* (pp. 49–76). New York: Wiley.

Christensen, A., & Jacobson, N. S. (2000). *Reconcilable differences.* New York: Guilford Press.

Cook, J., Tyson, R., White, J., Rushe, R., Gottman, J., & Murray, J. (1995). Mathematics of marital conflict: Qualitative dynamic modeling of marital interaction. *Journal of Family Psychology, 9,* 110–130.

Davies, P. C. W. (1991). *The mind of God.* New York: Simon & Schuster.

Gianino, A., & Tronick, E. Z. (1988). The mutual regulation model: The infant's self and interactive regulation and coping and defensive capacities. In T. M. Field, P. M. McCabe, & N. Schneiderman (Eds.), *Stress and coping across development* (pp. 47–70). Hillsdale, NJ: Erlbaum.

Goldfried, M. R., & D'Zurilla, T. J. (1969). A behavioral-analytic model for assessing competence. In C. D. Spielberger (Ed.), *Current topics in clinical and community psychology* (Vol. 1). New York: Academic Press.

Gottman, J. M. (1979). *Marital interaction: Experimental investigations.* New York: Academic Press.

Gottman, J. M. (1993). The roles of conflict engagement, escalation or avoidance in marital interaction: A longitudinal view of five types of couples. *Journal of Consulting and Clinical Psychology, 61,* 6–15.

Gottman, J. M. (1996). *A clinical manual of marital therapy.* Unpublished, The Gottman Institute, Seattle, WA.

Gottman, J. M. (1999). *The marriage clinic*. New York: Norton.

Gottman, J. M., Coan, J., Carrère, S., & Swanson, C. (1998). Predicting marital happiness and stability from newlywed interactions. *Journal of Marriage and the Family, 60*, 5–22.

Gottman, J. M., & Levenson, R. W. (1992). Marital processes predictive of later dissolution: Behavior, physiology, and health. *Journal of Personality and Social Psychology, 63*, 221–233.

Gottman, J. M., & Levenson, R. W. (2000). Predicting the timing of divorce: Results of a 14-year longitudinal study. *Journal of Marriage and the Family*.

Gottman, J. M., McCoy, K., Coan, J., & Collier, H. (1996). The Specific Affect Coding System (SPAFF) for observing emotional communication in marital and family interaction. In J. M. Gottman (Ed.), *What predicts divorce? The measures*. Mahwah, NJ: Erlbaum.

Gottman, J. M., & Notarius, C. I. (2001). Decade review paper on observing marital interaction. *Journal of Marriage and the Family*.

Gottman, J. M., & Roy, A. K. (1990). *Sequential analysis of observational data*. New York: Cambridge University Press.

Hahlweg, K., Schindler, L., Revenstorf, D., & Bengelmann, J. C. (1984). The Munich marital study. In K. Hahlweg & N. S. Jacobson (Eds.), *Marital interaction: Analysis and modification* (pp. 3–26). New York: Guilford Press.

Jacobson, N. S., & Gottman, J. M. (1999). *When men batter women*. New York: Simon & Schuster.

Jacobson, N. S., Gottman, J. M., Gortner, E., Berns, S., & Shortt, J. W. (1996). Psychological factors in the longitudinal course of battering: When do the couples split up? When does the abuse decrease? *Violence and Victims, 11*, 371–392.

Krokoff, L. J., Gottman, J. M., & Haas, S. D. (1989). Validation of a rapid couples interaction scoring system. *Behavioral Assessment, 11*, 65–79.

McCrady, B. S., Stout, R., Noel, N., Abrams, D., & Nelson, H. (1991). Comparative effectiveness of three types of spouse involved alcohol treatment: Outcomes 18 months after treatment. *British Journal of Addiction, 86*, 1415–1424.

Murray, J. D. (1989). *Mathematical biology*. Berlin, Germany: Springer-Verlag.

Notarius, C. I., Benson, P. R., Sloane, D., Vanzetti, N. A., & Hornyak, L. M. (1989). Exploring the interface between perception and behavior: An analysis of marital interaction in distressed and nondistressed couples. *Behavioral Assessment, 11*, 39–64.

O'Farrell, T. J. (1995). Marital and family therapy. In R. K. Hester & W. R. Miller (Eds.), *Handbook of alcoholism treatment approaches: Effective alternatives* (pp. 195–220). Boston: Allyn & Bacon.

Patterson, G. R. (1982). *Coercive family process*. Eugene, OR: Castalia.

Rosenblatt, P. C. (1994). *Metaphors of family systems theory*. New York: Guilford Press.

Rubin, M. E. (1977). *Differences between distressed and nondistressed couples in verbal and nonverbal communication codes*. Unpublished doctoral dissertation, Indiana University, South Bend.

Terman, L. M., Buttenwieser, P., Ferguson, L. W., Johnson, W. B., & Wilson, D. P. (1938). *Psychological factors in marital happiness*. New York: McGraw-Hill.

Thibaut, J. W., & Kelley, H. H. (1959). *The social psychology of groups*. New York: Wiley.

von Bertalanffy, L. (1968). *General systems theory*. New York: Braziller.

Weiss, R. L. (1980). Strategic behavioral marital therapy: Toward a model for assessment and intervention. In J. P. Vincent (Ed.), *Advances in family intervention, assessment and theory* (Vol. 1, pp. 229–271). Greenwich, CT: JAI Press.

Weiss, R. L., Hops, H., & Patterson, G. R. (1973). A framework for conceptualizing marital conflict. In L. A. Hamerlynck, L. C. Handy, & E. J. Marsh (Eds.), *Behavior change: Methodology, concepts, and practice* (pp. 309–342). Champaign, IL: Research Press.

Wile, D. (1992). *After the fight*. New York: Guilford Press.

Zilbergeld, B. (in press). *Great sex after 45*. New York: Simon & Schuster.

CHAPTER 16

Cognitive Therapy with Couples

MARK A. WHISMAN AND LAUREN M. WEINSTOCK

In a 1999 public opinion poll by Bennett, Petts, and Blumenthal, 99% of Americans reported that loving family relationships are extremely (91%) or somewhat (9%) important to them (as cited in Bogenschneider, 2000). Over 50% of marriages in the United States, however, ended in divorce (Martin & Bumpass, 1989). Developing effective forms of couple therapy, therefore, is important for treating relationship dissatisfaction and for decreasing rates of marital dissolution.

A myriad of factors have been evaluated in the onset, maintenance, and treatment of relationship problems, including intrapersonal, interpersonal, and environmental influences (as reviewed by Bradbury, Fincham, & Beach, 2000). One important intrapersonal factor has been the study of cognitions in relationship functioning and couple therapy. In this chapter, we provide an overview of the history of cognitive approaches to working with couples, discuss the theoretical constructs on which these approaches are based, and discuss the major methods of assessment and intervention. We conclude with a review of the research evaluating cognitive therapy with couples.

HISTORY OF COGNITIVE THERAPY APPROACHES WITH COUPLES

The role of cognitive functioning in the treatment of relationship problems has been a primary focus in the work of Aaron T. Beck and Albert Ellis and their respective colleagues. Following the success of cognitive therapy as a treatment for depression (Beck, Rush, Shaw, & Emery, 1979), there have been many applications of Beck's cognitive therapy as a treatment for a variety of problem behaviors, including relationship dissatisfaction. Detailed information about the application of Beck's cognitive theory and treatment as applied to relationship difficulties can be found in A. T. Beck (1998) and Dattilio and Padesky (1990).

According to the cognitive perspective, relationship problems are the result of the same type of cognitions that typify other emotional or behavioral problems. Specifically, relationship difficulties arise from negative schemas, which function as cognitive maps to help people operate in their social environment. Schemas are conceptualized as stable cognitive structures and cognitive generalizations, derived from past experience, that organize and guide the processing of information about oneself, one's partner, and one's relationship. Environmental events, in this case, relationship events or partner behaviors, activate these schemas, which in turn elicit stream-of-consciousness "automatic thoughts" and associated emotional and behavioral responses. Relationship difficulties also arise from cognitive distortions people make about their ongoing experience. There are many different types of cognitive distortions, and the interested reader is referred to A. T. Beck et al. (1979) for a complete discussion of these distortions. Among the most common distortions associated with relationship difficulties are dichotomous thinking (viewing situations in terms of categories versus continua; e.g., "My relationship is a failure" versus "We have some problems"), mindreading (believing one knows what others are thinking or feeling; e.g., "My partner doesn't love me"), and magnification/minimization (magnifying the negative or minimizing the positive in evaluations of experience; e.g., "Because my partner wasn't interested in sex last night she will never want to have sex with me").

A second cognitive approach to couples therapy is provided by Ellis and colleagues, who have applied Rational-Emotive Therapy (RET) as a treatment for relationship problems (Ellis, Sichel, Yeager, DiMattia, & DiGiuseppe, 1989). According to the RET perspective, relationship problems (as well as emotional and behavioral problems) are the result of irrational thinking, which is defined as "thinking that is highly exaggerated, inappropriately rigid, illogical, and especially, absolutist" (Ellis et al., 1989, p. 17). That is, when people "start with unrealistic expectations and then rigidly demand that their idealistic goals *must* be satisfied" (p. 13), disturbance in the relationship is likely to result. Ellis and colleagues discussed several kinds of irrational thinking that they believed would be particularly related to relationship disturbance. Demandingness refers to the irrational belief

that one requires (rather than desires) things from one's partner or relationship, and is most commonly revealed by "should" or "must" statements. Neediness refers to the irrational belief that one absolutely requires certain things from a partner or relationship to be happy and feel good about oneself. Low frustration tolerance refers to the irrational belief that bad feelings are intolerable and that one should not have to suffer them. Awfulizing refers to the irrational belief of catastrophizing (i.e., exaggerating the negative aspects) when things are not the way one believes they are supposed to be. Finally, damning oneself or others occurs when people associate their value as a person with how their relationships are going.

Although both Beck and Ellis share a common perspective that cognitions are influential in determining people's emotional and behavioral reactions to events, and although both approaches focus on helping people identify and modify these cognitions, the two approaches are not identical. Specifically, Beck's approach is based on collaborative empiricism: collaborative because the therapist and client work together, empirical because cognitions are changed when people collect data to evaluate the evidence for and against current and alternative beliefs. In comparison, Ellis's approach relies more heavily on therapists' ability to persuade and convince people regarding the irrationality of their beliefs.

The cognitive approaches of Beck and Ellis have been incorporated into other approaches to couple therapy. One approach, behavioral couple therapy, discussed in detail elsewhere (e.g., Baucom & Epstein, 1990; Jacobson & Margolin, 1979; Weiss & Perry, this volume), focuses primarily on improving the quality of life at home through increasing the frequency of caring (i.e., rewarding) behaviors, and teaching communication and problem-solving skills. However, from the onset, this approach has also included cognitive aspects of working with couples. For example, in their classic treatment manual, Jacobson and Margolin discussed the importance of the role of cognition in the assessment and treatment of relationship problems. However, cognitive interventions in these earlier writings remained fairly vague. Furthermore, cognitive assessment and intervention were not at the forefront of this approach. An early component analysis of behavioral couple therapy by Jacobson (1984) evaluated the relative effectiveness of the "two major components" (p. 295) of this treatment: behavior exchange and communication/problem-solving training.

The importance of a cognitive conceptualization and treatment of relationship dissatisfaction in the behavioral tradition has increased over time. For example, along with behavior and emotion, cognition is one of the three foci in Baucom and Epstein's (1990) treatment manual on cognitive-behavioral couple therapy. These authors have taken the constructs developed by Beck and Ellis and translated them into a relationship cognition framework. According to this perspective, five types of cognitive phenomena are important in the development and maintenance of relationship dissatisfaction: standards, assumptions, expectancies, selective attention, and attributions. Research evaluating the association between these five types of cognition and relationship outcomes is reviewed later in this chapter.

Whereas the cognitive therapies of Beck and Ellis (and their incorporation into behavioral couple therapy) share many features in common, a different approach to working with cognitions and relationship problems can be found in Cognitive Family Therapy (CFT), developed by Waring (1988). This approach, which derives from Kelly's (1955) personal construct theory, is based on the theory that mutual and reciprocal cognitive self-disclosure will result in changes in marital intimacy and, in turn, improvements in marital functioning. Through asking a series of why questions (e.g., "Why aren't you close?"), therapists encourage couples to discuss their ideas, beliefs, and theories about why they are having problems with their

relationship, as well as to discuss their views as to the impact of their parents' marriages on their own relationship. As evident in this short review of these approaches, there are several differences between Waring's approach and the other cognitive approaches to working with relationship difficulties. Waring, Barnes, and Woods (1990) discussed several of these differences. For example, CFT differs from the other cognitive approaches primarily in terms of "what specific conscious thoughts are disclosed, to whom they are disclosed and for what reason" (p. 35). First, in CFT, personal constructs are disclosed to one's partner and the therapist "to facilitate greater understanding and closeness" (p. 35). Thus, in comparison to the cognitive therapy of Beck or Ellis, in CFT there is no attempt to alter cognitions. Second, CFT explicitly avoids the expression of emotion, as it is believed that "disclosure of underlying affect would lead to criticism, hostility, and emotional distance" (p. 41). By contrast, Beck's and Ellis's approaches encourage emotional expression. Third, the therapist is relatively passive in CFT, whereas he or she is very active in Beck's and Ellis's approaches. Because of these key differences in theory and intervention, this approach is not discussed in further detail in this chapter.

THEORETICAL FOUNDATION FOR COGNITIVE THERAPY WITH COUPLES

In this section, the empirical research on relationship cognitions and relationship outcomes is reviewed. Our goal is to review the major findings regarding cognitions and relationship outcomes. Thus, we were not attempting to be comprehensive in this review and have included only relationship cognitions that have been the focus of several studies.

As formulated by A. T. Beck et al. (1979), a main component of the cognitive therapeutic approach is a focus on the information-processing mechanisms that serve as coding systems for the individual and that guide in the selection, integration, interpretation, and storage of information from the environment. Derived largely from this notion, Baucom, Epstein, Sayers, and Sher (1989) developed a typology of five cognitive constructs that have been shown to be central to an understanding of marital adjustment: standards (long-standing beliefs that focus on the characteristics the relationship and the partner should have), assumptions (beliefs that focus on the way oneself, one's partner, and one's relationships actually operate), selective attention (the process of perceiving only certain marital events or characteristics of one's partner), expectancies (predictions about the future of the relationship), and attributions (causal explanations for why certain events occur in the relationship). A full discussion of the five cognitive constructs follows.

STANDARDS

Standards represent a stable set of beliefs concerning the way relationships and partners should operate. Contrasted with assumptions (described below), standards serve an evaluative function in that a person employs such beliefs or rules to delineate "acceptable limits" for characteristics of the partner and of the relationship (Baucom, Epstein, Rankin, & Burnett, 1996). Moreover, standards likely influence a person's behavior within the relationship as well as how the person processes partner behavior and ongoing events. Examples of standards include the belief that partners should be able to mind read (i.e., sense each other's thoughts and feelings without overt communication) and the belief that people should be "perfect" sexual partners. According to cognitive theory, the degree to which this standard is met influences the person's satisfaction with the partner. It is important to note that standards are not necessarily problematic (Baucom et al.,

1989). However, theory suggests that standards can become maladaptive if they become too extreme or if they are not met (Baucom et al., 1989; Baucom, Epstein, Daiuto, et al., 1996; Baucom, Epstein, Rankin, et al., 1996).

Recently, investigators have suggested that it is useful to categorize relational standards along the dimensions of boundaries, power, and investment for each spouse (Baucom, Epstein, Daiuto, et al., 1996; Baucom, Epstein, Rankin, et al., 1996). Standards that concern boundaries focus on the degree to which a person endorses cooperation and sharing between partners, as opposed to the promotion of independent functioning. The power-control dimension involves the degree to which partners believe they must engage in compromise and mutual influence, as opposed to the exertion of effort to change the other's views to comply with one's own. Finally, standards that reflect the investment dimension involve the degree to which each partner contributes to the relationship. Such investment concerns the exchange of positive and negative behaviors between partners.

Research evidence validating relational standards as salient cognitive constructs in romantic relationships is growing. In fact, all three dimensions of boundaries, power, and investment standards have been shown to predict marital function (Baucom, Epstein, Daiuto, et al., 1996; Baucom, Epstein, Rankin, et al., 1996). More specifically, spouses who are more relationship-focused (i.e., those who report standards for minimal boundaries, egalitarian approaches to power and control, and high investment) score higher in marital adjustment. Earlier studies that did not focus on the boundaries, power, and investment dimensions per se also indicated that standards are important correlates of marital adjustment. More specifically, Epstein and Eidelson (1981) found that unrealistic standards and assumptions regarding relationships were more predictive of marital distress and low involvement in therapy than were irrational beliefs about individual functioning. Baucom,

Epstein, Daiuto, et al. (1996) found that level of unmet standards, as well as level of resultant emotional upset over unmet standards, predicted greater "active-response" patterns of engaging in hurtful behaviors to create distance from one's partner. Likewise, Baucom, Epstein, Rankin, et al. (1996) reported that level of unmet standards was associated with numerous indices of relational distress. It is important to note, however, that the results reported in this study did not find that extreme standards and emotional response to unmet standards predict marital adjustment.

ASSUMPTIONS

Whereas standards are beliefs about what relationships and partners should be like, assumptions are beliefs about the way oneself, one's partner, and one's relationship actually are. Beliefs such as "The sexes are inherently different" and "Partners cannot change" provide examples of the types of unrealistic assumptions that individuals may develop regarding their close relationships (Eidelson & Epstein, 1982). Such assumptions not only serve to create a cognitive structure for organizing information relevant to the partner and the marriage, but they also serve to guide interpretation of new events and partner behavior. Individuals who hold such unrealistic assumptions are likely to make biased attributions regarding partner behavior and to feel more hopeless about the future of the marriage (Baucom, Epstein, & Rankin, 1995). However, assumptions are not necessarily maladaptive. It is when the assumptions become inaccurate or unrealistic that the processing and interpretation of new events can become distorted (Baucom et al., 1989).

Assumptions can be broken down into two categories: personae and scripts (Baucom et al., 1989). Those made in the form of personae focus on aspects of the partner and how partners relate to one another. Examples of personae may take the form of assumptions regarding the way one's partner typically behaves, how men and women operate, and how men and women relate to one another (Baucom et al., 1995). Assumptions made in the form of scripts, however, focus on patterns of events that occur in a given relationship. For example, an individual may develop a script that outlines the sequence of events that typically unfolds during conflictual moments within the relationship.

The role of assumptions in relationship adjustment remains relatively untested. However, limited empirical findings provide some support for the notion that unrealistic assumptions are related to marital dissatisfaction. Two separate studies (Eidelson & Epstein, 1982; Epstein & Eidelson, 1981) found that the more spouses endorsed the beliefs that disagreement is destructive to the relationship and that their partners cannot change, the more likely they were to believe that therapy would not ameliorate their own marital problems. Spouses who endorsed these unrealistic assumptions also demonstrated a preference for individual over marital therapy (Eidelson & Epstein, 1982; Epstein & Eidelson, 1981), a greater desire to end the relationship (Eidelson & Epstein, 1982), and a decreased chance of improvement through therapy (Eidelson & Epstein, 1982; Epstein & Eidelson, 1981). Eidelson and Epstein also found that the assumption that the sexes are different predicted poor marital adjustment. In a more recent study, Bradbury and Fincham (1993) found that greater endorsement of unrealistic assumptions and standards was correlated with negative problem-solving behavior.

SELECTIVE ATTENTION

The application of selective attention to close relationships stems from the notion that perceptions about the relationship or one's partner contribute to level of relationship adjustment. That is, it is both the underlying belief systems (i.e., standards and assumptions) and the active processing and interpreting of relevant information that allow for a full understanding of cognition as it relates to relationship function. If partners selectively attend, or focus on only certain aspects of the relationship or partner, it is likely that they will miss other relevant information that can aid in the process of interpreting events in the relationship. As such interpretations will likely be incorporated into existing cognitive structures (e.g., assumptions), it is important that the individual have access to all available information. Baucom et al. (1989) comment that the process of selective attention in close relationships results in a distorted and often dissatisfying understanding of the relationship or particular event in the relationship. It is likely, therefore, that a negative and distorted understanding of the relationship will be incorporated into the individual's relationship or partner schemas.

Research in the area of social cognition has demonstrated that individuals fall susceptible to selective attention processes when they are fatigued or emotionally stressed or when existing cognitive structures direct such processes. Further, selective attention appears to be automatic in that people are unlikely to be aware that they are processing only a limited subset of available information (Baucom et al., 1989). It is therefore likely that selective attention will have a particularly powerful effect on relationship function because partners already experience distress when such processes take over, and partners are often unaware of the underlying cognitive processes that influence their views toward one another and the relationship.

Empirical studies provide support for the importance of selective attention in understanding relationship functioning. Studies that have asked people to report partner behavior over a 24-hour period have demonstrated that spouses often have differing perceptions of what has occurred during that time (e.g., Christensen, Sullaway, & King, 1983). In fact, when Jacobson and Moore (1981) asked couples to report whether certain events had occurred over the previous 24 hours, the rate of disagreement between spouses was greater than 50%. Reports of past behavior have also been shown to differ between objective raters and spouses (Robinson & Price, 1980). That is, when couples were asked to rate their behaviors, their reports corresponded to the reports of a trained observer only 50% of the time. Moreover, agreement between the rater and the spouses was lower among distressed couples than among nondistressed couples. Disagreement over the occurrence of past events and behaviors within couples is also greater for distressed than for nondistressed spouses (e.g., Christensen et al., 1983; Jacobson & Moore, 1981).

Expectancies

Past learning experiences are likely to guide one's predictions regarding future relationship functioning and partner behavior. Such expectancies allow a person to anticipate certain events and behaviors within the relationship and to respond accordingly. Consequently, if partners develop inaccurate expectancies or expectancies for negative outcomes in the relationship, the resultant behavior is likely to be guided by misinformation or negatively valenced motivation. As such, theory suggests that expectancies may sometimes serve to promote or perpetuate relationship distress.

Social learning theorists have identified two types of expectancies: those of outcome and those of efficacy (Bandura, 1977). Outcome expectancies focus on predictions that certain behaviors will result in a particular set of responses or outcomes, and are likely to take an if-then format (Baucom et al., 1989). That is, expectancies can involve anticipated responses of oneself to partner behavior (e.g., "If she contradicts me in front of the children, I will storm out of the room"), of the partner to one's own behavior (e.g., "If I ask him to clean up the kitchen, he will refuse and yell at me"), or responses to joint behavior (e.g., "If we avoid discussion of our problems, we will continue to resent one another"). Efficacy expectancies, however, focus on estimating the probability that a person will be able to carry out whatever actions are necessary to bring about a particular outcome. Relevant to this discussion, investigators have identified relational efficacy, or the expectancy among partners that they will be able to successfully resolve relationship problems, as an important construct in understanding relationship adjustment (Vanzetti, Notarius, & Nee-Smith, 1992).

A growing body of literature provides empirical support for the notion that expectancies are related to relationship adjustment as well as to problem-solving behavior in the relationship and to attributions for relationship problems. Vanzetti et al. (1992) found that dissatisfied spouses reported more negative expectancies and fewer positive expectancies for partner behavior than did satisfied spouses. Pretzer, Epstein, and Fleming (1991) reported that low efficacy expectancies regarding the resolution of marital problems were associated with both marital distress and depression. Finally, Vanzetti et al. found that spouses who reported low relational efficacy expectancies were more likely to attribute positive partner behavior to situational factors and to attribute negative partner behavior to dispositional factors.

ATTRIBUTIONS

Attributions reflect a person's explanations for relationship events and partner behavior and are the most heavily researched of the cognitive constructs presented in this chapter (for a review, see Bradbury & Fincham, 1990). Attributions often have been investigated along the internal-external, global-specific, and stable-unstable dimensions originally presented in

the reformulated learned helplessness theory of depression (Abramson, Seligman, & Teasdale, 1978). As reviewed by Bradbury and Fincham (1990), a large body of evidence suggests that dissatisfied spouses rate negative marital events or partner behavior as more internal, global, and stable, whereas attributions for positive partner behavior focus more on specific situational factors that are unstable over time and externally influenced. In comparison, satisfied partners attribute positive events to dispositional factors that are internal, global, and stable, whereas negative events are often viewed as specific to the situation. The classification of attributions along internal-external, global-specific, and stable-unstable dimensions may be related to the evidence that marital dissatisfaction and depression often co-occur (Whisman, 2001). However, the association between attributions and marital satisfaction does not appear to be an artifact of depression nor of depressed mood (e.g., Bradbury, Beach, Fincham, & Nelson, 1996; Fincham, Beach, & Bradbury, 1989).

Investigators have also explored attributional styles that focus on dimensions of partner intent (positive versus negative), blameworthiness, motivation (selfish versus unselfish), attitude (positive versus negative), and a lack of love. As reviewed by Bradbury and Fincham (1990), empirical evidence supports an association between relationship dissatisfaction and attributions of negative partner intent, blameworthiness of the partner, selfish partner motivation, and a negative attitude toward the respondent. Attributions that focus on a lack of love from one's partner also appear to be related to relationship dissatisfaction (Epstein, Pretzer, & Fleming, 1987), though additional studies must be conducted to confirm this finding.

Despite the large body of literature that has focused on attributional processes, several questions regarding their function in close relationships remain. For one, the findings described above are correlational in nature; as such, it is difficult to imply a direction of causality among attributional processes and relationship adjustment. However, there is growing evidence that attributions are indeed predictive of longitudinal changes in marital satisfaction (Fincham & Bradbury, 1993; Fincham, Harold, & Gano-Phillips, 2000).

ASSESSMENT AND INTERVENTION STRATEGIES

In the sections that follow, a cognitive approach to working with relationship dissatisfaction based on Beck's cognitive therapy is highlighted. Although the discussion is restricted to cognitive assessment and intervention, it is important to emphasize that use of these interventions is integrated into a framework of modifying behaviors, including the use of methods such as increasing caring behaviors and companionship activities and training in communication and problem solving. However, because these behavioral interventions are covered elsewhere in this volume (see Weiss & Perry, this volume), this discussion is limited to cognitive assessment and intervention.

Assessing Dysfunctional Relationship Cognitions

There are several methods for assessing cognitions in close relationships. First, a variety of self-report measures are available. For example, Fincham and Bradbury's (1992) Relationship Attribution Measure assesses causal and responsibility attributions. Likewise, Baucom, Epstein, Rankin, et al. (1996), Epstein and Eidelson (1981), and Vanzetti et al. (1992) have developed self-report measures to assess dysfunctional relationship beliefs, including standards, assumptions, and expectancies. These and other self-report measures of cognitions have been used in empirical research on understanding the nature of the association between relationship cognitions and relationship outcomes (e.g., satisfaction, stability) and have been used as outcome measures evaluating the efficacy of cognitive couple therapy (described later in this chapter). Standardized assessment of relationship cognitions (and other domains) is a useful and efficient method for collecting information on couples' functioning. The interested reader is referred to Bradbury's (1995) paper on assessing fundamental domains of marriage and to other resources on marital assessment (e.g., Patterson, 1999) to learn about and select measures for routine assessment of cognitions.

Treatment Format for Cognitive Therapy with Couples

Cognitive therapy with couples is designed to be time limited and short term, with a typical length of treatment between 15 and 20 (50-minute) sessions. The treatment is based on the assumption that modifying dysfunctional relationship cognitions will result in improved views of one's partner and the relationship, as well as reduced intensity and frequency of negative affective and behavioral reactions to the partner.

Sessions begin with the therapist working with clients to set the agenda for the session, identifying what will be covered during the session. The agenda can be introduced in a simple, conversational tone, by saying "My plan for today is to do X, W, and Z. Is there anything else you want to make sure we cover today?" During the early phases of treatment, the therapist will likely set the agenda and ask the couple if there is anything they would like to add or modify in the agenda. Over the course of treatment, however, the couple should become increasingly active in setting the agenda for the session.

A typical session agenda will include the following components (J. S. Beck, 1995). First, the therapist asks for a brief update since the previous session and a check on each partner's overall evaluation of the relationship. The therapist asks partners to rate their relationship during the week on a 1 to 10 scale; this type of rating can also be used to evaluate partners' satisfaction with the major problem areas in their relationship, such as money and communication. In addition to providing a snapshot view of the couple's perspective on the relationship for the week, this information can be used to track their progress over the course of treatment. Second, the therapist briefly checks on their perceptions and understanding of the previous session. Knowing that they are going to be asked about the previous session encourages partners to think about the session during the week and helps the therapist identify and correct any misperceptions. Third, the therapist reviews the homework from the previous session. A major tenet of cognitive therapy is that homework is essential for generalization and maintenance of the skills learned in treatment (A. T. Beck et al., 1979). In addition to discussing what they did for their homework, the therapist asks the couple what they learned from doing it and tries to connect this with the themes of treatment. If the couple had difficulty completing the homework, reasons for the difficulty are identified and troubleshooting is done to identify ways to address these difficulties (for a discussion of methods to promote homework adherence, see Detweiler & Whisman, 1999).

Next, the major topics for the session are presented and discussed. For example, topics may include socializing the couple to cognitive therapy, introducing methods for identifying or modifying automatic thoughts or core beliefs, and identifying and working on a particular problem. After covering the major topics for the session, the therapist works with the couple in setting new homework for the upcoming week. The homework should be specific (e.g., "Complete the three-column thought record when you are angry" versus "Work on becoming more

aware of your automatic thoughts"). A written handout describing the homework should be provided as a method for enhancing homework adherence (Detweiler & Whisman, 1999). The session ends with a summary: Asking partners to summarize the major points covered and provide feedback about the session, including whether there was anything that bothered or upset them, helps to solidify learning and identify and correct potential misunderstandings that may have occurred during the session.

INTERVENTIONS FOR IDENTIFYING AND MODIFYING DYSFUNCTIONAL RELATIONSHIP COGNITIONS

It is important in the early stages of treatment to socialize and educate clients regarding the cognitive model. This is done through a discussion of how people's thoughts about a situation lead to their emotional and behavioral response to that situation. Ideally, the explanation of the cognitive model uses examples of clients' own experiences, obtained, for instance, by having them recall a recent time when they were feeling bad about one another or their relationship. Furthermore, clients' expectations for therapy are addressed by discussing with them that through learning to identify and modify their thoughts, they will be able to overcome their current relationship difficulties and reduce the likelihood of future problems.

After socializing clients to cognitive therapy, treatment proceeds to help them learn to identify and later to modify their dysfunctional relationship cognitions. Under the cognitive model, cognitions are ordered in a hierarchical fashion, and treatment begins with the outer or surface-level cognitions. Thus, cognitive therapy begins with identification of partners' *automatic thoughts*. These are the automatic cognitive responses people have to ongoing events in their lives. It is important to first define and discuss the nature of automatic thoughts. Following this, people are taught to begin to become aware of their own automatic thoughts. In Beck's cognitive therapy, the "basic question" for identifying cognitive activity, including automatic thoughts, is "What was going through your mind just then?" (J. S. Beck, 1995). This is preferred to the question "What were you thinking just then?" because the latter is likely to result in people limiting their description to thoughts, whereas the former is likely to result in people also including descriptions of images and other cognitive activity. For example, following a criticism by her husband, a woman began to sob. When asked what was going through her mind, she recalled an image of herself as a child being criticized by her mother. In discussing this image, she was able to articulate her thoughts of being inadequate and her belief that there was something wrong with her. Thus, because people are often not consciously aware of their cognitions, it is important to begin with a general question that can tap different types of cognitive activity.

An important question facing couple therapists is when to assess for and intervene with relationship cognitions. For example, if a couple is talking about a problem in their relationship, the therapist must decide among various options, including whether to let them continue uninterrupted to collect information on the content and process of their problem solving, intervene to teach them communication and problem-solving skills, or interrupt the discussion and assess, educate, and intervene in terms of cognition. A particularly important indicator for working with cognitions is change in affect, as indicated by change in nonverbal (e.g., facial expression, posture) or verbal (e.g., voice tone or inflection) behavior. As discussed elsewhere (e.g., J. S. Beck, 1995; Safran, Vallis, Segal, & Shaw, 1986), it has been proposed that certain cognitions are accessible only when the person is experiencing the same affective state that is characteristic of when the person is experiencing the problem. Thus, a *change in affect* may

indicate the presence of "hot" cognitions; an "affective reaction may be due to the fact that one has tapped into an associative network of related memories and images and emotions" (Safran et al., 1986, p. 521). Consequently, a change in affect is the single most important marker for cognitive intervention. In particular, the therapist needs to look for affective reactions that are larger than anticipated, given the content of what the couple is talking about. For example, if a husband has a strong affective reaction to what his wife just said, and that reaction is greater than what one would think other people would have in a similar situation, it is likely that the statement has triggered an important cognition for the husband. Therefore, when changes in affect are noted during a session, particularly affective reactions that are stronger than anticipated, the therapist should routinely interrupt the discussion and ask the person who had the reaction what was going through his or her mind at that time.

The distinction between "hot" and "cold" cognitions and the emphasis on working primarily with hot cognitions distinguishes this approach (i.e., Beck's cognitive therapy) from the cognitive work described and evaluated by researchers who have incorporated cognitive interventions into behavioral couple therapy. We assert that by not focusing on hot cognitions, prior empirical evaluations of the additive effects of cognitive interventions into traditional behavioral couple therapy have not provided an adequate test of the potential impact of cognitive therapy. A detailed review of the efficacy of cognitive therapy is presented later in this chapter.

In working with couples, hot cognitions often naturally arise in the course of a session as couples interact around problem areas in their relationships. However, for other couples, there are situations that create a considerable amount of distress that do not spontaneously occur in therapy sessions. For example, a person might be upset by a partner's flirting behavior at a party, whereas someone else might be upset by a partner's diminished interest in sex. Although these situations occur outside the therapy session, they can still be the focus of cognitive assessment and intervention within a session. In these cases, the couple is asked to imagine the situation as vividly as possible; they are then asked to describe what goes through their minds as they imagine the situation. Alternatively, a couple can role-play the situation, making their automatic thoughts more accessible. The important point is that therapists should be on the lookout for affectively laden cognitions, which can occur spontaneously or can be elicited through imagery, role play, or other methods.

Once couples are able to identify their automatic thoughts in session, we commonly ask them to begin to monitor their cognitions between sessions. We believe it is important for people to practice the skills learned in therapy in order for them to generalize. Between sessions, couples are asked to use the Dysfunctional Thought Record (DTR; J. S. Beck, 1995; A. T. Beck et al., 1979), a worksheet that includes the following five columns: situation, automatic thought(s), emotion(s), adaptive response, and outcome. Couples begin by completing the first three columns of the DTR. Specifically, when they are feeling unpleasant emotions (e.g., anger, sadness, anxiety), they first write down their automatic thought and rate the degree to which they believe this thought (on a 1 to 10 scale). They write this down first, because if they are unable to complete the rest of the DTR, they will have at least completed the most critical part of the record. In addition to their automatic thought(s), they are to write down the situation that elicited their reaction and what they were feeling at the time, rated on a 1 to 10 scale. The use of a rating scale for rating intensity of thoughts and emotions helps people see that their thoughts and emotions are on a continuum, which is particularly beneficial for individuals who tend to see things in an all-or-nothing fashion.

Couples are told to complete the DTR while they are feeling an unpleasant emotion or as soon as possible afterward. The rationale for this is to elicit people's automatic thoughts, rather than the reconstructed thoughts or interpretations of what they are thinking, which is more likely to occur if they wait until later to complete the thought record. Couples are asked to bring their DTR to read and discuss in the next session.

In addition to these methods for helping couples become aware of automatic thoughts, other ways of assessing cognitions that may be contributing to their relationship difficulties are used. For example, a therapist can be aware of spontaneously occurring attributions that couples make that can be the target for assessment and intervention. Holtzworth-Munroe and Jacobson (1988) showed that people could be trained to detect spontaneous attributions that occurred during couples' problem-solving interactions. Specifically, they showed that coders could detect occurrence of attributional activity in terms of instances of "causal conjunctives": "words or phrases such as 'because,' 'the reason that,' 'due to,' 'since,' or 'consequently'" (p. 105). In similar fashion, these types of phrases can be used as markers for a person's spontaneously occurring attributions. Furthermore, clinicians can become aware of and track other types of relationship cognitions such as expectancies and standards. Ellis's irrational beliefs can be recognized by words such as "must," "always," "should," and "have to." The spontaneous occurrence of such statements can be seen as markers for additional exploration about the nature and magnitude of the belief.

After partners are able to identify and monitor their automatic thoughts and accompanying relationship cognitions, they are ready to begin to modify these cognitions. Interventions for modification of automatic thoughts is discussed in the next section of this chapter, but before moving on, a discussion of the assessment of core beliefs is warranted. In Beck's cognitive theory, cognitions are organized in a hierarchical fashion, with automatic thoughts representing surface cognitions that are elicited by ongoing experiences and that are closest to conscious awareness. Underlying these automatic thoughts, however, are *underlying assumptions* or *core beliefs*, which are the most fundamental level of beliefs and can be identified by their globality, rigidity, and over-generalizability (J. S. Beck, 1995). Between the automatic thoughts and core cognitions are intermediate beliefs, including standards, assumptions, and expectancies. Thus, the hierarchical organization of cognitions is V-shaped; insofar as there are multiple automatic thoughts at the top of the V, fewer intermediate beliefs, and a limited number of core beliefs at the base.

Safran et al. (1986) have proposed a set of guidelines for identifying and selecting core cognitive targets for assessment and intervention. The first guideline that may indicate the presence of core cognitive processes is self-referent cognitions: those cognitions that specifically refer to some evaluation of the self, such as "I am unlovable" or "I am incapable." Because Safran and colleagues were writing with respect to individual therapy, it is important to add that cognitions that specifically refer to the partner or to the relationship are also likely to be important cognitions for couple therapists to consider. For example, beliefs such as "He is a failure" and "Our relationship is hopeless" may also represent core beliefs.

The second guideline identified by Safran and colleagues (1986) that may indicate the presence of core cognitions refers to common themes. Although ideographic assessment is crucial for assessing the presence of particular relationship cognitions for a particular individual or couple, there are themes that may be particularly common in dissatisfied couples. In particular, theoretical and empirical writings suggest that themes of love (or intimacy) and power (or respect) are likely to be central to many dissatisfied couples (Krokoff, 1990;

Raush, Barry, Hertel, & Swain, 1974). Thus, couple therapists are advised to listen for cognitions that show that a person is viewing his or her partner's behavior in terms of lack of love, caring, or affection (e.g., "She doesn't love me any more"; "He is going to leave me") or domination and lack of equality or power (e.g., "He makes all the important decisions"; "I can't do anything right"), as these themes may reflect core cognitive processes. The third guideline for identifying core cognitions is to look for cognitions that exhibit cross-situational consistency. That is, patterns or regularities in partner's cognitions or in consistencies in the types of situations or events that distress a partner likely tap into core cognitions.

The primary method for identifying core cognitions is the use of the *downward arrow* (Burns, 1980). After a partner has articulated an automatic thought, the therapist asks about the meaning of the thought. As discussed by J. S. Beck (1995), there are two ways of asking about meaning that are likely to get at different levels of cognitions. First, asking "What does this thought mean *to* you?" is likely to elicit intermediate beliefs (e.g., assumptions, standards, and expectancies); asking "What does this thought mean *about* you?" (or "your partner" or "your relationship") is likely to elicit core beliefs. In some cases, the person is able to articulate a core cognition with one question; in other cases, the therapist will need to continue to ask meaning questions until one or more important cognitions are uncovered. Variations of the meaning question include "What is the worst (or most distressing) part about X?" and "What are the implications of X if it is true?"

After partners are able to identify their cognitions, treatment can proceed to modification of cognitions. Before discussing methods of intervention, however, an important caveat is needed. Novice therapists often move too quickly to encourage people to change their cognitions. The risk, however, is that people may feel they have not been adequately understood or validated. When working with distressed individuals, who often believe that their partner misunderstands them, making sure that people feel understood is of particular importance. Therefore, therapists are encouraged to summarize and validate partners' thoughts before proceeding to work on modifying them. It is useful to ask people if they have been understood and if it is okay to move on to challenging the beliefs before doing so.

Once a partner has identified an automatic thought and is ready to work on modifying it, the therapist can proceed to work with the person in changing this cognition. There are several ways of modifying cognitions, and therapists are encouraged to be creative and flexible in their use of these methods. Therefore, the following descriptions are offered as examples of ways of modifying cognitions; a more comprehensive listing can be found elsewhere (e.g., J. S. Beck, 1995).

First, therapist and partner can work together to evaluate the evidence regarding the cognitions. To do so, they first discuss "What is the evidence that supports this thought?" Cognitions do not develop in a vacuum, and it is often helpful for individuals as well as partners to consider and review the basis for the thought. Such a discussion can often engender positive feelings from partners, as they hear the person discussing experiences that contributed to the cognition, which in turn helps the partner see the person in a different light. Although the cognition is important in its own right, for a person to be able to modify the cognitions the therapist works with the person to answer, "What is the evidence against this thought?" Some people are able to generate responses to this question fairly easily; others will need help from the therapist and/or the partner to assist them in generating counterevidence, at least during early stages of modifying a particular cognition.

A second method for evaluating cognitions is through constructing an alternative explanation for the event. That is, therapists can work with partners in coming up with other ways of explaining an upsetting event, such as a negative partner behavior. For example, a wife complained that her husband did not spend much time with their newborn. She attributed his behavior to lack of interest in her and in the family, which was making her increasingly despondent. The therapist helped her generate alternative explanations for his behavior, such as the fact that he was working longer hours to bring home extra income to pay for the nursery they had just added in their house, which meant that he was not home as much and was often very tired when he was at home. Generating alternative, benign explanations for a partner's behavior often results in a person becoming happier with the partner and the relationship.

A third method for modifying cognitions is decatastrophizing. People often imagine the worst possible outcome and overestimate the likelihood that the worst outcome will occur. For such people, it is often helpful to ask them to articulate their worst fear (e.g., "What is the worst thing that could happen?"). Once they describe their worst fear, the therapist can work with them in determining whether they could survive it. Thus, although they may not want a particular outcome to occur, this intervention helps them to see that they could survive it and that it would not be as bad as they imagine. For example, one husband's biggest fear was that his wife would have an affair, which he said would "kill" him. Consequently, he kept seeking reassurance that she was not having an affair and was hesitant to make any requests for change in the relationship out of fear that she would have one. The therapist helped him decatastrophize this fear by asking him to think of the worst possible outcome, which for him was that she would leave him. The therapist then discussed with him how he had dealt with endings of other important relationships in his life. He was able to talk about feeling sad and depressed after a relationship had ended, but eventually being able to move on with his life. He was also able to think of other people who had been through a divorce and who had eventually been able to live happy and productive lives. The therapist was able to work with him further in deciding that although this would certainly be unpleasant and not what he wanted, he would be able to survive the end of the relationship if it were to occur. Consequently, he was able to reduce his reassurance seeking and become more genuine in the relationship by being honest with his wife about problems he saw in their marriage. In addition to reevaluating the outcome following the worst-case scenario, it is also helpful for people to evaluate the probability of the worst-case scenario actually occurring, as many people tend to overestimate the likelihood of negative events.

A fourth method for assessing beliefs is to evaluate the advantages and disadvantages of a belief. It may be difficult to determine the veracity of some beliefs. In these cases, it is often helpful for a therapist to work with a partner in examining the pros and cons of continuing to hold a belief, and then work to minimize the advantages and emphasize and maximize the disadvantages. For example, a woman strongly held the belief that her partner would eventually leave her. Because this was a future-oriented belief, it was difficult for the therapist to make any headway with challenging the belief through other means. The woman therefore was encouraged to examine the advantages and disadvantages of her belief that her partner would leave her. Among the former were the benefits of not being surprised and getting hurt less if he did leave her, whereas among the latter were the disadvantages of not being able to trust him, not being able to make long-term plans together, and, most important for her, a considerable deal of anxiety and worry. After weighing these and other pros and cons, she decided that it was more advantageous to give up the belief than to continue to hold on to it.

A fifth method for evaluating beliefs is to consider what you would tell a friend or family member in a similar situation. People often hold very different belief systems for themselves compared to those they hold for other people.

For example, people often have higher standards and expectancies for themselves, their partners, and their relationships than they do for others. A wife who had particularly high expectancies for herself was asked to write down all the things that she believed a "good wife" should do. In the following session, the therapist asked her to imagine that her married daughter had written this list and to consider what she would tell her daughter about these expectancies. When viewed from this perspective, she was able to see how unrealistic her beliefs were and how hard she had been on herself for not living up to these unattainable standards.

A sixth method is to conduct a behavioral experiment. Although experiments are appropriate for modifying nearly any type of relationship cognition, they are particularly important for cognitions associated with avoidance of situations that would provide disconfirming evidence. For example, people often avoid situations in which they feel afraid or anxious, which results in avoiding the very situations that would help to provide them an opportunity to challenge their views. Couples are told that just as scientists need to conduct experiments for testing their beliefs (i.e., theories), so also do partners need to conduct experiments to test their cognitions about their relationship. In creating a behavioral experiment, one or both partners create a situation in which to test out their cognitions and evaluate whether the outcome is what they had expected. For example, a man rarely shared his feelings with his wife; through identifying his automatic thoughts it was discovered that this was due to his belief that she would ridicule and belittle him if he talked about his feelings. This belief was tested in the session by having him talk to his wife about his fears that he had about their teenage son. Not only did she not ridicule him, his wife listened and reflected his feelings, which provided strong disconfirming evidence for the husband's belief. Such use of behavioral experiments is one aspect of Beck's cognitive therapy that sets it apart from Ellis's RET. These experiments are among the most powerful methods for modifying cognitions.

Over the course of a session or across several sessions, therapists are likely to identify many different cognitions. As each one is uncovered, the therapist must decide whether to work on a particular cognition. Here, the most important consideration is working with cognitions in a graded fashion. That is, therapists are advised to first help clients identify and modify their automatic thoughts, as they are the most easily recognized and corrected cognitions. Modifying automatic thoughts should not only bring some symptom relief, but should help to give people a sense of mastery before addressing intermediate and core beliefs. Secondary to this consideration, the following recommendations, adapted from J. S. Beck (1995), may help therapists decide whether to work with a particular cognition. Therapists should consider whether the cognition is directly related to the therapeutic goals of the session and/or the problem the couple is working on. If not, the cognition might best be tabled for a different time. Second, therapists should assess how strongly a person believes in the cognition. Compared to those that are only weakly endorsed, there is more room for change in cognitions that are strongly endorsed. Finally, therapists should consider how fundamental the cognition is. Cognitions that cut across situations are more likely to result in important change than are those associated with few situations.

Following a cognitive intervention, therapists should evaluate whether the intervention had its desired impact by checking whether the degree of belief in the cognition or the emotional reaction to the cognition has changed. If not, the therapist should adopt a different strategy in modifying the cognition until such change is observed.

As partners learn ways of modifying their beliefs in session, they are encouraged to practice these methods on their own between sessions.

Typically, this involves the use of the fourth and fifth columns in the DTR, which focus on the adaptive response and the outcome. Specifically, after identifying their beliefs, their emotional reaction, and the situation, partners are encouraged to come up with a more adaptive response to their distorted or negative cognition and to rate how much they endorse this adaptive response on a 1 to 10 scale. They can then write down the outcome, including a reevaluation of their mood. Completing this last column, which is designed to help people see the positive outcome of changing their cognitions, is particularly important for people who feel helpless about solving their problems and hopeless about the future of their relationship.

MAJOR PROBLEMS TREATED USING THIS APPROACH

Cognitive therapy with couples has primarily been applied as a treatment for marital and relationship dissatisfaction (or what would be labeled Partner Relational Problem, V61.1, in the fourth edition of the *Diagnostic and Statistical Manual of Mental Disorders;* APA, 1994). As discussed by Baucom, Shoham, Mueser, Daiuto, and Stickle (1998), an increase in marital adjustment or satisfaction is the primary criterion for evaluating the efficacy of couple therapy for relationship distress; and reviewed in a subsequent section of this chapter, cognitive therapy with couples has been shown to result in an increase in relationship satisfaction. In addition to the general category of relationship dissatisfaction, a variety of relationship problems are appropriate for this approach. In particular, cognitive therapy may be helpful for working with unrealistic expectancies, a common presenting problem for couples seeking therapy. For example, Whisman, Dixon, and Johnson (1997) found that in a national sample of practicing couple therapists, unrealistic expectations of the relationship or partner were reported to be the third most common problem seen in couples presenting for therapy, preceded only by communication and power struggles. In addition to relationship dissatisfaction in general and problems with relationship cognitions in particular, cognitive therapy with couples is an appropriate treatment for depression. Specifically, spouse-aided cognitive therapy (Emanuels-Zuurveen & Emmelkamp, 1997) and cognitive therapy with couples (Teichman, Bar-El, Shor, Sirota, & Elizur, 1995) have both been shown to effectively reduce depression among depressed spouses. Furthermore, insofar as they have been included in the practice of behavioral couple therapy, cognitive interventions have been shown to be helpful in treating depression, anxiety, and alcohol problems (as reviewed by Baucom et al., 1998).

CASE EXAMPLE

John and Mary were in their late forties when they sought treatment. They had been married for 24 years and had two children, both of whom were in college. Mary had recently returned to college to pursue a master's degree, after being a stay-at-home mom for the preceding 20 years. In their initial assessment, they reported that although there had been "ups and downs" in their relationship, they had both been generally satisfied with it until the time that Mary returned to school. Since then, they agreed that there had been an increase in the frequency and severity of their arguments, a decrease in their caring and affection toward one another, and an overall decrease in their relationship satisfaction. Questionnaire assessment indicated that their relationship satisfaction fell below standard cutoffs for relationship discord and that they were both experiencing moderate levels of depression.

After collecting an overview of the couple's views of the problems in their relationship and a description of their early relationship history (see Chapter 3 in Jacobson & Margolin, 1979),

the therapist explained the cognitive model to the couple, using an example from a recent disagreement that they had discussed in the first session. Specifically, the therapist asked them to describe the details of the argument (e.g., what led up to it, what they said to each other, how they were feeling) to access their cognitions at the time. He then asked them to recall what they were thinking at the time, and discussed how these beliefs were associated with the feelings and behaviors experienced during the argument. Both spouses acknowledged that the cognitive model made sense to them and that it was a different way of viewing their situation, given that they tended to blame one another for the problems in their relationship.

The first few sessions were devoted to teaching John and Mary to become aware of their cognitions through the use of the DTR when they were feeling upset about each other or about the relationship. In reviewing their responses to the DTR, a pattern emerged in which Mary would become upset when John would fail to ask her about her day or when he would talk about things that needed to be done around the house. Her automatic thoughts included "He isn't interested in what I am doing" and "He doesn't understand how much work I have to do." In comparison, John was most likely to become upset when Mary spent time studying in the evenings, rather than spending time with him. His automatic thoughts included "She cares only about her work" and "She is not interested in me."

After becoming aware of their automatic thoughts, John and Mary were taught ways of challenging and modifying these cognitions. For example, Mary worked on coming up with alternatives as to why John didn't ask her about her day (e.g., she often had late classes and didn't return home until the evening; he had a lot on his own mind regarding a problem he was having at work), and John worked on collecting evidence that Mary was not interested in her work only (e.g., she spent time with him on Friday nights; they were in therapy to improve their relationship). Furthermore, they agreed to make some behavioral changes in their relationship to challenge their automatic thoughts. For example, John agreed to ask Mary about her day when she got home from school, and Mary agreed to spend some time with John before beginning her studies in the evening.

Treatment then moved to helping the couple become aware of their underlying assumptions and core beliefs through the use of the downward arrow. Consistent with our earlier discussion of the importance of working with "hot" cognitions, the therapist was observant for changes in one partner's mood, which can serve as an important marker for accessible cognitions. During one session, Mary was enthusiastically discussing with the therapist a class assignment that she was completing. The therapist noticed that John looked very sad and that there were tears in his eyes as he listened to his wife talk about her project. The therapist asked John what was going through his mind, and he replied, "I remember that's how she used to look when she talked about us." The therapist used the downward arrow to establish the meaning of this statement. John reported that he feared she didn't love him as much as she did before, which in turn would mean that she might leave him. Thus, through asking him about the meaning of his automatic thoughts, the therapist was able to uncover John's underlying belief that he would be abandoned. Likewise, in a different part of the session, John was talking about how hard it was for him when Mary spent time studying on the weekend. The therapist noticed that Mary appeared to become increasingly withdrawn. When the therapist asked her what was going through her mind, she replied, "John doesn't appreciate all the work I have to do; he just doesn't get it." Through her responses to the downward arrow, Mary discussed how this thought meant that he didn't appreciate her developing her own interests, which in turn meant that he wouldn't be able to accept

her emerging identity apart from the family, which in turn meant that they were incompatible and, therefore, that they would end their relationship. Thus, both partners were dealing with the same underlying belief that the relationship might end. It was difficult for both Mary and John to acknowledge these core beliefs, but both expressed some relief at finally being able to discuss their biggest fears about their relationship.

The couple came to the next session reporting that there had been a turning point in their relationship. Mary had gone to visit their son at college over the weekend, but John had been unable to go. Neither had recalled how long it had been since they had been apart for two days. During the weekend, both John and Mary realized how much they missed each other and how much they wanted to stay together. When Mary returned on Sunday, they had a long talk, during which they discussed their fears of the ending of their relationship and their clear desire to stay together and work on improving the relationship. Both believed that the other truly wanted to remain in the relationship. Their core beliefs challenged and modified, Mary and John were able to continue work on recognizing and modifying other, less central beliefs, including making behavioral changes that served to reinforce their adaptive views on their changing relationship.

In this case example, this couple benefited from learning to recognize and modify their automatic thoughts. The therapist conceptualized that these automatic thoughts were largely being driven by their core belief that the relationship was going to end and, consequently, that each would be abandoned. The fortuitous separation allowed them to temporarily experience what it would be like to be apart, which was a negative experience for both. The conversation they had following this naturally occurring "experiment" provided convincing evidence for each of them that the other was committed to staying in the marriage. Had this weekend separation not occurred, the therapist would have worked with the couple to address the underlying assumption that their relationship was going to end. The key to this and any other cognitive intervention, however, would have been to work with the couple at collecting evidence that would be convincing to them (versus what the therapist would find convincing). Furthermore, if the couple decided to separate, through the use of the downward arrow, the therapist would help Mary and John identify the meaning that this separation would have for them (e.g., "It would mean I was a failure"; "It would mean I was unlovable"; or "It would mean I would never be able to be happy again") and would work to modify whatever negative beliefs were held by each partner.

EFFICACY OF COGNITIVE THERAPY WITH COUPLES

Cognitive therapy with couples, as presented in this chapter, has not yet been the focus of empirical investigation. However, other cognitive approaches to working with relationship dissatisfaction have been explored with mixed success. These other approaches have been applied as adjuncts to already existing treatments (most notably, behavioral couple therapy), as well as unique treatments that focus on various cognitive constructs (e.g., standards, attributions, irrational beliefs, or some combination). Although results from the existing literature suggest that a cognitive approach to the treatment of marital dissatisfaction is more effective than no treatment at all, only about 50 to 65% of those who are treated appear to demonstrate significant gains (e.g., Baucom & Lester, 1986; Baucom, Sayers, & Sher, 1990; Halford, Sanders, & Behrens, 1993). Moreover, treatments that incorporate a cognitive approach appear to be equally as effective in generating improvement in levels of marital satisfaction as therapies that do not adopt a cognitive focus (Wesley & Waring, 1996). Thus, investigators currently recognize the need for additional research to clarify

the effectiveness of cognitive therapy for relationship dissatisfaction. Such research is likely to aid in the refinement of a cognitive approach and in the identification of those who might benefit most from its application. To provide a fuller understanding of the current status of cognitive therapy in the area of close relationships, a review of the treatment efficacy research follows; a more detailed review can be found in Baucom et al. (1998).

The application of cognitive therapy to relationship dissatisfaction has been mostly within the context of an enhanced behavioral couples therapy (BCT). The impetus for the addition of a cognitive component to BCT came from the findings that BCT appears to be effective in moving only 35 to 40% of treated couples from the distressed to the nondistressed range of marital adjustment (Jacobson et al., 1984). It has therefore been theorized that the enhancement of BCT with a cognitive component might aid in the promotion of greater treatment gain. In one study that explored the use of cognitive restructuring as an adjunct to BCT, Baucom and Lester (1986) randomly assigned 24 couples to three experimental conditions: BCT alone, BCT plus cognitive restructuring, and a wait-list control group. The cognitive component of the combined treatment focused on both partners' attributions and expectancies. Results indicated that couples who were randomly assigned to the two treatment conditions demonstrated significant improvements on levels of marital satisfaction at the termination of the 12-week treatment and at 6-month follow-up. A direct comparison of the two treatment groups, however, indicated that there were no significant differences on outcome measures between BCT alone and the enhanced BCT treatment.

In a subsequent study, Baucom et al. (1990) compared a BCT alone condition to BCT plus cognitive restructuring (CR), BCT plus emotional expressiveness training (EET), BCT plus CR and EET, and a wait-list control group among 60 couples. The CR component focused on attributions and unrealistic standards, and the EET component focused on the expression of emotion and development of effective listening skills. After 12 weeks of treatment, results indicated that couples assigned to all four treatment groups demonstrated greater improvement in marital adjustment compared to couples in the control condition. However, comparisons between treatment conditions indicated that the addition of CR and EET did not appear to enhance BCT effectiveness.

In a research paradigm similar to that described above, Halford et al. (1993) compared BCT alone to an enhanced BCT (EBCT) condition among 26 couples. The EBCT evolved from the studies that had been conducted by Baucom and colleagues in that it incorporated their cognitive restructuring techniques and a component that focused on affect exploration. Halford et al. found that BCT and EBCT were equally effective in generating positive outcomes. Couples in both treatment conditions demonstrated significant increases in self-report marital satisfaction, as well as decreases in interactional negativity, unrealistic cognitions, and negative affect. Moreover, both treatments appeared to generalize their effects to the home environment (as measured by the coding of couple interactions in the home).

Other investigators also have explored the efficacy of cognitive therapy alone in the treatment of marital discord with similar results. In one such study, Huber and Milstein (1985) compared a cognitive restructuring only treatment for marital discord to a wait-list control group. The investigators found that efforts aimed at modifying unrealistic beliefs about marriage, oneself, and one's partner were effective in increasing marital satisfaction. That is, couples in the experimental group demonstrated greater treatment gains than those in the control condition. In a similar study, Emmelkamp et al. (1988) compared cognitive restructuring alone to a communication skills training condition. Cognitive restructuring

focused on the identification of causal attributions that distressed couples gave for relationship problems, as well as on the correction of maladaptive attributions. Emmelkamp et al. reported that both treatments were equally effective in decreasing target problems identified at the beginning of treatment.

From a review of the literature, it is apparent that various cognitive approaches to the treatment of relationship dissatisfaction have been investigated with equivocal success. Though such approaches appear to be more effective than no treatment at all, the mechanisms of change by which such treatments produce improvement are currently undetermined. Given the diversity of approaches described above, it is currently difficult to generate firm conclusions regarding cognitive approaches for marital dissatisfaction. As investigators have identified five relationship cognition constructs (standards, assumptions, expectancies, attributions, and selective attention) that appear to be associated with marital dissatisfaction (Baucom et al., 1989), it is recommended that future studies explore treatment in the context of this inclusive cognitive model. Further, we believe that the cognitive approaches evaluated to date may not have provided a powerful test of Beck's cognitive therapy approach to working with couples. In particular, the distinction between "hot" and "cold" cognitions is an important one, and our reading of the outcome literature suggests that most evaluations of cognitive interventions have focused on the latter, whereas Beck's approach emphasizes the former.

It is important to note the substantial overlap that might result from both cognitive and behavioral approaches. The findings of equal efficacy described above may reflect the reciprocal relationship between cognition and behavior. In fact, results from the studies conducted by Baucom and colleagues (Baucom & Lester, 1986; Baucom et al., 1990) indicated that females in behavioral treatment demonstrated significant change in both behavior *and* cognition at posttreatment.

Moreover, Emmelkamp et al. (1988) reported changes in both cognition and behavior among couples enrolled in a strict cognitive condition and for those enrolled in a communication skills training condition.

Finally, investigators have noted that random assignment of participants to study groups in the investigations described above might have resulted in diluted treatment effects. That is, random assignment restricts the matching of client needs to treatments, as is employed in most treatment settings. Consequently, the impact of moderators in determining efficacy of cognitive therapy for marital dissatisfaction has yet to be explored. Anecdotal evidence suggests that certain couples might benefit more from an approach that includes a cognitive component, whereas others might benefit more from a strict behavioral approach (Baucom & Lester, 1986; Baucom et al., 1990). Additional efficacy studies are necessary to identify moderating factors and to determine their impact on an effective cognitive approach to couple therapy.

SUMMARY

In this chapter, the sizable and growing body of literature supporting the importance of cognitive aspects of romantic relationships has been reviewed, as well as the theoretical and empirical bases of several cognitive perspectives on working with cognitions in couple therapy. A detailed approach to cognitive therapy that is based on this literature has been described and its impact on relationship function has been provided. Results from several studies suggest that cognitive approaches for relationship dissatisfaction are more effective than no treatment, but similar in effectiveness to other approaches to working with relationship problems. We assert that the impact of couple therapy can be enhanced by targeting a broader array of cognitions and by paying closer attention to the interplay between cognition and

emotion. Thus, there is a need for continued research into cognitive functioning and treatment of relationship dissatisfaction.

REFERENCES

Abramson, L. Y., Seligman, M. E. P., & Teasdale, J. D. (1978). Learned helplessness in humans: Critique and reformulation. *Journal of Abnormal Psychology, 87,* 102–109.

American Psychiatric Association. (1994). *Diagnostic and statistical manual of mental disorders.* (4th ed.). Washington, DC: Author.

Bandura, A. (1977). *Social learning theory.* Englewood Cliffs, NJ: Prentice-Hall.

Baucom, D. H., & Epstein, N. (1990). *Cognitive-behavioral marital therapy.* New York: Brunner/Mazel.

Baucom, D. H., Epstein, N., Daiuto, A. D., Carels, R. A., Rankin, L. A., & Burnett, C. K. (1996). Cognitions in marriage: The relationship between standards and attributions. *Journal of Family Psychology, 10,* 209–222.

Baucom, D. H., Epstein, N., & Rankin, L. A. (1995). Cognitive aspects of cognitive-behavioral marital therapy. In N. S. Jacobson & A. S. Gurman (Eds.), *Clinical handbook of couple therapy* (pp. 65–90). New York: Guilford Press.

Baucom, D. H., Epstein, N., Rankin, L. A., & Burnett, C. K. (1996). Assessing relationship standards: The Inventory of Specific Relationship Standards. *Journal of Family Psychology, 10,* 72–88.

Baucom, D. H., Epstein, N., Sayers, S., & Sher, T. G. (1989). The role of cognitions in marital relationships: Definitional, methodological, and conceptual issues. *Journal of Consulting and Clinical Psychology, 57,* 31–38.

Baucom, D. H., & Lester, G. W. (1986). The usefulness of cognitive restructuring as an adjunct to behavioral marital therapy. *Behavior Therapy, 17,* 385–403.

Baucom, D. H., Sayers, S. L., & Sher, T. G. (1990). Supplementing behavioral marital therapy with cognitive restructuring and emotional expressiveness training: An outcome investigation. *Journal of Consulting and Clinical Psychology, 58,* 636–645.

Baucom, D. H., Shoham, V., Mueser, K. T., Daiuto, A. D., & Stickle, T. R. (1998). Empirically supported couple and family interventions for marital distress and adult mental health problems. *Journal of Consulting and Clinical Psychology, 66,* 53–88.

Beck, A. T. (1998). *Love is never enough: How couples can overcome misunderstandings, resolve conflicts, and solve relationship problems through cognitive therapy.* New York: Harper & Row.

Beck, A. T., Rush, A. J., Shaw, B. F., & Emery, G. (1979). *Cognitive therapy of depression.* New York: Guilford Press.

Beck, J. S. (1995). *Cognitive therapy: Basics and beyond.* New York: Guilford Press.

Bogenschneider, K. (2000). Has family policy come of age? A decade review of the state of U.S. family policy in the 1990s. *Journal of Marriage and the Family, 62,* 1136–1159.

Bradbury, T. N. (1995). Assessing the four fundamental domains of marriage. *Family Relations, 44,* 459–468.

Bradbury, T. N., Beach, S. R. H., Fincham, F. D., & Nelson, G. M. (1996). Attributions and behavior in functional and dysfunctional marriages. *Journal of Consulting and Clinical Psychology, 64,* 569–576.

Bradbury, T. N., & Fincham, F. D. (1990). Attributions in marriage: Review and critique. *Psychological Bulletin, 107,* 3–33.

Bradbury, T. N., & Fincham, F. D. (1993). Assessing dysfunctional cognition in marriage: A reconsideration of the Relationship Belief Inventory. *Psychological Assessment, 5,* 92–101.

Bradbury, T. N., Fincham, F. D., & Beach, S. R. H. (2000). Research on the nature and determinants of marital satisfaction: A decade in review. *Journal of Marriage and the Family, 62,* 964–980.

Burns, D. D. (1980). *Feeling good: The new mood therapy.* New York: Signet.

Christensen, A., Sullaway, M., & King, C. E. (1983). Systematic error in behavioral reports of dyadic interaction: Egocentric bias and content effects. *Behavioral Assessment, 5,* 129–140.

Dattilio, F. M., & Padesky, C. A. (1990). *Cognitive therapy with couples.* Sarasota, FL: Professional Resource Exchange.

Detweiler, J. B., & Whisman, M. A. (1999). The role of homework assignment in cognitive therapy for depression: Potential methods for enhancing adherence. *Clinical Psychology: Science and Practice, 6,* 267–282.

Eidelson, R. J., & Epstein, N. (1982). Cognition and relationship maladjustment: Development of a measure of dysfunctional relationship beliefs. *Journal of Consulting and Clinical Psychology, 50,* 515–720.

Ellis, A., Sichel, J. L., Yeager, R. J., DiMattia, D. J., & DiGiuseppe, R. (1989). *Rational-emotive couples therapy.* New York: Pergamon Press.

Emanuels-Zuurveen, L., & Emmelkamp, P. M. (1997). Spouse-aided therapy with depressed patients. *Behavior Modification, 21,* 62–77.

Emmelkamp, P. M. G., van Linden, S. C., van den Heuvell, C., Ruphan, M., Sanderman, R., Scholing, A., et al. (1988). Cognitive and behavioral interventions: A comparative evaluation with clinically distressed couples. *Journal of Family Psychology, 1,* 365–377.

Epstein, N., & Eidelson, R. J. (1981). Unrealistic beliefs of clinical couples: Their relationship to expectations, goals, and satisfaction. *American Journal of Family Therapy, 9,* 13–22.

Epstein, N., Pretzer, J. L., & Fleming, B. (1987). The role of cognitive appraisal in self-reports of marital communication. *Behavior Therapy, 18,* 51–69.

Fincham, F. D., Beach, S. R., & Bradbury, T. N. (1989). Marital distress, depression, and attributions: Is the marital distress-attribution association an artifact of depression? *Journal of Consulting and Clinical Psychology, 57,* 768–771.

Fincham, F. D., & Bradbury, T. N. (1992). Assessing attributions in marriage: The Relationship Attribution Measure. *Journal of Personality and Social Psychology, 62,* 457–468.

Fincham, F. D., & Bradbury, T. N. (1993). Marital satisfaction, depression, and attributions: A longitudinal analysis. *Journal of Personality and Social Psychology, 64,* 442–452.

Fincham, F. D., Harold, G. T., & Gano-Phillips, S. (2000). The longitudinal association between attributions and marital satisfaction: Direction of effects and role of efficacy expectations. *Journal of Family Psychology, 14,* 267–285.

Halford, W. K., Sanders, M. R., & Behrens, B. C. (1993). A comparison of the generalization of behavioral marital therapy and enhanced behavioral marital therapy. *Journal of Consulting and Clinical Psychology, 61,* 51–60.

Holtzworth-Munroe, A., & Jacobson, N. S. (1988). Toward a methodology for coding spontaneous causal attributions: Preliminary results with married couples. *Journal of Social and Clinical Psychology, 7,* 101–112.

Huber, C. H., & Milstein, B. (1985). Cognitive restructuring and a collaborative set in couples' work. *American Journal of Family Therapy, 13,* 17–27.

Jacobson, N. S. (1984). A component analysis of behavioral marital therapy: The relative effectiveness of behavior exchange and communication/problem-solving training. *Journal of Consulting and Clinical Psychology, 52,* 295–305.

Jacobson, N. S., Follette, W. C., Revenstorf, D., Baucom, D. H., Hahlweg, K., & Margolin, G. (1984). Variability in outcome and clinical significance of behavioral marital therapy: A reanalysis of outcome data. *Journal of Consulting and Clinical Psychology, 52,* 497–504.

Jacobson, N. S., & Margolin, G. (1979). *Marital therapy: Strategies based on social learning and behavior exchange principles.* New York: Brunner/Mazel.

Jacobson, N. S., & Moore, D. (1981). Spouses as observers of the events in their relationship. *Journal of Consulting and Clinical Psychology, 46,* 269–277.

Kelly, G. A. (1955). *The psychology of personal constructs.* New York: Norton.

Krokoff, L. J. (1990). Hidden agendas in marriage: Affective and longitudinal dimensions. *Communication Research, 17,* 483–499.

Martin, T. C., & Bumpass, L. L. (1989). Recent trends in marital disruption. *Demography, 26,* 37–51.

Patterson, T. (1999). *The couple and family clinical documentation sourcebook: A comprehensive collection of mental health practice forms, handouts, and records.* New York: Wiley.

Pretzer, J., Epstein, N., & Fleming, B. (1991). The Marital Attitude Survey: A measure of dysfunctional attributions and expectancies. *Journal of Cognitive Psychotherapy, 5,* 131–148.

Raush, H. J., Barry, W. A., Hertel, R. K., & Swain, M. A. (1974). *Communication, conflict, and marriage.* San Francisco: Jossey-Bass.

Robinson, E. A., & Price, M. G. (1980). Pleasurable behavior in marital interaction: An observational study. *Journal of Consulting and Clinical Psychology, 48,* 117–118.

Safran, J. D., Vallis, T. M., Segal, Z., & Shaw, B. F. (1986). Assessment of core cognitive processes in cognitive therapy. *Cognitive Therapy and Research, 10,* 509–526.

Teichman, Y., Bar-El, Z., Shor, H., Sirota, P., & Elizur, A. (1995). A comparison of two modalities of cognitive therapy (individual and marital) in treating depression. *Psychiatry, 58,* 136–148.

Vanzetti, N. A., Notarius, C. I., & NeeSmith, D. (1992). Specific and generalized expectancies in marital interaction. *Journal of Family Psychology, 6,* 171–183.

Waring, E. M. (1988). *Enhancing marital intimacy through facilitating cognitive self-disclosure.* New York: Brunner/Mazel.

Waring, E. M., Barnes, S. M., & Woods, G. J. (1990). Comparing cognitive family therapy with cognitive behaviour modification and cognitive therapy for depression. *Psychiatric Forum, 15,* 33–42.

Wesley, S., & Waring, E. M. (1996). A critical review of marital therapy outcome research. *Canadian Journal of Psychiatry, 41,* 421–428.

Whisman, M. A. (2001). The association between marital dissatisfaction and depression. In S. R. H. Beach (Ed.), *Marital and family processes in depression: A scientific foundation for clinical practice* (pp. 3–24). Washington, DC: American Psychological Association.

Whisman, M. A., Dixon, A. E., & Johnson, B. (1997). Therapists' perspectives of couple problems and treatment issues in couple therapy. *Journal of Family Psychology, 11,* 361–366.

CHAPTER 17

Behavioral Couples Therapy

ROBERT L. WEISS AND BARBARA ANN PERRY

Behavioral couples therapy (BCT) has been marked from its initial appearance in the late 1960s and early 1970s by an unbridled emphasis on the empirical study of processes related to marital conflict. From its beginning as behavior marital therapy (BMT), it immodestly offered a single voice that promised answers to the field of marital therapy. It was precisely this promise, "Better living through behavioral psychology," that characterized the *Zeitgeist* of that time. What began as a single-minded dedication to "truth"—to be revealed by adherence to the principles of learning—is today more accurately construed as a consortium of behaviorally based marital therapies. It would be incorrect to suggest that behavioral couples therapy today is a single, unified, identifiable approach to relationship distress. The simple learning (conditioning) principles and strict adherence to teaching skills, both of which were seen as quintessential for BMT, no longer figure as prominently. Yet, even in the early BMT publications, strict reliance on learning technology was more limited than "outsiders" believed. Recognition of the complexities of marital interactions was present almost from the beginning.

This chapter seeks to provide a brief overview and update of the influences that have led to what today may seem like a panoply of behaviorally based approaches to couples therapy. BCT has not so much embraced eclecticism—by indiscriminately taking bits and pieces of various approaches and creating a melange of techniques—as it has shifted its emphasis from the external control of behavior to internal mediating factors now thought to underlie behavior change. Although still maintaining a recognizable adherence to behavioral tenets and reflecting no less an acceptance of the mandates identified with self-correcting empirical science, the doctrinaire "purity" of the approach is more apparent than real. It is also worth noting that BCT grew in large part from the clinical experiences of marital researchers who were also marital therapists. Although BCT has a strong empirical research heritage, it is also the case that clinician researchers were writing about marital complexities. Perhaps the field would have developed quite differently had this hands-on clinical influence not been as ubiquitous as it was and still is. The intent of this chapter is to provide a clinically relevant overview of those aspects of BCT that best reflect the thinking that underscores the applications suggested by current approaches. In doing so, the focus is on historical features of the approaches, conceptual and methodological issues, relevant assessment and intervention modalities, a detailed case illustration, and an overview of target problems and outcome effectiveness.

HISTORY OF THE THERAPEUTIC APPROACH

BCT initially began with relatively isolated reports of case studies describing techniques based on learning theory applied to persons who happened to be married. (See Gottman, 1979; Weiss & Heyman, 1990; Weiss & Wieder, 1982, for a more detailed historical account of developments in BCT.) Among the earliest reports were those illustrating the use of stimulus control techniques for controlling a husband's intrusive thoughts of his wife's infidelity (Goldiamond, 1965), and those showing how wives could use response contingent reinforcement procedures for modifying husband behaviors (Goldstein & Francis, 1969). Characteristically, these early examples focused on a single spouse and not on the interaction of the pair. BCT began to acquire an identity of its own when the focus of published reports shifted to the *processes* that described the ongoing interactions of spouses. On the one hand, the works of Liberman (1970) and Patterson and Reid (1970), employing reinforcement theory to families and couples, broadened the ecological context by addressing the complexity of marital interactions, as these were thought of at that time (see also Patterson, Weiss, & Hops, 1976). On the other hand, Stuart (1969, 1980) effected a blend of reinforcement theory,

social psychology, and systems theories in his approach to couples, with his original paper entitled "Operant Interpersonal Treatment for Marital Discord" (1969). Concepts and ideas such as social exchange (Thibaut & Kelley, 1959) reciprocity, coercion (Patterson & Reid, 1970), and quid pro quo exchanges (Jackson, 1965) found their way into these early BCT reports.[1] But from a strict operant reinforcement perspective, the work of Azrin, Naster, and Jones (1973) offered a sequenced approach for bringing spouses' behaviors under reinforcing control (e.g., through the use of contingency contracts).[2]

Patterson and Hops (1972) reported a marital treatment case based on intervention techniques being developed at that time by a collaboration of Oregon researchers and clinicians (Gerald R. Patterson, Hyman Hops, Robert L. Weiss, and Robert C. Ziller). In the following year, Weiss, Patterson, and Hops (1973) presented a hallmark, systematic approach to BCT. In 1977, Neil Jacobson (then a graduate student at the University of North Carolina), replicated the essentials of the Oregon BCT program. Jacobson and Gayla Margolin (a former Weiss student) wrote what today remains the standard manual for behavioral marital therapy that typifies the BCT thinking of that decade (Jacobson & Margolin, 1979).

In 1980, Stuart presented a more fully developed behavioral view of marital therapy, again based on behavioral, social psychological, and systems theory constructs. Learning-based interest in the broader contexts of human interactions, as reflected in the phrase "social learning," was expressed in the influential works of Alfred

---

[1] Although Jackson used quid pro quo marital exchanges metaphorically in describing the rules of relationships, behavioral writers adopted it quite literally to mean reciprocity in behavioral exchanges.

[2] In an attempt to provide therapists with a wider range of contracting options, "good faith contracts" were designed to place the reinforcing contingencies with each spouse, thereby creating parallel contract arrangements rather than those controlled by spouse-dependent reciprocity (Weiss, Birchler, & Vincent, 1974).

Bandura (1977) and Gerald Patterson (Patterson & Reid, 1970). Proponents of social learning theory differed among themselves as to what specific constructs were brought into play; for example, Bandura emphasized the more cognitive aspects of person-environment interactions. However, it was clear that affect, behavior, and cognitions had to be included in considering the impact of the environment on the person.

The decade of the 1970s drew to a close with the presentation of the Oregon Marital Studies Program (OMSP) Behavioral Systems Model (Weiss, 1978, 1980). Papers depicting this model set forth a modular approach to assessment and intervention for cases of marital distress. Among the salient features of the OMSP model are: (1) Marital adjustment was defined as accomplishments; (2) assessment was based on how well a couple was meeting the requisite accomplishments within specific contexts of interaction (e.g., affection, companionship, household management); and (3) a distinction was drawn between interventions that reflected efficacy or outcome expectations (after Bandura, 1977). The latter refers to the distinction between cognitive restructuring (e.g., beliefs that one can do something) and skills training (e.g., learning which behaviors lead to which outcomes).

Among the next generation of exemplars of the BCT tradition are four bona fide treatment guides for marital therapy (written for therapists, not couples) that best reflect the prospects for this approach: Jacobson and Margolin's (1979) *Marital Therapy: Strategies Based on Social Learning and Behavioral Exchange Principles;* Jacobson and Christensen's (1996) *Integrative Couple Therapy: Promoting Acceptance and Change;* Halford's (2001) *Brief Couple Therapy: Helping Partners Help Themselves* (see also the chapter by Weiss & Halford, 1996, "Managing Marital Therapy: Helping Partners Change"); and Baucom and Epstein's (1990) *Cognitive-Behavioral Therapy.* The section on intervention that follows draws on the influences these approaches have had on how martial therapy is structured

within this behavioral framework. In keeping with accounts of the history of BCT, the next section considers BCT in retrospect.

THEORETICAL CONSTRUCTS EMBODIED IN BCT

RADICAL SITUATIONALISM IN RETROSPECT

In a highly readable, comprehensive description of the evolution of BCT, Halford (1998) traces the shift from what might be labeled "radical situationalism" to today's explicit emphasis on person variables. The core of BCT, reflected in operant theory, was the centrality of reinforcing contingencies in understanding behavioral exchanges. The place to look for these reinforcing contingencies was in the overt behaviors of spouses, with "overt" being the operative term here. Early BCT embraced the tenets of behavioral psychology, which at that time focused on external rather than internal or dispositional determinants of behavior. Table 17.1 summarizes the underlying assumptions of behavior therapy, most of which are still germane to models of BCT.

The operant learning model proposed by Skinner (1953) served as a template for emphasizing the situational or environmental control of behavior, which was applied directly to marital interaction, conflict, and accord. The roles of shaping, contingency control, and extinction were central to this thinking. Not only did the consequences of responses (reinforcing contingencies) play a central role, but also situations themselves were factors that controlled integrated sequences of interactions. In their description of the coercion hypothesis, Patterson and Reid (1970) proposed the process by which dysfunctional marital interactions are developed and maintained. Accordingly, marital interactions are shaped by the behavioral consequences each spouse provides the other, that is, through the *joint* unfolding of positive

Table 17.1 Ten underlying assumptions of behavior therapy.

1. All behavior, normal and abnormal, is acquired and maintained in identical ways (i.e., according to the same principles of learning).
2. Behavior disorders represent learned maladaptive patterns that need not presume some inferred underlying cause or unseen motive.
3. Maladaptive behavior, such as a symptom, is itself the disorder, rather than a manifestation of a more basic underlying disorder or disease process.
4. It is not essential to discover the exact situation or set of circumstances in which the disorder was learned; these circumstances are usually irretrievable anyway. Rather, the focus should be on assessing the current determinants that support and maintain the undesired behavior.
5. Maladaptive behavior, having been learned, can be extinguished (i.e., unlearned) and replaced by new learned behavior patterns.
6. Treatment involves the application of the experimental findings of scientific psychology with an emphasis on developing a methodology that is precisely specified, objectively evaluated, and easily replicated.
7. Assessment is an ongoing part of treatment, as the effectiveness of treatment is continuously evaluated and specific intervention techniques are individually tailored to specific problems.
8. Behavioral therapy concentrates on here-and-now problems, rather than uncovering or attempting to reconstruct the past. The therapist is interested in helping the client identify and change current environmental stimuli that reinforce the undesired behavior to alter the client's behavior.
9. Treatment outcomes are evaluated in terms of measurable changes.
10. Research on specific therapeutic techniques is continuously carried out by behavioral therapists.

Source: Goldenberg & Goldenberg, 2000, p. 267.

and negative reinforcement. On the one hand, any behavior of Spouse A is learned (i.e., becomes more probable) when it effectively suppresses or otherwise effectively terminates Spouse B's annoying behavior (e.g., nagging). On the other hand, when Spouse B's annoying behavior stops, B is negatively reinforced by virtue of having removed the threat provided by Spouse A (positive reinforcement increases the probability of an associated response, whereas negative reinforcement increases the probability of a response occurring that reduces an associated aversive stimulus). This juxtaposition of positive and negative reinforcement patterns served as a model for the development of marital conflict patterns (e.g., Weiss, Patterson, & Hops, 1973).

Clearly, these earlier formulations represented functionalism at its best: focusing on what spouses were *doing* that produced either favorable or unfavorable outcomes. This functionalism was also captured in notions of *behavior*

exchange (quid pro quo) and *cost-benefit* models. Contracting became synonymous with BMT (e.g., Stuart, 1969). Spouses were instructed to effect changes in one another's behaviors by various contingency-based contracts (e.g., Weiss, Birchler, & Vincent, 1974). Quite simply, spouses themselves were uniquely important in effecting behavior change.

As noted previously, Weiss (1978) presented a performance-based model that highlighted marital accomplishments. A series of modular components defined marital accomplishments (e.g., objectification, support/understanding, problem solving, and behavior change), which were posited as necessary to a complete theory of marital adjustment. Within each module were specific assessment and intervention tactics that dealt with situations, communication, and benefits. Assessment and intervention techniques were either created anew or appropriated from existing marital literature to address the three subsections of each module.

Thus, in the objectification module, the focus was on defining with operational clarity the roles of situations, communication, and benefits. For example, assessments were carried out to determine how situations in the lives of a given couple conspired to foster either arguments or closeness. Likewise, assessment and intervention techniques were developed to enhance the processes of objective (i.e., denotative) communication and to develop (for each spouse) menus of self- and partner-relationship benefits. With some notable exceptions, earlier forms of BCT stressed situational and performance-based elements as part of assessment and marital intervention. BCT was synonymous with the teaching of communication and problem-solving skills.

RADICAL SITUATIONALISM: PROSPECT

Radical situationalism is, for the most part, a thing of the past in BCT quarters. This is now an era of "compassionate behavior change": a kinder, friendlier behavioral couples therapy. Today, *within-person* sources of change are embraced widely, even though their proponents vociferously claim that they remain identified with the "behavioral" in BCT. A Martian would be reasonably confused if told that he, she, or it was reading *behavioral* marital therapy literature, for frequently, not only the shadow but the persona of psychodynamic (object relations) theory appears in current writings!

The claim that BCT has metamorphosed is supported by two clear developments: one emphasizing self-regulation techniques (e.g., Halford, 1998; Weiss & Halford, 1996), the other emphasizing cognitive-affective changes in individual reactivity to partner behaviors, referred to as "acceptance and change" (Christensen & Jacobson, 1999; Jacobson & Christensen, 1996). A common theme in these newer BCT approaches is an explicit recognition of the roles of emotion, maladaptive cognitive processes, and methods for fostering within-person regulatory processes

(e.g., self-regulatory metaskills; Halford, 2001). The emphasis is almost exclusively on self-change (in the context of the relationship), in contrast to earlier forms of intervention that stressed techniques for partner change. In both of these approaches (acceptance/change and self-regulation), the writers utilize constructs from emotion-focused therapy (Greenberg & Johnson, 1988) and insight-oriented therapy (e.g., Snyder & Wills, 1989). Both recognize that change can occur only by taking account of affect, behaviors, and cognitions of each individual. A considerable effort is devoted to intervention strategies and tactics likely to change attributions as well as rigidly held notions of self-efficacy. Both of these approaches fully recognize the pain spouses feel, and both use a variety of techniques to join the spouses. Both utilize assessment data to develop a working model of the relationship, which is then used to promote self-regulation metaskills, such as self-appraisal, self-goal-setting, and evaluation (Halford, 2000); additionally the model is used as the basis for teaching more traditional negotiation and communication skills (Christensen & Jacobson, 1999). Both therapies are true exemplars of compassion for how spouses experience marital difficulties, yet they retain their behavioral roots by using information generated from empirical studies.

Finally, rounding out the description of developments in BCT, the contributions of John Gottman (this volume) are essential. Although initially not directly focused on techniques of marital therapy (Gottman, 1979), Gottman continues to provide an important subtext to the behavioral approaches considered in this chapter. The defining characteristics of BCT, as mentioned previously, have been a strong commitment to the development and empirical study of constructs and techniques. The functionalism of the behavioral approach is best represented in Gottman's systematic studies of how marital interactions unfold based on the behavioral patterns displayed in spouses' interactions.

Using observational (i.e., behavioral coding of couples' affect) and psychophysiological (e.g., heart rate, skin conductance) measures taken during couples' interactions, Gottman has been able to identify within-couple patterns that, for various samples, are predictive of divorce (discussed next).

METHODS OF ASSESSMENT AND INTERVENTION

CONCEPTUAL BACKGROUND

Perhaps the single distinguishing feature of BCT is the central role of assessment. Unlike diagnosis, assessment is concerned with behavioral resources (competencies and deficiencies) that focus on intervention. Behavioral assessment of marital adjustment, whether based on self-report or the observations of trained observers, always informs goals for intervention. In this sense, assessment and intervention are two sides of the same coin. This largely reflects BCT's view that interventions require evidence that something intended actually occurred and that desired change resulted. As already noted, in the earlier behavioral tradition, the importance of patterns of interactions was strongly emphasized, which meant focusing on external rather than internal events. Relationships developed and changed largely through the interdependent unfolding pattern of consequences of responding to one another. In studying marital conflict and accord, the focus is on the interaction of partners, and great emphasis is placed on the specific behavioral events that are occurring. The thoughts and attributions of each partner are less important than the quality of what they do to and for one another. Similarly, self-report assessment measures that were developed by the early BCT contributors were largely focused on what the partners did and how they observed their own and their partner's behavior. Before considering some of the specific assessment devices developed in the behavioral tradition, a larger conceptual issue, namely, the targets of assessment, is discussed next.

A QUESTION OF TARGETS

The status of therapy outcome variables has remained a troublesome issue in the area of marital research and therapy (Weiss & Margolin, 1986). Whether classifying couples as maritally distressed for research purposes, or specifying the desired outcome of successful intervention, the nature of the dependent variable remains unclear. Simply stated, nothing like the *Diagnostic and Statistical Manual of Mental Disorders (DSM-IV)* is available to specify *objective* criteria for marital adjustment. For example, the distinction between marital stability and satisfaction can actually blur how we determine intervention outcome. If a couple end their relationship right after ending therapy, is this automatic evidence of outcome failure?

Similarly, the field has relied on a variety of assessment instruments (most often, self-report measures), some that are long established and some newly developed (see Christensen, 1987; Weiss & Margolin, 1986). From the point of view of rich theoretical development, self-reports of marital satisfaction are insufficient for understanding what satisfaction is based on. The *conceptual* challenge for BCT therapists and researchers is not so much that couples may report increased marital satisfaction after therapy, but rather, knowing which performance elements ensure such outcomes. From a true behavioral perspective, the alternative ("It does not matter what they do, only what they think") is unacceptable; there has to be a tie to behavior.

Toward this end (specifying a behavioral basis for marital functioning), behavioral observation of marital interaction has been the assessment lynchpin for BCT researchers.

Behavioral observation has a rich empirical history (e.g., Heyman, 2001), beginning with the various versions of the Marital Interaction Coding System (MICS), originally developed by the Oregon group (e.g., Weiss & Summers, 1983), and does not rely on theoretical constructs. Almost without exception, the code books used to define constructs for what coders are trained to record while observing an interaction have not been based on an explicit theory of marital adjustment (Weiss & Frohman, 1985; Weiss & Heyman, 1990, 1997). Thus, although there have been numerous studies showing behavioral differences between couples who report greater or lesser marital satisfaction, these differences are not driven by theoretical formulations. Even today, among the more sophisticated observational approaches (e.g., Gottman, 1994), there is little theory to guide what one should observe. Among researchers in this area, Gottman has been most consistent in his attempts to develop a general theory of marital adjustment based on much prior empirical work and new findings from multilevel measurements of couples' interactions (Gottman, Swanson, & Murrary, 1999).

The result of this atheoretical tradition has meant that the major outcome measure for marital research and therapy relies on some variant of reported marital satisfaction. Therapists and researchers view spouses as in the best position to decide whether they are satisfied, and generally they have accepted self-report. From the beginning of BCT, the epistemological questions have been: What behaviors are needed for a couple to report marital satisfaction? How do spouses *know* their satisfaction? There are two components of reported satisfaction: a sentiment or evaluative component and a behavioral or performance-based component. Fincham and Linfield (1997) proposed that the evaluative component comprises orthogonal positive and negative dimensions, which spouses can reliably rate. It might be expected that there will be a high degree of correspondence between what

spouses report as their level of satisfaction and the transactions that make up their daily marital interactions. Instances of supportiveness, exchanges of positives, and providing comfort and understanding (to name a few possibilities) should be mirrored in higher levels of positive sentiment. Yet, studies have shown low levels of correlation between sentiment and behavior (Johnson & O'Leary, 1996; Weiss, 1980; Wills, Weiss, & Patterson, 1974), and the door has opened to questioning why behaviors do not impact satisfaction more than they appear to. Indeed, this disconnect between behavior and satisfaction led to the "sentiment override" hypothesis (Fincham, Garnier, Gano-Phillips, & Osborne, 1995; Weiss, 1980), which states that marital satisfaction as sentiment acts as a filter, such that high levels of satisfaction are likely to override instances of negative (e.g., disconfirming) relationship behaviors. The area is ripe for further theoretical development.

REPRESENTATIVE SELF-REPORT ASSESSMENT DEVICES AND BCT PRACTICE

In this section, selected validated, qualitative self-report measures that were either developed specifically for clinical practices of BCT or have proven useful in BCT applications are reviewed (see Christensen, 1987, and Weiss & Margolin, 1986 for other reviews).

Marital Status Inventory
MSI is a straightforward self-report measure of potential for divorce (Weiss & Cerreto, 1980). Spouses indicate whether each of 14 items, ranging from having had occasional thoughts of divorce (usually after arguments) to having taken formal steps to initiate divorce (e.g., consulting an attorney), are true or false for them. The items range from cognitive to behavioral actions, representing steps that sequentially would lead to an increased commitment to divorce. Studies have shown that individual

scores equal to or greater than four keyed items are very indicative of high risk for divorce.

Areas of Change Questionnaire

The original ACQ assessed two aspects of the degree to which each spouse desired a change in the other, as well as how correctly each perceived the degree of change desired by the other (Weiss & Birchler, 1975). Thirty-four items covering a range of topics (affection, companionship, finances, household chores, etc.) are presented in a standard format: "I want my partner to . . ." or "It would please my partner if I . . . paid bills on time . . . expressed his/her (my) emotions more clearly." Responses can range from *very much more* (+3), through *no change* (0), to *very much less* (−3). The combined score of each person's desired change is an indication of marital dissatisfaction (i.e., the greater the desired change, the less satisfaction).

The disparities between the change desired by one spouse and the perception of desired change by the other are often an important revelation for spouses during feedback. For instance, just learning that one has incorrectly assumed that an item was important to the other can be used to illustrate the adverse effects of "mindreading."

Proponents of self-regulation and acceptance viewpoints have modified the ACQ by refocusing on the self as the agent of change. Thus, the emphasis becomes whether greater or lesser change in one's own behaviors would lead to greater relationship harmony.

Miscellaneous Quantitative Measures

The following measures are frequently used in BCT work, but are not specifically identified with BCT.

The Dyadic Adjustment Scale (DAS; Spanier, 1976) is the most widely used measure of marital adjustment. A considerable amount of this test is based on whether respondents indicate perceived agreement with one another. That is, the construct of marital satisfaction is defined in terms of spouses agreeing with one another on marital issues (e.g., leisure time, finances). In addition, the DAS contains a single sentiment item that asks in general how satisfied a person is with the marriage. The DAS is typically used as an outcome measure.

The Conflict Tactics Scale (CTS; Straus, 1979) is a useful screen for spouse abuse. As part of an assessment battery, it clearly indicates the therapist's willingness to consider whether and to what extent abuse is an issue in a relationship.

Because martial distress and depression co-occur with a high degree of regularity, it is wise to assess extent of depressive symptoms (e.g., Beach, Sandeen, & O'Leary, 1990). A number of self-report measures of depressive symptoms can serve this purpose, although the Beck Depression Inventory (BDI; Beck, Ward, Mendelson, Mock, & Erbaugh, 1961) has been used widely in marital therapy studies as a screen for self-reported affect dysregulation.

Qualitative Measures

Techniques included here are those for relationship assessment that do not lend themselves readily to quantitative scoring, or for which no clinical norms exist. Nonetheless, they are quite consistent with the underlying philosophies of BCT.

The Spouse Observation Checklist (SOC; Weiss & Perry, 1983) is most closely identified with the behavioral approach to couples work. The SOC was an attempt to turn spouses into behavioral observers (albeit untrained participant-observers). Each spouse is instructed to record the frequency of occurrence of events from a broadly based catalogue of daily interactions, and to indicate whether they were pleasing or displeasing. These recordings are made daily, usually over a period of two weeks. The SOC offers an inventory of the benefits each person provides the other (pleasing events). This information is used subjectively to further enhance the positive goods and services they can exchange.

Self-Reporting of Relationship
Strengths and Weaknesses

It is useful to allow spouses to present their views of their relationship in an unstructured reporting form. Based on a listing of potential problem areas (see Table 17.2), each person is asked to identify three areas from the problem list that represent areas of relationship strength (those they feel they are handling well) and three areas that reflect relationship areas of felt weakness. For each of the resulting six areas, spouses write a few sentences for the individual issues selected and note how each relates to a relationship strength *and* to a relationship weakness. (Table 17.4, as part of the Case Example, below, provides an example of this format.) The challenge here is twofold: Couples must be able to discriminate what is working for them as well as what is not working for them. They also need to be able to reflect on each category in terms of how it is satisfying *and* annoying. The results of this assignment are most enlightening. For example, if a person is unable to list strengths, only many weaknesses, clearly the need will be to expand, as it were, his or her ability to recognize that behaviors

Table 17.2 Sample of problem areas used with strengths and weaknesses.

Potential Problem Areas Concerning Marital Adjustment

Running Household, Family Economics, and Family Living
1. Finances and money management.
2. Household management and decision making (meals, shopping, household chores, transportation).
3. Husband's work.
4. Wife's work.
5. Child care and training.
6. Family recreation and leisure time.
7. Adult recreation and leisure time.
8. Friendships.

Value and Philosophy
9. Education.
10. Religion.
11. Traditional versus contemporary outlook.
12. Politics.
13. Charity.

Person Factors
14. Temperament and personality differences.
15. Affection and closeness.
16. Acceptance-rejection.
17. Sexual adjustment (including contraception).
18. Jealousy and extramarital affairs.
19. Personal habits.
20. Personal improvement.
21. Health.
22. Kinship responsibilities.
23. Husband's mother.
24. Husband's father.
25. Wife's mother.
26. Wife's father.
27. Other relatives and dependents.

are not simply good or bad. The need is to become better at differentiating strengths and weaknesses in self and other. Spouses may also damn with faint praise by acknowledging, for example, that the other is good at turning off the lights at night. Some spouses will take this opportunity of free responding to write far more than intended in the allotted space (typically, 3.5 inches each for the strength and weakness sections). In any event, the rationale of this exercise is to facilitate individuals to make behavioral discriminations about their relationship and to force themselves to see strengths even in problematic interactions. This approach can be adapted to focusing on one's own strengths and weaknesses, thus making it consistent with Halford's (2001) emphasis on self-appraisal, discussed previously.

Behavioral Observation

As noted earlier in our discussion of conceptual issues in assessment, behavioral observation has been closely associated with BCT, although generally, it has been reserved for use with couples in clinical research settings due to the need for trained coders (cf. Heyman, 2001; Weiss & Heyman, 1997). However, office applications are possible using either home video or simply audiotape recording. After identifying various areas of conflict, the couple is instructed to attempt to reach a resolution of the issue either without the therapist being present (preferably) or with the therapist agreeing to remain a silent observer. Based on data from Gottman's (1994) latest research with groups of couples, it is particularly useful to identify those affects and behavioral patterns that have been predictive of poor marital outcome. The caveat is that these affects and interaction patterns are based on aggregated data, and predictions for any individual couple are much more uncertain. Table 17.3 summarizes findings for individual affects, coded by the Specific Affect Coding System (SPAFF; Gottman, McCoy, Coan, & Collier, 1996). Table 17.3 also lists interaction patterns based on coded observations of stimulus-response sequences that capture how each person responds to the behavior of the other as the interaction unfolds.

Although somewhat controversial, Gottman et al. (1998) did not find that displays of anger or good communication skills (e.g., active listening, paraphrasing, and reflection) were statistically discriminating of those couples who did or did not divorce. Another well-established finding, that distressed relative to nondistressed

Table 17.3 Specific affects and interaction patterns that do or do not predict divorce.

Affects that do:
- Defensiveness.
- Contempt.
- Belligerence.

Affects that do not:
- Anger per se, not destructive.
- Active listening, not predictive and very rare.

Patterns that do:
- Wife negative startup.
- Husband not accepting influence.
- Husband fails to de-escalate wife's low-intensity negative affect.
- Wife fails to de-escalate husband's high-intensity negative affect.
- Failure of husband to respond to wife's soothing.

Source: Based on Gottman et al. 1998.

couples display higher rates of negative reciprocity in their interactions (cf. Weiss & Heyman, 1997) was similarly not predictive of marital outcome.

INTERVENTION

Thus far, this chapter has described a multifaceted approach to BCT. The descriptions of BCT-based interventions must be more general and cover typical aspects of the different approaches, and it is not possible to present a treatment manual in this chapter. As noted in the previous section, treatment manuals are currently available. In this section on intervention, the aim is to provide the common elements that define BCT.

BCT does not assume that the duration of therapy is unlimited. Whether marital therapy is best thought of as crisis intervention or therapy of a longer duration, it is clear that within the various approaches, identifiable goals are necessary. Sessions may be spread out over time and not necessarily be held weekly, but the course of therapy ranges from 6 to 10 months. The major phases are intake, formalized assessment, feedback, planned intervention, and (usually) maintenance/follow-up.

Intake
Although there are many different approaches to conducting intakes, in BCT the focus typically is on generating agreement about a reasonable course of action in light of the couple's stated goals. Problems are first discussed dyadically, then separately with each spouse, ending with a summary by the therapist with both spouses present. An important distinction is made between *process* and *content* of initial interviews. Because a considerable amount of information can be gained efficiently from various self-report measures, the initial session provides the couple with (1) hands-on experience about the context of intervention (while socializing spouses to

the therapy process), and (2) a living example that shows the therapist patterns of their interaction. The interview provides an inventory of problem areas and attempted solutions. The notion is included in the socialization process that this and possibly the next few sessions are not so much aimed at bringing about desired changes as they are designed for creating an understanding of the relationship that will be formalized in a subsequent feedback session.

The distinction between assessment and therapy is absolutely essential in CBT approaches. Involving the spouses in their own evaluation process is a precursor to what will follow. Thus, when an individual wishes to expound in great detail about the history of a particular issue, the therapist can mark it as "received" and gently move on to the other items that constitute their problem inventory. Even if the spouses are unable to agree on the "problem," they are at least exposed to the inventory that reflects their partner's and their own issues. The inventory method also makes it easier to avoid the blame-justification pattern couples usually display.

The distinction between evaluation and intervention also provides a structure that lends authority to how the relationship will be viewed for intervention. The test results provide a platform from which to discuss possible interventions. Functionally, however, intervention proceeds almost from the very first moments of contact, because therapist empathy and ability to join the couple reflectively and the structure of the contact itself are all therapeutic. In some instances, such initial contacts may be sufficient to help individuals mobilize their resources and attain a better adjustment. In essence, the intake provides direction and also screens for possible safety issues.

Feedback
The specifics of the all-important feedback session vary depending on the specific version of BCT being considered. Common to all

approaches, however, is the therapist's overview of the relationship, using the results of the assessment tests as a guide. For example, the test results may appear to be at odds with the interview impressions. Thus, if there is a disconnect between test scores (e.g., indicating very high risk of divorce) and interview impressions (e.g., "We fully intend to stay together"), it is essential to address this discrepancy in negotiating a therapeutic contract. Noting that the couple is "statistically divorced" based on test results presents a focal issue for therapy planning. In this instance, and in general, testing is highly reactive in bringing about changes in how the couple view their situation.

Most often, the BCT therapist will try to summarize the couple's relationship blueprint, which has been referred to as the thematic structure (schema) or working theory of their relationship. Such models of relationship functioning highlight how each spouse is trying to accomplish what appears to be opposing and/or irreconcilable goals. The problem is how they have gone about solving their differences and how solutions themselves have become stumbling blocks. (The solution being the problem is a major tenet in "strategic therapy," as described by Haley, 1963.) How therapists create the relationship blueprint differs most among BCT practitioners. For example, Halford (2000) and Jacobson and Christensen (1996) place considerable emphasis on developing the affective, intrapersonal, family of origin factors that may have gone into shaping the "problem." Other BCT approaches single out communication and problem-solving skill deficits as instrumental, so that intervention begins directly with skills training. In 1980, Weiss presented a model that falls between these extremes. The emphasis was on how, by addressing relational efficacy expectations, one could overcome "resistance" to spouse's acceptance of behavioral skills training. Efficacy expectations (cognitions and their associated affects) define what is possible to change, and this depends greatly on how one explains a partner's behavior (causal attributions). The approach suggested by Weiss for dealing with efficacy expectations that impede change was based largely on systems theory. For example, making contextual changes via reframing ensures that behaviors will take on new meanings. For BCT, defining the self-efficacy piece as an occasion for cognitive restructuring was new, even though cognitive restructuring was already familiar as a cognitive-behavioral therapy technique for change. The recommendation was to use many of the common techniques of strategic therapy. The desired effect is to dislodge the predictable, stereotyped patterns spouses engage in and to allow for new awareness.

In summary, feedback based on structured assessment is step 1 in planning intervention. Whether one is using the sophisticated psychophysiological and behavioral observation technology employed by Gottman, or the less costly self-report measures developed in the tradition of BCT, the objective remains the same: "Here is how I see your relationship, in a way that I can present to you collaboratively and that allows us to implement a plan of action." For example, Jacobson and Christensen (1996) develop a theme or a story of the couple's relationship that sets the stage for explaining how their current attempts to adjust to one another cause the difficulty. The object of these feedback tactics is to externalize the problem as something that is impeding the success of the relationship. The problem can be viewed more readily from the perspective of acceptance. Alternatively, as a result of self-appraisal, one can set individual change objectives, as in Halford's (2001) self-regulation approach. The feedback session also serves to contain expressions of futility and confusion frequently observed in couples by providing structure for ensuing sessions.

Continued Intervention Sessions

Throughout this chapter, both conceptual and practical facets of intervention are discussed. The role of feedback has been described by detailing how planning for intervention is based on assessment information in specific BCT models. A common element seen among BCT practitioners is the use of cognitive restructuring and behavioral skills training designed to foster increased self-reliance in the context of the dyad. The ultimate goal is to *enhance individual functioning in the context of the dyad.* This applies whether dealing with (1) spouses' attributions, standards, beliefs, and expectations; (2) problems with affect regulation; (3) difficulties in assessing the contribution of situational "causes" of unsatisfactory interchanges; (4) rigid cognitions about the relationship; or (5) repetitive unskilled communication patterns and attempts to provide emotional support. This objective differs from the goals of individual therapy in that here, the focus is how one functions with an intimate partner. The BCT therapist strives to accomplish individual changes aimed at enhancing accord between partners (including viewing one's interactions differently). It is critical to note that the responsibility for change lies ultimately within the person/dyad, and that not all interventions will achieve the goal of maintaining the relationship. In fact, a desirable outcome may be separation or divorce if individual functioning is to be enhanced.

CASE EXAMPLE

The case of Cynthia and Walt illustrates many elements of a behaviorally based approach and indicates how couples may choose to modulate the amount of therapy they wish to utilize. The couple had been seen over a period of four months for 12 sessions: two joint assessment, two individual, and eight joint intervention sessions.

SESSION 1

Cynthia and Walt, a middle-aged couple (52 and 54 years, respectively), married for 30 years, described their reasons for coming as "lack of intimacy" and "communication difficulties." Cynthia was quite upset about their differences in how they spent time and money. Walt felt that Cynthia had a sexual dysfunction. They also stated that they were very uncomfortable with disagreements. They agreed that Cynthia was especially attached to a younger adolescent daughter who was still at home; they also had a son who was attending college.

Walt was a small business owner and Cynthia described her career as being a homemaker. They agreed that she focused almost exclusively on the children and household management. They described their relationship coming apart after the birth of their first child. They reported not having had sex for months. There was no physical violence, and frequent arguments resulted in each going to "their separate corners."

They were very concerned about appearances and confidentiality. They displayed considerable difficulty talking and showed considerable shyness and embarrassment in sessions. There was relatively little in-session blaming of one another. Both were very tearful throughout the initial session. They said they both wanted very much to stay together. Within the prior six months they had terminated marital therapy that had lasted for 26 sessions. They felt that it was not helpful because it seemed to lack a focus. They also had sought couple therapy 10 to 15 years earlier. Asked about the goals they sought from therapy, they described wanting a "healthy, happy, fun relationship." They were unable to be specific about this.

Their response to inquiries about how they met was recited in a factual manner (they met in college), with little spontaneity indicating positive reminiscences. Because of their dysphoric affect and difficulty talking, they were each given a BDI during the initial interview. The therapist said that before giving them a sense of what she thought might be helpful, she wanted to assess their depression, and suggested that the best way to do this would be for each of them to complete a form. Their scores on the BDI indicated moderate depressive symptoms.

The therapist offered a preliminary summary of what the couple had presented. They seemed to be leading parallel lives and were shown a diagram of circles with a very small area of overlap. They wanted to be happy but didn't know how to accomplish this, and found it difficult to be specific about what would be positive. The absence of sex clearly indicated they had grown apart, and this was distressing for both of them. Their arguments were wearing them down, and their communication was not effective. They responded to the therapist's concern about their being depressed by indicating that they both thought it was relationship-based (thus ruling out more severe clinical depression). The affects and sequences indicative of divorce as depicted in the Gottman et al. (1998) study (see Table 17.3) were notably lacking from their patterns of interaction. Sadness and formality seemed much more the rule for them than hostile belligerence.

They were offered a plan that included (1) first completing assessment forms at home; (2) a second joint assessment session, using the forms to further develop how they relate to one another; (3) individual sessions; and (4) a joint feedback session where they and the therapist would plan the next steps of therapy if they decided to continue.

SESSION 2: JOINT ASSESSMENT

The following information, based on their assessment forms, was available before the scheduled second joint session (husband and wife are listed respectively):

DAS scores of 60 and 70, clearly in the distressed range (scores above 100 indicate increasing marital satisfaction).

MSI scores of 1 and 0 (score of 4 or more is indicative of high divorce potential).

ACQ of 12 and 8 (total 20), indicating moderate to significant relationship distress.

Table 17.4 presents the information generated by the Marital Strengths and Weakness free report form (please refer to the potential problem areas, Table 17.2, from which Cynthia and Walt chose their items). There was not much agreement on potential problem areas, and Cynthia failed to mention sex. In the table, both the weakness and the strength items are presented in decreasing orders of negativity/positivity. Within each cell, both strength and weakness items are indicated in italics according to the valence of the cell (e.g., if the cell describes a problem area, the weakness items are in italics).

The therapist briefly summarized the strengths and weaknesses that were based collectively on these self-report data. For example, the MSI supported other signs of marital stability: There was evidence of strong regard for the relationship, and they shared a strong sense of family, although there also were considerable indications of tension and hurt feelings.

Using information based on their description of relationship strengths, the therapist decided to assess behaviorally and to begin communication skills training. They were first asked to talk to one another by guessing what each had written about the other's strengths. They were then told to tell each other what each other had written. Their responses were subdued but mildly positive, showing some sense of relief. They were then instructed to take a negative weakness item and rephrase it as a request. For example, in Cynthia's Temperament and Personality area, she said Walt was distracted and didn't listen well. She was asked to state what she wanted him to do, using more behavioral (pinpointed) language. Although ostensibly a simple communication exercise, it became extremely emotional for them to do. They were struck with the sadness of what they "had lost" (i.e., what they used to be able to do and no

Table 17.4   Case example: Husband's and wife's listing of areas of marital strength and weaknesses.

Husband	*Wife*
−1 Sexual Adjustment *Lack of diversity; "dirty."* *Rejects my sexual foreplay.* [Nothing as strengths]	−1 Temperament/Personality *Moody, unfriendly.* *Doesn't let others lead.* *Doesn't listen well.* Loyal and trustworthy. Generally a nice guy.
−2 No entry	−2 Acceptance/Rejection *Opposing opinion = rejection.* *Withdraws from family gatherings.* Rejects weakness in others. Rarely speaks poorly of other. Highly self-motivated.
−3 Adult Recreation/Leisure *No new activities.* *"Does not like to dance."* "Allows me to enjoy activities I like." Once convinced to do activity, she participates.	−3 Affection/Closeness *Doesn't show he is pleased with me.* *Only shows pleased if leads toward sexual goals.* Wants very much to have a close intimate relationship.
+1 Child Care *Very child-oriented.* *Provided strong religious basis.* "Smothers children." Controlling.	+1 Child Care *Loves his children.* *Shares with them.* Distances himself. Not enough interest in their daily activities.
+2 Finance/Money Management *Good budgeting management.* *Stays within monthly income.* Doesn't allow children to manage theirs. Doesn't try to save money.	+2 Finance/Money Management *Provides well.* *Concerned about the future.* Only interested in big picture. Fails to disclose all money matters.
+3 Traditional/Contemporary *Provides a religious basis for family.* *Very consistent values.* No experimentation. Doesn't allow for creativity in life.	+3 Traditional/Contemporary *Wonderful provider.* *Very goal-oriented.* (I) believe my identity lost . . . he doesn't understand. His work is not as important as mine.

Note: −1 = Most problematic; +1 = Most satisfying; −2 = Next most problematic; +2 Next most satisfying; etc. Categories are those each spouse selected; items in italics consistent with category rating as either problematic or satisfying.

longer seemed able to do). The session ended with an explanation that this was a sample of the efforts that they would be asked to make if they continued therapy.

The decision to meet individually was based on Walt's claim that Cynthia had a sexual dys-function, their reluctance to talk as a couple, and their continued depressive affect.

Cynthia's manner seemed to suggest that she wanted out of the relationship, even though her MSI score indicated otherwise. In her individ-ual session, she indicated that Walt was "very moody" and that when he was angry, she withdrew and stopped talking. She didn't want sexual intimacy because she felt she was not respected for what she contributed to the family. She didn't ask anyone to do anything for her and she felt guilty if she did ask. If Walt suggested helping her do something, such as vacuuming, she got angry because he had to ask and that was supposed to be her job. She indicated that a personal issue she faced was what to do with her life when her last child went off to college. She also felt she "had gotten lost somewhere over the years" and that she had "always been wife and mother before thinking of myself." She asserted that she was not thinking of leaving Walt and that the relationship was important to her, but she said, "He is not a good friend; I can't confide in him."

Walt's individual session paralleled his wife's. He believed his depression was only because of problems with the relationship. He was interested in a number of activities (e.g., fishing, working with horses, hunting) but felt she was not interested in any of them. He felt that her only interests were the kids, "she's not a companion," she didn't share his interests and didn't do things with him. He had stopped talking about work because he felt she was critical of the way he handled the business. He felt rejected by her and he could find nothing that would make her happy. He said, "I have devoted my life to her and she doesn't seem to appreciate that."

FEEDBACK SESSION AND FIRST INTERVENTION

The following points were offered during the feedback session:

> They had been leading parallel lives for 15 years, since the birth of their first child.
> She did kids; he did business.
> There was no adult, couple-focused interaction.

They were very conflict-avoidant.

They engaged in considerable mindreading, making assumptions about rejection that result in withdrawal.

They had a limited number of joint adult activities.

Both were showing symptoms of depression due to their relationship struggles.

It was not enough to reduce the negatives between them, they must also increase the positives of their interactions (based on the "sine wave" concept of satisfaction).[3]

Based on the Oregon model (Weiss, 1980), a therapy plan was described that would enable them to talk more clearly to one another (e.g., pinpointing, differentiating between problem solving and emotional expression, making effective opening statements, nonverbal active listening skills, paraphrasing), to achieve supportive goals, and to develop problem-solving skills. It was understandable that they were not sexually accommodating to one another given the extent to which they were misunderstanding one another's intentions and rarely had interactions other than about their home and children.

It was purposely left unsaid that Cynthia had sexual problems and that he was overly sensitive to rejection. These were considered to be individual problems and not highlighted at this point. The couple agreed to continue with therapy, which included a commitment to six to eight weeks, with the provision that they would reevaluate their progress and their goals for therapy at that time. Thereafter, the session moved into intervention mode, beginning with communication skills training.

---

[3] The pleasure sine wave (Weiss, 1980) proposes a theoretical function of how events are related either to increases in *satisfaction* or increases in *dissatisfaction*. Thus, the absence of annoyances in a relationship is not the same as the presence of pleasurable (appetitive) events. The absence of annoyances decreases dissatisfaction, but this does nothing to enhance satisfaction.

The therapist created a series of topics, written on individual 3 x 5 cards, based on content derived from the self-report and assessment interviews. The objective was to give the couple a positive experience in making statements to one another and to correct instances of nonproductive reactions. For homework, they were assigned brief reading material on common communication faults and examples of better communication skills. They also agreed to plan and engage in a joint activity with another couple on the following Saturday night.

SESSIONS 2 AND 3 INTERVENTION

By the second intervention session, they reported feeling much better. They had been very compliant in doing the reading assignments but were less diligent in arranging to spend time together. Additional communication training was focused on avoiding mindreading and seeing rejection when it was not intended.

By the third session, it became obvious that they could follow therapist-generated instructions, but were unable to initiate assignments on their own. Walt saw Cynthia as "supersensitive" and disapproving of him. He mindread her intent and magnified what he saw as her disapproval. As an example, if there was a mechanical failure in the household, he would conclude that she blamed him for it, when in fact that was not her view at all. Actually, she felt that he was very competent in handling these types of problems and was grateful that he was such a good "handyman."

The therapist had earlier provided information about a couples sexuality enhancement group, and avoided the notion that Cynthia was the sexually dysfunctional person. Because they had not followed up on reading the brochures or exploring it further, the therapist suggested that perhaps they were not yet ready to address their sexual issues.

They were scheduling meetings with each other and enjoyed that activity. During the session, they both filled out personal calendars and seemed bound to them; if it wasn't written on both calendars, it didn't happen. They also scheduled joint activities that they planned to undertake. These activities were based on a menu of possibilities that they created together of things they would like to do if they had 20 minutes, two hours, a day, or a weekend together. Although they were pleased with this new development, the therapist did not see this as actually helping them develop spontaneity in their relationship, but rather as a beginning step in reestablishing "togetherness."

SESSION 4 INTERVENTION

They agreed that the negativity and conflict had decreased and that they were communicating more. However, there was no increase in their joint activities or in their affectionate behaviors. Walt mentioned that perhaps he was more interested in sex than Cynthia was, and that he would never push her into something that only he wanted. Cynthia said that she wanted sex but that it was difficult for her to feel sexual when they were not sharing other interests during the day. She also indicated that perhaps she had low sexual desire caused by an imbalance in her hormones and thought she would see a physician for evaluation.

The plan for the next session was to have read materials on sensate focus provided by the therapist. They expressed great interest in doing the reading.

SESSION 5 INTERVENTION

This session was devoted to reviewing the sensate focus materials, addressing the possibilities for failure, what could go right, what problems there might be with their setting, and generally to make the entire set of procedures more acceptable. The therapist had also asked the couple to schedule a joint pleasurable activity (previous assignment), but Walt misinterpreted this to mean sexual intimacy. He initiated sexual contact, was rebuffed, and reacted by blaming himself for it. (They had been cautioned not to have intercourse.)

This disclosure led to a consideration of how they would know each was interested in sexual contact and how they would go about initiating it. Walt's tendency to operate on old (past) information in interpreting her behavior and not responding to cues she gave him was labeled an important point for both of them to attend to. That is, he was to ask how she felt rather than assuming he knew, and she was to be more verbal and specific about how she felt at different times, especially if she felt warmly toward him. In light of Walt's tendency to take responsibility for failures, the therapist told him his "job" was to avoid mindreading and check with Cynthia about what she was truly thinking. This was an epiphany for him, as he realized that this was something he could do that fit his concept of problem solving.

At this point, the therapist assigned the first stage of the sensate focus exercise, again emphasizing touching but no contact with erogenous areas. They agreed to schedule two to four sessions on their own.

SESSION 6 INTERVENTION

In reviewing the sensate focus assignment for the previous week, the couple reported doing two sessions. They first felt "embarrassed," mildly uncomfortable, and awkward, in part because they kept their clothes on. The second attempt went much better. Sometime later, and not as part of a sensate focus exercise, they did have sex and it went very well.

They "loved the idea" of sensate focus; it gave them the structure and tools they wanted from therapy. They came up with their first spontaneous idea: mini-sensate focus sessions where they rubbed feet and backs. They chose their own homework assignments: four full and eight mini-sensate focus sessions over the next two weeks, plus increased instances of affectionately touching during the day that was not geared toward sexual activity. They were to continue joint activities as a couple and with friends.

SESSION 7 INTERVENTION

The couple had done their self-assigned tasks and were very positive about how things were going. They were again enthused with the sensate focus exercises and were spending more time together. They expressed a concern over their son's returning home for a several-week stay, and they didn't feel sure how they would manage time to themselves. That is, they were not sure they would "feel safe" being more physically affectionate with each other or in scheduling sensate focus sessions if either child was in the house.

In addition to continuing sensate focus exercises and increasing their adult time together, a "new" problem emerged: What happens when their daughter leaves for college? Walt was concerned that Cynthia would distance herself from him. Walt already had plans for what he thought Cynthia should do (e.g., start her own business), but Cynthia was able to tell him that, though she appreciated his suggestions, she was considering several other options. The therapist pointed out that starting a new business might lead to increased separation between them. Overall, they felt that things had been going well. They were unable to schedule their next appointment due to vacations, but they were comfortable leaving open the time of the next session.

Two months later, Walt called to say that they "had fallen off the wagon" and that they wanted to resume therapy.

SESSION 8 INTERVENTION

In reestablishing contact, the couple discussed how they had had one sexual encounter that was painful for Cynthia and that Walt had reverted to mindreading and feeling responsible. Cynthia was okay with what had happened, but he felt it was a big problem. They had gradually decreased their joint activities prior to this experience because they had stopped scheduling them. When they missed one scheduling session, both assumed the other would set up a new one, but neither of them initiated another planning session. Walt then assumed that Cynthia "really didn't want to" be more engaged with him in their relationship.

Another problem emerged after a long evening of watching TV when they undertook their sensate focus session and it went poorly. Their pleasuring sessions typically occurred at the end of long and busy days when they were exhausted. They now agreed that they would turn the TV off two hours earlier to share talk time and thus be more awake and enthused about engaging in intimate activities.

Two persistent problems were apparent: Walt's continuing to focus on himself as being the cause of problems and his catastrophizing small incidents, and their time to foster togetherness being limited to scheduled appointments on their calendars. They were unable to keep their next appointment because of extended family illnesses.

HIGHLIGHT SUMMARY

A number of strategic decisions were made in planning and executing the intervention for this couple, based on the initial assessment. Three things dictated a focus on the present rather than on past history: their concerns about confidentiality and appearances, the fact that they wanted "tools" for specific goals (in light of their previous dissatisfaction with marital therapy), and their formal demeanor (e.g., throughout, Walt spoke of "intimacy" instead of "sex" or "intercourse"). Besides developing better communication, one of the therapist's immediate goals was to increase a sense of togetherness. Another

goal was to not focus the attention on Cynthia as having a sexual dysfunction (unless, as therapy progressed, she appeared to need a formal medical/sexual functioning evaluation).

As is usually the case with skills-based intervention, maintaining gains outside of therapist influence was difficult. Walt's tendency to revert to old ways of mindreading and the couple's rigid reliance on scheduling togetherness were persistent impediments to change. However, this couple had years of experience maintaining a structured pattern of interaction, and it seemed best to view their need for structure as a strength (that they were unlikely to change) and to look for ways to enhance their relationship within that framework. Thus, the therapist did not directly confront their use of calendars and their inability to be spontaneous with each other.

As their arguing and conflict decreased, therapy in this modality did open up new vistas for them, and they did experience an increased sense of togetherness and happiness. Because this is a fairly recent case, there are no current follow-up data on this couple. Their pattern throughout therapy was to modulate just how much and how frequently they would participate, and it is likely that they will request additional sessions.

A possibility for future sessions would be to help Walt target his mindreading and catastrophizing. Walt appears to have some of the typical depressive cognitions that would respond well to cognitive-behavioral methods. Cynthia also needs to be more proactive in the relationship and provide clearer cues for Walt to generate positive comments and encouragement.

MAJOR PROBLEMS TREATED

BCT traditionally has been associated with a wide range of both individual and relationship-based problems. The distinction is made between marital therapy that is relationship-focused and partner-assisted therapy. In the first, the problem is addressed as part of what might be called relationship adjustment. The focus is the ongoing nature of the relationship, even though one person may be more clinically involved (e.g., a wife who is more depressed than her husband). The emphasis is on a relationship-based problem. The second category refers to a clinical problem that pertains primarily to one individual in a relationship and that exists almost independently of the relationship. For example, agoraphobia may be a serious problem for one spouse and therapy may include the assistance of the other spouse, but not necessarily with the expectation that by treating the relationship, the agoraphobia will be diminished. Perhaps the portability of the problem makes the distinction: One could be agoraphobic in any of the marriages in partner-assisted treatment.

For complete reviews of major problems treated with the behavioral approach and of the effectiveness of BCT approaches, please refer to Baucom, Shoham, Mueser, Daiuto, and Stickle (1998), Halford (2001, Chapter 2), and Christensen and Heavey (1999). Baucom et al. sought to identify those empirically supported couple and family interventions shown to be effective in treating various forms of marital distress and adult mental health problems.

Among the more salient problems treated by BCT approaches are depression, alcohol abuse, and sexual dysfunctions. It is still not clear whether BCT is appropriate for marital abuse, as safety issues are paramount and the risk of prolonging an abusive relationship through ongoing marital therapy must be a legitimate source of concern (see Holtzworth-Munroe, Rehman, Marshall, & Meehan, in this volume).

The comorbidity of depression and marital distress makes it mandatory to determine whether, in any given case, depression is a significant factor and, if indicated, whether it is relationship-based. As noted by Christensen and Heavey (1999) in their review, at least two studies have indicated that BCT is not the treatment of choice for depressed women in maritally

nondistressed relationships. Comparisons are made in various studies of BMT, cognitive therapy (CT), and combined BMT and CT. Generally, CT treatment for depression does little to enhance marital satisfaction, although BMT for depressed couples who also show marital distress is relatively effective in improving marital adjustment. The combined treatment resulted in the least improvement for depressed women in distressed marriages (Baucom et al., 1998).

BCT treatment of problem drinking (alcohol abuse) has been studied extensively in the systematic research of O'Farrell and associates (O'Farrell, 1993) in Project CALM (Counseling for Alcoholic Marriages). The approach embodies clear behavioral steps in a manualized treatment approach. The program includes both an individual couple and subsequent couples' group sessions, skills building exercises for increasing exchanges of positive behaviors, communication effectiveness, and problem solving. In addition, partner-assisted disulfiram contracts are included, which may obscure the efficacy of the BCT components. One of the functional aspects of Project CALM is the focus on negative consequences of drinking, in addition to the more typical alcohol consumption measures. In keeping with behavioral approaches, the program has a built-in relapse-prevention module, which assumes that the cues for drinking will become an important part of treatment. Baucom et al. (1998) view this approach as promising but are not yet willing to include it among the demonstrated effective treatments.

Spouse abuse and physical aggression have also been a target of BCT approaches, though recognizing that a conjoint focus is not always the modality of choice. In light of the threat of serious physical harm, implicitly encouraging a couple to stay together may be compromising a partner's safety. Heyman and Neidig (1997) describe Physical Aggression Couples Treatment for marital aggression, but it does not involve standard marital therapy. The objective of the first half of the program "is to eliminate violence in the home. Period" (p. 589). The focus of the second half of the program is more traditionally like BCT and is directed toward improving communication skills and "negotiating more equitable marriage contracts" (p. 589). Holtzworth-Munroe et al.'s chapter (this volume) also cautions that violence must be contained before beginning BCT.

The manifestations of sexual dysfunction in marital relationships are as complex as they are varied. A study by Zimmer (1987) included maritally distressed couples in which wives reported orgasmic, arousal, and desire disorders, and a high percentage of husbands also reported some form of sexual dysfunction. The aim of the study was to determine whether the addition of BCT would be effective (e.g., communication and conflict resolution skills training) prior to undertaking a Masters and Johnson program. Although the gains in the combined group exceeded those in the Masters and Johnson alone and control conditions, attrition was higher for more maritally distressed couples. As seen next, the degree of initial marital distress is a critical factor in determining likely success of BCT interventions. At this time, it may be more a clinical assumption than an empirically based conclusion that BCT approaches facilitate amelioration of sexual dysfunction when combined with targeted sexual interventions.

EFFECTIVENESS OF BCT

History will show that BCT's legacy is its commitment to empirically testing the efficacy and effectiveness of its methods. To this end, there have been a number of conceptual and methodological advances in how to measure successful outcome. In addition to the Baucom et al. (1998) critical review and analysis of empirically validated marital and family therapies (including non-BCT approaches), a number of meta-analyses are also available (e.g., Christensen & Heavey, 1999; Dunn & Schwebel, 1995; Hahlweg

& Markman, 1988; Shadish et al., 1993). The concept of clinical significance (Jacobson & Truax, 1991) is among the most cogent ideas to emerge from discussions in the effectiveness literature. It involves two steps: A reliable change index is computed for each couple by normalizing their pre- to posttreatment change score given on a measure by the standard error of measurement for that measure. The difference must exceed the "noise level" or unreliability of the criterion measure to determine whether the difference is statistically significant. Having thus established that an individual couple has made a statistically significant improvement, the issue is whether they have moved from the range of distressed scores to that of nondistressed scores. Thus, it is not sufficient to show statistical difference from pre- to posttherapy; one must also show that the couple is no longer distressed. Using this highly conservative criterion, one can determine the percentage of couples who benefited within a single study. Most often, efficacy and effectiveness are assessed by means of meta-analytic procedures using effect sizes based on treated versus control group comparisons (e.g., Christensen & Heavey, 1999). As Halford (2001) observes: "Despite the replication and magnitude of the observed effects of behavioral couple therapy, there are significant limitations to the effects of BCT. Approximately 25 to 30% of couples show no measurable improvement with BCT . . . and although one-third improve somewhat, they still report significant marital distress" (p. 30). Similar considerations influenced Jacobson and Christensen to modify BCT.

Thus, it can be asked whether the glass is half-empty or half-full. In one sense, many couples *do* benefit from BCT approaches, based on results of many efficacy studies. However, very little is known about effectiveness because, until very recently, there have been no broad-based BCT effectiveness studies. An important distinction between efficacy and effectiveness applies when attempting to evaluate any intervention. Efficacy refers to showing a clinically significant change under fairly strictly controlled conditions, whereas effectiveness asks whether a treatment succeeds in real-world settings (i.e., without a priori selection of clients and therapists). In the face of ubiquitous comorbidity encountered in clinical practice, effectiveness is the more stringent criterion of utility. Efficacy results often fail to hold up in the more demanding venue of agencies.

Jacobson, Christensen, Prince, Cordova, and Eldridge (2000) reported preliminary results from a random assignment treatment comparison. This study is a prelude to a large-scale multisite investigation[4] of their integrative behavioral couple therapy, IBCT and traditional behavioral couple therapy (TBCT). Because of their small sample sizes, the authors did not test for differences between treatments. Descriptively, however, the percentages of couples who either improved (statistically significant pre- to posttreatment) or recovered (based on clinically significant change) were 64% and 80%, respectively, for the TBCT and IBCT groups. The outcome measures were based on two empirically validated self-report measures: the DAS (Spanier, 1976) and the Global Distress Scale (Snyder, 1979).

Halford, Osgarby, and Kelly (1996) report a quasi-experimental (nonrandom assignment of couples) study of their self-regulatory couple therapy. Based on their work and a study by Worthington et al. (1995), couples were shown to have benefited (on follow-up) from 3 sessions of treatment as much as those receiving 15 sessions of traditional BCT. Thus, there is preliminary evidence that couples can benefit from assessment, goal setting, and, in the case of Halford et al., these two interventions plus reading a BCT couples guide.

Larger-scale effectiveness studies remain to be done, but based on the manner in which BCT approaches have committed to empirical testing, it is reasonable to conclude that the glass is half-full and clinical as well as nondistressed couples benefit greatly from behavioral approaches.

SUMMARY

This chapter reviewed BCT in retrospect and prospect. Changes in the behavioral perspective on couples therapy, especially more recent adaptations, were briefly summarized, noting the influences of a much broadened social learning perspective. BCT evolved from an empirical tradition initially grounded in principles of learning and was increasingly influenced by cognitive and social learning theories of change. The chapter highlighted numerous connections with the research literature that helped define the newer approaches to BCT. The interplay between assessment and intervention characterizes all variations of BCT. Various conceptual issues faced when doing behavioral assessment were discussed. A case example illustrated specific assessment options and methods of intervention. Examples of problems treated with BCT and the effectiveness of these types of interventions were briefly discussed. BCT remains a viable empirically studied intervention dealing with couple distress. Effectiveness studies are ongoing and the initial findings argue well for the utilization of BCT.

---

[4] The larger investigation more closely approximates the requirements of an effectiveness study by (1) employing licensed practitioners as therapists and (2) not deselecting couples for individual disorders (personal communication, A. Christensen, December 12, 2000).

REFERENCES

Azrin, N., Naster, B., & Jones, R. (1973). Reciprocity counseling: A rapid learning based procedure for marital counseling. *Behavior Research and Therapy, 11,* 365–382.

Bandura, A. (1977). *Social learning theory.* Englewood Cliffs, NJ: Prentice Hall.

Baucom, D. H., & Epstein, N. (1990). *Cognitive-behavioral marital therapy.* New York: Brunner/Mazel.

Baucom, D. H., Shoham, V., Mueser, K., Daiuto, A. D., & Stickle, T. R. (1998). Empirically supported couple and family therapy interventions for marital distress and adult mental health problems. *Journal of Consulting and Clinical Psychology, 66,* 53–88.

Beach, S. R. H., Sandeen, E. E., & O'Leary, K. D. (1990). *Depression in marriage.* New York: Guilford Press.

Beck, A., Ward, C., Mendelson, M., Mock, J., & Erbaugh, J. (1961). An inventory for measuring depression. *Archives of General Psychiatry, 4,* 561–571.

Christensen, A. (1987). Assessment of behavior. In K. D. O'Leary (Ed.), *Assessment of marital discord* (pp. 130–157). Hillsdale, NJ: Erlbaum.

Christensen, A., & Heavey, C. L. (1999). Intervention for couples. *Annual Review of Psychology, 50,* 165–190.

Christensen, A., & Jacobson, N. S. (1999). *Reconcilable differences.* New York: Guilford Press.

Dunn, R. L., & Schwebel, A. L. (1995). Meta-analytic review of marital therapy outcome research. *Journal of Family Psychology, 9,* 58–69.

Fincham, F. D., Garnier, P. C., Gano-Phillips, S., & Osborne, L. N. (1995). Preinteraction expectations, marital satisfaction, and accessibility: A new look at sentiment override. *Journal of Family Psychology, 9,* 3–14.

Fincham, F. D., & Linfield, K. J. (1997). A new look at marital quality: Can spouses feel positive and negative about their relationship? *Journal of Family Psychology, 11,* 489–502.

Goldenberg, I., & Goldenberg, H. (2000). *Family therapy: An overview* (5th ed.). Belmont, CA: Brooks/Cole.

Goldiamond, I. (1965). Self-control procedures in personal behavior problems. *Psychological Reports, 17,* 851–868.

Goldstein, J. K., & Francis, B. (1969, October). *Behavior modification of husbands by wives.* Paper presented at the National Council of Family Relations annual meeting, Washington, DC.

Gottman, J. M. (1979). *Marital interaction: Experimental investigations.* New York: Academic Press.

Gottman, J. M. (1994). *What predicts divorce?* Hillsdale, NJ: Erlbaum.

Gottman, J. M., Coan, J., Carrère, S., & Swanson, C. (1998). Predicting marital happiness and stability from newlywed interactions. *Journal of Marriage and the Family, 60,* 5–27.

Gottman, J. M., McCoy, K., Coan, J., & Collier, H. (1996). The Specific Affect Coding System (SPAFF). In J. M. Gottman (Ed.), *What predicts divorce? The measures* (pp. 1–220). Hillsdale, NJ: Erlbaum.

Gottman, J. M., Swanson, C., & Murray, J. (1999). The mathematics of marital conflict: Dynamic mathematical nonlinear modeling of newlywed marital interaction. *Journal of Family Psychology, 13,* 3–19.

Greenberg, L. S., & Johnson, S. M. (1988). *Emotionally focused therapy for couples.* New York: Guilford Press.

Hahlweg, K., & Markman, H. J. (1988). Effectiveness of behavioral marital therapy: Empirical status of behavioral techniques in preventing and alleviating marital distress. *Journal of Consulting and Clinical Psychology, 56,* 440–447.

Haley, J. (1963). *Strategies of psychotherapy.* New York: Grune & Stratton.

Halford, W. K. (1998). The ongoing evolution of behavioral couples therapy: Retrospect and prospect. *Clinical Psychology Review, 18,* 613–633.

Halford, W. K. (2001). *Brief therapy for couples: Helping partners help themselves.* New York: Guilford Press.

Halford, W. K., Osgarby, S. M., & Kelly, A. B. (1996). Brief behavioural couples therapy: A preliminary evaluation. *Behavioural and Cognitive Psychotherapy, 24,* 263–273.

Heyman, R. E. (2001). Observation of couple conflicts: Clinical assessment applications, stubborn truths, and shaky foundations. *Psychological Assessment, 13,* 5–35.

Heyman, R. E., & Neidig, P. H. (1997). Physical aggression couples treatment. In W. K. Halford & H. Markman (Eds.), *Clinical handbook of marriage and couples intervention* (pp. 589–617). New York: Wiley.

Jackson, D. D. (1965). Family rules: Marital quid pro quo. *Archives of General Psychiatry, 12,* 589–594.

Jacobson, N. S., & Christensen, A. (1996). *Integrative couple therapy: Promoting acceptance and change.* New York: Norton.

Jacobson, N. S., Christensen, A., Prince, S. E., Cordova, J., & Eldridge, K. (2000). Integrative behavioral couple therapy: An acceptance-based, promising new treatment for couple discord. *Journal of Consulting and Clinical Psychology, 68,* 351–355.

Jacobson, N. S., & Margolin, G. (1979). *Marital therapy: Strategies based on social learning and behavioral exchange principles.* New York: Brunner/Mazel.

Jacobson, N. S., & Truax, P. (1991). Clinical significance: A statistical approach to defining meaningful change in psychotherapy research. *Journal of Consulting and Clinical Psychology, 58,* 12–19.

Johnson, P. I., & O'Leary, D. K. (1996). The behavioral components of marital satisfaction: An individualized assessment approach. *Journal of Consulting and Clinical Psychology, 64,* 417–423.

Liberman, R. P. (1970). Behavioral approaches to family and couple therapy. *American Journal of Orthopsychiatry, 40,* 106–118.

O'Farrell, T. J. (Ed.). (1993). A behavioral marital therapy couples' group program for alcoholics and their spouses. In *Treating alcohol problems: Marital and family interventions* (pp. 170–209). New York: Guilford Press.

Patterson, G. R., & Reid, J. B. (1970). Reciprocity and coercion: Two facets of social systems. In C. Neuringer & J. Michael (Eds.), *Behavior modification in clinical psychology* (pp. 133–177). New York: Appleton-Century-Crofts.

Patterson, G. R., Weiss, R. L., & Hops, H. (1976). Training of marital skills: Some problems and concepts. In H. Leitenberg (Ed.), *Handbook of behavior modification and behavior therapy* (pp. 242–254). Englewood Cliffs, NJ: Prentice Hall.

Shadish, W. R., Montgomery, L. M., Wilson, P., Wilson, M. R., Bright, L., & Okwumabua, T. (1993). Effects of family and marital psychotherapies: A meta-analysis. *Journal of Consulting and Clinical Psychology, 61,* 992–1002.

Skinner, B. F. (1953). *Science and human behavior.* New York: Macmillan.

Snyder, D. K. (1979). Multidimensional assessment of marital satisfaction. *Journal of Marriage and the Family, 41,* 813–823.

Snyder, D. K., & Wills, R. M. (1989). Behavioral versus insight-oriented marital therapy: Effects on individual and interspousal functioning. *Journal of Consulting and Clinical Psychology, 57,* 39–46.

Spanier, G. B. (1976). Measuring dyadic adjustment: New scales for assessing the quality of marriage and similar dyads. *Journal of Marriage and the Family, 38,* 15–28.

Straus, M. A. (1979). Measuring intrafamily conflict and violence: The Conflict Tactics Scales (CT). *Journal of Marriage and the Family, 41,* 75–88.

Stuart, R. B. (1969). Operant interpersonal treatment for marital discord. *Journal of Consulting and Clinical Psychology, 33,* 675–682.

Stuart, R. B. (1980). *Helping couples change: A social learning approach to marital therapy.* New York: Guilford Press.

Thibaut, J. W., & Kelley, H. H. (1959). *The social psychology of groups.* New York: Wiley.

Weiss, R. L. (1978). The conceptualization of marriage from a behavioral perspective. In T. J. Paolino & B. S. McCrady (Eds.), *Marriage and marital therapy: Psychoanalytic, behavioral and systems theory perspectives* (pp. 165–239). New York: Brunner/Mazel.

Weiss, R. L. (1980). Strategic behavioral marital therapy: Toward a model for assessment and intervention. In J. P. Vincent (Ed.), *Advances in family intervention, assessment and theory* (Vol. 1, pp. 229–271). Greenwich, CT: JAI Press.

Weiss, R. L., & Birchler, G. B. (1975). *Areas of change.* Unpublished manuscript, University of Oregon, Eugene.

Weiss, R. L., Birchler, G. B., & Vincent, J. P. (1974). Contractual models for negotiating training in marital dyads. *Journal of Marriage and the Family, 36,* 321–330.

Weiss, R. L., & Cerreto, M. C. (1980). The Marital Status Inventory: Development of a measure of dissolution potential. *American Journal of Family Therapy, 8,* 80–86.

Weiss, R. L., & Frohman, P. (1985). Behavioral observations: Not through a glass darkly. *Behavioral Assessment, 7,* 309–316.

Weiss, R. L., & Halford, W. K. (1996). Managing couples therapy. In V. Van Hasselt & M. Hersen (Eds.), *Sourcebook of psychological treatment manuals for adults* (pp. 489–537). New York: Plenum Press.

Weiss, R. L., & Heyman, R. E. (1990). Marital discord. In A. Bellack & M. Hersen (Eds.), *International handbook of behavior modification* (2nd ed., pp. 475–501). New York: Plenum Press.

Weiss, R. L., & Heyman, R. E. (1997). Marital interaction. In W. K. Halford & H. Markman (Eds.), *Clinical handbook of marriage and couples intervention* (pp. 13–35). New York: Wiley.

Weiss, R. L., & Margolin, G. (1986). Assessment of marital conflict and accord. In A. R. Ciminero, K. S. Calhoun, & H. E. Adams (Eds.), *Handbook for behavioral assessment* (pp. 561–600). New York: Wiley.

Weiss, R. L., Patterson, G. R., & Hops, H. (1973). A framework for conceptualizing marital conflict: A technology for altering it, some data for evaluating it. In L. D. Handy & E. L. Mash (Eds.), *Behavior change: Methodology concepts and practice* (pp. 309–342). Champaign, IL: Research Press.

Weiss, R. L., & Perry, B. A. (1983). The Spouse Observation Checklist. In E. E. Filsinger (Ed.), *A sourcebook of marriage and family assessment* (pp. 65–84). Beverly Hills, CA: Sage.

Weiss, R. L., & Summers, K. J. (1983). The Marital Interaction Coding System–III. In E. E. Filsinger (Ed.), *A sourcebook of marriage and family assessment* (pp. 85–115). Beverly Hills, CA: Sage.

Weiss, R. L., & Wieder, G. B. (1982). Marital and family distress. In A. Bellack, M. Hersen, & A. Kazdin (Eds.), *International handbook of behavior modification and therapy* (pp. 767–809). New York: Plenum Press.

Wills, T. A., Weiss, R. L., & Patterson, G. R. (1974). A behavioral analysis of the determinants of marital satisfaction. *Journal of Consulting and Clinical Psychology, 42,* 802–811.

Worthington, E. L., McCullough, M. E., Shortz, J. L., Mindes, E. J., Sandage, S. J., & Chaartrand, J. M. (1995). Can couples assessment and feedback improve relationships? Assessment as a brief relationship enrichment procedure. *Journal of Counseling Psychology, 42,* 466–475.

Zimmer, D. (1987). Does marital therapy enhance the effectiveness of treatment for sexual dysfunction? *Journal of Sex and Marital Therapy, 13,* 193–209.

CHAPTER 18

Treating Violence in Couples

Amy Holtzworth-Munroe, Uzma Rehman,
Amy D. Marshall, and Jeffrey C. Meehan

HISTORY OF APPROACH TO COUPLE VIOLENCE

Types of Couple Violence

Researchers and clinicians increasingly acknowledge that couple violence is a heterogeneous phenomenon. A consensus is growing that marital aggression can be differentiated into at least two types. One type, severe physical aggression (O'Leary, 1993) or patriarchal terrorism (Johnson, 1995), is probably what most people imagine when they think of battering. It is usually studied among samples of batterers entering domestic violence treatment programs or samples of battered women seeking help at shelters (Straus, 1999). This type of violence is characterized by severe male violence, with less severe female violence or severe wife violence perpetrated primarily for self-defense. It involves a high risk of wife injury and a high degree of wife fear; it probably functions to control

and dominate the wife. The second type of aggression, called mild physical aggression (O'Leary, 1993) or common couple violence (Johnson, 1995), is studied among newlywed, community, and, sometimes, marital therapy samples (Straus, 1999). It involves more bidirectional violence, with both spouses engaging in physical aggression that is mild to moderate in severity and frequency. Relative to more severe aggression, it is believed to be less likely to cause fear in the wife, to endanger her, or to be used to control her.

Clinical experience suggests that the second type of physical aggression will be seen more often than the first among couples seeking marital therapy. Thus, our conjoint therapy recommendations are geared toward couples experiencing mild physical aggression because, as discussed later, conjoint treatment may be inappropriate for couples experiencing severe husband violence. Even when dealing with mild aggression, however, it is inappropriate to discount the potential of any physical aggression to have negative and injurious consequences. At this time, we are unable to predict which couples experiencing low levels of aggression will escalate to increasingly severe and dangerous levels of violence versus which couples will either maintain a low level of violence or cease their aggression. Thus, the occurrence of any physical aggression in a relationship is a serious problem deserving attention in therapy.

PREVALENCE OF COUPLE VIOLENCE

Survey data from nationally representative samples suggest that, each year, one out of every eight husbands engages in physical aggression against his wife and up to two million women are severely assaulted by their male partner (Straus & Gelles, 1990). Aggression often begins early in a relationship; for example, researchers studying engaged couples find that about one-third of the men have used physical aggression against their fiancees (Leonard & Senchak; 1996; O'Leary et al., 1989). Husband physical aggression is even more prevalent among couples seeking marital therapy; in such samples, over 50% of the husbands have engaged in physical aggression against their wives in the past year (Holtzworth-Munroe et al., 1992; O'Leary, Vivian, & Malone, 1992).

Women also engage in physical aggression in intimate relationships. Indeed, surveys of nationally representative samples do not find significant differences between men and women in rates of spousal aggression (Straus & Gelles, 1986; Straus, Gelles, & Steinmetz, 1980). Similarly, among marital therapy clinic samples, up to 86% of partner aggression is reciprocal, with both partners engaging in primarily low levels of physical aggression (Cascardi, Langhinrichsen, & Vivian, 1992). As discussed below, although it is important for marital therapists to help both spouses end their use of aggression, husband violence is viewed as a more serious problem than wife violence because it results in more negative consequences.

STABILITY OF VIOLENCE

Findings from longitudinal studies suggest that once violence has occurred in a relationship, it may continue, particularly if the initial violence is severe or frequent. This has been found in two studies of newly married couples. First, O'Leary et al. (1989) found that if one had engaged in physical aggression against a partner at premarriage and at 18 months after marriage, the conditional probability of engaging in further aggression at 30 months was 0.72 for women and 0.59 for men. Similarly, Quigley and Leonard (1996) found that among husbands who had engaged in physical aggression in the first year of marriage, 76% engaged in further violence in the next two years of marriage; the risk increased to 86% among the most severely violence men.

Similar findings are found in studies of nationally representative samples. Feld and Straus (1989) found that among husbands who had committed three severe assaults in the year prior to the study, 67% continued their violence in the following year. Aldarondo (1996) found that from the first to the second year of his longitudinal study, 39% of violent men continued their violence, and from the second to the third year, 44% continued their violence. Unfortunately, 37% of the husbands who had discontinued violence initially resumed violence by the second follow-up assessment.

Which men are the most likely to continue their violence? Research suggests that, compared to men who cease their violence, persistently aggressive men were more likely to be younger, unemployed, have a lower family income, and engage in more frequent and severe fights with their spouse (Aldarondo & Kaufman Kantor, 1997; Aldarondo & Sugarman, 1996). As is evident from the O'Leary et al. (1989) findings cited above, a substantial number of wives also continue their physical aggression against their partners. However, researchers have not yet studied predictors of reassault by wives.

Differing Consequences of Male and Female Violence

Although the rates of female physical aggression are comparable to those of male physical aggression, husband violence has more severely negative physical and psychological consequences. Given the greater size and strength of men, they are more likely to physically injure their partner (Browne, 1993). For example, in one nationally representative sample, 3% of women reported needing medical attention due to a physical injury, compared to only 0.4% of men (Stets & Straus, 1989). Similarly, in a study of couples presenting for marital therapy, Cascardi et al. (1992) found that whereas most violence between husbands and wives was reciprocal, wives were more likely to sustain severe injuries. In another study, the wives in violent relationships were significantly more fearful of their partner than were the men (Cantos, Neidig, & O'Leary, 1993).

Psychological Impact of Husband Violence on Women and Children

Husband violence is associated with serious psychological effects for both battered women and their children. Relative to comparison samples, battered women are at particular risk to experience symptoms of Posttraumatic Stress Disorder and depression. Whereas most of this research has examined women experiencing severe husband violence, some researchers have studied the consequences of husband violence among women seeking marital therapy. The results of these studies suggest that, relative to women in nonaggressive relationships, women in aggressive relationships were still more likely to report clinical levels of depressive symptomatology (Cascardi et al., 1992). In addition, in a study of

newlyweds, Quigley and Leonard (1996) found that wives who experienced husband physical aggression over the first three years of marriage reported higher levels of depressive symptomatology than women whose husband was consistently nonviolent or who desisted from violence during this same time period.

Empirical evidence also indicates that children from maritally violent homes are at risk for behavior problems, emotional distress, and impaired social and academic functioning (Holtzworth-Munroe, Jouriles, Smutzler, & Norwood, 1998; Margolin, 1998). Research groups, such as Jouriles and colleagues at the University of Houston and Sullivan and colleagues at Michigan State University, are currently conducting research on the efficacy of interventions for children of battered women.

Effects of Marital Violence on Relationship Functioning

Studies of newlywed samples have demonstrated that the presence of physical aggression in early marriage is a predictor of later relationship problems. O'Leary et al. (1989) found that individuals who were married to a stably aggressive spouse (aggressive at more than one point in time) were less satisfied with their marriage than individuals married to a nonaggressive spouse. In addition, among this same sample, husbands' premarital aggression longitudinally predicted both wives' steps toward divorce and lower marital adjustment (Heyman, O'Leary, & Jouriles, 1995). Similarly, Quigley and Leonard (1996) found that the presence of stable husband physical aggression in the first three years of marriage was associated with a decline in the wife's marital satisfaction. Rogge and Bradbury (1999) found that whereas negative marital communication led to marital dissatisfaction, the presence of interspousal physical aggression among newlywed couples predicted relationship dissolution.

The Related Problem of Psychological Aggression

Increasingly, researchers also are examining psychological aggression as an important correlate and predictor of physical abuse. Initial studies indicate that behaviors such as swearing and name calling commonly occur among all couples (Barling, O'Leary, Jouriles, Vivian, & MacEwan, 1987). The widespread nature of these behaviors raises the question of whether such behavior can be labeled abusive or only become abusive when they reach a certain level of severity and frequency. Alternatively, such behaviors may become abusive in the context of a physically violent relationship as such actions may carry an additional threat when they have previously preceded violence.

Psychological aggression is a correlate of physical aggression, even among less severely violent samples. For example, Cascardi, O'Leary, Lawrence, and Schlee (1995) reported that, among couples seeking marital therapy, relative to nonabused women, women who had experienced husband violence reported their husband to be significantly more coercive and psychologically aggressive. In addition, psychological abuse has damaging consequences for battered women, with 72% of severely battered women reporting that emotional abuse has a more negative impact on them than physical abuse (Follingstad, Rutledge, Berg, Hause, & Polek, 1990). Finally, psychological aggression may predict the onset of physical aggression; Murphy and O'Leary (1989) found that husbands' use of psychological aggression at 18 months after marriage predicted physical aggression 30 months after marriage.

Need to Increase Therapist Awareness of the Problem

Given the prevalence of marital violence, it is likely that most marital therapists will treat violent couples even if they do not specialize in the treatment of physical aggression. However, many therapists have never received formal training regarding this problem, and two studies conducted by Harway, Hansen, and Cervantes (1997) demonstrate reason for concern. In the first, over 350 family and marital therapists were presented with a description of one of two actual cases involving family violence; though not depicted in the vignette, in reality, one of these cases had ended in the husband killing the wife. Therapists were asked what they would do with these cases. Forty percent of the respondents did not acknowledge family violence as a problem, and 55% did not suggest any intervention for the violence. It was unclear whether the therapists were unable to identify indicators of violence or recognized violence as a potential problem but were unable to suggest appropriate interventions. Thus, Harway et al. asked over 400 psychologists to read a case in which family violence was directly implicated. Respondents were asked how they would have intervened. The results showed that 50% of the responding therapists did not generate appropriate interventions. These data strongly demonstrate the need for greater awareness among clinicians regarding how to assess and treat cases of marital violence. The present chapter is designed to provide a basic background on this problem.

THEORETICAL CONSTRUCTS

This section briefly reviews some prominent theories of husband violence, which are often divided into three groups based on their level of analysis: the intrapersonal, interpersonal, or sociocultural causes of violence. Most recent theories include two or more levels of analysis; theories presented herein are based on their primary component. Theories suggesting the potential usefulness of couples therapy and behavioral-cognitive approaches in treating marital violence are also addressed.

INTRAPERSONAL THEORIES

Intrapersonal theories of husband violence assume that characteristics of the individual increase his risk of engaging in physical aggression. Bandura (1973, 1976) outlined a social learning theory of aggression that has been applied to husband violence (D. G. Dutton, 1995; O'Leary, 1988). In this model, aggressive behavior is acquired through learning, including observational learning in one's family or subculture, symbolic learning through, for example, television, and direct experience. Through this learning, particular stimuli are associated with and elicit aggression. The aggression elicitors most typically discussed in the marital violence literature include aversive wife behavior, anticipation of positive consequences, such as relief from tension, and factors unique to the subjective perspective of the aggressor, such as unfounded jealousy. Aggression is then maintained through rewards, including tangible rewards, social and status rewards, and self-reinforcement. As behavior is regulated by its consequences, this theory allows that aggression may be punished by aversive consequences or extinguished by withdrawing reward. Thus, therapists are advised to regard marital violence as a learned behavior and to examine and change the stimuli eliciting aggression and the balance of positive to negative consequences received for aggression.

Another intrapersonal theory that lends itself well to the interventions introduced below is the social information-processing model (Holtzworth-Munroe, 2000). In the first step of social information processing, decoding, one must perceive and interpret the relevant social stimuli in a situation. Misconstrual of social stimuli may occur due to factors such as distraction, inattention, unrealistic expectations, faulty attributions, anger, or alcohol use. In the second stage, response generation and selection, one must consider possible behavioral responses and choose a response. In the third stage, enactment, one must carry out the chosen response and monitor it to see if it has the expected impact. This monitoring will then be used to adjust future behavior. Each of these steps must be successfully completed for one to respond competently in a social interaction. Incompetent responses may escalate a conflictual situation and increase the risk of violence. As reviewed below, violent husbands evidence skills deficits at each of these three stages, suggesting that a focus on social and conflict resolution skills is an appropriate target for interventions with maritally violent men.

INTERPERSONAL THEORIES

Interpersonal theories of husband violence, such as family systems theory, focus on the interaction patterns between spouses. In family systems theory, the marital relationship is a system defined by repeated patterns of interaction between spouses. As events occur, the marital relationship system works to maintain a state of homeostasis or balance (Day, 1995). Thus, marital violence is a product of all the interdependent parts of a relationship. Each reaction is a precipitant in a continuous causal chain of interactions that maintain homeostasis. Marital violence is, therefore, a product of dysfunctional interactions in which both spouses contribute to an escalation of tension. Although numerous system characteristics of battering relationships have been identified, including inflexible family rules and tight boundaries between the relationship and the outside world, the communication patterns of violent relationships have been the subject of most empirical research and this work is reviewed below. Such data suggest the potential usefulness of communication and problem-solving training to break negative patterns of communication and reduce inequity between partners. It should be noted, however, that feminist critics maintain that family systems theory both ignores the existence of unequal power relationships in marriage and implies that the wife is responsible for the violence (Bograd, 1988).

SOCIOCULTURAL THEORIES

The broadest level of theoretical analysis is that of sociocultural theories, which maintain that marital violence exists because violent and patriarchal societies encourage the use of violence as a means of dominating women (Dobash & Dobash, 1979). Feminist theories suggest that violence against women is caused by a patriarchal social organization in which men possess greater power and privilege and an ideology that legitimizes them. Contributing to male dominance are men's economic advantage, adherence to traditional gender roles, and the accepted use of violence to settle disputes. Husband violence is assumed to be supported by society through factors such as peer support, lack of police response to reports of domestic violence, and minimal criminal sentences for domestic violence offenders.

As reviewed in Gelles and Straus (1979) and Bersani and Chen (1988), other sociocultural theories of violence have been proposed. For example, it has been suggested that the uneven distribution of violence in society is a function of differential cultural norms concerning violence and related issues, such as values regarding masculinity, the worth of life, and the meaning of honor. Others suggest that when resources, such as status and income, are lacking, violence may be used to maintain dominance or may be due to the frustration associated with few opportunities for achievement, power, or prestige. Some sociological theories assume that people will commit crimes, including violence, if social controls do not restrain them.

Theories at this level of analysis may have few direct implications for therapy with violent couples, yet they can be useful in the therapist's conceptualization of husband violence. For example, the therapist may wish to view violence in the context of the power difference based on gender inherent in many marriages (Vivian & Heyman, 1996) or may wish to consider the subculture in which the couple live and the stressors confronted in their lives.

RESEARCH ON MARITALLY VIOLENT HUSBANDS

A brief review of available data on the correlates of husband violence will familiarize therapists with risk factors for violence and alert them to relevant issues in conceptualizing cases and planning interventions. The brief summary below is based on more extensive reviews by Holtzworth-Munroe and colleagues (Holtzworth-Munroe, Bates, Smutzler, & Sandin, 1997; Holtzworth-Munroe, Smutzler, & Bates, 1997) and Schumacher et al. (2001).

BACKGROUND CORRELATES OF HUSBAND VIOLENCE

The factors reviewed here generally cannot be direct targets of intervention. Nonetheless, understanding these risk factors may increase the chances of identifying violent couples and help therapists consider intervention modifications with them (e.g., changing assignments for men with neuropsychological deficits).

Demographically, younger age, lower socioeconomic status, and cohabitation (as opposed to dating or marriage) are all related to an increased risk of male partner aggression; of these, young age is the strongest correlate of violence. Although higher rates of aggression have been found among Black and Hispanic couples than Caucasian couples, group differences often disappear when factors such as socioeconomic level and urbanicity are controlled.

Childhood experiences are correlated with later adult perpetration of intimate partner violence. For instance, in a large, longitudinal study, children from lower socioeconomic backgrounds were at risk for perpetrating partner aggression in young adulthood, and the most powerful predictors of such aggression were lower educational attainment and childhood conduct problems or juvenile delinquency (Magdol, Moffitt, Caspi, & Silva, 1998). In addition, data from numerous studies suggest that witnessing and experiencing violence in the childhood home are correlates of later male engagement in adult intimate aggression.

In a relatively new line of research, men who are violent with their partner are found to be more likely than nonviolent men to have suffered a head injury and may have neuropsychological deficits reflecting problems in the frontal lobes, which would interfere with impulse control and planning.

CORRELATES OF HUSBAND VIOLENCE THAT MAY BE AMENABLE TO TREATMENT

Social Factors

In one large study, level of social support resources was inversely related to the probability of intimate aggression in men (Magdol et al., 1997). Not all friends, however, are equal, and data suggest that association with peers who support the use of aggression or are involved in delinquent behavior may be risk factors for men to engage in relationship violence.

Attitudes and Beliefs

Attitudes supportive of the use of violence are positively correlated with spousal abuse (Sugarman & Frankel, 1996). Interestingly, sex-role beliefs and attitudes toward egalitarianism in relationships have not emerged as strong predictors of intimate aggression (Sugarman & Frankel, 1996). In contrast, there is increasing evidence that hostile and adversarial attitudes toward women are related to husband violence.

Power

Consistent with feminist theories, some have posited that men become violent when the feel entitled to power in their relationship and that they use violence to maintain their power. Others have argued that men become violent when they desire power but perceive themselves to be powerless.

Skills

Based on the social information-processing model, a series of studies demonstrate that, relative to nonviolent men, violent husbands display social skills deficits (Holtzworth-Munroe, 2000). For example, when presented with hypothetical marital conflict vignettes, violent men are more likely than nonviolent men to attribute hostile intentions to their wife's negative actions and to provide less competent, more aggressive responses. They are also less likely to generate competent responses when asked what would be the "best" thing to do in these situations.

Psychological Problems

Violent husbands are more likely than nonviolent men to report symptoms of depression and other psychological problems such as anxiety, mania, and psychotic disorders. In addition, antisocial and borderline personality characteristics are more common in violent men. Alcohol intoxication is a common factor in many incidents of intimate aggression, and husbands' premarital alcohol use predicts future husband aggression in newlywed samples. Also, illegal drug use is associated with severe husband-to-wife violence.

Violent men are also more angry and hostile than nonviolent men, both in general and toward their partner. As reviewed below, observational studies of marital interactions also consistently find that violent couples display more hostility than nonviolent couples.

Some theories suggest that men who are highly dependent on or anxiously attached to their wife are jealous and hypervigilant to any threats to the relationship and use violence in a rage when they fear the loss of the wife

(D. G. Dutton, 1995). The findings are somewhat mixed, but violent men have been found to score higher than nonviolent men on measures of jealousy, spouse dependency, and fearful or preoccupied attachment styles.

Subtypes of Maritally Violent Men

Although the above outlines general differences between maritally violent and nonviolent men, recent research has made it clear that samples of maritally violent men are heterogeneous. Based on a review of batterer typologies, Holtzworth-Munroe and Stuart (1994) suggested that, using three descriptive dimensions—(1) severity and frequency of husband violence; (2) generality of husband violence inside or outside of the home; and (3) the husband's psychopathology or personality disorder—three subtypes of batterers could be identified: (a) Family-only batterers engage in the least marital violence, the least violence outside the home, and evidence little or no psychopathology; (b) dysphoric/borderline batterers engage in moderate to severe wife abuse, but their violence is primarily confined to the wife; this group is psychologically distressed and evidence borderline personality characteristics; and (c) generally violent/antisocial batterers engage in the highest levels of marital and extrafamilial violence and evidence characteristics of Antisocial Personality Disorder.

Using a developmental model, Holtzworth-Munroe and Stuart (1994) predicted that family-only batterers would evidence the lowest levels of risk factors for violence. The violence of this subtype was proposed to result from a combination of stress (personal and/or marital) and low-level risk factors such as lack of relationship skills. Thus, during escalating marital conflicts, these men engage in physical aggression. Following such incidents, however, their low levels of psychopathology, combined with their relatively positive attitudes toward women and negative attitudes toward violence, lead to remorse and help prevent their aggression from

escalating. In contrast, dysphoric/borderline batterers were presumed to come from a background involving parental abuse and rejection. As a result, these men have difficulty forming stable, trusting relationships; instead, they are highly dependent and fearful of losing their wives. When frustrated, their borderline personality organization, anger, and insecure attachment lead to violence against the wife. Finally, generally violent/antisocial batterers were predicted to resemble other antisocial, aggressive groups, with high levels of many risk factors (such as impulsivity and lack of social skills), and their marital violence was seen as one part of their general use of aggression and engagement in antisocial behavior.

Recent batterer typologies have found subtypes similar to the above (Holtzworth-Munroe, Meehan, Herron, Rehman, & Stuart, 2000). Researchers have not yet studied the question of how different subtypes of batterers fare in conjoint couples therapy, but it appears that family-only batterers may be the only group for whom conjoint treatment is appropriate. These men are the least violent and have the fewest risk factors for violence, and these risk factors (such as social skills deficits) may be amenable to conjoint therapy. Indeed, in the Holtzworth-Munroe et al. (2000) study, the family-only group closely resembled a comparison group of nonviolent/distressed husbands, the usual target of conjoint therapy.

RESEARCH ON DYADIC-LEVEL VARIABLES

Two dyadic-level correlates of husband violence that may be amenable to conjoint therapy are briefly reviewed.

MARITAL DISTRESS

Couples experiencing husband violence typically are less satisfied with their marriage than nonviolent couples. It was originally assumed that marital dissatisfaction leads to conflict and ultimately to aggression (O'Leary, 1996). However, recent longitudinal studies of newlyweds suggest that the temporal order may be different—that male physical aggression in an otherwise satisfying relationship leads to a decline in wife marital satisfaction (Heyman et al., 1995; Quigley & Leonard, 1996) and relationship dissolution (Rogge & Bradbury, 1999).

Marital Communication

In studies comparing the marital problem discussions of violent and nonviolent couples, the findings are generally consistent. Violent husbands display more negative behaviors, including hostile and provocative forms of anger such as contempt and belligerence. Relative to nonviolent couples, violent couples demonstrate more negative reciprocity, and this pattern often escalates. Violent couples also engage in more demanding and withdrawing behavior, particularly husband demand-wife withdraw communication, than nonviolent couples.

Data from longitudinal studies indicate that whereas premarital communication negativity may predict marital dissatisfaction (Rogge & Bradbury, 1999), it may not predict husband violence (Smith, Vivian, & O'Leary, 1991). However, in a longitudinal study of husbands who were moderately to severely violent, men who displayed more negativity in a marital problem discussion were less likely than others in the sample to decrease their level of violence over time (Jacobson, Gottman, Gortner, Berns, & Shortt, 1996).

ASSESSMENT

Assessment of Physical Aggression

As discussed above, over half of couples seeking marital therapy have experienced husband physical aggression in the prior year. However, therapists may fail to detect the presence of physical aggression because couples often do not spontaneously report it as a presenting problem. O'Leary et al. (1992) found that only 6% of wives reported violence as a presenting problem on an intake form. Yet, during individual interviews that included direct questioning about marital violence, 44% of these wives reported husband violence. This figure rose to 53% when the wives were asked to complete a self-report behavior checklist measure, the Conflict Tactics Scale (CTS; Straus, 1979), suggesting that a behavioral checklist may reveal more aggression than an interview. Ehrensaft and Vivian (1996) also found that about half of spouses reporting mild husband physical aggression on the CTS had not mentioned this aggression during a marital therapy intake interview, and approximately one-quarter of spouses reporting severe husband physical aggression on the CTS had not mentioned this during an interview. When the couples were asked why they did not report violence at intake, the most common reasons given were that the violence was not considered a problem, the violence was unstable or infrequent, or the violence was perceived to be a secondary problem that would resolve when primary relationship problems were addressed.

These data clearly indicate that a structured instrument such as the CTS should be routinely administered to all couples seeking therapy to increase the likelihood of detecting husband violence. Indeed the most efficient way to assess for the presence of marital violence is to administer the CTS to both spouses and to ask them to complete it individually and privately. The CTS lists 19 behaviors, each of which is listed twice: once with regard to what the spouse completing the measure did to his or her partner and once with regard to what the partner did to him or her. Spouses report the occurrence and frequency in the prior year of each behavior; they also indicate whether a behavior has ever occurred in their relationship. The CTS includes items assessing psychological and physical aggression. As spouses often provide incongruent reports regarding the occurrence of specific violent behaviors, either partner's report of violence should be accepted as valid and assessed further.

The CTS was recently revised, created the Revised Conflict Tactics Scale (CTS2; Straus, Hamby, Boney-McCoy, & Sugarman, 1996). Both the psychological and aggression scales of the CTS were expanded to include new items, and new scales were added to assess sexual coercion and physical injury. The CTS2's assessment of sexual coercion and injury from violence may provide a good way to broach such sensitive topics, as it may be easier for spouses to first encounter these questions on a form than in a face-to-face interview. However, these changes come at the cost of decreased efficiency of administration, as the CTS2 contains 78 items.

Although the CTS and CTS2 are the most widely used self-report measures of marital violence, they have a number of shortcomings. An important limitation is that these measures do not assess the context of violence, such as the events leading to violence, the sequence of events during a violent incident, the aggressor's intentions, the partner's responses, or consequences of the violence; these variables may be important in understanding the role violence plays in a relationship. To assess context, therapists need to conduct interviews. We recommend conducting separate interviews with each spouse so that each, particularly frightened wives, may respond more honestly. Issues to be assessed include the behaviors leading to violence; the sequence of violent actions; the severity of violence and resulting injuries; actions following the violence, as possible reinforcers or punishers for violence; the involvement of third parties, such as police; and potential danger to others, including children. This assessment should also focus on

issues that may help to determine whether conjoint treatment is appropriate for a couple, including the level of the wife's fear for her safety and each spouse's motivation to enter conjoint treatment and to remain in the relationship. In addition, therapists should try to ascertain each partner's willingness to acknowledge that the physical aggression is a problem and to take responsibility for his or her own violent actions. Expressions of remorse and previous attempts to deal with the aggression should be assessed.

If severe or frequent violence is reported, the potential lethality of the situation should be assessed immediately. Information should be gathered regarding the presence of guns or other weapons in the home, recent escalations in violence, direct and indirect threats of lethality, level of the wife's fear, and whether substance use is associated with the violence. If the therapist determines that the likelihood of continued violence and/or lethality is present, he or she should immediately discuss safety planning with both spouses individually and jointly. The discussion with the husband should focus on the seriousness of the problem and on developing a series of emergency steps that can be taken to prevent his use of violence. These may include time-outs, calling the therapist or a crisis line, and understanding the need for safety planning on the part of the wife. Discussion with the wife should include developing a detailed and individualized plan for situations in which she may fear for her safety. Such discussions should cover practical issues such as how she can get herself and her children out of the home; finding a safe place where she can go, such as a relative's or friend's home or a shelter; and how she can get quick access to items such as car keys, money, and important documents. The wife should also be informed of appropriate local resources, including shelters and social service agencies, and of legal options available to her in her geographic area.

ASSESSING OTHER RELEVANT ISSUES

Psychological abuse often accompanies physical abuse and is a predictor of physical violence. Thus, therapists may prefer to administer more comprehensive measures of psychological abuse than the CTS and CTS2, such as the Psychological Maltreatment of Women Inventory (Tolman, 1999).

For wives, the psychological consequences of the violence, particularly PTSD and depressive symptoms, should be assessed. Similarly, the couple should be asked about the effects of their conflicts on children in the home and about any problems the children may be experiencing.

Therapists may wish to assess correlates of husband violence based on the research findings reviewed above and the need to identify appropriate targets for intervention. For example, therapists might assess such factors as a husband's level of anger and hostility, using the State-Trait Anger Expression Inventory (Spielberger, 1988); jealousy and dependency, using the Interpersonal Jealousy Scale (Mathes & Severa, 1981) and the Spouse Specific Dependency Scale (Rathus & O'Leary, 1997); attitudes toward women, using the Hostility toward Women Scale (Check, Malamuth, Elias, & Barton, 1985); and attitudes toward violence, using the Attitudes toward Violence Questionnaire (Riggs & O'Leary, 1996). Therapists may find it useful to assess men's communication and relationship skills, using such measures as the Spouse Specific Assertion/Aggression Scale (Rosenbaum & O'Leary, 1981), hypothetical marital conflict situation vignettes (Anglin & Holtzworth-Munroe, 1997), or the observation of marital interactions. Substance use and abuse and other manifestations of psychopathology by both partners should be carefully assessed. In addition, therapists may find it helpful to screen for subtypes of violent husbands using the Holtzworth-Munroe and Stuart (1994) typology, by assessing the severity of husband violence, generality of violence, and type of psychopathology/personality disorders.

DECIDING WHETHER CONJOINT THERAPY IS APPROPRIATE

After completing a thorough assessment and dealing with any necessary safety planning, therapists must decide whether to proceed with conjoint therapy or refer the individual spouses to gender-specific treatments (GST), which involve separate men's and women's groups. GST, in which men are seen in batterer treatment programs (see below), is the treatment format most commonly used for treatment of domestic violence. In fact, many state standards for batterer treatment programs of men court-ordered to treatment recommend that batterers be treated in groups of men, and indicate that conjoint treatment of the couple is inappropriate. For example, Section 4.5 of the Massachusetts State Standards states, "Any form of couples or conjoint counseling or marriage enhancement weekends or groups are inappropriate initially . . . couples counseling shall not be considered a component of batterer treatment" (Massachusetts Guidelines and Standards, 1994; p. 13).

Potential Disadvantages and Advantages to Conjoint Treatment

There is concern that seeing both partners in therapy and focusing on such issues as the couple's communication patterns may imply that the husband's violence is caused by both partners, rather than being the batterer's sole responsibility. An additional concern is that the wife may not feel comfortable expressing herself in the presence of the batterer and may fear further violence if she is honest about the level of violence she experiences or her desire to end the relationship. Also, there is concern that the process of discussing difficult relationship problems could increase husband anger and conflict and thus increase the risk of husband violence.

In contrast, there are many potential advantages to the conjoint treatment format. First is the ability to obtain a more accurate picture of the violence, given that the husband's and wife's reports may differ significantly. Second, therapists can ensure that both spouses understand the therapist's conceptualization of violence and how techniques should be implemented. Some interventions go more smoothly when both spouses are present to hear the rationale and procedures for them; for example, it is useful for both partners to understand what an appropriate time-out involves. Third, a husband may be less likely to use therapy to further abuse his wife when his wife has also heard what the therapist says; in contrast, in batterers' treatment, some men go home and tell their wife such things as "My therapist told me that it's your fault I'm violent." Conjoint therapy also allows couples to postpone volatile discussions until the therapy sessions and to avoid escalating arguments at home until they are better trained to discuss such problems. Fourth, given that physical violence often occurs in the context of an argument between partners (O'Leary, Heyman, & Neidig, 1999), direct intervention to decrease negative communication in conjoint treatment may decrease violence by changing the interactional patterns that precede it. Fifth, most couples presenting for marital therapy have experienced bidirectional violence, and self-defense accounts for fewer than 20% of these cases (Cascardi & Vivian, 1995); this suggests that both partners may benefit from learning to control their use of physical aggression. Finally, although husband violence often can have severe physical and psychological effects, many women seeking marital therapy are not experiencing that high a level of violence, nor are they fearful of participating in treatment with their husband (O'Leary et al., 1999). In many cases, these wives are seeking conjoint therapy and wish to remain in their relationship.

Guidelines for Deciding Whether Conjoint Treatment Is Appropriate

No existing research could be found that provides empirically based rules for deciding whether conjoint treatment is appropriate.

However, three studies have examined the efficacy of couple's therapy with violent couples and an examination of the subject exclusion criteria used in these studies may provide suggestions for guidelines. Similarly, examination of the additional steps these researchers took to protect wife safety suggests procedures to follow when working with aggressive couples.

Harris, Savage, Jones, and Brooke (1988) compared conjoint treatment to GST and a wait-list control group. For a couple to be eligible for the study, the wife had to indicate, in an individual interview, that she wanted to remain in the relationship and that she did not feel endangered by her partner's knowledge that she had discussed his violence with a counselor. Additionally, the husband had to exhibit no psychotic symptoms, serious brain injury, psychopathic disturbance, or substance abuse that was not being treated concurrently. Intake workers helped the wives construct individualized safety plans and provided them with information about community resources for battered women.

O'Leary et al. (1999) compared couples therapy to GST. This research group used extensive screening criteria to protect the safety of the wives, including couples in the study only if they met the following criteria: (1) the wife did not report sustaining injuries that required medical attention; (2) the wife reported in a private interview that she would feel comfortable in conjoint treatment; (3) the wife was not afraid of living with her husband; (4) the husband did not meet criteria for alcohol dependence; (5) neither spouse reported psychotic symptoms nor met criteria for psychopathology severe enough to interfere with participation; and (6) the husband had to admit the perpetration of at least one act of physical aggression.

Brannen and Rubin (1996) also compared conjoint therapy for husband violence to gender-specific groups. In contrast to the other two studies, Brannen and Rubin did not exclude couples based on the severity of husband violence or alcohol abuse; they offered couples therapy to a sample of men court-ordered to treatment after arrest. However, precautions were taken to ensure the wives' safety. For instance, a separate orientation was provided for the wives, during which they were given a 24-hour emergency phone number as well as phone numbers for law enforcement officials and shelters. In addition, husbands and wives completed weekly reports concerning psychological and physical abuse or threats. If any indication of a threatening situation existed, follow-up calls and additional help were provided for the wife.

Other clinicians and researchers also have discussed possible guidelines to use in determining when conjoint therapy is inappropriate for violent couples (Holtzworth-Munroe, Beatty, & Anglin, 1995; O'Leary, 1996). Most agree that severity of violence and danger to the wife are critical factors and that conjoint treatment is appropriate only for low to moderate levels of aggression if the wife is not perceived to be in danger of imminent physical harm. Related to this, the wife must not fear the husband, must feel comfortable in therapy with him, and must not feel so intimidated or dominated by him that she can't be honest in therapy. In addition, both partners must be interested in staying in the relationship. In essence, a conjoint format is most suitable for couples who believe that physical aggression is a problem and are willing to work toward a nonviolent relationship. It is inappropriate if one spouse does not acknowledge the existence or problematic nature of violence in the relationship, or is not willing to take steps to reduce the violence to include removing weapons from the home, seeking drug/alcohol treatment, or temporarily separating.

ALTERNATIVES TO CONJOINT THERAPY

If conjoint therapy is inappropriate, both husband and wife should be given referrals to other sources of help. Such referrals can be explained by telling a couple that the level of violence is too severe to begin conjoint treatment, based on concerns about safety and the possible escalation of violence. The belief that each partner is responsible for his or her own behavior and must take steps to end it should also be conveyed. Therapists can offer to reevaluate the appropriateness of conjoint therapy after the spouses have each sought appropriate assistance elsewhere (see referral suggestions below) and after the husband has completed a domestic violence treatment program.

Referrals for Battered Women

Referrals to support groups for battered women and advocacy services may be important because battered women are often not able to consider long-term options or deal with the trauma of violence until they obtain adequate support and resources. A recent study demonstrated that such advocacy can significantly reduce a woman's likelihood of future abuse. Sullivan and Bybee (1999) tested a 10-week intervention program in which undergraduate students assisted battered women leaving a shelter to develop individualized safety plans and obtain needed community resources such as legal assistance, employment, housing, child care, transportation, financial assistance, and health care. Over a two-year follow-up period, women who received the advocacy experienced less violence in their intimate relationships, fewer depressive symptoms, and more social support; they were also more effective in obtaining resources on their own than women who had not received advocacy services. Once such issues are addressed, a woman in a violent relationship may address other issues, including trauma symptoms and long-term planning in traditional therapy (M. A. Dutton, 1996).

Referrals for Male Batterers

If a couple does not appear to be appropriate for conjoint treatment, therapists should refer the husband to GST. This gives both spouses the clear message that the husband is responsible for his violence and for learning to become nonviolent. It also serves as a test of a man's willingness to change. For example, in some cases, wives have chosen to leave their violent husband on seeing that he does not follow a recommendation to seek GST.

Many communities offer batterer treatment programs that usually involve a mixture of men referred by the legal system or other therapists and self-referred men. There are numerous examples of GST in the literature (D. G. Dutton & Golant, 1995; Malloy, McCloskey, & Monford, 1999). These programs range widely in length, from 6 to 52 weeks. A group format is most commonly used. The expectation is that some men may be more willing to listen to their peers than to therapists, and that men at more advanced stages of change may provide positive examples, confrontation, and support for other men. Additionally, group therapy may help men avoid feelings of isolation and is also cost-effective. Male and female cotherapists are preferred to model a respectful male-female relationship and to provide differing perspectives on important issues. Many states have adopted standards regarding issues such as program length and format, and it is wise to consider local guidelines in making therapy referrals.

GST for violent husbands typically involves a combination of feminist theory and cognitive-behavioral techniques. GST material taken from the feminist perspective includes examination of the role of aggression and other forms of abusive behavior in maintaining a male's control of his partner, sex roles, and patriarchal power. From the cognitive-behavioral perspective, psychoeducational techniques including anger management, time-outs, and communication skills training are used.

The effectiveness of GST for partner violence has not been clearly established. In a pessimistic review of studies evaluating the effectiveness of court-ordered treatment of husband violence, Rosenfeld (1992) concluded that, overall, men who are arrested and ordered to treatment appear to recidivate at rates equivalent to men who are arrested and not sent to treatment. In contrast, Davis and Taylor (1999) concluded that more recent and more methodologically rigorous studies suggest that treatment is significantly more effective than no treatment in reducing violence. However, not all of the studies they reviewed are convincing. For example, in the largest study to date, Dunford (2000) studied over 800 Navy men and assessed four conditions: (1) cognitive-behavioral gender-specific batterer treatment program for violent husbands; (2) a group in which the same type of treatment was offered but wives were also invited to participate (most did not); (3) a condition in which the men were told that monthly checks for further violence would be conducted and, if further violence occurred, their commanding officer would be notified and appropriate steps would be taken; and (4) a control group that involved safety planning with the wife. At a one-year follow-up, the GST men's groups did not lead to lower recidivism rates than any of the other conditions, raising questions about the necessity of intervention programs. However, across all four treatment conditions evaluated, approximately two-thirds of the men ended their physical aggression.

In conclusion, the effectiveness of batterer treatment programs has not yet been definitively established. Nonetheless, appropriate referral of violent husbands to treatment programs continues to be recommended, in the absence of empirically demonstrated effective alternatives.

INTERVENTION: CONJOINT TREATMENT PROCEDURES

SETTING OF GOALS AND THERAPY CONTRACTS

Before beginning conjoint treatment with a couple with partner violence, couples need to be made aware of the therapist's expectations and goals for treatment. Specifically, couples should be clearly informed that cessation of husband violence is one of the primary goals of treatment.

Many couples are surprised by a therapist's concern regarding their aggression and wish to dismiss it as excessive, despite careful assessment of aggression during intake procedures.

Thus, as part of an effort to motivate couples to change, it is important to review a series of reasons underlying concern about aggression. Although the current level of aggression may be low, any level of physical aggression always carries a risk of injury, and it is useful to describe relevant cases. One example is a man who pushed his wife with no intent to hurt her, but as the floor was wet that day, she slipped and hit her head on the kitchen counter, suffering a concussion. It can be helpful to explain that although research demonstrates that some couples cease their aggression or maintain low levels of aggression, there is evidence that many couples escalate their levels of aggression. Unfortunately, as we cannot predict which couples are at risk for continuing or escalating aggression, therapists need to assume that every aggressive couple is at risk for escalating violence. Similarly, if a couple has risk factors for violence such as psychological aggression, excessive substance use, or violence in the family of origin, it should be explained that these factors may also cause violence to escalate. To further motivate the couple to work on aggression, any possible negative consequences of the aggression that have occurred should be discussed. For example, often, spouses are concerned about their children's awareness of their fights and wish to model better conflict resolution for them. Finally, therapists should explain that without a direct focus on ending the aggression, there is a risk that the therapy itself may escalate the aggression because the couple will be asked to discuss difficult topics likely to engender anger and frustration. Some couples avoid aggression by not discussing sensitive topics, but in therapy, the couple will be asked to address these issues. Thus, it is vital to ensure that aggression won't occur in the course of discussions during treatment.

Treatment should focus first on helping the partners to control their behavior when angry; once anger management skills are learned, they will be in a safer position to engage in problem solving regarding their major presenting problems. At this point, most couples are willing to agree to a treatment plan that will initially focus on anger management and controlling aggression.

In many cases, both partners have used physical aggression. It is then acknowledged that both must take responsibility for their own aggression and its consequences. Therapists point out that violence is a learned behavior and a choice, and that each spouse must take responsibility for stopping his or her physical aggression. We also emphasize that husband violence will be a particular target of treatment because it carries greater risk of physical injury and negative psychological effects.

It is critical to consider safety plans with both spouses. In addition, both should be asked to prevent precipitating further physical aggression, for example, by discussing heated issues only in public or in therapy sessions. They also need to lessen the danger of injury by, for instance, removing guns from the home. Both spouses should be asked to make a "no violence" contract with and agree to report any incidents of physical aggression to the therapist. The therapist should regularly ask about the occurrence of any physical aggression and explain that further occurrences of aggression will lead to a reexamination of the level of danger and the reasons the treatment plan is not working. In some cases, continuing or worsening violence indicates the need for termination of conjoint treatment and referral of the spouses to GST specializing in relationship violence. This message is an important motivator, demonstrating to couples how concerned the therapist is about their aggression.

This model uses a behavioral-cognitive and two-pronged approach: anger recognition and management, and communication and problem-solving skills. These parallel the treatment protocols for other existing conjoint treatment programs for partner violence and relationship aggression (Geffner, Mantooth, Franks, & Rao, 1989; Heyman & Neidig, 1997).

ANGER MANAGEMENT

The first set of skills introduced in conjoint treatment for physical aggression usually involves anger management. It is explained to couples that the term "anger management" is a misnomer, as anger is a natural emotion; rather, the therapist tries to help spouses manage their aggressive and abusive behavior when angry. In most cases, one to three full therapy sessions are devoted to anger management, followed by attention to these skills in subsequent sessions. Given the lower levels of aggression among couples in this type of conjoint therapy, this protocol provides adequate coverage of treatment for problems with anger. Procedures are borrowed from previous programs for anger management (Novaco, 1976), batterer treatment (Hamberger & Hastings, 1988; Saunders, 1989), and conjoint therapy for relationship aggression (Heyman & Neidig, 1997).

RECOGNITION OF ANGER

Spouses must first be able to identify their anger to manage and control it. The therapist should solicit examples from each spouse regarding how he or she experiences anger and help both to identify the physical, cognitive, and behavioral cues that accompany anger. Physical cues include changes such as flushing, tenseness, rapid heart beat, and sweating. Cognitive cues are best described as "hot thoughts" or "anger up statement," and can be broken into categories such as labeling ("She's so stupid"), hostile attributions ("She did that just to spite me"), catastrophizing ("Now my whole life is ruined"), and should

statements ("She should have known better than to do that"). Behavioral cues consist of the ways anger is expressed, including facial expressions, verbalizations, and motor behavior such as tapping fingers, slamming doors, and violence. It is important to point out to clients how anger (a feeling) differs from aggression (a response to having this feeling).

Next, the therapist asks each spouse to construct a personalized anger continuum from the least to the most extreme anger he or she experiences, using a line marked from 1 to 10. To facilitate an appreciation for the different intensities of anger, the therapist helps clients to label key anchor points along the line ("frustrated"/ "angry"/"furious"/"no longer in control of behavior and in danger of using aggression"). The therapist should guide the discussion so that physical, cognitive, and behavioral signs of anger are listed for each of these key points along the continuum.

Anger logs are introduced as an important ongoing homework assignment. On the anger log, spouses report the details of one or more episodes during the week when they feel angry. They record the situation, the intensity of the anger (from 1 to 10), and the physical, cognitive, and behavioral anger cues experienced. Partners are instructed to keep these anger logs and, across situations and weeks, to look for patterns in their anger (when and with whom they are angry and how they know they are angry). They can also be helped to identify high-risk situations for arguments and aggression. For example, one couple discovered after several weeks that their major fights occurred when the husband was running late while they were preparing to go out together.

TIME-OUTS

The first skill taught for managing anger is taking a time-out to avoid engaging in aggression during conflicts. Some couples have a difficult time accepting time-outs because this procedure may involve leaving a fight; this runs counter to beliefs that one should never walk away from a fight but should stay until insight or resolution is reached. In such cases, it is important for the therapist to help the couple compare the risk of continued aggression to the temporary suspension of the discussion of a heated issue. Couples may have avoided discussing issues for years and there is a danger that time-outs can be used to continue this pattern. In either situation, it is important that both spouses understand that a time-out does not permanently end discussion of the problem; they can discuss the issues calmly after the time-out or, if this is impossible, they can bring the issue to therapy. Many couples initially respond negatively to the term time-out, having heard it applied to the discipline of children. Accordingly, the procedure can be introduced using analogies to the time-outs taken during sporting events and as a chance to regroup and collect one's composure before making a costly mistake that could lose the game.

Time-outs have several components. First, partners must recognize their anger and take responsibility both for acknowledging it and for taking a time-out. In addition, they need to inform the partner by saying, "I am beginning to feel angry and I need to take a time-out." Each part of that statement is discussed in detail. By using an "I" statement one takes responsibility for one's feelings, acknowledging anger without blaming the spouse. This statement also involves calmly announcing a time-out rather than just leaving the discussion. A rule that neither spouse can tell the other when to take a time-out is useful; otherwise, this may quickly become another weapon of abuse. However, some women report situations in which they fear their husband's anger and he does not take a time-out. In this case, another version of time-out can be implemented in which either spouse can take a time-out for any negative feeling that is likely to make further discussion unproductive.

The time-out statement includes another important component: notifying the spouse when one will return. This is necessary to prevent abuse of time-outs, as when a man left home for three days and nights during a "time-out." One to three hours is usually necessary to calm down for men in batterer treatment programs. With couples in marital therapy, spouses often need less time (15 minutes to 1.5 hours). Thus, a half-hour period is initially recommended on a trial basis. The full time-out statement becomes "I am beginning to feel angry and I need to take a half-hour time-out."

After announcing the time-out, the partner is advised to leave the area where the argument was occurring. Ideally, he or she should leave the house or apartment, as the partner may get more angry listening in another room. In some situations, such as a woman taking a time-out late at night, this rule needs to be modified. Couples should be asked to consider how they would take time-outs in problematic situations, such as when they are in the car or in public.

During a time-out, spouses are encouraged to engage in techniques aimed at decreasing anger, such as mediation, relaxation techniques, and physical exercise. It is also helpful to teach couples "cool thoughts" or "anger down statements" that can be used to deescalate anger. Activities to be avoided during a time-out include those that may further escalate the anger or be dangerous in an angry state, such as alcohol use, aggressive exercising (e.g., chopping wood), driving, and ruminating about the argument.

At the end of the specified time, the spouse taking the time-out must either return or contact the partner and take another time-out. After the time-out is over, partners should continue discussing the problem. The couple is encouraged to take another time-out if needed or to suggest another time (including therapy) in which to continue discussing the problem.

The act of taking a time-out can be awkward for many couples, and it is helpful to have them practice in sessions and at home. Using a time-out log, clients should write down incidents in which a time-out was used, including the argument that led to the time-out, how the time-out was implemented, and what happened afterward. Therapist debriefing of these incidents can often pinpoint problems in the use of time-outs and identify problem areas in the relationship that may be amenable to problem solving.

It is useful to ask couples to take a time-out during therapy sessions in which they are becoming angry, providing them with in vivo training. In such cases, the therapist usually suggests that they take a short time-out. One spouse makes the time-out statement and leaves the room. The therapist also should leave the room and go to a neutral place to avoid being drawn into an alliance with either spouse. Both the partner and the therapist should return at the agreed upon time. At that point, the therapist can help review the time-out from both partners' perspectives: What steps did the partner taking the time-out use to calm down? Did the partner who did not take the time-out feel abandoned or angry that the conversation was cut short? Such discussions often help to elucidate potential problems with time-out, allowing the couple and therapist to brainstorm better methods.

OTHER ANGER MANAGEMENT SKILLS

Many methods of managing anger are covered in the time-out procedure, but it is often necessary to further develop these methods. Such discussions should focus on learning to manage the three components of anger discussed during anger recognition. For example, relaxation, slow breathing, and exercise can manage physical signs of anger; self-statements can be modified in response to cognitive signs of anger; and communication skills can be taught to counter behavioral signs of anger. Once these skills are taught, the weekly anger logs should be modified to include an additional section regarding the steps the spouse took to manage each of the three components of anger. Anger logs and time-out logs can be combined and should be monitored for many weeks or for the entire course of therapy.

COMMUNICATION AND PROBLEM-SOLVING SKILLS

Once couples are managing their anger more appropriately and have not engaged in further aggression, it is appropriate to begin communication and problem-solving skills training. The couple is often eager to do so because attention to their presenting problems may have been delayed for the few weeks of anger management training. At this point, techniques derived from behavioral marital therapy (BMT; Jacobson & Margolin, 1979) can be used. These methods are briefly presented here.

The topic is introduced by asking the couple to discuss reasons why good communication is important for a couple; these could include to avoid misunderstandings or to build intimacy. It is also noted that there are good and bad times to communicate. Bad times to talk should be discussed, such as in front of the television, while tending to a child, or while fatigued. The therapist should acknowledge that problems do arise at times when good communication is not possible. In such instances, the couple may choose not to tackle the problem at that time and to set a specific future time when the problem can be discussed; it is not sufficient for couples to simply decide that they talk "sometime in the future." After ground rules for good times to communicate have been established, the next stage is to practice the skills involved in the two parts of communication: listening and speaking.

Nonverbal Listening
It is helpful to ask clients to identify nonverbal cues that indicate that they are either being listened to or not. Cues indicative of a good

listener include making eye contact, turning toward the speaker, leaning forward, and nodding at appropriate points in the speaker's narrative. This point can also be made by having therapists model first poor, then good nonverbal listening with each client and ask for their thoughts and feelings during each portion. Spouses should then practice good nonverbal listening with one another.

Verbal Listening and Paraphrasing

The distinction between good and bad verbal listening is somewhat subtle, and it is often helpful for the therapist to model poor verbal listening to clients' stories. Poor verbal listening includes frequent interruptions for comments and questions that are tangential or move the topic of conversation away from what the speaker had intended; mindreading, sentence finishing, and incorrect paraphrasing are often involved. Paraphrasing is a good place to start learning good verbal listening skills. It should be emphasized that paraphrasing is not a part of normal communication and is not to be used in all conversations, but is useful in conversations when one needs to be heard accurately by one's spouse; discussions of topics that could lead to arguments are good examples. Paraphrasing feels unnatural, but its unnatural structure prevents escalation of conflicts by slowing down the discussions and preventing misunderstandings.

Paraphrasing involves careful listening; the listener should not be preparing what to say in response to the speaker. Initially, repeating what was said word-for-word reduces the possibility of misinterpretations. Then, the listener should check for accuracy. If the paraphrasing was accurate, the conversation can go on; if not, the speaker can correct what was said, and the listener should paraphrase this correction. Sometimes, the listener will feel overwhelmed by the amount of information given by the speaker; the listener should then be trained to request a break to paraphrase what had been said up to that point.

Expressing Feelings

Although speaking involves a large number of skills, that of expressing feelings must be emphasized. It is important to distinguish between thoughts and feelings; for instance, "I feel you should take out the garbage" is a thought, not a feeling. A person's feelings are his or her own responsibility. Therefore, statements that begin "You made me feel" or "It made me feel" are unsuitable; instead, "I" statements should be used. To help clients label their feelings, the therapist supplies a list of feeling words as a guide. This list can also help clients replace the use of vague feeling words, such as "good" or "bad," with more precise, informative, or "softer" emotions, such as "disappointed" or "rejected." Therapists may want to discuss how men tend to have more difficulty with this exercise than women, and that women usually are more socialized to pay attention to and express their feelings. For some men, anger is one of the few emotions they feel comfortable sharing, and these men should be helped to generate other feeling words. Assigning a feeling log for homework, in which clients identify feelings and their intensity over the course of a week, may be a useful exercise.

After completing these exercises in the sessions, homework might include one spouse telling a story to the other, using the appropriate feeling words for the situation. The listener then paraphrases the story, making sure to identify correctly the feelings expressed. Spouses then switch roles. Stories should not involve negative feelings about the relationship or spouse because it is too difficult to practice new listening skills while being criticized.

Problem Solving

Clients should be informed that this problem-solving structure will seem artificial and stilted, and there is no pretense that it resembles the naturalistic problem discussions of happily married couples. Instead, based on observational studies documenting the negative interaction patterns of distressed couples, the problem-solving format is designed to eliminate these destructive behaviors. As a result, the structure of problem solving can prevent the escalation of discussions into arguments and keep couples on-task.

Therapists should inform partners that a collaborative approach to problem solving is critical, and that each must be willing to accept responsibility for his or her contributions to the problem and for changing behavior. Part of this collaboration involves being able to overlook the short-term costs in a problem-solving solution for the long-term gains of an improved relationship. Additionally, problems should be thought of as mutual, not a problem of solely one spouse or the other. The problem-solving format is divided into two parts: problem definition and problem solution.

The problem definition component builds on the skills already introduced. The general format is as follows: Spouse A, "I like it when you ____, but when you _____, I feel _____." Spouse B paraphrases A, checks for accuracy, and then accepts responsibility for some aspect of the problem. Spouse A paraphrases the new information in B's statement, checks for accuracy, then A accepts responsibility for some aspect of the problem. Spouse B paraphrases the new information in A's last statement and checks for accuracy.

The positive statement at the beginning puts the problem in context by reminding both spouses of some positive aspect of their relationship. It also makes complaints easier for the listener to hear because it reduces the possibility that the listener will become defensive. The complaint should be as specific as possible, preferably focusing on explicit behaviors. In this way, it will be easier for the spouse to make changes and for the results of these changes to be clearly visible to both spouses. Derogatory labels ("You are insensitive"), overgeneralizing and exaggerating ("You always do this"), mindreading ("You did that on purpose"), and defining the other's feelings ("You are overly sensitive") are to be avoided. Examples of problem behaviors can be

given, but "kitchen sinking" (bringing up every instance of transgression) is to be avoided because it can escalate the discussion into an argument. The complainer should use the appropriate feeling words in the problem definition because the partner may be unaware of his or her feelings about the situation. When softer words are used, feeling statements can generate sympathy in spouses.

Perhaps the most difficult portion of the problem definition format is the acceptance of responsibility by both spouses. This is especially true for the complainer, who often has not considered his or her role in the problem. The acceptance of responsibility enhances a couple's collaborative efforts. Admission of responsibility should be truthful, but should not include possible solutions to the problem because these might cut off discussion of other possible solutions.

Once a problem definition has been generated and understood by both, the couple can move to the problem solution phase. This is divided into brainstorming, solution evaluation, contract development, and troubleshooting. In brainstorming, both partners list as many possible solutions to the problem as they can. Because of a tendency for violent couples to blame one another, the first proposed solution offered by each partner should involve something that he or she can personally do to change the problem. After an extensive list of possible solutions has been generated, the couple should evaluate the solutions one at a time, discussing the advantages and disadvantages of each. After listing the pros and cons of a solution, the couple should decide whether to eliminate it, keep it, modify it, or hold it until other solutions have been considered.

Once all possible solutions have been evaluated, the remaining ideas should be combined into a contract. The contract should be as specific as possible, including who will be doing what and when. It can include ways that spouses can remind each other of the contract, such as with notes on the refrigerator. Contracts should also include a time for periodic review, an evaluation of how well the solutions have worked, and making changes or adjustments as necessary. This step is highly useful because one spouse is often resistant to agree to a solution unless guaranteed that changes can be made if they are not working.

The last phase of problem solution is troubleshooting, which entails thinking about potential problems that might arise when implementing the contract. For instance, if a contract is about who makes dinner on a given night, the therapist should ask: What would happen if one spouse is sick or out of town? Couples should include in the contract ideas for how to handle potential problems. After they have acquired the problem-solving skills and applied them to minor and then moderate-size problems in their relationship, remaining therapy sessions involve applying these methods to their major presenting problems.

OTHER THERAPEUTIC INTERVENTIONS

At this point in therapy, other interventions or methods may be considered to address additional problems. For example, many aggressive couples benefit from some sessions of parent training in which they learn to discipline their children in nonaggressive ways. In addition, many couples need a more direct focus on restoring positive interactions to their relationship, using behavior exchange methods (Jacobson & Margolin, 1979) or exercises such as caring days (Stuart, 1980) or simply planning dates together. Some couples may need more specific help with sexual problems. Referrals to specialists should be considered at this point.

Therapist and couple jointly review the progress they have made on presenting problems and new problems identified during the course of therapy on a regular basis (every four to five sessions). They then adjust the therapy plan to make sure that all of these problems are addressed before termination. After violence has been eliminated, the major issues have been addressed, and the skills taught are being successfully applied, the therapist moves to less frequent meetings, initially every other week and then once a month. The therapist then becomes a consultant to the couple, who are now managing their problems on their own, and helps them to anticipate upcoming stressors or major life changes.

CASE EXAMPLE

Tom and Jan had been married six years and had one child, a 4-year-old son. This was Jan's first marriage; she was 32 years old. Tom was 60, and this was his fourth marriage; he had three adult children from his previous marriages. Tom was currently unemployed and depressed about this, as he worried that he was "too old" to get another job in his field. Jan was pursuing a part-time undergraduate degree at the local university, and since Tom's unemployment, she had begun a part-time job. Both were quite stressed by Tom's unemployment and their resulting financial problems. They sought therapy at a clinic providing very low-cost services to students.

In their initial conjoint interview, the couple reported seeking therapy because of communication problems and an increasing number of arguments. They reported fighting about a variety of issues, including money and sex. Tom wanted sex more frequently than Jan and was afraid that Jan was "no longer sexually interested" in him. The other major issue was the discipline of their child. Tom felt that Jan was too lenient as a parent, but Jan feared that Tom's anger would scare their son and set a bad example for him. Tom repeatedly noted his desire to make this marriage work and discussed the fact that he was beginning to "feel like a failure in marriage." In the initial interview, the therapist asked how bad their arguments got and whether there had been any physical contact during these conflicts. They both reported that they had each used physical aggression, but that there had never been any injuries or fear on either of their parts. Specifically, Tom had once grabbed Jan's arm and once blocked the door, both times to prevent her from leaving a fight. In response, in both situations, Jan had pushed or hit Tom with an open hand on the chest to move him out of the way and leave. Both incidents had occurred in the prior year.

Given the pattern of Tom's pursuing and Jan's trying to leave, the therapist considered the possible relevance of research on violent men's attachment insecurity and jealousy. The therapist thus asked the couple about jealousy, and was told that it was a major problem. Tom, being much older than Jan, was afraid that she would leave him for a younger man and had begun to monitor her activities and worry about whom she was with; he would ask her to report her daily activities and whom she saw and spoke with each day. Jan resented this and felt that Tom was trying to control her. No other obvious psychological abuse was reported, although both spouses engaged in name calling and swearing during heated arguments.

On the CTS, which was completed by the spouses before the second session, they each reported the same two incidents of aggression that had already been discussed. In the individual interviews, Jan told the therapist that the first time Tom stopped her from leaving, she had been "slightly afraid," but because he had let her leave when she hit him, she was no longer fearful of him and was confident that he would let her leave when fights escalated. Safety planning was discussed; Jan felt confident of her ability to leave a fight and had a friend with whom she and her child could stay if necessary. She was given phone numbers for the local battered women's support group and crisis line, but insisted that she was not interested in pursuing

these options because the violence she experienced was "not that serious." She did report concern that Tom would "get angry and hit" their son, but stated that this had never happened. She expressed a strong desire to try to work on improving their relationship and was concerned by Tom's recent statements that "this marriage will fail like all my others did."

In his individual interview, Tom admitted to engaging in physical aggression in his previous marriages, at levels similar to that in his current marriage. He reported that his previous aggression had also occurred in situations in which he was trying to prevent his wife from leaving. He claimed that jealousy had not been a problem in his previous relationships, because his ex-wives had been closer to him in age. He said that he was concerned about his aggression and was willing to work on it in therapy. He made the point that Jan's aggression also wasn't acceptable; the therapist agreed, and was able to help Tom acknowledge why Jan had more to fear than he did, based on their difference in size and strength.

In the third feedback session, the therapist expressed concern about the level of physical aggression, noting that similar behaviors had occurred in Tom's previous relationships and her concern that the aggression would continue and perhaps escalate if not directly addressed. The therapist explained the rationale for the two-pronged therapy approach she was recommending: addressing anger and aggression first and then moving onto communication and problem-solving training to address the couple's original presenting problems. The couple expressed some concern that spending time on anger and violence would delay getting to their "real" problems, but basically understood and accepted the rationale for such a delay. They also made a verbal "no violence" contract with the therapist.

The first few sessions of therapy focused on identifying anger, keeping anger logs, and learning ways to lower levels of anger. One full session was spent on time-outs. The first non-compliance with homework occurred following this session, with the couple returning without having taken any practice time-outs and claiming that they did not need them because they were getting along much better. The therapist convinced them to take some practice time-outs. The following session, the couple came to the session separately and were quite angry with one another. The evening before, they had had a major fight regarding how to discipline their son. After their anger levels had already exceeded the ideal point for a time-out, Jan had tried to take a time-out, but rather than using the recommended statement, she had announced, "I'm taking a goddamn time-out now because you are being so unreasonable. So leave me alone!" At that point, Tom had announced that she had not taken time-out properly and stepped in front of her to prevent her from leaving. Jan hit him on the abdomen with an open hand and ran out the door. Tom did not pursue her, and they had not spoken again until arriving for the therapy session. They were both still very angry.

After learning this, the therapist asked them to take a time-out during the session. She prompted the couple to use the correct phrasing and to carefully consider how they each would calm down during the time-out. Twenty minutes later, the session reconvened, and the therapist debriefed the time-out. Tom was able to recognize how much he feared his wife's leaving him. Jan acknowledged her desire to leave problems unsolved when she became too angry and that she often "chose to punish" Tom by avoiding any further discussion of the problem after the argument was over. The time-out taken during the session had helped them each to calm down and, for the first time, they acknowledged that time-outs might be useful.

The therapist revisited the issue of recurring aggression after the couple was calm and the time-out had been discussed. The couple and

therapist considered various options for dealing with the aggression, including possible referral to a more specialized program. After some discussion, the therapist and couple agreed to continue conjoint therapy and to spend additional time in each session on managing behavior when angry, rather than changing the full focus of therapy to communication skills training, as had originally been planned.

For the next eight sessions, half of each session was spent learning communication and problem-solving skills and the other half was devoted to debriefing anger logs, use of time-outs, and further exploration of the role of anger in the relationship and ways to control behavior when angry. In particular, Tom found relaxation training and cognitive restructuring regarding his jealous thoughts to be very useful. Jan began regular physical exercise and found that the anger logs helped her to identify high-risk situations, which primarily involved Tom criticizing her parenting.

At this point, no further violence had occurred and the couple began to use therapy sessions to systematically solve their major relationship problems using the problem-solving format. The therapist insisted that they problem-solve the issue of Tom's jealousy, and they came up with an elaborate but seemingly effective solution to that problem, including Jan's letting Tom know that she cared and Tom taking steps to manage his jealousy. Over the next several weeks, they reported that the contract was going well. Five therapy sessions were devoted to parent training to help the couple develop parenting skills and a consensus about child discipline. In particular, Jan was helped to become more consistent and Tom learned nonangry ways to discipline.

At this point, Tom was offered a job in a distant city and the couple used problem solving to make their decision to move. Jan decided to take a semester off from school and then resume her education at a college near where they were moving. In the last few therapy sessions, the couple both reported being very pleased with the progress they had made. They believed that their relationship was much stronger than it had been before therapy and that they were better parents. They accepted referrals to both a marital therapist and an anger management program in the city where they were moving, but did not plan to pursue either immediately. No follow-up information was obtained from this couple.

This case illustrates a relatively successful application of the model for treating partner violence. The therapist was initially concerned about the appropriateness of conjoint therapy, due to the husband's history of having been physically aggressive in several relationships and his level of jealousy. However, Jan did not report fear of Tom and expressed a desire to remain in the relationship, and Tom was willing to take responsibility for his aggression and agreed that it was an appropriate therapy goal.

The therapist again had questions about the therapy plan after aggression occurred so early in therapy and following several weeks devoted to anger control. However, this crisis led to an excellent chance for in vivo learning of time-out and its effectiveness as a technique to avoid violence. In addition, once calm, the couple expressed genuine regret about the incident and were willing to spend more time on the problem of aggression. After that, therapy progressed relatively smoothly and the couple made important gains in learning skills and solving presenting problems. The premature termination of therapy was not ideal because the couple had not had much time to practice implementing their newly acquired skills without direct therapist input. However, the couple was pleased with their progress and felt relatively confident that they would be able to handle future problems on their own. Most important, they now shared the therapist's concern regarding physical aggression and had made an agreement to seek additional therapy immediately if aggression recurred.

RESEARCH EXAMINING THE EFFECTIVENESS OF CONJOINT THERAPY FOR COUPLES EXPERIENCING HUSBAND PHYSICAL AGGRESSION

Three research teams have published studies examining the effectiveness of conjoint therapy with couples experiencing husband violence, and compared conjoint treatment to GST.

In the earliest study, Harris et al. (1988) recruited over 70 couples who had experienced husband violence and requested therapy at a family service agency. Random assignment to treatment conditions was used. Some couples were assigned to a couples counseling program that explicitly addressed violence as the primary relationship problem. In this study, it appears that couples were seen individually. The other treatment condition involved a combination of gender-specific and couples groups held weekly after the gender-specific group meeting.

Subject attrition from the study was extremely high. Across both treatment conditions, 35% of the sample never began treatment. A large number of couples who began treatment did not complete it; attrition was 67% in the couples conditions and 16% in the gender-specific condition. Attrition continued after treatment and at the 6 to 12-month posttherapy follow-up assessment, only 28 of the original sample could be interviewed. The follow-up data indicated that the two treatment conditions were equally effective in reducing the husbands' physical violence (based on wife report) and in improving the subjects' sense of psychological well-being.

Brannen and Rubin (1996) recruited a sample of couples who were referred to batterers treatment by the court system and who had indicated a desire to remain in their current relationship. As noted above, marital therapists may not have access to such a group because many state standards for batterer treatment programs indicate that conjoint treatment is inappropriate for court-mandated violence clients. Couples were randomly assigned to either couples group treatment, in which several couples jointly attended the groups, or to gender-specific group intervention, in which husbands attended a men's group for batterers and wives attended a group for battered women. The conjoint therapy was specifically designed to address husband violence as a primary problem. Forty-two of the 49 couples who began treatment completed it. In contrast to the Harris et al. (1988) study, six of the seven batterers who dropped out of treatment were in the gender-specific intervention condition. There were few differences in outcome across the two types of treatment. Follow-up data collected at six months posttreatment showed no significant differences between the two groups in level of recidivism, and in both therapy conditions, 90% of the subjects reported that they were violence-free. Among men with no history of alcohol abuse, neither treatment was more effective than the other. Among men with a history of alcohol abuse (all of whom were also involved in a court-monitored Antabuse program), the couples treatment was more effective than GST. These researchers also examined one of the major criticisms of couples treatment: that such a format may endanger the abuse victim and compromise her safety. Specifically, weekly data were gathered to monitor safety of program participants, assessing any ongoing abuse. Over the course of treatment, six instances of physical and emotional abuse were reported; two involved couples assigned to the conjoint treatment, and four were among couples assigned to GST. These data suggest that women in couples treatment were not in more danger than women in GST.

In the most recent study, O'Leary et al. (1999) carefully selected couples to be randomly assigned to either group conjoint therapy or GST. Participants responded to a newspaper ad offering free therapy to couples experiencing low levels of physical aggression. Thus, it is not clear how generalizable these study findings are to couples seeking marital therapy, who, as reviewed above, usually do not identify violence as a presenting problem. As in the other studies, the conjoint therapy did not employ standard marital therapy, but focused directly on the problem of marital violence (Heyman & Neidig, 1997). A total of 75 couples were randomly assigned to one treatment condition or the other. Only 37 couples completed treatment and dropout rates did not differ significantly between the two treatment conditions. Both treatment approaches resulted in statistically significant changes in men's violence and psychological abuse, but neither appears to have been particularly effective because more than 70% of the men engaged in physical aggression during the follow-up period. Regarding the comparison of the conjoint and GST groups, there were no differences in rates of physical aggression outcome according to treatment format. In addition, at the end of treatment, there were no treatment differences in husbands' psychological aggression, wives' depressive symptomatology, or wives' marital adjustment. Marital adjustment was better at follow-up for husbands in the conjoint therapy condition. Finally, based on regular checks of safety issues, it was found that women in the conjoint treatment did not report fear of their husband during therapy and did not report that therapy discussions led to physical aggression.

Thus, across the three available studies, no difference in outcome favored either gender-specific or conjoint therapy. The samples included couples who were interested in remaining together and willing to enter conjoint therapy and may resemble couples likely to be seen by marital therapists. However, in these studies, the couples were seeking help for husband violence and most couples seeking marital therapy do not report husband violence as a presenting problem. In addition, a specialized couples treatment addressing the man's violence directly was used in all of these studies. In two of them (Brannen & Rubin, 1996; O'Leary et al., 1999), a group format was used for the couples therapy. Thus, these data do not support the use of standard marital therapy for individual couples to reduce male violence.

The results of these studies also do not allow conclusions to be drawn regarding whether dropout rates will be higher from conjoint or gender-specific treatments. However, the data suggest that for carefully screened couples, conjoint treatment is as effective as the more widely used GST approach. Yet, the poor outcome in the O'Leary et al. (1999) study raises questions about the potential effectiveness of either treatment approach.

SUMMARY

Physical aggression is a common problem among couples seeking marital therapy. Most therapists, after they screen for violence, will find that over half the couples seeking help report the occurrence of husband aggression in the prior year. Familiarity with theories of partner violence and research on the correlates of such aggression will help therapists assess potentially important aspects of the problem and better understand the potential causes and consequences of violence for aggressive couples they treat. Sensitivity to such issues during the assessment phase will help therapists decide whether conjoint treatment is appropriate for a given couple. Current data suggest that conjoint therapy with a direct and specific focus on eliminating husband violence may be as effective as the more widely used gender-specific treatments, although the current data are mixed regarding how effective such interventions will be. In general, a cautious and informed approach is suggested, focusing on controlling abusive behaviors and training in communication and problem-solving skills to help couples end the violence in their relationships.

REFERENCES

Aldarondo, E. (1996). Cessation and persistence of wife assault: A longitudinal analysis. *American Journal of Orthopsychiatry, 66,* 141–151.

Aldarondo, E., & Kaufman Kantor, G. (1997). Social predictors of wife assault cessation. In G. Kaufman Kantor & J. L. Jasinski (Eds.), *Out of darkness: Contemporary perspectives on family violence* (pp. 183–193). Thousand Oaks, CA: Sage.

Aldarondo, E., & Sugarman, D. B. (1996). Risk marker analysis of the cessation and persistence of wife assault. *Journal of Consulting and Clinical Psychology, 64,* 1010–1019.

Anglin, K., & Holtzworth-Munroe, A. (1997). Comparing the responses of violent and nonviolent couples to problematic marital and nonmarital situations: Are the skill deficits of violent couples global? *Journal of Family Psychology, 11,* 301–313.

Bandura, A. (1973). *Aggression: A social learning analysis.* Englewood Cliffs, NJ: Prentice-Hall.

Bandura, A. (1976). Social learning analysis of aggression. In E. Ribes-Inesta & A. Bandura (Eds.), *Analysis of delinquency and aggression* (pp. 203–231). Hillsdale, NJ: Erlbaum.

Barling, J., O'Leary, K. D., Jouriles, E. N., Vivian, D., & MacEwen, K. E. (1987). Factor similarity of the Conflicts Tactics Scale across samples, spouses and sites. *Journal of Family Violence, 2,* 37–53.

Bersani, C. A., & Chen, H. T. (1988). Sociological perspectives in family violence. In V. B. Van Hasselt, R. L. Morrison, A. S. Bellack, & M. Hersen (Eds.), *Handbook of family violence* (pp. 57–86). New York: Plenum Press.

Bograd, M. (1988). How battered women and abusive men account for domestic violence: Excuses, justifications, or explanations? In G. T. Hotaling, D. Finkelhor, J. T. Kirkpatrick, & M. A. Straus (Eds.), *Coping with family violence: Research and policy perspectives* (pp. 60–70). Newbury Park, CA: Sage.

Brannen, S. J., & Rubin, A. (1996). Comparing the effectiveness of gender-specific and couples groups in a court-mandated spouse abuse treatment program. *Research on Social Work Practice, 6,* 405–424.

Browne, A. (1993). Violence against women by male partners: Prevalence, outcomes, and policy implications. *American Psychologist, 48,* 1077–1087.

Cantos, A. L., Neidig, P. H., & O'Leary, K. D. (1993). Men's and women's attributions of blame for domestic violence. *Journal of Family Violence, 8,* 289–303.

Cascardi, M., Langhinrichsen, J., & Vivian, D. (1992). Marital aggression: Impact, injury, and health correlates for husbands and wives. *Archives of Internal Medicine, 152,* 1178–1184.

Cascardi, M., O'Leary, K. D., Lawrence, E. E., & Schlee, K. A. (1995). Characteristics of women physically abused by their spouses and who seek treatment regarding marital conflict. *Journal of Consulting and Clinical Psychology, 63,* 616–623.

Cascardi, M., & Vivian, D. (1995). Context for specific episodes of marital violence: Gender and severity of violence differences. *Journal of Family Violence, 10,* 265–293.

Check, J. V. P., Malamuth, N. M., Elias, B., & Barton, S. A. (1985, April). On hostile ground. *Psychology Today,* 56–61.

Davis, R. C., & Taylor, B. G. (1999). Does batterer treatment reduce violence? A synthesis of the literature. In L. Feder (Ed.), *Women and domestic violence* (pp. 69–93). Binghamton, NY: Haworth Press.

Day, R. D. (1995). Family-systems theory. In R. D. Day, K. R. Gilbert, B. H. Settles, & W. R. Burr (Eds.), *Research and theory in family science* (pp. 91–101). Pacific Grove, CA: Brooks/Cole.

Dobash, R. E., & Dobash, R. P. (1979). *Violence against wives.* New York: Free Press.

Dunford, F. W. (2000). The San Diego Navy experiment: An assessment of interventions for men who assault their wives. *Journal of Consulting and Clinical Psychology, 68,* 468–476.

Dutton, D. G. (1995). *The domestic assault of women: Psychological and criminal justice perspectives.* Vancouver, Canada: University of British Columbia Press.

Dutton, D. G., & Golant, S. K. (1995). *The batterer: A psychological profile.* New York: Basic Books.

Dutton, M. A. (1996). Working with battered women. *In Session: Psychotherapy in Practice, 2,* 63–80.

Ehrensaft, M. K., & Vivian, D. (1996). Spouses' reasons for not reporting existing physical aggression as a marital problem. *Journal of Family Psychology, 10,* 443–453.

Feld, S. L., & Straus, M. A. (1989). Escalation and desistance of wife assault in marriage. *Criminology, 27,* 141–161.

Follingstad, D. R., Rutledge, L. L., Berg, B. J., Hause, E. S., & Polek, D. S. (1990). The role of emotional abuse in physically abusive relationships. *Journal of Family Violence, 5,* 107–120.

Geffner, R., Mantooth, C., Franks, D., & Rao, L. (1989). A psychoeducational conjoint therapy approach to reducing family violence. In P. L. Caesar & L. K. Hamberger (Eds.), *Therapeutic interventions with batterers: Theory and practice* (pp. 103–133). New York: Springer.

Gelles, R. J., & Straus, M. A. (1979). Determinants of violence in the family: Toward a theoretical integration. In W. R. Burr, R. Hill, F. I. Nye, & I. L. Keiss (Eds.), *Contemporary theories about the family* (Vol. 1, pp. 549–581). New York: Free Press.

Hamberger, L. K., & Hastings, J. E. (1988). Skills training for treatment of spouse abusers: An outcome study. *Journal of Family Violence, 3,* 121–130.

Harris, R., Savage, S., Jones, T., & Brooke, W. (1988). A comparison of treatments for abusive men and their partners within a family-service agency. *Canadian Journal of Community Mental Health, 7,* 147–155.

Harway, M., Hansen, M., & Cervantes, N. N. (1997). Therapist awareness of appropriate intervention in treatment of domestic violence: A review. *Journal of Aggression, Maltreatment, and Trauma, 1,* 27–40.

Heyman, R. E., & Neidig, P. H. (1997). Physical aggression couples treatment. In W. K. Halford & H. J. Markman (Eds.), *Clinical handbook of marriage and couples interventions* (pp. 589–617). Chichester, England: Wiley.

Heyman, R. E., O'Leary, K. D., & Jouriles, E. N. (1995). Alcohol and aggressive personality styles: Potentiators of serious physical aggression against wives? *Journal of Family Psychology, 9,* 44–57.

Holtzworth-Munroe, A. (2000). Social information processing skills deficits in maritally violent men: Summary of a research program. In J. P. Vincent & E. N. Jouriles (Eds.), *Domestic violence: Guidelines for research-informed practice* (pp. 13–36). London: Jessica Kingsley.

Holtzworth-Munroe, A., Bates, L., Smutzler, N., & Sandin, E. (1997). A brief review of the research on husband violence, Part I: Maritally violent versus nonviolent men. *Aggression and Violent Behavior, 2,* 65–99.

Holtzworth-Munroe, A., Beatty, S. B., & Anglin, K. (1995). The assessment and treatment of marital violence: An introduction for the marital therapist. In N. S. Jacobson & A. S. Gurman (Eds.), *Clinical handbook of marital therapy* (2nd ed., pp. 317–339). New York: Guilford Press.

Holtzworth-Munroe, A., Jouriles, E., Smutzler, N., & Norwood, W. D. (1998). Victims of domestic violence. In A. S. Bellack & M. Hersen (Eds.), *Comprehensive clinical psychology* (Vol. 9, pp. 325–339). Oxford, England: Pergamon Press.

Holtzworth-Munroe, A., Meehan, J. C., Herron, K., Rehman, U., & Stuart, G. L. (2000). Testing the Holtzworth-Munroe and Stuart (1994) batterer typology. *Journal of Consulting and Clinical Psychology, 68,* 1000–1019.

Holtzworth-Munroe, A., Smutzler, N., & Bates, L. (1997). A brief review of the research on husband violence, Part III: Sociodemographic factors, relationship factors, and differing consequences of husband and wife violence. *Aggression and Violent Behavior, 2,* 285–307.

Holtzworth-Munroe, A., & Stuart, G. L. (1994). Typologies of male batterers: Three subtypes and the differences among them. *Psychological Bulletin, 116,* 476–497.

Holtzworth-Munroe, A., Waltz, J., Jacobson, N. S., Monaco, V., Fehrenbach, P. A., & Gottman, J. M. (1992). Recruiting nonviolent men as control subjects for research on marital violence: How easily can it be done? *Violence and Victims, 7,* 79–88.

Jacobson, N. S., Gottman, J. M., Gortner, E., Berns, S., & Shortt, J. W. (1996). Psychological factors in the longitudinal course of battering: When do the couples split up? When does the abuse decrease? *Violence and Victims, 11,* 371–392.

Jacobson, N. S., & Margolin, G. (1979). *Marital therapy: Strategies based on social learning and behavior exchange principles.* New York: Brunner/Mazel.

Johnson, M. P. (1995). Patriarchal terrorism and common couple violence: Two forms of violence against women. *Journal of Marriage and the Family, 57,* 283–294.

Leonard, K. E., & Senchak, M. (1996). Prospective prediction of husband marital aggression within newlywed couples. *Journal of Abnormal Behavior, 105,* 369–380.

Magdol, L., Moffitt, T. E., Caspi, A., Newman, D. L., Fagan, J., & Silva, P. A. (1997). Gender differences in rates of partner violence in a birth cohort of 21-year-olds: Bridging the gap between clinical and epidemiological approaches. *Journal of Consulting and Clinical Psychology, 65,* 68–78.

Magdol, L., Moffitt, T. E., Caspi, A., & Silva, P. A. (1998). Developmental antecedents of partner abuse: A prospective-longitudinal study. *Journal of Abnormal Psychology, 107,* 375–389.

Malloy, K. A., McCloskey, K. A., & Monford, T. M. (1999). A group treatment program for male batterers. In L. VandeCreek & T. L. Jackson (Eds.), *Innovations in clinical practice: A source book* (Vol. 17, pp. 377–395). Sarasota, FL: Professional Resource Press.

Margolin, G. (1998). Effects of domestic violence on children. In P. K. Trickett & C. J. Schellenbach (Eds.), *Violence against children in the family and the communication* (pp. 57–101). Washington, DC: American Psychological Association.

Massachusetts Guidelines and Standards for Certification of Batterers' Treatment Program. (1994). *May revision.* Boston.

Mathes, E. W., & Severa, N. (1981). Jealousy, romantic love, and liking: Theoretical considerations and preliminary scale development. *Psychological Reports, 49,* 23–31.

Murphy, C. M., & O'Leary, K. D. (1989). Psychological aggression predicts physical aggression in early marriage. *Journal of Consulting and Clinical Psychology, 57,* 579–582.

Novaco, R. W. (1976). Treatment of chronic anger through cognitive and relaxation controls. *Journal of Consulting and Clinical Psychology, 44,* 681.

O'Leary, K. D. (1988). Physical aggression between spouses: A social learning theory perspective. In V. B. Van Hasselt, R. L. Morrison, A. S. Bellack, & M. Hersen (Eds.), *Handbook of family violence* (pp. 31–55). New York: Plenum Press.

O'Leary, K. D. (1993). Through a psychological lens: Personality traits, personality disorders, and levels of violence. In R. J. Gelles & D. R. Ioseke (Eds.), *Current controversies in family violence* (pp. 7–29). Newbury Park, CA: Sage.

O'Leary, K. D. (1996). Physical aggression in intimate relationships can be treated within a marital context under certain circumstances. *Journal of Interpersonal Violence, 11,* 450–452.

O'Leary, K. D., Barling, J., Arias, I., Rosenbaum, A., Malone, J., & Tyree, A. (1989). Prevalence and stability of marital aggression between spouses:

A longitudinal analysis. *Journal of Consulting and Clinical Psychology, 57,* 263–268.

O'Leary, K. D., Heyman, R. E., & Neidig, P. H. (1999). Treatment of wife abuse: A comparison of gender-specific and couples approaches. *Behavior Therapy, 30,* 475–505.

O'Leary, K. D., Vivian, D., & Malone, J. (1992). Assessment of physical aggression against women in marriage: The need for multimodal assessment. *Behavioral Assessment, 14,* 5–14.

Quigley, B. M., & Leonard, K. E. (1996). Desistance of husband aggression in the early years of marriage. *Violence and Victims, 11,* 355–370.

Rathus, J. H., & O'Leary, K. D. (1997). Spouse-Specific Dependency Scale: Scale development. *Journal of Family Violence, 12,* 159–168.

Riggs, D. S., & O'Leary, K. D. (1996). Aggression between heterosexual dating partners: An examination of a causal model of courtship aggression. *Journal of Interpersonal Violence, 11,* 519–540.

Rogge, R. D., & Bradbury, T. N. (1999). Till violence does us part: The differing roles of communication and aggression in predicting adverse marital outcomes. *Journal of Consulting and Clinical Psychology, 67,* 340–351.

Rosenbaum, A., & O'Leary, K. D. (1981). Marital violence: Characteristics of abusive couples. *Journal of Consulting and Clinical Psychology, 49,* 63–71.

Rosenfeld, B. D. (1992). Court-ordered treatment of spouse abuse. *Clinical Psychology Review, 12,* 205–226.

Saunders, D. G. (1989). Cognitive and behavioral interventions with men who batter: Application and outcome. In P. L. Caesar & L. K. Hamberger (Eds.), *Treating men who batter: Theory, practice and programs* (pp. 77–98). New York: Springer.

Schumacher, J. A., Feldbau-Kohn, S., Smith Slep, A. M., & Heyman, R. E. (2001). Risk factors for male-to-female partner physical abuse. *Aggression and Violent Behavior, 6,* 281–352.

Smith, D. A., Vivian, D., & O'Leary, K. D. (1991). The misnomer proposition: A critical reappraisal of the longitudinal status of "negativity" in marital communication. *Behavioral Assessment, 13,* 7–24.

Spielberger, C. D. (1988). *Manual for the State-Trait Anger Expression Inventory.* Odessa, FL: Psychological Assessment Resources.

Stets, J. E., & Straus, M. (1989). The marriage license as a hitting license: A comparison of assaults in dating, cohabitating, and married couples. *Journal of Family Violence, 4,* 161–180.

Straus, M. A. (1979). Measuring intra family conflict and violence: The Conflict Tactics (CT) scales. *Journal of Marriage and the Family, 41,* 75–88.

Straus, M. A. (1999). The controversy over domestic violence by women: A methological, theoretical, and sociology of science analysis. In X. B. Arriaga & S. Oskamp (Eds.), *Violence in intimate relationships* (pp. 17–44). Thousand Oaks, CA: Sage.

Straus, M. A., & Gelles, R. J. (1986). Societal change and change in family violence from 1975 to 1985 as revealed by two national surveys. *Journal of Marriage and the Family, 48,* 465–479.

Straus, M. A., & Gelles, R. J. (1990). *Physical violence in American families: Risk factors and adaptations to violence in families.* New Brunswick, NJ: Transaction.

Straus, M. A., Gelles, R. J., & Steinmetz, S. K. (1980). *Behind closed doors: Violence in the American family.* Garden City, NY: Doubleday.

Straus, M. A., Hamby, S. L., Boney-McCoy, S., & Sugarman, D. B. (1996). The Revised Conflict Tactics Scales (CTS2): Development and preliminary psychometric data. *Journal of Family Issues, 17,* 283–316.

Stuart, R. B. (1980). *Helping couples change: A social learning approach to marital therapy.* New York: Guilford Press.

Sugarman, D. B., & Frankel, S. L. (1996). Patriarchal ideology and wife-assault: A meta-analytic review. *Journal of Family Violence, 11,* 13–40.

Sullivan, C. M., & Bybee, D. I. (1999). Reducing violence using community-based advocacy for women with abusive partners. *Journal of Consulting and Clinical Psychology, 67,* 43–53.

Tolman, R. M. (1999). The validation of the psychological maltreatment of women inventory. *Violence and Victims, 14,* 25–37.

Vivian, D., & Heyman, R. E. (1996). Is there a place for conjoint treatment for couple violence? *In Session: Psychotherapy in Practice, 2,* 25–48.

CHAPTER 19

Cognitive-Behavioral Therapy with Gay and Lesbian Couples

CHRISTOPHER R. MARTELL AND THOMAS E. LAND

HISTORY OF THERAPEUTIC APPROACH

The issues same-gender couples face have only recently become the focus of behavioral research. Consequently, much of what is known about work with gay and lesbian couples has been garnered from studies with small sample sizes and from anecdotal reports. Purcell, Campos, and Perilla (1996) suggest that *cultural, client,* and *therapist* factors must be explored when discussing competence-based therapy with gay and lesbian clients. These three factors dominate this chapter's presentation of cognitive-behavioral couple therapy with same-gender couples. They are factors therapists should consider when doing what must be done with couple therapy for same-gender couples:

The authors would like to thank Andrew Christensen, Ph.D., and G. Dorsey Green, Ph.D., for reviewing early drafts of this work. We also gratefully acknowledge Virginia Rutter for editorial assistance. Correspondence concerning this chapter should be addressed to Christopher R. Martell, Associates in Behavioral Health, 818 12th Avenue, Seattle, Washington, 98122. Electronic mail may be sent via Internet to martellc@u.washington.edu.

translate the heterosexual model into the gay and lesbian experience.

Politically and culturally, same-gender couples receive little and uncertain support. The legal status of same-gender couples is in a greater state of flux than ever before. The Vermont State Legislature signed a civil union bill into law in May 2000, allowing same-gender couples to have rights similar to those of heterosexual married couples. In California, Proposition 22 (put before voters in March 2000) prohibits the state from recognizing a gay or lesbian union, even if other states, like Vermont, support such unions. Same-gender couples often note, with a sense of futility and anger, that nontraditional heterosexual couples (e.g., long-term cohabitors) are afforded the protection of the law even when family, religion, and culture are hostile toward their union. The rituals of marriage, during which heterosexual couples experience the pinnacle of religious and cultural support for their union, are seldom available to same-gender couples. For those couples who agree to have a formal commitment ceremony, most churches balk and family members often boycott. Needless to say, notices such as "The grooms are registered at Neiman Marcus" are unlikely to appear in any local newspaper. This lack of support means that same-gender couples exist with fewer institutional supports than cross-gender couples.

Therapist factors and the approach of the mental health establishment toward homosexuality also influence the state of couple therapy for same-gender couples. In the twentieth century, homosexuality moved from being a criminal offense, to a mental illness, to an alternative lifestyle. This transition is far from complete. Seventeen of the United States still maintain "antisodomy" laws that criminalize homoerotic behavior. There are also those in the therapeutic community (Nicolosi, 1991) who treat homosexuality as a psychiatric disorder, despite its elimination as a mental disorder in the *Diagnostic and Statistical Manual of Mental Disorders*, third edition (*DSM-III* American Psychiatric Association, 1980). On the other hand, the American Psychological Association has taken further steps toward elimination of the notion of pathology by publishing guidelines for psychologists working with gay, lesbian, and bisexual clients. The guidelines mandate therapy that is positive and affirming (American Psychological Association, 2000).

Applications of Treatments Developed on Heterosexual Couples Applied to Gay and Lesbian Couples

Because same-gender couples are excluded from many treatment outcome studies, most therapies for gay and lesbian couples follow the general protocols from treatments that have been primarily validated on heterosexual couples. Researchers argue that inclusion of same-gender couples would add confounding variables, and funding agencies fail to mandate this key element of diversity in study populations. However, the exclusion of same-gender couples in couple therapy research is an arbitrary, if not heterosexist decision. Heterosexism is defined as a belief

system or ideology that denigrates or stigmatizes any nonheterosexual form of behavior or identity (Herek, 1995). The American Couples Survey (Blumstein & Schwartz, 1983) is one example of just how rich the observations are about all couple types when same-gender and cross-gender partners are included. The bias toward legally married couples in the therapy literature usually prevents adequate analysis of the application of various treatments to the wide variety of relationships. This obscures necessary changes in the treatment that are required with people of different sexual orientations (Martell, 1999). Therefore, it is up to therapists to adapt what has been learned in the laboratory with heterosexual couples to their work with same-gender couples. For now, therapists must rely on information gathered mostly from heterosexual couples and translate it to suit gay and lesbian couples until a substantial literature on the unique needs of this population is accumulated.

Similarities and Differences between Same-Gender and Heterosexual Couples

The American Couples Survey (Blumstein & Schwartz, 1983) was one of the first to gather normative data on same-gender couples. Prior to the publication of their data, stereotypes and myths about same-gender couples suggested that these relationships were short lived and transient. In this survey, even gay men and lesbians were skeptical about the longevity of relationships. Relationships were not expected to last, nor were couples integrated in the larger lesbian and gay community. Still, Blumstein and Schwartz found a robust sample of same-gender couples who remained committed to each other over time, despite the almost total absence of social, religious, and legal support. These findings mirrored the longevity of cohabiting heterosexual couples. Among differences found, the survey suggested that gay couples have sex less frequently than married couples after 10 years together, and that they more frequently develop agreements about nonexclusive sexual behavior than married heterosexual or lesbian couples.

As researchers studying couple interactions, albeit not couple therapy, began to include gay and lesbian couples in longitudinal studies, their work provided information on a fairly large sample of gay and lesbian couples. These studies focused on themes and issues that predicted success in long-term relationships. Kurdek (1992a) looked at samples of lesbian and gay couples and compared them with samples of heterosexual married couples. He reported that interactions regarding issues of intimacy, power, personal flaws, personal distance, social concerns, and distrust were more alike than different among the three types of couples. The most frequent sources of disagreement for all three types were issues centering on intimacy and power. Kurdek (1994) found that the top five areas of conflict for both lesbian and gay couples were (1) managing finances, (2) driving style, (3) affection/sex, (4) being overly critical, and (5) division of household chores. For all couple types, arguments about intimacy predicted current relationship dissatisfaction but not long-term dissatisfaction. Arguments related to power were associated with immediate and long-term relationship dissatisfaction. Heterosexual couples were more likely to argue about social issues than were either gay or lesbian couples. Gay and lesbian couples were more likely to argue about distrust than were heterosexual couples. The pattern of similarities and differences in this work suggests that therapeutic strategies developed with heterosexual couples need not be extensively modified for same-gender couples, though certain considerations must be taken into account.

The first longitudinal study of gay and lesbian couple interaction that included observation of actual interactions was completed at the University of Washington (Gottman, personal communication, November 23, 1999; Gottman et al., in press). Gottman noted that lesbian and gay couples did not appear significantly different from heterosexual couples in communication styles.

They were more autonomous than heterosexual couples and more positive in their interactions. However, the same predictors of relationship dissolution were found in same-gender as in cross-gender couples (Kurdek, 1991, 1992b, 1998). Gottman (personal communication, July 16, 2000) found that male couples were more comfortable than either heterosexual or lesbian couples with regard to discussing sexual behavior. (The study was limited by a small sample size, however, and generalizations must be made cautiously.)

There is cultural prejudice against same-gender couples' parenting of children (Crawford & Solliday, 1996; McLeod & Crawford, 1998), although lesbian couples experience less cultural opposition than gay men. Gay men may choose either to adopt or to father children with a surrogate. Gay men and lesbians occasionally choose to coparent children, though the parents tend to not live in the same household. Some gay men and lesbians have children as products of earlier heterosexual marriages or relationships. The manner in which same-gender couples acquire and provide homes for their children may differ from the heterosexual family, but their ability to provide good parenting to their children has been repeatedly demonstrated in the literature (Allen & Burrell, 1996; Cramer, 1986; Golombok & Tasker, 1996; Patterson, 1996a, 1996b).

There are multiple cultural, ethnic, and racial factors that come into play with all couples, and therapist training may give short shrift to this kind of diversity just as it does to sexual diversity. Nevertheless, we know that no two couples are exactly alike, just as no two individuals in a couple are exactly alike. Gay, lesbian, and bisexual persons of color bring experiences to their relationships, and therapists must be aware of this richness of backgrounds. For example, definitions of family and community vary from culture to culture (Greene & Boyd-Franklin, 1996b; Morales, 1996). African American lesbian couples face "triple jeopardy" as members of multiple oppressed groups: women, African

Americans, and lesbians (Greene & Boyd-Franklin, 1996a, 1996b). Therapists must be sensitive to cultural differences in religious values, the importance of family, and the reliance on support from the community (Fukuyama & Ferguson, 2000). Gender roles also differ according to culture (Morales, 1996), and gender-role identity varies widely among couples. Therapists may be more effective when they consider the impact of multiple counternormative statuses belonging to non-White same-gender couples.

Structural forms of discrimination add stress to same-gender relationships. For example, in most states, these couples do not have the privilege of sharing insurance benefits. The lack of domestic partner insurance benefits often adds stress to couples. Problems with immigration may keep the couple separate or necessitate occasional trips to home countries to meet immigration laws. Heterosexual married couples do not face these problems.

The context in which individuals are raised and acquire beliefs about the world impacts them throughout their lives. This socialization context varies from culture to culture as well as among families of similar cultures. As their contexts change, people's learned behavior and beliefs may no longer apply. People from sexual minorities, who are seldom raised in environments that support the viability of alternative sexuality, will face major shifts in their understanding as they mature. Clinicians must take a truly idiographic position when working with same-gender couples to accommodate for the shifting contexts in which these couples live.

THE GAY AND LESBIAN COUPLE IN THE LARGER CULTURAL SYSTEM

Even within a cognitive and behavioral framework, it is important to be aware of the larger system in which a couple functions. Same-gender couples exist within a nonsupportive or hostile social milieu. The current literature does not support the common wisdom that same-gender couples in nonclinical samples have greater relationship difficulties than their heterosexual counterparts. Stereotypic images of gay men present them as internally phobic about homosexuality, promiscuous, and unable to maintain intimacy; images of lesbians depict them as fused and too quick to form intimate attachments. There is controversy about the assumption of enmeshment and fusion in lesbian couples (Iguarta, 1998; Pardie & Herb, 1997). Neither this assumption nor those of gay male internalized heterosexism (or so-called homophobia) and disengagement have been consistently validated (Meyer & Dean, 1998). The incidence of internalizing negative cultural attitudes about homosexuality in nonclinical samples of gay men is less than in clinical populations. Internalized heterosexism, when it exists, is usually correlated with an adverse mental health outcome (Gonsiorek, 1988) and is related to difficulty with intimacy. Some individuals may continue to display internalized heterosexist attitudes even after they have identified themselves as gay, lesbian, or bisexual (Herek & Glunt, 1995). Nevertheless, clinicians are cautioned to recognize that internalized homophobia continues to be an invalidated stereotype regardless of individual clients who hold negative ideas about their homosexuality.

Lifestyle devaluation by families of origin is common for same-gender couples (Blumstein & Schwartz, 1983; Brown, 1995). Thus, they may experience difficulty integrating their partner into their biological family. This lack of integration has been shown to be unrelated to couple satisfaction (Green, Bettinger, & Zacks, 1996). Therapists should not assume that all individuals need to disclose their sexuality to their family of origin. The concept of family as a source of social support may extend to many biologically unrelated individuals in the lives of gay and lesbian people; social support is more important for couples than biology or blood kinship. However, when partners need to disguise their relationship around relatives or employers, conflicts can arise when one partner finds this behavior unacceptably deceitful.

The unique developmental experiences of gay and lesbian people and the cultural prejudice against them influence therapy more than specific differences among same-gender or cross-gender couples. Therapist sensitivity to the subcultural differences resulting from being nonheterosexual is the most important requirement in doing therapy with same-gender couples. Utilizing established therapies makes sense given so few differences among same-gender and cross-gender couples, but doing so without understanding the often harsh realities of being gay or lesbian in current culture is potentially detrimental.

THEORETICAL CONSTRUCTS

We have observed that several couple therapies are useful with all distressed couples. However, the differences and similarities among gay and lesbian couples and heterosexual couples suggest minor alterations to the type of therapy conducted with either type of couple. The most important alteration is to be sensitive to the particular cultures of gay and lesbian clients, including their sexual, ethnic, and racial cultures. In the remainder of this chapter, the predominant treatment models of cognitive and behavioral couple therapy are discussed with suggestions for modifications of these methodologies to accommodate gay and lesbian clients. Three models are considered: behavioral couple therapy, cognitive therapy, and integrative behavioral couple therapy. The theoretical constructs on which these three models are based are presented first. Then, each therapy is briefly described, suggestions for combining elements of the types of therapies are discussed, and case examples are used to illustrate how to select therapeutic techniques for a particular couple. These therapies represent empirically validated treatments that have particular and distinct advantages for adapting to same-gender couples.

TRADITIONAL BEHAVIORAL COUPLE THERAPY

Behavioral couple therapy (BCT; Jacobson & Margolin, 1979) is based on the premise that reciprocity is important for good relationships. When couples focus on other-directed change, it is likely to damage the relationship. Therefore, a primary component of BCT is developing a collaborative set between partners. Each partner is encouraged to consider his or her role in creating and maintaining problems and to take personal and unilateral responsibility for making changes that can increase relationship satisfaction.

BCT follows the principles of social learning theory (Bandura, 1977) and of behavior exchange. Social learning theory developed from the premise that there is a continuous reciprocal interaction between behavioral and environmental determinants of psychological functioning. Personal variables, such as expectations and other cognitive phenomena, are considered part of the reciprocal interaction. Environment influences psychological and behavioral responses, and the person also influences the environment.

COGNITIVE THERAPY

Cognitive therapy (CT) for couples (Beck, 1988; Dattilio & Padesky, 1990) is based on the premise that couple communication is often tangled due to misinterpretations and faulty expectations regarding relationships. It derives from individual cognitive therapy. Cognitive therapists teach both partners to evaluate their beliefs and recognize cognitive distortions. Awareness of situations during which negative schema are activated and utilization of behavioral communication training also characterize cognitive couple therapy. The application to gay and lesbian couples is implied and discussed briefly by Dattilio and Padesky (1990). According to them, issues such as negative beliefs about self, stress over the loss of friends and loved ones during the AIDS epidemic, lack of social support, and isolation are issues more often facing gay and lesbian than heterosexual couples. These issues are amply addressed by standard CT.

Both BCT and CT are primarily change-oriented therapies. As such, they have been shown to be highly successful at helping couples change dysfunctional patterns of communication and behavior. Both models focus on skills training. Couples learn new tactics for communicating and problem solving; they learn to identify and correct irrational or unbalanced beliefs and begin to practice new behaviors. As BCT has developed, it has embodied more cognitive aspects (Baucom & Epstein, 1990). CT has always included behavioral experiments for both individuals and couples (Beck, Rush, Shaw, & Emery, 1979).

INTEGRATIVE BEHAVIORAL COUPLE THERAPY

Recent models of couple therapy have emphasized both change and acceptance in couple work. Integrative behavioral couple therapy (IBCT; Christensen & Jacobson, 2000; Jacobson & Christensen, 1996) is based on the premises that (1) all couples will face incompatibilities; (2) there are limits on change to address those incompatibilities; and (3) acceptance (as well as change) is important in dealing with incompatibilities. As a way of fostering acceptance, IBCT therapists try to create an atmosphere that allows couples to communicate in a manner leading to greater acceptance. IBCT is less oriented toward skills training than BCT or CT, and relies on natural contingencies to maintain new behaviors.

The theories proposed by cognitive and behavioral couple therapists generally apply to

same-gender couples, but certain considerations facilitate treatment success. Same-gender couples do not differ from heterosexual couples in their search for loving companionship or in their attempts to weather the occasional emotional storm. The research suggests that same-gender couples are more intimate, more flexible, and more egalitarian than heterosexual couples (Kurdek, 1998). However, gay and lesbian couples tend to end their relationships more frequently than do heterosexual couples (Blumstein & Schwartz, 1983; Kurdek, 1998).

CT provides an excellent tool for helping couples examine their beliefs about the viability of long-term relationships. Because few norms and expectations are available, gay and lesbian couples must create their own structure, rituals, and parameters to guide them in forming family units. BCT can help the couple learn to negotiate the boundaries of the relationship. IBCT may be particularly applicable, with its emphasis on acceptance of the partner and looking for differences as opportunities for greater intimacy. Instead of feeling the absence of perceived relationship rituals, couples can understand and embrace the freedom they have to define their relationship in a fashion that is acceptable to both partners. The couple will need to recognize and cope with pressure to conform to a heterosexual cultural standard, challenging beliefs and expectations that a same-gender relationship should blindly mimic heterosexual marriage.

METHODS OF ASSESSMENT AND INTERVENTION

Clinicians customarily develop a case conceptualization (Persons, 1989; Turkat, 1985) with every couple. Under a behavioral assessment model, case conceptualization allows the clinician to note the generic problems a couple faces and to assess the presence and strength of the unique social and cultural forces that shape the daily lives of same-gender couples. The clinician also gathers information to determine whether a more cognitive or more behavioral approach best suits the case. Generally, it is wise first to examine the extent to which cognitive distortions regarding relationships are impacting the couple (see the case of Sharon and Colleen, below). Selecting standard CT when these distortions are significant may be useful. However, when couples have very different personality styles and acceptance is an important part of the intervention, IBCT may be indicated (see the case of Ted and Robert, following). In most cases, behavior exchange and communication training can be helpful to couples, and these techniques are compatible with CT and IBCT. Case conceptualization and the use of predominantly cognitive or behavioral interventions depend on the assessment and the therapist's understanding of these methodologies. Data suggesting prescriptive therapies purely based on specific client problems do not exist at this time.

Many inventories that have been developed to measure couple satisfaction have been developed for heterosexual couples with gender references used accordingly. This heterosexist language limits the utility of these measures with same-gender couples. Using such measures denigrates, insults, and alienates gay and lesbian individuals. Measures that are gender-neutral and refer to partner rather than to husband, wife, or spouse are appropriate for same-gender couples.

The Dyadic Adjustment Scale (DAS; Spanier, 1976) is one of the most widely used scales for assessing couple satisfaction and is presented in a gender-neutral format. The DAS was developed to measure four factors: dyadic consensus, dyadic satisfaction, dyadic cohesion, and affectional expression. Using a sample of both heterosexual and same-gender couples, Kurdek (1992a) evaluated the four-factor theory of the DAS and concluded that there is limited support for the multidimensional nature of the

scale. He found that the DAS may in fact measure two levels of relationship adjustment: relationship satisfaction and factors that determine relationship satisfaction. The DAS is a good measure of overall couple satisfaction.

A new scale in development, the Frequency and Acceptability of Partner Behavior Scale (Christensen & Jacobson, 1997), measures the frequency of both positive and negative behaviors and the acceptability to each partner of those behaviors. For example, partner A may rate the number of times that partner B confided in him or her as occurring only once per month, and may then rate this as highly unacceptable. Each partner is then asked to rank order five areas of most concern. This gender-neutral scale provides the therapist with important information regarding how each partner believes the other is behaving toward him or her, and how distressed he or she is by such interactions. Psychometric data regarding this scale are currently being gathered and preliminary findings are being summarized (Doss & Christensen, 1999).

The Conflict Tactics Scale (CTS; Straus, 1979; Straus, Hamby, Boney-McCoy, & Sugarman, 1996), which refers to individuals as partners, is an important measure to screen for the possibility of domestic violence. Therapists are encouraged to always meet individually with each partner in a couple to assess the individual's level of distress and presence of psychopathology, to rule out domestic violence, and to find out about any undisclosed extrarelational affairs. The individual interviews with each partner are ideal for following up on the CTS (e.g., exploring further an incident of violence that the client endorsed).

Many individual inventories that are gender-free may be useful to the couple therapist. Therapists taking a more cognitive approach may use the Attributional Style Questionnaire (Seligman, Abramson, Semmel, & von Baeyer, 1979). This allows a greater understanding of each partner's belief system. For heterosexual couples, there is a high correlation between depression and relational distress (Jacobson, Dobson, Fruzzetti, Schmaling, & Salusky, 1991). Although this finding may not hold true for same-gender couples, a measure of depression such as the Beck Depression Inventory (Beck, Ward, Mendelson, Mock, & Erbaugh, 1961) may be useful. Case conceptualization relies heavily on the therapist developing a sound formulation about the problem areas, behavioral patterns, and beliefs about relationships experienced by the couple. Interviews alone do not provide enough normative information for therapists, and use of these assessment tools contributes to a thorough and valid treatment plan.

Therapeutic Strategies Modified for Gay and Lesbian Couples

Whether the therapist uses a predominantly behavioral or a cognitive approach to treating same-gender couples, the cultural factors that impact gay and lesbian people must be considered and therapists need to be flexible. Requirements of sexual exclusivity on the part of the couple and assumptions about involvement of the biological family in the couple's relationship and about gender-specific behaviors must be reconsidered with same-gender couples. These simple modifications in a therapist's understanding of what it means to be a same-gender couple can make therapy more effective.

The subject of sexuality can be approached openly with sufficient knowledge regarding sexual behaviors, values, and attitudes unique to the gay and lesbian communities. For example, gay men may hold different values regarding monogamy than either heterosexual or lesbian couples (Blumstein & Schwartz, 1983; Wilson, 1994). Many gay men desire long-term, monogamous relationships, but there are also couples in committed, long-term relationships for whom the absence of sexual monogamy is an accepted but complicated issue. Although

monogamous and nonmonogamous male couples show no significant differences in relationship satisfaction (Blasband & Peplau, 1985), male couples may have a different understanding of the meaning of monogamy than do heterosexual couples. For example, it would be naïve for a therapist who asks if a male couple is monogamous to accept a simple yes as an adequate response. A couple who is monogamous in the same city may have an explicit or tacit contract for nonmonogamy when traveling separately and still consider themselves monogamous. Therapists working with same-gender couples should consider the issues of honesty and trust of greater importance than sexual monogamy, depending on the values held by a particular couple. Therapists working with male couples must ensure that they are not imposing personal sexual values on their clients or invalidating couples' sexual behaviors and values. This is especially true because gay male sexuality continues to be condemned by major segments of our culture.

CT is an effective tool to balance a couple's divergent expectations regarding their relationship. CT for couples incorporates communication training with methods of Socratic questioning, identification of cognitive distortions, and modification of automatic thoughts and underlying beliefs. Behavioral techniques such as behavior exchange and problem-solving training (Jacobson & Margolin, 1979) can help to increase the reinforcement skills of each partner and improve a couple's ability to resolve conflicts.

Behavior exchange is usually an initial intervention because it is very useful in creating a collaborative set. Each partner in the couple is asked to commit to certain behaviors that he or she will do for the partner as a means of pleasing the partner rather than pleasing the self. Neither partner is asked to do anything that would be repulsive, overly burdensome, or demeaning. The partners are asked to develop lists of behaviors and to commit to implementing the behaviors over a specified period of time. Communication and problem-solving training emphasize instruction in active listening strategies and in operationally defining problems and brainstorming solutions.

IBCT (Jacobson & Christensen, 1996) contains components of behavioral and experiential therapies. It is less structured than standard behavioral therapies. The therapist frequently intervenes by reformulating statements made by either partner. During the initial intervention, the therapist develops a case formulation identifying the major themes that create problems for the couple. The therapist then attempts to gain an understanding of how the couple becomes polarized around the themes, and examines the reasons a couple is particularly vulnerable when behaviors based on these themes predominate. Couples' acceptance of the IBCT formulation is critical for effective therapy. When the couple agrees to the model proposed by the therapist, a common language emerges for discussing problems as they occur. IBCT, like other cognitive or behavioral therapies, is primarily focused on the present. The past is used to hypothesize reasons for partners behaving in a particular fashion and the major content of therapy sessions consists of debriefing situations that occur for the couple during the period between therapy sessions. Couples are usually seen on a weekly basis. Three major interventions used in IBCT are empathic joining, unified detachment, and tolerance interventions. Empathic joining techniques are used to promote softer disclosures from partners. Unified detachment allows the couple to work together to resolve a problem that is regarded as a dyadic issue rather than as the fault of one partner. Tolerance interventions are used to help the couple become desensitized to and tolerate behaviors that are resistant to change.

Therapists are very active during sessions. Empathic joining interventions require the therapist to be keenly aware of possible vulnerabilities left undisclosed during a couple's conflict. The therapist would then turn to each member of the couple and discuss the softer feelings present. For example, one partner may express great anger at not having been called when the other was going to be late from work. However, as well as anger there may be sadness or hurt because the partner feels devalued when not called. The therapist would try to have the couple discuss these emotions rather than continue to argue over the incident.

Unified detachment is an IBCT technique in which the therapist helps the couple see a given problem as independent of either partner rather than place blame on one partner or the other. Problems become opportunities for increasing intimacy through working together toward resolution. The couple comes to see a problem as something that happens to them, rather than something they do to each other. The problem is seen as a pattern of behavior or a trap that both people are in and is seen as an "it." This method prevents blaming and allows the couple to discuss problems in a less accusatory or defensive manner.

All people enter relationships with an idiosyncratic behavioral repertoire. Helping a couple to form a strong collaborative set (Jacobson & Margolin, 1979) in which they both are willing to try to change is critical to a successful outcome. An equally important role for the therapist is helping both partners understand that some behaviors, idiosyncratic to one partner, may never change, no matter how much the other wishes it. When certain characteristics of a person are impervious to change, the partner is encouraged to learn to tolerate some level of the behavior. Helping couples empathize with one another, recognize problems as a mutual challenge, and tolerate one another's behavior are the primary means by which IBCT therapists promote acceptance.

IBCT includes specific tolerance interventions intended to help couples deescalate arguments or lessen distress over intransigent (but not abusive) differences. Typical tolerance interventions consist of the therapist asking the clients to fake the negative behavior or of the therapist emphasizing the positive aspects of negative behavior. An example of the former is a therapist asking each partner to say or do something that the other partner has identified as distressing during a time when there is no emotional investment. In one case, Elaine would become silent and annoyed when she got in a discussion with her partner, Kay. Kay would then get very intense and speak loudly and rapidly on the topic. This behavior on Kay's part was identified in the session, and Kay was asked to do this at a time when she wasn't feeling "intense" and to do so for only a couple of minutes before telling Elaine that this behavior was part of a "faking assignment." Elaine, on the other hand, would use the expression "Oh, whatever" when she felt dismayed at Kay. This made Kay furious because she felt discounted. Elaine was given the assignment of responding to Kay by saying "Oh, whatever" even when she was very interested in continuing the conversation with Kay. The couple was told that this assignment would help them recognize reactions to their behavior and possibly desensitize the partner to the behavior as it occurred. IBCT does not incorporate paradoxical methods, and the couple is told what to expect, including possible paradoxical functions of the faking negative behavior assignment.

Empathic joining, unified detachment, and tolerance exercises help couples gain greater understanding of each other, work together to resolve problems without blaming, and desensitize partners to behaviors that habitually cause problems. There is a reasonable presentation order for the exercises: Empathic joining is used first, as it is likely to have the greatest impact on the couple, softening their responses to one another. Unified detachment is then used if there are issues the couple face but tend to blame on each other. Tolerance exercises are assigned when couples are trapped in behavior patterns they are unable to change.

MAJOR SYNDROMES, SYMPTOMS, AND PROBLEMS TREATED

When couples enter therapy because they want help resolving their problems, most cases will meet criteria for the *DSM-IV* code V61.1, Partner Relational Problem (American Psychiatric Association, 1994). In these cases, the therapist assesses the problem areas causing difficulty for the couple and decides on the order of interventions. A logical course is to begin therapy with behavior exchange techniques and gain a better understanding of the attitudes and beliefs that may interfere with relational satisfaction. Using IBCT to promote acceptance and change may lead to greater maintenance of therapy gains, although the data are not conclusive on this matter (Jacobson & Christensen, 1996). Therapy can progress smoothly when the primary problem is the relationship itself, and is not complicated by other Axis I or Axis II disorders.

Another V-code diagnosis that may apply, particularly due to the AIDS epidemic, is *DSM-IV* code V61.9, Relational Problem Related to a Mental Disorder or General Medical Condition. This diagnosis is given when a couple is seeking therapy because the physical or mental illness of one or both partners is adding stress to the relationship. The V-code is used for the couple, and the primary physical diagnosis or the *DSM-IV* psychiatric diagnosis is given to the appropriate partner in the couple. Although there is evidence that some psychological problems such as depression may be successfully treated with couple therapy (Prince & Jacobson, 1995), therapists must exercise caution in such an undertaking. A careful case conceptualization is critical when deciding whether couple therapy is to be the primary treatment or is used as an adjunct treatment to individual psychotherapy and/or pharmachotherapy.

Cognitive-behavior therapy (CBT) has been applied to personality disorders (Beck, Freeman, & Associates, 1990; Linehan, 1993) with both individuals and groups. CBT can also be applied to couples when one or both partners demonstrate Axis II symptoms. For example, using IBCT, each partner's perspective is elicited when working with couples on the borderline spectrum. Purely cognitive models can be used to assist clients with paranoid tendencies, or a schema-focused approach can be employed when an Axis II disorder is present. Helping a couple to identify core schema activated during a particular interaction may assist them in working through problems in a healthier fashion. An emphasis on both change and acceptance is necessary when one or both members of a couple manifest severe psychopathology.

Cognitive restructuring, communication/problem-solving training, and acceptance techniques can all be used to help couples facing one partner's specific behavior problems, though clinicians should not become focused on one partner's problems more than the interaction of the two. Battering is a behavioral problem that is not amenable to this approach, and therapists are generally cautioned to avoid treating batterers with couple therapy (see Holtzworth-Monroe, Rehman, Marshall, & Meehan, this volume). The victim should be provided with a safety plan and the perpetrator should be referred for individual therapy; in some cases, the legal system may become involved. The risk of increasing violence is great if premature attempts are made to have the couple openly discuss difficulties (Jacobson & Gottman, 1998). Therapists must be alert to domestic violence in lesbian couples and resist the idea that only men batter, thereby overlooking dangerous situations for women in same-gender relationships. Behavioral problems not involving physical violence can be treated with CBT. In some cases, individual therapy is indicated as well as couple therapy, provided that therapists coordinate care.

Cognitive-behavioral interventions are problem-specific, and case formulations should be based on operationally defined problem lists. Couples can then work together to solve or accommodate a variety of problem behaviors. Although outcome data clearly indicate that not all couples are successfully treated, goal-focused methodologies lend themselves to creative applications and enhance the possibility of decreasing behavioral problems in couples.

CASE EXAMPLES

ROBERT AND TED

Robert was a 55-year-old, gay White male who had been divorced for one year from a woman to whom he was married for 20 years. Although Robert had occasionally engaged in sexual activities with men during his marriage, he did not self-identify as gay until one year and six months prior to coming to therapy. He met his partner, Ted, at a gay bar while he was in the process of divorce but was still living with his wife. Robert and Ted had been together for six months when they came to therapy. Ted was 53 years old, also a gay White male. Eight months before meeting Robert, Ted had ended a 20-year relationship with a man. He described his former relationship as having been "sexless and abusive"; his partner kept a tight rein on him and would not let him socialize with other gay men. Robert, on the other hand, had been the family patriarch in a very traditional, religiously fundamentalist, heterosexual marriage.

Diagnosis and Assessment
Robert and Ted each completed the DAS prior to their first meeting with the therapist. They showed only mild distress, with respective DAS scores of 91 and 88. Although both were in counseling with individual therapists, only Robert met the criteria for an Axis I disorder and had been diagnosed with Adjustment Disorder with Depressed Mood. During individual

interviews, each denied the presence of physical altercations; in fact, they rarely argued. Both agreed that they did not want to maintain a monogamous relationship, and they openly disclosed sexual experiences that happened outside of the partnership. The primary area of conflict for them, however, was that Ted maintained an ongoing sexual relationship with a man named Derek. Robert had met Derek, recognized that the relationship was primarily of a sexual nature, and felt that the ongoing interactions with Derek threatened his relationship with Ted.

Case Formulation

In reviewing the main themes that were evident with Ted and Robert, the primary theme was one of trust and dependency. Robert had been in a very traditional heterosexual marriage for 20 years. He had followed the rules of the larger culture and maintained his marriage even though he never felt satisfied with this assumed identity. Because Robert's wife had allowed herself to be in a subservient role, he had never experienced an intimate adult relationship with someone who would strongly state opinions, insist on asserting individuality, and suggest very clear boundaries. He now found himself in such a relationship with Ted. Ted, on the other hand, had tried to partner with another man who subscribed to a nuclear family, monogamous ideal. Although he and his former partner had no sexual relationship for the last 16 years, Ted rarely strayed outside of the relationship for sexual gratification. His domineering former partner controlled his every move. Yet Ted remained in this relationship, subsuming his own desires and wishes to those of his partner. When this relationship ended, Ted vowed never to be in a sexless, powerless relationship again.

Treatment Approach and Rationale for Its Selection

The therapist in this case had expertise in both IBCT and CT. After conducting interviews with Robert and Ted, the therapist decided that taking an IBCT approach would be useful. IBCT is well suited for this couple because there is no insistence on one member giving up an affair provided there is full disclosure to the partner. Nonmonogamy is an accepted standard in the gay community, and monogamy was not a part of Robert and Ted's value system. The therapist needs to be available to help couples negotiate these very difficult issues and work on increasing intimacy and satisfaction in their primary relationship. Because therapists must try to work with couples within the framework of the couple's contract with each other (in this case, nonmonogamy), this issue was accepted as a characteristic of the relationship rather than a problem.

The therapist noted the similarities to their former relationship experiences and their current problems. These were polarized around the issues of Derek and of Robert's struggle with jealousy. The therapist tried to promote both empathic joining and unified detachment and formulated their difficulties in developmental terms. It was suggested that both men were developing true self-expression but that they were at very different stages in that process. Robert was just accepting life as a gay man, and being in a relationship with another man was a liberating experience. Although he still maintained some attachment to the ideal of sexual monogamy, he felt freed of the trap he had been in by entering a gay relationship. Ted also was experiencing new liberation. He wanted a loving, emotionally committed partnership, but freedom for Ted meant being able to find sexual pleasure inside and outside of the relationship. He was resistant to any infringement on this new freedom in the same way that Robert was resistant to his earlier pretense of heterosexuality.

These beliefs could indicate more cognitively oriented couple therapy. However, in Robert and Ted's case, the nonconfrontational, acceptance-oriented process of IBCT was considered by the therapist to be more useful. Both men experienced a great deal of invalidation in their lives, and one of the primary goals of IBCT is to promote validation. Also, IBCT relies more on increasing the possibility that natural contingencies of positive reinforcement will maintain treatment gains rather than on rule-governed behavior and arbitrary reinforcement. Both traditional BCT and CT primarily involve skill training and are rule-governed approaches.

Reference to Existing Treatment Protocols
The treatment with Ted and Robert followed the general guidelines put forth in Jacobson and Christensen (1996). In this case, the issues regarding Derek provided the couple with an opportunity to increase their trust and empathy. They were able to recognize that Derek was not the issue, though Ted's use of a date with Derek as a method of punishing Robert was significant. Consequently, the act of punishing one's partner or being manipulative became the focus for behavior change. When Robert expressed feeling unloved because Ted had spent time with Derek, Robert's experience of being second class became the focus of treatment. The therapist helped Ted to see the rational consequences of having an extrarelational affair, such as Robert's increasing fear of abandonment or Robert's questioning whether he was "good enough" for Ted. Robert was helped to recognize that he had used the traditional control over his former wife as avoidance, preventing her from doing anything that would increase his fears of abandonment. It was never necessary for him to learn to manage his fears in prior relationships. Robert needed to build trust in Ted's reliability. Ted needed to learn that he could negotiate with Robert rather than rebel if he thought Robert was becoming too controlling.

Posttermination Synopsis and Reflections
Treatment with Robert and Ted involved 12 sessions. Both reported that they had gained a greater respect for one another as a result of therapy. They were uncertain whether their relationship would last over the long term but reported that they were better able to discuss problems rationally and were more likely to validate each other's points of view. Ted became willing to put Robert first if choosing between Derek and Robert when making plans was necessary. Robert developed a greater capacity for expressing his desires to Ted without excessive emotion or ultimatums.

SHARON AND COLLEEN

Sharon and Colleen sought couple therapy three months into their relationship. They met on a women's soccer team and had been friends for six months prior to dating. Both had known the other's previous girlfriend, as they were involved in similar sports teams. Sharon and Colleen decided to cohabit after dating for two months and had been living in their new apartment for one month prior to the beginning of therapy. They came from very different cultural backgrounds: Colleen's family was middle class and suburban; Sharon was raised in an urban, multiracial, working-class family.

Diagnosis and Assessment
At the time that Sharon and Colleen were first seen in therapy, both had DAS scores in the distressed range. Colleen's individual therapist, who diagnosed her with Major Depressive Disorder, had made the referral. Colleen also had characteristics of Paranoid Personality Disorder, although she did not meet criteria for a *DSM-IV* diagnosis. In a clinical interview, she demonstrated a passive-dependent style and used avoidance as a primary response in coping with distress. Colleen raised her voice and broke objects during arguments. She never threw anything, nor had she ever become physically aggressive with Sharon, but her verbal aggressiveness was of considerable concern to both Sharon and the therapist. Sharon was distressed over relationship problems but did not meet criteria for an individual psychiatric diagnosis.

The main issues that Colleen and Sharon faced concerned separation and autonomy.

Due to Colleen's frequent fears that she would be deceived, she was hypervigilant to any of Sharon's inconsistencies. Colleen frequently tried to entrap Sharon and badger her to confess previously denied behaviors. For example, if Colleen came home and heard a message on the answering machine from one of Sharon's friends thanking her for a nice time at coffee, she might ask "So, did you buy coffee today or did you take your thermos to work?" In an attempt to avoid conflict, Sharon might provide a half-truth, saying that she brought her thermos but not that she had met her friend at a coffee shop. Colleen would then become enraged and accuse Sharon of lying and possibly having an affair. She would then play the answering machine message for Sharon and say "I've told you never to lie to me. How can I ever trust you again?" This pattern of interaction repeated itself in several different contexts. Despite an idyllic courtship, Sharon and Colleen were fighting on a daily basis by the time they entered therapy. Sharon became increasingly passive in the relationship and Colleen more demanding as her fears of being deceived increased.

Case Formulation
Several problem behaviors noted in the first two sessions were appropriately addressed in couple therapy. Neither Sharon nor Colleen used good communication skills when discussing problems: Colleen became accusatory, routinely interrupting Sharon; Sharon lacked assertiveness and avoided confrontations either by fragmentary disclosure or withdrawal. Both women held unrealistic beliefs about relationships. Colleen believed that a partner should spend 100% of nonworking time with her, and Sharon should give up all other acquaintances. Sharon believed that conflict with Colleen would inevitably lead to violence, as it had in her family of origin. Each woman believed that the other should understand her better because she was a woman, and each had a tendency to expect the

other to read her mind. Colleen needed to increase her emotional control skills. Her aggressive behavior toward inanimate objects when she was angry frightened Sharon and confirmed Sharon's fears regarding the possibility of violence in the relationship.

Treatment Approach and Rationale for Its Selection
Sharon and Colleen's therapist chose to work within a standard cognitive-behavioral framework. A skills training approach was considered the most useful tactic because of this couple's rigidity of beliefs and lack of behavior control. Colleen's lack of empathic ability mandated training in communication and problem-solving skills. Highly structured sessions that followed a clear agenda minimized the impact of Colleen's paranoia. Both Sharon and Colleen agreed that they needed to communicate differently and that each held troublesome assumptions about relationships. It was difficult to help Colleen overcome her belief that Sharon was unfaithful. Behavioral experiments were developed to eliminate Colleen's deceptive tactics. Cognitive couples therapy was considered to be a useful adjunct to Colleen's individual treatment for depression based on the literature supporting the utility of CT for depression (Dobson, 1989).

Reference to Existing Treatment Protocols
The treatment with Colleen and Sharon did not require modification of existing protocols with couples. Communication/problem-solving training (Jacobson & Margolin, 1979), and cognitive components of therapy (Dattilio & Padesky, 1990) were both used. Colleen and Sharon were asked to read the self-help book *Love Is Never Enough* (Beck, 1988), which served as a guide for CT. Cognitive and behavioral techniques were used in overlapping fashion rather than singularly. The agenda was set during each therapy session. Colleen and Sharon used problem-solving and communication skills training during the sessions and the therapist would point

out when one was being overly accusatory or nonassertive. When it was clear that there were cognitive distortions interfering with successfully working on a particular issue, the therapist asked the couple to examine the evidence supporting or refuting that particular belief. The couple then devised behavioral experiments to test cognitions in conjunction with assigned practice sessions while continuing the communication/problem-solving exercises at home.

Posttermination Synopsis and Reflections
Colleen and Sharon continued therapy for 28 sessions. At the time of termination, they had reduced the number of arguments that they had on a weekly basis by 50%. Although Colleen still struggled with jealousy and distrust, she learned to express her concerns to Sharon in a positive and collaborative manner. Sharon learned to state clearly and completely what she had done during the day and began to assert her need to have friends outside the relationship. They compromised on this critical issue. Colleen reluctantly agreed to Sharon's outside friendships and agreed to use thought-stopping and reframing to deal with her fears of abandonment and the jealousy those fears produced. Sharon agreed to inform Colleen if she were going out with a friend and would tell her where she was and when she would be home. Although this was not ideal, it allowed Sharon to begin socializing outside the relationship and provided Colleen a means for dealing with her belief that Sharon might be unfaithful.

EFFICACY AND EFFECTIVENESS DATA

BCT has been amply documented in the research literature, attesting to its efficacy (Baucom, Shoham, Meuser, Daiuto, & Stickle, 1998; Christensen & Heavey, 1999). A reanalysis of the outcome data on BCT suggested that the therapy demonstrates improvement in only 50%

of cases, and that even fewer of those who show improvement (about 33%) move into the nondistressed range of functioning (Jacobson et al., 1984). The addition of CT to BCT has been shown to be superior to minimal treatment controls (Baucom & Epstein, 1990). Early studies demonstrating that CT might enhance behavioral therapy for couples (Margolin & Weiss, 1978) were not supported by later findings (Baucom & Epstein, 1990). Jacobson and Christensen (1996) hypothesized that the addition of acceptance components would improve the effectiveness and generalizability of BCT. Preliminary investigations into this theory have shown promise for the model. Couples treated with IBCT, compared with those treated with BCT, have been shown to interact differently over time, expressing softer emotions and being less blaming of their partner (Cordova, Jacobson, & Christensen, 1998). A study of 21 couples randomly assigned to either BCT or IBCT (Jacobson, Christensen, Prince, Cordova, & Eldridge, 2000) demonstrated that both husbands and wives receiving IBCT reported greater increases in marital satisfaction than those receiving BCT.

Currently, a large multisite study is underway at the University of California–Los Angeles and at the University of Washington comparing traditional BCT and integrative couple therapy. As mentioned earlier, few studies have specifically included gay and lesbian couples. Assumptions regarding the effectiveness of these techniques with gay and lesbian couples are extrapolated from the literature that demonstrates few differences between same-gender and heterosexual couples. Future research should include same-gender couples in samples approximate to the number of same-gender couples in the general population. Non-White same-gender couples and same-gender couples from mixed racial, ethnic, and religious backgrounds should also be included to improve understanding of therapeutic complexities involving these populations. At this point, we assume that therapists can successfully conduct standard cognitive or cognitive-behavioral therapy with same-gender couples, provided they free themselves from adherence to heterosexist beliefs when working with this population.

Cognitive and behavior therapies have been demonstrated to be useful with couples. Three specific methodologies—BCT, CT, and IBCT—all have empirical support. Research on gay and lesbian couples demonstrates that there are many similarities to heterosexual couples, although differences have also been discovered that are relevant to couple therapy. Clinicians have relied on data from studies of heterosexual couples when applying cognitive-behavioral techniques to same-gender couples because few data have been collected on these pairs in clinical outcome studies. Researchers have been studying communication styles, relationship longevity, and areas of conflict in same-gender couples since the early 1980s, but the inclusion of sexual orientation as a demographic variable in outcome studies is still needed. Providing that clinicians consider the sociological and cultural differences between same-gender and heterosexual couples, they can use standard, empirically validated techniques. Until future research suggests alternatives, the main requirement is that therapists maintain acceptance of the legitimacy of same-gender unions and be cognizant of these couples' similarities to and differences from heterosexual couples while not relying on stereotypes or unsupported assumptions.

REFERENCES

Allen, M., & Burrell, N. (1996). Comparing the impact of homosexual and heterosexual parents on children: Meta-analysis of existing research. *Journal of Homosexuality, 32*(2), 19–35.

American Psychiatric Association. (1980). *Diagnostic and statistical manual of mental disorders* (3rd ed.). Washington, DC: Author.

American Psychiatric Association. (1994). *Diagnostic and statistical manual of mental disorders* (4th ed.). Washington, DC: Author.

American Psychological Association. (2000). *Guidelines for psychotherapy with lesbian, gay, and bisexual clients.* Washington, DC: Author.

Bandura, A. (1977). *Social learning theory.* Englewood Cliffs, NJ: Prentice-Hall.

Baucom, D. H., & Epstein, N. (1990). *Cognitive-behavioral marital therapy.* New York: Brunner/Mazel.

Baucom, D. H., Shoham, V., Meuser, K. T., Daiuto, A. D., & Stickle, T. R. (1998). Empirically supported couple and family interventions for marital distress and adult mental health problems. *Journal of Consulting and Clinical Psychology, 66,* 53–88.

Beck, A. T. (1988). *Love is never enough.* New York: Harper & Row.

Beck, A. T., Freeman, A., & Associates. (1990). *Cognitive therapy of personality disorders.* New York: Guilford Press.

Beck, A. T., Rush, A. J., Shaw, B. F., & Emery, G. (1979). *Cognitive therapy of depression.* New York: Guilford Press.

Beck, A. T., Ward, C. H., Mendelson, M., Mock, J. E., & Erbaugh, J. K. (1961). An inventory for measuring depression. *Archives of General Psychiatry, 4,* 561–571.

Blasband, D., & Peplau, L. A. (1985). Sexual exclusivity versus openness in gay male couples. *Archives of Sexual Behavior, 14*(5), 395–412.

Blumstein, P., & Schwartz, P. (1983). *American couples.* New York: Morrow.

Brown, L. S. (1995). Therapy with same sex couples: An introduction. In N. S. Jacobson & A. S. Gurman (Eds.), *Clinical handbook of couple therapy* (pp. 274–291). New York: Guilford Press.

Christensen, A., & Heavey, C. L. (1999). Interventions for couples. *Annual Review of Psychology, 50,* 165–190.

Christensen, A., & Jacobson, N. S. (1997). *Frequency and acceptability of partner behavior.* Unpublished questionnaire. (Available from Andrew Christensen, University of California, Department of Psychology, Los Angeles, CA 90095).

Christensen, A., & Jacobson, N. S. (2000). *Reconcilable differences.* New York: Guilford Press.

Cordova, J. V., Jacobson, N. S., & Christensen, A. (1998). Acceptance versus change interventions in behavioral couples therapy: Impact on couples' in-session communication. *Journal of Marriage and Family Counseling, 24*, 437–455.

Cramer, D. (1986). Gay parents and their children: A review of research and practical implications. *Journal of Counseling and Development, 64*, 504–507.

Crawford, I., & Solliday, E. (1996). The attitudes of undergraduate college students toward gay parenting. *Journal of Homosexuality, 30, 63*–77.

Dattilio, F. M., & Padesky, C. A. (1990). *Cognitive therapy with couples.* Sarasota, FL: Professional Resource Exchange.

Dobson, K. S. (1989). A meta-analysis of the efficacy of cognitive therapy for depression. *Journal of Consulting and Clinical Psychology, 57*, 414–419.

Doss, B. A., & Christensen, A. (1999). *Marital couples' reports of partner behavior: Gender differences in frequency and acceptability.* Paper presented at the 33rd annual convention of the Association for Advancement of Behavior Therapy, Toronto, Ontario, Canada.

Fukuyama, M. A., & Ferguson, A. D. (2000). Lesbian, gay, and bisexual people of color: Understanding cultural complexity and managing multiple oppressions. In R. M. Perez, K. A. DeBord, & K. J. Bieschke (Eds.), *Handbook of counseling and psychotherapy with lesbian, gay, and bisexual clients* (pp. 81–105). Washington, DC: American Psychological Association.

Golombok, S., & Tasker, F. (1996). Do parents influence the sexual orientation of their children? Findings from a longitudinal study of lesbian families. *Developmental Psychology, 32, 3*–11.

Gonsiorek, J. C. (1988). Mental health issues of gay and lesbian adolescents. *Journal of Adolescent Health Care, 9*, 114–122.

Gottman, J. M., Levenson, R. W., Swanson, C., Swanson, K., Tyson, R., & Yoshimoto, D. (in press). Observing gay, lesbian and heterosexual couples' relationships: Mathematical modeling of conflict interaction. *Journal of Homosexuality.*

Green, R.-J., Bettinger, M., & Zacks, E. (1996). Are lesbian couples fused and gay male couples disengaged? Questioning gender straightjackets. In J. Laird & R.-J. Green (Eds.), *Lesbians and gays in couples and families: A handbook for therapists* (pp. 185–230). San Francisco: Jossey-Bass.

Greene, B., & Boyd-Franklin, N. (1996a). African American lesbians: Issues in couples therapy. In J. Laird & R.-J. Green (Eds.), *Lesbians and gays in couples and families: A handbook for therapists* (pp. 251–271). San Francisco: Jossey-Bass.

Greene, B., & Boyd-Franklin, N. (1996b). African American lesbian couples: Ethnocultural considerations in psychotherapy. In M. Hill & E. D. Rothblum (Eds.), *Couples therapy: Feminist perspectives* (pp. 49–60). New York: Haworth Press.

Herek, G. M. (1995). Psychological heterosexism in the United States. In A. R. D'Augelli & C. J. Patterson (Eds.), *Lesbian, gay, and bisexual identities over the lifespan: Psychological perspectives* (pp. 321–346). New York: Oxford University Press.

Herek, G. M., & Glunt, E. K. (1995). Identity and community among gay and bisexual men in the AIDS era: Preliminary findings from the Sacramento Men's Health Study. In G. M. Herek & B. Greene (Eds.), *AIDS, identity, and community: The HIV epidemic and lesbian and gay men* (pp. 55–84). Thousand Oaks, CA: Sage.

Iguarta, K. J. (1998). Therapy with lesbian couples: The issues and the interventions. *Canadian Journal of Psychiatry, 43*(4), 391–396.

Jacobson, N. S., & Christensen, A. (1996). *Integrative couple therapy: Promoting acceptance and change.* New York: Norton.

Jacobson, N. S., Christensen, A., Prince, S. E., Cordova, J. V., & Eldridge, K. (2000). Integrative behavioral couple therapy: An acceptance-based, promising new treatment for couple discord. *Journal of Consulting and Clinical Psychology, 68*, 351–355.

Jacobson, N. S., Dobson, K., Fruzzetti, A. E., Schmaling, K. B., & Salusky, S. (1991). Marital therapy as a treatment for depression. *Journal of Consulting and Clinical Psychology, 59*(4). 547–557.

Jacobson, N. S., Follette, W. C., Revenstorf, D., Baucom, D. H., Hahlweg, K., & Margolin, G. (1984). Variability in outcome and clinical significance of behavioral marital therapy: A reanalysis of outcome data. *Journal of Consulting and Clinical Psychology, 52*, 497–504.

Jacobson, N. S., & Gottman, J. M. (1998). *When men batter women: New insights into ending abusive relationships.* New York: Simon & Schuster.

Jacobson, N. S., & Margolin, G. (1979). *Marital therapy: Strategies based on social learning and behavior exchange principles.* New York: Brunner/Mazel.

Kurdek, L. A. (1991). The dissolution of gay and lesbian couples. *Journal of Social and Personal Relationships, 8*(2), 265–278.

Kurdek, L. A. (1992a). Dimensionality of the Dyadic Adjustment Scale: Evidence from heterosexual and homosexual couples. *Journal of Family Psychology, 6*(1), 22–35.

Kurdek, L. A. (1992b). Relationship stability and relationship satisfaction in cohabiting gay and lesbian couples: A prospective longitudinal test of the contextual and interdependence models. *Journal of Social and Personal Relationships, 9*(1), 125–142.

Kurdek, L. A. (1994). Areas of conflict for gay, lesbian and heterosexual couples: What couples argue about influences relationship satisfaction. *Journal of Marriage and the Family, 56*(11), 923–934.

Kurdek, L. A. (1998). Relationship outcomes and their predictors: Longitudinal evidence from heterosexual married, gay cohabiting, and lesbian cohabiting couples. *Journal of Marriage and the Family, 60,* 553–568.

Linehan, M. M. (1993). *Cognitive-behavioral treatment of Borderline Personality Disorder.* New York: Guilford Press.

Margolin, G., & Weiss, R. L. (1978). Comparative evaluation of therapeutic components associated with behavioral marital treatments. *Journal of Consulting and Clinical Psychology, 46,* 1476–1486.

Martell, C. R. (1999). Behavior therapy and sexual minorities: Thoughts on progress and future directions. *Behavior Therapist, 22*(10), 194–195.

McLeod, A., & Crawford, I. (1998). The postmodern family: An examination of the psychosocial and legal perspectives of gay and lesbian parenting. In G. M. Herek (Ed.), *Stigma and sexual orientation: Understanding prejudice against lesbians, gay men, and bisexuals* (pp. 211–222). Thousand Oaks, CA: Sage.

Meyer, I. H., & Dean, L. (1998). Internalized homophobia, intimacy, and sexual behavior among gay and bisexual men. In G. M. Herek (Ed.), *Stigma and sexual orientation: Understanding prejudice against lesbians, gay men, and bisexuals psychological perspectives on lesbian and gay issues* (Vol. 2, pp. 160–186). Thousand Oaks, CA: Sage.

Morales, E. (1996). Gender roles among Latino gay and bisexual men: Implications for family and couple relationships. In J. Laird & R.-J. Green (Eds.), *Lesbians and gays in couples and families: A handbook for therapists* (pp. 272–297). San Francisco: Jossey-Bass.

Nicolosi, J. (1991). *Reparative therapy of male homosexuality.* Northvale, NJ: Aronson.

Pardie, L., & Herb, C. R. (1997). Merger and fusion in lesbian relationships: A problem of diagnosing what's wrong in terms of what's right. *Women and Therapy, 20*(3), 51–61.

Patterson, C. (1996a). Lesbian and gay parenthood. In M. Bornstein (Ed.), *Handbook of parenting* (pp. 255–274). Hillsdale, NJ: Erlbaum.

Patterson, C. (1996b). Lesbian mothers and their children: Findings from the Bay Area Families Study. In J. Laird & R.-J. Green (Eds.), *Lesbians and gays in couples and families: A handbook for therapists* (pp. 420–437). San Francisco: Jossey-Bass.

Persons, J. B. (1989). *Cognitive therapy in practice: A case formulation approach.* New York: Norton.

Prince, S. E., & Jacobson, N. S. (1995). Couple and family therapy for depression. In E. E. Guham & W. R. Leber (Eds.), *Handbook of depression* (pp. 404–424). New York: Guilford Press.

Purcell, D. W., Campos, P. E., & Perilla, J. L. (1996). Therapy with lesbians and gay men: A cognitive behavioral perspective. *Cognitive and Behavioral Practice, 3*(2), 391–415.

Seligman, M. E. P., Abramson, L. Y., Semmel, A., & von Baeyer, C. (1979). Depressive attributional style. *Journal of Abnormal Psychology, 88,* 242–247.

Spanier, G. B. (1976). Measuring dyadic adjustment. *Journal of Marriage and the Family, 38,* 15–28.

Straus, M. A. (1979). Measuring intrafamily conflict and violence: The Conflict Tactics Scale. *Journal of Marriage and the Family, 41,* 75–88.

Straus, M. A., Hamby, S. L., Boney-McCoy, S., & Sugarman, D. B. (1996). The Revised Conflict Tactics Scale (CTS2): Development and preliminary psychometric data. *Journal of Family Issues, 17*(3), 283–316.

Turkat, I. D. (Ed.). (1985). *Behavioral case formulation.* New York: Plenum Press.

Wilson, E. (1994, August). Gay sex and sexuality. *The Advocate, 661–662,* 16–24.

GROUP PSYCHOTHERAPY

CHAPTER 20

Rational-Emotive-Behavior Group Therapy

WINDY DRYDEN

HISTORY OF RATIONAL-EMOTIVE-BEHAVIOR THERAPY

A brief general overview of the historical development of rational-emotive-behavior therapy (REBT) and its development as an approach to group therapy is presented in this opening section. REBT was originated in 1955 by Albert Ellis, an American clinical psychologist. Ellis was initially trained in psychoanalysis, but was disappointed in the efficacy of this method and its shorter, less intensive variants. After experimenting with other therapeutic approaches in the early 1950s, Ellis created a form of therapy that brought together a number of different strands and blended them into an integrative whole. The two major strands were the Stoic view of Epictetus (1890), enshrined in his famous dictum "People are disturbed not by things, but by their views of things" (cognitive strand), and the behavioral view of John L. Watson (1919) and others that stressed that the best way to overcome fears is to act against them (behavioral strand).

These two strands showed that REBT (known at the time as rational therapy, RT) was one of the first approaches in what is now known as the cognitive-behavioral tradition in psychotherapy. At first, when Ellis presented his ideas to a field dominated by psychoanalytic thinkers and practitioners, he received strong criticism in the form of what can now be seen as predictable attacks from this quarter: that his therapy was too superficial, that it neglected the client's past, that it was too intellectual and diminished the importance of the emotions, and that the relationship that REBT urged its therapists to adopt with their clients completely downplayed the transferential nature of this relationship. Undaunted, Ellis continued to promulgate his ideas in print and at conferences and gradually attracted a growing number of enthusiastic followers and collaborators. At the suggestion of one of these collaborators, Robert Harper, in 1961 Ellis changed the name of his therapeutic approach from rational therapy to rational-emotive therapy (RET). He did this for two reasons: to silence his critics, who wrongly claimed that RT neglected clients' emotions, and to distance his approach from another, albeit lesser known therapeutic approach known as rational therapy that was based on Marxist philosophy.

The twin concepts of rationality and emotion were emphasized in Ellis's first major book-length work on REBT, *Reason and Emotion in Psychotherapy* (Ellis, 1962), which is generally regarded today as a classic work.

Ellis's work came to the fore in the late 1960s and early 1970s when behavior therapists were discovering the importance of cognitive factors (e.g., Lazarus, 1971). However, because of different priorities, Ellis did not grasp an opportunity that could have taken REBT to the forefront of the cognitive-behavioral movement. Behavior therapy has always stressed the importance of undertaking research to test both the validity of theoretical constructs and the efficacy of therapeutic methods, but because Ellis had never held a full-time academic appointment, he did not personally initiate and coordinate a research program to test his ideas.

This opportunity was fully taken by another pioneer in the cognitive-behavioral tradition, Aaron T. Beck, the originator of cognitive therapy. Based full-time in the Department of Psychiatry at the University of Pennsylvania and unencumbered by a clinical caseload, Beck, beginning in the 1960s and continuing into the 1970s and 1980s, initiated and coordinated a research program to test his cognitive theories of depression and anxiety and the efficacy of cognitive therapy for these two disorders. As his work became more widely known, Beck also attracted first-rate young researchers to work with him and, as a consequence, cognitive therapy has attracted far more research funds than REBT has; its reputation within the academic community has advanced accordingly and attracted the scientific attention of some of the world's leading psychotherapy researchers.

By contrast, much REBT research has been conducted by American Ph.D. candidates; when it has been carried out by established researchers, these scientists have lacked the research funds to carry out studies of the caliber of studies by cognitive therapy researchers.

Having said this, there is a substantial REBT research literature that will be reviewed later in this chapter.

Because REBT failed to capitalize on the research opportunities provided by the growing interest in the cognitive-behavioral therapies that occurred in the late 1960s and early 1970s, its development during those years and subsequently has occurred therapeutically. Thus, REBT has been practiced with children, adolescents, and adults experiencing a wide variety of clinical and nonclinical problems in individual therapy, couple therapy, family therapy, and group therapy; the last is the focus of this chapter. In addition, thanks to the training efforts of what is now known as the Albert Ellis Institute for Rational Emotive Behavior Therapy, REBT is now practiced throughout the world.

Another feature of the historical development of REBT has been Ellis's skill at showing how REBT contributes to popular trends of the day in the field of psychotherapy. For example, when the encounter group movement was prominent in the 1960s, Ellis outlined the REBT approach to encounter groups and marathon groups in particular (Ellis, 1969). Later, when various quasitherapeutic organizations like est, Lifespring, and Forum were being promoted as large group intensives, Ellis and his colleagues devised REBT intensives. In the 1980s, when the psychotherapy integration movement was attracting much attention largely because of the efforts of the Society for the Exploration of Psychotherapy Integration, Ellis (1987) wrote an article showing that REBT was indeed an integrative psychotherapeutic approach. In the past decade, constructivist and postmodern perspectives on psychotherapy have come to the fore, and true to form, Ellis (Ellis, 1997; Ellis & Yeager, 1989) wrote significant papers outlining REBT's contribution to both perspectives. Thus, although Ellis has never contributed significantly to the research literature on psychotherapy, he has, almost single-handedly, ensured that the REBT presence was felt whenever a significant trend in psychotherapy took center stage. Even when a trend emerged with which Ellis significantly disagreed (e.g., transpersonal psychotherapy), Ellis, and thus REBT's, voice was to be heard lambasting the trend (Ellis & Yeager 1989). Ellis refers to himself as a propagandist for REBT, and this certainly becomes clear in studying his list of publications. He rarely turns down an invitation to write on this subject, and he has responded to many published criticisms of REBT, whether they have come from outside REBT (e.g., Bernard & DiGiuseppe, 1989) or from within its fold (e.g., Dryden, 1996a).

Amid all this activity, Ellis decided once again to change the name of his therapy. As mentioned earlier, the original approach was called rational therapy and was changed in 1961 to rational-emotive therapy to counter arguments that RT neglected clients' emotions. Then suddenly, in 1993, Ellis decided to change the name again to rational-emotive-behavior therapy to silence critics who claimed, wrongly, that RET neglected clients' behavior. This did nothing to damper Ellis's ardor for spreading the REBT word.

As the above indicates, one of the features of REBT's development over the years has been the indefatigable efforts of its founder, Albert Ellis. Earlier, it was argued that Ellis failed to initiate and coordinate a research program into REBT theory and practice. Instead, he has chosen to promulgate REBT and ensure that its views on significant trends of the day are known. In addition to maintaining a heavy clinical caseload over the years, Ellis has also traveled widely both in North America and throughout the world, giving REBT workshops and presentations, and he regularly serves on the faculty of the Albert Ellis Institute's many training courses both in New York and elsewhere. At the time of this writing, Ellis is 87 and still is active in promulgating REBT. His prediction that he will "die in the saddle" will probably come true.

DEVELOPMENT OF REBT AS AN APPROACH TO GROUP THERAPY

REBT has been practiced in group therapy format in several different ways, but it was Ellis who was the first to run groups based on REBT principles. He did so in 1959, partly at the request of his clients, although at first he was reluctant to do so. His reluctance was based on his experiences of psychoanalytic groups, which he saw as being both ineffective and inefficient. However, when he began to run REBT groups, he quickly saw that his initial reluctance was misplaced. He soon began to run several groups and has done so ever since. Ellis's early groups were what might be called ongoing, semiopen outpatient groups that met once a week. Clients had to commit themselves to the group for a minimum period and had to give the group reasonable notice before leaving it. A new client could join the group, assuming that there was a vacancy and that the necessary commitment was given. Since those early days, REBT group therapy has developed through innovation, and the following formats are currently employed by REBT group therapists:

Ongoing, Semi-Open Outpatient Group

Although most of these groups (described previously) are heterogeneous in composition (in the sense that clients have a variety of different problems), some REBT group therapists run these groups along homogeneous lines, where clients share similar problems (e.g., anxiety or eating disorders).

Time-Limited, Closed, Problem- or Theme-Based Group

By definition, these groups are homogeneous in nature because they are based on a client problem (e.g., anger) or a theme (e.g., developing self-acceptance). The membership of the time-limited group is closed, first, to encourage group cohesion, particularly when there is no set therapeutic curriculum and the group is more open-ended. The second reason is to ensure that the therapeutic curriculum (when the group is based on one) is followed without needless repetition. As illustrated later in this chapter, when this type of group is based on a curriculum, it is important that all clients attend each session because crucial information is presented and applied to each member present. If the group were open, then whenever a new member joined the group, the group therapist would have to begin each session presenting material that would be new to the joining member but well understood by the established members.

REBT Marathon Encounter Groups

In the late 1960s, Ellis (1969) pioneered and ran REBT marathon encounter groups, which shared many of the features of other marathon encounter groups at the time (with their emphases on experiential exercises and person-to-person encounter). These groups also focused on processing participants' beliefs about the many emotion-laden situations they faced during the marathon group and disputed group members' irrational beliefs when they were uncovered, and on encouraging participants to take risks based on rational thinking.

REBT Women's Groups

REBT women's groups were pioneered by Janet Wolfe (1995), who, with sex educator Peggy Kellogg, began to run REBT sexuality groups for women in the early 1970s at the Institute for Rational Living. Later in that decade, Wolfe teamed up with Iris Fodor to run REBT assertiveness training groups for women and since then has run and inspired others to run a host of different REBT women's groups.

Hospital-Based Group REBT Program

In the hospital-based group REBT program, in-clients and day clients attend a group therapy program run on REBT principles. The author is associated with one such program, which offers two REBT-oriented groups a day for clients. Groups may be problem-, skills-, or agenda-based, with specific groups on anxiety, depression, anger/assertion, and dealing with relationships. In skills-based groups, clients are taught how to (1) assess their problems using the ABC framework (discussed in the next section); (2) dispute their irrational beliefs; (3) use a variety of imagery, behavioral, and emotive techniques to weaken their conviction in their irrational beliefs and to strengthen their conviction in their rational beliefs; and (4) confront and overcome obstacles to psychotherapeutic change. In agenda-based groups, clients are all given an opportunity to discuss and deal with specific aspects of their problems.

Problems of Living Large-Scale Group

For many years, Ellis has run what has become known as his "Friday night workshop." During this experience, Ellis interviews (one at a time) two volunteers from an audience of 50, 100, or even more people on one of their "problems in living." After Ellis has worked with the person for about 30 minutes, he invites the audience to comment on the process and to share relevant experiences from their own lives. A lively, but surprisingly therapeutic debate often ensues (Dryden & Backx, 1987).

Rational Emotive Behavior Intensives

In 1983, Ellis devised and began to hold nine-hour-long intensive groups run along REBT lines. These groups are highly structured, divided into the following six learning modules, each lasting 1 hour 15 minutes: The ABCs of REBT and the Disputing of Irrational Beliefs, Perfectionism and Unconditional Self-Acceptance, Dealing with Anger and Rage, Dealing with the Dire Need for Love and Approval, Dealing with Low Frustration Tolerance, Goal Setting and Homework.

Each learning module begins with a short lecture followed by an experiential exercise; it concludes with a period of sharing and feedback on the lecture and the exercise. At the end of the intensive, participants will have been given much valuable information on psychological disturbance and its remediation, taught a number of REBT's major cognitive, emotive, and behavioral techniques, and helped to devise an individualized self-help program based on what they have learned during the intensive.

In addition, REBT has been used in group-based education programs in educational, workplace, and nonclinical settings, as is shown later in this chapter.

THEORETICAL CONSTRUCTS ON WHICH REBT IS BASED

REBT is based on a number of theoretical principles, which can be divided into principles that account for psychological disturbance and its perpetuation, and principles that account for therapeutic change and guide the practice of the therapy.

How REBT Construes Psychological Disturbance and Its Perpetuation

It was mentioned earlier that REBT has roots in Stoic philosophy, and Epictetus' famous dictum was quoted: "People are disturbed not by things, but by their views of things." A reformulation of this Stoic view is at the core of the REBT conceptualization of psychological disturbance. The REBT version is: "People are disturbed, not by things, but by their rigid and extreme views of things." REBT holds that rigid and extreme beliefs are at the core of psychological disturbance, and REBT group therapists encourage group members to challenge and change those irrational beliefs. Group members are encouraged to acquire and develop the type of alternative flexible and nonextreme beliefs (rational beliefs) that are at the core of psychological health.

Irrational Beliefs and Their Rational Alternatives
Irrational beliefs are evaluative ideas that have the following characteristics: They are rigid or extreme, inconsistent with reality, illogical or nonsensical, and yield dysfunctional consequences. On the other hand, rational beliefs have the following characteristics: They are flexible or nonextreme, consistent with reality, logical or sensible, and yield functional consequences. REBT theory posits four irrational beliefs and their rational alternatives.

Demands are rigid ideas that people hold about how things absolutely must or must not be. Demands can be placed on oneself (e.g., "I must do well"), on others (e.g., "You must treat me well"), or on life conditions (e.g., "Life must be fair"). Ellis's view is that of all the irrational beliefs, it is these demands that are at the very core of psychological disturbance. The healthy alternative to a demand is a full preference.

Full preferences are flexible ideas that people hold about how they would like things to be without demanding that they have to be that way. Full preferences can relate to oneself (e.g., "I want to do well, but I don't have to do so"), others (e.g., "I want you to treat me well, but unfortunately, you don't have to do so"), or life conditions (e.g., "I very much want life to be fair, but unfortunately, it doesn't have to be the way I want it to be"). Again, Ellis's position is that of all the rational beliefs, it is these full preferences that are at the very core of psychological health.

Awfulizing beliefs are extreme ideas that people hold as derivatives from their demands when these demands aren't met (e.g., "I must do well and it's terrible if I don't"; "You must treat me well and it's awful when you don't"; "Life must be fair and it's the end of the world when it's not"). An awfulizing belief stems from the demand that things must not be as bad as they are, and is extreme in the sense that the person believes at the time one or more of the following: Nothing could be worse; the event in question is worse than 100% bad; and no good could possibly come from this bad event. The healthy alternative to an awfulizing belief is an anti-awfulizing belief.

Anti-awfulizing beliefs are nonextreme ideas that people hold as derivatives from their full preferences when these full preferences aren't met (e.g., "I want to do well, but I don't have to do so. It's bad if I don't do well, but not terrible"; "I want you to treat me well, but unfortunately you don't have to do so. When you don't treat me well, it's really unfortunate, but not awful"; "I very much want life to be fair, but unfortunately, it doesn't have to be the way I want it to be"). An anti-awfulizing belief stems from the full preference that one would like things not to be as bad as they are, but that doesn't mean that they must not be, and this full preference is nonextreme in the sense that the person believes at the time one or more of the following: Things could always be worse; the event in question is less than 100% bad; and good could come from this bad event.

Low frustration tolerance beliefs are extreme ideas that people hold as derivatives from their demands when these demands aren't met (e.g., "I must do well, and I can't bear it if I don't"; "You must treat me well, and it's intolerable when you don't"; "Life must be fair, and I can't stand it when it's not"). A low frustration tolerance stems from the demand that things must not be as frustrating or uncomfortable as they are, and is extreme in the sense that people believe at the time one or more of the following: They will die or disintegrate if the frustration or discomfort continues to exist; they will lose the capacity to experience happiness if the frustration or discomfort continues to exist; and the frustration or discomfort is not worth tolerating. The healthy alternative to a low frustration tolerance belief is a high frustration tolerance belief.

High frustration tolerance beliefs are nonextreme ideas that people hold as derivatives from their full preferences when these full preferences aren't met (e.g., "I want to do well, but I don't

have to do so. When I don't do well, it is difficult to bear, but I can bear it and it's worth bearing"; "I want you to treat me well, but unfortunately, you don't have to do so. When you don't treat me well, it's really hard to tolerate, but I can tolerate it and it's worth it to me to do so"; "I very much want life to be fair, but unfortunately, it doesn't have to be the way I want it to be. If life is unfair, that's hard to stand, but I can stand it and it is in my best interests to do so"). A high frustration tolerance belief stems from the full preference that it is undesirable when things are as frustrating or uncomfortable as they are, but unfortunately, things don't have to be different. It is nonextreme in the sense that the person believes at the time one or more of the following: I will struggle if the frustration or discomfort continues to exist, but I will neither die nor disintegrate; I will not lose the capacity to experience happiness if the frustration or discomfort continues to exist, although this capacity will be temporarily diminished; and the frustration or discomfort is not worth tolerating.

Depreciation beliefs are extreme ideas that people hold about themselves, others, and the world as derivatives from these demands when these demands aren't met (e.g., "I must do well and I am a failure if I don't"; "You must treat me well and you are a bad person if you don't"; "Life must be fair and the world is bad if it isn't"). A depreciation belief stems from the demand that I, you, or things must be as I want them to be. It is extreme in the sense that the person believes at the time one or more of the following: One can legitimately be given a single global rating that defines one's essence rated, and one's worth is dependent on conditions that change (e.g., my worth goes up when I do well and goes down when I don't do well; the world can legitimately be given a single rating that defines its essential nature, and the value of the world varies according to what happens within it (e.g., the value of the world goes up when something fair occurs and goes down when something unfair happens); one can be rated on the basis of a single personal aspect; and the world can be rated on the basis of one of its aspects. The healthy alternative to a depreciation belief is an acceptance belief.

Acceptance beliefs are nonextreme ideas that people hold as derivatives from their full preferences when these full preferences aren't met (e.g., "I want to do well, but I don't have to do so; when I don't do well, I am not a failure: I am a fallible human being who is not doing well on this occasion"; "I want you to treat me well, but unfortunately, you don't have to do so. When you don't treat me well, you are not a bad person, but a fallible human being who is treating me poorly"; "I very much want life to be fair, but unfortunately, it doesn't have to be the way I want it to be. If life is unfair, it is only unfair in this respect and doesn't prove that the world is a rotten place. The world is a complex place where many good, bad, and neutral things happen"). An acceptance is nonextreme in the sense that the person believes at the time one or more of the following: One cannot legitimately be given a single global rating that defines one's essence, and one's worth is not dependent on conditions that change (e.g., my worth stays the same whether or not I do well; the world cannot legitimately be given a single rating that defines its essential nature, and the value of the world does not vary according to what happens within it (e.g., the value of the world stays the same whether fairness exists or not); it makes sense to rate discrete aspects of a person and of the world, but it does not make sense to rate a person or the world entirely on the basis of these discrete aspects.

The Effects of Irrational Beliefs and Their Rational Alternatives

Holding irrational beliefs about life's adversities has a number of deleterious effects on a person's psychological functioning. First, they lead the person to have one *or more* unhealthy negative emotions, such as anxiety, depression, guilt, shame, hurt, unhealthy anger, unhealthy jealousy, and unhealthy envy. Second, irrational beliefs lead the person to act in a number of self, other-, and relationship-defeating ways. Third, irrational beliefs have an impairing impact on the person's cognitive functioning: They lead the person to think unrealistically about self, others, and the world. For example, irrational beliefs are often the breeding ground for what cognitive therapists call cognitive distortions. Thus, if you believe that you must perform well in public and you think that you haven't, you are likely to think in a variety of distorted ways, for example, mindreading (e.g., "I'm sure that the audience thinks that I made a fool of myself"), overgeneralization ("I'll always do poorly in public situations"), and minimization ("There were no redeeming features to my presentation"). Irrational beliefs also have an effect on the person's attentional and memory systems. Thus, when there is a possibility that a threat may occur to something of value in an individual's personal domain and the person holds an irrational belief about the threat, that person's attention will be drawn to the existence of the threat. The person may then exaggerate the chances that the threat will occur and the nature of the threat itself. Also, when the person has experienced a significant loss to his or her personal domain and holds an irrational belief about this loss, the person will tend to remember other losses rather than the gains that he or she has experienced in life.

By contrast, holding rational beliefs about the same adversities has a number of productive effects on a person's psychological functioning. First, these beliefs lead the person to have healthy negative emotions, such as concern, sadness, remorse, disappointment, sorrow, healthy anger, healthy jealousy, and healthy envy. Second, rational beliefs lead the person to act in a number of self-, other-, and relationship-enhancing ways. Third, rational beliefs have a constructive impact on the person's cognitive functioning; thus, they lead the person to think realistically about self, others, and the world. In particular, this helps the person to accept that good, bad, and neutral things can result from the adversity that he or she is facing.

How Individuals Perpetuate Psychological Disturbance

Once clients have made themselves disturbed, they may easily perpetuate their disturbance in the following ways:

1. By denying that they have disturbed feelings.
2. By failing to take responsibility for their psychological disturbance and thinking that other people or external events cause this disturbance.
3. By thinking that their past has caused their present disturbed feelings and that insight into their past is necessary to change these present feelings.
4. By not realizing that irrational beliefs are at the core of psychological disturbance, and therefore not knowing that psychotherapeutic change is predicated on changing these beliefs.
5. By acting in ways that reinforce their irrational beliefs.
6. By disturbing themselves about their original disturbance.
7. By thinking that identifying their irrational beliefs is sufficient to change them.
8. By thinking that understanding why their irrational beliefs are irrational and why their rational beliefs are rational is sufficient to surrender the former and acquire the latter.
9. By thinking that disputing their irrational beliefs without acting in ways that are consistent with their rational beliefs is sufficient to promote psychological change.
10. By thinking that occasionally acting in ways that are consistent with their rational beliefs is sufficient to effect psychological change.

HOW REBT CONSTRUES PSYCHOTHERAPEUTIC CHANGE

The rational-emotive-behavioral view of the person is basically an optimistic one, because although it posits that humans find it easy to think irrationally about matters that are important to them, REBT also holds that humans have the capacity to choose to work toward changing this irrational thinking and its self-defeating effects, and that the most elegant and long-lasting changes that humans can effect are ones that involve the philosophical restructuring of irrational beliefs. Change at this level can be specific or general. Specific philosophical change means that individuals change their irrational absolutistic demands (musts, shoulds) about given situations to rational relative preferences. General philosophic change involves people adopting a nondevout attitude toward life events in general.

To effect a philosophical change at either the specific or general level, people need to do the following:

1. Realize that, to a large degree, they create their own psychological disturbances, and that although environmental conditions can contribute to their problems, they are generally of secondary consideration in the change process.
2. Recognize that they do have the ability to significantly change these disturbances.
3. Understand that emotional and behavioral disturbances stem largely from irrational, absolutistic, dogmatic beliefs.
4. Detect their irrational beliefs and discriminate between them and their rational alternatives.
5. Dispute these irrational beliefs using the logico-empirical methods of science.
6. Work toward the internalization of their new rational beliefs by employing cognitive, emotive, and behavioral methods of change; in particular, ensuring that their behavior is consistent with their rational beliefs.

7. Continue this process of challenging irrational beliefs and using multimodal methods of change for the rest of their lives.

When people effect a philosophic change at B in the ABC model, they often are able to spontaneously correct their distorted inferences of reality (overgeneralizations, faulty attributions, etc.) that can be viewed as cognitions (Wessler & Wessler, 1980). However, they often need to challenge these distorted inferences more directly, as REBT has always emphasized (e.g., Ellis, 1962) and as cognitive therapists more recently have also stressed (Beck, Rush, Shaw, & Emery, 1979). REBT therapists hypothesize that people are more likely to make a profound philosophical change if they first assume that their inferences are true and then challenge their irrational beliefs, rather than if they first correct their inferential distortions and then challenge their underlying irrational beliefs. However, this hypothesis requires full empirical inquiry.

People can also make direct changes of the situation at A. Thus, rather than changing one's cognitions about a negative activating event, one could remove oneself from the event, directly change it in some way, or distract oneself from it by focusing on a different aspect of the event or on another event entirely.

People can change their behavior to effect inferential and/or philosophical change. Thus, one could change one's behavior to elicit a different (more positive) response from someone who was acting in a negative way toward one. In this way, one could change the A and/or form a new, more positive inference about A. When one changes one's behavior to promote philosophic change, it is important to actually face the negative event at A to give oneself the opportunity of thinking rationally in the face of this negative event.

REBT therapists prefer to help their clients make profound philosophical changes at B, but they do not dogmatically insist that their clients make such changes. If it becomes apparent that clients are not able to change their irrational beliefs, REBT therapists endeavor to help them either to change A directly (by avoiding the troublesome situation or by behaving differently) or to change their distorted inferences about the situation.

VIEW ON THE THERAPEUTIC RELATIONSHIP

REBT offers a very definite view on the practice of therapy with respect to the therapeutic relationship, therapist style, and therapeutic intervention. In dealing with this topic here, group therapy is specifically addressed.

The optimal relationship between therapist and client in REBT is one of informed allies. Ideally, the client should be informed about REBT, its mode of practice in group therapy, and the client's role as a group member, and, of course, the therapist should be informed about his or her role. As allies, they will share an understanding of and agree to pursue the client's goals for change, they will implement their roles in carrying out activities to facilitate goal achievement, and they will have a suitably well-bonded relationship that will enable these activities to be carried out smoothly and skillfully. The hallmarks of this relationship are that clients experience the therapist as understanding of their feelings and of the roots of their problems, genuine in the therapeutic encounter, and accepting of them as a fallible human being. The REBT view is that these core conditions are desirable, rather than necessary or sufficient, for client change to occur. They are important to the extent that they help both parties to engage productively in the tasks of REBT. This, of course, is an ideal picture; in reality, there will be many threats to this relationship that need to be dealt with if client change is to occur (Ellis, 1985; Neenan & Dryden, 1996).

The picture is complicated in group therapy, where it is important that members experience one another as empathic, genuine, and accepting of one another and that they help each other engage in the tasks of REBT (an example of this point is clearly demonstrated in the first illustrative case, described later in the chapter). When client noncooperation is apparent, the group therapist will help particular clients to see the irrational beliefs they hold that are interfering with their cooperative participation in the group process. But, as will be discussed later, the dominant focus in the group is on members' problems in their daily lives outside the group, rather than on their relationships with one another within the group.

VIEW ON THERAPIST STYLE

The preferred therapist style in group REBT is active-directive. The therapist is active in interventions and directs group members to the irrational beliefs that underpin their disturbed feelings and unconstructive behavior. REBT can be seen as an educational approach to psychotherapy in that the group therapist teaches group members the REBT model of disturbance and psychotherapeutic change and invites them to use this model to understand and address their psychological problems. As such, Ellis sees effective REBT group therapists as being authoritative (but not authoritarian) teachers who are clear communicators and who help group members understand how they disturb themselves and what they can do to undisturb themselves. In doing so, effective REBT group therapists use either Socratic and didactic teaching methods or a mixture of the two, depending on the learning style of individual clients.

REBT group therapists tend to favor an informal therapeutic style characterized by the discriminate use of humor and self-disclosure. However, they are prepared to vary their style according to the group member with whom they are working. Still, REBT group therapists take their roles very seriously. This is demonstrated by the rigorous way they focus on their main

therapeutic task: to help group members overcome their psychological problems by identifying, challenging, and changing their irrational beliefs and to act in ways that are consistent with their developing rational beliefs.

VIEW ON GROUP THERAPEUTIC INTERVENTION

REBT group therapy is a structured process in which the therapist ensures that all group members are given an opportunity to discuss their problems. Some REBT therapists emulate their cognitive therapy colleagues and set an agenda at the beginning of the group session to facilitate structured interaction and to help with time allocation. This emphasis on individual attention occurs in all REBT groups, with the exception of the Problems in Living workshops and the REBT intensives (described earlier), which are both too large to permit such attention. Because every group member is given individual attention, the REBT view is that this process is best facilitated at the outset by the therapist. Thus, the early interaction is between the group therapist and the individual group member discussing his or her problem. After a while, other group members make their points either of their own accord or at the suggestion of the therapist, who might say something like "Who would like to comment on what Bill has just said?" or "What does the group think of what Brenda has just said?" Thus, much of the REBT group process is taken up by "therapy in the group" interactions (between group member and group therapist) and "therapy by the group" interactions (between a group member and other group members). However, even in the latter interactions, the group therapist plays a gatekeeping role, ensuring that unhelpful interactions are kept to a minimum.

This gatekeeping role of the REBT therapist is a central one and warrants further consideration. It often happens, for example, when group members are endeavoring to help a particular member whose problem is under discussion, that they either give that person practical advice on how to solve the problem or offer the group member a different perspective with which to view the situation. Assuming the gatekeeping role, the REBT group therapist listens carefully to the advice or perspective being offered and intervenes to correct bad or damaging advice and unhelpful perspectives (if other group members do not do this first). The therapist then assists the whole group as well as the particular group member to see the belief core of the latter's problem while the sensible aspects of the advice or perspective are being put forward. Here is an example of the latter:

Stephen, one of the group members, has been discussing his feelings of guilt about hurting his mother's feelings.

STEPHEN: So, that sums it up. I'm guilty about saying no to my mother because I might hurt her feelings.

BRUCE: But, you don't hurt your mother's feelings. She hurts her own feelings by the beliefs that she holds about you saying no to her.

THERAPIST (after a pause to see who would take up Bruce's point):   That's a valid perspective, Bruce, but that won't help Stephen get over his problem of guilt.

BRUCE: Why won't it?

THERAPIST: Can anybody see why it won't?

MARY: Because Stephen thinks that he can hurt his mother's feelings.

BRUCE (jumping in):   When he can't, which is the point I made earlier.

THERAPIST (deciding to make the point himself because he doesn't think that any other group member will):   But in REBT, we start by assuming temporarily that Stephen can and indeed has hurt his mother's feelings. We do this because doing so helps us to identify, challenge, and change his underlying irrational beliefs that lead to his guilt. Then, Stephen will be over his feelings of guilt and in a better frame of mind to

discuss whether he can or cannot hurt his mother's feelings.

The point has been made in this section that therapy takes place in the group by the therapist and by the group members working with one another. In contrast, there is little emphasis on "therapy of the group" interventions that tend to occur in *some* (but not in all) forms of psychodynamic group therapy. Here, the therapist's task is to observe the overall functioning of the group and to make interpretations of the observed phenomena based on a theoretical (psychoanalytical) understanding of what goes on in such groups. The focus is on the group as a whole and not on the problems of individual group members. By contrast, in REBT group therapy, the definite emphasis is on these problems.

METHODS OF ASSESSMENT AND INTERVENTION

In this section, methods and issues concerning assessment of clients who are suitable for different REBT groups are discussed and exclusion criteria that help to ensure that unsuitable clients are not placed in these groups are outlined. The major interventions used are also described.

ASSESSMENT

Assessment for REBT group therapy has two main purposes. First, assessment is done for therapeutic purposes, when the key issue concerns placing the client in a group because it is considered that REBT group therapy (in one of its formats) is the treatment of choice for the individual concerned. Here, the emphasis is on inclusive criteria. Second, assessment is done primarily for pragmatic purposes. At the Albert Ellis Institute, REBT groups are run largely for pragmatic purposes, such as for financial reasons or to reduce long waiting lists. The emphasis is on exclusion criteria, such as clients being assigned to REBT group therapy unless there is a good reason not to do so.

The chief way of assessing clients' suitability for REBT groups is by interview, where the client's problems are identified, views on therapy are determined, and the nature of REBT groups is explained. This interview is an assessment interview and not a therapy interview, as no therapeutic interventions are made. However, the Albert Ellis Institute requires that prospective group clients have at least one session of individual therapy to determine the individual's reaction to REBT interventions, particularly when they are made in a group session. Whichever type of interview is preferred, the purpose is to include or exclude that person from group REBT.

Inclusion Criteria
The following are criteria to include a client in a REBT group:

1. *The person wishes to join a REBT group.* Clients understand the REBT approach to their problems and think that it will be helpful to them, especially in a group session.
2. *The person is able to participate constructively in a structured group.* Clients are able and willing to focus on specific problems and discuss these in a group setting; to share therapeutic time with other group members; to help other group members as well as be helped by them.
3. *The person prefers a structured approach to address problems and wishes to have some time allocated every session to a discussion of them.* In some other approaches to group therapy, time is devoted each session to a discussion of the problems of a small number of group members; this discussion is relatively unstructured. This approach

suits some clients, but it does not suit others. Those who prefer a more structured approach (where they have an opportunity every session to discuss their problems) are good candidates for REBT group therapy.
4. *The person's problems are particularly suited to a group approach.* For clients being assessed for a time-limited, closed, problem- or theme-based group, it is important that they have the target problem. Clients must want help for the problem and be willing to put other problems on the "back burner" or deal with these problems in concurrent individual therapy. Clients being assessed for an ongoing, semiopen, outpatient group can have a variety of problems. Interpersonal problems lend themselves particularly to this type of group because such problems become manifest in the group interaction and can be explored in the here and now. Membership of a heterogeneous, ongoing, semiopen outpatient group is determined more by exclusion factors with respect to presenting problems (see following text) than inclusion factors.

Exclusion Criteria
The following are considered to be sound reasons to exclude a client from joining a REBT group:

1. *The person does not wish to join a REBT group.* Sometimes, clients are referred for REBT group therapy by a consultant psychiatrist who has made the referral without explaining the nature of this approach. When this group is explained to them, they indicate that they do not wish to join such a group.
2. *It is predicted that the person will not be able to make therapeutic use of the structured nature of group REBT.* Some individuals appear too undisciplined, talkative, or manic to use the structured ABC framework of

problem assessment or intervention, to respond to other group members, or to listen silently and attentively when other group members are discussing their problems.

3. *The person is likely to be too withdrawn to participate.* Clients who are autistic, schizoid, or severely socially anxious are likely to respond to the interactive nature of REBT group therapy by withdrawing and not participating. Such clients who do join the group usually drop out when they are confronted (even gently) by other group members concerning their nonparticipation.

4. *The person is unable to share therapeutic time with other group members.* Sometimes, clients are too demanding of the therapist's time to participate constructively in a structured REBT group, where the amount of time that can be allocated to any one member is limited. Such clients often respond unconstructively to this fact of REBT group culture and are best seen in individual therapy until they can share therapeutic time with others.

5. *The person does not want to help others.* Membership in a therapy group is predicated on the notion that the members have some interest in helping others as well as being helped by them. Some clients, however, though interested in being helped by the group therapist and by the other group members, have no interest in helping others. Consequently, they are not good candidates for REBT group therapy until they develop such an interest.

6. *The person is likely to be too hostile or too impatient to be a cooperative group member.* Clients whose anger problem makes them likely to respond with overt hostility to attempts by the group leader or by group members to cooperate with the structured nature of the REBT group process are not good candidates for this type of group therapy, nor are clients who are inordinately impatient and find it extraordinarily difficult to wait their turn to discuss a problem or to remain attentive to others when they have had their turn.

7. *The nature of the client's problem means that group REBT is contraindicated.* Not all client problems can be productively responded to in REBT group therapy. For example, those with severe Posttraumatic Stress Disorder (PTSD) are not good candidates for group REBT because they need extended sessions of individual therapy to ensure sufficient imaginal exposure to enable emotional processing to occur. The exception to this is where the group is devoted to the treatment of specific types of PTSD, in which case, a group protocol can be devised for the treatment of this problem. For other client problems, the presence of other group members may inhibit self-disclosure to the extent that the therapist does not get a full enough picture to help the person.

It may happen that the assessment does not reveal that a client is unsuitable for REBT group therapy and this turns out to be the case after the person joins the group. When this happens, clients are shown how to be more effective members of the group. If this does not work, they are told that they will have to leave the group and enter individual REBT until they can function effectively in the group setting.

INTERVENTION

As stressed earlier, REBT group therapy interventions are largely therapist-led, at least until group members have learned how to use REBT with one another. Then the therapist increasingly takes a back seat, serving as a consultant to the group and intervening (1) when it becomes apparent that group members are off track in their attempts to help a particular member with a problem; (2) when members give poor or damaging advice or suggest un-helpful homework assignments; and (3) when members focus only on the practical aspects of the person's problem, overlooking its psycho-logical aspects (particularly the person's irra-tional beliefs).

When the therapist does intervene, it is usu-ally to direct a group member's attention to his or her irrational beliefs and how the member can challenge and change them. In doing so, the therapist chooses among various methods.

ABC Framework Analysis

When individual group members discuss a problem, the therapist will give them a brief time to discuss it in their own way, but will then encourage them to give a specific example of this problem and to analyze this event using REBT's ABC framework: A = Activating event (the aspect of the situation that the group mem-ber was most disturbed about); B = irrational beliefs about A; and C = emotional, behavioral, and thinking consequences of B. The ABC framework helps structure group members' discussion of their problems; without this framework, members might ramble and use group time unproductively.

Disputing Specific and Core Irrational Beliefs

After helping individual members to assess their problems, the therapist takes the lead to help them dispute their irrational beliefs. Ini-tially, group members are helped to dispute specific irrational beliefs (held in specific situa-tions about specific As). Later in the group pro-cess, members are helped to dispute their core irrational beliefs (held about a variety of situa-tions, e.g., thinking they have been rejected).

As DiGiuseppe (1991) noted, disputing irra-tional beliefs involves the group therapist (in the first instance) asking individual members whether their irrational beliefs (specific and core) are true or false, logical or illogical, and functional or dysfunctional and to provide reasons for their responses. A discussion then ensues in which the therapist and other group members engage the person in a debate about these beliefs until the person understands that these irrational beliefs are false, illogical, and dysfunctional and that his or her rational alter-native beliefs are true, logical, and functional.

Homework Assignments

Unless group members act on their new rational belief, they will not truly believe them and the new belief will not influence their emotions; thus, their behavior and thinking will not im-prove. Consequently, a feature of REBT groups is the homework assignment, where members resolve to capitalize on the therapeutic work they have done in the group session by doing something between sessions. The following are common homework assignments suggested in REBT group therapy:

Bibliotherapy: Group members read REBT-based self-help material to help them better understand a rational concept and how to im-plement it in their own life.

Cognitive homework: Group members use one of a number of cognitively oriented written homework forms to practice disputing their irrational beliefs and to deepen their convic-tion in rational beliefs.

Emotive homework: Group members practice one or more emotive techniques to deepen conviction in their rational beliefs, such as using forceful, rational self-statements, dis-puting on audiotape their irrational defenses of their irrational beliefs, and using rational-emotive imagery to rehearse their rational beliefs while vividly imagining negative events at A about which they usually disturb themselves.

Behavioral-cognitive homework: Clients rehearse their rational beliefs while acting in ways that are consistent with them. The conjoint use of behavioral and cognitive techniques, where clients face negative activating events, practice thinking rationally in the face of such events, and refrain from doing anything to feel comfortable in the moment, is the most potent homework assignment used by REBT group therapists.

Correcting Cognitive Distortions

Cognitive distortions are negative, unrealistic ways of making sense of situations that we face and the implications of facing them. They include distorted inferences of events at A (in the ABC framework) and distorted cognitive consequences at C of irrational beliefs at B. Examples of cognitive distortions at A include "My boss will fire me"; "People will laugh at me if I make a mistake in my presentation tomorrow"; and "My sister hates me for doing well on the test." Although these inferences may be true, they are distorted in the absence of evidence supporting them. Examples of cognitive distortions (shown in italics) at C include always/never thinking (*"I will never get another job* when my boss fires me"); magnification ("People who laugh at my mistake at the presentation *will tell others and everyone will know that I made a fool of myself"*), and overgeneralization ("Because my sister hates me for doing well on the test, *everyone will hate me when I do well"*). Again, these thoughts are distorted in the absence of supporting evidence.

REBT argues that cognitive distortions at A and C largely stem from irrational beliefs; therefore, it is best to help group members to dispute their irrational beliefs before helping them to correct these distortions. Indeed, REBT group therapists often have to intervene with other members who rush in to correct their fellow group members' cognitive distortions instead of helping them first to dispute their irrational beliefs. Correcting cognitive distortions involves asking members to adopt an objective standpoint and provide evidence for and against their (distorted) thoughts at A and those at C. It also involves asking clients to form more realistic inferences at A and more realistic cognitive consequences at C.

As stated earlier, REBT group therapists first target irrational beliefs for change before disputing cognitive distortions. They do this because disputing group members' irrational beliefs helps them to adopt the objective standpoint necessary to correct their cognitive distortions. However, because REBT is a flexible approach to therapy, there may be times when the therapist will target cognitive distortions for change before disputing irrational beliefs.

Skill Training and Role-Play Methods

Skill training methods can be used when group members have various skill deficits. The group is particularly useful when these deficits are interpersonal in nature (e.g., assertion, dating, and conversational skills) because other group members who are competent in these skills can give advice and can serve as good models in role-play scenarios. Then the member is given the opportunity to practice the targeted skill with one of the other group members playing a significant other.

Role-play methods can also be used to encourage members to rehearse a behavioral-cognitive homework assignment before putting it into practice between sessions. Other members play relevant people in the group member's real life. The main purpose of role play is to give group members practice at skill development and rehearsal of relevant behaviors, and the feedback that participants give one another at the end of role plays and skill practice scenarios can be particularly therapeutic. Throughout the skill practice sessions and role-play scenarios, the therapist is alert for the presence of any irrational beliefs that may be impeding the group; when these are found, they are disputed after the scenario has finished.

Role-play methods can also be used to help group members strengthen their conviction in their rational beliefs. Thus, a person can play the role of his or her "rational self" while the other group members can, one at a time, play the role of his or her "irrational self" and encourage the person to think irrationally. The group member's task is to persuasively respond to these irrational attacks. The therapist intervenes to keep the exercise on track and to prevent other group members from overwhelming the targeted member with too many arguments.

Advice Giving and Problem Solving

Group members give much advice during the REBT group process. Indeed, if left to the members themselves, advice giving would be their most frequently used group intervention. Given this reality, the REBT group therapist is vigilant when such advice is given and intervenes to counter bad and potentially damaging advice. The therapist helps the member concerned to focus instead on identifying, challenging, and changing the irrational beliefs that underpin his or her psychological problem, and then encourages the member to engage in practical problem solving instead. This involves the group member clarifying the practical problem to be solved, brainstorming possible solutions, evaluating each solution, choosing the best one, and overcoming obstacles to implementing the chosen solution. The other members are encouraged to play an active role in this process, which is overseen by the therapist.

CURRICULUM OF A TIME-LIMITED, CLOSED, THEME-BASED GROUP

In this section, a curriculum of a 10-session educationally based self-acceptance group run over 10 weeks is outlined from the point of view of the group therapist's tasks (Dryden, 1996b).

Session 1: Why Self-Acceptance and Not Self-Esteem

Ask group members to introduce themselves to the group; explain any guidelines that you want group members to follow; consider the concept of self-esteem and its disadvantages; consider the concept of self-acceptance and its advantages; stress the value of homework assignments; assign the first task (see relevant chapters in Dryden, 1999, which review the ideas covered in this session).

Session 2: Goals and Problem Assessment

Review the previous week's homework assignment; set goals with group members; analyze a specific example of self-depreciation for each group member using the ABC framework; set the next homework assignment (this asks group members to identify and analyze another situation in which they depreciated themselves using the ABC framework).

Session 3: Questioning Demands, Self-Depreciation Beliefs, and Their Healthy Alternatives

Review the previous week's homework assignment; teach group members how to question their demands and related self-depreciation beliefs as well as the healthy alternatives to these beliefs; assign homework designed to help group members practice their new questioning skills.

Session 4: The Rational Portfolio Method

Review the previous week's homework assignment; teach the rational portfolio technique (a technique requiring group members to devise as many arguments as they can, outlining why their demands and self-depreciation beliefs are irrational and why their full preferences and self-acceptance beliefs are rational); set the next homework task (completion of a single rational portfolio).

Session 5: The Zig-Zag Technique and Explaining the Nature of Belief Change

Review the previous week's homework assignment; teach the zigzag technique (a technique to strengthen rational beliefs by responding to self-made attacks on them); explain the nature of belief change; set the next homework task; conduct a midgroup review.

Session 6: Three Emotive Techniques to Facilitate Change

Review the previous week's homework assignment; teach group members a number of techniques, such as the taperecorded version of the zigzag technique, the use of forceful self-statements, and rational-emotive imagery, all designed to help them further weaken their conviction in their irrational beliefs and strengthen conviction in their rational beliefs; set the next homework tasks (to practice the three techniques taught in the session).

Session 7: The Conjoint Use of Cognitive and Behavioral Techniques

Review the previous week's homework tasks; provide a rationale for the conjoint use of behavioral and cognitive techniques; set the next homework task (this involves the conjoint use of behavioral and cognitive techniques); teach mental rehearsal of behavioral-cognitive tasks; identify and overcome obstacles to carrying out behavioral-cognitive tasks.

Session 8: More Cognitive-Behavioral Tasks and Shame-Attacking Exercises

Review the previous week's homework task; set other behavioral-cognitive tasks as a homework assignment; provide a rationale for shame-attacking exercises (i.e., to practice accepting oneself for doing something "shameful" in public), and suggest that group members carry out one such task as an additional assignment.

Session 9: Distorted Inferences: How to Challenge These Products of Irrational Beliefs

Review the previous week's homework tasks; teach the group the effect of beliefs on the way they think; teach the group how to challenge distorted inferences; set the next homework

assignment (list of strengths and weaknesses while in a self-accepting frame of mind).

Session 10: Ending, Evaluation, and Beyond

Review the previous week's homework task; evaluate the progress made by each group member; give members the self-acceptance quiz; elicit feedback from group members on the group; help group members to maintain and extend their gains.

MAJOR SYNDROMES, SYMPTOMS, AND PROBLEMS TREATED

In the final section of this chapter, the empirical status of REBT as a therapeutic approach is briefly reviewed, drawing on research reviews on this model. Unfortunately, there are no reviews of the effectiveness of REBT group therapy, but because research shows that group therapy is at least as effective as individual therapy (Bergin & Garfield, 1994), there is no reason to suppose that this will be different for REBT.

REBT group therapy is a useful therapeutic arena for clients with a variety of syndromes, symptoms, and problems. To illustrate this variety, Table 20.1 lists relevant articles on REBT group therapy that have been published in the journal sponsored over the years by the Albert Ellis Institute for REBT, originally known as *Rational Living* (1966–1983), subsequently called the *Journal of Rational-Emotive Therapy* (1983–1987) and then the *Journal of Rational-Emotive and Cognitive-Behavior Therapy* (1988-present). This list is illustrative rather than comprehensive.

As can be seen in Table 20.1, group REBT has been used with a broad variety of problems and syndromes as well as with a broad client population. As with many other group treatments, REBT group therapy is best suited to those who are able to share time with the group therapist, who can concentrate on the problems of others

Table 20.1 Articles on REBT group therapy, 1966–1998.

Rational Living

- 1966: Group therapy with hospitalized psychotic clients (Gullo, 1966).
- 1967: Group therapy with alcoholics (Sherman, 1967).
- 1972: Group therapy with unselected outpatient psychiatric clients (Maultsby, Stiefel, & Brodsky, 1972).
- 1973: A structured approach to group counseling with couples with marriage problems (McClellan & Stieper, 1973).
- 1974: Group therapy with university students with speech anxiety problems (Straatmayer & Watkins, 1974).
- 1976: Group therapy with elementary school students with test anxiety (Warren, Deffenbacher, & Brading, 1976).
- 1977: REBT group therapy with clients in a partial hospitalization setting (Lefkovitz & Davis, 1977).

Journal of Rational-Emotive Therapy

- 1984: Group therapy with non-assertive university students (Thorpe, Freedman, & McGalliard, 1984).
- 1985: Structured group therapy with clients with low self-esteem (Ponzoha & Warren, 1985).
  Group therapy with high school females with bulimia (Harvill, 1985).
- 1987: Group therapy with a "mixed" population of psychiatric inpatients: Neurotic, psychotic and adjustment disorder (Jacobsen, Tamkin, & Blount, 1987).
  Rational behavior problem solving as a group career development intervention for persons with mental and physical disabilities (Farley, 1987).

Journal of Rational-Emotive and Cognitive-Behavior Therapy

- 1988: Group therapy with women with mid-life transition or "empty-nest" problems (Oliver, 1988).
  Group therapy with clients with divorce-related dysphoria (Malouff, Lanyon, & Schutte, 1988).
  REBT in a group-based therapeutic community with clients with substance abuse problems (Yeager, DiGiuseppe, Olsen, Lewis, & Alberti, 1988).
- 1989: Group therapy with women with premenstrual syndrome (Morse, Bernard, & Dennerstein, 1989).
  Group therapy with university students with interpersonal anxiety (Vestre & Judge, 1989).
- 1990: Group therapy with clients with social anxiety (DiGiuseppe, McGowan, Sutton Simon, & Gardner, 1990).
- 1992: An REBT group therapy-based inpatient program with clients with major depression and a variety of personality disorders (Nottingham & Neimeyer, 1992).
- 1993: Education-based REBT training groups in the workplace (Grieger & DiMattia, 1993).
  Group therapy for preventing and coping with stress among safety officers (Kushnir & Malkinson, 1993).
  Group therapy with Conduct Disorder and Attention-Deficit Hyperactivity Disorder adolescents (Morris, 1993).
- 1995: A group-based parent education program with nonclinical parents (Joyce, 1995).
  REBT women's groups (Wolfe, 1995).
- 1995: Group therapy with a variety of offenders (Bernard, 1995).
- 1997: Group-based stress management with clients with chronic fatigue syndrome (Balter & Unger, 1997).
  Group therapy with post-stroke clients (Alvarez, 1997).
  Group-based parent education for stressed mothers of young children with Down Syndrome (Greaves, 1997).
- 1998: REBT group therapy and problem solving with children with social skills deficits (Flanagan, Povall, Dellino, & Byrne, 1998).
  Group therapy to increase the performance of high school students in mathematics (Shannon & Allen, 1998).

as well as their own, and who are willing to help others as well as receive help themselves. Effective REBT group therapy, then, requires clients who are free from severe psychiatric disturbance.

CASE EXAMPLES

In this section, the practice of REBT group therapy is presented through an excerpt from an ongoing, semiopen outpatient group and by presenting the curriculum of a time-limited, closed, theme-based group. This group has eight members and one therapist (the author). It has been meeting for three months, and each session lasts for two hours. The practice in running this type of group is to set an agenda at the beginning of the session so that it is known at the outset what each group member is intending to discuss. It is also common to encourage all group members to discuss an issue in each group session; each person in the group has about 15 minutes to discuss an agenda item and to report back briefly the homework assignment. In this excerpt, Norman is explaining why he hasn't done his homework assignment, which was to speak to Sarah, a woman he is interested in romantically but whom he is anxious about approaching.

NORMAN: . . . So I was too busy to seek out Sarah this week, but things are easier for me next week, so I'll do it then.

FREDA: Norman, I don't buy that. You said you were too busy, but earlier, when speaking to Steve, you said that you also spent a lot of time surfing the Net this week.

STEVE: That's right, Norman, you did say that. Admit it, you copped out.

NORMAN: All right, I copped out.

FREDA: Why did you cop out?

NORMAN: Because I was scared to talk to Sarah.

KATE: But, we discussed the reasons why you were scared last week.

NORMAN: I guess I forgot what those reasons were.

STEVE: I remember what they were. You're scared of talking to Sarah because you tell yourself that you . . .

THERAPIST (interrupting): Hold on, Steve, you're making life a bit too easy for Norman. Let him figure out why he's scared. Well, Norman, what's the famous question that I suggest people ask themselves when they're feeling disturbed?

(One of the roles of the REBT group therapist is to ensure that group members don't "rescue" other group members. "Doing the work" for a group member when that member is capable of doing that work for himself or herself is one way of "rescuing" that member.)

NORMAN: What am I demanding?

THERAPIST: That's right, so what were you demanding about speaking to Sarah that led you to put off speaking to her?

NORMAN: Sarah must not reject me.

THERAPIST: That's right. Now, how can you challenge that demand?

(Norman goes on to challenge his demand. His full preference and the self-acceptance belief that is derived from it are: "I don't want Sarah to reject me, but I'm not immune from rejection. I can accept myself as a fallible human being if she does." This is consistent with reality, logical, and healthy. Then Freda makes an interesting observation.)

FREDA: But, Norman, I think that there's something else going on here.

THERAPIST (after Norman doesn't respond): Go on Freda.

FREDA: Well, aren't you putting off speaking to Sarah because even if you rehearse that rational belief, you'll still feel uncomfortable, and you'd rather feel comfortable in the moment and not risk rejection than feel uncomfortable in the moment and possibly get rejected.

THERAPIST: And possibly getting what you want.

NORMAN: I never thought of that.

ROBERT: Does that mean that Freda's right?

NORMAN: I guess so.

THERAPIST: You don't sound convinced.

NORMAN: No, Freda's right. I just don't want to admit it.

THERAPIST: So how are you going to deal with that obstacle?

NORMAN: By asking myself: "What am I demanding?" about being uncomfortable.

THERAPIST: Excellent.

(With the group's help, Norman goes on to see that he needs to challenge his demand for comfort when he speaks to Sarah. He agrees to speak to her in the coming week while rehearsing his rational beliefs about the possibility and the reality of being uncomfortable.)

This excerpt shows some of the features of an ongoing REBT group:

1. It is highly interactive. There are few silences and no prolonged silences.
2. After the group has met for a while, group members speak up quite readily and find it quite easy to confront one another, usually in a helpful way. When the confrontation is unhelpful, the therapist usually intervenes.
3. The therapist serves as a gatekeeper and intervenes to facilitate constructive intrapersonal and interpersonal communication. In this excerpt, the therapist intervenes to ensure that one group member doesn't do the work for another when the latter is quite capable of doing the work for himself. Instead, the therapist intervenes to prompt Norman to do the work that he can do for himself with minimal prompting.

4. After the group has met for a while and its members have become used to applying the REBT model to their own problems, members can come up with insightful REBT-inspired comments to explain, for example, why other members aren't progressing as well as they could and what they can do about it.

RESEARCH ON THE EFFECTIVENESS OF REBT

The first controlled study of REBT was published in 1957 by Ellis, who compared the results he had obtained from using classical psychoanalysis, psychoanalytically oriented psychotherapy, and rational-emotive therapy. It was hardly an unbiased study and its positive results are not to be taken too seriously. However, starting in the 1960s and continuing into the 1980s, more than 1,000 outcome studies have been done on REBT and on closely related cognitive-behavioral therapies. The great majority of these controlled studies have shown that, when compared to a control group, clients treated with REBT or with a form of cognitive-behavior therapy that is an essential part of REBT fare significantly better than those who are not so treated. Outcome studies have been reviewed by Hajzler and Bernard (1991), Hollon and Beck (1994), and Lyons and Woods (1991). Such studies, testing the use of REBT and cognitive-behavior therapy derived from REBT, continue to proliferate, most indicating that treatment methods that consist of REBT procedures help clients or subjects significantly more than control groups.

In addition to empirical studies that tend to back the main therapeutic hypotheses of REBT, hundreds of other controlled experiments have been published that indicate that many of the main theoretical hypotheses of REBT—especially its ABC theory of human disturbance—now have considerable experimental backing. Also, hundreds more research studies present evidence that many of the REBT-favored therapeutic techniques, such as active-directive therapy, direct disputing of irrational ideas, the use of rational or coping statements, and the employment of psychoeducational methods, have distinct effectiveness. Ellis (1979) has cited hundreds of these studies in his comprehensive review of the REBT-oriented literature. If his review were brought up to date, it would now include hundreds of additional studies that present empirical confirmation of many of the most important REBT theories and therapeutic applications.

REBT does not have undisputed evidence of the validity of its theories or the effectiveness of its practice. Like all other major systems of psychotherapy, it is still lacking in these respects; considerable further research needs to be done to validate its major hypotheses. Although its treatment methods have been tested many times against the methods of other kinds of psychotherapy and against nontreated control groups and they have usually been proven adequate, they have not often been compared to the procedures of other popular forms of cognitive-behavior therapy. Numerous experimental studies remain to be done in this area.

SUMMARY

In this chapter, the underlying theory of REBT, its practice in a variety of different group therapy formats, and a cautious review of its effectiveness have been presented. Given that REBT is a leading approach within the cognitive-behavior therapy tradition, it shares the strengths of that tradition. It is suitable for managed care, can be cautiously viewed as an empirically supported treatment (EST), and satisfies the current demand for brief outcome-based interventions. However, REBT has distinctive features within the cognitive-behavior therapy tradition, and there is a need for more empirical research to be carried out on these distinctions if REBT is to be regarded as an EST in its own right and not just because of its place within the broader cognitive-behavioral paradigm.

REFERENCES

Alvarez, M. F. (1997). Using REBT and supportive psychotherapy with post-stroke clients. *Journal of Rational-Emotive and Cognitive-Behavior Therapy, 15*, 231–245.

Balter, R., & Unger, P. (1997). REBT stress management with clients with chronic fatigue syndrome. *Journal of Rational-Emotive and Cognitive-Behavior Therapy, 15*, 223–230.

Beck, A. T., Rush, A. J., Shaw, B. F., & Emery, G. (1979). *Cognitive therapy of depression*. New York: Guilford Press.

Bergin, A. E., & Garfield, S. L. (Eds.). (1994). *Handbook of psychotherapy and behavior change*. New York: Wiley.

Bernard, M. E. (Ed.). (1995). Rational emotive and cognitive behavioral therapy with offenders. *Journal of Rational-Emotive and Cognitive-Behavior Therapy, 13*, 211–282.

Bernard, M. E., & DiGiuseppe, R. (Eds.). (1989). *Inside rational-emotive therapy*. San Diego, CA: Academic Press.

DiGiuseppe, R. (1991). Comprehensive cognitive disputing in RET. In M. E. Bernard (Ed.), *Using rational-emotive therapy effectively* (pp. 173–196). New York: Plenum Press.

DiGiuseppe, R., McGowan, L., Sutton Simon, K., & Gardner, F. (1990). A comparative outcome study of four cognitive therapies in the treatment of social anxiety. *Journal of Rational-Emotive and Cognitive-Behavior Therapy, 8*, 129–146.

Dryden, W. (Ed.). (1996a). Rational emotive behavior therapy: Critiques from within. *Journal of Rational-Emotive and Cognitive-Behavior Therapy, 14*, 3–78.

Dryden, W. (1996b). Teaching the principles of unconditional self-acceptance in a structured group setting. In R. Bayne, I. Horton, & J. Bimrose (Eds.), *New directions in counselling*. London: Routledge.

Dryden, W. (1999). *How to accept yourself*. London: Sheldon.

Dryden, W., & Backx, W. (1987). Problems in living: The Friday night workshop. In W. Dryden (Ed.), *Current issues in rational-emotive therapy* (pp. 154–170). London: Croom Helm.

Ellis, A. (1957). Outcome of employing three techniques of psychotherapy. *Journal of Clinical Psychology, 13,* 344–350.

Ellis, A. (1962). *Reason and emotion in psychotherapy.* Secaucus, NJ: Lyle Stuart.

Ellis, A. (1969). A weekend of rational encounter. In A. Burton (Ed.), *Encounter* (pp. 112–127). San Francisco: Jossey-Bass.

Ellis, A. (1979). Rational-emotive therapy: Research data that support the clinical and personality hypotheses of RET and other modes of cognitive-behavior therapy. In A. Ellis & J. M. Whiteley (Eds.), *Theoretical and empirical foundations of rational-emotive therapy* (pp. 101–173). Monterey: CA: Brooks/Cole.

Ellis, A. (1985). *Overcoming resistance: Rational-emotive therapy with difficult clients.* New York: Springer.

Ellis, A. (1987). Integrative developments in rational-emotive therapy (RET). *Journal of Integrative and Eclectic Psychotherapy, 6,* 470–479.

Ellis, A. (1990). Is Rational-Emotive Therapy (RET) "rationalist" or "constructivist"? In W. Dryden (Ed.), *The essential Albert Ellis* (pp. 114–141). New York: Springer.

Ellis, A. (1997). Post-modern ethics for active-directive counseling and psychotherapy. *Journal of Mental Health Counseling, 18,* 211–225.

Ellis, A., & Yeager, R. J. (1989). *When some therapies don't work: The dangers of transpersonal psychology.* New York: Prometheus Books.

Epictetus. (1890). *The collected works of Epictetus.* Boston: Little, Brown.

Farley, R. C. (1987). Rational behavior problem-solving as a career development intervention for persons with disabilities. *Journal of Rational-Emotive Therapy, 5,* 32–42.

Flanagan, R., Povall, L., Dellino, M., & Byrne, L. (1998). A comparison of problem solving with and without rational emotive behavior therapy to improve children's social skills. *Journal of Rational-Emotive and Cognitive-Behavior Therapy, 16,* 125–134.

Greaves, D. (1997). The effect of rational-emotive parent education on the stress of mothers of young children with Down syndrome. *Journal of Rational-Emotive and Cognitive-Behavior Therapy, 15,* 249–267.

Grieger, R. M., & DiMattia, D. (Eds.). (1993). RET in the workplace. Parts 1 & 2. *Journal of Rational-Emotive and Cognitive-Behavior Therapy, 11,* 3–119.

Gullo, J. M. (1966). Counseling hospitalized clients. *Rational Living, 1*(2), 11–15.

Hajzler, D., & Bernard, M. E. (1991). A review of rational-emotive outcome studies. *School Psychology Quarterly, 6,* 27–49.

Harvill, R. (1985). Bulimia: Treatment of purging via systematic rational restructuring. *Journal of Rational-Emotive Therapy, 3,* 130–137.

Hollon, S. D., & Beck, A. T. (1994). Cognitive and cognitive-behavioral therapies. In A. E. Bergin & S. L. Garfield (Eds.), *Handbook of psychotherapy and behavior change* (pp. 428–466). New York: Wiley.

Jacobsen, R. H., Tamkin, A. S., & Blount, J. B. (1987). The efficacy of rational-emotive group therapy in psychiatric clients. *Journal of Rational-Emotive Therapy, 5,* 22–31.

Joyce, M. R. (1995). Emotional relief for parents: Is rational-emotive parent education effective? *Journal of Rational-Emotive and Cognitive-Behavior Therapy, 13,* 55–75.

Kushnir, T., & Malkinson, R. (1993). A rational-emotive group intervention for preventing and coping with stress among safety officers. *Journal of Rational-Emotive and Cognitive-Behavior Therapy, 11,* 195–206.

Lazarus, A. A. (1971). *Behavior therapy and beyond.* New York: McGraw-Hill.

Lefkovitz, P. M., & Davis, H. J. (1977). Rational-emotive therapy in a partial hospitalization setting. *Rational Living, 12*(2), 35–38.

Lyons, L. C., & Woods, P. J. (1991). The efficacy of rational-emotive therapy: A quantitative review of the outcome research. *Clinical Psychology Review, 11,* 357–390.

Malouff, J. M., Lanyon, R. I., & Schutte, N. S. (1988). Effectiveness of a brief group RET treatment for divorce-related dysphoria. *Journal of Rational-Emotive and Cognitive-Behavior Therapy, 6,* 162–171.

Maultsby, M. C., Stiefel, L., & Brodsky, L. (1972). A theory of rational behavioral group process. *Rational Living, 7*(1), 28–34.

McClellan, T. A., & Stieper, D. R. (1973). A structured approach to group marriage counseling. *Rational Living, 8*(2), 12–18.

Morris, G. B. (1993). A rational-emotive treatment program with Conduct Disorder and Attentional-Deficit Hyperactivity Disorder adolescents. *Journal of Rational-Emotive and Cognitive-Behavior Therapy, 11*, 23–134.

Morse, C., Bernard, M. E., & Dennerstein, L. (1989). The effects of rational-emotive therapy and relaxation training on premenstrual syndrome: A preliminary study. *Journal of Rational-Emotive and Cognitive-Behavior Therapy, 7*, 98–110.

Neenan, M., & Dryden, W. (1996). *Dealing with difficulties in rational emotive behavior therapy.* London: Whurr.

Nottingham, E. J., IV, & Neimeyer, R. A. (1992). Evaluation of a comprehensive inpatient rational-emotive therapy program: Some preliminary data. *Journal of Rational-Emotive and Cognitive-Behavior Therapy, 10*, 57–81.

Oliver, R. (1988). "Empty nest" or relationship restructuring? A rational-emotive approach to a mid-life transition. *Journal of Rational-Emotive and Cognitive-Behavior Therapy, 6*, 102–117.

Ponzoha, C., & Warren, R. (1985). Self-acceptance techniques for structured groups. *Journal of Rational-Emotive Therapy, 3*, 36–43.

Shannon, H. D., & Allen, T. W. (1998). The effectiveness of a REBT training program in increasing the performance of high school students in mathematics. *Journal of Rational-Emotive and Cognitive-Behavior Therapy, 16*, 197–209.

Sherman, S. H. (1967). Alcoholism and group therapy. *Rational Living, 2*(2), 20–22.

Straatmeyer, A. J., & Watkins, J. T. (1974). Rational-emotive therapy and the reduction of speech anxiety. *Rational Living, 9*(1), 33–37.

Thorpe, G. L., Freedman, E. G., & McGalliard, D. W. (1984). Components of rational-emotive imagery: Two experiments with non-assertive students. *Journal of Rational-Emotive Therapy, 2*(2), 11–19.

Vestre, N. D., & Judge, T. J. (1989). Evaluation of self-administered rational-emotive therapy programs for interpersonal anxiety. *Journal of Rational-Emotive and Cognitive-Behavior Therapy, 7*, 141–154.

Warren, R., Deffenbacher, J. L., & Brading, P. (1976). Rational-emotive therapy and the reduction of test anxiety in elementary school students. *Rational Living, 11*(2), 26–29.

Watson, J. L. (1919). *Psychology from the standpoint of a behaviorist.* Philadelphia: Lippincott.

Wessler, R. A., & Wessler, R. L. (1980). *The principles and practice of rational-emotive therapy.* San Francisco: Jossey-Bass.

Wolfe, J. (1995). Rational emotive behavior therapy women's groups: A twenty year retrospective. *Journal of Rational-Emotive and Cognitive-Behavior Therapy, 13*, 153–170.

Yeager, R. J., DiGiuseppe, R., Olsen, J. T., Lewis, L., & Alberti, R. (1988). Rational-emotive therapy in the therapeutic community. *Journal of Rational-Emotive and Cognitive-Behavior Therapy, 6*, 211–235.

CHAPTER 21

A Skills-Training Approach to Relationship Education in Groups

W. KIM HALFORD

At the beginning of committed relationships, couples almost universally report high relationship satisfaction (Bradbury, 1998; Markman, 1991; Markman & Hahlweg, 1993). However, the average relationship satisfaction declines each year over at least the first 10 years of the relationship, with a substantial proportion of couples reporting dramatic declines in satisfaction that often are associated with contemplation or enactment of separation (Glenn, 1998). Deteriorating relationship satisfaction and separation are associated with a range of adverse mental and physical outcomes for partners and their children (Burman & Margolin, 1992; Halford, Kelly, & Markman, 1997).

Relationship education developed as an attempt to promote mutually satisfying couple relationships and to prevent relationship breakdown (Hunt, Hof, & DeMaria, 1998). Such education often is offered in a group format, and this chapter describes the application of a skills training approach that is delivered in a group format. The chapter begins with a description of the development of this approach and then describes the key theoretical constructs under-

lying skills-based relationship education. This is followed by a section on methods of assessment and intervention and a case example of a couple attending a group relationship education program. The final section is a review of empirical evidence on the effectiveness of relationship education.

HISTORY OF MAJOR APPROACHES TO RELATIONSHIP EDUCATION

Relationship education developed from the work of religious marriage celebrants such as priests, rabbis, and ministers who offered brief counsel to marrying couples (Hunt et al., 1998). In the early 1950s, religious organizations, in particular the Catholic Church, began to offer structured relationship education programs in a group format for marrying couples (Hunt et al., 1998). In the mid-1950s in the United States (Hunt et al., 1998), Australia (Harris, Simons, Willis, & Barrie, 1992), and other Western countries, secular organizations also began to offer programs. By the late 1990s, between one-quarter and one-third of marrying couples in the United States, Australia, and Britain were attending some form of relationship education (Halford, 1999; Simons, Harris, & Willis, 1994; Sullivan & Bradbury, 1997). The diversity of currently available programs can be seen as falling into three broad categories: awareness, inventories, and skills training.

AWARENESS

Awareness approaches emphasize the transmission of information, clarification of expectations, and increasing couples' awareness of key relationship processes that influence relationship outcomes. Some programs include demonstration of relevant relationship skills such as communication, but in general, active training in these skills does not occur. From the available surveys of relationship education, it would seem that the majority of couples who participate receive this form of education (Harris et al., 1992; "To Have and to Hold," 1998).

A limitation of the awareness programs is that many of the approaches have grown from the providers' practical experience of delivering marriage and relationship education, and do not draw on conceptual models or research available in the relevant literature. Many have been developed locally by practitioners, and often the exact content and process of the programs are not well documented (Halford, 1999). The consequent lack of standardization of these programs means that they cannot readily be evaluated in scientific research.

INVENTORIES

A second category of relationship education programs is inventory-based programs. The most widely used inventories are PREPARE (Olsen, Fournier, & Druckman, 1996) and the

Facilitating Open Couple Communication Understanding and Study (FOCCUS; Markey & Micheletto, 1997). In these programs, each partner completes a self-report inventory that assesses a broad range of couple functioning dimensions, and the couple is provided with systematic feedback about the results of that assessment.

The scores on both PREPARE (Fowers & Olsen, 1986; A. Larsen & Olsen, 1989) and FOCCUS (Williams & Jurich, 1995) predict relationship satisfaction and separation in couples across the first five years of marriage. However, there are no published studies that have utilized a controlled evaluation of inventory-based programs. Inventory programs like PREPARE and FOCCUS have the advantage of being clearly structured and, hence, amenable to scientific evaluation. Furthermore, they do target factors shown to predict relationship outcomes. However, a presumption underlying these approaches is that awareness will promote better couple coping. As Silliman, Stanley, Coffin, Markman, and Jordan (in press) point out, identification of relationship weaknesses or differences between partners may be counterproductive unless couples are helped to deal effectively with the issues identified. For example, feedback on divergent expectations may lead to profitable discussion, but couples lacking conflict management skills may be unable to resolve these differences.

SKILLS TRAINING

The third broad category of relationship education is skills training programs. There are a number of such programs, including Guerney and colleagues' Relationship Enhancement program (Guerney, 1977, 1987; Guerney & Maxson, 1990), Markman and colleagues' Premarital Relationship Enhancement Program (PREP; Markman, Stanley, & Blumberg, 1994), and the Couples Communication program (Miller, Wackman, &

Nunnally, 1976). In each of these programs, couples receive instruction on key relationship skills. Instruction is a mixture of lectures, demonstrations, and audiovisual presentations. Couples also receive opportunities to practice these skills and receive feedback from educators. In most programs, couples undertake assignments between sessions, which provide an opportunity for participants to practice applying skills in their relationship.

The various skills training programs have a number of content areas in common. For example, positive communication, conflict management, and positive expressions of affection are included in Relationship Education, PREP, and Couple Communication (Guerney, 1977; Markman et al., 1994; Miller et al., 1976). There also are significant variations. For example, in PREP, most emphasis is placed on reduction of destructive conflict, as this is argued to be central to the prevention of relationship problems (Markman et al., 1994). In Relationship Education, the development of partner empathy receives very strong emphasis (Guerney, 1977), whereas this has less emphasis in PREP.

THEORETICAL CONSTRUCTS

Historically, the design of many relationship education programs developed independently from psychological research on the influences on relationship satisfaction and stability. This is unfortunate, as there is very important research-based information on the influences on relationship outcomes, particularly from longitudinal studies of the course of relationships. There are over 120 published studies assessing psychological variables and the longitudinal course of couple relationship satisfaction and stability (Karney & Bradbury, 1995). Bradbury (1995) adapted the stress-vulnerability-coping model to offer a heuristic model by which this comprehensive literature can be summarized. In addition to this literature, a large number of studies have examined sociodemographic variables and their relationship to the satisfaction and stability of couple relationships (Glenn, 1998; J. Larson & Holman, 1994). Halford (1999) modified and extended Karney and Bradbury's (1995) model to incorporate these sociodemographic factors and suggested that there are four broad classes of variables that impact on the trajectory of relationship satisfaction over time: adaptive processes within the couple system, life events impinging on the couple, enduring individual characteristics of the partners, and contextual variables.

ADAPTIVE COUPLE PROCESSES

Adaptive processes refer to the cognitive, behavioral, and affective processes that occur during couple interaction. Certain deficits in these adaptive processes seem to predispose couples to relationship problems. More specifically, deficits in communication and conflict management behaviors observed in engaged couples prospectively predict divorce and relationship dissatisfaction over the first years of marriage (Gottman, Coan, Carrere, & Swanson, 1998; Markman, 1981; Markman & Hahlweg, 1993). Dysfunctional communication in engaged couples also predicts the development of verbal and physical aggression in the relationship in the first few years of marriage (Murphy & O'Leary, 1989; O'Leary et al., 1989), at least for mild to moderate severity aggression. Furthermore, relationship aggression often is established early in the relationship and usually continues and escalates once established (Murphy & O'Leary, 1989; O'Leary et al., 1989).

It is noteworthy that the communication deficits observed in some engaged couples do not correlate with their reported relationship satisfaction at the time (Markman & Hahlweg, 1993; Sanders, Halford, & Behrens, 1999). It seems that these communication difficulties do not stop couples from forming committed relationships, but the difficulties may predispose them to develop relationship problems later (Pasch & Bradbury, 1998). In couples who have been married for some time, these same communication difficulties predict deterioration in relationship satisfaction and decreased relationship stability (Gottman, 1993, 1994).

The beliefs and expectations individuals have when entering into relationships and marriage constitute another predictor of the risk of relationship distress in the first few years of marriage (Olsen & Fowers, 1986; Olsen & Larsen, 1989). Couples characterized by unrealistic expectations and beliefs in areas such as importance of communication, appropriate methods of conflict resolution, importance of family and friends, and gender roles have higher rates of erosion in relationship satisfaction than couples not so characterized. Negative attributions, in which partners ascribe blame for relationship problems to stable, negative characteristics of their spouse, also prospectively predict deterioration in relationship satisfaction (Fincham & Bradbury, 1991).

Finally, certain patterns of emotional expression are predictive of relationship problems. Showing contempt, disgust, fear, or emotional withdrawal toward one's partner during interaction is predictive of relationship deterioration and taking steps toward separation (Gottman, 1994). Thus, certain behavioral, cognitive, and affective characteristics of couples' adaptive processes predate, and prospectively predict, relationship problems.

LIFE EVENTS

Life events refer to the developmental transitions and the acute and chronic circumstances that impinge on the couple or individual partners. Relationship problems are more likely to develop during periods of high rates of change (Karney & Bradbury, 1995). For example, the transition to parenthood often is associated with a decline in couple relationship satisfaction (Cowan & Cowan, 1992). However, some couples report that the transition to parenthood enhances relationship satisfaction and commitment (Cowan & Cowan, 1992). Similarly, partners who successfully support each other through stressful events, such as a severe illness, often report that the experience brings them closer together (Halford, Scott, & Smythe, 2000). Thus, significant life events have the potential to either increase or decrease relationship satisfaction.

Couples with less robust adaptive processes are believed to be particularly vulnerable to the negative effects of a range of stressful events (Markman, Halford, & Cordova, 1997). In particular, couples who lack communication skills or who have inflexible or unrealistic expectations of relationships find it hard to adapt to major life transitions. For example, couples in which the woman was recently diagnosed with breast or gynecological cancer, and who have poor communication and ineffective mutual support, show deterioration in their relationship and poor individual coping with the cancer (Halford, Scott, et al., 2000).

INDIVIDUAL CHARACTERISTICS

Individual characteristics refer to the stable personal factors that each partner brings to a relationship (Bradbury, 1995). Whereas most normal personality variations do not seem to contribute much variance to relationship satisfaction (Gottman, 1994; Karney & Bradbury, 1995), high neuroticism and insecure attachment style both are associated with increased risk for relationship problems (Feeney & Noller, 1996; Karney & Bradbury, 1997).

High levels of education, high income, and high-status occupation all are associated with increased chance of relationship satisfaction and stability (Glick, 1984; Kurdek, 1991, 1993; Martin & Bumpass, 1989; Mott & Moore, 1979).

The reasons for these effects are not entirely clear. A possible explanation is that the relationships of poor and less educated couples have greater cumulative exposure to stresses such as financial and health problems. This exposure may produce greater risk for relationship problems (Kurdek, 1993).

Psychological Disorder

A major risk indicator for relationship distress is a psychological disorder. Higher rates of relationship problems consistently are reported in people with psychoses (Halford, 1995), depression, alcohol abuse, and some anxiety disorders (Emmelkamp, De Haan, & Hoogduin, 1990; Halford, Bouma, Kelly, & Young, 1999; Halford & Osgarby, 1993; O'Farrell & Birchler, 1987; Reich & Thompson, 1985; Ruscher & Gotlib, 1988; Weissman, 1987). The link between individual and couple problems is complex. For instance, relationship problems and individual problems can exacerbate each other (Halford, Bouma, et al., 1999). In addition, certain personal characteristics may dispose people to both individual and relationship problems. For example, deficits in interpersonal communication and negative affect regulation predict the onset of both alcohol abuse (Block, Block, & Keyes, 1988), and relationship problems (Markman & Hahlweg, 1993). Such deficits might precipitate the co-occurrence of relationship and alcohol problems.

Relationship History

Several aspects of the partners' relationship history are predictive of relationship satisfaction and stability. For example, negative family-of-origin experiences increase the chance of relationship problems (J. Larson & Holman, 1994). In particular, parental divorce is associated with higher rates of marital problems in their offspring when they become adults (DeGraaf, 1991; Glenn & Kramer, 1987; Glenn & Shelton, 1983), as is violence in the family of origin (e.g., Burgess, Hartman, & McCormack, 1987; Mihalic

& Elliott, 1997; Riggs, O'Leary, & Breslin, 1990; Stets & Straus, 1990; Stith & Farley, 1993; Straus et al., 1980; Widom, 1989).

The mechanisms by which parental divorce or aggression impact on subsequent adult relationships is becoming clearer. Exposure to parental divorce is associated with more negative expectations of marriage (Black & Sprenkle, 1991; Gibardi & Rosen, 1991) and with observable deficits in communication and conflict management in couples prior to marriage (Sanders et al., 1999). Adult offspring of parents who were aggressive toward each other also show deficits in communication and conflict management skills in their dating and marital relationships (Halford, Sanders, & Behrens, 2000). Negative expectations and communication deficits may well be learned from the parents' relationship; subsequently, this learned behavior impacts negatively on the adult relationships of the offspring.

The history of the current relationship also is predictive of relationship satisfaction and stability. Specifically, the longer and better couples know each other before marriage, the greater the reported relationship satisfaction after marriage (Birchnell & Kennard, 1984; Kurdeck, 1991, 1993). However, cohabitation before marriage is associated with increased risk of relationship distress and separation (Balakkrishnan, Rao, Lapierre-Adamcyk, & Krotski, 1987; Janus & Janus, 1993; Trussel & Rao, 1987). Choosing to cohabit is associated with a variety of factors, such as low religiosity, uncertainty about committing to the relationship, and negative perceptions of marriage. Any of these or other variables might account for the high risk of relationship breakdown for couples who cohabit before marriage.

CONTEXTUAL VARIABLES

Couple relationships occur within a cultural context that defines how marriage and other couple relationships are supposed to be. Although there are certain general assumptions shared across Western cultures, there also are important variations among those cultures. For example, German couples without relationship problems engage in a level of verbal negativity similar to that of distressed Australian couples (Halford, Hahlweg, & Dunne, 1990), suggesting that greater levels of negativity are more acceptable and less dysfunctional in the German cultural context. Even within one country there is great diversity in acceptable relationship behavior. Winkler and Doherty (1983) found that verbal conflict was reported as more common in New York couples who were born in Israel than in Anglo couples living in New York. However, verbal conflict was less often associated with physical aggression or relationship distress in the Israeli-born couples than in the Anglo couples. Thus, the cultural appropriateness and functional impact of behavior varies considerably, even within Western cultures.

It can be important to assess the cultural context within which relationship standards develop and may be reinforced. Partners who differ in their ethnic, racial, or cultural background often differ in their expectations and beliefs about relationships (Jones & Chao, 1997). This diversity in partner assumptions and beliefs can be a source of great strength for a relationship when the partners are able to draw on the wisdom and strengths of different cultural traditions. At the same time, substantial differences in expectations can be a significant source of conflict between the partners (Jones & Chao, 1997). Marriages in which partners have very different cultural backgrounds break down at slightly higher rates than other marriages (Birchnall & Kennard, 1984; Kurdeck, 1991; White, 1990).

Although the partner role is central to most adults in couple relationships, this is not the only relationship or role they each have. Other relationships and roles are part of the context in which couple interaction occurs, and these can impact in a positive or negative manner on the couple relationship. For example, work often

provides extra stimulation and ideas to enrich the relationship, but work demands also can compete for time with the partner (Thompson, 1997). Friends may provide support and shared activities that complement the relationship and reduce the chance of excessive dependence on the spouse; however, friendships also can take away time from the partner. Parenting, sports, hobbies, and community service activities all have the capacity to enrich or erode relationship quality.

There are consistent findings that approval of one's spouse and relationship by friends and extended family are predictive of better relationship satisfaction and stability (Booth & Johnson, 1988; Kurdek, 1991). At the same time, there is evidence that excessive intrusion by family on selection of dating partners and subsequent mate selection can signal later relationship problems (Benson, Larson, Wilson, & Demo, 1993).

IMPLICATIONS OF THEORY FOR THE PRACTICE OF RELATIONSHIP EDUCATION

The influences on relationship satisfaction summarized above have implications for the targeting, timing, and content of relationship education. With respect to the targeting of relationship education, it is evident from the preceding review that there is a broad range of risk variables that predict relationship outcomes. This range of variables can be conceptualized as falling into two categories: static risk indicators and dynamic risk factors. Static risk indicators cannot be changed at the time of intervention. For example, family-of-origin experiences are static variables that predict risk of relationship problems. In contrast, dynamic risk factors can be changed. For example, relationship expectations and couple communication predict risk of relationship problems and can be changed by relationship education.

Many risk indicators can be measured relatively easily. For example, parental divorce, age, previous marriages, and the presence of children can be assessed by simple questions. Assessment of these risk indicators can help couples or educators to assess the relative risk level of particular couples for relationship problems. Thus, these indicators allow targeting of relationship education toward those couples who may benefit most.

Risk factors, such as poor couple communication and unrealistic relationship expectations, often are more time-consuming to assess and therefore are less suitable for easily identifying couples most likely to benefit from relationship education. For example, negative affect in observed communication is a reliable predictor of relationship distress, but requires sophisticated audiovisual recording equipment and highly trained raters to conduct the assessment. However, some dynamic risk factors are reliably associated with certain risk indicators. For example, parental divorce and aggression in the family of origin are associated with negative communication in engaged couples (Halford, Sanders, et al., 2000; Sanders et al., 1999). Thus, easily assessed risk indicators such as the presence of parental divorce and aggression are markers of likely negative communication. Negative communication can then be targeted in relationship education, as improvements in communication in couples who are at high risk of relationship problems have been shown to help couples sustain relationship satisfaction (Halford, Sanders, & Behrens, in press). In summary, certain easily assessed risk indicators can be used to direct relationship education to couples who are at highest risk of relationship distress.

A second major implication of theory on relationship satisfaction and stability concerns the timing of when relationship education is offered. Traditionally, it has been offered to couples when they enter committed relationships, most often, just before marriage (Hunt, Hof, & DeMaria, 1998). The available research affirms that entry to marriage is a good time for relationship education. In the early years of marriage, many couples find that their initial overwhelming attraction

to their partner moderates, new relationship roles and routines need to be developed, and means of negotiating conflict need to be evolved (Huston, McHale, & Crouter, 1986; Veroff, Douvan, & Hatchett, 1995). Furthermore, across the first four to five years of marriage, relationship satisfaction declines in an approximately linear fashion (Huston et al., 1986; Karney & Bradbury, 1997; Veroff et al., 1995). About one-third of all divorces in the United States occur in the first five years of marriage (National Center for Health Statistics, 1991).

In addition to the time of marriage, a number of other life events and developmental processes that couples experience are associated with the onset of relationship problems. For example, the transition to parenthood, relocation, major illness, and unemployment all are associated with increased risk of relationship distress (Belsky & Kelly, 1994; Gagnon, Hersen, Kabacoff, & van Hasselt, 1999; J. Larson & Holman, 1994). Relationship education that assists couples to make these challenging life transitions, just prior to or as they are experiencing them, could help couples to sustain relationship satisfaction and commitment.

A third major implication of theory regarding relationship satisfaction and stability is that some couples have special needs in relationship education. One important example is couples who form stepfamilies. In stepfamilies, there is a particularly high rate of conflict over parenting (Cissna, Cox, & Bochner, 1990), and special challenges arise in negotiating the parenting arrangements, particularly with respect to the role of stepparents in major decisions and discipline of children (Visher & Visher, 1991). Therefore, effective interventions to promote satisfying couple relationships within stepfamilies need to address the relationship of the stepparent with the children and help couples to negotiate mutually acceptable parenting arrangements (Lawton & Sanders, 1994).

A second example of couples with special needs is when at least one partner has an individual psychological disorder that impacts on the relationship, such as alcohol abuse or depression (Halford, Bouma, et al., 1999). In such couples, helping the partner with the disorder to change his or her behavior is likely to be an important element of promoting a mutually satisfying relationship. For example, encouraging a heavy drinker to moderate drinking, using a brief intervention consisting of motivational interviewing, goal setting, and coping with high-risk situations, might enhance long-term relationship satisfaction and stability.

METHODS OF ASSESSMENT AND INTERVENTION

The content and process used in running a skills-based relationship education program are described in this section. The focus is on a program called Couple Commitment and Relationship Enhancement (Couple CARE) that was developed by the author with colleagues (Halford, Moore, Wilson, Burrows, & Farrugia, 1999). Couple CARE builds on the ideas of pioneers in relationship education, for example, Markman and colleagues (1994) in PREP and Guerney (1977) in the Relationship Enhancement program. Common to each program is a multisession, small-group format, with a focus on development of key relationship skills that are associated with relationship satisfaction and stability. Couple CARE, like PREP, is aimed at relationship enrichment and prevention of relationship problems in couples currently satisfied with their relationship.

In addition to the skill acquisition emphasized in most skills-based relationship education programs, Couple CARE includes the promotion of self-regulation as an explicit goal. The self-regulatory approach is based on the assumption that each partner in a relationship needs to be able to implement *self-change* to enhance the relationship (Halford, 2001; Halford & Moore, in press; Halford, Sanders, & Behrens,

1994). Self-change is seen as engaging a series of self-regulation metaskills, including self-assessment of contributions to the relationship, self-selection of personal goals to enhance the relationship, attempts at self-directed behavior change to achieve those goals, and self-evaluation of the effects of behavior change. In a self-regulatory approach, the aim is to teach partners how to self-direct relationship change in a manner that will sustain mutual satisfaction in the long term.

Typically, relationship education is run with small groups of couples, but it can be delivered to individual couples in self-directed learning formats without face-to-face contact with leaders (Halford & Moore, in press). Although the group format is the focus of this chapter, within this format there is considerable variety of delivery modes. Groups may be run across a weekend or as weekly sessions across a number of weeks. To assist in skill acquisition, it probably is necessary to provide couples with the opportunity to apply skills away from the training sessions and to review those applications in subsequent sessions.

ASSESSMENT

It is my experience that group relationship education works best when the leader knows the couples and their goals for relationship education, and when the couples in any given group are relatively homogeneous with respect to their relationship education needs. Consequently, before commencing group relationship education, an initial assessment and screening session is conducted with each couple. In that session, one aim is to get to know the couple and find out their relationship education goals. A second aim is to screen for factors that contraindicate using this approach for that couple. A third aim is to assess any special needs the couple may have that will need attention during relationship education.

The assessment session typically consists of a conjoint interview, brief individual interviews with each partner, and completion of some self-report inventories. In the conjoint interview, the couple are asked about their relationship history to establish how long they have been together, any particular challenges they face in their relationship, and whether they have children. They also are asked about their goals in attending relationship education. In the individual interviews, inquiries are made about previous relationships, prior history of any psychological or psychiatric treatment, and the occurrence of aggression in the current or previous relationships. Approximately 25% of marrying couples report an episode of violence in their relationship in the previous 12 months (McLaughlin, Leonard, & Senchak, 1992; O'Leary, Malone, & Tyree, 1994); the occurrence of aggression early in the relationship predicts relationship breakup in the first few years of marriage (Rogge & Bradbury, 1999). Consequently, it is important to know if aggression is occurring and, if it is, to assess the level of risk of injury to partners, particularly the woman.

In Couple CARE, couples complete a selection of self-report measures prior to commencing relationship education. Spanier's (1976) Dyadic Adjustment Scale (DAS) is part of this initial assessment. The DAS is a 32-item global self-report measure of relationship satisfaction. Scores of 90 or less indicate significant relationship distress. Couples who are experiencing significant relationship distress should not be included in a relationship enhancement and prevention program. For couples who are currently quite satisfied in the relationship, it can be upsetting to have couples who have major distress engage in conflict in the group. Furthermore, distressed couples are better served by attending conjoint therapy rather than group relationship education sessions.

Individuals with a severe psychological disorder may require specific assistance, and partners are routinely assessed for individual problems. The Depression Anxiety Stress Scale (DASS; Lovibond & Lovibond, 1995) is a 21-item self-report measure that provides a sound assessment of depression, anxiety, and stress. Elevations for either partner into the severe clinical range on any of the subscales of the DASS suggest that work with the couple alone, rather than in a group, is advisable. The Alcohol Use Disorders Test (Saunders, Aasland, Babor, de la Fuente, & Grant, 1993) is a 10-item screening measure of hazardous and harmful drinking; a score of 8 or more on this scale indicates hazardous drinking levels. Drinking in the harmful range (approximately 40 standard drinks per week for men or 20 for women, or the presence of binge drinking) indicates that individual treatment with the drinking partner is advisable before the couple enters a group relationship education program.

CONTENT OF RELATIONSHIP EDUCATION

As noted earlier, the content covered in Couple CARE is similar to that covered in PREP, in that the emphasis throughout the program is on active training in key skills associated with relationship satisfaction and stability. A distinctive characteristic of Couple CARE, however, is a focus on self-directed change. The content of Couple CARE falls into six units, summarized in Table 21.1. The initial session is focused on relationship goal setting. To that end, couples develop a shared relationship goal statement, which we refer to as their *relationship vision*. Development of this vision involves having couples discuss a number of dimensions of expectations about relationships, such as their desired degree of closeness versus autonomy, gender role, power and control, and styles of communication. People discuss memories of their family of origin with their partner, and how those and other important relationships may have shaped their relationship expectations. Couples consider the strengths and

Table 21.1   Content of couple CARE, a six-session relationship education program.

Module	Detail of Content
1	*Introduction and goal setting:* Introduction of leader(s) and couple(s); overview of program; rationale for skills training focus of program; identification of key behavioral domains promoting relationship intimacy; review of relationship expectations, development of relationship goals; intimacy enhancement through self-directed goal setting.
2	*Communication:* Review of key communication skills; guided self-evaluation of current communication skills; self-directed selection of communication enhancement goals and practice of implementation of those skills; self-directed goal setting and definition of homework task to enhance communication.
3	*Intimacy:* Review of communication homework tasks, and self-directed further goal selection and definition of further homework task; review of factors promoting intimacy; assessing partner support, expressions of caring, reviewing individual and joint activities; self-directed change plan.
4	*Conflict management:* Review intimacy enhancement tasks; introduction to the concept of the patterns of conflict and effective conflict management; negotiation with partner about relationship rules for managing conflict; self-directed goal setting for effective management of conflict; introduction to the concept of flexible gender roles, couple review of current gender roles, self-directed goal setting for future gender-role flexibility.
5	*Sexuality:* Review of communication homework task; review of the role of sexuality in relationship intimacy; couple discussion and goal setting to enhance sexual intimacy; introduction to the concept of partner support, self-directed goal setting to enhance partner support; self-directed definition of homework tasks to implement selected goals in areas of sexuality or partner support.
6	*Managing change:* Review of homework tasks; self-directed selection of any further goals to enhance relationship functioning; introduction of issue of maintenance of relationship functioning; self-directed identification of future life events impacting on relationship; planning to promote relationship adaptation to predictable life events. Closure.

weaknesses they believe they bring to the current relationship, and develop a shared set of relationship goals. The leader helps couples define specifically and concretely their vision of a good relationship, which then becomes a basis for developing self-change goals that help them move toward that defined vision.

An important element of all skills-based relationship education programs is communication skills training. The elements that constitute adaptive communication in a relationship are likely to vary across relationships and across settings (Halford, Gravestock, Lowe, & Scheldt, 1992). Consequently, in Couple CARE, individuals self-select goals for enhancing their own communication from an array of available skills, and self-evaluate their own, rather than their partner's, communication. In practice, couples first are asked to have a discussion with each other. Next, each partner self-assesses their

communication during the discussion, using a checklist of potentially helpful communication behaviors set out in Table 21.2. After completing that form, each partner identifies for himself or herself specific communication behaviors to improve to enhance their communication. This does not mean that the leader avoids responsibility for helping the partners determine goals. Rather, the leader helps both partners to accurately self-evaluate their current communication and to develop specific, self-selected goals for enhancing communication.

Conflict management is another important element of Couple CARE. Once couples have a reasonable level of communication skills, they can use these skills to better manage conflict. As part of the session on conflict, there is a discussion of the different settings in which conflict may occur and of the fact that there are some settings in which it is easier to have a

Table 21.2 Communication skills self-evaluation form.

NAME: _____ DATE: _____

The aim of this form is for you to identify your strengths and weaknesses in communication and to select goals for improvement. Rate each of the skills below using this code:

         0   - Very poor use of skill
         1   - Unsatisfactory use of skill
         2   - Satisfactory use of skill, but room for improvement
         3   - Good use of skill
     N/A - Not applicable

Skill	0	1	2	3	N/A
Specific descriptors					
Self-disclosure					
Clear expression of positives					
Assertive expression of negatives					
Attending to partner					
Minimal encouragers					
Reserving judgment					
Asking questions					
Summarizing content					
Paraphrasing feelings					
Positive suggestions					

Self-identified strengths in communication: _____

_____

Self-identified weaknesses in communication: _____

_____

productive discussion than others. Couples are asked to consider the times, places, and circumstances in which they could most productively talk about difficult topics. Couples also are educated about the common maladaptive patterns of couple interaction around conflict, such as the demand-withdraw and mutual avoidance patterns. They are helped to identify their own usual pattern of interaction around conflict, and then self-select goals that will help them to avoid unhelpful patterns of interaction.

To maintain relationship satisfaction over time, it is important that couples prepare themselves for changes in their relationship produced by major life transitions. In Couple CARE, couples are asked to rate the likelihood of various life events occurring in the next one or two years, and the probability that if those events occur, they might have a negative effect on their relationship. They identify the ways an event such as birth of a child, loss of a job, or a change of work circumstances might impact the relationship. Partners self-select goals they believe would help them adapt in a relationship-maintaining way to these transitions. For example, a number of couples have identified that they may have reduced opportunities for having couple time once they have children. They have then set individual goals, such as ensuring that child care is available or cultivating activities they can do at home, which will increase their chance of having shared enjoyable time together when they have young children.

In summary, the focus in Couple CARE is on developing the relationship metaskills of couples. Providing information about influences on relationship satisfaction as well as active training in key relationship skills are central to Couple CARE, but couples are particularly encouraged to develop their ability to monitor their contributions to the relationship and to set and implement goals for achieving the vision they have identified. In this way, the learning is tailored to the individuals for their particular relationship, in a fashion that encourages individual responsibility for making the relationship strong and that provides a structure for achieving goals and ongoing relationship enhancement.

APPLICATION OF RELATIONSHIP EDUCATION

The targeting of relationship education to couples can be undertaken in a variety of ways. Three possibilities often described in the prevention research area are referred to as universal, selective, and indicated programs. Universal prevention refers to any program that is available to all members of a defined population in an effort to reduce the overall prevalence of a problem within a defined community (Muñoz, Mrazek, & Haggerty, 1996). In the context of relationship education, universal targeting includes any attempt to engage all people either entering or in committed relationships. Selective prevention refers to specifically recruiting individuals who currently have no measurable problem but who are at high risk for future problems. For example, relationship education might be offered selectively to couples who experienced parental divorce or violence in the family of origin, or who married at a young age. Indicated prevention refers to early intervention with individuals with emerging relationship problems that have not yet developed into severe relationship distress. For example, education might be offered to couples who engaged in low level relationship aggression but who are not severely distressed, to try to prevent the development of severe problems later.

We offer Couple CARE in groups to couples in the early stages of committed relationships and who currently report being happy. We recommend individual conjoint therapy rather than Couple CARE if the couple currently are distressed, if they are aggressive toward each other, or if either partner has an individual psychological disorder. Although we offer Couple

CARE universally, in our outreach we target couples who are at high risk for relationship problems. This is based on our research findings, reviewed in greater detail later, that high-risk couples seem to benefit more than low-risk couples from relationship education (Halford et al., in press).

CASE EXAMPLE

Lyn (41) is a sales representative and Graham (47) is a self-employed builder who have been married for one year. This couple had some markers for being at high risk of developing relationship problems, but at the time of presentation for relationship education, both reported high relationship satisfaction. In the initial interview, Lyn and Graham each said that they were very much in love with their spouse, that their communication was good, and that they enjoyed a wide range of activities together. Consistent with these verbal reports, on the DAS, Lyn scored 117 and Graham scored 121, reflecting a high level of current relationship satisfaction. Individually and conjointly, each partner expressed commitment to making the relationship a mutually satisfying one, but also expressed concern about being able to sustain their current level of satisfaction.

Both partners had been married before. Lyn was married to John at age 25 and divorced at age 31. Lyn and John had no children. Lyn described John as an aloof and distant man who had been unexpressive of his feelings. She reported that her relationship with John was polite and civil but lacked intimacy and passion. Although on numerous occasions, Lyn had suggested to John that they seek relationship counseling, he had refused to do so. Lyn left John, feeling that the marriage was emotionally barren.

Graham was married to Denise when he was 19 years of age. They were divorced when Graham was 44. Graham and Denise had three children, now ranging in age from 11 to 17 years. They currently live with Denise but spend every second weekend and each Wednesday night at Graham and Lyn's home. Graham reported that Denise had suffered from depression after the birth of their first child, and he felt the relationship was never the same after that. He reported that she had been very critical of him through the last 10 years of their marriage. He coped with this negativity by avoiding discussions with her and working very long hours in his business. Four years previously, he felt the arguments between them were intolerable and were affecting the children, so he left. Graham also reported that he managed stress poorly, often resorted to being introverted, and that he was concerned that his lack of emotional expressiveness and his withdrawal would place his relationship with Lyn under strain in the long term.

Lyn had met Graham two years earlier through an advertisement she placed in the personal section of a metropolitan newspaper. They dated for 12 months before moving in together and married a few months after that. In the conjoint interview, both partners were asked what had attracted them to the other and how their relationship had developed. They were both very positive about each other and described a high level of commitment to the relationship.

When asked to describe the goals they hoped to achieve from participating in relationship education, Lyn stated that she wanted them to review their relationship experiences to prevent them from making the same mistakes they had made in the past. She also wanted to learn to manage stress more effectively, as she felt she became terse with Graham when under pressure at work. Graham wanted to learn to communicate his feelings more effectively and to prevent work stress from interfering in his relationship with Lyn.

Lyn and Graham attended a Couple CARE group with three other couples that ran as six weekly two-hour sessions and covered the content listed in Table 21.1. In the section on family of origin and previous relationship experiences, Lyn related that her parents had separated when she was 7 years old, and that she had seen little of her father since the separation. She mentioned that her mother had three different live-in relationships with men during Lyn's adolescence. Two of these men Lyn had seen being violent toward her mother, and Lyn speculated that her experiences had led her to be very angry toward men and that this had contributed to the breakdown of her first marriage. In discussion, Lyn indicated that two strengths she brought to her current relationship were a realistic appraisal that long-term relationships needed effort, and a commitment to making the relationship with Graham better than other relationships she had experienced. She also stated a desire to learn to express dissatisfaction in her relationship with Graham with less anger.

Graham related that his father had placed enormous importance on providing money for the family, a priority that Graham attributed to his father's growing up during the Great Depression of the 1930s. Graham felt he had internalized this value, which had led him to work very hard in his business all his adult life. Graham felt a strength he brought to the relationship with Lyn was that he was a hard worker and was setting them up for a financially comfortable future. At the same time, he felt very stressed about work, believed he worked too many hours, and wanted to learn to manage his stress better. The other couples in the group also discussed their prior relationship experiences and their goals. One goal several couples mentioned was enhancing quality couple time. Graham and Lyn had not mentioned this goal specifically, but decided to add this to their goals.

The second session focused on communication, and each couple discussed their day to that point. After the discussion, each partner self-assessed communication skills using the checklist shown

in Table 21.2. At the end of the exercise, each person reported to the larger group on a strength he or she had as a communicator, and one skill each would like to work on. As people reported, they were assisted in making their self-assessments specific and accurate and in formulating observable communication improvement goals. For example, Graham stated that he wanted to improve his expression of feelings. After questions from the leader about what feelings he wanted to express, he reported that he wanted to compliment Lyn more often. Lyn reported that she felt she was good at expressing herself, but that she interrupted Graham too often. In response to that comment, Lyn was asked what she wanted to do instead of interrupting. She stated a goal of letting Graham finish his comments and asking him open-ended questions to ensure that she understood what he was saying. Couples were then asked to have a second conversation, with the aim of implementing their self-change goals during the communication. The couples then reviewed if they had implemented their self-change goals and what effect changes in the communication had on the interaction. Finally, couples were asked to have a further discussion between sessions and to self-evaluate their communication at that time.

Session 3 focused on intimacy. Before they commenced the work on intimacy, couples reported on the discussions they had during the week and their self-evaluations of their communication during those discussions. Graham and Lyn both reported success in implementing their self-selected goals to enhance their communication. They identified two shared goals for enhancing the intimacy in their relationship: mutual support of each other regarding the stress of work, and having more quality time together as a couple. The group had a brief discussion on how partners support each other with work stress. After hearing these ideas, Lyn and Graham resolved to do three specific things to help support each other with stress: talk at least twice a week about work issues, spend time on the weekends having fun away from work, and give each other regular massages.

The fourth session, on management of conflict, began with each couple discussing a difficult issue in their relationship. During this exercise, the leader observed that Lyn's voice became raised and that Graham turned away from Lyn. They acknowledged they were both irritated with each other, and the process of interaction was discussed. Both agreed that Lyn had become critical of Graham, and he had then refused to talk. They reported that this was a common pattern when they talked about difficult issues. After discussion, they decided to attempt to change this conflict management pattern.

The leader suggested to the group that the speaker-listener technique is useful to overcome many conflict management problems. In this technique, one person becomes the speaker, whose role it is to speak as clearly and specifically as possible about the issue. The listener focuses intently on what the speaker says, and tries, through summaries and questions, to understand the speaker's viewpoint. The listener may not disagree or offer an opinion. Once the speaker is satisfied that he or she has been heard by the listener, the partners exchange roles. Each of the couples tried to use this technique in their discussion. Lyn and Graham had some difficulty initially in doing the task, but with coaching from the leader, they managed to talk this issue through. Both partners were then asked what they would try to do differently in the future when having difficulty with conflict. Each reported that they wanted to use the speaker-listener structure to help them listen more effectively. We identified an issue for them to discuss at home (the weekly budget, about which they often disagreed), and they agreed to tape the discussion for review in the next session.

In session 5, Graham and Lyn's tape was reviewed. They had done quite well in discussing the issue of the weekly budget, though they had not followed strictly the speaker-listener roles. The leader asked each partner to identify what he or she was doing right to help the conversation proceed. Lyn identified that she was speaking more slowly and pausing more to let Graham express his opinions. Graham reported that he was focusing on what Lyn said and asking questions to help him understand. The couple each stated goals of maintaining these changes, and we identified another topic (how Graham disciplined his children) for them to discuss in the following week. The main part of session 5 was on sexuality. Graham and Lyn both believed their sex life was good. Their stated goal in this area was to have a few weekends a year away together to add romance to their sex life.

The final session focused on managing change. Lyn and Graham identified that the major change likely to affect them over the next 12 months was Lyn's moving from half- to full-time work. She reported some trepidation about coping with full-time work. They discussed a range of strategies they could use to support her. Graham identified that for him to do more of the household chores would be helpful to ease the burden on Lyn. They also reaffirmed their earlier resolutions to have time together and to talk regularly about work issues.

The experience of Graham and Lyn is representative of the experience of many couples seen in relationship education. They reported that their relationship was highly satisfying for each of them. They were able to discuss the strengths and weaknesses of their current relationship without acrimony. At the same time, the systematic review of their relationship across the areas covered in Couple CARE enabled them to be specific about actions to take to improve some aspects of their relationship. The couple identified goals for relationship enhancement in all of the six sessions they attended, and they implemented self-directed change to address these goals during the program. The group discussion and suggestions from other couples provided ideas for Lyn and Graham to consider. The leader facilitated group discussion, structured the self-directed learning exercises, and helped partners define specific goals and develop concrete action plans to achieve those goals.

RESEARCH ON RELATIONSHIP EDUCATION

There are a large number of research studies evaluating marriage education and enrichment as well as numerous reviews and meta-analyses of that evidence (Bagarozzi & Rauen, 1981; Bradbury & Fincham, 1990; Christensen & Heavey, 1999; Dyer & Halford, 1998; Giblin, Sprenkle, & Sheehan, 1986; Guerney & Maxson, 1990; Hahlweg & Markman, 1988; Sayers, Kohn, & Heavey, 1998; Van Widenfelt, Markman, Guerney, Behrens, & Hosman, 1997). The conclusions drawn by reviewers of research on the effects of marriage and relationship education diverge quite markedly, even when examining the same evidence. For example, Guerney and Maxson, commenting on the meta-analysis of outcome studies undertaken by Giblin et al., concluded, "There is no doubt that, on the whole, enrichment programs work and the field is an entirely legitimate one" (p. 1133). In contrast, Bradbury and Fincham concluded from the results of the same meta-analysis: "Prevention programs have not yet been shown to produce lasting changes in relationships" (p. 397).

Given the diversity of conclusions drawn by reviewers of the evidence, it is important to analyze the available data carefully to establish exactly what effects have been demonstrated with which programs for which couples. There is a general finding that most couples who complete competently run premarriage education programs report high satisfaction with the programs (Harris et al., 1992). This is evident across information and awareness, inventory, and skills training programs (Halford, 1999).

A 1985 meta-analysis of 85 relationship education and enhancement programs found an average effect size of .44 across all education programs and relationship outcome measures (Giblin et al., 1985), which by convention is a moderate-size effect (Cohen, 1997). The Giblin et al. meta-analysis included all available studies, whether or not they were published; no studies were excluded on methodological grounds. Most studies lacked any sort of control group, and only a very small number of the studies included any follow-up results, hence, most studies included in this meta-analysis failed to meet usual scientific standards of evaluation. In contrast, Hahlweg and Markman (1988) conducted a meta-analysis that included only seven studies, but all of these were published controlled trials. Moreover, they focused their review on programs that included relationship skills training. They found a mean effect size of .79 for education programs relative to controls. Thus, a large effect size was found in the highest-quality studies.

Both the Giblin et al. (1985) and Hahlweg and Markman (1988) meta-analyses found differences in effect sizes as a function of type of measure used to assess change. Observational measures of relationship skills showed substantially larger differences between groups than self-report measures of relationship satisfaction (.76 versus .35 in Giblin et al., and 1.51 versus .52 in Hahlweg & Markman). Furthermore, Giblin et al. found greater effect sizes for self-report measures classified as assessing relationship skills (.63) than for measures classified as assessing relationship satisfaction (.34). Thus, since the mid- to late 1980s, it has been well established that relationship education produces large improvements in relationship skills in the short term, and that there are small short-term increases in relationship satisfaction. However, given that marriage and relationship education is designed to prevent relationship problems from developing, it is important to focus on studies that evaluate the effects of education on

Table 21.3 Prevention of relationship distress: summary of controlled trials.

Author	Subjects	Intervention	Measures	Key Findings
Avery et al., 1980; Ridley, Jorgensen, Morgan, & Avery, 1982	54 couples	Guerney Relationship Enhancement program (RE)	SR of relationship satisfaction and quality; OBS (for 37 couples only) audiotape of couple "request for change" interaction.	RE couples improved in communication and relationship adjustment from pre- to posttest. Increases in communication skills maintained at 6-month follow-up. No follow-up data reported on perceived relationship adjustment.
Halford, Sanders, & Behrens, in press	83 couples stratified into high and low risk based on parental divorce or violence.	Couple CARE, a group 6-session program, compared to an awareness control condition.	Self-reported relationship satisfaction; observed couple communication.	High-risk couples showed sustained gains in communication to 1-year follow-up. High-risk couples receiving Couple CARE showed higher satisfaction at 4-year follow-up than high-risk control couples. Low-risk couples did not benefit from Couple CARE.
Hahlweg et al., 1998	81 couples	EPL ("German" PREP) plus segment on Christian marriage	SR of relationship satisfaction; OBS: videotape of couple problem-solving interaction.	EPL couples improved in communication skills and nonverbal positivity from pre- to posttest, and maintained gains at 1-, 3-, and 5-year follow-ups. No differences between groups on relationship satisfaction at posttest, but EPL couples demonstrated significantly higher relationship satisfaction at 3- and 5-year follow-up.
Markman et al., 1988; Markman et al., 1993	114 couples	PREP	SR of relationship satisfaction; OBS: videotape of couple problem-solving interaction.	PREP couples showed significant gains in communication at posttest, maintained to 1.5- and 3-year follow-up. PREP couples relationship satisfaction greater at 1.5- and 3-year follow-ups. Males maintained higher relationship satisfaction through 4- and 5-year follow-ups.
Miller et al., 1975	32 couples	Minnesota Couples Communication Project (MCCP)	OBS: audiotape of couple interaction over planning task.	Compared to controls, MCCP couples significantly improved in communication skills.
Renick et al., 1992*	24 couples	PREP	SR of relationship satisfaction; OBS: videotape of couple problem-solving interaction.	Compared to Engaged Encounter controls, PREP couples increased in communication skills from pre- to posttest. PREP couples showed trend toward increase in relationship satisfaction at 2-month follow-up.

(continued)

Table 21.3   *(Continued)*

Author	Subjects	Intervention	Measures	Key Findings
Van Widenfelt, Hosman, Schaap, & van der Staak, 1996	67 couples with history of parental divorce	"Dutch" PREP plus family-of-origin session.	SR of problem intensity, problem-solving efficacy, and relationship satisfaction.	All couples deteriorated over time on all measures; no evidence of effect of PREP.
Wampler & Sprenkle, 1980	52 couples	MCCP	SR of relationship quality; OBS: audiotape of couple problem-solving interaction.	MCCP couples improved in communication skills significantly more than attention-only and control couples and increased in perceived relationship quality. increases in perceived relationship quality maintained at 6-month follow-up, but improvements in communication skills were not maintained.

*Not from original source. Most detailed published report. *Note:* SR = Self-report measures; OBS = Observational measures; PREP = Premarital Relationship Enhancement Program; RCCT = Randomized controlled trial.

relationship satisfaction and stability over periods of years, focusing particularly on the effects on couples who initially are satisfied in their relationships.

There are only eight controlled trials that evaluated relationship education programs for currently satisfied couples entering committed relationships, and that also include follow-up assessments at six months or more. These studies are summarized in Table 21.3. All these programs consisted of between four and eight face-to-face group sessions each of two to three hours duration. These evaluations were of skills-based programs, with almost all of them focusing on PREP or a variant of PREP.

SUMMARY

Across studies, there is a consistent finding that, relative to no intervention or minimal intervention controls, couples participating in relationship education programs do acquire the targeted skills (Avery, Ridley, Leslie, & Milholland, 1980; Markman, Floyd, Stanley, & Storaasli, 1988; Markman & Hahlweg, 1993; Miller, Nunnally, & Wackman, 1975; Renick, Blumberg, & Markman, 1992; Wampler & Sprenkle, 1980). Long-term follow-up of the maintenance of acquired skills has been investigated less, but three recent studies show maintenance of acquired skills over a period of some years (Hahlweg, Markman, Thurmair, Eckert, & Engel, 1998; Halford et al., in press; Markman, Renick, Floyd, Stanley, & Clements, 1993). However, attenuation of training effects was reported to occur over a 5- to 10-year period in the only study to have follow-up data over that period of time (Stanley, Markman, St. Peters, & Leber, 1995).

The most meaningful index of the efficacy of relationship education is the long-term effects. Unfortunately, only four studies have follow-ups of more than 12 months. Markman and colleagues have found in two studies that skills-based relationship education was associated with enhanced relationship satisfaction or functioning two and five years after marriage (Hahlweg et al., 1998; Markman et al., 1993). The latter study also found that at five-year follow-up, the intervention couples reported significantly fewer instances of spousal physical violence than control couples. A third study using an almost identical education program did not replicate these results (Van Widenfelt et al., 1996). The Van Widenfelt et al. study differed from the Markman studies in that high-risk couples were targeted. This finding may indicate limitations in developing relationship education programs solely through research with universal populations. Neither the Markman nor Hahlweg study was a true randomized controlled trial. In the Markman study, couples were randomly assigned to be offered or not offered the relationship education program. Only about one-third of couples offered the program agreed to participate. In the Hahlweg study, couples chose whether to undertake the skills-based relationship education program or a standard church-provided program. So there is a degree of self-selection into the education condition in both these studies.

The fourth study was a randomized controlled trial of a skills-based relationship education program similar to PREP, with relationship satisfaction and stability data collected through to four-year follow-up (Halford et al., in press). A unique aspect of this study was that couples were classified into high or low risk for relationship problems on the basis of negative family-of-origin experiences (parental divorce or interparental violence). Those couples completing relationship education had significantly higher relationship satisfaction at four-year follow-up than control couples, but this effect was evident only for couples at high risk for relationship problems. The possibility that relationship education may have differential effects for different couples needs replication, but suggests that some couples may benefit more from relationship education than other couples.

In summary, the effects of skills-based relationship education programs on relationship skills are well established; the programs produce increases in skills that are sustained for at least the first few years of a committed relationship. There is some evidence that PREP and

its variants prevent the erosion of relationship satisfaction over time, but these effects may be limited to couples at high risk for relationship distress. The needs of couples with special challenges to address in their relationship, such as individual problems in a partner or formation of stepfamilies, require additional research attention. Also, relationship education could be developed further by examining the effect of relationship education with couples at points of relationship change other than the transition into the relationship.

REFERENCES

Avery, A., Ridley, C., Leslie, L., & Milholland, T. (1980). Relationship enhancement with premarital dyads: A six month follow-up. *American Journal of Family Therapy, 8,* 23–30.

Bagarozzi, D. A., & Rauen, P. I. (1981). Premarital counseling: Appraisal and status. *American Journal of Family Therapy, 9,* 13–27.

Balakkrishnan, R. R., Rao, K. V., Lapierre-Adamcyk, E., & Krotski, K. J. (1987). A hazard model analysis of covariates of marriage dissolution in Canada. *Demography, 24,* 395–406.

Belsky, J., & Kelly, J. (1994). *Transition to parenthood.* New York: Delacorte Press.

Benson, M. J., Larson, J., Wilson, S. M., & Demo, D. H. (1993). Family of origin influences on late adolescent romantic relationships. *Journal of Marriage and the Family, 55,* 663–672.

Birchnall, J., & Kennard, J. (1984). Early and current factors associated with poor quality marriages. *Social Psychiatry, 19,* 31–40.

Black, L. E., & Sprenkle, D. H. (1991). Gender differences in college students' attitudes toward divorce and their willingness to marry. *Journal of Divorce and Remarriage, 15,* 47–60.

Block, J., Block, J. H., & Keyes, S. (1988). Longitudinally foretelling drug usage in adolescence: Early childhood personality and environmental precursors. *Child Development, 59,* 336–355.

Booth, A., & Johnson, D. R. (1988). Premarital cohabitation and marital success. *Journal of Family Issues, 9,* 255–272.

Bradbury, T. N. (1995). Assessing the four fundamental domains of marriage. *Family Relations, 44,* 459–468.

Bradbury, T. N. (Ed.). (1998). *The developmental course of marital dysfunction.* New York: Cambridge University Press.

Bradbury, T. N., & Fincham, F. D. (1990). Preventing marital dysfunction: Review and analysis. In F. D. Fincham & T. N. Bradbury (Eds.), *The psychology of marriage: Basic issues and applications* (pp. 375–401). New York: Guilford Press.

Burgess, A. W., Hartman, C. R., & McCormack, A. (1987). Abused to abuser: Antecedents of socially deviant behaviors. *American Journal of Psychiatry, 144,* 1431–1436.

Burman, B., & Margolin, G. (1992). Analysis of the association between marital relationships and health problems: An interactional perspective. *Psychological Bulletin, 112,* 39–63.

Christensen, A., & Heavey, C. L. (1999). Interventions for couples. *Annual Review of Psychology, 50,* 165–190.

Cissna, K. N., Cox, D. E., & Bochner, A. P. (1990). The dialectic of marital and parental relationships within the stepfamily. *Communication Monographs, 57,* 44–61.

Cohen, J. (1997). *Statistical power analysis for the behavioral sciences* (Rev. ed.). New York: Academic Press.

Cowan, C. P., & Cowan, P. A. (1992). *When partners become parents.* New York: Basic Books.

DeGraaf, A. (1991). De invloed van echtscheiding van de ouders op demografisch gedrag van de vrouw [The impact of divorced parents on women's demographic behavior]. *Maandststistiek van de Bevolking, 39,* 30–38.

Dyer, C., & Halford, W. K. (1998). Prevention of relationship problems: Retrospect and prospect. *Behaviour Change, 15,* 107–125.

Emmelkamp, P. M. G., De Haan, E., & Hoogduin, C. A. I. (1990). Marital adjustment and Obsessive-Compulsive Disorder. *British Journal of Psychiatry, 156,* 55–60.

Feeney, J., & Noller, P. (1996). *Adult attachment.* Thousand Oaks, CA: Sage.

Fincham, F. D., & Bradbury, T. N. (1991). Marital conflict: Towards a more complete integration of research and treatment. In J. P. Vincent (Ed.), *Advances in family intervention, assessment and theory* (Vol. 5, pp. 1–24). Greenwich, CT: JAI Press.

Fowers, B. J., & Olsen, D. H. (1986). Predicting marital success with PREPARE: A predictive validity study. *Journal of Marital and Family Therapy, 12,* 403–413.

Gagnon, M. D., Hersen, M., Kabacoff, R. I., & Van Hasselt, V. B. (1999). Interpersonal and psychological correlates of marital dissatisfaction in late life: A review. *Clinical Psychology Review, 19,* 359–378.

Gibardi, L., & Rosen, L. A. (1991). Differences between college students from divorced and intact families. *Journal of Divorce and Remarriage, 15,* 175–191.

Giblin, P., Sprenkle, D. H., & Sheehan, R. (1985). Enrichment outcome research: A meta-analysis of premarital, marital, and family interventions. *Journal of Marital and Family Therapy, 11,* 257–271.

Glenn, N. D. (1998). The course of marital success and failure in five American 10-year cohorts. *Journal of Marriage and the Family, 60,* 569–576.

Glenn, N. D., & Kramer, K. B. (1987). The marriages and divorces of the children of divorce. *Journal of Marriage and the Family, 49,* 811–825.

Glenn, N. D., & Shelton, B. A. (1983). Pre-adult background variables and divorce: A note of caution about over-reliance on variance. *Journal of Marriage and the Family, 45,* 405–410.

Glick, P. C. (1984). Marriage, divorce, and living arrangements. *Journal of Family Issues, 5,* 7–26.

Gottman, J. M. (1993). The role of conflict engagement, escalation, and avoidance in marital interaction: A longitudinal view of five types of couples. *Journal of Consulting and Clinical Psychology, 61,* 6–15.

Gottman, J. M. (1994). *What predicts divorce? The relationship between marital processes and marital outcomes.* Hillsdale, NJ: Erlbaum.

Gottman, J. M., Coan, J., Carrère, S., & Swanson, C. (1998). Predicting marital happiness and stability from newlywed interactions. *Journal of Marriage and the Family, 60,* 5–22.

Guerney, B. G. (1977). *Relationship enhancement.* San Francisco: Jossey-Bass.

Guerney, B. G. (Ed.). (1987). *Relationship enhancement manual.* Bethesda, MD: Ideal.

Guerney, B. G., Jr., & Maxson, P. (1990). Marital and family enrichment research: A decade review and a look ahead. *Journal of Marriage and the Family, 52,* 1127–1135.

Hahlweg, K., & Markman, H. J. (1988). Effectiveness of behavioral marital therapy: Empirical status of behavioral techniques in preventing and alleviating marital distress. *Journal of Consulting and Clinical Psychology, 56,* 440–447.

Hahlweg, K., Markman, H. J., Thurmair, F., Eckert, V., & Engel, J. (1998). Prevention of marital distress: Results of a German prospective longitudinal study. *Journal of Family Psychology, 12,* 543–556.

Halford, W. K. (1995). Marriage and the prevention of psychiatric disorder. In B. Raphael & G. D. Burrows (Eds.), *Handbook of preventive psychiatry* (pp. 121–138). Amsterdam: Elsevier.

Halford, W. K. (1999). *Australian couples in Millennium Three: A research development agenda for marriage and relationship education.* Canberra, Australia: Department of Family and Community Services.

Halford, W. K. (2001). *Brief couples therapy: Helping partners help themselves.* New York: Guilford Press.

Halford, W. K., Bouma, R., Kelly, A. B., & Young, R. (1999). The interaction of individual psychopathology and marital problems: Current findings and clinical implications. *Behavior Modification, 23,* 179–216.

Halford, W. K., Gravestock, F., Lowe, R., & Scheldt, S. (1992). Toward a behavioral ecology of stressful marital interactions. *Behavioral Assessment, 13,* 135–148.

Halford, W. K., Hahlweg, K., & Dunne, M. (1990). The cross-cultural consistency of marital communication associated with marital distress. *Journal of Marriage and the Family, 52,* 109–122.

Halford, W. K., Kelly, A., & Markman, H. J. (1997). The concept of a healthy marriage. In W. K. Halford & H. J. Markman (Eds.), *Clinical handbook of marriage and couples intervention* (pp. 3–12). Chichester, England: Wiley.

Halford, W. K., & Moore, E. (in press). Relationship education and the prevention of relationship problems. In A. S. Gurman (Ed.), *Clinical handbook of couple therapy* (3rd ed.). New York: Guilford Press.

Halford, W. K., Moore, E., Wilson, K., Burrows, T., & Farrugia, C. (1999). *Couple Commitment and Relationship Enhancement (Couple CARE): A guidebook for enhancing your relationship.* Brisbane, Australia: Griffith University, School of Applied Psychology.

Halford, W. K., & Osgarby, S. M. (1993). Alcohol abuse in individuals presenting for marital therapy. *Journal of Family Psychology, 11,* 1–13.

Halford, W. K., Sanders, M. R., & Behrens, B. C. (1994). Self-regulation in behavioral couples therapy. *Behavior Therapy, 25,* 431–452.

Halford, W. K., Sanders, M. R., & Behrens, B. C. (2000). Repeating the errors of our parents? Family of origin spouse violence and observed conflict management in engaged couples. *Family Process, 39,* 219–235.

Halford, W. K., Sanders, M. R., & Behrens, B. C. (in press). Can skills training prevent relationship problems in at-risk couples? Four-year effects of a behavioral relationship education program. *Journal of Family Psychology.*

Halford, W. K., Scott, J., & Smythe, J. (2000). Couples and cancer. In K. Schmaling & T. Sher (Eds.), *Couples and illness* (pp. 135–170). Washington, DC: American Psychological Association.

Harris, R., Simons, M., Willis, P., & Barrie, A. (1992). *Love, sex and water skiing: The experience of premarriage education in Australia.* Adelaide: University of South Australia, Center for Human Resource Studies.

To have and to hold: Strategies to strengthen marriage and relationships. (1998). Canberra, Australia: House of Representatives Standing Committee on Legal and Constitutional Affairs.

Hunt, R., Hof, L., & DeMaria, R. (1998). *Marriage enrichment: Preparation, mentoring, and outreach.* Philadelphia: Brunner/Mazel.

Huston, T. L., McHale, S., & Crouter, A. (1986). When the honeymoon's over: Changes in the marital relationship over the first year. In R. L. Gilmour & S. W. Duck (Eds.), *The emerging field of personal relationships* (pp. 109–132). Hillsdale, NJ: Erlbaum.

Janus, S. S., & Janus, C. C. (1993). *The Janus report on human sexuality.* New York: Wiley.

Jones, A. C., & Chao, C. M. (1997). Racial, ethnic and cultural issues in couples therapy. In W. K. Halford & H. J. Markman (Eds.), *Clinical handbook of marriage and couples intervention* (pp. 157–178). Chichester, England: Wiley.

Karney, B. R., & Bradbury, T. N. (1995). The longitudinal course of marital quality and stability: A review of theory, method and research. *Psychological Bulletin, 118,* 3–34.

Karney, B. R., & Bradbury, T. N. (1997). Neuroticism, marital interaction, and the trajectory of marital satisfaction. *Journal of Personality and Social Psychology, 66,* 413–424.

Kurdek, L. A. (1991). Marital stability and changes in marital quality in newlywed couples: A test of the contextual model. *Journal of Social and Personal Relationships, 8,* 27–48.

Kurdek, L. A. (1993). Predicting marital dissolution: A 5-year prospective longitudinal study of newlywed couples. *Journal of Personality and Social Psychology, 64,* 221–242.

Larsen, A. S., & Olsen, D. H. (1989). Predicting marital satisfaction using PREPARE: A replication study. *Journal of Marital and Family Therapy, 15,* 311–322.

Larson, J. H., & Holman, T. B. (1994). Premarital predictors of marital quality and stability. *Family Relations, 43,* 228–237.

Lawton, J. M., & Sanders, M. R. (1994). Designing effective behavioral family interventions for stepfamilies. *Clinical Psychology Review, 14,* 463–496.

Lovibond, S. H., & Lovibond, P. F. (1995). *Manual for the Depression Anxiety Stress Scale.* Sydney, Australia: Psychology Foundation of Australia.

Markey, B., & Micheletto, M. (1997). *Instructor manual for FOCCUS.* Omaha, NE: Archdiocese of Omaha.

Markman, H. J. (1981). The prediction of marital distress: A five-year follow-up. *Journal of Consulting and Clinical Psychology, 49,* 760–762.

Markman, H. J. (1991). Backwards into the future of couples therapy and couples therapy research: A comment on Jacobson. *Journal of Family Psychology, 4,* 416–425.

Markman, H. J., Floyd, F. J., Stanley, S. M., & Storaasli, R. D. (1988). Prevention of marital distress: A longitudinal investigation. *Journal of Consulting and Clinical Psychology, 56,* 210–217.

Markman, H. J., & Hahlweg, K. (1993). The prediction and prevention of marital distress: An international perspective. *Clinical Psychology Review, 13,* 29–43.

Markman, H. J., Halford, W. K., & Cordova, A. D. (1997). A grand tour of future directions in the study and promotion of healthy relationships. In W. K. Halford & H. J. Markman (Eds.), *Clinical handbook of marriage and couples interventions* (pp. 695–716). Chichester, England: Wiley.

Markman, H. J., Renick, M. J., Floyd, F. J., Stanley, S. M., & Clements, M. (1993). Preventing marital distress through communication and conflict management training: A 4- and 5-year follow-up. *Journal of Consulting and Clinical Psychology, 61,* 70–77.

Markman, H. J., Stanley, S. M., & Blumberg, S. L. (1994). *Fighting for your marriage: Positive steps for preventing divorce and preserving a lasting love.* San Francisco: Jossey-Bass.

Martin, T. C., & Bumpass, L. L. (1989). Recent trends in marital disruption. *Demography, 26,* 37–51.

McLaughlin, I. G., Leonard, K. E., & Senchak, M. (1992). Prevalence and distribution of premarital aggression among couples applying for a marriage licence. *Journal of Family Violence, 7,* 309–319.

Mihalic, S. W., & Elliott, D. (1997). A social learning theory model of marital violence. *Journal of Family Violence, 12,* 21–47.

Miller, S., Nunnally, E., & Wackman, D. (1975). Minnesota Couples Communication Program (MCCP): Premarital and marital groups. In D. Olsen (Ed.), *Treating relationships* (pp. 21–40). Lake Mills, IA: Graphic.

Miller, S., Wackman, D. B., & Nunnally, E. W. (1976). A communication training program for couples. *Social Casework, 57,* 9–18.

Mott, F. L., & Moore, S. F. (1979). The causes of marital disruption among American women: An interdisciplinary perspective. *Journal of Marriage and the Family, 41,* 355–365.

Muñoz, R. F., Mrazek, P. J., & Haggerty, R. J. (1996). Institute of Medicine report on prevention of mental disorders: Summary and commentary. *American Psychologist, 51,* 1116–1122.

Murphy, C. M., & O'Leary, K. A. (1989). Psychological aggression predicts physical aggression in early marriage. *Journal of Consulting and Clinical Psychology, 57,* 579–582.

National Center for Health Statistics. (1991). *Advance report of final marriage statistics, 1988* (Monthly Vital Statistics Report 39). Hyattsville, MD: Public Health Service.

O'Farrell, T. J., & Birchler, G. R. (1987). Marital relationships of alcoholic, conflicted, and nonconflicted couples. *Journal of Marital and Family Therapy, 13,* 259–274.

O'Leary, K. D., Barling, J., Arias, I., Rosenbaum, A., Malone, J., & Tyree, A. (1989). Prevalence and stability of physical aggression between spouses: A longitudinal analysis. *Journal of Consulting and Clinical Psychology, 57,* 263–268.

O'Leary, K. D., Malone, J., & Tyree, A. (1994). Physical aggression in early marriage: Pre-relationship and relationship effects. *Journal of Consulting and Clinical Psychology, 62,* 594–602.

Olsen, D. H., Fournier, D. G., & Druckman, J. M. (1996). *PREPARE.* Minneapolis, MN: Life Innovations.

Olsen, D. H., & Fowers, B. J. (1986). Predicting marital success with PREPARE: A predictive validity study. *Journal of Marital and Family Therapy, 12,* 403–413.

Olsen, D. H., & Larsen, A. S. (1989). Predicting marital satisfaction using PREPARE: A replication study. *Journal of Marital and Family Therapy, 15,* 311–322.

Pasch, L. A., & Bradbury, T. N. (1998). Social support, conflict, and the development of marital dysfunction. *Journal of Consulting and Clinical Psychology, 66,* 219–230.

Reich, J., & Thompson, W. D. (1985). Marital status of schizophrenic and alcoholic patients. *Journal of Nervous and Mental Disease, 173,* 499–502.

Renick, M. J., Blumberg, S., & Markman, H. J. (1992). The Prevention and Relationship Enhancement Program (PREP): An empirically-based preventive intervention program for couples. *Family Relations, 41,* 141–148.

Ridley, C. A., Jorgensen, S. R., Morgan, A. C., & Avery, A. W. (1982). Relationship enhancement with premarital couples: An assessment of effects on relationship quality. *American Journal of Family Therapy, 10,* 41–48.

Riggs, D. S., O'Leary, K. D., & Breslin, F. C. (1990). Multiple correlates of physical aggression in dating couples. *Journal of Interpersonal Violence, 5,* 61–73.

Rogge, R. D., & Bradbury, T. N. (1999). Till violence does us part: The differing roles of communication and aggression in predicting adverse marital outcomes. *Journal of Consulting and Clinical Psychology, 67,* 340–351.

Ruscher, S. M., & Gotlib, I. H. (1988). Marital interaction patterns of couples with and without a depressed partner. *Behavior Therapy, 19,* 455–470.

Sanders, M. R., Halford, W. K., & Behrens, B. C. (1999). Parental divorce and premarital couple communication. *Journal of Family Psychology, 13,* 60–74.

Saunders, J. B., Aasland, O. G., Babor, T. F., de la Fuente, J. R., & Grant, M. (1993). Development of the Alcohol Use Disorders Identification Test (AUDIT): WHO collaborative project on early detection of persons with harmful alcohol consumption: II. *Addiction, 88,* 791–804.

Sayers, S. L., Kohn, C. S., & Heavey, C. (1998). Prevention of marital dysfunction: Behavioral approaches and beyond. *Clinical Psychology Review, 18,* 713–744.

Silliman, B., Stanley, S. M., Coffin, W., Markman, H. J., & Jordan, P. L. (in press). Preventive interventions for couples. In H. Liddle, D. Santisteban, R. Levant, & J. Bray (Eds.), *Family psychology intervention science.* Washington, DC: American Psychological Association.

Simons, M., Harris, R., & Willis, P. (1994). *Pathways to marriage: Learning for married life in Australia.* Adelaide: University of South Australia, Centre for Research in Education and Work.

Spanier, G. B. (1976). Measuring dyadic adjustment: New scales for assessing the quality of marriage and similar dyads. *Journal of Marriage and the Family, 37,* 15–28.

Stanley, S. M., Markman, H. J., St. Peters, M., & Leber, B. D. (1995). Strengthening marriages and preventing divorce: New directions in prevention research. *Family Relations, 44,* 392–401.

Stets, J. E., & Straus, M. A. (1990). The marriage licence as a hitting license: A comparison of dating, cohabiting and married couples. In M. A. Straus & R. J. Gelles (Eds.), *Physical violence in American families: Risk factors and adaption to violence in 8415 families* (pp. 131–164). New Brunswick, NJ: Transaction.

Stith, S. M., & Farley, S. C. (1993). A predictive model of male spousal violence. *Journal of Family Violence, 8,* 183–201.

Straus, M. A., Gelles, R., & Steinmetz, S. K. (1980). *Behind closed doors: Violence in the American family.* New York: Doubleday.

Sullivan, K. T., & Bradbury, T. N. (1997). Are premarital prevention programs reaching couples at risk for marital dysfunction? *Journal of Consulting and Clinical Psychology, 65,* 24–30.

Thompson, B. M. (1997). Couples and the work-family interface. In W. K. Halford & H. J. Markman (Eds.), *Clinical handbook of marriage and couples intervention* (pp. 273–290). Chichester, England: Wiley.

Trussel, J., & Rao, K. U. (1987). Premarital cohabitation and marital stability: A reassessment of the Canadian evidence. *Journal of Marriage and the Family, 51,* 535–544.

Van Widenfelt, B., Hosman, C., Schaap, C., & van der Staak, C. (1996). The prevention of relationship distress for couples at risk: A controlled evaluation with nine-month and two-year follow-ups. *Family Relations, 45,* 156–165.

Van Widenfelt, B., Markman, H. J., Guerney, B., Behrens, B., & Hosman, C. (1997). Prevention of relationship problems. In W. K. Halford & H. J. Markman (Eds.), *Clinical handbook of marriage and couples interventions* (pp. 651–678). Chichester, England: Wiley.

Veroff, J., Douvan, E., & Hatchett, S. J. (1995). *Marital instability: A social and behavioral study of the early years.* Westport, CT: Praeger.

Visher, E. B., & Visher, J. S. (1991). Therapy with stepfamily couples. *Psychiatric Annals, 21,* 462–465.

Wampler, K. S., & Sprenkle, D. (1980). The Minnesota Couple Communication Program: A follow-up study. *Journal of Marriage and the Family, 42,* 577–585.

Weissman, M. M. (1987). Advances in psychiatric epidemiology: Rates and risk for major depression. *American Journal of Public Health, 77,* 445–451.

White, L. K. (1990). Determinants of divorce: A review of research in the eighties. *Journal of Marriage and the Family, 52,* 904–912.

Widom, C. S. (1989). Does violence beget violence? A critical examination of the literature. *Psychological Bulletin, 106,* 3–28.

Williams, L., & Jurich, J. (1995). Predicting marital success after five years: Assessing the predictive validity of FOCCUS. *Journal of Marital and Family Therapy, 21,* 41–153.

Winkler, I., & Doherty, W. J. (1983). Communication style and marital satisfaction in Israeli and American couples. *Family Process, 22,* 229–237.

CHAPTER 22

Culturally Sensitive Cognitive-Behavioral Therapy for Depression with Low-Income and Minority Clients

JASON M. SATTERFIELD

In 1990, the World Health Organization listed depression as the fourth leading cause of disability worldwide and the societal cost as rising. By 2020, the disability caused by depression will be second only to heart disease (Murray & Lopez, 1996). Many models used to understand this rise in depression and its less than optimal response to treatment have turned to sociological explanations, namely, the role of stress and diminishing social supports in an increasingly crowded and competitive multicultural world. Treatment models have simultaneously evolved to include culturally bound manifestations of this devastating illness and the need to develop a wider range of more flexible and culturally appropriate interventions.

This chapter presents a culturally sensitive cognitive-behavioral group model designed to treat depression in low-income and minority clients—a population at high risk for depression and poor treatment response. First, a brief overview examines the relationships among minority identity, socioeconomic status, and mental health as a means of identifying depressogenic factors and opportunities for clinical interventions. A history of multicultural therapy models and how they relate to group psychotherapy and cognitive-behavioral therapy (CBT) is also discussed. Second, basic theoretical constructs behind CBT for depression, CBT in groups, and knowledge helpful for developing cultural sensitivity are reviewed. The third section provides specifics of the group structure and content along with suggestions regarding management of group processes and group administration. Following that is a description of the syndromes, symptoms, and diagnoses best treated with this modality. The final section presents excerpts from a case example and data from multicultural pilot groups used to test the effectiveness of this model.

HISTORY OF CULTURALLY SENSITIVE GROUP CBT

The racial, ethnic, and economic composition of the United States is undergoing an unprecedented transformation. In 1995, the U.S. Bureau of the Census estimated that by the year 2000, 33% of the population would be people of color. By 2050, the Bureau estimates 50% of the population will be people of color, with the largest gains in the Latino population (U.S. Bureau of the Census, 1995). Despite the economic prosperity enjoyed by much of the country over the past decade, the lowest-income sector of our communities is also rapidly expanding (Healey, 1995; Holmes, 1996; Schnitzer, 1996; U.S. Bureau of the Census, 1996). In fact, the growing income inequalities in the United States now outstrip those in any other industrialized nation (Holmes, 1996; Kerbo, 1996). Although poverty cuts across cultural and ethnic lines, the proportion of poor individuals among Blacks and Hispanics is more than three times higher than among Whites and is especially high in female-headed households (Danziger, Sandefur, & Weinberg, 1994; Wilson, 1991). Consequently, significant adaptations to our traditional mental health services seem essential if psychology and allied professions are to adequately meet the changing needs of our increasingly multicultural and economically stratified society.

MINORITY STATUS AND MENTAL HEALTH

The relationship between race or ethnicity and mental illness is complex and poorly understood. Research bias, culturally constrained diagnostic categories, and societal confounds such as socioeconomic status (SES) and discrimination make significant clarification unlikely. All racial minorities in the United States have lower incomes, less education, and higher unemployment than Whites. At first glance, racial or ethnic minorities seem to suffer from higher rates of both depression and anxiety than do Caucasians; however, after controlling for differences in education, income, and employment, many of these differences disappear despite the greater stress often encountered due to minority status (Williams & Harris-Reid, 1999).

Many minorities are also recent immigrants who must manage the stress of learning a new culture and possibly a new language in addition to the stress of minority status and probable poverty. Even high-functioning, well-educated immigrants sometimes find themselves employed in menial, low-paying jobs because of an inability to speak the language or effectively negotiate a foreign culture. This loss of status and self-esteem can increase their risk for psychopathology. Depending on their country of origin, the process of immigration can often be traumatic and likely to engender depression or other stress-related disorders. Second-generation minorities often find themselves negotiating two cultures: that of the majority and also that of their dependent parents and local minority communities. Their financial resources may be further drained by having to provide for themselves and for less acculturated family members.

SOCIOECONOMIC STATUS AND MENTAL HEALTH

SES is one of the strongest known determinants of variations in health status, even after controlling for access to health care (Adler et al., 1994). It appears that stressors endemic to the experience of poverty damage both physical and mental health. This social and economic phenomenon should be of special interest to the mental health field given the relatively stable, inverse relationship between SES and psychopathology (Bruce, Takeuchi, & Leaf, 1991; Dohrenwend et al., 1992; Holzer et al., 1986;

Kessler et al., 1994; Saraceno & Barbui, 1997). More specifically, poor adults have a 1.92 greater probability for the development of a new Axis I psychiatric disorder than the non-poor, even after controlling for gender, ethnicity, and other demographic variables (Bruce et al., 1991). Depressive symptoms are especially prevalent in lower-SES clients, independent of ethnicity (Biafora, 1995; Roberts, 1987). The Epidemiological Catchment Area study found that respondents whose household income was below $17,500/year were 16 times more likely to meet criteria for Major Depression than those with incomes over $35,000/year (Eaton et al., 1997). Of special concern is the growing phenomenon of persistent poverty, where cumulative and sometimes unavoidable adversity significantly enhances risks for depression and other psychopathology even further (R. A. Turner & Lloyd, 1995).

MENTAL HEALTH SERVICES ACCESS AND UTILIZATION

Unfortunately, minority and low-income individuals have less access and lower utilization rates for mental health care than do majority or high-income individuals. The U.S. Census Bureau (2000) estimates that 33.4% of minorities have no health insurance coverage, in contrast to 11% of non-Hispanic White adults. One in three individuals living below the poverty level have no insurance. Given the lack of insurance coverage and the high correlation between minority status and poverty, most minority clients simply cannot afford needed services.

Even if access is available, utilization research suggests that low-income and minority clients are less likely to seek out and/or remain in mental health services regardless of need (Cheung & Snowden, 1990; Dworkin & Adams, 1987; S. Sue, 1977). S. Sue, McKinney, & Allen (1976) found a 23% dropout after the first session, with 70%

dropping out by session 10. Organista, Muñoz, and González (1994) found a 58% dropout rate in depression groups for low-income clients, compared to the mean premature termination rate of 35% taken from a review of the group therapy literature (Bostwick, 1987). Conversely, good education and high SES have been found to predict continuation of treatment (Rabin, Kaslow, & Rehm, 1985). Although overall rates of outpatient mental health treatment utilization increased for low- and middle-income African Americans from 1981 to 1993, this increase came from a greater reliance on general medicine providers and not a greater use of mental health providers (Cooper-Patrick et al., 1999).

Parron (1982) explains problems with minority health care utilization by highlighting deficiencies in availability, accessibility, acceptability, and accountability of current mental health services. Other service use frameworks have looked to predisposing factors (e.g., race, gender, education, age), enabling factors (e.g., income, perceived availability, cost, transportation), and perceived need for help to better understand the access and utilization problems in the low-income and minority communities (Yeatts, Crow, & Folts, 1992).

DEVELOPING MULTICULTURAL PERSPECTIVES FOR MENTAL HEALTH

Attempts to answer the call for more culturally sensitive and effective mental health services have included ethnic and linguistic matching, teaching therapists "cultural competence" for work with specific ethnic groups, and more general cultural sensitivity training for therapists (Hall, 1997; Leong, 1986; Organista, 2000; Pinderhughes, 1989; S. Sue, 1998). Ideally, services might combine the best from all three approaches: providing ethnic or linguistic match when possible and/or desired, training providers in concrete cultural details of the predominant groups likely to be served, and giving providers the general skills of cultural awareness and sensitivity that can be applied when any issue of difference arises.

Although results have been equivocal, the preponderance of ethnic and linguistic matching studies show improved attendance, satisfaction, and clinical outcomes when the race and language of the client matches that of the mental health provider (S. Sue, 1998; Takeuchi, Uehara, & Maramba, 1999). However, the issue of attempting to match the ethnicity of client and provider has raised both practical and political concerns. Practically speaking, matching is simply not feasible given the different demographic composition of providers and clients. As of 1994, only 4% of the membership of the American Psychological Association were persons of color (Bernal & Castro, 1994). In 1993, only 9.4% of U.S. Americans with doctorates in psychology and only 8% of full-time psychology faculty were minorities. It is also unclear exactly what a "match" would mean: Even within a given ethnicity, there can be a great variety of subcultures that may or may not work well together. Politically speaking, the policy encourages treatment segregation. As history has shown, separate often does not mean equal, particularly when treatment resources are distributed by a racially different governing body.

Another approach to meeting our growing need for culturally appropriate treatment has been the push to develop cultural competence for treating a given ethnic or racial group. These programs often target the largest ethnic groups in a local demographic area and strive to teach cultural and/or language specifics to local providers. Useful and insightful programs have been developed for work with Latinos (Falicov, 2000; Organista, 2000), Asian Americans (Lee, 2000; Leong, 1986), African Americans (Jackson & Greene, 2000; Randall, 1994), women (Comas-Díaz & Greene, 1994; Davis

& Padesky, 1989), gays and lesbians (Purcell, Campos, & Perilla, 1996), and others. Although helpful, this approach requires a provider to become "competent" in a potentially limitless number of cultures and runs the risk of spreading cultural stereotypes by minimizing intracultural differences.

Cultural sensitivity training is perhaps the most adaptable but least specific way to answer the need for new services. Growing from the philosophical perspectives of postmodernism and constructivism (Lyddon & Weill, 1997; Mahoney, 1991; Neimeyer, 1993), these models recognize the inherently value-laden and often biased nature of traditional theories of psychotherapy and human change and how these might not be helpful to persons of different cultural backgrounds. Several general guidelines currently exist that are meant to stimulate thought, increase multicultural sensitivity, and provoke empirical study and validation. The American Psychological Association (APA, 1993) created "Guidelines for Providers of Psychological Services to Ethnic, Linguistic, and Culturally Diverse Populations" and has published multiple works from their Office of Ethnic Minority Affairs. Other guidelines and models include the ethnomedical model (Alladin, 1999), the Dimensions of Personal Identity (Arredondo et al., 1996), Cultural Humility Training (Tervalon & Murray-García, 1998), and the guidelines of the Association for Multicultural Counseling and Development (D. W. Sue, Arredondo, & McDavis, 1995). Most of the guidelines and training models include exercises to (1) increase cultural self-awareness, (2) begin building cultural knowledge, and (3) create highly flexible skills needed to build a helpful relationship with clients who may be from very different backgrounds. Specific examples of each of these three goal areas are found in Table 22.1. Further guidelines for awareness building and sensitivity training can be found in Pinderhughes (1989) and Palmer and Laungani (1999).

Table 22.1 Selected examples from the goal areas of cultural sensitivity training.

Cultural Awareness

- Heterogeneous training groups to inspire cultural reflection and self-awareness. Explore personal feelings of being different, being powerful/powerless, stereotypes, and participation in oppression.
- Being aware of how a client self-identifies, including race, ethnicity, culture, gender, sexual orientation, and religion, and where this "places" client in the present majority culture, including socioeconomic status and education.
- Noticing the elements of difference between client and therapist and how this may affect rapport, trust, judgment, and explicit/implicit manifestations of power.
- Being aware of culturally bound diagnostic categories and the cultural "myopia" of most treatment modalities.

Cultural Knowledge

- Knowing the social and political contexts that create and perpetuate oppression.
- Identifying and understanding the daily wearing stressors of being a minority or impoverished.
- Knowing a client's culturally bound conceptions of illness, health, and treatment or healing.
- Understanding the basic history and development of a particular culture and the functionality of its beliefs.

Cultural Skills

- Learning to manage the inherent anxiety of interacting with someone who is different.
- Learning to acknowledge and manage the feelings that arise from having participated in or been victim of various manifestations of discrimination and bias.
- Learning how to question clients about their cultural perspectives in a way that is open and nonjudgmental.

GROUP PSYCHOTHERAPY, CBT, AND CULTURAL SENSITIVITY

Culturally driven adaptations to specific forms of therapy and particular theoretical orientations have begun to take form. Salvendy (1999) and Nakkab and Hernandez (1990) offer useful perspectives on how cultural heterogeneity among treatment group members and between the group leader and group members impacts group dynamics and necessitates changes in group leadership style. They argue for a greater flexibility in traditional group rules that tend to discourage therapist self-disclosure or socializing and emphasize the role of the group as a "cultural broker." They suggest special attention to different ways of thinking about personal boundaries, trust, power differentials, and respect for authority and elders and how these might impact the formation and stability of a group.

Clinical guidelines and treatment manuals written by frontline cognitive-behavioral therapists offer useful ways to develop both cultural competence and cultural sensitivity in the context of individual and group CBT (Azocar, Miranda, & Dwyer, 1996; Organista, 2000; Padesky & Greenberger, 1995; Randall, 1994; Satterfield, 1998). CBT basic concepts may be culturally bound, but sensitive and flexible applications of these constructs may translate into acceptable and effective treatment for underserved populations. Practical suggestions for these adaptations are discussed in greater detail next.

THEORETICAL CONSTRUCTS FOR CULTURALLY SENSITIVE CBT DEPRESSION GROUPS

The theoretical constructs behind this group intervention are numerous and have been derived from a variety of different orientations. Those mentioned in greatest detail are divided into three sections: the basic theoretical constructs behind CBT for depression; the application of these basic CBT constructs in the context of group treatment; and the multicultural awareness, knowledge, and sensitivity required to deliver group CBT to minority and low-income clients.

BASIC CBT CONSTRUCTS

Depression is conceptualized using a diathesis-stress model, where a diathesis (e.g., cognitive or attributional style) interacts with stress (e.g., minority or poverty stress) to produce the onset of a depressive disorder (Beck, 1967). Depression is thought to be maintained or exacerbated by subsequent reductions in activities and social contacts (i.e., positive reinforcements) and/or increasingly unbalanced negative thinking. More in keeping with interpersonal therapy (IPT) for depression, careful attention is given to the role of an individual's interpersonal and social environments and any role transitions that may have occurred (Klerman, Weissman, Rounsaville, & Chevron, 1984).

The CBT interventions target the three domains thought to maintain or exacerbate depressive disorders: activity scheduling, promoting cognitive balance, and improving social supports. Cognitive diatheses thought to have a role in the onset of the depressive disorder are addressed throughout each of the three domains. Many of the culturally sensitive group interventions were adapted from *Control Your Depression* (Lewinsohn, Muñoz, Youngren, & Zeiss, 1986) and influenced by other sources (Beck, Rush, Shaw, & Emery, 1979; Burns, 1980; Freeman, Pretzer, Fleming, & Simon, 1990; Greenberger & Padesky, 1995; Satterfield, 1994; Yalom, 1985). For a more detailed look at the theoretical underpinnings of CBT for depression, see Dobson and Steinman (this volume).

CBT AND GROUP PROCESS

A special sensitivity to group process was added to the more traditional CBT model in the hope that specific attention to group dynamics and cohesion would create a more attractive and acceptable group for low-income and minority clients. The group format was thought to provide better opportunities for normalization, acculturation, and social support among other "curative" group factors (Yalom, 1985). The goal was to provide quality CBT group therapy *through* the group rather than simply *in* a group format (Satterfield, 1994; Whitney & Rose, 1989). The theoretical constructs of group cohesion, multilevel interventions (isomorphisms), and a here-and-now focus are discussed below.

The definition and understanding of group cohesion has grown more sophisticated over the past few years (Braaten, 1991; Budman, Soldz, Demby, Davis, & Merry, 1993; Budman et al., 1989; Kaul & Bednar, 1986). Group cohesion has been equated roughly with the therapeutic alliance in individual therapy. It manifests itself differently, depending on the stage of the group. Multiple studies and meta-analyses of group cohesion have shown a strong positive correlation among cohesion, performance, symptom reduction, and other clinical outcomes (Budman et al., 1987, 1989; Evans & Dion, 1991; Hand, Lamontagne, & Marks, 1976). Although cohesion is important in every group, it was thought to be critical for low-income and minority clients, who are at high risk of prematurely discontinuing treatment and who typically feel they are not valued and do not belong. Although homogeneous groups tend to become cohesive and reach stable working stages more quickly, racial heterogeneity does not preclude cohesion and can act as a catalyst that opens discussion of central issues of self-worth, belonging, cultural identity, and acculturation. As long as the group leader can facilitate basic communication and safety, the greater variety of worldviews provides all assembled with novel opportunities and ideas.

In a group setting, interventions can target the individual, a dyad or pair, a subgroup, or the group as a whole. Limited research suggests that the selective use of these multiple layers of interaction can facilitate cohesion, modeling, group and personal growth, and clinical outcomes (Dies, 1993; Falloon, 1981; Hand et al., 1976; Karterud, 1989; Kaul & Bednar, 1986). For example, more group-as-a-whole interventions are used in the early stages of the group to foster a sense of group identity and ownership of the group. Dyadic interventions are used for new members to create an immediate subgroup and facilitate identification and modeling. Subgroups are used to complete in-session homework assignments and brainstorm disputations of automatic thoughts. Individual work includes homework assignments and weekly check-ins.

Although the focus in these short-term groups is on the alleviation of depressive symptoms and improvement in real-world functioning, the here-and-now opportunities of group therapy are especially important. Group interactions often evoke feelings of inferiority, anger, insecurity, and other "hot" emotions, which the cognitive therapist can use as poignant, here-and-now examples in the service of cognitive restructuring. Hollon and Shaw (1979) further show that groups can elicit important negative inferences that might not come to light during individual therapy; that is a member of a multicultural group has many more opportunities for negative self-comparisons and subsequent interventions. Here-and-now group interactions also provide a natural arena to test social hypotheses, practice newly acquired social skills or acculturated behaviors, and create a "therapeutic mirror" showing the objective social consequences of a patient's actions and beliefs.

THEORETICAL CONSTRUCTS AND KNOWLEDGE FOR CULTURAL SENSITIVITY

To best understand and meet the needs of low-income and minority clients, it is essential first to become aware of the inherently biased beliefs often held by therapists, clients, and traditional CBT.

Client Beliefs and Experiences

Given the diversity of the low-income and minority communities, no given set of beliefs regarding depression or psychological treatment is possible, and few empirically based surveys exist to offer guidance. However, literature reviews, focus groups, and past clinical encounters offer useful insights (Friedman, Patterson, & Gomez, 1983; Heitler, 1976; Lorion, 1974; Schnitzer, 1996).

A greater than average number of psychosocial stressors are endemic to the experience of poverty and influence the development and maintenance of a client's beliefs. These stressors include unemployment, physical illness, substandard housing or homelessness, caregiver stress, high divorce rates, prejudice and discrimination, family disintegration, and lack of transportation or child care (Eaton & Muntaner, 1999). Given these frequently occurring stressors, feelings of hopelessness, devaluation, disempowerment, and stigmatization are common. Many low-income clients have ceased the struggle to find work or improve their condition as one door after another has been closed. It becomes difficult not to internalize societal prejudices that label many low-income persons unintelligent, immature, criminal, drug abusing, or lazy. The alternative is to externalize the causes of stressors, which may preserve self-esteem but take away a sense of control. The cycle of negative experiences, beliefs, and expectations becomes a downward spiral as low-income individuals endure more and more negative, devaluing experiences and become less able to cope with objectively severe stressors. Active coping efforts and attempts to control their environment are diminished because clients are either too depressed from internalizing their situation or too hopeless because causes are viewed as external and unchangeable (Eaton & Muntaner, 1999; Uumoto, 1986).

Low-income and minority clients frequently report accumulated negative experiences with health care providers and other authority figures and institutions who either act disrespectfully or unempathically or are simply unable to provide adequate treatment or relief. Treatment often begins with the client already on the defensive, expecting not to be believed, understood, or relieved. These fears might be exacerbated in the mental health setting, where the client fears additional stigma, stereotyping, or characterological blame. Clients are afraid to develop trust or hope due to past negative perceptions and experiences that suggest these are luxuries they cannot afford. Clients may implicitly search for evidence that confirms these negative beliefs or behave in ways to confirm these negative self-fulfilling prophecies. In other words, a missed phone message or lost referral might become "proof" that, once again, the client will not be respected and taken seriously.

Heitler (1976) and others suggest that low-income clients expect the clinician to be active, somewhat directive, and advice-giving. Formality, therapeutic neutrality, and a nonsymptom-focused approach might be alienating. Clients expect symptom relief in a relatively short time and appreciate demonstrations of practical interventions. Failure to address these expectations, regardless of their reality, might result in low client satisfaction and premature terminations.

Although race, ethnicity, and economic standing are intimately connected, it is important to be aware that negative stressors tied to race but independent of SES do still regularly occur. Although major episodic experiences of racially motivated violence and discrimination may have declined, more "minor" but wearing experiences occur daily in the lives of minority clients. In a comparison of major and minor experiences with discrimination, Williams and colleagues found that it was the minor daily experiences with discrimination that most impacted mental and physical well-being (Williams et al., 1999). Discrimination in both its overt and subtle forms greatly impacts client beliefs about therapy and depression and their expectations about the trustworthiness of the group leader and other

group members. Issues regarding trust will undoubtedly impact group self-disclosure and the development of cohesion.

Great diversity exists in culturally bound beliefs regarding the causes and treatment of mental illness or stress. Some cultures emphasize spiritual explanations for depression; others focus on somatic symptoms and have virtually no concept of an "emotional disorder." The presence of a psychiatric disorder and the need for treatment can be drastically stigmatizing and require special interventions to make treatment acceptable and effective. The best practice usually involves the development of special cultural knowledge and competence in the cultures most likely to be represented in a given group. Reality requires a mixture of specific cultural competence paired with an ability to elicit and respond to culturally bound beliefs in clients from unfamiliar cultures.

Clients who have immigrated experience the triple stressors of being a minority, of the immigration itself, and of acculturation. These clients often develop a sense of "cultural bereavement" because social supports, stabilizing routines, favorite activities, and positive reinforcers have all been lost (Nakkab & Hernandez, 1990). Clients are faced with the challenge of learning a new language, finding employment and financial stability, and learning new cultural norms and ways of behaving while maintaining their sense of identity and sources of self-esteem. This challenging balancing act is one that few majority, nonimmigrants can understand. The acceptance of mental health group treatment might further wound an already damaged sense of self if depression is seen as a moral failing or if group attendance and self-disclosure are seen as "losing face" around others.

Therapist Beliefs and Experiences
Even well-intentioned therapists often harbor countertherapeutic beliefs and expectations about their low-income and minority clients. In the now classic New Haven study, surveyed mental health providers regarded lower-class

clients as crude, volatile, passive, apathetic, and uninterested in clinical improvement (Hollingshead & Redlich, 1958). Although this study took place nearly 50 years ago, this "blaming the victim" mentality has not been eliminated. Frustrated therapists may still see low-income clients as disorganized, irresponsible, entitled, or simply unwilling to work for their own mental health (Schnitzer, 1996). Of special importance are the attributions therapists make regarding the "countertherapeutic behaviors" of their low-income clients, such as when they miss appointments, show up late, or do not complete homework assignments. Stable attributions that habitually place blame on the client breed therapist resentment and frustration and impair therapist motivation to "go the extra mile." The extraordinary day-to-day demands low-income clients face in a sometimes unimaginably chaotic life (e.g., the struggle to provide adequate food and shelter, the demands of low-income single motherhood, concerns for personal safety) are easily overlooked by many therapists.

To successfully facilitate a culturally sensitive group for depressed low-income and minority clients, the group leader must have special self-awareness, competence to explore and manage diversity, and the flexibility to change technique. First, leaders must be aware of their own culture, biases, and participation in societal discrimination (Palmer & Laungani, 1999; Pinderhughes, 1989). Although one may strive to be "a blank slate" or "color blind," these goals are simply unrealistic and perhaps harmful. Based on personal and cultural experiences, therapists will have preexisting (and perhaps well-defended) ideas about African Americans, women, gays, and others. The less individual information is available on a given client, the more one is likely to fall back on stereotypes. As Laungani (1999) states, "Stereotypes are the hooks on which people hang their initial impressions and observations" (p. 43). Part of the process of running a culturally sensitive group involves first becoming aware of the cultural biases and stereotypes one currently embraces.

Skillful questioning about a client's cultural background requires special technique and sensitivity. The leader needs to know what words will elicit useful information and how far to pursue this line of questioning. Some clients may resent having to educate their group leader unless cultural inquiries are clearly justified (Padesky & Greenberger, 1995). The leader must also recognize and neutralize the internal anxiety created by interacting with clients of a different race or culture. Leaders must be aware of how their personality, appearance, and choice of therapeutic modality may be experienced by others. Ideally, leaders will have the flexibility to think in terms of clinical hypotheses or best guesses rather than set formulations or foregone conclusions that are closed to revision (S. Sue, 1998). This flexibility includes the ability to accept innovation and try nonstandard practices, such as using judicious self-disclosure, giving and accepting advice, accepting small gifts, and allowing out-of-group socializing. Other specific means of preparation and modification of techniques are discussed in the following section on assessment and intervention.

Culturally Bound CBT Beliefs and Biases

CBT was initially developed in a Western industrialized medical setting in the late 1960s and early 1970s. Its primary philosophical roots are closely connected to modern, scientific notions of rationality and logic. Inherent to CBT is the Western conceptualization of the self as an autonomous, free-willed individual with the capacity for personal control of factors within and outside of the self. CBT values willpower, determination, assertiveness, independence, open verbal communication, linear organization, productivity, and efficient management of time and resources. A CBT therapist and client "collaborate," and dissent is tolerated or even encouraged. The client becomes a "naïve scientist" who develops hypotheses about his or her mood, then collects "data" to either confirm or disconfirm these hypotheses. Hypotheses are then adapted and the "research" or therapy continues in the spirit of the scientific method.

These cultural biases inherent to CBT are not necessarily helpful or harmful. It is essential, however, for the CBT practitioner to be aware of these assumptions and how they may be received by minority or non-Western clients. It is also essential to use the cultural assumptions of CBT as organizing and guiding principles that can be changed, adapted, or even discarded if necessary. For example, although this treatment modality does emphasize rational cognition, it is ultimately the "pragmatic utility, rather than the bedrock validity" of cognition that is most important (Mahoney, 1988, p. 5). Padesky and Greenberger (1995) and Persons (1989) offer other examples of how to bend the assumptions of CBT to meet the needs of diverse clients.

METHODS OF ASSESSMENT AND INTERVENTION

The following CBT group treatment model was developed over a number of years at San Francisco General Hospital's (SFGH) Depression Clinic, founded by Ricardo Muñoz, Jeanne Miranda, and others. This clinic served a predominately low-income and minority population with group and individual counseling in English and Spanish. The following assessment procedures and group treatment specifics should be considered a work in progress and are written broadly to facilitate easy adaptation to other populations. A more detailed description of the group content and goals can be found in Miranda, Schreckengost, and Heine (1992).

RECRUITMENT AND PROGRAM DEVELOPMENT

Without sufficient access and utilization, even a superior treatment program cannot be effective. Mental health services must be accessible and acceptable for persons not familiar with the concepts of depression or mental illness and for those who attach a powerfully negative stigma to mental health treatment. Because each clinic and clientele can have different needs, it is best to initially survey the demographic makeup of potential clients and enlist the help of community leaders and organizations. Neighborhood meetings, focus groups, church socials, and contact with cultural experts can provide useful information on what types of services will be most acceptable and how to best market them. The location of the clinic also plays a role in the initial acceptability and accessibility of services. Clinics near public transportation or other familiar medical clinics ease transportation problems and other anxieties. Clinics that provide privacy and comfort while still being located in minority neighborhoods are more likely to be accepted. Because clients are likely to see their primary care doctors in their neighborhood clinics, this is fertile ground to reach depressed, underserved patients. Regular outreach and education are provided for the primary care physicians and nurses to improve the detection of Major Depression and to teach ways to successfully present or "sell" a referral to a client. Although important, other techniques of initial recruitment/outreach, community education, and culture-specific treatment adaptations are beyond the scope of this chapter (Dumka, Garza, Roosa, & Stoerzinger, 1997; Thompson, Neighbors, Munday, & Jackson, 1996; Yeatts et al., 1992).

ASSESSMENT AND INTAKE

The initial management of the referral and intake are critical in establishing a successful connection due to the reservations new clients might have about mental health services. Ideally, referrals should come from a prepared and respected figure who can begin the "sell" for the group even before the intake is scheduled.

Matching for language and ethnicity is particularly helpful in these initial stages, when any connection is quite tenuous. At the SFGH Depression Clinic (now the SFGH Division of Psychosocial Medicine), a clinic volunteer (sometimes a past client or community member) escorts the client from the primary care clinic to the nearby depression program to set up the appointment in person. New clients can immediately interact with multicultural and multilingual staff in an office setting with culturally sensitive decor. Clients are called with a reminder the night before their initial appointment and encouraged to share any questions or reservations. Clients without phones are sent letters and postcards. Clinicians problem-solve with clients about transportation, child care, and other obstacles to attendance often encountered by low-income and minority clients.

Low-income and minority clients might have greater difficulty with regular attendance; thus clinicians need a high tolerance for no-shows. Missed appointments can be followed by both personal letters and phone calls with offers for assistance. Intake clinicians should consult with the referring nurse or physician to assist in connecting with hard-to-reach or ambivalent clients; for example, intake appointments can be scheduled immediately after a medical appointment. At times, home visits can be used to develop rapport with a client and explain services. No-shows or difficulties in establishing initial contacts should not automatically be considered resistance or noncompliance. For clients who are not interested or ready for treatment, referring providers can use a stages-of-change model and motivational interviewing techniques to better prepare clients for future treatment (Miller & Rollnick, 1991). Consultation and recommendations to referring providers who assist in this process can be offered.

Clients may have little familiarity with the mental health system or may mistrust the intentions of mental health providers. A greater degree of structure, open disclosure, and a clear intake rationale accompanied by treatment choices help to educate clients and build rapport. Intake workers must constantly monitor themselves for feelings of power or superiority during the intake, and evaluate a client's level of comfort through special attention to paralinguistic clues, such as sighs and vocal intonation. Treatment often begins by assisting clients with case management issues, such as completing Social Security paperwork or applying for general assistance. These practical considerations should be mentioned in the intake, as patients are constantly evaluating the benefits of treatment. These pragmatic and essential services can help demonstrate the use and benevolence of the program and to prepare clients for treatment.

In the current model, an intake includes a full diagnostic screen for all major Axis I disorders using the English or Spanish Prime-MD (Spitzer, Williams, Kroenke, & Linzer, 1994). Although at times laborious, this degree of completeness is essential in evaluating appropriateness for group treatment and formulating treatment plans to include all comorbidities. A typical assessment must also include a significant look at any current psychosocial stressors, including financial, minority status, and acculturative stresses and concurrent medical illnesses. All family and social supports should be documented and the client's preferences or values in including them in treatment should be elicited. When assessing psychosocial and cultural variables, it is important not to err in either direction: feigning color blindness or obsessively mining for cultural details from a sense of guilt. Further areas of inquiry that may be useful in tailoring treatment to a client's needs are found in Table 22.2.

PREGROUP TRAINING

Special attention should be given to the early stages of treatment, as negative outcome-related

Table 22.2　Sample assessment and intake areas of inquiry.

Diagnostic screening.

Client's language skills.

Specific ethnic and cultural identity.

Client's model of illness and treatment.

Current and past social supports.

Client's short-term and long-range goals.

Role of family in client's illness and treatment.

Past and current psychosocial stressors as defined by client's culture.

Culture and the expression of symptoms.

Experiences with poverty, race, discrimination, and prejudice.

events often occur early in the treatment process (Jacobs, Charles, Jacobs, Weinstein, & Mann, 1972). An individual pregroup training session following the diagnostic intake and screening alleviates anxiety, reduces premature attrition, and improves outcomes (Beutler, Crago, & Arizmendi, 1986; Dies & Teleska, 1985; Orlinsky & Howard, 1986; Piper, Debane, Bienvenu, & Garant, 1982; Piper & Perrault, 1989; Vinogradov & Yalom, 1990; Yalom, 1985). Typical pregroup training sessions include basic education about group roles and process, rationale for treatment, introduction of group rules and guidelines, role inductions, and the installation of hope. All information should be presented in accessible language that ideally uses feedback from past clinic clients. Group therapy can be framed as a special hands-on class to help with everyday stress and acculturation issues, and thus may help clients accept group treatment. Clients should be explicitly told whether the group is racially and culturally homogeneous and asked for their reactions.

The goal of the culturally sensitive pregroup session is to significantly address the issue of acceptability by explicitly and experientially addressing beliefs about therapy and to enhance a clinic's accountability; this also creates a forum for clients to evaluate and alter services they receive as needed. These goals can be achieved in part through the following procedures:

1. Provide verbal and written information and explain the client's diagnosis and treatment format in familiar terms.
2. Explain and provide the rationale for CBT, making explicit links to client-specific stressors.
3. Familiarize clients with the clinic and ethnically diverse staff, using moderate self-disclosure to create identifications.
4. Foster a sense of collaboration, empowerment, and accountability by frequently asking for feedback.
5. Give clients forms and direct phone numbers to voice opinions, and sign a written contract specifying services offered.
6. Elicit and address client expectations/goals (e.g., a "wish list") and concerns regarding therapy and the group.
7. Perform a "role induction" procedure in the actual group room, demonstrating what to expect and how to behave in group.
8. Instill hope using personal success stories from past group graduates who closely match the current client.

When possible, all pregroup training sessions should be performed by the assigned group facilitator to foster rapport and increase the likelihood of attendance at the first group meeting.

Culturally Sensitive Group CBT Intervention

After completing the one or two sessions required for assessment and pregroup training, clients are assigned to one of several ongoing treatment groups. Clients commit to weekly group meetings for a total of 16 weeks. Specific group structure, general considerations, role of the facilitator, and group content are discussed in the following paragraphs.

Group Structure

Clients attend 16 weekly, two-hour, partially manualized group sessions. Each group is composed of 6 to 10 clinically depressed clients with one junior and one senior group facilitator. The group consists of three four-week modules focusing on activities, thoughts, and social contacts. In the last four weeks, clients repeat their first module and do treatment review and relapse prevention. Clients complete a Beck Depression Inventory (BDI; Beck, Ward, Mendelson, Mock, & Erbaugh, 1961) before each session and more comprehensive measures at pre-, mid-, and posttreatment, and at three-month follow-up intervals. The explicit treatment contract, shorter time frame, and definite end point enhance the pragmatic focus, speed therapeutic work, improve commitment to treatment, and match low-income clients' expectations more closely. The detailed clinical measures are a way to provide important clinical feedback to clients and the program and are used to shape future interventions based on individual and group needs.

Clients are given a group manual containing an outline and homework forms for the 16 sessions (Muñoz, Miranda, & Satterfield, 1996). Members can add or alter pages to create a more personalized manual to keep and review after treatment ends. Basic group guidelines and suggestions for group behavior are listed in the manual, but each group is given the power and control to create their own group rules. As mentioned earlier, the group manual was adapted from *Control Your Depression* (Lewinsohn et al., 1986) and influenced by other sources (Beck et al., 1979; Burns, 1980; Freeman et al., 1990; Greenberger & Padesky, 1995; Satterfield, 1994; Yalom, 1985). The manual was written using understandable language with examples reflecting common problems of low-income and minority life (e.g., no money or transportation to do pleasant activities, stressors of immigration). With the manual, clients know what to expect at each session and are invited to become a part of the treatment planning process.

The group format is partially open. If space allows, new members can enter the group at the beginning of each four-week module, and senior members can "graduate" at the end of any given module. Pragmatically, this model allows programs to better manage client flow and reduce wait-list time. Clinically, senior group members often "sell" the group to incoming members by sharing the initial feelings they had when joining the group and the progress they have made over the past several sessions. Senior members also help teach CBT skills to newer members and are thus able to further solidify their grasp of the material while bolstering self-esteem and self-efficacy. Newer clients thus feel more welcome and hopeful, and this facilitates greater group cohesion, modeling, and skill learning. Group facilitators purposefully pair senior with newer members to encourage this teaching and sharing through explicit exercises and implicit statements that highlight similarities between two individuals or among members of the group as a whole. Ethnic matching is used when a client appears especially ambivalent about treatment. This pairing and provision of social support provides a powerful experience of caring and mentorship that indirectly disconfirms depressogenic beliefs about unlovability and worthlessness.

General Considerations

Group structure, content, and in-session exercises should be used to foster group cohesion as soon as possible. Although clients will likely be heterogeneous in some respects, special effort can be made to initially highlight their similarities (e.g., diagnosis, psychosocial stressors, family issues, anxieties). Great effort should be expended to keep the client in treatment by first using group members and the draw of social support, then moving to a more one-on-one level of outreach. In this partially open group model, a "buddy" or senior group member is paired with a new member to aid in the transition to group and to speed identification and cohesion. Shared group tasks, such as creating activity schedules, are used to create a sense of cooperation and mutual struggle. Therapists use their alliance to and knowledge of each individual (established in the pregroup training sessions) to begin building dyads and subgroups and then move to group-as-a-whole interventions (e.g., creating a group identity by using "we" statements, specifying uniqueness of this particular group). In general, the facilitator needs to have good "dynamic sizing" skills and know when to generalize and be inclusive versus individualize and be exclusive (S. Sue, 1998). The therapist models self-disclosure in the beginning of each treatment module by sharing appropriate personal information and assisting clients to do so with the group. It should be understood that some clients fear possible bias or stereotyping if they self-disclose. Others may feel pressure to withhold potentially negative or stigmatizing information about themselves if they are seen as "representatives" of their given culture. New members are explicitly told that participation is a personal choice. If a member fails to attend a session, a personalized "missing you" letter can be signed by each consenting member and mailed to the absent member before the next group.

The group keeps a practical focus in helping clients cope with everyday problems; however, here-and-now group interventions are utilized when appropriate. Here-and-now interventions (i.e., discussing immediate group events in the present moment) are important because of their power to actively demonstrate CBT concepts and provide skills practice while clients are affectively aroused. Here-and-now interventions are relevant because group is conceptualized as a microcosm of the clients' broader social domain and problems from the "there-and-then" often manifest in the group's here-and-now. Examples of here-and-now interventions include capturing automatic thoughts during group role plays, expressing anger at other members and negotiating conflict, and openly discussing the anxiety inherent in termination.

Role of the Facilitator

The facilitator is seen as the client's personal advocate. In between session contact, case management interventions, brief family meetings, home visits, and consultation with primary care providers may all be a part of standard treatment. As with other CBT groups, the therapist facilitates group work by collaboratively setting an agenda and moving the group through relevant exercises to build coping skills and examine depressogenic thinking. The facilitator reinforces participation by giving repeated depression measures and helping clients chart their progress and adapt their treatment as needed. In the process-sensitive group format, the therapist attends to both the CBT content and group process and uses the two synergistically. In other words, the group process is used to demonstrate and vitalize the CBT content (Satterfield, 1994).

For facilitators to perform this difficult role and continue in their personal process of cultural exploration and discovery, regular clinic meetings and staff training opportunities are essential. Clinicians must recognize and evaluate the reality and usefulness of personal expectations regarding therapy with low-income and minority clients and the attributions made when things do not proceed as desired (Murdock & Altmaier, 1991; Persons, 1989). The detection and treatment of burnout should be incorporated into the standard operating procedures of any practice involving low-income and minority clients. Burnout is common, perhaps unavoidable at times, but it can be alleviated with the same cognitive-behavioral skills used with clients (Farber, 1990; Grosch & Olsen, 1994; Raquepaw & Miller, 1989). Finally, work with low-income and minority clients often requires a flexibility and openness not typically taught in training institutions; thus, unusual methods are needed for unusual circumstances (Azocar et al., 1996; Schnitzer, 1996).

Group Content

The goals of the activities module are to demonstrate the link between activities and mood, monitor and increase daily activities, improve recognition and recall of seemingly minor yet reinforcing daily activities, and collectively brainstorm on how to increase culturally acceptable activities given the limitations of poverty, medical illnesses, and unsafe neighborhoods. In-session exercises include creating lists of free local events and cultural activities, identifying obstacles to increased activity, rehearsing behaviors, balancing the interdependent needs of self versus others, and reducing stress. Homework includes regular monitoring of daily moods and activity levels and exercises on goal setting. Clients practice basic problem-solving skills of identifying a problem (e.g., finding affordable housing), listing alternatives (e.g., applying for federal assistance, searching the rental ads), weighing pros and cons, and devising a solution. Clients with a strong religious background often include spiritual activities and growth in their treatment of depression and frame these active interventions as "serving a higher power."

In the social contact module, clients learn and test the connection between social contacts and mood. Each client diagrams and evaluates his or her social support network. Facilitators should be sensitive to varying degrees of collective versus individualist orientations and how the social support network exercise might draw different responses. There is no correct type or amount of support, but rather an evaluation of how effective the clients' current support system is in meeting their specific needs. Common Western judgments about enmeshment or detachment should be applied judiciously, and perhaps not used at all. Recent immigrants may find this exercise particularly difficult, as many of them have left their entire social support

network behind. Classes can then focus on how to increase the size of the network and how to enhance existing relationships. Exercises include social skills training, assertiveness, and conflict resolution. Clients are asked to think about how these Western skills may or may not seem appropriate to their cultural background. Adaptations are encouraged and analyzed in terms of their relative utility. Role plays of relevant social situations (e.g., conflict with a welfare worker) and here-and-now group examples are used whenever possible. Clients practice giving and receiving positive and negative feedback from other members and "try on" different cultural communication norms. Members often spontaneously record the names and numbers of graduating group members to maintain social contacts after the group ends. In contrast to standard group models, between-session and posttreatment socializing is not discouraged. Most members have few or no social contacts and benefit greatly from the new contacts made in the group. The group is used as a way to forge healthy connections, and new relationships are seen as opportunities to practice new social and communication skills.

The thoughts module explores the link between positive and negative cognition and mood, with an emphasis on the functionality of a thought and not necessarily its rationality. The ideas of the "management of reality" and "balancing one's thoughts" are central. Group members often ask themselves, "Does this thought help me or hurt me? Why is it there? Do I want to do anything about it? What can I do about it?" Exercises include Ellis's ABCD (Activating event, Belief, Consequences, Disputation; Ellis & Grieger, 1977), "yes . . . but," thought stopping, and reframing. Clients are taught basic skills of scheduling worry time, using distractions, identifying unbalanced thinking, and beginning to uncover underlying assumptions and compensatory strategies. All skills are taught and practiced repeatedly in a relaxed, low-pressure atmosphere. Clients initially find it much easier to challenge one another's thoughts, then move to challenge their own. Nearly all clients put their homework (e.g., ABCD or dysfunctional thought record) on a chalkboard during each group. Although this initially raises anxiety for some members, it soon becomes part of the group culture and greatly improves adherence, modeling, and social reinforcement. Clients with low literacy skills are assisted by a more literate group member, who acts as a volunteer tutor.

Clients repeat a modified version of their first module during the last four weeks. This time is used to review concepts and skills and to prepare a postgroup coping plan. This review is especially important in eliciting automatic thoughts about self-efficacy and beliefs about the future and in specifying both short- and long-range goals. Members are encouraged to view realistically continuing stressors such as living in high-crime neighborhoods and to create lists of coping strategies to challenge feelings of helplessness. Continuing members are able to witness and participate in the "graduation process" to better prepare them for their own upcoming termination.

Periodic "class reunions" allow members to reconnect and to review important CBT concepts. Clinical measures are readministered and clients who relapse can reenroll in an ongoing group or be referred for other treatment. These data may be shared with the primary care provider, particularly if pharmacotherapy is part of the client's treatment plan.

MAJOR SYNDROMES, SYMPTOMS, AND PROBLEMS TREATED

Like individual CBT, CBT groups have been used successfully for a wide range of psychopathology and other psychosocial problems, including Major Depression, anxiety, bulimia, schizophrenia, substance abuse/dependence, and chronic pain (Garner, Fairburn, & Davis,

1987; Heimberg, Salzman, Holt, & Blendell, 1993; National Institute on Drug Abuse [NIDA], 1999; Organista et al., 1994; Romano, Quinn, & Halmi, 1994; J. A. Turner, Clancy, McQuade, & Cardenas, 1990; Wykes, Parr, & Landau, 1999). In the realm of affective disorders, most research supports CBT groups for mild to moderate Major Depression, but promising results have also been found for Bipolar Disorder and Dysthymia (McCullough, 2000; Rothbaum & Astin, 2000). Recent research with individual CBT suggests that a group CBT modality may also be appropriate as an adjunctive treatment for severe depression and for depressed clients with serious comorbid medical conditions such as cancer and myocardial infarction (Antoni et al., 2001; Buselli & Stuart, 1999; DeRubeis, Gelfand, Tang, & Simons, 1999).

CASE EXAMPLE

Paula W. is a 54-year-old, single, African American woman on Social Security disability for chronic obstructive pulmonary disease, diabetes mellitus, morbid obesity, and depression. She lives with and cares for two of her grandchildren in a one-bedroom apartment in San Francisco public housing. She was referred for a depression treatment group by a nurse practitioner in her community primary care clinic. Paula refused antidepressant medications, citing fear of side effects and an already complex medication regimen. Clinical excerpts below detail Paula's progression from the initial assessment and intake until the three-month postgroup follow-up. Because the excerpts focus on only one group member, most interventions described are at the individual intervention level. It is important to keep in mind the multiple levels of intervention ranging from individual to dyad to subgroup to group as a whole.

Paula was scheduled for a two-session assessment and intake that included the Prime-MD (Diagnostic and Statistical Manual of Mental Disorders [DSM] structured interview), symptom-focused questionnaires (Beck Depression Inventory [BDI], Beck Anxiety Inventory [BAI], Hopelessness Scale), and pregroup training. The intake and pregroup training were performed by a young, male, Causcasian postdoctoral fellow who would also be one of her two group cofacilitators. Paula met *DSM-III-R* criteria for Major Depression with a history of polysubstance dependence in remission for over 10 years. Her symptom measures placed her in the moderately depressed range. The etiology and formulation of her current depression closely followed cognitive-behavioral theory and included the causal role of how the childhood abuse and neglect she had been subjected to created her core beliefs of unlovability and worthlessness. This cognitive template in interaction with severe stressors throughout her life gave rise to the behavioral, emotional, and neurovegetative symptoms that constitute depression. The stressors of low-income living, minority status, gender, medical illness, and extreme familial chaos were given central importance. Paula was reminded that Major Depression is not an inevitable outcome of high stress, although the two are often correlated.

Paula met the criteria for Major Depression and did not have any diagnoses that might preclude her participation in group, such as psychosis or antisocial personality, and was thus offered pregroup training and a position in an ongoing group. It was thought that the social support provided in group and the opportunities for modeling and skill building would be of special importance for her. The following illustrative excerpts were taken from her intake, her first group session, her eighth group session, and the first section of her last group module (session 9).

INTAKE EXCERPT

THERAPIST: Welcome, Ms. W. Thank you for coming in today. I know it's not easy coming all the way from where you live. . . . I would first like to share some things we need to do today and in our next appointment and why they're important to get done. Before we dive into that, I wanted to see if there's something specific you wanted to make sure we get to today.

PAULA: Well, just feeling better, I guess. I'm wondering what you're going to do.

THERAPIST: Good. I want you to feel better too, and I'm glad you're wondering and asking questions. You are welcome to wonder or ask questions at anytime you want, and you deserve an answer. One of the things we'll talk about today is what your goals are—what's most important to accomplish so you can feel better. That's usually different for different people, so later I'd like to hear what feeling better means for you and your life. [Goes on to list the agenda items and flow of the session.] Is there anything else we should add to that list? [They proceed through the structured diagnostic interview and move to an overview of treatment and goal setting.]

THERAPIST: Ms. W, thank you for all the information you shared with me today. I know it's not easy to talk about some of this stuff. Just as your doctor thought, you do have what we call clinical depression. We'll spend some time talking about what that means to us and how it is treated here in our clinic. I can even give you some things written by depression experts to take home and read, if you'd like. But in a way, you're an expert here too—an expert on yourself and how this thing we're calling depression affects your life. I'd like to eventually put all of our expertise together and come up with the best plan to get you where you need to go. Do you feel comfortable sharing your expertise about yourself? [They talk about her psychosocial environment, relevant stressors, being Baptist, her drug-addicted children, and her multiple medical symptoms.] Ms. W, before we get any further, I wanted to say something about the focus of our clinic. As you probably noticed, we have all sorts of staff and all sorts of patients here from a lot of different cultures—we're just lucky that way. We think everybody has something important to contribute, no matter where they come from. I've learned, though, that I shouldn't make assumptions. What I see and think and feel as a White man from the Midwest might be very different from you—that can be a real strength as long we can communicate about our differences. Do you think your race and culture is important here? Is it related to depression? Would you be willing to talk about it with me?

PAULA: You got all day? [laughs]

THERAPIST: [laughs] Sounds like you have a lot to say. Good. I want to hear it.

PAULA: I wouldn't be here if I wasn't Black and poor. I'd probably be in your chair asking you questions or at least in some private downtown doctor's office getting all sorts of attention. That's the truth, and there ain't nothing you or I can do about it.

THERAPIST: I think I'm getting what you mean, but tell me more. This sounds like something you feel very strongly about.

PAULA: Let's just say that if I had the keys to your house and your car, I wouldn't be so depressed. No disrespect, but I'm just telling it like it is.

THERAPIST: No disrespect taken. Do you think that has to do with me being White or with my income or me being male or maybe something else?

PAULA: All of them. If I didn't have to worry about money, I wouldn't be so depressed, and even if I was, I could afford any treatment I wanted. If I wasn't a Black woman, I'd have money. That and if I wasn't so fat.

THERAPIST: You know, Ms. W, you're right. Black women usually do have lower incomes than White men, and it's not right. Having medical illnesses and being overweight makes it harder for you to earn a living too. You do have more to deal with—more stress, more discrimination, more sexism. And money is a really big worry for a lot of folks, just like you said. People have to have decent food, shelter, clothing, and comfort—"keys to a good house." I want to suggest there may be something else going on too. You have all that to deal with because of your race and gender, but you have a lot of medical illnesses too—diabetes, heart disease, lung disease, and the illness we're going to treat here, clinical depression. We think of it like a medical disease, and stress brings it on or makes it worse—kind of like smoking makes your lung disease worse or eating sugary foods can make your diabetes worse, but it wasn't just sugar that gave you diabetes. For you, I'm hearing that a big source of your stress—and something that will affect your depression—is being an overweight Black woman on a fixed income in this society. The stress contributes to your depression, but we're not just talking about everyday depression or feeling blue. We're talking about a medical illness—clinical depression—*plus* all that stress.

PAULA: Yeah, that makes sense. How are you going to fix that?

THERAPIST: Part of what we'll do in treatment is to provide support and try to come up with ways to deal with the stress, even though society's not likely to change anytime soon. . . . I'll be one of your group leaders, and the other leader is an older Latino man. The other group members are depressed too and will be able to relate to what you're going through. They are Latino, African American, Caucasian, men and women. How will it feel for you to work with such a mixed group?

PAULA: We can give it a try.

The preceeding exchange was obviously filled with affect and beliefs that were not fully explored. One goal of the intake is to demonstrate the therapist's sense of cultural humility and respect for the client's unique cultural background while trying to provide some basic education and containment. These issues were again touched on in the second intake session and pregroup training, further priming them for discussion in the treatment group.

GROUP SESSION 1: ACTIVITIES MODULE PART 1

The agenda for session 1 was:

1. Complete BDI and start progress chart.
2. Group therapy: format, rules, rationale.
3. What is depression? (didactics)
4. What is CBT?
5. Introductions (cohesion building).
6. How activities affect mood.
7. Homework: Daily Mood Scale and Activity Checklist.

Paula's group was composed of six other members who were racially heterogeneous and two cofacilitators (one junior and one senior). Paula was one of two new members; the other five pre-existing members were at various points of completion in their 16-session cycle. The group facilitators purposefully made comments that paired Paula with a slightly older African American woman already in the group and pointed out Paula's similarities to the existing group members. Group-as-a-whole interventions were used in abundance, and existing group members read from the manual, explained how the BDI is completed, and so on to demonstrate their easy mastery of the material and their empowerment in the group. Paula described her initial problem with activity level, and the group facilitator made efforts to connect her with other members and elicit their experiences and support:

PAULA: I don't feel like doing anything. I watch TV from 18 to 20 hours a day, in between naps. I don't get out of the house unless I go to a doctor's appointment, and sometimes I miss them too. It's a big problem. I can't walk from here to there without getting out of breath. It's all this weight. It's just sickening, and I

have no one to blame but myself. I just keep eating and eating and eating.

THERAPIST: I know Jack and Mattie [other group members] are having a really hard time with weight too. And Linda sometimes wears her oxygen to group. What do you folks think? Have you been able to change your activity level despite your weight or shortness of breath? How did your activity level affect your mood?

GROUP SESSION 8: THOUGHTS MODULE PART 4

The agenda for this session was:

1. Complete BDI and add to progress chart.
2. Review last week's homework: Daily Mood Scale, Thought Checklist, ABCD.
3. What are deeper beliefs and how do they make you feel?
4. Practice more ABCDs.
5. Summary and preventing relapse.
6. Saying goodbye to graduates.
7. Homework and new members for next week.

This was the last session of Paula's second module (Session 8 of 16). At this time, one member had completed all 16 sessions and was going to terminate after this group. Members were encouraged to discuss their thoughts and affect about graduation and helped to understand the link between the two. Graduating members were encouraged to share their feelings about the group and its multicultural nature. Each graduate was also encouraged to provide written and/or verbal feedback to the group facilitators after the group has ended.

Group members used their new skills in balancing thoughts to come up with the most helpful ways to think about graduation. They also used their newly acquired attention to cognition as a way to identify here-and-now group beliefs, such as "I should be loved by everyone in this group"; "I'm so much slower than everyone else here"; and "When I graduate, I'll still be terribly depressed." The group joined together to "balance" or rewrite each of these cognitions on the chalkboard. At this midpoint in treatment for Paula, her depression scores had decreased by nearly half and she was ready to take an active role in breaking in new members at the beginning of the next module.

Paula described her efforts at keeping thought records: "You got me wanting to think right now. You know, wondering how I can think about it different so everything seems more all right. I did my ABCD thing on my daughter and it worked! I was mad and depressed at her, but after my homework, I decided to tell her about it and I did. We ended up eating fish together and turning off the TV. If I can do it, you can do it too. Don't worry about graduating. I don't think I'm so worried now either, as long as I can keep up my homework."

SESSION 9: SOCIAL CONTACTS MODULE PART 1

The agenda for this session was:

1. Complete BDI and add to progress chart.
2. Group overview for new members.
3. What is depression?
4. What is CBT?
5. Introductions.
6. How people affect our mood.
7. Homework: Daily Mood Scale and Social Activity Checklist.

This group was just past Paula's midpoint in treatment and her last unique treatment module. Her final four weeks would be a repeat of her first (activities) module, with a special focus on how to maintain her gains and solidify her new knowledge. The group content first explains the meaning of "social support" and its various manifestations in emotional or concrete forms. Participants provide further examples of

supportive and unsupportive behaviors. Each participant diagrams a social support network using himself or herself as the center of a series of concentric circles, with distance from the center indicating degree of closeness. Members share ideas on how to increase their support networks and about the common problems they encounter when meeting new people or trying to deepen existing relationships, and include stereotypes about being low-income and/or minority.

The final excerpt is taken from Paula's sixteenth and final session. Her depression scores had fallen into the nonsignificant range, she had begun to lose weight, and she was far more hopeful about her future.

THERAPIST: Paula, I'm looking at your progress chart and it looks like you're a lot less depressed than when you started 16 weeks ago.

PAULA: Yeah, that's the truth. I never would've believed it.

THERAPIST: What do you think happened?

PAULA: I didn't really think I was depressed until I got in here. I thought it was going to be a bunch of baloney. I thought I didn't belong at first, but after being with you all and working through this book, I learned a lot about myself. I'm understanding myself much better than I did before. I'm learning a lot of things I didn't know just by listening to you guys talk. Instead of just going home and being depressed or arguing with my daughter, I wonder what my group would say— what you guys would do—and I do it. I'm active now. I can stand up for myself now. I'm even doing those ABCDs still.

THERAPIST: And how do you feel about graduating after today?

PAULA: I'm not so sure about going out in the world on my own, but I don't want this to be a crutch too. I've started looking forward to every Thursday group, and I'm going to miss this place. This was my safe haven. I wish it could last forever, and I know I'm going to cry. I learned how I was cutting everyone off and how good it feels to let people in again. I'm different now. I take the bus to group and walk home. I walk all the time. I never did that before. I've seen all of you change and I bet you can see it in me too. I never would've thought such a group of people could do all this, but we did. I can't give myself an A, but I think I get a B + .

Paula's depression scores remained in the nonsignificant range at her three-month follow-up and she had continued to lose weight. Her family problems continued, along with the stressors of being low-income, Black, and female, but she was far better equipped to face them. Given the chronic nature of depression and her life stressors, it is likely Paula will need to reenroll in the future or at least have semiregular "booster" sessions to maintain her gains.

RESEARCH ON CULTURALLY SENSITIVE CBT DEPRESSION GROUPS

A significant and impressive body of literature has demonstrated the efficacy of CBT for depression in both group and individual formats (e.g., Beutler et al., 1987; Dobson, 1989; Elkin et al., 1989; Free, Oei, & Sanders, 1991; Organista et al., 1994; Shaffer, Shapiro, Sank, & Coghlan, 1981). Research also suggests that low-income clients respond well to present-focused, concrete interventions such as those found in CBT (Acosta, Yamamoto, & Evans, 1982; Azocar et al., 1996; Heitler, 1976; Lorion, 1974; Organista, Dwyer, & Azocar, 1993; Organista et al., 1994).

Relatively little research has addressed the issue of CBT's cultural sensitivity and its effectiveness with low-income and minority patients. Although studies that specifically address these issues are needed, it appears that CBT is also effective for these underserved populations, but

changes in depression may be lower in magnitude and dropout rates are higher (Organista et al., 1994; Randall, 1994).

Pilot data on this particular group model have been encouraging. Twenty-three low-income, primary care clients who met *DSM-III-R* diagnostic criteria for Major Depressive Episode were enrolled in the pilot group study. Many clients had concomitant diagnoses of medical disorders, anxiety, recent substance abuse, and personality disorders, reflecting a real-world client sample. The sample was 47% African American, 35% Caucasian, 12% Latino, and 6% "other"; 52% were male and ages ranged from 19 to 57; average income was $441 per month.

Of clients enrolled in the pilot group treatment program, 74.6% completed all 16 sessions, yielding a dropout rate of 25.4%. This is in contrast to Organista et al. (1994), who worked with similar clients in the same clinic and showed a 58% group dropout rate. The standard dropout rate for most group psychotherapy is 35% (Bostwick, 1987). Pilot group clients averaged being only 2.89 minutes late for each 90-minute session.

Brief satisfaction surveys showed high client satisfaction and group cohesion. Over 90% of pilot group clients endorsed the statements "I nearly always felt included by the group" and "I liked group very much." Over 80% endorsed "The group was very helpful in treating my depression" and "The other members were an important part of my treatment."

Similar to the research of Organista et al. (1994), changes in BDI scores were more modest than reported with middle-income majority clients. On average, pilot clients showed a 33.03% reduction in depressive symptoms at completion of the group. More encouragingly, pilot clients showed a 29.78% reduction in BDI scores at a three-month follow-up. This represented a modest improvement over our clinic's average BDI reduction of 27.7% from pre- to posttreatment, including treatment completers and dropouts (Organista et al., 1994).

To ascertain whether this level of symptom reduction was clinically significant, measures of social activity level and pleasant activities (Muñoz & Ying, 1993) and hopelessness (Beck, Weissman, Lester, & Trexler, 1974) were included. Pilot group clients were found to be 16.2% more behaviorally active, 24.5% more socially active, and 33.3% less hopeless. Gains were maintained at a three-month follow-up.

SUMMARY

The CBT group structure, content, and explicit focus on cultural sensitivity and group dynamics appear to greatly improve retention of low-income and minority clients and modestly improve clinical outcomes that were maintained at a three-month follow-up. Parron's (1982) concerns with availability, accessibility, acceptability, and accountability were addressed by using flexible group models to reach more clients, coordinating and consulting with primary care clinics for referrals, altering appointment scheduling and the outreach system, providing reminders and removing obstacles to attendance, making treatment more acceptable by using pregroup training by diverse staff and altering group content and format, capitalizing on natural group processes, and allowing clients ample opportunities to provide feedback and see their feedback in use.

CBT in groups with low-income and minority populations has demonstrated its acceptability to the clients it serves as well as its effectiveness in solving real problems. Although grounded in Western rational thought, CBT can be adapted to match the needs of heterogeneous client populations. Concepts and procedures from multicultural psychology can be integrated into the basic CBT model. Service and delivery systems can be adapted to meet both resource limitations and the special needs of different client populations. CBT is a comprehensive application of empirically driven procedures, and calls on clinicians to be flexible and to use multimodal methods in assessment, treatment planning, and implementation.

REFERENCES

Acosta, F., Yamamoto, J., & Evans, L. (1982). *Effective psychotherapy for low-income and minority patients.* New York: Plenum Press.

Adler, N., Boyce, W., Chesney, M., Cohen, S., Folkman, S., Kahn, R., et al. (1994). Socioeconomic status and health: The challenge of the gradient. *American Psychologist, 49,* 15–24.

Alladin, W. (1999). Models of counselling and psychotherapy for a multiethnic society. In S. Palmer & P. Laungani (Eds.), *Counselling in a multicultural society* (pp. 90–112). London: Sage.

American Psychological Association. (1993). Guidelines for providers of psychological services to ethnic, linguistic, and culturally diverse populations. *American Psychologist, 48*(1), 45–48.

Antoni, M. H., Lehman, J. M., Kilbourn, K. M., Boyers, A. E., Culver, J. L., Alferi, S. M., et al. (2001). Cognitive-behavioral stress management intervention decreases the prevalence of depression and enhances benefit finding among women under treatment for early-stage breast cancer. *Health Psychology, 20*(1), 20–32.

Arredondo, P., Toporek, R., Brown, S. P., Jones, J., Locke, D. C., Sanchez, J., et al. (1996). Operationalization of the multicultural counseling competencies. *Journal of Multicultural Counseling and Development, 24,* 42–78.

Azocar, F., Miranda, J., & Dwyer, E. V. (1996). Treatment of depression in disadvantaged women. *Women and Therapy, 18*(3), 91–105.

Beck, A. T. (1967). *Depression: Causes and treatment.* Philadelphia: University of Pennsylvania Press.

Beck, A. T., Rush, J. A., Shaw, B. F., & Emery, G. (1979). *Cognitive therapy of depression.* New York: Guilford Press.

Beck, A. T., Ward, C. H., Mendelson, M., Mock, J., & Erbaugh, J. (1961). An inventory for measuring depression. *Archives of General Psychiatry, 4,* 561–571.

Beck, A. T., Weissman, A., Lester, D., & Trexler, L. (1974). The measurement of pessimism: The

Hopelessness Scale. *Journal of Consulting and Clinical Psychology, 42,* 861–865.

Bernal, M., & Castro, F. (1994). Are clinical psychologists prepared for service and research with ethnic minorities? *American Psychologist, 49,* 797–805.

Beutler, L. E., Crago, M., & Arizmendi, T. G. (1986). Research on therapist variables in psychotherapy. In S. L. Garfield & A. E. Bergin (Eds.), *Handbook of psychotherapy and behavior change* (2nd ed., pp. 257–310). New York: Wiley.

Beutler, L., Scogin, F., Kirkish, P., Schretlen, D., Corbishley, A., Hamblin, D., et al. (1987). Group cognitive therapy and alprazolam in the treatment of depression in older adults. *Journal of Consulting and Clinical Psychology, 55,* 550–556.

Biafora, F. (1995). Cross-cultural perspective on illness and wellness: Implications for depression. *Journal of Social Distress and the Homeless, 4*(2), 105–129.

Bostwick, G. (1987). "Where's Mary?" A review of the group treatment dropout literature. *Social Work with Groups, 10*(3), 117–131.

Braaten, L. J. (1991). Group cohesion: A new multidimensional model. *Group, 15*(1), 39–55.

Bruce, M. L., Takeuchi, D. T., & Leaf, P. J. (1991). Poverty and psychiatric status: Longitudinal evidence from the New Haven Epidemiologic Catchment Area study. *Archives of General Psychiatry, 48,* 470–474.

Budman, S. H., Demby, A., Feldstein, M., Redondo, J., Scherz, B., Bennett, M. J., et al. (1987). Preliminary findings on a new instrument to measure cohesion in group psychotherapy. *International Journal of Group Psychotherapy, 37*(1), 75–94.

Budman, S. H., Soldz, S., Demby, A., Davis, M. S., & Merry, J. (1993). What is cohesiveness? An empirical examination. *Small Group Research, 24*(2), 199–216.

Budman, S. H., Soldz, S., Demby, A., Feldstein, M., Springer, T., & Davis, M. S. (1989). Cohesion, alliance and outcome in group psychotherapy. *Psychiatry, 52,* 339–351.

Burns, D. D. (1980). *Feeling good: The new mood therapy.* New York: Signet.

Buselli, E. F., & Stuart, E. M. (1999). Influence of psychosocial factors and biopsychosocial interventions on outcomes after myocardial infarction. *Journal of Cardiovascular Nursing, 13*(3), 60–72.

Cheung, F. K., & Snowden, L. R. (1990). Community mental health and ethnic minority populations. *Community Mental Health Journal, 26,* 277–291.

Comas-Díaz, L., & Greene, B. (1994). *Women of color: Integrating ethnic and gender identities in psychotherapy.* New York: Guilford Press.

Cooper-Patrick, L., Gallo, J. J., Powe, N. R., Steinwachs, D. M., Eaton, W. W., & Ford, D. E. (1999). Mental health service utilization by African Americans and Whites: The Baltimore Epidemiologic Catchment Area follow-up. *Medical Care, 37*(10), 1034–1045.

Danziger, S. H., Sandefur, G. D., & Weinberg, D. H. (1994). *Confronting poverty: Prescriptions for change.* Cambridge, MA: Harvard University Press.

Davis, D., & Padesky, C. (1989). Enhancing cognitive therapy with women. In A. Freeman & K. Simon (Eds.), *Comprehensive handbook of cognitive therapy* (pp. 535–557). New York: Plenum Press.

DeRubeis, R. J., Gelfand, L. A., Tang, T. Z., & Simons, A. D. (1999). Medications versus cognitive behavior therapy for severely depressed outpatients: Mega-analysis of four randomized comparisons. *American Journal of Psychiatry, 156*(7), 1007–1013.

Dies, R. R. (1993). Research on group psychotherapy: Overview and clinical applications. In A. Alonso & H. Swiller (Eds.), *Group therapy in clinical practice* (pp. 473–518). Washington, DC: American Psychiatric Press.

Dies, R. R., & Teleska, P. A. (1985). Negative outcome in group psychotherapy. In D. T. Mays & C. M. Franks (Eds.), *Negative outcome in psychotherapy and what to do about it* (pp. 118–141). New York: Springer.

Dobson, K. S. (1989). A meta-analysis of the efficacy of cognitive therapy for depression. *Journal of Consulting and Clinical Psychology, 57,* 414–419.

Dohrenwend, B., Levav, I., Shrout, P. E., Schwartz, S., Naveh, G., Link, B. G., et al. (1992). Socioeconomic status and psychiatric disorders: The causation-selection issue. *Science, 255,* 946–952.

Dumka, L. E., Garza, C. A., Roosa, M. W., & Stoerzinger, H. D. (1997). Recruitment and retention of high-risk families into a preventive parent training intervention. *Journal of Primary Prevention, 18*(1), 25–39.

Dworkin, R. J., & Adams, G. L. (1987). Retention of Hispanics in public sector mental health services. *Community Mental Health Journal, 23,* 204–216.

Eaton, W. W., Anthony, J. C., Gallo, J., Cai, G., Tien, A., Romanoski, A., et al. (1997). Natural history of Diagnostic Interview Schedule/*DSM-IV* Major Depression: The Baltimore Epidemiologic Catchment Area follow-up. *Archives of General Psychiatry, 54*(11), 993–999.

Eaton, W. W., & Muntaner, C. (1999). Socioeconomic stratification and mental disorder. In A. V. Horwitz & T. L. Scheid (Eds.), *A handbook for the study of mental health: Social contexts, theories, and systems* (pp. 259–283). Cambridge, MA: Cambridge University Press.

Elkin, I., Shea, M. T., Watkins, J. T., Imber, S. D., Sotsky, S. M., Collins, J. F., et al. (1989). National Institute of Mental Health Treatment of Depression Collaborative Research Program: General effectiveness of treatments. *Archives of General Psychiatry, 46,* 971–982.

Ellis, A., & Grieger, R. (1977). *Handbook of rational emotive therapy.* New York: Holt, Rinehart and Winston.

Evans, C. R., & Dion, K. L. (1991). Group cohesion and performance: A meta-analysis. *Small Group Research, 22,* 175–186.

Falicov, C. J. (2000). *Latino families in therapy: A guide to multicultural practice.* New York: Guilford Press.

Falloon, I. (1981). Interpersonal variables in behavioral group therapy. *British Journal of Medical Psychology, 54,* 133–141.

Farber, B. A. (1990). Burnout in psychotherapists: Incidence, types, and trends. *Psychotherapy in Private Practice, 8*(1), 35–44.

Free, M., Oei, T., & Sanders, M. (1991). Treatment outcome of a group cognitive therapy program for depression. *International Journal of Group Psychotherapy, 41,* 533–547.

Freeman, A. M., Pretzer, J. L., Fleming, B., & Simon, K. (1990). *Clinical applications of cognitive therapy.* New York: Plenum Press.

Friedman, L. C., Patterson, G. K., & Gomez, R. R. (1983). A socioeconomic minority: The poor and mental health care. *American Journal of Social Psychiatry, 3*(2), 19–25.

Garner, D. M., Fairburn, C. G., & Davis, R. (1987). Cognitive-behavioral treatment of bulimia nervosa: A critical appraisal. *Behavior Modification, 11*(4), 398–431.

Greenberger, D., & Padesky, C. A. (1995). *Mind over mood: A cognitive therapy treatment manual for clients.* New York: Guilford Press.

Grosch, W. N., & Olsen, D. C. (1994). *When helping starts to hurt: A new look at burnout among psychotherapists.* New York: Norton.

Hall, C. C. I. (1997). Cultural malpractice: The growing obsolescence of psychology with the changing U. S. population. *American Psychologist, 52*(6), 642–651.

Hand, I., Lamontagne, Y., & Marks, I. M. (1976). Group exposure in vivo for agoraphobics. *British Journal of Psychiatry, 124,* 588–602.

Healey, J. F. (1995). Hispanic Americans: Colonization, immigration, and ethnic enclaves. In J. F. Healey (Ed.), *Race, ethnicity, gender, and class: The sociology of group conflict and change* (pp. 341–401). Thousand Oaks, CA: Pine Forge Press.

Heimberg, R., Salzman, D., Holt, C. S., & Blendell, K. (1993). Cognitive-behavioral group treatment for social phobia: Effectiveness at five-year follow-up. *Cognitive Therapy and Research, 17*(4), 325–339.

Heitler, J. B. (1976). Preparatory techniques in initiating expressive psychotherapy with lower-class, unsophisticated patients. *Psychological Bulletin, 83*(2), 339–352.

Hollingshead, A. B., & Redlich, F. C. (1958). *Social class and mental illness.* New York: Wiley.

Hollon, S., & Shaw, M. (1979). Group cognitive therapy for depressed patients. In A. Beck, A. Rush, B. Shaw, & G. Emery (Eds.), *Cognitive therapy of Depression* (pp. 328–353). New York: Guilford Press.

Holmes, S. A. (1996, June 20). Income disparity between poorest and richest rises: Trend in U. S. confirmed—New report by Census Bureau shows gap is at its widest since World War II. *The New York Times,* pp. A1, A18.

Holzer, C. E., Shea, B. M., Swanson, J. W., Leaf, P. J., Myers, J. K., George, L., et al. (1986). The increased risk for specific psychiatric disorders among persons of low socioeconomic status. *American Journal of Social Psychiatry, 6,* 259–271.

Jackson, L. C., & Greene, B. (2000). *Psychotherapy with African American women: Innovations in psychodynamic perspectives and practice.* New York: Guilford Press.

Jacobs, D., Charles, E., Jacobs, T., Weinstein, H., & Mann, D. (1972). Preparation for treatment of the disadvantaged patient: Effects on disposition and outcome. *American Journal of Orthopsychiatry, 42,* 666–674.

Karterud, S. (1989). A study of Bion's basic assumption groups. *Human Relations, 42,* 315–335.

Kaul, T. J., & Bednar, R. L. (1986). Experiential group research: Results, questions, and suggestions. In S. L. Garfield & A. E. Bergin (Eds.), *Handbook of psychotherapy and behavior change* (3rd ed., pp. 671–714). New York: Wiley.

Kerbo, H. R. (1996). *Social stratification and inequality: Class conflict in historical and comparative perspective* (3rd ed.). New York: McGraw-Hill.

Kessler, R. C., McGonagle, K. A., Zhao, S., Nelson, C. B., Hughes, M., Eshleman, S., et al. (1994). Lifetime and 12-month prevalence of *DSM-III-R* psychiatric disorders in the United States. *Archives of General Psychiatry, 51,* 8–19.

Klerman, G. L., Weissman, M. M., Rounsaville, B. J., & Chevron, E. S. (1984). *Interpersonal psychotherapy of depression.* Northvale, NJ: Aronson.

Laungani, P. (1999). Culture and identity: Implications for counselling. In S. Palmer & P. Laungani (Eds.), *Counselling in a multicultural society* (pp. 35–70). London: Sage.

Lee, E. (2000). *Working with Asian Americans.* New York: Guilford Press.

Leong, F. T. (1986). Counseling and psychotherapy with Asian-Americans: Review of the literature. *Journal of Counseling Psychology, 33*(2), 196–206.

Lewinsohn, P. M., Muñoz, R. F., Youngren, M. A., & Zeiss, A. M. (1986). *Control your depression* (Rev. ed.). New York: Simon & Schuster.

Lorion, R. P. (1974). Patient and therapist variables in the treatment of low-income patients. *Psychological Bulletin, 81*(6), 344–354.

Lyddon, W. J., & Weill, R. (1997). Cognitive psychotherapy and postmodernism: Emerging themes and challenges. *Journal of Cognitive Psychotherapy: An International Quarterly, 2*(2), 75–90.

Mahoney, M. J. (1988). Constructive metatheory: I. Basic features and historical foundations. *International Journal of Personal Construct Psychology, 1,* 1–35.

Mahoney, M. J. (1991). *Human change processes.* New York: Basic Books.

McCullough, J. P. (2000). *Treatment for chronic depression: Cognitive Behavioral Analysis System of Psychotherapy* (CBASP). New York: Guilford Press.

Miller, W. R., & Rollnick, S. (1991). *Motivational interviewing: Preparing people to change addictive behavior.* New York: Guilford Press.

Miranda, J., Schreckengost, J., & Heine, L. (1992). Cognitive-behavioral group treatment for depression. In M. McKay & K. Paleg (Eds.), *Focal group psychotherapy* (pp. 135–162). Oakland, CA: New Harbinger.

Muñoz, R. F., Miranda, J., & Satterfield, J. M. (1996). *Coping with problems in life.* Unpublished manuscript, University of California San Francisco.

Muñoz, R. F., & Ying, Y. W. (1993). *The prevention of depression: Research and practice.* Baltimore: Johns Hopkins University Press.

Murdock, N. L., & Altmaier, E. M. (1991). Handbook of social and clinical psychology: The health perspective. *Pergamon General Psychology Series, 162,* 563–578.

Murray, C. J. L., & Lopez, A. D. (1996). *The global burden of disease: A comprehensive assessment of mortality and disability from diseases, injuries, and risk factors in 1990 and projected to 2020.* Cambridge, MA: Harvard University Press.

Nakkab, S., & Hernandez, M. (1990). Group psychotherapy in the context of cultural diversity. *Group, 22*(2), 95–103.

National Institute on Drug Abuse. (1999). *Principles of drug addiction treatment* (NIH Publication No. 99–4180). Bethesda, MD: National Institutes of Health.

Neimeyer, R. A. (1993). Constructivism and the cognitive psychotherapies: Some conceptual and strategic contrasts. *Journal of Cognitive Psychotherapy: An International Quarterly, 7,* 159–171.

Organista, K. C. (2000). Latinos. In J. R. White & A. S. Freeman (Eds.), *Cognitive-behavioral group therapy for specific problems and populations* (pp. 218–303). Washington, DC: American Psychological Association.

Organista, K. C., Dwyer, E. V., & Azocar, F. (1993, October). Cognitive behavioral therapy with Latino outpatients. *Behavioral Therapist,* 229–233.

Organista, K. C., Muñoz, R. F., & González, G. (1994). Cognitive-behavioral therapy for depression in low-income and minority medical outpatients: Description of a program and exploratory analyses. *Cognitive Therapy and Research, 18*(3), 241–259.

Orlinsky, D. E., & Howard, K. I. (1986). Process and outcome in psychotherapy. In S. L. Garfield & A. E. Bergin (Eds.), *Handbook of psychotherapy and behavior change* (3rd ed., pp. 311–381). New York: Wiley.

Padesky, C. A., & Greenberger, D. (1995). *Clinician's guide to "Mind over Mood."* New York: Guilford Press.

Palmer, S., & Laungani, P. (1999). *Counselling in a multicultural society.* London: Sage.

Parron, D. L. (1982). An overview of minority group mental health needs and issues as presented to the President's Commission on Mental Health. In F. V. Muñoz & R. Endo (Eds.), *Perspectives on minority group mental health* (pp. 3–22). Washington, DC: University Press of America.

Persons, J. B. (1989). *Cognitive therapy in practice: A case formulation approach* (pp. 194–213). New York: Norton.

Pinderhughes, E. (1989). *Understanding race, ethnicity, and power: The key to efficacy in clinical practice.* New York: Free Press.

Piper, W. E., Debane, E. G., Bienvenu, J., & Garant, J. (1982). A study of group pretraining for group psychotherapy. *International Journal of Group Psychotherapy, 32,* 309–325.

Piper, W. E., & Perrault, E. L. (1989). Pretherapy preparation for group members. *International Journal of Group Psychotherapy, 39,* 17–34.

Purcell, D. W., Campos, P. E., & Perilla, J. (1996). Cognitive-behavioral interventions with lesbians and gay men. *Cognitive and Behavioral Practice, 3,* 391–415.

Rabin, A. S., Kaslow, N. J., & Rehm, L. P. (1985). Factors influencing continuation in a behavioral therapy. *Behavior Research and Therapy, 23,* 695–698.

Randall, E. J. (1994). Cultural relativism in cognitive therapy with disadvantaged African American women. *Journal of Cognitive Psychotherapy: An International Quarterly, 8*(3), 195–207.

Raquepaw, J. M., & Miller, R. S. (1989). Psychotherapist burnout: A componential analysis. *Professional Psychology: Research and Practice, 20*(1), 32–36.

Roberts, R. E. (1987). Epidemiological issues in measuring preventive effects. In R. F. Muñoz (Ed.), *Depression prevention: Research directions* (pp. 45–75). San Francisco: Hemisphere.

Romano, S. J., Quinn, L., & Halmi, K. (1994). Cognitive-behavioral group psychotherapy for bulimia nervosa: Clinical considerations and group format. *Eating Disorders: Journal of Treatment and Prevention, 2*(1), 31–41.

Rothbaum, B. O., & Astin, M. C. (2000). Integration of pharmacotherapy and psychotherapy for Bipolar Disorder. *Journal of Clinical Psychiatry, 61*(Suppl. 9), 68–75.

Salvendy, J. T. (1999). Ethnocultural considerations in group psychotherapy. *International Journal of Group Psychotherapy, 49*(4), 429–464.

Saraceno, B., & Barbui, C. (1997). Poverty and mental illness. *Canadian Journal of Psychiatry, 42,* 285–290.

Satterfield, J. M. (1994). Integrating group dynamics and cognitive-behavioral groups: A hybrid model. *Clinical Psychology: Science and Practice, 1*(2), 185–196.

Satterfield, J. M. (1998). Cognitive behavioral group therapy for depressed, low-income minority clients: Retention and treatment enhancement. *Cognitive and Behavioral Practice, 5,* 65–80.

Schnitzer, P. K. (1996). "They don't come in!" Stories told, lessons taught about poor families in therapy. *American Journal of Orthopsychiatry, 66*(4), 572–582.

Shaffer, C. S., Shapiro, J., Sank, L. I., & Coghlan, D. J. (1981). Positive changes in depression, anxiety, and assertion following individual and group cognitive behavior therapy intervention. *Cognitive Therapy and Research, 2,* 149–157.

Spitzer, R. L., Williams, J. B., Kroenke, K., & Linzer, M. (1994). Utility of a new procedure for diagnosing mental disorders in primary care: The Prime-MD 1000 study. *Journal of the American Medical Association, 272*(22), 1749–1756.

Sue, D. W., Arredondo, P., & McDavis, R. J. (1995). Multicultural counseling competencies and standards. In J. Ponterotto (Ed.), *Handbook of multicultural counseling* (pp. 624–644). Thousand Oaks, CA: Sage.

Sue, S. (1977). Community mental health services to minority groups. *American Psychologist, 32,* 616–624.

Sue, S. (1998). In search of cultural competence in psychotherapy and counseling. *American Psychologist, 53*(4), 440–448.

Sue, S., McKinney, H. L., & Allen, D. B. (1976). Predictors of the duration of therapy for clients in the community mental health system. *Community Mental Health Journal, 12*(4), 365–375.

Takeuchi, D. T., Uehara, E., & Maramba, G. (1999). Cultural diversity and mental health treatment. In A. V. Horwitz & T. L. Scheid (Eds.), *A handbook for the study of mental health: Social contexts, theories, and systems* (pp. 550–565). New York: Cambridge University Press.

Tervalon, M., & Murray-García, J. (1998). Cultural humility versus cultural competence: A critical distinction in defining physician training outcomes in multicultural education. *Journal of Health Care for the Poor and Underserved, 9*(2), 117–125.

Thompson, E. E., Neighbors, H. W., Munday, C., & Jackson, J. S. (1996). Recruitment and retention of African American patients for clinical research: An exploration of response rates in an urban psychiatric hospital. *Journal of Consulting and Clinical Psychology, 64*(5), 861–867.

Turner, J. A., Clancy, S., McQuade, K. J., & Cardenas, D. D. (1990). Effectiveness of behavioral therapy for chronic back pain: A component analysis. *Journal of Consulting and Clinical Psychology, 58*, 573–599.

Turner, R. A., & Lloyd, D. A. (1995). Lifetime traumas and mental health: The significance of cumulative adversity. *Journal of Health and Social Behavior, 36*, 360–376.

U.S. Bureau of the Census. (1995). *Statistical abstracts of the U. S.* (115th ed.). Washington, DC: Author.

U.S. Bureau of the Census. (1996). *A brief look at postwar income inequality.* Washington, DC: Author.

U.S. Bureau of the Census. (2000). *Current population survey.* Washington, DC: Author.

Uumoto, J. M. (1986). Examination of psychological distress in ethnic minorities from a learned helplessness framework. *Professional Psychology: Research and Practice, 17*(5), 448–453.

Vinogradov, S., & Yalom, I. (1990). *A concise guide to group psychotherapy.* Washington, DC: American Psychiatric Press.

Whitney, D., & Rose, S. D. (1989). The effect of process and structured content on outcome in stress management groups. *Journal of Social Service Research, 13*(2), 89–105.

Williams, D. R., & Harris-Reid, M. (1999). Race and mental health: Emerging patterns and promising approaches. In A. V. Horwitz & T. L. Scheid (Eds.), *A handbook for the study of mental health: Social contexts, theories, and systems* (pp. 295–314). Cambridge, MA: Cambridge University Press.

Wilson, W. J. (1991). Studying inner-city social dislocations: The challenge of public agenda research–1990 presidential address. *American Sociological Review, 56*, 1–14.

Wykes, T., Parr, A., & Landau, S. (1999). Group treatment of auditory hallucinations: Exploratory study of effectiveness. *British Journal of Psychiatry, 175*, 180–185.

Yalom, I. (1985). *The theory and practice of group psychotherapy* (3rd ed.). New York: Basic Books.

Yeatts, D. E., Crow, T., & Folts, E. (1992). Service use among low-income minority elderly: Strategies for overcoming barriers. *Gerontologist, 32*(1), 24–32.

CHAPTER 23

Cognitive/Behavioral Group Therapy with Older Adults

HELEN M. DEVRIES AND DAVID W. COON

The effectiveness of cognitive-behavioral therapy (CBT) for a variety of mental health disorders in older adults has been well documented (Coon, Rider, Gallagher-Thompson, & Thompson, 1999; DeVries & Gallagher-Thompson, 2000; Gallagher & Thompson, 1982; Gatz, Fiske, Fox, McCallum, & Wetherell, 1998; Scogin & McElreath, 1994; Teri & McCurry, 2000; Thompson, 1996). In particular, use of CBT in the treatment of depression, anxiety disorders, sleep disorders, and caregiver distress has shown much promise for enhancing quality of life for at-risk older adults. Most studies of CBT with older adults have used individual treatment models (e.g., Gallagher-Thompson & Steffen, 1994; Thompson, Coon, Gallagher-Thompson, Sommer, & Koin, 2001; Thompson, Gallagher, & Breckenridge, 1987). However, there is growing interest in developing treatment approaches that employ a group format in the use of CBT. Most studies of group CBT with older adults have focused on two types of group approaches: traditional therapy groups and psychoeducational groups (e.g., Beutler et al., 1987; Teri & McCurry, 2000; Thompson

et al., 2000). Although both approaches use similar techniques, there are some significant differences. In psychoeducational approaches, classes are highly structured, with specific topics predetermined for each session. The length of time for the course of treatment is planned to coincide with the amount of material to be covered. The key issues of the participants are addressed only to the extent that they are relevant to the material being presented in the class. In therapy groups, there is more emphasis on the individual issues of each client, with a more expansive range of issues being addressed (Thompson et al., 2000).

Both approaches, however, emphasize the acquisition of cognitive and behavioral skills for the management of negative emotions. In both types of group CBT, participants are expected to maintain records of automatic thoughts and are taught to recognize unhelpful/dysfunctional thoughts and to challenge these thoughts or replace them with more helpful/functional thoughts. Behavioral change tactics are also taught, with participants learning to set behavioral goals, monitor frequency of targeted behaviors, identify antecedents and consequences around the targeted behavior, and modify antecedents and/or consequences to reinforce behavioral change.

In addition to being potentially more cost-effective, group approaches to treatment offer several advantages for older adults. Toseland (1995), in his book, *Group Work with the Elderly and Family Caregivers,* indicates several of these advantages. First, groups have the potential for providing a sense of belonging and affiliation that helps counter the social isolation and loneliness sometimes experienced in late life: "Well-functioning groups provide a warm, familiar, friendly, and supportive environment for mutual sharing, and responsive social contact with peers" (p. 17). Second, group participation offers an opportunity for older adults to have their experiences validated and affirmed: "Sharing mutual experiences helps older adults to feel that they are not alone with their concerns, that their thoughts, feelings, and experiences are not unusual or deviant" (p. 18). Third, groups provide a more objective and emotionally detached perspective that can help the older adult put problematic experiences in perspective. Fourth, they allow members to engage in multiple roles in which they can both give and receive support. Fifth, groups provide opportunities for interpersonal learning by providing multiple sources of feedback, a range of alternative perspectives, creative ideas, and new insights, and help with the transition to new roles. Finally, groups offer opportunities to learn and share new information and support in resolving problems.

In addition, Thompson et al. (2000) suggest that CBT groups and psychoeducational groups based on CB principles provide a learning-focused approach that can (1) reduce stereotypes and the associated stigma that elders may associate with psychotherapy; (2) offer older adults the opportunity to actively collaborate with leaders to develop individualized strategies to meet their diverse needs in light of their potentially complex situations and comorbid conditions; and (3) be beneficial for elders on fixed income given CB's time-limited nature.

THEORETICAL CONSTRUCTS

CBT is a well-established treatment modality that employs both cognitive and behavioral techniques in the design of interventions. It is beyond the scope of this chapter to describe CBT in detail (for a detailed description of one CB approach, see Coon, Rider, et al., 1999; Dick, Gallagher-Thompson, Coon, Powers, & Thompson, 1996; Thompson, 1996). However, it is important to articulate the assumptions that are common to all CB approaches to treatment, whether in individual or group format.

First, CBT assumes a relationship among thoughts/beliefs, emotions, and behavior. What one believes about an event or experience will impact how one feels and behaves in that situation. Likewise, the activities/behaviors that one engages in will affect mood and thoughts. Thus, a depressed person, for example, is often caught in a downward spiral of negative thoughts that lead to more depressed feelings and disengagement from pleasant and meaningful activities.

A second assumption is that changing behaviors and thoughts will result in changes in mood. By identifying and changing negative/dysfunctional thoughts and increasing participation in meaningful activities, the depressed person will experience improvement in mood. Therefore, much of the work of CBT is aimed at teaching the skills needed to change the dysfunctional thinking and behaviors that contribute to negative mood. The consequence of teaching these skills is an increase in the individual's sense of self-efficacy, competency, and coping abilities. As individuals learn to recognize the impact their own unhelpful thinking patterns have on their negative mood, they feel empowered and are able to change negative mood more effectively.

Finally, all CBT approaches utilize a set of common techniques to help clients learn the skills for managing and changing negative mood. These techniques include monitoring mood and/or target behavior, monitoring dysfunctional thoughts, challenging dysfunctional thoughts, developing skills for altering dysfunctional thoughts or problem behavior, and practicing new skills.

METHODS OF ASSESSMENT

A key assessment issue is the appropriateness of the prospective client for group CBT. In addition to getting a clear understanding of the origins and nature of the presenting problem and its effect on the participant's current functioning, several domains of functioning need to be evaluated before determining the suitability of a particular older adult for this treatment modality.

Physical Limitations: The first domain to assess is that of physical limitation. Limitations that might prevent group participation include, but are not limited to, sensory losses (such as hearing loss) that would make it impossible to interact with a group, aphasia that would make verbal communication difficult, and extreme frailty that would make participation in a group too physically exhausting.

Cognitive Impairment: It is important to evaluate if there is any cognitive impairment that would limit the individual's ability to carry out the tasks of CBT (e.g., mood monitoring, recognition of dysfunctional thoughts). Assessment of cognitive status is critical because impairment in this domain has major impact on the individual's ability to participate in treatment. Specific areas of assessment include auditory comprehension, memory, and reading/writing capacity. There are several good cognitive screening measures (e.g., Folstein Mini Mental Status Exam, Cognistat)

that are helpful in determining cognitive status. (It is beyond the scope of this chapter to review cognitive assessment procedures. Two excellent articles that address this issue are Kaszniak, 1996; La Rue & Watson, 1998).

Social Constraints: It is important to know if there are social situations or concerns that would limit the older adult's ability to participate in group CBT. For example, does the older adult have dependable transportation to sessions? Often, older adults do not drive at night or at all and must rely on public transportation or family members for rides. This needs to be determined before sessions begin. Also, it is important to assess the client's attitude toward mental health services. Many older adults distrust or misunderstand mental health services and feel stigmatized by the prospect of participating in psychotherapy.

Severe Pathology and Suicide Risk: Clients who are in acute crisis do not make good candidates for group therapy. It is important to screen out clients who are experiencing severe pathology until they are stabilized and out of crisis and to evaluate a client for suicidal ideation and plans. The highest rate of completed suicides is among older adults, which suggests that suicide risk often is not evaluated in this population. Clearly, an actively suicidal client is not appropriate for group therapy until the suicide risk has been decreased.

In addition to these formal areas of assessment, the therapist should be sensitive to more subtle factors that might interfere with effective treatment of the older client. Although there is a growing literature on CB approaches with racial and ethnic minority clients (e.g., Casas, 1988; Iwamasa, 1996; Organista & Muñoz, 1996; Paradis, Friedman, Hatch, & Ackerman, 1996), little is known about the effectiveness of CB-based group approaches with racial and ethnic minority elders (Gallagher-Thompson, Arean, et al.,

2000; Organista, 2000; Thompson et al., 2000). Information regarding cultural traditions, beliefs, and values as well as health and mental health beliefs and practices, including alternative or nontraditional practices, is important to gather as part of the initial assessment. In multicultural applications of CB, there exists a need for close attention to cultural influences traditionally ignored in treatment (Organista, 2000). This approach suggests the need for a creative process emanating from CB principles that tailors CB-based group interventions to culturally relevant engagement strategies, problem areas, intervention strategies, and homework. Without current research to effectively inform therapists, CB groups are warranted that will promote bicultural competency rather than mainstream skills, that conceptualize and address problems with regard to cultural norms, and that foster social change strategies, such as skill development, that empower clients to challenge oppressive social situations (Organista, 2000).

Working with older adults involves some of the same kinds of concerns and need for sensitivity that therapists encounter when they work with ethnically or culturally diverse clients. Most older adults in the cohort born before 1935 are not familiar with group psychotherapy. Thus, it is necessary to socialize the older adult into the process of therapy and what to expect. This might include clarifying goals and expectations and establishing ground rules for group participation. In addition, it is helpful to familiarize older adults with the assumptions of CBT and the model that will be used in therapy. This demystifies the process and helps ensure more cooperation and participation by the client. Once therapy has begun, it is important to adapt the format and pace of therapy to a level that is comfortable for older clients. These modifications might involve the use of multimodal presentation of information, including auditory and visual presentation; a slower pace for introducing new information, with several repetitions

and reviews; and sensitivity to cohort-specific word meanings.

MAJOR SYNDROMES AND PROBLEMS OF OLDER ADULTS AND APPROACHES TO INTERVENTION

DEPRESSION

Depression is the most common mental health problem experienced by older adults (Wolfe, Morrow, & Fredrickson, 1996). Despite this fact, the prevalence rate for mood disorders in older adults is actually lower than that for younger adults. The highest risk group for depression in late life exists in those who are institutionalized or hospitalized. Yet, even among this group, the rates of depression are lower than in similarly hospitalized younger adults (Wolfe et al., 1996).

There are several group CBT manuals for the treatment of depression in older adults. Yost, Beutler, Corbishley, and Allender (1986) have published a detailed manual for treating depression in older clients using group CBT. Dick, Gallagher-Thompson, Coon, et al. (1996) and Dick, Gallagher-Thompson, and Thompson (1996) have developed CBT client and therapist treatment manuals for late-life depression built on the work of Beck (Beck, Rush, Shaw, & Emery, 1979) and Lewinsohn (Lewinsohn, Muñoz, Youngren, & Zeiss, 1986) that can be adapted for use with groups. Regardless of the actual format for conducting group therapy, all approaches rely on the techniques of CBT to help clients identify and change problematic thoughts and behaviors. The group facilitator plays an active role, especially in the early phase of treatment, in teaching group members to understand the model and to develop skill in applying the CB techniques to their own situations.

The actual course of group CBT begins with an introduction of the CB model of depression and the relationship among mood, thoughts and beliefs, and behavior. An initial task in this phase of therapy is to help clients identify specific issues that will be helpful for them to address in reaching their overall goal of improved mood. The challenge for the therapist is to help older adults develop concrete and measurable steps that will serve as evidence that they are reaching their target goal. Each member of the group should define the goals that are unique to his or her situation. The advantage of a group format is that members can assist each other in defining their goals and can serve as models to help those who might be having a difficult time identifying appropriate and measurable goals.

Usually, homework assignments in this initial phase include monitoring mood and behaviors during the week. This homework task teaches clients to record their mood on a daily basis, to record situations or events associated with the mood, and to track changes during the day or week. A commonly used approach to mood monitoring is to use a Daily Mood Rating Form, which asks clients to rate their mood each day. The rating scale ranges from 1 ("very depressed") to 5 ("so-so") to 9 ("very happy"). Each day, individuals indicate their mood score for that day and then in the next column, indicate why they felt this way (what situation or event triggered this mood). Clients bring these forms to each session and share them with each other. As they discuss their mood ratings with each other, they begin to become aware of the relationship between mood changes and pleasurable and nonpleasurable activities.

Once members see the connection between events and mood, the therapist is able to foster the awareness that individuals have some capacity to increase the frequency of pleasant events in their lives. This capacity conveys the potential to control one's mood. The knowledge that they can generate pleasant events in their lives often gives hope and increases a sense of self-efficacy in depressed persons. The task associated with this awareness is to increase the frequency of pleasant events in which the older adult engages. A useful tool to help older adults identify the kinds of activities that might enhance their mood is the Older Person's Pleasant Events Schedule (Gallagher & Thompson, 1981). This is a 66-item self-report inventory that assesses seven domains with potential for enjoyment for an older adult: nature, social, thoughts and feelings, recognition from others, giving to others, competence, and leisure activities. The measure assesses both the degree of enjoyment associated with a specific activity and the frequency with which the client engages in that activity. When scores are plotted on a graph, clients can easily see which activities give the most enjoyment and which are engaged in most frequently. If there is a discrepancy between the level of pleasure associated with an activity and the frequency of participation, the client can then target specific behaviors to increase so as to enhance positive mood. Thus, highly pleasurable events should be increased if their frequency is rated low. Similarly, if activities that bring little pleasure are engaged in more frequently, they may be decreased and time allotted to do something more pleasurable.

After group members have defined their goals and have learned how to monitor mood, the next step is to instruct them on specific CB techniques, such as keeping a record of dysfunctional thoughts. Older adults tend to prefer a modification of the Dysfunctional Thought Record (Beck et al., 1979) called the Daily Record of Unhelpful Thoughts. This form consists of several columns that record the situation (the event that led to unpleasant emotions), the automatic unhelpful thoughts (the negative thoughts that accompanied the event), the feelings, and some possible challenges to the unhelpful thoughts (more helpful alternative thoughts). At first, group members record only the first three items (situation, automatic thoughts, feelings). As they learn about the types of dysfunctional thoughts that contribute to negative mood, they can begin to note the specific thoughts that might be contributing to their own depression. Group members can be very helpful to each other in identifying unhelpful thinking patterns and in developing challenges to these thought patterns. As older adults practice this process through frequent repetition, they begin to be able to detect and challenge automatic thoughts before they contribute to serious negative emotions.

In addition to these core tools, there are a variety of other CB techniques frequently integrated into treatment for depression and other late-life concerns, including relaxation exercises, problem-solving skills, imagery exercises, scheduling of "worry time," and "becoming a scientist" (i.e., doing experiments to confirm or refute hypotheses about oneself or significant others; Beck et al., 1979; Coon, Rider, et al., 1999; Dick, Gallagher-Thompson, Coon, et al., 1996; Gallagher & Thompson, 1981; Lewinsohn et al., 1986).

In the later phase of therapy, the therapist spends less time teaching cognitive and behavioral strategies and more time addressing particular problems that individual group members actually experience in using the techniques while trying to incorporate the techniques into their daily lives. All group members learn to adapt and implement the techniques in their own situation. Over time, the therapist becomes less active as a teacher of new information and more active in providing support and facilitating constructive interaction among group members. Homework remains an essential part of group CBT throughout the entire course of therapy and is used to teach and reinforce adaptive coping skills. Obstacles to homework compliance should always be addressed in a straightforward manner that encourages group members to become interested in figuring out how the homework can help them. It is important not to stigmatize or criticize those who have problems with homework, but rather to work collaboratively to identify homework activities relevant to their individual goals and likely to be completed between sessions. Some

older clients dislike the term "homework," and once again, therapists are encouraged to work collaboratively to identify language useful to the client. Therapists can effectively use the input of group members to identify creative assignments for participants as well as rename the term. Recent examples of word substitutes that were identified by our older clients are experiments, practice, journal writing, mind exercises, and practice sheets.

Overall, the course of group CBT moves from a highly structured format in which topics are planned in advance and content is consistent and uniform for all group members to a more individualized emphasis that shapes homework assignments to each group member's needs and goals. Each session follows a similar format, with homework review always beginning the session. Group members are invited to share their homework in greater detail with each other and compare their experiences. As a result of the discussion, the therapist can clarify a skill or technique, develop a new homework assignment, or problem solve with those experiencing difficulty carrying out assignments. Groups always end with a review of material covered and tasks accomplished during the session.

Termination time lines for most CB-based groups are identified at the outset of treatment. However, termination usually involves the development of a maintenance plan or "survival guide" for each group member that includes identification of situations and triggers that lead to distress and the delineation of specific strategies and techniques that encompass the skills learned in therapy that can be used after the group ends. Danger signals for possible relapse or problem recurrence are highlighted in the guide, and procedures are developed and rehearsed outlining what the group member might do in the event that danger signals are experienced, including the development of a contact list of resources relevant to the older client's problems.

The use of CB psychoeducational "classes" is a particularly effective way to provide early intervention and prevention strategies to those at risk for developing depression. For example, older adults who are at high risk for depression include those who have experienced a significant loss (particularly death of a spouse), those who have a chronic illness, and those who are caring for a physically or cognitively impaired family member. For these at-risk individuals, a class format is attractive because it minimizes any stigma associated with mental health services, teaches skills for coping effectively with known stressors unique to their situation, and provides social support and reinforcement from others going through similar situations (Coon, Rider, et al., 1999; Thompson et al., 2000).

ANXIETY DISORDERS

Compared to other types of mental health problems, the incidence of anxiety symptoms is relatively high among older adults (Zarit & Zarit, 1998). The actual prevalence rate is difficult to determine because anxiety symptoms may co-exist with other diagnoses, such as depression or dementia, as well as in conjunction with a medical illness (Fisher & Noll, 1996). One of the difficulties of accurate diagnosis is that anxiety symptoms are often confused with somatic symptoms, such as chest pain, rapid heart rate, headache, and gastrointestinal symptoms, which are associated with a variety of medical disorders. Consequently, many older adults experiencing anxiety symptoms do not receive treatment.

Anxiety in older adults, when it is diagnosed, is often treated pharmacologically by a primary care physician. Use of benzodiazepines is common (Scogin, 1998). In fact, anxiolytic medication is more likely to be prescribed for older adults experiencing anxiety symptoms than for younger adults experiencing similar symptoms (Fisher & Noll, 1996). Scogin, however, notes

several possible concerns in the use of anxiolytic drugs with older adults, including contributing to cognitive impairment, sedation, troublesome interactions with other medications, and physical dependence.

Although CBT for anxiety disorders has been studied in younger adults, far fewer studies have looked at the use of CBT with older adults diagnosed with an anxiety disorder. Despite this paucity of information, there are some indications that a combination of behavioral and cognitive techniques can be helpful to patients experiencing Generalized Anxiety Disorder, Posttraumatic Stress Disorder (PTSD), and panic attacks (Fisher & Noll, 1996). Therapy groups that emphasize skill building through such CBT techniques as progressive muscle relaxation, guided imagery, monitoring dysfunctional thoughts, and thought-stopping show promise in decreasing levels of anxiety. These techniques are particularly suited for group instruction and practice. As in other group approaches, participants can benefit from the social support and encouragement of the other members. For patients with specific phobias, the traditional approach has been to use systematic desensitization and exposure therapy. For some older adults, these approaches may be contraindicated if the person is physically frail or has dementia. There is a great need for further development and evaluation of psychosocial approaches to the treatment of anxiety in older adults, particularly in light of the possible risks of pharmacological interventions.

SLEEP DISORDERS

Older adults frequently complain of disturbance in their sleep patterns, with various studies indicating prevalence rates of 12 to 25% for adults over the age of 65 (Knight & Satre, 1999). The most common complaints include difficulty falling asleep, frequent awakenings during the night, early morning awakening, and light or poor quality sleep (Bootzin, Epstein, Engle-Friedman, & Salvio, 1996). The diagnostic challenge is to differentiate between normal age-related changes in sleep patterns and those that indicate a sleep disturbance of significant concern.

Like older adults experiencing anxiety symptoms, those experiencing sleep difficulties are likely to complain to primary care physicians, who frequently either assume it is a normal part of aging and so ignore the problem or prescribe sleep medications. Mellinger, Balter, and Uhlenhuth (1985) report that in a survey of adults experiencing sleep disturbances, a large percentage (69%) were 50 to 79 years old. This statistic is most likely higher among older adults in nursing homes. Bootzin et al. (1996) state, "Not only do older adults consume disproportionate amounts of sleep medication, but persons living in institutions may have such medications prescribed and continued with little regard for the nature of the sleep disorder or the effects of the medication on sleep" (p. 399). Unfortunately, the use of hypnotics poses substantial risk for older adults experiencing chronic sleep problems. In particular, the risk of addiction is of grave concern, with severe rebound insomnia the consequence of long-term use, especially of benzodiazepines (Bootzin et al., 1996).

Use of sleep medications is recommended only when all other approaches to treatment have been tried and shown to be ineffective (Nielsen, Nordhus, & Kvale, 1998). Short-term, nonpharmacological approaches have been developed as alternative and more appropriate treatments for sleeping difficulties in older adults (Lacks & Morin, 1992; Lichstein & Reidel, 1994). Recommended treatment approaches include sleep restriction, sleep education, stimulus control, cognitive restructuring, and relaxation training (Bootzin et al., 1996; Gatz et al., 1998). Sleep restriction seeks to increase sleep efficiency by limiting the amount of time spent in bed, with the goal of increasing the ratio of time spent sleeping to time spent awake while in the bed. Sleep education teaches older adults about the normal changes in sleep patterns associated with aging and instructs them in ways to enhance sleep-inducing behaviors. Stimulus control teaches people to alter the sleep environment to foster rapid sleep onset by eliminating activities in the bedroom that serve as cues for staying awake (eating, TV watching, reading). Cognitive restructuring uses cognitive techniques to challenge faulty assumptions about sleep. Relaxation training helps the older adult reduce physiological impediments to sleep. For older adults, passive exercises that focus on deep breathing and guided imagery tend to be very effective.

Several group CBT approaches to the treatment of late-life sleep disorders have been described (Epstein, 1994; Morin, Kowatch, Barry, & Walton, 1993). Morin et al. described a group CBT approach for older adults with sleep problems that combines many of the recommended cognitive and behavioral elements mentioned earlier. Their approach involved an eight-week group intervention aimed at changing maladaptive sleep habits and altering dysfunctional beliefs and attitudes about sleeplessness. Maladaptive sleep patterns were altered by interventions that provided stimulus control instructions, which focused on altering behaviors that prevent consistent sleep-wake cycles and on strengthening bedroom cues for sleep. Examples of stimulus control instructions included: Lie down only when you are sleepy; Do not use your bed for anything except sleep (e.g., don't read, eat, or watch television in bed); Get up at the same time every morning, regardless of how much you have slept during the night; and Avoid daytime naps.

Dysfunctional beliefs about sleep are common in older persons with insomnia (Morin, Stone, Trinkle, Mercer, & Remsberg, 1992), and the second component of Morin, Kowatch, et al.'s (1993) intervention focused on identifying and challenging problematic beliefs about sleeplessness. An example of unhelpful thinking is that one must get at least eight hours of sleep at night or one will not be able to function the next day. Morin and associates (1992) noted that in treating insomnia, there are several types of dysfunctional beliefs that respond to cognitive restructuring. These include misconceptions about the causes of insomnia or the consequences of poor sleep, unrealistic sleep expectations, and false beliefs about sleep-enhancing behaviors. Intervention involved providing accurate information and the rehearsing of alternative belief statements.

GRIEF/BEREAVEMENT

Loss and bereavement are common experiences in late life. Epidemiological data indicate that there are approximately 12 million widowed men and women in the United States (McKibbin, Koonce-Volwiler, Cronkite, & Gallagher-Thompson, 2000). In addition to spousal bereavement, older adults experience loss of friends and family members on a regular basis. Other loss experiences are common in multiple domains, including role loss or change, loss of income, loss of physical and cognitive function, and, eventually, loss of one's own life (Thompson et al., 2000). Most older adults adapt reasonably well to these losses without need for professional intervention (Gallagher, Breckenridge, Thompson, & Peterson, 1983; Lund, 1989). However, inhibited or chronic grief reactions may occur with some older adults and should be evaluated and treated. Prigerson et al. (1995) suggest that complicated grief is associated with such symptoms as thinking about the person so much that it creates disruptions in daily routines, being drawn to places associated with the deceased person, feeling lonely or bitter,

avoiding reminders of the person, being upset by memories of the person, and being angry about the person's death. If these symptoms occur frequently over an extended period of time and disrupt the person's daily functioning, then the person is considered to be experiencing a complicated grief reaction.

Of particular concern is the increased risk of suicide among widowed persons (Blazer, 1991). Studies of bereaved persons suggest that the greatest psychological impact occurs within the first several months, with gradual improvement over time (Thompson, Gallagher, Cover, Gilewski, & Peterson, 1989). Those who continue to experience high levels of psychological distress one to two years after the death of their spouse may require psychological intervention to help them adjust to their loss (Thompson, Gallagher-Thompson, Futterman, & Peterson, 1991). Unresolved spousal bereavement seems to be associated with decreased physical and mental well-being and increased mortality (Klausner & Alexopoulos, 1999). Of particular concern is the increased risk for a serious depressive disorder for those who are unable to adjust to their loss. The presence of symptoms such as hopelessness, denial of feelings, cognitive distortions regarding the loss, excessive self-blame, unrealistic view of the future or person lost, and psychomotor retardation may indicate that a serious depressive disorder has developed (Thompson et al., 2000). Symptoms of anxiety disorders or PTSD following a significant loss might also indicate the presence of a pathological grief reaction (McKibbin et al., 2000).

In his book *Grief Counseling and Grief Therapy*, Worden (1991) has a section on grief and the elderly. He identifies multiple features of grief in the elderly that should be assessed and included in any intervention approach. These include such issues as multiple losses, loneliness, role adjustment, and personal death awareness. He suggests several approaches to intervention that might be appropriate in a group format, such as support groups, reminiscing groups, and skill building groups or classes involving learning to manage new responsibilities. Use of psychoeducational classes to provide early intervention for at-risk elders might be very helpful in facilitating the grief process and preventing complicated grief reactions.

Unfortunately, there are few published studies of group interventions designed to assist older adults during the bereavement process. The most commonly known intervention is widow-to-widow support groups for assisting with the grieving process (Silverman, 1969). CBT group interventions for bereaved older adults have not been well documented. Most rely on Beck's model of CBT. Specifically, the focus is on helping group members to identify unhelpful thoughts, to become aware of the relationship between thoughts and emotions, and to develop some skill in cognitive restructuring. Azhar and Varma (1995) described a group CBT approach that incorporated a religious component into the intervention for widows who self-identified with a common religion. Religious texts were used to help challenge unhelpful or inaccurate core beliefs. This approach raises the issue of cultural sensitivity in assessing what is appropriate in a given individual's reaction to and understanding of loss.

One of the most striking findings of research into the grief processes of older adults is that the first several months are the most stressful, and that the level of adjustment to the loss that occurs in those early months will influence long-term adjustment (Lund, 1989). The implication is that interventions need to be available early in the bereavement process and then continue over a relatively long period of time. This does not mean that all bereaved older adults need to participate for a long time. Rather, assistance should be available for different phases of the grief process so that the older adult may participate when ready. For some, that will be early in the process; for others, it will be much later.

CAREGIVING

Family caregiving has increased dramatically and will continue to do so as individuals with chronic illness or disability live longer. Until the last quarter of the past century, few survived into old age. Today, however, many are living well into their 70s, 80s, and even 90s with chronic medical conditions that limit daily functioning or require high levels of support and care. Families have traditionally provided the majority of care for older family members, with spouses and daughters or daughters-in-law providing the bulk of the care (National Alliance for Caregiving, 1997; Stone, Cafferta, & Sangl, 1987). However, the demographic changes in the aging population indicate that families must provide care for longer periods of time for more frail or disabled relatives than in the past. These long-term responsibilities place extraordinary demands on family caregivers and may strain financial, emotional, and physical resources.

Many studies have documented the stressful nature of caregiving (Anthony-Bergstone, Zarit, & Gatz, 1988; Gallagher, Rose, Rivera, Lovett, & Thompson, 1989; Kiecolt-Glaser, Dura, Speicher, Trask, & Glaser, 1991; Schulz, Visintainier, & Williamson, 1990). Specifically, caregivers report experiencing more symptoms of psychological distress and receive more psychiatric diagnoses compared to the general population and to appropriate control groups (Schulz et al., 1990). Reviews of the caregiving literature indicate that caregiver burden is correlated with a range of psychological problems, such as depression, anxiety, hostility, and poorer self-reported physical health (Bourgeois, Schulz, & Burgio, 1996; Schulz, O'Brien, Bookwala, & Fleissner, 1995). In addition, caregivers report frequent use of psychotropic medications to manage depression and other forms of psychological distress (Schulz et al., 1995).

In response to the growing body of literature documenting caregiver burden, a broad variety of programs and services to address these concerns have been developed. Most commonly, caregivers have been encouraged to participate in support groups. However, caregiving is a long-term process that requires a series of adjustments over the course of the caregiving "career" (Pearlin, 1993). Thus, the kind of clinical intervention that is most appropriate will depend on the phase of caregiving. Pearlin describes three stages of caregiving: the initial phase, assuming the role of caregiver; the middle phase, dealing with the extensive caregiving tasks; and the late phase, resumption of normal life after death of care recipient.

Psychoeducational approaches to intervention with distressed caregivers have been described in the caregiving literature (Bourgeois et al., 1996; Gallagher-Thompson, 1994; Gallagher-Thompson & DeVries, 1994; Gallagher-Thompson, Lovett, et al., 2000). These interventions can be used in any of the phases of caregiving, with the content aimed at the specific challenges associated with that particular phase. Most psychoeducational programs are based on CB theory and focus on the development of specific skills designed to enhance adaptive coping. Psychoeducational approaches are frequently carried out in a group format rather than in individual counseling, which contributes an element of social support to the process. However, caregiving involves entire families and strategies aimed at assisting only the primary caregiver may be only partially effective. Zarit and Zarit (1998) emphasize the importance of family meetings, in addition to specific interventions targeting the primary caregiver, to address caregiver distress and burnout.

Based on extensive experience developing and evaluating psychoeducational interventions for caregivers, Gallagher-Thompson, Arean, et al. (2000) note that interventions are most successful when the following conditions are met: (1) length of time for group is limited to no more than 8 to 10 weeks (long enough to foster learning of new skills, but short enough to accommodate caregivers' demanding schedules); and

(2) the focus is on teaching a relatively small number of coping skills (better to teach fewer skills in depth than overwhelm caregivers with too much information). Gallagher-Thompson and colleagues have described in detail several group CBT psychoeducational interventions for caregivers, including a Life Satisfaction Class (Thompson, Gallagher, & Lovett, 1992), a Problem-Solving Class (Gallagher, Thompson, Silven, & Priddy, 1985), and a Coping with Frustration Class (Gallagher-Thompson & DeVries, 1994; Gallagher-Thompson et al., 1992). Currently, work is being done to develop and evaluate the effectiveness of group CBT interventions with ethnic minority caregivers (Gallagher-Thompson, Arean, et al., 2000). All of these approaches incorporate behavioral and cognitive techniques to enhance caregiver's coping and emotional well-being. (Treatment manuals for these psychoeducational classes are available from Gallagher-Thompson.)

CHRONIC ILLNESS

Most adults over the age of 65 experience at least one type of chronic illness. Prevalence estimates of chronic illness in older adults range from 50 to 86% (Knight & Satre, 1999). Specifically, epidemiological data indicate that approximately 85% of persons age 75 to 79 have osteoarthritis, 59% of persons in their 70s or 80s have chronic obstructive pulmonary disease, 32% of those over age 75 have some form of heart disease, and 39% of those over 65 have hypertension (Cavanaugh, 1990; Mongan, 1990; Ries, 1990). The consequence of chronic illness for the individual often means permanent changes in lifestyle to accommodate restrictive medical schedules and regimens. In addition, many must endure chronic pain and adjustment to physical limitations.

The psychological impact of chronic illness may strain coping resources and challenge the person's sense of self-worth and control.

Negative beliefs about changes in body image, competence, and sense of self increase the risk for psychological distress, particularly depression. In fact, rates of depression in chronically ill older adults have been found to be as high as 59% (Knight & Satre, 1999). Several studies have found that suicidal ideation and behavior in the elderly are associated with medical illness and increased functional disability (Frierson, 1991; Zautra, Maxwell, & Reich, 1989). Others have argued that depression in the medically ill is associated with the disability that accompanies the physical illness rather than the illness alone (Zeiss, Lewinsohn, Rohde, & Seeley, 1996). In either case, comorbidity of medical and psychological problems is common. Blazer (1991) found a high rate of depression among older medical inpatients (up to 40%) and also among older medical outpatients. Clearly, medical and psychological problems impact each other (Haley, 1996): Chronic illness can affect psychological well-being; decreased psychological well-being can affect the experience of and response to medical illness.

An approach to treatment that addresses both the medical and the psychosocial aspects of their illness is greatly to patients' advantage. In particular, psychological interventions that increase compliance with beneficial medical regimens and reduce negative psychosocial consequences of the illness are most helpful in reducing risk of depression and other psychological disorders. Group CBT is an ideal way to address either or both of these treatment goals. In addition to the benefits of cognitive and behavioral strategies for coping with illness, the group format provides the possibility of increased social support, models of coping, and timely feedback as group members seek to change behavior or challenge unhelpful thinking.

Unfortunately, there have been few studies describing group CBT with older medically ill patients. A few have described CBT approaches that show promise in reducing depression in geriatric medical populations (both inpatient and outpatient), in managing chronic pain, and in limiting excess disability (Arean & Miranda, 1996; Cook, 1998; Lopez & Mermelstein, 1995; Rybarczyk et al., 1992; Widner & Zeichner, 1993). These approaches rely on a combination of behavioral techniques (increasing pleasant events, relaxation techniques, problem solving) and cognitive techniques (cognitive restructuring, distraction, pleasant imagery, calming self-statements). Any psychosocial intervention for medically ill patients requires active collaboration with other health providers to the older adult to ensure the most comprehensive and appropriate treatment.

CASE EXAMPLES

CASE EXAMPLE 1

Mrs. M. is an 82-year-old married woman who is the primary caregiver for her 86-year-old husband with dementia. She self-referred to a CB psychoeducational class for distressed caregivers. Mrs. M. reported that she was frightened of her husband, who had become verbally abusive and threatening; felt misunderstood by her children, who blamed her for mismanaging their father; and felt generally overwhelmed by her situation. She wanted to place her husband in the nursing home associated with their retirement community but felt that her children would not agree and that she would feel guilty for doing so. She had always played a supportive role to her husband and felt that she was disrespectful and inappropriate for taking over so many responsibilities for him. In turn, he accused her of stealing his money and plotting against him. The physical care for him was becoming too difficult for her. He fought her when she tried to help him shower and dress. She had a slight build and was physically frail. She was afraid of falling when her husband fought her attempts to assist him.

On the urging of several friends in her retirement community, she enrolled in our psychoeducational class for caregivers of cognitively impaired family members. The class met for two hours per week for eight weeks and was held at a social service agency in the downtown area of a major city. The purpose of the class was to teach cognitive and behavioral skills for coping with the frustrations of caregiving. Specific skills included relaxation training (based on deep breathing and guided imagery), recognition and challenging of unhelpful thoughts, and assertiveness skills. Mrs. M. responded very positively to the relaxation exercises, but struggled with keeping a record of unhelpful thoughts. She could identify situations that were upsetting and the feelings she experienced, but found it difficult to identify the accompanying thoughts. This is where other group members were helpful: They shared their thought records with her to give her models, encouraged her attempts to track her thoughts and feelings, and applauded her successful efforts. She responded very positively to these supportive efforts and began to keep a record to bring to class each week. The result was that she began to recognize her many self-blaming and belittling comments (e.g., "I always make him so angry"; "I'll never be good at taking care of him"; "I've always been so stupid. I can't get anything right"). She began to challenge these unhelpful thoughts and replace them with more adaptive ones (e.g., "I'm doing the best I can"; "Most of the time I manage him okay"; "I'm learning a lot about how to take care of things"). The assertiveness component of the class helped her to recognize that she had a right to get some help with the caregiving from her children and to begin to explore when and how she might place her husband in the long-term care facility at her retirement community.

All of these skills were encouraged and supported by the group. Mrs. M. made significant gains in improving her mood and in her optimism about getting help with her caregiving responsibilities and gained a new sense of self-efficacy about her caregiving role. She was very responsive to the group's affirmation and reinforcement of her efforts to learn new skills. These gains would have taken longer and been less dramatic without the encouragement of the group. In fact, it is doubtful she would have had the motivation to persevere in her attempts to identify unhelpful thoughts and challenge those thoughts without the support of the group.

The impact of the group environment and collaboration on her enjoyment of and benefit from the class was even more striking. She traveled to the class each week with two friends from the suburban retirement community where she lived. The two friends were considerably younger than she (68 and 71 years) and were also caring for their spouses who had dementia. The trip to the class required the use of public transportation and a travel time of about 30 minutes. This trip might have been an overwhelming obstacle if faced alone, but instead became an "outing" with her two friends. Following the class every week, several class members would go together for lunch at a local restaurant. During the week, her friends at the retirement community and other class members would phone to see how she was doing and encourage her efforts. Clearly, the group format served as a positive social support as she learned and implemented new skills. Mrs. M's experience portends well for the effectiveness of a group CB format for distressed older adults.

CASE EXAMPLE 2

Mr. R., a retired 73-year-old Mexican American office manager, suffered a mild stroke 17 months after the loss of his male partner of 32 years. He was referred by his geropsychiatrist almost nine months poststroke to a time-limited CB-based group therapy for older adults struggling with depression. During the intake process, he reported suffering from a number of major depressive episodes in his life. For many years, he had accepted these episodes as "part of who I am," but almost seven years earlier, at the suggestion of his doctor and with the support of his partner, he began seeing the geropsychiatrist and started taking antidepressants. He had lived with his male lover for the last half of his life, but he considered himself bisexual, having always been attracted to both sexes and having been married to a childhood sweetheart for almost eight years until she was killed in a car accident when he was 27. He described himself as having "gay, straight, and in-between" friends, and credited his partner with helping him adjust to his sexuality. He had grown up a "first-generation U.S. citizen" with extremely negative stereotypes about sex and his sexual attractions. Moreover, he described himself as having lived in a Mexican American community that very narrowly defined what it meant to be "a man."

Mr. R.'s recent stroke had left him with slight speech impediment (especially when he got excited, agitated, or frustrated and tried to speak quickly) as well as a slight short-term memory problem. Since his partner's death and the stroke, he had isolated himself more and more and found it difficult to complete chores or connect socially. He expressed concern about whether he should tell the group about his relationship with his partner and, ultimately, decided it was "none of their business," referring to his partner as his "close friend" or "best friend and roommate."

This particular CB-based group focused on encouraging members to identify and engage in pleasant activities and identifying negative thinking patterns that particularly interfered with engagement in pleasurable activities. In the first few sessions, Mr. R. appeared, to some group members, uninterested in "getting down to business" and seemed to "avoid" his problems by engaging in too much "small talk," or *platica*, as he later referred to it. In collaboration with the therapist, Mr. R. spoke to the group

about his uneasiness with starting right out with his treatment goals and his struggles, particularly relative to speech and memory. The therapist and group encouraged him to discuss *platica* and its importance in his feeling connected to the group and in facilitating his progress. He was also encouraged to examine his thinking about this group discussion as homework and to ask himself how to balance his expectations with the goals he hoped to accomplish. Group members also discussed their own concerns about memory and supported his developing flashcards to remember CB tenets, detailed activity schedules to include in his pocket calendar, and assertiveness skills to ask others to repeat information until he "got it down."

Interestingly enough, Mr. R. noticed that some members often arrived before the group started, and he decided to help set up the room and check in or engage in small talk with those members who arrived early. Later on, he realized that the group's discussion of his small talk, his decision to come to group early, and the homework assignment to examine his thinking around the issue had increased his comfort level with the group. His comfort actually increased to the point that he was able to describe his "former roommate" as his "life partner." He also acknowledged that his coming early to group and the group meeting itself had become a "challenging" yet pleasurable event on his weekly activity schedule.

The group also encouraged Mr. R. to examine the evidence around his concerns regarding how he was viewed by his friends since his stroke and the death of his partner. While two other widowed group members shared similar experiences of the "world being made of couples," all the group members challenged Mr. R. to check out his assumptions about what his friends actually thought about him, his interests, and his capabilities. Mr. R. quickly learned that several friends thought he wanted to be left alone after he stopped returning their calls. He realized that both he and his friends had missed one another's company when they didn't check in with one another but engaged in "mindreading" instead. Mr. R. responded quickly to the group's suggestions based on CB principles and began to engage in more pleasant social and individual activities.

Mr. R.'s improvement was evident in the number of activities he pursued, the alleviation of his depressive symptoms, and in his active pursuit of a physician-sanctioned exercise program and diet. Moreover, near the end of the group, he began dating again, meeting several dating partners through reengagement with his social network. Prior to termination, Mr. R. completed a maintenance guide incorporating the strategies he found most useful from this group experience (e.g., activity schedules, flash cards, and cognitive restructuring techniques). He was also encouraged to continue to use the maintenance guide, its resources and referrals consistently, as well as to attend the regularly scheduled medication management appointments with his geropsychiatrist to maintain his therapeutic gains.

OUTCOME RESEARCH

Most studies of CBT with older adults have focused on individual approaches, but there is encouraging preliminary data suggesting the efficacy of group CBT in treating a number of later-life psychological problems. For instance, the August 2000 issue of *Clinical Psychology Review* provides an overview of assessment and treatment issues for older adults. Specifically, the issue identifies promising group CBT approaches for the treatment of depression (Kemp, Corgiat, & Gill, 1992), anxiety disorders (Stanley, Beck, & Glassco, 1996), and sleep disorders (Morin et al., 1993). Preliminary work is also being done to develop appropriate group interventions for individuals with early-stage dementia to reduce risk of depression and to develop coping strategies (Snyder, Quayhagen,

Shepherd, & Bower, 1995; Teri & Gallagher-Thompson, 1991).

Teri and McCurry (2000), in a very detailed review of empirically evaluated psychosocial treatments with older adults, state that CBT (both individual and group) has been the subject of the most empirical research. These studies have found CB, psychodynamic, and reminiscence therapies to be effective in decreasing depression; some evidence suggests that improvements in CB conditions are better maintained at follow-up than other treatment conditions. However, additional long-term follow-up studies are needed to state this with confidence.

Moreover, in a comprehensive review of empirically validated interventions for older adults, Gatz and her colleagues (1998) designated a treatment modality as "well established" or "probably efficacious," depending on whether the approach met the criteria for empirically validated treatments established by the Task Force on Promotion and Dissemination of Psychological Procedures appointed by the Division of Clinical Psychology of the American Psychological Association. Although their analysis found that the majority of empirically studied treatment approaches focused on individual therapy, there were some data available on group approaches. They conclude that CBT, including CBT-based group interventions, was "probably efficacious" for the treatment of a variety of disorders in older adults, including depression, sleep disorders, and caregiver burden (Gatz et al., 1998). Teri and McCurry (2000) found empirical evidence for group-based CBT's efficacy with various medical illnesses, including hearing loss and osteoarthritis, as well as among long-term care residents experiencing acute adjustment problems (Dhooper, Green, Huff, & Austin-Murphy, 1993; Dye & Erber, 1981).

For depressed outpatients, Fry (1984) found group CBT effective in both immediate and delayed treatment forms, significantly reducing depressive symptoms in geriatric subjects. Arean and colleagues (Arean & Miranda, 1996), in a study of 75 older adults with Major Depressive Disorder, compared problem-solving group therapy, reminiscence group therapy, and a wait-list condition. Individuals in both therapy conditions showed significant reductions in depression compared to the control group, although the problem-solving group showed significantly greater reductions at the end of treatment and at three-month follow-up. In another study, Beutler and his fellow researchers (Beutler et al., 1987) compared group cognitive therapy plus alprazolam support, alprazolam support alone, cognitive therapy plus placebo support, and placebo support alone. They found that patients assigned to group cognitive therapy relative to non-group therapy subjects improved in self-reported depressive symptoms and objective sleep efficiency. In contrast, no differences between alprazolam and placebo were found, regardless of whether patients received group cognitive therapy. Moreover, much lower dropout and dissatisfaction rates were noted among patients assigned to the study's cognitive therapy conditions.

Psychoeducational classes for the treatment of a range of psychological problems in older adults have also shown promise, including the treatment of insomnia (Morin, Culbert, & Schwartz, 1994), the management of chronic pain (Cook, 1998), and the treatment of distress and burden in family caregivers (Gallagher, Lovett, & Thompson, 1988; Gallagher-Thompson, Lovett, et al., 2000).

With regard to caregivers, CB-based groups have been effective in reducing burden; improving family functioning, communication, and problem-solving; and alleviating caregiver depression and psychological distress (Gallagher-Thompson, Lovett, et al., 2000). However, results vary depending on a variety of patient and caregiver individual differences (Coon, Schulz, & Ory, 1999; Schulz et al., 1995). More specifically, in a recent study of caregivers to physically frail and/or cognitively impaired elders conducted by Gallagher-Thompson and her colleagues (Gallagher et al., 1988; Gallagher-Thompson, Lovett, et al., 2000), participants in psychoeducational classes designed to increase pleasant events reported greater reductions in caregiver depression and burden when compared to either a problem-solving class or a wait-list control condition. Participants in both classes reported more frequent use of cognitive or behavioral coping strategies and less subjective burden from pre- to postintervention when compared to the wait-list condition.

Similarly, participants in a Coping with Frustration class culturally tailored to meet the needs of Hispanic/Latino family caregivers of dementia victims reported significantly fewer depressive symptoms and showed a trend for increased control of feelings of anger and frustration, compared to those on a wait-list who did not improve on any measure of distress (Gallagher-Thompson, Arean, Rivera, & Thompson, in press). McCurry and colleagues (McCurry, Logsdon, Vitiello, & Teri, 1998) randomized dementia caregivers with sleep disturbance to one of three conditions: group behavioral treatment, individual behavioral treatment, or wait-list control. Caregivers in the individual and group treatments were taught a combination of behavioral strategies to improve sleep (sleep hygiene, stimulus control, and sleep compression) as well as education about caregiver resources and behavior problem management. Caregivers in the two treatment groups had significant improvements in self-reported quality of sleep after treatment and at three-month follow-up compared to wait-list subjects, although there were no differences in caregiver depression, caregiver burden, or patient problem behavior as a result of intervention assignment (McCurry et al., 1998). Generally, family caregivers also endorse high levels of satisfaction with these approaches, reporting increased self-efficacy in general or with regard to managing caregiving problems (Haley, Levine, Brown, &

Bartolucci, 1987; Steffen, Gallagher-Thompson, Zeiss, & Willis-Shore, 1994; Toseland, Rossiter, & Labrecque, 1989).

SUMMARY

CB group therapy shows promise as a treatment option for many disorders of late life (Teri & McCurry, 2000; Thompson et al., 2000). Although more empirical studies are needed to document outcome efficacy for group CBT, especially with regard to the maintenance of initial gains, preliminary findings indicate that group CBT is effective in the treatment of some common psychological disorders in older adults, including depression, chronic pain associated with medical conditions, sleep disorders, and family caregiver distress. Clearly, new research needs to more adequately address the diversity of the aging process and the heterogeneity of the older adult population. A wide variety of research opportunities into the applicability of CBT group interventions exist from treatment for those with mild cognitive impairment, those suffering from a variety of chronic illnesses, substance abusers, and those struggling with nursing home adjustment.

The vast majority of clinical outcome research with older adults has been conducted on the efficacy of CBT with a very narrow range of patients (i.e., predominantly White, middle- to upper-class individuals). Results from these studies may not generalize to elders from other racial, ethnic, and socioeconomic backgrounds. CBT provides a compatible clinical backdrop to develop, incorporate, and investigate successful strategies to use within cultural groups as well as to appropriately tailor for effectiveness across different groups (Higgins et al., in press). We encourage clinical researchers' future efforts to (1) examine the impact of cultural beliefs, values, and practices on treatment outcome; (2) uncover modifications necessary to account for the distinct learning histories,

language, and cultural practices of diverse elders; and (3) help establish treatment guidelines for diverse populations of elders. Further empirical research is needed to establish the efficacy of CBT for ethnically and culturally diverse individuals in general as well as for diverse older adult populations.

REFERENCES

Anthony-Bergstone, C. R., Zarit, S. H., & Gatz, M. (1988). Symptoms of psychological distress among caregivers of dementia patients. *Psychology and Aging, 3,* 245–248.

Arean, P., & Miranda, J. (1996). The treatment of depression in elderly primary care patients: A naturalistic study. *Journal of Clinical Geropsychology, 2,* 153–160.

Azhar, M., & Varma, S. (1995). Religious psychotherapy as management of bereavement. *Acta Psychiatrica Scandinavica, 91,* 233–235.

Beck, A. T., Rush, J., Shaw, B., & Emery, G. (1979). *Cognitive therapy of depression.* New York: Guilford Press.

Beutler, L., Scogin, F., Kirkish, P., Schretlen, D., Corbishley, A., Hamblin, D., et al. (1987). Group cognitive therapy and alprozolam in the treatment of depression in older adults. *Journal of Consulting and Clinical Psychology, 55,* 550–556.

Blazer, D. G. (1991). Suicide risk factors in the elderly: An epidemiological study. *Journal of Geriatric Psychiatry, 24,* 175–190.

Blazer, D. G. (1993). *Depression in late life* (2nd ed.). St. Louis, MO: Mosby-Yearbook.

Bootzin, R. R., Epstein, D., Engle-Friedman, M., & Salvio, M. A. (1996). Sleep disturbances. In L. L. Carstensen, B. A. Edelstein, & L. Dronbrand (Eds.), *The practical handbook of clinical gerontology* (pp. 398–422). London: Sage.

Bourgeois, M., Schulz, R., & Burgio, L. (1996). Interventions for caregivers of patients with Alzheimer's disease: A review and analysis of content, process and outcomes. *International Journal of Aging Human Development, 43,* 35–92.

Casas, J. (1988). Cognitive behavioral approaches: A minority perspective. *Counseling Psychologist, 16,* 106–110.

Cavanaugh, J. C. (1990). *Adult development and aging.* Belmont, CA: Wadsworth.

Cook, A. (1998). Cognitive-behavioral pain management for elderly nursing home residents. *Journals of Gerontology: Series B, Psychological Sciences and Social Sciences, 53B*(1), 51–59.

Coon, D., Schulz, R., & Ory, M. (1999). Innovative intervention approaches with Alzheimer's disease caregivers. In D. Biegel & A. Blum (Eds.), *Innovations in practice and service delivery across the lifespan* (pp. 295–325). New York: Oxford University Press.

Coon, D. W., Rider, K., Gallagher-Thompson, D., & Thompson, L. (1999). Cognitive-behavioral therapy for treatment of late-life distress. In M. Duffy (Ed.), *Handbook of counseling and psychotherapy with older adults* (pp. 487–510). New York: Wiley.

DeVries, H., & Gallagher-Thompson, D. (2000). Assessment and crisis intervention with older adults. In F. Dattilio & A. Freeman (Eds.), *Cognitive-behavioral strategies in crisis intervention* (2nd ed., pp. 196–215). New York: Guilford Press.

Dhooper, S., Green, S., Huff, M., & Austin-Murphy, J. (1993). Efficacy of a group approach to reducing depression in nursing home elderly residents. *Journal of Gerontological Social Work, 20,* 87–100.

Dick, L., Gallagher-Thompson, D., Coon, D., Powers, D., & Thompson, L. W. (1996). *Cognitive-behavioral therapy for late-life depression: A patient's manual.* Stanford, CA: VA Palo Alto Health Care System and Stanford University.

Dick, L., Gallagher-Thompson, D., & Thompson, L. (1996). Cognitive behavioral therapy. In R. Woods (Ed.), *Handbook of the clinical psychology of aging* (p. 509–544). New York: Wiley.

Dye, C., & Erber, J. (1981). Two group procedures for the treatment of nursing home patients. *Gerontologist, 21,* 539–544.

Epstein, D. R. (1994). *A behavioral intervention to enhance the sleep-wake patterns of older adults with insomnia.* Unpublished doctoral dissertation, University of Arizona, Tucson.

Fisher, J. E., & Noll, J. P. (1996). Anxiety disorders. In L. L. Carstensen, B. A. Edelstein, & L. Dronbrand (Eds.), *The practical handbook of clinical gerontology* (pp. 304–323). London: Sage.

Frierson, R. (1991). Suicide attempts by the old and the very old. *Archives of International Medicine, 151,* 141–144.

Fry, P. S. (1984). Cognitive training and cognitive behavioral variables in the treatment of depression in the elderly. *Clinical Gerontologist, 3*(1), 25–45.

Gallagher, D., Breckenridge, J., Thompson, L., & Peterson, J. (1983). Effects of bereavement on indicators of mental health in elderly widows and widowers. *Journal of Gerontology, 38,* 565–571.

Gallagher, D., Lovett, S., & Thompson, L. W. (1988). *Increasing life satisfaction class for caregivers: Class leaders' manual.* Palo Alto, CA: Department of Veterans Affairs Medical Center.

Gallagher, D., Rose, J., Rivera, P., Lovett, S., & Thompson, L. W. (1989). Prevalence of depression in family caregivers. *Gerontologist, 29,* 449–456.

Gallagher, D., & Thompson, L. (1981). *Depression in the elderly: A behavioral treatment manual.* Los Angeles: University of Southern California Press.

Gallagher, D., & Thompson, L. (1982). Treatment of Major Depressive Disorder in older adult outpatients with brief psychotherapies. *Psychotherapy: Theory, Research and Practice, 19,* 482–490.

Gallagher, D., Thompson, L. W., Silven, D., & Priddy, M. (1985). *Problem solving for caregivers: Class leaders' manual.* Palo Alto, CA: VA Palo Alto Health Care System and Stanford University School of Medicine.

Gallagher-Thompson, D. (1994). Direct services and interventions for caregivers: A review of extant programs and a look to the future. In M. H. Cantor (Ed.), *Family caregiving: Agenda for the future* (pp. 102–122). San Francisco: American Society on Aging.

Gallagher-Thompson, D., Arean, P., Coon, D., Menendez, A., Takagi, K., Haley, W. E., et al. (2000). Development and implementation of intervention strategies for culturally diverse caregiving populations. In R. Shulz (Ed.), *Handbook on dementia caregiving populations* (pp. 151–185). New York: Springer.

Gallagher-Thompson, D., Arean, P., Rivera, P., & Thompson, L. (in press). Reducing stress in Hispanic family caregivers using a psychoeducational intervention. *Clinical Gerontologist.*

Gallagher-Thompson, D., & DeVries, H. (1994). Coping with frustration classes: Development and preliminary outcomes with women who care for relatives with dementia. *Gerontologist, 34,* 545–552.

Gallagher-Thompson, D., Lovett, S., Rose, J., McKibbin, C., Coon, D., Futterman, A., et al. (2000). Impact of psychoeducational interventions on distressed family caregivers. *Journal of Clinical Geropsychology, 6*(2), 91–110.

Gallagher-Thompson, D., Rose, J., Florsheim, M., Jacome, P., DelMaestro, S., Peters, L., et al. (1992). *Controlling your frustration: A class for caregivers.* Palo Alto, CA: Department of Veterans Affairs Medical Center.

Gallagher-Thompson, D., & Steffen, A. M. (1994). Comparative effects of cognitive-behavioral and brief psychodynamic psychotherapies for depressed family caregivers. *Journal of Consulting and Clinical Psychology, 62,* 543–549.

Gatz, M., Fiske, A., Fox, L. S., McCallum, T. J., & Wetherell, J. L. (1998). Empirically validated psychological treatments for older adults. *Journal of Mental Health and Aging, 4*(1), 9–46.

Haley, W. H. (1996). The medical context of psychotherapy with the elderly. In S. Zarit & B. Knight (Eds.), *Psychotherapy and aging: Effective interventions with older adults* (pp. 221–240). Washington, DC: American Psychological Association.

Haley, W. H., Levine, E., Brown, S., & Bartolucci, A. (1987). Stress, appraisal, coping and social support as predictors of adaptational outcome among dementia caregivers. *Psychology and Aging, 2,* 323–330.

Higgins, A., Coon, D. W., Solano, N., Kinoshita, L., McCallum, T. J., D'Andrea, J., et al. (in press). Behavioral and cognitive interventions for late life depression: Special issues in the treatment of older adults. *Journal of Clinical Geropsychology.*

Iwamasa, G. (1996). On being an ethnic minority cognitive behavioral therapist. *Cognitive and Behavioral Practice, 3*(2), 235–254.

Kaszniak, A. (1996). Techniques and instruments for assessment of the elderly. In S. Zarit & B. Knight (Eds.), *A guide to psychotherapy and aging: Effective clinical interventions in a life-stage context* (pp. 163–220). Washington, DC: American Psychological Association.

Kemp, B. J., Corgiat, M., & Gill, C. (1992). Effects of brief cognitive-behavioral group psychotherapy with older persons with and without disabling illness. *Behavior Health, and Aging, 2,* 21–28.

Kiecolt-Glaser, J. K., Dura, J. R., Speicher, C. E., Trask, O. J., & Glaser, R. (1991). Spousal caregivers of dementia victims: Longitudinal changes in immunity and health. *Psychosomatic Medicine, 53,* 345–362.

Klausner, E., & Alexopoulos, G. (1999). The future of psychosocial treatments for elderly patients. *Psychiatric Services, 50,* 1198–1204.

Knight, B. G., & Satre, D. (1999, Summer). Cognitive behavioral psychotherapy with older adults. *Clinical Psychology: Science and Practice, 6*(2), 188–203.

Lacks, P., & Morin, C. M. (1992). Recent advances in the assessment and treatment of insomnia. *Journal of Consulting and Clinical Psychology, 60,* 586–594.

La Rue, A., & Watson, J. (1998). Psychological assessment of older adults. *Professional Psychology: Research and Practice, 29,* 5–14.

Lewinsohn, P., Muñoz, R., Youngren, M., & Zeiss, A. (1986). *Control your depression.* Englewood Cliffs, NJ: Prentice-Hall.

Lichstein, K. L., & Reidel, B. W. (1994). Behavioral assessment and treatment of insomnia: A review with an emphasis on clinical application. *Behavior Therapy, 25,* 659–688.

Lopez, M., & Mermelstein, R. (1995). A cognitive-behavioral program to improve geriatric rehabilitation outcome. *Gerontologist, 35,* 696–700.

Lund, D. A. (1989). *Older bereaved spouses: Research with practical applications.* New York: Hemisphere.

McCurry, S., Logsdon, R., Vitiello, M., & Teri, L. (1998). Successful behavioral treatment for reported sleep problems in elderly caregivers of dementia patients: A controlled study. *Journals of Gerontology: Series B, Psychological Sciences and Social Sciences, 53B*(2), 122–129.

McKibbin, C. L., Koonce-Volwiler, D., Cronkite, R. C., & Gallagher-Thompson, D. (2000). Psychological, social, and economic implications of bereavement among older women. In B. Sherr & J. S. St. Lawrence (Ed.), *Women, health and the mind* (pp. 151–171). New York: Wiley.

Mellinger, G. D., Balter, M. B., & Uhlenhuth, E. H. (1985). Insomnia and its treatment: Prevalence and correlates. *Archives of General Psychiatry, 42,* 225–232.

Mongan, E. (1990). Arthritis and osteoporosis. In B. Kemp, K. Brummel-Smith, & J. W. Ramsdell (Eds.), *Geriatric rehabilitation* (pp. 91–105). Austin, TX: ProEd.

Morin, C. M. (1993). *Insomnia: Psychological assessment and management*. New York: Guilford Press.

Morin, C. M., Culbert, J. P., & Schwartz, S. M. (1994). Nonpharmacological interventions for insomnia: A meta-analysis of treatment efficacy. *American Journal of Psychiatry, 151*, 1172–1180.

Morin, C. M., Kowatch, R. A., Barry, T., & Walton, E. (1993). Cognitive-behavior therapy for late-life insomnia. *Journal of Consulting and Clinical Psychology, 61*(1), 137–146.

Morin, C. M., Stone, J., Trinkle, D., Mercer, J., & Remsberg, S. (1992). Dysfunctional beliefs and attitudes about sleep among older adults with and without insomnia complaints. *Psychology and Aging, 8*, 463–467.

National Alliance for Caregiving. (1997). *Family caregiving in the U.S.: Findings from a national survey.* Washington, DC: National Alliance for Caregiving and American Association of Retired Persons.

Nielsen, G., Nordhus, I., & Kvale, G. (1998). Insomnia in older adults. In I. Nordhus, G. VandenBos, S. Berg, & P. Fromholt (Eds.), *Clinical geropsychology*. Washington, DC: American Psychological Association.

Organista, K. C. (2000). Latinos. In J. R. White & A. S. Freeman (Eds.), *Cognitive-behavioral group therapy for specific problems and populations* (pp. 218–303). Washington, DC: American Psychological Association.

Organista, K. C., & Muñoz, R. F. (1996). Cognitive behavioral therapy with Latinos. *Cognitive and Behavioral Practice, 3*(2), 255–270.

Organista, K. C., Muñoz, R. F., & Gonzales, G. (1994). Cognitive behavioral therapy for depression in low-income and minority medical outpatients: Description of a program and exploratory analyses. *Cognitive Therapy and Research, 18*(3), 241–259.

Paradis, C., Friedman, S., Hatch, M., & Ackerman, R. (1996). Cognitive behavioral treatment of anxiety disorders in Orthodox Jews. *Cognitive and Behavioral Practice, 3*(2), 271–288.

Pearlin, L. I. (1993). The social contexts of stress. In L. Goldberger & S. Breznitz (Eds.), *Handbook of stress: Theoretical and clinical aspects* (3rd ed., pp. 303–315). New York: Free Press.

Prigerson, H., Frank, E., Kasly, S., Reynolds, C., Anderson, B., Zubenko, G., et al. (1995). Complicated grief and bereavement-related depression as distinct disorders: Preliminary empirical validation in elderly bereaved spouses. *American Journal of Psychiatry, 152*, 22–30.

Ries, A. L. (1990). Pulmonary rehabilitation. In B. Kemp, K. Brummel-Smith, & J. W. Ramsdell (Eds.), *Geriatric rehabilitation* (pp. 107–120). Austin, TX: ProEd.

Rybarczyk, B., Gallagher-Thompson, D., Rodman, J., Zeiss, A., Gantz, F. F., & Yesavage, J. S. (1992). Applying cognitive-behavioral psychotherapy to the chronically ill elderly: Treatment issues and case illustration. *International Psychogeriatrics, 4*(1), 127–140.

Schulz, R., O'Brien, A., Bookwala, J., & Fleissner, K. (1995). Psychiatric and physical morbidity effects of dementia caregiving: Prevalence, correlates and causes. *Gerontologist, 35*, 771–791.

Schulz, R., Visintainier, P., & Williamson, G. M. (1990). Psychiatric and physical morbidity effects of caregiving. *Journals of Gerontology: Series B, Psychological Sciences and Social Sciences, 45*, 181–191.

Scogin, F. R. (1998). Anxiety in old age. In I. H. Nordhus, G. R. VandenBos, S. Berg, & P. Fromholt (Eds.), *Clinical geropsychology* (pp. 205–210). Washington, DC: American Psychological Association.

Scogin, F., & McElreath, L. (1994). Efficacy of psychosocial treatment for geriatric depression: A quantitative review. *Journal of Consulting and Clinical Psychology, 62*(1), 69–74.

Silverman, P. R. (1969). The widow-to-widow program: An experiment in preventive intervention. *Mental Hygiene, 53*, 333–337.

Snyder, L., Quayhagen, M. P., Shepherd, S., & Bower, D. (1995). Supportive seminar groups: An intervention for early stage dementia patients. *Gerontologist, 35*, 691–695.

Stanley, M. A., Beck, J. G., & Glassco, J. D. (1996). Treatment of generalized anxiety in older adults: A preliminary comparison of cognitive-behavioral and supportive approaches. *Behavior Therapy, 27*, 565–581.

Steffen, A., Gallagher-Thompson, D., Zeiss, A., & Willis-Shore, J. (1994). *Self-efficacy for caregiving:*

Psychoeducational interventions with dementia family caregivers. Paper presented at the annual meeting of the American Psychological Association, Los Angeles.

Steuer, J. L., Mintz, J., Hammen, C. L., Hill, M. A., Jarvik, L. S., McCarley, T., et al. (1984). Cognitive-behavioral and psychodynamic group psychotherapy in treatment of geriatric depression. *Journal of Consulting and Clinical Psychology, 52,* 180–189.

Stone, R., Cafferata, G. L., & Sangl, G. (1987). Caregivers of the frail elderly: A national profile. *Gerontologist, 27,* 616–626.

Teri, L., & Gallagher-Thompson, D. (1991). Cognitive-behavioral interventions for treatment of depression in Alzheimer's patients. *Gerontologist, 31,* 413–416.

Teri, L., & McCurry, S. M. (2000). Psychosocial therapies. In C. E. Coffey & J. L. Cummings (Eds.), *Textbook of geriatric neuropsychiatry* (2nd ed., pp. 861–890). Washington, DC: American Psychiatric Press.

Thompson, L. W. (1996). Cognitive-behavioral therapy and treatment for late-life depression. *Journal of Clinical Psychology, 57*(Suppl. 5), 29–37.

Thompson, L. W., Coon, D. W., Gallagher-Thompson, D., Sommer, B., & Koin, D. (2001). Comparison of desipramine and cognitive behavioral therapy in the treatment of late-life depression. *American Journal of Geriatric Psychiatry, 9*(3), 225–240.

Thompson, L., Gallagher, D., & Breckenridge, J. (1987). Comparative effectiveness of psychotherapies for depressed elders. *Journal of Consulting and Clinical Psychology, 55*(3), 385–390.

Thompson, L. W., Gallagher, D., Cover, H., Gilewski, M., & Peterson, J. (1989). Effects of bereavement on symptoms of psychopathology in older men and women. In D. Lund (Ed.), *Older bereaved spouses: Research with practical applications* (pp. 17–24). New York: Hemisphere.

Thompson, L. W., Gallagher, D., & Lovett, S. (1992). *Increasing life satisfaction: Class leaders' and participant manuals.* Palo Alto, CA: VA Palo Alto Health Care System and Stanford University School of Medicine.

Thompson, L. W., Gallagher-Thompson, D., Futterman, A., & Peterson, J. (1991). The effects of late-life spousal bereavement over a thirty-month interval. *Psychology and Aging, 6,* 434–441.

Thompson, L. W., Powers, D., Coon, D. W., Takagi, K., McKibbin, C., & Gallagher-Thompson, D. (2000). Older adults. In A. Freeman & J. White (Eds.), *Cognitive behavioral group therapy for specific problems and populations* (pp. 235–261). Washington, DC: American Psychological Association.

Toseland, R. W. (1995) *Group work with the elderly and family caregivers.* New York: Springer.

Toseland, R., Rossiter, C., & Labrecque, M. (1989). The effectiveness of three group intervention strategies to support family caregivers. *American Journal of Orthopsychiatry, 59*(3), 420–429.

Widner, S., & Zeichner, A. (1993). Psychological interventions for the elderly chronic pain patient. *Clinical Gerontologist, 13,* 3–18.

Wolfe, R., Morrow, J., & Fredrickson, B. L. (1996). Mood disorders in older adults. In L. L. Carstensen, B. A. Edelstein, & L. Dronbrand (Eds.), *The practical handbook of clinical gerontology* (pp. 274–303). London: Sage.

Worden, J. W. (1991). *Grief counseling and grief therapy: A handbook for the mental health practitioner* (2nd ed.). New York: Springer.

Yost, D., Beutler, L., Corbishley, A. M., & Allender, J. (1986). *Group cognitive therapy: A treatment approach for depressed older adults.* New York: Pergamon Press.

Zarit, S. H., & Zarit, J. M. (1998). *Mental disorders in older adults: Fundamentals of assessment and treatment.* New York: Guilford Press.

Zautra, A. J., Maxwell, B. M., & Reich, J. W. (1989). Relationship among physical impairment, distress, and well-being in older adults. *Journal of Behavioral Medicine, 12,* 543–557.

Zeiss, M. M., Lewinsohn, P. M., Rohde, P., & Seeley, J. R. (1996). Relationship of physical disease and functional impairment to depression in older people. *Psychology and Aging, 11,* 572–581.

SPECIAL TOPICS

CHAPTER 24

Behavioral Supervision

RONA L. LEVY

THEORETICAL BASIS

DISTINGUISHING COGNITIVE-BEHAVIORAL SUPERVISION FROM OTHER FORMS OF SUPERVISION

Clinicians who approach the treatment of their clients from a cognitive-behavioral (CB) perspective will also likely approach many of their other professional (and personal as well, but that is beyond the scope of this paper) activities, including supervision, from this same perspective. Some of the most basic principles of a CB perspective include (1) choosing methods that have demonstrated empirical success; (2) an "experimental" approach to choosing methods when it is not apparent which method has demonstrated success in the situation at hand; (3) a recognition of the importance of both cognitions and behavior in bringing about individual change; and (4) an awareness of how the fundamentals of social learning theory are applied to CB practice. These fundamentals can be simplistically reduced to the idea that individuals generally engage in activities they find rewarding or that remove aversive conditions, and do not continue to engage in activities for

which they are punished or that they do not find rewarding. Of course, the devil is always in the details, and intelligent practitioners applying these details understand the complexities of these conditions in real life. Nevertheless, they are solid guiding principles for the cognitive-behaviorist.

Putting this background in the context of supervision from a CB perspective leads to supervision based on these fundamental principles. It will differ from supervision by someone whose approach does not adhere to these principles. However, the line distinguishing who is cognitive-behavioral and who is not is often blurred. To the extent that supervisors who do not call themselves cognitive-behavioral accept any basic CB principles (such as rewarding desirable performance), their supervision is likely to have similarities to a CB approach. Further, CB and non-CB supervisors often engage in similar activities but provide different theoretical rationales for their activities.

Consider the following situation. A supervisee discusses with her supervisor how her client's reactions to her often seem to come "out of the blue." The supervisor says that he knows the supervisee is always thinking she is stupid.

The supervisee may feel she has done nothing to bring on this reaction. Psychodynamic supervisors would explain the concept of transference and would explain how this concept applies in this clinical situation. Psychodynamic supervisors are likely to have their antennae out for possible instances of transference in their interactions with supervisees. This is likely to be a central concept in their work with supervisees. CB supervisors may analyze the situation using the concept of stimulus generalization, derived from empirical research. They know that if a stimulus (person) is similar to a stimulus the person has encountered in the past, the individual will react in a way that will increase reward, or decrease aversive consequences, with the prior stimulus. CB supervisors may explain this phenomenon with clients to their supervisees and possibly be aware of it in their own interactions with supervisees. A focus on transference is less likely to be central for CB practitioners, as the research has not been sufficiently developed to outline clear implications of this phenomenon.

The author has been an instructor and supervisor of graduate social work students for approximately 30 years, having also written extensively on methods for the enhancement of adherence to recommendations, particularly medical recommendations (Levy & Feld, 1999; Shelton & Levy, 1981). These strategies to enhance *patient* adherence should also be used to increase the likelihood that *practitioners* will follow practice protocols, including adherence-enhancement protocols. It seems that these enhancers are a natural fit for supervision recommendations, as supervision is ultimately a process where one attempts to support others in engaging in certain activities. Hence, the series of recommendations starting on page 570 for increasing the effectiveness of supervision by increasing the supervisee's likelihood of following specific recommendations. They have been adapted from recommendations for the enhancement of adherence to medical recommendations;

much of the literature is drawn from this field, as most of the adherence work has occurred in medicine. However, their application to the area of supervision of others is logical and fairly straightforward.

REASONS FOR NONADHERENCE

A number of factors have been shown to be associated with individuals not following through on recommendations. Major factors include the person giving the recommendation (for simplicity, this individual will be referred to as the supervisor henceforward), the type of request, and, in medicine, factors associated with the illness. Supervisors can affect adherence through their interactional style and specifics of how requests are made (Dajani, 1996). Characteristics of the request, such as duration and complexity, can affect adherence (Peura, 1998). Finally, positive effects such as the absence or reduction of negative stimuli following more desirable client behavior can contribute to adherence (Dajani, 1996).

As Donovan and Blake (1992) note, individuals are likely to carry out a cost-benefit analysis of actions as they weigh the costs/risks of each action against the benefits they perceive. Thus, an apparently irrational act of noncompliance from the doctor's/supervisor's point of view may be a very rational action from the patient's/supervisee's point of view. Haynes, Taylor, and Sackett (1979) summarized reasons patients gave for their nonadherence across a number of studies. Their summary provides a useful starting point for looking at possible strategies to improve adherence to supervisory recommendations. Drawing from that list, supervisees' reasons for their nonadherence can be grouped into three categories:

1. *Supervisees do not have adequate skills or knowledge to follow a regimen.* Reasons patients gave for nonadherence that fall in this category include poor instruction, incorrect or inadequate

information on medications or appointments, and lost appointment slips. Simply stated, individuals cannot follow through on an assignment if they do not know what they are supposed to do or how or when they are supposed to do it. Thus, as will be emphasized later, a supervisor should never assume, without some form of check, that a supervisee knows how to carry out an assignment. Unfortunately, with the current time pressures on many organizations, there is often insufficient time for adequate supervisory education and adherence instruction. In the author's practica settings, each student is expected to receive a minimum number of supervised hours, but on occasion, students have mentioned that they do not have this much contact with their supervisors. They often are too uncomfortable to raise this issue with their supervisor. Field liaison faculty address this problem immediately when they become aware of it.

2. *Supervisees do not believe they will be helped by the activity, or do not accept the activity because they do not believe its value will outweigh its costs.* Continuing to extrapolate from studies with patients in the medical literature, reasons given by patients that fall within the category of acceptance or beliefs include feeling dissatisfied with the clinician or treatment, believing they were getting incorrect or inappropriate medication, receiving contradictory advice from friends, not believing the treatment was helping or believing it was making them worse (e.g., side effects), improving and believing that further reason for treatment is unnecessary, feeling dissatisfied with clinical procedures (e.g., amount of time spent waiting), having alternative health care beliefs, obtaining contradictory information from the Internet, and feeling indifferent or experiencing "lack of will-power." This last phrase seems quite vague and should be replaced by a more useful explanation, such as that the individual does not see the reward for adherence. This type of explanation would provide a direction for possible corrective action. Cultural norms also may play a major

role in patient acceptance of interventions, as Zuckerman, Guerra, Drossman, Foland, and Gregory (1996) have shown by demonstrating differences between Hispanics and non-Hispanic Whites in health care-seeking behaviors related to bowel complaints.

3. *Supervisees' environment is not supportive of or interferes with adherence.* Reasons patients gave for nonadherence that fall within this category are financial need, sickness, child care problems, transportation difficulties, employment or housework interference, being asleep when medications should be taken, lack of family support or illness in the family, and loss of the medication. Keeping an appointment may be extremely costly to a woman who has no child care arrangements or transportation, limited finances, and an employer who may penalize or even fire her if she takes time off from work. In other words, there may be environmental barriers for supervisees such as schedule conflicts, which must be addressed if the supervisor is interested in reducing potential nonadherence.

STRUCTURING THE SUPERVISION SESSION

The supervisor must recognize that *adherence-enhancement activities must be a focus of supervisory contact.* This point is critical. Adherence-enhancement must not be merely adjunctive to supervision: It should be viewed as central. Thus, when meeting with the supervisee, the supervisor should be focused on what the supervisee should do outside the immediate situation. The following suggests how this may be accomplished.

INITIAL CONTACT

At the beginning of supervision, the supervisor should inform supervisees of the rationale for activities when away from the supervisor, so they understand what is expected and agree to work independently. These activities may be thought of as homework, and it should be stressed that adherence to homework assignments is the basis of effectively learning the material being taught.

MEETINGS

Meetings should begin with a review of the homework given during the previous appointment. The supervisor should go over any difficulties that were encountered, attempt to address them, and, consistent with the recommendations below, praise success. If a supervisee has been asked to read some material and take notes on what was read, for example, the supervisor should take time to clarify and review information that has been recorded. Supervisees who put a good deal of time and energy into preparing such material are typically interested in discussing this information and should be positively reinforced for their efforts. If subsequent homework seems indicated, time is then needed to cover what the supervisee will be doing during the time between this meeting and the next.

If the homework was not accomplished as requested, the portion that was finished or attempted should be acknowledged. Supervisor and supervisee should work together to problem-solve ways to correct difficulties.

Each meeting should conclude with a review of homework and any additional appropriate adherence-enhancement recommendations.

ADHERENCE-ENHANCEMENT RECOMMENDATIONS

Recommendations to enhance adherence constitute a checklist for the supervisor to consider when developing a protocol for supervisory activities. Addressing all of these suggestions may not be feasible when homework assignments are discussed at each meeting. However, they are offered as useful tools for increasing the likelihood of adherence. The more recommendations that are followed, the greater the chances for supervisory effectiveness. The supervisor can anticipate that certain adherence-enhancing techniques will be most appropriate for a given problem and should have a protocol in place that involves several staff. For example, all supervisees may be asked to practice an intake role play with another supervisee, read an informational pamphlet on depression, role-play their activity with the supervisor, make a public commitment to do the assignment, and then make a follow-up phone call to the supervisor's voice mail regarding adherence questions prior to the next supervisory meeting.

As with many situations in medicine and psychology, *preventing nonadherence is far easier and more effective than treating nonadherence.* Therefore, ideally, these methods should be used early in supervisory contact to establish a pattern of adherence.

RECOMMENDATION 1

The quality of the supervisor-supervisee relationship is critical: Supervisees should believe in their supervisors as well as in the value of the assignment for their education and clinical effectiveness.

Supervisees must believe that the supervisor is competent, that the assigned task is useful, that it is acceptable to others, that it has a high probability of successful completion, and that the entire educational program is valuable. Supervisors should take the time to elicit supervisees' beliefs, fears, and expectations regarding adherence; questions should be encouraged. Good rapport is critical, as it is likely to elicit greater adherence. Drossman and Olden, among others, have written extensively on this (Drossman, 1997, 1999; Olden, 1998, in press). In addition, attention to gender issues is extremely important for the development of good relationships whenever recommendations are made (Toner, 1994).

Homework interactions should not be unidirectional: Supervisees should help select assignments. Supervisors can introduce the collaboration with a question such as "What do you think would be a good way to keep track of ?" Or the supervisor may offer a range of assignments from which the supervisee can choose. Cecil and Killeen (1997), among others, have demonstrated that when physicians exhibited less control dominance, as observed during videotaped encounters, there was an increase in patient compliance and satisfaction.

The term "active patient orientation" was coined by Schulman (1979), who also demonstrated increased adherence among patients who were active participants in the treatment planning process. It is also an approach that is sensitive to gender issues. First, supervisees should have an increased perception of control. No one is making them do this; they have chosen to do the assignment and are thus more likely to follow through. Second, supervisees will have selected assignments that they can imagine occurring in their own world. This fact reduces the possibility that, after reflecting on an assignment, a supervisee will think, "My supervisor doesn't really know how difficult it would be to do that," and then fail to adhere. Herxheimer (1998) stresses the importance of doctors and patients sharing the same goals in taking medicine, with a shift in patient attitude from compliance to concordance. This call for a collaborative approach is cited elsewhere (Crespo-Fierro, 1997; Oleske, 1998; Pathare & Paton, 1997).

Supervisees should feel comfortable renegotiating assignments. For example, a supervisee may be willing to schedule a role play with a colleague and phone in his or her success, but may ask to renegotiate the time limit on preparatory reading. Such negotiation may prevent the supervisee from dropping all recommendations.

Supervisees need to believe in the value of the educational process. In medicine, Herxheimer (1998) notes the need for increasing patients' knowledge and understanding of side effects. Peura (1998) suggests that clinicians may increase the effects of treatment in certain patients by helping to dispel long-held inaccurate beliefs about the causes of their illness. After the desired task is determined, supervisees should be asked their reaction to the assignment. This intensive discussion will provide the opportunity to further enact other adherence-enhancement steps, such as more direct training, if needed. Written materials, such as readings on the effectiveness of practicing role plays, may assist in supervisees' commitment to the task. In addition, some people benefit from listening to relevant audio or videocassettes.

RECOMMENDATION 2

The supervisor should be sure assignments contain specific details about the desired behavior. Assignments should specify how, when, where, and for how long the assignment is to be done. Studies in the medical literature show considerable variation in the interpretation of doctors' instructions (typically, medication taking). In one study (Mazzulo, Lasagna, & Griner, 1974), it was found that patients had many different interpretations of apparently simple instructions such as "Take four times a day." Does this mean with meals, before meals, evenly spaced? Does careful timing matter? Peura (1998) suggests that failure to eradicate infection may be due to small variations in the dosing or timing of medications.

When asking supervisees to keep an ongoing record of an activity, supervisors could ask where they plan to keep their monitoring sheet. This encourages them to plan the specific details of how they will do this assignment. Many men, for example, prefer to keep a 3×5 card in a shirt pocket. Supervisees can be encouraged to do their recording as close as possible in time to when the event of interest occurred. Otherwise, they may forget to record it and are more likely to record inaccurately.

One way to accomplish this goal is to provide a specific outline of a supervisee's responsibilities so that the chances of misinterpretation are reduced. However, simplicity should not be sacrificed for specificity. Extreme detail and complexity may actually make a behavior too difficult (Haynes et al., 1979). For example, it would not be helpful to suggest a specific phrase for supervisees to use to greet a patient each time. It would be better to suggest that supervisees have some greeting planned with which they are comfortable, and which may vary with the situation and leave the exact format to their discretion.

RECOMMENDATION 3

The supervisor should ask the supervisee to rehearse cognitively and then behaviorally any appropriate assignments. Having supervisees take time during a supervisory session to actually imagine carrying out the assignment can lead to several positive results. First, supervisees may imagine possible difficulties, which could then be problem-solved. For example, if a client does not respond in the way the supervisee hoped, what would happen next? Supervisees may also ask clarifying questions regarding confusing aspects of the assignment. Finally, rehearsing a difficult activity in the atmosphere of the office, with the support of the supervisor readily available, may be an easy first step to completing the assignment.

In addition to rehearsing cognitively in the office, several techniques for cognitive rehearsal outside of the supervisor's office have also been recommended. With Suinn's (1972a, 1972b) approach, the supervisee is asked to carry out a specific cognitive strategy just before engaging in a self-directed assignment. This procedure asks the supervisee to *relax,*

visualize (the successful completion of the regimen), and *do* (the regimen). For example, supervisees who experience stress before an activity would be asked to first relax immediately before the event, then to visualize successfully completing the event, and then to do, or initiate, the response. Meichenbaum's (1977) self-instructional training provides similar rehearsal technique.

RECOMMENDATION 4

The supervisor should provide direct skill training. A frequent mistake is the assumption that the supervisee has the skills necessary to complete the desired task. It is therefore wise to practice the behavior in the office before asking supervisees to engage in the task in the natural social environment. This practice is particularly recommended in cases where the assigned behavior is so complex that verbal instructions alone are inadequate. For example, when suggesting that supervisees engage in a verbal interaction process, such as conducting an assessment, showing empathy, or acknowledging reinforcement, it is useful to have them demonstrate the skill. Rehearsal strategies have been used as effective components of adherence-enhancement strategies for a wide range of behaviors, including physician adherence to adherence-enhancement protocols (Schlundt, Quesenberry, Pichert, Lorenz, & Boswell, 1994).

Direct skill training involves a chain of events that, depending on the skill level, may need repeating. In its complete form, an instructional chain consists of the following behaviors:

1. The supervisor assesses the level of supervisee skills relevant to the upcoming assignment (skill training is not always necessary).
2. If the decision is made to proceed with skill training, the supervisor begins by giving the supervisee verbal and written instructions.

3. The supervisor models the skill, if appropriate.

4. The supervisee then imitates the skill, with coaching, prompting, and reward for approximations toward the desired goal.

For example, consider the case of an anxious supervisee who is almost constantly in interaction with clients. She was asked to take "brief relaxes" throughout her day. She was told this could even be done in a face-to-face interaction. She expressed doubt about how she could do this, so it was determined that skill training was appropriate. The supervisee was given verbal and written instructions (e.g., "Take a slow deep breath, exhale slowly, let your tension be released"). The supervisor then modeled this behavior, demonstrating that this relaxation did not need to interrupt their interaction. Finally, the supervisee was asked to perform the behavior, with appropriate feedback from the supervisor.

RECOMMENDATION 5

Adherence should be rewarded. Social learning theory teaches us that the rate of adherence, like all behavior, is influenced by the consequences that immediately follow adherence behavior (Davidson & Davidson, 1980). Missed opportunities to reward adherence may lead to a decrease in the frequency and duration of home practice activities and an overall reduction in effectiveness.

There are a number of reward opportunities for encouraging supervisees to adhere to prescribed tasks. The sources of reward can be the supervisor, supervisees themselves, or significant others.

Supervisor Reinforcement

Because supervisees may not gain immediate reward from persons in their social environment, they should always be told in advance that the criterion for success is the execution of the behavior (adherence) and not the outcome of adherence. The supervisor, at least initially, is frequently the most important source of reward. The supervisor should keep a careful record of all prescribed assignments and refer to this record when speaking with supervisees. Supervisees should never have to "fish" for reinforcement by reminding the supervisor of what they were asked to do.

Initially, supervisees should be reinforced for all approximations to desirable adherence efforts. For example, if a supervisee is asked to keep detailed records of interactions with clients, but did this only for interactions with some clients, he or she should be rewarded for the records that were kept. Shaping of the supervisee's performance can then be carried out by rewarding gradually closer approximations to the assignment (see next recommendation).

Supervisors can also make use of other media, such as e-mail, to deliver reward. An e-mail offers the opportunity to provide social reward to supervisees in a natural setting. Phone calls may also be appropriate, if supervisor and supervisee agree on this method. Whenever possible, phone calls should be made at a scheduled time, preferably after completion of a task rather than when there is difficulty in doing the task. Supervisees can be instructed to call when they finish a difficult task, not "whenever the homework doesn't go well." Thus, although problems arising from homework should be acknowledged and receive empathy, the emphasis remains on the positive aspects of performance of assigned tasks.

Reward structures should be clearly outlined. Supervisors may use a written statement that outlines the benefits of adherence and the costs of nonadherence (Gambrill, 1977; Steckel & Swain, 1977). Although this format (sometimes called a contract) can require extra time and effort to construct, it can provide the additional structure and contingencies needed to foster the completion of home activities. In addition, contracts provide clear-cut criteria for achievement of the stated therapeutic activities. Although the use of contracts has generally been found to be effective, a comparison of which individuals and with whom it would be best to use a contract is difficult and has not yet been empirically tested. At present, the best recommendation is to provide an abbreviated contract for all supervisees asked to do homework. For tasks with extensive or particularly difficult protocols, a more extensive contract may be warranted.

Contracts can be unilateral or bilateral. In a unilateral contract, supervisees obligate themselves to complete the homework and are rewarded for such completion. Bilateral contracts specify the obligations and the mutual rewards for each of the parties involved. Contracts should be very specific, determined by negotiation, and fully understood and accepted by the supervisee. Successful contracts have short-range, written goals, and both supervisor and supervisee keep a copy.

Other elements of a successful contract include the following:

1. A very clear and detailed description of the homework.
2. Specification of the reward gained if the homework is completed.
3. Provision for consequences for failure to complete the assignment within a specified time limit or behavior frequency.
4. Specification of the means by which the contract response is to be observed, measured, and recorded.
5. An arrangement whereby the delivery of rewards follows the response as quickly as possible.

A range of reinforcers are available to the supervisor. These include verbal praise, written letters of praise sent to agency directors or school personnel and included in the supervisee's file, special lunches, time off, and other small tokens of appreciation (e.g., a box of mints for supervisees who like mints) accompanied by praise.

Supervisee Reward

Another important source of reward is the supervisee himself or herself. Self-reward is vital to the success of homework and may actually be the key to maintaining therapeutic behaviors after treatment has been terminated. Supervisees should be encouraged to set up specific external rewards, or internal ones in which they tell themselves they are pleased with their accomplishment (Johnson, 1971).

Reinforcement from Significant Others

Involving others in the supervisee's training can be a very effective part of supervision. Other supervisees, supervisors, or friends selected by the supervisee can help in various ways to support completion of homework assignments (Levy, 1983, 1985). Other persons' participation may even be formalized by building it into a contract. For example, the supervisor might say, "I will take you and Joan (the supervisee's peer) to lunch if . . ."

Brownell and colleagues (Brownell, Heckerman, Westlake, Hayes, & Monti, 1978; Brownell & Stunkard, 1981; Wilson & Brownell, 1978) have systematically involved partners of overweight spouses in weight-reduction programs, with mixed results. Each week, as clients are given homework assignments, partners are given their own homework assignments, many of which include rewards to the overweight partner for adherence to assignments.

RECOMMENDATION 6

Whenever possible, the supervisor should begin with smaller activities that are likely to be successful, and then gradually increase these to the desired goal. This technique is sometimes referred to as the "foot in the door" technique (Freedman & Fraser, 1966; Lepper, 1973). Supervisees are first asked to complete a small request. If the request is adhered to and rewarded, they are then more likely to complete a subsequent larger task. Ideally, the beginning assignment should be simple and require relatively little effort on the part of the supervisee. Each assignment is carefully planned to be within the supervisee's skill repertoire. For example, if something supervisees are asked to do is different from their usual practice, such as assessing for multiple areas with which they are only minimally familiar, supervisees may be asked to try to assess for one or two new areas to start. Monitoring provides another example where the stepwise procedure may be useful. If an ultimate goal is to have supervisees record something throughout their practice day, they could begin by selecting a two-hour period when recording might be easy.

It is a good idea to keep requests as simple as possible. Raz and Elchanan (1995) compared the effects of prescribing penicillin V 1.0 g twice daily to 0.5 g four times daily. Adherence in the former group was 90%, compared to 58% in the latter group. Symptom resolution was also significantly better in the twice-daily group.

RECOMMENDATION 7

The supervisor should work with supervisees to set up a system that will remind supervisees of the assignment. The supervisor should take steps to ensure that supervisees are reminded to carry out an assignment at the appropriate time and place. One cue to assignment adherence that can be carried into the natural environment is a copy of the written assignments. Supervisors may use either a photocopy of their own record, made in session when assignments are given, or they might utilize NCR (no carbon required) pads when writing down assignments. Thus, the supervisor and the supervisee immediately get a copy. Supervisees may then be asked to post this assignment list in a convenient place. Another useful technique is to create a place on appointment cards where assignments are to be recorded. The following can be printed on the

back of cards: "Between now and _____ you have been asked to _____." If the list is long and will not fit on the card, simply write "complete assignments on your assignment sheet."

E-mails and other reminder forms, in addition to being rewards, may also be useful to remind and prompt supervisees (Levy & Claravall, 1977; Mazzulo et al., 1974). Other individuals in the supervisee's environment (with the supervisee's suggestions) can be enlisted to provide needed reminders at appropriate times. Various devices have been used as aids to adherence, including programmable watches and calendars (Epstein & Cluss, 1981). Telephone calls, automated messages, mailed cards, and computer messages have all been effectively employed to increase adherence rates across a range of behaviors (Dexter et al., 1998; Hawe, McKenzie, & Scurry, 1998; Liew, Capra, Makol, Black, & Shinefield, 1998; O'Brien & Lazenbnik, 1998; Roter et al., 1998).

RECOMMENDATION 8

The supervisee should make an overt commitment to adhere. Overt commitments, such as verbalizations of a concrete plan, serve two purposes. First, they provide considerable evidence about how someone intends to act. Such information can provide a basis for further discussion if it appears that the supervisee may not intend to adhere to assignments. One of the best ways to predict adherence is to simply ask supervisees whether they intend to adhere to the assigned outside activity. The supervisor may also ask for specifics, such as frequency and duration.

Second, an overt commitment serves to enhance the likelihood of adherence. In many situations, such a commitment, if given verbally and in writing, is sufficient to bring about completion of assignments (Levy, 1977; Levy & Clark, 1980; Levy, Yamashita, & Pow, 1979). However, despite assurances from supervisees that they intend to do the assignment, the supervisor may doubt the accuracy of the prediction. In some cases, a supervisee may repeatedly promise to engage in a task and fail to follow through. As with reminders, the evidence is mixed on the relationship between overt commitment and improvement in adherence rates (Shelton & Levy, 1981). Yet, it requires so little to simply ask a supervisee "Will you do it?" that it seems useful to use this technique in all situations, along with other techniques that may be appropriate.

RECOMMENDATION 9

The supervisor should try to anticipate and reduce the negative effects of adherence. Efforts should be made to anticipate barriers to adherence in the natural environment and facilitate the integration of the assignment into the supervisee's normal activities. For example, the supervisor could ask supervisees for a plan if they forget to cover certain areas during an assessment. Many pitfalls can be avoided by following some of the strategies already discussed. For example, supervisees who have received thorough training in performing a task are likely to find it less difficult. Supervisees who have tried techniques such as Meichenbaum's (1977) or Johnson's (1971) self-reward system are less dependent on external rewards, as they generate their own intrinsic reward. Thus, a supervisee who performs a very difficult task (such as making it to early clinics on time for a week when chronic lateness has been a problem) can be encouraged to say something like "Good for me! That was tough, but I did it." Even if persons around them are less rewarding (e.g., roommates who have to be quiet so supervisees can sleep at night), supervisees can self-reward.

Sometimes, easy modifications can help avoid punishment for adherence. One supervisee reported that it was difficult to put her yellow monitoring sheets on her desk to monitor her task completion. She said she worked in an office where people were always writing on white sheets of paper, and if she pulled out a yellow sheet, people would know that it was something different. This was handled by simply copying the form on white sheets of paper.

RECOMMENDATION 10

Adherence should be closely monitored by as many sources as possible. Monitoring may include direct or indirect assessment of the supervisee's adherence behavior. It may be carried out by the supervisee (self-monitoring), by someone in the supervisee's environment who has the opportunity to observe adherence (or nonadherence) behavior, or both.

Monitoring is important because problems can affect a supervisee's reporting of events, such as forgetting or response bias, including the desire to look good to the supervisor. If the supervisor cannot directly observe adherence, he or she must rely on some system of monitoring to determine that it has occurred and whether congratulations or further instructions are appropriate. Monitoring can also provide several direct benefits to supervisees. They can engage in self-reward when monitored data are good and will also be made more aware of the importance of the task being assigned.

When the assignment is to ask a client about specific areas, adherence can be self-monitored by having supervisees count the areas they ask about. Adherence can also be comonitored by having the client, if appropriate, count the number of areas inquired about. If available to the supervisor, trained observers in the supervisee's environment may be used. Other methods, discussed in Gordis (1979) and Dunbar (1979), may also be used to monitor adherence, including data from "permanent products" (e.g., physical consequences of a behavior, such as notes written during a session) or mechanical devices (e.g., devices that keep track of how long tape-recorders have been played). For both ethical and practical reasons, supervisees should be involved in the planning of any methods used to monitor their behavior.

When monitoring for adherence is conducted by the supervisee, several issues arise. Self-monitoring may be reactive; that is, it may actually change the behaviors being observed (Barlow, Hayes, & Nelson, 1984). This change is usually in the desired direction for clinical goals, although in a small minority of cases, reactivity may pose a problem if the supervisor is conducting supervision research and interested in valid nonreactive data. Another issue when using self-monitoring is accuracy. It would certainly be undesirable if the supervisor were rewarding the supervisee for covering certain assessment areas, as reported on the supervisee's self-monitoring sheet, if the supervisee were not actually accomplishing these tasks. In this case, the supervisee would be rewarded for inaccurate recording. Thus, it is important for the supervisor to know how to determine and enhance the accuracy of the data received from supervisee self-reporting.

Monitoring by others raises many of the same issues as self-monitoring. Monitoring by others may also be reactive, and could thus be utilized by the supervisor to affect adherence in a desirable direction. Observers also need to be trained in accurate recording methods. Finally, the supervisor needs to be aware of factors that can affect the accuracy of information, such as observer bias in recording data.

In working with supervisees or other persons to set up adherence enhancements such as monitoring, reward, and reminders, supervisors need to be aware of the importance of viewing these activities as assignments for themselves (or staff). In other words, supervisors need to monitor and reward their own appropriate supervision behaviors, and may need to gradually and consistently shape good supervision behavior in themselves.

A final consideration: Some supervisees may not need or may be resistant to this type of supervision. As with everything, "the devil is always in the details," and the way the supervision is implemented will, of necessity, vary with the experience and personality of both the supervisor and supervisee. The extent to which a supervisor spends time on each recommendation will need to be individually determined. For example, a supervisee with considerable experience in an area may become irritated if every detail of a recommendation is spelled out. If the supervisor errs and irritation (or resistance) is sensed, direct discussions of preferred methods of working together usually are helpful. Some recommendations, however, are unlikely to evoke resistance. For example, all individuals find reinforcement gratifying, and a wise supervisor will praise supervisees for a job well done. The form this reinforcement takes will vary for the person, as it does in all interpersonal relationships.

CASE EXAMPLE

Dean was a second-year M.S.W. student. He began a placement working with adolescents in a residential treatment facility. He was assigned to work with one young man, Andy, who was very negative about anything related to school. Dean met with his new supervisor, Mr. Roberts, and started the meeting by stating that he had no idea how to begin with Andy. The supervisor wanted Dean to conduct an assessment with Andy, which would include obtaining information such as what he likes to do in school, what bothers him about school, what he would be doing if he could imagine an ideal situation for himself, what he says to himself when he is participating in school activities, and whether he has difficulty understanding and/or doing school work.

Mr. Roberts began his time with Dean by building a relationship and asking him about his own interests and experiences. He tried to bolster Dean's confidence in his expertise by outlining some of his own general background and clinical experience (Recommendation 1). Mr. Roberts outlined how he likes to work with supervisees. He stated that he would like to make suggestions for Dean to practice between their sessions, and that it was very important for Dean to follow through on these, as they were an important basis for success together (Structuring the Supervision Session).

As they started to talk about the type of assessment Dean should obtain from Andy, Mr. Roberts said to Dean, "I think you should ask Andy the following questions . . ." (Recommendation 2). Mr. Roberts asked Dean first to imagine himself asking Andy each of these questions. He then asked Dean to role-play asking these questions, with Mr. Roberts playing Andy (Recommendation 3). Mr. Roberts gave corrective feedback to Dean, as appropriate, about how he did in the role play (Recommendation 4). Because he felt there was some need to do so, Mr. Roberts modeled the activity again and repeated the cycle, giving feedback to Dean again. Mr. Roberts was careful at this time not to give Dean all possible recommendations for his assessment of Andy. Rather, he made a few suggestions and expected to add to these in subsequent meetings with Dean (Recommendation 6).

Mr. Roberts asked Dean what he might use that would help him remember the points he should cover. When Dean suggested some kind of checklist, Mr. Roberts worked with him to develop a written interview schedule to which Dean could refer and on which he was asked to record assessment information obtained during his session with Andy (Recommendation 7). Mr. Roberts asked Dean to bring a copy of this record to their next session together (Recommendation 10). Mr. Roberts asked Dean if he could think of any other problems that might arise to prevent him from asking Andy these questions. Dean suggested that Andy may be hostile. At that point, Mr. Roberts engaged in another role play, where Dean was Andy and Mr. Roberts responded to Andy. Dean was then given a chance to practice what Mr. Roberts had demonstrated (Recommendation 9). Mr. Roberts concluded the meeting by reviewing and summarizing all the assignments to which Dean had agreed and confirming with Dean that he would follow through on these (Recommendation 8 and Structuring the Supervision Session).

At their next meeting, Mr. Roberts began by asking Dean for the record he had kept and how he felt the assessment assignment went (Structuring the Supervision Session). Mr. Roberts commended Dean for following through on the assignment, including bringing in the monitoring form and trying to follow the assignment (Recommendation 5). He spent some time with Dean refining the assignment, such as including additional aspects that were not part of the original task. These encompassed more complex assessment questions to be addressed to Andy that, in the interest of starting small and gradually increasing difficulty and complexity, were not part of the original assignment. Mr. Roberts structured subsequent meetings the same way. That is, he first began with a review of assignments completed with appropriate reward for any approximations to the assignment, worked with Dean to develop new assignments, built in the adherence factor in giving the recommendations, and concluded with a review of assignment given.

SUMMARY

Supervision involves facilitating another individual in carrying out certain clinical tasks in a particular way. Improved supervisee adherence lies in the behavior of the supervisor. Supervisors may begin with a careful assessment of factors that can affect adherence. In learning about the supervisee, the supervisor should obtain information relevant to three reasons of possible nonadherence: (1) the supervisee's skills and knowledge, (2) the supervisee's belief system, and (3) the supervisee's environment supports.

Supervision sessions should include attention to the activities of the supervisee outside of the supervisor's office. Supervisees should be informed about the importance of adherence to their successful training experience. The first part of each follow-up meeting where adherence is a major issue should be spent reviewing homework given during the prior meeting. The rest of the meeting should include time spent on homework assignments and adherence-enhancement recommendations that are selected with sensitivity to the three problem categories previously stated. A checklist of these recommendations is useful to cue supervisors to address each of the points. Assuming that adherence will lead to therapeutic benefits for clients, these recommendations can increase the likelihood that supervisees will generate more positive outcomes for their clients.

One limitation concerning these suggestions is that most of them have not been tested in the context of supervisory activities. However, all of the recommendations have empirical support in the clinical realm, which can reasonably be extrapolated to supervision. For example, behavior that is rewarded is likely to increase, and behavior that is punished is likely to decrease (Davidson & Davidson, 1980). Nevertheless, the author concurs completely that further research on adherence is needed in the area of supervision.

Another concern is the potential cost, both of time and of money, that may be involved in implementing many of these suggestions. The author recognizes that initially it may be time consuming to engage in these techniques. However, although such an analysis is beyond the scope of this paper, research in medicine has demonstrated the cost-benefit value of adherence. Windsor et al. (1993) did a formal cost-benefit analysis determining the value of one health education program, and found ranges from a cost of $1 to a benefit of $6.72, and from a cost of $1 to a benefit $17.18. Murphy and Coster (1997) have suggested that evidence-based

practice guidelines provide a means of measuring outcomes related to health status and cost-benefit issues. This is a convincing argument, and further research is encouraged on the cost and impact of compliance-enhancement strategies in general and supervision in particular.

REFERENCES

Barlow, D. H., Hayes, S. C., & Nelson, R. O. (1984). *The scientist practitioner.* New York: Pergamon Press.

Brownell, K. D., Heckerman, C. L., Westlake, R. J., Hayes, S. C., & Monti, P. M. (1978). The effects of couples training and partner cooperativeness in the behavioral treatment of obesity. *Behavioral Research and Therapy, 16,* 323–333.

Brownell, K. D., & Stunkard, A. J. (1981). Couples training, pharmacotherapy, and behavior therapy in the treatment of obesity. *Archives of General Psychiatry, 38,* 1224–1229.

Cecil, D. W., & Killeen, I. (1997). Control, compliance, and satisfaction in the family practice encounter. *Family Medicine, 29*(9), 653–657.

Crespo-Fierro, M. (1997). Compliance/adherence and care management in HIV disease. *Journal of the Association of Nurses AIDS Care, 8,* 31–43.

Dajani, A. S. (1996). Adherence to physicians' instructions as a factor in managing streptococcal pharyngitis. *Pediatrics, 97*(Suppl. 6), 976–980.

Davidson, P. O., & Davidson, S. M. (1980). *Behavioral medicine: Changing health lifestyles.* New York: Brunner/Mazel.

Dexter, P. R., Wolinsky, F. D., Gramelspacher, G. P., Zhou, X. H., Eckert, G. J., Waisburel, M., et al. (1998). Effectiveness of computer-generated reminders for increasing discussions about advance directives and completion of advance directive forms: A randomized, controlled trial. *Annals of Internal Medicine, 128*(2), 102–110.

Donovan, J. L., & Blake, D. R. (1992). Patient non-compliance: Deviance or reasoned decision-making? *Social Science Medicine, 34*(5), 507–513.

Drossman, D. A. (1997). Psychosocial sound bites: Exercises in patient-doctor relationship. *American Journal of Gastroenterology, 92,* 1418–1423.

Drossman, D. A. (1999). Psychosocial factors in the care of patients with gastrointestinal disorders. In T. Yamada (Ed.), *Textbook of gastroenterology* (pp. 638–659). Philadelphia: Lippincott-Raven.

Dunbar, J. M. (1979). *New directions in patient adherence* (pp. 41–57). Lexington, MA: Lexington Books.

Epstein, L. H., & Cluss, P. A. (1981). A behavioral medicine perspective on adherence to long-term medical regimens. *Journal of Consulting and Clinical Psychology, 50*, 950–971.

Freedman, J. L., & Fraser, S. C. (1966). Compliance without pressure: The foot-in-the-door technique. *Journal of Personality and Social Psychology, 195–202.*

Gambrill, E. D. (1977). *Behavior modification.* San Francisco: Jossey-Bass.

Gordis, L. (1979). Conceptual and methodologic problems in measuring patient adherence. In R. B. Haynes, D. W. Taylor, & D. L. Sackett (Eds.), *Adherence in health care* (pp. 23–45). Baltimore: Johns Hopkins University Press.

Hawe, P., McKenzie, N., & Scurry, R. (1998). Randomised controlled trial of the use of a modified postal reminder card on the uptake of measles vaccination. *Archives of Disease in Childhood, 79*(2), 136–40.

Haynes, R. B., Taylor, D. W., & Sackett, D. L. (1979). *Adherence in health care.* Baltimore: Johns Hopkins University Press.

Herxheimer, A. (1998). Many NSAID users who bleed don't know when to stop: Uncomprehending "adherence" is dangerous. *British Medical Journal, 316*(7130), 492.

Johnson, S. M. (1971). Self-observation as an agent of behavioral change. *Behavior Therapy, 2*, 488–497.

Lepper, M. R. (1973). Dissonance, self-perception and honesty in children. *Journal of Personality and Social Psychology, 25*, 65–74.

Levy, R. L. (1977). Relationship of an overt commitment to task adherence in behavior therapy. *Journal of Behavior Therapy and Experimental Psychiatry, 8*, 25–29.

Levy, R. L. (1983). Social support and adherence: A selective review and critique of treatment integrity and outcome measurement. *Social Science and Medicine, 17*, 1329–1338.

Levy, R. L. (1985). Social support and adherence: Update. *Journal of Hypertension, 3*(Suppl. 1), 45–49.

Levy, R. L., & Claravall, V. (1977). Differential effects of a phone reminder on patients with long and short between-visit intervals. *Medical Care, 15*, 435–438.

Levy, R. L., & Clark, H. (1980). The use of an overt commitment to enhance adherence: A cautionary note. *Journal of Behavior Therapy and Experimental Psychiatry, 11*, 105–107.

Levy, R. L., & Feld, A. D. (1999). Increasing patient adherence to gastroenterology treatment and prevention regimens. *American Journal of Gastroenterology, 94*(7), 1733–1742.

Levy, R. L., Yamashita, D., & Pow, G. (1979). Relationship of an overt commitment to the frequency and speed of adherence with decision making. *Medical Care, 17*, 281–284.

Liew, T. A., Capra, A. M., Makol, J., Black, S. B., & Shinefield, H. R. (1998). Effectiveness and cost-effectiveness of letters, automated telephone messages, or both for under immunized children in a health maintenance organization. *Pediatrics, 10*(4), E3.

Mazzulo, S. M., Lasagna, L., & Griner, P. F. (1974). Variations in interpretation of prescription assignments. *Journal of the American Medical Association, 227*, 929–931.

Meichenbaum, D. H. (1977). *Cognitive-behavior modification: An integrative approach.* New York: Plenum Press.

Murphy, J., & Coster, G. (1997). Issues in patient compliance. *Drugs, 54*(6), 797–800.

O'Brien, G., & Lazenbnik, R. (1998). Telephone call reminders in an adolescent clinic. *Pediatrics, 101*(6), E6.

Olden, K. W. (1998). Approach to the patient with irritable bowel syndrome. In T. A. Stern, J. B. Herman, & P. L. Slaven (Eds.), *MGH guide to psychiatry in primary care* (pp. 113–120). New York: McGraw-Hill.

Olden, K. W. (in press). *Psychosocial aspects of gastroenterology: Doctor-patient interactions.*

Oleske, J. (1998). Antiretroviral therapy and medical management of pediatric HIV infection. *Pediatrics, 102*(Suppl. 4), 1005–1062.

Pathare, S. R., & Paton, C. (1997). ABC of mental health: Psychotropic drug treatment. *British Medical Journal, 315*(7109), 661–664.

Peura, D. (1998). Helicobacter pylori: Rational management options. *American Journal of Medicine, 105*(5), 424–430.

Raz, R., & Elchanan, G. (1995). Penicillin V twice daily vs. four times daily in the treatment of streptococcal pharyngitis. *Infectious Disease in Clinical Practice, 4,* 50–54.

Roter, D. L., Hall, J. A., Merisca, R., Nordstrom, B., Cretin, D., & Svarstad, B. (1998). Effectiveness of interventions to improve patient compliance: A meta-analysis. *Medical Care, 36*(8), 1138–1161.

Schlundt, D. G., Quesenberry, L., Pichert, J. W., Lorenz, R. A., & Boswell, E. J. (1994). Evaluation of a training program for improving adherence promotion skills. *Patient Education Counseling, 24*(2), 165–173.

Schulman, B. (1979). Active patient orientation and outcomes in hypertensive treatment. *Medical Care, 17,* 267–280.

Shelton, J. L., & Levy, R. L. (1981). *Behavioral assignments and treatment adherence.* Champaign, IL: Research Press.

Steckel, S. B., & Swain, M. A. (1977). Contracting with patients to improve adherence. *Hospitals, 51,* 81–84.

Suinn, R. M. (1972a). Behavior rehearsal for ski racers. *Behavior Therapy, 3,* 308–310.

Suinn, R. M. (1972b). Removing emotional obstacles to learning and performance by visuo-motor behavior rehearsal. *Behavior Therapy, 3,* 308–310.

Toner, B. (1994). Cognitive-behavioral treatment of functional somatic syndromes: Integrating gender issues. *Cognitive and Behavioral Practice, 1,* 157–178.

Wilson, G. T., & Brownell, K. D. (1978). Behavior therapy for obesity including family members in the treatment process. *Behavior Therapy, 9,* 943–945.

Windsor, R. A., Lowe, J. B., Perkins, L. L., Smith-Yoder, D., Artz, L., Crawford, M., et al. (1993). Health education for pregnant smokers: Its behavioral impact and cost benefit. *American Journal of Public Health, 83*(2), 201–206.

Zuckerman, M. J., Guerra, L. G., Drossman, D. A., Foland, J. A., & Gregory, G. G. (1996). Health care-seeking behaviors related to bowel complaints. Hispanics versus non-Hispanic Whites. *Digestive Disorder Science, 41,* 77–82.

CHAPTER 25

Ethical Issues

TERENCE PATTERSON AND MICHAEL C. GOTTLIEB

In this chapter, the authors, both very involved in the area of ethics in psychotherapy, address ethical dilemmas commonly presented in cognitive/behavioral/functional (C/B/F) approaches. The first part, written by Terrance Patterson, identifies the historical context of ethical criticisms of C/B/F approaches and views them as misperceptions. The second part, written by Michael Gottlieb, examines boundary issues in depth and urges that ethical issues be viewed on a continuum, within a context, and from a multicultural perspective.

ETHICAL PRINCIPLES APPLIED TO COGNITIVE/BEHAVIORAL/ FUNCTIONAL APPROACHES: HISTORICAL PATTERNS AND MISPERCEPTIONS

Ethical and legal violations in the mental health field have been highly visible during the past decade in the practice of psychotherapy. Among the issues that have received the most attention are violations of confidentiality, incompetence,

client abandonment, therapist substance abuse and other impairments, fraud, false advertising, and multiple relationships. Reasons for the increased attention include the proliferation of new approaches and practitioners, and the increased attention that has been paid to the specification and enforcement of the ethical and legal codes themselves. Indeed, it appears that the number of violations reported and adjudicated have begun to decrease recently, but it is still important to elucidate the areas of psychotherapy practice that raise ethical concerns.

In particular, theoretical orientation in relation to ethical judgments has received little attention. Although some major approaches, such as behavior therapy and isolated techniques such as paradoxical and strategic interventions, have received some scrutiny, the dimensions of various approaches that should be considered in making ethical decisions remain unclear.

Behavior therapy has been criticized as "mechanistic, Machiavellian, and manipulative" (Glynn, Mueser, & Liberman, 1989, p. 60). Practices that have been addressed from an ethical perspective include behavioral control (Glynn et al., 1989; Lutzker & Campbell, 1994; Stuart,

1975), directives (Ellis, 1997), and ethical relativism (Kitchener, 1996). Much criticism has been directed at traditional behavioral approaches in general (Leslie, 1997) and toward work with severely disturbed or disabled patients, often in inpatient settings (Leduc, Dumais, & Evans, 1990). Concerns about client rights (Sheldon, 1982; Van Houten, Axelrod, Bailey, & Favell, 1988), the ability to give informed consent (McLean, 1980; Ringen, 1996), and definitions of deviance (Greenspoon, 1987; Ross, 1977; Silverstein, 1977) have made traditional behavior therapy a frequent target. Although the early practice of behavior therapy typically has been misunderstood and frequently underexplained, many of the practices criticized have subsequently been modified, particularly with outpatients who have less severe disturbances.

Most discussions of ethical principles applied to psychotherapy inherently pertain to approaches that involve transference, insight, and medium- to long-term nondirective, nonproblem-focused treatments. It becomes apparent that the same issues are not relevant in an approach in which a specific behavior is addressed collaboratively between therapist and client for a short time. For example, although it is not the optimal ethical practice to have a posttermination, nonromantic social relationship with a high-functioning client many years after five sessions of problem-focused treatment, it is apparent that there is a different quality to that relationship than with a patient who has been in four years of twice-weekly analysis. It does seem appropriate, however, that in comparing these situations, different judgments might be made about the ethics of the posttherapy relationship.

In this chapter, an argument is not advanced for or against revision of ethical standards, but rather an attempt is made to elucidate aspects of the practice of C/B/F therapy that should be considered in making decisions about ethics. As with all ethical judgments, there will be a few that are black or white, whereas most will remain in the gray area in which the therapist must assume responsibility for a decision that ultimately does no harm and is in the best interests of the client.

DISTINCTIVE FEATURES OF C/B/F THERAPY RELATED TO ETHICS

Before describing the components that are unique to behavior therapy, the author wishes to state emphatically that the case is *not* being made that C/B/F approaches should be exempt from ethics codes or common standards of care. The frequent criticisms of behavior therapy from an ethical perspective are addressed, particularly those aspects that are not black or white according to current standards, and therefore often result in behavior therapy's being misunderstood.

Another aspect of the dilemma in which techniques rooted in behavior therapy are sometimes viewed as ethically questionable is that behavioral methods are often used by practitioners of other approaches out of context. Imagery and rehearsal are two techniques that are grounded in behaviorism and used in other therapies, frequently without adequate assessment or follow-up. In a similar fashion, inadequate training or supervision of behavioral techniques can result in their misapplication (Stein, 1975). In addition, practices that are commonly used in specific cultures are considered inappropriate in others (Kaslow, 1998). Thus, techniques applied inappropriately or out of context may erroneously create an impression that the techniques themselves violate ethical standards.

ETIOLOGY

Theories regarding the causes of psychopathology in psychodynamic models involve early experiences, trauma, and other phenomena and are often viewed as requiring intensive, long-term analysis. Rather than being remediated in the short-term by redecision, for example, as in cognitive therapy, or through social conditioning or self-monitoring as in behavior therapy, disorders presented in psychodynamic therapy are often viewed as ameliorable only in treatment involving an intense relationship with the therapist (e.g., Cashdan, 1988). This use of the medical model of psychotherapy typically involves the therapist as the object of transference who is somewhat aloof (e.g., Tarachow, 1964); the patient is the one to be "cured." Although practitioners using the various psychodynamic models approach therapy differently, the concept of the therapist as expert who will uncover the early origins of pathology and promote insight to cure psychopathology in the long term is part of this traditional model of psychotherapy.

When shorter-term, more collaborative models such as C/B/F therapy are used, there is less need for the therapist to be the expert. The origins of problems are viewed as more contextual, multidetermined, and under the control of the client. The problem is generally formulated in terms of faulty learning, improper conditioning, skill deficits, or inadequate reinforcement. Thus, the more *recent* and *skill-driven* components of problem formulation in C/B/F approaches allow for a less mysterious, more cooperative style in which assessment, treatment, and the logistics of therapy are developed jointly between therapist and client. Clients are usually made aware of the causal attributions of the therapist because they participate actively in empirical treatments and self-monitor their progress. There is less reliance, therefore, on the therapist to analyze transferential relationships and deterministic etiology or to wait for insight to develop. Clients *know* when they are making progress, because in most instances, it is observable and measurable, and therefore, the therapy is briefer (e.g., Bandura, 1969; Dobson, 1988).

As a result of the vast difference in the etiological formulation of disorders between psychodynamic (and other traditional) therapies and that of C/B/F approaches, the nature of the relationship and the objectives and length of treatment are different in the C/B/F model. These inevitably need to be considered in making ethical decisions.

The Therapist-Client Relationship
The therapist-client relationship in behavior therapy is inherently ideographic and collaborative. Functional assessment and related approaches require that the context of the client's presenting problem be specified in detail, and that treatment address deficits, strengths, reinforcers, and other contingencies that pertain to the target behavior. The identification of specific distorted cognitions and other patterns maintaining undesired behaviors is intrinsic to the behavioral repertoire. Behavioral researchers, appreciating the idiosyncrasies of individual behavior, often prefer single-case experimental designs, which depend on a great deal of client self-monitoring.

In behavior therapy, there is functional understanding of the unique context of the client's situation, and the therapist is not an object of transference and a blank slate for projection of the client's unconscious. This allows for a direct, collaborative relationship between client and therapist. The problem to be addressed, the methods to be used, the time frame likely to be needed, and a concrete evaluation procedure are discussed openly, directly, and frequently with the client and included as part of a "contract" in a signed informed consent. There is no need for the therapist to determine unilaterally whether personality integration or resistance is occurring, or for a therapeutic formulation to be kept from the client in the interests of a cure. Similarly, aloofness is not a common characteristic of the therapist-client relationship in C/B/F approaches.

Due to the straightforward, collaborative, empirical nature of the client-therapist relationship in behavior therapy, ethical guidelines such as those regarding dual relationships should be evaluated in context. For instance, although the principle of *integrity* (Kitchener, 1996) should always be upheld and the power differential between client and therapist should never be abused, there may be situations in which a casual social relationship may develop with impunity between a therapist and client who previously have been involved professionally in short-term, problem-focused treatment. This is particularly true if it is clear that the therapist will no longer be consulted for this problem, both parties regard each other as equals, and they encounter each other in the course of a hobby or recreational interest. Although these circumstances may well occur with clients who have been in other kinds of therapy, they may be more common and straightforward in C/B/F treatment. The second part of this chapter addresses the ambiguity of dual relationships in greater detail.

Objectives

In the broadest sense, the objectives of all psychotherapy are the same: to assist clients to function at their own highest level. In practice, the major approaches have very different goals (Glynn et al., 1989; Patterson, 1999). Psychodynamic approaches seek to integrate the personality through insight; humanistic models seek growth and expression; and C/B/F therapy seeks to change cognitions and behaviors. Glynn et al. (1989) state that "adherence to the specification of problems and goals is the *characteristic in itself* that distinguishes behavioral therapy from the other approaches" (p. 59).

The term "symptom substitution" has been used to incriminate behavioral approaches as being limited in their effect, as it has been posited that when one dysfunctional behavior is removed, another will surface in its place (Weitzman, 1967). In fact, there is no empirical evidence for this, nor for the premise that devel-

opment of insight or expression of affect *in itself* promotes lasting behavioral change. Similarly, there is no evidence that longer treatment, which is usually associated with psychodynamic and more traditional humanistic approaches, produces either greater change or longer-lasting effects. With regard to the objectives of therapy, then, ethical standards are applicable to the extent that research can demonstrate the effectiveness of a particular approach in producing specific outcomes. An approach that links assessment and treatment directly to outcomes desired by the client adheres most closely to optimal ethical standards.

Assessment

The nature of assessment, a general term denoting a systematic evaluation of the client, differs among the various forms of C/B/F therapy, but usually involves self-report, observation, validity probes, and other empirical measures. C/B/F therapists generally do not use traditional diagnostic measures such as *Diagnostic and Statistical Manual of Mental Disorders (DSM)* categories or the Mental Status Exam (MSE), unless required to do so in a specific setting for insurance or monitoring purposes. Behavior therapy itself is founded on functional assessment (Strosahl & Jacobson, 1986), an empirical procedure that seeks to identify the antecedents and consequences of behavior and to develop a plan to modify contingencies that maintain dysfunctional behaviors and establish or strengthen new ones. Functional deficits and strengths are identified and specified; compared to *DSM* classifications, there is a de-emphasis on categories of disorders and an accentuation of description and quantification of the statements and the behaviors of the client.

Whatever the relative merits of functional versus traditional forms of assessment, there is no doubt that the traditional method is more widely used across mental health disciplines and approaches to therapy. Behavioral assessment often becomes a target of criticism for its overall lack of use of traditional categories of pathology; indeed, the behavioral clinician who is unaware of *DSM* nomenclature is at a disadvantage in communicating with many professional colleagues. Such lack of traditional classification is frequently viewed as constituting an inadequate diagnostic scheme, although behavior therapists view functional assessment as primary, essential information. Clear, behaviorally anchored formulations of problems are usually more understandable to clients and consultees. Ethically, neither method is superior, and each can make claims to being either more descriptive of an individual client's situation (behavioral assessment) or more consistent with common standards of care (traditional *DSM* and MSE). The only clearly unethical use of any form of assessment is its failure to account for the client's true condition or to indicate an appropriate treatment plan.

Duration

The issue of duration as it pertains to ethics in behavior therapy is related to therapy objectives and problem etiology. Behavior therapy at times may be protracted. Although treatment for a disorder such as a specific phobia may be completed within six sessions, follow-up to enhance self-monitoring and maintenance of new behaviors may be scheduled intermittently over a period of six months or more. In instances where a therapist engages a client for a combination of assessment, exploration, and supportive therapy using a behavioral model, the duration of treatment may be extended for many months. Thus, although it is true that behavior therapy is typically brief therapy, the length of treatment is not confined to a discreet number of continuous weekly sessions, and the duration depends on the functional assessment. In essence, treatment planning addresses the client's presenting problem and may be expanded or shortened according to the progress

being made. The axiom often proposed that "longer therapy is deeper therapy" is unsubstantiated (Glynn et al., 1989) and is based on theoretical constructs rather than empiricism.

Emphasis on Prescribing Change and In Vivo Approaches

This aspect is perhaps the most controversial one in behavior therapy as it pertains to ethical principles, and is often misunderstood (Leslie, 1997; Woolfolk & Richardson, 1992). Unlike person-centered or psychoanalytic approaches, which do not make direct recommendations for the client to engage in specific activities, behavior therapy requires the therapist to be direct and prescriptive. Newer techniques, such as "prescribing the symptom" or "paradoxical intervention" (Ascher, 1989; Dowd & Truitt, 1988), are often assumed to be similar in procedure and intent to behavioral techniques, but they do not reflect the contextual, systematic components integral to behavior therapy. Without detouring into the various features of these two techniques, approaches related to C/B/F therapy and their ethical implications are now explored.

By focusing on behaviors (or cognitions or patterns), C/B/F approaches inevitably examine client activities that produce undesired results and seek those that will be more positive. Both implicitly and explicitly, specific behaviors must be decreased or eliminated and others increased (reinforced). A thorough functional assessment specifies the dimensions of each process and clarifies for the client the unintended consequences of both eliminating the undesired behavior and gaining the new one (iatrogenic effects). For example, a couple therapist who is not trained in using C/B/F approaches systematically may prescribe that a couple having violent arguments go home and have at least two of these arguments daily to see their absurdity and to essentially "burn out" on them. Although there may be some instances when this would be appropriate, a thorough assessment of the history and nature of these arguments and the function they have in the relationship may strongly contraindicate such a prescription and may prevent serious injury or fatality from occurring. Conversely, a therapist may encourage a couple to decrease violent arguments and to increase direct, positive communication with each other; consequently, they find they miss the intensity of their earlier interactions and decide that they have very little that is positive to communicate. This outcome poses a risk for the therapist, who, while actively discouraging arguments and recommending clear communication practices, has actually "prescribed" specific behaviors that produce outcomes that are not entirely satisfactory to these clients. Thus, it is clear that direct prescriptions in therapy must be used in the context of their function and consequences and be thoroughly understood by the therapist who uses them.

These risks may occur for therapists of other orientations as well, but they are prominent for behavior therapists, who, after a period of assessment and collaboration with the client, often prescribe procedures for clients to follow. C/B/F therapy follows ethical guidelines closely, in comparison with other orientations that "prescribe the symptom" out of context. C/B/F therapy involves clients collaboratively in treatment planning and evaluates a procedure following its implementation; thus, it attenuates the possibility of undesired consequences.

Similar concerns have been raised about other in vivo approaches in which there is an expectation for a client to engage in procedures suggested by the therapist during the treatment session. An example of this is behavioral rehearsal, a technique pioneered in behavior therapy. Following a thorough functional assessment and specification of target behaviors in collaboration with the client, a behavior therapist will shape desired behaviors through successive approximations. A clinician untrained in the contextual approach to this method might exert pressure on a client to implement strategies in an untimely or inappropriate manner. Other in-session practices associated with behavior therapy include desensitization, implosion, and the use of emotive imagery. By virtue of being directive, live, and often intense, these behavioral methods must be implemented in the context of a comprehensive assessment and treatment plan to avoid harm to clients and charges of malpractice. In systematic C/B/F treatment, the degree of client discomfort is continuously monitored and is within the client's control at all times.

Behavioral Control Using Operant Techniques
Much of the ethical criticism directed toward the use of operant conditioning in behavior therapy dates back to original articles on the use of aversive conditioning (Vizueta, 1979), response elimination, punishment (Matson & Kazdin, 1981), and time-out (Gast & Nelson, 1977; Neisworth & Madle, 1976) in inpatient settings. A great deal of faultfinding has also been directed at behavioral control in the schools (Graham-Clay & Reschly, 1987; O'Leary & O'Leary, 1977; Valenti, 1997). Glynn et al. (1989) observed emphatically that "behavior therapy mandates *shared control*" (p. 64). The criticisms are worth noting, however, because they continue to influence both public and professional impressions of behavior therapy.

To review briefly, aversive conditioning is the presentation of an unpleasant stimulus following an undesirable response in order to eliminate that response. Although it is often misused, it continues to be an effective and ethical procedure in behavior therapy, and remains an alternative to the preferred use of positive reinforcement of the desired behavior. Response elimination involves the gradual reduction to eradication of a behavior following reaction to a stimulus. Much criticism has focused on the elimination of a behavior from the repertoire of a client who may already have skill deficits. However, as indicated earlier, a functional analysis first attempts to reinforce desired behaviors, and only secondarily attempts to eliminate those that may be injurious, annoying, or otherwise dysfunctional to the client and his or her setting. A core focus of C/B/F therapy is the strengthening of existing skills and existing functional cognitions.

Another behavioral practice that has been criticized and misunderstood from an ethical perspective is *time-out* (Gast & Nelson, 1977; Neisworth & Madle, 1976). Whether applied to children or behaviorally disordered adults, a thorough functional assessment must always be done according to the client's level of development. This leads to a treatment plan that reflects appropriate duration, setting, and inclusion of relevant reinforcers. The complete term is *time-out from positive reinforcement*, referring to a reinforcer that increases a behavior that is undesired under specific circumstances. Specifically, it actually refers to removal of the client from the response environment (Smolev, 1971).

For example, when a 3-year-old who is having tantrums is placed in a room with nothing he desires and nothing related to the behavior itself on a timely and consistent basis, the behavior is often reduced or eliminated. As soon as quietness or calm behavior is apparent, it is then important to reinforce that behavior through praise or another functional response. Because time-out has in practice been too long, too short, or inconsistent, or possibly because it has been viewed as harsh punishment, this effective tool has been criticized as ineffective or inhumane. However, this technique has long been applied appropriately in both clinical and nonclinical settings, and is a highly ethical procedure that allows many clients to learn appropriate behavior and be socialized more effectively.

Thus far, criticisms of behavior therapy have addressed the issues of causation, assessment, objectives, duration, the therapist-client relationship, prescription of change, in vivo approaches, behavioral control, and other aspects. In one way or another, these criticisms have been based on the implication that behavior therapy involves unethical practices due to its difference from traditional therapeutic procedures, or on misunderstanding. On closer examination, it can be seen that other therapies share many techniques with behavior therapy, which are often implemented out of context or in a condensed format. Other comments are based on the earliest, misperceived, or most restrictive forms of behavior therapy. Viewed from a wider philosophical perspective, it must be acknowledged that all forms of psychotherapy attempt to control behavior in some form. The basic question is whether clients are informed and involved about the therapeutic process, whether appropriate assessment, treatment planning, and intervention procedures are used, and whether the outcomes achieved are in the client's best interests.

MAJOR PROBLEMS TREATED USING A C/B/F APPROACH

One of the major dilemmas resulting in the criticism of C/B/F approaches is that cognitive, behavioral, and functional techniques are not identified as such and are not implemented properly when used in other orientations. Behaviorism (the general category) has been applied in the broadest sense to every orientation and with virtually every presenting problem, disorder, and syndrome in the mental health field, often inappropriately or inadequately. Besides having a long history, C/B/F methods make more use of technology and research than any other form of psychotherapy (Rapp, 1984); thus, more techniques are *borrowed* from the C/B/F model than from others. Once the objective of behavior change is established, C/B/F techniques can fit into numerous other models. Thus, the reliance on empirical data and their dissemination through extensive research have resulted in behavior therapy's being associated with nearly every problem and used in some fashion in many other models in psychotherapy.

As mentioned earlier, many of the misconceptions about behavior therapy arose when it was utilized for the inpatient treatment of severely mentally ill patients. Although inpatient applications are still extremely viable and procedures have advanced greatly, discussion in this section is focused on the widespread contemporary use of C/B/F approaches in outpatient settings. The ethical aspects pertaining to behavior therapy as addressed earlier in this chapter are discussed in relation to treating problems commonly addressed in therapy.

Anxiety Disorders
Anxiety in its various forms, including generalized and specific anxiety, Obsessive-Compulsive Disorder, and phobia, has been a frequent focus of behavior therapy (Barlow, 1988; Berkovec, 1993). Because these disorders involve the physical, emotional, and cognitive realms, anxieties generally lend themselves to empirical observation. Although other approaches are used, it is commonly accepted that behavioral methods such as systematic desensitization, cognitive restructuring, self-monitoring, and environmental modification are efficient and effective in diminishing anxiety. Anxiety lends itself well to measurement on a continuum of frequency and intensity, and the behavioral practice of ameliorating rather than eliminating the problem entirely is widely used. Thus, established C/B/F techniques often can accomplish the objective of diminishing anxiety-related behaviors in a relatively short period of time.

In reviewing the features of behavior therapy delineated earlier, it appears that, whereas the actual etiology of anxiety in its historical context may be relevant in assessing the problem, the most critical features are the antecedents and consequences that maintain the disorder in the present (Wolpe & Lazarus,

1966). Assessment thus becomes a functional matter, in that only those environmental factors that pertain to the current problem are salient. The sole objective of treatment is to diminish anxiety to the extent possible. For a specific anxiety or phobia, this may involve as few as three to six sessions. The evaluation and follow-up determine whether the disorder is functionally autonomous or generalized to other anxiety problems, and whether the short-term gains will be maintained.

The nature of the therapist-client relationship is vital to the collaboration, trust, and compliance that develop in the treatment of anxiety and other behavioral disorders. For example, the therapist typically is explicit in directing an obsessive-compulsive client to self-monitor regularly, to engage in self-defined pleasurable activities, and to attempt to either increase or decrease the target behaviors incrementally at certain times. These methods may be rehearsed both covertly and overtly during the therapy session, and assignments for between sessions are routinely given. There is no doubt that behavior is being *controlled* during this process, but it is inevitably accomplished collaboratively with the client and involves thorough assessment, treatment planning, and evaluation in the context of a congenial relationship. The relationship can be friendly and collaborative while it remains systematic and focused.

Depression
Depression is the most common disorder treated in psychotherapy and has long been a focus of C/B/F treatment (Beck, 1967). Because of its multifaceted etiology, depression frequently has other manifestations. Conduct Disorder in children and marital conflict in adults are often viewed as evidence of depression, and inferential, construct-based therapies seek to uncover the "deeper" roots in childhood and personality structure. This takes time, and although it may be effective, it is a more circuitous route than a behavior therapy approach.

The general approach to depression under a C/B/F model is to take a complete history, identify the antecedents and consequences of the target behavior, and employ procedures that diminish depressive behaviors and reinforce pleasurable ones. This may include many common behavioral techniques such as self-management (Rehm, 1984); positive reinforcement (Tennov, Jacobson, & Trinidad, 1976); differential reinforcement of other behaviors, which rewards proximate behaviors (Homer, 1980); social skill training (Reisinger, 1974); and the Premack principle, which pairs target behaviors with frequently occurring activities (Robinson & Lewinsohn, 1973). Treatment also involves contextual issues such as developmental stages, sociocultural aspects, significant relationships, and the overall balance among social, emotional, and physical aspects of the client's life. The critical factor to be addressed is modification of *the depression-related behavior itself.* Aspects such as history, insight, personality, and the therapist-client relationship may be used as tools to achieve efficient, effective amelioration of the depression, but they are not in themselves primary objectives of treatment. As with the treatment of anxiety, the nature of the therapist-client relationship is a key factor in C/B/F approaches to depression.

The numerous criticisms of the use of a C/B/F approach in the treatment of depression, such as its being superficial, temporary, or likely to generate other symptoms, have been unfounded. In fact, cognitive-behavioral treatment with medication, besides being one of the most researched clinical areas in recent decades, has become widely acknowledged to be highly effective across the spectrum of mood disorders (Muñoz, Ying, Perez-Stable, & Miranda, 1993; Murphy, Carney, Knesevich, & Wetzel, 1995; Persons, Davison, & Tompkins, 2001). Part of the C/B/T argument for effectiveness in treating depression is based on the specificity with which depressive behaviors are identified. Typically, first depression is targeted for treatment; then, if other symptoms are part of a larger constellation of a depressive disorder, those behaviors are targeted for amelioration as well. This focused, comprehensive approach is more direct, observable, and measurable than deductive methods that infer causality and may not address and evaluate the depression directly.

Substance Abuse and Eating Disorders
The treatment of addiction to substances has undergone many metamorphoses, ranging from an emphasis on morality, to psychopathology, to its identification as a disease. The most common lay approaches to substance abuse, twelve-step programs, include strong spiritual and social elements as well as behaviorally based methods. In fact, whereas some psychotherapies might explore broader and deeper dimensions of substance abuse, behavior therapy focuses on the substance abusing behaviors themselves. When an adjunctive treatment program is needed, it is included in the treatment plan. In fact, it might be considered unethical not to do so. Standard C/B/F techniques such as relapse prevention (Marlatt, 1985), systematic desensitization, self-monitoring, relaxation training, and cognitive restructuring are commonly used to address abuse-related behaviors.

Similar approaches are applicable to treating eating disorders (Agras et al., 1989; Agras & Apple, this volume; Touyz, 1998). In fact, the famous "family lunch session" used by Minuchin (1974) in structural family therapy is a direct application of response prevention, behavioral rehearsal, and psychoeducation. Conversely, the common analytic inference of the etiology of eating disorders as a disturbance between the anorectic patient and the parent exemplifies the indirect, deductive approach and, in isolation, ignores the immediate behaviors maintaining the disorder. Most popular commercial weight-loss programs today rely on social support, self-monitoring, and psychoeducation.

Family, Couple, and Child Relational Problems
In examining approaches used in assessment and treatment of parent and child relational problems, including family dysfunction, marital conflict, and child behavior disorders, it is apparent that the entire range of therapeutic modalities has been used (Guerin, 1976). Here too, it appears that most effective approaches have integrated C/B/F techniques, at times in piecemeal fashion. Family and couple therapy was derived from psychoanalytic and systems theories, and its earliest applications were adaptations of analytic methods to relational systems. Imaginative, eclectic techniques evolved form physics, anthropology, mathematics, drama, existential and humanistic philosophy, and elsewhere (Bateson, 1972; Haley, 1963; Kaslow, 1990; Satir, 1967). Here too criticism was made of direct approaches as being superficial and temporary. Psychodynamic therapists viewed family intervention as the basis for individual personality restructuring.

Except for the pure analytic family therapies, techniques such as role rehearsal, flooding, behavioral prescription, self-monitoring, communication training, and even functional analysis are commonly employed. One of the earliest descriptions of behavioral technology applied to marital therapy was by Jacobson and Margolin (1979). Later, differentiation was made between individual and marital therapy for such disorders as depression (Jacobson, Dobson, Fruzzetti, Schmaling, & Salusky, 1991) and agoraphobia (Arnow, Taylor, Agras, & Telch, 1985). The most prominent science-based approach to the treatment of couples today is described by Gottman (this volume). The current integration of behavior therapy with cognitive therapy and related concepts, known as *acceptance and commitment therapy*, is described by Christensen and Jacobson (2000) and in this volume by Hayes, Pankey, Gifford, Batten, and Quiñones.

Among the most powerful attractions to many therapists-in-training were the immediacy and directness of the techniques used by charismatic innovators in family therapy. These procedures expanded the repertoire of relational therapists exponentially, yet they were sometimes applied in an unethical manner. Techniques such as symptom prescription, psychodrama, regression, physical manipulation, and confrontation were often taught and applied inappropriately. Many direct approaches, such as rehearsal, flooding, and self-monitoring, are associated with a C/B/F model, but they are often implemented poorly, and their use has been criticized as not going "deep" enough, ignoring client defenses, and as harmful to clients. In practice, improper use of C/B/F procedures in couple and family therapy frequently ignores functional assessment and a thorough application of systematic procedures to target behaviors.

Children have also been treated successfully under a C/B/F model for numerous behavioral problems (D. S. Bennett & Gibbons, 2000; Evans, 1999). One area in the family/child area that must be addressed critically is that of non-behavioral treatment of individual children for behavioral problems. The most common abuse has been the long-term treatment of children without employing direct, contextual approaches. Specifically, the use of psychodynamic approaches such as insight, transference, and play therapy in isolation frequently ignores the active involvement of parents, teachers, and others. Essential components of functional assessment and skills training that have been highly successful in treating behavioral problems have also been frequently ignored. A persistent refusal to employ these approaches may produce iatrogenic effects (e.g., the inadvertent reinforcement of parent noninvolvement) and the ensuing breach of the principle of *beneficence* (Kitchener, 1996) that underlies the various professional codes of ethics.

In the area of family and child relational problems, as with others, behavioral treatment is the most researched modality (Alexander, Holtzworth-Munroe, & Jameson, 1993; Pinsof, 1989). Clinical trials under the C/B/F model often include treatment manuals and research reports on detailed systematic procedures and the impact of microtechniques on target behaviors. Clinically significant differentiation of the indications for marital therapy versus individual therapy has been amply demonstrated, and substantial evidence of the effectiveness of family interventions in the treatment of schizophrenia, substance abuse, and juvenile behavioral disorders is evident in the literature. In essence, no other approach in family therapy has opened itself to detailed scrutiny as much as the C/B/F model. A close examination not only of effectiveness but also of therapeutic thoroughness reveals that criticisms of family and child C/B/F treatment pertaining to ethics are based largely on misunderstanding and faulty application of techniques and inadequate training in behavioral methods.

A CONTROVERSY REGARDING BOUNDARY MANAGEMENT

The issue of establishing boundaries in psychotherapy has been hotly debated for nearly 25 years. The controversy first arose regarding sexual misconduct by the therapist in the context of traditional psychotherapy relationships; it later expanded to include other, more subtle issues such as nonsexual multiple relationships and sexual harassment. Interestingly, the argument seldom focused on theoretical orientation per se. Few writers ever discussed the possibility that adherence to one theoretical orientation or another could lead to differential vulnerability for boundary violations.

Nevertheless, there seems always to have been a subtle and unstated assumption that boundary violations were more likely to occur in those types of therapies that involve a higher degree of self-disclosure on the part of patient and/or therapist and that last over longer periods of time. This notion was recently supported by Tubbs and Pomeranz (2001), who

suggested that ethical infractions in C/B/F approaches might be fewer due to their brief and more structured nature. For the most part, C/B/F approaches received little attention in this respect, despite the fact that they can present unique dilemmas with regard to boundary management.

Recently, questions regarding boundary management in C/B/F approaches have been raised by Lazarus (1994, 1998, 2001) and Williams (1997). Their work has produced much criticism (B. E. Bennett, Bryan, VandenBos, & Greenwood, 1990; Borys, 1994; Brown, 1994; Gabbard, 1994; Gottlieb, 1994; Gutheil, 1994). We examine the issues from a broader international perspective. First, we provide a brief historical review. Next we discuss some models that have been developed to assist in general ethical decision making and those more directly related to boundary issues. The arguments of Lazarus and Williams are then presented as well as the criticisms of their position. The chapter concludes with guidelines C/B/F clinicians may wish to consider for developing their own ethical practice policies that focus on maintenance of appropriate boundaries within our cultural context and that minimize iatrogenic risk.

A BRIEF HISTORY

Health professionals have long contended that sexual contact between psychotherapists and their patients is unethical (Bouhoutous, Holroyd, Lerman, Forer, & Greenberg, 1983; Karasu, 1980; Widiger & Rorer, 1984). As early as 1977, Holroyd and Brodsky discussed the harmful effects of sexual involvement of clinicians with their patients. This work was later supported by the work of Bouhoutous et al., L. S. Brown (1988), and Feldman-Summers and Jones (1984). Because of the potentially serious consequences (Pope & Vetter, 1992), such behavior has been specifically prohibited for mental health professionals (e.g., American

Psychological Association [APA], 1992; American Association of Marital and Family Therapy [AAMFT], 2001; National Association of Social Workers [NASW], 1996). Subsequently, a debate arose regarding other, more complex types of boundary violations, such as sexual relationships with former patients (e.g., Gottlieb, Sell, & Schoenfeld, 1988; Sell, Gottlieb, & Schoenfeld, 1986), sexual relations with students, sexual harassment (Fitzgerald, 1997), and nonsexual dual relationships (Roll & Millen, 1981).

The most recent revision of the Ethical Principles of Psychologists and Code of Conduct (APA, 1992) made numerous efforts to directly address many of these issues. It specifically defines and prohibits sexual harassment (sec. 1.11), other types of harassment (sec. 1.12), harm (sec. 1.14), multiple relationships (sec. 1.17), exploitation, (sec. 1.19), sexual intimacies with current clients (sec. 4.05) and former clients (sec. 4.07), treatment of former lovers (sec. 4.06), and generally misusing one's influence (sec. 1.15). From these provisions it can readily be deduced that it is the practitioner's responsibility to (1) be sensitive to these issues; (2) refrain from entering into a relationship if doing so is likely to cause harm; (3) be very cautious when establishing professional relationships with those with whom one has a preexisting relationship; and (4) resolve conflicts that do arise from the standpoint of the client's best interest (Staal & King, 2000). With all these standards and guidelines, it would appear that the issue of boundary management for mental heath clinicians was very clear. Nevertheless, the issue continues to be debated regarding behavior in other contexts, such as posttherapy relationships that are nonsexual (Anderson & Kitchener, 1998), business relationships (Lamb et al., 1994), interpersonal relationships in rural communities (Faulkner & Faulkner, 1997; Schank & Skovholt, 1997), and relationships in confined communities, such as the military (Staal & King, 2000). This debate continues because ethical standards are seldom absolute or

rigid; they acknowledge that some multiple relationships may be unavoidable in certain situations and that they are not necessarily harmful (Gottlieb, 1993; Staal & King, 2000). In the following section, we address the efforts that have been made to develop guidelines to manage such relationships.

GUIDELINES FOR DECISION MAKING

Practicing C/B/F therapies at times presents dilemmas regarding multiple relationships and boundary management. In an effort to assist clinicians in this regard, numerous ethical decision-making models have been proposed. Four are briefly reviewed here. The earliest effort to develop an ethical decision-making model was by Kitchener (1984). She recommended that clinicians who are presented with an ethical dilemma begin with their own ordinary moral sense and the facts of the situation. The combination of these two elements will lead to an immediate and intuitive judgment that then must be critically evaluated through reasoned judgment and use of ethical principles and professional rules and codes.

Haas and Malouf (1989) expanded Kitchener's (1984) work by developing a more complex flow chart that incorporated additional elements: developing a plan, determining if the plan will satisfy the needs of the affected parties, asking if the plan raised new ethical dilemmas, and evaluating the plan once implemented. Handelsman (1998) developed a more complex model that emphasized the moral values and personal feelings of the clinician. His model includes the Haas and Malouf elements and adds a degree of useful introspection.

These models represented significant advances in our thinking regarding ethical decision making, but they are general in nature and less helpful in specific situations, such as those involving boundary management. To address that issue, Gottlieb (1993) developed a decision-making model specifically to consider questions of exploitation and boundary violations in situations of potential dual relationships. The model began by asking the practitioner to evaluate the existing professional relationship along the dimensions of power, duration, and clarity of termination. The clinician then was asked to do a similar analysis of the new or contemplated relationship. The model offered a flow chart by which to determine those relationships that would entail low risk for the consumer and those that would involve greater risk. For example, making a speech on child rearing to a PTA meeting generally is not a barrier to having a subsequent social relationship with someone in the audience due to the brief nature of the contact, the clarity of termination, and the rather small power differential. On the other hand, engaging in long-term insight-oriented psychotherapy precludes any other type of relationship due to the long-standing and ongoing nature of the relationship and the great power differential between therapist and client. In this connection, Pope (1994) and Koocher, Norcross, and Hill (1998) offer convenient checklists clinicians may find helpful in these situations.

BOUNDARIES

The work noted above has provided a basis for recent research specifically devoted to boundary issues. Smith and Fitzpatrick (1995) defined treatment boundaries as "a therapeutic frame which defines a set of roles for the participants" (p. 499). It includes structural elements such as time, place, money, and the content of therapy, that is, what actually takes place between clinician and client (Smith & Fitzpatrick, 1995). They go on to note several principles that underpin the concept of boundaries. These include abstinence or avoidance of selfish gratification, neutrality regarding the events in a client's life outside the therapeutic context, and respect for autonomy of the client (Smith & Fitzpatrick,

1995). The importance of maintaining boundaries has been well stated by Pope (1994): Establishing safe, reliable, and useful boundaries is one of the most fundamental responsibilities of the therapist. The boundaries must create a context in which therapist and patient can do the work of therapy. They must form an environment in which the patient may experience and give voice to the most intense, unexpected, and powerful feelings, impulses, images, fantasies, and longings in the presence of another person, yet never be at undue risk for exploitation. They must accord reasonable privacy so that the patient is free to discuss what seems most embarrassing, undesirable, disgusting, frightening, or taboo (p. 70).

One may think of the variety of possible boundary transgressions along a continuum ranging from minimal and of no harm to those that place clients at great risk for injury. In this regard, Smith and Fitzpatrick (1995) distinguish between boundary crossing and boundary violation. Boundary crossing entails departures from commonly accepted clinical practice that may or may not benefit the client, such as accepting a Christmas gift. Boundary violations, on the other hand, are a departure from accepted practice that places the client at serious risk.

The wide variety of theoretical orientations and therapeutic techniques available to clinicians today poses a problem for those attempting to define appropriate boundaries of their clinical practice. For example, psychodynamically oriented clinicians probably would never consider seeing a client outside of the office. On the other hand, a C/B/F clinician would consider it perfectly appropriate to have a meal outside the office with a client suffering from a social phobia for the purpose of in vivo exposure. Smith and Fitzpatrick (1995) conclude that it is our obligation to distinguish those interventions that violate a particular theoretical position from those that would place clients at risk for harm.

From this body of work there seems to have developed a broad consensus that establishing boundaries are a fundamental part of the therapeutic process; it is the clinician's responsibility to institute and maintain such rules to protect clients, and clinicians must do what they can to anticipate and avoid behavior that could potentially do harm. However, in recent years, some have challenged these ideas.

DISSENTING VOICES

Arnold Lazarus

Arnold Lazarus (1994), one of the pioneers of behavioral psychology, has written that psychology's ethical principles, and particularly its most recent revision (APA, 1992) as well as many risk management procedures (e.g., B. E. Bennett et al., 1990), could be "taken too far . . . and backfire" (p. 256), fostering needlessly restrictive treatment of clients by clinicians. He went further and suggested that in some cases, rigid adherence to such rules was ridiculous, potentially harmful, and could even result in treatment he described as "dehumanizing" (p. 256). That is, following the ethics code and related risk management procedures could lead to the construction of artificial boundaries to such a rigid or excessive degree that they might compromise therapeutic effectiveness and even be inhumane. He asserted that it is safer to "go by the book" (p. 260) and adhere to inflexible rules rather than think for oneself but that "it doesn't hurt to temper the rules and regulations with a touch of common sense" (p. 258). Such a position appears responsible and reasonable until one examines some of his examples.

Much of Lazarus's criticism was directed toward psychoanalytic practitioners, yet many examples can be applied to common practice situations that might arise regardless of one's theoretical orientation. They include asking a patient for a ride to the service station where Lazarus's car was being repaired; having a consultation with the mother of a patient over lunch in a restaurant; socializing and playing tennis with certain clients; and treating relatives and friends.

It should come as no surprise that Lazarus was soundly criticized from numerous quarters. B. E. Bennett et al. (1990) agreed that therapy should not be conducted in a "cookbook" fashion (p. 264), but they expressed fear that Lazarus's position could influence less experienced clinicians to minimize the importance of boundary issues. They delicately concluded that, "when a driver does not heed the warning signs and wanders over the center line, all vehicles are in danger" (p. 266).

Borys (1994) emphasized that ethical rules regarding boundaries were established as a matter of client protection. Although she agreed that "mindless rule following" could be "ineffective and stultifying" (p. 268), she took exception to Lazarus's "extensive latitude" (p. 267) regarding the rules. She reviewed in some detail the meaning of boundaries, especially in the case of trauma survivors, noting that the boundaries served beneficial purposes in the treatment process and that even the most seemingly benign decisions could backfire and cause damage to clients. She concluded that becoming stultified was most likely a function of not understanding the rules and their rationale, and that a clinician who understood boundaries as a means of promoting effective treatment would find them to be allies in the treatment process.

Brown (1994) suggested that Lazarus (1994) had located the problem incorrectly. She argued that there was a failure of mainstream psychology to appreciate the power dynamics in therapy relationships; that boundary violations often arose due to impulse, not thoughtful consideration; and that such decisions could further imbalance an already imbalanced relationship, thereby putting the clinician in a position of even greater power than he or she would have had otherwise.

Gabbard (1994) criticized Lazarus (1994) for appearing to presume that a client's positive response confirmed the wisdom of crossing certain boundaries and for taking the position that observing boundaries was primarily a means of reducing clinician anxiety regarding liability rather than a matter of honoring client welfare. He noted that even nonsexual boundary violations could be harmful and concluded that Lazarus was oversimplifying the complexities inherent in dual roles. Gottlieb (1994) raised issues regarding a seeming failure of Lazarus to structure the relationship from the outset, similarly to Gabbard, and for not considering the potentially complex consequences of dual relationships. He noted that clinical judgment and ethical decision making were inextricably bound and that Lazarus seemed to fail to take account of this complex relationship. Finally, he suggested that "going by the book" was often more difficult, time-consuming, and complex than simply making judgments at the time that such situations arose.

Gutheil (1994) accused Lazarus (1994) of unfairly counterposing risk management and humane interventions and argued that good intentions do not necessarily lead to good outcomes; that Lazarus did not differentiate boundary crossing and boundary violation; and that even behavior many of us would agree to be innocent can still lead to a clinician's being sued.

Later, Lazarus (1998) made an effort to explain his earlier position. He spoke quite personally of his formative years in South Africa and how differently society was organized. In doing so, he helped the reader understand more fully the reasons he had taken such a controversial position. He noted that due to his large extended family, seeking professional services outside the family would have been almost unthinkable because family members looked out for one another and provided "personal, tender and affectionate caring. Impartiality, neutrality, and objectivity were synonyms for distance and indifference . . . would I consult a stranger for

medical services or turn to one of my uncles?" (p. 22). He recounted his difficulty in being separated from his extended family when he emigrated to the United States and how he established new relationships after his arrival. He noted with some pride that a good friend performed surgery on him and that two former clients were members of the surgical team. He tempered his approach by offering the suggestion that instead of a rule that one should never treat family or friends, it is advisable to be cautious about doing so when the client suffers from significant psychopathology. This argument is based on the notion that the behavioral techniques utilized would be the same regardless of who the client was; therefore, one's preexisting relationship would not change the nature of the treatment.

Lazarus (1998) emphasized that he was not suggesting a laissez-faire or indiscriminate approach to practice. Rather, he advocated a case-by-case, nondogmatic process of deciding when and when not to enter into secondary relationships because there are no clear-cut, truly sensible guidelines and large gray areas remain.

Most recently, Lazarus (2001) continued his argument by reiterating that ethical provisions regarding multiple relationships are excessively stringent. He went further and claimed that "regulatory boards incorrectly believe that they can protect consumers by declaring all forms of dual relations as synonymous for 'exploitation' and 'harm,' and by asserting that most dual relationships inevitably lead to sex with a client" (p. 16). He contended that decisions regarding such matters should be negotiable and made on a case-by-case basis within "the confines of strict professionalism." He concluded by noting that rather than instilling fear, we should be teaching students how to navigate these complex waters.

Critique. Lazarus makes several arguments that should be supported. First, we agree that instilling fear in students and colleagues is not helpful (Handelsman, Knapp, & Gottlieb, in press) and that we should encourage them to develop skills to manage professional boundaries. Second, Lazarus is technically correct that there is no evidence that rules against exploitation prevent abuse. Third, some multiple relations are beneficial, such as faculty who may play many roles with students.

Although much of the criticism against Lazarus has been well placed, one point has been lost. Each critic has attacked Lazarus based on standards that exist in the United States. From that perspective, Lazarus does make recommendations that are troubling and could lead to boundary problems for clinicians and/or their supervisees. When Lazarus speaks fondly of his background in South Africa, he is not being critical only of our ethics codes, but of how relationships are constructed in contemporary American culture.

His position has recently been supported in a thought-provoking article (Sampson, 2000). Sampson argued that American culture supports a highly individualistic emphasis on interpersonal relationships that is based in early Protestant Christianity. Features of this position include high degrees of self-sufficiency, autonomy, and responsibility for oneself such that we are responsible not just for our successes but for our failures as well. He contrasted this notion with Rabbinic Judaism, which views interpersonal relations along a continuum of autonomy/relatedness. The implication of this work is that cultural values shape social norms and that our views as Americans should not be privileged over those of other cultures. This point has been supported by F. Kaslow (1998), who reports how differently boundary issues are perceived in countries that do not share our cultural values.

Sampson (2000) and Kaslow (1998) raise serious questions about the assumption that our cultural values are universal and the personal cost that may ensue for each of us from a too stringent interpretation. This is a worthy debate, and Lazarus should be considered an important part of it. We acknowledge that cultural differences may lead to different ethical decisions and that what may be inappropriate in one culture may be quite acceptable in another. As family psychologists, we wish for a culture that values more collective and interdependent relationships. However, prescription is beyond our scope here, and this discussion is centered on the professional issues confronted predominantly in the United States and other Western societies that espouse similar professional codes of ethics.

Martin Williams

Williams (1997) argued that "there are two distinct and contradictory positions regarding boundaries in psychotherapy" (p. 238). He noted that although ethical concerns dictate a need for careful maintenance of boundaries, practices of certain theoretical orientations argue that some boundaries should be routinely crossed. He concluded that boundary maintenance and theoretical orientation "do not coexist well" (p. 238). He went on to express concern that well-intentioned C/B/F clinicians could appear to be violating community standards when judged by someone who "holds a conservative view of boundaries" (p. 238), and he worried that behavioral and eclectic clinicians may be at risk for state regulatory board sanction or lawsuit by virtue of their techniques alone. He then selectively reviewed the literature with emphasis on the issue of boundaries in psychodynamically oriented psychotherapy. For example, he noted that the concept of boundary violations had supplanted "transference abuse," implying that this change was due to its "greater courtroom utility" (p. 240) because it was "free from the criticism that it derives from psychoanalysis" (p. 240). He concluded that "the reliable occurrence of such harm has not been established" (p. 241) with regard to nonsexual boundary violations.

In a section on behavior therapy, Williams (1997) reminded the reader that behaviorism and humanism share a common origin of rebellion against psychoanalysis and then explained how modeling in behavioral therapies is a type of self-disclosure. He went on to state, "Nothing in the theory of behavioral therapy would or should preclude socializing with patients, taking meals with them, giving them gifts, or treating them at their homes, schools or offices. Hugging patients might increase the therapist's potency as a reinforcer" (p. 244). He concluded this section by noting some of the criticisms of Lazarus (1994) mentioned above and quoted him as saying, "One of the worst professional or ethical violations is that of permitting current risk management principles to take precedence over humane interventions" (Lazarus, 1994, p. 244). Williams concluded with three points: (1) strict boundary maintenance should not be considered as a minimum standard of care; (2) the complex endeavor of psychotherapy cannot easily be delimited by a simplistic and restrictive set of rules; and (3) to restrict flexibility can only increase the likelihood of damage awards in court and the stagnation of the practice of psychotherapy.

Critique. Williams is quite correct that the psychotherapeutic process is complex. He is also right to argue that prohibiting flexibility and innovation would be harmful and that regulation should not stifle scientific progress. He agrees with Lazarus that there is no empirical evidence that certain types of multiple relationships cause harm ipso facto. He notes correctly that there is nothing in the behavioral tradition that should automatically preclude taking meals with clients, treating them in their homes, offering hugs, or socializing. However, the fact that there is nothing in the behavioral tradition to preclude such activities does not mean that such behavior is always beneficial or a good practice. Unfortunately, he does not

seem to take the context of such interactions into account.

By arguing as he does, Williams seems to be saying that if one is a C/B/F clinician, it is not necessary to worry about relational complications or transferential issues. Were C/B/F approaches as narrowly confined as they were in the past, it is probably true that distortions of professional relationships would be less likely. Unfortunately, Williams does not take into account the wide variety of venues in with C/B/F clinicians work, the different populations whom they treat where such issues may create boundary problems, or the widespread use of C/B/F methods by clinicians from other orientations.

Since their inception, behavioral and later cognitive therapies have revolutionized the psychotherapeutic endeavor. Today, C/B/F clinicians work in virtually all settings and provide an extraordinarily wide variety of empirically based services. One result of this expansion is that C/B/F clinicians are faced with a high degree of complexity in their daily clinical work (Gottlieb & Cooper, in press), involving provision of a large number of different therapeutic services to the same clients intermittently, perhaps over long periods of time.

One who reads the work of Lazarus and Williams might begin to wonder if practicing C/B/F therapy is a prudent endeavor. Are C/B/F clinicians lacking something in their training? Are they differentially vulnerable to ethics complaints and licensure attack for practicing within their theoretical orientation? In our view, nothing could be further from the truth.

First, there is no regulatory bias against C/B/F clinicians. Similarly, there is nothing in the APA *Ethical Principles and Code of Conduct* (1992) or those of any other profession to support such notions. Rather, the APA ethical principles represent an atheoretical consensus by the profession regarding appropriate professional behavior. The code was literally written and edited by hundreds of colleagues of all theoretical orientations before it was adopted, and no one orientation is privileged over another. Second, it is obvious that theoretical orientation may lead to differences in boundary management policies. For example, it is hard to argue that a C/B/F clinician's home visit to evaluate an agoraphobic would be construed as a boundary violation. The issue, then, is not whether C/B/F clinicians cross boundaries more than clinicians of other theoretical orientations; boundary crossing is not generally problematic. Rather, ethical problems may arise when boundaries are violated and clients are harmed as a result. Therefore, the clinical question is how to match therapeutic modality to patient needs (B. E. Bennett et al., 1990). To borrow from Paul (1967): *When, under what circumstances, and with what types of clients are various boundary crossings beneficial and under which circumstances might they be harmful?* In approaching the problem from this perspective, the clinician properly focuses on what is best for the client rather than on the implementation of a particular theoretical or personal point of view.

Clinicians of all theoretical persuasions must at times modify their approach and/or subordinate their theory to patient welfare. The fact that there is nothing in C/B/F therapy that says that one cannot socialize with a patient does not mean that it is necessarily advisable. Ethical principles are derived from theories of biomedical ethics (e.g., Beauchamp & Childress, 1983), not from psychological theory, and ethics codes develop from a consensus of a profession regarding what our best practices should be as a matter of client welfare. To suggest that theoretical orientation should take precedence over client welfare is to seriously conflate the ethical issues involved. Theoretical orientation should never be placed ahead of patient welfare.

Third, it is certainly true that state board complaints and lawsuits often are filed by disturbed and/or disgruntled clients. That is precisely why, regardless of one's theoretical orientation,

all clinicians must carefully consider the consequences of their actions, and why risk management strategies have been developed. A fundamental aspect of this process, and the best risk management strategy of all, is taking into account the client's perspective on boundaries as part of a thorough clinical assessment. Trying to diminish the importance of risk management by arguing that it is simply a matter of mindless rule adherence and/or the avoiding of appearances is not helpful. Rather, it is important to educate students and colleagues about these issues and to help them adapt to current realities. Arguing about whether nonsexual boundary violations cause harm or not is beside the point. If they present a potential danger, they should be avoided as a matter of client welfare.

Finally, practicing from a C/B/F approach is a complex matter. Although many of the issues raised by Lazarus and Williams are not applicable to competent C/B/F clinicians, they are right to bring attention to potential pitfalls to which they may be vulnerable.

DEVELOPING AN ETHICS POLICY

The practice of C/B/F therapy is a complex matter, and, as knowledge is created, new clinical and ethical dilemmas will continue to arise. Risk management involves providing practitioners with the information needed for everyday decision making (B. E. Bennett et al., 1990). Ideally, the best clinical decision is the best ethical one as well as the best risk management strategy (Gottlieb, 1997). However, in the practice of C/B/F therapy, this ideal may be a moving target. Until the field is more settled and more specific guidelines are created, individual practitioners will be forced to rely on their own informed judgment. What follows is an exercise that C/B/F clinicians may find useful for identifying and managing various boundary issues that may arise in daily practice. By taking the steps listed below, clinicians can evaluate their practices, improve risk management, and reduce the potential for iatrogenic risk through the development of an individual ethics policy.

Individual clinicians are advised to study the ethical dilemmas that commonly occur in their practices and develop an individualized ethics policy to address them. Such a policy will certainly not resolve all the ethical dilemmas that may arise, but this practice may assist in avoiding problems. Another benefit of such a policy is that it may serve to sensitize clinicians to issues where some vulnerability may exist and help plan for managing them.

First, it is necessary to define one's practice. Such a definition includes describing one's specific theoretical orientation, practice setting, populations served, personal values, and any other factors that may be relevant. For example, an altruistic C/B/F clinician working in a free, inner-city community clinic with a Latino population will face boundary issues very different from those of a sole practitioner treating middle-class clients in the suburbs. Simply writing such a description may identify certain issues before proceeding further.

Second, it is necessary to determine what state laws, regulations, and/or institutional policies must be considered. In this connection, one must also refer to the ethics codes of one's professional organization as well as any relevant specialty guidelines. For example, a C/B/F clinician who works in a county juvenile facility is subject to all relevant state laws, including the mental health code, juvenile code, state licensing board requirements, professional organization ethics codes, and specific policies of the agency. Boundary maintenance may become particularly difficult if an ethics code conflicts with agency policy in certain respects.

Third, having assessed the type of practice one has and the regulations that are pertinent, what ethical dilemmas can be most reasonably anticipated? For instance, the director of a

hospital cognitive rehabilitation unit needs to consider institutional policies on how boundaries regarding confidentiality should be managed with family members when a client's competency is in question. The specialist in pain management who works on a pediatric oncology unit needs to think carefully about what types of relationships he or she will have with patients' parents.

Fourth, it is necessary to examine the specific practice under review. What ethical problems have arisen in the past? How frequently have they occurred? Have colleagues who work in the area of systematic desensitization, for example, had similar problems? Does the frequency or seriousness of the problem warrant a specific policy to address it? A cognitive therapist who specializes in treating depression and anxiety disorders finds that a relatively high percentage of her clients also suffer from personality disorders. She may then decide to revise her informed consent procedure to highlight boundaries regarding potentially demanding or intrusive behavior, such as after-hours telephone calls.

Fifth, are there unique elements to the practice that make certain dilemmas more likely? A behavioral marital therapist finds himself becoming increasingly involved in his clients' personal lives and feels a special need to reach out to young women who have been victims of domestic violence. After realizing this phenomenon, he establishes a consulting relationship with a trusted colleague to monitor his treatment of such women and feelings of overidentifying with the victims.

Sixth, it is helpful to brainstorm. After performing this exercise, practitioners should share their findings with others who do similar work. This step is more theoretical and abstract, but it may lead to discussion and discovery of issues previously not considered.

Seventh, an initial draft of the policy should be written and shared with coworkers, colleagues, administrators, and those in similar practice settings. A critical review should be requested from the recipients and revisions made as needed.

Eighth, once the policy has been revised, it should be shared with clients who are more functional and less distressed. They should be asked to review it and perform a critical analysis from their perspective. The policy should then be revised again as needed.

Ninth, the policy should be piloted with a sample of new clients. Feedback should be sought and revisions made as needed.

Tenth, the policy should be implemented.

Eleventh, in true C/B/F fashion, the policy should be reviewed at least annually in light of new scientific knowledge, ethical guidelines, laws, and regulations. Finally, if an obstacle arises at any step in the development of the policy, ethics consultation should be sought.

SUMMARY

Our review of the historical and contemporary ethical issues in C/B/F therapies leads to three general conclusions. First, C/B/F approaches have at times been misrepresented and misapplied. Second, using C/B/F therapies can lead to complex ethical dilemmas when differing treatment modalities are applied to diverse populations in various settings over long periods of time. Third, notable controversies remain unresolved regarding boundary management in C/B/F modalities.

We believe that the dilemmas raised in this chapter will diminish and become more clear as the field grows and develops. Until that time arrives, C/B/F practitioners must make every effort to anticipate the clinical and ethical complexities that accompany their work. In an effort to assist colleagues to think through such difficulties and to focus on boundary management, we propose that practitioners develop their own ethics policies in anticipation of the dilemmas that are most likely to arise in their practices.

In all cases, readers are urged to strive to do what is clinically indicated, is ethically appropriate, and represents good risk management. This is a difficult task, and we hope this discussion will prove fruitful in guiding practitioners through this complex area and will further adherence to the highest ethical standards.

REFERENCES

Agras, W. S., Schneider, J. A., Arnow, B., Raeburn, S. D., et al. (1989). Cognitive-behavioral and response-prevention treatments for bulimia nervosa. *Journal of Consulting and Clinical Psychology, 57*(2), 15–21.

Alexander, J. F., Holtzworth-Munroe, A., & Jameson, P. B. (1993). Research on the process and outcome of marital and family therapy. In A. E. Bergin & S. L. Garfield (Eds.), *Handbook of psychotherapy and behavioral change* (4th ed., pp. 595–630). New York: Wiley.

American Association of Marital and Family Therapy. (2001). *AAMFT code of ethics.* Washington, DC: Author.

American Psychological Association. (1992). Ethical principles of psychologists and code of conduct. *American Psychologist, 47*, 1597–1611.

Anderson, S. K., & Kitchener, K. S. (1998). Nonsexual post therapy relationships: A conceptual framework to assess ethical risks. *Professional Psychology: Research and Practice, 29*, 91–99.

Arnow, B. A., Taylor, C. B., Agras, W. S., & Telch, M. J. (1985). Enhancing agoraphobia treatment by changing couple communication patterns. *Behavior Therapy, 16*(5), 452–467.

Ascher, L. M. (1989). Paradoxical intention and recursive anxiety. In L. M. Ascher (Ed.), *Therapeutic paradox* (pp. 93–136). New York: Guilford Press.

Bandura, A. (1969). *Principles of behavior modification.* New York: Holt, Rinehardt and Winston.

Barlow, D. H. (1988). *Anxiety and its disorders: The nature and treatment of anxiety and panic.* New York: Guilford Press.

Bateson, G. (1972). *Steps to an ecology of mind.* New York: Ballantine Books.

Beauchamp, T. L., & Childress, J. E. (1983). *Principles of biomedical ethics* (2nd ed.). New York: Oxford University Press.

Beck, A. T. (1967). *Depression: Causes and treatment.* Philadelphia: University of Pennsylvania Press.

Bennett, B. E., Bryan, B. K., VandenBos, G. R., & Greenwood, A. (1990). *Professional liability and risk management.* Washington, DC: American Psychological Association.

Bennett, D. S., & Gibbons, T. A. (2000). Efficacy of child cognitive-behavioral interventions for antisocial behavior: A meta-analysis. *Child and Family Behavior Therapy, 22*(1), 1–15.

Berkovec, T. (1993). Efficacy of applied relaxation and cognitive-behavioral therapy in the treatment of Generalized Anxiety Disorder. *Journal of Consulting and Clinical Psychology, 61,* 611–619.

Borys, D. S. (1994). Maintaining therapeutic boundaries: The motive is therapeutic effectiveness and not defensive practice. *Ethics and Behavior, 4,* 267–274.

Borys, D. S., & Pope, K. S. (1989). Dual relationships between therapist and client: A national study of psychologists, psychiatrists and social workers. *Professional Psychology: Research and Practice, 20,* 283–293.

Bouhoutous, J., Holroyd, J. C., Lerman, H., Forer, B. R., & Greenberg, M. (1983). Sexual intimacy between psychotherapists and patients. *Professional Psychology: Research and Practice, 14,* 185–196.

Brown, L. S. (1988). Harmful effects of post termination sexual and romantic relationships between therapists and their former clients. *Psychotherapy: Theory, Research, Practice and Training, 25,* 249–255.

Brown, L. S. (1994). Concrete boundaries and the problem of literal minuends: A response to Lazarus. *Ethics and Behavior, 4,* 275–282.

Cashdan, S. (1988). *Object relations therapy: Using the relationship.* New York: Norton.

Christensen, A., & Jacobson, N. (2000). *Reconcilable differences.* New York: Guilford Press.

Dobson, K. (Ed.). (1988). *Handbook of cognitive-behavior therapies.* New York: Guilford Press.

Dowd, E. T., & Truitt, S. D. (1988). Paradoxical interventions in behavior modification. In M. Hersen & P. M. Miller (Eds.), *Progress in behavior modification* (pp. 96–130). Newbury Park, CA: Sage.

Ellis, A. (1997). Postmodern ethics for active-directive counseling and psychotherapy. *Journal of Mental Health Counseling, 19*(3), 211–225.

Evans, I. M. (1999). Child-focused behavioral assessment and modification. *Journal of Clinical Child Psychology, 28*(4), 493–501.

Faulkner, K. K., & Faulkner, T. A. (1997). Managing multiple relationships in rural communities: Neutrality and boundary violations. *Clinical Psychology: Science and Practice, 4,* 225–234.

Feldman-Summers, S., & Jones, G. (1984). Psychological impact of sexual contact between therapists or other health care practitioners and their clients. *Journal of Consulting and Clinical Psychology, 52,* 1054–1061.

Fitzgerald, L. F. (1997). But was it really sexual harassment? Legal, behavioral, and psychological definitions of the workplace victimization of women (pp. 7–8). In W. O'Donohue (Ed.), *Sexual harassment: Theory research and treatment.* Needham Heights, MA: Allyn & Bacon.

Gabbard, G. O. (1994). Teetering on the precipice: A commentary on Lazarus' "How certain boundaries and ethics diminish therapeutic effectiveness." *Ethics and Behavior, 4,* 283–286.

Gast, D. L., & Nelson, C. M. (1977). Legal and ethical considerations for the use of timeout in special education settings. *Journal of Special Education, 11*(4), 457–467.

Glynn, S. M., Mueser, K. T., & Liberman, R. P. (1989). The behavioral approach. In A. Lazarus (Ed.), *Outpatient psychiatry: Diagnosis and treatment* (2nd ed., pp. 59–68). Baltimore: Williams & Wilkins.

Gottlieb, M. C. (1993). Avoiding exploitive dual relationships: A decision making model. *Psychotherapy: Theory, Research, Practice and Training, 30,* 41–48.

Gottlieb, M. C. (1994). Ethical decision making, boundaries, and treatment effectiveness: A reprise. *Ethics and Behavior, 4,* 287–293.

Gottlieb, M. C. (1995). Ethical dilemmas in change of format and live supervision. In R. H. Mikesell, D. Lusterman, & S. H. McDaniel (Eds.), *Integrating family therapy: Handbook of family psychology and systems therapy* (pp. 561–570). Washington, DC: American Psychological Association.

Gottlieb, M. C. (1997). An ethics policy for family practice management. In D. T. Marsh & R. D. Magel (Eds.), *Ethical and legal issues in professional practice with families* (pp. 257–270). New York: Wiley.

Gottlieb, M. C., & Cooper, C. C. (in press). Ethical issues in integrative therapies. In J. Lebow (Ed.), *Comprehensive handbook of psychotherapy: Volume IV: Integrative and eclectic therapies*. New York: Wiley.

Gottlieb, M. C., Sell, J. M., & Schoenfeld, L. S. (1988). Social/romantic relationships with present and former clients: State licensing board actions. *Professional Psychology: Research and Practice, 19*, 459–462.

Graham-Clay, S. L., & Reschly, D. J. (1987). Legal and ethical issues. In C. A. Maher & S. G. Forman (Eds.), *A behavioral approach to education of children and youth: School psychology* (pp. 289–309). Hillsdale, NJ: Erlbaum.

Greenspoon, J. L. (1987). A behavioristic approach. In *Male and female sexuality: Psychological approaches* (pp. 109–128). Washington, DC: Hemisphere.

Guerin, P. J. (1976). Family therapy: The first twenty-five years. In P. J. Guerin (Ed.), *Family therapy theory and practice*. New York: Gardner Press.

Gutheil, T. G. (1994). Discussion of Lazarus's "How certain boundaries and ethics diminish therapeutic effectiveness." *Ethics and Behavior, 4*, 295–298.

Haas, L. J., & Malouf, J. L. (1989). *Keeping up the good work: A practitioner's guide to mental health ethics.* Sarasota, FL: Professional Resource Exchange.

Haley, J. (1963). *Uncommon therapy.* San Francisco: Jossey-Bass.

Handelsman, M. M. (1998). Ethics and ethical reasoning. In S. Cullari (Ed.), *Foundations of clinical psychology* (pp. 80–111). Needham Heights, MA: Allyn & Bacon.

Handelsman, M. M., Knapp, S. J., & Gottlieb, M. C. (in press). Positive ethics. In C. R. Snyder & S. J. Lopez (Eds.), *Handbook of positive psychology*. New York: Oxford University Press.

Holroyd, J. C., & Brodsky, A. M. (1977). Psychologists' attitudes and practices regarding erotic and nonerotic physical contact with patients. *American Psychologist, 32*, 893–899.

Homer, A. L., & Peterson, L. (1980). Differential reinforcement of other behavior: A preferred response elimination procedure. *Behavior Therapy, 11*(4), 449–471.

Jacobson, N. S., Dobson, K., Fruzzetti, A. E., Schmaling, K. B., & Salusky, S. (1991). Marital therapy as a treatment of depression. *Journal of Consulting and Clinical Psychology, 59*, 547–557.

Jacobson, N. S., & Margolin, G. (1979). *Marital therapy: Strategies based on social learning theory and behavior exchange principles.* New York: Brunner/Mazel.

Karasu, T. B. (1980). The ethics of psychotherapy. *American Journal of Psychiatry, 137*, 1502–1512.

Kaslow, F. W. (1990). *Voices in family psychology.* Newbury Park, CA: Sage.

Kaslow, F. W. (1998). Ethical problems in mental health practice. *Journal of Family Psychotherapy, 9*(2), 41–54.

Kitchener, K. S. (1984). Intuition, critical evaluation and ethical principles: The foundation for ethical decisions in counseling psychology. *Counseling Psychologist, 12*, 43–55.

Kitchener, K. S. (1996). Professional codes of ethics and ongoing moral problems in psychology. In W. O'Donohue & R. J. Kitchener (Eds.), *The philosophy of psychology* (pp. 361–371). London: Sage.

Koocher, G. P., Norcross, J. C., & Hill, S. (1998). *Psychologists' desk reference.* New York: Oxford University Press.

Lamb, D. H., Strand, K. K., Woodburn, J. R., Buchko, K. J., Lewis, J. T., & Kang, J. R. (1994). Sexual and business relationships between therapists and former clients. *Psychotherapy: Theory, Research and Practice, 31*, 270–278.

Lazarus, A. A. (1994). How certain boundaries and ethics diminish therapeutic effectiveness. *Ethics and Behavior, 4*, 255–261.

Lazarus, A. A. (1998). How do you like these boundaries? *Clinical Psychologist, 51*, 22–25.

Lazarus, A. A. (2001, January/February). Not all "dual relationships" are taboo: Some tend to enhance treatment outcomes. *National Psychologist, 16.*

Leduc, A., Dumais, A., & Evans, I. M. (1990). Social behaviorism, rehabilitation, and ethics: Applications for people with severe disabilities. In G. H. Eifert & I. M. Evans (Eds.), *Unifying behavior* therapy: Contributions of paradigmatic behaviorism. *Springer series on behavior therapy and behavior medicine* (Vol. 23, pp. 268–289). New York: Springer.

Leslie, J. C. (1997). Ethical implications of behavior modification: Historical and current issues. *Psychological Record, 47*(4), 637–648.

Lutzker, J. R., & Campbell, R. (1994). *Ecobehavioral family interventions in developmental disabilities.* Pacific Grove, CA: Brooks/Cole.

Margolin, G. (1982). Ethical and legal considerations in marital and family therapy. *American Psychologist, 37,* 788–801.

Marlatt, G. A. (Ed.). (1985). *Cognitive assessment and intervention procedures for relapse prevention.* New York: Guilford Press.

Matson, J. L., & Kazdin, A. E. (1981). Punishment in behavior modification: Pragmatic, ethical, and legal issues. *Clinical Psychology Review, 2,* 197–210.

McLean, P. D. (1980). The effect of informal consent on the acceptance of random treatment assignment in a clinical population. *Behavior Therapy, 11*(1), 129–133.

Minuchin, S. (1974). *Families and family therapy.* Cambridge, MA: Harvard University Press.

Muñoz, R. F., Ying, Y., Perez-Stable, E., & Miranda, J. (1993). *The prevention of depression: Research and practice.* Baltimore: Johns Hopkins University Press.

Murphy, G. E., Carney, R. M., Knesevich, M. A., & Wetzel, R. D. (1995). Cognitive behavior therapy, relaxation training, and trycyclic antidepressant medication in the treatment of depression. *Psychological Reports, 77*(2), 403–420.

National Association of Social Workers. (1996). *Code of ethics.* Washington, DC: Author.

Neisworth, J. T., & Madle, R. A. (1976). Time-out with staff accountability: A technical note. *Behavior Therapy, 7*(2), 261–263.

O'Leary, S. G., & O'Leary, K. D. (1977). Ethical issues of behavior modification research in schools. *Psychology in the Schools, 14*(3), 299–307.

Patterson, T. (1999). *The couple and family clinical documentation sourcebook.* New York: Wiley.

Paul, G. (1967). The strategy of outcome research in psychotherapy. *Journal of Consulting Psychology, 31,* 109–118.

Persons, J. B., Davidson, J., & Tompkins, M. A. (2001). *Essential components of cognitive-behavior therapy for depression.* Washington, DC: American Psychological Association.

Pinsof, W. M. (1989). A conceptual framework and methodological criteria for family process research. *Journal of Consulting and Clinical Psychology, 57,* 53–59.

Pope, K. S. (1994). *Sexual involvement with therapists.* Washington, DC: American Psychological Association.

Pope, K. S., Levenson, H., & Schover, L. R. (1979). Sexual intimacy in psychology training: Results and implications of a national study. *American Psychologist, 34,* 682–689.

Pope, K. S., Tabachnick, B. G., & Kieth-Spiegel, P. (1987). Ethics of practice: The beliefs and behaviors of psychologists as therapists. *American Psychologist, 42,* 993–1006.

Pope, K. S., & Vetter, V. A. (1992). Ethics dilemmas encountered by members of the American Psychological Association. *American Psychologist, 47,* 397–411.

Rapp, M. S. (1984). Ethics in behavior therapy: Historical aspects and current status. *Canadian Journal of Psychiatry, 29*(7), 547–550.

Rehm, L. P. (1984). Self-management therapy for depression. *Advances in Behavior Research and Therapy, 6,* 83–98.

Reisinger, J. J. (1974). The treatment of anxiety-depression via positive reinforcement and response cost. *Journal of Applied Behavior Analysis, 5,* 125–130.

Ringen, J. (1996). The behavior therapist's dilemma: Reflections on autonomy, informed consent, and scientific psychology. In W. O'Donohue & R. J. Uitchener (Eds.), *The philosophy of psychology* (pp. 352–361). London: Sage.

Robinson, J. C., & Lewinsohn, P. M. (1973). An experimental analysis of a technique based on the Premack principle for changing the verbal behavior of depressed individuals. *Psychological Reports, 32,* 199–210.

Roll, S., & Millen, L. (1981). A guide to violating an injunction in psychotherapy: On seeing acquaintances as patients. *Psychotherapy: Theory, Research and Practice, 18,* 179–187.

Ross, M. W. (1977). Paradigm lost or paradigm regained? Behavior therapy and homosexuality. *New Zealand Psychologist, 6*(1), 42–51.

Sampson, E. E. (2000). Reinterpreting individualism and collectivism: Their religious roots and monologic versus dialogic person-other relationship. *American Psychologist, 55,* 1425–1432.

Satir, V. (1967). *Conjoint family therapy.* Palo Alto, CA: Science and Behavior Books.

Schank, J. A., & Skovholt, T. M. (1997). Dual-relationship dilemmas of rural and small community psychologists. *Professional Psychology: Research and Practice, 28,* 44–49.

Sell, J. M., Gottlieb, M. C., & Schoenfeld, L. S. (1986). Ethical considerations of social/romantic relationships with present and former clients. *Professional Psychology: Research and Practice, 17,* 504–509.

Sheldon, J. (1982). Legal and ethical issues in the behavioral treatment of juvenile and adult offenders. In E. K. Morris & C. J. Braukmann (Eds.), *Behavioral approaches to crime and delinquency: A handbook of application, research, and concepts* (pp. 543–575). New York: Plenum Press.

Silverstein, C. (1977). Homosexuality and the ethics of behavioral treatment: Paper 2. *Journal of Homosexuality, 2*(3), 205–211.

Smith, D., & Fitzpatrick, M. (1995). Patient-therapist boundary issues: An integrative review of theory and research. *Professional Psychology: Research and Practice, 26,* 499–506.

Smolev, S. R. (1971). Use of operant techniques for the modification of self-injurious behavior. *American Journal of Mental Deficiency, 76*(3), 295–305.

Staal, M. A., & King, R. E. (2000). Managing a multiple relationship environment: The ethics of military psychology. *Professional Psychology: Research and Practice, 31,* 698–705.

Stein, T. J. (1975). Some ethical considerations of short-term workshops in the principles and methods of behavior modification. *Journal of Applied Behavior Analysis, 8*(1), 113–115.

Strosahl, K., & Jacobson, N. S. (1986). Training and supervision of behavior therapists. *Clinical Supervisor, 4*(1/2), 183–206.

Stuart, R. B. (1975). Challenges for behavior therapy: 1975. *Canadian Psychological Review, 16*(3), 164–172.

Tarachow, S. (1964). *An introduction to psychotherapy.* New York: International Universities Press.

Tennov, D., Jacobson, J., & Trinidad, J. (1976). Reinforcement procedures. *American Psychologist, 31*(11), 811–812.

Touyz, S. W. (1998). Ethical considerations in the implementation of behaviour modification programmes in patients with anorexia nervosa: A historical perspective. In W. Vandereycken & P. J. Beumont (Eds.), *Treating eating disorders: Ethical, legal and personal issues* (pp. 216–229). New York: New York University Press.

Tubb, P., & Pomeranz, A. M. (2001). Ethical behaviors of psychologists: Changes since 1987. *Journal of Clinical Psychology, 57,* 395–399.

Valenti, R. J. (1977). Ethical issues in applied behavior modification and implications for use in public school settings. *Southern Journal of Educational Research, 11*(3), 159–167.

Van Houten, R., Axelrod, S., Bailey, J. S., & Favell, J. E. (1988). The right to effective behavioral treatment. *Behavioral Analyst, 11*(2), 111–114.

Vizueta, A. (1979). Ethical considerations about the use of aversive stimulation in behavior therapy. *Revista Latinoamericana de Psicologia [Latin-American Review of Psychology], 11*(3), 403–409.

Weitzman, B. (1967). Behavior therapy and psychotherapy. *Psychological Review, 74*(4), 300–317.

Widiger, T. A., & Rorer, L. G. (1984). The responsible psychotherapist. *American Psychologist, 39,* 503–515.

Williams, M. H. (1997). Boundary violations: Do some contended standards of care fail to encompass commonplace procedures of humanistic, behavioral and eclectic psychotherapists? *Psychotherapy: Theory, Research, Practice and Training, 34,* 238–249.

Wolpe, J., & Lazarus, A. A. (1966). *Behavior therapy techniques.* New York: Pergamon Press.

Woolfolk, R. L., & Richardson, F. C. (1992). Behavior therapy and the ideology of modernity. In R. B. Miller (Ed.), *The restoration of dialogue.* Washington, DC: American Psychological Association.

Author Index

Subject Index